S0-CFC-301

FUNDAMENTALS OF MANAGEMENT SCIENCE

Efraim Turban
University of Southern California

Jack R. Meredith
University of Cincinnati

FUNDAMENTALS OF MANAGEMENT SCIENCE

1988 Fourth Edition

BPI
IRWIN
Homewood, Illinois 60430

Editor: Michael W. Junior
Developmental editor: Janette S. Stecki
Production manager: Bette Ittersagen
Production editor: Ann Cassady
Copyediting coordinator: Jean Roberts
Cover design: Tim Kaage
Cover photo: Michel Tcherevkoff ©
Compositor: Arcata Graphics/Kingsport
Typeface: 10½ x 12 Caledonia
Printer: Arcata Graphics/Halliday

ISBN 0-256-06256-0

Library of Congress Catalog Card No. 87-72395

Printed in the United States of America

2 3 4 5 6 7 8 9 0 H 5 4 3 2 1 0 9 8

To my mother, Devora

E. T.

To the memory of my parents, Blanche and Joyce Harvey

J. M.

Preface

Today, the techniques of management science are known to business leaders, urban planners, farmers, military strategists, space scientists, and public administrators in a host of fields. Words such as *systems, models, optimization, simulation,* and *cost-benefit* are now common in the public vocabulary. The need is thus great for an introductory text that explains, with a minimum of mathematics, how to *formulate* decision problems, how to *solve* them using management science concepts, and how to *apply* the solutions obtained.

As more complex models were developed in the field, relatively more attention was paid to the task of solving the models, while less emphasis was placed on the important phases of formulation and application. This book attempts to correct that deficiency by providing a comprehensive discussion of these two crucial phases. The book is organized in three parts: Foundations, The Tools, and Applications.

In Part I of the book, the foundations of the field are outlined. The reader is introduced to the topic of management science in Chapter 1. Its characteristics and processes are then outlined in Chapter 2, which focuses on the relation of management science to decision making.

Part II, The Tools, is concerned with formulating managerial problems from many different fields and finding solutions to them using management science models. The chapters are intentionally written to be independent of each other so the instructor may cover only the topics desired for the course. Chapters in this part of the book are typically divided into two sections: "Basics" and "Extensions." The book was written with the express aim of allowing coverage in a course ranging from one quarter (if only the "Basics" sections are covered) to two quarters (if the entire text is to be covered). The essence of each topic is presented in the former at a minimal level of mathematical sophistication—typically, only algebra or elementary statistics is needed. The sections in the "Extensions" elaborate on some of the basic models at a somewhat higher level of sophistication. These sections are typically also independent of each other and may thus be selected at will by the instructor for further class study. The mathematical and statistical background needed for the book, as well as a few additional topics (such as "present value"), are included in Appendix A, Mathematics, and in Appendix B, Statistics. Appendix C includes requisite tables for the text and, lastly, the *answers* (not solutions) to the even-numbered problems are given in Appendix D.

Each chapter in Part II typically begins with a brief episode showing the student how a particular decision problem arises. When possible, this example is carried throughout the chapter to illustrate the concepts being developed. We have attempted to present a variety of decision situations from a number of fields to emphasize the flexibility of the management science approach. Chapter 7 in particular presents a wide array of applications of linear programming, thus departing from the standard format of the chapters in Part II. In lieu of presenting the mathematical theorems and proofs that form the basis of many of the models, we appeal to intuitive reasoning and logic. These chapters each include a case to help the student apply the tools and techniques learned in the chapter to a realistic situation. The chapters then conclude with a glossary of chapter terms.

The sequence of the chapters progresses from general decision models (Chapters 3 and 4) through forecasting (Chapter 5), mathematical programming (Chapters 6–10), networks (Chapter 11), dynamic programming (Chapter 12), Markov analysis (Chapter 13), and inventory models (Chapter 14), and ends with the stochastic models of queuing (Chapter 15) and simulation (Chapter 16). Each chapter is as independent of the others as possible to provide the instructor with the flexibility of using selected chapters at will.

Part III, Applications, begins with an examination of the new tools of decision support systems (Chapter 17) and expert systems (Chapter 18). From there, the difficulty and process of implementation is addressed in Chapter 19. A detailed case study is then given in Chapter 20 to illustrate how to integrate the tools and techniques in a more realistic framework than the problems of Part II alone allow. The book concludes with an assessment of the future directions and areas of the application of management science in Chapter 21.

In the three years that have passed between the previous edition of this book and this one, we have witnessed the continuation of the revolution of the "personal" or microcomputer. This revolution will eventually result in a computer (or at least a computer terminal) on almost every manager's desk. Furthermore, several universities are already requiring students to own or have access to a computer.

This revolution will have a significant impact on the teaching of quantitative methods and management science. Students will work much more with computers and less with manual manipulation, while instructors will be able to introduce more complex, real-life problems into their teaching. Of course, other issues involving the use of computers, such as cost and security, will also arise and must be addressed.

For this reason, we decided in this new edition to emphasize the use of computers in teaching management science. Specifically, microcomputer software for use with *Fundamentals of Management Science* is now available. *MSS: The Management Science System* by Theron Nelson is a simple yet powerful collection of operations and management science programs for student use on the IBM PC. The package has many error detection and prevention features built into it to minimize common input errors. The input routines have all been designed to allow problems to be entered into the computer in the way they appear in the textbook. In other words, the student will generally not have to "prepare" the problem prior to typing in the program. All of the *MSS* programs are menu driven. Every effort has been made to take the guess work out of the use of these programs.

In addition, we address the role of computers in solving problems and conducting sensitivity ("what if") analyses in each chapter. Actual computer printouts are also included. A special appendix to Chapter 1 discusses the use of computers in management science. Details about general purpose software availability are provided in the *Instructor's Manual.*

The following are some of the major changes made in this edition. We have increased the number of chapters dealing with mathematical programming, particularly linear and goal programming, from three to five. The topic of goal programming was greatly expanded and several application examples are included in a new chapter. The decision support system chapter was updated and contains considerable new information. Also, a separate chapter on expert systems was added, as well as new sections in a number of areas such as visual simulation.

A greater international emphasis was added to the problems, examples, and cases to respond to the new American Assembly of Collegiate Schools of Business requirements in this area. And in addition to the wide selection of problems in the previous edition, we have added, replaced, or changed about 50 problems, bringing the total number of problems close to 500.

The *Instructor's Manual* includes extensive suggestions for organizing and teaching this course as well as complete answers to the problems and causes. A separate *Test Bank* provides comprehensive questions and problems in a multiple-choice format, on a chapter-by-chapter basis.

The number of persons to whom we owe thanks for their contributions to the development of this book defies enumeration. Of particular help in this edition were the suggestions and advice offered to us by A. J. Waltz, University of South Florida; Peter M. Ellis, Utah State University; Richard Ehrhardt, University of North Carolina, Greensboro; Fatollah Salimian, Salisbury State College, Pennsylvania; and Samuel Wagner, Franklin and Marshall College. We would also like to thank the reviewers of previous editions: James A. Bartos, Ohio State University: F. Douglas Holcombe, Marshall University; Michael Middleton, University of San Francisco; Thomas Tucker, University of Houston at Clear Lake; and Ross E. Lanser, San Jose State University. Special acknowledgment is made of the ideas and constructive suggestions of Carol Meredith in this and previous editions. Also, we gratefully acknowledge the extensive assistance of Donna Schaeffer and Sharon Turban in proofing the manuscript and galleys.

Efraim Turban
Jack Meredith

Contents

PART I
FOUNDATIONS *1*

1 **Introduction** *3*
- 1.1 What's It All About? ***4***
- 1.2 Definitions of Management Science, ***6***
- 1.3 The Characteristics of Management Science, ***7***
- 1.4 The Tools of Management Science, ***7***
- 1.5 Cutler-Hammer's Patent Decision, ***8***
- 1.6 Historical Development, ***9***
- 1.7 Extent of Use and Limitations, ***10***
- 1.8 Plan of the Book, ***13***
- 1.9 Review Questions, ***15***
- 1.10 Glossary, ***15***
- 1.11 References and Bibliography, ***15***
- 1.12 Appendix: Using the Computer, ***16***

2 **Management Science: Characteristics and Process** *19*
- 2.1 Introduction, ***20***
- 2.2 Decision Making: A Primary Focus, ***21***
- 2.3 The Scientific Approach, ***22***
- 2.4 The Systems Point of View, ***22***
- 2.5 An Interdisciplinary Approach, ***26***
- 2.6 Models, ***27***
- 2.7 Use of Computers, ***28***
- 2.8 Step 1: Definition of the Problem, ***29***

2.9 Step 2: Classification of the Problem, *31*
2.10 Step 3: Modeling (Formulation), *31*
2.11 Step 4: Solving the Model, *35*
2.12 Step 5: Model Validation and Sensitivity Analysis, *43*
2.13 Step 6: Implementation, *44*
2.14 Managerial Problems and the Tools of Management Science, *44*
2.15 Concluding Remarks, *49*
2.16 Problems, *49*
2.17 Review Questions, *49*
2.18 Glossary, *50*
2.19 References and Bibliography, *51*

PART II
THE TOOLS 53

3 **Decision Theory** *55*
Part A: Basics
3.1 Decision Analysis with Decision Tables, *58*
3.2 Classification of Decision Situations, *61*
3.3 Decisions under Certainty, *64*
3.4 Decisions under Risk, *00*
3.5 Decisions Trees, *72*
3.6 Computer Programs for Decision Tables and Trees, *80*
3.7 Concluding Remarks, *84*
3.8 Problems for Part A, *85*
Part B: Extensions
3.9 The Acquisition of Additional Information, *91*
3.10 The Value of Perfect Information, *93*
3.11 The Value of Imperfect Information, *96*
3.12 Decisions under Certainty, *102*
3.13 Use of Computers, *107*
3.14 Appendix: Calculating Revised Probabilities, *111*
3.15 Problems for Part B, *115*
3.16 Case I: The Condominium, *118*
Case II: Maintaining the Water Valves, *119*
Case III: The Air Force Contract, *120*
3.17 Glossary, *121*
3.18 References and Bibliography, *122*

4 **Utility and Game Theories** *123*
Part A: Basics
4.1 Utility and Decision Theory, *125*
4.2 Multiple Goals, *134*
4.3 Concluding Remarks, *139*

4.4 Problems for Part A, ***139***
4.5 Game Theory, ***142***
4.6 Concluding Remarks, ***157***
Part B: The Extensions
4.7 Problems for Part B, ***158***
4.8 Case: The Videotape Strategy, ***162***
4.9 Glossary, ***163***
4.10 References and Bibliography, ***163***

5 **Forecasting** *165*
Part A: Basics
5.1 The Forecasting Situation, ***167***
5.2 Judgmental Forecasting Methods, ***172***
5.3 Counting Methods, ***173***
5.4 Moving Averages and Exponential Smoothing, ***173***
5.5 Forecasting Errors, ***177***
5.6 Other Time-Series Methods, ***181***
5.7 Causal Methods, ***182***
5.8 Problems for Part A, ***184***
Part B: Extensions
5.9 Decomposition, ***186***
5.10 Computerization, ***203***
5.11 Concluding Remarks, ***203***
5.12 Problems for Part B, ***204***
5.13 Case: Bardstown Box Company, ***206***
5.14 Glossary, ***207***
5.15 References and Bibliography, ***208***

A Preview to Chapters 6–10 *209*

6 **Linear Programming—Foundations** *211*
Part A: Basics
6.1 The Nature of Linear Programming Problems, ***213***
6.2 Formulation, ***214***
6.3 General Formulation and Terminology, ***219***
6.4 The Graphical Method of Solution, ***224***
6.5 Utilization of the Resources—Slack and Surplus Variables, ***236***
6.6 Concluding Remarks, ***239***
6.7 Problems for Part A, ***240***
Part B: Extensions
6.8 The Simplex Method, ***242***
6.9 Computerization, ***257***
6.10 Special Situations in the Simplex Method, ***258***
6.11 Problems for Part B, ***266***

6.12 Case: The Daphne Jewelry Company, ***268***
6.13 Glossary, ***269***
6.14 References and Bibliography, ***270***

7 Linear Programming—Applications 272
7.1 Crude Oil Refining, ***273***
7.2 Paper Trimming, ***275***
7.3 Agriculture, ***276***
7.4 Finance (Banking), ***278***
7.5 Paper Manufacturing, ***280***
7.6 Marketing, ***281***
7.7 Auditing, ***282***
7.8 Hospital Scheduling, ***284***
7.9 Multiperiod Production Scheduling, ***286***
7.10 Solution of Game Theory Problems, ***287***
7.11 Concluding Remarks, ***292***
7.12 Problems, ***293***
7.13 References and Bibliography, ***298***

8 Topics in Mathematical Programming 299
Part A: Basics
8.1 Duality, ***301***
8.2 Sensitivity Analysis, ***311***
8.3 Computerization, ***321***
8.4 Problems for Part A, ***325***
Part B: Extensions
8.5 Integer Programming, ***331***
8.6 The Zero-One Model, ***335***
8.7 The Branch and Bound Method, ***338***
8.8 Nonlinear Programming, ***344***
8.9 Computer Programs, ***346***
8.10 Concluding Remarks, ***346***
8.11 Problems for Part B, ***347***
8.12 Case: Hensley Valve Corp., ***349***
8.13 Glossary, ***350***
8.14 References and Bibliography, ***351***

9 Goal Programming 352
Part A: Basics
9.1 Introduction, ***354***
9.2 The Basic Idea of Goal Programming, ***356***
9.3 Concepts for Goal Programming, ***356***
9.4 The Structure of Goal Programming, ***358***
9.5 Formulation: The Birch Paper Co., ***362***
9.6 Computerized Solution to the BIP Case, ***364***

9.7 Sensitivity Analysis, ***365***
9.8 Examples of Applications, ***367***
9.9 Problems for Part A, ***376***
Part B: Extensions
9.10 Graphical Solution, ***375***
9.11 Special Situations, ***377***
9.12 Setting up Goals, ***377***
9.13 Concluding Remarks, ***378***
9.14 Problems for Part B, ***378***
9.15 Case: Cartoy International, ***379***
9.16 Glossary, ***380***
9.17 References and Bibliography, ***381***

10 Distribution Models *382*
Part A: Basics
10.1 The Transportation Problem—Characteristics and Assumptions, ***384***
10.2 The Transportation Method, ***389***
10.3 Applications, ***402***
10.4 The Assignment Problem, ***405***
10.5 Concluding Remarks, ***413***
10.6 Problems for Part A, ***415***
Part B: Extensions
10.7 The Modified Distribution Procedure (MODI), ***420***
10.8 Degeneracy, ***425***
10.9 Use of Computers, ***429***
10.10 Problems for Part B, ***430***
10.11 Case I: Northeastern Blood Bank, ***432***
Case II: Greenhill's Federal Grant, ***433***
10.12 Glossary, ***434***
10.13 References and Bibliography, ***434***

11 Network Models *435*
Part A: Basics
11.1 Introduction to PERT and CPM, ***437***
11.2 Formulation: The Basic Inputs to PERT/CPM, ***442***
11.3 Solving PERT and CPM, ***443***
11.4 Event Analysis (Step 5), ***447***
11.5 Activity Analysis (Step 6), ***453***
11.6 Analysis and Application, ***458***
11.7 Problems for Part A, ***463***
Part B: Extensions
11.8 Estimate of Activity Time in PERT, ***467***
11.9 Finding the Probabilities of Completion in PERT (Risk Analysis), ***468***
11.10 The Critical Path Method (CPM): Cost-Time Relationships, ***472***
11.11 Other Network Methods, ***480***

11.12 Minimal Spanning Tree, *481*
11.13 Shortest Route, *483*
11.14 Maximum Flow, *487*
11.15 Computerization, *489*
11.16 Concluding Remarks, *494*
11.17 Problems for Part B, *497*
11.18 Case: The Sharon Construction Corporation, *501*
11.19 Glossary, *502*
11.20 References and Bibliography, *503*

12 Dynamic Programming 505
Part A: Basics
12.1 The Nature of Dynamic Programming, *507*
12.2 The Stagecoach Problem, *509*
12.3 Terminology and Structure, *513*
12.4 Allocation Processes, *517*
12.5 Concluding Remarks, *521*
12.6 Problems for Part A, *522*
Part B: Extensions
12.7 Probabilistic Problems, *525*
12.8 Mathematical Presentation and Optimization Techniques, *528*
12.9 The Knapsack Problem, *529*
12.10 Computerization, *534*
12.11 Problems for Part B, *534*
12.12 Case: The Personnel Director, *535*
12.13 Glossary, *535*
12.14 References and Bibliography, *536*

13 Markov Analysis 537
Part A: Basics
13.1 Markov Systems, *540*
13.2 Input Data: Transition Probabilities and Initial Conditions, *543*
13.3 State Probabilities, *545*
13.4 Steady State (Equilibrium), *552*
13.5 Managerial Applications, *556*
13.6 Concluding Remarks, *558*
13.7 Problems for Part A, *559*
Part B: Extensions
13.8 Absorbing States, *563*
13.9 Managerial Application, *566*
13.10 Use of Computers, *567*
13.11 Problems for Part B, *571*
13.12 Case: Springfield General Hospital, *572*
13.13 Glossary, *573*
13.14 References and Bibliography, *573*

14 Inventory Models *574*
Part A: Basics
14.1 Production/Inventory Systems, ***576***
14.2 The Structure of the Inventory System, ***579***
14.3 Inventory Costs, ***582***
14.4 The Economic Order Quantity Model, ***584***
14.5 Application of the EOQ Model, ***592***
14.6 Discussion of the EOQ Assumptions, ***595***
14.7 Inventory Systems, ***597***
14.8 Concluding Remarks, ***600***
14.9 Problems for Part A, ***601***
Part B: Extensions
14.10 Quantity Discounts, ***603***
14.11 Production Runs: Economic Lot Size (ELS), ***607***
14.12 Single-Period Inventories, ***612***
14.13 Material Requirements Planning (MRP), ***616***
14.14 Planned Shortages, ***621***
14.15 Safety Stocks and Service Levels, ***624***
14.16 Use of Computers, ***631***
14.17 Concluding Remarks, ***634***
14.18 Problems for Part B, ***634***
14.19 Case I: Visutech, ***637***
Case II: Emco Corporation, ***638***
14.20 Glossary, ***641***
14.21 References and Bibliography, ***642***

15 Waiting Lines *644*
Part A: Basics
15.1 The Queuing Situation, ***646***
15.2 The Managerial Problem, ***648***
15.3 The Methodology of Queuing Analysis, ***651***
15.4 The Arrival Process, ***652***
15.5 The Service Process, ***655***
15.6 The Waiting Line, ***657***
15.7 Queuing Models and Solution Approaches, ***658***
15.8 The Basic Poisson-Exponential Model ($M/M/1$ $FCFS/\infty/\infty$), ***661***
15.9 Cost Analysis of Queuing Systems, ***664***
15.10 Managerial Applications of Poisson-Exponential Queuing Systems, ***665***
15.11 Concluding Remarks, ***669***
15.12 Problems for Part A, ***671***
Part B: Extensions
15.13 Multifacility Queuing Systems ($M/M/K$ $FCFS/\infty/\infty$), ***675***
15.14 Other Queuing Situations, ***682***
15.15 Serial Queues, ***683***
15.16 Use of Computers, ***685***
15.17 Problems for Part B, ***688***

15.18 Case I: Newtown Maintenance Division, ***691***
Case II: A Queuing Case Study of Drive-In Banking, ***691***
15.19 Glossary, ***695***
15.20 References and Bibliography, ***696***

16 Simulation *697*
Part A: Basics
16.1 The General Nature of Simulation, ***699***
16.2 The Methodology of Simulation, ***703***
16.3 Types of Simulation, ***704***
16.4 The Monte Carlo Methodology, ***705***
16.5 Time Independent, Discrete Simulation, ***710***
16.6 Time Dependent, Discrete Simulation, ***718***
16.7 Risk Analysis, ***721***
16.8 The Role of Computers in Simulation, ***723***
16.9 Issues in Simulation, ***724***
16.10 Problems for Part A, ***726***
Part B: Extensions
16.11 Complex Queuing Situations, ***730***
16.12 Simulation with Continuous Probability Distributions, ***734***
16.13 Visual Interactive Simulation, ***737***
16.14 Heuristic Programming, ***742***
16.15 Business Games, ***745***
16.16 Corporate and Financial Planning Models, ***749***
16.17 System Dynamics, ***752***
16.18 Other Simulation Models, ***754***
16.19 Concluding Remarks, ***757***
16.20 Problems for Part B, ***757***
16.21 Case: Express A.G., ***763***
16.22 Glossary, ***764***
16.23 References and Bibliography, ***765***

PART III
APPLICATIONS *767*

A Preview to Chapters 17 and 18 *769*

17 Decision Support Systems *770*
17.1 Introduction and Definitions, ***772***
17.2 A Framework for Decision Support, ***772***
17.3 DSS Characteristics and Benefits, ***774***
17.4 The Evolution of Decision Support Systems, ***777***
17.5 The Structure of Decision Support Systems, ***777***
17.6 The Capabilities of DSS, ***781***
17.7 Construction Considerations, ***783***

17.8 A Group Decision Support System (GDSS), *786*
17.9 Examples of Applications, *787*
17.10 Example of a DSS Generator: IFPS, *790*
17.11 Concluding Remarks, *793*
17.12 Review Questions, *793*
17.13 Glossary, *794*
17.14 References and Bibliography, *794*

18 **Expert Systems** *795*
18.1 Introduction and Basic Concepts, *797*
18.2 The Structure of Expert Systems, *801*
18.3 How an Expert System Works, *803*
18.4 The Benefits of Expert Systems, *804*
18.5 Limitations of Expert Systems, *806*
18.6 Expert Systems and Management Science, *806*
18.7 Expert Systems Applications XCON, *810*
18.8 Concluding Remarks, *813*
18.9 Review Questions, *814*
18.10 Glossary, *814*
18.11 References and Bibliography, *815*

19 **Implementation** *817*
19.1 What Is Implementation? *818*
19.2 Project Viability, *822*
19.3 Other Project Particulars, *823*
19.4 Organizational Factors, *824*
19.5 Operational Factors, *826*
19.6 Behavioral Factors, *829*
19.7 Implementation Failure: A Case Study, *836*
19.8 Concluding Remarks, *837*
19.9 Review Questions, *837*
19.10 Case: Sunrise Electronics, *838*
19.11 Glossary, *839*
19.12 References and Bibliography, *840*

20 **A Case Application** *842*
20.1 Brunswick Corporation, *843*
20.2 Analysis, *848*
20.3 Solution by Incremental Analysis, *852*
20.4 Solution by Decision Tree, *855*
20.5 Solution by Simulation, *857*
20.6 Review Questions, *861*
20.7 References and Bibliography, *862*

21 **The Future of Management Science** *863*
21.1 The Past: Requirements for Growth, *865*
21.2 The Present: Extensions of MS, *866*

21.3 The Future: Effectiveness and Computerized Management Support Systems, *866*
21.4 Research Opportunities, *869*
21.5 Concluding Remarks, *870*
21.6 References and Bibliography, *871*

Appendix A: Mathematics *873*

Appendix B: Statistics *888*

Appendix C: Tables *901*

Appendix D: Answers to Even-Numbered Problems *904*

Index *911*

PART I

In the initial part of the text our aim is to provide a foundation on which to develop the topics in the rest of the book. We do this in two stages.

- Chapter 1 introduces the topic of management science and its wide applicability to decision making. The chapter concludes with an overview of the plan of the text.
- Chapter 2 is directed toward the management science process itself. The use of models to solve managerial problems is the essence of this approach and thus the focus of the chapter. The chapter then relates the management science tools to prototypal managerial problems and discusses their applicability.

FOUNDATIONS

1 Introduction

1.1 What's it all about?
1.2 Definitions of management science.
1.3 The characteristics of management science.
1.4 The tools of management science.
1.5 Cutler-Hammer's patent decision.
1.6 Historical development.
1.7 Extent of use and limitations.
1.8 Plan of the book.
1.9 Review questions.
1.10 Glossary.
1.11 References and bibliography.
1.12 Appendix: Using the computer.

This book is about the application of the scientific approach to an area basic to all managers and administrators: decision making. Management science can be a tremendous aid to the manager faced with decisions. It can sort out the complex array of data, show what is relevant and what is not, focus on the lack of certain crucial information, provide an objective basis of choosing the best (or a good enough) solution, and even quantify the manager's feelings and preferences for solution outcomes. In short, it can be used to make better decisions and improve the management of organizations.

This chapter begins with a definition of management science, and then presents its major characteristics and a description of its historical development. The chapter ends with a discussion of the applicability and limitations of management science.

LEARNING OBJECTIVES

The student should be able to:

a. Relate management to decision making and productivity.
b. Describe the complexity of today's managerial decisions.
c. Describe the inadequacy of traditional management tools.
d. Define and explain the term *management science.*
e. Identify the characteristics of management science.
f. Explain the development of management science tools and their relationship to managerial problems.
g. Trace the historical development of the field.
h. Describe the applicability and use of management science in a diversity of fields.
i. Name and discuss the major limitations of management science.

1.1 WHAT'S IT ALL ABOUT?

Before we delve into management science—what it is, what it can be used for, and what it cannot be used for—let us briefly look at the term *management.* **Management** is a *process* used to achieve certain *goals* through the utilization of *resources* (people, money, energy, materials, space, time). The resources are considered the inputs, and the attainment of the goals the output of the process. The degree of success of the manager's job is often measured by the ratio between the outputs and inputs. This ratio is an indication of the organization's **productivity.**

Productivity—a measure of success

Productivity is a major concern for any organization since it determines the well-being of the organization and its participants. Productivity is also one of the most important issues at the national level. National productivity is the sum of the productivities of all organizations and individuals, and it determines the standard of living, the employment rate, and the economic well-being of the country.

The level of productivity, or the success of management, depends on the execution of certain *managerial functions* such as planning, organizing, directing, and controlling. To carry out these functions, managers engage in a continuous process of making decisions. Therefore, *management* is considered by many as equivalent to *decision making.*

Decision making—art or science?

For years, managers have considered decision making to be a pure art—a talent acquired over a long period of time through experience (learning by "trial and error"). It has been considered an art because a variety of individual styles can be used in approaching and successfully solving the same type of managerial problems in actual business practice. These styles are often based on creativity, judgment, intuition, and experience rather than on the systematic analytical approach.

However, the environment in which management must operate is changing. Man has long since landed on the moon, and technological advancement dictates the pace of our life. Such advances in technology cannot possibly be made or sustained without concurrent advances in the systems of management. Such unusual strides have been possible only because the art of management has increasingly been supplemented by science.

The importance of a single decision

If one examines the reasons for bankruptcies of small and even large corporations, one frequently finds that the bankruptcy is the result of a single wrong decision. For example, many corporations expanded too fast during the economic boom of the early 1970s and then collapsed during the mid-70s recession. A good example was the giant W. C. Grant discount chain. Lack of cash flow led to its bankruptcy. Similarly, excess inventories caused huge losses and bankruptcies for several agricultural machinery manufacturers, as in the case of International Harvester.

Greater complexity and cost of errors

Business and its environment are more complex today than ever before, and the trend toward increasing complexity is continuing. Figure 1.1 shows the changes in the major factors (on the left) that have an impact on managerial decision making. The results (on the right) indicate that making decisions today is much more complicated than in the past for three reasons. First, the number of alternatives is usually much larger. Second, the consequences of the decisions are more difficult to predict due to increased uncertainty. Finally, the cost of making errors has become larger and larger, mainly due to the size of operations, automation, and a resulting chain-reaction situation in which the impact of an error may be felt in many places due to complex interrelationships.

FIGURE 1.1
Factors affecting decision making

Factor	*Trend*	*Results*
Technology	Increasing →	More alternatives to choose from
Information/computers	Increasing →	
Organizational size	Increasing →	Larger cost of making errors
Structural complexity	Increasing →	
Competition	Increasing ↗	
International stability	Decreasing →	More uncertainty regarding the future
Consumerism	Increasing →	
Government intervention	Increasing →	

To illustrate how critical the impact of a single error can be, consider the following example.

Polaroid's SX-70

In the early 70s, the management of Polaroid decided to invest millions of dollars in developing a new camera, SX-70. The justification for the huge investment was the anticipation of large profits from the sale of *film* for the camera. On July 2, 1975, the Dow Jones Industrial Average plunged almost 16 points and closed at a low for the year of 790. The major contributor to the fall was the drop in Polaroid, a once highly priced glamour issue, that fell 11⅜ points, a decline of 32 percent, in a single day! The drop was attributed to an announcement that the sales of SX-70 film were only one third of the company's projections. The plunge reduced the value of Polariod shares by more than $360 million overnight! The impact was so significant that even though Polaroid did not file for bankruptcy, its earnings declined for several years.

As a result of these trends and changes it is very difficult to rely on a trial-and-error approach to management, especially in decisions involving the factors shown in Figure 1.1. Managers must become more sophisticated—they must learn to utilize new tools and techniques that are being developed in their field. No one can imagine a successful physician using the medicines and equipment of the turn of the century. Yet, in management, one can find executives using management tools of that time.

Programmed decision making

The management science approach adopts the view that a substantial portion of decision making consists of (1) analyzing phenomena that can be measured, (2) determining relationships that can be represented quantitatively, and (3) determining cause-and-effect relationships, whose internal consistency can be tested experimentally. Thus, the objective of this approach is to bring as many management phenomena as possible into the domain of standardized or "programmed" decisions where solution techniques are already available. **Programmed decisions** then can be solved quickly with the aid of scientific tools and computers so that the manager can devote a larger portion of time to the qualitative aspects of the problems as well as to more complex decisions.

1.2 DEFINITIONS OF MANAGEMENT SCIENCE

Management science has had almost as many definitions as it has had practitioners. Indeed, it is practically an annual occurrence for the retiring presidents of the professional societies to give their personal definition in presidential addresses.

Two classical definitions, for example, are:

1. Operations research [management science] is the application of scientific methods, techniques, and tools to problems involving the operations of systems so as to provide those in control of the operations with optimum solutions to the problems.[1]
2. "[T]he application of the scientific method to the study of the operations of large, complex organizations or activities."[2]

In this text, **management science** is defined as: *The application of the scientific method to the analysis and solution of managerial decision problems.* Note that **operations research** is another term used almost inter-

[1] Churchman, Ackoff, and Arnoff ([2], page 9). (The number in the brackets refers to the listing in the References and Bibliography section at the end of each chapter.)

[2] The Committee on Operations Research of the National Research Council in Great Britain.

changeably with management science. Other names often used to connote more or less the same general area are operational research, operations analysis, quantitative analysis, quantitative methods, systems analysis, decision analysis, and decision science. The reason for so many names (most of which have their own professional societies) is that the entire field is relatively new and there is no general agreement yet on what body of knowledge it includes.

Other names

In addition to the formal definition of management science, and sometimes instead of such a definition, it is customary to list the special characteristics of the field.

1.3 THE CHARACTERISTICS OF MANAGEMENT SCIENCE

The major characteristics of management science are:

1. A primary focus on managerial decision making.
2. The application of the scientific approach to decision making.
3. The examination of the decision situation from a broad perspective; that is, the application of a *systems approach.*
4. The use of methods and knowledge from several disciplines.
5. A reliance on formal mathematical models.
6. The extensive use of electronic *computers.*

These characteristics will be discussed in detail in Chapter 2.

1.4 THE TOOLS OF MANAGEMENT SCIENCE

The characteristics of management science established the foundation on which the **tools** and **techniques** developed. The role of the management scientist can be viewed as that of a consultant, or a physician, who is called on to diagnose a problem, propose a treatment, and sometimes to perform the treatment. In such a capacity, the management scientist works with tools that enable him or her to analyze a problem (diagnosis), to predict the future development of the problem (prognosis), and to suggest the best treatment.

To understand how the management scientist works, let us compare him or her with a physician. When a patient comes to a doctor, the doctor performs a diagnosis. In most cases, the diagnosis will point to a common disease such as the flu. For such cases, the doctor will prescribe standard treatment (aspirin and rest). For more complicated diseases, the doctor will refer the patient to a specialist, who will conduct more tests and may prescribe a *special* treatment, if necessary.

A similar situation exists in management. Organizational problems are analogous to diseases. Some of these problems are fairly standard, for

Standard tools for recurring decision situations

example, the misallocation of scarce resources or the improper level of inventories. These *standard problems* can be treated with *standard* tools if the manager is informed and recognizes them. For certain types of allocation problems, a tool named linear programming was developed. For more complex allocation problems, the tools of integer programming and dynamic programming were developed. (The entire spectrum of tools is presented in Chapter 2 and is discussed in detail in Part II of this text.)

Borrowed tools

In addition to such tools, management scientists also use standard tools borrowed from other disciplines. For example, statistical tools are used in determining significant differences between proposed solutions, and forecasting models are used in predicting the consequences of proposed treatments. Similarly, econometric, financial, marketing, and organizational behavior models are frequently incorporated into the analysis. Finally, for complex problems, the management scientist may build special tools. Clearly, a manager must be aware of such tools and know when to call a specialist in. The application of one of these tools is illustrated in the next section.

Special tools for unique problems

1.5 CUTLER–HAMMER'S PATENT DECISION[3]

In 1974, Cutler-Hammer, Inc., was offered the opportunity of purchasing the defense market rights to a patent for a new type of flight safety system. The inventor wanted a quick response so he could offer the rights to other firms should Cutler-Hammer decline.

However, the market for the system was highly uncertain and Cutler-Hammer needed a way to factor this uncertainty into their decision. They decided to try a model called a "decision tree." A team of Cutler-Hammer and outside analysts spent two weeks developing the decision tree and augmenting the simplified model with three more complex subsidiary models.

The decision tree illustrated three choices open to Cutler-Hammer: accept the offer, decline the offer, or wait and seek a sublicense should the system be successful. If the option were accepted, there was, the team calculated, a 71 percent chance of obtaining a license agreement. If such an agreement could not be obtained, the firm stood to lose $125,000. But if the license was obtained, the chances of winning an initial defense contract were 15 percent. If the contract could not be won, the firm would lose $700,000. And if the first defense contract could be won, the chances of obtaining a follow-on contract worth $10.5 million were 25 percent. If the second contract could not be obtained, then at least Cutler-Hammer could obtain a sublicense, worth $3.5 million.

The purpose of the subsidiary models was to generate the values and their timing described above. One model determined yearly earnings

[3] Condensed from Ulvila and Brown ([14], pages 131–33).

and their present values. The second one considered timing, likely legislative actions that could affect the system, the competitive strength of competing systems, and the likelihood of a plane crash in the near future, to assess the probability of winning a defense contract. The third model considered the uncertainty in the number of units sold, their price, and the profit margin, to assess the probability distributions of contract earnings.

The results of the decision tree analysis, including the three subsidiary models, were shown, along with the decision tree, to top management in the form of risk profiles. In sum, if the option offer were accepted, there was a 60 percent chance of losing about $700,000, a 29 percent chance of losing about $125,000, and an 11 percent chance of gaining a return of about $5.25 million. The expected value of all these was about $100,000.

But if the wait-and-see approach were taken, there was a 94 percent chance of no gain or loss and a 6 percent chance of making about $830,000. The expected value here was about $50,000. Based on the results provided by these models, Cutler-Hammer management unanimously decided to adopt the wait-and-see approach instead of the high-risk option.

This application illustrates the importance of management science and the broad range of applicability of its tools. In the next section we describe the history and beginnings of management science.

1.6 HISTORICAL DEVELOPMENT

It is difficult to mark the "beginning" of management science. The scientific approach to management can be traced back to the era of the Industrial Revolution and even to much earlier periods. In the late 19th century, Frederick W. Taylor [12] formalized his **scientific management** approach, which marked the beginning of industrial engineering. There is evidence of the use of mathematical models at the turn of the century (e.g., Erlang's work on waiting line problems, Edison's work on war games, and the development of the inventory management Economic Order Quantity formula by Harris).

F. W. Taylor's scientific management

The use of math models

It was not until World War II that management science began to establish itself as a separate discipline, both in England (termed *operational research*) and in the United States (termed *operations research*). In order to maximize their war effort, the British government organized teams of scientific and engineering personnel to assist field commanders in solving perplexing strategic and tactical problems. They found that technically trained experts could solve problems outside of their normal professional competency. They asked biologists to examine problems in electronics, physicists to think in terms of the movement of people rather than the movement of molecules, mathematicians to apply probability theory to improve soldiers' chances of survival, and chemists to study equilibria in systems other than chemical. Teams of specialists studied problems ranging from the evaluation of cost and effectiveness of complete military systems

Cross-fertilization in science

(such as the defense system of a country) to the best allocation of depth charges in antisubmarine warfare.

The success of the British operational research teams led the United States to institute a similar effort in 1942 (small-scale projects dated back to 1937). The initial project involved the deployment of merchant marine convoys to minimize losses from enemy submarines.

From wartime use to industry

Following the war, operations research extended into industry—first into the process-type industries such as oil refineries, and steel and paper mills. These industries are characterized by large volumes of relatively few products. The savings were high since even a penny a unit on a large volume could total up to millions of dollars. In addition, a high capital-to-worker ratio in these automated industries meant relatively fewer employees, whose duties were mainly in supervision, control, and maintenance. Therefore, the employees showed little resistance to change.

The 40-year period after World War II saw a dramatic development and refinement of techniques, with a corresponding expansion to almost all industries and services. Furthermore, the complexity of managerial problems attacked by management science increased significantly, especially with the introduction of the technique of simulation and large, efficient computing systems. As the field grew, the name management science increased in popularity.

Trend toward public sector decision making

In the 1970s the use of management science expanded into large social and urban systems such as criminal justice, health care, and education. Then the 1980s introduced a new dimension into management science—its integration with management information systems. This integration is taking place in a rapidly developing area termed *decision support systems* (DSS). This topic is discussed in Chapter 17 of this book. Finally, recent developments in the area of artificial intelligence are providing the management scientist with additional tools, most notably expert systems (Chapter 18).

All of this development is evident in the management science departments that emerged at many universities, several of which grant a doctoral degree in the field. In the United States alone there are about 10,000 members in the related professional societies. About 15 English-language periodicals deal with theories and applications of management science.

1.7 EXTENT OF USE AND LIMITATIONS

While relatively few studies have been published on the extent and success of using management science, the research that has been published reveals impressive results. A detailed survey reported by the American Management Association [1] gives some indication of both the possible savings and the difficulties of measuring them. For example, of the 324 responding companies using management science, 130 reported "considerable improvement" and "appreciable net savings." Actual figures of $100,000

Dollar and other benefits surveyed

or more were reported by 17 companies, anticipated savings of $300,000 or more by 18 companies. Many indicated that directly measurable dollar savings were only a *small part* of the benefit obtained. Only two of the 324 companies indicated an intention to decrease management science activities, and not one indicated plans to discontinue using them.

Other surveys [4, 9, 10, 13], while failing to give savings figures, indicated that virtually all practitioners were satisfied with management science and planned to continue its use. Evidence of its benefits may also be seen in the constantly increasing rate of application of management science in industrial firms; some of the more common areas of application are shown in Table 1.1. One of these surveys ([13]) revealed that 44 percent of the largest U.S. industrial and service corporations have a management science unit at their corporate headquarters.[4]

TABLE 1.1
A comparative table of areas of application of management science techniques

	Survey			
Area of application	*AMA* [*1*] *1958* *n* = *631 firms* *(percent)*	*Hovey and Wagner* [7] *1958* *n* = *90 firms* *(percent)*	*Schumacher and Smith* [*10*] *1965* *n* = *65 firms* *(percent)*	*Gaither* [4] *1975* *n* = *275 firms* *(percent)*
Production	24	32	68	49
Long-range planning	23	39	55	No data
Advertising, sales, and marketing	25	14	20	16
Inventory	21	31	68	31
Transportation	15	18	41	8
Top management	15	No data	No data	No data
Research	14	No data	No data	No data
Finance	13	No data	No data	No data
Accounting	11	11	13	No data
Purchasing	8	No data	No data	No data
Personnel	8	No data	No data	No data
Quality control	No data	22	38	20
Maintenance	No data	11	24	19
Plant location	No data	10	24	11
Equipment replacement	No data	10	20	12
Packaging	No data	9	5	No data
Capital budgeting	No data	7	29	20
Percent of companies using management science	No data	42.6	61.5	48.4

Although most surveys indicated satisfaction with the techniques, there was some dissatisfaction with the wide gap that exists between theory

[4] As determined by a sample taken from *Fortune* magazine's list of the 500 largest corporations.

and application in management science (e.g., see Grayson [5]). Chapter 19 of this text deals with some of the reasons for the unsuccessful use of management science.

Management science, like any other management tool, is no substitute for good management. The manager must still decide what to investigate, what to do about the factors that cannot be quantified, and how to interpret the results of scientific analysis. Management science requires capable, well-qualified, and experienced personnel. It also frequently consumes a great deal of time and may become very costly. Attempting shortcuts by superficially examining the problems, or using inappropriate models or inaccurate data, may produce results that, if applied, will be far more costly than simply using the dictates of subjective judgment.

Only a costly tool?

The results of management science cannot be guaranteed; the potential benefits, however, may be enormous and well worth the time, effort, and expense required. The main arguments for and against its use are:

Management science—pro and con

For

1. Systematic and logical approach to decision making.
2. Helps communication within the organization through consultation with experts in various areas.
3. Permits a thorough analysis of a large number of alternative options.
4. Enables evaluation of situations involving uncertainty.
5. Allows decision maker to judge how much information to gather in a given problem.
6. Increases the effectiveness of the decision.
7. Enables quick identification of the best available solution.
8. Allows quick and inexpensive examination of a large (sometimes infinite) number of alternatives.
9. Enables experimentation with models, thus eliminating the cost of making errors while experimenting with reality.

Against

1. Time-consuming.
2. Lack of acceptance by decision makers.
3. Assessments of uncertainties are difficult to obtain.
4. Evaluates the decision in terms of a sometimes oversimplified model of reality.
5. Can be expensive to undertake, relative to the size of the problem.
6. Studies may be shelved for various reasons (see Chapter 19), resulting in an unproductive expense.

One question that managers frequently ask in discussions after lectures on management science is "Where have these techniques been applied consistently?" The list of applications is growing continuously. Examples of typical managerial problems where management science techniques have been applied are:

Areas of application

- Inventory control.
- Facility design.
- Product-mix determination.
- Portfolio analysis (of securities).
- Scheduling and sequencing.
- Merger-growth analysis.
- Transportation planning.
- Design of information systems.
- Allocation of scarce resources.
- Investment decisions (new plants and the like).
- Project management—planning and control.
- New product decisions.
- Sales force decisions.
- Market research decisions.
- Research and development decisions.
- Oil and gas exploration decisions.
- Pricing decisions.
- Competitive bidding decisions.
- Quality control decisions.
- Machine setup problems in production.
- Distribution decisions.
- Manpower planning and control decisions.
- Credit policy analysis.
- Research and development effectiveness.

Examples of such applications will be seen in the examples and problems throughout the chapters of this book.

1.8 PLAN OF THE BOOK

The text is divided into three parts (Figure 1.2): "Foundations," "The Tools," and "Applications."

Part I: Foundations

The *foundations* part consists of two chapters. Here in Chapter 1, the characteristics, the basic philosophy, and the history of management science have been presented. Chapter 2 provides the theoretical background of managerial decision making and the methodology of management science.

Part II: The tools

Part II presents the major (and some supporting) management science and statistical tools. In Chapters 3 and 4, the quantitative approach to decision making is considered, followed by Chapter 5 on forecasting, laying the basis for the management science tools and techniques presented in Chapters 6–16.

FIGURE 1.2
Organization of the book

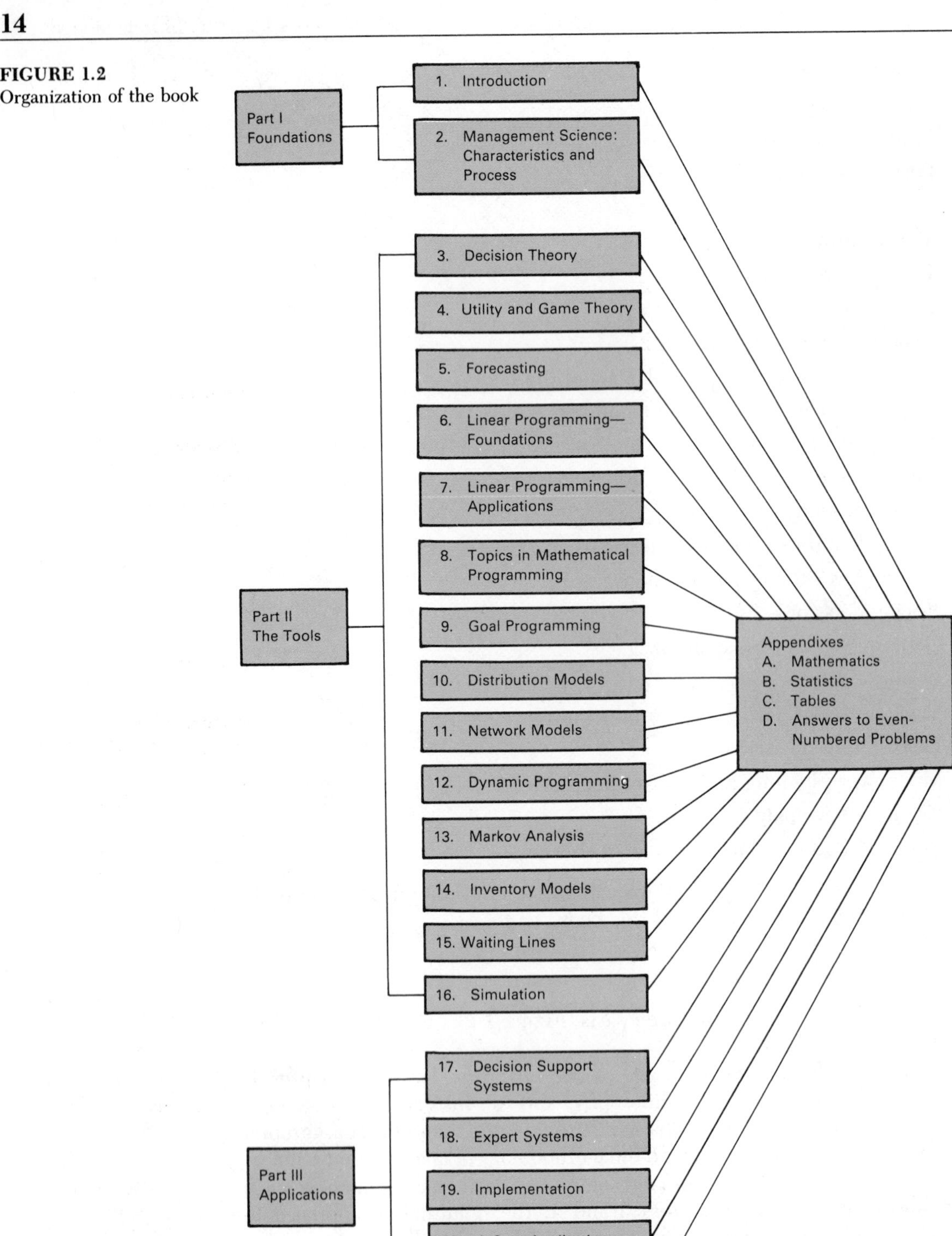

Part III: Applications

The last part of the book has been reserved for a discussion of the *application* of management science. Chapters 17 and 18 introduce the concepts of decision support and expert systems and Chapter 19 deals with the problems of implementation, in general and for a particular project. A detailed case study is then presented in Chapter 20 and addressed with three different management science tools. The text concludes with a general assessment of the future of management science in Chapter 21.

1.9 REVIEW QUESTIONS

1. Give an example that will illustrate the equivalence of management and decision making.
2. Explain why the management style of "trial and error" is becoming less and less attractive.
3. Explain why decision making today is more complex than 30 years ago.
4. Examine the definitions of management science. Can you give a personal example of a management science situation that will fit these definitions?
5. Explain how the standard tools of management science were developed.
6. Discuss the major advantages of management science.
7. Discuss the major disadvantages.
8. List some managerial problems that would seem amenable to management science techniques. List some that would *not*.

1.10 GLOSSARY

Management Mobilization of resources in order to attain the organization's goals.

Management science The application of the scientific approach to the analysis and solution of managerial decision problems.

Operations research Basically the same as management science (used interchangeably in this text).

Programmed decisions Standard or repetitive decision situations for which solution techniques are already available.

Productivity Ratio of outputs (results) to inputs (resources).

Techniques (tools) of management science Mathematical models specially developed to deal with standard managerial problems.

Scientific management A school of management thought headed by F. W. Taylor that focused on economic efficiency as the productive core of the organization.

1.11 REFERENCES AND BIBLIOGRAPHY

1. AMA Management Report No. 10. *Operations Research Considered*. New York: AMA, 1958.
2. Churchman, C. W.; R. L. Ackoff; and E. L. Arnoff. *Introduction to Operations Research*. New York: John Wiley & Sons, 1957.
3. Forgionne, G. A. "Corporate Management Science Activities." *Interfaces* 3 (June 1983), pp. 20–28.
4. Gaither, N. "The Adoption of Operations Research Techniques by Manufacturing Organizations." *Decision Sciences* 6 (1975), pp. 797–813.
5. Grayson, C. J., Jr. "Management Science and Business Practice," *Harvard Business Review* 51 (1973), pp. 41–48.
6. Hillier, F. S., and G. J. Lieberman. *Introduction to Operations Research*. 4th ed. San Francisco: Holden-Day, 1986.
7. Hovey, R. W., and W. H. Wagner. "A Sample Survey of Industrial Operations-Research Activities." *Operations Research* 6 (1958), pp. 878–81.
8. Larson, R. C., and A. R. Odoni. *Urban Operations*

Research, Englewood Cliffs, N.J.: Prentice-Hall, 1981.

9. Ledbetter, W., and J. Cox. "Are OR Techniques Being Used?" *Industrial Engineering,* September 1977, pp. 19–21.
10. Schumacher, C. D., and B. E. Smith. "A Sample Survey of Industrial Operations-Research Activities II." *Operations Research* 13 (1965), pp. 1023–27.
11. Simon, H. *The New Science of Management Decisions.* Rev. ed. Englewood Cliffs, N.J.: Prentice-Hall, 1977.
12. Taylor, F. W. *The Principles of Scientific Management.* New York: W. W. Norton, 1967.
13. Turban, E. "A Sample Survey of Operations Research Activities at the Corporate Level." *Operations Research* 20 (1972), pp. 708–21.
14. Ulvila, J. W., and R. V. Brown. "Decision Analysis Comes of Age." *Harvard Business Review,* September–October 1982, pp. 131–33.

1.12 APPENDIX: USING THE COMPUTER

In this text you will learn a lot about mathematical models, their formulation, and their solution. The various examples, homework problems, and even most of the cases have purposely been limited in size so that they are manageable for hand calculation. Most real-life problems, however, are much larger, so they require a substantially greater computational effort.

This problem is easily overcome by the use of the digital computer. The routine nature of the computational algorithms has led to computer programs that provide the results quickly and accurately, thereby allowing the user to devote more time to problem formulation and interpretation of the results. The user need not be an expert in computer operation or programming in order to solve most of the models in this book. However, users must understand the theory of the various algorithms and models so they can set up the problem properly and interpret the results supplied by the computer. The purpose of this appendix is to give a general overview regarding the use of computers in management science. Specific examples will be given in most of the forthcoming chapters.

Computer hardware and software

You will probably be working with one or more of the following types of computers someday:

a. Microcomputer ("personal" computer).
b. Mainframe (midsize or large) computer operating in an on-line or time-sharing mode.

a. Microcomputers

There have been dozens of microcomputers on the market starting with the Timex-Sinclair that sold for less than $100 and ending with complete systems such as IBM Personal Computers, Texas Instruments, Business Pro, and Apple MacIntosh that may cost, with their support systems, thousands of dollars. The microcomputer is a completely freestanding computer. When you use it, it is all yours; no sharing, no account number, no code to enter. Most software for micros is available on diskettes as "canned" or preprogrammed packages. Be sure that the diskette will fit the computer you will be using. There are dozens of such packages on the market. Your instructor has a list of several in the *Instructor's Manual.*

Once you have a diskette, you simply insert it in the disk drive of your machine. Microcomputers have a very simple start-up procedure (called booting or cold start). In many cases, all you have to do is turn on the computer. Since most diskettes include several programs, you will see a list of these programs (called a menu) when the program first starts. Using a code, you select the desired model (program) from the diskette, and it is loaded into the computer; you are then ready to enter the input data.

During the loading of the program, as well as during the data entry, you will conduct a "dialogue" with the computer. This is usually done through a series of questions asked by the computer and answers given by you. Many diskettes include most of the instructions necessary to input data; others may require a guide.

The form of the input data will differ, depending on the software package and the computer used. Usually they are very simple. The data for each program are input interactively (in dialogue with the computer). Sometimes input is done through a data statement (usually only on a mainframe). This is faster because you do not have to wait for the computer to tell you what to do. However, it is less convenient than the dialogue-interactive mode.

There are many simple rules for entering data (such as press "return" every time you type something). Such rules are available in your computer guide and the supporting software documentation.

b. On-line, time-shared mainframes

Mainframe computers are typically used on a time-sharing, interactive basis. Many terminals are connected and available in multiple locations. It is also possible to connect to such systems from a remote location via a telephone line (if a terminal and a modem are available).

In a time-sharing mode you must first learn how to access the computer and then the specific program you want. All communication is done directly with the computer, in a similar fashion as on the micro. The difference is that (1) the program is not on a diskette but is in the "library" or storage of the large computer and (2) you must usually pay for the service.

The initial access (usually called log-on) involves telling the computer your identification, a password, and the account to be charged. Sometimes you must enter additional information also, such as the number of the terminal from which you are communicating. Then you must usually tell the computer the name of the computer language (e.g., BASIC, APL) in which the program is written and the name of the program you desire (e.g., LINPRO for linear programming). Once the program is loaded you proceed in a similar manner as on the micro. The specifics of data entry depend on the software and hardware involved.

Output and interpretation

The output will differ from package to package. Examples of outputs and their interpretation are given in the corresponding chapters of this book.

The MSS(Nelson) package

The teaching and learning package for this edition of *Fundamentals of Management Science* includes a computer package on two diskettes, authored by T. Nelson. The package is called *The Management Science System* (MSS), and is published by BPI/Irwin, Homewood, Illinois (1988). The printouts in the chapters of this text are based on this package.

2

2.1 Introduction.
2.2 Decision making: A primary focus.
2.3 The scientific point of view.
2.4 The systems point of view.
2.5 An interdisciplinary approach.
2.6 Models.
2.7 Use of computers.
2.8 Step 1: Definition of the problem.
2.9 Step 2: Classification of the problem.
2.10 Step 3: Modeling (formulation).
2.11 Step 4: Solving the model.
2.12 Step 5: Model validation and sensitivity analysis.
2.13 Step 6: Implementation.
2.14 Managerial problems and the tools of management science.
2.15 Concluding remarks.
2.16 Problems.
2.17 Review questions.
2.18 Glossary.
2.19 References and bibliography.

Decision making, which is of prime interest to management science, can be viewed as a systematic process. Such a perspective enables the development of quantitative tools with which managers can make better decisions.

Chapter 2 reviews the general decision-making process and then discusses the characteristics that are common to the quantitative tools. Throughout the exposition of these topics, the foundation for the entire book is laid. Therefore, the material presented here should be considered as the backbone on which management science is constructed.

Management science: Characteristics and process

LEARNING OBJECTIVES

The student should be able to:

a. Distinguish among characteristics, process, and tools of management science.
b. Relate decision making to problem solving.
c. Follow the standardized process of problem solving.
d. Explain the logic and steps of the scientific approach.
e. Define the terms *systems* and *systems point of view.*
f. Describe the concept of the systems approach; define the components and boundaries of a system.
g. Distinguish between a system's effectiveness and its efficiency.
h. Describe the role of an interdisciplinary approach.
i. Define models and the types of models and understand their role.
j. Describe the structure of a mathematical model and define dependent, independent, and controllable variables.
k. Define and distinguish between normative and descriptive models.
l. Distinguish between nonprogrammed and programmed decision situations.
m. Discuss the relationship of management science to computers.
n. Explain the logic and steps of the management science approach.
o. Distinguish between nonprogrammed and programmed problems.
p. Describe the process of modeling (or formulating) a problem.
q. Define the concept of principle of choice.
r. Define the terms: *optimization*, *suboptimization*, and *satisficing*, and describe their interrelationships.
s. List the major solution techniques: numerical, enumerative, algorithmic, and analytical.
t. Define: *feasible*, *infeasible*, and unique solutions.
u. Describe *sensitivity analysis* and its purpose.
v. Describe how decision support systems and expert systems relate to management science.
w. List the major managerial problems and relate them to the appropriate management science tool.

2.1 INTRODUCTION

In this chapter management science is going to be examined from three perspectives: its *characteristics*, its *process*, and its *tools*.

The characteristics

1. A primary interest in managerial decision making.
2. The employment of a scientific approach.
3. Problems and decisions are viewed from a systems perspective.
4. An interdisciplinary framework is attempted.
5. Mathematical models are used.
6. Computers are very frequently employed.

These characteristics, which are exhibited to a greater or lesser degree in all management science projects, are discussed in Sections 2.2–2.7.

The process

Decision making as a process

Management science employs a systematic approach to decision making. This process is discussed in Sections 2.8–2.13.

The tools

The standard tools of management science were created basically as a response to certain repetitive managerial problems. These problems, the appropriate tools, and the relationship between the problems and the tools are discussed in Section 2.14.

2.2 DECISION MAKING: A PRIMARY FOCUS

Planning: A series of decisions

A *decision* is the conclusion of a *process* by which one chooses between two or more available alternative courses of action for the purpose of attaining a goal(s). The process is called *decision making.* According to Herbert A. Simon [12], managerial decision making is synonymous with the whole process of management. To illustrate the idea, let us examine the important managerial function of *planning.* Planning involves a *series of decisions* such as: What should be done? When? How? Where? By whom? Hence, planning implies decision making. Other functions of management such as organizing and controlling can also be viewed as composed of making decisions.

Decision making and problem solving

Decision making: A systematic process

A major premise of management science is that decision making, regardless of the situation involved, can be considered as a general systematic process, consisting of the following major steps:

1. Defining the problem.
2. Searching for alternative courses of action.
3. Evaluating the alternatives.
4. Selecting one alternative.

Much confusion exists between the terms *decision making* and *problem solving.* One way to distinguish between the two is to consider the entire process (steps 1–4 above) as *problem solving;* the specific step of "selecting an alternative" (step 4 above) is the *decision* or the *solution* to the problem. Another viewpoint is that steps 1–4 constitute decision making that ends with a recommendation, while problem solving further includes the implementation of the recommendation.

However, in the interest of consistency with many other texts, the terms *decision making* and *problem solving* will be considered as equivalent in this text and will be used interchangeably.

Regardless of its name, the process is similar to the general process of scientific analysis. This similarity provides the basis for the management science approach to decision making, as will be shown in the following section.

2.3 THE SCIENTIFIC APPROACH

The scientific approach (also known as the *scientific method*) is a formalized reasoning process to which many of the scientific discoveries since Descartes must be credited.[1] It consists of the following steps:

The steps of the scientific method

Step 1. The problem for analysis is defined, and the conditions for observation are determined.
Step 2. Observations are made under different conditions to determine the behavior of the system containing the problem.
Step 3. Based on the observations, a hypothesis is conceived that describes how the factors involved are thought to interact, or what is the best solution to the problem.
Step 4. To test the hypothesis, an experiment is designed.
Step 5. The experiment is executed, and measurements are obtained and recorded.
Step 6. The results of the experiment are analyzed, and the hypothesis is either accepted or rejected.

The six steps of the scientific method can be applied to decision making. For example, the *evaluation* of alternatives is done scientifically through *experimentation*. The overall relationship of the scientific approach to the decision-making process is shown in Figure 2.1.

Using the scientific approach to solve problems

Management science employs this scientific approach for the purpose of solving problems. For each of the steps outlined in Figure 2.1, certain methodologies have been developed. These management science methodologies are centered around the idea that problems should be viewed as systems.

2.4 THE SYSTEMS POINT OF VIEW

A system defined

The third characteristic of management science is its use of systems theory and analysis. A **system** is a collection of people, resources, concepts, and procedures that is intended to perform some identifiable function, or to serve a goal.[2] A clear definition of that function is most important.

[1] Descartes was a French philosopher and mathematician of the 17th century, considered the father of modern philosophy. He emphasized the use of reason as the chief tool of inquiry.

[2] In the remainder of this book the term *system* is going to be used to describe an organization, a part of an organization, or a problem under study.

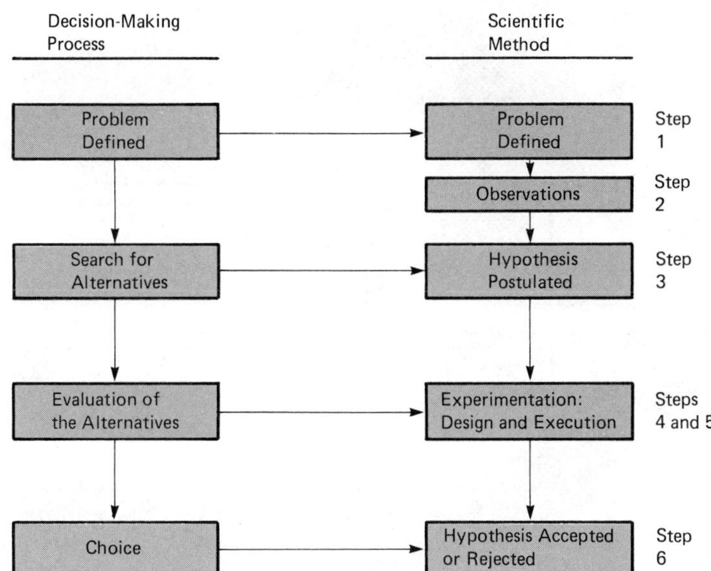

FIGURE 2.1
Relationship of the scientific approach to the decision-making process

The *purpose* of an air defense system, for instance, is to protect the targets on the ground, not just to destroy attacking aircraft or missiles.

A hierarchy of systems

The notion of *levels* (or a *hierarchy*) of systems reflects the fact that all systems are subsystems, since all are contained within some larger system. For example, a bank would include within itself *subsystems* such as: (1) the commercial loan department, (2) the consumer loan department, (3) the savings department, and (4) the operations department. Also the bank itself may be a subsidiary of a chain of banks; for example, the Bank of America, which is a subsystem of the California banking system, which is a part of the national banking system, which is a part of the national economy, and so on. The connections and interactions between the subsystems are termed interfaces.

The structure of a system

Systems as inputs, processes, and outputs

Systems are divided into three distinct parts: *inputs, processes,* and *outputs.* They are surrounded by an environment (Figure 2.2) and are frequently connected by a feedback mechanism.

Inputs Inputs include those elements that enter the system. Examples of inputs are raw materials to a chemical plant, or students to a university.

Processes All the elements necessary to *convert* the inputs into outputs are included in the processes. For example, in a chemical plant a process may include energy, operating procedures, materials handling, and the use of employees and machines. In a university a process may

FIGURE 2.2
The system and its environment

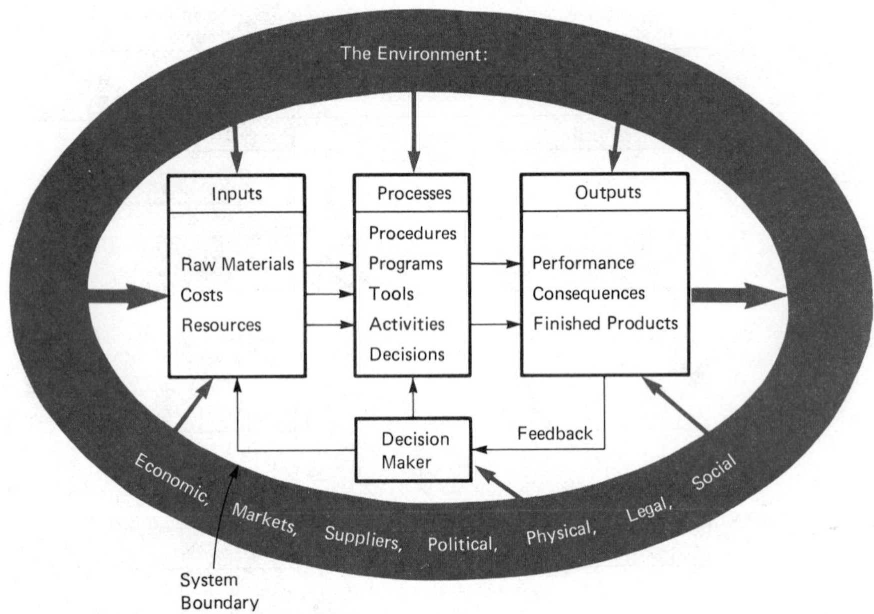

include teaching, learning, examinations, and the use of faculty, laboratories, and libraries.

Outputs Outputs describe the finished products or the consequences of being in the system. For example, fertilizers are one output of a chemical plant and graduates are the output of universities.

Feedback, the essence of control

Feedback. The flow of information to the decision maker concerning the system's output is called feedback. Based on this information, the decision maker can modify the inputs, or the processes, or both, as shown in Figure 2.2.

What is the environment?

The environment There are several elements that lie outside the system in the sense that they are not inputs, outputs, or processes. However, they have an impact on the system's performance and consequently on the attainment of its goals. These are termed the **environment.** One way to identify the elements of the environment is by answering two questions as suggested by Churchman [4]:

1. Is it possible to manipulate this element?
2. Does the element matter relative to the system's goals?

If and only if the answer to the first question is no, but to the second is yes, should the element be considered part of the environment. Environmental elements can be social, political, legal, physical, economic, and the like. For example, in a chemical plant, the suppliers, competitors, and customers are elements of the environment. In a university, the neighboring universities, the community, and the regional accrediting society represent some elements of the environment.

The boundary. A system is separated from its environment by a boundary. The system is inside the boundary while the environment lies outside. The boundaries may be physical (e.g., the system is a department in building C), or the boundary may be some nonphysical factor. For example, a system can be bounded by time, such as when we analyze an organization for a period of only one year.

When systems are being studied, it is often necessary to arbitrarily define the boundaries in order to simplify the analysis. Such boundaries are related to the concept of closed and open systems.

Closed and open systems Since every system can be considered a subsystem of another, the application of systems analysis may never end. Therefore, it is necessary, as a matter of practicality, to confine the analysis to defined boundaries. Such confinement is termed *closing* the system.

A *closed system* represents an extreme along a continuum; an *open system* is at the other extreme. The continuum reflects the degree of independence of the system. Closed systems are totally independent, while open systems are very dependent. A closed system is considered to be isolated from environmental influences. The system accepts inputs from the environment and may deliver outputs into the environment, but there are no interactions during the transformation process.

A special type of closed system is called a "black box." In a black box the inputs and outputs are well defined but the process itself is not specified. Managers frequently treat management science models and computer systems as black boxes. That is, they do not care *how* the models or the computer work; they only care about the results. They consider them as they would a telephone or an airplane; they use them but do not care how they function to achieve the effect they do.

Open systems exchange information, material, or energy with the environment. Living systems are the best examples of open systems. And most organizations are also open systems that continually adapt to changes in their environment.

Many of the management science models are confined to a closed system. Decision support systems, on the other hand, attempt to deal with systems that are relatively open. Such systems are more complex and analyzing them involves checking the impacts on the environment. In a closed system, however, it is not necessary to conduct such checks since it is assumed that the system is isolated from the environment.

The systems approach

Management science recognizes that a decision made in one segment of the organization may have a significant effect, not only on the operation of that particular segment, but on the operation of other segments as well. Therefore, when possible, the overall organizational point of view is adopted. Such an approach is termed a *systems point of view* or a *systems*

A systems viewpoint

approach. Further discussion of the systems approach is given in Section 2.11, where the concepts of optimization and suboptimization are presented.

System effectiveness and efficiency

Effectiveness is defined as the *extent to which goals are achieved.* It is thus concerned with the *results* or the *outputs* of a system. As such, effectiveness is synonymous with performance. Effectiveness is evaluated by *measures of effectiveness* (also known as measures of performance).

Effectiveness versus efficiency

Effectiveness is frequently confused with **efficiency.** Effectiveness measures the degree of a goal's attainment; efficiency measures how well resources are being utilized. Effectiveness does not necessarily imply efficiency. A system may be effective but very *inefficient* if it attains its goals but at tremendous expense. On the other hand, a system may be *efficient* (make best use of resources) but *ineffective* (not achieve its objectives).

Management science is interested in improving managerial decisions. At the extreme, an attempt is made to arrive at decisions that will result in the highest level of productivity (a situation called optimality).

Cost-benefit analysis

In many managerial systems, and especially those involving the delivery of human services (such as education, health, or recreation), the measurement of the system's effectiveness and efficiency constitutes a major problem. The reason for the difficulty is due to the existence of several, often nonquantifiable, goals, as well as the indirect costs and benefits that are involved. In recent years, several methodologies have been developed under the names of *cost effectiveness, cost-benefit analysis, benefit-cost ratios,* and *systems analysis* that attempt to measure the effectiveness and efficiency of such systems. For further discussion and references see Van Gigch [13].

The examination of a problem from a systems point of view enlarges the scope of the analysis and creates encouraging conditions for an interdisciplinary approach.

2.5 AN INTERDISCIPLINARY APPROACH

The team approach

Many managerial problems have physical, psychological, biological, mathematical, sociological, engineering, and economic aspects. By bringing together a team with a variety of backgrounds, new and advanced approaches to old problems are often obtained. The scientific mind from each discipline attempts to extract the essence of the problem and relate it structurally to other similar problems encountered in one's own particular field. Having drawn some analogies, the researcher can then determine if the problem under study is amenable to solution methods traditionally successful in his or her field. When scientists from several disciplines do this collectively, the pool of possible approaches is large enough to reinforce individual disciplines.

Therefore, many management science problems are attacked by teams (the average size is three persons). A team approach, however, has some potential dangers. Working as a committee, the team approach may suffer from the potential deficiencies and weaknesses of committees, such as inefficiency, compromised decisions, lack of leadership, and poor communication.

The problems of committees

Frequently, however, there is no economic justification for a team, in which case the "one-person show" is appropriate. Many problems are simple enough to be handled by a single qualified researcher, especially one with an interdisciplinary training. Also, thanks to the advance of computers, it is easier and cheaper than ever before to retrieve information about other disciplines, thus enabling even a person with minimal training in several disciplines to employ an interdisciplinary approach.

2.6 MODELS

The use of models, especially mathematical models, is the backbone of management science. A **model** is a *simplified representation* or abstraction of reality. It is usually simplified because reality is too complex to copy exactly and because much of the complexity is actually irrelevant to the specific problem. But these characteristics of *simplification* and *representation* are difficult to simultaneously achieve in practice. For example, a model can be simple but not then represent the true situation.

A model defined

Simplification and representation of reality

The representation of systems or problems through models can be done at various degrees of abstraction. Models are classified, according to their degree of abstraction, into three groups:

Iconic (scale) An **iconic model,** the least abstract, is a physical replica of a system, usually based on a different scale than the original. These may appear in three dimensions such as airplane, car, or bridge models to scale, or a production line. Photographs and computer icons are other types of iconic scale models but in only two dimensions.

Analog An **analog model** does not look like the real system but behaves like it. These are usually *two-dimensional* charts or diagrams; that is, they are physical models, but their shape *differs* from that of the system. Some examples are:

- Organization charts that depict structure, authority, and responsibility relationships.
- A map where different colors represent water or mountains.
- Stock market charts.
- Blueprints of a machine or a house.
- An oil dipstick.
- An hourglass.

Analog models are more abstract than iconic models.

Mathematical The complexity of relationships in some systems cannot be represented physically, or the physical representation may be cumbersome and take time to construct or manipulate. Therefore, a more abstract model is used with the aid of symbols. Most management science analysis is executed with the aid of **mathematical models** that utilize mathematical symbols. These are general rather than specific and can describe diverse situations. Furthermore, they can be easily manipulated for purposes of experimentation and prediction.

Management science uses mathematical models

The following are the major reasons why management science employs mathematical models.

a. The use of mathematical models enables the identification of a very large, sometimes almost infinite number of possible solutions. With today's advanced technology and communications, managers are faced with more and more alternatives.
b. Models enable the compression of time. Years of operations can be simulated in minutes or even seconds of computer time.
c. Manipulation of the model (changing variables) is much easier than manipulating the real system. Therefore, experimentation is easier.
d. The cost of making mistakes during a trial-and-error experiment is much smaller when done on the model.
e. Today's environment involves considerable uncertainty. The use of modeling allows a manager to take *calculated risks* in the decision-making process.
f. The cost of the modeling analysis is much lower than if a similar process was conducted with the real system.
g. Models enhance and reinforce learning.

The structure of the models and the process of their construction is discussed later in Section 2.10.

2.7 USE OF COMPUTERS

The last characteristic of management science is its common use of computers. Many managerial problems are complex, involving numerous interrelated variables. The search for and evaluation of alternative solutions, even when sophisticated models are involved, may become a gigantic computational project. In many cases, a manual or a hand calculator approach to the analysis is impractical or even impossible, since it may take more than a lifetime to solve the problem. Thus, many problems are solvable only with the aid of high-speed computational devices.

The need for high-speed computers

In addition to the use of the computer for the execution of the necessary calculations in solving the models, computers are also used in data collection, storage, retrieval, and analysis (e.g., identifying frequency distributions) and in the validation of the models. Computers are also used to assist the implementation using "what if" capabilities and graphical presentation, which make it easier for managers to understand and use the model results.

The use of computers has become closely associated with quantitative analysis and management science. Computers have the important advantage of being a relatively inexpensive means of rapid calculation and possess the accuracy and flexibility invaluable in experimenting with and solving managerial decision models.

Faster, cheaper, more accurate

The computer has provided a means for solving those problems that have long been quantifiable but computationally too complex or time-consuming for human calculation. Problems that would take months to solve manually can be solved in seconds using computers. Production and personnel scheduling, allocation of resources, blending of raw materials, investment, ordering materials, and other managerial activities can be reevaluated daily in light of current information. Previously, such activities could be reevaluated only weekly, monthly, or even annually. By the time decisions were made, the information on which they were based was often obsolete, so that poor consequences resulted.

Obsolete analyses in the past

As time passed, the availability of computers increased and the cost of processing data and computing results decreased. Thus, more and more use was made of computers in management science. It is therefore clear that the development of management science goes hand in hand with the use of computers.

The examples presented in this book are usually much simpler than real-life problems; therefore, they can often be solved manually. However, real-life problems will require a computer, so we have included a guide to computerization in each chapter of this book.

The management science process—A preview

It was demonstrated earlier that management science employs a scientific approach, and that rather than dealing with the organization or the problem itself, it deals with a representative mathematical model. In addition, the analysis is done from the perspective of a system, possibly by an interdisciplinary team. The question of exactly *what* this representation consists of and how it is conducted will be addressed in Chapters 3–16. In this chapter some general discussion of the *process* that management science follows will be presented as it relates to mathematical models.

The management science process is illustrated in Figure 2.3. The six-step process starts with the definition of the problem and ends with the implementation of a solution. The details of this process and the methodological problems that are involved in its execution are discussed in Sections 2.8–2.13.

2.8 STEP 1: DEFINITION OF THE PROBLEM

Since management science is primarily a quantitative discipline, it is necessary to employ numerical analysis from the beginning. By the

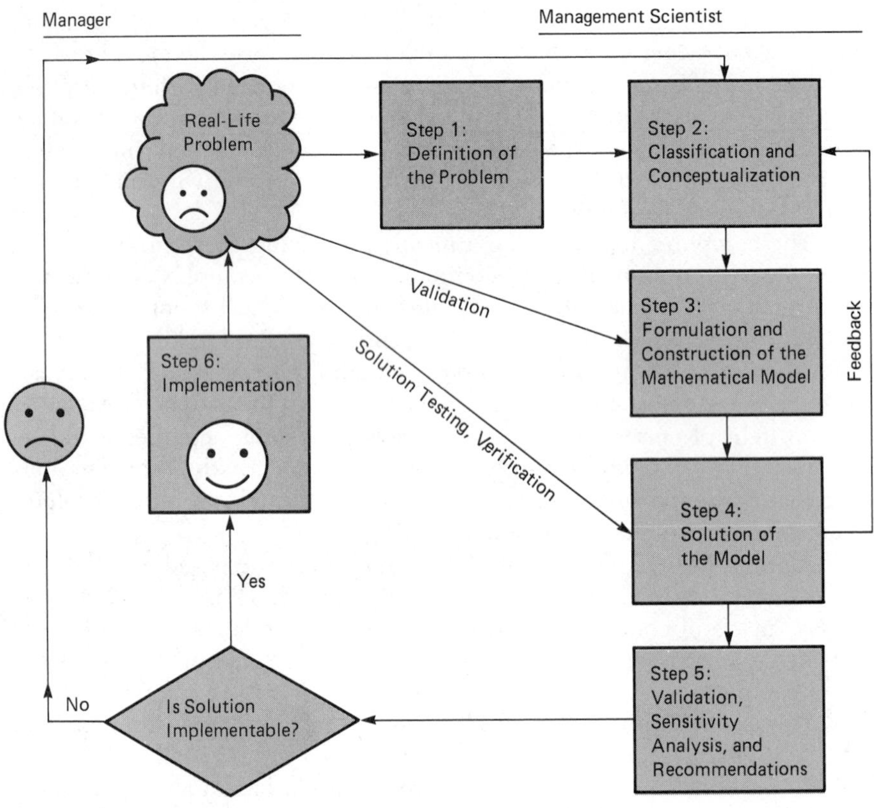

FIGURE 2.3 The process of management science

"definition of the problem" we mean recognizing that a problem exists, determining its magnitude, defining it precisely, and noting what its *symptoms* are. Often, what is described as a problem (e.g., excessive costs) may only be a *symptom* of a problem (e.g., improper inventory levels). Since so-called real-world problems are usually complicated by many interrelated factors, it is sometimes difficult to distinguish between symptoms and problems. However, it is necessary to properly identify and define the problem in order to solve it.

The existence of a problem in an organization can best be appraised by monitoring the productivity level. In order to do so, it is necessary to study the organization's inputs, processes, and outputs. The measurement of productivity, as well as the construction of the model, is based on data. The collection of existing data and the estimation of unavailable future data is one of the most difficult tasks of the management scientist. The following are some of the issues that arise during data estimation.

a. Outcome variables may occur over an extended period of time, with revenues (or profits) and expenses being recorded at different points of time. To overcome this difficulty a present-value approach should be used for all calculations involving future moneys. The issue of what interest rate to select for the discounting is a special concern and is usually addressed by the financial/accounting staff.

b. It is often necessary to use a subjective approach to data estimation. One such method is presented in Chapter 11, where optimistic, pessimistic, and most likely estimates are averaged (by using weights) to obtain an expected value.

c. It is assumed that the data used for the assessment and modeling are the same as that expected to prevail when the solution is later implemented. If not, it is necessary to predict the nature of the change and include it in the analysis as well.

Once the analysis is completed, it is possible to determine whether a problem really exists, where it is located, and how significant it is. These activities are part of the problem definition that precedes the problem classification.

2.9 STEP 2: CLASSIFICATION OF THE PROBLEM

This step involves the *conceptualization* of a problem in an attempt to classify it into a definable *category*. As mentioned earlier, problems can be classified into two major categories: *standard* (also called programmed) and *special* (called nonprogrammed).

Programmed versus nonprogrammed problems

Herbert A. Simon [12] has distinguished two extreme situations of decision problems. At one end of the spectrum are the well-structured problems that are *repetitive* and *routine* and for which a standard model has been worked out. These problems are called **programmed** because the method used to handle them is embodied in a series of consistent steps that can routinely be repeated. They are listed as *prototypal managerial problems* at the end of this chapter. Examples of such problems are weekly schedules of employees, monthly determination of products to produce, and selection of the best quantity of materials to be purchased. At the other end of the spectrum are the *ill-structured* or **nonprogrammed** problems that are novel and nonrecurrent. For example, acquisition and merger decisions, undertaking a research and development project, expanding a freeway, and opening a university are all nonprogrammed problems.

Programmed models for recurring problems

Ill-structured problems

In addition to classifying the problem into a major category, it is necessary to classify it into a precise prototype (described later). Only then is it possible to proceed with formulating the problem.

2.10 STEP 3: MODELING (FORMULATION)

Modeling or *formulating* the problem involves the conceptualization of the problem and its abstraction to a mathematical form. The dependent and independent variables are identified and the equations describing their

The role of assumptions

The need to simplify the problems in the model

The delicate art of modeling

relationships established. Simplifications are made, whenever necessary, through a set of *assumptions*. For example, a relationship between two variables may be assumed to be linear so that the problem will fit the model of linear programming. It is necessary to find a proper balance between the level of simplification of the model and the representation of reality. The simpler the model, the easier are the manipulations and the solutions, but the less representative it will be of the real problem.

The task of modeling is one of the most delicate and intricate in management science. It is a combination of art and science and involves a multitude of interrelated activities and methodological issues. The most important of these are:

a. The components of the model.
b. The structure of the model.
c. The mathematical relationships.
d. The validation of the model.

These topics are discussed next.

a. The components of mathematical models

Three types of model components

All mathematical models are comprised of three basic components: *result variables, decision variables,* and *uncontrollable variables.* These components are connected by mathematical (logical) relationships, as shown in Figure 2.4.

FIGURE 2.4
The general structure of a model

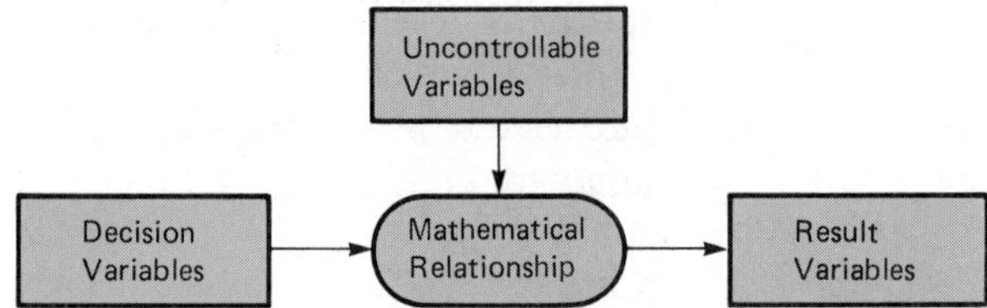

The result variables These reflect the *level of effectiveness* of the system. That is, they tell how well the system performs or attains its goals. Some of the more common result variables that are used in organizations to measure effectiveness are shown in Table 2.1. The result variables are **dependent** variables.[3] They also have other names that are often used in management science:

- Outputs of the system.
- Measures of performance.
- Measures of effectiveness.

---

[3] A dependent variable means that for the event described by this variable to occur, another event must occur first. In this case, the result variables depend on the occurrence of the decision and the uncontrollable variables.

- Payoffs.
- Outcomes.
- Objectives.

The decision variables The decision variables describe elements in the problem for which a choice must be made. These variables are *manipulable* and *controllable* by the decision maker. Examples are the quantities of products to produce, the number of units to be ordered, and the number of tellers to use in a bank (others are shown in Table 2.1). Decision variables are classified mathematically as *independent* variables or *unknown* variables. They are denoted by the letters x_1, x_2, and so on, or by x, y, z. The aim of management science is to find the best (or good enough) values of these decision variables.

The uncontrollable variables In any decision situation there are factors that affect the result variables but that are not under the control of the decision maker. Examples are the prime interest rate, building codes, tax regulations, and prices of supplies (others are shown in Table 2.1). Most of these factors are uncontrollable because they emanate from the environment surrounding the decision maker. These variables are also independent variables since they affect the dependent (result) variables.

TABLE 2.1
Examples of the components of models

Area	*Decision variables*	*Result variables*	*Uncontrollable variables*
Financial investment	Investment amounts Period of investment Timing of investment	Total profit Rate of return Earnings/share Liquidity	Inflation rate Prime rate Competition
Marketing	Advertising budget Number of models Zonal sales reps.	Market share Customer satisfaction	Disposable income Competitor's actions
Manufacturing	Production amounts Inventory levels Incentive plan	Total cost Quality level Spoilage	Machine capacity Technology Materials prices
Accounting	Audit schedule Use of computers Depreciation schedule	Data processing cost Error rate	Legal requirements Tax rates Computer technology
Transportation	Shipments	Total transport cost	Delivery distance Regulations
Services	Number of servers	Customer satisfaction	Demand for service

b. The structure of mathematical models

Mathematical expressions to tie the components together

The components of a mathematical model are expressed as variables. These are then tied together by sets of mathematical expressions such as equations or inequalities, thereby forming a system. Figure 2.5 is an example of such a model of a manufacturing system. In management science, however, the arrows in the picture are replaced by mathematical expressions.

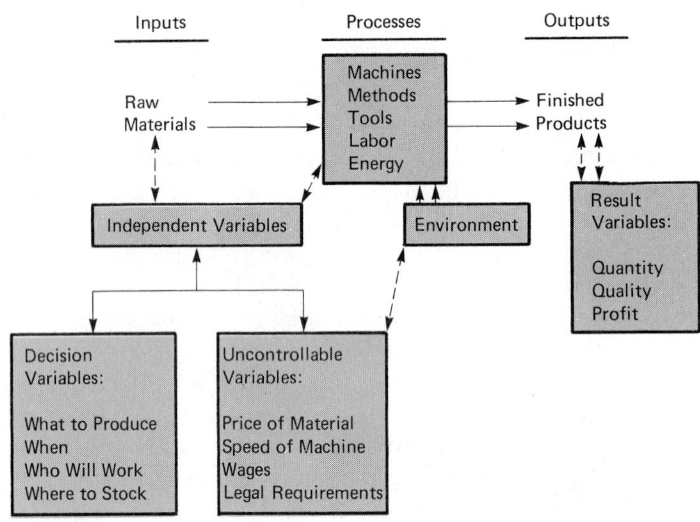

FIGURE 2.5
A manufacturing systems model

c. The mathematical relationships in the model

Two types of relationships

The mathematical relationships in a management science model may include two major parts: the *objective function* and the *constraints.*

The objective function The objective function expresses the dependent variables in the model as they relate to the independent variables. For example, an objective function may look like:

$$R = p_1x_1 + p_2x_2$$

where R symbolizes the total revenue to a manufacturer (dependent variable); x_1 and x_2 are the quantities of the two products that are produced and sold (decision variables); and p_1 and p_2 are the prices set by the marketplace (uncontrollable variables). The objective, or goal, is to maximize the revenue. Such an objective is usually limited by *constraints.*

The constraints The **constraints** express the limitations imposed on managerial systems due to regulations, competition, scarcity of resources, technology, or other uncontrollable variables. For example, a marketing constraint might be represented by:

$$x_1 + x_2 \leq 50$$

That is, the total quantity of the two products that can be sold is 50 or less.

Figure 2.6 illustrates this manufacturer's model. The model can be interpreted as: Find the value of the decision variables x_1 and x_2 such that the total revenue R (result variable) is maximized, subject to the marketing limitation and market prices, which are uncontrollable by the manufacturer.

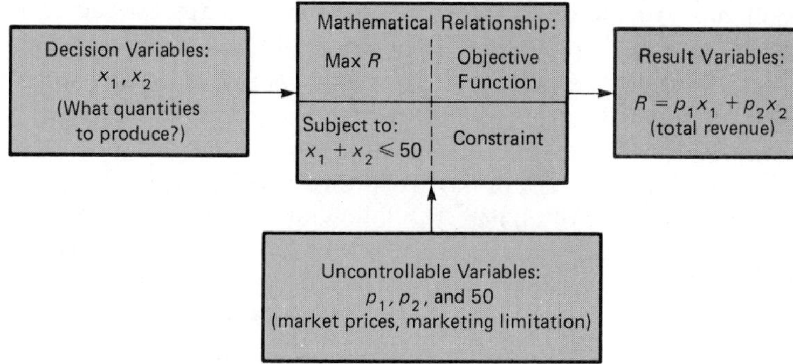

FIGURE 2.6
A model of a manufacturing situation

d. Validation of the model

After a model has been constructed, it is necessary to know how well it represents reality. That is, we need to know whether the model is internally correct in a logical and programming sense. This task is part of the model validation process, which is usually done after the model is completed and capable of yielding a solution. Validation will be discussed in Section 2.12 after the solution procedure is presented.

2.11 STEP 4: SOLVING THE MODEL

As previously stated, solution procedures to standard problems are well developed and computer codes exist for all of them. The user, therefore, is relieved of the task of developing these procedures. However, it is important that the user understand some of the concepts and the methodological issues that are involved in this step in order to properly understand what is happening and how to employ the computer results.

> Definition: A *solution* to a model means finding a specific set of values of the decision variables that result in a desirable output level.

In this section we will discuss the following issues:

a. Desirable output levels (criteria of choice, optimization, and suboptimization).
b. Model experimentation and evaluation.
c. Numerical versus analytical techniques.
b. Classification of solutions.

a. Desirable output levels

The solution procedure depends on the most desirable and economically feasible output level. Are we trying to get the best? Or will any acceptable result be sufficient? This issue is treated under the topic of the selection of a **principle of choice.**

The choice of a solution approach

Selection of a principle of choice A **principle of choice** refers to a decision regarding the acceptability of a solution approach. Is the best possible alternative sought, or will a "good enough" solution do? Are we willing to assume risk or do we prefer a conservative approach? Of the various principles of choice, the following are of prime interest:

The *best* way

Optimization. An optimal alternative is one that is demonstrably the *best* of *all* possible alternatives. To find it one should examine *all* alternatives and prove that the one selected is indeed the best.

In operational terms, **optimization** can be achieved in one of three ways:

1. Get the *highest level* (maximum) of goal attainment from a *given* set of resources (or at a given cost).
2. Find the alternative with the *lowest cost* (minimization of resources) that will fulfill a required level of goal(s).
3. Find the alternative with the highest *ratio* of goal attainment to cost (e.g., profit per dollar invested); in other words, maximize productivity.

Normative models

Optimization *prescribes* the course of action that the decision maker should take in order to achieve goals most efficiently. Therefore, models designed to optimize an objective are referred to as **normative** models. Such a model must possess a decision criterion for selecting the *best* (optimal) available alternative and proving that the selected alternative is indeed optimal.

Normative decision theory is based on the following assumptions:

The "economic man" assumptions

1. Man is an economic being whose objective is to maximize personal goals; that is, the decision maker is *rational.*
2. In a given decision situation, all alternative courses of action and their possible consequences are known.
3. The decision maker has an order of preference that enables him or her to rank the desirability of all consequences of the analysis.

Suboptimization. By definition, the use of optimization requires that the decision maker consider the impact of each alternative course of action on the entire organization. The reason for this is that a decision made in one area may have significant effects in other areas. Take as an example a production department that plans its own schedule. For that department it would be beneficial to produce only a few products but in large quantities to reduce manufacturing cost. However, such a plan may result in high and costly inventories and marketing difficulties due to lack of a variety of products.

Using a systems point of view affords consideration of the impact on the entire system. Thus, the production department should make its plans in conjunction with other departments. Such an approach, however, may require a complicated, expensive, and time-consuming effort. Therefore, as a matter of practice, the management scientist may "close" the system within narrow boundaries, considering only part of the organization under study. Such an approach is called *suboptimization.*

If a decision is made in one part of the organization *without paying attention* to the rest of it, then a solution that is *optimal* from the point of view of the part may be **suboptimal** from the point of view of the whole, producing inferior or even damaging results.

Optimal or suboptimal?

Suboptimization, however, may still be a very practical approach and therefore many problems are first approached from this perspective. The primary reason for this is that analyzing only a portion of a system allows some tentative conclusions to be made without getting bogged down in a deluge of details. Once a solution is proposed, its potential effects on the remaining departments of the organization can be checked. If no significant negative effects can be traced, the solution may then be considered optimal from a systems point of view.

The practicality of suboptimization

Advances in management science models and computers may ultimately allow an analysis of the complex *whole* readily and effectively in one evaluation; that is, to use an optimization approach. Until then, the use of suboptimization will continue as a very practical approach for complex problems.

Good enough or "satisficing." According to Simon [12], most human decision making, whether organizational or individual, involves a willingness to settle for a satisfactory solution, "something less than the best." In a **satisficing** mode the decision maker sets up an *aspiration* (desired) level of goals and then searches the alternatives until one is found that achieves this. The usual reasons for satisficing are lack of time or ability for optimization as well as an unwillingness to pay the price for the required information. An example of selecting a satisfactory alternative can be seen in a company that wants to sell some property. According to the optimization approach, the company should examine *all* offers and select the *highest* offer, assuming that its objective is to maximize the proceeds from the sale. In reality, this process is not followed. What the seller normally does is assess the market and set up a desired price (the aspiration level), say $55,000. The first buyer to offer $55,000 (or more) will get the property. If the seller is unsuccessful in getting a bid of $55,000 within a certain period, he or she will change the asking price, say to $53,000, which in essence means reducing the seller's level of aspiration or goal. If the seller then sells the property for at least $53,000, the seller is satisficing a new goal.

Satisficing to an aspiration level

Satisficing as a principle of choice is used in those management science tools that are labeled **descriptive.**

Descriptive models describe things *as they are.* Their major use in management science is to investigate the outcomes or consequences of various alternative courses of action, as reflected by the system's performance or effectiveness. However, since the descriptive analysis checks the effectiveness of the system for given conditions (or given alternatives) rather than for *all* conditions, there is no *guarantee* that an alternative selected with the aid of descriptive analysis is optimal.

Descriptive models

Descriptive models are usually applied in decision situations when normative models are not applicable. They are also used when the objective is to define the problem or to assess its seriousness rather than to select an alternative. Descriptive models are especially useful in *predicting the behavior* of the system under various assumptions.

Predicting behavior with descriptive models

Other principles of choice. In addition to optimization and satisficing, there are several other, less common, principles of choice. These will be discussed in Chapter 3.

b. Model experimentation and evaluation

Once the principle of choice is determined, the search for the "best" or a "good enough" alternative may begin. In general, this activity involves five steps:

1. Generate alternatives.
2. Predict the outcome of each alternative.
3. Relate outcomes to goals.
4. Compare the alternatives.
5. Select an alternative.

1. Generate alternatives The decision-making process as presented in Section 2.2 involves a search for alternative courses of action that are candidate solutions to the problem. In management science, such alternative courses of action may be either given or they may be generated by the model. In the first case, the model is used to *evaluate* the given alternatives; in the second case, it is used to generate and then evaluate alternatives.

Modeling to generate and/or evaluate alternatives

There are several methods of searching for alternatives; some require a greater, some a lesser, degree of creativity and ingenuity (e.g., see Harrison [7]). At the very least, the search process requires resources such as money, labor, and time. Since these are usually limited, the search must be terminated sooner or later. In some cases, the search may continue while an *evaluation* is proceeding. Consider, for example, the selection of a person to fill a position. Typically, candidates are evaluated and compared while the search continues.

2. Predict the outcome of each alternative In order to evaluate an alternative, it is necessary to predict its outcome. Predicting the outcomes of the alternatives requires *forecasting*, since most outcomes occur weeks or months *after* a decision has been made. This topic is treated as a separate subject later in the text (Chapter 5).

Outcomes versus goals

3. Relate outcomes to goals The value of an outcome is judged in terms of the goal's attainment. Sometimes an outcome is expressed directly in terms of a goal. For example, *profit* is an outcome while *profit maximization* is the goal, and both are expressed in dollar terms. In other cases, an outcome may be expressed in terms other than those of the goal. For example, the outcome may be in terms of machine downtime, while the goal can be expressed in terms of dollars. In such cases, it is necessary to transform the outcome so it is expressed in terms of the goal.

4. Compare the alternatives Once the previous activities have been completed, the decision maker can compare the alternatives and select one. Some of the difficult issues considered in this stage are:

Comparison difficulties

- *Multiple goals.* The models described in this book are frequently based on the analysis of one goal, such as "maximization of profit." In reality, several goals may exist simultaneously. Methods for overcoming this difficulty are discussed in Chapters 4 and 9.
- *Sensitivity to change.* The result variables may be particularly sensitive to changes or errors in some of the independent variables. The evaluation should check this sensitivity to avoid highly sensitive alternatives, as will be explained later in this chapter.
- *What constitutes a significant difference between alternatives?* In comparing alternatives, one may find that alternative A will bring $323,200, while alternative B will bring $323,150. Is alternative A superior to B? In theory, the answer is yes. Practically speaking, the two alternatives are basically the same. The accuracy of data is such that $50 out of $323,000 is *not* a significant factor.

  In general, it is important to determine when an alternative is indeed superior. Since we deal with models, we simplify reality. Alternative A will bring $50 extra but might make some employees unhappy. In this text, a choice is made based on quantitative factors only. In reality, other factors must be considered, especially when the difference seems to be small. (Statistical tests can be employed in certain cases to determine if a significant difference exists.)
- *What principle of choice to use?* The selection of a principle of choice must precede the actual decision. Should the decision maker attempt to find an optimal solution, or should a "satisfactory" solution be accepted if it can be derived much faster (and/or cheaper)? The principle of choice reflects the attitudes, policies, and objectives of the decision maker.

5. Select an alternative The process ends with a choice, namely the selection and recommendation of a solution (or an alternative course of action). The decision is based on the principle of choice determined earlier.

c. Numerical versus analytical techniques

Numerical techniques consist of a trial-and-error comparison of several proposed solutions. Each solution can be distinguished by its set of decision variables. The specific method to be used depends on the principle of choice and on the nature of the problem under consideration. Numerical techniques can yield either optimal or nonoptimal solutions.

Enumeration or algorithm?

The numerical techniques that yield optimal solutions consist of those that are based on *complete enumeration* and those that are based on *algorithms.*

Complete enumeration When one checks *every possible* solution (or values of the decision variables), he or she performs a complete **enumeration.** This technique is useful only when the number of alternatives is relatively small; otherwise, it is a lengthy, tedious, or even impossible approach.

Algorithms An **algorithm** is a step-by-step process of searching for the optimal solution by *gradually* improving each solution. Thus, in contrast to a complete enumeration where an exhaustive trial-and-error process is performed (*all* solutions are checked), an algorithm is a progressive trial-and-error process that checks only a *portion* of all feasible solutions.

Simulation and heuristics do not guarantee optimal solutions

The numerical techniques that yield nonoptimal solutions are basically those of *simulation* and *heuristics* (Chapter 16).

Heuristics **Heuristics** are step-by-step procedures or rules that in a finite number of steps, arrive at a good-enough solution. These rules are based on either experimentation or else sound, logical concepts. They are fast and easy to apply. Heuristics have received increasing attention since, in some cases, they are the only practical or economic way to solve complex management problems. For further discussion, see Chapter 16 and Zanakis [16]. Heuristics play an important role in the problem-solving procedures of expert systems.

An illustration To illustrate the use of numerical techniques, one might consider a control box. The box has knobs on it representing different independent controllable variables, and dials (gauges) representing the dependent variables that measure the system's effectiveness. The uncontrollable variables are built into the operation of the box through internal wiring. When the decision maker wants to explore the consequence of a given alternative course of action, he or she merely turns the knobs (each combination setting of the knobs represents an alternative course of action) and watches the dials.

An inventory control box

The illustration in Figure 2.7 represents a control box for an inventory model. The box has only one dial, representing the cost of inventory. This is the measure of the system's effectiveness. The knobs represent two controllable variables: x_1 is the number of orders placed each year and x_2 is the quantity of safety stock the company keeps. The decision maker, sitting in front of this box, would manipulate the knobs. For example, the decision maker may set $x_1 = 2$ orders per year and $x_2 = 400$ units of safety stock. Then the dial that shows the resulting cost, $7,000, can be observed.

Complete enumeration or an algorithm?

To find a solution in the case of *complete enumeration,* one will have to experiment with *all* combinations of the knobs. For example, $x_1 = 2$ and $x_2 = 400$ is one combination shown in Figure 2.7. Each time a combination is attempted, the inventory cost is recorded. When *all* possible combinations have been tried, the *optimal* solution can be identified.

In the case of using an *algorithm,* there is no need to check *all* alternatives; through previous experience, or a certain theory, one attempts to generate new combinations of knobs such that their resultant inventory

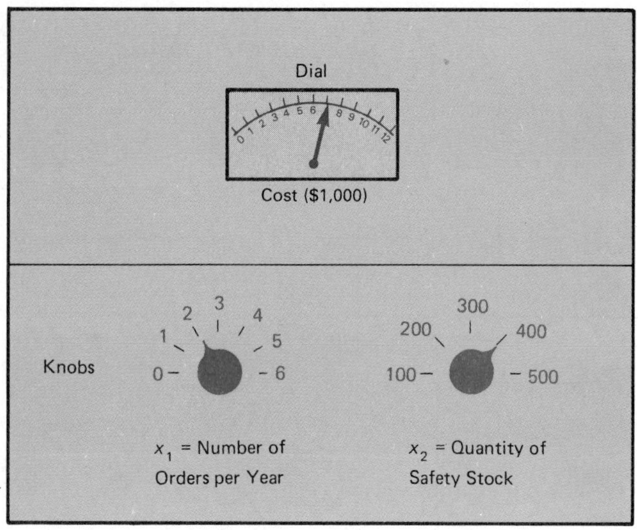

FIGURE 2.7
A control box for an inventory problem

cost is *continuously decreasing*. The time and cost of using an algorithm will be significantly less than that of complete enumeration since fewer combinations of knobs will be checked.

Finally, management can decide not to check all combinations of the knobs, but only some of them. Such a decision may be based on heuristics. In this case, the choice will be the best of those alternatives checked, but not necessarily the best inventory policy. This case is typical of the technique called **simulation,** where the solution is not guaranteed to be optimal.

Analytical approach for direct result

Analytical techniques **Analytical** techniques use mathematical formulas to directly (in one step) either *derive* an optimal solution or *predict* a certain result. As such, analytical models are *deductive* in character in contrast to the numerical procedures, which are essentially *inductive* in character.

The management science tools discussed in this text are classified in Figure 2.8, according to the solution techniques discussed above.

d. Classification of solutions

Solutions can be classified as being *feasible* or *infeasible, optimal* or *nonoptimal,* and *unique* or *multiple.*

Feasible

Feasible and infeasible solutions A *feasible* solution is one that satisfies *all* the requirements and constraints imposed on the problem. Violating one or more of these requirements results in an unacceptable, **infeasible** solution.

For example, there are many ways of getting dressed. As a matter of fact, there are *n*! (*n* factorial) different ways of getting dressed with *n*

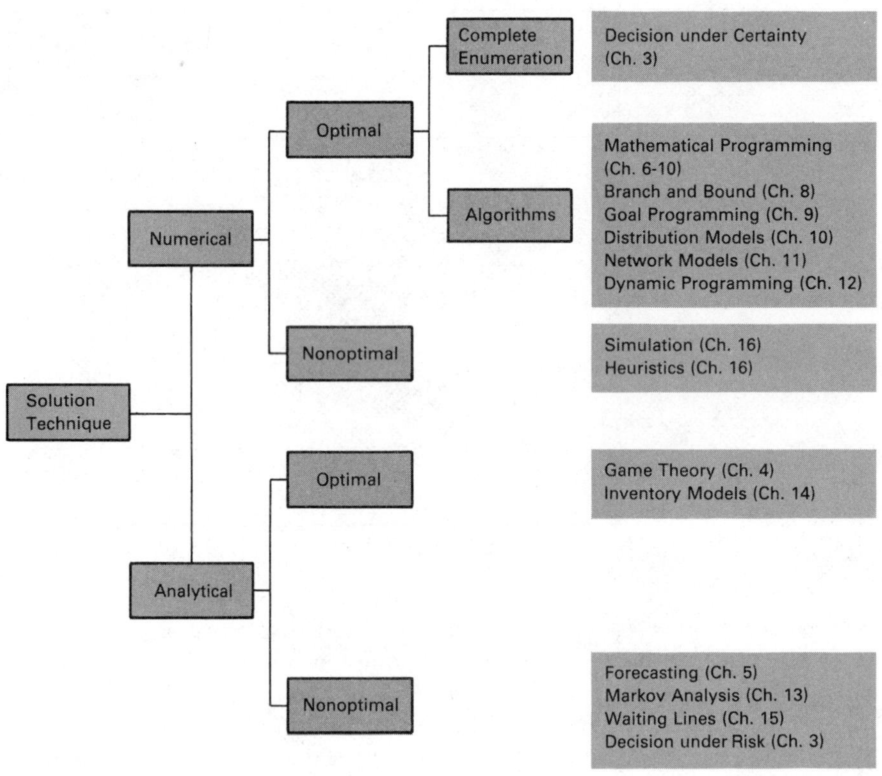

FIGURE 2.8
Model classification by solution technique

pieces of clothing. With $n = 10$ there are 3,628,800 different ways of getting dressed. Suppose that you want to determine the fastest way of getting dressed; do you have to check all 3,628,800 alternatives? Of course not! You can start with your socks, then shoes, then shirt, and so on. But you cannot put your socks on after your shoes are on—this is obviously an *infeasible* solution. By identifying the infeasible solutions early, it is possible to narrow down the number of alternatives requiring evaluation.

Infeasible solutions

Optimal

Optimal and nonoptimal solutions An *optimal* solution is the *best* of all feasible solutions. For a solution to be declared optimal there must be proof that *all* feasible solutions were checked and that the proposed solution is better than any other solution. A feasible solution that cannot be classified as optimal is considered *nonoptimal*.

Unique

Unique and multiple solutions If there exists only one optimal solution it is called *unique*. If two or more optimal solutions can be identified, then there exist *multiple* solutions. The latter case is usually preferred by managers since it gives them greater flexibility in implementing a solution. Mathematical models may not include some behavioral and qualitative factors. In comparing multiple solutions, management may include consideration of these variables, thus making the solution more acceptable.

2.12 STEP 5: MODEL VALIDATION AND SENSITIVITY ANALYSIS

After a model has been constructed, it is necessary to know how well the model represents reality. Often the accuracy of a model cannot be assessed until model solutions are generated. Validation requires answering such questions as: Are the predictions made by the model empirically accurate? and, Is the model representative of the system's behavior under real-world circumstances? A valid model should behave in a manner similar to the underlying phenomena.

The process of validation may be viewed as a two-step process. The first step is to determine whether the model is *internally* correct in a logical and programming sense. The second is to determine whether it represents the system (or phenomena) it is supposed to represent.

Model validation is necessary

One way to validate a model is to try it with different possible sets of data and see if the solutions resemble the historical behavior of the system. For example, if a model describes sales behavior as a function of interest rates, then it can be tested by "plugging in" several values of interest rates, say, 4, 5, . . . , 19 percent, examining what level of sales is predicted in each case, and comparing this to historical data. Obviously, if the model was unable to successfully describe historical occurrences, it should not be considered valid for making future predictions; therefore, adjustments are necessary in the model.

Another way to validate a model is to solve small problems and see if the results make sense to the user.

Sensitivity analysis for insight

Sensitivity analysis **Sensitivity analysis** is an attempt to help managers when they are uncertain about the accuracy or relative importance of their information. In sensitivity analysis the information in question is altered to find what effects, if any, changes will have on the output of the proposed solution to the problem. In other words, the purpose of sensitivity analysis is to determine the effect of *changes* in the independent variables on the values of the dependent variables. For example, an optimal solution that was based on an assumed prime interest rate of 7 percent may have prescribed an investment in real estate rather than in stocks or bonds. Suppose that the interest rate is 6 percent or 9 percent—is real estate still the best investment?

Of special interest are questions such as:

Questions a sensitivity analysis can answer

1. What change can occur in a certain independent variable before a change occurs in the recommended solution?
2. What is the magnitude of a change in the proposed solution resulting from a change in an independent variable(s)?
3. Which independent variables are most sensitive? That is, which variables will, when changed only slightly, cause the value of the dependent variables to change significantly? Which independent variables are insensitive?
4. Is a proposed solution highly sensitive? That is, does the solution include sensitive variables that, when changed slightly, will alter the

solution so that it will no longer be optimal? Conversely, insensitive solutions will hold with a wide range of variations in the independent variables.

Insensitive solutions are usually easier to implement since their predicted results are more certain to occur and since management can modify the proposed solution with a small loss in effectiveness of the system.

Sensitivity analyses may be performed in several ways, as will be discussed in later chapters. Of special interest are the "what if" and goal-seeking analyses discussed in Chapters 16 and 17.

2.13 STEP 6: IMPLEMENTATION

The management scientist's role does not end with the submission of a recommended solution. To complete the process, a solution must be implemented. Implementing a management science solution is a very difficult process; on many occasions it is harder to implement a solution than to build and solve a model. The fact is, many management science recommendations are not implemented. The reasons for this situation and a discussion of the things that can be done to help implementation are given in Chapter 19.

2.14 MANAGERIAL PROBLEMS AND THE TOOLS OF MANAGEMENT SCIENCE

Models for prototypal managerial problems

Throughout the history of management science, certain types of problems have been encountered repeatedly. The structure of these has been abstracted and analyzed so as to yield "prototype" problems. To handle these prototype problems, a set of standard solution procedures (also called *tools* or *techniques*) has been developed. Thus, whenever a management problem is recognized as a prototype problem, it can be molded into a standard format and the appropriate tool can be applied for its solution.

The prototypal managerial problems

Some common managerial problems discussed in this text are:

Competitive situations When the results of a decision are determined not only by one's own course of action but also by that of another decision maker, a competitive situation exists. This situation may be viewed as a game that each party attempts to win.

Allocation problems These problems arise when (1) there are a number of activities to be performed, (2) there exist two or more different ways to perform these activities, and (3) resources or facilities are scarce. The problem then is to find the best utilization of resources; namely, which activities to pursue and in what magnitude, so that effectiveness will be maximized.

Distribution problems Moving a commodity (e.g., oil or corn) from several sources to several destinations at minimum cost constitutes a *transportation problem.* Several types of problems (e.g., production scheduling) can be viewed and solved as transportation problems. A related topic is the *assignment problem,* in which certain items such as a person or an activity are to be assigned, on a one-to-one basis, to other items such as facilities or services. The objective is to minimize the cost or to maximize the effectiveness of the assignment.

Network problems Network problems describe flows of commodities, activities, information, or other resources between locations. For example, in the construction of a bridge, many activities, information, and resources flow as time passes. The problem is to find the best activity plan for such systems.

Inventory control The proper level of inventories of materials, money, finished products, or persons is a major problem in many organizations. The costs of carrying inventories are high, but inventories can result in large savings by preventing shortages, providing discounts on large quantities purchased or produced, eliminating changes in the level of production, and reducing ordering and setup costs. The problem is to find the proper level of inventory, which is determined by the decisions "when" and "how much" to order, that will minimize the total cost.

Waiting line problems Whenever persons or objects that require service arrive at a service facility, a waiting line is likely to occur, especially in rush periods. Typically, in such situations there is a waiting line during certain periods, but the facility may be idle during other "slack" periods.

In general, the larger the facility, the costlier its operation but the smaller the waiting time for service. The problem is to find the appropriate size of the facility as well as to determine its operating procedures (e.g., give priority to certain customers) in such a way as to minimize the sum of the relevant costs.

Predicting the behavior of a system Management is frequently interested in predicting the behavior of a system under different conditions or scenarios. While this is not classified as a prototype problem by itself, it can be used in constructing prototype procedures and/or evaluating solutions.

Other problems Several other managerial problems are of interest to management scientists. The most important are:[4]

- Sequencing (which task to do next) and routing (what part minimizes travel time between points).
- Maintenance (how often to repair) and replacement (which items, how often).
- Search (which items to consider first).
- Bidding (what strategy, how high or low).

---

[4] These are not discussed in the text. The interested reader is referred to Wagner [15].

Complex problems Complex problems may appear in any of the above areas (e.g., inventory or allocation) but their structure is not standard. Such problems need special attention and are classified as being "semistructured" or "unstructured."

The tools of management science

As indicated earlier, certain managerial problems were singled out for intensive study as they appeared more and more frequently in practice. These studies resulted in a body of tools and techniques developed specifically for solving certain managerial problems. Listed below are those tools of management science that are discussed in this text.

Decision tables Allocation and investment problems involving a relatively small number of possible solutions can be presented in a tabular form known as a decision table.

Decision trees The extension of decision tables for situations involving several decision periods takes the shape of a "tree."

Game theory Game theory provides a systematic approach to decision making in competitive environments and a framework for the study of conflict.

Forecasting To predict the outcome of managerial decisions, various forecasting approaches are employed. Many of these are based on statistics.

Mathematical programming Mathematical programming attempts to maximize the attainment level of one goal subject to a set of requirements and limitations. It has extensive use in business, economics, engineering, the military, and public service, mainly as an aid to the solution of allocation problems. In this text, the following models will be covered: *linear programming; transportation* and *assignment models; integer* and *goal programming.*

Branch and bound Branch and bound is a step-by-step procedure used when a *very large* (or even infinite) number of alternatives exist for certain managerial problems.

Network models This is a family of tools designed for the purpose of planning and controlling complex projects. The best known models are *PERT* (Program Evaluation Review Technique) and *CPM* (Critical Path Method).

Dynamic programming Dynamic programming is an approach to decisions that are basically sequential in nature or can be reformulated so as to be considered sequential. It is a very general and powerful tool.

Markov chains Markov chains are used for predicting the outcome of processes where systems or units change their condition over time (e.g., consumers change their preferences for certain brands).

Inventory models For certain types of inventory control problems, special models that attempt to minimize the cost associated with ordering and carrying inventories have been developed.

Waiting line (queuing) models For certain types of problems involving waiting lines, special models have been developed to predict the performance of service systems.

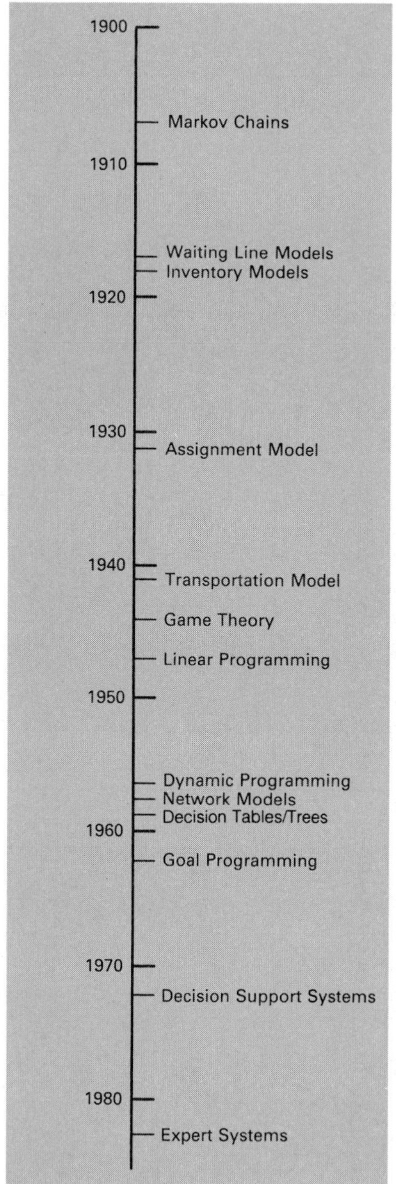

FIGURE 2.9
The evolution of management science tools

Simulation models For the analysis of complex systems when all other models fail, management science uses descriptive-type simulation models. Specifically, five types of models are presented in this text: (1) artificial intelligence, (2) heuristic programming, (3) management games, (4) systems simulation, and (5) Monte Carlo simulation.

Decision support systems Even though computerized, **decision support systems** are as much "approaches" to problems as "tools." They are designed to handle semistructured problems and can incorporate any of the other tools, especially mathematical programming and simulation.

TABLE 2.2
The major relationships between problems and tools

Chapter	3	3	4	5	6,7	8	9	10	11	12	13	14	15	16	17	18
Problem type \ *Tools*	*Decision tables*	*Decision trees*	*Game theory*	*Forecasting*	*Mathematical programming*	*Branch and bound*	*Goal programming*	*Transportation, assignment*	*PERT/CPM*	*Dynamic programming*	*Markov chains*	*Inventory*	*Waiting lines*	*Simulation*	*Decision support systems*	*Expert systems*
Allocation	X	X			X	X	X			X						
Distribution					X	X	X	X								
Network									X	X						
Competitive decision making			X											X		
Inventory					X					X		X		X		
Waiting lines													X	X		
Predicting a system's behavior	X	X		X							X		X	X		
Complex, semistructured, unstructured							X							X	X	X

Expert systems For particularly complex problems where judgment is essential, an applied tool of artificial intelligence, called an **expert system,** is available.

A plot of the historical evolution of these tools is given in Figure 2.9 to help you visualize their order of evolution and the growth in the foundations of the field.

The relationships between managerial problems and the tools

The one-to-one matching of a problem to a technique does not always hold. In some instances, a particular tool can be used for several prototype problems; and in other situations, one problem can be addressed with several tools. Although selection of a specific tool may depend on the specific problem, there are certain relationships that *usually* hold true. These are presented for structured problems in Table 2.2.

2.15 CONCLUDING REMARKS

Decision making is a complicated process consisting of certain steps and elements common to all decision situations. Such generalization makes it a potential subject for scientific analysis. The importance and complexity of the decision-making process has attracted investigators from several disciplines, resulting in various approaches to the study. One of these approaches is management science.

This chapter concludes the first part of the book, in which many concepts were described. In Part II, the various tools and techniques of management science will be presented.

2.16 PROBLEMS[5]

1. A European manufacturer of solar energy devices has two models available: Alpha, which costs $800 and sells for $1,000, and Beta, which costs $1,150 and sells for $1,500.
   a. The company's objective is profit maximization; write the objective function.
   b. The company's objective is to maximize sales in units; write the objective function in this case.
2. Express, mathematically, the following requirements and constraints for the preceding problem.
   a. The market for the Alpha devices is limited to no more than 400 units a month.
   b. The total number of devices produced will be at least 540 per month.
   c. Production capability is limited to no more than 720 units per month.
   d. The capital available for production is $50,000 per month.
3. A company has a $55,000 fixed cost in its Model T product. This model sells for $1,000, while its variable cost is $740. The company's goal is profit maximization. Write the objective function.

2.17 REVIEW QUESTIONS

1. What is the difference between making decisions and solving problems? Give an example.
2. Apply a scientific approach process to the following problems:
   a. Can vitamin C cure colds?
   b. Will a new product be accepted in the market?
   c. Should an airline add an additional flight between Chicago and New York?
3. Analyze a managerial system of your choice and identify the following:
   a. The components.
   b. The environment.
   c. The inputs.
   d. The system's goals.
   e. The decision variables.
4. What are some of the "measures of effectiveness" in a manufacturing plant; in a restaurant; in an educational institution; in the U.S. Congress?
5. Give an example of a managerial problem where an interdisciplinary team is desirable. Explain why.
6. Give an example of a mathematical model used by management.
7. What are some of the controllable and uncon-

[5] Answers to the even-numbered problems are given in Appendix D.

trollable variables in the following systems; automotive manufacturer, hospital, courthouse, airline, restaurant, hotel, bank, oil refinery, atomic power plant?

8. What is meant by an objective function?
9. Why are computers an integral part of management science? Under what conditions should computers *not* be used by a management scientist?
10. Give examples of three programmed decisions in an organization with which you are familiar.
11. Give examples of two nonprogrammed decisions in an organization.
12. Apply the management science process to the problem of deciding whether to open a new fast-food outlet. What should the principle of choice be?
13. The city of Toulouse in France is debating whether or not to build a public transportation system. What should the principle of choice be?
14. Compare and contrast normative versus descriptive approaches to decision making.
15. Give an example that illustrates the difference between optimization and suboptimization.
16. Distinguish between numerical and analytical solution techniques. Between an algorithm and a simulation.
17. Give an example to illustrate the simultaneous existence of several goals in organizations.
18. How can a model that predicts the movement of the Toyko stock market be validated?
19. Describe a situation that will demonstrate the meaning of sensitivity analysis.
20. Give an example of an infeasible solution.
21. Define a "unique" solution.
22. Describe the role of decision support systems in managerial decision making.

2.18 GLOSSARY

Algorithm A set of logical steps to follow to reach a solution.

Analog model A physical model in a different form from the actual system being modeled.

Analytical Considering the individual subparts of a system to deduce a result.

Constraints Limitations on actions.

Decision support system An advanced, responsive, easy-to-use computer system intended for complex managerial decisions.

Dependent variables System measures of effectiveness.

Descriptive Nonoptimizing; describes how a system operates.

Effectiveness The degree of goal attainment.

Efficiency Ratio of output to input.

Enumeration Listing of possible items to consider.

Environment Uncontrollable elements outside the system that affect it.

Expert system A form of artificial intelligence that incorporates the decision rules of an expert within the computer.

Heuristic A logical rule to efficiently search for "good enough" solutions.

Iconic model A physical, scaled replica.

Infeasible Not acceptable; can't be done.

Inputs The forms of resources introduced into a system for transformation into outputs.

Mathematical model A system of symbols and expressions to represent a real situation.

Model An abstraction of reality.

Normative Prescribes how a system *should* operate.

Numerical Trial-and-error inductive comparisons.

Optimization The best solution possible.

Outputs The result of a transformation process in a system.

Principle of choice The criterion for basing a choice among alternatives.

Programmed problems Repetitive, routine problems for which standard models have been developed.

Prototypal managerial problems Common organizational decision situations such as a "resource allocation" problem.

Satisfice A solution that is acceptable.

Sensitivity analysis Measuring the effect of a change in one variable on a proposed solution.

Simulation An imitation of reality.

Suboptimal Best for a subsystem of the total system.

System A set of elements that are considered to act as a single, goal-oriented entity.

2.19 REFERENCES AND BIBLIOGRAPHY

1. Ackoff, R. L., and F. Emery. *On Purposeful Systems*. Hawthorne, N.Y.: Aldine Publishing, 1972.
2. Aronofsky, J. S., ed. *Progress in Operations Research—The Relationship between Operations Research and the Computer*. New York: John Wiley & Sons, 1968.
3. Bonczek, R. H., W. Holsapple, and A. B. Whinston. "Computer-Based Support of Organizational Decision Making." *Decision Sciences* 10 (April 1979), pp. 268–91.
4. Churchman, C. West. *The Systems Approach*. Rev. ed. New York: Delacort Press, 1975.
5. ______. *The Design of Inquiring Systems*. New York: Basic Books, 1971.
6. Gass, S. I. *Decision Making, Models and Algorithms: A First Course*. New York: John Wiley & Sons, 1985.
7. Harrison, E. F. *The Managerial Decision-Making Process*. 2nd ed. Boston: Houghton Mifflin, 1981.
8. Kleijnen, J. P. C. "Computers and Operations Research: A Survey." *Computers and Operations Research* 3 (1976).
9. Mitroff, I. I., F. Betz, L. R. Pondy, and F. Sagasti. "On Managing Science in the Systems Age: Two Schemes for the Study of Science as a Whole Systems Phenomenon." *Interfaces* 4, no. 3 (1974), pp. 46–58.
10. Newell, A., and H. A. Simon. *Human Problem Solving*. Englewood Cliffs, N.J.: Prentice-Hall, 1972.
11. Saaty, T. L., and J. H. Alexander. *Thinking with Models*. Elmsford, N.Y.: Pergamon Press, 1981.
12. Simon, H. A. *The New Science of Management Decisions*. Rev. ed. Englewood Cliffs, N.J.: Prentice-Hall, 1977.
13. Van Gigch, J. P. *Applied General Systems Theory*. 2nd ed. New York: Harper & Row, 1978.
14. Verma, H. L., and C. W. Gross. *Introduction to Quantitative Methods—A Managerial Approach*. Santa Barbara, Calif.: Hamilton Publishing, 1978.
15. Wagner, H. M. *Principles of Operations Research*. 2nd ed. Englewood Cliffs, N.J.: Prentice-Hall, 1975.
16. Zanakis, S. H., and J. R. Evans. "Heuristic Optimization: Why, When, and How to Use It." *Interfaces*, October 1981, pp. 84–91.

PART II

THE TOOLS

In Part I of this text the foundations of management science were outlined. The management science process was described as centering around the formulation of managerial problems as mathematical models. In this part of the text we will present the most common standard models, which are termed the tools or the techniques of the management scientist. The chapters in Part II are typically divided into two sections: Basics and Extensions.

The Basics sections:

- Start with an illustrative example.
- Discuss the nature of the situation presented.
- Generalize the situation.
- Present the logic and methodology of the tool.
- Show, through example(s), how the tool is applied to the managerial problem.
- Summarize the material.
- Present problems for solution.

The Extensions sections usually include the theory behind the tool, other advanced topics, other applications, and more difficult problems.

At the end of each chapter there is a case study to illustrate the application of the tool and a comprehensive bibliography for further study.

3

Decision theory

PART A: BASICS

3.1 Decision analysis with decision tables.
3.2 Classification of decision situations.
3.3 Decisions under certainty.
3.4 Decisions under risk.
3.5 Decision trees.
3.6 Computer programs for decision tables and trees.
3.7 Concluding remarks.
3.8 Problems for Part A.

PART B: EXTENSIONS

3.9 The acquisition of additional information.
3.10 The value of perfect information.
3.11 The value of imperfect information.
3.12 Decisions under uncertainty.
3.13 Use of computers.
3.14 Appendix: Calculating revised probabilities.
3.15 Problems for Part B.
3.16 Case I—The condominium.
Case II—Maintaining the water valves.
Case III—The air force contract.
3.17 Glossary.
3.18 References and bibliography.

This chapter begins the presentation of the tools and techniques of management science. Thus, the general procedure of problem analysis, presented in Chapter 2, will now be put to work. The major content of this chapter is the use of decision tables and trees as tools for selecting alternatives. Managerial problems are then classified and the appropriate tools and techniques are divided into three major classes: decisions under certainty (deterministic), decisions under risk (probabilistic), and decisions under uncertainty. These three classes are discussed in detail here.

LEARNING OBJECTIVES

The student should be able to:

a. Describe the role and structure of decision matrices.
b. Define the terms: *state of nature, alternative course of action, payoff, feasible solution, probability of occurrence of a state of nature.*
c. Classify decisions into: certainty, uncertainty, and risk. Define these categories and understand their characteristics.
d. Describe the role of availability of information in decision making.
e. Relate the management science tools to decision categories.
f. Solve problems under certainty, using decision matrices.
g. Define objective and subjective probabilities.
h. Describe the concepts of expected value and expected opportunity loss (regret).
i. Compute decisions under risk using decision matrices and expected value.
j. Compute opportunity loss tables.
k. Describe the relationship between the value of information and its cost.
l. Discuss the structure of decision trees and their relationship to decision matrices.
m. Build decision trees for managerial problems and solve the trees.

Extensions

n. Compute the value of perfect information.
o. Describe the concepts of revised probabilities and imperfect information.
p. Define the concept of reliability in prediction.
q. Describe the structure of Bayes' formula.
r. Revise probabilities.
s. Solve problems involving decision trees and revised probabilities.
t. Compute the value of imperfect information.
u. Solve problems under uncertainty using the following criteria of choice: Laplace, minimax, maximax, Hurwicz, and minimax regret.
v. Discuss the shortcomings of the various criteria of choice.

PART A: BASICS

"The Dow Jones Industrial Average failed to hold above the 3000 mark," the ticker tape calmly proclaimed. Mary Golden, vice president of Friendly Trust Company, read the message on the ticker tape over and over again. She moaned to herself: "This is the sixth time in the last four months that the famous indicator has penetrated the magic 3000 mark but could not hold above it more than a few days." The major reason cited by most analysts for the weakness of the market was fear of an upcoming inflation and climbing interest rates. Mary was still in shock when the ticker tape brought another message: "City Bank of New York raised the prime rate by ¼ of 1 percent." This was too much for one day.

Mary was in charge of the Trust's investment department. She had just been authorized to invest a large sum of money in one (and only one) of three alternatives: corporate bonds, common stocks, or certificates of deposit (time deposits).

The Trust's objective is to maximize the yield on the investment over a one-year period. The problem is that the economic situation seemed to be uncertain and no one was able to predict the exact movements of the stock or even the bond markets. It was rather obvious to Mary that the yields (in percent of return on investment) depend on the state of the economy. Therefore, she consulted the economic research department. The researchers were not sure what the exact state of the economy would be after one year. However, they told Mary they expected the economy to be in one of three possible conditions (or states): solid growth, stagnation, or inflation. When asked for the likelihood of each condition, the researchers estimated a 50 percent chance for solid growth, a 30 percent chance of stagnation, and a 20 percent chance for inflation.

Mary examined the relationship between the yield on the possible investments and the state of the economy and concluded that past experience indicated the following trends:

1. *If* there is solid growth in the economy, bonds will yield 12 percent; stocks, 15 percent; and time deposits, 6.5 percent.
2. *If* stagnation prevails, bonds will yield 6 percent; stocks, 3 percent; and time deposits, 6.5 percent.
3. *If* inflation prevails, bonds will yield 3 percent; the value of stocks will drop 2 percent; and time deposits will yield 6.5 percent.

Mary examined all the above information and realized that the investment decision would not be simple at all.

3.1 DECISION ANALYSIS WITH DECISION TABLES

Characteristics of the investment problem

Mary's dilemma is a typical managerial investment problem. Mary, the *decision maker* in this case, must make a *choice* among several *courses of action*. She will attempt to evaluate the alternatives based on their yield during the next year, since the Trust's goal is to maximize its yield over that period. The difficulty is that there is *uncertainty* with respect to what is going to happen in the future. No matter which choice Mary makes, she is going to *assume some risk* that the future she has hoped for is not going to materialize. What is the degree of risk that she is assuming? How does it relate to the available alternatives? Can the risk be reduced? Can the risk be eliminated? *Decision theory*, a quantitative analysis procedure applied to decision making, attempts to answer such questions.

Decision theory for risk and uncertainty

The use of decision tables

The payoff table for analyzing data

The quantitative data of many decision situations can be arranged in a standardized tabular form known as a decision table (or a **payoff** table). The objective of doing so is to enable a systematic analysis of the problem. While not all decision situations are explicitly amenable to a tabular presentation, many concepts used in decision tables are common to all decision situations.

Decision tables typically contain four elements:

1. The alternative courses of action (decision variables).
2. The states of nature.
3. The probabilities of the states of nature.
4. The payoffs (results or outcomes).

Let us return to Mary's problem and arrange the information there as a decision table.

The alternative courses of action Decision making, by definition, involves two or more *options*, or **alternative courses of action,** also called strategies or alternatives. One, *and only one,* of these alternatives *must* be selected. The alternative courses of action are designated as a_1, a_2, . . . , a_n (sometimes d_1, d_2, . . . , d_n), where n is the number of available alternatives that may be either finite or infinite. For example, the decision to select a textbook for a particular class may involve numerous, but finite, alternatives. If, however, one were producing beer, the quantity of water to add to the mix may include, at least in theory, an infinite number of combinations. For example, one can add 2.1 gallons, 2.11 gallons, 2.111 gallons, and so on.

A finite number of alternatives

In this text, the alternatives are listed on the left side of the table, one to a row. In other books or computer programs they may be presented as columns.

In most operating circumstances, not all possible alternatives are considered, but only those within a limited range. This range may still leave an infinite number of alternatives to select from, as in beer making. There are, however, enough rules of good brewing to establish that the water added ought to be within the range of, say, 7 to 7.5 gallons to a 10-gallon barrel. This is the range of *feasible* solutions. It still leaves an infinite number of points between 7 and7.5, but one might decide to structure the alternatives in only tenths of gallons, thus reducing the number to only six (7, 7.1, 7.2, 7.3, 7.4, 7.5). Decision tables are then used when the number of alternatives is *finite* and usually small (e.g., less than 100).

Only feasible alternatives

In the investment problem there are three alternatives. They are listed on the left-hand side of the decision table (see Table 3.1). It is assumed that Mary will choose one of the given alternatives. The ability to generate alternatives depends on the creativity and imagination of the manager and the information available. A creative manager sees more alternatives than does a conservative one. For example, If Mary wants to consider investing in both stocks and bonds simultaneously, she can create more alternatives such as a_4: 50 percent stocks, 50 percent bonds; or a_5: 30 percent stocks, 70 percent bonds.

TABLE 3.1
Decision table (payoffs in percentage yield)

States of nature / *Alternatives (decision variables)*	.5	.3	.2	←*Probabilities (uncontrollable)*
	Solid growth s_1	*Stagnation* s_2	*Inflation* s_3	
a_1 *Bonds*	12	6	3	←*Payoffs*
a_2 *Stocks*	15	3	−2	
a_3 *Time deposits (CDs)*	6.5	6.5	6.5	

The states of nature At the top of the table, the possible **states of nature** (also called events or possible futures) are listed. They are generally labeled $s_1, s_2, \ldots, s_m$. In other texts they may be presented as rows. A state of nature can be a state of the economy (inflation), a weather condition (rain), a political development (election of a certain candidate), or other situation that the decision maker cannot control. In the investment example there are three states of nature that are the possible states of the economy: solid growth, stagnation, and inflation. The states of nature are usually *not* determined by the action of a single individual or an organization. They are basically the result of an "act of God," or the result of many forces pushing in various directions. The number of states of nature in decision tables is assumed to be finite and usually not large. Only one state of nature may occur at a time.

Uncontrollable futures

The probabilities of the states of nature A question may be asked: "What is the likelihood of these states of nature occurring?" Whenever it is possible to answer this question in terms of explicit chances (or probabilities), the information is recorded at the top of the table. The probabilities are given either in percent or in percentage fractions; for example, 50 percent = .5, 30 percent = .3. Since it is assumed that one *and only one* of the given states of nature will occur in the future, then the sum of the probabilities must always be one. This is expressed as:

One and only one state of nature will occur

$$p_1 + p_2 + \cdots + p_m = 1 \qquad (3.1)^1$$

where p_1 = Probability of s_1 occurring, p_2 = Probability of s_2 occurring, and so on. In Mary's example, $p_1 = .5$, $p_2 = .3$, and $p_3 = .2$. The subscript m designates the fact that m states of nature are considered.

The payoffs The payoff (or the *outcome*) associated with a certain alternative and a specific state is given in that cell within the body of the table located at the *intersection* of the alternative in question (given by a row) and the specific state of nature (given by a column). The payoff is designated by o_{ij} where i indicates the row and j the column. For example, in Table 3.1, if the decision maker selects alternative a_1 and future s_2 occurs, then the outcome of the decision is estimated as a payoff (yield) of 6 percent. The payoffs can be thought of as *conditional* since a specific payoff results from a specific state of nature occurring, but after a certain alternative course of action has been taken. An important point to remember is that the payoff is measured within a *specified* period (e.g., after one year). This period is sometimes called the *decision horizon.* Alternatively, a payoff can be the *present value* of several payoffs realized at different times in the future. Note that the payoffs must usually be forecasted (see Chapter 5). Payoffs can be measured in terms of money, market share, or other physical measures. The payoffs considered in most decisions are monetary. However, other consequences also will occur and should be taken into account once the quantitative answer is derived.

Conditional payoffs

The general structure of a decision table

Table 3.2 shows the general structure of decision tables.

The decision table as a model

In terms of the elements of mathematical models, the decision table can be described as:

Alternative courses of action	= Independent, decision variables.
States of nature	= Independent, uncontrollable parameters.
Probabilities of the states of nature	= Independent, uncontrollable parameters.
Payoffs	= Expected results.

[1] Alternatively the equation can be written as $\sum_{j=1}^{m} p_j = 1$.

TABLE 3.2
The decision table—general structure

Alternative courses of action	States of nature			
	p_1	p_2	. . .	p_m
	s_1	s_2	. . .	s_m
a_1	o_{11}	o_{12}	. . .	o_{1m}
a_2	o_{21}	o_{22}	. . .	o_{2m}
⋮	⋮	⋮	. . .	⋮
a_n	o_{n1}	o_{n2}	. . .	o_{nm}

Decision variables (rows $a_1 \ldots a_n$); *Uncontrollable parameters* (p and s rows); *Payoffs* (o_{ij} entries)

3.2 CLASSIFICATION OF DECISION SITUATIONS

Decision zones

Decision situations are frequently classified on the basis of what the decision maker knows (or believes) about the situation. It is customary to divide the degree of knowledge into three categories (see Figure 3.1), ranging from complete knowledge, on the left, to ignorance, on the right. Specifically, these categories are:

1. Certainty (complete information).
2. Risk (partial information).
3. Uncertainty (limited information).

Decision making under certainty

Deterministic decisions

In decision making under **certainty,** it is assumed that complete information is available so that the decision maker knows exactly what the outcome of each course of action will be. The decision maker thus becomes a perfect predictor of the future. For example, the alternative to invest in U.S. Savings Bonds is one in which it is reasonable to assume complete availability of information about the future return on the investment. Such situations are also termed **deterministic.** They occur most often with short time horizons. For example, with decisions whose impact will be felt after three months it is more reasonable to assume certainty than in a decision

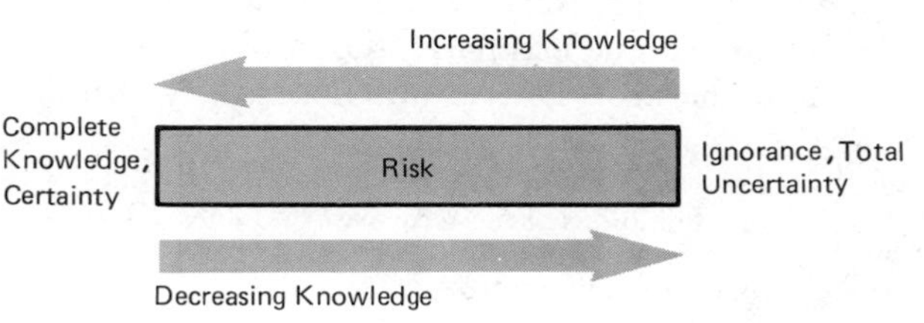

FIGURE 3.1
The zones of decision making

whose impact will be felt after two years. A substantial amount of knowledge and understanding of the behavior of the system under consideration is required to assumea state of certainty.

The decision table describing certainty is composed of a single column, since only one state of nature is assumed to occur. That is, only one possible payoff is associated with each decision alternative.

Decision making under risk

Probabilistic decisions

A decision under **risk** (also known as a *probabilistic* or **stochastic** decision situation) is one in which there could be two or more possible payoffs. For example, investing in stocks may result in an annual rate of return on investment of either 15 percent, 3 percent, or negative 2 percent, depending on the state of the economy. The reason there could be more than one payoff is that several possible states of nature are uncontrollable by the decision maker. If we assume that the *chance* of occurrence of each of the states of nature is known, then we say that the decision situation is *under risk*.

In risk situations, it is assumed that the long-run probabilities of occurrence of the given states of nature (and their conditional outcomes) are known or can be estimated. A classic example of such a situation is roulette. The roulette board is divided into 37 equal parts: 18 are black, 18 are red, and 1 is marked with zero. The player knows the probabilities of each state of nature represented by parts of the roulette field (e.g., 18/37 for red, 1/37 for zero). In making a decision, the player knows the long-run probability of winning the bet and therefore can assess the degree of risk assumed (termed a *calculated risk*).

Calculated risk

Less information is available than in decision making under certainty, since it is not definitely known which outcome will occur. The actual outcome depends on which *state of nature* occurs. For example, the number of umbrellas a store sells in a month depends on how much rain falls during the month. In this situation, it is often worthwhile for the decision maker to conduct a sensitivity analysis of the decision to determine how desirable the decision is under alternative outcomes.

Decision making under uncertainty

In decision making under **uncertainty,** the decision maker considers situations in which several outcomes are possible for each course of action.[2] However, in contrast to the risk situation, the decision maker *does not know,* or cannot estimate, the probability of occurrence of the possible states of nature. This is not necessarily the case of ignorance however,

Uncertainty or risk?

[2] The definitions of the terms *risk* and *uncertainty*, as presented here, were suggested by Professor F. H. Knight of the University of Chicago in 1933. Several other definitions can be found in the literature.

because he or she at least knows the possible states of nature. For example, it may be impossible to assess the probability of the success of a brand-new product. Thus, uncertainty situations contain even less information than risky situations.

The relationship between these decision situations and the different management science techniques, which are briefly introduced in Chapter 2 and which are discussed at length in Chapters 3–16, is shown in Table 3.3.

TABLE 3.3
The relationship between decision situations and management science techniques

Chapter	*Management science techniques*	*Decision situations*		
		Certainty	*Risk*	*Uncertainty*
3	Decision tables	X	X	X
3	Decision trees	X	X	
4	Game theory		X	X
5	Forecasting	X	X	
6,7	Linear programming	X		
8	Branch and bound	X		
8	Integer programming	X		
9	Goal programming	X		
10	Distribution (transportation, assignment)	X		
11	Maximum flow	X		
11	CPM	X		
11	Shortest route	X		
11	PERT		X	
12	Dynamic programming	X	X	
13	Markov chains		X	
14	Inventory	X	X	
15	Queuing		X	
16	Simulation	X	X	

The decision-making process

The classical definition of risk and uncertainty can be viewed from a different perspective by looking at the *process* of making a decision. This process consists of the following steps:

a. Consider the alternatives (opportunities) and the possible uncertainties concerning the anticipated consequences.

b. Draw a decision table (or a decision tree, as will be explained in Section 3.5).

c. Probabilities of each of the states of nature are assigned, either objectively or else through the decision maker's (or an expert's) subjective judgment. It is sometimes common to label decision making under risk as decision making under uncertainty but with known probabilities of the states of nature.

d. Evaluate the results in light of the criterion of choice.

e. Make the decision.

3.3 DECISIONS UNDER CERTAINTY

In decision making under certainty the situation can be mapped as a table with one payoff column (one state of nature). Therefore, in making a decision, all one has to do is to compare all the entries in the payoff column and select the alternative with the highest profit or lowest cost. The logic for such a choice is simple: There is no reason for doing otherwise. In executing such a comparison, one distinguishes between two cases:

Enumeration or search

1. When the number of alternatives is relatively small. In this case, an approach known as **complete enumeration** is used.
2. When the number of alternatives is large or even infinite. In this case, a selective search for the best solution is conducted with the aid of mathematical models.

Complete enumeration

Complete enumeration means examining every payoff, one at a time, comparing the payoffs to each other (e.g., in pairs), and discarding inferior solutions. The process continues until *all* payoffs are examined.

Example: Assignment of employees to machines A maintenance crew of three machinists is to be assigned to the repair of three machines, on a one-to-one basis, in a manner that minimizes repair time. Based on historical data, the supervisor knows the exact repair time, which varies with each person-machine match. The repair times, in hours, are shown in Table 3.4. (For example, if Jack works on machine A it takes him three hours to fix it; the repair time is the payoff in this case.)

TABLE 3.4
Repair times

Machinist \ *Machine*	A	B	C
Jack	3	7	4
Gene	4	6	6
Mel	3	8	5

Consider all possible matches

Solution All alternative assignments, with their appropriate total repair times, are shown in Table 3.5. Note that the decision table has only one column of payoffs (one state of nature).

By comparing the total repair times for *all* possibilities, it is found that alternative a_5 is the best, since the total repair time is the smallpest. Larger assignment problems have an extremely large number of possible solutions and are therefore solved by algorithms (as will be shown in Chapter 9) rather than by enumeration.

TABLE 3.5
Assignment payoffs

Alternatives	*Total payoff (total repair time)*	
a_1 Jack–A, Gene–B, Mel–C	$3 + 6 + 5 = 14$	
a_2 Jack–A, Gene–C, Mel–B	$3 + 6 + 8 = 17$	
a_3 Jack–B, Gene–A, Mel–C	$7 + 4 + 5 = 16$	
a_4 Jack–B, Gene–C, Mel–A	$7 + 6 + 3 = 16$	
a_5 Jack–C, Gene–B, Mel–A	$4 + 6 + 3 = 13$	←*Best*
a_6 Jack–C, Gene–A, Mel–B	$4 + 4 + 8 = 16$	

Computation with analytical models

While complete enumeration is an effective approach in many situations, there are two cases in which it does not work at all or works very poorly. The first is the case of an *infinite number of alternatives*. Managerial problems such as allocation of resources or blending liquid materials are examples of such situations. To cope with these problems, models such as linear programming (Chapter 6) have been developed.

Why use models?

The second case involves problems with a *finite but very large*, sometimes astronomical, number of alternatives. Such problems are frequently referred to as *combinatorial problems*. Several scheduling and sequencing problems are of this nature. In these cases, it is possible to enumerate all the alternatives, but it may take years to do so, even with the aid of high-speed computers. Special models such as branch and bound (Chapter 7), assignment (Chapter 10), dynamic programming (Chapter 12), and heuristic programming (Chapter 16) have been developed for effective solutions.

Combinatorial problems

Summary

Decision making under certainty involves the following steps:[3]

1. Determine the alternative courses of action.
2. Calculate (or assess) the payoffs, one for each course of action.
3. Select the one with the best payoff (e.g., largest profit or smallest cost), either by complete enumeration or by the use of an analytical model.

3.4 DECISIONS UNDER RISK

Decision situations in which the chance (or probability) of occurrence of each state of nature is known (or can be estimated) are defined as decisions

[3] For an extended discussion of decisions under certainty, see White [17].

Calculated risk

made under *risk*. In such cases the decision maker can assess the degree of risk that he or she is taking in terms of probability distributions. For example, a decision not to purchase fire insurance means that the decision maker takes a chance of perhaps 1 in 10,000 of losing all of his or her property in a fire.

The concept of probability in decision making

Probabilities in decision making should be viewed as a means of expressing the decision maker's judgment about an uncertain future. We all use phrases such as:

"There is a pretty good chance that interest rates will decline."
"It is more likely to rain today."
"It's not likely that mortgage rates will come down."
"We are not sure how our competitor will react."

Probabilities constitute a language similar to the above but more precise. By definition, a probability is the relative frequence of an event occurring when a situation is repeated many times under identical circumstances. But probabilities in managerial language are also used for one-time decision situations. For example, instead of saying that our new product has a pretty good chance of succeeding, we say that there is an 85 percent chance that the product will be a success.

Objective and subjective probabilities

There are two approaches to the assessment of the probabilities of the states of nature: objective and subjective.

History or experimentation for probabilities

Objective probability **Objective probabilities** can be derived either based on historical occurrences or based on experimentation. Alternatively, they can be derived with statistical formulas. For example, the probability of a "head" in the toss of a coin is computed statistically as one half because only two states of nature (a head or a tail) can occur; and assuming the coin is fair, there is an equal chance for each (i.e., 50 percent). Thus, the use of objective probabilities narrows the scope for judgment. Unfortunately, the use of objective probabilities requires several of the following crucial assumptions that restrict its use:

1. Objective probabilities are based on observation of past events, experimentation, or both. Therefore, in using objective probabilities for decision making, it must be assumed that future conditions will follow the same pattern as past conditions (or that a clear trend for future events has been established); otherwise, predictions of the future will be meaningless.
2. A necessary result of the assumption above is that the process observed must be stable.

3. It must be assumed that if a sample was observed for determining past behavior, it was large enough (statistically) and representative of the process under study.

Belief about the probabilities

Subjective probability The **subjective probability** approach measures the *degree of belief* in the likelihood of the future occurrence of a given outcome. Thus, such probabilities are a subjective appraisal of the nature of reality, in contrast to objective probabilities, which must be actual, countable, observable fact. Subjective probabilities are intuitive judgments about the probabilities of the states of nature, made by an individual(s) possessing experience with the phenomena involved. Subjective probability is used in cases in which objective probabilities cannot be used. The major problem with subjective probabilities is that different decision makers may give different estimates of the probabilities, and even change their estimates as a result of psychological, emotional, or other such factors.

Note: In either case we incorporate *judgment* into the decision process. For example, we must judge whether historical data is appropriate as a basis for using objective probabilities.

Solution approaches to decision making under risk

Several criteria

The most acceptable solution approach to decision making under risk is the use of **expected value** as a criterion of choice. Alternatively, the **expected opportunity loss** criterion may be used. Both lead to the same result. Other criteria are the **most probable state of nature** criterion and some of those used for decision making under uncertainty (such as minimax), which are discussed in Section 3.11.

An example of decision making under risk: How to beat inflation In the problem presented at the beginning of this chapter, Mary Golden was considering an investment for a trust fund in one of the following alternatives: a_1 = Corporate bonds, a_2 = Common stocks, or a_3 = Time deposits. Suppose that the Trust wants to invest in only *one alternative* with a delcared objective of maximizing the yield over a one-year period. The yield (in percent of return) will depend on the state of the economy,

TABLE 3.6
Yields (in percent) of investment alternatives

States of nature	.5	.3	.2	←*Probabilities*	
Alternatives	*Solid growth*	*Stagnation*	*Inflation*	*Expected value (percent)*	
a_1	12	6	3	8.4	←*Maximum*
a_2	15	3	−2	8.0	
a_3	6.5	6.5	6.5	6.5	

which can be either solid growth, stagnation, or inflation. The estimated yields under each alternative and state of the economy are shown in Table 3.6. The problem is to find the best investment alternative.

Solution approach A: The use of the expected payoff criterion This approach prescribes that the decision maker select the alternative with the best expected (average) payoff. This alternative should be selected each time the decision maker confronts the investment situation. Over the long run the average yearly yield will be the same as the expected payoff.

> The expected payoff of an alternative is the sum of all possible payoffs of that alternative, weighted by the probabilities of those payoffs occurring.

Maximizing expected yield

How to find the expected payoff. The expected payoffs are computed, one by one, for each alternative.

Step 1. Multiply each payoff by its corresponding probability. For example, in alternative a_1 of Table 3.6: $12 \times .5$, $6 \times .3$, and $3 \times .2$.

Step 2. Sum the results of the multiplications of step 1; the total is the expected payoff.[4]

For alternative a_1 in Table 3.6 the results are $E(a_1) = 12 \times .5 + 6 \times .3 + 3 \times .2 = 8.4$ percent, where $E(a_1)$ is the symbol designing expected value, E, of alternative a_1.

Repeating the process for alternatives a_2 and a_3, one gets:

$$E(a_2) = 15 \times .5 + 3 \times .3 - 2 \times .2 = 8.0 \text{ percent}$$
$$E(a_3) = 6.5 \times .5 + 6.5 \times .3 + 6.5 \times .2 = 6.5 \text{ percent}$$

The selection of an alternative. Once the expected payoffs for all alternatives are determined, only the newly formed column of expected payoffs need be considered (see the right-hand column of Table 3.6). This is the dependent (or result) variable of the decision model. If the problem is one of maximization, then the *highest* expected payoff is searched for, using complete enumeration. In minimization, the alternative with the *lowest* expected payoff is sought. In the investment (maximization) example, alternative a_1 has the highest expected yield, and therefore investing in

[4] In mathematical terms, let:

a_i = Alternative i
s_j = State of nature j
p_j = Probability that state of nature s_j will occur
o_{ij} = Payoff resulting from the selection of alternative a_i when s_j occurs

Then, the expected value $E(a_i)$ is:

$$E(a_i) = p_1 o_{i1} + p_2 o_{i2} + \cdots = \sum_j p_j o_{ij}$$

corporate bonds is recommended. The meaning of this choice is that the decision maker should invest in a_1, and only in a_1, each time that he or she is confronted with the decision. Furthermore, the average yearly yield, over the long run, per decision, is 8.4 percent. *Note:* The use of this criterion, when the payoffs are expressed in dollars, is called the **expected monetary value** or the EMV criterion.

EMV = expected monetary value

Solution approach B: The expected opportunity loss (EOL) criterion (also called the regret criterion) The basic idea of this criterion is that people frequently act to minimize their anticipated average (expected) **regret. Opportunity loss** is defined as the relative loss resulting from selecting an alternative, given that a particular state of nature occurred, as compared with the best alternative that could have been selected. For example, if Mary Golden invests in bonds (a_1) and solid growth occurs, she will regret not having invested in stocks (a_2), which would have been the best alternative. Since she will make 12 percent with the bonds versus 15 percent that she could have made with stocks, her regret, or opportunity loss, is 3 percent. Table 3.7 shows the complete opportunity loss data. Within each payoff column, each payoff is subtracted from the largest payoff in the column. Once the table is constructed, the *expected* regret is computed by the same method used in computing expected payoffs, and the alternative with the *smallest expected regret* is selected. This rule is true for *any* regret table, whether derived from profit or loss data. Regret is always bad and is to be avoided or minimized.

Minimizing expected regret

Note also that alternative a_1 was selected under both the opportunity loss criterion and the expected payoff criterion. This is *not* a coincidence. Both will *always lead* to the *same choice* since the mathematical operations are basically the same. The difference is only philosophical. These are merely two different explanations of why people make certain choices.

EOL and EMV give the same result

Solution approach C: The "most probable state of nature" criterion This criterion prescribes that as the decision maker confronts the various possible states of nature in a decision under risk, he or she ignores all but the most probable state. By doing so, the decision maker changes

Ignoring less likely outcomes

TABLE 3.7
Opportunity loss table (percent yield) of Table 3.6

States of nature / *Alternatives*	.5	.3	.2	←*Probabilities*	
	Solid growth	*Stagnation*	*Inflation*	*Expected regret*	
a_1	15 − 12 = 3	6.5 − 6 = .5	6.5 − 3 = 3.5	3 × .5 + .5 × .3 + 3.5 × .2 = 2.35	←*Smallest regret*
a_2	15 − 15 = 0	6.5 − 3 = 3.5	6.5 − (−2) = 8.5	0 × .5 + 3.5 × .3 + 8.5 × .2 = 2.75	
a_3	15 − 6.5 = 8.5	6.5 − 6.5 = 0	6.5 − 6.5 = 0	8.5 × .5 + 0 × .3 + 0 × .2 = 4.25	

the situation to a decision under assumed certainty. Some nonrepetitive decisions are treated with this principle. For example, decisions to embark on new ventures are sometimes made only on the basis of what will happen if the venture succeeds (assuming the chance for success is .8 or more), although there is almost always some chance for failure.

Example. Consider the investment decision of Table 3.6. According to the most-probable-state-of-nature criterion, the decision maker assumes that solid growth will occur since it has the largest chance of occurring. The other states of nature are ignored. Therefore, she will select a_2 since it will give her the largest yield (15 percent) in the event that solid growth will occur. However, if the decision maker is wrong, she may end with a yield of 3 or even lose 2. If this is a repeating situation, she will only make 8 (the expected value) over the long run.

One problem with this criterion is that it ignores the magnitude of some of the payoffs. For example, according to this criterion, a decision maker would choose a_1 over a_2 in the table below, no matter what the profits are under the s_2 column.

	$p_1 = .6$ s_1	$p_2 = .4$ s_2
a_1	10	10
a_2	8	500

Solution approach D: Criteria of choice for uncertainty In Part B of this chapter we introduce five criteria of choice for the case of uncertainty. These could be used for the case of risk as well. However, with the exception of nonrepetitive decisions, it is very unlikely that these criteria will be used, since they possess too many deficiencies and do not include the consideration of the risk level.

Note: Solution approach C ignores the relative magnitude of some of the outcomes, while solution approach D ignores the likelihood of each of the events occurring. The expected value criterion *combines* both the size of the consequences and their likelihood. Therefore, it is a superior criterion for most situations.

Notes on application

Nonrepetitive decisions The expected value approach is based on achieving the best payoff over the long run. For example, if the decision maker of Table 3.6 selects alternative a_1, he or she will make *either* a 12, 6, or 3 percent yield, each time the decision is made. Only over the *long* *run* will these yields average out to 8.4 percent. The question may thus be asked: Is there any justification in using an expected value approach for a one-shot, nonrepetitive decision?

There is at least one case in which the answer to this question is clearly yes. If a company is making several one-shot decisions whose payoff is more or less of the same magnitude, then the overall impact of using an expected value approach is similar to that of a repetitive decision. That is, repeating one decision 30 times, or making 30 decisions one time, results in the same mathematical expectation. In cases where an expected value cannot be justified, the criteria discussed in Section 3.12 (such as minimax) can be used, or the use of utilities, as shown in Chapter 4, may be a good approach.

Use of mathematical models The evaluation of decisions under risk is made by comparing (complete enumeration) *all* expected payoffs and selecting the best one. However, this may be a long and costly procedure if many alternatives and payoffs are considered. For these types of situations probabilistic mathematical models (such as those presented in Chapters 13–16) are available.

The use of utilities as payoffs This subject will be discussed in Chapter 4.

Dominance In certain cases, it is possible to eliminate some alternatives from evaluation because they are *inferior to* or *dominated by* other alternatives. For example, assume that alternative a_4 is added as an investment alternative to Table 3.6, where the yields are: 10 in the case of solid growth, 6 in the case of stagnation, and 2 in the case of inflation. If we compare this alternative (a_4) to a_1, we get:

	Solid growth	*Stagnation*	*Inflation*
a_1	12	6	3
a_4	10	6	2

It can clearly be seen that the decision maker should not consider a_4 at all, because no matter what state of nature occurs, the decision maker will be as well off or better with a_1. Thus, it is said that a_1 **dominates** a_4.

A note on the concept of risk

Last, in spite of the utility of the expected value as a decision criterion for risky situations, it is always advisable to also consider the *variability* of the payoffs. For example, it may not be worthwhile to select an alternative that has an insignificantly higher expected return if it also entails the possibility of significant loss. Thus, the variability of returns should always be considered.

Sensitivity analysis

Assume that our company is examining a venture in which we can make \$45,000 or lose \$15,000. Also assume that the company uses expected value as the criterion for decision making; if the EMV of this venture is larger than zero, the company will undertake the project, but if the EMV is zero, they will be indifferent.

Denote the probability of success by p. Therefore:

$$\text{EMV} = p(45{,}000) + (1 - p)(-15{,}000)$$

If we set EMV to zero and solve for p, we will get $p = .25$. That is, if the probability of success is larger than .25, the EMV will be larger than zero. By assumption, the company should undertake the project.

Now suppose that we have estimated the probability of success to be .60; obviously the company will undertake the project. Furthermore, the probability of success could drop all the way to .25 before the company would change its decision. As the probability approaches .25, the EMV gets smaller and smaller, shrinking to exactly zero at .25 and becoming *negative* for values less than .25. This value of $p = .25$ is called the **critical probability** and is used in what is known as a "what if" or sensitivity analysis of the recommended choice.

Summary

The use of the expected payoff criterion for making decisions under risk enables the decision maker to consider the risk involved in the decision. The expected payoff is the sum of individual payoffs weighted by their probabilities of occurrence. Other criteria of choice may be used, especially in nonrepetitive situations, such as maximum possible loss.

3.5 DECISION TREES

Decision making as discussed thus far has been limited to a single decision over one period of time. A decision was to be made at the beginning of the period, and the future consequences were estimated either in terms of the present value or the future worth of the results. All the information was presented in the form of a decision table. There are times, however, when a decision cannot be viewed as an isolated, single occurrence, but rather as the first of a sequence of several interrelated decisions over several future periods. Therefore, the decision maker must consider the whole series of decisions simultaneously. Such a situation is called a *sequential* or *multiperiod* decision process. Using decision tables to analyze these decisions becomes too cumbersome. The tool that was developed instead

Decision trees for sequential decisions

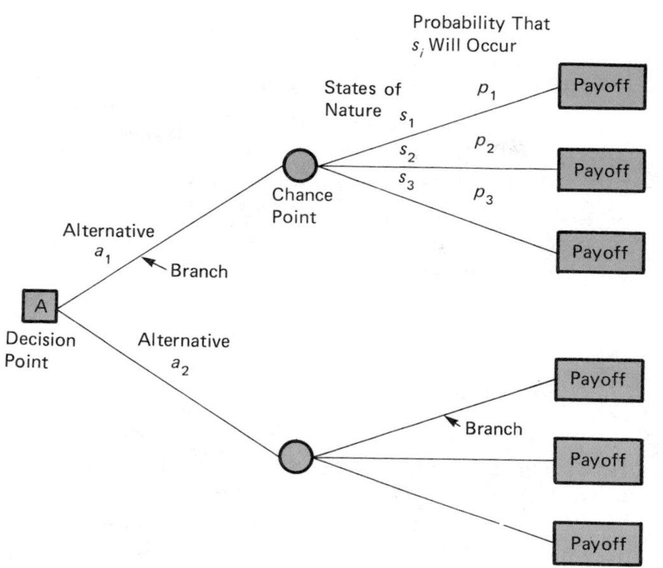

FIGURE 3.2
The general structure of a decision tree

is called a **decision tree,** which is basically a graphical exposition of decision tables in the form of a tree.[5]

Advantages

Decisions at a glance

Decision trees provide a graphical presentation of sequential decision processes. They show, at a glance, when decisions are expected to be made, what the possible consequences are, and what the resultant payoffs are expected to be.

Another advantage is that the results of the computations are depicted directly on the tree, simplifying the analysis.

The composition of a decision tree

A decision tree is composed of the following elements (see Figure 3.2): decision points, alternatives, chance points, states of nature, and payoffs.

Alternatives emerge from decision points

1. Decision points At a **decision point** (also called a decision node, act node, or decision fork), usually designated by a square, the decision maker must select *one alternative course of action* from a finite number of available ones. These are shown as **branches** or arcs emerging out of the right side of the decision point. When there is a cost associated with the alternative, it is written along the branch. An alternative not selected

[5] A similar but more complicated tool, *dynamic programming,* will be described in Chapter 12.

is *pruned*, designated by the symbol ‖. Each alternative branch may result in either a payoff, in another decision point, or in a chance point.

Events emerge from chance points

2. *Chance points* A **chance point** (also known as an event fork or chance node), designated by a circle, indicates that a chance event is expected at this point in the process. That is, one of a finite number of *states of nature* is expected to occur. The states of nature are shown on the tree as branches to the right of the chance points. Since decision trees depict decision making under risk, the assumed probabilities of the states of nature are written above the branches. Each state of nature may be followed by a payoff, a decision point, or by another chance point.

Constructing a tree

A tree grows to the right

A tree is started at the *left* of the page with a decision point. Once the decision point is constructed, all possible alternatives are drawn branching out to the right. Then, a chance point or other decision points are added, corresponding to events or decisions that are expected to occur after the initial decision. Each time a chance point is added, the appropriate states of nature, with their corresponding probabilities, branch out of it to the right. The tree continues to branch from left to right until the payoffs are reached. Figure 3.2 shows the general structure of a small tree. Larger trees involve a sequence of several decision and chance points, representing several decision periods, as shown later in both this section and in Section 3.11. The tree shown in Figure 3.2 represents a single decision and as such is equivalent to a decision table.

The process of constructing a tree may be divided conceptually into three steps:

a. Build a *logical tree,* which includes all decision points, chance points, and emerging arcs, arranged in chronological order.
b. Introduce the probabilities of the states of nature on the arcs, thus forming a *probability tree.*
c. Finally, add the conditional payoffs, thus forming the completed *decision tree.*

Example of the equivalence of decision trees and decision tables

Table-tree equivalence

Consider the situation in Table 3.8. (This problem was solved in Section 3.4 by computing the expected value of each alternative. Alternative a_1 was recommended with the highest expected value.) This table is presented as a decision tree in Figure 3.3.

Evaluating a tree In order to solve a tree, it is customary to divide it into segments. Two types of segments are considered: *decision points* with all their alternatives (Figure 3.4a), and *chance points* with all their emerging states of nature (Figure 3.4b).

The solution process starts with those segments ending in the final

TABLE 3.8
Table 3.1 reproduced

Alternatives \ States of nature	.5	.3	.2	
	Solid growth s_1	Stagnation s_2	Inflation s_3	Expected value
a_1 *Bonds*	12	6	3	8.4
a_2 *Stocks*	15	3	−2	8.0
a_3 *Time deposits*	6.5	6.5	6.5	6.5

payoffs, at the *right side of the tree,* and continues to the left, segment by segment, in the *reverse* order from which it was drawn.

Backward evaluation

1. *Chance point segments.* The *expected value* of all the states of nature emerging from a chance point must be computed (multiply payoffs by probabilities and sum up the results). The expected value is then written above the chance point inside a rectangle (labeled EMV in Figure 3.3). These expected values are considered as payoffs for the next branch to the left.

Chance segments use EMV

2. *Decision point segments.* At a decision point, the payoffs given (or computed) for each alternative are compared and the best one is selected. All others are disregarded. A disregarded alternative is marked by the symbol || directly on the branch (see Figure 3.3).

Decision segments

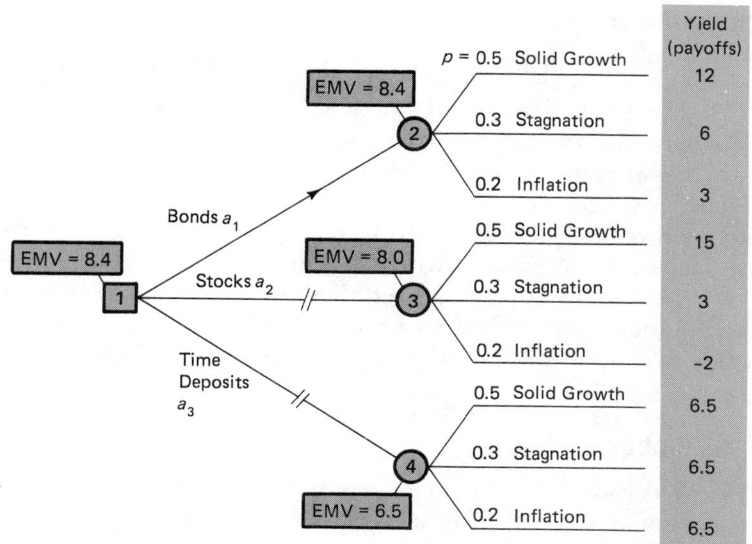

FIGURE 3.3
A decision tree for Table 3.8

FIGURE 3.4
Segments of a tree

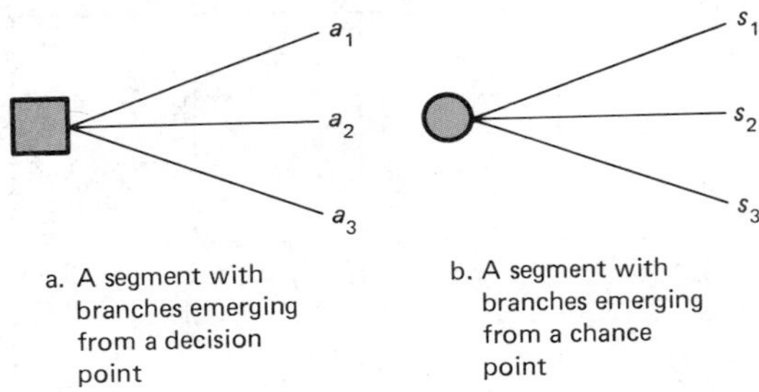

Thus, the decision maker *must* select one alternative at each *decision* point, and discard (prune) *all* other alternatives. The computation process continues from the right to the left. Pruning slowly reduces the size of the decision tree until only one alternative remains at the last decision point on the left side of the tree.

Evaluating the tree of Figure 3.3

Computations at a chance point The segments at the right are considered first. They are all chance points, and therefore *expected values* are computed. The expected values (designated in Figure 3.3 as EMV) are: For point **2:**

$$\text{EMV} = 12(.5) + 6(.3) + 3(.2) = 8.4.$$

For point **3:**

$$\text{EMV} = 15(.5) + 3(.3) - 2(.2) = 8.0.$$

For point **4:**

$$\text{EMV} = 6.5(.5) + 6.5(.3) + 6.5(.2) = 6.5.$$

Payoffs

The EMVs are entered, above each chance point, inside a rectangle. They are now considered as *payoffs* for the next step.

Computations at a decision point Figure 3.5 shows the situation in Figure 3.3 after EMVs for all chance points have been computed. At decision point 1, all alternatives are compared with the EMVs considered as payoffs. Alternative a_1 with the highest payoff is recommended.

The example just presented showed a decision tree for a single-decision period (equivalent to a decision table). However, decision trees are especially useful in multiperiod situations involving sequential decisions.

The multiperiod case

The multiperiod tree

Decision trees involving a sequence of decisions are nothing but a collection of smaller decision trees, each representing a single time period. All grow horizontally from left to right; the trunk is at the left and the

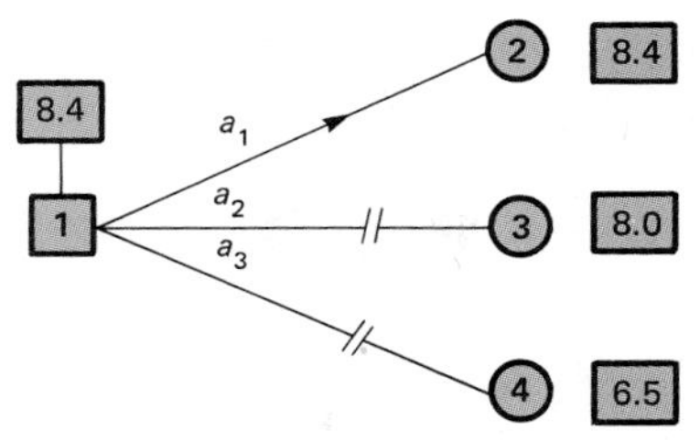

FIGURE 3.5 Computation at a decision point

branches at the right. The tree can be extended to the limit of forecasting ability.

Example The Microflange Company is facing heavy demand for one of its flanges. The existing manufacturing facility is presently working at full capacity on normal shifts. The firm has two options to meet the heavy demand: either instituting overtime, an option that will cost $2,000, or installing new machinery at a cost of $20,000. The choice between the options depends mainly on what happens to sales over the next two years. During the *first year,* management estimates that there is a 70 percent chance that sales will rise and a 30 percent chance that they will fall.

The information given so far is sufficient to start building a decision tree (Figure 3.6 points **1, 2,** and **3**). After one year of operation, managment will be faced with another decision, which will depend on the action taken initially, the events during the year, and the projection of second-year sales.

The decisions after one year Depending on the action at time zero and the states of nature, management could be at either point **4, 5, 6,** or **7.**

Decisions, decisions, decisions!

First decision point (4 in Figure 3.6). If a new machine had been installed at time zero and sales had risen, then management could either install a second machine or institute overtime. The decision at point **4** depends on the anticipated payoffs after two years. These depend on sales forecasts, which can be either high (20 percent chance), medium (70 percent), or low (10 percent). In the event that a second machine is installed, the anticipated payoffs are $80,000, $60,000, and $50,000, respectively.[6] This information is entered on the right side of the tree. The expected value is then computed ($63,000) and entered above chance point **8.**

However, if overtime is instituted, the profits are estimated to be $60,000 for high sales, $50,000 for medium sales, and $40,000 for low sales. This information is used to compute the expected value, which is then entered at chance point **9** in Figure 3.6 ($51,000).

Second decision point. If a new machine had been installed initially and sales had fallen, then the decision maker would be at point **5** after one year. At that point, management would have no choice but to use

[6] We assume that these figures and the rest of the payoffs and expenses in this problem are given in present values, so they can be combined and compared.

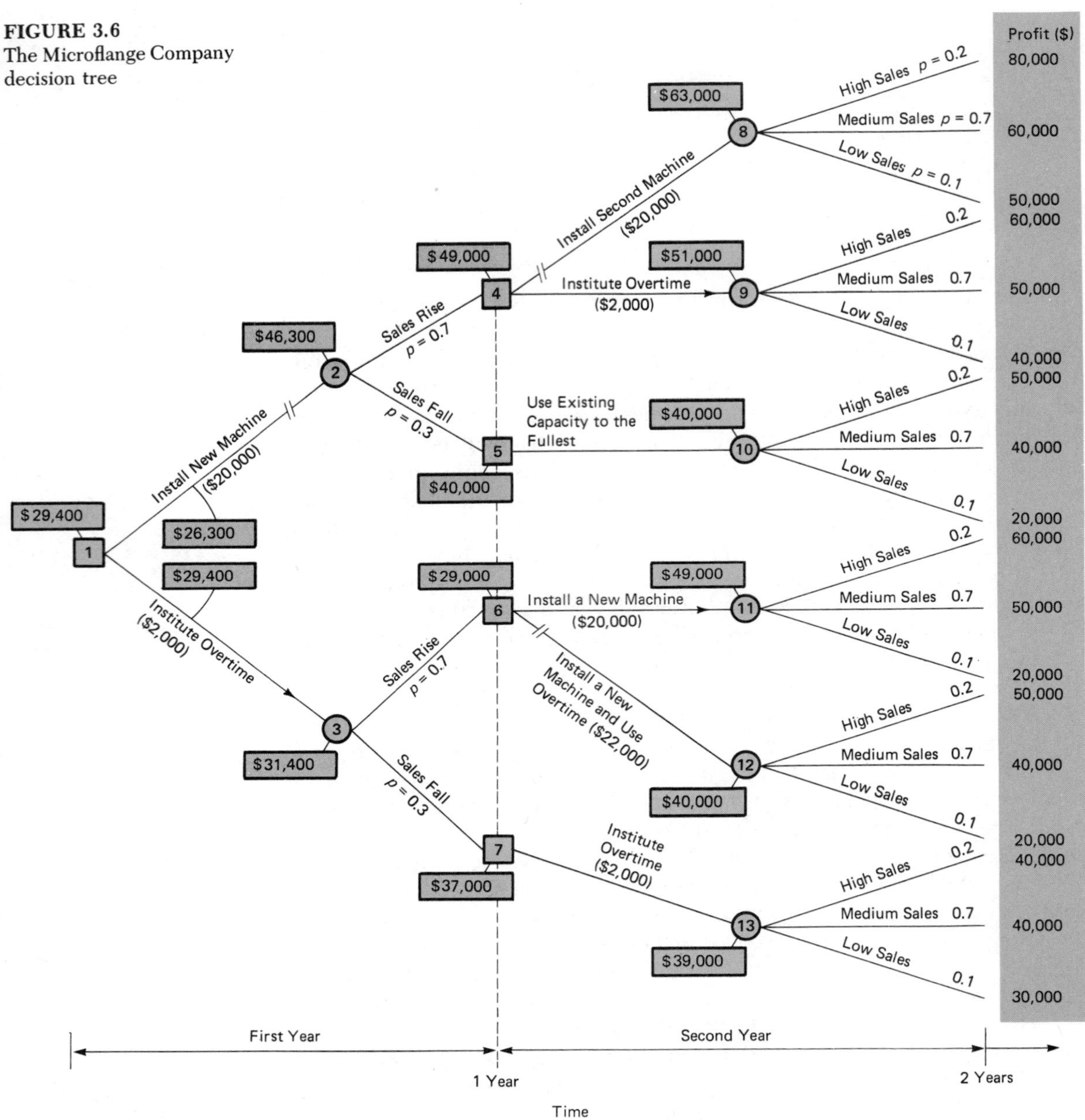

FIGURE 3.6
The Microflange Company decision tree

the existing capacities to the fullest extent. Anticipated results are shown on the tree at point **10**.

Third decision point. If overtime had been instituted initially and sales had risen, then management would be at decision point **6** with two alternatives open: install a new machine, or install a new machine *and* use overtime. The anticipated payoffs are shown at points **11** and **12**.

Fourth decision point. If overtime had been instituted initially and sales had fallen, then management would be at decision point **7** where only one alternative is assumed to be available: institute overtime. The anticipated results are shown at point **13.**

The problem is to find the best course of action the company should take *initially* and at *intermediate* stages, knowing all the information above.

Evaluation

Using the procedure previously outlined, the expected values at all chance points are computed (starting from the right).
For point **8:**

$$EMV = .2 \times 80{,}000 + .7 \times 60{,}000 + .1 \times 50{,}000 = \$63{,}000$$

For point **9:**

$$EMV = .2 \times 60{,}000 + .7 \times 50{,}000 + .1 \times 40{,}000 = \$51{,}000$$

Similarly, for the other points the EMVs are:

Point	(10)	(11)	(12)	(13)
EMV	\$40,000	\$49,000	\$40,000	\$39,000

Next, the computation moves leftward, thus reaching decision points **4, 5, 6,** and **7.**

Point 4. At this decision point the alternative of a second machine (\$63,000 − \$20,000 = \$43,000 profit) is compared with the alternative of overtime (\$51,000 − \$2,000 = \$49,000 profit). Since the latter is more profitable, it is selected, and the EMV of \$49,000 is entered above point **4.**

Point 5. There is only one alternative. The expected value of point **10** is thus recorded at point **5.**

Point 6. At this decision point there are two alternatives: install a new machine (\$49,000 − \$20,000 = \$29,000) or overtime plus new machine (\$40,000 − \$22,000 = \$18,000). The first one is better, and so an EMV of \$29,000 is recorded at point **6.**

Point 7. There is only one alternative at this point. The EMV from point **13,** \$39,000, is recorded (less the \$2,000 expense) at point **7.**

At this stage only the left side of the tree is considered. This information is presented in Figure 3.7.

Computation of the left side (Figure 3.7)

EMV of point **2** = .7 × \$49,000 + .3 × \$40,000 = \$46,300
EMV of point **3** = .7 × \$29,000 + .3 × \$37,000 = \$31,400

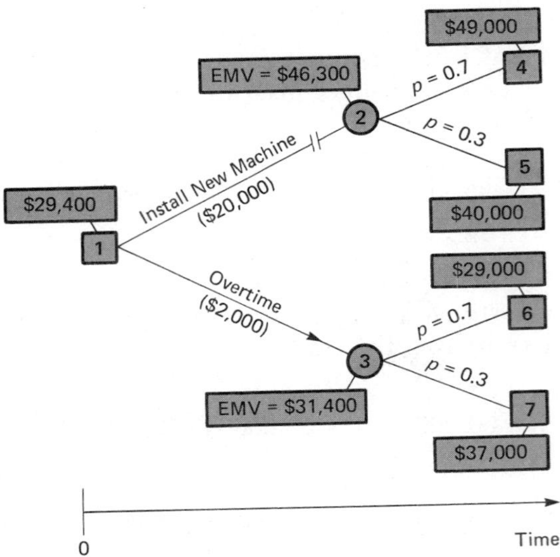

FIGURE 3.7
Left side of Figure 3.6

Finally, decision point **1** is considered:
The expected value of installing a new machine is:

$$\text{EMV} = \$46{,}300 - \$20{,}000 = \$26{,}200$$

The expected value with overtime is:

$$\text{EMV} = \$31{,}400 - \$2{,}000 = \$29{,}400$$

Thus, it is better to plan now on overtime, for an expected gain of $29,400. The final decision, therefore, is to use overtime this year and, *if* sales rise, install a new machine the second year. If sales fall, however, the overtime should be continued.

3.6 COMPUTER PROGRAMS FOR DECISION TABLES AND TREES

Computer programs for decision tables, sometimes referred to as "expected value analyses," consist of a variety of calculations and are available as a part of many standard statistical packages. Typical programs include:

Inputs

The decision table.

Outputs

The expected value of all alternatives and the identification of the best (optimal) one.

A computer printout of the problem presented in Tables 3.6 and 3.8 is given below, based on the MSS package.

EXPECTED MONETARY VALUE (EMV)

Problem Name: dt1

Decision Alternative	EMV	
a1	8.40	<---BEST
a2	8.00	
a3	6.50	

In addition, the computer will produce an analysis of perfect and imperfect information (see Part B of this chapter).

Computerized decision trees

Computerized decision tree analyses are commercially available from several vendors. A typical program includes:

Inputs

a. The decision points, the alternatives emerging from each, and the point at the end of each alternative.
b. Chance points, their branches (states of nature), and the ending point for each branch.
c. Terminal points with their respective payoffs.

Outputs

a. The alternative(s) selected.
b. The expected value of the best alternative.

A printout of the decision tree described in Problem 19 is shown below.

** INFORMATION ENTERED **

DECISION NODES

NODE	BRANCHES	ALTERNATIVE NUMBER	ENDING NODE
0	2	1	1
		2	3
2	2	3	6
		4	7
5	2	5	12
		6	13

CHANCE NODES

NODE	BRANCHES	PROBABILITY	ENDING NODE
1	2	.7	2
		.3	8
3	2	.4	4
		.6	5
4	3	.2	9
		.3	10
		.5	11

TERMINAL NODES

NODE	PAYOFF
6	-3500
7	-1500
8	-2500
9	-1500
10	-2000
11	-4500
12	-4000
13	-5000

** RESULTS **

SELECTED ALTERNATIVES:

5 4 1

EXPECTED PAYOFF:-1800

** END OF ANALYSIS **

Note:

1. Nodes are labeled from zero on and include the terminal points with their payoffs.
2. The initial expense is added to each payoff on the right-hand side (the terminal nodes).
3. A negative payoff implies a cost.

Special packages for decision analysis[7]

Several application software packages exist that can be considered as potentially useful decision aids. They can be incorporated into the decision

[7] Adapted from Turban [15].

analysis itself or be used to supplement it, either by providing input data (e.g., subjective judgments), or by "massaging" the output data of the decision support system (see Chapter 17). Representative examples are described below.

Expert Choice™ (Decision Support Software, McLean, Virginia) Expert Choice is a structured decision aid that allows users to graphically portray a complex decision analysis problem with multiple criteria for evaluation. An example of Expert Choice's site selection model is shown in Figure 3.8. A number of attributes are considered, each of which is assigned a subjective weight that indicates the importance of the attribute. Alternatives are then outlined as they relate to each attribute. As with several other micro programs, here too there are limitations on the number of attributes and alternatives.

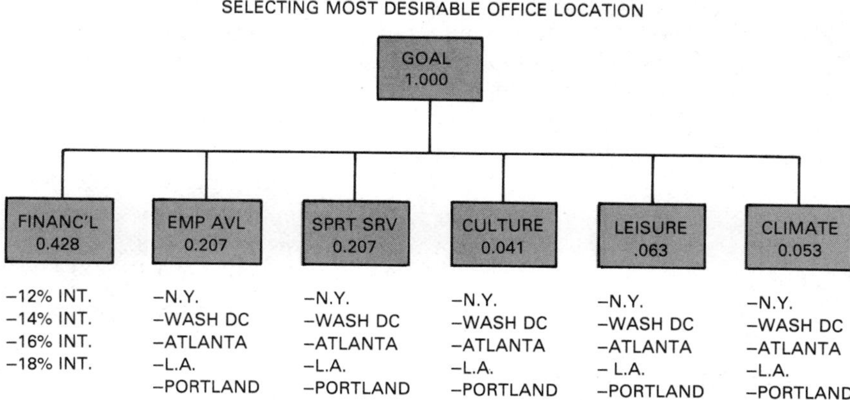

Courtesy Decision Support Software, McLeen, Virginia

FIGURE 3.8
Expert Choice site selection model

Decision Master™ (Generic Software, Inc., Bellevue, Washington) Decision Master helps the user make decisions involving multiple choices and multiple criteria for each choice. It also allows each criterion to be separately weighted and each choice/criterion to be individually rated.

Decision Aid™ (Computer Software Consultants, Inc., New York, New York) This managerial problem-solving decision aid consists of several components such as: personnel selection decision simulation; time series analysis and projections; multiple regression; statistical hypothesis testing; financial planning; and project management.

ORION™ (Comshare, Inc., Ann Arbor, Michigan) This package provides a data analysis system for marketing and financial managers. It offers sales forecasting, market share analysis, cash flow projections, quality control charting, and production scheduling.

Arborist™ (Texas Instruments, Dallas, Texas) Arborist is a tool for solving decision situations under risk that are presented as *decision trees.* Using extensive graphics, the program allows the user to view, over several windows, the entire decision tree and/or portions of it. The probabilities of the states of nature are entered numerically (or a "probability wheel" can be used to graphically assist in estimating probabilities). With direct interface to 1–2–3® from Lotus®, Arborist can be used for financial planning and investment analysis.

Lightyear™ (Lightyear, Santa Clara, California) Lightyear enables the user to weight different factors in a decision-making process. The weighing is done numerically, or by using a subjective rating (such as "good" and "excellent"). The program, which uses graphics extensively, enables easy "what if" sensitivity analysis.

Summary

The unique feature of decision trees is that they allow management to view the logical order of a sequence of decisions. They show a clear graphical presentation of the various alternative courses of action and their possible consequences. Using decision trees, management can also examine the impact of a series of decisions (multiperiod decisions) on the objectives of the organization. The graphical presentation helps in understanding the interactions among alternative courses of action, uncertain events, and future consequences.

The computations required in decision trees can usually be done manually; a computer is required only when extremely large and complicated trees are analyzed. For some practical aspects of implementation, consult Magee [10] and [11], and Ulvilla and Brown [16].

3.7 CONCLUDING REMARKS

Most managerial decisions are made in one of two decision environments that are presented in this chapter, namely *certainty* or *risk*. In decisions under certainty, the payoff, or the outcome of selecting an alternative, is assumed to be known. In decisions under risk, it is assumed that it is possible to assess the chances of various outcomes occurring but it is not possible to predict exactly which one will occur.

Decision theory has developed a methodology of analyzing managerial decisions. It uses a standard format, known as a decision (payoff) table, for arranging all the pertinent data of the situation.

In the case of certainty, the selection of the best alternative is made either by a comparison process called complete enumeration or with the aid of mathematical models. Mathematical models are used to conduct an efficient search among given alternatives, or sometimes even to generate the alternatives themselves. In either case, the choice is based on a rational selection of the *best* payoff.

In the case of risky decisions, the decision maker may use one of several available criteria for making a choice. Most acceptable is the search (again conducted by complete enumeration or mathematical models) for the alternative with the highest expected payoff.

Decision tables and trees are valuable tools to aid in decision making under risk. Decision trees also have the capability of solving sequential decisions involving different sets of decision alternatives and, in general, more complex decision situations.

Part B of this chapter discusses the third decision situation, that of uncertainty. The value of acquiring additional information about states of nature is also discussed.

3.8 PROBLEMS FOR PART A

1. The demand for Swiss watches is estimated as:

Number of units	*Probability*
20	.15
21	.20
22	.36
23	.19
24	.10

Find the expected revenue if the product sells for 399 francs.

2. An $800,000 property has a 1/10 of 1 percent chance of catching fire that will cause damages of $100,000; and 1/20 of 1 percent chance of catching fire that will completely destroy the property. Management decided to insure the property and it is reviewing two possible insurance policies:
   a. A policy with $50,000 deductible: that is, the insurance company covers all damages except the initial $50,000. The annual premium for such a policy is $750.
   b. A no-deduction (fully paid) policy with an annual premium of $1,000.

   If the company's objective is cost minimization, which policy should it purchase? Build both an opportunity loss table and a regular payoff decision table for the situation and solve both of them.

3. The table below shows the length of stay distribution in a Toronto hospital, in days.

Days	*Probability (percent)*	*Days*	*Probability (percent)*
2	3	6	15
3	5	7	25
4	5	8	20
5	10	9	10
		10	7

The hospital makes $120 net profit per day during the first four days of patients' stay, and $40 a day for the fifth day or more of stay. How much profit will the hospital make in one year (365 days) if it admits 20 patients per day, on the average?

4. Lemon Auto keeps detailed data on its car sales during the previous year. The table below summarizes these sales. For example, there were 15 days when no cars were sold at all.

	Number of days
No cars were sold	15
One car per day was sold	30
Two cars per day were sold	87
Three cars sold	141
Four cars sold	27
Total number of days observed	300

   a. Find the frequency distribution of the sales.
   b. Find the average number of cars sold daily.
   c. Find the yearly profit of Lemon Auto if the average profit per car is $237.

5. Fire insurance for a plant valued at $1 million costs $150.
   a. Should the company take the insurance if the chance of a fire that will destroy the plant is 1 in 10,000 (base your answer on expected value)?
   b. What factor(s) may change the decision?

6. You have been offered the chance to play a dice game in which you will receive $10 each time the point total of a toss of two dice is 4. If it costs you $1 per toss to participate, should you play or not?

7. A survey conducted over the last 20 years in Hamburg, Germany, indicated that in 8 of them the winter was mild, in 7 of them it was cold, and in the remaining 5 it was very cold.

A company sells 1,000 fur coats in a mild year, 1,300 in a cold year, and 2,000 in a very cold year.

Find the yearly expected profit of the company if a fur coat costs 85 deutsche mark (DM) and is sold to stores for 123 DM.

8. Find the best alternative in the following decision tables: a and b are *profits*, and c is *cost* data. Use both an expected value and an expected opportunity loss (EOL) approach.

a.

States of nature / *Alternatives*	.3	5	.2
	s_1	s_2	s_3
a_1	5	8	3
a_2	6	5	7

b.

States of nature / *Alternatives*	.6	.1	.2	.1
	s_1	s_2	s_3	s_4
a_1	3	5	8	−1
a_2	6	5	2	0
a_3	0	5	6	4

c.

States of nature / *Alternatives*	.1	.6	.3
	s_1	s_2	s_3
a_1	5	2	1
a_2	4	3	3
a_3	2	6	1

9. A marketing agent frequently flies from Montreal to Boston. She can use the airport bus, which costs \$3; but if she takes it, there is a .08 chance that she will miss the flight. A hotel limousine costs \$7, with a .96 chance of being on time for the flight. For \$15, she can use a taxi that will make 99 of 100 flights. Each time she catches the plane, she will conclude a business transaction, which will produce a profit of \$1,000; otherwise, she will lose it.

Which mode of transportation should the marketing agent use in order to maximize her profit?

10. The yearly demand for a seasonal item follows the distribution below:

Demand (units)	*Probability*
1,000	.20
2,000	.30
3,000	.40
4,000	.10

The manufacturer of the item can produce it by one of three methods:

a. Use existing tools at a cost of \$6 per unit.

b. Buy special equipment for \$1,000. The value of the equipment at the end of the year (salvage value) is zero. The variable cost, per unit produced, is \$3.

c. Buy special equipment for \$10,000, which can be depreciated over four years (one fourth of the value each year). The variable cost using this equipment is \$2 per unit produced.

Which method of production should the manufacturer follow in order to maximize profit? *Hint:* Compare total annual costs. Assume production must meet all demand.

11. A firm needs temporary business space. It can lease the desired space for \$5,000 for one year or \$9,000 for two years (all rent is paid in advance). Alternatively, it can rent the space for one year for \$5,000 and then if it wishes to rerent, pay \$5,500 on the first day of the second year as rent for the second year. The firm estimates that there is a 25 percent chance that they will have to depart from the city after one year. In that case, if they have rented the space for two years, they can sublet it for the second year. The chance of subletting is 60 percent, and they would receive \$5,500, paid on the first day of the second year. If they are unable to sublet the space, it will remain empty for the entire second year. The interest rate that the company uses for evaluating such decisions is 10 percent.

Should the company rent the space for one year or two? Why?

12. Greenwood Groceries buys fresh fruit daily for $1 a crate. Crates sold the same day bring $1.50 profit contribution, each. Crates that are not sold in a day are sold later as animal food for 25 cents, each. The demand for fruit fluctuates, according to the following distribution (data collected over the last 300 days):

Demand (number of crates)	*Number of days*
10	120
11	90
12	75
13	15
Total	300

a. How many crates should the store order if Greenwood wants to maximize profit from selling fruit? Use an expected value approach.

b. What will be the average daily profit?

13. An apartment building has eight washing machines. The probability of these machines failing in any given year is:

Number of machines failing during the year	*Probability*
3	.15
4	.30
5	.50
6	.05

Once a machine has failed, its repair will cost either $30, the minimum service charge, $70 for a moderate repair, or $120 for a major repair. The chance for a major repair is 36 percent, while for a moderate repair it is 44 percent for any washer.

Sears offers a prepaid one-year maintenance policy that costs $45 per machine.

a. Should the owner of the apartment building buy the maintenance insurance?

b. Assume that the cost of repair is evenly distributed over the year while the insurance premium is prepaid. How is your analysis affected by this assumption?

14. A consultant plans to work in Bolivia, where the exchange rate is 100 pesos for $1. He plans to be there for several months, and his expenses for the period are estimated at 250,000 pesos. A sky-rocketing inflation is temporarily in check while the government attempts to get a loan, the effect of which will be to lower the exchange rate by 10 percent (i.e., $1 = 90 pesos). If the loan is refused, the exchange rate will increase by 20 percent ($1 = 120 pesos). Suppose it is known that the probability of the government receiving the loan is .80. The consultant considers the following alternatives:

a_1 Immediately convert enough dollars into pesos to meet expenses for the entire period.

a_2 Wait until the loan is either granted or refused; in the meantine, hold dollars.

a_3 Hedge by converting part of the dollars to 125,000 pesos now and holding enough in dollars until the loan is either granted or refused, and then buy 125,000 additional pesos.

Assume that the decision on the loan is to be made prior to his arrival in the foreign country. Assume also that after the change in the exchange rate, the consultant will still need 250,000 pesos (regardless of the exchange rate).

If the consultant wants to minimize his dollar expense, which course of action should he take?

15. A common scene in many casinos is an old woman simultaneously playing two slot machines at a rate of 30 plays on each machine per hour. Assume that she plays the "dime" machines. The winning chances are given below (per play, per machine):

Winning prize	*Chance*
$10 (jackpot)	1 out of 400
$1	1 out of 100
50¢	1 out of 50
20¢	1 out of 10

a. Find the net gain (loss) of the woman during a four-hour period.

b. Compute the profit (loss) of the "house" from each machine in an hour.

c. The total cost of operating such a machine (including maintenance and depreciation) is $6 per day. The machine is played an average of 10 hours a day. Is the machine profitable?

c. How many plays an hour will have to be made for the casino to break even on each machine?

16. Given a decision situation with profit data:

p_i	.3	.7
	s_1	s_2
a_1	15	4
a_2	10	12
a_3	2	15

a. Find the best alternative using EMV.
b. Find the *range of probabilities* of s_1 within which the best alternative is still preferable.

17. Lime sales in Cuba are affected by both supply, which is determined by weather conditions, and demand, which is determined by the state of the economy. It is forecasted that the next year will be: cold (30 percent), mild (45 percent), warm (25 percent), and that the economy will be: stable (50 percent), in recession (30 percent), or else back in inflation.

Following are the historical annual lime sales (in kilograms):

Cold year: 200 kilos in a stable economy, 100 in a recession, 130 in inflation.
Mild year: 240 in a stable economy, 150 in a recession, 200 in inflation.
Warm year: 300 in either a stable or an inflationary economy, 200 kilos in a recession.

Find the average monthly value of sales if a kilo of limes sells for 170 pesos.

18. *a.* Write the following decision table in tree form:

Futures / *Alternatives*	*Fire*	*No fire*
Insure	$ 100	$100
Do not insure	$8,000	$ 0

These figures are cost data.
There is a .01 chance of a fire.
b. What action should an individual take to minimize cost?

19. Given the decision tree below, find the best alternative and its expected value. The outcomes shown are *costs* and the investment expenses are in parentheses.

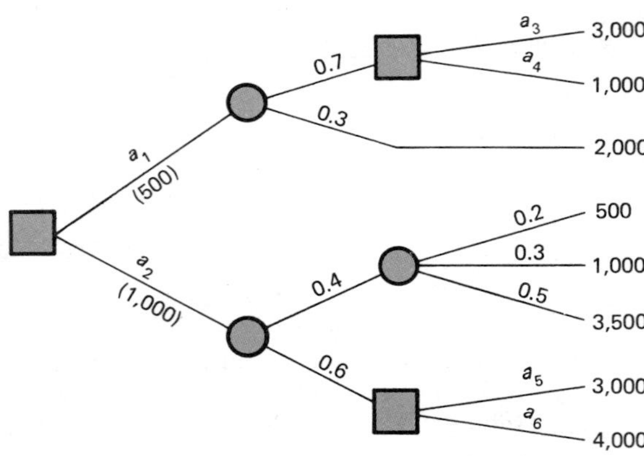

20. Given a decision tree, as shown in the figure below:
a. Write the equivalent table form.
b. Find the action that will minimize total cost (assume data are present values; use the tree presentation).

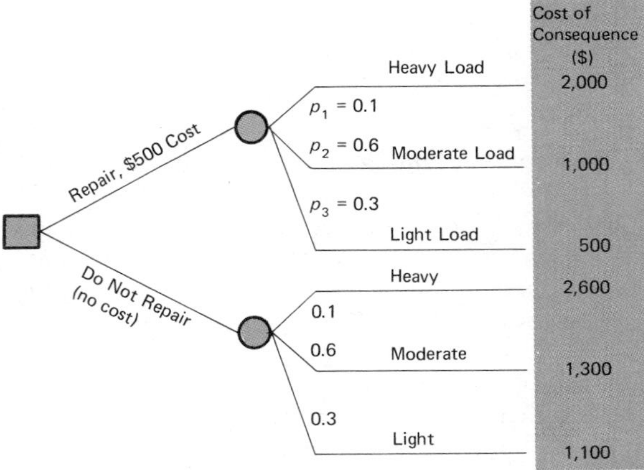

21. The future of solar energy in Africa depends on oil prices. The African Solar Company is considering the development of one of two possible home solar energy devices: Sun I and Sun II.

The anticipated profits as they relate to oil prices are shown in the table below:

	Oil price		
	High	*Very high*	*Extremely high*
Sun I	−50,000	73,000	500,000
Sun II	138,000	−100,000	60,000

The company economist estimates that the chances that oil prices will be high are 60 percent, very high 30 percent, and extremely high 10 percent. What device should the company develop if it is interested in maximizing profit?

a. Present as a decision tree.

b. Solve the tree; find the best alternative.

22. If you attend all class sessions, your probability of passing the course is .8; but if you only attend randomly, your probability of passing the course is .5. If you fail, you may take a makeup exam where the probabilities of passing are .6 if you attended in full and .1 if you attended at random. If passing the course is worth 5 credits, but, in terms of energy, attending full time "costs" 3 credits and attending randomly "costs" 1 credit, which attendance pattern should you adopt?

Note: Assume that all failing students will take the makeup exam. The utility of failing is zero.

23. An oil explorer, commonly called a wildcatter, must decide whether to drill a well or sell his rights to a particular exploration site. The desirability of drilling depends on whether there is oil beneath the surface. Before drilling, the wildcatter has the option of taking seismographic readings that will give him further geological and geophysical information. This information will enable him to deduce whether subsurface structures usually associated with oil fields exist in this particular location. However, some uncertainty about the presence of oil will still exist after seismic testing because oil is sometimes found where no subsurface structure is detected, and vice versa.

The wildcatter estimates that the cost of drilling a well would be $250,000 (in net present value terms, after making allowance for all taxes). The yield that would be expected from a typical oil well is estimated to be $1.2 million (in net present value terms, net of all taxes and operating costs, but excluding drilling costs). Siesmic tests would cost $50,000 per test.

The wildcatter could sell his rights for $230,000 before either drilling or testing. However, if he should decide to carry out seismographic readings and no subsurface structure is indicated, the site will be considered almost worthless by other wildcatters, in which case he will barely be able to sell the rights for $10,000. If substructure is indicated by the test, he can sell his rights for $300,000. If no oil is found, the value of the exploration site is considered to be zero.

The probability of getting oil from the site without any test is 30 percent. If he carries out the seismic test, he feels that the test will indicate subsurface structure with a 40 percent probability. In case of structure, he can drill with a 65 percent chance of finding oil. In the case of no structure, he can drill with a 75 percent chance of finding the well dry.

What should the wildcatter do? Draw a decision tree to solve the problem.

24. ABC's growth rate in past years has been slower than the average for the industry. The company is considering two alternatives to rectify the situation: (1) expand the number of product lines and (2) increase inventories for better service.

There is a 70 percent chance that the economy will go into a growth state, in which case there is an 80 percent chance for increased demand. If demand increases, a profit of $1 million is expected; however if demand does not increase, only $800,000 profit is anticipated. If inventories are increased, a profit of $900,000 is anticipated in case of high demand; otherwise $600,000 will be realized.

In the event the economy does not grow, a mild recession is anticipated. In this case, there is a 50–50 percent chance for either high or low demand. The profits are then estimated to be:

Expansion and high demand	$750,000
Expansion and low demand	600,000
Inventories and high demand	550,000
Inventories and low demand	400,000

Profit figures are forecast for after one year of operation.

A product expansion policy requires

$100,000 in cash now. Keeping inventories will cost $12,000 for the year, payable at year end. The company is using an interest rate of 10 percent for its analysis.

Should the company expand its products or work with inventories?

25. Todo Corp. operates two complex production lines on an eight-hour per day basis. These lines fail frequently due to the extensive workload. The daily probability of line no. 1 failing is .10 and that of line no. 2 is .15. When any line fails, the cost is 10,000 ¥ (yen) each hour; when both lines are down at the same time, the cost is 14,000 ¥ per hour.

The company is trying to decide whether to hire one or two repairpersons. The time for one person to repair a machine is five hours. If two are hired they can work either as a team or individually on separate machines. If they work as a team, the repair time reduces to three hours. If a repairperson costs 1000 ¥ per hour, what would you recommend Todo do?

26. A machine shop received an order for 2,000 units to be made on one of its automated machines. This is a multistation operation and once it is started, it runs without interruption. The machine shop makes $2 profit on each part of acceptable quality. Each unit that is classified as "defective" needs rework at a cost of $3.50 before it is considered "acceptable."

Historical data indicates that if the machine is used without any special preparation, it produces either 1 percent defectives (this happens 50 percent of the time), 2 percent defectives (this happens 30 percent of the time), 3 percent defectives (this happens 12 percent of the time), or 5 percent defectives in the remaining cases. With a minor adjustment that costs $42, the defective rate *above* 2 percent is reduced to 2 percent; with a major adjustment (cost $100), the defective rate is 1 percent.

What adjustment policy should the machine shop adopt in order to maximize profit?

PART B: EXTENSIONS

3.9 THE ACQUISITION OF ADDITIONAL INFORMATION

Examining the situations of certainty, risk, and uncertainty, it is clear that there is a difference between the three situations in terms of the amount of information available for making the decision. In the case of certainty, it is assumed that we have complete information. That is, each time an alternative is selected there is only one possible outcome, which is known. In the case of risk, there are several possible outcomes associated with each alternative, and their chances of occurring are assumed to be known. Finally, in the case of uncertainty, there are again several possible outcomes associated with each alternative, but the decision maker does not know the likelihood of each of these occurring. That is, there is even less information available than in risk. These situations are illustrated in Figure 3.9.

Situation	*Amount of information*
Certainty	Most
Risk	Some
Uncertainty	Least

FIGURE 3.9
The amount of information in decision situations

Of course, managers prefer to make decisions with as much information as possible. That is, they prefer to make decisions under certainty, if at all possible. Otherwise, they will accept risk. Only in extreme cases will they be willing to make decisions under uncertainty. For this reason, in many decision situations a subdecision has to be made: whether to attempt to acquire additional information.

The feasibility of acquiring more information

Whenever a decision about the acquisition of additional information is to be made, the following questions should be considered.

1. *What information is needed and is it available?* Only if one knows what information is needed and if the information is obtainable should one proceed.
2. *Is there time to acquire the information?* Again, only if the answer is affirmative should one continue.
3. *What is the quality of the information?* Information can have very different levels of quality or validity, particularly if it is available from different sources. This issue will be explored later.
4. *What is the value of the information?*
5. *What is the cost of the information?*
6. *Should the information be acquired?*

TABLE 3.9
Simple decision table

	.3 *Rain*	.7 *No rain*
Take umbrella	Dry, happy	Frustrated Why did I bring it?
Do not take umbrella	Wet, mad	Thankful

Our analysis here will be based on the assumption that additional information is available and that there is sufficient time to acquire and use it.

Information quality: Perfect versus imperfect information

Our discussion here will be limited only to information quality in terms of its accuracy, although there are several other dimensions of information quality that can also be important.

Perfect information Both perfect and imperfect information relate to decision making under risk. That is, the probability of an outcome, given a repetitive decision situation, is assumed to be known. For example, suppose you are about to make a decision on whether or not to bring an umbrella with you. A simplified decision table is shown in Table 3.9.

Assume that on an annual basis there is a 30 percent chance of rain each day. Based on this information, if we can quantify the outcomes in the table, we can use expected values to develop a *policy* that will tell us whether or not to take an umbrella.

However, it may make more sense to examine the weather every morning. This requires more information. If we can find a predictor who can tell us whether it will rain that day or not, and if such a predictor is always correct, then we are in a situation of deciding whether or not to acquire **perfect information.** This situation corresponds to Table 3.10A, which illustrates the relationship between what was predicted and what actually occurs.

TABLE 3.10
The quality of information in risk situations

A. Perfect

		Actual Rain	*Actual* No rain
Predicted	Rain	1	0
	No rain	0	1

B. Imperfect

		Actual Rain	*Actual* No rain
Predicted	Rain	.8	.2
	No rain	.2	.8

Note: The number of predictions may be the same as the number of states of nature (such as here) or it may be larger (for example, "not sure" can be a prediction).

Using perfect information, a risky decision can be converted into one of decision making under certainty. The only difference from certainty is that the probabilities of the states of nature, in the long run, cannot be changed. That is, several outcomes will occur in the long run.

Imperfect information Here the prediction is not perfect, as in Table 3.10B. Using imperfect information, the probability of each possible state of nature occurring is redetermined each time a decision must be made. This process changes the earlier predicted probabilities of the states of nature from their initial *(prior)* values to revised *(posterior)* values. With each additional prediction, the probabilities continue to be revised, with each posterior probability considered to be the **prior probability** for the next prediction. The statistical tool used to perform such an analysis is called **Bayes' theorem.** This process of revision is discussed in Section 3.11.

3.10 THE VALUE OF PERFECT INFORMATION

In decision making under risk, the decision maker operates with less information than in the case of decision making under certainty. One may ask the question: Suppose that additional information can be obtained; what will its value be to the decision maker? This discussion will be confined to the case where the obtained information changes the situation from one of risk to one of certainty. That is, the decision maker, prior to the time a decision is to be made, is assumed to acquire perfect information, information describing precisely which state of nature will occur next.[8] (The frequency distribution of occurrences of the states of nature does not change—one just learns with certainty *which* state will occur next.)

A crystal ball . . .

The decision maker faces two decisions when perfect information is involved. First, if the perfect information were available, which alternative should be selected? Second, should the perfect information be acquired? The second decision is based on the comparison of the benefit of the perfect information with its cost.

. . . for a price

Example

Let us analyze the investment decision presented in Table 3.6 as reproduced in Table 3.11.

The problem, solved by the expected value approach, indicated that the best alternative was a_1, yielding an average of 8.4 percent. Let us now assume that each percent of yield equals \$10,000; that is, a decision maker who uses the expected value as a criterion will make, over the long run, $8.4 \times \$10{,}000 = \$84{,}000$, per decision.

[8] Cases involving *imperfect* information are more complicated to analyze since the problem remains that of decision making under risk, with revised probabilities. Bayes' theorem (see Section 3.11) is used in such cases to compute the revised probabilities.

TABLE 3.11
The investment decision (in percent yield)

Alternatives \ States of nature	.5 Growth	.3 Stagnation	.2 Inflation	Expected value
a_1 *Bonds*	12	6	3	8.4
a_2 *Stocks*	(15)	3	−2	8.0
a_3 *Time deposit*	6.5	(6.5)	(6.5)	6.5

What alternative course of action should be selected, given perfect information? Assume that we deal with a repetitive situation; that is, the decision is made every year. Suppose that in advance of making a decision, a market research firm is able to predict, with certainty, the state of the economy that will prevail. Thus, the decision maker can make a choice with complete certainty. The choice depends on what the research firm predicts:

- If the research firm predicts growth, then the best choice is stocks (a_2).
- If the research firm predicts stagnation, the choice will be time deposit (a_3).
- If the prediction is for inflation, the choice will again be time deposit (a_3).

A varying choice

Note that, in contrast to the regular expected value situation where one alternative is selected, here the choice may vary among alternatives.

The expected payoff with perfect information. Assuming that the frequency distribution of the states of the economy does not change over the long run, then 50 percent of the time the research firm will predict that growth is the next state. The decision maker, now knowing in advance what is going to happen next, will select a_2 and realize a 15 percent yield. Similarly, 30 percent of the time stagnation will be predicted and the decision maker will make 6.5 percent by selecting a_3, and 20 percent of the time inflation will give 6.5 percent by selecting a_3. These choices are circled in Table 3.11. The decision maker's average (expected) yield will be:

$$.5 \times 15 + .3 \times 6.5 + .2 \times 6.5 = 10.75 \text{ percent}$$

Using the \$10,000 per 1 percent equivalence, the average return per decision will be \$107,500.

Should the perfect information be acquired: If we compare the expected yield with perfect information (\$107,500) with the expected yield under regular conditions (\$84,000) we see an improvement of \$23,500.

In general, decisions with perfect information yield much better results than decisions without it. The difference of $23,500 is called the **expected value of perfect information (EVPI)** and is used to answer the question of whether or not the perfect information should be acquired.[9]

EVPI

Note that EVPI is the average improvement in the objective function, per decision. If this figure is compared against the cost of acquiring the information, management can make a decision regarding the acquisition of the information. For example, if the research firm charges $15,000 per prediction, the investor stands to gain $23,500 − $15,000 = $8,500, on the average, by using the service. But if the marketing firm charges $23,500 or more for this service, then the arrangement would not be profitable.

What's the info worth?

Thus, the EVPI tells the decision maker the *upper limit* one should be willing to pay for "perfect predicting information"; information that is 100 percent reliable.

If the decision maker decides to buy the perfect information, the decision maker should, of course, wait for the (perfect) prediction and then make a choice accordingly.

Summary

To determine whether or not to purchase perfect information one should:

1. Compute the expected payoff *without* perfect information and select the best alternative.
2. Compute the expected payoff *with* perfect information, assuming the best selection of alternatives is made.
3. Compute the EVPI by subtracting (1) above from (2). (Reverse order for cost minimization.)[10]
4. If the difference is larger than the cost of the information, it should be purchased; otherwise, it should not.
5. The value of EVPI *must* be ≥ 0.

---

[9] The mathematical expression of the expected value of perfect information in the case of maximization is:

$$\text{EVPI} = \underbrace{\sum_{j=1}^{n} p_j (\max_i o_{ij})}_{\substack{\text{Expected yield with} \\ \text{perfect information}}} - \underbrace{\max_i \sum_{j=1}^{n} p_j o_{ij}}_{\substack{\text{Expected yield} \\ \text{without perfect} \\ \text{information}}}$$

where:

p_j = Probability of state of nature j
o_{ij} = The payoff when action a_i is taken and state of nature j occurs

[10] In the case of minimization:

$$\text{EVPI} = \begin{bmatrix}\text{Expected cost without} \\ \text{perfect information}\end{bmatrix} - \begin{bmatrix}\text{Expected cost with} \\ \text{perfect information}\end{bmatrix}$$

Note: The equivalence of EVPI and EOL

The expected value of perfect information (EVPI) in the investment example was $23,500 or 2.35 percent of yield. Examining Table 3.7, the reader will find that the expected regret or expected opportunity loss (EOL) of the *best alternative* is also 2.35 percent yield. Is this a coincidence? The answer is no! As a matter of fact the EVPI is *always equal* to the best (smallest) EOL.

EVPI = EOL

3.11 THE VALUE OF IMPERFECT INFORMATION

The value of perfect information is computed with the assumption that a perfect predictor exists. In other words, each time that a prediction for a state of nature is made, this prediction comes true. In reality, however, this is a very rare case. The typical case involves predictions which only rarely come true. Such a case is called prediction under imperfect (or sample) information, and it will be discussed next. However, before we turn to this topic it is necessary to review the Bayes' theorem of revised probabilities.

Bayes' theorem

Example American Ecology, Inc., estimates that its new product, E-3, has a .8 chance (80 percent) of being a winner. Thus, there is a .2 chance of its being a loser. However, before the company makes a production commitment it would like to further investigate the situation since these initial estimates (called "prior probabilities") may not be accurate. Hence, the possibility of calling on a market researcher to conduct a special survey of the market is being evaluated.

From previous experience it is known that such a special survey can either *predict success*, *predict failure*, or *be inconclusive*. Statistically, it is known that of all the new products that were successful, 70 percent of the time the surveys correctly predicted success *(S)*, 10 percent of the time they falsely predicted failure *(F)*, and 20 percent of the time they were inconclusive *(I)*. On the other hand, an examination of all the cases that were failures (losers) indicated that in 85 percent of these cases the surveys correctly predicted failure, in 10 percent they were inconclusive, and success was incorrectly predicted in the remaining 5 percent. This information is summarized in Table 3.12.

TABLE 3.12
Reliability of the surveys

	Actual state of products	
Results of survey	*Winners (W)*	*Losers (L)*
Predicted success *(S)*	.70	.05
Inconclusive *(I)*	.20	.10
Predicted failure *(F)*	.10	.85
Total	1.00	1.00

The probabilities in Table 3.12 are *conditional probabilities* and indicate the *reliability* of the surveys to prospective customers.[11] These conditional probabilities, which describe the *track record* of the forecaster, are not easy to obtain. They may be based on personal knowledge of the past accuracy of the forecaster, reports from other customers or users, or a simple subjective assessment. It is assumed that future prediction success will match that of the past.

Conditional probabilities

Using revised probabilities with imperfect information

Bayes' theorem is a procedure that is used when revising the probabilities of the states of nature for evaluating the subdecision regarding the acquisition of additional information needed to revise the prior probabilities. The **revised probabilities** depend on the nature of the additional information, which is found only after the information is acquired. For this reason, if we analyze a situation prior to the actual acquisition of the information, we cannot prescribe the best decision alternative. Instead, we derive a *decision policy* or *strategy*.

A policy; a strategy

A decision policy does not recommend a particular alternative as being the best. Instead, it recommends several specific alternatives, one for every possible outcome of the additional information.

The use of revised probabilities in assessing the acquisition of additional information involves the following nine steps:

Step 1. The decision situation is evaluated with the prior probabilities.
Step 2. Assuming that it is impossible to obtain perfect information, the possibility of acquiring partial information is checked.
Step 3. Revised (posterior) probabilities are computed, one for each possible outcome of the prediction.
Step 4. The probabilities of each of the research outcomes ("indicators") are computed.
Step 5. A decision tree is constructed.
Step 6. The tree is solved.
Step 7. The expected value of the additional information is computed.
Step 8. A decision on whether or not to acquire the information is made.
Step 9. An alternative in the original problem is selected.

Example The marketing department of Production Unlimited, Inc., is considering whether or not to develop a new product. All the relevant information is shown in Table 3.13.

Solution

Step 1. Initial evaluation. Using the prior probabilities, the expected values can be computed. Accordingly, the product *should not* be developed,

[11] A conditional probability is the probability of a certain event occurring *given* the occurrence of some other event (see Appendix B), which in our case is currently *unknown*.

TABLE 3.13
Marketing payoffs (dollars)

States of nature / Alternatives	.2 A	.5 B	.3 C	Expected value	
a_1 *Develop*	300,000	200,000	−600,000	−20,000	
a_2 *Do not develop*	0	0	0	0	← *Best*

since a loss of $20,000, on the average, is expected if the product is developed.

Step 2. Check track record. Since Production Unlimited is unable to obtain *perfect information,* they have decided to settle for less than perfect information. Thus, a consultant has been called on to predict, through a survey, what state of nature, in the consultant's opinion, will occur next. The consultant asks $50,000 for the survey. The track record of the consultant indicates that the consultant's surveys have the prediction reliabilities shown in Table 3.14. This information is called the *conditional probabilities* of the source.

TABLE 3.14
Consultant's reliability (conditional probability matrix)

Indicators	*Actual state of nature* A	B	C
Survey predicted *A* (call this prediction A_p)	$P(A_p \mid A) = .80$	$P(A_p \mid B) = .10$	$P(A_p \mid C) = .10$
Survey predicted *B* (call this prediction B_p)	$P(B_p \mid A) = .10$	$P(B_p \mid B) = .90$	$P(B_p \mid C) = .20$
Survey predicted *C* (call this prediction C_p)	$P(C_p \mid A) = .10$	$P(C_p \mid B) = \ \ 0$	$P(C_p \mid C) = .70$

For example, of all the past cases in which *B* actually occurred, 90 percent of the time the survey correctly predicted that *B* would occur, 10 percent of the time the wrong prediction of *A* was made, and 0 percent of the time the wrong prediction of *C* was made.

Note: In this analysis we assume that the quality of the predictions will stay the same in the future as it has been in the past. Also, the number of predictions (indicators) can be different than the number of states of nature. For example, the consultant can include "I do not know."

Step 3. Compute revised probabilities. Given (in Table 3.13) the prior probabilities, and the reliability of the survey (Table 3.14), the revised probabilities can be calculated with the aid of Equation 3.5 (see chapter appendix, Section 3.14).

For branch A_p:

$$P(A|A_p) = \frac{P(A)P(A_p|A)}{P(A)P(A_p|A) + P(B)P(A_p|B) + P(C)P(A_p|C)}$$

$$= \frac{.2 \times .8}{.2 \times .8 + .5 \times .1 + .3 \times .1} = \frac{.16}{.24} = .667$$

$$P(B|A_p) = \frac{.5 \times .1}{.5 \times .1 + .2 \times .8 + .3 \times .1} = \frac{.05}{.24} = .208$$

$$P(C|A_p) = \frac{.3 \times .1}{.3 \times .1 + .2 \times .8 + .5 \times .1} = \frac{.03}{.24} = .125$$

For branch B_p:

$$P(A|B_p) = \frac{.2 \times .1}{.2 \times .1 + .5 \times .9 + .3 \times .2} = \frac{.02}{.53} = .038$$

$$P(B|B_p) = \frac{.45}{.53} = .849$$

$$P(C|B_p) = \frac{.06}{.53} = .113$$

For branch C_p:

$$P(A|C_p) = \frac{.2 \times .1}{.2 \times .1 + .5 \times 0 + .3 \times .7} = \frac{.02}{.23} = .087$$

$$P(B|C_p) = 0$$

$$P(C|C_p) = \frac{.21}{.23} = .913$$

Step 4. Compute the indicator (marginal) probabilities. In order to determine whether or not to use the consultant, it is necessary to use the probabilities that the consultant's survey will actually predict events A_p, B_p, or C_p. These probabilities (derived above as the denominators of the Bayes' equations) are:

$$P(A_p) = .24$$
$$P(B_p) = .53$$
$$P(C_p) = .23$$

Step 5. Construct a decision tree. Management must now decide whether or not to use the consultant. Then they must decide about the new product (a_1–develop, a_2–do not develop). The situation is shown in the form of a decision tree in Figure 3.10.

Two decisions

The upper part of the tree shows the information presented in Table 3.13. The lower part of the tree presents the situation of using the consultant. There exist three branches: branch A_p for when the survey predicts A, branch B_p for when the survey predicts B, and branch C_p for when the

FIGURE 3.10
A decision tree for Bayes' analysis—general structure

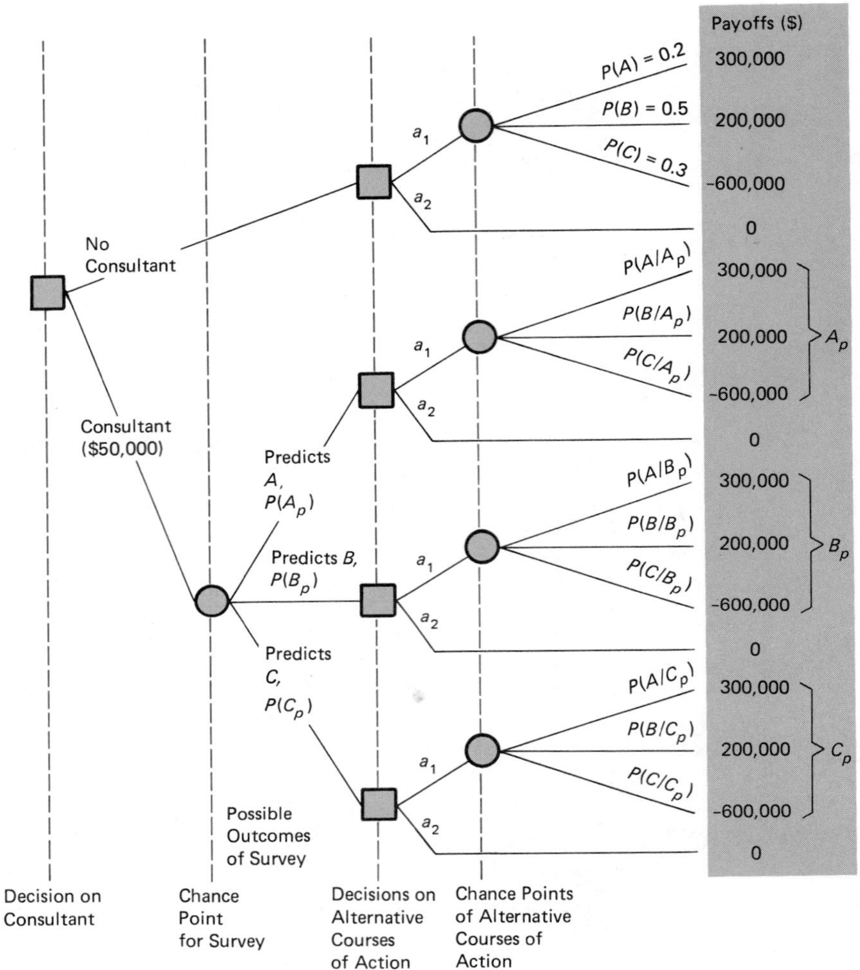

survey predicts C. The revised probabilities from step 3 and the indicator probabilities from step 4 are next entered on the tree (Figure 3.11).

Step 6. Solve the decision tree (Figure 3.11). The expected values at all chance points are computed. Then the best alternative at every decision point is selected. In this case, if the consultant is not used, the expected value (top branch) is zero. If the consultant is used, the expected value using posterior probabilities is:[12]

$$.24(\$166{,}700) + .53(\$113{,}400) + .23(\$0) = \$100{,}110$$

Step 7. Compute the expected value of imperfect information. We compute the **expected value** of the imperfect additional **(sample) information (EVSI)** using Equation 3.2 below.

[12] The numbers may not exactly total due to rounding.

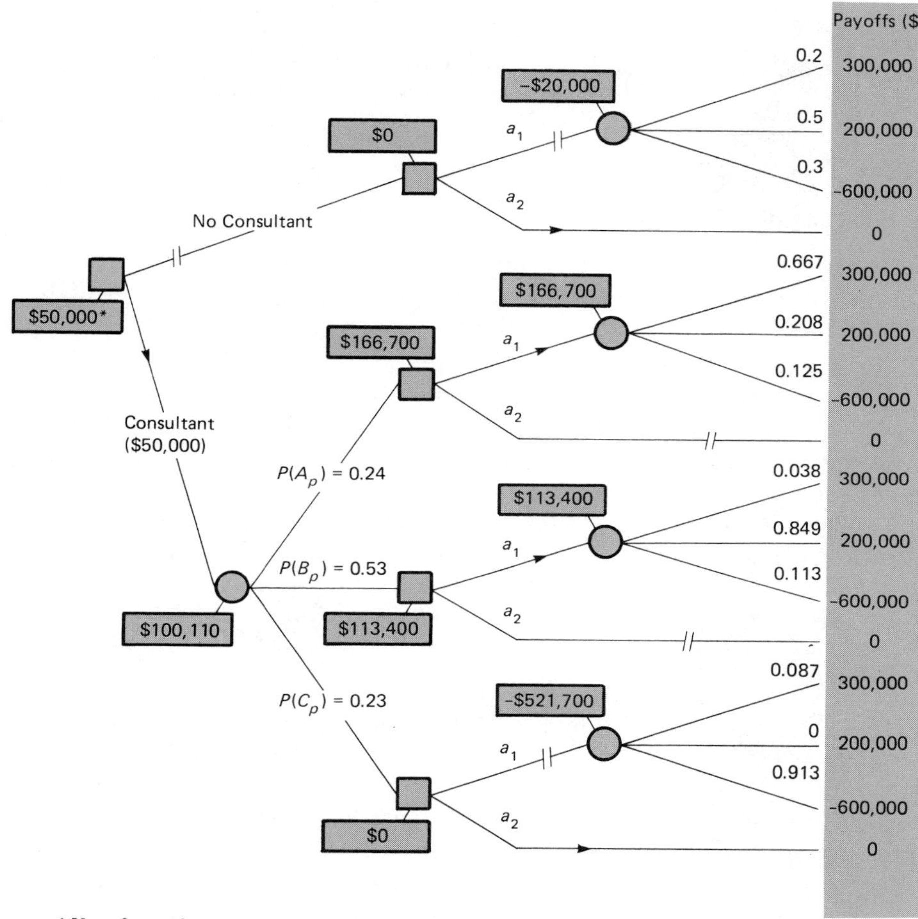

* Use of consultant is recommended.

FIGURE 3.11
Decision analysis with revised probabilities

Computing the value of imperfect (sample, survey, or partial) information

The value of imperfect information

The information computed in Bayes' analysis is less than perfect, since its prediction reliability is not 100 percent. Therefore, it is interesting to determine the value of such information. The expected value, per decision, of the imperfect sample or survey information (EVSI) is computed (for the case of maximization) as:[13]

EVSI

[13] In the case of minimization:

$$\text{EVSI} = \begin{bmatrix}\text{Best expected cost}\\ \text{using prior}\\ \text{probabilities}\end{bmatrix} - \begin{bmatrix}\text{Best expected cost}\\ \text{using revised}\\ \text{probabilities}\end{bmatrix}$$

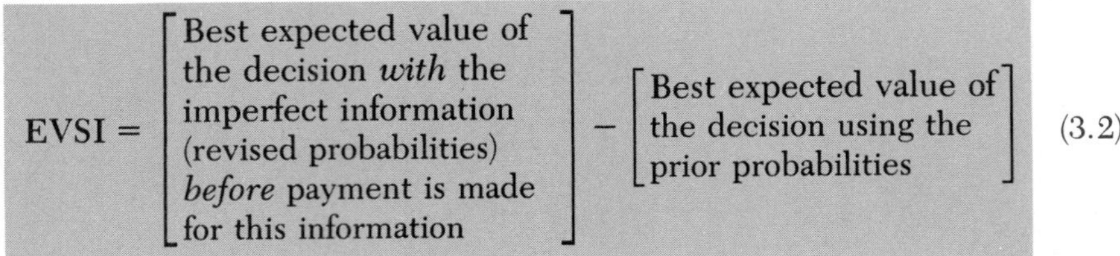

$$\text{EVSI} = \left[\begin{array}{l}\text{Best expected value of}\\ \text{the decision } \textit{with} \text{ the}\\ \text{imperfect information}\\ \text{(revised probabilities)}\\ \textit{before} \text{ payment is made}\\ \text{for this information}\end{array}\right] - \left[\begin{array}{l}\text{Best expected value of}\\ \text{the decision using the}\\ \text{prior probabilities}\end{array}\right] \quad (3.2)$$

In our example:

Expected value with imperfect information (revised probabilities) = 100,110

Expected value with prior probabilities = 0

Thus, EVSI = \$100,110 − 0 = \$100,110. As in the case of EVPI, here too we get an indication regarding the upper limit that management should be willing to pay for the additional information. Note that the expected value of imperfect information is *smaller than* the expected value of perfect information. The reason for this is that the imperfect information is less reliable. The value of perfect information serves as an *upper limit* for the value of imperfect information. The ratio of EVSI/EVPI is called the *efficiency* of the imperfect information.

Efficiency

Step 8. Decide whether or not to acquire the information. The expected value of the sample information is now compared with the cost of acquiring it.

If EVSI > Cost: Acquire the information
If EVSI < Cost: Do not acquire the information

In our case, EVSI = \$100,110 and the cost is \$50,000. Therefore, the information should be acquired.

Step 9. Select an alternative. If the consultant is not hired, select the alternative with the best expected value. If the consultant *is* hired, then wait for the additional information and then make a final decision. In our case, the decision policy is:

If the survey indicates A_p, select alternative a_1
If the survey indicates B_p, select alternative a_1
If the survey indicates C_p, select alternative a_2

Note: Comparing several consultants. In addition to the use of imperfect information for accepting or rejecting an opportunity to conduct research to gain additional information, one can use the methodology to select a research firm (or consultant) from among several. To do so, the track record of each contender is examined and the expected value of the sample information (EVSI) is compared against the cost.

3.12 DECISIONS UNDER UNCERTAINTY

In the condition of uncertainty, the decision maker recognizes different potential states of nature but cannot confidently estimate the probabilities

TABLE 3.15
Payoff table (percent of return on investment)

Alternatives \ States of nature	*Positive legislation and low competition* s_1	*Positive legislation and strong competition* s_2	*No legislation and low competition* s_3	*No legislation and strong competition* s_4
a_1 = *30 rooms*	10	5	4	−2
a_2 = *40 rooms*	17	10	1	−10
a_3 = *50 rooms*	24	15	−3	−20

of their occurrence.[14] This is an undesirable but often unavoidable situation. It may occur when one faces a completely new phenomenon (e.g., the 1973 energy crisis) or when a completely new product, process, or state of nature is under consideration. In many such situations even prominent experts cannot agree on the chances of the various states of nature occurring.

Example

The Palm Tree Hotel is considering the construction of an additional wing. Management is evaluating the possibility of adding 30, 40, or 50 rooms. The success of the addition depends on a combination of local government legislation and competition in the field; four states of nature are being considered. They are shown, together with the anticipated payoffs (in percent of yearly return on investment), in Table 3.15.

Management cannot agree on the probabilities of the states of nature. The problem is: how many rooms to build in order to maximize the return on investment.

No "right" answers

At the present time, decision theory does not provide a single best criterion for selecting an alternative under conditions of uncertainty. Instead, there are a number of different criteria, each with its justifications and limitations. The choice among these is determined by organizational policy, the attitude of the decision maker toward risk, or both.

Principle of choice by policy

Criteria of choice

Five criteria of choice are presented:

Laplace

1. The criterion of equal probabilities (Laplace) The user of this criterion assumes that all states of nature are *equally likely* to occur. Thus, equal probabilities are assigned to each. The expected values are then computed and the alternative with the highest expected payoff is selected.

Example. Using the example given in Table 3.15, probabilities of

[14] In the limiting case of uncertainty, called "ignorance," even the possible states of nature are not known. We will not consider this case here.

¼ are assigned to each of the *four* states of nature. The expected payoffs are:

$$E(a_1) = 1/4 \times 10 + 1/4 \times 5 + 1/4 \times 4 + 1/4 \times (-2) = 17/4$$
$$E(a_2) = 1/4(17 + 10 + 1 - 10) = 18/4 \text{ (largest expected yield)}$$
$$E(a_3) = 1/4(24 + 15 - 3 - 20) = 16/4$$

Thus, the best alternative is a_2, with an expected payoff of 18/4. The major argument against this criterion is that there is absolutely no reason to assume the probabilities are all equal. Such an assumption may be as erroneous as assuming one outcome in particular will occur.

Minimax

2. *Criterion of pessimism (maximin or minimax)* The user of this criterion is completely pessimistic, since he or she assumes that the worst will happen, no matter which alternative is selected. To provide protection, the decision maker should select the alternative that will give as large a payoff as possible under this pessimistic assumption (best of the worsts).

Example. Let us reproduce Table 3.15 as Table 3.16 (payoffs in percent yield).

Assume that the decision maker selects a_1; then the *worst* that can happen is a loss of 2 percent when s_4 occurs. Similarly, the worst for a_2 is -10, and for a_3 is -20 (the lowest number in the row is selected in the case of maximization). This information is entered into a new column labeled Worst. From this column, the best entry is then selected (-2 in the example). The decision maker maximizes the minimum payoffs, and therefore this criterion is labeled *maximin.*[15] The use of this criterion will guarantee the decision maker that in the *worst possible case* the loss will be 2.

One drawback of this criterion (which is also a drawback of all the remaining criteria) is that the decision is based on only a *small portion* of the available information. Thus, valuable information is completely disregarded, as shown in Table 3.17, which illustrates a deliberately exaggerated case (maximization).

TABLE 3.16
Pessimistic approach in the case of profit

States of nature / *Alternatives*	s_1	s_2	s_3	s_4	*Worst (minimum)*	*Best of worst (maximum of minimums)*
a_1	10	5	4	−2	−2	−2
a_2	17	10	1	−10	−10	
a_3	24	15	−3	−20	−20	

[15] In the case of cost minimization, the decision maker will minimize the maximum possible costs; that is, the decision maker will *minimax.*

TABLE 3.17
Profits under two alternatives

Alternatives \ States of nature	s_1	s_2	s_3	*Minimum (worst)*	
a_1	40,000	20,000	500	500	
a_2	550	520	510	510	←*Maximum (best)*

According to the criterion of pessimism, a_2 should be selected. The decision is based on the "minimum" column, which includes only one entry from each row. The rest of the data is ignored. In reality, most decision makers will pay attention to the remaining information and consequently not use this approach and select a_1 The pessimistic decision maker acts in a *superconservative* manner, paying attention only to the risks and completely neglecting the opportunities.

Neglects opportunities

Maximax

3. ***Criterion of optimism (maximax or minimin)*** An optimistic decision maker assumes that the very best outcome will occur and selects the alternative with the best possible payoff.

Larry Lucky

To do so, the decision maker searches for the best possible payoff for each alternative. These are placed in a new column to the right of the decision table. The alternative with the best payoff in this newly added column is then selected (best of bests).

Example. Reproducing the data of Table 3.15 in Table 3.18, the "best" column is created.[16] According to the maximax criterion, alternative a_3 would be selected.

TABLE 3.18
Maximax choice

Alternatives \ States of nature	s_1	s_2	s_3	s_4	*Best*	
a_1	10	5	4	−2	10	
a_2	17	10	1	−10	17	
a_3	24	15	−3	−20	24	←*Best of bests*

[16] If the data were costs, then the optimistic decision maker would select as best the *lowest* cost payoff for each alternative and then select the *lowest* of these lowests. Such an approach is labeled *minimin.*

Notice again that no attention is paid to most of the available information; only the highest payoff is considered. Thus, an optimistic decision maker is a gambler who *disregards* the risks and looks forward only to the opportunities.

The gambler

4. *Coefficient of optimism (Hurwicz criterion)* Most decision makers are not completely optimistic or completely pessimistic. Therefore, it was suggested, by Hurwicz, that a degree of optimism labeled alpha, α, be measured on a 0 to 1 scale (0 = completely pessimistic, 1 = completely optimistic). Hurwicz suggested that the best alternative is the one with the highest (in maximization) weighted value, where the weighted value, *WV*, for each alternative (row in the decision table) is expressed by:

Middle-of-the-road types

Hurwicz

$$(WV)_i = \alpha[\text{best } o_{ij}] + (1 - \alpha)[\text{worst } o_{ij}] \tag{3.3}$$

where o_{ij} is the payoff. Then, the best $(WV)_i$ is selected.

Example. Examining Table 3.18 with α given as .7 we get:

$$WV(a_1) = .7 \times 10 + (1 - .7) \times (-2) = 6.4$$
$$WV(a_2) = .7 \times 17 + (1 - .7) \times (-10) = 8.9$$
$$WV(a_3) = .7 \times 24 + (1 - .7) \times (-20) = 10.8 \leftarrow \text{(maximum)}$$

Thus, alternative a_3 is the best. *Note:* In the case of minimization, such as with costs, where the best is lowest, select the alternative with the *lowest WV*.

The major difficulty in applying this criterion is the measurement of alpha.[17] Note that use is made of more information than in minimax, yet only the two extreme payoffs are considered and the remaining information is ignored.

Savage's "regret"

5. *The criterion of regret (Savage's criterion)* The concept of regret is equivalent to the determination of *opportunity loss,* discussed in Section 3.4. Both concepts represent the important economic concept of *opportunity cost,* which indicates the magnitude of *the loss incurred by not selecting the best alternative.*

I wish I had done. . . .

A pessimistic approach

Savage argued that the decision maker should attempt to *minimize the largest anticipated regret.* That is, employ a **minimax** approach to the **regret** data (in a basically pessimistic manner).

Example. Let us use the hotel example of Table 3.15.

Solution:

Step 1. Build a regret (opportunity loss) table. This is done according to the method exhibited in Table 3.7. The result is shown in Table 3.19.

[17] One way to determine alpha has been suggested by Luce and Raiffa ([9], p. 283).

TABLE 3.19
Regret table for Table 3.15

Alternatives \ *States of nature*	s_1	s_2	s_3	s_4	*Largest regret (worst)*	
a_1	24 − 10 = 14	15 − 5 = 10	4 − 4 = 0	−2 − (−2) = 0	14	
a_2	24 − 17 = 7	15 − 10 = 5	4 − 1 = 3	−2 − (−10) = 8	8	← *Minimum*
a_3	24 − 24 = 0	15 − 15 = 0	4 − (−3) = 7	−2 − (−20) = 18	18	

Step 2. Minimax the regret. This is done by finding the worst (largest) regret in each row, and then selecting the lowest regret in the newly formed column.

Minimax regret

In the example the lowest regret is for alternative a_2. This selection guarantees that regardless of what happens, the decision maker will never have a regret larger than 8. Note again that use is made only of a small portion of the available information.

Note: The value of regret, by definition, can never be negative.

Summary

Decision making under uncertainty is more difficult than it is for risk or certainty. All five different criteria presented here have some deficiencies and will usually point to different selections of alternatives. In management, decision making under uncertainty should be avoided since the results can be disastrous. Instead, enough information should be acquired so that decisions can be made at least under calculated risk or, at best, under certainty.

3.13 USE OF COMPUTERS

Perfect information

An example of perfect information computer computations from Table 3.11 is shown in Nelson's DSS output below. The computations are self-explanatory.

THE EXPECTED VALUE OF PERFECT INFORMATION (EVPI)

Problem Name: Table 3.11

EMV without Perfect Information:	8.40
EMV with Perfect Information:	10.75

Problem Type: PAYOFF Maximization

EMV with PI	–	EMV without PI	=	EVPI
10.75		8.40		2.35

Imperfect information

The revision of probabilities using Bayes' theorem and its application for the decision regarding the acquisition of additional information is easily programmed for a computer. The following illustration follows the computations executed manually in Section 3.11. Furthermore, Nelson's MSS package is capable of conducting a comparative study in which the acquisition of information from several sources (vendors) is compared. The input to the program includes the original decision table (Table 3.13) and the source reliabilities (conditional probabilities) in Table 3.14.

To begin with, the program computes the expected value of the imperfect ("survey") information. This value is compared to the cost, and the net gain is computed. If several sources (vendors) are involved, the analysis includes a comparative study to identify the best one.

THE EXPECTED VALUE OF PERFECT INFORMATION (EVPI)

Problem name: NONE — Problem Type: PAYOFF Maximization

EMV with PI	–	EMV without PI	=	EVPI
160,000.00		0.00		160,000.00

THE EXPECTED VALUE OF SURVEY INFORMATION (EVSI) AND
THE EXPECTED NET GAIN FROM SURVEY INFORMATION (ENGSI)

EMV with SI	–	EMV without SI	=	EVSI	Survey Cost	ENGSI
99,999.99		0.00		99,999.99	50,000.00	49,999.99

The MSS package includes a routine for comparing several vendors of information. The program computes ENGSI for each vendor and selects the best one. Next, the revised (posterior) probabilities are depicted.

STATES OF NATURE				
INDICAT.	A	B	C	P(I)
Ap	0.6667	0.2083	0.1250	0.2400
Bp	0.0377	0.8491	0.1132	0.5300
Cp	0.0870	0.0000	0.9130	0.2300
P(Si)	0.2000	0.5000	0.3000	

Finally, the decision tree computation is performed and, optionally, a node-by-node analysis is given.

```
Problem Name: NONE                        Problem Type: Payoff Maximization
                        Total Nodes in Tree:    14

    Initial Tree Branch Selected: Imperfect Information Source # 1
                      Expected Value:       49,999.99
    If Information Indicator Ap
        Then Select Decision Alternative a1
                      Expected Value:      116,666.67
    If Information Indicator Bp
        Then Select Decision Alternative a1
                      Expected Value:       63,207.54
    If Information Indicator Cp
        Then Select Decision Alternative a2
                      Expected Value:      -50,000.00
                  DECISION TREE NODE INFORMATION


    Node Number:      1                        Type: Chance
Node is on tree branch:    a1              Expected Value:     -20,000.00

                  Branches     P(Si)       Payoff
                  --------     ------      ----------
                  A            0.2000      300,000.00
                  B            0.5000      200,000.00
                  C            0.3000     -600,000.00
```

Uncertainty

All the computation approaches described in this chapter are easily computerized, as shown by Nelson's MSS output below. (For the problem in Table 3.15.)

LAPLACE CRITERION VALUE (EQUAL P(Si) VALUES)

Problem Name: dt2

Decision Alternative	LaPlace Value	
A 1	4.25	
A 2	4.50	<---BEST
A 3	4.00	

MAXIMIN PAYOFF

Problem Name: dt2

Decision Alternative	Minimum Payoff	
A 1	−2.00	<---BEST
A 2	−10.00	
A 3	−20.00	

MAXIMAX PAYOFF

Problem Name: dt2

Decision Alternative	Maximum Payoff	
A 1	10.00	
A 2	17.00	
A 3	24.00	<---BEST

HURWICZ CRITERION (COEFFICIENT OF OPTIMISM)

Problem Name: dt2
ALPHA Value: 0.7000

Decision Alternative	Weighted Value	
A 1	6.40	
A 2	8.90	
A 3	10.80	<---BEST

SAVAGE'S CRITERION (MINIMAX REGRET)

Problem Name: dt2

Decision Alternative	Maximum Regret	
A 1	14.00	
A 2	8.00	<---BEST
A 3	18.00	

3.14 APPENDIX: CALCULATING REVISED PROBABILITIES

We use the example of Section 3.11 to show the calculation of revised probabilities.

Formulation Let $P(W)$ be the prior probability of the product being a winner. Given:

$P(W) = .80$
$P(L) = .20$ (the probability of the product being a loser)

The conditional probabilities of Table 3.12 are:

1. *In the event the product is actually a winner:*

$P(S|W) =$ Probability of the survey predicting success, given the product is actually a winner. $P(S|W) = .70$
$P(I|W) =$ The probability of the survey being inconclusive, given the product is actually a winner. $P(I|W) = .20$
$P(F|W) =$ The probability of the survey predicting failure, given the product is actually a winner. $P(F|W) = .10$

2. *In the event the product is actually a loser:*

$P(S|L) =$ Probability of the survey predicting success (given . . .) $= .05$
$P(I|L) =$ Probability that the survey is inconclusive (given . . .) $= .10$
$P(F|L) =$ Probability of the survey predicting failure (given . . .) $= .85$

The point to remember here is that all this information is known *before* the survey is actually taken.

Revision of the probabilities of the states of nature Suppose the survey is taken and it predicts success. The prior probability of $P(W)$ will be changed now to a posterior probability, $P(W|S)$, which is the probability of the product being a winner *given* that the survey predicts success. This probability can be computed by using the Bayes' formula for two variables as given in Equation 3.4:

$$P(W|S) = \frac{P(W)P(S|W)}{P(S)} = \frac{P(W)P(S|W)}{P(W)P(S|W) + P(L)P(S|L)} \tag{3.4}$$

This formula is adapted from the general formula for Bayes' theorem, Equation 3.5:

$$P(N_i|B) = \frac{P(N_i)P(B|N_i)}{\sum_{i=1}^{n} P(N_i)P(B|N_i)} = \frac{P(N_i)P(B|N_i)}{P(N_1)P(B|N_1) + P(N_2)P(B|N_2) + \cdots + P(N_n)P(B|N_n)} \tag{3.5}$$

where:

B = Outcome predicted by the research (or new information), which is, in our example, either success (S), inconclusive (I), or failure (F)
N_i = A possible state of nature (either a winner [W] or loser [L] in our example)
i = 1, 2, 3, . . . n, where n = The number of states (two states here, winner and loser)

Equation 3.5 states that the posterior probabilities of the states of nature (N_i: winner or loser), after observing some survey evidence (B: success, inconclusive, or failure), is proportional to the product of the prior probability of N_i and the conditional probability of B given state N_i.

Computing the revised probabilities

In the event the survey predicts success Using Equation 3.4 we get:

$$P(W|S) = \frac{.8 \times .7}{.8 \times .7 + .2 \times .05} = \frac{.56}{.57} = .9825$$

That is, the probability of a winner is increased from 80 to 98.25 percent due to the fact that the additional information predicted success. Similarly:

$$P(L|S) = \frac{P(L)P(S|L)}{P(L)P(S|L) + P(W)P(S|W)} = \frac{.2 \times .05}{.2 \times .05 + .8 \times .7} = \frac{.01}{.57} = .0175$$

It is possible to compute $P(L|S)$ in a shorter manner. Since the product can be either a winner or a loser, then $P(W|S) + P(L|S)$ must sum to 1.0. Therefore:

$$P(L|S) = 1 - P(W|S) = 1 - .9825 = .0175$$

An important question that one may ask is: What is the probability of the survey predicting success? This probability is designated $P(S)$ and is computed from Equation 3.6.

$$P(S) = P(W)P(S|W) + P(L)P(S|L) \tag{3.6}$$

Note that this value is exactly the denominator in Equation 3.4. In our example:

$$P(S) = .8 \times .7 + .2 \times .05 = .57$$

In the event the survey is inconclusive Using Equation 3.5 we get:

$$P(W|I) = \frac{P(W)P(I|W)}{P(W)P(I|W) + P(L)P(I|L)} = \frac{.8 \times .2}{.8 \times .2 + .2 \times .1} = \frac{.16}{.18} = .8889$$

Similarly:

$$P(L|I) = 1 - .8889 = .1111$$

Also, the probability of the survey predicting inconclusiveness, $P(I)$, is computed as .18 (the denominator of the $P(W|I)$ equation).

In the event the survey predicts failure

$$P(W|F) = \frac{P(W)P(F|W)}{P(W)P(F|W) + P(L)P(F|L)} = \frac{.8 \times .1}{.8 \times .1 + .2 \times .85} = \frac{.08}{.25} = .32$$

(Notice the drastic revision, from 80 percent to 32 percent!) And similarly,

$$P(L|F) = 1 - \frac{.08}{.25} = \frac{.17}{.25} = .68$$

The chance of the survey predicting failure, $P(F)$, is .25 (the denominator of the $P(W|F)$ equation).

What will the survey predict?

Revision without the survey

We showed that it is possible to revise the initial probabilities *without actually taking* the survey. Of course, the answers that we received are *conditional, depending on the outcome of the survey*. For example, *if* the survey predicts success, then the probability of having a winner, $P(W|S)$, is 98.25 percent, and so on. In decision making it is important to find out, *before* the survey is taken, the chance that the survey will predict success, failure, or will be inconclusive. In deriving the solution above it was found that:

$P(S)$ = Probability that the survey will indicate "success" = .57
$P(I)$ = Probability that the survey will be inconclusive = .18
$P(F)$ = Probability that the survey will indicate "failure" = .25

Note that since these are the only possible survey outcomes, they must sum to 1.0.

Figures 3.12 and 3.13 summarize the process and the results obtained in the example above.

FIGURE 3.12
Summary of the Bayes' process

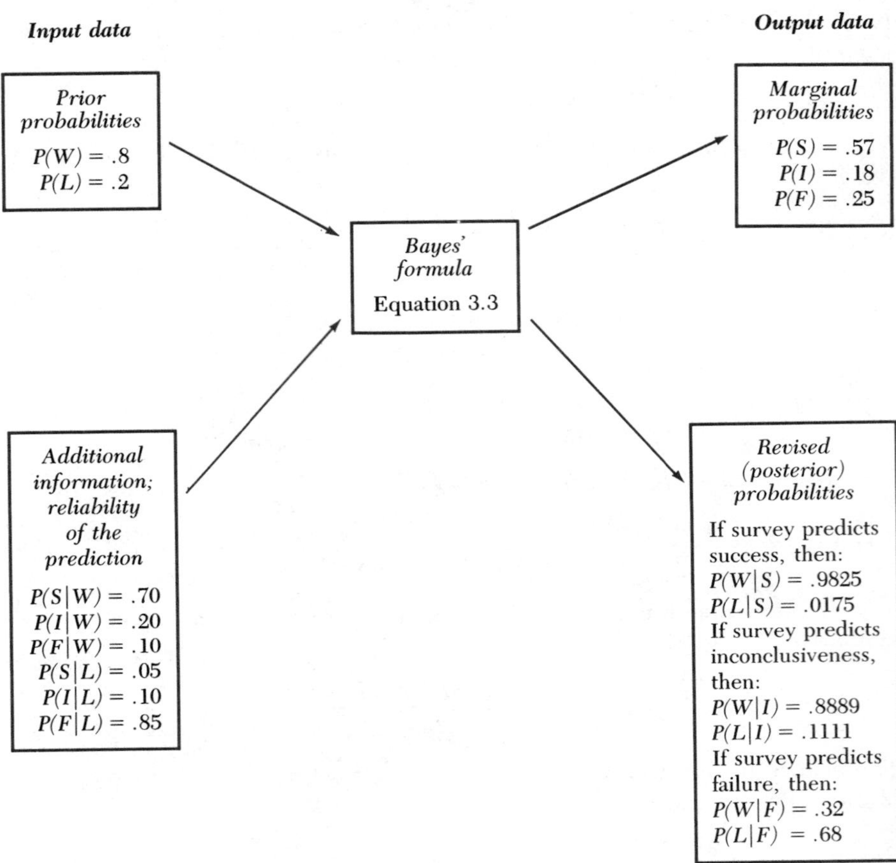

FIGURE 3.13
Tree representation of the Bayes' process

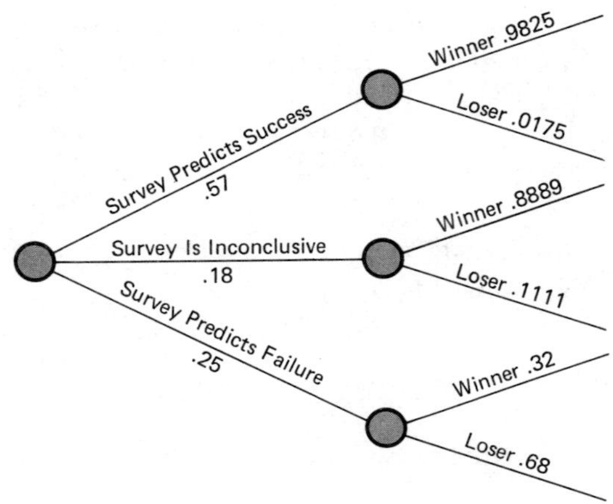

3.15 PROBLEMS FOR PART B

27. Find the expected value of perfect information in Problem 8 *(a)*, *(b)*, and *(c)*. Compare the results to the EOL.

28. Review problem 12. Assume that the store can buy information that will enable it to predict, with certainty, the daily demand. How much should the store be willing to pay for such information?

29. Review problem 14. Find the value of perfect information and comment on it.

30. Given two decision tables below, find the best alternative in each by the following criteria:

a. Laplace (equal probabilities).
b. Pessimism.
c. Optimism.
d. Coefficient of optimism (Hurwicz) with $\alpha = .4$.
e. Regret (Savage).

TABLE 1—Cost data

	s_1	s_2	s_3	s_4
a_1	5	8	3	1
a_2	7	4	5	2
a_3	3	6	6	4

TABLE 2—Profit data

	s_1	s_2	s_3
a_1	7	2	−1
a_2	3	6	2
a_3	0	3	8

31. Consider a decision in which the possible outcomes can be classified as either acceptable (x) or not acceptable (y). Given below is a payoff table.

Futures / *Alternatives*	s_1	s_2	s_3
a_1	x	x	y
a_2	x	y	x

a. If the probabilities of the futures, s_1, s_2, and s_3 are unknown (call them p_1, p_2, and p_3), which alternative would you select? Why?

b. Describe under what conditions the two alternatives would be of equal value to the decision maker.

Hint: Naturally, the utility of x is larger than that of y. Use the "expected value criterion." Assume a repetitive situation.

32. The manager of an advertising agency has to make a decision between three available programs (a_1, a_2, a_3). There are three possible futures that can be expected: s_1 = Market rises, s_2 = Market falls, s_3 = No change in the market. The manager can estimate the yields in each case (given in the table below, in percent of return) but cannot estimate the probabilities of the various futures occurring.

Futures / *Programs*	s_1	s_2	s_3
a_1	3	6	−1
a_2	8	5	4
a_3	−4	7	12

Which program will the manager select if he uses the following decision approaches:

a. Laplace (equal probabilities).
b. Pessimistic approach.
c. Optimistic approach.
d. Hurwicz criterion with $\alpha = .55$.
e. Minimax regret (Savage).

33. International Investor's Bank is evaluating two investment proposals involving 3 million lire. The first is to buy class A bonds with a 7.3 percent return. The second is to buy some land in Easton, Pennsylvania. The land is intended for development into an industrial park, in which case a 17 percent return is expected. However, the land is close to a planned new highway, and the government may purchase the land to build a rest area. In this case, the government will pay the bank 4.5 percent above the purchase price.

Assuming a one-year decision horizon, what would you advise the bank to do if the probability of the government action is unknown?

34. The probability of the government action in Problem 33 is unknown. However, there exists a theoretical probability that will make the two alternatives *equal.* Find that probability.

35. Review a decision made by an organization. Describe how the decision was made. Was the decision a case of certainty? Uncertainty? Risk? Could a decision table approach be applied? Why or why not?

36. It is said that managers will avoid making decisions under uncertainty. Why?

37. A patient calls her doctor complaining that she is sick. Based on the described symptoms and the knowledge of the kind of diseases currently epidemic in the city, the physician suspects that there is a 40 percent chance that the patient has disease D_1 and a 60 percent chance that she has disease D_2.

Upon arrival at the physician's office the patient is subjected to a test that has either a *negative* or a *positive* result.

The physician knows that there is a .6 likelihood that the results discovered in the test are associated with D_1. That is, in all past cases of D_1, the test was positive 60 percent of the time. Also, the physician knows that there is only a .2 likelihood that the results are associated with D_2.

a. Find the revised probabilities of D_1 and D_2. Assume that the patient has either D_1 or D_2.

b. What is the probability that a test will yield negative results?

38. Given a decision matrix (profits in thousands of dollars):

	S_1	S_2
a_1	5	8
a_2	9	3
a_3	−1	10

The probability of S_1 is .35 and that of S_2 is .65. A research company's track record showed that it had three predictions (p_1, p_2, and p_3) with respect to the states of nature as shown below.

	S_1	S_2
p_1	.8	0
p_2	.1	.1
p_3	.1	.9

a. Draw a decision tree for the situation, including the decision regarding the employment of the research company.

b. Show all revised (posterior) probabilities.

c. What is the probability of predicting P_3?

d. The research company charges $2,700 per prediction; would you advise using it?

39. The following is the payoff profit matrix for two alternate plans:

Futures / *Alternatives*	$p = .75$ Market receptive	$p = .25$ Market unfavorable
Plan a	$20,000	$6,000
Plan b	$25,000	$3,000

a. Which plan do you recommend adopting, using the expected value criterion?

b. What is the expected value of perfect information?

c. It is known from past experience that of all the cases when the market was receptive, a research company predicted it in 90 percent of the cases. In the other 10 percent they predicted an unfavorable market. Also, of all the cases when the market proved to be unfavorable, the research company predicted it correctly in 85 percent of the cases. (The other 15 percent of the cases they predicted it incorrectly.) Find the posterior probabilities of all states of nature.

d. Using the posterior probabilities, which plan would you recommend now?

e. How much should one be willing to pay (maximum) for the research survey?

40. Eeetee Phones of England can either make or purchase the electronic innards for its phones. The profits in thousands of dollars per year are given in the table below (the "track record" of the research group) for each of the alternatives and vary with the level of sales as shown (in pounds).

	Sales level			
	I: Low	*II: Mod*	*III: High*	*IV: Very high*
Make	−20	40	100	300
Buy	10	60	80	240

a. The probabilities of each of the sales levels are: .1, .2, .6, and .1 for levels I through IV. Build a decision tree, compute the EVPI, and find the best alternative.

b. A research study costing £3,000 can be bought. It may result in one of two conclusions, with the conditional probabilities given below. Should Eeetee purchase the research?

	I	*II*	*III*	*IV*
Conclusion A	.05	.25	.80	.90
Conclusion B	.95	.75	.20	.10

41. Management is considering replacing an energy-saving device with a new one. The new device has a probability of 60 percent of being superior to the old one. A testing service is called on to test it.

From experience it is known that when a new device was actually superior, the testing service predicted this superiority in 80 percent of the cases. However, when the new device was really inferior, the testing service predicted it to be superior 50 percent of the time.

a. Suppose a test is undertaken and superiority for the new device is predicted. What will management's revised probabilities be of the device being superior?

b. Suppose the test indicates that the device is inferior. How would the probabilities be changed now?

c. What is the probability that the test will indicate a superior device?

42. Use the decision situation below (profits in millions of dollars) in this problem.

	s_1	s_2	s_3	s_4	s_5
a_1	10	8	3	−2	12
a_2	−4	12	8	11	5
a_3	0	3	6	10	2
Probabilities	.2	.1	.3	.3	.1

Two vendors submit bids for conducting (imperfect) predictions. Vendor A wants $350,000 per prediction and Vendor B wants $600,000 per prediction. The conditional probabilities that reflect the anticipated reliability of the vendors are given below.

Vendor A

Indicator	s_1	s_2	s_3	s_4	s_5
I_1	.6	0	.1	0	0
I_2	.1	.7	0	.1	0
I_3	0	.2	.6	.1	0
I_4	.1	.1	0	.8	0
I_5	.1	0	.2	0	.9
I_6	.1	0	.2	0	.1

Vendor B

Indicator	s_1	s_2	s_3	s_4	s_5
I_1	.8	.1	0	.05	0
I_2	0	.8	.1	0	0
I_3	.1	0	.9	.05	.1
I_4	.1	0	0	.9	0
I_5	0	.1	0	0	.9

Use a computer to answer the following questions:

a. How much should the company pay, at the most, for perfect information?

b. Which vendor should they hire (if any) and why?

c. What is the chance that Vendor A will be inconclusive (indicator I_6)?

d. What is the chance that Vendor B will predict I_3?

e. Build the decision tree for Vendor A and show all the computations at the nodes.

f. List the revised probabilities for the five states of nature if Vendor A makes prediction I_2.

3.16 CASE I

THE CONDOMINIUM

It was a hot summer day in Mexico City and Dave Greenhouse was trying to make a decision before 5 P.M. Dave was in the business of buying repossessed condominium apartments from lending institutions such as savings and loan associations and banks. In the summer of 1980, during the recession, there were many such repossessions. The lending institutions' objectives were to get rid of the property as soon as possible. Dave would buy the apartments and then sell them, hopefully with a nice profit.

This time the Aztec Savings and Loan Association offered him three units (he must take all of them or nothing at a nonnegotiable price of P72,000 (pesos). It was the last day that the offer was valid and Dave knew that he must make a fast decision. He had already had the assets appraised. The estimated selling price that he could get for the units is shown below:

Unit 1. P26,900.

Unit 2. Twenty-five percent chance of P25,000, 50 percent chance of P26,000, and 25 percent of P27,000.

Unit 3. Thirty percent chance of P25,000, 40 percent of P26,000, and 30 percent chance of P27,000.

There was also a selling cost of P1,000 per unit (advertising, legal, financial, and so forth).

Dave hoped to sell the units within 60 days. This was the time limit the savings and loan association gave him to pay the P72,000; Dave estimated there was a 70 percent chance that he could do it. Any unit that was not sold within 60 days would be sold, for certainty, within the next 30 days. However, in that case there would be a financial charge for late payment of P440 per apartment.

Present the situation in a decision table and advise Dave on what to do.

CASE II

MAINTAINING THE WATER VALVES

With the 1978 passage of California's Proposition 13, local governments across the country became very cost conscious. Sharon Brown, Evergreen's city manager, was under continuous pressure to contain costs.

The city of Evergreen owns and operates its own water system. A major expense item is water valve repair. These valves are currently repaired by the city's maintenance department. In preparing next year's budget, the water system manager, Bill White, was faced with the following situation.

The average number of valves repaired in one year is 4,120. The average time needed to repair a valve is 42 minutes. It is estimated that the labor cost next year will be $14 an hour. Parts and supplies are estimated at $3 per valve. Overhead shop expenses are computed at 40 percent of the total labor and parts cost. Some of the valves being repaired also need reworking, because of poor material or mistakes made by employees. Historical data indicate that the percentage of repaired valves that need reworking varies according to the following distribution:

Reworking needed (percent)	*Probability*
3.0	.50
4.0	.40
4.6	.10

A reworked valve is 100 percent reliable because such valves go through a special quality control check. The reworking cost is estimated to be $20 per valve.

Last month, the city manager called in all her assistants and advised them about some cost containment programs that were soon to be implemented. Specifically, she requested they each check on the possibility of eliminating inefficient in-house services that could be contracted out. Accordingly, Bill White advertised the valve repair job on a contractual basis. Western Maintenance Corp. (WMC), a reputable company, came up with the lowest bid: a $38,000 flat yearly fee plus $5 a valve with all reworking done at no additional charge.

City manager Ms. Brown requested that Mr. White evaluate WMC's proposal in terms of possible dollar savings. Mr. White's response is given in the following memo:

> TO: Sharon Brown, City Manager
> FROM: William White, Manager,
> Water System
> SUBJECT: WMC's Proposal on Valve
> Repair Jobs
>
> After careful evaluation of the proposal, I recommend that the contract be awarded to WMC. However, due to the budget squeeze, I will not be able to reassign the employees involved to any other jobs. Therefore, I recommend that the contract be awarded to WMC if and only if they will hire all displaced employees.

Upon receipt of this memo, Sharon Brown called the president of WMC. His response was as follows:

> WMC is currently fully staffed, so hiring the city employees, some of whom are not highly skilled, will increase our cost. Therefore, WMC will be able to hire them only if the terms of the contract are changed to a flat fee of $40,000 plus $5 per valve, or else a $38,000 flat fee and $5.50 per valve.

Use a decision tree approach to advise Sharon Brown what to do.

a. Construct a decision tree and include the alternative of WMC not hiring the city employees.
b. Solve the tree; discuss the results.

c. Suppose the city agrees to the $40,000 flat fee and $5 per valve proposal, provided that the $40,000 is paid in four quarterly payments. The first payment is made with the signing of the contract. If Evergreen's cost of capital is 10 percent compounded quarterly, how will this affect the decision?

CASE III

THE AIR FORCE CONTRACT

Nova Aviation, Inc., is considering its bidding strategy for a U.S. Air Force contract. Because of the specialization of this job there is only one other contractor currently approved to bid on it, Sun Aircraft. The air force determines bid eligibility after lengthy investigation, and is, therefore, unlikely to approve of any additional contractors in the near future.

Due to the repetitive nature of such bids, Nova usually has special meetings to consider bidding strategy. They are considering two options: bidding "high" or bidding "low." Marketing Director Donna Scher explained the logic behind these options as follows:

"Our company's policy is to bid every time, while Sun's policy is to bid only 60 percent of the time. And we have only two choices: a high bid or a low one. If we bid high and Sun doesn't bid, we get the job and make $1.1 million profit. But if Sun bids, then we might get the contract or we might not, depending on their bidding level. All in all, our profit on a high bid averages out to zero when Sun bids. If we place a low bid, our per bid profit averages out to $500,000 *regardless* of Sun's action."

Steve Green, Nova's director of finance, thought for a few moments: "If what you say is true, it seems that we should bid 'high' whenever our competitor doesn't bid and 'low' whenever they do."

"Exactly," replied Ms. Scher. "But," said Steve, "how can we find out what Sun might do? We could try to buy this information from someone at Sun, but not only is that unethical, but probably illegal as well."

"Wait a minute," says Ms. Scher. "Suppose it were legal; how much should we offer for such information assuming it were 100 percent reliable?"

"That's a good question," replied Mr. Hunt, the company's president. "It seems to me, however, that we're getting off the track. What do you propose to do, Donna?"

"We could use an expected value approach to solve this problem," said Ms. Scher, "but that approach would assume that our competitor will behave in the future as they behaved in the past, and how can we make such an assumption? How can we know what they'll do?"

"Well," said the president, "we've tried before to predict their moves. Aviation Research Co. has provided such information before, at $100,000 a shot. Their track record isn't bad: of 30 times that Sun bid, Aviation Research predicted it correctly 24 times. On the other hand, of the 20 times that Sun didn't bid, Aviation called it right 17 times."

"What you're saying, Mr. Hunt," said Steve, "is that this research company isn't 100 percent reliable."

"You may infer that, but Aviation Research is still considered the best research company available in this market. Now it's getting late, and we have to make a decision."

You are Steve Green. Prepare a short report advising your boss how to handle this decision. Specifically, use the concepts of the value of perfect and imperfect information and decision policy. Work out the actual numerical values.

3.17 GLOSSARY

Alternative course of action An alternative of choice that is open to the decision maker.

Bayes' theorem A statistical process of revising prior probabilities based on additional information.

Branches (of a decision tree) Lines or arcs that emerge either from a decision point to designate alternatives, or from a chance point to designate states of nature.

Certainty The decision environment when there is only one possible payoff for a decision. This situation occurs when only one state of nature exists.

Chance point A circle on the decision tree designating that states of nature follow.

Coefficient of optimism, α A measure of willingness to assume risk. There exist two extremes: $\alpha = 0$, completely pessimistic; $\alpha = 1$, completely optimistic (gambler).

Complete enumeration A listing of all possible combinations and the comparison of their results.

Criterion of optimism A criterion of choice under uncertainty that assumes that the best is going to occur (maximax).

Criterion of pessimism A criterion of choice under uncertainty that assumes that the worst is coming. Thus, trying to select the best of the worsts (maximin).

Critical probability The probability of an event that results in the EMV of an alternative equal to a desired value.

Decision point A square on the decision tree that indicates that a choice is to be made (selection of an alternative course of action).

Decision tree A graphical representation of a sequence of interrelated decisions to be made under risk.

Deterministic Perfect knowledge of the outcome; certainty.

Dominance When one alternative is preferred to another because it is at least as good as the other and, in some outcome(s), better.

Equal probabilities (Laplace's) criterion of choice Criterion for decision making under uncertainty that assumes that the probabilities of all states of nature occurring are equal.

Expected monetary value (EMV) The average gain/loss for each alternative course of action. It is computed by weighting the payoffs by their probabilities of occurrence.

Expected opportunity loss (EOL). The average opportunity loss, or regret, per decision.

Expected value (EV) A weighted average (mean), found by weighting each possible payoff by its probability (relative frequency) of occurrence.

Expected value of perfect information (EVPI) The difference in expected payoff between making a decision under risk with an expected value approach and making a decision having perfect information about which state of nature is going to occur.

Expected value of sample (or survey) information (EVSI) The difference between the best expected value with posterior probabilities and the best expected value with prior probabilities. It is a measure of the maximum (or upper limit) value of the additional information.

Minimax regret A pessimistic criterion for decision making using the regret figures as payoffs; using this criterion one minimizes the maximum regret values.

Most probable state of nature A criterion of choice for decision making under risk that assumes that the state of nature with the highest probability will occur.

Objective probability Probability estimate based on hard data obtained from history or through experimentation (contrast with subjective probability).

Opportunity loss (or cost) The amount of loss attached to each possible outcome of an alternative, due to *not* selecting the best alternative.

Payoff The result of selecting an alternative course of action, given a specific state of nature occurring (also called outcome).

Perfect information The prior knowledge of exactly which state of nature will occur.

Prior probabilities The original probabilities of the states of nature prior to adjustments made as a result of acquiring additional information.

Regret See "Opportunity loss (or cost)."

Revised probabilities The probabilities of the states of nature after being adjusted with the aid of Bayes' theorem.

Risk A decision situation where several states of nature exist and their likelihood (probability) of occurrence is known.

State of nature Future event that impacts the result of a decision and is *not* under the control of the decision maker.

Stochastic A situation that involves risk; where the outcome is uncertain.

Subjective probability The probability estimate of a knowledgeable person that is based on judgment and intuition.

Uncertainty The decision environment in which several states of nature exist, but their chances of occurring are not known.

3.18 REFERENCES AND BIBLIOGRAPHY

1. Brown, Rex V.; Andrew S. Kahr; and Cameron Peterson. *Decision Analysis for the Manager.* New York: Holt, Rinehart & Winston, 1974.
2. Brown, R. V., et al. *Decision Analysis: An Overview.* New York: Holt, Rinehart & Winston, 1974.
3. Fishburn, P. C. *Utility Theory and Its Applications.* New York: John Wiley & Sons, 1970.
4. Harrison, E. F. *The Managerial Decision-Making Process.* Boston: Houghton Mifflin, 1975.
5. Holloway, C. A. *Decision Making under Uncertainty.* Englewood Cliffs, N.J.: Prentice-Hall, 1979.
6. Hertz, D. D. *Risk Analysis and Its Applications.* New York: John Wiley & Sons, 1982.
7. ________. *Practical Risk Analysis.* New York: John Wiley & Sons, 1983.
8. Hwang, C. L. and K. Yoon. *Multiple Attribute Decision Making: Methods and Applications: A State of the Art Survey.* New York: Springer-Verlag, 1981.
9. Luce, R. D., and H. Raiffa. *Games and Decisions.* New York: John Wiley & Sons, 1957.
10. Magee, J. F. "Decision Trees for Decision Making." *Harvard Business Review,* July–August 1964, pp. 126–38.
11. ______. "How to Use Decision Trees in Capital Investment." *Harvard Business Review,* September–October 1964, pp. 79–96.
12. Oxenfeldt, A. R. *A Basic Approach to Executive Decision Making.* New York: AMACOM, 1978.
13. Raiffa, H. *Decision Analysis.* Reading, Mass.: Addison-Wesley Publishing, 1970.
14. Starr, M. K., and M. Zeleny (ed.) *Multiple Criteria Decision Making.* New York: Elsevier North-Holland Publishing, 1977.
15. Turban, E. *Decision Support Systems and Expert Systems.* New York: Macmillan, 1988.
16. Ulvilla, J., and R. V. Brown. "Decision Analysis Comes of Age." *Harvard Business Review,* September–October 1982, pp. 130–141.
17. White, D. J. *Decision Methodology.* London: John Wiley & Sons, 1975.
18. Zionts, S. *Multiple Criteria Problem Solving: Proceedings in Buffalo, 1977.* New York: Springer-Verlag, 1978.

4

Utility and game theories

PART A: BASICS

4.1 Utility and decision theory.
4.2 Multiple goals.
4.3 Concluding remarks.
4.4 Problems for Part A.

PART B: EXTENSIONS

4.5 Game theory.
4.6 Concluding remarks.
4.7 Problems for Part B.
4.8 Case—The videotape strategy.
4.9 Glossary.
4.10 References and bibliography.

Extending the exposition of Chapter 3, this chapter now delves into additional topics and concepts of decision theory. It begins with the use of utility as a measure of payoffs and then moves to a discussion of the quantitative handling of multiple goals in decision situations.

In Part B, the issue of competitive decision making is addressed through what is called game theory. Zero-sum, nonzero-sum, and *N*-person games are all analyzed.

LEARNING OBJECTIVES

The student should be able to:

a. Describe the need for utility theory.
b. Build utility curves for money.
c. Solve decision problems under risk using utilities as payoffs.
d. Express multiple goals in terms of a single goal by several methods.

Extensions

e. Differentiate between competitive and noncompetitive decision situations.
f. List and define the special terminology developed for game theory
g. Discuss the underlying assumptions.
h. Classify the major types of games.
i. Solve pure strategy games.
j. Solve 2 × 2 mixed strategy games using formulas.
k. Reduce games by dominance.
l. Describe the structure of nonzero-sum and *N*-person games and the difficulties in solving such games.
m. Graphically present a two-person, zero-sum game of size 2 × 2.

PART A: BASICS

Paul sensed they were caught in a dilemma. All month he and his girlfriend had planned to go to the school's annual prom. They had even saved up the usual $20 per couple admission fee. But at the last minute the student council raised the fee to $30 to cover the unexpected costs of hiring a well-known dance band. That seemed to doom their plans. Then one of his friends, knowing their dilemma, jokingly offered them a coin-toss gamble. If the toss showed heads, they must pay him the $20 they had saved, but if it showed tails, he would pay them $12. At the time, Paul had laughed off the gamble since it was so obviously unfair. But now, Paul wondered—perhaps it wasn't such a foolish gamble after all.

4.1 UTILITY AND DECISION THEORY

Let us attempt to analyze the above situation with the expected value method presented in Chapter 3, as shown in Table 4.1. The payoffs represent the money left after the gamble.

Solution Using an expected payoff approach, Paul and his girl should reject his friend's offer, since the expected value of rejection is higher.

Analysis Before Paul and his girl reject the offer, they should do some thinking. If they consider the enjoyment they will have at the prom, they probably should accept the offer. The reason for this is that the $20 is of very little use to them, since it cannot get them to the prom; but if they win the gamble, they will have enough money ($20 + $12 = $32) to pay the admission fee and even buy a soft drink or two. What should actually be compared in this case are not the monetary values but the benefits or **utilities** that it has for Paul and his girl.

Expected monetary value or expected utility?

Discussion In the analysis of decision making under risk, the best alternative is usually selected by calculating and comparing the expected monetary values (EMV) of the various alternatives. However, there are at least three situations in which EMV is *not* likely to be a valid criterion. First, if the decision maker finds difficulty in expressing the values of some of the outcomes of his or her decisions in terms of monetary payoffs, then EMV cannot be used. Second, EMV assumes that the decision maker

EMV not valid in three cases

TABLE 4.1
The expected monetary payoff

Alternatives \ *States of nature*	.5 *Heads*	.5 *Tails*	*Expected payoff (EMV)*	
Accept offer	0	32	16	
Reject offer	20	20	20	← *Maximum*

is willing to risk losing money in the short run as long as he or she is better off in the long run. In reality, however, decision makers frequently act to *avoid* risk in the short run, particularly if there is any possibility whatsoever of incurring a large initial loss. Finally, EMV assumes a linear relationship between the amount of money and its value (or utility). For example, it is assumed that the value of $20,000 is twice that of $10,000. In reality, however, it has been observed that with an increase in the amount of wealth accumulated, the value of additional money decreases. (For example, the value of a dollar added to $10 is larger than that of one added to $1,000.)

For all these situations there is a need for a measure other than money that better describes how decision makers value possible outcomes.

The application of *utility* as a measure of the *value of an outcome* was proposed by Von Neumann and Morgenstern [17]. They suggested that each individual has a measurable preference among various choices available in risk situations. This preference is called *utility* and is measured in arbitrary units called **utiles.** By suitable questioning (an example will be given later), it is possible to determine a person's utility for various amounts of money. This is called a person's *utility* (or *preference*) *function*. The graph of this function offers a picture of the individual's attitude toward risk taking. Von Neumann and Morgenstern hypothesized that in any decision involving risk, a person will choose that alternative that maximizes his or her expected utility.[1]

Utiles

This idea is based on the following assumptions:

Utility a cardinal measure

1. Utility can be measured on a cardinal scale. That is, cardinal numbers (1, 2, and so on) can describe how many utiles constitute a payoff. For example, if a certain consequence, say a 5 percent share of the market, is twice as important as another consequence, say 6 percent profit, we describe the 5 percent share of the market as having twice as many utiles as the 6 percent profit.

Utilites are additive

2. Utilities of different objects can be added together (this is called the **additivity assumption**). For example, if object A is worth 10 utiles and object B is worth 5 utiles, then objects A and B together are worth 15 utiles.

Certainty equivalent Let us return to Paul's dilemma. Paul and his girl have two alternatives: accept the offer with an EMV of $16, or reject it and save the $20. Let us assume that they are *indifferent* between the two alternatives. That is, they are willing to accept the offer at $20 but they are not willing to pay *more* than $20. It is clear that the decision of how much to pay for this gamble is *subjective*. While they are willing to pay $20, someone else may be willing to pay even $25, while a third

[1] The mechanics of computing **expected utility** are the same as the mechanics of computing any expected value; namely, multiply the probabilities by the corresponding payoffs (this time given in units of utility called utiles) and add them up.

person may not be willing to pay more than $18. We call such a subjective valuation of a risky situation (a *gamble*) the **certainty equivalent (CE)** of the decision maker for that risky situation.

The concept of certainty equivalent enables us to classify decision makers into three types:

- EMV takers whose certainty equivalent = EMV.
- Risk takers whose certainty equivalent is *larger* than the EMV of the gamble (such as Paul and his girlfriend).
- Risk averters whose certainty equivalent is *smaller* than the EMV.

Risk premium We see that people's attitudes toward risk are related to the certainty equivalent (CE) and the EMV of the risk. The difference between these two is called the **risk premium (RP).**

$$\text{RP} = EMV - CE$$

In our example, RP = 16 − 20 = −$4. For a risk taker, the RP is negative since the CE > EMV. For a risk averter, the RP is positive. Why do people behave differently? For more insight into this issue let us look at the solution of the school prom case.

Solution of the school prom case using utilities

Let us examine the problem in utility terms: Since the $20 will not get Paul and his girl to the prom, it is of little value to them. We may arbitrarily assume that the $20 is worth 100 utiles. Losing the $20 will leave them with no money, a situation which is worth 0 utiles. However, the additional $12 is crucial, since they will have $32 and will then be able to go to the prom. Therefore, the $32 is extremely valuable—worth, say, 500 utiles. Now the decision situation can be reevaluated (see Table 4.2) in terms of utilities.

Using the **expected utility** (EU), they should *accept* the offer, since the expected utility in the case of "accept" is: .5(0) + .5(500) = 250 utiles, which is higher than the expected utility of "reject," which is .5(100) + .5(100) = 100.

TABLE 4.2
Expected utility (EU)

States of nature / *Alternatives*	.5 *Lose (heads)*	.5 *Win (tails)*	*EU*	
Accept	0	500	250	← *Maximum*
Reject	100	100	100	

Gambling versus insurance

The above example can explain why people gamble, that is, why they are willing to spend money to assume risk. The next example of utility will show why people insure themselves, that is, why they are willing to spend money to *avoid* risk.

Example: To insure or not to insure?

Insure or not?

Suppose that management is about to make a decision concerning fire insurance on a plant valued at $2 million. There is a chance of 1 in 2,000 (i.e., .0005) that a fire will destroy the plant during a one-year period. The annual premium for insurance is $1,500. Should the company insure or not? The situation is shown in the decision Table 4.3.

TABLE 4.3
Fire insurance, EMV outcomes

States of nature / *Alternatives*	.0005	.9995	*Expected cost (EMV)*	
	Fire	*No fire*		
Insure	$1,500	$1,500	$1,500	
Do not insure	$2,000,000	0	$1,000	← *Minimum cost*

According to the EMV, management should not insure. In the long run it will cost much more to insure than not to. However, since the situation is in the realm of uncertainty, there is a chance, although very small, that fire may even occur during the very first year. The loss of $2 million would probably bankrupt the company—a situation that management could not afford. Therefore, they will buy the insurance even though it has a larger expected monetary cost. If the same situation is analyzed in utility terms, it might look like this:

The $1,500 premium is worth −1 utile to the company; zero dollars is worth zero utiles. A loss of $2 million is worth −10,000 utiles. This information is entered in Table 4.4.

The results show that the expected utility of insuring is higher than that of not insuring; thus, the company will elect to insure.

TABLE 4.4
Fire insurance, EU outcomes

States of nature / *Alternatives*	.0005	.9995	*Expected utility (EU)*	
	Fire	*No fire*		
Insure	−1	−1	−1 utile	← *Maximum utility*
Do not insure	−10,000	0	−5 utiles	

Utility (preference) curves

From the discussion so far it is evident that the mechanics of using utilities as payoffs are similar to using money (or any other objective value such as yield) as payoffs. The only difference is that the expected value is expressed in terms of expected utility (EU), instead of expected monetary value (EMV). The biggest problem, however, is the assignment of utility values as a replacement for monetary values. The relationship between money and utility can be described graphically with the help of a curve termed the **utility curve** or *utility function*.

The EU

If a utility curve can be constructed, then one can read off the curve the utility values that correspond to any desired monetary values. The construction of the curve, therefore, is the key to the analysis. According to the Von Neumann–Morgenstern proposal, a curve can be constructed by measuring the attitude of the decision maker toward risk. Four such curves are shown in Figure 4.1. The shape of each curve is a function of the individual's attitude toward risk. Curve *a* describes a typical risk averse person and in curve *b*, a person who is poor but willing to gamble to improve his standard of living. The same person, once he has accumulated wealth, will become risk averse. Once a person's utility curve is known, then it is possible to replace any monetary value by its utility equivalent for that person.

Utility curves

Example

A decision table with three alternatives and three states of nature is shown in Table 4.5 (with payoffs given in dollars). The objective is to maximize profit. The problem is to select the alternative that will do so.

Solution by EMV Using expected monetary value, alternative a_1 with the largest EMV of \$6.6 is selected.

Solution by expected utility In order to evaluate the decision table in terms of utility, it is necessary to express *all* nine entries in the table

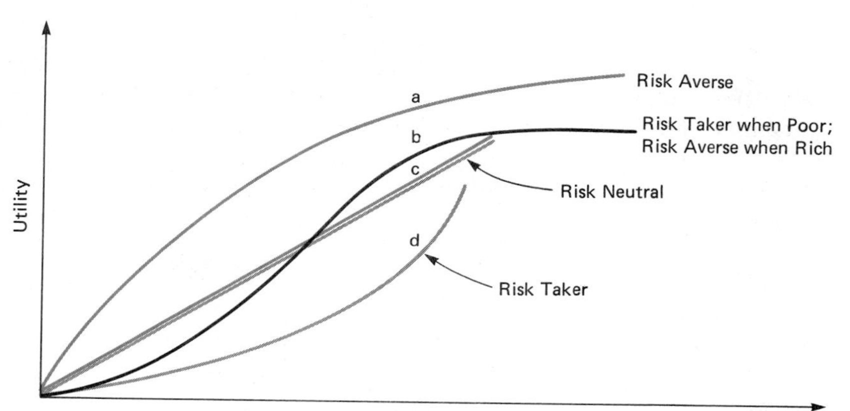

FIGURE 4.1
Different utility curves

TABLE 4.5 Decision table with profit figures

Alternatives \ States of nature	.2	.5	.3	EMV	
	s_1	s_2	s_3		
a_1	12	6	4	6.6	← *Maximum*
a_2	15	3	−2	3.9	
a_3	6.5	6.5	6.5	6.5	

in utiles. The question of how to do this can be answered with the aid of the decision maker's utility curve.

How to construct a utility curve

To illustrate how the decision maker's utility-of-money curve is obtained, let us first arbitrarily assign the value of 100 utiles to the highest outcome, \$15, and 0 utiles to the worst possible outcome, −\$2.[2] This data is graphed in Figure 4.2 (see points *A* and *B*). To build the utility curve, additional reference points are needed. The utility for \$12 will be derived in order to illustrate how to obtain additional points on the curve.

Constructing the utility curve

One way of doing this is to ask the decision maker, whose utility curve is to be constructed, to visualize a hypothetical gambling situation in which the decision maker has the option of investing:

A gamble

a. Either in a lottery ticket with two possible outcomes: winning \$15 (the highest outcome) or losing \$2 (the worst outcome).
b. Or in a project that is sure to yield \$12.

"Let's Make a Deal"

(The situation is similar to the former popular TV program "Let's Make a Deal.")

The decision whether or not to take the lottery ticket clearly depends on the chance of making the \$15; and it is a personal, subjective decision. Some people will prefer the lottery only if the odds of making \$15 are very high; others will take it with lower odds. The management scientist attempts, by trial and error, to find the "*chance* of making \$15," to be labeled *p*, that will make the decision maker *indifferent* between the two options.

Gambling or take the "sure thing"?

This is done in the following manner: First, the decision maker is asked if he or she *prefers* the \$12 certain return over the lottery ticket with an arbitrary probability of, say, $p = .80$. If the decision maker says yes, *p* is *increased* slowly to $p = .81$, $p = .82$, and so on, until the point

[2] One can use any other pair of numbers instead of 100 and 0, for example, 1 and 0.

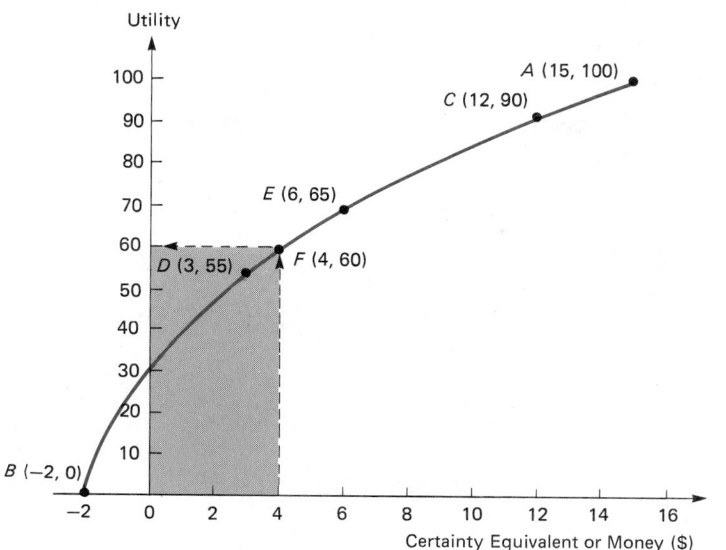

FIGURE 4.2
The utility-of-money curve

that the decision maker is *indifferent* between the sure return and the ticket. If the decision maker says no, the value of p is decreased slowly to the point where the decision maker expresses indifference. Since the decision maker is indifferent, the $12 alternative is equivalent to the gamble. Therefore, the $12 is called the *certainty equivalent* of the lottery ticket.

A point of indifference

Suppose that the analyst finds that at a probability of $p = .90$, the decision maker is indifferent between the two points. Given this information, the analyst can now find the decision maker's utility for $12, using the indifference Equation 4.1.

$$\text{Utility of a certain equivalent} = \text{Expected utility of the lottery} \quad (4.1)$$

In our case:

$$U(\$12) = pU(\$15) + (1 - p)U(-\$2)$$

The assigned values of 100 utiles to $15 and 0 utiles to −$2 are now introduced into Equation 4.1, as are the predetermined probability values:

$$U(\$12) = p(100) + (1 - p)0 = .9(100) + .1(0) = 90 \text{ utiles}$$

Thus, the utility of $12 is 90 utiles (point C in Figure 4.2).

Similarly, by the use of further hypothetical gambling situations (e.g., $6 for certain versus a lottery with a probability, p, of gaining a yield of $15 and $1-p$ of −$2), it is possible to obtain other values for the curve. Let us assume that the utility values for the additional points of $3 and $6 were found to be 55 and 65, respectively. These results are plotted in

TABLE 4.6
Utility values for the profits of Table 4.6

States of nature / Alternatives	.2		.5		.3		EMV	Expected utility (EU)	
	s_1		s_2		s_3				
	$	*Utiles*	$	*Utiles*	$	*Utiles*			
a_1	12	90	6	65	4	60	6.6	68.5	
a_2	15	100	3	55	−2	0	3.9	47.5	
a_3	6.5	70	6.5	70	6.5	70	6.5	70	← *Maximum EU*

Figure 4.2 (points *D* and *E*). Next, a continuous curve is constructed by connecting all computed points (each marked with a dot). This curve describes the decision maker's utility for money. Note that this decision maker is somewhat risk averse; more money has less utility for him or her than it has for a risk-taking decision maker (see Figure 4.1).

Risk taker or risk averse?

From this graph in Figure 4.2 it is possible to read the utility values for all the monetary payoffs of Table 4.5. These utility values are shown in Table 4.6. For example, to read the utility value of $4 in Figure 4.2, go from point 4 on the horizontal axis up (follow the arrows) to point *F*; then turn 90 degrees to the left and go to the utility axis (reaching it at 60). The coordinates of point *F* are thus 4 and 60, which means that $4 is equivalent to 60 utiles.

It is now possible to compute the expected utility value (EU) of the various alternatives.

$$\text{EU}(a_1) = 90(.2) + 65(.5) + 60(.3) = 68.5$$
$$\text{EU}(a_2) = 100(.2) + 55(.5) + 0(.3) = 47.5$$
$$\text{EU}(a_3) = 70(.2) + 70(.5) + 70(.3) = 70$$

The third alternative has the highest expected utility, and is therefore recommended.

A nonlinear relationship

Note that the alternative with the highest EMV (a_1), does not have the highest EU. This is not surprising, due to the nonlinear relationship that exists between monetary values and utility for this decision maker. Alternative a_1 is more speculative than a_3. The decision maker indicated, through personal preferences, that he or she is less likely to gamble. The shape of the utility curve tells us that this decision maker is averse to risk.

The concept of risk profile

In decision making under risk, we relate the possible results for each alternative to their respective probabilities. Such a presentation is called a **risk profile** and is slightly different from a decision table.

Example Given below are the risk profiles of two projects, A and B.

Project A

Possible result	*Probability*	*EMV*
−1,000	.1	−100
6,000	.6	3,600
10,000	.2	2,000
15,000	.1	1,500
	1.0	7,000

Project B

Possible result	*Probability*	*EMV*
0	.1	0
5,000	.5	2,500
10,000	.4	4,000
	1.0	6,500

The problem is to find which project should be selected for a decision maker with the utility-of-money curve shown (in thousands) in Figure 4.2.

Solution Using the utility curve, we can find the expected utility values of the two projects.

Project A

Result	*Utility*	*Probability*	*E(utility)*
−1,000	15	.1	1.5
6,000	65	.6	39.0
10,000	82	.2	16.4
15,000	100	.1	10.0
			66.9

Project B

Result	*Utility*	*Probability*	*E(utility)*
0	30	.1	3.0
5,000	63	.5	31.5
10,000	82	.4	32.8
			67.3

Project B is preferred over A even though its expected monetary value is lower ($6,500 versus $7,000 for project A).

Utility curves expressed as functions

Once utility curves are constructed, they can sometimes be expressed as a function, such as:

$$U(M) = 0.8M + \sqrt{9M}.$$

Here, the utility is algebraically related to the amount of money by a formula. For example, if $M = \$40{,}000$ then its utility will be:

$$\begin{aligned} U(40{,}000) &= .8(40{,}000) + \sqrt{360{,}000} \\ &= 32{,}600 \end{aligned}$$

Preference curves using probabilities

The utility curves constructed in this chapter show the relationship between utility and money (the certainty equivalent). The curves were structured by finding the certainty equivalent for gambles involving two possible outcomes, one with a probability of p and the other with a probability of $1-p$. We call such results *preference profiles.*

Preference (indifference) curves

To find the indifference points, we changed the values of p and kept the monetary values constant. Alternatively, it is possible to keep the value of p constant (say, at 50 percent) and change the value of the payoffs. Such an approach will result in a curve that looks like the utility but graphs the probabilities (on a scale of 0 to 1) rather than utility. This is called a *preference* (or *indifference*) curve. The mechanics of using this curve are similar to what we did in Table 4.6; namely, from the preference curve we derive probability values (instead of the utility values) and multiply them by the probabilities of the states of nature of the various alternatives. Then, instead of getting expected utilities, we get expected probabilities. The alternative with the *highest expected probability* is then selected.

Summary

Utility theory has been found to be a useful instrument in analyzing decision making under risk. While the theoretical value of the utility concept is apparent, its implementation is no simple task. Besides the frequent skepticism expressed by managers, several measurement problems must be overcome to obtain utility curves, for example, resolving issues of whether or not the curves remain stable over time.

4.2 MULTIPLE GOALS

No single goal

The analysis of management decisions aims at evaluating, to the greatest possible extent, how far each alternative advances management toward its goals. Unfortunately, managerial problems are seldom evaluated in terms of a single goal such as profit maximization. Today's management systems are becoming more and more complex, and a single goal is rare. Instead, managers want to attain simultaneous goals, some of which conflict with each other. Therefore it is often necessary to analyze each alternative in light of its potential impact on several goals.

For example, consider a profit-making firm. In addition to making money, the company wants to grow, to develop its products and its employees, to provide job security to its workers, and to serve the community. Managers want to satisfy the shareholders and at the same time enjoy high salaries and expense accounts, while employees wish to increase their take-home pay and fringe benefits. Needless to say, some of these goals complement each other while others are in direct conflict. Add to this social, legal, and ethical considerations and the system of goals begins to look quite complex.

Complementary and conflicting goals

The quantitative approach to decision theory is based on comparing a single measure of effectiveness. Therefore, it is necessary to transform, mathematically, the multiple goal problem into a single goal problem prior to the final comparison, or to develop another method of comparison.

A transformation is required

Before presenting a methodology for dealing with the **multiple goal** situation, it will be worthwhile to discuss some of the difficulties involved.

Some difficulties

1. It is usually difficult to obtain an explicit statement of the organization's goals.
2. Various participants assess the importance (priorities) of the various goals differently.
3. The decision maker may change the importance assigned to specific goals with the passage of time or in different decision situations.
4. Goals and subgoals are viewed differently at various levels of the organization and in various departments.
5. The goals themselves are dynamic in response to continuous changes in the organization and its environment.
6. The relationship between alternatives and their impact on goals may be difficult to quantify.

In spite of these difficulties, it is instructive to examine some methods that can be used to resolve the multiple goal situation. Five such techniques are outlined below.

Expression of goals as requirements (constraints)[3]

Goals as system requirements

This approach is used in linear programming. The most important (primary) goal is maximized (or minimized) and all other (secondary) goals are expressed in terms of system *requirements.*

Example Compudyne Corporation expresses its 1989 goals in the following manner: primary goal—cost minimization. All other goals are expressed as constraints:

1. Maintain *at least* a 15 percent market share.
2. Profit should be *no less* than $2 per share.
3. Sales volume should top last year's by *at least* 6 percent.
4. Consumer complaints should *not increase.*
5. Product quality should *not decrease.*
6. Employee turnover should *decrease* by 1 percent.

The model then proceeds to *minimize* the level of the primary goal while *satisfying* the secondary goals.

[3] See Chapter 6, 'Linear Programming,' for an application of this approach.

Conversion to a single scale

A single scale

Multiple goals can sometimes be expressed by a single measure such as dollars. In this case, all the outcomes, as well as the costs of the alternatives, should be expressed in the same measure.

Example: Change in maintenance policy Assume that a company is considering a change in its maintenance policy from weekly to biweekly preventive maintenance. The maintenance policy primarily affects breakdowns but also has an impact on maintenance costs, product quality, and spare parts inventory. In this case, it may be possible to express the effect of the two alternatives on the various goals (or measures of effectiveness) directly in dollar terms. For example, total weekly cost = \$3,000 for maintenance + \$600 for product quality losses + \$280 for breakdowns = \$3,880.

Expressing one goal in terms of another (trade-offs)

Goal trade-offs

Sometimes it is possible to express two or more goals in terms of one, by using trade-offs, thus again arriving at a single measure of effectiveness.

Example: Sales and profit increases The projected outcomes of two alternatives are shown in Table 4.7. The question is: Which alternative is better if both cost the same? To answer this question it is necessary to find a single measure of effectiveness.

TABLE 4.7
Two outcomes

Outcomes / *Alternatives*	*Sales increase*	*Profit increase*
a_1	\$50,000	9%
a_2	\$80,000	4%

Suppose management decides that each 1 percent increase in profit is worth a \$10,000 increase in sales. Then \$50,000 and \$80,000 sales increases are equivalent to a 5 percent and 8 percent increase in profit, respectively, as shown in Table 4.8.

TABLE 4.8
Combined outcomes

Outcomes / *Alternatives*	*Sales expressed as percent profit*	*Profit*	*Total*	
a_1	$\frac{\$50,000}{\$10,000} \times 1\% = 5\%$	9%	$5 + 9 = 14$	← *Maximum*
a_2	$\frac{\$80,000}{\$10,000} \times 1\% = 8\%$	4%	$8 + 4 = 12$	

TABLE 4.9
Multiple outcomes

Alternatives \ *Corporate goals*	*Profit*	*Market share*	*Sales**	*Cash reserves**
a_1	5%	18%	23	.6
a_2	3%	20%	30	.3

* In millions of dollars.

TABLE 4.10
Utility valuation of Table 4.9

Alternatives \ *Corporate goals*	*Profit*	*Market share*	*Sales*	*Cash reserves*	*Total utility*	
a_1	40	60	20	40	160	
a_2	25	80	28	30	163	← *Maximum*

Once the two outcomes are expressed in one measure, we can combine and compare them (14 for a_1, 12 for a_2), then select the most effective (a_1 in this case).

The trade-offs between sales and profits were linear in this example. But in other cases, the relationship may be *non*linear and it would be necessary to construct trade-off curves to accurately show the relationship between the result variables.

Using a utility or point system

The value of one goal in the previous example was expressed in terms of the other. Another method is to express all alternatives in terms of utiles.[4]

Example Two alternatives are considered in light of the attainment of the four different corporate goals shown in Table 4.9. Table 4.10 gives management's utility valuation of these goals.

Relative weights In the example just presented, utiles were assigned and totaled, assuming that all goals carry the same weight. However, in many organizations, objectives may carry different weights and priorities. Therefore, it is appropriate to adjust the utiles before totaling them.

[4] The approach presented in Section 4.1 can be used for assigning utiles. For other methods, see Fishburn [7].

A weighted sum

One way to treat such situations is to compute the weighted total of utiles. For example, Table 4.11 shows the problem of Table 4.10 with weights put on each goal.

TABLE 4.11
Weighted utilities

Goals	*Profit*	*Market share*	*Sales*	*Cash*	*Total weighted utility*
Weights	2.0	1.2	.4	.8	
a_1	40	60	20	40	192 ← *Maximum*
a_2	25	80	28	30	181.2

The total weighted utility is then computed, similar to the way that expected value is computed. Each utile is multiplied by its relative importance, and the results are totaled.

$$\text{For } a_1\text{: } 40(2) + 60(1.2) + 20(.4) + 40(.8) = 192$$
$$\text{For } a_2\text{: } 25(2) + 80(1.2) + 28(.4) + 30(.8) = 181.2$$

Thus, alternative a_1 is superior.

Delphi

A major problem in such an approach is assessing the relative importance, or priorities, of goals. Various methods such as ranking, pairing, allocating 100 points among the alternatives, and the like can be used. Also, the use of experts is recommended (e.g., via the **Delphi** method [11]). The interested reader is referred to Fishburn [7] and Chapter 5, next.

The point system

A well-known variation of the use of utility is the *point system*. A point system is used by many universities in admission decisions. For example, in order to be admitted into an MBA program, the university may require a minimum of 750 points. These points are computed by multiplying the student's grade point average by 100 (e.g., a B average is 3.0, or 300 points) and adding the result achieved on the Graduate Management Admission Test (GMAT). Banks also use a point system to determine loan eligibility, and some employers use a point system in their annual performance evaluation to determine various levels of merit increases.

Goal programming

A special method of treating certain multiple goal situations involving problems of linear programming is termed *goal programming*. According to this technique, goals are ranked in order of their importance. For example, profit may be more important than share of the market. Then allocation decisions are made such that the sum of the undesirable deviations from the goals is minimized. This topic is treated in detail in Chapter 9.

4.3 CONCLUDING REMARKS

The material presented in Part A of Chapter 4 is based on and supplemental to that of Chapter 3. Two topics were discussed. First, the use of *utility* theory was introduced, permitting subjective assessments of payoffs and the additivity of different payoffs. Second, the difficulty of measuring attainment level when *multiple goals* exist was emphasized, and some techniques for solving this problem were suggested. In Part B of the chapter we consider what is commonly called "decision making under competition," or game theory.

4.4 PROBLEMS FOR PART A

1. A manager expresses indifference between a certain profit of $5,000, and a venture with a 70 percent chance of making $10,000 and a 30 percent chance of making nothing. If the manager's utility scale was set at 0 utiles for $0, and 100 for $10,000, what is the utility index for $5,000? What is the risk premium?
2. The manager in Problem 1 is indifferent between a venture that has a 60 percent chance of making $10,000 and a 40 percent chance of making $1,000, and a sure investment that yields $5,000. Find the value of $1,000 in utiles for this manager. Find the risk premium.
3. Below are the results of a preference test given to an executive:
   a. The executive is indifferent between an investment that will yield a certain $10,000, and a risky venture with a 50 percent chance of $30,000 profit and a 50 percent chance of a *loss* of $1,000.
   b. The executive's utility function for money has the following shape:

Money ($)	−1,000	0	5,000	20,000	30,000
Utility	−2	0	10	20	30

   A new risky venture is proposed. The possible payoffs are *either* $0 or $20,000. The probabilities of the gain cannot be determined. Find what probability combination of $0 and $20,000 would make the executive indifferent to the certain $10,000.
4. A manager has an opportunity of investing $3,000 in a venture that has a .2 chance of making no profit, a .3 chance of making a $2,000 profit, a .2 chance of making a $4,000 profit, and a .3 chance of making a $6,000 profit. Her utilities for each of the outcomes are 0 for $0, .625 for $2,000, .875 for $4,000, and 1.000 for making $6,000. Draw the manager's utility curve and advise her on making the investment.
5. A Jamaican plant manager has a utility of 10 for $20,000, 6 for $11,000, 0 for $0, and −10 for a loss of $5,000.
   a. The plant manager is indifferent between receiving $11,000 for certain, and a lottery with a .6 chance of winning $5,000 and a .4 chance of winning $20,000. What is the utility of $5,000 for the manager? Construct the manager's utility curve.
   b. Using this curve, find the certainty equivalent for the following gamble (i.e., the amount of cash that will make the manager *indifferent* to the gamble below).

Payoff	*Probability*
$−2,000	.2
0	.3
3,000	.4
10,000	.1

   c. What probability combination of $0 and $20,000 would make the manager indifferent to the certain $11,000?
   d. The manager is facing a decision about buying a new production machine that can bring a net profit of $15,000 (80 percent chance) or a loss of $1,000 (20 percent chance); alternatively, the manager can use the old machine and make a $10,000 profit. Use the utility curve to find which alternative the manager should select. Specify all necessary assumptions.

6. A survey of 10 physicians, 50 patients, and 20 nurses shows that each group allocated 100 "units of worth" among the four stated objectives of a hospital as follows:

Objectives	*Physicians*	*Patients*	*Nurses*
A	10	30	20
B	20	20	20
C	50	30	20
D	20	20	40
Total	100	100	100

a. Assuming that all participants are considered to be equal, find the relative importance of the various objectives.
b. Assume that physicians are considered twice as important as nurses and nurses are three times as important as patients. Find the relative importance of the various objectives.

7. EDX Electronic Corporation, Limited, can produce either product A, which will result in a 23 percent share of the market and a net profit of 7 percent, or product B, which will result in increasing the company's share of the market to 27 percent and a net profit of 5.5 percent. If the company considers each percent of net profit as important as a 2 percent share of the market, which product should the company produce?

8. Given below are the results of three years of operations at Computer Services Corporation:

Measure	*1978*	*1979*	*1980*
Sales (in million $)	6.0	6.6	7.2
Share of market (%)	15.0	13.5	16.5
Net profit ($ per share)	2.0	1.8	1.4
Equity per share ($)	4.0	4.2	4.8

The company's stated policy is that the relative importance of the objectives is as follows:
a. Net profit is the most important objective.
b. Equity per share is half as important as net profit.
c. Sales are 1.2 times more important than equity per share.
d. Share of the market is .4 times as important as net profit.

Which year was the most successful for the company's operations? Use 1978 as the base year.

9. International University uses a mathematical model for the initial screening of law school applicants. The variables considered are:
a. The Law School Admission Test (LSAT), which has a possible score between 200 and 800.
b. Grade point average (GPA on a 0–4 scale).
c. An essay score of the LSAT that can vary from 0 to 80.
d. The undergraduate school attended by the applicant, which is evaluated between 1 (poor) and 5 (excellent).
e. The applicant's involvement in extracurricular activities, which is valued from 0 (nothing) to 10 (extremely active).

The weights for the variables are: LSAT = .4, GPA = .4, essay = .1, undergraduate school = .05, extra curricular activities = .05.

John and Mary applied to the school; the information available on both is given below:

	LSAT	*GPA*	*Essay*	*Undergraduate school*	*Extra activities*
John	500	3.8	60	2	6
Mary	600	3.0	72	4	6

Use a single measure of performance to evaluate the two candidates. Which candidate is better?

10. Goodsite International is searching for a worldwide location for their new plant. Three sites are under consideration. These sites and the attributes on which they are being judged are given in the table below. Devise a methodology that will enable the company to select the most appropriate site.

	Site		
Attribute	*Los Angeles*	*Spain*	*Japan*
Climate	Excellent	Good	Poor
Labor availability	Plenty	Poor	Average
Regulations	Stiff	Easy	Easy
Cost of operations	High	Low	Medium
Transportation	Good	Good	Excellent
Cost of land	Very high	Low	High

11. The utility curve for a manager is given as $U(M) = 1.1M + \sqrt{20M}$.
a. What is the attitude of this manager toward risk?

b. Will this manager prefer investing in project *P*1, where there is a 30 percent chance of making $1 million and a 70 percent chance of making $2 million; or in *P*2, where there is a 50-percent chance of making nothing and a 50-percent chance of making $4 million?

12. In the Cutler-Hammer example of Section 1.5, why was the alternative with the lower expected value selected?

PART B: EXTENSIONS

4.5 GAME THEORY

In 1943, General Kenney, commander of the Allied Air Forces in the Southwest Pacific, was faced with a problem. The Japanese were about to reinforce their army in New Guinea from their base in New Britain. Kenney's mission was to bomb and destroy the convoy of reinforcements. The Japanese had a choice of alternative sailing routes. They could either sail north of New Britain, where the weather was rainy and visibility poor for reconnaissance, or southward, where the weather was generally fair (see Figure 4.3). In either case, the journey would take three days. Kenney's problem was to decide where to concentrate the bulk of his reconnaissance aircraft to search for the convoy. The Japanese wanted their ships to have minimal exposure to enemy bombers and, of course, Kenney wanted as many days of bombing exposure as possible.

FIGURE 4.3
The convoy's alternatives

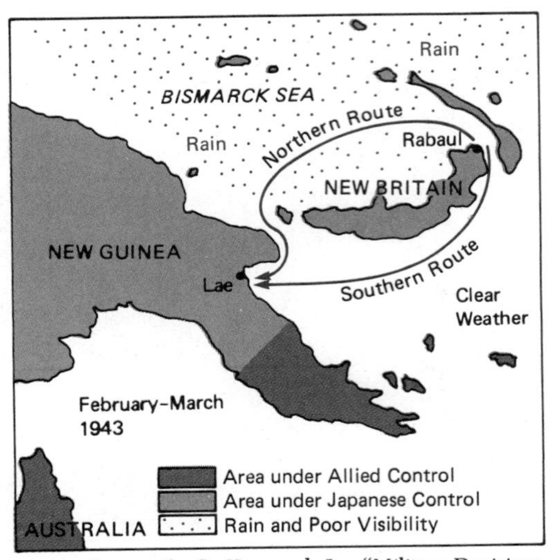

Source: O. G. Haywood, Jr., "Military Decisions and Game Theory." *Journal of the Operations Research Society of America* (November 1954), p. 366.

The following were the possible "days of bombing exposure":

1. If Kenney concentrated his aircraft on the northern route and the Japanese sailed north, the Japanese would not be found until the second day. There would thus be two days of exposure.
2. If Kenney concentrated on the northern route and the Japanese sailed south, they might easily be missed on the first day. There would again be two days of exposure.

3. If Kenney concentrated on the southern route and the Japanese sailed north, they would not be discovered until the third day, resulting in only one day of exposure.
4. If Kenney concentrated on the southern route and the Japanese sailed south, they would be sighted immediately for three full days of exposure.

The problem faced by both sides was what course of action to take.

The nature of game theory problems

Decision under conflict

The military situation just presented illustrates decision making *under* **conflict** or *competition*. Its main characteristic is that two or more decision makers are involved and the consequences (payoff) to each depends on the courses of action taken by all. Further, objectives do not coincide and may, as illustrated in the military example, be completely opposed. As a matter of fact, each party is usually trying to maximize his or her overall welfare at the expense of the others.

"Game" presentation

Such situations are similar to parlor and other types of games. For this reason the name *game theory* was adopted. Yet, situations analyzed with the aid of this tool are a far cry from "games." Marketing strategies, international military conflicts, labor-management negotiations, and potential mergers are just a few examples of real-life game theory problems.

The complexity of game theory problems

The presence of two or more decision makers with conflicting objectives makes decision making complex for mathematical analysis. The decision tables discussed in the previous chapter cannot handle such situations. Game theory thus evolved as a mathematical process for formally developing optimal strategies for problems under competition or conflict.

Methodology of game theory

Optimal strategies

The managerial situation, problem, or conflict is presented in game format. The decision makers are viewed as players. Game theory aims at prescribing optimal playing strategies for the participants. A **strategy** is defined as a complete, predetermined plan for selecting a course of action, under every possible circumstance.[5] An *optimal strategy* is the best among all possible strategies. In addition, the model computes the long-run payoffs or consequences of the decisions to all parties involved.

[5] This differs from the typical military or business definition, which outlines only the main aspects of a plan, leaving a certain amount of freedom for improvisation. In contrast, this definition contains all details as well as the overall plan.

Payoffs for strategies

Format, assumptions, and classification of games

The military conflict example will be used to illustrate the presentation of the basic format of games and the related terminology. In this section, the assumptions of games and their classifications will also be discussed.

The format of games and major assumptions Games are arranged in a standard format. Certain rules and regulations that express the assumptions apply, and a specially developed terminology is used. The major aspects of the format concern:

The game situation

1. *The number of participants (termed "players").* The military example involved two players. In other situations three, four, or more players may participate. A player can be a single individual or a group of individuals with the same objective.
2. *Timing.* It would have been easier for Kenney if he could have delayed his decision until the Japanese made their move (and vice versa). However, both had to decide simultaneously. *Simultaneous* decisions are assumed in all game situations.
3. *Conflicting goals.* Each party is interested in maximizing his or her welfare at the expense of the other.
4. *Repetition.* The military conflict is an example of a one-shot decision, which is termed a **play.** A series of repetitive decisions (plays) is called a **game.** It is generally assumed that most instances involve repetitive situations.
5. *Payoff.* The consequence of the decisions of the opponents in the military conflict was measured in terms of *days of bombing exposure.* Such results are called *payoffs.* The *average payoff per play* is termed the **value of the game.** A game whose value is zero is called a **fair game.**
6. *Information availability.* Both Kenney and the Japanese were aware of all pertinent information. In general, it is assumed that each player knows *all* possible courses of action (finite number) open to the opponent as well as *all* anticipated payoffs. The cost of collecting this information is not considered relevant to the formal analysis.

Games composed of repetitive plays

Zero value = Fair game

Presentation of games Games are presented either in tabular (termed *normal*) or tree (termed *extensive*) form, depending on preference and the type of analysis or experimentation to be performed.[6] Only the former is discussed here.

Tree or normal form

Normal form (a tabular presentation). A game is said to be in *normal form* when the entire sequence of decisions that must be made throughout the game is lumped together in a single strategy. This is the common form of games and the one used in this text. This form is limited to the case of two players.

An example of normal form presentation using the military conflict.

[6] A tree form presents a sequence of decisions based on accumulated information and previous decisions. For details see [12].

In this situation, there were two decision makers: Kenney, with two possible courses of action: a_1, concentrate of northern route, or a_2, concentrate on the southern route; and the Japanese, who had to decide either to sail north, (b_1), or south (b_2). The above situation is presented in normal form as a payoff table in Table 4.12.

TABLE 4.12
The military conflict as a game payoff table

Allies \ *Japan*	*North*, b_1	*South*, b_2
Northern, a_1	2	2
Southern, a_2	1	3

The payoff table

A game payoff table is similar to a decision payoff table (see Chapter 3). The difference between the two is that in a decision table, there is only one decision maker who makes decisions in uncertain environments, expressed as "states of nature." In the game table, on the other hand, there are two decision makers, one on the left and the other at the top. (For this reason, a decision table is sometimes viewed as a "one-player game against nature.") The information in the cells is the payoff (number of days exposure, in this case). A *positive* number means a *gain* to the player situated at the *left* side of the table ("Allies" in Table 4.12). This gain is the loss of the player situated at the top of the table (Japan). A negative number means a *loss* to the player situated at the left and a gain to the player at the top of the table.

Classification of games Games may be classified according to the number of players (e.g., two-person games, three-person games) and whether the game is *zero-sum* or *nonzero-sum*. These latter terms are defined next.

Your loss is my gain!

1. *Zero-sum games.* In **zero-sum games,** the winner(s) receives the entire amount of the payoff that is contributed by the loser(s). Such a game is always strictly competitive. The players' objective is to win as much as they can at the expense of the rival. That is, the players have diametrically opposed interests with regard to the outcome of the game. Zero-sum games with two decision makers are labeled "two-person, zero-sum games" and are the major subject of this chapter. Two assumptions are necessary for the analysis of these games:
   a. All two-person, zero-sum games are solvable.
   b. The utility functions of the players, with respect to the outcome of the game, are identical.[7] In other words, the payoffs are transferable to either player with the same value to each.

[7] This assumption is imperative for defining zero-sum games because if the utility functions of the competitors were not identical, the game would be of nonzero-sum type.

2. *Nonzero-sum games.* In a **nonzero-sum game** the gains of one player differ from the losses of the other (they can be either smaller or larger, but not equal). This means that some other parties in the environment may share in the gains or the losses. Therefore, nonzero-sum games, as will be illustrated later, are not strictly competitive, and there is sometimes a possibility of cooperation.

The solution tells us the best strategy and resulting payoff

Solving games A solution to game problems provides us with answers to these two questions:

1. What strategy should each player follow to maximize his or her welfare?
2. What will the payoff to each player be if the recommended strategy is followed?

Unfortunately, clear answers can be given only in a few instances of conflicts; namely, for two-person, zero-sum games. The following sections deal with such solutions. Two-person, zero-sum games are divided into two groups: those with a pure strategy solution and those with a mixed strategy solution.

Two-person, zero-sum games—pure strategy

A pure strategy versus a mixed strategy

The Allies-Japanese conflict presented earlier is an example of such a game. The term **pure strategy** refers to a prescribed solution in which one alternative is repeatedly recommended to each player, regardless of what the other player does. This is in contrast to a *mixed strategy,* where players change from alternative to alternative when the game is repeated.

Analysis of the Allies-Japanese conflict The Allies-Japanese conflict is reproduced in Table 4.13. It was assumed that each player knew the alternatives available to the opponent and the conditional number of "days of exposure" for each decision. Furthermore, since game theory assumes that the decision makers are rational, it is evident that the Allies will try to *maximize* the days of exposure while the Japanese will try to *minimize* them.

The Allies can get the maximum "days of exposure" (three) if they select a_2 and the Japanese select b_2. However, the Allies realize that the Japanese, being rational competitors, will not select b_2. The reason for this is that *no matter what the Allies do,* the Japanese will be at least as well off, or better off, selecting b_1 rather than b_2*!* If the Allies select a_1, the Japanese will be subjected to two days of bombing exposure regardless

TABLE 4.13
Allies-Japanese conflict
(Table 4.12 reproduced)

Japan / *Allies*	*North,* b_1	*South,* b_2
North, a_1	2	2
South, a_2	1	3

of whether they had taken b_1 or b_2. But if the Allies follow a_2, the Japanese choice of b_1 would subject them to only one day of exposure, as compared to three from b_2. Therefore, knowing that the Japanese will select b_1, the Allies will select a_1.

Another way to look at this situation is to assume that both competitors are extremely cautious in their decisions and instead of assuming risk, will take a conservative, or pessimistic, approach.

A pessimistic, or "minimax" approach

This approach, which is also called the *minimax* approach since it is based on the **minimax theorem,** implies that:

1. Both players determine the *worst possible payoff* associated with each of their alternatives.
2. Then, they each select that alternative that yields *the best* of these worst payoffs.

Solving the game

The choices of both players are illustrated in Table 4.14. The steps involved in solving the game of Table 4.14 using this approach are:

TABLE 4.14
Pessimistic selection

Allies \ *Japan*	b_1	b_2	*Row minimum (worst results to Allies)*	
a_1	②	2	②	← *Maximum (best of worst)*
a_2	1	3	1	
Column maximum (worst loss to Japan)	②	3		
	↑ *Minimum (best of worst)*			

For the Allies

Step 1. Find the *minimum* value in each row. That is, find the worst payoff for each course of action. In this example, the minimum is 2 in row a_1 and 1 in row a_2. Write them in a new column, at the right-hand side of the table.

Step 2. Select the row with the maximum of the minimums computed in step 1 as the best strategy. In this example, the highest value in the newly added third column is 2. Hence, the Allies should select a_1 (the northern route).

For the Japanese

Step 1. Find the maximum in each column. In this case, the maximum is 2 in column b_1 and 3 in column b_2. Write them in a new, bottom row.

Step 2. Select the column with the minimum of the maximums of step 1 as the best strategy. In this case, select the lower value in the third (bottom) row, which is 2. Hence, the Japanese should sail the northern route (alternative b_1).

Maximin and minimax

Another way of looking at this is to say that player A attempts to maximize his or her minimum gains ("maximin"), while player B attempts to minimize his or her maximum losses ("minimax"). In a pure strategy game, the maximin value *must equal* the minimax value.[8] (Notice that both solutions yield 2, which is circled in Table 4.14.)

Solution to the Allies-Japanese conflict The solution to a game answers two questions:

1. What strategy *should* each player follow? In the example:
   The Allies should follow a_1.
   The Japanese should follow b_1.
2. What will the ultimate outcome of the game *(value of the game)* be if the players follow the prescribed strategy? In the example: There will be two days of exposure. *Note:* This solution was actually adopted by both sides during the war, with a resultant two days of bombing exposure.

Some notes on a pure strategy game

Change in strategy. Since games are repetitive, both players may change their strategy. But in pure strategy games there is no incentive to change the prescribed strategy. Any player deviating from the prescribed strategy will find either no improvement or (usually) a worsening of payoffs.

Multiple solutions

Multiple solutions. It is possible for games to have several solutions. For example, the game presented in Table 4.15 has two solutions for player A (play a_2 and/or a_4).

TABLE 4.15
Multiple solution case

Player B

		b_1	b_2	b_3	*Minimum*	
	a_1	7	−1	2	−1	
	a_2	4	4	6	④	←*Maximum*
Player A	a_3	6	3	0	0	
	a_4	7	4	5	④	←*Maximum*
	Maximum	7	④ ↑ *Minimum*	6		

[8] Pure strategies exist only when the solution has reached a point of equilibrium or steady state, referred to as a saddle point. Therefore, pure strategy games are also called *saddle point* or *strictly determined* games. For a detailed discussion of saddle points, see Luce and Raiffa [12].

Dominance. An alternative course of action is said to **dominate** another when all the payoffs in the row (or the column) of that alternative are as good as *and at least one is better than* the corresponding payoffs of the other. For example, in Table 4.15, alternative a_4 is better than alternative a_3, for player A, no matter what player B does. Thus, alternative a_4 is said to *dominate* a_3.

A dominating alternative

Row dominance does not seem to exist, at first sight, in Table 4.14; but column b_1 dominates column b_2 for the Japanese. Thus, the table can be reduced to that shown in Table 4.16. *Now,* however, row a_1 dominates row a_2, resulting in the final solution of (a_1, b_1). Thus, row (column) dominance should always be *rechecked* if a column (row) has just been deleted by dominance.

TABLE 4.16
Reduced table

	b_1
a_1	②
a_2	1

Another example of dominance is given in Table 4.17. Alternative a_2 dominates a_3, but a_1 dominates both a_2 and a_3. Likewise, b_1 dominates b_2 but not b_3 or b_4 (b_3 also dominates b_2).

TABLE 4.17
Dominance illustration

		Player B			
		b_1	b_2	b_3	b_4
	a_1	3	3	3	4
Player A	a_2	2	3	2	1
	a_3	2	2	2	0

Payoffs. In the previous example, a positive payoff indicated a gain to A and a loss to B. Another method of indicating payoffs is to show the percent A receives of the total. For example, a payoff of 65 would indicate 65 percent of the payoff to A and 35 percent to B (see Problems 20 and 24).

Summary

Row dominance requires the dominating row to have entries that are larger than and/or equal to (with at least one entry larger than) the corresponding entries in the dominated row (since A is

Delete dominated alternatives

receiving the payoff). For column dominance, the entries must be smaller than and/or equal to (with at least one entry smaller than) the dominated column (since B is *losing* the payoff). Dominated rows and columns can be deleted from the table since they play no further role in the solution. This makes the table smaller and easier for further computations.

As can be seen in the examples, evaluation of dominance will result in a *solution* in the case of pure strategy games. Therefore, it could be used instead of minimax as a procedure for solving pure strategy games. However, a major objective of dominance is to reduce the size of the table when mixed strategy games (discussed next) are encountered. Mixed strategy games are much easier to solve if they can be reduced in size first.

Two-person, zero-sum games—mixed strategy

A mixed strategy

Some two-person, zero-sum games are not pure strategy games. The way to judge if a game is one of pure strategy or not is to try to solve it by the pessimistic approach. If the "best of the worst" value is *the same* in value and sign for both players (as was shown to be the case in Table 4.14), the game is a pure strategy game. Otherwise, it is necessary to treat the game as requiring a **mixed strategy.**

A marketing example Two competing companies are about to make a decision regarding an investment in a new promotional campaign. Company A considers two alternative courses of action:

$$a_1 = \text{Advertise in all media}$$
$$a_2 = \text{Advertise in newspapers only}$$

Company B considers two alternatives:

$$b_1 = \text{Run a sweepstake}$$
$$b_2 = \text{Run a big sale}$$

If company A advertises in all media and company B runs a sweepstake, then company A will increase its share of the market, at the expense of B, by 4 percent. If A advertises in all media and B runs a big sale, A will lose 1 percent of the market. If A advertises in newspapers only and B runs a sweepstake, A will lose 2 percent; and if A advertises in newspapers only and B runs a big sale, then A will gain 1 percent.

It is assumed that the above information is known to both companies. Furthermore, it is assumed that the objective of the companies is to maintain as large a share of the market as possible. The information is summarized in Table 4.18.

Note again that positive numbers mean a gain to A (and consequently a loss to B) and negative numbers imply a loss to A and a gain to B.

TABLE 4.18
A marketing problem

B / A	b_1 *Run a sweep-stake*	b_2 *Run a big sale*
a_1 *Advertise, all media*	4	−1
a_2 *Advertise, newspaper only*	−2	1

Analysis of the marketing example game Suppose that a pessimistic approach is attempted (see Table 4.19) for this problem. The solution recommends that player A use a_1 and that player B use b_2. Note that the maximum value for player A of −1 (circled) is *not* equal to the minimum value for player B of 1. Assume that on the first play player A selects alternative a_1 (his proposed maximin) and player B selects alternative b_2 (his proposed minimax). As soon as A finds out that B is consistently playing b_2, player A's next move will be a shift to a_2, since he will receive a larger payoff than by playing a_1. When B finds out that A has shifted to a_2, he will shift to b_1. Then, as A finds out about this shift, he will change back to a_1, and so on.

Minimax ≠ Maximin

TABLE 4.19
Minimax approach to the marketing problem

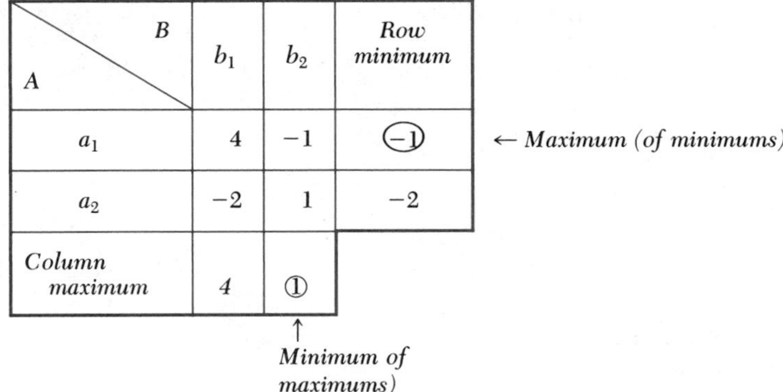

B / A	b_1	b_2	*Row minimum*	
a_1	4	−1	(−1)	← *Maximum (of minimums)*
a_2	−2	1	−2	
Column maximum	4	(1)		
		↑ *Minimum of maximums)*		

Both players will soon find out that:

1. It is better to shift from alternative to alternative (*mix* the alternatives) rather than play the same one all the time as with a pure strategy approach.
2. They should practice maximum secrecy with their plans so that the opponent will not be able to guess the next move.
3. The average payoff is determined by the fraction of time (proportion) that each of the alternatives is played, and there is a certain fraction that is best for each player.

Maintain secrecy

TABLE 4.20
Solving a mixed strategy game (c_{ij} = payoff)

Player B

Proportions		(q)	$(1 - q)$
	Choices	b_1	b_2
Player A (p)	a_1	$c_{11} = 4$	$c_{12} = -1$
$(1 - p)$	a_2	$c_{21} = -2$	$c_{22} = 1$

Randomly mix choices

The above points elaborate the basic idea of mixed strategy games. The best strategy in such a game is a *random selection* of all alternatives that conform, in the long run, to predetermined proportions.[9] These proportions are designed by a frequency distribution. For example, the prescribed solution for player A may be to select alternative a_1 for 20 percent of the time and alternative a_2 for 80 percent of the time. Then, out of a series of, say, 10 decisions, player A should select a_1 twice and a_2 eight times. The sequence of the decisions must be randomly determined, however, to maintain secrecy.[10]

Summary

A solution to a mixed strategy problem includes:

1. *Computation of the best proportion mix of the alternatives.*
2. *Computation of the value of the game*, which is the expected (average) gain or loss, per play, to player A.

Analytical solution to a mixed strategy game with two choices open to each player (2 × 2 game) Let us consider the data in Table 4.18 for illustrating a mixed strategy game. This information is reproduced in Table 4.20 with corresponding generalized symbols.[11]

Calculating the expected payoff

Solution. Let us assume that player B plays alternative b_1 consistently and player A plays a_1 in p of the cases and a_2 in $(1 - p)$ of the cases. The *expected payoff* (V_1) to player A is then (using an expected value formula and treating the proportion as probabilities):

[9] The mixed strategy approach is based on expected value. (See Chapter 3 for discussion.)

[10] One way to assure random choice in repetitive games is to take 10 pieces of paper and write a_1 on 2 of them and a_2 on 8 of them. Then mix them up in a container and, without looking, draw one piece of paper for the first play. Return the paper and draw a second piece for the next play, and so on. For other ways of random selection, see Chapter 16.

[11] With two choices, the proportions for A could be denoted as p_1 and p_2; however, since $p_1 + p_2 = 1$ or $p_2 = 1 - p_1$, there is only one unknown, which is designated as p in this case. A similar designation is made for B, using q instead of p.

$$V_1 = p(4) + (1 - p)(-2)$$

Similarly, when B plays b_2 consistently, the expected payoff to A is:

$$V_2 = p(-1) + (1 - p)(1)$$

Player A desires to mix his strategies so that player B cannot reduce A's gain by shifting strategies. To do so, the expected payoff to A when B plays either strategy b_1 or strategy b_2 should be the same. By doing so, A becomes *independent* of B's decision. B can mix b_1 and b_2 in any proportion and A will receive the guaranteed minimum. That is, the two expected payoffs V_1 and V_2 must be equal:

$$\overbrace{p(4) + (1 - p)(-2)}^{V_1\text{, when B plays } b_1} = \overbrace{p(-1) + (1 - p)(1)}^{V_2\text{, when B plays } b_2}$$

or:

$$\begin{aligned} 4p - 2 + 2p &= -p + 1 - p \\ 8p &= 3 \\ p &= 3/8 \end{aligned}$$

That is, the proportion for a_1 is $3/8$ and for a_2 is $1 - 3/8 = 5/8$.

The general case. The requirement that $V_1 = V_2$ yields the following equation:

$$pc_{11} + (1 - p)c_{21} = pc_{12} + (1 - p)c_{22}$$

Rearrangement of this equation yields the following:

$$p = \frac{c_{22} - c_{21}}{c_{11} - c_{12} - c_{21} + c_{22}} \tag{4.2}$$

In our example, the proportion p, for playing a_1, is prescribed for player A:

$$p = \frac{1 - (-2)}{4 - (-1) - (-2) + 1} = \frac{3}{8}$$

and the proportion for playing a_2 is:

$$1 - p = 1 - \frac{3}{8} = \frac{5}{8}$$

Thus, player A should choose alternative a_1 in $3/8$ of the plays and alternative a_2 for the remaining $5/8$ of the plays. Of course, alternatives should be "mixed" randomly. Similarly, for player B, the proportion q of playing b_1 is derived by equation $V_1 = V_2$ for the columns, which, in this case, yields the following equation:

$$qc_{11} + (1 - q)c_{12} = qc_{21} + (1 - q)c_{22}$$

Computing B's proportions

or:

$$q = \frac{c_{22} - c_{12}}{c_{11} - c_{12} - c_{21} + c_{22}} \tag{4.3}$$

In our example:

$$q = \frac{1 - (-1)}{4 - (-1) - (-2) + 1} = \frac{2}{8} = .25$$

and the proportion for playing b_2 is $1 - q = .75$. Thus, player B should randomly mix his strategies, so that in the long run b_1 is chosen 25 percent and b_2 is chosen 75 percent of the time the game is played.

Calculating the value of the game

The value of the game. Once p and q are established, the *value of the game*, V, can be determined. Assuming that player A plays with the prescribed probability p, his or her payoff (expected average reward per play) can be found using *one* of the following four equations:[12]

$$\begin{array}{ll} \text{either} & V = pc_{11} + (1 - p)c_{21} \\ \text{or} & V = pc_{12} + (1 - p)c_{22} \\ \text{or} & V = qc_{11} + (1 - q)c_{12} \\ \text{or} & V = qc_{21} + (1 - q)c_{22} \end{array} \tag{4.4}$$

In our example:

$$V = \frac{3}{8} \times 4 + \frac{5}{8} \times (-2) = \frac{1}{4}$$

$$V = \frac{3}{8} \times (-1) + \frac{5}{8} \times 1 = \frac{1}{4}$$

$$V = \frac{1}{4} \times 4 + \frac{3}{4} \times (-1) = \frac{1}{4}$$

$$V = \frac{1}{4} \times (-2) + \frac{3}{4} \times 1 = \frac{1}{4}$$

Thus, the value of the game is ¼. Since a game matrix is in terms of the payoff to A, there is an expected gain of ¼ to A and an expected loss (per play) of ¼ to B. To summarize the solution for our example:

Player A: Play a_1 ⅜ of the time and a_2⅝ of the time.
Player B: Play b_1 ¼ of the time and b_2 ¾ of the time.

The value of the game is ¼; that is, A's expected gain is ¼ and B's expected loss is ¼.

---

[12] A good check is to compute V in alternate ways. In a correct solution, the results must be the same.

TABLE 4.21
Table 4.18 reproduced

		Player B	
		b_1	b_2
Player A (p)	a_1	4	−1
$(1 - p)$	a_1	−2	1

A solution procedure for games larger than 2 × 2 is presented in Chapter 7.

Graphical solution

The graphical method can be used to solve games where one of the players has two alternatives and the other has three or more alternatives. (For details, see Williams [18].) A more general method that can handle games of any size is transformation to linear programming.

Consider the game shown in Table 4.21, which is the marketing game solved previously by the analytical method. Assume that player B plays b_1 all the time. What will the value of such a game be to player A? The value will depend on what A does. If A plays a_1 all the time, the value will be 4. If A plays a_2 all the time, the value will be −2; and if A mixes his or her choice with a proportion p, then the *expected value* of the game will be $V_1 = 4p - 2(1 - p)$, or $6p - 2$. Similarly, if B plays b_2 all the time, the value of the game to A will be $-p + (1 - p)$, or $-2p + 1$.

The values $V_1 = 6p - 2$ and $V_2 = -2p + 1$ can be represented graphically by straight lines. These lines are shown in Figure 4.4.

Construction of the lines The horizontal axis, which represents the proportion of time that A will play a_1, is constructed first, starting with $p = 0$ on the right side up to $p = 1$ on the left side. Every point on the horizontal axis represents the proportion mix between a_1 and a_2. At the far left ($p = 1$), player A will choose a_1 all the time, while at the other end ($p = 0$), alternative a_2 is played all the time. At any other point there is a mix of the two alternatives. For example, at $p = 1/3$, the mix consists of choosing a_1 for 1/3 of the time and a_2 for 2/3 of the time.

Plotting the strategies

The vertical axis represents the payoff to player A. The scaling of this axis is set arbitrarily (e.g., 1″ = 3 percent of the market). Now, two straight lines are plotted, each corresponding to one of B's alternatives, in the following way: For the payoff resulting from B playing b_1 all the time, a *straight line* is drawn from 4 percent on the left side to −2 percent on the right side. This is the line $V_1 = 6p - 2$.[13] Note that 4 percent is

[13] The line has the following meaning: If we set $p = 0$, then player A plays a_2 all the time with a payoff of −2. If $p = 1$, then the payoff is $(6 \times 1) - 2 = 4$, which is achieved when A plays a_1 all the time.

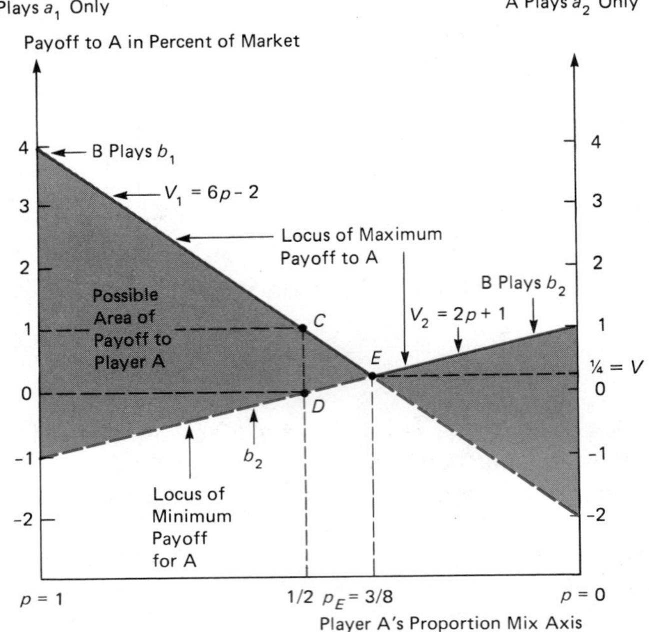

FIGURE 4.4
Player A's strategy mix

in cell c_{11} and that -2 is in cell c_{21} of Table 4.21. Next, a straight line is drawn from the situation in which B plays b_2 all the time: from -1 percent on the left to 1 percent on the right (these figures are in the b_2 column), describing the line $V_2 = -2p + 1$.

Let us now examine the case in which A mixes his or her alternatives, say, .5 of a_1 and .5 of a_2 (i.e., at a point $p = ½$). The value of the game may be either 1 percent (.5 times 4 percent plus .5 times -2 percent) if B sticks to b_1; or 0 (.5 times -1 percent plus .5 times 1 percent) if B plays b_2. These values are shown as points C and D, respectively, in Figure 4.4. If B mixes the choices, the payoff will be between 1 and 0 (graphically shown as the line CD).

The boundaries as payoffs

The shaded area represents the entire feasible area of expected payoffs when p varies between 0 and 1. Player A will try to look for a payoff on the *upper boundary* of this feasible area (bold line), which is the locus of maximum payoffs to A. Player B will try to establish the payoff at the *lower boundary* (broken line) of the feasible area (locus of minimum payoffs to A). For example, if player A tries to get 4 percent by playing a_1 all the time, then B will find out and play b_2 all the time; thus A will lose 1 percent instead of gaining 4 percent. The same situation holds true for every point on the boundary except E. At that point, *no matter what B does,* the payoff to A is the maximum possible for that value of p_E. However, it is also equal to the minimum payoff; that is, point E is the lowest on the upper boundary and the highest on the lower boundary at the same time.

The proportion p_E can be read off the horizontal axis as 3/8; that is, A should play a_1 for 3/8 of the time (and therefore a_2 for 5/8 of the time). The value of the game is found at point E and can be read off the vertical axis as $V = 1/4$ percent.

In a similar manner, it is possible to present B's situation on an additional chart. It will reveal that B's best strategy is to mix b_1 for 1/4 of the time and b_2 for 3/4 of the time. To sum up, the solution of this game is:

$$p = 3/8 \text{ (play } a_1\text{);}$$
$$1 - p = 5/8 \text{ (play } a_2\text{);}$$
$$q = 1/4 \text{ (play } b_1\text{); and}$$
$$1 - q = 3/4 \text{ (play } b_2\text{).}$$

The average gain to player A is 1/4 (B loses 1/4).

4.6 CONCLUDING REMARKS

The reader, now familiar with the major concepts and rules of game theory, can appreciate some of the roadblocks in applying it to real situations of conflict. Concepts such as moves, strategies, complete information, payoff matrix, and simultaneous decisions are theoretical idealizations with intuitive meaning but very little practicability. It seems that even the two-person, zero-sum game, the only game model currently completely solved mathematically, is oversimplified. Moreover, even if the assumptions of a given conflict are more or less reasonable and the model replicates reality, behavioral problems such as convincing the players that their best interests lie in using the proportion-mix strategy approach may interfere with any analytical solution.

Game theory only provides a starting point for the study and analysis of conflicts because real-life conflicts are much more complex. Realizing this, one may ask: "Why study game theory if its application is so limited?" The answer is:

Novel way to analyze conflict

1. Game theory stimulates us to think about conflicts in a novel way. It helps form a framework for working on complex problems. Concepts such as strategy and payoff give valuable orientation to those who must think about complicated conflict situations.
2. Game theory leads us to see why the existing theory is inadequate. It stimulates us to think and to look around for better solutions, thereby initiating further research.
3. The theory is applicable to almost any type of conflict (military, economic, political, and social, to name a few).

4. The game formulation often helps explain much of the phenomena being observed.
5. Game theory formulations and solutions may give decision makers a better understanding of the intricacies of life and help explain social behavior.

Although many of the accomplishments of game theory are of a rather conceptual or general nature, its ideas, methodology, and vocabulary have become part of the daily thinking and language of many decision makers in a broad spectrum of activities ranging from corporation board meetings to top-level political conferences. Perhaps the best evidence that game theory has come of age is the publication of the periodical *International Journal of Game Theory,* the first journal wholly devoted to game theory. Another encouraging bit of evidence is RAND Corporation's bibliography [1] listing over 400 papers and books, many of which are related to applications of game theory.

4.7 PROBLEMS FOR PART B

13. Find the best strategy (strategies) for each player in the following two-person, zero-sum games. Also find the value of the game to both players. Circle the points of maximin and minimax.

a.

	b_1	b_2
a_1	1	3
a_2	7	4

b.

	b_1	b_2
a_1	−1	0
a_2	1	3

c.

	b_1	b_2	b_3
a_1	1	−2	3
a_2	−2	−5	−3
a_3	−1	−6	−5

d.

	b_1	b_2	b_3	b_4	b_5
a_1	3	3	1	6	0
a_2	−1	1	2	0	8
a_3	6	−3	2	1	4
a_4	5	3	3	6	4

14. Two companies are competing in a duopolistic market.[14] Both attempt to increase their share of the market, which is now equally divided. Company A plans to have a weekly advertising campaign that can increase its share of the market by 3 percent (of the total market) if company B does nothing. Company B, however, plans a

[14] A market with only two competitors.

weekly price cut that will result in a 4 percent gain to B if A does nothing and 1 percent gain to B if A uses the advertising campaign. No change in the market is forseen if both companies do nothing.

a. Arrange the problem in a payoff table.

b. Suggest the best strategy for each company to follow.

15. Solve the following game:

	b_1	b_2
a_1	3	−2
a_2	1	5

16. Given below is a payoff table for two manufacturers, A and B, competing in one market. Each has to make a decision between two alternatives.

B / A	b_1	b_2
a_1	−2	3
a_2	1	0

a. Assuming that this is a repetitive decision, what is the best policy for the manufacturers?

b. Let the figures in the payoff table be percentage of change in market share; what will the average gain (loss) to each manufacturer be?

c. As a manager of company B, would you follow the prescribed strategy? Why or why not?

17. A and B play a game in which each has three coins. A has a 2-cent coin, a nickel, and a dime. B has a penny, a nickel, and a dime. Each selects one of his coins without knowledge of the other's choice. If the sum of the two coins adds to an odd number, A wins B's coin. If the sum is an even number, B wins A's coin.

a. Arrange the payoff table.

b. Find the best strategy for both players.

c. If you had to play the game, would you rather be A or B? Why?

18. Check the following payoff table for dominance:

	b_1	b_2	b_3	b_4	b_5
a_1	−3	4	3	2	0
a_2	2	1	4	6	3
a_3	2	1	3	5	1
a_4	1	6	−4	3	1
a_5	2	1	3	4	1

Show the reduced matrix.

19. Given three game tables:

TABLE 1

	b_1	b_2
a_1	3	−2
a_2	−3	0

TABLE 2

	b_1	b_2
a_1	5	0
a_2	−1	2

TABLE 3

	b_1	b_2
a_1	6	−4
a_2	−6	0

Solve the games. What can you conclude about the relationship among the three games in this case?

20. Two French companies plan a TV advertising campaign for a competitive product. TV ads run during four basic periods: morning *(M)*, afternoon *(A)*, evening *(E)*, and night *(N)*. Advertising time is available in units; company A can afford one unit only, and company B can afford two units. Thus, company A has four choices, advertise in *M*, *A*, *E*, or *N*, while company B has 10 alternatives as shown below:

		B									
		M(2)	*A*(2)	*E*(2)	*N*(2)	*M*(1) *A*(1)	*M*(1) *E*(1)	*M*(1) *N*(1)	*A*(1) *E*(1)	*A*(1) *N*(1)	*E*(1) *N*(1)
	M	.30	.25	.20	.30	.25	.20	.30	.20	.25	.25
A	*A*	.35	.25	.20	.40	.30	.25	.30	.20	.25	.30
	E	.40	.30	.25	.50	.30	.35	.35	.25	.30	.35
	N	.25	.20	.10	.25	.20	.15	.20	.15	.20	.20

The payoff table shows the conditional share of the market captured by company A. For example, if A uses one unit in the morning and B uses two units in the morning, then A gets 30 percent of the market and B gets the remaining 70 percent.

It is assumed that the objective of each company is to maximize its share of the market and that the cost of advertising is the same per unit.

View this situation as a zero-sum game.

a. What action should each company take?

b. How will the market then be divided?

21. Two companies compete in a market and consider promotional campaigns. If both advertise simultaneously, the market share will remain unchanged and both will lose the expenses of the campaign that are estimated by company A to equal 9 units of utility and by B to equal 11 units. If neither advertises, there will be no change in the market (i.e., no change in utility). If A advertises and B does not, A will gain 6 units, B will lose 14 units. If B advertises and A does not, B will gain 8 units and A will lose 14 units. What strategy should the two companies follow?

a. Present the problem in game form. Write two payoff tables: one for company A and one for company B.

b. Solve by minimax. Assume that the companies do not communicate with each other. Comment on the results.

c. Assume that the companies communicate and cooperate prior to the decision. What will they do then?

d. What could be the difference between a one-shot decision and a repetitive decision in the noncooperative case (part [*b*])?

22. Any farmer's dilemma is how much to plant each season. Several factors contribute to the dilemma. In the first place, nature is merciless and he (or she) who plants does not know how much he will be able to reap. Second, there are many farmers competing in the market and there is little cooperation between them with regard to the amount planted. Third, the market is also merciless. There is an upper limit to quantities that can be sold, and prices drop very rapidly as quantities increase. If a farmer plants large quantities (which means large expenses), he may suffer a huge loss if prices drop. On the other hand, if he plants small quantities, he may lose the opportunity for making large profits. A farmer's dilemma can be presented as a two-person game if we envision all other farmers as one competitor. Let us assume that nature's influence is negligible and that the farmer's problem is whether to plant on a small scale (100 acres) or on a large scale (250 acres). We assume for simplicity that the other farmers will plant either on a small scale (2,000 acres) or on a large scale (5,000 acres).

There are four possible consequences in this situation:

a. All farmers, including ours, plant on a small scale. In that case, there will be 2,100 acres planted and the profit per acre will be $100.

b. All farmers plant on a large scale. The total planted acreage will be 5,250, and the profit per acre will be $10.

c. Our farmer plants 100 acres; the others plant 5,000 acres. The profit per acre will be $12.

d. Our farmer plants 250 acres, and the rest plant 2,000 acres. The expected profit is $90 per acre.

(1) Present the problem in matrix form (two matrices, one for our farmer and one for the "other" farmers).

(2) Solve using the minimax approach. Assume no communication.

(3) Solve assuming communication and cooperation.

23. Two competing companies consider the advertising alternatives below. The table shows the alternatives and the percent increase in market share for company A. One percent of the share of the market is considered equal to $10,000.

		B				
		B_1	B_2	B_3	B_4	B_5
A	A_1	1	0	−1	−8	−9
	A_2	5	3	5	−7	−3
	A_3	7	−1	1	7	9

Find:

a. The optimal strategy of each company.

b. The average, per period, monetary gain (loss) to company B.

24. Recent suburban development in the city of MidAmerica resulted in the construction of three new shopping centers: Eastland, Westland, and Northland. The location of these centers and the number of shoppers expected in each, per week, is shown below.

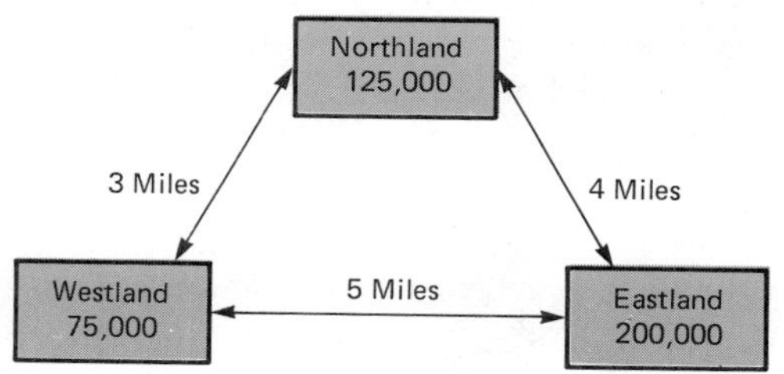

Both Burgerqueen (BQ) and McBurger (MB) are each planning to open a restaurant in the new section of MidAmerica, and both must soon decide on the exact location. The location decision is a top secret at both companies. However, a reputable independent market research company provided both of them with the following data:

a. If BQ is closer to a shopping center than MB, then 80 percent of the business in that center will be captured by BQ.

b. If MB is closer to a shopping center than BQ, then BQ will get 30 percent of the business there, leaving 70 percent for MB.

c. If both BQ and MB open a restaurant at the same distance from a shopping center, then MB will capture 55 percent and BQ will get 45 percent of the market.

(1) Set up the problem as a game.

(2) Find the best strategies for the two companies.

(3) Assume that 10 percent of all shoppers eat at a fast-food restaurant. Find how many shoppers will eat in each establishment during the first week of operation if the optimal locations are selected.

25. Examine Figure 4.4 and graphically find the best strategy and payoff to player B if player A plays:

a. a_2 80 percent of the time.

b. a_2 20 percent of the time.

26. Show a graphical solution for the pure strategy case (the Allies-Japan case) of Table 4.14 and explain the difference between it and mixed strategy.

4.8 CASE

THE VIDEOTAPE STRATEGY

The Soonie Company is a manufacturer of videotapes. Being a leader in its field, the company runs national ads comparing its products to those of Pany, its major competitor. Soonie uses three advertising strategies: a_1—a direct attack on their competitor; a_2—an indirect attack; and a_3—no attack at all.

Pany is a more conservative company. It uses these advertising strategies: b_1—"our products are of the highest quality"; b_2—"our products give you more for your money"; and b_3—"sure, you can buy other products, but. . . ."

Soonie's advertising budget amounts to hundreds of thousands of dollars annually. Basic ad strategy decisions are made monthly. Recent sales results indicate that the company's market share actually fluctuates too much and has periodic sharp declines. In its last meeting, the board of directors asked Soonie's president to study the situation.

Ann White, the newly appointed director of marketing research, was authorized to investigate the problem. Using computerized time series and regression analyses, she attempted to find the relationship between advertising policies and sales levels. After analyzing historical data for the past few years (videotapes are relatively new products), she decided there was no correlation between the two. Then she realized that Soonie's market share also depended on Pany's strategy. However, it was impossible to know exactly what the competition had in mind in the past.

"We should record what level of ads Pany uses," Ann thought to herself. For a moment she felt hopeless. Then she called a meeting of all key sales representatives, asking them to indicate how Soonie's ads pulled in relation to various strategies used by Pany. Ad effectiveness was based on the following four-point scale: 4 = excellent; 3 = good; 2 = fair; and 1 = poor.

Although the sales reps disagreed on several of the possible results, she constructed an average response that looked like this:

If Soonie employs strategy a_1 and Pany employs b_1, the response to Soonie's strategy is *good*. Similarly, for the other possibilities the results were:

If Soonie employs	*If Pany employs*	*The results for Soonie*
a_1	b_2	Excellent
a_1	b_3	Fair
a_2	b_1	Poor
a_2	b_2	Good
a_2	b_3	Fair
a_3	b_1	Fair
a_3	b_2	Good
a_3	b_3	Excellent

A quick review of these results indicated that there was no one superior strategy. Poor to fair results were possible for each of Soonie's alternatives. "I can see now why my computerized programs failed to show any conclusive results. I wish we had a better information system."

At this point, the company's president called Ann and requested "specific recommendations for future ad strategies." For a moment Ann thought that she should tell him that she had found no relationship between strategy and sales level. Then she figured that this was probably not true.

What should Ann do? Consider such factors as the lack of collusion between the competitors, possible cooperation between the competitors, and overall market size.

4.9 GLOSSARY

Additivity assumption (of utilities) The utility of two or more items equals the sum of the utilities of the individual items.

Certainty equivalent (CE) A subjective evaluation of the monetary worth of a gamble to a decision maker.

Conflict A decision situation where the payoff is conditioned on the decisions made by two or more decision makers with conflicting objectives.

Dominance A case where one decision alternative is superior to another alternative under all circumstances.

Expected utility (EU) The long-run average utility per decision.

A fair game A game whose value is zero.

A game A series of repetitive decisions (plays).

Minimax theorem The theorem that is the basis for the solution to the two-person, zero-sum game. The theorem maintains that each player acts to maximize his or her minimum possible gain (or minimize his or her maximum loss.)

Mixed strategy A case where the decision maker should change the alternative courses of action at random, according to a predetermined proportion.

Multiple goals A situation in which the impact of a decision is evaluated for several goals simultaneously.

Nonzero-sum game A game where the winner(s) receives either less or more than what the loser(s) contributed.

***N*-person game** A conflict involving more than two decision makers.

A play One move (one decision) in a game.

Preference theory A measure of attitude toward risk using probabilities of a gamble.

Pure strategy A case where the best strategy is to repeatedly stick to one decision alternative no matter what the opposition does.

Risk premium The attitude toward risk, as measured by the difference between EMV and CE.

Risk profile A list of the payoffs and probabilities for each alternative.

Strategy A complete, predetermined plan for selecting the appropriate course of action for every possible circumstance.

Two-person game A conflict with two parties.

Utile A unit of measurement of utility.

Utility The subjective value of the outcome to the decision maker.

Utility curve The relationship between the quantity of money and its benefit to the decision maker.

Value of the game The average payoff per play.

Zero-sum game A game where the winner(s) receives, and the loser(s) contributes, the entire amount at stake.

4.10 REFERENCES AND BIBLIOGRAPHY

1. *A Bibliography of Selected RAND Publications: Game Theory.* Santa Monica, Calif: The RAND Corp., Sb-1039, October 1971.
2. Bacharach, M. *Economics and the Theory of Games.* Boulder, Colo: Westview Press, 1977.
3. Bell, R. I. *Having It Your Way: The Strategy of Settling Everyday Conflicts.* New York: W. W. Norton, 1977.
4. Bowen, K. C. *Research Games: An Approach to the Study of Decision Process.* New York: Halsted Press, 1978.
5. Buchler, I. R., and H. G. Nutini. *Game Theory in the Behavioral Sciences.* Pittsburgh: University of Pittsburgh Press, 1969.
6. Davis, M. D. *Game Theory: A Nontechnical Introduction.* New York: Basic Books, 1970.
7. Fishburn, P. C. *Utility Theory for Decision Making.* New York: John Wiley & Sons, 1970.
8. Harsanyi, J. C. *Rational Behavior and Bargaining Equilibrium in Games and Social Situations.* New York: Cambridge University Press, 1977.
9. Hertz, D. D. *Risk Analysis and Its Applications.* New York: John Wiley & Sons, 1982.
10. Keeney, R., and H. Raiffa. *Decisions with Multi-*

ple Objectives, Preferences, and Value Trade-offs. New York: John Wiley & Sons, 1976.

11. Linstone, H. A., and M. Turoff, eds. *The Delphi Method*. Reading, Mass.: Addison-Wesley Publishing, 1975.
12. Luce, R. D., and H. Raiffa. *Games and Decisions*. New York: John Wiley & Sons, 1957.
13. Schrage, L. *Linear Programming Model with LINDO*. Palo Alto, Calif.: The Scientific Press, 1981.
14. Shakun, M. G., ed. "Game Theory and Gaming," a special issue of *Management Science* 18, no. 5 (January 1972).
15. Shubik, M. *The Uses and Methods of Game Theory*. New York: Elsevier North-Holland Publishing, 1975.
16. Steuer, R. E. *Multiple Criteria Optimization: Theory, Computation, and Applications*. New York: John Wiley & Sons, 1986.
17. Von Neumann, J., and O. Morgenstern. *Theory of Games and Economic Behavior*. 3rd ed. Princeton, N.J.: Princeton University Press, 1953.
18. Williams, J. D. *The Complete Strategyst*. Rev. ed. New York: McGraw-Hill, 1966.
19. Yu, P. L. *Multiple Criteria Decision Making: Concepts, Techniques, and Extensions*. New York: Plenum Press, 1985.

5

PART A: BASICS

5.1 The forecasting situation.
5.2 Judgmental forecasting methods.
5.3 Counting methods.
5.4 Moving averages and exponential smoothing.
5.5 Forecasting errors.
5.6 Other time-series methods.
5.7 Causal methods.
5.8 Problems for Part A.

PART B: EXTENSIONS

5.9 Decomposition.
5.10 Computerization.
5.11 Concluding remarks.
5.12 Problems for Part B.
5.13 Case—Bardstown Box Company.
5.14 Glossary.
5.15 References and bibliography.

Managers, in their decision-making activities, must be able to anticipate the future under various scenarios. They need to be able to predict the demand for their products and services, the probable development of new technology for their operations, cost trends, changes in lead time, the reactions to decisions they are contemplating, and so on. These all involve forecasting, the topic of this chapter. In some situations, data are lacking and a "qualitative" forecast must be made. In other situations, data may be plentiful and a quantitative, or statistical, forecast is possible.

In this chapter we will consider both qualitative and quantitative forecasts and describe various approaches or models under each category. In Part A we will focus on the qualitative approaches first and then consider some of the statistical models. Part B then develops some of the more complex approaches, finishing up with a presentation of the software packages available for forecasting.

Forecasting

LEARNING OBJECTIVES

The student should be able to:

a. List the types of the major forecasting approaches and their characteristics.
b. Describe the need for forecasting and the role it plays in decision making.
c. Describe the nature of qualitative, time series, and causal forecasts, and when each type should be used.
d. Describe the major qualitative forecasting methods.
e. Solve problems using exponential smoothing and moving averages.
f. Distinguish between the accuracy of different forecasting methods and compute it through the use of bias and MAD values.
g. Describe the causal forecasting methodology.

Extensions

h. Describe the decomposition process of time-series analysis.
i. Employ time-series analysis for decomposing data and for forecasting.
j. Describe a linear trend model and perform a linear regression analysis.
k. Define correlation.
l. Describe the concept of leading and lagging indicators.
m. Describe the concept of "seasonal index."
n. Compute seasonal indices.

PART A: BASICS

Bill Jacobs, administrator for the Lakeland City Health Center, was feeling frustrated in his attempts to predict next quarter's demand for service at his center, expressed in terms of *patient visits*. Lakeland City Health Center is a federally funded health clinic that serves the needs of the citizens of Lakeland, Florida. The federal government requires that the center prepare a budget request each quarter for the coming quarter. The request is based largely on the forecast of demand for specific services during the next quarter. The center is currently in its fourth year of operation and is presently preparing its staffing plan for the upcoming quarter.

Demand data are available for each of the four quarters of the preceding three years and for the first two quarters of the current year. Bill has, in the past, tried using the last quarter's demand to predict the next quarter's demand for the center. He has also tried using the average of all past demand. Neither of these two approaches has proved satisfactory. The use of the last quarter's demand as a predictor of the next quarter's demand produced erratic forecasts. For example, using this method, he predicted (and staffed, scheduled, and purchased for) a demand of 3,500 visits for the second quarter of 1984, when about 8,000 visits actually resulted. (Overtime and rush orders reached a peak during this quarter.) Then he predicted 8,000 visits for the third quarter when only 5,500 visits materialized. Clearly this method could not sort out the fluctuations in the demand data and were therefore deemed unsatisfactory.

Bill had then turned to using the average of all demand data to predict the next quarter's demand. For the fourth quarter of 1984 he had predicted a demand of 5,667, when about 10,000 actually occurred. Bill recognized that this averaging method produced forecasts that smoothed out the fluctuations, but did not adequately respond to any growth or reduction in the demand trend. As a matter of fact, the averaging method performed progressively worse as the amount of data increased. At this point, Bill had decided that he needed a more sophisticated tool for prediction.

We will return to Bill's situation and some other models he might consider a bit later in this chapter.

5.1 THE FORECASTING SITUATION*

The management science process is centered around decision making. As the reader may recall, such a process involves choosing an alternative course of action by evaluating the possible consequences of the choice. Although the choice is made today, the *forecast* consequences occur some-

* Portions of this chapter are adapted from Jack R. Meredith, *The Management of Operations*, 3rd ed. (New York: John Wiley & Sons, 1987), pp. 74–105. Copyright © 1987 John Wiley & Sons, Inc. Reprinted by permission.

time in the future (perhaps a year or more). Therefore, the quality of the decision depends in large part on the quality of the forecast.

Our opening case dealt with a forecast of *demand*. As the reader may imagine, demand data are used in several management science models such as inventory, decision tables and trees, queuing (the arrival rate), transportation, and linear programming. Bill's problem is that the historical data fluctuate in what seems to be (at least at first sight), an irregular fashion. Furthermore, Bill is not sure how to relate the future to the past.

The uses of forecasts

The major use of forecasting, as it relates to management science, is to predict the value of the model input data, as well as the logical relationship of the model, at some time in the future. The future time of interest depends on "when" we want to evaluate our options. For example, in a regular investment decision we may be interested in prices a year from today, while in a capital investment decision we may be interested in projected prices during the next five years. Generally speaking, we distinguish between two types of forecasts: *(a)* short run (up to one year), where the forecast is used mainly in deterministic models and *(b)* long run (beyond one year), where the forecast is used in both deterministic and probabilistic models.

Forecasting models and methods

There exist many types of forecasting models because forecasting is an extremely difficult task. What is going to happen in the future depends, in many cases, on a multiplicity of factors, most of which are uncontrollable. Furthermore, data availability, accuracy, cost, and the time required to make the forecast also play an important role.

Forecasting methods can be grouped in several ways. One classification scheme distinguishes between formally recognized forecasting techniques (formal) and informal approaches such as intuition, spur-of-the-moment guesses, and seat-of-the-pants predictions. Our attention in this chapter will be directed to the formal methods.

Formal methods can be divided into four categories: *judgment methods*, *counting methods*, *time-series methods*, and *association* or *causal methods*. Figure 5.1 lists these various categories. Those methods described in this chapter include the appropriate section number. Each of the categories are briefly discussed below.

Judgment methods Judgment methods are those based on subjective estimates and expert opinion, rather than on hard data. They are often used for long-range forecasts, especially where external factors (e.g., technological or political developments such as the 1973 OPEC oil crisis) may

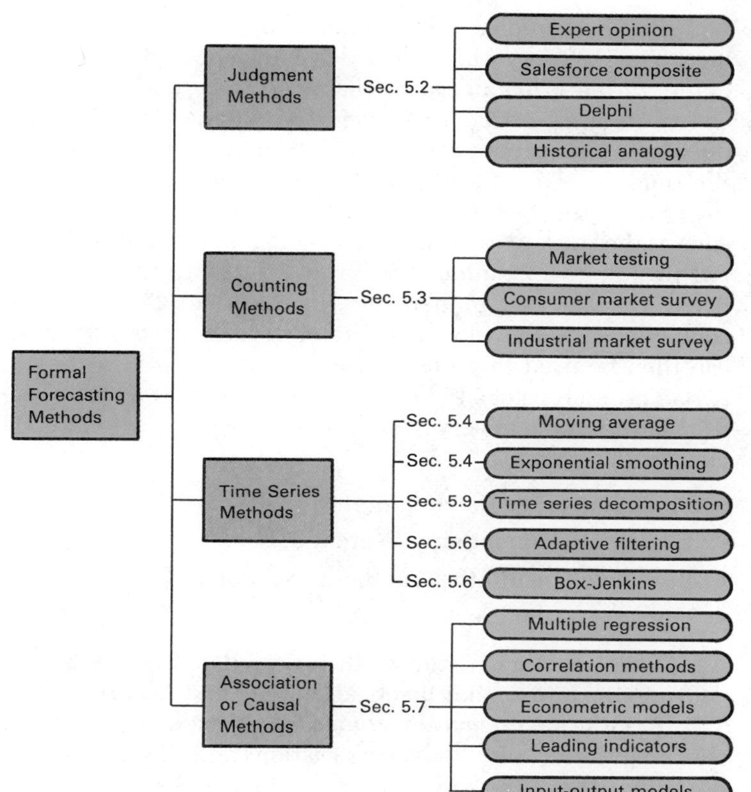

FIGURE 5.1 Classification of forecasting methods*

play a significant role. They also are used where historical data are very *limited* or *nonexistent,* such as in new product/service introductions.

Counting methods Counting methods involve some kind of experimentation or surveys of a sample with an attempt to generalize about the entire market. These methods are primarily used for forecasting demand for products/services, a part of marketing research.

The next two types of forecasting methods are quantitative in nature. They are based on hard data and are thus generally considered more objective than the previous types. They typically use historical data and are commonly divided between time-series and causal methods.

Time-series analysis A **time series** is a set of values of some business or economic variable, measured at successive (usually equal) intervals of time. For example, quarterly sales of a firm make up a time series, as does the yearly growth of people in a city, the weekly demand for hospital beds, and so on.

If, for example, we recorded the number of automobiles sold each month of 1988 by the Schroeder Oldsmobile Co. and kept those data points *in the order in which they were recorded,* the 12 numbers would constitute a *12-period time series.* We undertake *time-series analysis* in decision making because we believe that knowledge of *past behavior* of the time series might help our understanding of (and therefore our ability to predict) the behavior of the series in the future. In some instances, such as the stock market, this assumption may be unjustified, but in managerial planning we assume that (to some extent, at least) history will repeat itself and that past tendencies will continue. Time-series analysis efforts conclude with the development of a *time-series forecasting model* that can then be used to predict future events.

The analysis of a time series can be done by a host of methods ranging from fairly simple to very complicated. The following methods are described later in this chapter:

- Moving average (Section 5.4).
- Exponential smoothing (Section 5.4).
- Box-Jenkins and other methods (Section 5.7).
- Decomposition (Section 5.9).

These methods analyze historical data and essentially project this data into the future; they do not attempt to find any cause-effect relationship.

Association or causal methods Association or **causal** methods include data analysis for finding data associations and, if possible, cause-effect relationships. They are more powerful than the time-series methods, but they are also more complex. Their complexity comes from two sources. First, they include more variables, some of which are external to the situation. Second, they employ sophisticated statistical techniques for segregating the various types of variables. Causal approaches are most appropriate for midterm (between short and long-term) forecasting. These methods, described in Section 5.7, usually require a computer for their execution.

Generally speaking, judgment and counting methods, which are subjective in nature, are used in those cases where quantitative methods are inappropriate or cannot be used. Time pressure, lack of data, or lack of money may prevent the use of a quantitative model. Complexity of historical data (due to interactions or fluctuations, for example) may also inhibit the use of hard data.

Factors influencing the choice of forecasting method

The method chosen to prepare a forecast depends on a number of factors.

The historical data available If historical data are available, a quantitative forecasting method can be used. Attempting to forecast without a history is almost as useful as using a crystal ball. The history need not be long, complete, or even for exactly the same item as is being forecast. But some historical database should be located if at all possible. If data are not available, an experiment can sometimes be conducted to generate the needed information.

The money and time available The greater the limitations on time or money available for forecasting, the more likely it is that an unsophisticated method will have to be used. In general, management desires to use that forecasting method that minimizes the total cost of making the forecast and the cost of an *inaccurate* forecast. Costs of forecasting inaccuracy include the cost of making a wrong decision: for example, the costs of over- or understocking or producing an item; the costs of under- or overstaffing, and the intangible and opportunity costs associated with loss of customer/client goodwill because an item was not available. This trade-off situation is depicted in Figure 5.2. The best forecasting method is the one for which the combined costs are minimized but, since some of these costs are difficult if not impossible to measure, a "best" method is difficult to determine.

With the advent of computers and preprogrammed forecasting routines, the cost and time of statistical forecasts based on historical data has been reduced significantly. It therefore has become more cost effective for organizations to conduct more sophisticated forecasts, and the optimum forecasting method has thus shifted to the right in Figure 5.2.

The accuracy required If, for whatever reasons, the forecast must be very accurate, highly sophisticated and expensive methods are called for. Typically, very long-range (3–10 years) forecasts require the least accuracy, while very short-range (one week to a few months) forecasts require great accuracy, since detailed plans and actions are based on these short-range projections.

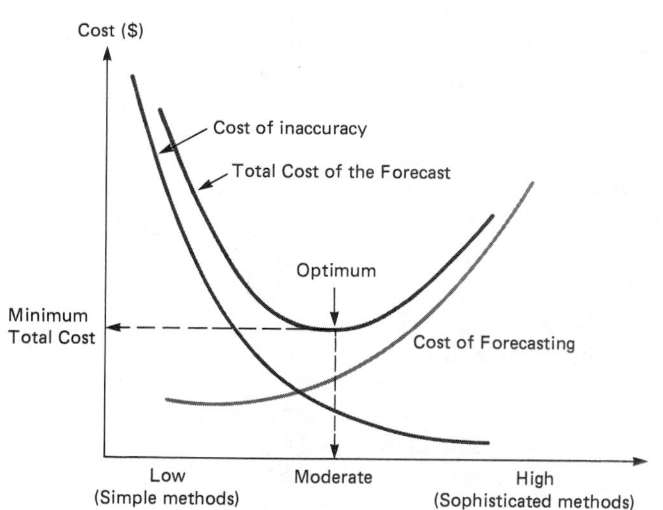

FIGURE 5.2
The costs of forecasting accuracy

5.2 JUDGMENTAL FORECASTING METHODS

Some of the most significant decisions made by organizations, for example, new product decisions, are made on the basis of judgment. Judgment forecasts are made using information such as expert opinion, or analyses of demand information for similar products or services that have been previously introduced and for which historical data are available. An example of the latter method, known as *historical analogy,* was the use of demand data for black-and-white television sets to predict the slope of the demand curve for color TV sets. Two judgmental forecasting methods are particularly common; these are expert opinion and Delphi.

Forecasting by historical analogy

Expert opinion

Using expert judgment

Consider, for example, a company that has introduced, over the years, several dozen different consumer goods. It is conceivable that the experience of key managers, particularly those associated with the marketing of the products, could provide better forecasts of costs, prices, or the demand for another new product than any surveys of the potential market. In fact, this is often the case, and methods have been developed to probe this expert knowledge. As "two heads are better than one," most expert judgment methods rely on the formation of a panel of experts who reach a consensus or compromise forecast based on their individual experiences and judgment.

The problems with committees

But panel or committee solutions to the forecasting problem are sometimes biased in favor of the opinion of one dominant member. Either that member is a better salesperson of his or her own ideas, is more "expert" than fellow committee members (perhaps others on the panel simply believe this, whether it is fact or not), or is simply more verbal than others on the panel. This bias may result in forecasts that are not good or as well thought out as predictions based on *all* of the information available from the committee members. There exist several methods to improve the work of committees, one of which is the Delphi method.

Delphi

Using Delphi to improve expert forecasts

One method for combining individual experts' forecast opinions is called **Delphi.** The Delphi method was developed by the RAND Corporation as a technique for group forecasting that would eliminate the undesirable effects of interaction between members of the group. The experts need not meet face-to-face, nor need they know who the other experts are. The method generally begins by having each expert provide individual written forecasts, along with any supporting arguments and assumptions. These forecasts are submitted to the Delphi coordinator, who edits, clarifies, and summarizes the data. These data are provided as feedback to the experts along with a *second round* of questions. Questions and feedback continue in writing for several rounds, becoming increasingly more specific,

Rounds of questions are employed

until consensus among the panel members is either reached or until the experts do not change their forecasts any more.

The Delphi method allows the benefits of multiple opinions and communication between group members of diverse opinions and assumptions, but avoids the negative effects of dominant behavior and stubbornness to change one's mind that are often associated with committee solutions. For more details, see Linstone [8].

5.3 COUNTING METHODS

Counting methods of forecasting employ experiments and surveys, usually based on representative samples of the entire population. The purpose is to generalize from the sample to the entire population. Of special interest are market surveys and market testing.

The market survey and market testing

New products and services are often subjected to extensive *market research* before a final decision is made regarding the introduction of this new output. Such devices as the telephone survey, the mail questionnaire, consumer panels, and test markets are used to ascertain estimates of value, perceived quality, and demand. For example, both the Nielson TV ratings, and the Gallup public opinion poll are based on sample surveys of public attitudes and behavior.

Test marketing can also provide data over a long period of time to track changes in shopping and/or buying trends (called *longitudinal research*). A test market is usually some specific geographical region that is selected because it represents some segment of the organization's overall market for the new output. The test market requires that the product or service actually be introduced into the limited test area. Test marketing provides management with information about actual consumer behavior rather than simply consumer attitudes, opinions, or intentions, since there are often great differences between a consumer's attitudes and his or her actions.

As with consumer market surveys, it is also possible to conduct *industrial* market surveys. Here the subjects are vendors, purchasing agents, and other individuals who are more knowledgeable than consumers.

5.4 MOVING AVERAGES AND EXPONENTIAL SMOOTHING

The two simplest time-series analysis methods are **moving averages** and **exponential smoothing.** These methods can be used to make forecasts directly, or can be incorporated in the decomposition process (see Section 5.9).

Table 5.1 presents Bill Jacobs's historical data for the Lakeland City Health Center. For illustration, the data are also plotted in Figure 5.3.

TABLE 5.1
Patient demand for the Lakeland City Health Center

Year	*Quarter*	*Period number*	*Number of patient visits*
1984	1	1	3,500
	2	2	8,000
	3	3	5,500
	4	4	10,000
1985	1	5	4,500
	2	6	6,000
	3	7	3,000
	4	8	5,500
1986	1	9	5,000
	2	10	9,500
	3	11	7,500
	4	12	15,000
1987	1	13	13,500
	2	14	17,500

As you remember, Bill had decided he needed a more sophisticated forecasting methodology than just using last period's demand or the average of all the previous periods.

Moving averages

Using only the last few periods to average

To overcome the deficiency of using a simple average, the moving average technique generates the next period's forecast by averaging the actual demand for only the last *n* (*n* is often in the range of 4 to 7) time

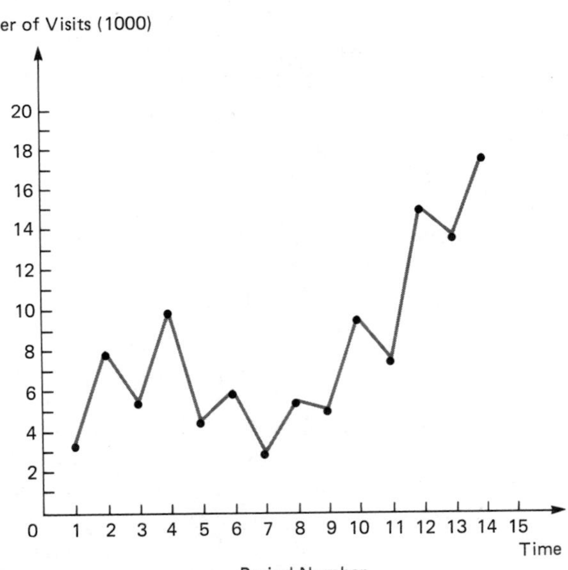

FIGURE 5.3
Plot of Lakeland's quarterly demand

periods, rather than for all the periods such as in a simple average. Any data older than n are thus ignored. The choice of the value for n is usually based on the expected seasonality in the data, such as four quarters, or 12 months, in a year. Such a choice will effectively neutralize the impact of any seasonality in the data. If n must be chosen arbitrarily, then it should be based on the value that best describes the historical data when used in the model.

Mathematically, the moving average is computed as:

$$F_{t+1} = \frac{1}{n} \sum_{i=(t-n+1)}^{t} D_i \tag{5.1}$$

where:

t = Period number for the *current* period
F_{t+1} = Forecast of demand for the *next* period
D_i = Actual demand in period i
n = Number of periods of demand to be included (known as the "order" of the moving average)

For example, to forecast demand for the next quarter of this year (i.e., quarter 3 of 1987 or period 15 in Table 5.1) using a moving average of order four (that is, $n = 4$), Bill would compute:

$$F_{14+1} = \frac{1}{4} \sum_{i=14-4+1}^{14} D_i$$

or:

$$F_{15} = \frac{1}{4} \sum_{i=11}^{14} D_i$$

$$F_{15} = (D_{11} + D_{12} + D_{13} + D_{14})/4$$

$$F_{15} = (7{,}500 + 15{,}000 + 13{,}500 + 17{,}500)/4$$

$$F_{15} = 13{,}375$$

The forecast for the next quarter, using a moving average forecast of order four, would therefore be 13,375 visits.

The moving average as a compromise

The moving average is a *compromise* between the last period's demand and the simple average, both of which the administrator has rejected as being unsatisfactory. The number of periods to be averaged in the moving average is dependent on the specific situation. If too few periods are included in the average, the forecast will be similar to the forecast obtained when only the last period's demand had been used as the forecast. Using too many periods in the moving average will result in a forecast similar to the forecast obtained when the simple average was used.

Exponential smoothing

Achieving the two objectives by exponential smoothing

As noted above, we generally want to use the most current data, and at the same time, use enough historical observations to smooth out random fluctuations. One technique perfectly adapted to meeting these two objectives is exponential smoothing.

The computation of a forecast using exponential smoothing is carried out with the following equation. If we consider demand data, for example,

$$\text{New demand forecast} = (\alpha)\text{ current demand} + (1-\alpha)\text{ previous demand forecast}$$

or:

$$F_{t+1} = \alpha D_t + (1-\alpha)F_t \tag{5.2}$$

where α is a **smoothing constant** that must be greater than or equal to zero but less than or equal to 1. The other symbols are illustrated in the diagram below.

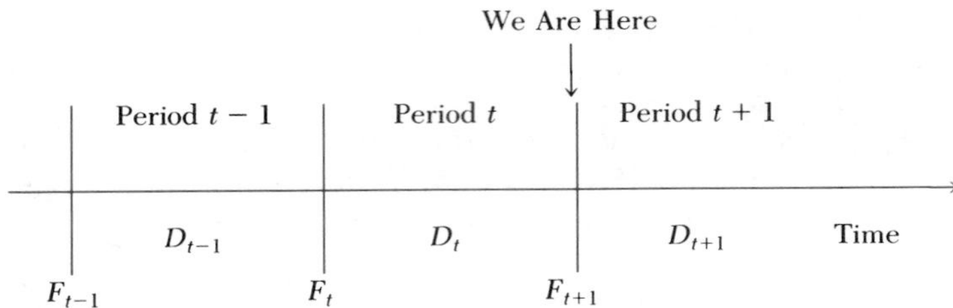

Note that Equation 5.2 is iterative in nature. That is, the previous solution (for F_t) is used to obtain the next solution (for F_{t+1}). If we substitute into Equation 5.2 the equation for F_t, and keep substituting back in the same fashion, we can obtain the equation that led to the name *exponential smoothing*. This is shown in Equation 5.3.

$$F_{t+1} = \alpha D_t + \alpha(1-\alpha)D_{t-1} + \alpha(1-\alpha)^2 D_{t-2} + \alpha(1-\alpha)^3 D_{t-3} + \cdots + \alpha(1-\alpha)^{t-1}D_1 \tag{5.3}$$

If we consider a value of α of 0.1, Equation 5.3 becomes:

$$F_{t+1} = .1D_t + .09D_{t-1} + .081D_{t-2} + .073D_{t-3} + \cdots$$

and for a value of 0.5 it becomes:

$$F_{t+1} = .5D_t + .25D_{t-1} + .125D_{t-2} + .063D_{t-3} + \cdots$$

Thus, the exponentially decreasing contributions of earlier demands to the latest forecast can be clearly seen.

The smoothing constant as a weighting factor

The smoothing constant α can be interpreted as the *weight* assigned to the last (i.e., the current) data point. The higher the weight assigned to this current demand, the greater the influence this point has on the

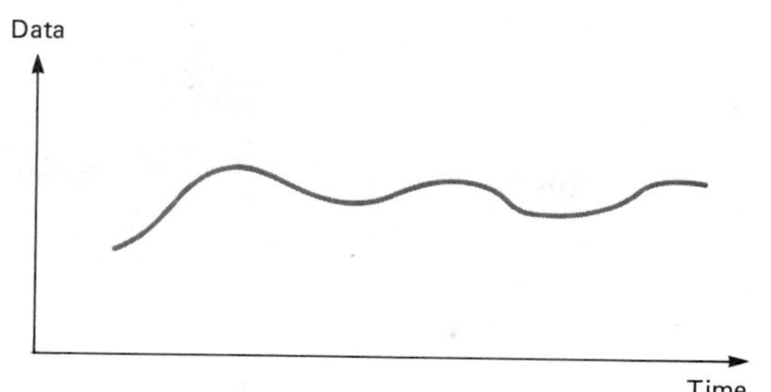

FIGURE 5.4
Data exhibiting low variability (use high α)

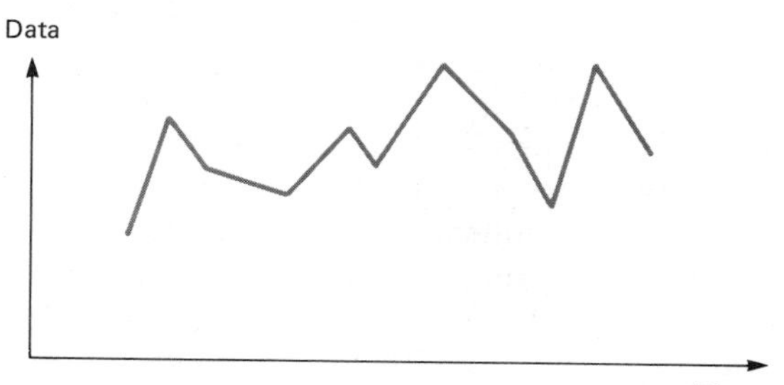

FIGURE 5.5
Data exhibiting high variability (use low α)

forecast. For example if α is equal to 1, the demand forecast for the next period will be equal to the value of the current demand, the approach Bill used earlier.

Our objective in exponential forecasting (also called *smoothing*) is to choose the value of α that results in the best forecasts. With a large α, exponential smoothing will produce forecasts that react quickly to fluctuations. Generally speaking, larger values of α are used in situations in which the data can be plotted as a rather smooth curve, such as Figure 5.4. If, on the other hand, the data look more like Figure 5.5, a lower value of α should be used. A small value of α weights historical data more heavily than current data and therefore will produce forecasts that do not react as quickly to possibly random changes in the data. The appropriate value of α is, like n, usually determined through a trial-and-error process; values typically lie in the range of 0.01 to 0.30.

5.5 FORECASTING ERRORS

There are very few instances of perfect forecasting. Most forecasts tend to be somewhat, or significantly, incorrect. It is important to assess the quality of a forecast by comparing later actual results to the forecast. This comparison then tells us about the magnitude of the forecast errors and the quality of the forecasting method.

The two most common methods of measuring forecast error are the mean absolute deviation (**MAD**) and the **bias.**

$$\text{MAD} = \frac{1}{n} \sum_{i=1}^{n} |F_i - D_i| \tag{5.4}$$

$$\text{Bias} = \frac{1}{n} \sum_{i=1}^{n} (F_i - D_i) \tag{5.5}$$

where:

F_i = Forecast of demand in period i
D_i = Actual demand in period i
n = Number of periods of data analyzed

Very different effects

Though very similar in appearance, these two methods measure different forecasting effects. Since the MAD only sums absolute values of errors, both positive and negative errors add to the sum and the average size of the error is determined. This gives the manager a sense of the *accuracy* of the forecasting model. A manager might use this knowledge by saying: "Our forecasts are typically only accurate within 10 percent; we should prepare for being either 10 percent *above* or *below* the forecast."

The bias, on the other hand, tells whether the forecast is typically too low or too high, and by how much. A manager knowing this might say: "We are almost always forecasting 10 percent too low; we had better make an extra 10 percent to hedge against this potential error." That is, MAD tells the average size of the error and bias tells the direction. As mentioned earlier, the best forecast methods will exhibit the least error measurements.

Example Suppose that two methods of forecasting are tested against data for a four-month period. Method A gave forecasts for January through April of 102, 107, 106, and 113, respectively; Method B gave 104, 105, 107, 110; and the actual results were 103, 106, 106, and 111. The MAD for Method A would be $(|102 - 103| + |107 - 106| + |106 - 106| + |113 - 111|)/4 = 1$; and the bias would be $[(102 - 103) + \ldots]/4 = 0.5$. For Method B the MAD is also 1, but the bias is 0 (check the data). Thus, Method B is the better of the two.

It may well happen that one forecasting method has a smaller MAD but a larger bias, or vice versa. In such cases, the circumstances of the situation must be considered to determine whether MAD or bias is the most important measure.

A tracking signal

The MAD is sometimes used as a **tracking signal** in certain **adaptive forecasting** models (see reference [15]). Briefly, adaptive forecasting models *self-adjust* by increasing or decreasing the smoothing constant α in the exponential smoothing method when the tracking signal becomes too large.

Let us now use exponential smoothing to forecast demand for the Lakeland City Health Center example. We will use two different smoothing factors and calculate the MAD and bias in the forecasts to determine the

TABLE 5.2
Actual and exponentially forecast values of quarterly demand for the Lakeland Health Center (data in thousands)

Year	*Quarter*	*Actual* *D*	*Forecast* ($\alpha = 0.1$) *F*	*Forecast* ($\alpha = 0.3$) *F*
1984	1	3.5		
	2	8.0	3.50	3.50
	3	5.5	3.95	4.85
	4	10.0	4.11	5.05
1985	1	4.5	4.69	6.53
	2	6.0	4.68	5.92
	3	3.0	4.81	5.95
	4	5.5	4.63	5.06
1986	1	5.0	4.71	5.19
	2	9.5	4.74	5.14
	3	7.5	5.22	6.44
	4	15.0	5.45	6.76
1987	1	13.5	6.40	9.23
	2	17.5	7.11	10.51
	3	?	8.15	12.61

best one. Table 5.2 presents the actual historical data for patient visits to the Lakeland City Health Center and the exponentially smoothed forecasts for the corresponding periods using α values of 0.1 and 0.3. Since there was no data on which to base a forecast for period one F_1 (the forecast that would have been made in period zero), some value must be selected. We let F_1 be equal to D_1, the actual value of the series in period one. Then F_2 is computed (using $\alpha = 0.1$).

$$\begin{aligned} F_2 &= \alpha D_1 + (1 - \alpha)F_1 \\ F_2 &= 0.1 \times 3.5 + (1 - 0.1) \times 3.5 \\ &= 0.35 + 0.9(3.5) \\ &= 3.5 \end{aligned}$$

In the same manner, we compute F_3 as:

$$\begin{aligned} F_3 &= 0.1(8) + 0.9(3.5) \\ &= 3.95 \end{aligned}$$

The computations for the exponentially smoothed forecasts continue for each period using the previous forecast and the value of the current observation. The current data is weighted by α and the historical data (all of which is embodied in the previous period's forecast) by $(1 - \alpha)$. As can be seen from Table 5.2, F_{15}, the forecasts for the next quarter, using each of the two α values, are 8,150 and 12,610 emergency services, a considerable difference.

Table 5.3 presents the quarterly data needed for the computation of the final MAD and bias for the two forecasts.

Comparing values of α

As indicated by the MAD calculations, the error is quite high with either value of α, though 0.3 seems the better of the two. This is because

TABLE 5.3 Calculation of the forecast errors

Year	Quarter	*Algebraic difference (Forecast − Actual)* $\alpha = 0.1$	*Algebraic difference (Forecast − Actual)* $\alpha = 0.3$	*Absolute difference |Forecast − Actual|* $\alpha = 0.1$	*Absolute difference |Forecast − Actual|* $\alpha = 0.3$
1984	1				
	2	− 4.50	− 4.50	4.50	4.50
	3	− 1.55	− 0.65	1.55	0.65
	4	− 5.89	− 4.95	5.89	4.95
1985	1	+ 0.19	+ 2.03	0.19	2.03
	2	− 1.32	− 0.08	1.32	0.08
	3	+ 1.81	+ 2.95	1.81	2.95
	4	− 0.87	− 0.44	0.87	0.44
1986	1	− 0.29	+ 0.19	0.29	0.19
	2	− 4.76	− 4.36	4.76	4.36
	3	− 2.28	− 1.06	2.28	1.06
	4	− 9.55	− 8.24	9.55	8.24
1987	1	− 7.10	− 4.27	7.10	4.27
	2	−10.39	− 6.99	10.39	6.99
	Sum	−46.50	−30.37	50.50	40.71
	Mean	Bias = − 3.57	Bias = − 2.33	MAD = 3.88	MAD = 3.13

the exponential smoothing model is fairly simple and, as such, does not consider seasonal and trend impacts, which *are* considered by time-series decomposition analysis (Section 5.9). The large negative value of the bias indicates that most of the error is due to negative bias in the model, in this case consistently forecasting too low or "lagging" the demand (a characteristic of the simpler exponential forecasting models such as this one). This result is also seen in Figure 5.6, which shows the actual demand data and the forecast values using $\alpha = 0.1$ and $\alpha = 0.3$. Notice, for example, that the downturn after quarter 4 and the upturn after quarter 9 are detected more quickly by the $\alpha = 0.3$ model, as we have indicated should be the case. You may notice that both models lag behind the upward trend after quarter 9. In general, if values of alpha greater than 0.3 seem to give the best results, then exponential forecasting should probably not be used. A smoothing model like the one presented in Equation 5.2 is best used in situations where demand fluctuates around an overall level trend. If the trend is increasing or decreasing, other models are usually more appropriate.

Lagging

Other measures of error

Several other methods are used to measure forecasting errors. Some are variants of MAD and bias. Various computer programs (see Section 5.10) offer some of the following additional methods.

a. The mean percentage deviation: This is just the bias converted to a percentage. Each error $F_i - D_i$ is replaced by $100[(F_i - D_i)/D_i]$.

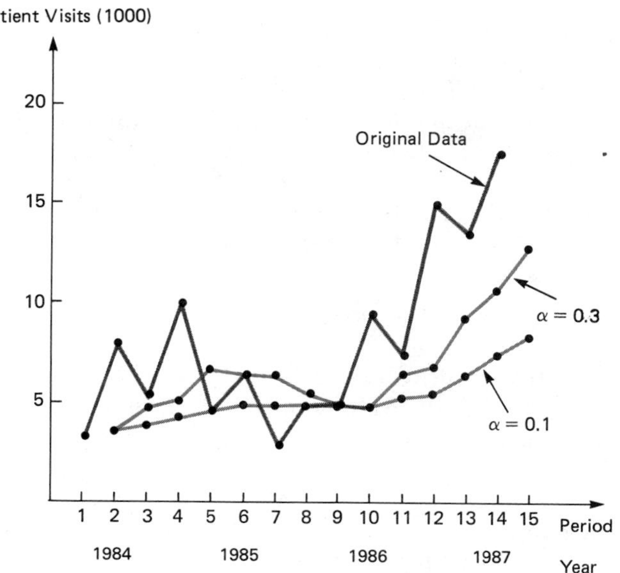

FIGURE 5.6
Plot of actual data and exponential forecasts

Being dimensionless, this measure enables comparisons among different series of forecasts.

b. The mean absolute percentage deviation: This is the MAD converted to a percentage. Each absolute value $|F_i - D_i|$ is replaced by $100\,|F_i - D_i|/D_i$. This measure also enables dimensionless comparisons among forecasts.

c. The mean squared deviation: This measure is computed by averaging the squares of the separate deviations $(F_i - D_i)^2$. Squaring the deviations has the same effect as taking their absolute value, but it also penalizes large errors much more than small ones. This property could be important in practice, where small deviations are much easier to handle than large ones. The resulting measure is in square units.

d. The standard error: This measure is based on the squared deviations also, but takes the mean as $n - 2$ (the 2 comes from the two estimates of the regression line, the slope and the intercept) instead of dividing by n, and then takes the square root of the average to get a measure in the same units as D.

5.6 OTHER TIME–SERIES METHODS

In addition to simple moving averages and exponential smoothing, there exist several other methods. For example, *adaptive filtering* is a type of weighted combination of actual and estimated outcomes, systematically altered to reflect underlying data patterns. *Time-series extrapolation* involves predicting outcomes based on the extension of a least squares (regression) function fitted to a data series with time as an independent variable. A very popular method is *time-series decomposition*, presented later in Section 5.9.

Box-Jenkins is a complex, computer-based, iterative procedure that produces an autoregressive, integrated moving average model, adjusted for trend and seasonal factors (these factors will be described in Part B of this chapter). Box-Jenkins (see references [1] and [4]) estimates appropriate weighting parameters, tests the model, and repeats the cycle as appropriate. To some degree, the Box-Jenkins method can be considered a causal model.

5.7 CAUSAL METHODS

Considering the factors that cause volume

In the previous section we saw that demand could be related to time; that is, the volume changed as time changed. While a relationship existed, we could not say for sure that time *caused* the changes in demand. There are factors other than time that are often related to volume and, in fact, these factors often cause, or at least precede, the volume or demand changes.

Marriages as a predictor of housing demand

For example, increases in single-family housing starts during a given quarter might be highly related to the number of new marriages during the previous quarter. While marriages do not directly *cause* new houses to be purchased, it is logical to argue that marriages (which cause new households to form) are a major precondition to new housing starts. Figure 5.7 illustrates the likely relationship between new marriages (the independent variable) and single-family housing starts. This figure indicates a rather close relationship between the two variables. The variables are thus said to be highly *correlated.* Correlation-based forecasts predict values based on historic patterns of covariation between variables. The relationship between housing starts in one quarter and marriages in a previous quarter is an example of a *logical* association. Many causal models use such "leading indicators" to predict upcoming events.

Predictor variables

The least squares regression method (used in Section 5.9 to determine the linear time-series trend) can also be used to estimate a trend-predicting

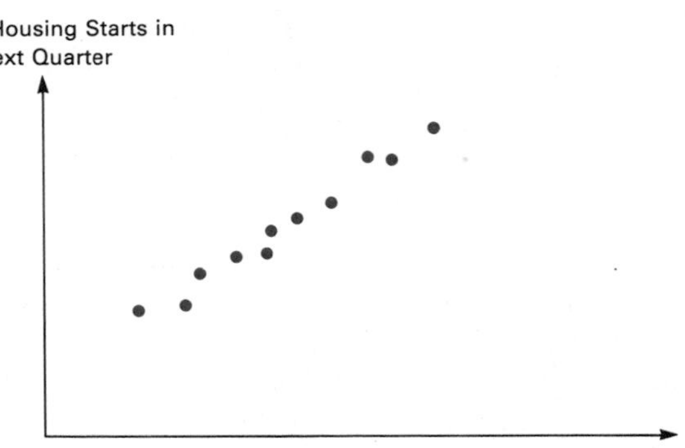

FIGURE 5.7
Plot of marriages versus housing starts showing the close relationship

equation for new housing starts. As opposed to correlation methods, regression models estimate values by a predictive equation derived by minimizing the residual variance of one or more predictor variables. The linear equation:

$$Y'_X = a + bX \qquad (5.5)$$

would be interpreted as:

Y'_X = The predicted number of new housing starts
a = The Y-axis intercept
b = The slope
X = The number of new marriages in the previous quarter

This linear regression methodology can be extended to situations in which more than one explanatory variable is used, called **multiple regression,** to explain the behavior of the dependent variable Y. For example, in addition to the number of marriages, the employment rate in the previous quarter might also explain a great deal of the change in housing starts. The regression equation would be of the form:

Including many causative factors through multiple regression and correlation analysis

$$Y'_{X_1X_2} = a + b_1X_1 + b_2X_2 \qquad (5.6)$$

where:

$Y'_{X_1X_2}$ = The predicted number of housing starts based on new marriages *and* and the employment rate
a = The Y-axis intercept
b_1 and b_2 = The slopes (rates of change in Y') with respect to X_1 and X_2
X_1 and X_2 = The number of marriages and the employment rate, respectively, in the previous quarter

A number of extensions of regression methodology are used in causal forecasting. One is the **econometric model.** In many cases, the dependent and independent variables used in forecasting models are *interdependent.* That is, sales may be a function of personal income and personal income a function of sales. Econometric models take these interrelationships into consideration by formulating, not one regression equation, but a series of simultaneous regression equations that relate the data to all of the interdependent factors, many of which are also predicted by the model.

Econometric models

A different type of causal model is the *input-output* approach. Here, interindustry demands are analyzed to determine the net effect on each industry of all the other industries combined. A forecast of total demands on each and all of the industries is then computed in one overall solution. The model is particularly useful for determining expected *changes* in demands due to changes in other industries. However, the complexity of causal models and the corresponding time and data required for their construction is an impediment to their use.

Input-output models

5.8 PROBLEMS FOR PART A

1. How many periods (n) should be included in a moving average for each of the following sets of data?
   a. Hourly fire alarms.
   b. Daily output from a 40-hour per week manufacturer.
   c. Monthly sales.
   d. Quarterly earnings.
   e. Daily sales from a 24-hour convenience food store.
   f. Weekly bank deposits.
2. Plot the following data and then calculate and plot a moving average of order $n = 3$, order $n = 4$, and order $n = 5$.

Period	1	2	3	4	5	6	7	8	9	10
Data	6	5	5	4	5	3	2	4	3	3

3. Use the data from periods 6 to 10 in Problem 2 to make an exponential forecast for period 11. Try three values of smoothing constants, alpha of 0.05, 0.30, and 0.90. Start with $F_1 = 6$. Compare to the moving average forecasts obtained from the answers to Problem 2.
4. Make an exponential forecast for period 5 with two values of alpha, 0.05 and 0.60, given the data below. Start with $F_1 = 32$. Compare the results.

Period	1	2	3	4
Data	32	14	41	10

5. Calculate the MAD and bias for periods 7 through 10 of the six forecasts in Problems 2 and 3 to determine the best forecast method.
6. Use the data in Problem 4 to calculate the MAD and bias for the two sets of forecasts of periods 2 through 4. How do they compare?
7. To give the flexibility of emphasizing different portions of a time series, a *weighted* moving average is sometimes used, where each data point in the moving average has its own weight (between 0 and 1.0) and all the weights sum to 1.0. For example, a four-period moving average might weight the oldest data point only by 0.1, the next oldest by 0.2, the second most recent by 0.3, and the most recent by 0.4, thus acting much like exponential smoothing. Use these weights to calculate a forecast for the Lakeland City Health Center.
8. Recompute the exponential forecast for the Lakeland City Health Center using an alpha of 0.3, but use the MAD as a tracking signal. Whenever the MAD exceeds 3.0, switch to an alpha of 0.8. When the MAD drops to less than 3.0, return to an alpha of 0.3. Plot the result on Figure 5.6. Is this method of "adaptive smoothing" more accurate than simple exponential smoothing for this data?
9. A conceptually simple method of adaptive smoothing is known as "Chow's Method." With this approach, after the actual demand is known for the forecast period, one recalculates the forecast two times using an alpha 0.05 larger and 0.05 smaller than what was previously used. Using the best result of the three, one then forecasts the next period, using the value that performed best in the last period. Starting with an alpha of 0.3, try this approach on the Lakeland City Health Center data of Table 5.2 and plot the results on Figure 5.6. How does this method compare with the others?
10. Given below is a list of actual data for 15 periods and a computer printout of simple linear regression with forecasts for each period. Calculate the MAD, bias, mean percentage deviation, mean absolute percentage deviation, mean squared deviation, and standard error of the forecast.

PERIOD (X)	ACTUAL (Y)	FORE-CAST (Y)	ERROR	% ERROR
1	0.50	0.90	−0.40	80.42
2	1.50	1.36	0.14	9.56

PERIOD (X)	ACTUAL (Y)	FORE-CAST (Y)	ERROR	% ERROR
3	2.25	1.81	0.44	19.51
4	3.00	2.27	0.73	24.48
5	3.25	2.72	0.53	16.31
6	3.50	3.17	0.33	9.30
7	3.50	3.63	−0.13	3.68
8	3.50	4.08	−0.58	16.67
9	3.75	4.54	−0.79	21.01
10	4.00	4.99	−0.99	24.81
11	4.75	5.45	−0.70	14.67
12	5.50	5.90	−0.40	7.29
13	6.50	6.36	0.14	2.22
14	7.50	6.81	0.69	9.20
15	8.25	7.26	0.99	11.94

	COEFFICIENT
INTERCEPT (A)	.447619
SLOPE (B)	.454464

PART B: EXTENSIONS

5.9 DECOMPOSITION

Time-series decomposition is a procedure that separates a time series of past values into four components: (1) *trend T*, (2) *seasonal variation S*, (3) *cyclical variation C*, and (4) *random (unexplained) variation R*. Then each of the first three components is *extrapolated* into the future to form the basis for a forecast through recombination of the components. A brief description of the four components follows.

The trend (T)

The **trend** component refers to the long-term direction or secular movements in which the graph describing a time series appears to be going over a long interval of time. Figure 5.8 illustrates three fairly common trends.

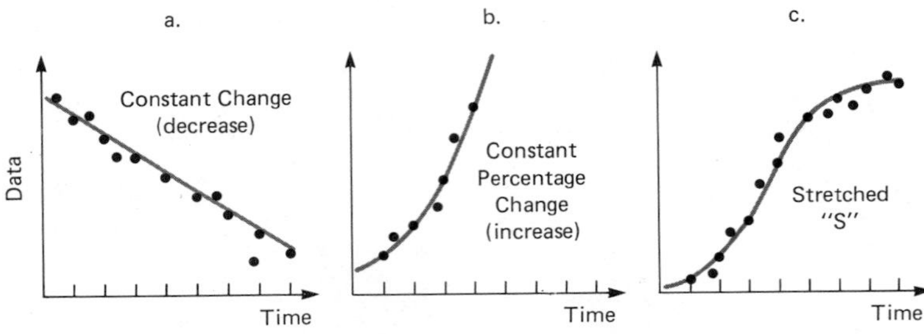

FIGURE 5.8
Three common trends

Straight-line trend

A straight-line or "linear" trend showing a constant amount of *change*, as in Figure 5.8a, could be an accurate fit to the historical data over some *limited range* of time, even though it might provide a rather poor fit over an entire time series. For example, the **life cycle** curve in Figure 5.8c could be approximated by three separate straight trend lines, as shown in Figure 5.9. Over each of these shorter ranges, a straight line provides a good approximation to the actual curve.

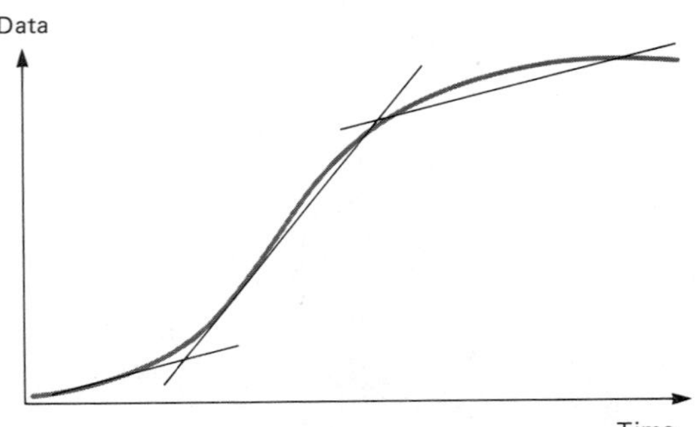

FIGURE 5.9
Straight trend approximation of stretched S growth curve

Figure 5.8b illustrates the situation of a constant *percentage* change. Here, change in the data depends on the current level of the data rather than being constant each period, as in Figure 5.8a. Figure 5.8c indicates a nonlinear trend line known as the **"stretched S"** or life cycle growth curve.

Nonlinear trends

The seasonal (S)

Seasonal fluctuations result primarily from nature, but are also brought about by human behavior. Snow tires and antifreeze enjoy brisk demand during the winter months, while sales of golf balls and bikinis peak in the spring and summer months. Of course, seasonal demand often *leads* or *lags* (i.e., precedes or follows) the actual season. For example, the production season to meet retailer's demand for Christmas goods is August through September. Sales of "heart-shaped" boxes of candy and Christmas trees are brought about by events that are controlled by humans. The *seasonal* variation in events need not be related to the seasons of the year, however. For example, fire alarms in New York City reach a "seasonal" peak at 7 P.M. and a seasonal low at 7 A.M. every day. And restaurants reach three "seasonal" peaks every day at 7.30 A.M., 12:30 P.M., and about 8 P.M. A typical seasonal is shown in Figure 5.10.

The bases for seasonal variation

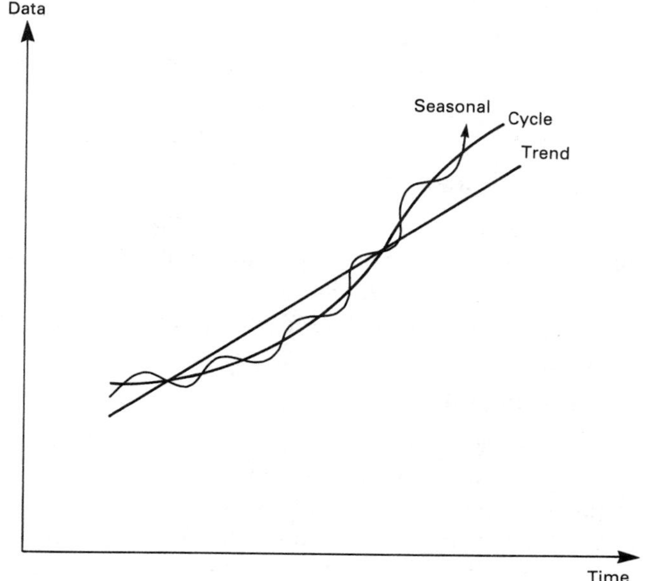

FIGURE 5.10
Seasonal variation superimposed on a trend and cycle

The cycle (C)

The **cycle** component is only obvious in time series that span several years. A cycle can be defined as a *long-term oscillation* or swing of the data points about the trend line over a period of at least three complete

Long-term cycles

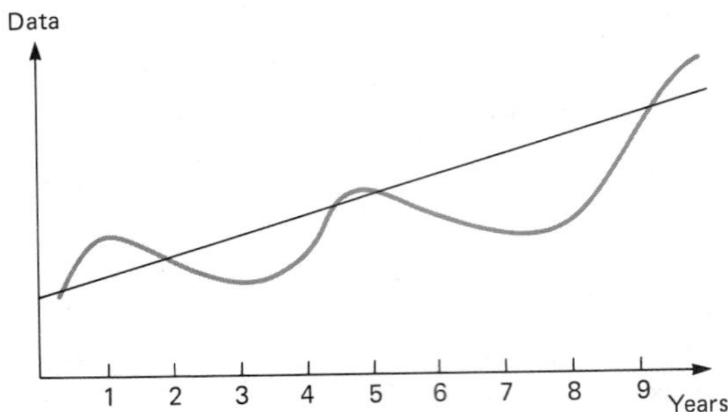

FIGURE 5.11
Typical cycles

sets of seasonals. National economic cycles of boom times and depressions, and periods of war and peace are examples of such cycles. Figure 5.11 presents two complete cycles and the underlying straight-line trend of a time series where no yearly seasonal is assumed to exist. Note that the oscillations around the trend line are *not* symmetrical, as they seldom are in actual time series.

Cycles, particularly business cycles, are often difficult to explain, and economists have spent considerable effort in research and speculation about their causes and frequency. Identification of a cyclic pattern in a time series requires the analysis of a long set of data. For example, only two cycles were completed in nine years for the time series shown in Figure 5.11. For most short-term forecasting the cycle component is not considered because it is difficult to predict the direction of the cycle in the short run. For further details, see reference [13].

Random variation (R)

Random variation is unpredictable

Random variations are, as the name implies, without specific assignable cause and without pattern. Random fluctuations can usually be explained after the fact, such as the increase in energy consumption due to abnormally harsh weather conditions, but cannot be systematically predicted.

The decomposition procedure

There are several approaches to decomposition and several ways that each component can be estimated. The procedure illustrated here is a fairly common one; its major steps are shown in Figure 5.12.

Our approach is based on the multiplication of the components in order to get the forecast; that is, it is assumed that the time series variable Y is a product of the variables T, C, S, and R.

$$Y = T \times C \times S \times R \tag{5.7}$$

Some statisticians prefer to consider Y as the sum of $T + C + S + R$. We will not use this approach.

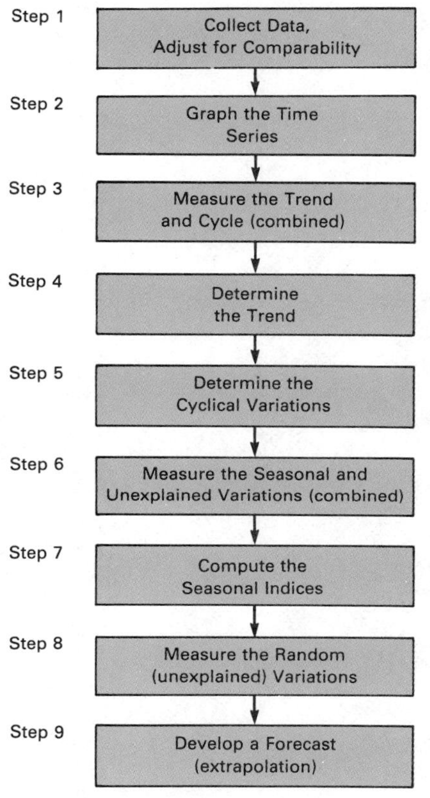

FIGURE 5.12
The decomposition process

The details of the procedure are as follows:

Step 1. Collection and adjustment of data The data must be reliable and in line with the purpose of the analysis. Data must be adjusted for any special situations (e.g., leap years versus regular years).

Step 2. Graphing the time series It is helpful to graph the data of the time series, noting qualitatively the presence of a long-term trend, cyclical variations, seasonal variations, and large random variations.

Example (adapted from Plane [11]):

The Mercantile Stores Company, Inc. (MSC), is a chain of retail department stores. The sales figures of MSC for the period 1980–1987 are shown in Table 5.4. Since the sales are in terms of dollars, the data are adjusted to reflect the changes in the value of the dollar. Alternatively, sales can be shown in terms of units sold whenever possible, assuming that the units do not change much over time. The data are broken down into quarters.

Graph shows trend and seasonals

The data are graphed in Figure 5.13. From this graph it is evident that seasonal variations exist. It is also clear that there is an upward trend. The other variations (cyclical and random) are not visible from the graph.

TABLE 5.4
MSC sales (in 1980 dollars)

Year	*Quarter*	*Sales (\$ millions)*
1980	1	48.6
	2	54.2
	3	59.8
	4	79.8
1981	1	49.5
	2	56.0
	3	63.5
	4	85.5
1982	1	54.7
	2	59.9
	3	65.0
	4	89.0
1983	1	57.0
	2	63.9
	3	68.6
	4	94.2
1984	1	58.7
	2	67.1
	3	74.2
	4	102.8
1985	1	65.3
	2	72.3
	3	78.3
	4	111.2
1986	1	72.1
	2	82.0
	3	91.6
	4	127.5
1987	1	82.3
	2	92.0
	3	96.7
	4	134.9

Although it is not necessary to graph the data, it can be very helpful to do so. The graph of Figure 5.13 was generated by a computer.

Step 3. Measure the trend and the cycle (combined) Once the data are collected, adjusted, and graphed, they are ready to be processed. If a computer is used (Section 5.10), then this is the time to enter the data into it. Here, the manual approach is illustrated, so the reader can understand what is being done by the computer. In step 3, we separate the trend and the cycle from the seasonal and random variations.

One way to execute this separation is to use annual data as the basis for computation. Such a separation will eliminate seasonal differences and most of the random variations. However, in order to compare these annualized values to the original quarterly observations, they must be made comparable in both magnitude and timing. The annualized values can be made comparable in size by converting the annual total to a monthly or

Annualize the data

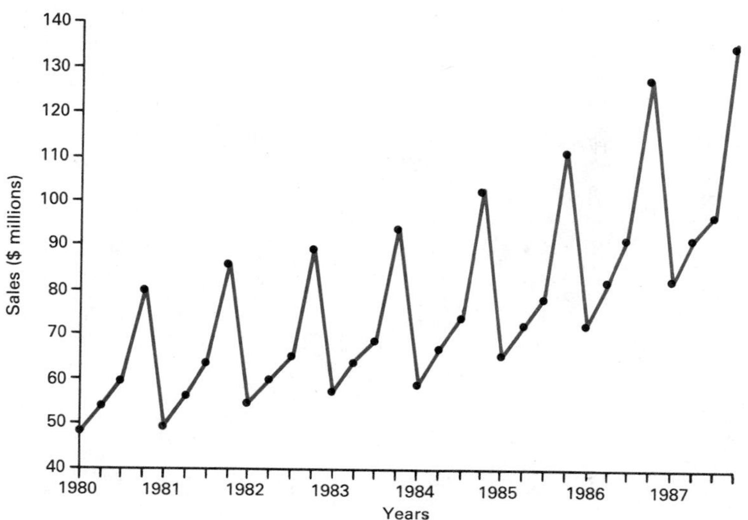

FIGURE 5.13
A graph of the data

quarterly average (dividing the total by 12 or 4). The following procedure assures that the annualized values and the original observations are comparable both in size and in timing.

Calculate a 12-month or 4-quarter *moving average*. This is done, for quarterly data, by averaging the first four quarters (quarters 1 through 4). Then, the oldest quarter (1) is dropped and quarter 5 is added instead, and so on. Each average is placed in time at the midpoint of the dates of the included observations. Thus, the first average refers to a point in time midway between the dates of the second and third quarterly observations, the second is a point between the third and fourth quarters, and so on.

Example

The moving average for MSC is shown in column 2 of Table 5.5. Note that the column of the moving average is shown one-half line offset from the sales data because the moving average represents the average value for the middle of the time span. Since each average is constructed over a one-year period, each value is two quarters from both the beginning and the end of that time span.

Center the moving average

The moving average shown in column 2 of Table 5.5 is not a "typical" value for any quarter, so the next step is to center the moving average as in column 3. This centering is accomplished by averaging two adjacent averages in column 2 of Table 5.5. This centered moving average is shown in column 3. The first value in this column represents the centered moving average for the third quarter of 1980. Note that the first period for which a centered moving average is available is not the first period for which raw data are available. When quarterly data are used, two quarters are lost at the beginning and again at the end of the data.

TABLE 5.5
Moving average for MSC

Year	Quarter	(1) Sales ($ millions)	(2) Moving average	(3) Centered moving average	(4) Ratio of sales to moving average (1) ÷ (3)
1980	1	48.6			
	2	54.2			
			÷ 4 = 60.60		
	3	59.8		÷ 2 = 60.71	0.9850
			60.82		
	4	79.8		61.05	1.3071
			61.28		
1981	1	49.5		61.74	0.8017
			62.20		
	2	56.0		62.91	0.8902
			63.62		
	3	63.5		64.27	0.9880
			64.92		
	4	85.5		65.41	1.3071
			65.90		
1982	1	54.7		66.09	0.8276
			66.28		
	2	59.9		66.72	0.8978
			67.15		
	3	65.0		67.44	0.9638
			67.72		
	4	89.0		68.22	1.3046
			68.72		
1983	1	57.0		69.17	0.8241
			69.62		
	2	63.9		70.27	0.9093
			70.92		
	3	68.6		71.14	0.9643
			71.35		
	4	94.2		71.75	1.3129
			72.15		
1984	1	58.7		72.85	0.8058
			73.55		
	2	67.1		74.62	0.8992
			75.70		
	3	74.2		76.52	0.9697
			77.35		
	4	102.8		78.00	1.3179
			78.65		
1985	1	65.3		79.16	0.8249
			79.68		
	2	72.3		80.73	0.8956
			81.78		
	3	78.3		82.63	0.9476
			83.48		
	4	111.2		84.69	1.3130
			85.90		
1986	1	72.1		87.56	0.8234
			89.22		
	2	82.0		91.26	0.8985
			93.30		
	3	91.6		94.58	0.9685
			95.85		
	4	127.5		97.10	1.3131
			98.35		
1987	1	82.3		98.98	0.8315
			99.62		
	2	92.0		100.55	0.9150
			101.48		
	3	96.7			
	4	134.9			

The need to center the moving average resulted from the choice of an even number of quarters (four) as the basis for the computation. A choice of an odd number would eliminate the need to center the data. However, using a four-quarter moving average has a statistical advantage over the use of three or five quarters.

Column 4 of Table 5.5 shows the ratio of each quarterly value to the centered moving average. This column will be used in the computation of the seasonal and the random variations in steps 6–8.

Step 4. Separating the effect of the trend (T) The moving average, as computed in column 3 of Table 5.5, contains both trend and cyclical movements. Our task is to separate the two. First, the trend is to be

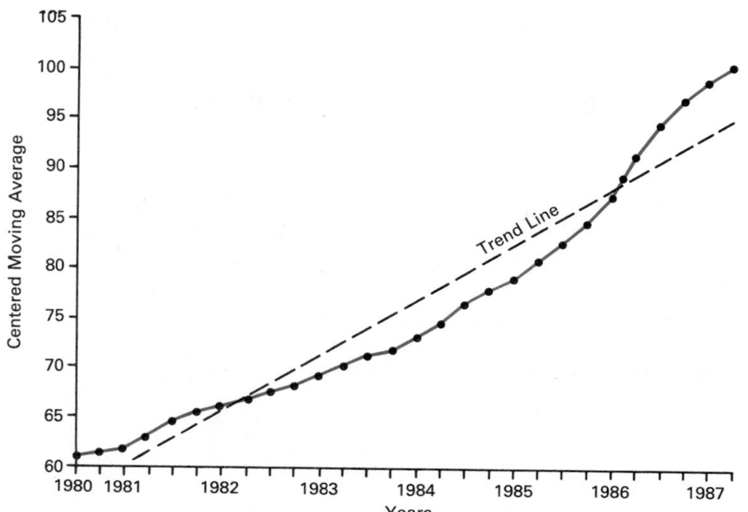

FIGURE 5.14
Drawing a freehand trend line

separated. Several methods exist for determining the trend. Two popular methods are the *freehand* and the *least square.*

Two ways to find the trend

a. *Freehand:* This method is most straightforward; it involves the freehand fitting of a smooth line that, in the judgment of the forecaster, is a good fit to the moving average. This method is simple but not accurate. Furthermore, projections that are made on the basis of this graphical approach can be even less accurate. A freehand fit is demonstrated in Figure 5.14. The data are from column 3 of Table 5.5.

b. *Least-square (regression) analysis:* If the trend line appears to be linear, as in Figure 5.8a, or if it is possible to segment the trend line into linear portions, as in Figure 5.9, then the method of linear regression can be used.

As indicated earlier, the trend is the long-run direction of the series of data. In our example, the trend (Figure 5.14) appears to follow a straight line; that is, to be a linear trend with respect to time. In order to project this linear trend into the future, we must first estimate the parameters of the trend line. The parameters of the straight line that must be estimated are the Y-axis intercept and the slope of the line. The *Y-axis intercept* is the value of Y where the trend line crosses the Y-axis (at $X = 0$). The *slope* is the amount of change in Y for a one-period change in X. There are several procedures for estimating the slope and intercept of a straight line from the observed values of X and Y, but **least squares regression** is the most widely used method.[1] The equation that we will use to forecast

The intercept and slope of the trend line equation

[1] The method derives its name from the way in which the parameters of the line are estimated. That is, the method minimizes the sum of the squares of the vertical deviations between the trend line and the original data points.

the trend into the future is known as the *estimated regression equation*, and is shown as:

Least squares regression most commonly used for trend determination

$$T_x = a + bX \tag{5.8}$$

where:

T_x = The trend *forecasted* value of sales Y for period number X
a = The estimate of the Y-axis intercept
b = The estimate of the slope of the line
X = The period number
Y = Actual sales (historical data)

The two equations used to determine a and b are:

$$b = \frac{\Sigma XY - n\overline{X}\overline{Y}}{\Sigma X^2 - n\overline{X}^2} \tag{5.9}$$

and

$$a = \overline{Y} - b\overline{X} \tag{5.10}$$

where:

ΣXY = X times Y for each period, summed over all of the periods
ΣX^2 = X squared for each period, summed over all of the periods
$\overline{X}$ = The average of the X values
$\overline{Y}$ = The average of the Y values
n = The number of periods of data used in the regression

Using least squares regression for the MSC Corp.

Using the data from column 3 of Table 5.5, we can compute the slope and the intercept of the trend equation. To simplify the computations, we will arrange the data into four columns, as shown in Table 5.6. The numbers in column 3 are simply column 1 numbers squared and the numbers in column 4 are computed by multiplying the numbers in column 1 by the corresponding number from column 2. To compute the slope of the regression line *(b)* we need the average of column 1, which is:

$$\overline{X} = \frac{\Sigma X}{n} = \frac{406}{28} = 14.5$$

and the average of column 2, which is:

$$\overline{Y} = \frac{\Sigma Y}{n} = \frac{2126.12}{28} = 75.93$$

In addition, we need the total of columns 3 and 4. In our algebraic notation, ΣXY is the sum of column 4.

TABLE 5.6
Least squares trend data

Quarter number X	*Sales (\$ millions)* Y	X^2	XY
1	60.71	1	60.71
2	61.05	4	122.10
3	61.74	9	185.22
4	62.91	16	251.64
5	64.27	25	321.35
6	65.41	36	392.46
7	66.09	49	462.63
8	66.72	64	533.76
9	67.44	81	606.96
10	68.22	100	682.20
11	69.17	121	760.87
12	70.27	144	843.24
13	71.14	169	924.82
14	71.75	196	1004.50
15	72.85	225	1092.75
16	74.62	256	1193.92
17	76.52	289	1300.84
18	78.00	324	1404.00
19	79.16	361	1504.04
20	80.73	400	1614.60
21	82.63	441	1735.23
22	84.69	484	1947.87
23	87.56	529	2013.88
24	91.26	576	2190.24
25	94.58	625	2364.50
26	97.10	676	2524.60
27	98.98	729	2672.46
28	100.55	784	2815.40
$\Sigma X = 406$	$\Sigma Y = 2126.12$	$\Sigma X^2 = 7714$	$\Sigma XY = 33442$

The slope can then be computed by using Equation 5.9.

$$\begin{aligned} b &= \frac{33442 - 28(14.5)75.93}{7714 - 28(14.5)^2} \\ &= 1.43 \end{aligned}$$

which means that the sales volume is, on the average, increasing by \$1.43 million every quarter.

The Y-axis intercept is computed from Equation 5.10.

$$\begin{aligned} a &= 75.93 - 1.43(14.5) \\ &= 55.20 \end{aligned}$$

which means that the initial sales volume at time $X = 0$ would have been \$55.20 million.

The forecasting equation for the trend in sales volume is therefore (in millions of dollars):

$$T_x = 55.20 + 1.43X$$

Step 5. Computing the cycle In step 4 we showed how to find T, either by freehand or by finding the values of T for each quarter. If the freehand method is used, then one can read the values directly from the graph. If regression is used, one can calculate the value of T for each quarter. Table 5.7 shows the values of T, by quarter (in column 3), as calculated from the regression equation. For example, the value for the third quarter of 1980 ($X = 1$) is:

$$T_1 = 55.20 + 1.43(1) = 56.62$$

and for the "last" quarter (the 28th):

$$T_{28} = 55.20 + 1.43(28) = 95.24$$

TABLE 5.7
Computing the trend and the cycle

Quarter X	*Centered moving average* CMA	*Trend* T	*Cycle* $C = CMA/T$
1*	60.71	56.62	1.07
2	61.05	58.05	1.05
3	61.74	59.48	1.04
4	62.91	60.91	1.03
5	64.27	62.34	1.03
6	65.41	63.77	1.03
7	66.09	65.20	1.01
8	66.72	66.64	1.00
9	67.44	68.07	0.99
10	68.22	69.50	0.98
11	69.17	70.93	0.98
12	70.27	72.36	0.97
13	71.14	73.79	0.96
14	71.75	75.22	0.95
15	72.85	76.65	0.95
16	74.62	78.08	0.96
17	76.52	79.51	0.96
18	78.00	80.94	0.96
19	79.16	82.37	0.96
20	80.73	83.80	0.96
21	82.63	85.23	0.97
22	84.69	86.66	0.98
23	87.56	88.09	0.99
24	91.26	89.52	1.02
25	94.58	90.95	1.04
26	97.10	92.38	1.05
27	98.98	93.81	1.06
28	100.55	95.24	1.06

* Quarter 1 is the third quarter of 1980.

Notice also that in column 2 we reproduced the values of the centered moving average (CMA). We can now calculate the values of C as:

$$C = \text{CMA}/T \tag{5.11}$$

For example, for the third quarter ($X = 1$) we get:

$$C = 60.71/56.62 = 1.07$$

Using this approach, the cyclical movements are expressed as a percentage of the trend. The results appear in column 4 of Table 5.7.

A mild cycle

As shown in Figure 5.15, the cyclical movements are fairly mild and the span of the cycle covers quite a few years. The trend line in Figure 5.15 is shown by the horizontal 100 percent line.

Step 6. *Measuring the combined effects of seasonal and random variations* The decomposition method assumes that the original data are the product of $T \times C \times S \times R$. Previously, we assumed the value of $T \times C$ to be the centered moving average. Therefore, the value of $S \times R$ can be calculated as:

Separating the components

$$S \times R = \frac{T \times C \times S \times R}{T \times C} = \frac{\text{Original data}}{\text{Centered Moving Average}}$$

This computation was done in column 4 of Table 5.5. Note that the value $S \times R$ is thus expressed as a *percentage* of the corresponding moving average.

Step 7. *Compute the seasonal variations* The term *seasonal variation* can apply to any repetitive pattern in a time series where the interval of time to completion of the pattern is one year or less. Thus, the term

Repetitive patterns

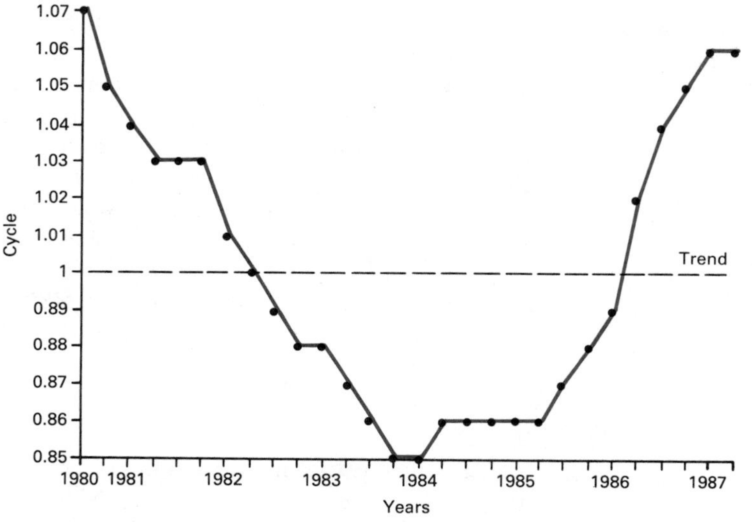

FIGURE 5.15
Graphing the cycle

could be used to describe not only a monthly or quarterly pattern within a year, but also a weekly pattern within a month, a daily pattern within a week, or even an hourly pattern within a day. By observing the graph of our original data, it seems that we do have quarterly variations.

In order to compute the value of S, we regroup the $S \times R$ values (column 4 in Table 5.5) by period. That is, all first quarters together, all second quarters, and so on. This is shown in Table 5.8.

TABLE 5.8
Quarterly ratios of sales to centered moving average

	Quarter			
Year	*1*	*2*	*3*	*4*
1980			0.9850	1.3071
1981	0.8017	0.8902	0.9880	1.3071
1982	0.8276	0.8978	0.9638	1.3046
1983	0.8241	0.9093	0.9643	1.3129
1984	0.8058	0.8992	0.9697	1.3179
1985	0.8249	0.8956	0.9476	1.3130
1986	0.8234	0.8985	0.9685	1.3131
1987	0.8315	0.9150		

The next task is to find a typical value of the quarterly indices. There are several ways to proceed in finding this value. For the case of Mercantile Stores, it might be appropriate to simply take the arithmetic mean of the entries in each quarter. However, it is usually considered to be more reasonable to construct a modified mean. A modified mean is found by striking out the highest and lowest value for each quarter, and averaging the remaining values. This is done in order to remove the influences of any unusual quarter. But when an unusually high (low) value is removed, it is necessary to remove the lowest (highest) value as well, so that the mean of the remaining values still represents a useful measure of central tendency. If the data are highly volatile, it might be desirable to strike out two or even three low values and a similar number of high values, depending on the number of years of data.

Drop extreme values

The modified mean for Mercantile Stores is constructed in Table 5.9. For each column, the highest and lowest values are struck out. The remaining values are averaged. Since they do not total precisely to 4.00, they have next been adjusted so that their total is 4 (within the limit of rounding) by multiplying each modified mean by four and dividing by the actual total of modified means. These adjusted modified means, expressed as seasonal indices, are shown in the last row of Table 5.9.

Normalize the means

Seasonal adjustment of data

The seasonal indices computed in Table 5.9 will be used to compute the random variations (R). However, they can also be used to adjust the

TABLE 5.9 Computation of seasonal indices

	Quarter			
Year	*1*	*2*	*3*	*4*
1980			0.9850	1.3071
1981	~~0.8017~~	~~0.8902~~	~~0.9880~~	1.3071
1982	0.8276	0.8978	0.9638	~~1.3046~~
1983	0.8241	0.9093	0.9643	1.3129
1984	0.8058	0.8992	0.9697	~~1.3179~~
1985	0.8249	0.8956	~~0.9476~~	1.3130
1986	0.8234	0.8985	0.9685	1.3131
1987	~~0.8315~~	~~0.9150~~		
Modified total	4.1058	4.5004	4.8513	6.5532
Modified mean	0.82116	0.90008	0.97026	1.31064
Adjusted modified mean	0.821	0.900	0.970	1.310
Seasonal index	82.116	90.008	97.026	131.064

Calculations:

Total of modified means = 0.82116 + 0.90008 + 0.97026 + 1.31064 = 4.00214
Adjusted modified means:

(1) $0.82116 \times \frac{4.0}{4.00214} = 0.821$ (3) $0.97026 \times \frac{4.0}{4.00214} = 0.970$

(2) $0.90008 \times \frac{4.0}{4.00214} = 0.900$ (4) $1.31064 \times \frac{4.0}{4.00214} = 1.310$

original data. This is done by dividing the original data by the appropriate index, multiplied by 100. For example, for the first quarter we get:

$$\frac{48.6 \times 100}{82.1} = 59.2$$

This adjustment can also be done on forecast data for any desired time period in the future, as will be shown later.

There are other more sophisticated methods of seasonal adjustment, too. Almost all economic time series published by the U.S. government are available in seasonally adjusted form. Although the basic concepts of seasonal adjustments in this chapter are used in seasonally adjusted time series published by federal agencies, there may also be gradual changes in the pattern of seasonality. For example, as construction activity changes in character, the construction that is increasing may have a different seasonal pattern than the construction that is decreasing. This causes a change over time in the seasonal indices. If such a time series is encountered, a crude refinement for changing seasonal patterns may be accomplished by plotting the ratio of the time series value to the centered moving average (for a particular quarter or month) for the various years in the data. Then a trend line may be fitted either visually or by the method of least squares

A trend in seasonality

TABLE 5.10
The random variations

Quarter X	*Random* R
1	1.016
2	.998
3	.978
4	.989
5	1.019
6	.998
7	1.010
8	.998
9	.994
10	.996
11	1.005
12	1.010
13	.994
14	1.002
15	.983
16	.991
17	1.000
18	1.006
19	1.006
20	.995
21	.977
22	1.002
23	1.004
24	.998
25	.998
26	1.002
27	1.014
28	1.017

to aid in projecting future seasonal indices for that period. However, these procedures should be used with care.

Step 8. Measuring the random (unexplained) variations In step 6 we identified the value $S \times R$; to compute R all we have to do is to divide this value by the seasonal index S. For example, for quarter 1 we get:

$$R = \frac{S \times R}{S} = \frac{0.9850}{0.97} = 1.016$$

Table 5.10 shows the random values for quarters 1 through 28. In our example, the random variations are fairly small and the forecaster may wish to ignore them. However, these variations may be considered in the forecast through a risk analysis approach. This approach will be demonstrated in the next step.

Risk analysis

Step 9. Develop a forecast The decomposition procedure for a time series is reversed in order to predict future values of the time series. As always, it is cautioned that any prediction is better thought of as a projection from past data. If the basic forces underlying the time series change, the future values of the time series may not reflect the behavior indicated by past values.

There are several methods of developing the forecast. One of them is briefly introduced next.

Let us assume that we would like to forecast the demand for the year 1990 and for each quarter of that year. Since we labeled the third quarter of 1980 as 1 in order to calculate the centered moving average, then the last quarter of 1987 is 30. Therefore, the four quarters of 1990 are numbered as 39, 40, 41, and 42. The computation involves four operations.

Four steps in making the forecast

a. Compute the trend line (extrapolation into the future)

The trend line was computed in step 4 as a linear equation:

$$T = 55.20 + 1.43x$$

where x designates the appropriate quarter. Using this equation for the four quarters, we get:

1st quarter 1990 (39); $y = 55.20 + 1.43(39) = 110.97$
2nd quarter 1990 (40); $y = 55.20 + 1.43(40) = 112.40$
3rd quarter 1990 (41); $y = 55.20 + 1.43(41) = 113.83$
4th quarter 1990 42); $y = 55.20 + 1.43(42) = 115.26$

b. Seasonal adjustment

The trend projections for 1990 are now each multiplied by the appropriate seasonal index:

1st quarter 1990 = $(.821)110.97 = 91.11$
2nd quarter 1990 = $(.900)112.40 = 101.16$
3rd quarter 1990 = $(.970)113.83 = 110.42$
4th quarter 1990 = $(1.310)115.26 = 150.99$

c. Cyclical adjustment

The seasonally adjusted data can now be adjusted for the **cyclical** variation. This is a most difficult task since the cyclical movements are of an irregular nature. One approach is to use a freehand extrapolation of the business cycle. Another approach is to consult experts in the field. The cyclical adjustment can be made for each quarter or for the entire year. This is perhaps the most difficult judgmental task in the entire process. The projection of where the economic cycle will be at any given time in the future is based on information from general economic predictions and perceptions of the relationship between these conditions and the series being forecast. This forecast is done in a percentage.

Judgment is needed

Using a freehand prediction (see Figure 5.15) we establish the cyclical adjustments for the four quarters as:

1st quarter 1990 = .97
2nd quarter 1990 = .96
3rd quarter 1990 = .95
4th quarter 1990 = .96

These figures are multiplied by the seasonally adjusted data. The result $T \times S \times C$ is:

1st quarter 1990 = 91.11 × .97 = 88.38
2nd quarter 1990 = 101.16 × .96 = 97.11
3rd quarter 1990 = 110.42 × .95 = 104.90
4th quarter 1990 = 150.99 × .96 = 144.95

d. Inclusion of the random variations: Risk analysis

The *R* values computed in step 8 (Table 5.10) are used to construct a cumulative probability distribution that describes the uncertainty surrounding the forecasts based on *T*, *S*, and *C*. The cumulative probability distribution for our case is shown in Figure 5.16a.

Forecast variability

The forecaster can now perform a risk analysis by combining the $T \times S \times C$ information with the data in Figure 5.16a. We illustrate such a combination for the first quarter of 1990 in Fig. 5.16b. Notice that the forecast for the first quarter of 1990 was calculated as $88,380,000. This value is aligned with the value of 1.00 in Figure 5.16b. The range of sales in this quarter is therefore predicted to be between 86.17 (i.e., 88.38 × .975) and 90.15 (88.38 × 1.020). In our case, the range is fairly narrow since the random variations are minimal. In other cases, one may see a distribution of plus or minus 20 percent or more around the mean. In such a case, the actual plans will be determined by the corporate attitude toward risk. Finally, all dollar values should, of course, be adjusted for inflation.

FIGURE 5.16
Risk analysis based on *R* values

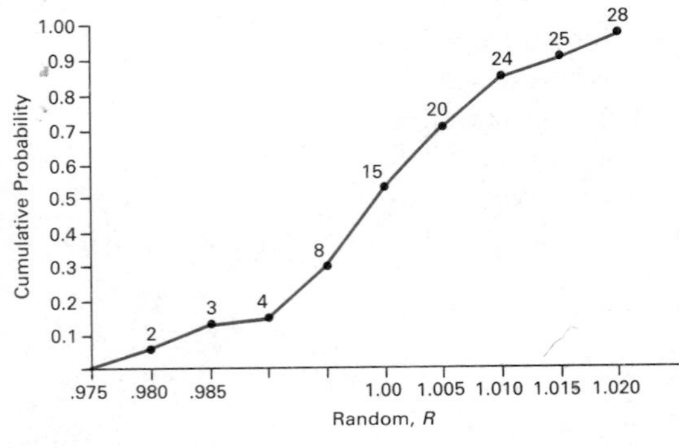

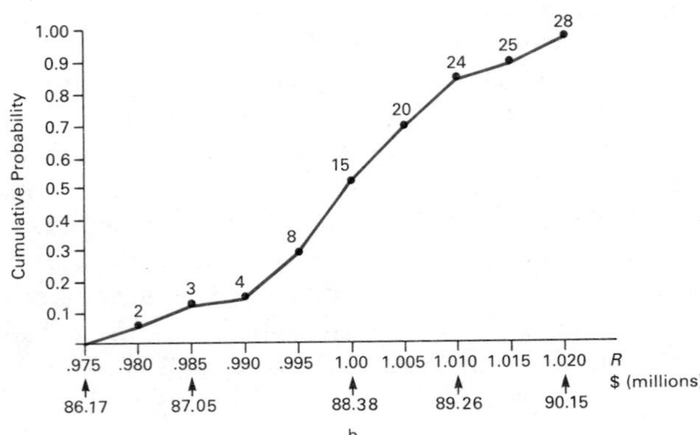

5.10 COMPUTERIZATION

Forecasting methods easily lend themselves to computerization, and indeed, dozens of software packages are available on the market for any type of computer.

Table 5.11 includes 11 representative software packages for the personal computer. In addition, many of the standard statistical packages include routines for forecasting. Many of the packages are flexible, allowing users to include their own judgmental values.

TABLE 5.11
Representative micro forecasting packages

Name	*Vendor*
Autobox, BOXX™	Automatic Forecasting Systems, Inc. (Hatboro, Pa.).
EXEC*U*STAT™	EXEC*U*STAT Inc. (Princeton, N.J.).
Forecast Master™	Scientific Systems, Inc. (Cambridge, Mass.).
Forecast Plus™	Walonick Associates (Minneapolis, Minn.).
Futurcast™	Futurion Assoc, Inc. (Pittsburg, Calif.).
Micro TSP™	McGraw-Hill (New York, N.Y.).
Soritec Econometrics™	The Soritec Group (Springfield, Va.).
SPSS/PC +™	SPSS, Inc. (Chicago, Ill.).
Systat™	Systat Inc. (Evanston, Ill.).
The Forecasting Edge™	Human Edge Software (Palo Alto, Calif.).
1,2,3 Forecast™	1,2,3 Forecast (Salem, Oreg.).

5.11 CONCLUDING REMARKS

This chapter described the need and uses of forecasts and the factors that influence the choice of the most appropriate forecasting approach. The various forecasting approaches—qualitative, counting, time-series analysis, and causal—were described and illustrated.

The most common types of qualitative forecasting approaches are market surveys, expert opinion, and Delphi. Time-series analysis includes moving averages, exponential smoothing, decomposition models, and Box-Jenkins. Causal forecasting methods consist of multiple regression, econometric models, and input-output. These complex models take much data and time for construction and are best made by skilled experts in this field using computers.

Measures of forecast accuracy include the mean absolute deviation (MAD) and bias. The MAD measures the average error, ignoring whether the error is positive or negative, of a set of forecasts compared to the actual result. The bias is almost the same thing but includes the sign (direction) of the error, positive errors meaning the forecast was too high. The forecasting method with the smallest MAD and bias is best.

5.12 PROBLEMS FOR PART B

11. Develop a linear regression equation to predict demand in the future from the data below.

Demand	23	24	31	28	29
Year	1979	1980	1981	1982	1983

12. Determine the linear regression trend equation and seasonals for the data below.

Units	5	4	3	5	6	5	4	6
Quarter	1	2	3	4	5	6	7	8

13. Determine in Problem 11 if odd-numbered years are different from even-numbered years by calculating "seasonals" for each.

14. Predict quarter 10 in Problem 12 by linear regression and seasonals and calculate the current MAD and bias.

15. Develop a demand regression equation for the data below and predict demand at a price of $4 and a price of $9.

Price, $	7	6	8	5
Demand	1,050	1,100	1,020	1,130

16. *a.* Demand for snow tires in Toronto depends on the snowfall, with the history for the last 10 years given below. Use the data to develop a linear regression equation for snow tire demand. Calculate the MAD and the bias and predict 1985 demand, if weather forecasters predict 22 inches of snowfall.

Year	*Snowfall (inches)*	*Demand*
1975	25.0	2050
1976	27.6	1944
1977	22.4	2250
1978	24.0	1700
1979	28.2	1842
1980	22.2	2404
1981	23.4	1756
1982	25.2	1780
1983	23.8	2144
1984	24.6	1862

b. A friend in the used auto business thinks you might get a better forecast by considering the possibility that demand *lags* snowfall by a year. That is, consider the possibility that demand is related to the snowfall in the *previous* year and develop a new regression equation, MAD, bias, and 1985 prediction. Is the result better or worse?

17. Given the following toy store data on "Rube's Triangle," a toy for children from 5 to 85 years:

Month	J	F	M	A	M	J	J	A	S	O
Demand (000s)	0.2	0.5	1.0	2	4	8	25	45	59	66

a. Forecast November demand by a three-month moving average.

b. Forecast November demand by exponential forecasting with an alpha of 0.3.

c. Forecast November demand by linear regression.

d. Plot the data and the linear trend line from (*c*). What does it look like is happening / Can you intuitively forecast November?

18. Vollo, Inc., of Sweden, is preparing a prediction of its U.S. sales for 1995. The information is as follows:

Quarter	*Trend line*	*Cycle*	*Seasonal index*
Winter	80,000	1.05	.70
Spring	88,000	1.10	.90
Summer	96,000	1.00	1.10
Fall	104,000	.90	1.30

Calculate the number of units to be produced each quarter for the U.S. market.

19. The cyclical residuals of the Japanese demand for black-and-white TVs are given below.

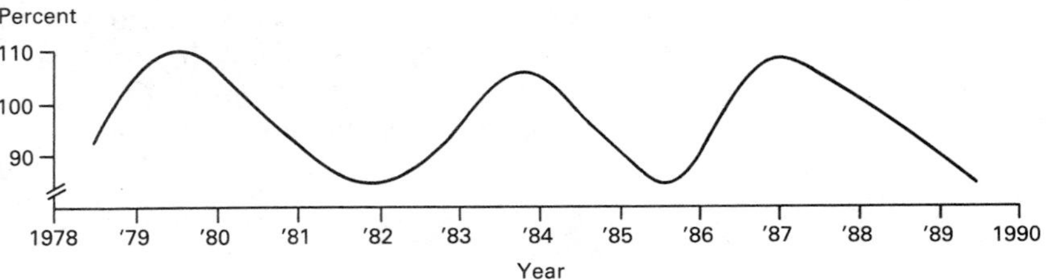

a. Estimate the cyclical values of the demand for the years 1989, 1990, and 1991.

b. The trend line for demand is forecast (in thousands of units) by the equation $y = 50 + 10x$, where x is the time ($x = 0$ in 1979) and y is the annual demand. The quarterly seasonal percent indices are quarter 1—92; quarter 2—106; quarter 3—110; and quarter 4—98. Predict the demand for each quarter of 1990.

c. Given the cumulative distribution of the unexplained variation curve below, find the probability of demand being 140,000 units or less in 1989.

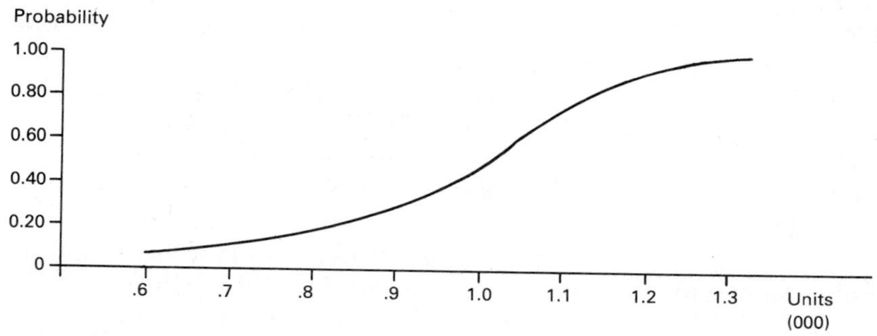

20. The sales history of Swedish Machine Parts, Ltd. is given in units below:

	Period	*Value*		*Period*	*Value*		*Period*	*Value*
1977	1	456.00		16	494.00		31	520.00
	2	543.00	1981	17	490.00		32	514.00
	3	457.00		18	550.00	1985	33	506.00
	4	486.00		19	502.00		34	588.00
1978	5	444.00		20	510.00		35	510.00
	6	534.00	1982	21	570.00		36	503.00
	7	478.00		22	500.00	1986	37	550.00
	8	596.00		23	492.00		38	600.00
1979	9	468.00		24	512.00		39	534.00
	10	550.00	1983	25	502.00		40	512.00
	11	487.00		26	594.00	1987	41	545.00
	12	490.00		27	513.00		42	612.00
1980	13	488.00		28	510.00		43	542.00
	14	560.00	1984	29	498.00		44	542.00
	15	499.00		30	593.00			

Use a computer package to find:

a. The forecast for period 45 by exponential smoothing ($\alpha = 0.3$).

b. Period 45 forecast by centered moving average.

c. The trend equation.

d. The seasonal indices.

e. The cycle.

f. Random variations.

g. Predict quarter 1 of 1995 and quarter 2 of 1996.

h. Predict the total for 1977.

5.13 CASE

BARDSTOWN BOX COMPANY

Bardstown Box Company is a small, closely held corporation located in Bardstown, England. The stock of the company is divided among three brothers, with the principal shareholder being the founding brother, Bob Wilson. Bob formed the company 20 years ago when he resigned as a salesman for a large corrugated box manufacturer.

Bob attributes his success to the fact that he can better serve the five-district area that he considers "his territory" than can any of his large competitors. Bardstown Box supplies corrugated cartons to many regional distilleries and to several breweries. Also, standard-size boxes are printed to order for many small manufacturing firms in the region. Bob feels that the large box manufacturers cannot economically provide this personal level of service to his accounts.

Bob recognizes the danger of becoming too dependent on any client and has enforced the policy that no single customer can account for over 20 percent of sales. Two of the distilleries account for 20 percent of sales each, and hence are limited in their purchases. Bob has convinced the purchasing agents of these two companies to add other suppliers, since this alternative supply protects them against problems Bardstown might have in shipping, paper shortages, or labor problems.

Bardstown currently has over 600 customers with orders ranging in size from a low of 100 boxes to blanket orders for 50,000 boxes per year. Boxes are produced in 16 standard sizes with special printing to customers' specifications. Bardstown's printing equipment limits their print to two colors. The standardization and limited printing allows Bardstown to be price competitive with the big producers but they also provide the service for small and "emergency" orders that large box manufacturers cannot provide.

Such personal service, however, requires tight inventory control and close production scheduling. So far, Bob Wilson has always forecast demand and prepared production schedules through experience, but because of the ever-growing number of accounts and changes in personnel in customer purchasing departments, the accuracy of his forecasting has been rapidly declining. The number of back orders is on the increase, late orders are more common, and inventory levels of finished boxes are on the increase. A second warehouse has recently been leased due to the overcrowded conditions in the main warehouse. Plans are to move some of the slower moving boxes to the leased space.

There has always been an increase in demand for boxes prior to the Christmas holiday season, when customers begin stocking for holiday promotional demand. Such seasonality in demand has always substantially increased the difficulty of making a reliable forecast.

Bob Wilson feels that it is now important to develop an improved forecasting method. It should take both customer growth and seasonality into consideration. Bob believes that if such a method can be applied to forecasting total demand, it can also be used to forecast demand for the larger customers; the requirements of the smaller customers could then be integrated to smooth production and warehousing volume.

Bob has compiled the following demand data.

Month	Sales (in thousands of boxes)				
	1979	*1980*	*1981*	*1982*	*1983*
January	12	8	12	15	15
February	8	14	8	12	22
March	10	18	18	14	18
April	18	15	13	18	18
May	14	16	14	15	16
June	10	18	18	18	20
July	16	14	17	20	28
August	18	28	20	22	28
September	20	22	25	26	20
October	27	27	28	28	30
November	24	26	18	20	22
December	18	10	18	22	28
	195	216	209	230	265

Questions for discussion

1. Develop a forecasting method for Bardstown and forecast total demand for 1984.
2. How might Bob improve the accuracy of the forecast?
3. Should Bob's experience with the market be factored into the forecast? How?

5.14 GLOSSARY

Adaptive forecasting A method that automatically changes the smoothing constant in relation to model error.

Bias A tendency to always be high (or low), a measure of error.

Causal Identifying events that cause other events.

Cycle A long-term variation around the trend.

Delphi A special qualitative methodology for group forecasting.

Econometric model A quantitative forecasting approach used in economics.

Exponential smoothing Weighting a set of data with exponentially decreasing coefficients.

Least squares regression Estimation of a data series by minimizing the deviations of the estimate from the actual.

Life cycle analysis, stretched S A generalized, four-stage life-imitating model.

MAD Mean absolute deviation, a measure of forecasting error.

Moving average An average of only the last *n* data points.

Multiple regression The use of a number of independent variables to make a prediction of the dependent variable.

Random Unpredictable; occurring by chance.

Seasonal A regular periodic variation around the trend.

Smoothing constant The weight attached to the latest data point in an exponential smoothing model.

Tracking signal The measuring of forecast error to determine prediction accuracy.

Time series A data series that changes with time.

Trend The long-term direction of a series of data.

5.15 REFERENCES AND BIBLIOGRAPHY

1. Box, G. E. P., and G. M. Jenkins. *Time Series Analysis: Forecasting and Control*. San Francisco: Holden-Day, 1970.
2. Chambers, J. S., S. K. Mullick, and D. D. Smith. "How to Choose the Right Forecasting Technique." *Harvard Business Review*, July–August 1971, pp. 45–74.
3. Georgoff, D. M., and R. G. Murdick. "Manager's Guide to Forecasting." *Harvard Business Review*, January–February 1986, pp. 110–20.
4. Hoff, J. C. *A Practical Guide: Box-Jenkins Forecasting*, Belmont, Calif.: Lifetime Learning Publications, 1983.
5. Hogarth, R. M., et al. "Forecasting and Planning: An Evaluation." *Management Science* 27 (1981), pp. 115–38.
6. Levenbach, H., and J. P. Cleary. *The Beginning Forecaster*. Belmont, Calif.: Lifetime Learning Publications, 1982.
7. ________. *The Professional Forecaster*. Belmont, Calif.: Lifetime Learning Publications, 1982.
8. Linstone, H. A., and M. Turoff. *The Delphi Method: Techniques and Applications*. Reading, Mass.: Addison-Wesley Publishing, 1975.
9. Mahmoud E. "Accuracy in Forecasting." *Journal of Forecasting*, April–June 1984.
10. Makridakis, S., and S. C. Wheelwright. *The Handbook of Forecasting: A Manager's Guide*. New York: John Wiley & Sons, 1982.
11. Plane, D. R. *Business and Economic Statistics*. Rev. ed. Plano, Tex.: Business Publications, 1981.
12. Thomopoulos, N. T. *Applied Forecasting Methods*. Englewood Cliffs, N.J.: Prentice-Hall, 1980.
13. Valentine L. M., and C. A. Dauten. *Business Cycles and Forecasting*. Cincinnati: South-Western Publishing Co., 1983.
14. Wheelwright, S. C., et al. *Forecasting Methods for Management*. 2nd ed. New York: John Wiley & Sons, 1977.
15. Whybark, D. C. "A Comparison of Adaptive Forecasting Techniques." *The Logistics and Transportation Review* 8 (January 1973), pp. 13–26.
16. Wood, D., and R. Fields. *Forecasting for Business: Methods and Applications*. London: Longman Business Series, 1976.

A preview

MATHEMATICAL PROGRAMMING

Mathematical programming is the name for a family of tools designed to help solve managerial problems in which the decision maker must allocate scarce (or limited) resources among various activities to optimize a measurable goal. For example, distribution of machine time (the resource) among various products (the activities) is a typical allocation problem. Allocation problems usually display the following characteristics and necessitate making certain assumptions.

CHARACTERISTICS

1. A limited quantity of economic resources (such as labor, capital, machines, or water) is available for allocation.
2. The resources are used in the production of products or services.
3. There are two or more ways in which the resources can be used. Each is called a solution or a program. (Usually the number of ways is very large, or even infinite.)
4. Each activity (product or service) in which the resources are used yields a return (or reward) in terms of the stated goal.
5. The allocation is usually restricted by several limitations and requirements called constraints.

ASSUMPTIONS

1. Returns from different allocations can be compared; that is, they can be measured by a common unit (such as dollars or utility).
2. The return from any allocation is independent of other allocations.
3. The total return is the sum of the returns yielded by the different activities.
4. All data are known with certainty.
5. The resources are to be used in the most economical manner.

Chapters 6–10

The allocation problem can generally be stated as: Find the way of allocating the limited resources to various activities so the total reward will be maximized. Allocation problems, typically, have a large number of possible alternative solutions. Depending on the underlying assumptions, the number of solutions can be either infinite or finite. Usually, different solutions yield different rewards. Of the available solutions, one (sometimes more than one) is the *best*, in the sense that the degree of goal attainment associated with it is the highest (i.e., total reward is maximized). This is referred to as the optimal solution.

A survey would find that many, or even most, problems in organizations are related to the allocation of resources (money, people, time, power, space, equipment). The reasons for this are that the resources are limited, there are many ways of allocation, it is difficult to measure the contribution of the allocation to the goals, and there is disagreement concerning the importance of the results. Mathematical programming provides a relatively unbiased approach to this allocation problem.

The field of mathematical programming that is covered in this text includes:

Linear programming—foundations (Chapter 6) Linear programming deals with allocation problems in which the goal (or objective) and all the requirements imposed on the problem are expressed by linear functions (see Appendix A).

Linear programming—applications (Chapter 7) This chapter presents a variety of example applications for which linear programming is most appropriate.

Integer linear programming (Chapter 8) When the requirement that some or all of the decision variables must be integers (whole numbers) is added to a linear programming problem, it becomes one of integer (linear) programming. Integer programming can also be used as an auxiliary tool for solving a host of difficult managerial problems.

Nonlinear programming (Chapter 8) Mathematical programming problems, where the goal and/or one or more of the requirements imposed on the problem are expressed by nonlinear functions (see Appendix A), are referred to as nonlinear programming problems.

Goal programming (Chapter 9) This is a variant of linear programming that is used when multiple goals exist.

Distribution problems (Chapter 10) The transportation of a commodity from sources of supply to destinations, at minimum cost (or maximum profit), and the assignment of workers (or equipment) to jobs are examples of what are termed *distribution problems*. These are also a special case of linear programming.

Linear programming can be used to solve a diversity of problems involving networks (Chapter 11), dynamic programming subproblems (Chapter 12), competitive games (Chapter 4), and inventories (Chapter 14).

The uses of mathematical programming, especially of linear programming, are so common that "canned" computer programs can be found today in just about any organization that has a computer. A glance at almost any issue of a professional or trade journal reveals the many applications of mathematical programming. To date, thousands of examples of successful applications have been published. For instance, the petroleum industry makes extensive use of linear programming techniques, and integer programming is increasingly applied to the complex problems of scheduling operations. Process industries such as chemicals, food, steel, and rubber are known as especially heavy users of mathematical programming.

6

Linear programming—foundations

PART A: BASICS

6.1 The nature of linear programming problems.
6.2 Formulation.
6.3 General formulation and terminology.
6.4 The graphical method of solution.
6.5 Utilization of the resources—Slack and surplus variables.
6.6 Concluding remarks.
6.7 Problems for Part A.

PART B: EXTENSIONS

6.8 The simplex method.
6.9 Computerization.
6.10 Special situations in the simplex method.
6.11 Problems for Part B.
6.12 Case–The Daphne Jewelry Company.
6.13 Glossary.
6.14 References and bibliography.

Linear programming (LP) is one of the best known tools of management science. Perhaps the most general statement of its objective is that it is used to determine an optimal allocation of an organization's limited resources among competing demands. There are many managerial problems that can be considered allocation problems. These range from product-mix and blending problems to bus scheduling and dietary planning.

Linear programming deals with a special class of allocation problems; namely, those in which all the mathematical functions in the model are linear.

Part A of this chapter presents the general formulation of the LP problem and the graphical technique for its solution. In Part B, the simplex method of solution, a most efficient algorithm of linear programming, is presented. Some important extensions of linear programming are then presented in Chapters 8–10.

LEARNING OBJECTIVES

The student should be able to:

a. Describe the nature of allocation problems such as product-mix and blending.
b. Describe the structure of an LP problem and, specifically, the concepts of objective function, constraints, and nonnegativity.
c. List the assumptions of the model.
d. Discuss the concept relating to solutions in linear programming (feasible, optimal, infeasible, multiple, and unbounded).
e. Formulate simple LP problems.
f. Describe and use the graphical method for solving LP problems.
g. Describe the concepts of slack and dual variables.
h. Properly address situations involving allocation of resources in the optimal solution; compute values for slack and surplus variables.

Extensions

i. Describe the general logic of the simplex method.
j. Build a simplex tableau and describe its components.
k. Solve problems by the simplex method.
l. Describe special situations in linear programming such as degeneracy, unbounded solutions, and multiple solutions.

PART A: BASICS

The Sekido Corporation—Part I

Suji Okita and his wife Keiko were heartily enjoying their dinner of fresh shrimp, their first unhurried meal in days. Final tests had just been successfully completed on the new "slit matrix" television projection system Suji had developed, and the outlook was encouraging. "They'll be installing the system on two models for initial sales next week," he was saying to Keiko. "I wish we had a larger work force, more machine time, and better marketing capabilities; I'm sure we could make considerably more profit. But even as it is, we don't know how many of each model to produce."

Keiko was thinking about her problem at the Toshida Paint Company. A new, expensive, special-purpose paint, Sungold, was becoming very popular, and the production manager had asked Keiko to see if she could find a combination of two new ingredients, code-named Alpha and Beta, that would result in an equivalent brilliance and hue but at less cost than the original ingredients. She felt confident she could.

Keiko did not realize that her problem, a typical *blending* problem, was in many ways equivalent to Suji's, a typical *product-mix* problem.

6.1 THE NATURE OF LINEAR PROGRAMMING PROBLEMS

Two prototype LP problems

Allocation problems appear in several forms. Two of the most common are the **product-mix problem** faced by Suji and the **blending problem** faced by Keiko.

The product-mix problem

Maximize profit with fixed resources

Product-mix type problems are among the most common in linear programming. They are especially important in planning and scheduling situations. In a product-mix problem, there are two or more *products* (also called *candidates* or *activities*) such as TV models in the previous example, competing for limited resources such as limited production capacity. The problem is to find out *which products* to include in the production plan *and in what quantities* these should be included (product mix) in order to maximize profit, market share, or some other such goal.

Allocating scarce resources

Although a solution to a product-mix problem does specify the quantities to be produced, what it tells more generally, in effect, is *how to allocate* scarce resources. This is because the technology of production is given and once a decision has been made on the products and quantities to produce, a determination is made of what resources to use (allocate) and in what quantities.

The blending problem

Blending problems involve the determination of the *best blend* of available ingredients to form a certain quantity of a product under strict specifications. The best blend means the least-cost blend of inputs required to meet a designated level of output or given specifications. Blending problems are especially important in the process industries such as petroleum, chemicals, and food, and in fields where a certain level of service is desired at minimum cost. The decision maker must determine the ingredients to use and in what quantities.

In this respect, the blending problem is similar to the product-mix problem. However, the objectives usually differ. In the product-mix problem, the profit derived from selling the products made from the given amount of resources is to be maximized. In blending, the cost of the ingredients is to be minimized, while adhering to certain specifications and using certain ingredients (resources). In the *blending* problem, an attempt is made to use *as few resources as possible* to provide *a given product* (or service) level.

Minimize resource use to obtain a fixed output

Therefore, a blending problem is also considered a problem of allocating resources in the best manner, and in both cases we try to achieve the highest ratio of outputs to inputs; that is, to maximize productivity.

6.2 FORMULATION

The linear programming model

Management science models, as the reader may recall, are composed of three components: the *decision* (controllable) variables, the *environment* (uncontrollable) parameters, and the *result* (dependent) variables. The LP model is composed of the same components, but they assume different names, as shown in Figure 6.1.

a. The decision variables The decision variables in LP depend on the type of LP problem being considered. They can be the quantities of

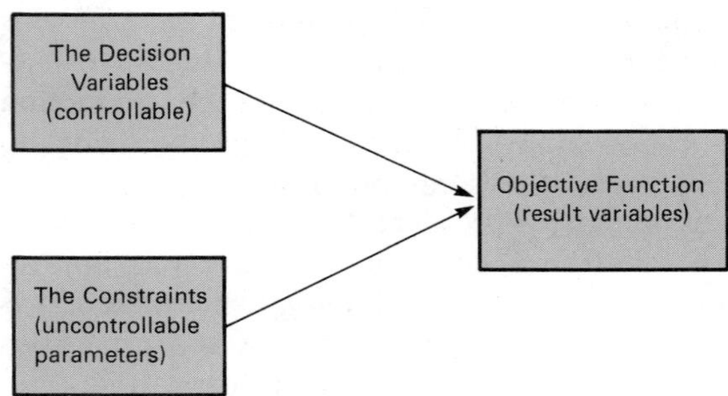

FIGURE 6.1 The linear programming model

the resources to be allocated, or the number of units to be produced. The decision maker is searching for the value of these unknown variables (usually denoted by x_1, x_2, . . . or x, y, and z) that will provide an **optimal solution** to the problem.

b. The objective function A linear programming model attempts to optimize a single goal, written as a **linear function;** for example, total profit = $5x_1 + 7x_2 + 1x_3$. That is, it attempts to find either the maximum level of a desirable goal, such as total share of the market or total profit, or the minimum level of some undesirable outcome, such as total cost.

c. The constraints The decision maker is searching for the values of the decision variables that will maximize (or minimize) the value of the objective function. Such a process is usually subject to several uncontrollable restrictions, requirements, or regulations that are called **constraints.** These constraints are expressed as linear inequalities and/or equations.

Two examples

Let us return to the product-mix and blending problems and present both with the relevant data. Then, we will formulate both problems in the general structure of the linear programming model.

Example: The product-mix (maximization) problem

The two models of color TV sets produced by the Sekido Corporation, Suji's employer, will be designated as A and B. The company is in the market to make money; that is, its objective is profit maximization. The profit realized is \$300 from set A and \$250 from set B. Obviously, the more sets produced and sold, the better. The trouble is that there are certain limitations that prevent Sekido Company from producing and selling thousands of sets daily. These limitations are:

1. Availability of only 40 hours of labor each day in the production department (a labor constraint).
2. A daily availability of only 45 hours of machine time (a machining constraint).
3. Inability to sell more than 12 sets of model A each day (a marketing constraint).

Sekido's problem is to determine *how many sets of each model to produce each day so that the total profit will be as large as possible.* Note that Sekido produces only a small number of sets each day due to the specialized manufacturing process required for these sets. In solving this problem, the above limitations and the known technology of manufacturing must be taken into consideration.

The linear programming approach is divided into two steps: first, the problem is set up or *formulated*, and then the model is solved.

Formulation of the product-mix problem

Decision variables

The decision variables The decision variables in this case are:

x_1 = The number of sets of model A to be produced daily
x_2 = The number of sets of model B to be produced daily

Objective function

The objective function The daily profit realized from selling sets of model A is $300x_1$ (i.e., the profit per unit times the number of units). Similarly for model B, a profit of $250x_2$ will be realized. The total profit, z, is, therefore, $300x_1 + 250x_2$. This total profit is called the **objective function.**

Remember that Sekido wishes to maximize the total profit; that is, it wants to maximize the value of the objective function z.

The constraints on the system The limitations on the system are given as:

Constraints

1. Labor constraint. The production department has only 40 hours of labor available each day to manufacture both models. It is known that each set of model A, being of higher quality, requires two hours of labor, whereas each set of model B requires only one hour. This limitation can be expressed as:

Demand for labor				Supply
Total labor for model A		Total labor for model B		Total labor available
$2x_1$	$+$	$1x_2$	$\leq$	40

Note that the less-than-or-equal-to sign ($\leq$) is used. That is, 40 hours is the *available* capacity, which does not necessarily have to be used in full. Also note that all variable coefficients are included (e.g., 0 and 1) to follow "standard LP form."

2. Machine time constraint. There are up to 45 machine-hours available per day. Machine processing time for one unit of model A is one hour and for one unit of model B, three hours. This limitation can be expressed as:

$$1x_1 + 3x_2 \leq 45$$

3. Marketing constraint. It is only possible to sell *up to* 12 units of model A each day. This can be expressed as: $1x_1 \leq 12$; that is, x_1 is smaller than or equal to 12. This constraint is written in standard form as:

$$1x_1 + 0x_2 \leq 12$$

4. Nonnegativity constraint. Finally, it is impossible to produce a negative number of sets; that is, both x_1 and x_2 must be **nonnegative** (zero or positive). This constraint is expressed as:

Nonnegativity

$$1x_1 \geq 0, \quad 1x_2 \geq 0$$

In summary, the problem is to find the best daily production plan (or program) so that the total profit will be maximized.[1]

The problem, then, can be summarized in standard form as follows. Find x_1 and x_2 that maximize z, the objective function, subject to constraints.

maximize $z = 300x_1 + 250x_2$
subject to:
$2x_1 + 1x_2 \leq 40$ (labor constraint)
$1x_1 + 3x_2 \leq 45$ (machine time constraint)
$1x_1 + 0x_2 \leq 12$ (marketing constraint)
$1x_1 + 0x_2 \geq 0$
$0x_1 + 1x_2 \geq 0$ (nonnegativity constraints in standard form)[2]

We shall return to the solution of this problem later.

Example: The blending problem (minimization)

In preparing Sungold paint, it is required that the paint have a brilliance rating of at least 300 degrees and a hue level of at least 250 degrees. Brilliance and hue levels are determined by two ingredients: Alpha and Beta. Both Alpha and Beta contribute equally to the brilliance rating, one ounce (dry weight) of either producing one degree of brilliance in one case of paint. However, the hue is controlled entirely by the amount of Alpha, one ounce of it producing three degrees of hue in one case of paint. The cost of Alpha is 45 cents per ounce, and the cost of Beta is 12 cents per ounce. Assuming that the objective is to minimize the cost of

[1] Since production continues day after day, it is not necessary to complete all sets at the end of the day; that is, a fractional number of sets is permissible (e.g., 5.73 sets). However, had it been necessary to complete all sets by the end of the day, additional constraints limiting x_1 and x_2 to whole numbers would have been added. Such an addition changes the problem to one of *integer programming.*

[2] In later sections of this book, we *may not* write these constraints in the formulation of problems. However, they are always implied, and the reader should remember their existence. Also, in most LP computer programs, it is not necessary to input these constraints; they are automatically assumed.

FIGURE 6.2
The blending problem

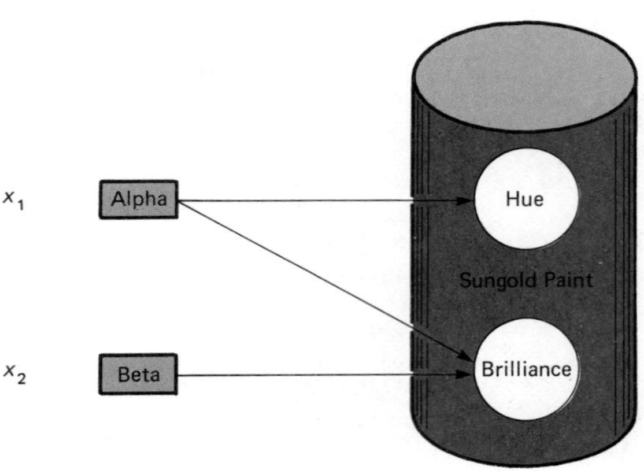

the resources, then the problem is to find the quantity of Alpha and Beta to be included in the preparation of each case of paint.[3] The problem is shown graphically in Figure 6.2

Formulation of the blending problem

Decision variables

The *decision variables* are:

x_1 = Quantity of Alpha to be included, in ounces, in each case of paint
x_2 = Quantity of Beta to be included, in ounces, in each case of paint

Objective function

The objective is to minimize the total cost of the ingredients required for one case of paint. Since the cost of Alpha is 45 cents per ounce, and since x_1 ounces are going to be used in each case, then the cost per case is $45x_1$. Similarly, for Beta the cost is $12x_2$. The total cost is, therefore, $45x_1 + 12x_2$, and as our objective function, it is to be *minimized* subject to the constraints of the following specifications:

Constraints

1. To provide a brilliance rating of at least 300 degrees in each case. Since each ounce of Alpha or Beta increases the brightness by one degree, the following relationship exists:

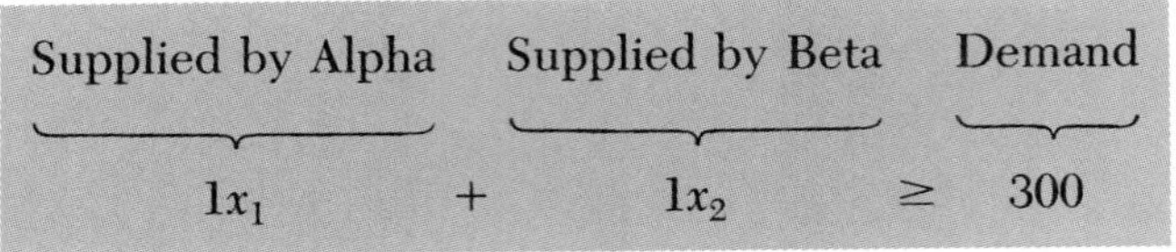

[3] An optimal answer for one case of paint will remain optimal for any number of cases as long as the relationships are linear. The total quantity of paint to be produced is, of course, larger than one case, and it is determined mainly by the demand and the manufacturing technology.

2. To provide a hue level of at least 250 degrees. The effect of Alpha (alone) on hue can similarly be written as:

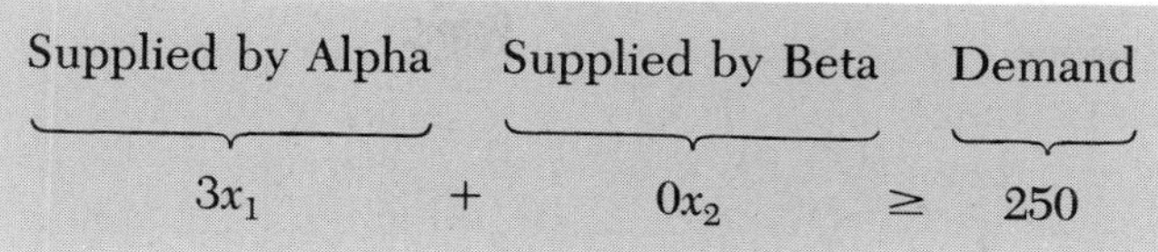

$$\underbrace{3x_1}_{\text{Supplied by Alpha}} + \underbrace{0x_2}_{\text{Supplied by Beta}} \geq \underbrace{250}_{\text{Demand}}$$

In summary, the blending problem is formulated as follows. Find x_1 and x_2 that:

minimize $z = 45x_1 + 12x_2$
subject to:
$1x_1 + 1x_2 \geq 300$ (brightness specification)
$3x_1 + 0x_2 \geq 250$ (hue specification)

As mentioned before, the nonnegativity requirement will not be stated.

The blending problem is going to be solved later in the chapter. At this time, the reader may note that the blending problem is very similar in structure to the product-mix problem. One difference, however, is that here we wish to minimize the value of the objective function, while in the product-mix problem we were maximizing the objective function.

Note: In our example, all the maximization constraints are of the less than or equal to ($\leq$) type, and all the minimization constraints are of the greater than or equal to ($\geq$) type. In reality, when we deal with larger problems, we find all types of constraints, $\leq$, $\geq$, and $=$ in both types of problems, as will be demonstrated later.

6.3 GENERAL FORMULATION AND TERMINOLOGY

In the previous section, two classical managerial problems were formulated. Let us now generalize the formulation.[4]

---

[4] The problem area has been of interest to economists and mathematicians for a long time. The pioneering work in formulating the LP problem was done by the Russian economist L. V. Kantorovich. Several other economists, such as T. C. Koopmans, R. Dorfman, W. W. Cooper, A. Charnes, H. W. Kuhn, and A. W. Tucker, were important contributors to the area. But the person who should get most of the credit for the breakthrough in solving linear programming is George B. Dantzig (in 1947).

Formulation of a linear programming (LP) problem

Every LP problem is composed of:

LP components

Decision variables The variables whose values are unknown and are searched for. Usually they are designated by x_1, x_2, and so on.

Objective function This is a mathematical expression, given as a linear function, that shows the relationship between the decision variables and a *single goal* (or objective) under consideration. The objective function is a measure of goal attainment. Examples of such goals are total profit, total cost, share of the market, and the like.

Multiple goals

If the managerial problem involves multiple goals, one can use the following two-step approach.

1. Select a primary goal whose level is to be maximized or minimized.
2. Transform the other goals into constraints, which must only be satisfied.

For example, one may attempt to maximize profit (the primary goal) subject to a growth rate of at least 12 percent per year (a secondary goal).

An alternative approach is to combine several goals into one (e.g., through trade-offs, as discussed in Chapter 4). Such an approach is more complicated.

Optimization Linear programming attempts to either maximize or minimize the values of the objective function.

Profit or cost coefficients The coefficients of the variables in the objective function (e.g., 300 and 250 in the product-mix example or 45 and 12 in the blending problem) are called the profit (or cost) coefficients. They express the *rate* at which the value of the objective function increases or decreases by including in the solution one unit of each of the decision variables.

Constraints The maximization (or minimization) is performed subject to a set of constraints. Therefore, linear programming can be defined as a *constrained optimization problem.* These constraints are expressed in the form of linear inequalities (or, sometimes, equalities). They reflect the fact that resources are limited (e.g., in a product-mix problem) or they specify the product requirements (e.g., in a blending problem).

Input-output (technology) coefficients The coefficients of the constraints' variables are called the *input-output* coefficients. They indicate the rate at which a given resource is depleted or utilized. They appear on the left-hand side of the constraints.

Capacities The capacities (or availability) of the various resources, usually expressed as some upper or lower limit, are given on the *right-hand side* of the constraints. The right-hand side also expresses minimum requirements.

Nonnegativity The standard format of linear programming (shown in footnote 5) includes the nonnegativity inequalities. They are needed for the simplex solution procedure and to communicate the fact that negative values of physical quantities do not exist.

Example

These major components of a linear programming model[5] are illustrated for the blending problem (discussed in the previous section).

Find: x_1 and x_2 that will minimize the value of the linear objective function:

Decision variables

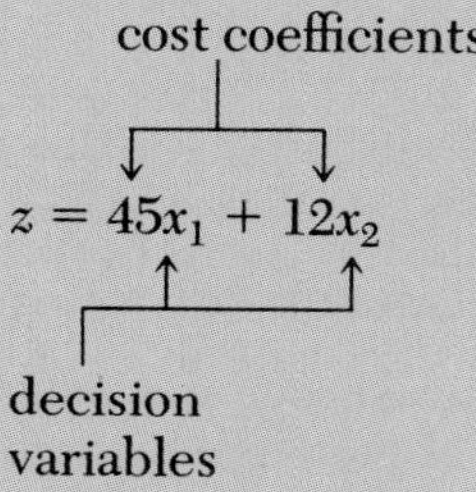

Objective function

subject to the linear constraints:

$$1x_1 + 1x_2 \geq 300$$
$$3x_1 + 0x_2 \geq 250$$

input-output coefficients — capacities or requirements

Constraints

---

[5] The general linear programming problem can be presented in the following mathematical terms. Let:

a_{ij} = The input-output coefficients
c_j = The cost (profit) coefficients
b_i = The capacities (right-hand side)
x_j = The decision variables

Find a vector $(x_1, \ldots, x_n)$ that minimizes (or maximizes) a linear objective function $F(x)$ where:

$$F(x) = c_1x_1 + c_2x_2 + \cdots + c_jx_j + \cdots + c_nx_n \qquad (6.1)$$

subject to the linear constraints:

$$\left.\begin{array}{l} a_{11}x_1 + a_{12}x_2 + \cdots + a_{1n}x_n \leq b_1 \\ a_{21}x_1 + a_{22}x_2 + \cdots + a_{2n}x_n \leq b_2 \\ \ldots \quad \ldots \quad \ldots \quad \ldots \quad \ldots \\ a_{i1}x_1 + a_{i2}x_2 + \cdots + a_{in}x_n \leq b_i \\ \ldots \quad \ldots \quad \ldots \quad \ldots \quad \ldots \\ a_{m1}x_1 + a_{m2}x_2 + \cdots + a_{mn}x_n \leq b_m \end{array}\right\} \qquad (6.2)$$

and the nonnegativity constraints:

$$x_1 \geq 0,\ x_2 \geq 0,\ \ldots \qquad (6.3)$$

Nonnegativity

and subject to the nonnegativity of the decision variables: $x_1 \geq 0$; $x_2 \geq 0$

Advantages of linear programming

Linear programming is a tool that can be used to solve allocation-type problems. Such problems are very common and extremely important in organizations. Their solution is difficult due to the fact that an infinite number of feasible solutions may exist. Linear programming not only provides the optimal solution, but does so in a very efficient manner. Further, it provides additional information concerning the value of the resources that are allocated, as will be discussed in Chapter 8.

Limitations of linear programming due to assumptions

The applicability of linear programming is limited by several assumptions. As in all mathematical models, assumptions are made for reducing the complex real-world problem into a simplified form. The major assumptions are summarized below.

Eight limiting assumptions

Certainty It is assumed that all data involved in the linear programming problem are known with certainty.[6]

Linear objective function It is assumed that the objective function is linear. This means that per unit cost, price, or profit are assumed to be unaffected by changes in production methods or quantities produced or sold.

Linear constraints The constraints are also assumed to be linear. This means that all the input-output coefficients are considered to be unaffected by a change of methods, quantities, or utilization level.

Nonnegativity Negative activity levels (or negative production) are not permissible. It is required, therefore, that all decision variables take nonnegative values.

Additivity It is assumed that the total utilization of each resource is determined by adding together that portion of the resource required for the production of each of the various products or activities. The **assumption of additivity** also means that the effectiveness of the joint performance of activities, under any circumstances, equals the sum of the effectiveness resulting from the individual performance of these activities.

Divisibility Variables can, in general, be classified as continuous or discrete. Continuous variables are subject to *measurement* (e.g., weight, temperature), whereas discrete variables are those that can be counted: 1, 2, 3, . . . In linear programming, it is assumed that the unknown variables x_1, x_2 . . . , are continuous, that is, they can take any fractional value. If

[6] In problems under risk, the expected value of the input data can be considered as a constant, thus enabling the treatment of risky situations by linear programming. (For details, see Dantzig [4].)

the variables are restricted to whole numbers and thus are indivisible, a problem in **integer programming** exists (see Chapter 8).

Independence Complete independence of coefficients is assumed, both among activities and among resources. For example, the price of one product has no effect on the price of another.

Proportionality The requirement that the objective function and constraints must be linear is a proportionality requirement. This means that the amount of resources used, and the resulting value of the objective function, will be proportional to the value of the decision variables.

Solving linear programs

A set of decision variables, each having a value, is called a *solution*. For example, $x_1 = 5$ and $x_2 = 0$ is a solution for the Sekido Corporation problem. Proposed solutions to a linear programming problem that *satisfy all the constraints* are called *feasible*. The collection of **feasible solutions** is called the **feasible solution space** or **area.** Any proposed solution that violates one or more of the constraints is termed **infeasible.**

Feasible or infeasible?

The major task in applying linear programming is the formulation of the problem. Once a problem has been formulated, one of several available methods of solution can be applied. Normally, this is done with the aid of a computer. With the exception of Karmarkar's Algorithm, described below, of all the solution methods, only two have a significant value. They are (1) the *graphical method,* whose main purpose is to illustrate the concepts involved in the solution process; and (2) the general, computationally powerful **simplex method** and its variants. In Section 6.4 the graphical method is illustrated; the simplex method is presented in Part B.

The simplex method

Two new procedures for solving linear programming problems have recently been reported. The first, reported in 1979, is called the ellipsoid algorithm and the second, reported in 1984, is known as Karmarkar's algorithm.

The Ellipsoid Algorithm This method was developed by a Russian mathematician, L. G. Khachian, and was first described in a report in 1979 [5]. The approach involves shrinking an ellipsoid that surrounds the feasible solution space until it converges on the optimum solution. Its advantage was purported to be that it solved problems in a period of time-related linearly to the complexity of the problem, rather than exponentially, as is characterized by the simplex method. However, in practice, it was found that the linear increase was so great that it provided no major improvement over the simplex method for most practical-sized problems.

Karmarkar's Algorithm In this method, the algorithm moves to a point *within* the solution space instead of on the boundary, and creates sequences of spheres that converge to the optimum vertex. It, too, solves LP problems in a linear amount of time, but is much more efficient for large problems than either the Ellipsoid Algorithm or the simplex [8,9,10].

Testing is currently proceeding with the new algorithm, and the applications look very promising.

6.4 THE GRAPHICAL METHOD OF SOLUTION

A graphical solution

The graphical method is used mainly to illustrate certain characteristics of LP problems and to help in explaining the simplex method. The only case where it has a practical value is in the solution of small problems with two decision variables (such as x_1 and x_2) and only a few constraints, or, problems with two constraints and only a few decision variables.[7]

Example: A maximization problem

In order to illustrate the graphical method, let us reproduce the product-mix problem discussed previously:

$$\text{maximize } z = 300x_1 + 250x_2$$

subject to:

$$2x_1 + 1x_2 \leq 40 \quad \text{((labor constraint)}$$
$$1x_1 + 3x_2 \leq 45 \quad \text{(machining constraint)}$$
$$1x_1 + 0x_2 \leq 12 \quad \text{(marketing constraint)}$$

Since there are only two decision variables, the problem can be graphically treated in a two-dimensional space.

Graphical analysis

Originated by Descartes

The plotting of algebraic equations and **inequalities** in terms of geometric lines and curves was initiated by the French philosopher Descartes in the 17th century. Two straight lines intersecting at right angles are used as a reference and points are located by giving two coordinates (distances from each of the lines). The plane formed by the two lines is divided into four regions called quadrants. An example of such a system is shown in Figure 6.3. We use x_1 and x_2 to designate the lines. Sometimes x and y are used instead.

Since the nonnegativity constraints appear in all linear programming problems, we are limited to the 1st quadrant only ($x_1 \geq 0$, $x_2 \geq 0$). The graphical solution procedure consists of two phases: *(a)* graphing the feasible area, and *(b)* identifying the optimal solution.

Graphing the feasible area

The graphical method starts with the graphing of a *feasible* area within which a search for the optimal solution is to be conducted. The feasible

[7] In the latter case, duality theory (Chapter 8) is used to transform the problem into one with two decision variables prior to the use of the graphical method. Problems with three decision variables can be solved graphically, but the graphical method is a cumbersome process to use in that situation.

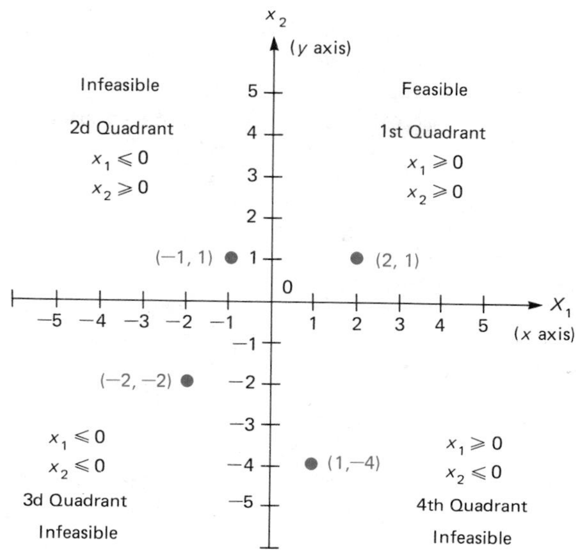

FIGURE 6.3
Feasible and infeasible quadrants on the two-dimensional grid.

Graphing the constraints

area is established through graphing all of the inequalities and equations that describe the constraints.

Graphing the first (labor) constraint (Figure 6.4) This is expressed as $2x_1 + 1x_2 \leq 40$. The steps in drawing the constraint are:

Step 1. Since an inequality of the type *less than or equal to* has, in effect, two parts, we will first consider only the equality part of the

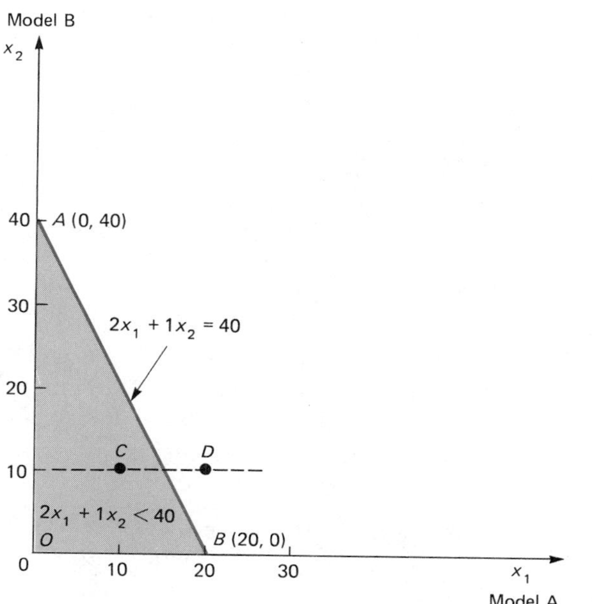

FIGURE 6.4
The first constraint

constraint. In our example, it will be $2x_1 + 1x_2 = 40$. Since an equation can be shown graphically as a straight line (linear function in a two-dimensional space), it is sufficient to find the coordinates of two points to graph the entire equation as a line. To do so, x_1 is first set to zero (i.e., do not produce TV model A). This will yield a point where the equation $2x_1 + 1x_2 = 40$ intersects the x_2 axis (point A in Figure 6.4).[8] When we set $x_1 = 0$, then $2(0) + x_2 = 40$, or $x_2 = 40$. This solution means that if only model B sets are produced, it will be at a rate of 40 per day. Thus, point A will have the coordinates of (0, 40). Similarly, if x_2 is set to zero, then:

$$2x_1 + 0 = 40$$

or:

$$x_1 = 20 \text{ (produce 20 units of model A)}$$

This is shown as point B (20, 0) in Figure 6.4.

Step 2. Joining points A and B by a straight line is a representation of the equation $2x_1 + x_2 = 40$. However, it is not just the equation that is of interest, but also the inequality $2x_1 + x_2 \leq 40$. This inequality is represented by an *area* below and to the bottom left of the equality (Figure 6.4).[9] This area represents all the combinations that use 40 or less units of labor.

Inequality represents an area

How to find the side of the constraint on which the feasible area is located There are several methods that can be used to find the location of the feasible area.

Method A. Take an arbitrary point and check if it is feasible. If the point is feasible, then the entire area is feasible. For example, point C in Figure 6.4, which is inside the area, has coordinates of (10, 10). If we substitute these coordinates into the constraint $2x_1 + 1x_2 \leq 40$, we get $2(10) + 1(10) = 30$. Since 30 is smaller than 40, the point is in the feasible area. Point $D = (20, 10)$, on the other hand, is not feasible, since $2(20) + 1(10) = 50$.

Method B. Use the following rules:

- If the constraint does not pass through the origin, then: For $\leq$ constraints, the feasible area will be on the side of the line that is *closer* to the origin (0, 0). For example, point C in Figure 6.4.
- For $\geq$ constraints, the feasible area will be on the side that is *away* from the origin. For example, if the line in Figure 6.4 had been $2x_1 + x_2 \geq 40$, then point D would have been in the feasible area.
- If the constraint goes through the origin, use Method A.

---

[8] The equation describing the x_2 axis is $x_1 = 0$; that is, any point *on* the x_2 axis will have a coordinate of $x_1 = 0$ and an appropriate x_2 coordinate.

[9] Note that the area *includes* the line, since the inequality includes the "=" sign. (That is, it is not a "strict" inequality.)

The inequality area in Figure 6.4 would normally include negative values of x_1 and x_2, except for the fact that in linear programming, negative values are excluded by the nonnegativity constraints $x_1 \geq 0$ and $x_2 \geq 0$. The end result is a feasible area inside (and including the boundary of) the triangle *O–A–B* in Figure 6.4 (shaded). Note that this shaded area includes an infinite number of solution combinations of models A and B, all of which meet the labor limitation.

Graphing the second (machine time) constraint Similarly, the shaded area *O–C–D* in Figure 6.5 represents the area of feasible solutions for the machining constraint $1x_1 + 3x_2 \leq 45$. This area is constructed as follows:

Step 1. The equation portion of the inequality is considered:

$$1x_1 + 3x_2 = 45$$

Step 2. x_1 is set to zero. Solving for x_2 we get:

$$x_2 = 15 \text{ (point } C\text{)}$$

Step 3. x_2 is set to 0. Solving for x_1:

$$x_1 = 45 \text{ (point } D\text{)}$$

Finally, points *C* and *D* are connected by a straight line, and the feasible area is then to the *left* of, and including, the line.

Graphing the third (marketing) constraint Next, the equality part $x_1 = 12$ of the marketing constraint $x_1 \leq 12$ is plotted as a straight line, vertically from point *E* and parallel to the x_2 axis (Figure 6.6). Again, the feasible area is left of, and including, the line.

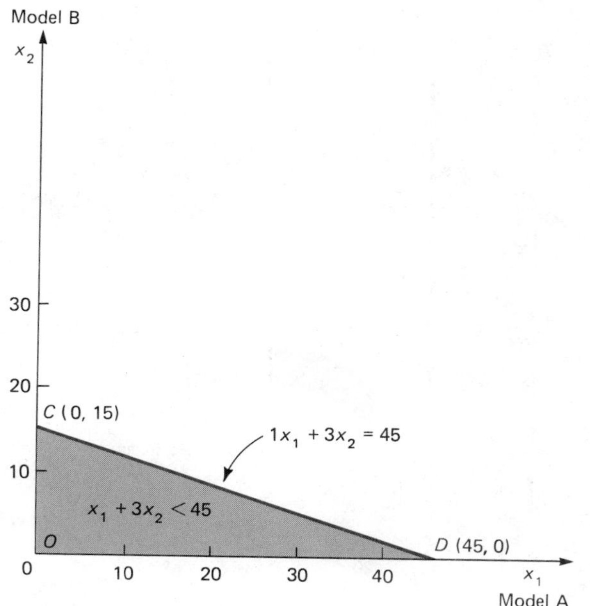

FIGURE 6.5
The second constraint

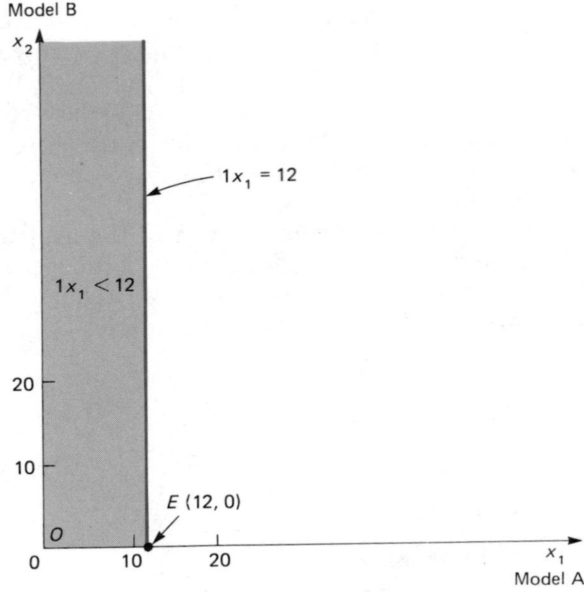

FIGURE 6.6
The third constraint

Combining the constraints Once all the constraints have been drawn, they can be put on one graph. As a matter of practicality they can be built on one graph from the beginning. We used the three graphs of Figures 6.4, 6.5, and 6.6 for instructional purposes only. The combination of all constraints is shown in Figure 6.7. The shaded area *O–C–G–E* is

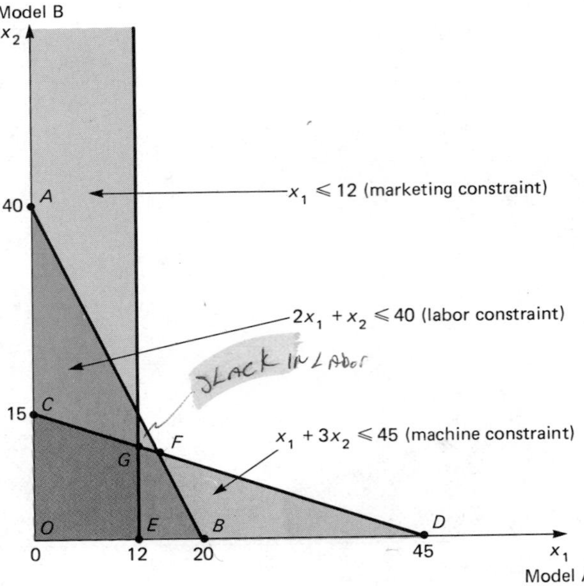

FIGURE 6.7
All three constraints simultaneously

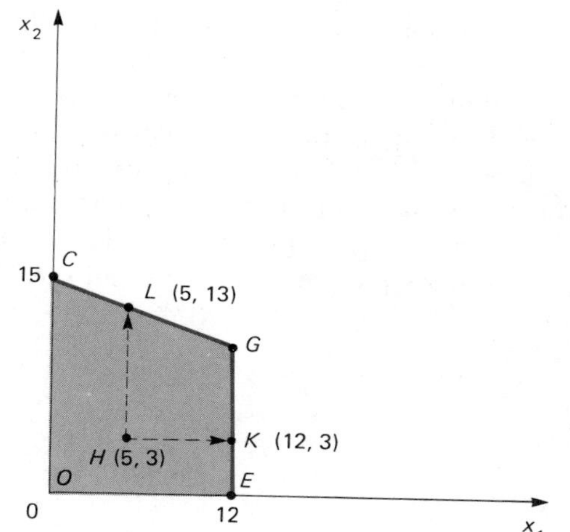

FIGURE 6.8
The feasible area

the area that is to the lower left of all equations simultaneously. Therefore, any solution in this area is *feasible* with respect to *all* the constraints. To put it another way, solutions in this area do not violate any of the constraints. This area, including the boundary, is called the feasible solution space and is reproduced in Figure 6.8.

Feasible—the area within *all* constraints

Identifying an optimal solution

Any point in the shaded area of Figure 6.8 and its boundary is a feasible solution. Since there are an infinite number of points in this area, there are an *infinite number of feasible solutions* for this problem. To find an optimal one, it is necessary to identify a solution (point) in the feasible area that maximizes the profit (objective) function.

Infinite number of possible solutions

How can this task be accomplished? Let us examine a feasible solution inside the feasible area of Figure 6.8; say, point *H*. This point is a solution plan that calls for five sets of model A ($x_1 = 5$) and three sets of model B ($x_2 = 3$). This solution is not optimal, since production of x_1 can be increased from point *H* to point *K* (12 units of x_1 and 3 of x_2), resulting in a higher profit. Notice that such an increase may continue only until we are limited by a constraint. Similarly, point *L*, where more x_2 is produced that at *H*, will result in a higher profit than point *H*.

The reason that both points *K* and *L* are better than point *H* is because both yield a higher profit, since the coefficients of the objective function are positive (more units, more profit). It can, however, be shown that no matter what sign the coefficients of the objective function have, there will always be at least one point somewhere on a boundary of the feasible area that is *superior* to any point inside the area. Therefore, an optimal solution to a linear programming problem can *never* be inside the feasible area but must be on a boundary. Furthermore, it can be shown that an optimal solution must be at a corner (called a **vertex**) where two (or more)

On the boundary

constraints intersect.[10] Therefore, an efficient search for an optimal solution need only consider corner points (O, C, G, and E in our case). Two methods can be used for such a search.

To a corner

Enumeration

*1. **Enumeration of all corner points*** In this method, the solution values at all the corner points are compared. This is done by determining the coordinates of all corner points and then computing and comparing the values of the objective function at these points. Let us demonstrate: For points O, C, and E, the exact coordinates can be read directly from Figure 6.8, as given below:

Point	x_1	x_2
O	0	0
C	0	15
E	12	0
G	?	?

For point G, the approximate coordinates can be read from the graph, or exact coordinates can be computed as follows: Point G is at the intersection of two straight lines. Therefore, the value at point G (as given by x_1 and x_2) must be the same for the two intersecting lines. Such a value can be found by simultaneously solving the two intersecting linear equations, one of which describes the marketing constraint and the other the machine time constraint.[11] In this case:

$$\text{Equation 1:}\quad 1x_1 = 12 \qquad \text{(marketing constraint)}$$
$$\text{Equation 2:}\quad 1x_1 + 3x_2 = 45 \qquad \text{(machine constraint)}$$

The solution is simple in this situation, since the value of one decision variable, x_1, is already known to be 12. This value is introduced into Equation 2, which can then be solved. We get:

$$1x_1 + 3x_2 = 12 + 3x_2 = 45, \quad \text{or} \quad 3x_2 = 33, \quad \text{or} \quad x_2 = 11$$

Therefore, the coordinates of point G are (12, 11).

Identify the best corner

Now the profits at each corner point can be calculated, using the objective function $300x_1 + 250x_2$. The results are shown in Table 6.1.

The point that yields the greatest profit is point G. The optimal solution, therefore, is to produce 12 units of TV model A and 11 units of TV model B. The total profit is \$6,350.

The process of comparing profits at all corner points may be very lengthy, since in larger linear programming problems many corners exist.

[10] If only one optimal solution exists, it must be on a vertex. If more than one optimal solution exists, then *at least* two optimal solutions *must* be on two adjoining vertices, and the others will be on the boundary connecting them.

[11] For methods of solving simultaneous equations, see Appendix A.

TABLE 6.1
Profit values at corner points

Point (corner)	*Solution coordinates*	*Total profit* $300x_1 + 250x_2 =$
O	(0, 0)	300 (0) + 250 (0) = 0
C	(0, 15)	300 (0) + 250(15) = $3,750
E	(12, 0)	300(12) + 250 (0) = $3,600
G	(12, 11)	300(12) + 250(11) = $6,350 ←*Maximum*

The second graphical method that can be used for the search of the corners is more efficient.[12] This method is presented next.

2. The use of isoprofit (constant profit) lines According to this procedure, the optimal solution can be found by using the *slope* of the objective function as a guide. Let us illustrate.

Slope of the objective function

In examining solution H (5, 3) in Figure 6.8, it was indicated that better solutions are available [e.g., K (12, 3)]. The question is: In what direction should one move to find better solutions? The answer to this question is found from the objective function. If the objective function (a profit function in our example) is graphed and the direction of increasing profit is identified, then when one starts moving the profit function in that direction, the profit will increase and increase. The limit to the increase is reached when the function touches some point(s) on the boundary of the feasible area (if the feasible area is bounded).[13] This point is then an optimal solution. The graphical method accomplishes this task in a systematic fashion.

Graphing an objective function. The graphing of the profit function may at first appear difficult because profit functions (such as $z = 300x_1 + 250x_2$) describe an infinite number of equations that depend on the value of z and, therefore, cannot be presented as a single line. To overcome this difficulty, a *family* of linear equations, called **isoprofit lines,** is built by assigning various values to z (where z is the total profit).[14] Graphically, such a family can be plotted as many lines *parallel* to each other (see Figure 6.9).[15] The location of each line depends on the value of z.

Isoprofit lines

Let us assume that $z = 1{,}500$.[16] In this case, the profit equation $300x_1 + 250x_2 = 1{,}500$ can be drawn as a straight line exactly in the same manner as the equality constraints were drawn. This line intersects

[12] The simplex method (see Section 6.8) is a nongraphical procedure for efficiently conducting a similar search.

[13] A feasible area may be unbounded from one or more sides. For a treatment of such cases, see Dantzig [4].

[14] An isoprofit line is a line (a collection of points), each of whose points designates a solution with the *same* profit.

[15] In a cost minimization problem these are termed *isocost* lines.

[16] Any arbitrary profit figure will work. However, it is simple to pick a profit number that gives an integer as an answer to x_1 when we set $x_2 = 0$, and vice versa. A good choice is to use a number that is divided easily by the coefficients of both variables. For example, $1{,}500 \div 300 = 5$, and $1{,}500 \div 250 = 6$.

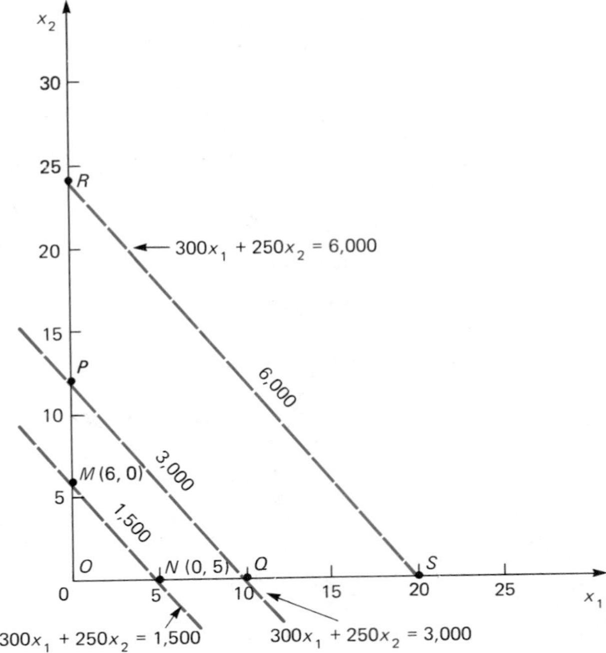

FIGURE 6.9 Family of isoprofit equations $z = 300x_1 + 250x_2$

the x_1 axis at point N in Figure 6.9 (where $x_2 = 0$ and $x_1 = 5$) and the x_2 axis at point M where $x_1 = 0$ and $x_2 = 6$). Point N tells us how many units of product x_1 *alone* are required to produce a profit of \$1,500. Since the profit contribution per unit of product x_1 is \$300, the answer is 1,500 $\div$ 300 = 5 units of x_1. Similarly, since the per unit profit contribution of x_2 is \$250, it takes 6 units of x_2, if only x_2 is produced (as indicated by point M), to produce a profit of \$1,500. All points on the isoprofit line MN are within the shaded area, representing feasible solutions, each giving a total profit of \$1,500 (see Figure 6.9).

In a similar fashion, other isoprofit lines could be drawn, yielding different levels of profits. For example, line PQ in Figure 6.9 represents a \$3,000 isoprofit level, and the line RS represents a \$6,000 isoprofit level. An examination of lines MN, PQ, and RS shows that they are *parallel* to each other. Note also that profit levels increase as the isoprofit lines get *farther away* from the origin (point O).

Moving parallel

Farthest away from the origin

A little reflection will show that an even higher profit can be achieved if additional isoprofit lines can be drawn farther away from the origin. The question is: Where is the farthest *isoprofit* line? Let us see how this question can be answered.

Finding the optimal solution(s). The feasible area is reproduced from Figure 6.8 as Figure 6.10. Superimposed on the figure is the isoprofit line MN.

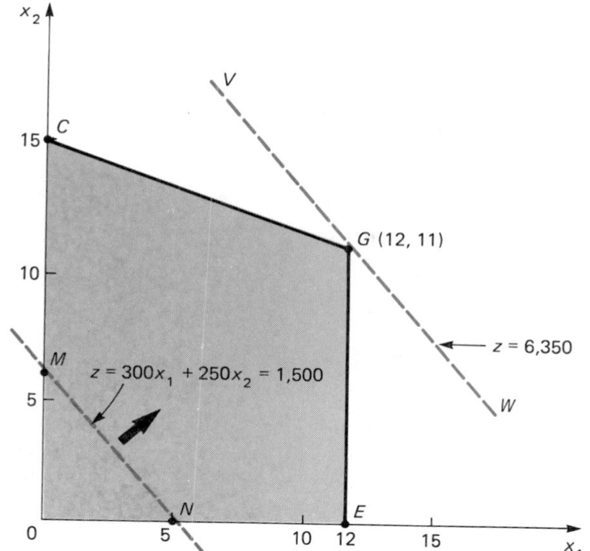

FIGURE 6.10
Moving to an optimal solution

Now, if one starts building parallel isoprofit lines in the northeast direction (see the heavy arrow), these lines will represent higher and higher profits. We shall now show how to build such parallel lines and how to find the farthest possible isoprofit line.

To build parallel lines to *MN*, take a ruler and a 90-degree triangle. Hold the ruler perpendicular to line *MN* and keep one side of the triangle on the line *MN*. To find the farthest isoprofit, move the triangle slowly to the northeast until the point where it is about to leave the feasible area (shaded in Figure 6.10).

The optimal solution

In our example, the farthest isoprofit line *(VW)* hits point *G*, which is declared the *optimal solution*. The coordinates of this point were previously computed as 12 and 11. The value of the objective function at that point is $300(12) + 250(11) = 6{,}350$. Therefore, line *VW* designates an isoprofit line $z = 6{,}350$.

A vertex or a boundary?

When employing the above method, one of two cases may be expected. First, the farthest isoprofit line may intersect one corner point, providing a single optimal solution. Second, the farthest isoprofit line may coincide with one of the boundary lines of the feasible area. (This second case is discussed in more detail in Section 6.10). This procedure reaffirms the previous comment that an optimal solution must be on the boundary and

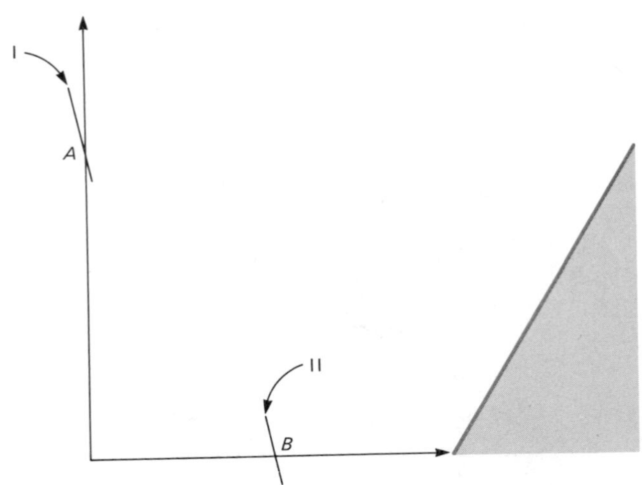

FIGURE 6.11
A "closer" optimal point

not inside the feasible area and that the optimal solution must always occur at a vertex.[17]

Binding constraint

Note that if the optimal values of x_1 and x_2 are introduced into the inequality constraints, the solution will fully utilize only the second and the third resources. That is, the labor constraint is not *binding*. This can be clearly seen in Figure 6.7 where the labor constraint does not intersect at the optimal point. In general, any constraint that does not intersect on the optimal vertex is *not* fully utilized.

Note: The isoprofit line that results in an optimal solution is not necessarily the line on the farthest point from the origin. That is, while a point may be the farthest from the origin, the optimal line may or may not go through this point (depending on the slope of the line). For example, in Figure 6.11, isoprofit line II is much "closer" to the origin than line I. Yet line II passes through the optimal solution at point B (maximization).

Example: A minimization problem

Minimization

The graphical method can be used for minimization problems in a manner similar to the maximization case. To illustrate, let us examine the *blending problem* discussed earlier.

The problem is reproduced below:

$$\text{minimize } z = 45x_1 + 12x_2$$
subject to:
$$1x_1 + 1x_2 \geq 300$$
$$3x_1 + 0x_2 \geq 250$$

[17] If only one solution exists.

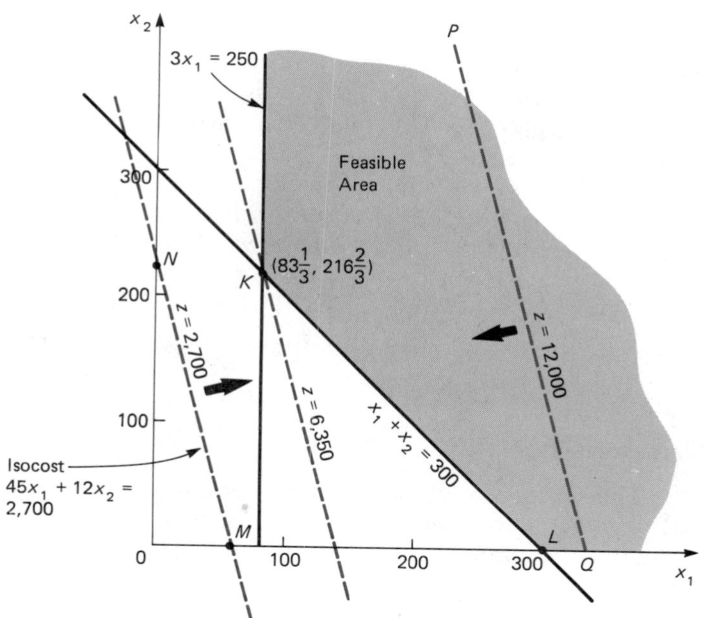

FIGURE 6.12
The blending problem

To begin with, the inequality constraints are considered equations. They are drawn in Figure 6.12. Since the inequalities are of the *greater-than-or-equal-to* type, the feasible area is formed by considering the area to the *upper right* side of each equation (away from the origin, the shaded area in Figure 6.12). Next, a family of lines that represents various levels of the objective function is drawn (broken lines in Figure 6.12). These lines, in the minimization case, are called **isocost** lines.

Isocost lines

In the diagram, a value of $z = 2{,}700$ is arbitrarily selected. The isocost equation is:

$$45x_1 + 12x_2 = 2{,}700$$

This isocost line is shown as line *MN* in Figure 6.12; note that the line *does not* intersect the feasible solution space. Therefore, this isocost line must be moved *toward* the feasible area until it first intersects a point (or points) in this region (point *K*).[18] The coordinates of point *K* can be read from the graph, or they can be computed as the intersection of the two linear equations. The solution for point *K* is:

$$x_1 = 83\tfrac{1}{3}$$
$$x_2 = 216\tfrac{2}{3}$$

[18] If the isocost line is constructed inside the feasible area, like line *PQ* in Figure 6.12, then the search moves in the direction of the arrow, toward the origin. Since the objective is cost minimization, we search for the *lowest* level isocost that is still feasible.

The solution

This means that for every case of the finished paint, the following raw materials should be used: 83⅓ ounces of Alpha at a cost of 45 cents × 83⅓ = 3,750 cents; and 216⅔ ounces of Beta at a cost of 12 cents × 216⅔ = 2,600 cents. The total cost is, therefore, 3,750 cents + 2,600 cents = 6,350 cents.

Equality means *on* the line.

Graphing an equality Thus far we have graphed only inequalities. If a constraint appears as an equality, then the feasible region of solutions is not an area any more, but a *line segment,* directly on the line describing the equality constraint.[19]

6.5 UTILIZATION OF THE RESOURCES—SLACK AND SURPLUS VARIABLES

Slack variables

The optimal solution for the product-mix problem calls for $x_1 = 12$ and $x_2 = 11$. Let us examine now what will happen to the constraints if the optimal solution is used.

1. The labor constraint

This constraint is expressed as:

$$\overbrace{2x_1 + 1x_2}^{\text{Demand for labor}} \leq \overbrace{40}^{\text{Supply of labor}}$$

Introducing the optimal values we get:

$$2(12) + 1(11) = 35 \text{ hours}$$

Slack variables

That is, the demand for labor is 35 hours, while the supply is 40. Therefore, there would be 40 − 35 = 5 hours of unused labor potential. This unused supply is called *slack*. The slack must take only nonnegative values; that is, it can be either zero or positive. Designating this slack by s_1 (where the 1 designates the first constraint), the labor constraint can be rewritten as

$$2x_1 + 1x_2 + s_1 = 40$$

transforming the constraint into an equality. The solution for s_1 is:

$$s_1 = 40 - (2x_1 + 1x_2) = 40 - 2(12) - 1(11) = 5$$

In general, in the optimal solution, any smaller-than-or-equal-to constraint will have a slack that can be either 0 or positive.

[19] Mathematically, an equality constraint can also be expressed as two inequalities. For example, $2x_1 + 5x_2 = 30$ is the same as $2x_1 + 5x_2 \geq 30$ *and* $2x_1 + 5x_2 \leq 30$. Sometimes it is more desirable to use the latter approach in formulating an equality.

2. *The machine constraint*

Similarly, the machine slack variable can be inserted into the constraint as:

$$x_1 + 3x_2 + s_2 = 45$$

Substituting the values of the optimal solution and solving for s_2:

$$s_2 = 45 - (1x_1 + 3x_2) = 45 - 12 - 33 = 0$$

In this case, the machine time is *fully utilized* (no slack exists). A fully utilized constraint is also called a *binding* constraint and constitutes a *bottleneck* in the organization's operations. A binding constraint is a line that passes through the optimal point on the graph.

Full utilization: No slack

3. *The marketing constraint*

Similarly:

$$1x_1 + s_3 = 12$$

Solving:

$$s_3 = 12 - 1x_1 = 12 - 12 = 0$$

The implication again is that there is no slack; the constraint is being exactly met.

Note: A glance at Figures 6.7 and 6.10 will show that a constraint with zero slack intersects the optimal solution point. A constraint with positive slack *does not* intersect the point of the optimal solution.

Surplus variables

Any larger-than-or-equal-to constraint has a surplus variable.

Example 1

Given:

$$2x_1 + 3x_2 \geq 50$$

Let the optimal solution be:

$$x_1 = 12;\ x_2 = 11$$

Introducing these values into the left side of the inequality, we get:

$$2(12) + 3(11) = 57$$

The value of the left side of the inequality is larger than the value of the right side. The difference, 7, in this case, is called a **surplus variable.** It indicates by how much the requirements of the right-hand side are exceeded (overachievement). That is, a surplus variable shows by how much certain minimum specifications are exceeded.

Surplus variable

A surplus variable can either be positive or zero. It is written as:

$$2x_1 + 3x_2 - s_4 = 50$$

Notice again that the inequality has been changed to an equality. Introducing the values of the decision variables and solving for s_4:

$$s_4 = (2x_1 + 3x_2) - 50 = 2(12) + 3(11) - 50 = 7$$

Example 2

Taking the first constraint of the blending problem:

$$1x_1 + 1x_2 - s_1 = 300$$
$$s_1 = 1x_1 + 1x_2 - 300 = 83\tfrac{1}{3} + 216\tfrac{2}{3} - 300 = 0$$

The value of the surplus is zero, which indicates that the minimum specification is just being met.

Note 1: A linear programming inequality constraint can be multiplied or divided by a constant without changing the optimal solution. For example, the inequality $3x_1 + 6x_2 \geq 15$ can be rewritten $x_1 + 2x_2 \geq 5$. However, if this is done, the magnitude of the surplus (or slack) variable will be changed. Therefore, one *should not* change the original constraints. The slack and surplus variables also play an important role in the simplex method, as will be seen in Part B of this chapter.

Note 2: The addition of slack and surplus variables helps standardize the LP problem, as required by the simplex method (see Section 6.8).

Summary

Each smaller-than-or-equal-to constraint has a slack variable whose value is either positive or zero. Each larger-than-or-equal-to constraint has a surplus variable whose value is either positive or zero. Each equality constraint has neither slack nor surplus. Any constraints that intersect at the point of the optimal solution have neither slack nor surplus; that is, they have zero slack or surplus.

Farming with linear programming software

Farmers and other businesspeople have always faced problems of finding the best feed mix for their chickens, the best blend for their products, or the best route for their trucks. Though the big companies with mathematicians on their staffs could solve these problems on their large mainframe computers, small businesses had to guess at the right answers.

Now, however, software is available for these people on the personal computer and it is helping them in many ways. The user-friendly software helps ordinary folk frame their problem in a linear programming format so it can be solved easily and quickly. Sometimes the user is asked to put the problem in the format of a spreadsheet, with which many people are familiar.

A number of firms are offering this software in various options and at a variety of prices, ranging from \$100 to \$1,000. Some packages are specifically oriented to farming, trucking, and other specific industries, and are thus that much more user friendly.

A Chicago nurse, for example, is saving her hospital over \$100,000 a year in overtime costs by better scheduling its nurses. And a Texas rancher is saving his cattle during drought periods by feeding them more inexpensive cottonseed rather than alfalfa hay. A New York coal wholesaler is able to meet customers' demands for a particular ash, sulfur, and heating value in their coal with a cheaper mix.

But the use of these programs isn't limited to the small user, either. The president of Newfoundland Energy, for example, now solves his firm's regular purchasing decision regarding what crudes to buy on a personal computer rather than the company mainframe, thereby saving thousands of dollars of expensive computer time.

Source: "The Right Mix: New Software Makes the Choice Much Easier," *The Wall Street Journal,* March 27, 1987.

6.6 CONCLUDING REMARKS

Linear programming is a powerful tool of management science, designed to solve allocation problems. Such problems appear in dozens of forms and complications. The major difficulty is that there are an infinite number of feasible solutions; therefore, finding the optimal or the *best of all* possible solutions is not usually possible by complete enumeration. Linear programming is a model that enables an efficient search for the optimal solution.

Linear programming models the allocation problem with two parts: a linear objective function that is to be maximized or minimized, and a set of linear constraints that describes the limitations and requirements subject to which the maximization or minimization is attempted.

The model is solved by an efficient algorithm called the simplex method. This method is presented in Part B of this chapter. The graphical method that was presented in Part A is very restricted in use. Part B of this chapter (as well as Chapters 8 and 9) deals with various topics and extensions that relax some of the limiting assumptions, enabling linear programming to be applied to a wide range of situations.

6.7 PROBLEMS FOR PART A[20]

1. Nitron Corp. of Canada produces two products. Profit for product A is \$60; for product B, \$50. Each must pass through two machines, P and Q. Product A requires 10 minutes on machine P and 8 minutes on machine Q. Product B requires 20 minutes on machine P and 5 minutes on machine Q. Machine P is available 200 minutes a day, while machine Q is available 80 minutes a day. The company must produce at least two units of product A and five of product B each day. Units that are not completed in a given day are finished the next day; that is, a portion of a product can be produced in the daily plan. What is the most profitable daily production plan?
   a. Formulate.
   b. Solve graphically (specifically show all constraints and the objective function as well as the optimal solution).
   c. How should the resources be allocated?

2. Given:

   maximize $z = 5x_1 + 5x_2$
   subject to:
   (1) $1x_1 + 2x_2 \leq 30$
   (2) $1x_1 + 1x_2 \leq 19$
   (3) $8x_1 + 3x_2 \leq 120$

   a. Solve the problem graphically.
   b. If the problem has more than one optimal solution, explain why this is so and list all the optimal solutions.
   c. Find the slacks, or surpluses, or both, on all constraints.

3. Given a set of constraints:

   (1) $10x_1 + 8x_2 \leq 120$
   (2) $5x_1 + 5x_2 \geq 30$
   (3) $1x_1 \geq 2$
   (4) $1x_2 \leq 10$
   (5) $1x_2 \geq x_1$

   a. Graphically display the feasible area.
   b. Compute the coordinates of all feasible corner (intersection) points.
   c. If the objective function is:

   maximize $z = 5.5x_1 + 3x_2$

   find the value of the objective function at all corner points. Which corner point is the best one?
   d. Graphically draw the slope of the objective function. Confirm the findings of part *(c)*.
   e. Find the slacks/surpluses on all constraints.
   f. Suppose the objective function is:

   minimize $z = 5.5x_1 + 3x_2$

   What will the optimal solution be?

4. Given:

   maximize $z = 8x_1 + 6x_2$
   subject to:
   (1) $5x_1 + 2x_2 \leq 60$
   (2) $2x_1 + 4x_2 \leq 48$
   (3) $3x_1 \geq 15$
   (4) $5x_1 - 4x_2 \leq 40$

   a. Graphically show the feasible solution area.
   b. Compute the coordinates of all intersecting feasible corners.
   c. Find the optimal solution.
   d. Find the value of the objective function.
   e. Find the slacks/surpluses on all constraints.
   f. Suppose that the last constraint is changed to a strict equality. What will the optimal solution be now?

5. A store sells men's and ladies' tennis shoes. It makes a profit of \$1 a pair on the men's shoes and \$1.20 a pair on the ladies'. It takes two minutes of a salesperson's time and two minutes of a cashier's time to sell a pair of men's shoes. It takes three minutes of a salesperson's time and one minute of a cashier's time per pair of women's shoes. The store is open eight hours per day, during which time there are two salespersons and one cashier on duty. How much of the salespersons' and the cashier's time should be allocated to the men's and ladies' shoes and how many shoes should the store sell in order to maximize profit each day? What is the profit?
   a. List all the assumptions that are necessary to formulate this as a linear programming problem.

[20] A large number of LP problems for formulation and computer solution are available in Part B of this chapter, as well as in Chapters 7 and 8.

b. Formulate as a linear programming problem.
c. Solve graphically.

6. A knitting machine can produce 1,000 pairs of pants or 3,000 shirts (or a combination of the two) each day. The finishing department can handle either 1,500 pairs of pants or 2,000 shirts (or a combination of the two) each day. The marketing department requires that at least 400 pants be produced each day. The company's stated objective is profit maximization.
a. If the profit from a pair of pants is \$4 and that derived from a shirt is \$1.50, how many of each type should be produced? Solve graphically.
b. If the profit from a shirt is \$2, what should be the *minimum* profit derived from selling a pair of pants that will justify production of pants only?
c. Examine the solutions to *(a)* and *(b)* and interpret the difference between them. Can this interpretation be generalized to all LP graphical solutions?

7. The owner of Black Angus Ranch of Australia is trying to determine the correct mix of two types of beef feed, A and B, which cost 50 cents and 75 cents per pound, respectively. Five essential ingredients are contained in the feed, as shown in the table below, which also indicates the minimum daily requirements of each ingredient:

	Percent per pound of feed		
Ingredient	*Feed A*	*Feed B*	*Minimum daily requirement (pounds)*
1	20	25	30
2	30	10	50
3	0	30	20
4	24	15	60
5	10	20	40

Find the least-cost daily blend for the ranch; that is, how many pounds of feed A and feed B will be included in the mix? (Solve graphically.)

8. Korean Valves, Inc. produces drainage valves. Two alternative production lines are available. The company just received an order for producing 1,000 Mark I valves. Line 1 can produce the valves at a rate of 15 minutes for each valve. The production capacity on line 2 is 5 valves per hour. Line 1 is available, for this order, for not more than 200 hours at 80,000 won an hour. Line 2 is available, for this order, for not more than 170 hours at 50,000 won an hour.
Find the best production plan.
a. Formulate in two different ways. (*Hint:* In one of the ways, the decision variables are in terms of hours.)
b. Solve graphically.
c. Discuss the best allocation of resources.

9. *a.* Given a constraint $3x_1 + 5x_2 - 1x_3 \leq 80$; the optimal solution is: $x_1 = 5$, $x_2 = 6$, $x_3 = 1$; find the slack on this constraint.
b. Given a constraint $5x_1 + 2x_2 + 8x_3 \geq 120$; the optimal solution is: $x_1 = 20$, $x_2 = 10$, $x_3 = 0$; find the surplus on this constraint.

10. Given two LP graphical solutions; the optimal solution is marked by x. In each case find:
a. Which constraints are redundant.
b. Which constraints will have a slack.
c. Which constraints will have a surplus.

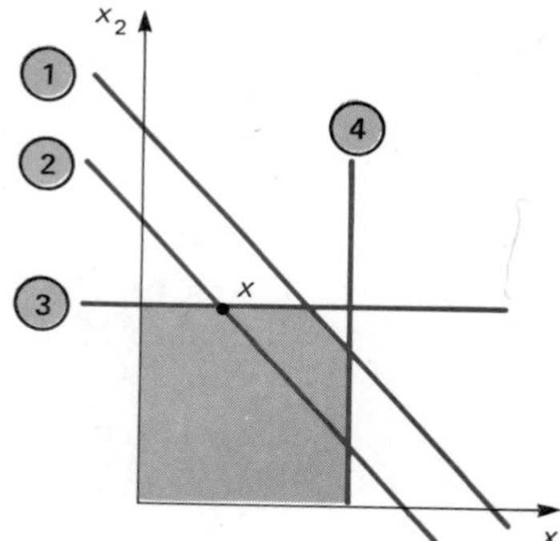

a. Maximization

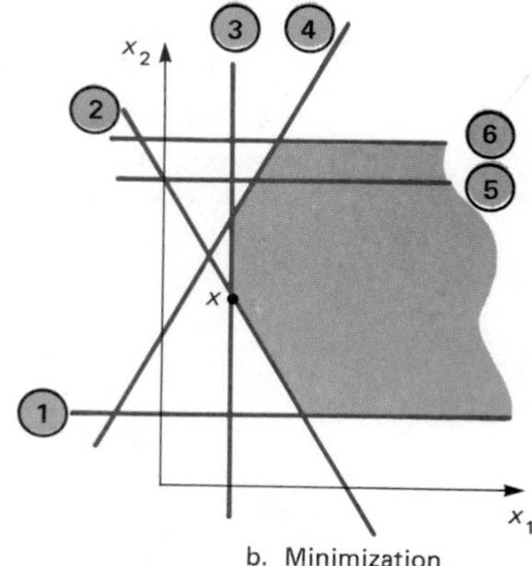

b. Minimization

PART B: EXTENSIONS

6.8 THE SIMPLEX METHOD

LP in 1947

The simplex method is an **iterative** algorithm for efficiently solving large linear programming problems.[21] It was first developed in 1947 by G. B. Dantzig [4] and his associates in the U.S. Department of the Air Force. Some revisions in the method have since been made in order to increase computational efficiency, but the basic approach remains the same. The simplex method and its variations have now been programmed and coded for practically all makes and types of computers. Before launching into the simplex process, however, it will be worthwhile to spend some time visualizing, in graphic terms, what the simplex process does algebraically.

The simplex method

Graphical explanation of the simplex process

It was pointed out during the graphical solution procedure that the search for an optimal solution can be limited to only the corner points of the feasible solution space. This was easy enough to do by hand for a problem with only two variables and three constraints, but for larger problems a more efficient procedure for identifying and evaluating corner points is necessary. This is one of the main objectives of the simplex method.

Moving to adjacent corners

In the simplex method, the search usually starts at the origin and moves to that *adjacent corner* that increases (for maximization problems) the value of the objective function the most. Upon reaching such a corner, the search moves to an even better corner adjacent to the new one. The process continues until no further improvement is possible. To illustrate this process in two dimensions, we reproduce Figure 6.7 as Figure 6.13. The search starts at the origin O and moves to corner C (corner C has a profit of \$3,750 versus \$3,600 at corner E, see Table 6.1) and then to the optimal point, corner G.

Optimality by iteration

The simplex process must always reach the optimum solution (if a solution exists) because in each iteration the objective function improves and there are only a finite number of corner points in the feasible solution space. Also, the optimum will be reached regardless of which direction the process starts. In Figure 6.13, for example, going first to point E would not have affected the ultimate solution, nor the number of iterations, though in other situations different routes will result in a different number of iterations.

---

[21] The iterative simplex procedure obtains an optimal solution by sequentially improving the previous solution. The improvement procedure follows the same steps each time; that is, it "iterates" through the same process in each pass.

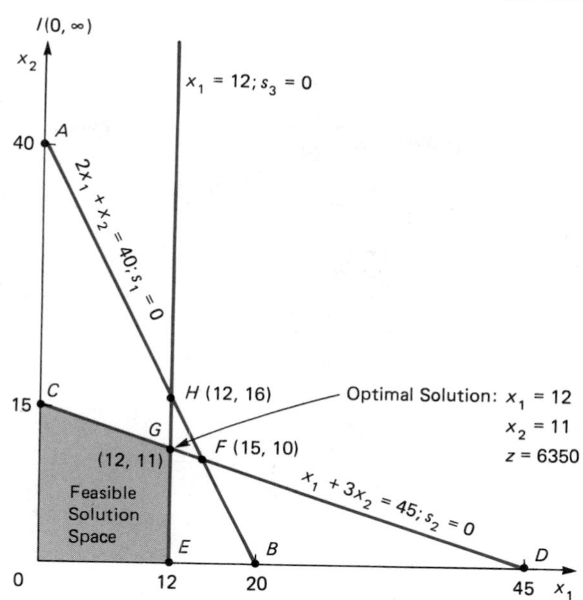

FIGURE 6.13
The product-mix problem (basic solution points)

The simplex process

The computational process of the simplex involves six steps, as depicted in Figure 6.14. These steps are:

Step 1. Standardize the problem into a linear programming tableau.
Step 2. Generate an initial solution, called a **basis.**
Step 3. Test the solution for optimality. If the solution is not optimal, improve it (go to step 4); otherwise go to step 6.

The improvement of a nonoptimal solution is done in two steps:

The steps

Step 4. Identify one variable that will leave the basis and one variable that will enter the basis.
Step 5. Generate an improved solution. The improved solution is checked for optimality. If it is not optimal, then steps 4 and 5 are repeated. If it is optimal, step 6 is undertaken.
Step 6. Find if more than one optimal solution exists.

This process guarantees that an optimal solution, if it exists, will be found in a finite number of iterations. The process will be illustrated through a product-mix example.

Example Let us reproduce the product-mix problem that was previously solved graphically.

FIGURE 6.14
Schematic presentation of the simplex method

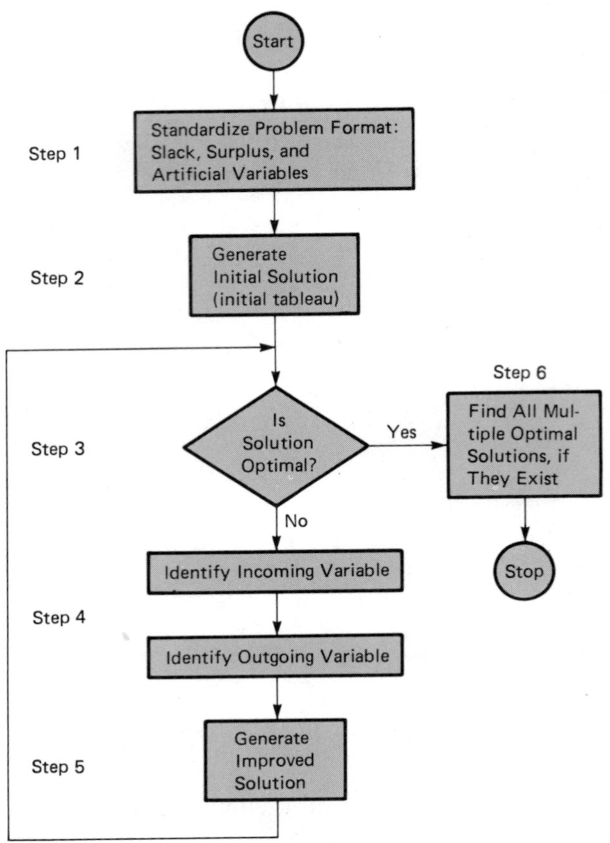

$$\text{maximize } z = 300x_1 + 250x_2$$
subject to:
$$2x_1 + 1x_2 \leq 40$$
$$1x_1 + 3x_2 \leq 45$$
$$1x_1 + 0x_2 \leq 12$$

The graphical solution of the problem is shown in Figure 6.13.

Step 1: Standardize the problem

A standard form

Since only corner points of the feasible solution space are to be checked, and since these points are defined by the intersection of equations, it is necessary to convert the inequalities in the problem statement into equations in order to find the coordinates of the intersecting points. Such a conversion depends on the type of constraints involved.

Constraints with inequalities of the smaller-than-or-equal-to type

A "slack" variable is added to each of these type constraints. For example, the labor constraint in the product-mix problem is:

Slack variable

$$2x_1 + 1x_2 \leq 40$$

Adding a slack variable:

$$2x_1 + 1x_2 + 1s_1 = 40$$

where s_1 = Slack of labor and $s_1 \geq 0$.

For example, if it was decided to produce 5 type-A sets and 15 type-B sets, then the total required labor hours would be:

$$2 \times 5 + 1 \times 15 = 25$$

However, 40 labor hours are available. Therefore, the unused portion of the labor hour supply, that is, the *slack*, s_1, is 15 hours. Note that a negative slack is not allowed. For instance, producing 20 type-A and 15 type-B sets would result in a "slack" of -15 hours. That is, 15 more labor hours would be required than are available, which is unacceptable. Lastly, note that if *no* sets, either A or B, were produced ($x_1 = x_2 = 0$ is a common starting point in the simplex procedure), then the slack s_1 would be 40:

$$2 \times 0 + 1 \times 0 + 1s_1 = 40$$

Constraints with inequalities of the larger-than-or-equal-to type

Let us examine the blending constraint $x_1 + x_2 \geq 300$. Once a solution is found and the values of the variables are introduced into the constraint, then the left side can be either equal to *or* larger than 300. In the latter case, there will be a *surplus*. Let us call it s_2. It is possible, therefore, to write the inequality $x_1 + x_2 \geq 300$ as:

Surplus variable

$$1x_1 + 1x_2 - 1s_2 = 300$$

where $s_2 \geq 0$.

For example, if 160 ounces of Alpha and 150 ounces of Beta are used in the blend, then:

$$160 + 150 - 1s_2 = 300$$

or the surplus, s_2, is 10. This solution would mean that it is more profitable to exceed the minimum specification than to meet it exactly.

Artificial variables

However, if no Alpha or Beta is produced ($x_1 = x_2 = 0$, a starting point in the simplex), then the equation $1x_1 + 1x_2 - 1s_2 = 300$ will result in the solution $s_2 = -300$, which is not allowable. Neither a slack nor a

Artificial variable

surplus can be negative. To overcome this difficulty, an auxiliary variable, called an **artificial variable,** is introduced into the equation. This allows us to form the initial basis. The constraint is then written as:

$$1x_1 + 1x_2 - 1s_2 + 1a_2 = 300$$

where a_2 is the artificial variable for the constraint ($a_2 \geq 0$). When x_1, x_2, and s_2 are set to zero, then $a_2 = 300$.

Penalty of M

Since the sole objective of the artificial variable is to simply form an initial basis, it does not have any physical meaning and must be kept out of any final solution. To prevent such a variable from entering the optimal solution, a very large penalty (usually denoted by the symbol M) is assigned as a coefficient to the corresponding variable in the objective function.[22] This, then, keeps the artificial variable from ever being an attractive alternative solution. An example will be given later.

Constraints with an equality

Consider a constraint given as an equality, say:

$$3x_1 + 1x_2 = 10$$

If, as an initial simplex solution, the two variables x_1 and x_2 are set to zero, a value of $0 = 10$ is obtained, which is unacceptable. This difficulty is again solved by adding an artificial variable:

$$3x_1 + 1x_2 + a_3 = 10$$

Then, when x_1 and x_2 are set to zero, $a_3 = 10$. Again, a penalty of M must be assigned to a_3 in the objective function to preclude using a_3 in the final solution, because a_3 has no physical meaning. We will return to this issue of artificial variables and how to handle them in the simplex in Section 6.10.

Once the constraints have been modified, the problem can then be written in a standard form.

Example a: The product-mix problem. Since all the constraints in this example are of the type $\leq$, then it is necessary to add three slacks, one for each constraint (s_1 = slack on labor, s_2 = slack on machine time, and s_3 = marketing slack). *The slack variables will have a coefficient of zero in the objective function* because "producing" slack (i.e., not using a resource) does not generate any profit, nor does it have any costs. The problem then, can be written in a *standard form* as shown in Table 6.2.

TABLE 6.2
Standard form for the product-mix problem

Objective function:	maximize	$z = 300x_1 + 250x_2 + 0s_1 + 0s_2 + 0s_3$
subject to:	(1)	$2x_1 + 1x_2 + 1s_1 + 0s_2 + 0s_3 = 40$
	(2)	$1x_1 + 3x_2 + 0s_1 + 1s_2 + 0s_3 = 45$
	(3)	$1x_1 + 0x_2 + 0s_1 + 0s_2 + 1s_3 = 12$

[22] The magnitude of M should be large enough to *ensure* that the artificial variable will be so undesirable that it will never enter a solution.

Example b: The blending problem. The blending problem was formulated as:

$$\begin{aligned}&\text{minimize } z + 45x_1 + 12x_2\\&\text{subject to:}\\&\quad 1x_1 + 1x_2 \geq 300\\&\quad 3x_1 + 0x_2 \geq 250\end{aligned}$$

Since the constraints are of the larger-than-or-equal-to type, it is necessary to add both surplus and artificial variables. The resulting standard form is shown in Table 6.3. The surpluses have a coefficient of zero in the objective function because they incur no cost. However, to ensure that the artificial variables are kept out of the final solution, they are given a large cost penalty of $+M$ in the objective function (use $-M$ in a maximization problem).

TABLE 6.3
Standard form for the blending problem

Objective function:	minimize	$z = 45x_1 + 12x_2 + 0s_1 + 0s_2 + Ma_1 + Ma_2$
subject to:	(1)	$1x_1 + 1x_2 - s_1 + a_1 = 300$
	(2)	$3x_1 + 0x_2 - s_2 + a_2 = 250$

Before proceeding to step 2, let us explain, again in graphical terms, what the simplex method does once the problem is written in standard form.

Basic variables and a basis

The product-mix maximization problem, as presented in Table 6.2, consists of a system of three linear equations describing the constraints and a family of isoprofit functions (the objective function). To determine corner points, the intersection coordinates of the constraints must be calculated. In order to do so it is necessary to solve the three linear equations simultaneously.

Note that there exist five unknown variables: x_1, x_2, s_1, s_2, and s_3; on the other hand, there are only three equations. A solution to a system of linear equations requires that the number of equations equal the number of variables; otherwise there will be an infinite number of solutions. To overcome this problem, two of the five variables are set to zero. Then it is possible to solve the system of linear equations for the three remaining variables. In general, two cases are distinguished.

Basic solutions

The *basis*

1. Solutions with exactly m variables, where m is the number of constraints, are called *basic solutions*. The m variables in these solutions are called **basic variables** and they constitute the *basis* of the solution. The remaining variables have values of zero.
2. Solutions that include more than m nonzero variables are called *nonbasic* solutions.

TABLE 6.4
The 10 possible bases for the product-mix problem

Basis no.	Variables in the solution					*Corner points in Figure 6.13*	*Feasible?*
	x_1	x_2	s_1	s_2	s_3		
1	0	0	40	45	12	*O*	Yes
2	0	40	0	−75	12	*A*	No
3	0	15	25	0	12	*C*	Yes
4	0	∞	−∞	−∞	0	*I*	No
5	20	0	0	25	−8	*B*	No
6	45	0	−50	0	−33	*D*	No
7	12	0	16	33	0	*E*	Yes
8	15	10	0	0	−3	*F*	No
9	12	16	0	−15	0	*H*	No
10	12	11	5	0	0	*G*	Yes

Feasible—Infeasible

The *basic* solutions can be further divided into two groups: *feasible* and *infeasible*. The *feasible solutions* are those that satisfy *all* the constraints; that is, they are in the *feasible* area and the value of *all* their variables must be nonnegative.

Basic feasible

The simplex procedure searches for *basic feasible solutions* only (the corner points of the feasible area). In large linear programming problems, such solutions are a small part of all basic solutions. Thus, the amount of search is much less than that required by complete enumeration of all corner points.

Graphical illustration: The product-mix problem (from Figure 6.13) With three equations and five unknowns, there are 10 possible ways of setting two of the variables to zero and solving the remaining three variables. Thus, there are 10 bases listed in Table 6.4.

Each of these bases is a *basic solution*, as shown in Figure 6.13. But only the corner points *O*, *C*, *G*, and *E* have nonnegative values for *all five* variables in Table 6.4.[23] Therefore, only *these* corner points (listed in Table 6.5) constitute the *feasible* basic solutions of Table 6.4. The search for an optimal solution is now narrowed from 10 points to 4.

Notice in Table 6.5 that each succeeding corner includes all but one of the same basic variables, though their *values* may differ. That is, *C* has two of the basic variables (s_1 and s_3) that *O* has and has x_2 replacing s_2, and *G* has the same basis as *C* except for x_1 replacing s_3. And in *E*, s_2 replaces x_2 of *G*. Returning to the origin *O*, s_3 replaces x_1 of *E*. Therefore, each pair of succeeding bases represents *adjacent* corners of the feasible solution space in Figure 6.13.

This, then, will be the solution procedure of the simplex method. The search starts with a solution at the origin, *O*. Then it moves to an adjacent corner where the objective function achieves the largest initial

[23] Slack variables cannot take negative values either and therefore points such as *A* and *H* correspond to infeasible solutions.

TABLE 6.5
The feasible corner points (basic feasible solutions)

Corner	x_1	x_2	s_1	s_2	s_3
O	0	0	40	45	12
C	0	15	25	0	12
G	12	11	5	0	0
E	12	0	16	33	0

improvement. It continues on from corner to corner, improving the value of the objective function each time. At some point, no further improvement will be possible, signaling the attainment of the optimal solution. *Note:* In some cases, the origin is not a feasible starting solution. This situation is handled in a special way, as will be shown later.

Step 2: Generate an initial solution

The expression of the LP problem in the standard form of step 1 suggests an easy initial solution that is both basic and feasible. For example, the product-mix problem expressed in Table 6.2 has three constraint equations and five variables. Thus, there must be 5 − 3 = 2 nonbasic variables with zero values and 3 basic variables to solve for. Reproducing these equations:

$$
\begin{aligned}
2x_1 + 1x_2 + 1s_1 &= 40 \\
1x_1 + 3x_2 + 1s_2 &= 45 \\
1x_1 + 0x_2 + 1s_3 &= 12
\end{aligned}
$$

A natural solution to this set of equations would be to set x_1 and x_2 as the nonbasic variables with s_1, s_2, and s_3 as the basic variables. This is because x_1 and x_2 appear in more than one equation, whereas s_1, s_2, and s_3 each appear only once and in different equations and can thus be solved easily. Setting $x_1 = x_2 = 0$ and solving for s_1, s_2, and s_3:

$$s_1 = 40,\ s_2 = 45,\ s_3 = 12$$

The resulting profit is found from the objective function as:

$$
\begin{aligned}
z &= 300x_1 + 250x_2 + 0s_1 + 0s_2 + 0s_3 \\
&= 300(0) + 250(0) + 0(40) + 0(45) + 0(12) = 0
\end{aligned}
$$

The Gauss-Jordan method

Obtaining such a simple initial solution is, of course, the purpose of starting the simplex solution process with a standard format. The simplex process then *continues to maintain* this simplified solution format through the *Gauss-Jordan method* of solving simultaneous equations (see Section A5 of Appendix A). That is, each iteration of the simplex involves again expressing the set of equations such that each basic variable appears in only one, a different one, of the equations. This is not as difficult as it may sound, because the simplex begins from such a point (as in Table 6.2) and then switches only *one* of the basic variables for one of the nonbasic

FIGURE 6.15
A tableau explanation

	List of basic variables ↓ *Basis*	*Coefficients of objective function* ↓ *Unit profits*	*Quantity in solution* ↓ *Quantity*	*Main body:* *Decision variables* x_1	x_2	*Slack (surplus) variables* s_1	s_2	s_3
Basic Rows	s_1	0	40	2	1	[1]	0	0
	s_2	0	45	1	3	0	[1]	0
	s_3	0	12	1	0	0	0	[1]
c_j row (coefficients of objective function)				300	250	0	0	0
z_j row (new coefficient: per unit "losses")				0	0	0	0	0
$c_j - z_j$ row (the evaluator)				300	250	0	0	0

variables, as we saw in Table 6.5. Thus, reexpressing the equations in this special form only requires eliminating the new basic variable from all but one equation.

To facilitate the required manipulations of the equations, the simplex process makes use of a specialized adaptation of the standard LP form shown in Table 6.2. This adaptation is called a "tableau" *(tabulated coefficients).*

The structure of a tableau

Figure 6.15 illustrates the initial tableau of the product-mix problem. Explanations of its major parts are included.

Discussion

Notice that the tableau includes three rows, one for each constraint. This correspondence will be maintained throughout the entire simplex manipulations.

The main body of the tableau corresponds to the standard format of the problem, as shown in Table 6.2. Notice, however, that the variables are not repeated in each row but are summarized on the top. Also notice that the right-hand side quantities have been shifted to the left. The column "Basis" identifies the proposed initial solution variables ("boxed" in the table).

The z_j row. The row denoted z_j is labeled "per unit 'losses.'" It shows the amount of profit the objective function will be *reduced* by when one unit of the variable, in each column, is brought into the basis. Initially, all z_j's have values of zero. The reason for this is that only slack variables are in the first tableau and their coefficients in the objective function are always initially zero. If there had been $\geq$ or $=$ constraints in this problem, then some of the z_j's would have had nonzero values.

Each value in this row is found as follows:

Rule: Multiply the elements in the "Unit Profits" column by the corresponding elements of the main body, on a variable-by-variable basis, and total the results. For example, the z_j for column x_2 is: $0(1) + 0(3) + 0(0) = 0$.

The evaluator row: $c_j - z_j$. The bottom row, $c_j - z_j$, shows the *net* impact on the value of the objective function of bringing one unit of each of the column variables into the basis. The c_j's tell us how much will be gained while the z_j's tell us how much will simultaneously be lost. If the difference between the two is *positive,* then the value of the objective function can be *increased* by introducing one unit of the variable into the solution. In maximization problems, this is an indication of a possible *improvement;* that is, if one (or more) of the $c_j - z_j$ values is positive, then the solution is *not optimal.* This is the basis of the analysis to be conducted in step 3.

Economic interpretation. The value $c_j - z_j$ represents the *opportunity cost* of not having one unit of the corresponding variable in the solution. That is, it shows the marginal impact on the value of the objective function. (The value $c_j - z_j$ of the slack variables is related to the concept of the *dual variables* to be presented in Chapter 8.)

The value of the objective function z. Finally, the value of the objective function can be computed by multiplying each "Unit profit" by its corresponding quantity, and then totaling the results. For example, the value of the objective function (total profit) in Figure 6.15 is:

$$0(40) + 0(45) + 0(12) = 0$$

Step 3: Test for optimality

This test is made by examining the $c_j - z_j$ row in the tableau and using the following rule.

Rule for optimality

For an optimal solution of a maximization problem, it is sufficient if all the coefficients of the $c_j - z_j$ row are nonpositive (either zero or negative).

TABLE 6.6
The initial product-mix tableau (I)

	Basis	Unit profits	Quantity	x_1 (Incoming)	x_2	s_1	s_2	s_3	Ratio
	s_1	0	40	2	1	1	0	0	40/2 = 20
	s_2	0	45	1	3	0	1	0	45
Outgoing	s_3	0	12	①	0	0	0	1	12
	c_j (unit profits)			300	250	0	0	0	
	z_j (unit losses)			0	0	0	0	0	
	$c_j - z_j$			300	250	0	0	0	

That is, if bringing any other variable into the basis can only either decrease the profit or leave it unchanged, then the current solution must be optimal. Since both coefficients of x_1 and x_2 are positive in the $c_j - z_j$ row of Table 6.6, then introducing either x_1 or x_2 into the basis will *increase* the profit. Therefore, the current solution is *not* optimal.

Since the solution is not optimal, it can be improved. The improvement is done by:

- Identifying the incoming variable.
- Identifying the outgoing variable.
- Building the improved tableau.

Step 4: Identify the incoming and outgoing variables

In order to illustrate this step, the initial tableau of the product-mix problem is presented in Table 6.6. The improvement is done by an exchange of variables: one incoming, one outgoing.

Incoming

The incoming variable First, *an incoming variable* (currently nonbasic, to be changed to a basic variable) is chosen by inspecting the $c_j - z_j$ row of the current solution for that variable with the *largest positive* coefficient. In this example, therefore, x_1, with a coefficient of 300, is chosen. This is also known as the *pivot column*.

Rule for determining the incoming variable (in maximization)

Select the column with the largest positive coefficient in the $c_j - z_j$ row.[24]

[24] It is not mandatory to select the column with the largest positive coefficient. Any column with a positive $c_j - z_j$ is a good candidate. However, it is customary to use the column with the largest value.

The outgoing variable Once the incoming variable has been identified, it is necessary to identify the outgoing variable, called *the pivot row.*

Outgoing

The procedure for determining the *outgoing basic variable* (either s_1, s_2, or s_3 in the example) is somewhat more involved. In essence, the outgoing variable is that basic variable that is first reduced to zero as x_1 (the incoming variable) increases from zero. This is done as follows. For each basis row in the tableau, form the ratio of the "Quantity" to the coefficient of the incoming variable. In this case, the incoming variable is x_1, so the three ratios are 40/2 = 20, 45/1 = 45, and 12/1 = 12, which are listed in the rightmost column of the tableau. Select the row with the smallest nonnegative ratio. That ratio will preserve the nonnegativity of all the variables in the solution. (Negative ratios indicate no limit for the incoming variable.) This row's basic variable will be the *outgoing* variable. In Table 6.6 the smallest positive ratio is 12, so the outgoing variable is s_3.

The coefficient of the incoming variable in the outgoing row is called the *pivot element,* 1 in Table 6.6, and is circled for later reference.

Pivot element

The above procedure is summarized in the following rule.

Rule for determining the outgoing variable

Look down the column of the incoming variable and consider only positive elements (coefficients). Then, divide the quantity of each constraint by the corresponding coefficient in the column of the incoming variable. The row with the smallest ratio is selected as the outgoing row.

Step 5: Generate an improved solution

The solution is improved by introducing the incoming variable into the basis and removing the outgoing variable.[25] This is done row by row on the old tableau, forming, in the process, a new one.

The procedure starts with transforming the row of the outgoing variable, then the other basis rows, and finally transforming the c_j, z_j, and $c_j - z_j$ rows.

Transformation of the outgoing row

Rule: Divide the main body elements and the "Quantity" of the outgoing row by the pivot element.

[25] The mathematics executed in this step involve solving the new set of equations in the improved tableau. The Gauss-Jordan procedure (Appendix A) is applied through the special structure of the simplex method.

TABLE 6.7
First improved solution—Tableau II

Basis	Unit profits	Quantity	x_1	x_2	s_1	s_2	s_3	Ratio
s_1	0	16	0	1	[1]	0	−2	16
s_2	0	33	0	③	0	[1]	−1	11
x_1	300	12	[1]	0	0	0	1	limit = ∞
c_j			300	250	0	0	0	
z_j			300	0	0	0	300	
$c_j - z_j$			0	250	0	0	−300	

Since the coefficient is 1 in this case, the row is unchanged. Note that in the new row, x_1 replaces s_3 is the "Basis" column, and is thus boxed; as a result, the unit profit has been changed from 0 to 300. This information is now entered into the improved tableau (Table 6.7).

Transformation of the other rows

The transformation, again, deals only with the columns of the main body and the "Quantity." The process involves three activities:

1. Identify the coefficient at the intersection of the row to be transformed and the incoming column. For example, the coefficient for the first row in Table 6.6 is 2; for the second one it is 1.
2. Multiply this number, in turn, by every element of the transformed outgoing row (the new third row here).
3. Subtract the result of the second activity from the old row (to be transformed) to derive the new transformed row.

Example: Transforming the first row

The coefficient for this row in the incoming column is 2.

	Quantity	x_1	x_2	s_1	s_2	s_3
The new third row (Table 6.7)	12	1	0	0	0	1
The row to be transformed (first row, Table 6.6)	40	2	1	1	0	0
Minus: 2 × New third row	−24	−2	0	0	0	−2
Result: New first row (Table 6.7)	16	0	1	1	0	−2

This is the first row in the improved tableau (Table 6.7). Notice that the "Basis" and the "Unit profits" are transformed unchanged. The reason for this is that s_1 remains a basis variable.

Example: Transforming the second row

Here, the coefficient is 1 and the mathematical manipulations are:

	Quantity	x_1	x_2	s_1	s_2	s_3
Second row	45	1	3	0	1	0
Minus: 1 × New third row	−12	−1	0	0	0	−1
Result: New second row (Table 6.7)	33	0	3	0	1	−1

Transformation of the c_j row

This row is transformed unchanged (always).

Computing the new z_j row

Multiply the "Unit profits" in each row by the main body column coefficients and sum the results.

For the value in Table 6.7 under column:

$$
\begin{array}{ll}
x_1 & 0(0) \;\; + 0(0) \;\;\; + 300(1) = 300 \\
x_2 & 0(1) \;\; + 0(3) \;\;\; + 300(0) = 0 \\
s_1 & 0(1) \;\; + 0(0) \;\;\; + 300(0) = 0 \\
s_2 & 0(0) \;\; + 0(1) \;\;\; + 300(0) = 0 \\
s_3 & 0(-2) + 0(-1) + 300(1) = 300
\end{array}
$$

Computing the new $c_j - z_j$ row

Simply subtract z_j from c_j.

Computing the new value of the objective function

The improved solution calls for $s_1 = 16$, $s_2 = 33$, and $x_1 = 12$ ($x_2 = 0$ and $s_3 = 0$ being nonbasic variables). The value of the objective function is thus:

$$z = 12(300) + 16(0) + 33(0) = \$3{,}600$$

Step 3 (repeat): Test for optimality

The new solution must now be tested for optimality. It can be seen that the variable x_2 in the new $c_j - z_j$ row has a *positive coefficient;* therefore, the current solution is not optimal.

Step 4 (repeat): Identify incoming and outgoing variables

The incoming variable

In Tableau II (Table 6.7), x_2 has the largest positive coefficient in the $c_j - z_j$ row (250) and therefore it is the *incoming variable.*

The outgoing variable

Since the incoming variable is x_2, the ratios are:

$$\text{For constraint 1: } \frac{16}{1} = 16$$

$$\text{For constraint 2: } \frac{33}{3} = 11 \leftarrow \textit{Smallest}$$

$$\text{For constraint 3: } \frac{12}{0} = \text{limit at } \infty$$

The second row has the smallest nonnegative ratio. This row contains the variable s_2 as a basic variable ("boxed" in Table 6.7). Hence, the variable s_2 is the outgoing variable. The exchange of x_2 for s_2 is equivalent to a move from corner E to corner G in Figure 6.13.

Note: The existence of a zero in the body of the tableau indicates that this variable provides no limit to the value of the incoming variable—it could increase without limit toward infinity.

Step 5 (repeat): Generate an improved solution

The rows of the tableau of the *old solution* (Tableau II, Table 6.7) are transformed one at a time to a *new solution* (Tableau III, Table 6.8).

TABLE 6.8
Second improved solution—Tableau III

Basis	*Unit profits*	*Quantity*	x_1	x_2	s_1	s_2	s_3	*Ratio*
s_1	0	5	0	0	[1]	−⅓	−⅔	
x_2	250	11	0	[1]	0	⅓	−⅓	
x_1	300	12	[1]	0	0	0	1	
c_j			300	250	0	0	0	
z_j			300	250	0	250/3	650/3	
$c_j - z_j$			0	0	0	−250/3	−650/3	

Step 3 (repeat): Test of optimality

It is optimal!

Inspection of the new $c_j - z_j$ row in Table 6.8 reveals that there are no positive coefficients; hence, the second improved solution is optimal.

Interpretation of the results

The results of Table 6.8 can be read as follows:

The constraint rows

The solution values of the variables are:

Row (3) $x_1 = 12$: Produce 12 model A sets.
Row (2) $x_2 = 11$: Produce 11 model B sets.
Row (1) $s_1 = 5$: Constraint 1 has a slack of 5; that is, only 35 hours of labor out of 40 hours will be utilized.

Note that all basic variables have a coefficient of 1. The other coefficients, for example, $-1/3$ in constraint 1 with s_2, are called the *ratios of substitution* between the row and column variables. They designate the trade-offs that occur when a nonbasic variable becomes a basic variable.

Ratios of substitution

The value of the objective function (profit)

The final profit can be calculated as:

$$0(5) + 250(11) + 300(12) = \$6{,}350$$

Step 6: Check for other optimal solutions

It is important to know if only one optimal solution exists (unique solution) or if there is more than one. **Multiple optimal solutions** allow management greater flexibility in implementing a solution.

The check for other optimal solutions is simple. If the coefficient of one of the *nonbasic* variables in the final $c_j - z_j$ row is zero, then multiple optimal solutions exist. A coefficient of zero means that this variable can enter the basis, creating another feasible solution, but with the *same* value of the objective function. If two solutions exist, then there must be an infinite number of optimal solutions that are linear combinations of these two solutions (on the line joining them). In Table 6.8, there are no zero coefficients of nonbasic variables; hence, there is only one optimal solution to this problem.

6.9 COMPUTERIZATION

Real-life LP problems are almost always too large and complex for graphical or manual simplex solutions. Therefore, they are solved with computers and usually include slack, dual, and sensitivity analyses. Dozens of LP packages exist and are commercially available for both microcomputers and mainframes. Virtually all computer manufacturers and software companies also offer LP packages.

As an example of an LP computer routine, we will use the Sekido product-mix example presented in the beginning of this chapter. (See Figures 6.16 and 6.17.)

First, the computer asks the user questions regarding the input data. An example of such a dialogue is given in Figure 6.16 with the user's responses shown in color. Note that the nonnegativity constraints are omitted, since this information is preprogrammed in the computer.

Once the data have been entered, the computer repeats, if desired, the "information entered" (so that any corrections can be made) and then

FIGURE 6.16
LP computer program: Entering data

```
LINEAR PROGRAMMING INPUT SCREEN
IS IT MAX OR MIN?
MAX
ENTER THE OBJECTIVE FUNCTION:
300X1 + 250X2
ENTER THE CONSTRAINTS:
2X1 + 1X2 ≤ 40
1X1 + 3X2 ≤ 45
1X1 + 0X2 ≤ 12

DO YOU WISH TO ENTER ANOTHER ROW (Y/N)?
NO
NUMBER OF VARIABLES: 2          NUMBER OF CONSTRAINTS: 3
```

computes and prints the results. The printout in Figure 6.17 provides the complete solution, as discussed in this chapter, plus the shadow prices (dual's variables), to be discussed in Chapter 8. In addition, the value of the "reduced cost" is provided. This tells us how much the value of the objective function will be penalized when we enter into the optimal solution one unit of a decision variable not currently in the optimal solution. Additional information provided by the program will be shown and discussed in Chapter 8, as well as a discussion of the availability of other LP packages. The MSS package used to generate this printout has several additional output options, such as showing the simplex tableaux, that can be requested.

6.10 SPECIAL SITUATIONS IN THE SIMPLEX METHOD

There are several special linear programming situations that require adjustments in the simplex procedure. Nine are described below.

The simplex method: Minimization

Two ways to solve

The simplex method solves minimization problems in essentially the same manner as it solves maximization problems. There are two alternative approaches for minimization problems.

Direct approach The first approach is to solve the problem as a minimization problem directly, but this requires a slight change in the simplex procedure. The method of solving a minimization problem is basically the same as with a maximization problem, except that all the coefficients in the $c_j - z_j$ row should be *positive* for the optimality test and the incoming variable is that variable in the $c_j - z_j$ row with the most *negative* coefficient (provides the greatest reduction, per unit, for minimization). This method will not be pursued here.

Conversion The second approach is to convert the problem into a maximization problem, solve it as a maximization problem, and then translate the results in the light of the minimization objective.

FIGURE 6.17
LP computer program: Solution

```
**OPTIMAL SOLUTION**

                              SOLUTION SUMMARY
                           PROBLEM NAME: 1p1

                      OBJECTIVE FUNCTION VALUE: 6350
```

VARIABLE NAME	SOLUTION QUANTITY	REDUCED COST
X1	12	0
X2	11	0

CONSTRAINTS ANALYSIS

CONSTRAINT NUMBER	RHS VALUE	SLACK OR SURPLUS	SHADOW PRICE
1	40	5	0
2	45	0	33.33
3	12	0	216.66

Since minimizing a function is equivalent to maximizing the *negative* of that function, the only change required in order to convert a linear programming problem for minimization to maximization (or vice versa) is to multiply the objective function by -1. The constraints remain untouched.

Example 1. Given:

$$\text{minimize } z = 2x_1 - 5x_2$$

The problem is converted to:

$$\text{maximize } w = -2x_1 + 5x_2$$

When the solution is obtained (say, $x_1 = 12$, $x_2 = 3$) the results should be substituted back into the *original* minimization objective function to obtain the minimized value of z; $z = 2(12) - 5(3) = 9$.

Example 2. Given:

$$\text{minimize } z = 5x_1 + 1x_2 - 2x_3$$

The problem is converted to:

$$\text{maximize } w = -5x_1 - 1x_2 + 2x_3$$

Example: Solving the blending problem To illustrate this approach, as well as to demonstrate the procedure for handling artificial variables, the blending problem of Part A will be solved, starting from the standard form in Table 6.3. First, however, the objective function must be converted to maximization:

$$\text{maximize } w = -45x_1 - 12x_2 - 0s_1 - 0s_2 - Ma_1 - Ma_2$$

where M is a very large number (e.g., 1,000 or 10,000).

The equivalent tableau is given in Table 6.9. Note the inferiority of the initial "profit" solution (value of the objective function).

$$-M(300) - M(250) = -550M$$

TABLE 6.9
Tableau for the blending problem

Basis	*Unit profits*	*Quantity*	x_1	x_2	s_1	s_2	a_1	a_2	*Ratio*
a_1	$-M$	300	1	1	-1	0	[1]	0	300
a_2	$-M$	250	③	0	0	-1	0	[1]	250/3
c_j			-45	-12	0	0	$-M$	$-M$	
z_j			$-4M$	$-M$	M	M	$-M$	$-M$	
$c_j - z_j$			$-45 + 4M$	$-12 + M$	$-M$	$-M$	0	0	

The tableaus in Tables 6.10 and 6.11 illustrate the solution process. It is suggested that the reader follow the calculations through on his or her own to ensure a complete understanding, not only of the minimization process and handling artificial variables, but of the simplex procedure itself.

Tableau III represents an optimal solution, since all the coefficients in the $c_j - z_j$ row are negative or zero ($12 - M$ is a large negative number). The answer is thus:

$$x_1 = 83.33 \text{ ounces of Alpha}$$
$$x_2 = 216.67 \text{ ounces of Beta}$$
$$\text{"Profit"} = -12(216.67) - 45(83.33) = -6350 \text{ cents or}$$
$$\text{Cost} = -\text{"Profit"} = 6{,}350 \text{ cents.}$$

Note that once an artificial variable leaves the basis, it will never enter again because of the large penalty of M associated with it (1,000 could have been used here instead of M).

TABLE 6.10
Second (improved) tableau (II)

Basis	*Unit profits*	*Quantity*	x_1	x_2	s_1	s_2	a_1	a_2	*Ratio*
a_1	$-M$	216.67	0	①	-1	⅓	[1]	$-$⅓	216.67
x_1	-45	83.33	[1]	0	0	$-$⅓	0	⅓	limit = ∞
c_j			-45	-12	0	0	$-M$	$-M$	
z_j			-45	$-M$	M	$(15 - M/3)$	$-M$	$(-15 + M/3)$	
$c_j - z_j$			0	$-12 + M$	$-M$	$(M/3 - 15)$	0	$(15 - 4M/3)$	

TABLE 6.11
Third (optimal) tableau (III)

Basis	Unit profits	Quantity	x_1	x_2	s_1	s_2	a_1	a_2	Ratio
x_2	−12	216.67	0	[1]	−1	⅓	1	−⅓	
x_1	−45	83.33	[1]	0	0	−⅓	0	⅓	
c_j			−45	−12	0	0	$-M$	$-M$	
z_j			−45	−12	12	11	−12	−11	
$c_j - z_j$			0	0	−12	−11	$(12 - M)$	$(11 - M)$	

TABLE 6.12
Tie for incoming variable

	x_1	x_2	x_3	$x_4 \ldots$
$c_j - z_j$	7	4	7	−15

(? with arrows pointing to x_1 and x_3)

Two incoming variables

If two or more variables have the same largest coefficient in the $c_j - z_j$ row (see Table 6.12), then either may be arbitrarily chosen as the incoming variable. This will not affect the final solution.

Two outgoing basic variables (degeneracy)

The situations presented thus far had the property that the number of variables in the solution was the same as the number of constraints (not counting the nonnegativity constraints). If the number of positive variables in the solution is *less* than the number of constraints, the solution is "degenerate." An example of **degeneracy** occurs when three or more constraints intersect in the solution of a problem with two variables. This is shown in Figure 6.18.

In the simplex procedure, degeneracy occurs when two ratios tie for smallest (see Table 6.13). The problem is: Which of the two should go? Again, the choice for outgoing basic variable may be made arbitrarily

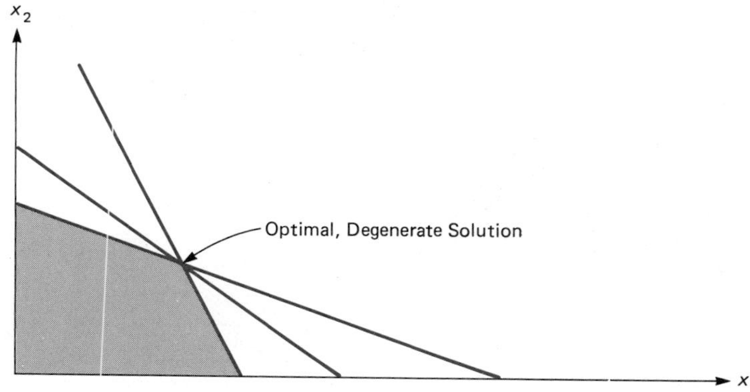

FIGURE 6.18
Degeneracy in a two-variable problem

TABLE 6.13
Example of degeneracy in a tableau

Tie for outgoing variable:

Basis	*Unit profits*	*Quantity*	x_1	x_2	x_3		s_1	s_2	*Ratio*	
s_1	—	50	0	0	① ←	?	[1]	2	50/1 = 50 ←	*Minimum?*
x_1	—	200	[1]	0	④ ←		0	1	200/4 = 50 ←	
x_2	—	250	0	[1]	2		0	5	250/2 = 125	
$c_j - z_j$			0	0	3		0	1		

Improved tableau with s_1 arbitrarily selected as outgoing variable:

Basis	*Unit profits*	*Quantity*	x_1	x_2	x_3	s_1	s_2	*Ratio*
x_3	—	50	0	0	[1]	1	2	
x_1	—	0	[1]	0	0	−4	−7	
x_2	—	150	0	[1]	0	−2	0	
$c_j - z_j$			0	0	0	−3	−5	

Final solution: $x_3 = 50$, $x_1 = 0$ (just like nonbasic variables), $x_2 = 150$.

without affecting the final solution. However, care must be exercised to recognize that the other basic variable (the one *not* selected as outgoing), even though having a new value of zero in the basis, is *still* a basic variable and is thus carried throughout the simplex calculation.

Unbounded solutions

An infinite value

Graphically, in this case, the feasible solution space extends indefinitely (Figure 6.19). The result in the simplex is that there is no outgoing basic variable; the ratios are either infinite or negative (see Table 6.14). Therefore, the optimal solution is infinite. This result usually means that an error was made, the problem was misstated, or an incorrect assumption was made.

TABLE 6.14
No outgoing variable

Basis	*Unit profits*	*Quantity*	x_1	x_2	s_1	s_2	*Ratio*
s_1	—	180	1	−1	[1]	0	180/−1 (ignore)
s_2	—	55	5	0	0	[1]	55/0 limit = ∞
$c_j - z_j$			−2	3	0	0	

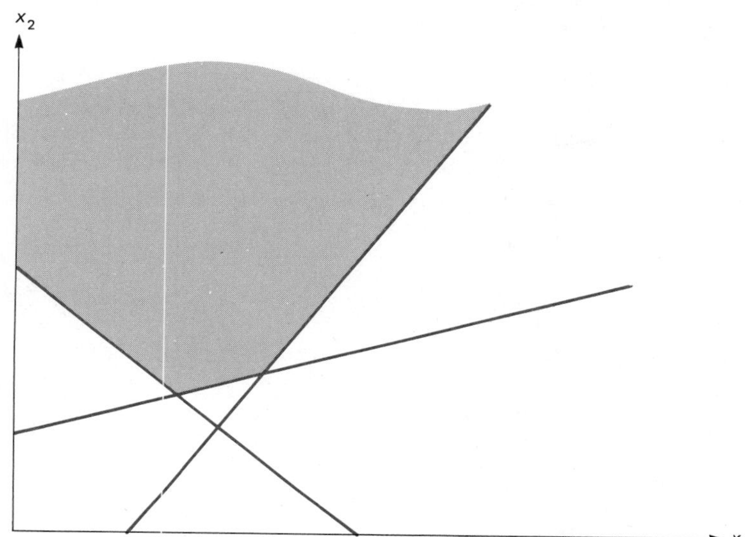

FIGURE 6.19
An unbounded maximization problem

Unconstrained variables

Negative solutions

Occasionally a problem arises when some of the variables are *not* constrained to be nonnegative; that is, one or more of the decision variables may be allowed to be negative. In this case, the problem statement is modified slightly before employing the simplex (which *requires* that all variables be nonnegative). The modification is to replace the unconstrained variable, say, x_i, throughout the problem statement with the difference of two variables $(y_i - w_i)$, where both $y_i \geq 0$ and $w_i \geq 0$. The optimal simplex solution will then either have $y_i = 0$, in which case $x_i = -w_i$; or else $w_i = 0$ and $x_i = y_i$.

For example, suppose the following problem statement is given and x_2 is a temperature (° F) that may be either positive or negative.

$$
\begin{aligned}
&\text{maximize } z = 40x_1 + 65x_2 - 8x_3 \\
&\text{subject to:} \\
&\quad 1x_1 + 1x_2 + 1x_3 \geq 1000 \\
&\quad 2x_1 + 0x_2 - 1x_3 \leq 783 \\
&\quad 1x_1 + 0x_2 + 0x_3 \geq 0 \\
&\quad 0x_1 + 0x_2 + 1x_3 \geq 0
\end{aligned}
$$

Then the problem would be recast as:

$$
\begin{aligned}
&\text{maximize } z = 40x_1 + 65y - 65w - 8x_3 \\
&\text{subject to:} \\
&\qquad 1x_1 + 1y - 1w + 1x_3 \geq 1000 \\
&\qquad 2x_1 + 0y + 0w - 1x_3 \leq 783 \\
&\text{and} \quad x_1, \quad y, \quad w, \quad x_3 \geq 0
\end{aligned}
$$

Negative right-hand quantity (b_i)

If one of the b_i quantities is negative, then by multiplying the entire constraint by -1 the constraint will be in proper form. Note that if the constraint was an inequality, multiplying by -1 will *reverse* the direction of the inequality ($\geq$ instead of $\leq$, and vice versa), which may thereby necessitate adding an artificial variable to obtain an initial basis.

For example, if one of the constraints in a problem is:

$$1x_1 - 2x_2 + 1x_3 \leq -10$$

then multiplying by -1 yields:

$$-1x_1 + 2x_2 - 1x_3 \geq 10$$

Adding *surplus* and artificial variables further results in:

$$-1x_1 + 2x_2 - 1x_3 - 1s_1 + 1a_1 = 10$$

No feasible solution

No solutions

In some cases, there will not be a feasible solution to the problem. Graphically, no solution space that simultaneously satisfies all constraints exists—See Figure 6.20. The clue to this situation, when using the simplex process, is that the "optimal" solution will still contain an *artificial* variable and the value of the $c_j - z_j$ row will still be on the order of $-M$ (see Table 6.15 on page 265).

Multiple optimal solutions

This solution is shown, for a maximization case, in Figure 6.21. The objective function, when moved as far as possible from the origin to the

FIGURE 6.20
No feasible solution space (shaded regions are infeasible)

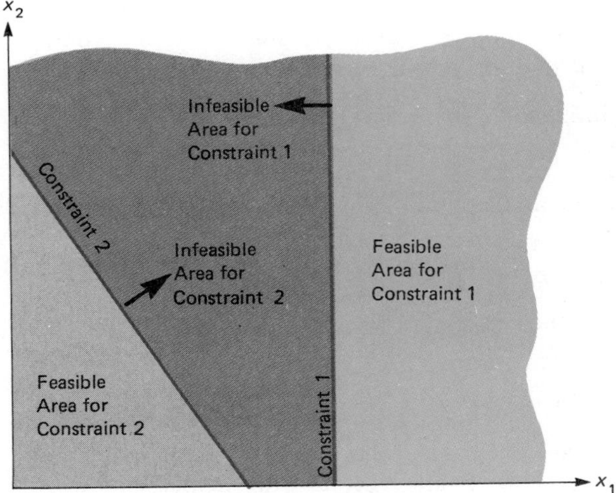

Basis	Unit profits	Quantity	x_1	x_2	s_1	s_2	a_1	a_2	Ratio
x_2	—	370	2	[1]	6	−1	0	0	
a_2	—	120	1	0	2	0	−3	[1]	
$c_j - z_j$			$(-M - 6)$	0	−17	$-2M$	−8	0	

TABLE 6.15
No feasible solution

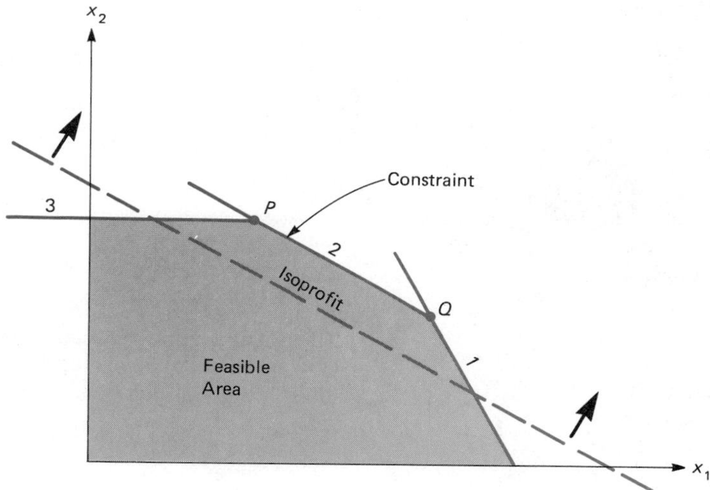

FIGURE 6.21
Multiple solutions case

right, does not touch a corner point, but rather a line segment between two points (P and Q in Figure 6.21). This happens when the isoprofit line is parallel to an "active" (binding) constraint (2 in Figure 6.21). In such a case, there are optimal solutions both at corner P, at corner Q, and at an infinite number of points on the line segment PQ.

This situation can be recognized in the simplex procedure by the fact that one of the nonbasic variables in the $c_j - z_j$ row will have a value of zero (see Table 6.16). Hence, a nonbasic variable may be brought into the solution basis, thereby creating a new solution with the same value of the objective function.

Basis	Unit profits	Quantity	x_1	x_2	s_1	s_2	Ratio
x_2	—	6	2	[1]	2	0	6/2 = 3
s_2	—	18	6	0	3	[1]	18/3 = 6
$c_j - z_j$			−3	—	0	0	

TABLE 6.16
The multiple solutions situation

Redundant constraint

A constraint that does not intersect the feasible area of solutions is called **redundant.** It can be removed from the problem without affecting the solution. The constraint $2x_1 + 1x_2 \leq 40$ in Figure 6.13 illustrates such a constraint. Note that a redundant constraint will *not* affect the solution nor the simplex process.

6.11 PROBLEMS FOR PART B

11. Solve by the simplex method:

a. maximize $z = 8x_1 + 6x_2$
subject to:

$$\begin{aligned} 4x_1 + 2x_2 &\leq 60 \\ 2x_1 + 4x_2 &\leq 48 \\ 1x_1 \quad\quad &\geq 5 \\ 3x_2 &\geq 5 \end{aligned}$$

b. minimize $z = 2x_1 + 4x_2 + x_3$
subject to:

$$\begin{aligned} 1x_1 + 2x_2 - 1x_3 &\geq 5 \\ 2x_1 - x_2 + 2x_3 &= 2 \\ -1x_1 + 2x_2 + 2x_3 &\geq 1 \\ 1x_3 &\leq 2 \end{aligned}$$

12. COM Food Corporation specializes in menu preparation for Philippine restaurants, institutions, and individual families. The major idea of the program is to provide an adequate (and tasteful) diet at a minimal cost. Given below is a *simplified* diet problem.

The minimum daily nutrient requirements for a certain group of adults are:

Calories	2,860
Protein	80 grams
Iron	15 milligrams
Niacin	20 milligrams
Vitamin A	20,000 units

A menu, when recommended by COM Food, must supply *at least* these minimum daily requirements. In this simplified problem, we shall assume that COM Food prepares one menu only. (In actual cases, a different menu would be prepared for every day of the week, or even every day of the month.)

Given below is a table of foods and prices (Philippine pesos per pound) offered to the customers.

Food	*Price per pound (pesos)*
Beef	1.00
Butter	.79
Bread	.26
Carrots	.15
Halibut	.80
Eggs	.34
Cheese	1.10

The quantities of calories, protein, iron, and calcium included in each 100 grams of the above foods are given below:

	Food	*Calories*	*Protein*	*Iron (mg)*	*Niacin (mg)*	*Vitamin A (units)*
A	Beef	309	26.0	3.1	4.1	0
B	Butter	716	.6	0	1	3,330
C	Bread	276	8.5	.6	.9	—
D	Carrots	42	1.2	.6	.4	12,000
E	Halibut	182	26.2	.8	10.5	0
F	Eggs	162	12.8	2.7	.3	1,140
G	Cheese	368	21.5	.5	.4	1,240

Find the least-cost food mix of the daily menu that satisfies minimum daily requirements.

a. Set up the problem as a linear program.
b. How many foods will be included in the optimal solution? Why? (Answer this *before* attempting to solve the problem.)
c. Review your answer to *(b)*. Under what circumstance(s) will the answer to *(b)* be different?
d. Solve the problem: Give the quantities of the foods to be included and the total daily cost. (A computer is recommended.)
e. In what nutritional elements will you have a surplus? In what quantities?
f. The customers are unhappy with the proposed menu solution since it does not in-

clude beef and it includes too much bread and eggs, so the following requirements are imposed:

(1) The menu must include at least 100 grams of beef.

(2) The menu should not include more than 500 grams of bread and 200 grams of eggs.

Resolve the problem and find the optimal menu now. What is the additional cost and in what nutritional elements will there be a surplus? (How much?)

13. Western Swiss Machine shop makes deluxe and regular skis on a weekly schedule for the area skiing enthusiasts. They have a contract with Apple Hill to supply 18 regular pairs of skis per week. They also sell both regular and deluxe skis to local sporting goods stores. A deluxe pair of skis requires 40 minutes for roughing and 20 minutes for finishing, while a regular pair of skis requires 20 minutes for roughing and 26⅔ minutes for finishing. With only 1,000 minutes for roughing and 800 minutes of finishing time available per week and a profit realization of 4 SFr (Swiss francs) and 3 SFr for the deluxe and regular, respectively, what weekly mix of the two types of skis should be produced to meet the contract's requirement and maximize profits?

a. Formulate as a linear program in two *different ways*.

b. Solve graphically (the formulation with the three constraints).

c. Solve by the simplex method.

14. Given:

$$\begin{aligned} &\text{minimize } z = 5x_1 + 4x_2 \\ &\text{subject to:} \\ &\quad 4x_1 + 2.5x_2 \geq 60 \\ &\quad 2x_1 + 5x_2 \geq 60 \\ &\quad 5x_1 + 4x_2 \geq 82 \end{aligned}$$

a. Solve the problem graphically.

b. Explain the uniqueness of the problem.

c. Solve the problem by the simplex method.

d. How is the uniqueness of this problem reflected in the simplex procedure?

e. Assume that the second constraint is changed to $2x_1 + 6x_2 \geq 60$. What will the impact of this change be? How will it be reflected in the simplex solution now?

15. The Indian Valve Company is developing an alloy to be used in the manufacture of valves. The research department has determined that the alloy can be formed by mixing the alloying metals of iron, nickel, and chrome, provided that the proportions of the materials fall within certain limits. The chemists have set the following proportional limits on the quantities of iron, nickel, and chrome that may be used.

Limit	*Iron*	*Nickel*	*Chrome*
Upper	5	1*	—
Lower	3	1*	—
Upper	3	—	1*
Lower	2	—	1*
Upper	—	1*	3
Lower	—	1*	3

* Base.

The upper limit means that, for example, *no more* than 5 parts of iron should be used for each part of nickel; the lower limit means that at least 3 parts of iron should be used for each part of nickel, and so on.

If the unit costs of iron, nickel, and chrome are 1, 2, and 3 rupees, respectively, what is the lowest-cost mixture per unit of alloy that will satisfy the quality requirements?

a. Formulate as a linear programming problem.

b. Solve (use a computer).

16. Given a problem:

$$\begin{aligned} &\text{maximize } z = 5x_1 + 3x_2 \\ &\text{subject to:} \\ &\quad 4x_1 + 2x_2 \leq 10 \\ &\quad 2x_1 + 2x_2 \leq 8 \end{aligned}$$

Solve the problem by the simplex method and/or graphically.

17. Solve Problem 16, adding a third constraint: $1x_1 \geq 2$.

18. Solve Problem 16 if the $\leq$ sign in the first constraint is changed to an equality (=).

19. Solve Problem 16 if the constraint $4x_1 + 2x_2 \leq 10$ is replaced by $1x_1 - 1x_2 \leq -1$.

20. Solve Problem 16 if both constraints are replaced by:

$$\begin{aligned} 1x_1 - 1x_2 &\leq -1 \\ 1x_1 &\leq 1 \end{aligned}$$

21. Solve Problem 16 if the additional constraint $1x_1 \geq 3$ is added.

6.12 CASE

THE DAPHNE JEWELRY COMPANY[26]

The Daphne Jewelry Company markets the bulk of its products through seven salespersons operating in seven separate sales territories (on a one-to-one basis). This is due to the fact that other area salespersons use Daphne's products only as a supplement to some other distributor's line. The seven leading salespersons follow just the opposite practice, using the products of other manufacturers to augment the Daphne line. For this reason the firm sets periodic sales quotas only for these persons.

The firm sells nine product lines. These are listed in Table 1, where each column shows how $1 in sales in each of the seven territories is distributed among the various product lines. For example, the .07 coefficient for the first product, belts, indicates that on the average, 7 cents of every dollar's worth of merchandise sold in territory 1 is generated by belts. These distributions were found to be quite stable over time, regardless of the size of the account.

TABLE 1
Dollar distribution value of sales for nine products in seven territories

	Sales territory						
Product lines	*No. 1*	*No. 2*	*No. 3*	*No. 4*	*No. 5*	*No. 6*	*No. 7*
1. Belts	.07	.02	.01	.15	.18	.15	.00
2. Buckles	.05	.00	.00	.10	.10	.07	.00
3. Package goods	.20	.35	.30	.25	.25	.25	.50
4. Necklaces	.07	.07	.07	.10	.15	.10	.03
5. Earrings	.15	.15	.15	.15	.15	.15	.15
6. Bracelets	.10	.20	.10	.10	.10	.10	.05
7. Gold stone	.18	.10	.17	.10	.05	.05	.12
8. Hematite	.15	.08	.17	.02	.02	.10	.12
9. Job turquoise	.03	.03	.03	.03	.00	.03	.03
Total	1.00	1.00	1.00	1.00	1.00	1.00	1.00

The market potential of each sales territory for the next planning period is presented in Table 2. This is Daphne's estimate of "potential" demand for its products next year for each of the seven territories at the present level of advertising. These demand forecasts were based upon past sales records, information gathered from trade associations and governmental agencies, as well as independent forecasts made by consulting firms that specialize in economic analysis of trade areas.

TABLE 2
Daphne's market potential in each of seven selling areas

Sales territory	*Market potential (maximum)*
No. 1	$ 225,000
No. 2	135,000
No. 3	150,000
No. 4	100,000
No. 5	210,000
No. 6	80,000
No. 7	250,000
Total	$1,150,000

The cost of a dollar's worth of merchandise required in the production of each product line, together with the corresponding sales commission paid on each dollar of sales, is depicted in

[26] Case developed by Dr. Malcolm Golden, University of Miami, and by Dr. Alan Parker, Florida International University. Reproduced with permission.

TABLE 3
Material costs and sales commission for nine product lines

Product lines	*Cost of $1 in merchandise*	*Sales commission on $1 in merchandise*
1–6 inclusive	$.50	$.15
7–9 inclusive	.67	.10

TABLE 4
Product line capacity

Product line	*Product line capacity*
1	$ 70,000
2	20,000
3	210,000
4	70,000
5	150,000
6	100,000
7	150,000
8	150,000
9	30,000

Table 3. The production capacity of the nine product lines is given in Table 4.

During recent years the company's sales and profits have been growing very slowly. Last year the company netted about $200,000 on sales of about $650,000. Mr. Brown, the president of Daphne Jewelry, was not pleased with the results. He felt there was a large quantity of unutilized production capacity as well as market potential. Mrs. Grant, the vice president of marketing, disagreed with Brown's assessment. She felt that the company was at or near optimal operating conditions, and that very little could be done within the framework of the existing conditions.

Last Monday, the president called the executive management team and requested proposals for improving the situation. The vice president for marketing suggested an increase in marketing efforts, especially in territories 2, 4, and 6, where current market potential is the lowest. The vice president for production suggested increasing production of those product lines that yield the highest return. The controller suggested dropping the least profitable products or territories, or both. The president was reluctant to accept any of these suggestions, since both the market potential and the production capacity were underutilized. Furthermore, the specific marketing plan proposed violated the production capabilities, while the proposed increase in certain product lines violated the marketing capabilities.

The president finally decided to call upon a management scientist who was asked to prepare a report to include the following items:

a. Evaluate the existing situation; determine if the company is indeed close to optimal operating conditions.
b. Analyze the marketing and production proposals brought forth by the vice presidents and the controller.
c. Submit other proposals; determine their feasibility and profitability.
d. Analyze the pricing and commission policies; submit recommendations.

6.13 GLOSSARY

Additivity assumption An assumption in LP that the returns are independent of each other and can be added together proportionally.

Allocation problem A problem involving the best allocation of scarce resources, commonly solved by LP.

Artificial variable A fictitious constraint parameter used in the simplex to obtain an initial solution.

Basic variable One of the variables currently in the basis.

Basis A solution in m variables of a system of m equations in n unknowns, where $n \geq m$. The other n–m variables have the value zero.

Blending problem One of the two major types of LP problems: minimizing the cost of a given output.

Constraints Restrictions on the problem solution arising from limited resources, policy requirements, and so on.

Degeneracy A situation in the simplex where a basic variable takes on the value zero, just like a nonbasic variable.

Divisibility assumption An assumption in LP that the resources are infinitely divisible, an unrealistic assumption when considering items such as automobiles or people.

Feasible area The solution space or region that satisfies all the constraints simultaneously.

Feasible solution A solution inside or on the boundary of the feasible area.

Inequality constraint A restriction on some combination of the variables such that they must be greater than, less than, or equal to a particular value.

Infeasible solution A solution that violates at least one constraint.

Integer programming A programming approach that recognizes the indivisibility of one or more of the decision variables.

Isocost (isoprofit) lines Lines of constant cost (profit) on a graph, each line parallel to the others.

Iteration One pass through an algorithmic process, such as the simplex.

Linear function A mathematical expression in which the variables appear in separate terms and raised to the first power.

Multiple optimal solutions When alternative optima exist.

Nonnegativity constraint The restriction in LP that all decision variables must be positive or zero.

Objective function The statement of the goal of the program (the result variable) in mathematical form.

Optimal solution The best of all feasible solutions.

Product-mix problem One of the two basic forms of LP problems: maximizing the output with given resources.

Redundant constraint A constraint that does not affect the feasible region or solutions.

Simplex method A particular algorithm for solving programming problems stated as linear functions that only investigates feasible corner points of the solution space.

Slack variable A variable representing the difference between the use of a resource and its availability.

Surplus variable A variable representing the difference between the use of a resource and a minimum requirement.

Unbounded solution A solution involving the infinite use of some resource.

Vertex A corner point of the solution space corresponding to the intersection of two or more constraints.

6.14 REFERENCES AND BIBLIOGRAPHY

1. Anderson, D. R., D. J. Sweeney, and T. Williams. *Linear Programming for Decision Making.* St. Paul, Minn.: West Publishing, 1974.
2. Bazaraa, M. S., and J. J. Jarvis. *Linear Programming and Network Flows.* New York: John Wiley & Sons, 1977.
3. Best, M. J., and K. Ritter. *Linear Programming: Action Set Analysis and Computer Programs.* Englewood Cliffs, N.J.: Prentice-Hall, 1985.
4. Dantzig, G. B. *Linear Programming and Extensions.* Princeton, N.J.: Princeton University Press, 1963.
5. Friendly, J. "Shazam! A Shortcut for Computers." *New York Times,* November 11, 1979, p. E7.
6. Gass, S. I. *An Illustrated Guide to Linear Programming.* New York: McGraw-Hill, 1970.
7. Ignizio, J. P. *Linear Programming in Single and Multiple Objective Systems.* Englewood Cliffs, N.J.: Prentice-Hall, 1982.
8. Hooker, J. N. "Karmarker's Linear Programming Algorithm." *Interfaces,* July–August 1986, pp. 75–90, and January–February 1987, p. 128.

9. Karmarker, N. "A New Polynomial-time Algorithm for Linear Programming." *Combinatorica,* 4., no. 4, 1984, pp. 373–95.

10. Kolata, G. "A Fast Way to Solve Hard Problems." *Science,* September 21, 1984, pp. 1379–80.

11. Kolman, B., and R. E. Beck. *Elementary Linear Programming with Applications.* New York: Academic Press, 1980.

12. Laidlaw, C. D. *Linear Programming for Urban Development and Plan Evaluation.* New York: Praeger Publishers, 1972.

13. Lee, S. M. *Linear Optimization for Management.* New York: Petrocelli-Charter, 1976.

14. Lev, B., and H. J. Weiss. *Introduction to Mathematical Programming.* New York: Elsevier North-Holland, 1982.

15. Levin, R. L., and R. P. Lamone. *Linear Programming for Management Decisions.* Homewood, Ill.: Richard D. Irwin, 1969.

16. Loomba, N. P. *Linear Programming: A Managerial Perspective,* 2nd ed. New York: Macmillan, 1976.

17. Loomba, N. P., and E. Turban. *Applied Programming in Management.* New York: Holt, Rinehart & Winston, 1974.

18. Machol, R. E. *Elementary Systems Mathematics: Linear Programming for Business and Social Sciences.* New York: McGraw-Hill, 1976.

19. Rothenberg, R. *Linear Programming.* New York: Elsevier North-Holland, 1980.

20. Taha, H. A. *Operations Research: An Introduction.* 4th ed. New York: Macmillan, 1987.

7

7.1 Crude oil refining.
7.2 Paper trimming.
7.3 Agriculture.
7.4 Finance (banking).
7.5 Paper manufacturing.
7.6 Marketing.
7.7 Auditing.
7.8 Hospital scheduling.
7.9 Multiperiod production scheduling.
7.10 Solution of game theory problems.
7.11 Concluding remarks.
7.12 Problems.
7.13 References and bibliography.

The power and richness of linear programming are demonstrated in this chapter through 10 diverse examples. In addition, the formulation of complex and difficult situations is illustrated in many of the examples. The problems at the end of the chapter are intended to enhance formulation skills.

Linear programming—applications

LEARNING OBJECTIVES

The student should be able to:

a. Perceive which decision situations satisfy the assumptions of linear programming, and which do not.
b. Appreciate the richness of application of the linear programming approach.
c. Be able to formulate appropriate complex decision situations as linear programs.
d. Understand the application of linear programming in general to managerial decisions and problems.

7.1 CRUDE OIL REFINING

CAM Oil Company produces four products in its refinery: gasoline, heating oil, jet fuel, and lubricating oil. These products are made from four available crude oils. The process is schematically shown in Figure 7.1.

The first three crudes are processed in unit I; the fourth crude is processed in either unit I or unit II. Only unit II is capable of producing lube oil in addition to the other three products.

Resources (input) availability (in barrels per week)

Crude 1 and 3: up to 200,000 each
Crude 2: up to 150,000
Crude 4: up to 250,000

Input-output coefficients Table 7.1 shows the input-output relationship between crudes (inputs) and products (outputs). These are the yields. For example, a barrel of crude 1 yields .5 barrels of gasoline, .3 barrels of heating oil, and .1 barrels of jet fuel.

Marketability Each week, CAM can sell up to 250,000 barrels of gasoline; 120,000 barrels of heating oil; 30,000 barrels of lube oil; and 100,000 barrels of jet fuel.

Profit For each barrel of crude 1 refined, CAM realizes 15 cents profit, crude 2 brings 20 cents per barrel, crude 3 brings 11 cents per

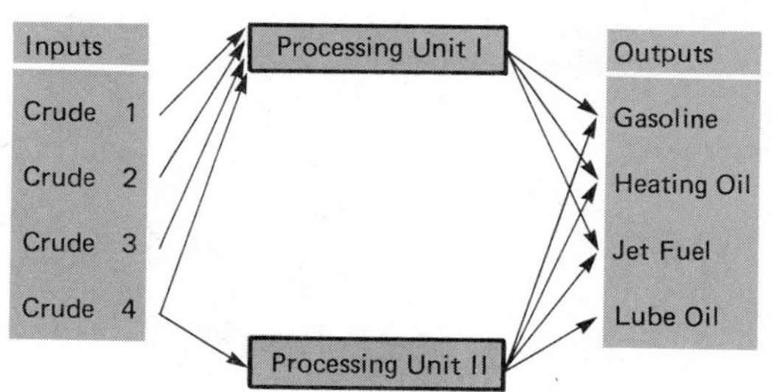

FIGURE 7.1
CAM Oil Company

TABLE 7.1
Input-output coefficients

	Gasoline	*Heating oil*	*Lube oil*	*Jet fuel*	*Loss*
Unit I					
Crude 1	.5	.3	0	.1	.1
2	.4	.2	0	.2	.2
3	.6	.2	0	.1	.1
4	.5	.1	0	.2	.2
Unit II					
Crude 4	.4	.1	.3	.1	.1

barrel, and crude 4 brings 20 cents per barrel if processed in unit I and 30 cents per barrel if processed in unit II. The objective of CAM is to maximize profits. The problem is: How much crude oil of each available type should CAM refine each week to meet the profit maximization objective?

Formulation

1. ***Define the decision variables***

They are (all in barrels per week):

$$\begin{aligned} x_1 &= \text{Amount of crude 1 to be processed} \\ x_2 &= \text{Amount of crude 2 to be processed} \\ x_3 &= \text{Amount of crude 3 to be processed} \\ x_4 &= \text{Amount of crude 4 to be processed in unit I} \\ x_5 &= \text{Amount of crude 4 to be processed in unit II} \\ (x_4 + x_5 &= \text{Amount of crude 4 processed}) \end{aligned}$$

2. ***The objective function to be maximized is the total profit:***

$$\text{maximize } z = 15x_1 + 20x_2 + 11x_3 + 20x_4 + 30x_5$$

3. ***The constraints***

Crude availability:

$$\begin{aligned} 1x_1 &\le 200{,}000 \\ 1x_2 &\le 150{,}000 \\ 1x_3 &\le 200{,}000 \\ 1x_4 + 1x_5 &\le 250{,}000 \end{aligned}$$

Technology and marketability:

$$\begin{aligned} .5x_1 + .4x_2 + .6x_3 + .5x_4 + .4x_5 &\le 250{,}000 \quad \text{(for gasoline)} \\ .3x_1 + .2x_2 + .2x_3 + .1x_4 + .1x_5 &\le 120{,}000 \quad \text{(heating oil)} \\ .3x_5 &\le 30{,}000 \quad \text{(lube oil)} \\ .1x_1 + .2x_2 + .1x_3 + .2x_4 + .1x_5 &\le 100{,}000 \quad \text{(jet fuel)} \end{aligned}$$

The problem has thus been formulated and can be solved as an LP problem.

The optimal (computerized) solution

$$x_1 = 150{,}000 \text{ barrels}$$
$$x_2 = 150{,}000 \text{ barrels}$$
$$x_3 = 0$$
$$x_4 = 150{,}000 \text{ barrels}$$
$$x_5 = 100{,}000 \text{ barrels}$$
$$\text{Total profit} = 11{,}250{,}000 \text{ cents} = \$112{,}500 \text{ (each week).}$$

Moral: Even a few pennies per barrel can make you a millionaire if you use linear programming and happen to own an oil company!

7.2 PAPER TRIMMING

The Northwestern Paper Company produces rolls of paper, 12 inches wide × 1,000 feet long. These standard rolls are purchased by many of its clients. However, some clients prefer to receive special sizes; namely, 2-inch, 3½-inch, or 5-inch rolls, all 1,000 feet long. The minimum amount of rolls required is 500 of 2-inch, 2,000 of 3½-inch, and 1,500 of 5-inch rolls. The special rolls can be cut out of the 12-inch standard rolls.

TABLE 7.2
Paper trimming alternatives

	Size of rolls			
Alternatives	*2-inch*	*3½-inch*	*5-inch*	*Waste*
1	6	0	0	0
2	1	0	2	0
3	2	2	0	1
4	0	2	1	0
5	3	0	1	1
6	4	1	0	½

The company is considering six cutting alternatives, each of which results in one inch of waste or less. These are shown in Table 7.2 which lists the number of rolls in each cutting alternative. Find the best cutting program to minimize the waste.

Formulation

1. ***The decision variables***

Let x_1 = Number of 12-inch rolls to be cut according to alternative 1, x_2 = Number of rolls to be cut according to alternative 2, and so on.

2. ***The objective function to be minimized is the "total waste":***

$$\text{minimize } z = 0x_1 + 0x_2 + 1x_3 + 0x_4 + 1x_5 + \tfrac{1}{2}x_6$$

3. ***The constraints***

$$6x_1 + 1x_2 + 2x_3 + 0x_4 + 3x_5 + 4x_6 \geq 500$$ (which reflects the minimum requirement for 2-inch rolls)

$$2x_3 + 2x_4 + 1x_6 \geq 2{,}000$$ (for 3½-inch rolls)

$$2x_2 + 1x_4 + 1x_5 \geq 1{,}500$$ (for 5-inch rolls)

Solution (by computer)

$$x_1 = 41.67,\ x_2 = 250,\ x_3 = 0,\ x_4 = 1{,}000,\ x_5 = 0,\ x_6 = 0$$

Total waste (objective function) is zero. This solution will result in exactly 500 rolls of 2-inches, 2,000 rolls of 3½ inches, and 1,500 rolls of 5 inches.

7.3 AGRICULTURE

Sam Green just acquired a five-acre orange grove in South Florida. The U.S. Department of Agriculture recommends that orange groves be fertilized twice a year. The quantities of chemicals recommended by the Agriculture Department, per acre, per application of fertilizer, are:

Nitrogen—at least 20 lbs.
Phosphoric acid—at least 25 lbs.
Potash—at least 30 lbs.
Chlorine—no more than 36 lbs.

Fertilizers are sold on the market under various brands, in standard bags of either 25 lbs. or 50 lbs. Each brand is designated by a system of three numbers. For example, 8–10–6 means that each bag contains 8 percent (by weight) nitrogen, 10 percent phosphoric acid, and 6 percent potash.

Sam is shopping for fertilizers, determined to pay as little as possible; at the same time, he wants to follow the recommendations of the Agriculture Department.

The fertilizers currently available on the market are:

Brand	*Designation*	*Cost/bag*	*Chlorine content (percent)*	*Weight*
A	4–6–8	$5.50	8	50 lbs.
B	8–8–8	6.00	6	50 lbs.
C	6–6–20	5.00	5	25 lbs.

Find:

a. How many bags of each type Sam should buy each year.
b. Sam's yearly budget for fertilizers.
c. The excess amount of chemicals that the grove will receive each year.

d. The actual amount of chlorine provided to the grove yearly, as compared to the recommended amount.

Formulation

This blending-type problem can be formulated in two different ways, depending on the definition of the decision variables. The problem is first solved for one application of the fertilizers per acre.

Formulation A

1. ***The decision variables***

These are the number of pounds of each of the fertilizers, that is:

x_1 = No. of pounds of brand A, per application, per acre
x_2 = No. of pounds of brand B, per application, per acre
x_3 = No. of pounds of brand C, per application, per acre

2. ***The objective function***

Each pound of brand A costs: 5.50/50 = .11
Each pound of brand B costs: 6.00/50 = .12
Each pound of brand C costs: 5.00/25 = .20

Therefore, the objective function for total cost, z, is:

$$z = .11x_1 + .12x_2 + .20x_3$$

and it is to be *minimized.*

3. ***The constraints***

a. Provide at least 20 pounds of nitrogen. Nitrogen is provided by the three fertilizers according to the percentage designated; that is:

$$\underbrace{.04x_1}_{\text{provided by brand A}} + \underbrace{.08x_2}_{\text{provided by brand B}} + \underbrace{.06x_3}_{\text{provided by brand C}} \geq 20$$

b. Provide at least 25 pounds of phosphoric acid. Similarly:

$$.06x_1 + .08x_2 + .06x_3 \geq 25$$

c. Provide at least 30 pounds of potash. Similarly:

$$.08x_1 + .08x_2 + .20x_3 \geq 30$$

d. Provide no more than 36 pounds of chlorine. Similarly:

$$.08x_1 + .06x_2 + .05x_3 \leq 36$$

The solution (by computer)

$$x_1 = 0$$
$$x_2 = 285.71$$
$$x_3 = 35.71$$
$$z = \$41.43$$

Note that this solution, even for five acres, results in a noninteger number of bags. Thus, the problem is really one of "integer programming," a topic we will address in Chapter 8.

Another formulation of this problem, intended to get around the integer difficulty, is given below. Can you see why this formulation is no better than the one in A in solving the integer difficulty?

Formulation B

1. ***The decision variables***

They are the number of bags of each brand:

y_1 = No. of bags of brand A, per acre, per application
y_2 = No. of bags of brand B, per acre, per application
y_3 = No. of bags of brand C, per acre, per application

2. ***The objective function***

$$\text{minimize } z = 5.5y_1 + 6.0y_2 + 5.0y_3$$

3. ***The constraints***

The nitrogen constraint:

$$.04(50)y_1 + .08(50)y_2 + .06(25)y_3 \geq 20$$

The student is encouraged to complete the formulation of this problem.

7.4 FINANCE (BANKING)

Palmetto National Savings & Loan makes five kinds of loans. These loans, with the yearly interest rate charged to customers, are shown in the table below:

Type of loan	*Interest charged (percent)*
Commercial loans	15
Home mortgage (first mortgage)	10
Home improvements	13.6
Home mortgage (second mortgage)	14
Short-term revolving loan	18

The bank has $53 million in available funds. Its objective is to maximize yield on investment.

The demand for funds

The demand for short-term revolving loans never exceeds \$5 million. All other demands are unlimited.

Policies and regulations

a. Home improvement loans cannot be higher than 20 percent of first mortgage loans.
b. Commercial loans must be smaller than or equal to the second mortgage loans.
c. The bank must invest at least 60 percent of the loans outstanding (total loans) in mortgages.
d. For safety reasons, there must be at least \$2 invested in first mortgage loans for every dollar invested in second mortgage loans.
e. Short-term loans cannot exceed \$5 million.

Find the best bank fund allocation plan.

Formulation

1. ***The decision variables***

x_1 = Dollars invested in commercial loans
x_2 = Dollars invested in first mortgages
x_3 = Dollars invested in home improvements
x_4 = Dollars invested in second mortgages
x_5 = Dollars invested in short-term loans

2. ***The objective function***

Total yearly yield, $z = .15x_1 + .10x_2 + .136x_3 + .14x_4 + .18x_5$, which is to be maximized.

3. ***The constraints***

Monthly availability: $1x_1 + 1x_2 + 1x_3 + 1x_4 + 1x_5 \leq 53{,}000{,}000$
Policy a: $1x_3 \leq .2x_2$
b: $1x_1 \leq 1x_4$
c: $1x_2 + 1x_4 \geq .6(1x_1 + 1x_2 + 1x_3 + 1x_4 + 1x_5)$
d: $1x_2 \geq 2x_4$
e: $1x_5 \leq 5{,}000{,}000$

The solution (derived by computer)

$x_1 = 10{,}900{,}000$
$x_2 = 21{,}800{,}000$
$x_3 = 4{,}360{,}000$
$x_4 = 10{,}900{,}000$
$x_5 = 5{,}000{,}000$
$z = 6{,}838{,}808$

7.5 PAPER MANUFACTURING

A paper mill produces two types of paper: paper for books and paper for magazines. Each ton of paper for books requires 2 tons of spruce and 3 tons of fir; each ton of paper for magazines requires 2 tons of spruce and 2 tons of fir. The company must supply at least 25,000 tons of paper for books and 100,000 tons of paper for magazines a year. The yearly availability of materials is 278,000 tons of spruce and 426,000 tons of fir. The marketing department requires that the amount of paper manufactured for magazines be at least 1.5 times that which is manufactured for books. Each ton of paper for books is sold for $750, while that for magazines is sold for $685 per ton. The cost of spruce is $100 per ton, while a ton of fir costs $112.

Find:

a. The most profitable production plan.
b. The best use of the resources.
c. The annual profit.

Formulation

1. *The decision variables*

x_1 = Paper produced for books (in tons)
x_2 = Paper produced for magazines (in tons)

2. *The objective function*

Cost of materials for books: 2(100) + 3(112) = 536
Revenue = 750. Thus, gross profit = 750 − 536 = $214 per ton

Cost of materials for magazines: 2(100) + 2(112) = 424
Revenue = 685. Thus, gross profit = 685 − 424 = $261 per ton

The objective function is:

$$\text{maximize } z = 214x_1 + 261x_2$$

3. *The constraints*

$2x_1 + 2x_2 \leq 278{,}000$ (spruce availability)
$3x_1 + 2x_2 \leq 426{,}000$ (fir availability)
$1x_1 \geq 25{,}000$ (supply requirement)
$1x_2 \geq 100{,}000$ (supply requirement)
$1x_2 \geq 1.5x_1$ *or:* $1.5x_1 - x_2 \leq 0$ (marketing requirement)

The solution

a. The optimal solution is:

$$x_1 = 25{,}000$$
$$x_2 = 114{,}000$$

b. The spruce is used in full (slack = 0).
The fir is only partially utilized.
(There is a slack of 123,000 tons.)

c. The annual gross profit is z = \$35,104,000 (before processing expenses).

7.6 MARKETING

The Everglade Shoe Company plans to allocate some or all of its monthly advertising budget of \$82,000 in the Miami Metropolitan area. It can purchase local radio spots at \$120 per spot, local TV spots at \$600 per spot, and local newspaper advertising at \$220 per insertion.

The company's policy requirements specify that the company must spend at least \$40,000 on TV and allow monthly newspaper expenditures up to either \$60,000 or 50 percent of the TV expenditures, whichever is most profitable, overall, for the company.

The payoff from each advertising medium is a function of the size of its audience. The general experience of the firm is that the values of insertions and spots in terms of "audience points" (an arbitrary unit), are as given below:

Radio	40 audience points per spot
TV	180 audience points per spot
Newspapers	320 audience points per insertion

Find the optimal allocation of advertising expenditures among the three media.

Formulation

1. ***The decision variables***

x_1 = No. of spots allocated to radio
x_2 = No. of spots allocated to TV
x_3 = No. of insertions allocated to newspapers

2. ***The objective function***

$$\text{maximize } z = 40x_1 + 180x_2 + 320x_3$$

3. ***The constraints***

$$(1)\quad 120x_1 + 600x_2 + 220x_3 \leq 82{,}000$$
$$(2)\quad 600x_2 \geq 40{,}000$$

and either:

$$(3a)\quad 220x_3 \leq 60{,}000$$

or:

$$(3b) \qquad 220x_3 \leq 300x_2$$

and x_1, x_2, x_3 are integers.

The solution

The problem must be solved twice, once for each set of "either/or" constraints, and the better solution selected.

Either:

$$x_2 = 66\tfrac{2}{3},\ x_3 = 190.9,\quad z = 73{,}090.9 \text{ for } (3a)$$

or:

$$x_2 = 91.1,\ x_3 = 124.24,\ z = 56{,}157.6 \text{ for } (3b)$$

The first solution is better. Rounding to integers:

$$x_2 = 66$$
$$x_3 = 191$$
$$z = \$73{,}000$$

Note: Another approach is to use 0–1 auxiliary variables, as in Section 8.6.

7.7 AUDITING

Arthur and Son, P.A., is an auditing firm that conducts both financial and operational audits. Arthur can conduct 90 financial audits (FAs) per year if he spends full time on just FAs, *or* 180 operational audits (OAs) per year full time, or any linear combination of both.[1] Son works up the reports on Arthur's audits for the customer firms. Son can prepare 180 financial audit reports or 150 operational audit reports per year, or any linear combination thereof. The office staff can handle no more than 160 reports of any kind, per year. Arthur and Son have calculated that to keep their association solvent they must produce at least 30 FAs and 50 OAs each year.

The profit from each FA has averaged \$720 in the past and for each OA has been about \$650. How many FAs and OAs should Arthur and Son attempt to conduct each year to maximize their firm's profits?

Formulation

1. The decision variables

$$y = \text{Number of FAs}$$
$$x = \text{Number of OAs}$$

[1] A linear combination means that since the capacity required for 1 FA is the same as that for 2 OAs (90 to 180 ratio), then Arthur can conduct such combinations as 89 FAs plus 2 OAs, or 88 FAs plus 4 OAs, and so on.

2. *The objective function z, to be maximized*

$$\text{maximize } z = 720y + 650x$$

3. *The constraints*

The formulation of the constraints is more complicated. To show how they are derived, let us graph the situation for Arthur (Figure 7.2).

Arthur can conduct 90 FAs at maximum capacity. This information is shown as point *A*, that is, zero OAs and 90 FAs. Similarly, point *B* (180, 0) designates that Arthur can conduct 180 OAs and zero FAs at maximum capacity. The straight line connecting points *A* and *B* indicates all other possible combinations for Arthur. For example, point *C* designates 90 OAs and 45 FAs. The problem is to find the equation of the straight line that designates the constraint. From geometry it is known that if the coordinates of two points are (x_1, y_1) and (x_2, y_2), then the equation of the straight line connecting these two points is:

$$y = \frac{y_2x_1 - y_1x_2}{x_1 - x_2} + \left(\frac{y_1 - y_2}{x_1 - x_2}\right)x \tag{7.1}$$

Thus, the equation of the straight line between (0, 90) and (180, 0) is:

$$y = 90 - \left(\frac{90}{180}\right)x = 90 - .5x$$

or:

$$y + .5x = 90$$

and the inequality constraint is:

$$y + .5x \leq 90$$

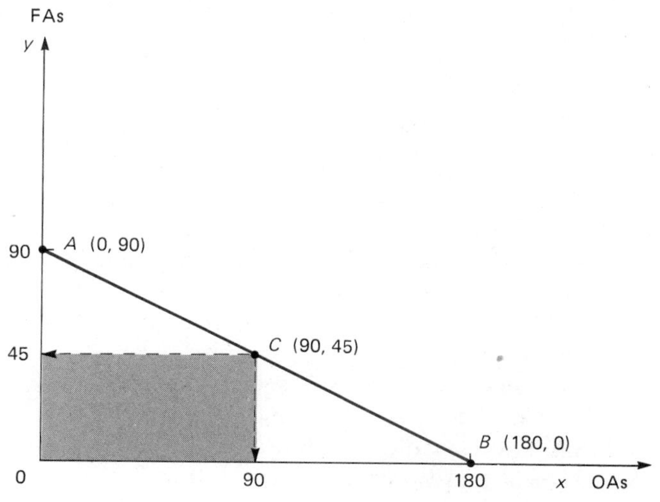

FIGURE 7.2
Capacity of Arthur

Similarly, for Son:

$$y + 1.2x \leq 180$$

The office staff and solvency constraints are expressed as:

$$\begin{aligned} y + x &\leq 160 \\ y &\geq 30 \\ x &\geq 50 \end{aligned}$$

Summary of formulation

$$\begin{aligned} &\text{maximize } 720y + 650x \\ &\text{subject to:} \\ &\quad 1y + .5x \leq 90 \\ &\quad 1y + 1.2x \leq 180 \\ &\quad 1y + 1x \leq 160 \\ &\quad 1y \geq 30 \\ &\quad 1x \geq 50 \end{aligned}$$

The solution of this problem is $y = 30$, $x = 120$, and the maximum profit = \$99,600.

7.8 HOSPITAL SCHEDULING

Palm General Hospital is concerned with the staffing of its emergency department. A recent analysis indicated that a typical day may be divided into six periods. In each period a different demand level, measured by "cases," is experienced.

Time period	*Average number of cases*
7 A.M.–11 A.M.	80
11 A.M.– 3 P.M.	60
3 P.M.– 7 P.M.	120
7 P.M.–11 P.M.	60
11 P.M.– 3 A.M.	40
3 A.M.– 7 A.M.	20

Past experience indicates that one emergency room (ER) nurse is required to handle every 2.5 cases each hour. Thus, for example, between 7 A.M. and 8 A.M. there is a need for eight nurses to handle the 20 cases (80 cases per 4 hours).

ER nurses work in shifts of eight hours. The normal shifts are: 7 A.M.–3 P.M.; 3 P.M.–11 P.M.; and 11 P.M.–7 A.M. However, three nurses said that they are willing to start an eight-hour shift at 11 A.M., if necessary, and two said that they will start a shift at 7 P.M., if asked.

Find the least-cost schedule that will assure complete coverage of the emergency room. Make any necessary assumptions.

Formulation

The problem is to find the minimum number of nurses, assuming that they all receive the same wages. Thus, the least cost schedule means the minimum number of nurses.

1. ***The decision variables***

x_1 = Number of nurses starting at 7 A.M.
x_2 = Number of nurses starting at 11 A.M.
x_3 = Number of nurses starting at 3 P.M.
x_4 = Number of nurses starting at 7 P.M.
x_5 = Number of nurses starting at 11 P.M.

2. ***The objective function***

$$\text{minimize } z = x_1 + x_2 + x_3 + x_4 + x_5$$

3. ***The constraints***

To structure the constraints, it is necessary to assume first that the demand in each time period is constant regardless of the hour observed. This enables the computation of the minimum number of required nurses:

Time period	7–11	11–3	3–7	7–11	11–3	3–7
Required nurses	8	6	12	6	4	2

The demand constraints thus are:

$$\begin{aligned} 1x_1 &\geq 8 \text{ (for the 7 A.M.–11 A.M. time period)} \\ 1x_1 + 1x_2 &\geq 6 \text{ (for 11–3)} \\ 1x_2 + 1x_3 &\geq 12 \text{ (for 3–7)} \\ 1x_3 + 1x_4 &\geq 6 \text{ (for 7–11)} \\ 1x_4 + 1x_5 &\geq 4 \text{ (for 11–3)} \\ 1x_5 &\geq 2 \text{ (for 3–7)} \end{aligned}$$

The supply constraints are:

$$\begin{aligned} x_2 &\leq 3 \\ x_4 &\leq 2 \end{aligned}$$

4. ***The optimal solution (derived by computer) is:***

$$x_1 = 8,\ x_2 = 3,\ x_3 = 9,\ x_4 = 2,\ x_5 = 2,$$

for a total of 24 nurses.

7.9 MULTIPERIOD PRODUCTION SCHEDULING

Linear programming can be used to determine a production schedule over several production periods in cases of fluctuating demand for a product. The following example illustrates such a situation.

Calpal is a small manufacturer of a special engineering workstation. The company operates one plant with a monthly capacity of 3,000 units. In addition, 750 units can be produced on an overtime basis, which is 30 percent more expensive, on the average. The labor cost when producing on regular time is \$1,000; it is \$1,300 on overtime (per workstation produced).

The company may use inventories to reduce fluctuations in production, but carrying inventories costs money (see Chapter 14). The cost of carrying one finished unit in inventory is \$80 per unit per month.

Management is preparing a six-month production plan with the following stipulations:

a. All demand must be met according to the following schedule.

Month	*Units*
1	2,500
2	3,200
3	3,800
4	3,500
5	5,000
6	3,000

b. There should be no inventory left at the end of the sixth month.
c. There is no inventory at the present time.

The problem is to find the production schedule for the next six months that minimizes total cost.

Formulation

The decision variables

x_i = Quantity produced in month i, on a regular time basis, for $i = 1,2,3,4,5,6$
y_i = Quantity produced on overtime in month i
v_i = quantity in inventory at the end of month i; note that $v_6 = 0$

The objective function

$$\text{minimize } z = 1{,}000(x_1 + x_2 + x_3 + x_4 + x_5 + x_6) + 1{,}300(y_1 + y_2 + y_3 + y_4 + y_5 + y_6) + 80(v_1 + v_2 + v_3 + v_4 + v_5)$$

The constraints

a. Production is limited to 3,000 units/month on a regular basis. Six constraints express this limitation.

$$x_1 \leq 3{,}000,\ x_2 \leq 3{,}000,\ x_3 \leq 3{,}000,\ x_4 \leq 3{,}000,\ x_5 \leq 3{,}000,\ x_6 \leq 3{,}000$$

b. Similarly, we have the following overtime limitations:

$$y_1 \leq 750,\ y_2 \leq 750,\ y_3 \leq 750,\ y_4 \leq 750,\ y_5 \leq 750,\ y_6 \leq 750$$

c. Six constraints (one for each month) can be written to show how the demand is to be met. For month 1:

$$x_1 + y_1 - v_1 = 2{,}500$$

That is, the total produced in regular and overtime, minus what we carry on for the future, must equal the demand.

Similarly, for months 2–6 we get:

$$\begin{aligned} x_2 + y_2 - v_2 + v_1 &= 3{,}200 \\ x_3 + y_2 - v_3 + v_2 &= 3{,}800 \\ x_4 + y_4 - v_4 + v_3 &= 3{,}500 \\ x_5 + y_5 - v_5 + v_4 &= 5{,}000 \\ x_6 + y_6 - 0 + v_5 &= 3{,}000 \end{aligned}$$

Solution

The solution involves 17 decision variables and 18 constraints; it is left as a homework exercise for the student.

Note: This problem can be expanded in the real world to include variable monthly production capability, back orders (unfilled orders) and their penalties, variable costs, and so on. When more complexity is added, linear programming may not be a sufficient tool and we may need to employ a more powerful tool such as dynamic programming (Chapter 12) or simulation (Chapter 16).

7.10 SOLUTION OF GAME THEORY PROBLEMS

In order to demonstrate the use of linear programming in solving games, an example of a 2 × 2 game solved in Chapter 4 will be used. Linear programming, however, can be used with two-person, zero-sum games of any size, within practical limits. The example is reproduced as Table 7.3.

The solution involves two stages:

a. If negative values exist, it becomes necessary to "scale up" all entries by adding a fixed number to them. (The scaling does not affect the optimal solution except to increase its value by the number added to

TABLE 7.3

B / A	b_1	b_2
a_1	4	−1
a_2	−2	1

TABLE 7.4

B / A	b_1	b_2
a_1	7	2
a_2	1	4

each cell). Scaling will make all entries either zero or positive.[2] In our case, 3 is added to all cells, as shown in Table 7.4.

b. Transformation into linear programming form. Each game can be transformed to either a maximization or a minimization form.

Example: Transformation to a minimization problem

Let us look at the problem from the point of view of player A. Player A wants to design her game in such a manner that *at least* a payoff u is guaranteed. Assume that she mixes a_1 and a_2 with proportions p_1 and p_2. Then, the above requirement can be written as two inequalities:

Step 1. Write the inequalities (constraints)

$7p_1 + 1p_2 \geq u$ (The expected gain, when player B plays b_1 all the time, is at least as large as u.)

$2p_1 + 4p_2 \geq u$ (The expected gain, when player B plays b_2 all the time, is at least as large as u.)

The coefficients of each of the two inequalities are determined by reading each column of the game matrix, starting with the first.

Step 2. Divide the inequalities by u The result is:

$$\frac{7p_1}{u} + \frac{1p_2}{u} \geq 1$$
$$\frac{2p_1}{u} + \frac{4p_2}{u} \geq 1 \tag{7.2}$$

Step 3. Introduce auxiliary variables Now, let us introduce two new variables, x_1 and x_2, whose values, by definition, are given as:

$$x_1 = \frac{p_1}{u} \quad \textit{and} \quad x_2 = \frac{p_2}{u} \tag{7.3}$$

[2] In scaling for a linear programming computer solution, it is generally wise to scale in such a way as to produce as many zeros as possible, to reduce computer calculation and to save storage space. But here we deliberately scaled up so that zeros are avoided in order to illustrate a more general example.

Having introduced the new variables into Equation 7.2, the constraints can now be rewritten as:

$$7x_1 + 1x_2 \geq 1$$
$$2x_1 + 4x_2 \geq 1$$

Step 4. Construct the objective function Because player A has only two courses of action to choose from, there are only two proportions to consider (p_1 and p_2) whose sum equals 1 ($p_1 + p_2 = 1$).

Now, divide the equation $p_1 + p_2 = 1$ by u. The result is:

$$\frac{p_1}{u} + \frac{p_2}{u} = \frac{1}{u}$$

Introducing the auxiliary variables x_1 and x_2, we obtain:

$$x_1 + x_2 = \frac{1}{u} \qquad (7.4)$$

Player A would like to have no less than u, but she would also like u to be as high as possible, or to maximize u. This is equivalent to minimizing $1/u$ or to minimizing $x_1 + x_2$. Hence, the problem can now be formulated from player A's perspective.

Step 5. Formulate the linear programming problem The result of the previous step is the objective function.

$$\text{minimize } w = x_1 + x_2$$

The objective function is subject to the constraints derived in step 3.

$$7x_1 + 1x_2 \geq 1$$
$$2x_1 + 4x_2 \geq 1$$

Step 6. Solve the linear programming problem The optimal solution is:

$$x_1 = \frac{3}{26} \quad \text{and} \quad x_2 = \frac{5}{26}$$

A linear programming presentation for player B can be generated similarly. (This time the objective function is to be *maximized*.)

$$\text{maximize } z = y_1 + y_2$$
subject to:
$$7y_1 + 2y_2 \leq 1$$
$$1y_1 + 4y_2 \leq 1$$

where y_1 and y_2 are auxiliary variables:

$$y_1 = \frac{q_1}{u}; \quad y_2 = \frac{q_2}{u}$$

The optimal solution for this problem is:

$$y_1 = \frac{1}{13}$$

$$y_2 = \frac{3}{13}$$

Step 7. ***Find the proportion mix*** In order to find the proportions (p for player A, q for B) of the mixed strategy, a *transformation ratio, t,* is defined as:

Transformation ratio

$$t = \sum y_i = \sum x_j \qquad (7.5)$$

In our case, we get:

$$t = \sum y_i = \frac{1}{13} + \frac{3}{13} = \frac{4}{13}$$

or:

$$t = \sum x_j = \frac{3}{26} + \frac{5}{26} = \frac{8}{26} = \frac{4}{13}$$

Now, all y_i's and x_j's are divided by the transformation ratio to get the proportion mix for both players.

For player A:

$$p_j = \frac{x_j}{t} \qquad (7.6)$$

In the example:

$$p_1 = \frac{3/26}{4/13} = \frac{3}{8}$$

$$p_2 = \frac{5/26}{4/13} = \frac{5}{8}$$

For player B:

$$q_1 = \frac{y_i}{t} \qquad (7.7)$$

In the example:

$$q_1 = \frac{1/13}{4/13} = \frac{1}{4}$$

$$q_2 = \frac{3/13}{4/13} = \frac{3}{4}$$

Step 8. Finally, the value of the game is computed Using Equation 7.8:

$$V = \frac{1}{t} - k \tag{7.8}$$

where k is the number added while scaling up.

In our case, $k = 3$ and $t = 4/13$, thus $1/t = 13/4$ and V is:

$$V = \frac{13}{4} - 3 = \frac{1}{4}$$

Summary of the solution:

Player A: Play a_1 3/8 of the time, a_2 5/8 of the time.
Player B: Play b_1 1/4 of the time, b_2 3/4 of the time.
A gains in each play, on the average, 1/4 from B.

Computerization

Since it is possible to convert any game into a linear programming problem that has a very efficient computational solution procedure (the simplex method), then this procedure could be followed for all games, especially mixed strategy games. Another advantage of the conversion to linear programming is that, because of the "primal-dual" relationship (a concept we will describe in Chapter 8), it is sufficient to solve only one LP problem to find the strategy of both players.

One of the options available in the LINDO program [11] is a game theory presentation. The following example illustrates such a solution as well as the primal-dual relationship.

Example[3]

Given the game problem below:

		B	
		b_1	b_2
	a_1	4	−6
A	a_2	−5	8
	a_3	3	−4

[3] Condensed from LINDO [11].

The resultant LP problems are:

For A

maximize G
subject to:
(1) $1p_1 + 1p_2 + 1p_3 = 1$
(2) $4p_1 - 5p_2 + 3p_3 \geq G$
(3) $-6p_1 + 8p_2 - 4p_3 \geq G$

where G is the minimum expected profit, and p_i is the proportion to play a_i

For B

minimize L
subject to:
(1) $1q_1 + 1q_2 = 1$
(2) $4q_1 - 6q_2 \leq L$
(3) $-5q_1 + 8q_2 \leq L$
(4) $3q_1 - 4q_2 \leq L$

where L is the maximum expected loss, and q_i is the proportion to play b_i

Solution (computer printout)

For A | *For B*

Value of the objective function = 0.2

Variable	*Value*	*Variable*	*Value*
G	0.20	L	0.20
p_1	0.00	q_1	0.60
p_2	0.35	q_2	0.40
p_3	0.65		

Slacks and Duals

Constraint	*Slack*	*Dual*	*Constraint*	*Slack*	*Dual*
1	0	0.2	1	0	−0.20
2	0	−0.6	2	0.2	0.00
3	0	−0.4	3	0	0.35
			4	0	0.65

It is clear from this example that it is sufficient to solve *only one* player's LP problem. The dual's variables give the proportion mix for the second player.

Nonzero-sum games

Certain categories of nonzero-sum games can also be transformed to linear programming problems. For details, see LINDO [11].

7.11 CONCLUDING REMARKS

The 10 examples of applications presented in this chapter illustrate some of the wide range of applications of linear programming. Many other applications can be found throughout business, engineering, government, economics, science, and almost every field. The problems in Section 7.12 provide additional examples of this diversity.

However, linear programming is even more powerful than has been demonstrated so far. The solution to LP problems can also provide important supplementary information. This will be demonstrated in Chapter 8, where the topics of duality and sensitivity analysis are addressed.

7.12 PROBLEMS

1. Carlo's International manufactures blue jeans. Three brands are considered: A, B, and C. The manufacture of brand A requires 2 minutes machine time, 30 minutes labor, and costs $7. Brand B requires 2.5 minutes machine time, 40 minutes labor, and costs $10 to produce. Finally, brand C, the top of the line, requires 3 minutes machine time, 1 hour labor, and costs $13 to produce. Brand A sells for $12, brand B for $14, and brand C for $20.

   The company works on a weekly schedule of five days, with two shifts of 7.5 hours (net time) each. It has four machines available for production and 50 employees on each shift. Its weekly manufacturing budget is $10,000. Its declared objective is profit maximization.

   a. Formulate the problem as a linear program.
   b. Solve the problem (use the computer).

2. The Swiss Construction Company is building roads on the side of the Alps. It is necessary to use explosives to blow up the underground boulders to make the surface level. There are three ingredients (A, B, C) in the explosive used. It is known that at least 10 grams of the explosive must be used to get results. If more than 20 grams are used, the explosion will be too damaging. Also, for an explosion, at least ¼ gram of ingredient C must be used for every gram of ingredient A, and at least 1 gram of ingredient B must be used for every gram of ingredient C. The costs of ingredients A, B, and C are 6 Swiss francs (SFr), 18 SFr, and 20 SFr per gram, respectively. Find the least-cost explosive mix necessary to produce a safe explosion.

3. Westcan Corporation is considering producing five different types of small computers that yield the following unit profits:

Type	A	B	C	D	E
Net profit ($000)	16	8	11	6	10

   The company has $1 million capital to invest in production and a capability of 10,000 working days.

   The capital and labor requirements for each product are given below.

Type	*Required capital per unit ($000)*	*Required per unit working days*
A	20	200
B	15	120
C	16	150
D	10	80
E	14	100

   Formulate as a linear program to find the best production plan:

   a. If the company's objective is *profit maximization.*
   b. If the company's objective is to produce the *maximum number of total units* (of all types together).

4. Sun Electric can produce three chips:
   A, which costs $6 per unit and sells for $9 per unit.
   B, which costs $5 per unit and sells for $6 per unit.
   C, which costs $8 per unit and sells for $9 per unit.

   The company's declared objective is profit maximization. The company is planning a monthly production schedule. The marketing department requires the production of at least 100 units of chip C and no more than 1,000 units of chip A. The production department cannot produce more than 4,000 units of all chips. Products are made on the "chipping" machine, which can produce 20, 30, or 40 units of chips A, B, or C, respectively, per hour. The machine is available for up to 100 hours each month. The marketing department also requires that there be at least twice as many units of B as of C in the monthly schedule. The finance department has set an upper budget of $15,000 for the schedule.

   How many units of A, B, and C should the company produce?

5. Atlantic Chemical produces three products, A, B, and C, which can be extracted and blended from three ores: b_1, which costs \$2 a ton and up to 1,000 tons of which is available a month; b_2, which costs \$1.50 a ton and up to 800 tons a month are available; and b_3, which costs \$3 a ton and is available in unlimited quantities. The company wishes to determine how much of each product to make from the available ores so as to maximize the profit from the overall operation. The requirements on the ores are as follows:

Product A requires: 5 tons b_1, 10 tons b_2, 10 tons b_3.
Product B requires: 7 tons b_1, 8 tons b_2, 5 tons b_3.
Product C requires: 10 tons b_1, 5 tons b_2, no tons b_3.
} Per ton of product

Sales price per ton: A = \$130, B = \$140, C = \$100.

a. What important assumption, which is not usually implied in an LP problem, is necessary to formulate this problem in LP terms?

b. Formulate as a linear programming problem.

6. A French market research firm wishes to conduct home visit interviews according to the quotas specified in the first column of the following table:

Type of household	*Responding calls (quota)*	*Probability of response to calls* Morning	*After-noon*	*Eve-ning*
Single person	50	.1	.1	.5
Married, no children	100	.5	.4	.7
Married, children	150	.75	.6	.9

Since not all persons are at home at the time of the visit and not all persons cooperate, there is only a certain "probability of response" to the home visits (calls).

The following requirements are imposed:

a. The total number (responding and nonresponding) of morning calls must not exceed the total number of afternoon calls.

b. The total number of responding evening calls must be at least 20 percent and no more than 30 percent of the total number of all responding calls.

c. An evening call costs twice as much as a morning or an afternoon call.

Decide how the calls should be distributed among the three types of households (by the three times during the day) such that the *expected* quotas are fulfilled at minimum cost. Formulate only.

7. Glades Discount Store is opening a new department with a storage area of 10,000 square feet. Management considers four products for display.

Product A:
Costs \$55, sells for \$80, and requires 24 square feet per unit for storage.

Product B:
Costs \$100, sells for \$130, and requires 20 square feet per unit for storage.

Product C:
Costs \$200, sells for \$295, and requires 36 square feet per unit for storage.

Product D:
Costs \$300, sells for \$399, and requires 50 square feet per unit for storage.

It is required that at least 10 units of each product be on display. The company's objective is profit maximization.

Find out how many units of each product should be on display if the company has \$600,000 available for purchasing the product. Formulate as a linear programming problem (assuming divisibility of the products; that is, ignore the fact that the answer should be in integer form).

8. The Canadian Safety Council has allocated \$500,000 for projects designed to prevent automobile accidents. Four proposals were submitted: (*a*) TV advertisements, (*b*) teenage safety education, (*c*) improved airbags, and (*d*) enforcement of driving laws. The projects are expected to result in the reduction of both fatalities and property damage, as shown in the table below.

Project	*Expected reduction in fatalities per \$1,000*	*Average property damage averted per \$1,000*
a	.25	300
b	.32	500
c	.15	0
d	.28	250

The council has decided that no single project will be awarded more than \$250,000. They also wish to award at least \$50,000 for teenage education. Finally, they want to award at least \$1 for improved airbags for each dollar awarded for TV advertisements. The federal government, for internal analysis purposes, has assessed the average value of a human life as being \$400,000.

a. Assume that the council's only objective is fatality prevention. Formulate as a linear programming problem to find the best fund allocation.

b. Reformulate the problem for the case that *both* fatalities and damage aversion are the objectives of the funds' allocation.

9. Korea National Bank is preparing to invest up to 5 billion won of its cash reserves. The bank is considering the following alternatives:

Alternative	*Expected rate of return (percent)*	*Risk factor*
U.S. Treasury securities	7.6	0
Corporate bonds	8.9	1
Loans to corporations	10.3	2
Stocks	14.0	5

The expected return is measured in percent over one year. The risk factor is a projection for next year, based on experience.

The bank's investment policy requires that:

a. The amount loaned to corporations will not exceed the amount invested in U.S. Treasury securities.

b. The *weighted* risk factor will not exceed 1.9.

c. For every won invested in stocks, there will be at least 0.5 won invested in U.S. Treasury securities.

d. The amount invested in stocks will not exceed 25 percent of the total amount invested.

Find the investment portfolio that will maximize the bank's return on investment.

(*Hint:* To find the weighted risk factor, multiply the amounts invested in the corresponding risk factor and divide by the total investment.)

10. Paint Fair Company advertises its weekly sales in newspapers, television, and radio. Each dollar spent in advertising in newspapers is estimated to reach an exposure of 12 buying customers, each dollar in TV reaches an exposure of 15 buying customers, and each dollar in radio reaches an exposure of 10 buying customers. The company has an agreement with all three media services according to which it will spend not less than 20 percent of its total money actually expended in each medium. Further, it is agreed that the combined newspaper and television budget will not be larger than three times the radio budget.

The company has just decided to spend no more than \$17,000 on advertising. The problem is: How much should the company budget for each medium if it is interested in reaching as many buying customers as possible?

11. The minimum daily requirement of vitamin D for patients following surgery is 180 units, while the maximum amount of B_{12} that they may receive is 150 units. The hospital dietitian is considering liver and steak for the daily diet. Each pound of liver costs \$1.50, while a pound of steak costs \$4.00. On the average, two ounces of liver and five ounces of steak provide the minimum daily need of vitamin D. An ounce of liver yields 30 units of vitamin D and 20 units of vitamin B_{12}.

A pound of steak yields 480 units of B_{12} and an undetermined amount of vitamin D. (*Hint:* You can find it yourself.)

Find the least-cost diet, per patient, per day. *Note:* There are 454 grams in a pound and 16 ounces in a pound.

12. Sunoil sells two types of Gasohol: regular and premium. Gasohol is prepared by mixing gasoline and alcohol.

Sunoil can buy up to 100,000 barrels per week of gasoline at \$40 per barrel, and up to 12,000 barrels per week of alcohol at \$47 per barrel. Regular Gasohol is made by blending 9 portions of gasoline with one portion of alcohol, while premium Gasohol is made of 87 percent gas and 13 percent alcohol.

Each barrel is equivalent to 42 gallons. A gallon of regular Gasohol sells for \$1.35 and a gallon of premium Gasohol sells for \$1.43.

The company must provide at least 600,000 gallons of premium and 1 million gallons of regular each week. In addition, the amount of regular Gasohol produced must be at least twice the amount of premium produced.

Find the most profitable production plan. *Note:* This problem can be formulated either with two or with four decision variables.

Find:

a. The quantities of gasoline and alcohol used.
b. The quantities of regular and premium produced.
c. The total cost.
d. The total profit.

13. Sherwood Acres, a central Kentucky farm, grows tobacco and soybeans on its 350 acres of land. An acre of soybeans brings a $150 profit and an acre of tobacco brings a $500 profit. Because of state agricultural regulations, no more than 150 acres can be planted in tobacco. Each acre of tobacco requires 100 mh of labor over the growing season and each acre of soybeans requires 20 mh. There are 16,000 mh of labor available during the growing season. How many acres should be planted in tobacco and how many in soybeans to maximize profit?

14. Robin, Inc., produces two different concrete products with the following price and input data.

	Selling Price ($)	*Input Requirements: Material (lb)*	*Power Consumed (kWh)*	*Labor (hr)*
Construction blocks	0.75	4	0.2	0.04
Decorative blocks	1.75	3	0.2	0.10

Labor cost is $5 per hour, materials cost $0.05 per pound and power costs $1.00 per kWh. If the company is limited to

100,000 lb of material
9000 kWh of power
1200 hr of labor

and if demand for decorative blocks is at most 3500 units, what quantity of each block should be produced to maximize profit?

15. Given a game:

$$A \overset{B}{\begin{bmatrix} 2 & 5 \\ 3 & 1 \\ 0 & 3 \end{bmatrix}}$$

a. Convert the game to a linear programming problem for both players.
b. Solve both games by the simplex method (or use a computer). Show the relationship between the two solutions.

16. Given the two-person, zero-sum games:

a.

A \ B		
	4	−2
	−3	5

b.

A \ B			
	2	1	4
	−1	3	0
	2	−1	3
	1	4	−1

Write the equivalent linear programming problems for both (*a*) and (*b*). Find the optimal strategies and the value of the game.

17. Change the following linear programming problems into game form.

a. maximize $z = 3x_1 + 3.5x_2$
subject to:
$1x_1 + 2x_2 \leq 4{,}000$
$4x_1 + 3x_2 \leq 12{,}000$

b. minimize $w = 2x_1 + 1x_2$
subject to:
$3x_1 + 2x_2 \geq 20$
$1x_1 + 3x_2 \geq 16$

1. Bazaraa, M. S., and J. J. Jarvis. *Linear Programming and Network Flows*. New York: John Wiley & Sons, 1977.
2. Ignizio, J. P. *Linear Programming in Single and Multiple Objective Systems*. Englewood Cliffs, N.J.: Prentice-Hall, 1982.
3. Kolman, B., and R. E. Beck. *Elementary Linear Programming with Applications*. New York: Academic Press, 1980.
4. Laidlaw, C. D. *Linear Programming for Urban Development and Plan Evaluation*. New York: Praeger Publishers, 1972.
5. Lee, S. M. *Linear Optimization for Management*. New York: Petrocelli-Charter, 1976.
6. Lev, B., and H. J. Weiss. *Introduction to Mathematical Programming*. New York: Elsevier North-Holland, 1982.
7. Loomba, N. P. *Linear Programming: A Managerial Perspective*. 2nd ed. New York: Macmillan, 1976.
8. Loomba, N. P., and E. Turban. *Applied Programming in Management*. New York: Holt, Rinehart & Winston, 1974.
9. Machol, R. E. *Elementary Systems Mathematics: Linear Programming for Business and Social Sciences*. New York: McGraw-Hill, 1976.
10. Rothenberg, R. *Linear Programming*. New York: Elsevier North-Holland, 1980.
11. Schrage, L. *Linear, Integer, and Quadratic Programming with LINDO*. 3rd. ed. Palo Alto, Calif: Scientific Press, 1986.

8

PART A: BASICS

8.1 Duality.
8.2 Sensitivity analysis.
8.3 Computerization.
8.4 Problems for Part A.

PART B: EXTENSIONS

8.5 Integer programming.
8.6 The zero-one model.
8.7 The branch and bound method.
8.8 Nonlinear programming.
8.9 Computer programs.
8.10 Concluding remarks.
8.11 Problems for Part B.
8.12 Case–Hensley Valve Corp.
8.13 Glossary.
8.14 References and Bibliography.

The linear programming model addressed in Chapters 6 and 7 is a special case of the broad field of mathematical programming. This chapter focuses on some extensions of linear programming and other models of mathematical programming. Part A of the chapter is devoted to two interesting extensions of linear programming: duality and sensitivity analysis.

Part B of the chapter discusses the concepts of integer programming, where the solution must be in integer units (14 persons, 3 airplanes, and so on). In addition, a solution technique called branch and bound is presented. Finally, the technique of nonlinear programming, where the objective function and/or the constraints cannot be expressed in linear terms, is briefly discussed.

Topics in mathematical programming

LEARNING OBJECTIVES

The student should be able to:

a. Define duality and describe its major properties.
b. Write the dual to a LP problem.
c. Describe and discuss the economic interpretation of the dual.
d. Describe the relationship between dual and slack (surplus) variables.
e. Use the dual variables for making managerial decisions.
f. Describe the concept of sensitivity analysis.
g. Perform simple sensitivity analyses.

Extensions

h. Formulate integer programming problems.
i. Solve integer programming problems graphically and by rounding.
j. Describe the concept of cost of indivisibility.
k. Define branch and bound and describe how the technique works (specifically, the setting of the bounds).
l. Solve simple problems with branch and bound.
m. Describe the structure of a nonlinear programming problem.
n. Define quadratic programming.

PART A: BASICS

The Sekido Corporation—Part II

The optimal daily production plan suggested by Suji Okita (12 units of type A TV sets and 11 of type B) was submitted to Sekido's executive committee for approval. During their weekly Monday morning meeting, the members of the committee raised the following questions:

1. Should additional resources (labor, machine time) be committed to the production of these TV sets? If so, how much?
2. If the available supply of Sekido's resources should happen to change, what effect will it have on the company's profit?
3. Would it be worthwhile to increase Sekido's marketing effort to increase potential sales from 12 to 13, 14, or even more? How much should the company be willing to invest in such a promotion?
4. What is the best production plan if some of the input variables (per unit profits, production technology) change?
5. How does the restriction of producing a whole number of units affect the results?

Upon returning home, Suji found that Keiko was faced with similar questions at her office. For example: What effect will certain changes in the paint specifications have on the total production cost? And what will happen to the optimal blending plan if other objectives are also considered?

Three very useful extensions of linear programming can be used to answer these and similar questions:

- Duality.
- Sensitivity analysis.
- Integer programming.

8.1 DUALITY

With every linear programming maximization problem there is an associated minimization problem, and vice versa. Therefore, linear programming problems exist in pairs. The original problem is called the **primal**, while the complementary problem is termed the **dual.**

The primal—the dual

Duality plays an important role for these reasons:

1. The dual problem has an *important economic interpretation.*
2. *Several theories* that are used to develop methods for efficient computational shortcuts to the simplex method are based on the concept of duality.

An important economic interpretation

3. In some cases, the use of the dual helps *overcome some computer capacity limitations.*
4. Some special procedures developed for *testing optimal solutions* are based on duality.

Theoretically, the dual problem is the same problem as the primal, but mathematically transformed. Therefore, the solution of the primal (by the simplex method) gives the solution to the dual, and vice versa.

Major properties

The following are some properties of duality:

1. If the primal is a maximization problem, the dual is a minimization problem, and vice versa.
2. An optimal solution to the dual exists only when the primal has an optimal solution (and vice versa).
3. The value of the objective function of the optimal solution in both problems is the same.
4. The dual of the dual is the primal.
5. The solution of the dual problem can be obtained from the solution of the primal problem, and vice versa (if solved by a procedure such as the simplex method.)

Formulation of the dual to a maximization problem—an example

The product-mix problem discussed in Chapter 6 is reproduced below as the *primal:*

$$\text{maximize } z = 300x_1 + 250x_2$$
subject to:
$$2x_1 + 1x_2 \le 40 \quad \text{(labor constraint)}$$
$$1x_1 + 3x_2 \le 45 \quad \text{(machine time constraint)}$$
$$1x_1 + 0x_2 \le 12 \quad \text{(marketing constraint)}$$

Writing the dual

The objective. Since the original problem calls for *maximization*, the dual will be a *minimization* problem.

The decision variables. For each constraint in the primal, there is one decision variable in the dual. Thus, there will be, in this example, three variables to be denoted u_1, u_2, and u_3. The dual variable's coefficients can be either positive, zero, or negative.

One-to-one correspondence

The objective function. Remember that each dual variable corresponds to a constraint in the primal. The coefficient of each variable in the objective function of the dual is equal to the right-hand side (capacity, b_i) of the corresponding constraint in the primal. For example, the capacity of the labor (first) constraint in the primal is 40; thus the coefficient of u_1 in the dual's objective function is 40. The objective function for the dual is:

$$\text{minimize } w = 40u_1 + 45u_2 + 12u_3$$

The constraints.[1] For each decision (unknown) variable in the primal, there is a corresponding constraint in the dual. Since there are two primal variables, there will be two constraints in the dual. The right-hand side of the dual's constraints is the same as the corresponding coefficients of the objective function in the primal. For example, the coefficient of the *first* variable in the primal objective is 300, and so will be the right-hand side of the dual's *first* constraint.

The coefficients of the constraints in the dual are formed from the coefficients of the primal's constraints by writing each column of these coefficients as a row. The coefficients of the primal's constraints are:

$$\begin{matrix} 2 & 1 \\ 1 & 3 \\ 1 & 0 \end{matrix}$$

With each column written as a row, the result is:[2]

Previous first column:	2	1	1
Previous second column:	1	3	0

Thus, the dual's constraints are:

$$\begin{aligned} 2u_1 + 1u_2 + 1u_3 &\geq 300 \\ 1u_1 + 3u_2 + 0u_3 &\geq 250 \end{aligned}$$

Note that the signs of the inequalities are $\geq$ since all the constraints in the primal were of the $\leq$ standard format.

Standardization of the primal

The primal problem presented earlier contained only $\leq$ type constraints, and it was to be maximized. If a primal problem deviates from such a structure, it must then be transformed into the required standard format.

Example 1

Given a primal:

$$\begin{aligned} &\text{minimize } y = 3x_1 + 4x_2 - 2x_3 \\ &\text{subject to:} \\ &\quad (1)\quad 1x_1 + 2x_2 - 3x_3 \geq 40 \\ &\quad (2)\quad 3x_1 + 5x_2 + 1x_3 \leq 50 \\ &\quad (3)\quad 0x_1 + 3x_2 + 2x_3 = 30 \end{aligned}$$

[1] Before structuring the dual constraints, all primal constraints should be transformed to $\leq$ in maximization; $\geq$ in minimization. This transformation process will be discussed soon.

[2] If the coefficients of the primal are written in the form of a matrix, then the matrix of the coefficients in the dual is the *transpose* (see Appendix A) of the matrix in the primal.

Step 1. If the objective function is to be minimized, convert it into maximization by multiplying it by -1.
We get:

$$\text{maximize } z = -3x_1 - 4x_2 + 2x_3$$

Step 2. Multiply each $\geq$ constraint by -1 in order to convert it to a $\leq$ type.

Constraint 1 thus becomes:

$$-1x_1 - 2x_2 + 3x_3 \leq -40$$

Step 3. Split each equality constraint into two inequalities; one $\leq$ and the other $\geq$. (Mathematically, an equation is equivalent to two inequalities, one $\leq$ and one $\geq$.)

Thus, constraint 3 is expressed as:

$$\begin{aligned} &(3a) \quad 0x_1 + 3x_2 + 2x_3 \leq 30 \\ &(3b) \quad 0x_1 + 3x_2 + 2x_3 \geq 30 \end{aligned}$$

However, since constraint $3b$ is of the $\geq$ type, it has to be multiplied by -1 in order to convert it to a $\leq$ type.

Conclusion

The standardized or canonical form

The original problem can now be rewritten as:

Standardized primal

$$\begin{aligned} &\text{maximize } z = -3x_1 - 4x_2 + 2x_3 \\ &\text{subject to:} \\ &(1) \quad -1x_1 - 2x_2 + 3x_3 \leq -40 \\ &(2) \quad 3x_1 + 5x_2 + 1x_3 \leq 50 \\ &(3a) \quad 0x_1 + 3x_2 + 2x_3 \leq 30 \\ &(3b) \quad 0x_1 - 3x_2 - 2x_3 \leq -30 \end{aligned}$$

Dual

$$\begin{aligned} &\text{minimize } w = -40u_1 + 50u_2 + 30u_3 - 30u_4 \\ &\text{subject to:} \\ &-1u_1 + 3u_2 + 0u_3 + 0u_4 \geq -3 \\ &-2u_1 + 5u_2 + 3u_3 - 3u_4 \geq -4 \\ &3u_1 + 1u_2 + 2u_3 - 2u_4 \geq 2 \end{aligned}$$

Example 2

In the previous example, a primal minimization problem was converted to a standard maximization problem and then its dual was derived. Alternatively, the primal problem can be standardized as a minimization problem where all the constraints are of the $\geq$ type. Let us examine another example.

Given a primal:

$$\begin{aligned} &\text{minimize } z = 2x_1 + 3x_2 - 1x_3 \\ &\text{subject to:} \\ &(1) \quad 5x_1 + 1x_2 + 1x_3 \geq 20 \\ &(2) \quad 2x_1 + 1x_2 + 3x_3 = 24 \\ &(3) \quad 1x_1 + 2x_2 - 1x_3 \leq 18 \end{aligned}$$

Standardization. Constraints 2 and 3 are not in the required form.
Step 1. Split constraint 2 into two constraints:

$$\begin{aligned} &(2a) \quad 2x_1 + 1x_2 + 3x_3 \leq 24 \\ &(2b) \quad 2x_1 + 1x_2 + 3x_3 \geq 24 \end{aligned}$$

Multiply (2*a*) by −1 to reverse the direction of the inequality:

$$(2a) \quad -2x_1 - 1x_2 - 3x_3 \geq -24$$

Step 2. Reverse the inequality of constraint 3 by multiplying it by −1:

$$(3) \quad -1x_1 - 2x_2 + 1x_3 \geq -18$$

Now the standardized primal and its dual can be written:

Standardized primal

minimize $z = 2x_1 + 3x_2 - 1x_3$

subject to:

(1) $5x_1 + 1x_2 + 1x_3 \geq 20$

(2*a*) $-2x_1 - 1x_2 - 3x_3 \geq -24$

(2*b*) $2x_1 + 1x_2 + 3x_3 \geq 24$

(3) $-1x_1 - 2x_2 + 1x_3 \geq -18$

Dual

maximize $w = 20u_1 - 24u_2 + 24u_3 - 18u_4$

subject to:

$5u_1 - 2u_2 + 2u_3 - 1u_4 \leq 2$

$1u_1 - 1u_2 + 1u_3 - 2u_4 \leq 3$

$1u_1 - 3u_2 + 3u_3 + 1u_4 \leq -1$

Summary

The primal-dual relationship is shown pictorially in Figure 8.1.[3] The dual, once formulated, can be solved as any regular linear program-

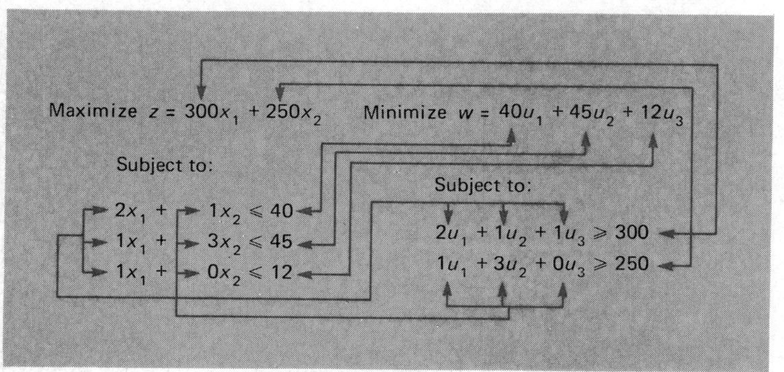

FIGURE 8.1
The primal-dual relationship

[3] The general form of the primal-dual relationship is:

Primal

maximize $z = \sum_{j=1}^{n} c_j x_j$

subject to:

$$\sum_{j=1}^{n} a_{ij} x_j \leq b_i$$

for $i = 1, 2, \ldots, m$ and $j = 1, 2, \ldots, n$

Dual

minimize $w = \sum_{i=1}^{m} b_i u_i$

subject to:

$$\sum_{i=1}^{m} a_{ij} u_i \geq c_j$$

ming problem (e.g., using the simplex method). In addition, the use of the simplex method automatically gives the solution to the dual when the primal is being solved.

Solution to the dual

The dual problem, once formulated, can be solved like any other linear programming problem. However, given a simplex solution to the primal, it is not necessary to solve the dual, since the final tableau of the primal's solution provides *both* the optimal values of the primal and the dual problems.

Let us reproduce the final tableau of the product-mix problem (Table 6.8) in Table 8.1.

The optimal solution to the dual problem can be read directly in the $c_j - z_j$ row of the tableau since $u_j = -(c_j - z_j)$. The column s_1, which is related to the first constraint, has a $c_j - z_j$ value of zero; that is, $u_1 = 0$. Similarly, $u_2 = 250/3$ (take the negative of the value shown) and $u_3 = 650/3$. Since the dual problem has two constraints, it has two surplus variables, t_1 and t_2, whose values can also be found in the primal's optimal tableau. Examining the $c_j - z_j$ row in the tableau, we see that its value is zero under the x_1 column; that is, the surplus t_1 of the first dual's constraint (which is associated with the primal x_1 variable) is zero. Similarly, the surplus t_2 of the second dual's constraint is zero.

Note: In solving dual problems, irregularities may be encountered, such as negative right-hand "Quantity" values in the constraints. Special extensions of the simplex method, such as the dual-simplex algorithm, can then be used. For details, see [3, 5, or 6].

Finding the dual values without the simplex

It is possible to find the value of the dual's variables without resorting to the simplex tableau or even writing the dual problem. This approach can be particularly useful when the graphical method is used.

TABLE 8.1
Reproduction of Table 6.8

Basis	*Unit profit*	*Quantity*	x_1	x_2	s_1	s_2	s_3
s_1	0	5	0	0	1	−1/3	−5/3
x_2	250	11	0	1	0	1/3	−1/3
x_1	300	12	1	0	0	0	1
c_j			300	250	0	0	0
z_j			300	250	0	250/3	650/3
$c_j - z_j$			0	0	0	−250/3	−650/3
Dual's solution:			t_1	t_2	$-u_1$	$-u_2$	$-u_3$

Step 1. Solve the problem (graphically, if it has only two decision variables). Compute the value of the objective function (z_{original}). Then, for each dual variable:

Step 2. Increase the right-hand side of the relevant constraint by one unit.

Step 3. Resolve the problem with the new value of the constraint and compute the value of the objective function (z_{new}).

Step 4. The dual's value is then:

$$z_{\text{new}} - z_{\text{original}}$$

Economic interpretation of the dual (product-mix example)

The meaning of the dual's variables The dual variables, u_i, are also called the **shadow prices,** the **marginal values** of the constraints, or the *opportunity costs* per unit of each resource (constraint) presented in the primal. These imaginary prices can be used for making various managerial decisions such as examining the profitability of purchasing additional resources and evaluating the trade-offs among them.

Shadow prices

The dual variables measure the change in the value of the objective function of the primal when one additional unit of a specific resource is added. If, for example, machine capacity is increased from 45 hours (the current machine time available) to 46 hours, the total profit will increase by $u_2 = 250/3 = \$83\frac{1}{3}$.[4] Similarly, if the marketability of model A is increased from 12 sets to 13 sets, the total profit will increase by $u_3 = 650/3 = \$216\frac{2}{3}$.

Thus, the $\$83\frac{1}{3}$ can be viewed as the value of one unit of machine time (marginal value of the resource). Therefore, the total value of the resource "machine time" is $83\frac{1}{3} \times 45 = \$3,750$. Similarly, the value of one unit of "marketability" is $u_3 = 650/3$; the total value of marketability is therefore $12 \times 216\frac{2}{3} = \$2,600$. However, if labor availability is increased from 40 to 41 units, there will be *no gain* ($u_1 = 0$). The reason is that *labor is not utilized in full* at present; this is clearly shown by the fact that $s_1 = 5$ (i.e., slack in labor exists). A resource that is not fully utilized is considered a *free good* and obviously an increase in its supply will not increase profits.

Marginal values

Free good

The total value of all resources is therefore the value of machine time + marketability + labor time: $\$3,750 + \$2,600 + 0 = \$6,350$, which is exactly the value of the objective function in both the primal and the dual.

The interpretation of the objective function of the dual When the dual's unit value of the resources is multiplied by the available quantities (right-hand side of the constraints), a total value function is constructed as follows:

[4] Provided that the structure of the optimal solution remains unchanged; that is, that the same variables participate in the optimal solution. See the next section (sensitivity analysis) for further discussion.

$$\text{Total value of labor} = u_1 \left(\frac{\text{Dollars}}{\text{Hour}}\right) \times 40 \text{ hours} = \$40u_1$$

$$\text{Total value of machine} = u_2 \left(\frac{\text{Dollars}}{\text{Hour}}\right) \times 45 \text{ hours} = \$45u_2$$

$$\text{Total value of marketing} = u_3 \left(\frac{\text{Dollars}}{\text{Unit}}\right) \times 12 \text{ units} = \$12u_3$$

The total value of all resources is $40u_1 + 45u_2 + 12u_3$.

The objective of the manufacturer is to *minimize* the value of the resources used. Therefore, the dual's objective function is: minimize $z = 40u_1 + 45u_2 + 12u_3$. This minimization is subject to two constraints.

The interpretation of the constraints It is given that one unit of TV model A requires two hours of labor, one hour of machine time, and one unit of marketing effort. Investing *less than* these quantities will result in less than one unit of model A. Since the *profit* (or *contribution margin*) made from such a TV is \$300, it can be said that the value of the invested resources *must* be *at least* \$300, or $2u_1 + 1u_2 + 1u_3 \geq 300$.

Similarly, the constraint for model B is:

$$1u_1 + 3u_2 \geq 350$$

Marginal contribution

Remember that these values are accounting or shadow price values that do not measure *cost* but measure potential, *marginal contribution* to profit.

The relationship between the dual's variables and the objective function The dual variables, by definition, measure the change in the value of the objective function of the primal when the right-hand side of the primal's constraints are changed by one unit. The following relationship thus exists between the two:

Right-hand side	*If dual variable is*	*Then objective function value will*
add one unit	positive	increase by the amount of the dual
add one unit	negative	decrease by the amount of the dual
add one unit	zero	remain unchanged
delete one unit	positive	decrease by the amount of the dual
delete one unit	negative	increase by the amount of the dual
delete one unit	zero	remain unchanged

Notes:

- There is one dual variable for every constraint in the primal.
- If the change in the right-hand side is less than one unit, then the change in the objective function will be proportional. For example, if

the right-hand side increased by .5, then the value of the objective function will increase by one half of the value of the dual variable.

- If the change in the right-hand side is more than one unit, then the change in the objective function will be proportionally greater. Such a change can be made only up to a certain limit, as will be discussed in the coming section on sensitivity analysis.

The relationship between the dual variables and the slack (surplus) variables One dual variable exists for each constraint. It was shown earlier that each constraint will also have either a slack or a surplus variable. The question is: What kind of relationship exists between the two types of variables? To understand this relationship, one should review the economic interpretation of the dual variables. As stated, a dual whose value is zero signifies a free good for the constraint (or resource) it represents. Such a case occurs when the resource is *not* fully utilized; that is, when it has a slack. In general, the following relationships, known as the *Kuhn-Tucker conditions*, exist for each constraint:[5]

Kuhn-Tucker conditions

		Dual		*Primal's slack or surplus*
Condition 1	If:	0	Then:	Positive
Condition 2	If:	Nonzero	Then:	0

Note that when the dual is *nonzero*, the resource is fully utilized (no slack or surplus). The reason for this is that if a constraint is fully utilized and one increases the supply of this constraint (right-hand side), it should increase the profit (in the case of maximization). Increasing the supply of a nonfully utilized resource (one with a slack) will not do any good; that is, the value of the objective function will not be changed.

Managerial applications

Management can use the dual for decisions regarding addition, deletion, and trade-offs of resources.

Example 1: Adding machine capacity Suppose that management is considering the expansion of the available machine time. The estimated daily cost is $50 per hour increase. Should management expand? In order to answer this question, one of two approaches may be used.

Consider the cost of the change

[5] Whenever there is a unique optimal solution and the problem is nondegenerate.

1. Re-solve the problem, changing the machine constraint to $x_1 + 3x_2 \leq 46$; keep all other data unchanged. The new solution calls for $x_1 = 12$, $x_2 = 11⅓$, and $z = 6{,}433⅓$. Since the addition to profit, $6{,}433⅓ - 6{,}350 = \$83⅓$, is larger than the \$50 required investment, it should be recommended.
2. Use the dual. Since the "worth" of machine time, $u_2 = \$83⅓$, is larger than the investment, the investment should be recommended.
3. If a change of one unit is recommended, then it makes sense to add even more. The limit for the change is given by a sensitivity analysis.

Example 2: Cut back in resources Suppose the advertising budget is cut so that only 11 rather than 12 units of model A can be sold each day. What is the impact on profit? The marketing people claim that it is \$300 per day, since the profit contribution of model A is \$300 per unit. The fact is that it is only $u_3 = \$216⅔$. The reason for this is that reducing x_1 to 11 releases one unit of machine time that enables the production of one third of model B (from 11 to 11⅓). Such a change is worth \$83⅓, as seen before. Therefore, the net impact is \$300 − \$83⅓ = \$216⅔.

Example 3: Should capacity be changed? Given: The solution $x_1 = 5$, $x_2 = 1$, $z = \$50$ to a linear programming maximization problem. The problem includes a space constraint of $3x_1 + 5x_2 \leq 20$ (ft^2) with a corresponding dual variable value of \$1.80. Management is considering changing the space availability. An increase in availability costs \$2 per ft^2; a decrease in availability reduces expenses by \$1.60. What should management do and why?

If management increases the available space, the cost increase will be \$2 per ft^2, while the contribution to profit will only be \$1.80. Therefore, this is not advisable. If management decreases the available space, the contribution to profit will decrease by \$1.80, while the expenses will be reduced by only \$1.60. Therefore, this is not advisable either. Thus, management should not change the space availability.

Note: Using our definition, the shadow price gives the *maximum price that should be paid to obtain one additional unit of the resource* (over the relevant range). However, one should be careful when determining this maximum price. It should include only those costs of making the changes that have not been included in the calculation of the per unit contribution of the basic decision variables (the coefficients of the objective function).

The reason for this is that by expanding the resources, we create more products; some of the cost of creating the resources (the variable cost) is included in the cost of the unit, as expressed in the objective function. (The coefficients of the objective function are computed on a per unit basis: Contribution = Revenue − Cost.) Therefore, the decision of whether or not to increase the resource should consider only the nonvariable cost of increasing that resource (which is not reflected in the objective function).

8.2 SENSITIVITY ANALYSIS

The optimal solution to a linear programming problem is based on a set of assumptions and on forecasting of future data such as prices. In a **deterministic model,** there is no provision for risk or uncertainty. Therefore, it is important for management to know *what* will happen to the optimal solution *if* changes occur in the input data on which the LP model is based. The technique to address this issue is called **sensitivity analysis.**[6]

The name *sensitivity analysis* derives from the fact that an analysis is made to find out how sensitive the optimal solution is to changes in the input data. There are two approaches for conducting sensitivity studies.

1. ***A trial-and-error approach*** According to this approach, one may change the input data, hence forming a new problem. Then the problem is solved from the beginning and the results are compared with that of the old problem. This process is repeated for all desired changes. The deficiency of this approach is that it may become very lengthy, since there are large numbers of possible changes in the data. Another possible deficiency is that resolving a problem may be very expensive, especially for large-scale problems.

2. ***Use of an analytical approach*** When an analytical approach is used, there is no need to completely resolve the LP problems each time a change is made. Furthermore, information such as the "permissible range of change," which is directly provided by the analytical approach, can be provided by the trial-and-error approach only after an extremely lengthy experimentation period. The analytical approach finds the effects on the optimal solution of each of the following changes, one at a time, in the input data:

- Changes in the coefficients in the objective function.
- Changes in the right-hand "quantity" side of the constraints.
- Changes in the input-output coefficients in the constraints.
- Adding or deleting a constraint.

It should be noted that the optimal solution may be changed in various ways: the value of the objective function (but not the basis) may be changed, its composition (the basic variables) may be changed, or the solution may become infeasible.

Changes in the coefficients of the objective function

Changes in the coefficients of the objective function are basically *product pricing* decisions. Two important managerial questions can be answered by the analysis:

[6] Other names are "optimality analysis," "postoptimality analysis," "what-if analysis," and in some cases "parametric programming."

- When does a price (or profit) *decrease* of a product, currently in the optimal solution (a basic variable), justify discontinuing its production?
- How much of a price (or profit) *increase* in a product, currently *not* in the optimal solution, justifies its production (inclusion in the optimal plan)?

Similar questions regarding price ratios and limits can also be answered.

Graphical explanation of the changes in the coefficients

Example 1: The product-mix problem. Let us reproduce the product-mix problem:

$$\text{maximize } z = 300x_1 + 250x_2$$
subject to:

$$\begin{aligned} 2x_1 + 1x_2 &\leq 40 \\ 1x_1 + 3x_2 &\leq 45 \\ 1x_1 + 0x_2 &\leq 12 \end{aligned}$$

The decision as to whether or not the optimal solution should include a particular product, and how much, depends on its relative contribution to profit, as expressed in the objective function. In graphical terms, such a decision depends on the *slope* of the objective function. Let us examine the optimal graphical solution to the product-mix problem (Figure 8.2).

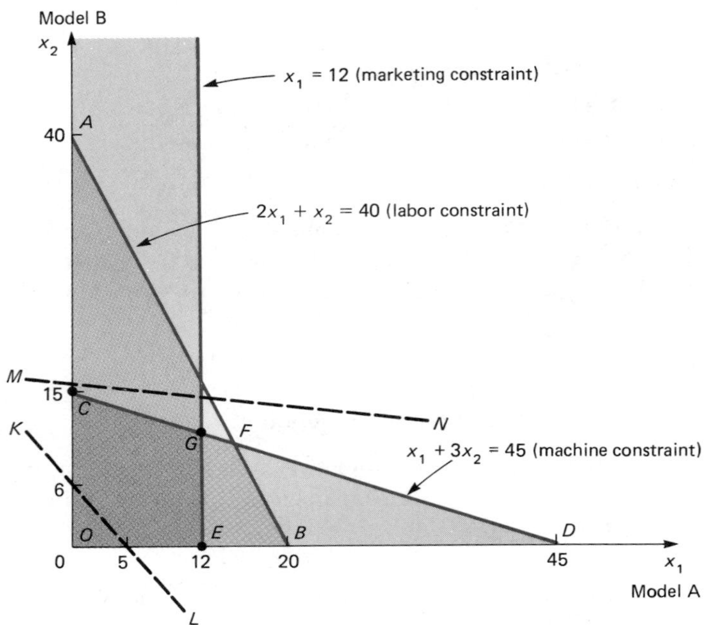

FIGURE 8.2
Solution to the product-mix problem

The existing objective function (line *KL*) yields a solution at point *G* (12 units of x_1 and 11 of x_2). However, if we change the slope of the objective function so it is parallel to line *MN*, then the optimal solution will be at point *C* (produce 15 of x_2). The slope of the objective function can change if the coefficient of x_1 changes, the coefficient of x_2 changes, or the ratio between the coefficients of x_1 and x_2 is changed.

A change in solution from point *G* to point *C* will be achieved when the coefficient of x_2 is more than three times that of x_1. The reason for this is that with a ratio of exactly one to three, the objective function will be parallel to the machine constraint *CD*, with both points *C* and *G* being optimal. A smaller x_2/x_1 ratio means that *G* is the solution; a larger ratio means that *C* is the solution.

Limits on the coefficients

Consider Figure 8.2. The current solution involves both product A (i.e., x_1) and B (x_2). Assume that the profit contribution of x_1 remains 300, while the profit contribution of x_2 increases. This increase will change the slope of line *KL* toward that of *MN*. When the profit contribution reaches 900 (exactly 3 times 300), the line will be parallel to *CD* and both points *C* and *G* will be in the optimal solution. Thus, 900 is the upper limit of the coefficient of x_2. If the profit contribution of B is *more* than 900, the solution will then be at point *C*. On the other hand, the solution may move from point *G* to point *E* (produce A only). For this to happen, assuming that the profit contribution of x_1 remains 300, the profit contribution of x_2 would have to decrease to *below* zero. If the profit contribution of x_2 is *exactly* zero, then both points *G* and *E* will be optimal. Thus, the upper limit on the coefficient of x_2 is 900, while the lower limit is zero.

Let us now consider the variable x_1. If the coefficient of x_2 remains 250, then the *lower* limit of the coefficient of x_1 is 83⅓ (i.e., ⅓ of 250). If the profit contribution of x_1 becomes *less* than 83⅓, then x_1 will not appear in the optimal solution (which will move to point *C*).

The upper limit on x_1 is the amount required to move the solution from *G* to *E*. This can happen only if the coefficient of x_2 is negative. Since the coefficient of x_2 is 300, then no matter what the coefficient of x_1, point *G* will be superior to *E*. Thus, the upper limit of x_1 is ∞.

The limits on x_1 and x_2 are summarized in the computer printout of Section 8.3. These limits are computed by the use of the simplex method, as will be illustrated next.

Note: The example so far has dealt only with products that are in the solution. However, assume that the optimal solution was at point *C* to begin with (product x_2 only). Again, by figuring the appropriate slope, it would have been possible to figure the necessary increase in the coefficient of x_1 that would result in the inclusion of x_1 in the optimal solution.

The graphical analysis is limited, of course, to two decision variables. A similar analysis is possible using the simplex method.

Use of the simplex method

The aim of the sensitivity analysis presented here is to find the *range* of no change in the composition of the basis. The range is composed of two limits: lower and upper. As long as a variable's coefficient is within this range, the current optimal solution will remain unchanged, though the objective function will change in value. Should the coefficient go above or below these limits, there will be a change in the basis and optimal solution. The limits of the range that were explained graphically above will now be computed with the help of the simplex tableau.

Example 2: Given a product-mix problem:

$$\begin{aligned}&\text{maximize } z = 5x_1 + 4.5x_2 + 1x_3\\ &\text{subject to:}\\ &\quad 15x_1 + 15.8x_2 + 0x_3 \le 150\\ &\quad 5x_1 + 6.4x_2 + 15x_3 \le 77\\ &\quad 0x_1 + 2.8x_2 + 11.8x_3 \le 36\end{aligned}$$

The optimal tableau of this problem is shown below.

Basis	*Unit profits*	*Quantity*	x_1	x_2	x_3	s_1	s_2	s_3
x_1	5	10	1	1.053	0	.067	0	0
x_3	1	1.8	0	.076	1	−0.22	.067	0
s_3	0	15.12	0	1.924	0	.258	−.773	1
c_j			5	4.5	1	0	0	0
z_j			5	5.342	1	.311	.067	0
$c_j - z_j$			0	−.842	0	−.311	−.067	0

The simplex approach distinguishes between an analysis of the coefficients of basic variables and nonbasic variables.

Analysis of basic variables The analysis will be conducted on products x_1 and x_3, which are in the basis.

Analysis for x_1

Step 1. Copy the $c_j - z_j$ row of the optimal solution.
Step 2. Copy the x_1 row; enter it just below the $c_j - z_j$ row.
Step 3. Divide each $c_j - z_j$ row entry, *for variables not in the solution* (x_2, s_1, and s_2) by the associated variable a_{ij} from the x_1 row.

	x_1	x_2	x_3	s_1	s_2	s_3
$c_j - z_j$ row	0	−.842	0	−.311	−.067	0
x_1 row	1	1.053	0	.067	0	0
$\dfrac{c_j - z_j \text{ row}}{x_1 \text{ row}}$	—	$\dfrac{-.842}{1.053} = -.8$	—	$\dfrac{-.311}{.067} = -4.64$	$\dfrac{-.067}{0} = -\infty$	—

Conclusion

The smallest positive number in the last row of the table tells by how much the profit of x_1 can be increased before the solution is changed. Since there are no positive values, there is no limit; that is, infinity (∞).

The *largest negative number (smallest absolute value)*, $-.8$ in this case, indicates by how much the coefficient of x_1 can be decreased without changing the solution.

The range. These two numbers constitute the range within which the price of x_1 can be changed from the current level of 5. The lower limit is $5 - 0.8 = 4.2$, and the upper limit is $5 + \infty = \infty$.

Analysis for x_3

	x_2	s_1	s_2
$c_j - z_j$ row	$-.842$	$-.311$	$-.067$
x_3 row	$.076$	$-.022$	$.067$
$\dfrac{c_j - z_j \text{ row}}{x_3 \text{ row}}$	$\dfrac{-.842}{.076} = -11.09$	$\dfrac{-.311}{-.022} = 14.13$	$\dfrac{-.067}{.067} = -1$

The largest negative number is -1.
The smallest positive number is 14.13.

The range is:

$$\text{Lower limit} = 1 - 1 = 0$$
$$\text{Upper limit} = 1 + 14.13 = 15.13$$

Interpretation

a. If the profit contribution of x_3 exceeds 15.13, then s_1 will enter into the solution; if this happens, then x_1 (the only other product in the solution) will not be produced and the optimal solution will involve producing only x_3.

b. For product x_3 to be removed from the solution (s_2 would enter), its price contribution will have to be less than zero (i.e., negative). A similar interpretation would be made for variable x_1.

Summary

The preceding analysis is generalized in Equations 8.1 and 8.2.

$$\text{Upper limit} = \text{minimize}\left[c_i + \frac{c_j - z_j}{a_{ij}}\right] \quad \text{for all } a_{ij} < 0 \qquad (8.1)$$

$$\text{Lower limit} = \text{maximize}\left[c_i + \frac{c_j - z_j}{a_{ij}}\right] \quad \text{for all } a_{ij} > 0 \tag{8.2}$$

where:

c_i = Profit contribution of basic variable i
j = Index of nonbasic variable j
a_{ij} = Substitution ratio, in the optimal tableau, between basic variable i and nonbasic variable j

Range for nonbasic variables

If there is a variable, j, not participating in the optimal basis, then, in order for this variable to be included in the optimal solution, its coefficient in the objective function will have to change from the existing c_j to a new level, c_j (new). This level is given by Inequality 8.3.

$$c_j\,(\text{new}) \geq z_j \tag{8.3}$$

Computations

The only nonbasic decision variable is x_2 (with a coefficient c_2). By using Inequality 8.3:

$$c_2\,(\text{new}) \geq z_2 = 5.342$$

That is, if the profit contribution of x_2 increases from 4.5 to over 5.342, then x_2 will be included in the solution.

This is the *upper limit* on the range of c_2. There is no *lower limit* on the range of c_2 because this is a maximization problem. Therefore, a coefficient of x_2 lower than the existing 4.5 will make it *even less desirable*.[7]

Capacity changes (changes in the right-hand "Quantity" side of the constraints)

The right-hand side of the constraints expresses the capacities, or limitations of the resources, or it makes explicit certain requirements. Management may be interested in finding out the effect of changes in these values (b_i's) on the optimal solution. Such a change may not affect the optimal solution, may change the composition of the basis, or may affect only the value of the objective function (same basis variables with different values). Of special interest is the impact on the dual's variables. Graphically, a change in any b_i is shown as a movement of the constraint, *parallel to itself*.

[7] Essentially, the lower range for nonbasic variables, in maximization, is $-\infty$.

Example

Given:

$$\begin{aligned}&\text{maximize } z = 3x_1 + 4x_2\\&\text{subject to:}\\&\quad (1)\ 3x_1 + 5x_2 \le 15\\&\quad (2)\ 2x_1 + 1x_2 \le 8\\&\quad (3)\ 0x_1 + 1x_2 \le 2\end{aligned}$$

The graphical solution of this problem is shown in Figure 8.3, where point C is the optimal solution. Moving a binding constraint (such as 1 or 2) will change the location of the optimal solution. For example, if the capacity of constraint 2 is increased from 8 to 9 (line ST), then the optimal solution will move to point G. On the other hand, slightly moving constraint 3 will not affect the optimal solution at all (since the constraint is not binding). However, moving it further may change the location of the optimal solution. Management may be interested in finding the range of such changes. For example, moving constraint 2 more to the right will result in a situation where the solution is at point F (5 units of x_1, 0 of x_2). This will happen when the capacity of constraint 2 is 10; that is, 10 is the upper limit on constraint 2.

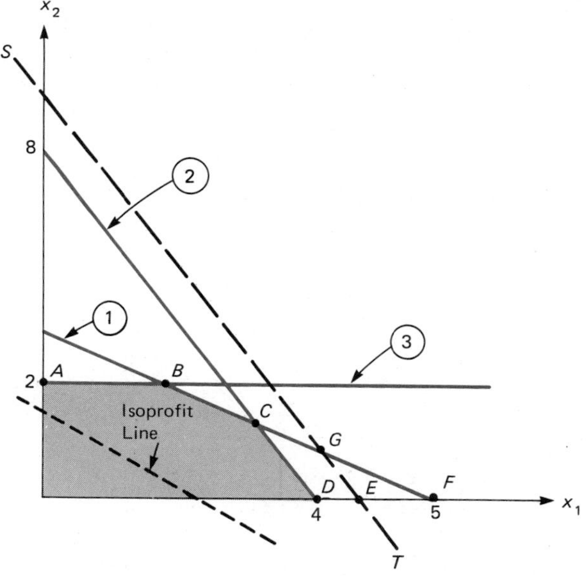

FIGURE 8.3 Changes in capacity

Use of the simplex method to determine the range of b_i

Range of feasibility

The dual variable, as shown earlier, can tell management the impact on the objective function of a marginal (one unit) change in the right-hand-side values (b_i's). If a change in one unit is desirable, then management may want to find if a change of two, three, or more units is feasible with respect to the dual variable. Specifically, management would like to know the range of b_i over which the dual variable (shadow price) will remain valid.

The simplex method is going to be used in the following manner:

Step 1. List the "Quantity" column of the optimal table.
Step 2. List the substitution ratios of the constraint whose range of b_i is analyzed.
Step 3. Divide the Quantity by the substitution ratio.
Step 4. Identify the smallest positive and the largest negative results.

Example

Let us analyze the product-mix problem that was solved graphically (Figure 8.3). The optimal simplex solution is given in Table 8.2.

TABLE 8.2
Optimal simplex solution of the product-mix problem

Basis	*Unit profit*	*Quantity*	x_1	x_2	s_1	s_2	s_3
x_1	3	3.57	1	0	−.143	.714	0
s_3	0	1.143	0	0	−.286	.428	1
x_2	4	0.857	0	1	.286	−.428	0
$c_j - z_j$			0	0	−.714	−.428	0

Analysis for the first constraint

Quantity	s_1	Q/s_1
3.57	−.143	−24.96
1.143	−.286	− 3.99
.857	.286	3.00

The smallest positive Q/s_1 (3.00 in our case) tells us how much the existing $b_1 = 15$ can be decreased.

The largest negative Q/s_1 (3.99 in our case) tells us by how much the existing $b_1 = 15$ can be increased. Thus, the *range* over which b_1 can be changed is:

Lower limit = 15 − 3.00 = 12.00
Upper limit = 15 + 3.99 = 18.99

Analysis for the second constraint

Quantity	s_2	Q/s_2
3.57	.714	5
1.143	.428	2.67
.857	−.428	−2

Lower limit = 8 − 2.67 = 5.33
Upper limit = 8 + 2 = 10.00

Analysis for the third constraint

This is not a binding constraint, therefore the upper limit on b_3 is ∞. Since there is slack on this constraint, adding more capacity will not do us any good.

Quantity	s_3	Q/s_3
3.57	0	∞
1.143	1	1.143
.857	0	∞

Upper limit = ∞
Lower limit = 2 − 1.143 = 0.857

The logic of the analysis

Introducing a positive slack into a constraint is equivalent to reducing the value of the right-hand side by the value of the slack. For example, in the constraint:

$$5x_1 + 2x_2 + s_1 = 20$$
$$\text{if } s_1 = 2\text{, then } 5x_1 + 2x_2 = 18$$

The same is true for a negative slack.

Thus, introducing a slack is equivalent to decreasing (increasing) the right-hand side. Therefore, in order to determine the *range* of the right-hand side, one should determine the maximum amount of slack (positive and negative) that can be introduced. This is done by analyzing the slack (surplus) of each constraint in the final simplex tableau. The maximum amount that can be introduced is found by:

The smallest positive Q/slack ratio, which tells us how much the value of the right-hand side can be *decreased.*

The largest negative Q/slack ratio, which tells us how much the value of the right-hand side can be *increased.*

Capacity limits

As an alternative to direct analysis of the b_i's, one can use the dual's objective function coefficients. Since the capacity values in linear programming are equivalent to the coefficients of the objective function of the dual, it is possible to conduct a sensitivity analysis of the primal's b_i's by writing the dual problem and conducting a sensitivity analysis on the coefficients of the objective function. Such a treatment would then establish upper and lower limits on the b_i's. These limits are very important since they tell management how much a capacity limit can be changed before the existing optimal basis changes.

Changes in the input-output ("technology") coefficients of the constraints

A change in the input-output coefficients (left-hand side) of the constraints is equivalent to either changing the slope of the constraint (in the case of two decision variables) or moving the constraint parallel to itself (if the ratio of the coefficients remains the same). As a result of such a change, the area of feasible solutions will be changed. The impact on the optimal solution depends on the magnitude of the change. An analytical treatment of this topic is beyond the scope of this text. (The interested reader should consult references [1, 3, 4, or 6].)

Adding or deleting constraints

The addition of a new constraint can lead to one of the following results. First, the constraint may be redundant in the sense that it does not further restrict the feasible solution set. In that case, the optimal solution remains the same. Second, the constraint may decrease the feasible area, but the optimal solution will remain the same. Third, the additional constraint may reduce the feasible area so as to make the current optimal solution *infeasible*, thereby creating the need for finding a new optimal solution.

To find the impact of an added constraint on the optimal solution, all one has to do is to insert the value of the variables of the optimal solution into the new constraint. If the constraint is *not* violated, it belongs to the first or the second result above, and there is no change in the optimal solution. If the constraint is violated, then the problem must be resolved.

When deleting a constraint, one should check if the constraint is fully utilized (zero slack or surplus). If the answer is yes, the problem must be resolved; otherwise, there will be no change in the optimal solution.

8.3 COMPUTERIZATION

Most real-life problems are too large or complex for a graphical or manual simplex solution. Therefore, they are solved with the aid of computer programs. Dozens of computer programs are available from software companies, computer manufacturers, textbook publishers, and universities. As with other software, LP packages were developed both for mainframe and for mini- and microcomputers.

The inputs to the computer are typically simple: the objective function and the constraints. The most common outputs include:

a. The value of the decision variables.
b. The value of the objective function.
c. The value of the slack and surplus variables.
d. The value of the dual's variables.
e. Limited sensitivity analysis.

Example 1

In Section 8.2, we examined the following product-mix problem using both a graphical solution and the simplex approach.

$$\begin{aligned} &\text{maximize } z = 3x_1 + 4x_2 \\ &\text{subject to:} \\ &\quad 3x_1 + 5x_2 \le 15 \\ &\quad 2x_1 + 1x_2 \le 8 \\ &\quad 0x_1 + 1x_2 \le 2 \end{aligned}$$

Data input The data input to the linear programming problem are sufficient for the sensitivity analysis. All the user has to do is to request "sensitivity analysis" from the menu.

Solution The computer printout (Table 8.3) includes three parts: solution and dual, right-hand side ranging, and objective function ranging. The analysis follows.

Interpretation of the results

The solution is divided into four parts.

a. Variable solution This solution includes:

1. The value of the objective function.

$$z = 14.14286$$

2. The value of the decision variables.

$$x_1 = 3.571 \qquad x_2 = 0.457$$

TABLE 8.3
Sensitivity analysis

SOLUTION SUMMARY

PROBLEM NAME: TYPE: MAXIMIZATION

OBJECTIVE FUNCTION VALUE: 14.14286

VARIABLE NAME	SOLUTION QUANTITY	REDUCED COST
X1	3.571429	0
X2	.8571428	0

CONSTRAINT ANALYSIS

CONSTRAINT NUMBER	RHS VALUE	SLACK OR SURPLUS	SHADOW PRICE
1	15.000	0	.7142858
2	8.000	0	.4285713
3	2.000	1.142857	0

SENSITIVITY ANALYSIS—RIGHT HAND SIDE RANGING
PROBLEM NAME TYPE: MAXIMIZATION

ROW NO.	LOWER LIMIT	CURRENT RHS	UPPER LIMIT	OUTGOING LOWER	VARIABLE UPPER
1	12	15	19	X2	SLK-3
2	5.333333	8	10	SLK-3	X2
3	.8571428	2	NO LIMIT	SLK-3	NONE

SENSITIVITY ANALYSIS—OBJECTIVE FUNCTION RANGING
PROBLEM NAME: TYPE: MAXIMIZATION

VAR. NAME	LOWER LIMIT	CURRENT VALUE	UPPER LIMIT	INCOMING LOWER	VARIABLE UPPER
X1	2.4	3	8.0	SLK-2	SLK-1
X2	1.5	4	5	SLK-1	SLK-2

3. Reduced cost (coefficient of sensitivity). This coefficient measures how much the cost per unit must be decreased (or profit per unit increased) to bring another variable not currently in the solution into the solution.

b. Constraint analysis Here all the constraints are listed with their slack (surplus) and shadow (dual) prices. Notice that if the slack is zero, the shadow price is non-zero; if the slack is non-zero, then the shadow price is zero.

c. ***Right-hand side ranging*** We consider each column in turn.

1. Row number: This refers to the number of the constraint, in the same sequence that it was entered in the problem.
2. Lower limit: The minimum level, a lower limit, in the current right-hand side (RHS) value of a constraint that is possible before the value of the corresponding shadow price is changed. In other words, the downward range over which the shadow price associated with the constraint remains valid.
3. Current value: This is the value of the RHS of the original problem or the most current version of the problem, for each constraint.
4. Upper limit: The maximum level of the current RHS value of a constraint that is possible before the value of the shadow price is changed. The upper value is 19 for constraint no. 1.
5. Outgoing variable, lower: The current basis variable that will be forced out of the solution if the lower limit is violated. In other words, if more than an allowable amount of decrease is removed from the RHS of the constraint, this variable will leave the solution.
6. Outgoing variable, upper: The current basis variable that will be forced out of the solution if the upper limit is violated.

d. Sensitivity analysis—objective function ranging We consider each column in turn.

1. Variable name: This is the name assigned to the decision variable (e.g., x_1)
2. Lower limit: The limit to which the coefficients in the objective function can be reduced (one at a time) without changing the current optimal solution. For example, if the profit contribution of variable #1 (currently 3) goes below 2.4, at least one of the variables in the currently optimal solution will change.

TABLE 8.4
Computer solution for example 2

SOLUTION SUMMARY

PROBLEM NAME: TYPE: MAXIMIZATION

OBJECTIVE FUNCTION VALUE: 51.8

VARIABLE NAME	SOLUTION QUANTITY	REDUCED COST
X1	10	0
X2	0	.8422222
X3	1.8	0

CONSTRAINTS ANALYSIS

CONSTRAINT NUMBER	RHS VALUE	SLACK OR SURPLUS	SHADOW PRICE
1	150.000	0	.3111111
2	77.000	0	6.666667E-02
3	36.000	14.76	0

SENSITIVITY ANALYSIS—RIGHT HAND SIDE RANGING

PROBLEM NAME: TYPE: MAXIMIZATION

ROW NO.	LOWER LIMIT	CURRENT RHS	UPPER LIMIT	OUTGOING LOWER	VARIABLE UPPER
1	93.71187	150	231	SLK-3	X3
2	50	77	95.76261	X3	SLK-3
3	21.24	36	NO LIMIT	SLK-3	NONE

SENSITIVITY ANALYSIS—OBJECTIVE FUNCTION RANGING

PROBLEM NAME: TYPE: MAXIMIZATION

VAR. NAME	LOWER LIMIT	CURRENT VALUE	UPPER LIMIT	INCOMING LOWER	VARIABLE UPPER
X1	4.200422	5	NO LIMIT	X2	NONE
X3	0	1	15	SLK-2	SLK-1
X2	NO LIMIT	4.5	5.34	NONE	X2

3. Current value: The current value of the coefficient for the variable in the objective function.
4. Upper limit: The maximum level of a coefficient, expressed as an upper limit, that is possi-

ble without changing the current optimal solution. For example, the upper limit for variable x_1 is 8.

5. Incoming variable, lower: The current nonbasis variable that will enter the optimal solution if the maximum decrease is violated.
6. Incoming variable, upper: The current nonbasis variable that will enter the optimal solution if the maximum increase is violated.

Example 2

Let us examine the product-mix problem discussed in Section 8.2. Given:

$$\begin{aligned}
&\text{maximize } z = 5x_1 + 4.5x_2 + 1x_3\\
&\text{subject to:}\\
&\quad 15x_1 + 15.8x_2 + 0x_3 \leq 150\\
&\quad 5x_1 + 6.4x_2 + 15x_3 \leq 77\\
&\quad 0x_1 + 2.8x_2 + 11.8x_3 \leq 36
\end{aligned}$$

The computer solution printout is given in Table 8.4.

Interpreting the output

The first part of the table lists the variables, their values in the optimal solution, and their coefficients in the objective function. Notice that the second variable is not in the solution and, therefore, has a nonzero value in the last column.

The objective function coefficients explanation is given in the text (Section 8.2) for this example. Notice, however, that there are differences in the values of the limits. The reason is that the computer program used is accurate only to two decimal places, while the manual solution is more accurate (in this case). Rounding errors tend to accumulate in a computer and this can be a major problem in computer applications.

The interpretation of the right-hand side analysis is the same as in the previous example.

8.4 PROBLEMS FOR PART A

1. Write the dual to the blending problem given in Section 6.2. Solve graphically.
2. Write the dual to Problem 6.11a. Solve by the simplex method. Compare to the simplex solution of the primal.
3. Given a linear programming problem:

$$\begin{aligned}
&\text{minimize } z = 6x_1 + 5x_2\\
&\text{subject to:}\\
&\quad (1)\ 4x_1 + 8x_2 \geq 80\\
&\quad (2)\ 6x_1 + 4x_2 \geq 100\\
&\quad (3)\ 5x_1 + 5x_2 \geq 95\\
&\quad (4)\ 6x_1 + 3x_2 \geq 110
\end{aligned}$$

a. Write the dual to the problem.
b. Solve the dual by the simplex method (or by computer).
c. What is the solution of the primal? (Answer *without* solving the primal.)
d. What is the total value of each constraint?

4. Write the dual to the following problems:

a. maximize $5x_1 + 3x_2 + x_3$
subject to:
$$5x_1 + 3x_2 \leq 50$$
$$2x_2 + x_3 \geq 20$$
$$2x_1 + 3x_2 - x_3 = 26$$

b. minimize $6x_1 - 2x_2$
subject to:
$$3x_1 + 4x_2 \geq 50$$
$$x_1 + 2x_2 = 20$$
$$2x_1 + 3x_2 \leq 45$$

5. The solution to a linear programming minimization problem is $x_1 = 8$, $x_2 = 3$, $x_3 = 5$, $z =$ \$84. There is a raw material constraint that is expressed as:

$$7x_1 + 3x_2 - x_3 \leq 60$$

The dual variable of this constraint is −\$2.6. Management is considering changing the availability of the raw material. Increasing the availability costs \$2.50 per unit, while decreasing raw material by one unit reduces expenses by \$2.70. What would you advise management to do and why?

6. Given a *LP* problem:

minimize $z = 300x_1 + 800x_2$
subject to:

$$(1)\quad 2x_1 + 2x_2 \leq 1$$
$$(2)\quad 4x_1 + 2x_2 \geq 1$$
$$(3)\quad 10x_1 + 20x_2 \geq 6$$
$$(4)\quad x_1 + x_2 = 1/2$$

a. Solve the problem graphically and by the simplex method.
b. Which of the constraints are fully utilized?
c. Use the shadow prices to find the impact on the objective function of the following changes:
(1) Increase the right-hand side of constraint 1 by .5.
(2) Decrease the right-hand side of constraint 1 by .1.
(3) Increase the right-hand side of constraint 2 by .1.
(4) Decrease the right-hand side of constraint 2 by .5.
(5) Decrease the right-hand side of constraint 3 by .5.
(6) Increase the right-hand side of constraint 4 by .1.

d. Verify the answer to *(b)* through observation of the graphical solution.

7. Write the dual to Problem 6. Solve by computer. Compare to the results of Problem 6.

8. Given the *LP* problem:

maximize $z = 5{,}000x_1 + 4{,}000x_2$
subject to:
$$x_1 + x_2 \geq 5$$
$$x_1 - 3x_2 \leq 0$$
$$10x_1 + 15x_2 \leq 150$$
$$20x_1 + 10x_2 \leq 160$$
$$30x_1 + 10x_2 \geq 135$$

Find:
a. The lower and upper limits of the coefficients of the basic variables.
b. The limit on the coefficients of the nonbasic variables.
c. The upper and lower limits of all five right-hand side constraints.

9. Given:

maximize $z = 2.5x_1 + 2.25x_2 + .5x_3$
subject to:
$$7.5x_1 + 7.9x_2 \leq 75$$
$$2.5x_1 + 3.2x_2 + 7.5x_3 \leq 38.5$$
$$1.4x_2 + 5.8x_3 \leq 18$$

Find:
a. How much should the profit coefficient of x_2 be increased in order for it to be included in the optimal solution?
b. How much can the profit of x_1 be decreased without it dropping out of the optimal solution?
c. Change the right-hand side of the first constraint to 45; what impact will such a change have on the solution? Change it to 46 and check again. What can you conclude from the results?

10. Given a linear programming problem:

maximize $z = 70x_1 + 30x_2$
subject to:

$$2x_1 + x_2 \leq 1$$
$$x_1 + 8x_2 \leq 4$$

a. Solve graphically.

b. What price coefficient should the product, currently not in the optimal solution, have in order to be included in the optimal solution?

c. How much can the right-hand side of constraint 2 change before the optimal solution is changed? What will the impact of the change be?

d. How much can the coefficient of x_1 in constraint 1 change before the optimal solution is changed?

e. What will be the impact of the following additional constraint on the solution:

$$2x_1 + 5x_2 = 4$$

11. Refer to the blending problem in Chapter 6 (Figure 6.12).

a. What price will x_1 have to assume in order for it to be eliminated from the optimal solution?

b. What change in the brightness requirement needs to occur in order to change the optimal solution?

c. What change in the coefficients of the hue constraint (a_{ij}) must occur in order to change the optimal solution?

12. Given a LP problem:

FORMULATION

MAXIMIZATION PROBLEM

3.75X1 + 7.63X2 + 8.07X3

SUBJECT TO

1.5X1 + 2X2 + 1X3 ≤ 9600

4X1 + 5X2 + 10X3 ≤ 38400

1X1 + 1.5X2 + 1X3 ≤ 6000

0X1 + 1X2 + 0X3 ≥ 1000

0X1 + 0X2 + 1X3 ≥ 3000

** RESULTS **

SOLUTION SUMMARY

PROBLEM NAME: TYPE: MAXIMIZATION

OBJECTIVE FUNCTION VALUE: 37028.4

VARIABLE NAME	SOLUTION QUANTITY	REDUCED COST
X1	0	2.354
X2	1680	0
X3	3000	0

CONSTRAINTS ANALYSIS

CONSTRAINT NUMBER	RHS VALUE	SLACK OR SURPLUS	SHADOW PRICE
1	9600.000	3240	0
2	38400.000	0	1.526
3	6000.000	480	0
4	1000.000	680	0
5	3000.000	0	7.19

SENSITIVITY ANALYSIS—RIGHT HAND SIDE RANGING
PROBLEM NAME: TYPE: MAXIMIZATION

ROW NO.	LOWER LIMIT	CURRENT RHS	UPPER LIMIT	OUTGOING LOWER	VARIABLE UPPER
1	6360	9600	NO LIMIT	SLK-1	NONE
2	35000	38400	40000	SUR-4	SLK-3
3	5520	6000	NO LIMIT	SLK-3	NONE
4	NO LIMIT	1000	1680	NONE	SUR-4
5	2760	3000	3340	SLK-3	SUR-4

SENSITIVITY ANALYSIS—OBJECTIVE FUNCTION RANGING
PROBLEM NAME: TYPE: MAXIMIZATION

VAR. NAME	LOWER LIMIT	CURRENT VALUE	UPPER LIMIT	INCOMING LOWER	VARIABLE UPPER
X2	4.6875	7.63	NO LIMIT	X1	NONE
X3	NO LIMIT	8.07	15.26	NONE	SUR-5
X1	NO LIMIT	3.75	6.10	NONE	X1

This is a product-mix problem with:

X1 = Units of budget
X2 = Units of regular
X3 = Units of deluxe

Constraint:

(1) cutting (minutes)
(2) sewing (minutes)
(3) packing (minutes)
(4) marketing (units)
(5) marketing (units)

O.F. value in dollars

Answer the following questions:

a. Should management increase the capacity of sewing by 10 hours if the cost of such a change is $120? Why or why not?
b. The cost of making one unit of a "budget" is $10. What should this product sell for in order to be included in the solution?
c. What is the utilization (in percent) of the cutting department?
d. Which constraints are not fully utilized?
e. Can you have a production plan of product X2 (regular) only? Why or why not?
f. Can you have a production plan of product X3 only? Why or why not?
g. What will be the total profit if we make 2,990 units of deluxe (instead of 3,000) in the optimal manner?
h. Why is there "no limit" on the RHS analysis of constraint 4?

13. Refer to Problem 7 in Chapter 6. The current solution is: $x_1 = 181.8$; $x_2 = 109.1$.

a. Assume that the cost coefficient of x_1 is 50. What must the cost coefficient of x_2 be for:
(1) The solution to be at *D* (the intersection of constraints 3 and 5)?
(2) The solution to be at *A* (the intersection of constraint 2 with the x_2 axis)?
b. Describe, with examples, two ways to reduce the total cost.
c. Which constraints will have a dual variable?

14. Given a linear programming problem:

minimize $z = 50x_1 + 80x_2 + 15x_3 + 180x_4$
subject to:

$$300x_1 + 1{,}000x_2 + 10x_3 + 1{,}500x_4 \geq 2{,}500 \quad \text{(color)}$$
$$20x_1 + 110x_2 + 10x_3 + 0x_4 \geq 200 \quad \text{(strength)}$$
$$15x_1 + 10x_2 + 8x_3 + 48x_4 \geq 100 \quad \text{(weight)}$$
$$x_1 \leq 2; \quad x_2 \leq 1.5$$

and the computerized solution below, find the quantities of the four ingredients x_1, x_2, x_3, and x_4 that will provide sufficient color, strength, and weight to a blend but still minimize the overall cost. Answer the following questions.

a. What will the total cost of the blend be?
b. How much will the blend weigh?
c. Which ingredients are not included in the solution?
d. What should the cost of the absent ingredient(s) be to be included in the solution?
e. How strong is the blend going to be?
f. What is the utilization level of constraint 4?
g. Suppose that we introduce into the blend one additional pound of x_1; what will the total cost be?
h. Why is the dual of constraint 4 equal to zero?
i. Refer to the RHS ranging; why is there no limit on constraint 2? On constraint 4?
j. Why is there an upper and lower limit on constraint 5, but not on 4?
k. How much can we save by *decreasing* the color requirement by 10 percent?
l. What will happen if the cost of ingredient 4 is increased 10 percent? What if it is increased 20 percent?
m. What is the meaning of the outgoing variables sur-2 and x_4 in constraint 3 (upper and lower)?
n. What is the meaning of incoming variable lower = slk-5 and upper = x_1 for x_4?

SOLUTION SUMMARY

PROBLEM NAME: TYPE: MINIMIZATION

OBJECTIVE FUNCTION VALUE: 335.2344

VARIABLE NAME	SOLUTION QUANTITY	REDUCED COST
X1	0	4.296865
X2	1.5	0
X3	6.901043	0
X4	.6206597	0

CONSTRAINTS ANALYSIS

CONSTRAINT NUMBER	RHS VALUE	SLACK OR SURPLUS	SHADOW PRICE
1	2500.00	0	.0625
2	200.00	34.01042	0
3	100.00	0	1.796875
4	2.00	2	0
5	1.50	0	.46875

SENSITIVITY ANALYSIS—RIGHT HAND SIDE RANGING
PROBLEM NAME: TYPE: MINIMIZATION

ROW NO.	LOWER LIMIT	CURRENT RHS	UPPER LIMIT	OUTGOING LOWER	VARIABLE UPPER
1	1606.25	2500	3316.25	X4	SUR-2
2	NO LIMIT	200	234.0104	NONE	SUR-2
3	73.87999	100	815.0004	SUR-2	X4
4	0	2	NO LIMIT	SLK-4	NONE
5	1.254696	1.5	2.405063	SUR-2	X4

SENSITIVITY ANALYSIS—OBJECTIVE FUNCTION RANGING
PROBLEM NAME: TYPE: MINIMIZATION

VAR. NAME	LOWER LIMIT	CURRENT VALUE	UPPER LIMIT	INCOMING LOWER	VARIABLE UPPER
X4	179.3165	180	202	SLK-5	X1
X3	1.2	15	15.16364	SUR-3	SLK-5
X2	NO LIMIT	80	80.46875	NONE	SLK-5
X1	45.7	50	NO LIMIT	X1	NONE

PART B: EXTENSIONS

8.5 INTEGER PROGRAMMING

Jack Smith, the administrator of Southern General Hospital, just returned from a meeting with the hospital board. He was in a gloomy mood since the board only approved funds for a minor expansion, \$210,000, to be used for not more than 10 hospital beds. He wanted to make the most of this authorization; that is, to get as much additional income as possible to improve the hospital's cash flow situation. So he called his assistant, Ruth, and asked her advice. There were two places where the additional beds could be added—in ward A and/or ward B. Each additional bed in ward A would generate \$20 profit a day, versus \$25 in ward B. For a moment he thought of placing all the additional beds in ward B; however, he remembered that the board insisted on at least two beds for ward A. Also, the expansion would cost \$24,600 per bed in ward B and only \$20,000 per bed in ward A. Thus, he could add more beds in ward A. The problem, therefore, was how many beds to add to each ward (say, x_1 to ward A and x_2 to ward B).

A minor expansion

With all this information, Jack instructed Ruth to go to work on the problem. Ruth, having just completed a course in management science, immediately realized that she was dealing with an allocation problem. As she formulated it, she was very pleased to find out that it was linear, as follows:

$$\text{maximize } z = 20x_1 + 25x_2$$

subject to:

$$1x_1 + 1x_2 \leq 10 \text{ (total bed limitation)}$$
$$\$20{,}000x_1 + \$24{,}600x_2 \leq 210{,}000 \text{ (budget constraint)}$$
$$1x_1 + 0x_2 \leq 2 \text{ (at least two beds in ward A)}$$

With only two variables and three constraints, it seemed natural to try the graphical method (Figure 8.4). Ruth did so, and found an optimal solution of 2 beds in ward A and 6.9 beds in ward B, with a total daily profit of \$212.50 (point P in Figure 8.4). Examining the solution, Ruth immediately realized that she was dealing with an integer programming problem, since 6.9 beds is obviously not feasible. Before she had a chance to reexamine the solution she was surprised by Jack.

"I don't know what they teach you there at school, but you have been working on the problem for more than half an hour; let me try it." At that stage Ruth had no choice but to look at Jack's attempt. Jack rationalized that in this case there are only a few alternatives; they are listed in Table 8.5. Obviously, alternatives a_0 and a_1 should not be considered, since there must be at least two beds in ward A. He also realized that alternatives a_2, a_3, a_4, a_5, a_6, and a_7, exceeded the available budget. Left with only alternatives a_8, a_9, and a_{10}, he computed their profits and declared: "It is best to build eight beds in ward A and two in ward B; it will cost

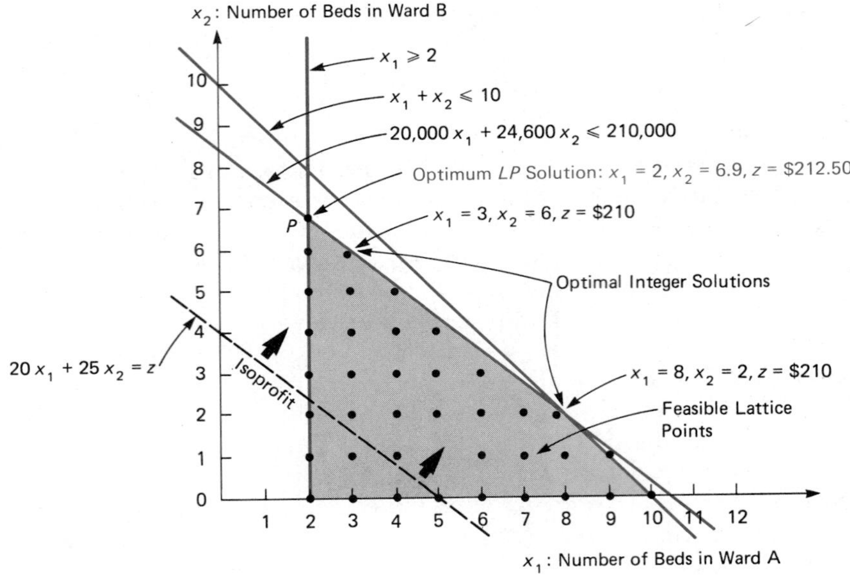

FIGURE 8.4
Geographical approach to bed allocation.

us \$209,200, and it will generate a daily profit of \$210. As you see, we do not need your linear programming."

Ruth returned, disheartened, to her desk. After all, why spend time on linear programming? Nevertheless, she decided to return to the graphical solution. As she examined the points marked with a • in Figure 8.4 (feasible integer solution points), it took her only a moment to notice that there was another solution. She called Jack and declared: "To get a daily profit of \$210, it is sufficient to build only six beds in ward B and three in A at

TABLE 8.5
Bed alternatives

Alternatives	*Beds in ward A*	*Beds in ward B*	*Required expenses*	*Daily profit*
a_0	0	10	\$246,000	(infeasible)
a_1	1	9	241,000	(infeasible)
a_2	2	8	236,800	(infeasible)
a_3	3	7	232,200	(infeasible)
a_4	4	6	227,600	(infeasible)
a_5	5	5	223,000	(infeasible)
a_6	6	4	218,400	(infeasible)
a_7	7	3	213,800	(infeasible)
a_8	8	2	209,200	\$210
a_9	9	1	204,600	\$205
a_{10}	10	0	200,000	\$200

a total cost of $207,600,[8] a savings of $1,600 in the required investment."[9] Jack was surprised; he checked and rechecked and finally admitted that the investment in "that linear programming course" was perhaps not so worthless.

Integer programming—the basics

The case just presented is an illustration of an **integer programming** problem. A mathematical programming problem which requires that some or all of the decision variables appearing in the optimal solution must be nonnegative whole numbers (such as 0, 1, 2, . . .), is classified as an integer programming problem. In other words, an **indivisibility** requirement is imposed either on all of the decision variables (an **all-integer** case) or on some of the decision variables (a **mixed-integer** case). Many practical problems involve integers. For example, it is impossible to have 2.7 elevators in a building, to admit 12.6 patients to a hospital, or to have 30.3 seats in a classroom.

An indivisibility

Mixed integers

Adding the indivisibility requirement results in additional constraints. This means that the optimal integer solution will be either inferior (the usual case) or at best as good as the optimal noninteger solution. In other words, there is a cost attached to imposing the indivisibility requirement. For example, in the optimal noninteger LP solution to the hospital expansion problem, a daily profit of $212.50 is expected, $2.50 more than in the all-integer solution. This difference is called the *cost of indivisibility*.

Cost of indivisibility

Integer programming is important not only because it allows us to solve practical problems with indivisibility requirements, but also because it can be used as a computational tool in the solution of several complicated problems that cannot otherwise be solved (or cannot otherwise be solved effectively). For example, many nonlinear as well as combinatorial problems can be reduced to integer programming form.[10] (For details, see Ignizio [6], Loomba and Turban [9], or Salkin [11].)

When the indivisibility requirement is added to a regular linear programming problem, the result is an *integer* (linear) *programming* problem.[11]

---

[8] Notice that here there are two (and only two) optimal integer solutions. The reader may recall that in LP, when more than one optimal solution exists, there are an infinite number of optimal solutions.

[9] Ruth and Jack's solutions are both optimal from a mathematical point of view. However, Ruth's solution is superior, since it requires less capital outlay. (The cost of capital outlay was disregarded in the formulation.) Multiple optimal solution situations give management greater flexibility of implementation, since they can consider factors not expressed in the formal model.

[10] A combinatorial problem consists of finding, from among a finite set of feasible solutions (usually very large), a solution that optimizes the value of the objective function.

[11] When the indivisibility requirement is added to a *nonlinear* programming problem, the result is integer-nonlinear programming, a rather complex situation that will not be discussed in this text.

Methods of solution

Complete enumeration

Complete enumeration What Jack attempted to do in the hospital expansion case was to list all possible solutions, eliminate those that violate the constraints, and select the best solution by comparing the net profits. Such a process is called an *enumeration;* and if *all* feasible solutions are checked, it is termed a **complete enumeration.** What Jack did was to assume that he should enumerate only the alternatives involving 10 beds (a partial enumeration), neglecting alternatives of 9 or fewer beds.

Since most integer programming problems have a finite number of feasible solutions, these can be solved by complete enumeration. To do so it is necessary to assign all possible integer values to all variables and to check all possible feasible solution combinations to determine that combination which yields the best value of the objective function. In cases with a small number of variables and possible combinations, this method is efficient. However, in many practical problems there is a very large number of possible solution combinations and the enumeration method is therefore impractical.

The zero-one algorithm

Branch and bound

There is one special case in which complete enumeration might be used to advantage. In several business and economic decision problems there are only two possible courses of action for every alternative under consideration, such as invest or not invest, accept or reject. For such cases, an implicit enumeration search, named the *zero-one algorithm,* has been developed (discussed in Section 8.6). This method has, for example, been used in the problem of allocating funds to research and development projects and found to be very efficient with as many as 50 projects. Enumeration efforts, in general, may be reduced with the **branch and bound** approach (to be discussed later in this chapter).

Rounding the noninteger solution A practical approach to an integer programming problem in some cases is to solve it as a regular linear programming problem and then round off the optimal results. The major advantage of such an approach is the saving of time and cost that would have been required for formulating and solving an integer programming model. The major disadvantage of the rounding approach is that the resultant solution may differ significantly from the optimal integer solution and, furthermore, may even be infeasible.

While the infeasibility problem can be avoided when rounding, by making sure that the constraints are not violated, it is impossible to tell offhand how close the rounded solution is to the optimal integer one. However, it is possible to tell how close the rounded integer solution is to the regular noninteger solution. If the difference between the two is not large, there is very little sense in investing time and money in an attempt to identify the optimal integer solution.[12]

[12] The logic for this approach is that the optimal integer solution must be in between the noninteger solution and the rounded solution. If the difference between these two is small, then the difference between the rounded and the true optimal integer solution is minimal.

A variant of the rounding method is the *trial-and-error* approach, in which one enumerates *selected* feasible integer solutions in the neighborhood of the optimal LP solution. For example, using this approach, Ruth would have investigated the solutions: (8,1) [i.e., $x_1 = 8$, $x_2 = 1$], (7,2), (6,3), (9,1), and (10,0). **Trial and error**

The graphical method Integer programming problems with either two unknown variables or two constraints can be solved by the graphical method. Its major advantages are its simplicity and its applicability for solving both the all-integer and mixed-integer problems. Ruth used this method in the hospital expansion case.

The graphical approach for integer programming problems is similar to the graphical approach for solving regular linear programming problems; the difference lies in the nature of the *feasible solution spaces* for the two problems (see Figure 8.4). Whereas in the linear programming case the set of feasible solutions is a *space* bounded by the linear constraints, in integer programming the feasible area is a collection of *all-integer points.* Once such points are marked, the isoprofit line is moved away from the origin until it covers the last lattice points in the feasible area—points (3,6) and (8,2) in Figure 8.4.[13] **The feasible solution space**

Branch and bound This is a special type of enumeration procedure and is discussed in Section 8.7.

Use of linear programming Some integer problems, such as the transportation problem with integer data, can be solved as regular LP problems with guaranteed integer solutions.

More complicated methods A host of more complicated methods are available for larger and more complex problems. All require computers. For a discussion, see [5], [11], or [12]. Of special interest are the methods based on Gomory's "cutting plane" algorithm (see [4] and [12]). According to these methods, a feasible solution area is constructed by sequentially adding constraints that eliminate or "cut" infeasible areas from the original solution space. Thus, the solution region converges to the area circumscribed by the extreme lattice points. Dynamic programming (Chapter 12) can also be used to solve certain types of integer programming problems. Finally, heuristic methods (Chapter 16) have also been developed for special integer programming problems. **Cutting planes**

8.6 THE ZERO-ONE MODEL

A special and important application of integer programming is the case where the value of the decision variables is limited to two "logical" variables. For example, a variable may be either yes or no, or match or no-match. These are symbolized by the values 0 and 1 and known as **zero-one variables.** Jensen [7] includes a computer program to solve these problems. The MSS package solves these problems as regular integer programming problems. **Logical variables**

[13] A lattice point here refers to a point with all-integer coordinates.

Examples

a. ***Research and development (R&D) or capital budgeting*** Companies frequently face the situation of selecting one or more R&D projects or investment opportunities among several competing projects. For example, consider the list below. If $25 million is available, which projects should be selected?

Competing projects	*Cost ($ million)*	*Expected utility*
Crime prevention (x_1)	5	20
Housing improvement (x_2)	20	18
Health care center (x_3)	12	13
Geriatric research (x_4)	7	30
Gifted child education (x_5)	4	15

Formulation. Each decision variable can assume one of two values, either 0 (not selected) or 1 (selected). Thus $x_1 = 0$ means not to select the crime prevention project. The objective function is:

$$\text{maximize } z = 20x_1 + 18x_2 + 13x_3 + 30x_4 + 15x_5$$

subject to:

$$5x_1 + 20x_2 + 12x_3 + 7x_4 + 4x_5 \leq 25$$

and

$$x_i = 0,1 \text{ for all } i$$

b. ***The knapsack problem*** Four items are considered for loading on an airplane. The weights and values of the items are shown below. Which items should be loaded on a plane whose capacity is 11 tons to maximize the value of the cargo transported?

Item	*Weight (tons)*	*Value*
A	2	18
B	4	25
C	5	30
D	3	20

Formulation. The decision variables are 0 (do not load) or 1 (load). The objective function is:

$$\text{maximize } z = 18x_A + 25x_B + 30x_C + 20x_D$$

subject to:

$$2x_A + 4x_B + 5x_C + 3x_D \leq 11$$

and

$$x_i = 0,1 \text{ for all } i$$

Note: A variation of this problem is solved by dynamic programming in Section 12.9.

c. *The fixed-charge problem* Many real-life problems involve a combination of fixed and variable costs. The fixed costs are incurred only if certain projects are undertaken or a certain capacity level is exceeded. A common example is machine scheduling.

Example. Eastland Corp. is planning to produce at least 900 pollution control valves. Three production lines are available with the setup costs, unit processing (variable) costs, and capacities given below. Find which lines to use in order to minimize the total cost.

Line	*Setup cost*	*Unit processing cost*	*Maximum capacity*
A	$850	$20	500
B	150	58	700
C	520	36	620

Formulation. Let x_A, x_B, and x_C represent the quantities to be produced on lines A, B, and C; d_A, d_B, and d_C indicate whether a line is to be used (1) or not (0). The objective function is

$$\text{minimize } z = \underbrace{(850d_A + 150d_B + 520d_C)}_{\text{Fixed cost}} + \underbrace{(20x_A + 58x_B + 36x_C)}_{\text{Variable cost}}$$

subject to:

$$\begin{aligned} x_A + x_B + x_C &\geq 900 \\ x_A &\leq 500d_A \\ x_B &\leq 700d_B \\ x_C &\leq 620d_C \end{aligned}$$

and

$$d_i = 0,1 \text{ for all } i$$

(*Note:* This problem is actually a mixed-integer programming problem, since only *some* of the variables are restricted to zero or one values.)

d. *Capacity planning* A company is considering whether to expand a warehouse or not. If so, the amount of the expansion, x, should be at least 2,000 units, but not more than 10,000. Disregarding other information, this condition can be written as two constraints:

$$\begin{aligned} &(1)\ x - 10{,}000d \leq 0 \\ &(2)\ x - 2{,}000d \geq 0 \end{aligned}$$

where:

$$d = 0,1$$

Now, if $d = 1$ in the solution, then x can assume any value between 2,000 and 10,000. But if $d = 0$ in the solution, then $x = 0$.

e. Mutually exclusive constraints In many real-life situations, an optimization is to be made subject to one constraint (or a set of constraints) or another, but not both. In this case, the problem can be separated into two or more problems, each solved separately, and then the one with the highest payoff selected. Or, an elegant integer-programming approach can be used. For example:

$$\begin{aligned}
&\text{maximize } 5x_1 + 7x_2 \\
&\text{subject to either:} \\
&\quad 2x_1 + x_2 \leq 5{,}000 \\
&\text{or:} \\
&\quad 3x_1 + 7x_2 \leq 14{,}000 \\
&\text{or:} \\
&\quad 5x_1 + 6x_2 \leq 12{,}500
\end{aligned}$$

The integer programming presentation is:

$$\begin{aligned}
&\text{maximize } 5x_1 + 7x_2 + 0d_1 + 0d_2 + 0d_3 \\
&\text{subject to:} \\
&\quad 2x_1 + x_2 \leq 5{,}000 + Md_1 \\
&\quad 3x_1 + 7x_2 \leq 14{,}000 + Md_2 \\
&\quad 5x_1 + 6x_2 \leq 12{,}500 + Md_3 \\
&\quad d_1 + d_2 + d_3 = 1
\end{aligned}$$

where M is a very large number compared to the RHS values (say, 100,000) and d_1, d_2, and d_3 are either 0 or 1. This is another mixed-integer programming problem, since only the ds are required to have integer values.

f. Assignment The assignment problem in Chapter 10 uses 0–1 variables when it is converted into a linear program. (See Chapter 10 for details.)

8.7 THE BRANCH AND BOUND METHOD

The branch and bound method is an intelligent search procedure for either an optimal or, with less computational effort, a close-to-optimal solution to certain managerial problems, including all-integer and mixed-integer problems.

The process in general

Dividing into subproblems

The process consists of dividing a problem into two or more *subproblems* and setting two *bounds* on the value of the objective function. The manner of determining bounds depends on the type of problem. A distinction is then made between *feasible bounding solutions* and *infeasible bounding solutions*. The subproblems are then solved. All subproblems whose objective functions are worse than the established feasible bounds are

Employee \ Machine	Mill (x)	Lathe (y)	Drill (z)
Jim (a)	0	3	2
Bill (b)	2	4	1
Joe (c)	2	1	3

TABLE 8.6
An assignment problem

eliminated from further consideration. The remaining subproblems are used to modify the bounds and then subdivided and investigated. The process is repeated until no further subdivision is possible, at which point the optimal (or near optimal) solution has been reached.

Example Let us illustrate by solving a problem of finding the best assignment of three employees to three machines on a one-to-one basis. Table 8.6 shows the profits (determined from prior experience) derived from assigning each employee to each machine. For example, if Jim is assigned to a drilling machine, a profit of 2 is realized.

Solution First, the maximum possible profit is computed. To do so, the highest possible profit in the first row, which is 3, is selected; accordingly, Jim is assigned to the lathe (a to y, or ay). Next is the second row; 4 is the highest profit. Therefore an assignment of b to y is made. Similarly, c is assigned to z. The profit for this assignment (ay, by, cz) is: $3 + 4 + 3 = 10$. This solution is *infeasible* since two employees were assigned to machine y, violating the one-to-one requirement. (If this solution had been feasible, it would also have been optimal and the problem would have been solved.) This solution, with the highest possible profit, is now used as the *upper bound* (UB), an infeasible bound in this case.

Upper bound

First branching

By changing *one assignment* in the *infeasible solution*, and leaving the others the same, three new problems are formed. Suppose a change in the assignment to the milling machine (x) is chosen; then three subproblems will involve assigning a, b, and c consecutively to x. First, a is assigned to x. The original assignments of b and c (by, cz) are kept. This solution is feasible with a value of 7 (see Figure 8.5). Being a feasible solution, it is declared the *first lower bound* (LB). Since the LB is less than the UB, we continue. Second, b is assigned to x. In this case the (feasible) solution is: ay, bx, and cz, with a value of 8. Since this is a better feasible solution than the previous one, the previous solution is dropped. Finally, c is assigned to x with the solution: cx, ay, and by (which is infeasible) with a value of 9.

The original problem has now been partitioned into three new problems, with a best (but infeasible) solution of 9 instead of 10. Therefore, 9

FIGURE 8.5
First branching

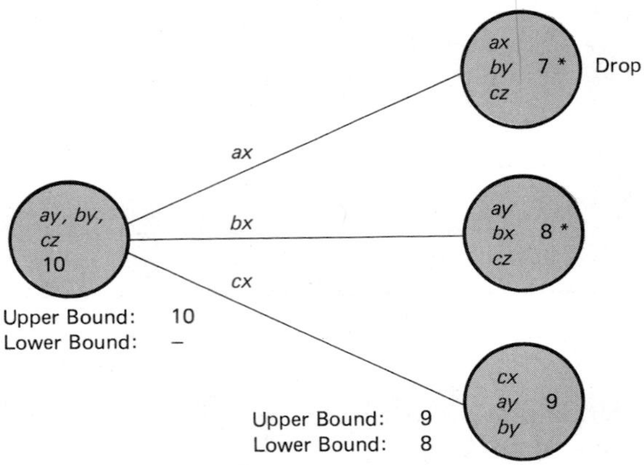

becomes the *new upper bound.*[14] It is still an infeasible solution, but it has a value closer to the feasible area than the previous upper bound had. The optimal solution must now be between the *lower bound* of 8 and the *upper bound* of 9. Now the *ax* solution can be dropped from further consideration since it is *below* the lower bound.

Lower bound

Second branching

The next branching is from *cx,* since this is the current best but infeasible solution. This time two branches are possible, *ay* and *by* (see Figure 8.6).

Again, solutions whose value is less than the current lower bound are dropped; thus, *ay* with a profit of 6 is dropped. Since no further

FIGURE 8.6
Second branching

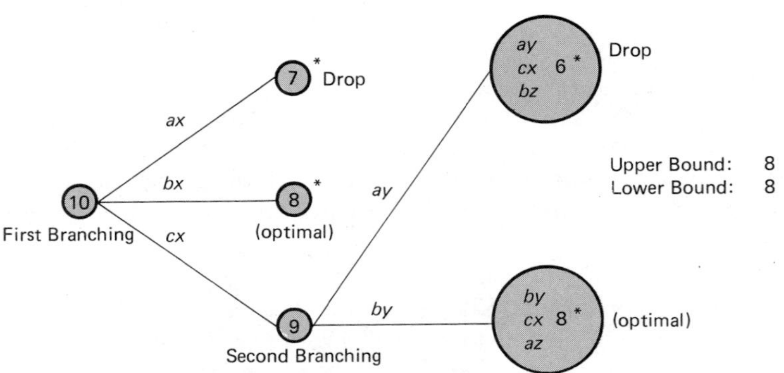

[14] New bounds are generated at each branching because the partitioning of the problem *totally replaces* the previous problem.

branching is possible (only feasible solutions remain and feasible solutions are not partitioned), the optimal solution has been reached. At that point, the old UB is replaced with the new one (8); at the optimal solution UB = LB. Here, two optimal solutions with a profit of 8 have been identified:

1. *b* to *x*, *a* to *y*, *c* to *z*.
2. *c* to *x*, *b* to *y*, *a* to *z*.

Flexibility of branch and bound

The procedure for bounding is very flexible—in the example above, for instance, the initial upper bound could have been found by selecting the largest value in each *column* rather than in each row.

Use in solving integer programming problems

The branch and bound technique can be used to solve integer programming problems. The first step is to solve the problem by linear programming without paying attention to the integer requirements. Then, if the solution is noninteger, a branching procedure is employed. This procedure splits the problem into two subproblems, based on two integer values that are immediately above and below the noninteger value. Assume, for instance, that a variable x_2 in the LP solution equals 2.25; then the problem is divided into two subproblems by introducing two new constraints: $x_2 \geq 3$ and $x_2 \leq 2$, one constraint in each branch.

Example The Worthy Company is a large manufacturer of household appliances. Recently, its board of directors approved $25 million for constructing additional plants and/or warehouses. The construction of each warehouse will cost $2 million, and management does not want more than eight warehouses. The construction of each plant will cost $4 million, and management does not plan to construct more than five. It is estimated that each warehouse will contribute $31,000 per month to the company's profit, while each plant will contribute $60,000 per month. The problem is to determine the optimal number of plants and warehouses. Since fractions of plants or warehouses cannot be built, the problem is an integer programming one.

Formulation. The problem can be stated as follows (data are in thousands of dollars):

$$\begin{aligned}
&\text{maximize } z = 31x_1 + 60x_2\\
&\text{subject to:}\\
&\quad 2x_1 + 4x_2 \leq 25\\
&\quad x_1 \leq 8\\
&\quad x_2 \leq 5
\end{aligned}$$

and both x_1 and x_2 must be nonnegative integers, where:

$$\begin{aligned}
x_1 &= \text{Number of warehouses}\\
x_2 &= \text{Number of plants}
\end{aligned}$$

Solution

Step 1. The optimal, noninteger solution is:

$$x_1 = 8 \text{ warehouses}$$
$$x_2 = 2.25 \text{ plants}$$
$$z = 383 \text{ (thousand dollars) profit}$$

The solution is not acceptable since x_2 is not an integer. The value of $z = 383$ is set as the initial *upper bound.*

Step 2. The next step is to set a lower bound. The lower bound, in the case of maximization, must be *feasible.* (Remember that the upper bound is usually *not* feasible.) One way to find a feasible solution is to *round* the optimal one, making sure that the constraints are not violated. The rounded solution is: $x_1 = 8$; $x_2 = 2$; $z = 368$. The value $z = 368$ is set as the LB.

Step 3. Compare the UB and LB. If they are equal, stop. This is the optimal solution. Otherwise, go to step 4.

Step 4. Branch from the node with the current UB. That is, branch from the noninteger (infeasible) solution. In this case, there is only one noninteger variable (x_2), and therefore we branch from this variable. In general, however, branching is done from the variable farthest from being integral. The branching results in two subproblems. In our case, since $x_2 = 2.25$, the branching results in subproblems with $x_2 \leq 2$ and $x_2 \geq 3$.

The two subproblems created are:

Subproblem A

$$\begin{aligned} &\text{maximize } z = 31x_1 + 60x_2 \\ &\text{subject to:} \\ &\quad 2x_1 + 4x_2 \leq 25 \\ &\quad x_1 \leq 8 \\ &\quad x_2 \leq 5 \\ &\quad x_2 \geq 3 \\ &x_1, x_2 \text{ are integers} \end{aligned}$$

Subproblem B

$$\begin{aligned} &\text{maximize } z = 31x_1 + 60x_2 \\ &\text{subject to:} \\ &\quad 2x_1 + 4x_2 \leq 25 \\ &\quad x_1 \leq 8 \\ &\quad x_2 \leq 5 \\ &\quad x_2 \leq 2 \\ &x_1, x_2 \text{ are integers} \end{aligned}$$

Optimal solution for subproblems A and B:

For subproblem A: $x_1 = 6.5$, $x_2 = 3$, and $z = 381.5$
For subproblem B: $x_1 = 8$, $x_2 = 2$, and $z = 368$.

This information is shown in Figure 8.7 in tree form. The search of subproblem B is stopped, since it has the all-integer feasible solution $z = 368$, which equals the lower bound established earlier. Subproblem A is searched further, since it has a *noninteger solution* and the value of its objective function is greater than the current lower bound of 368. Thus, it is possible that the optimal integer solution to A will yield a value of z larger than 368. The second *upper bound* is set to 381.5, replacing the initial upper bound of 383.

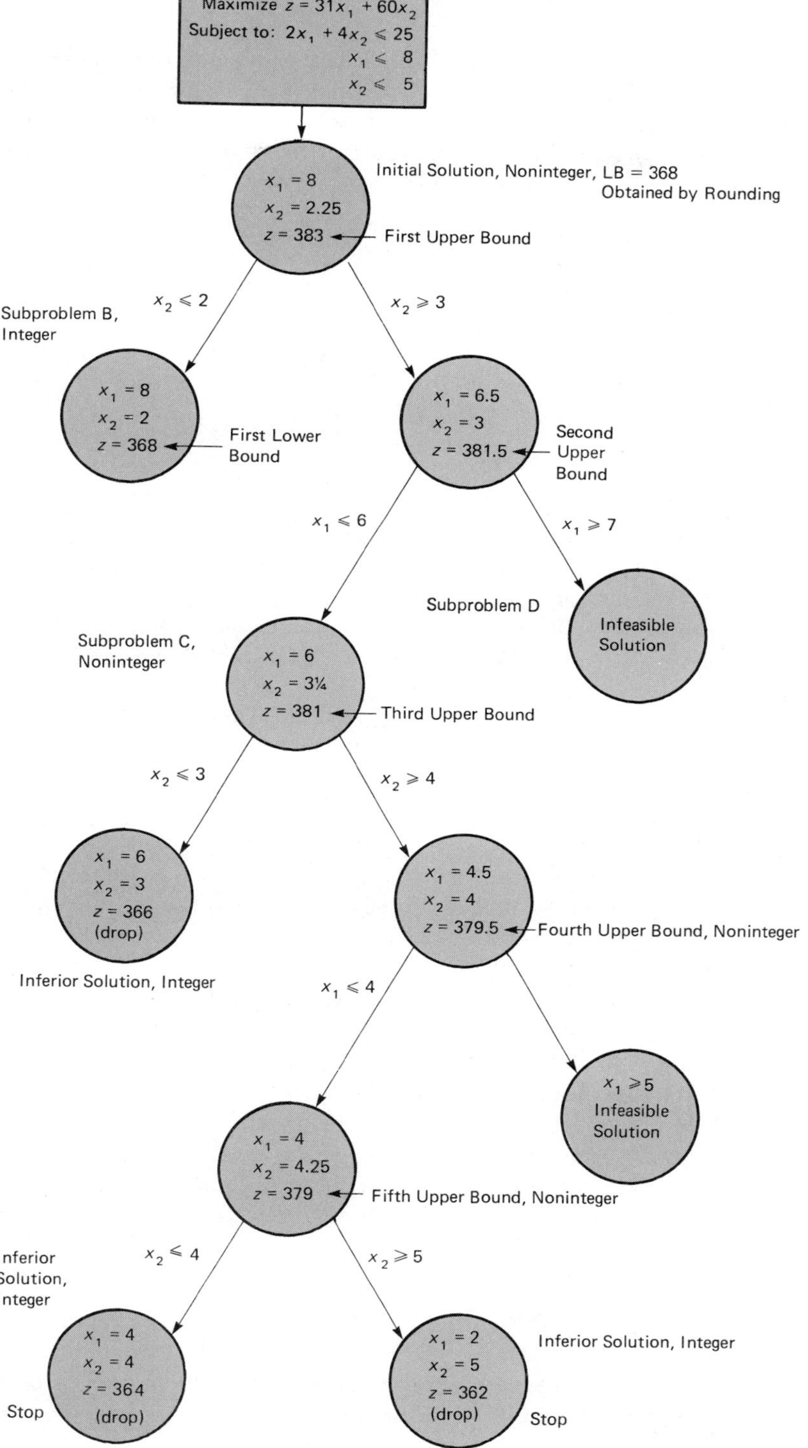

Maximize $z = 31x_1 + 60x_2$
Subject to: $2x_1 + 4x_2 \leq 25$
$x_1 \leq 8$
$x_2 \leq 5$
$x_1 = 8$
$x_2 = 2.25$
$z = 383$
Initial Solution, Noninteger, LB = 368
Obtained by Rounding
First Upper Bound
$x_2 \leq 2$
$x_2 \geq 3$
Subproblem B,
Integer
$x_1 = 8$
$x_2 = 2$
$z = 368$
First Lower
Bound
$x_1 = 6.5$
$x_2 = 3$
$z = 381.5$
Second
Upper
Bound
$x_1 \leq 6$
$x_1 \geq 7$
Subproblem D
Infeasible
Solution
Subproblem C,
Noninteger
$x_1 = 6$
$x_2 = 3¼$
$z = 381$
Third Upper Bound
$x_2 \leq 3$
$x_2 \geq 4$
$x_1 = 6$
$x_2 = 3$
$z = 366$
(drop)
Inferior Solution, Integer
$x_1 = 4.5$
$x_2 = 4$
$z = 379.5$
Fourth Upper Bound, Noninteger
$x_1 \leq 4$
$x_1 \geq 5$
Infeasible
Solution
$x_1 = 4$
$x_2 = 4.25$
$z = 379$
Fifth Upper Bound, Noninteger
Inferior
Solution,
Integer
$x_2 \leq 4$
$x_2 \geq 5$
$x_1 = 4$
$x_2 = 4$
$z = 364$
(drop)
Stop
$x_1 = 2$
$x_2 = 5$
$z = 362$
(drop)
Stop
Inferior Solution, Integer

FIGURE 8.7
Branch and bound solution

Next, the solution of subproblem A is branched into two other subproblems: subproblem C, where an additional constraint of $x_1 \leq 6$ is added; and subproblem D, where an additional constraint of $x_1 \geq 7$ is added. The reason for adding these constraints is that since $x_1 = 6.5$ is noninteger, then the feasible integer solution *must* be with either $x_1 \leq 6$ *or* $x_1 \geq 7$.

Subproblem C	*Subproblem D*
maximize $z = 31x_1 + 60x_2$	maximize $z = 31x_1 + 60x_2$
subject to:	subject to:
$2x_1 + 4x_2 \leq 25$	$2x_1 + 4x_2 \leq 25$
$x_1 \leq 8$	$x_1 \leq 8$
$x_2 \leq 5$	$x_2 \leq 5$
$x_2 \geq 3$	$x_2 \geq 3$
$x_1 \leq 6$	$x_1 \geq 7$
x_1, x_2 are integers	x_1, x_2 are integers

Subproblem D has no feasible solution, since any value for x_1 (only ≥ 7 and ≤ 8 are considered) will violate the constraints $x_2 \geq 3$ and $2x_1 + 4x_2 \leq 25$ and, therefore, its solution is not considered. Subproblem C has a noninteger solution with a new third *upper bound* of $z = 381$ (see Figure 8.7). The process is continued until no further branching is possible, or until the new upper bound becomes equal to or smaller than the *lower bound.* In this case, the process stops with integer feasible solutions that are inferior to the lower bound $z = 368$; and, therefore, the optimal solution is:

$$x_1 = 8, x_2 = 2, \quad \text{and} \quad z = 368$$

Notes: (1) In our example, the lower bound was not changed. Usually the lower bound will change, increasing in value toward the upper limit. (2) If two noninteger solutions (J and K) result from a branching, use the one with the largest z value for the next branching (say, J). If the branching of J results in a noninteger problem with a z value lower than that of K, then it is necessary to branch from problem K as well.

Branch and bound can be efficiently coded into a computer routine (e.g., IBM's MPSX/370); it works well in problems containing a few integer-valued variables. However, in problems with large numbers of integer-valued variables and in cases where the noninteger solution is far from optimal, then the number of required iterations may be too large for efficient application. For such cases, a more complicated procedure is required (see Salkin [11]).

8.8 NONLINEAR PROGRAMMING

A **nonlinear programming** problem is a mathematical programming problem in which the objective function and/or one or more of the constraints are nonlinear.

Nonlinear functions

Functional relationships that contain such terms as $2x^3$, $\log 1/x$, $2e^x$, as well as discontinuous functions, are termed *nonlinear functions*. In general, any functional relation that does not meet linearity conditions (see Appendix A) is considered nonlinear.

Nonlinear functions

Examples of nonlinear programming problems

1. minimize $z = 3x^2 - 2y$ (Nonlinear objective function and linear constraints)
   subject to:
   $$3x + 4y \geq 12$$
   $$x - y \geq 3$$
2. minimize $z = 2xy - \frac{2}{x}$ (Nonlinear objective function and nonlinear constraints)
   subject to:
   $$3x^2 + 2y \leq 100$$
   $$x + y^3 \leq 80$$
3. maximize $z = 5x + 7y$ (Linear objective function and nonlinear constraints)
   subject to:
   $$x^2 + 2y^3 \leq 65$$
   $$2x^2 + y \leq 50$$

Solution methods As opposed to the simplex method, which is a general method for solving linear programming problems, there is no general method for solving *all* nonlinear programming problems. Instead, various computational techniques, some of which are mathematically complicated, have been developed to solve different categories of nonlinear programs. These special computational methods are limiting factors in the use of nonlinear programming.

In this text we will not solve any nonlinear programming problems. For methods of solution, see Avriel [2], Loomba and Turban [9], or Zangwill [13].

Quadratic programming

Some of the less complicated types of nonlinear problems are those involving **quadratic programming.** These deal with the problem of minimizing a quadratic (second degree) objective function, subject to linear constraints.[15] Many practical problems can be formulated as quadratic programs. Fairly efficient solution techniques have been developed for quadratic programming problems but are beyond the scope of this text. See Avriel [2] and Minoux [10].

[15] Examples of quadratic functions are:

$$x_1^2;\ (x_1 - 2)^2;\quad \text{and}\quad x_1^2 + x_2^2 - 2x_1 + x_2$$

8.9 COMPUTER PROGRAMS

There exist many computer programs for mathematical programming. A representative list is given in Table 8.7. The list includes integer and certain nonlinear programming models.

TABLE 8.7
Representative programs for mathematical programming

MP1-MP8: Eight programs for different mathematical programming models. SCI Computing, Wilmette, Ill.
LINDO, GINO, VINO: LINDO Systems, Inc., Chicago, Ill.
MPS III: Ketron, Inc., Arlington, Va.
MPSX: IBM, Armonk, N.Y.
GAMS/MINOS: Stanford University, Stanford, Calif.
LP 83: Sunset Software, San Marino, Calif.

Integer programming example

The MSS package includes an integer programming routine based on the cutting plane method. Given below is the solution to Jack Smith's problem of Section 8.5. The solution is self-explanatory.

OPTIMAL LINEAR SOLUTION VALUE: 212.76
OPTIMAL INTEGER SOLUTION VALUE: 210

VARIABLE NAME	LINEAR SOLUTION	INTEGER SOLUTION
X1	2	3
X2	6.91	6

8.10 CONCLUDING REMARKS

Several important extensions of linear programming have been presented in this chapter. First, duality and sensitivity analysis, an integral part of any real-world application of LP, were presented in Part A of the chapter.

Many real-world problems impose integer requirements on the decision variables. For such cases, integer programming must be used. This procedure is less efficient than the regular simplex method and requires innovative approaches for solutions. A related methodology, the branch and bound technique, can be used to solve integer programming problems. Finally, many other complex problems are nonlinear in nature, but their complex solution procedures are beyond the scope of this text.

8.11 PROBLEMS FOR PART B

15. Graphics, Inc., is considering several potential sites for its manufacturing plants. The proposed locations are shown in the table below, together with the estimated costs (per unit shipped) to their five existing distribution centers. The supply at each proposed plant is currently considered unlimited with identical variable manufacturing costs. However, the monthly fixed cost at each plant varies. Find where the plants should be constructed and the monthly shipment to minimize the total cost. *Hint:* Use auxiliary variables.

Proposed locations	*Distribution centers* A	B	C	D	E	*Monthly fixed costs*
Chicago	6	8	3	8	5	8,000
Denver	10	4	5	12	8	11,000
Los Angeles	4	8	6	15	9	12,000
Miami	12	8	9	4	7	7,500
New York	11	5	6	8	7	8,900
Monthly demand	100	120	150	80	60	

16. Given:

$$\text{maximize } z = x_1 + x_2$$
subject to:
$$2x_1 + x_2 \leq 5$$
$$x_1 + 2x_2 \leq 5$$
$$x_1, x_2 \text{ integer}$$

a. Solve by complete enumeration.
b. Solve graphically.
c. Solve by rounding the noninteger LP solution.
d. Find the cost of indivisibility.

17. The navy is considering three types of attack aircraft to equip its carriers; a supersonic type, a subsonic type, and a boost glide type. The effectiveness of any air vehicle to the fleet is determined by the expected military value of targets the aircraft can "kill" during military engagements of a certain length. These have been estimated for the three types mentioned as follows:

Type	*Expected value of target "killed"*
Supersonic	30
Subsonic	24
Boost glide	25

The following numbers of aircraft could be accommodated if the entire deck is allocated to one specific type.

Type of aircraft	*Number of full deck*
Supersonic	60
Subsonic	120
Boost glide	160

In other words, the deck can contain (if full) 60 supersonic, or 120 subsonic, or 160 boost glide, or any linear combination of these types.

Personnel requirements and monthly maintenance costs are as follows:

Type	*Personnel per aircraft*	*Maintenance cost per aircraft*
Supersonic	15	$5,000
Subsonic	13	3,000
Boost glide	17	6,000

A carrier has facilities for 1,500 personnel, and the navy's monthly maintenance budget for aircraft is $650,000 per carrier.

The problem is to find how many of each of the three types of aircraft should be purchased per carrier in order to maximize the value of the attack capability of a carrier. Formulate as an integer programming problem: Define the decision variables, establish the objective function, and determine the constraint relationships. (Formulate only.)

18. Canadian Aviation Company organizes summer charter flights from Toronto to London. The company uses three types of aircraft whose operating cost and capacities are shown below.

Type of aircraft	*Passenger capacity*	*Cost per flight*	*Maximum possible flights*	*Required crew*
M-1	100	$ 6,000	15	4
M-2	180	8,000	12	12
M-3	270	10,000	6	17

The company can spare a crew of only 140 for the entire mission. Thirty-two hundred students signed up for the summer, each paying $110.

All students *must* be flown. Find how many flights of each type should be used in order to maximize profit.

Formulate as a mathematical program. (Do not solve.)

19. Venezuela-Colombia Hospital has recently modernized one of its operating rooms so that it now contains the very latest in a variety of equipment. Only two types of operations are considered. The hospital desires to schedule as many operations as possible in this room, which can handle up to 12 operations type A, or 30 operations type B (or any linear combination) per day. Each A-type operation requires 4 pints of blood, and each B-type operation requires 5.5 pints of blood. The hospital has a blood inventory of 100 pints. At least 7 type A operations and no more than 20 type B operations should be performed. Find the best possible schedule.
    a. Set up the problem as an integer linear program.
    b. Solve the problem graphically and show the feasible area.
    c. Comment on the resource utilization in the optimal solution.
    d. Suppose that the value of each operation of type A is three times as important as that of type B. Reformulate, solve the problem, and comment on the result.

20. The Singapore Mower Blade Company wishes to market a deluxe and a regular model lawn mower blade. The deluxe requires 5 units of carbon steel and 8 units of alloy steel per 150 blades, while the regular blade requires 10 units of carbon steel and no alloy steel per 150 blades. Due to market conditions (recent boom), the company is left with only 300 units of carbon steel and 200 units of alloy steel. The deluxe blade also requires 2 hours of grinding time and 1.25 hours of finishing time per 150 blades, while the regular needs 1 hour of grinding and .5 hours of finishing. The grinding department states that it has at most 50 hours available in the time period concerned, and the finishing department can contribute 30 hours toward the production of the blades.
    a. How can the firm maximize profit if $2 profit from a deluxe blade and $1.50 from a regular blade is realized? (Solve graphically.)
    b. What is the best production plan if an *integer number of batches* must be produced? (Solve graphically.)

    Hint: Formulate the problem in batches of 150 blades.

21. Flamingo Computing Corporation manufactures two types of small computers, A and B. The company can produce up to seven computers a week. Of its 10 available production teams, 2 are required for the production of each computer type A every week and 3 are required for the production of each computer type B.

    The company profit (in thousands of dollars) for each unit of type A sold is $8 - 2x_1$ (where x_1 is the amount sold of type A) and $5 - x_2$ for each unit of type B. All computers must be completed by the end of each week.

    The problem is to find the most profitable weekly production plan for the company. (Formulate only; do not solve.)

22. Solve Problem 16 by branch and bound.

23. Given an assignment problem: The cost of assigning jobs A, B, and C to machines M, N, O, and P is shown below.

    Find the best assignment. Solve by branch and bound.

Job \ *Machine*	*M*	*N*	*O*	*P*
A	6	7	5	9
B	8	5	6	7
C	10	8	5	6

24. In branch and bound:
    a. Discuss the role of the lower bound in minimization problems.
    b. Discuss the role of the upper bound in minimization problems.
    c. At what point can branches be dropped from consideration?
    d. Discuss three ways of bounding the assignment example in Section 8.7. Which is best?

25. Explain why the value of the objective function in a product-mix integer programming problem can never exceed that of a similar linear programming problem where there is no integer requirement.

26. Give an example that will illustrate a case where there exists a linear programming problem that has a *noninteger* optimal solution valued z, and an integer requirement is imposed on the problem. The optimal integer solution also has a value of z, exactly the same as the noninteger solution. That is, the cost of indivisibility is zero. Use a graphical presentation.

27. Hong Kong Computers is looking for potential sites for their warehouses. The expected construction time is two years and the available funds are $50 million the first year and $36 million the second year. The projected costs and returns (all in present values) are shown in the table below for four potential locations. The company wishes to maximize the projected return value. Formulate as an integer program using 0–1 variables.

	Projected cost (millions, $)		
Site	*Year 1*	*Year 2*	*Projected return (points value)*
A	12	15	100
B	20	31	160
C	17	30	150
D	32	15	155

28. Consider a zero-one model for the R&D or capital budgeting problem. Assume that you have five projects like the ones in example *a* of Section 8.6. Now assume that there are *additional constraints*, as expressed below. Write the equalities (or inequalities) for these constraints:
    a. Any two of the first four projects *must* be undertaken.
    b. Projects x_1 and x_3 must be taken simultaneously or not taken at all.
    c. Project x_1 will be undertaken *only* if x_3 is undertaken but x_3 is *not* conditional on x_1 (i.e., you can have x_3 without x_1, but you cannot have x_1 unless x_3 is undertaken).

8.12 CASE

HENSLEY VALVE CORP.

It was Monday morning and the weekly meeting of the Executive Committee was in full swing. There were two primary items on the agenda and both directly affected Hensley's profit margin.

Agenda Item A: The Proposed Tax Increase on Diesel Fuel.

Agenda Item B: Record Interest Rates.

"Gus, as regional manager in our largest selling region, what will be the result of our raising prices to offset this possible increase in our trucking costs?"

"Well J. B., it certainly won't help our sales effort. Valve JBH-1 is only marginally profitable now, but takes twice the time to sell as our more profitable JBH-2s. I'm afraid a price increase might wipe out the viability of our JBH-1 valves altogether."

"That's what I was afraid of, too. Pat, how about the effect of that cancellation of the second NC machine we were hoping would help our productivity? I know you were counting on that to increase our output rate, but with the latest two big jumps in the prime rate we simply can't afford it at this time."

"Yes, I realize that, J. B. I certainly hadn't expected the prime rate to go quite this high. Basically, our output rates will remain limited, especially on old line 3, which produces the JBH-1 and -2 valves. Given the limited floor space and equipment and working three shifts on this line, we can still produce at most 600 JBH-1s or 100 JBH-2s a week, or any combination in-between. I wondered if it would be worthwhile to have Tim Moran in our controller's office look at the interacting effect of all these changes? It seems that since so many things are happening at once, it may be best to totally change our product mix as well as our prices."

"I agree, Pat. It seems appropriate to undertake a complete contingency analysis of what we should do given any specific change in the market or combination of changes. I'll work up a memo to Tim this afternoon."

MEMO

TO: Tim Moran, Controller's Assistant
FROM: J. B. Hensley, President
SUBJECT: Reanalysis of Product Line

Please undertake a review of our JBH-1 and -2 valves for the next meeting of the Executive Committee on Monday morning. For this purpose you may assume their profitability to be $10 and $40 each, respectively. We have figured that a JBH-1 takes, on average, 4 hours to sell and a -2 takes 2 hours to sell. Sales has at most 1,000 hours a week available. Check with Pat Johnson for production figures on line 3. Items we would specifically like to know include:

- Given our limited capacities, how many of each valve should we currently be producing and selling to maximize our profits?
- What is an extra hour of sales time worth?
- At what hour sales effort is it not worth producing JBH-1s any longer?
- What is an increase in the capacity of line 3 worth?
- At what JBH-1 profitability will only JBH-1s be worth producing?
- What will be the effect on the solution of improving the JBH-1 marketing effort so it only takes 2.5 hours to sell a unit? What per unit investment is this worth?

Please add any other information you find to be relevant. Thank you.

8.13 GLOSSARY

All-integer An integer programming problem where *all* the decision variables must be whole numbers.

Branch and bound An intelligent search procedure for optimal or near-optimal solutions.

Branching Dividing a managerial problem into subproblems.

Complete enumeration A comparison of *all* possible solution values.

Deterministic model A model where all parameters are assumed to be known with certainty, such as LP.

Dual problem A linear programming complementary problem that is associated with an original linear programming (primal) problem.

Indivisibility A requirement that the values of a variable be restricted to whole numbers.

Integer programming A mathematical programming problem which requires that some or all of the decision variables be whole numbers.

Marginal value The additional return from having one more unit available.

Mixed integer An integer programming problem where some but not all of the decision variables must be whole numbers.

Nonlinear programming A problem approach used when the objective function and/or one or more constraints are nonlinear.

Primal problem An original linear programming problem.

Quadratic programming A mathematic programming problem with a quadratic (second degree) objective function and linear constraints.

Sensitivity analysis An analysis of the impact of changes in the input data to a linear programming problem on its optimal solution.

Shadow price The value that is added to the value of the objective function when one unit is added to a linear programming constraint (right-hand side). This value equals the *dual variable* of the resource.

Zero-one variables Logical variables that must take a value of either 0 or 1.

8.14 REFERENCES AND BIBLIOGRAPHY

1. Anderson, D. R., D. J. Sweeney, and T. Williams. *Linear Programming for Decision Making*. St. Paul, Minn.: West Publishing, 1974.
2. Avriel, M. *Nonlinear Programming: Analysis and Methods*. Englewood Cliffs, N.J.: Prentice-Hall, 1976.
3. Bradley, S. P., et al. *Applied Mathematical Programming*. Reading, Mass.: Addison-Wesley Publishing, 1977.
4. Gal, T. *Postoptimal Analysis, Parametric Programming, and Related Topics*. New York: McGraw-Hill, 1979.
5. Garfinkel, R., and G. L. Nemhauser. *Integer Programming*. New York: John Wiley & Sons, 1972.
6. Ignizio, J. P. *Linear Programming in Single and Multiple Objective Systems*. Englewood Cliffs, N.J.: Prentice-Hall, 1982.
7. Jensen, P. *Microsolve Operations Research*. San Francisco: Holden-Day, 1983.
8. Lev, B., and H. J. Weiss. *Introduction to Mathematical Programming*. New York: Elsevier North-Holland Publishing, 1982.
9. Loomba, N. P., and E. Turban. *Applied Programming in Management*. New York: Holt, Rinehart & Winston, 1974.
10. Minoux, M. *Mathematical Programming*. New York: John Wiley & Sons, 1986.
11. Salkin, H. *Integer Programming*. Reading, Mass.: Addison-Wesley Publishing, 1975.
12. Taha, H. A. *Integer Programming: Theory, Applications and Computers*. New York: Academic Press, 1975.
13. Zangwill, W. I. *Nonlinear Programming: A Unified Approach*. Englewood Cliffs, N.J.: Prentice-Hall, 1969.

9

Goal programming

PART A: BASICS

9.1 Introduction.
9.2 The basic idea of goal programming.
9.3 Concepts for goal programming.
9.4 The structure of goal programming.
9.5 Formulation: The Birch Paper Co.
9.6 Computerized solution to the BIP case.
9.7 Sensitivity analysis.
9.8 Examples of applications.
9.9 Problems for Part A.

PART B: EXTENSIONS

9.10 Graphical solution.
9.11 Special situations.
9.12 Setting up goals.
9.13 Concluding remarks.
9.14 Problems for Part B.
9.15 Case—Cartoy International.
9.16 Glossary.
9.17 References and bibliography.

Linear programming applications can be found in hundreds of organizations worldwide. However, when the applications become more complex, especially when several competing objectives must be considered simultaneously, there is a need for a more powerful tool. One technique for dealing with such cases is called goal programming (GP), the subject of this chapter.

LEARNING OBJECTIVES

The student should be able to:

a. Understand the need for goal programming.
b. Describe the concepts and terminology used in goal programming.
c. Comprehend the structure of goal programming.
d. Formulate a problem as a goal programming problem.
e. Use a software package to solve a goal program and understand its output.
f. Conduct a sensitivity analysis for goal programming.

Extensions

g. Use the graphical procedure to solve small goal programming problems.
h. Handle additional restrictions on existing constraints in two different ways.
i. Understand the use of goal programming in setting objectives for workers.

The Birch Paper Company

The Birch Paper Company (BIP) is composed of three divisions. Division A makes paperboard that is sold to divisions B and C and the outside market. Division B produces boxes that are sold to division C and to the outside market. Division C makes two specialty paper products that are sold to Sears Roebuck & Co. The company's production plan was determined in the past by a linear programming model. This approach permitted profit maximization. However, the approach created temporary working capital and cash reserve difficulties. As a result, the credit rating of the company was lowered and the company stock lost 15 percent of its value in one month. Cash reserves and working capital requirements were then imposed, but as a result, profits declined. The angry shareholders forced the CEO to resign. The three division heads, Bill, Gill, and Will, decided to discard the linear programming model in an attempt to improve the situation, but they were unable to agree on an alternative plan.

The matter was aggravated when Patricia Gray, the corporate chief financial officer (CFO), pushed for even stricter financial requirements. The division managers blamed Patricia for adding to their troubles. Patricia replied that this was nonsense: "You make the production decisions, and if you cannot improve profitability, you should go."

It was the first day of work for Donna Beer, the newly appointed CEO, when she was thrown into the midst of a heated debate between Bill and Will, who were blaming each other for a production problem. Donna paused for a moment to consider the following:

- Why was the LP model discarded?
- Can a substitute model be used?
- What will happen if the cash reserves and working capital requirements are increased or reduced?

Donna realized that the job of the CEO may not be as easy or as pleasant as many people think.

Source: This case is based on the Harvard Business School case Birch Paper Company. The GP application was suggested by R. P. Manes, "Birch Paper Company Revisited: An Exercise in Transfer Pricing," *Accounting Review* 45 (July 1970), pp. 565–72; and S. Kinory, "Goal Programming and Managerial Decision Making," *Management International Review* 18, no. 2 (1978), pp. 101–9.

9.1 INTRODUCTION

Multiple goals

Donna's case highlights several important issues. First, BIP's situation involves **multiple goals,** an issue previously discussed in Chapter 4. In practice, many decisions are made subject to multiple criteria where a "satisfactory" solution is sought, rather than an optimal one. Second, the requirements and constraints in the real world are not always rigid; that is, deviations from targets may be acceptable, especially when trade-offs are permitted. Finally, the BIP situation seems to have many of the characteristics of linear programming (for example, general structure, assumptions). However, the LP solution was ineffective. What is needed is a modified approach to the simplex method. The approach that is used to handle such situations is called **goal programming** (GP). Beforewe present the technique, let us examine the differences between problems that can be solved by linear programming and those that require the GP approach.

Linear programming is structured with a single objective function that is to be optimized. In the formulation discussed so far, either one objective existed or, if there were several objectives, one was expressed in the objective function while the remaining objectives were expressed as constraints. For example, maximizing profit could be the primary objective, subject to at least a 10 percent share of the market (a secondary objective). Since most organizations possess several (sometimes even conflicting) goals, it is often difficult to determine which goal to maximize and which goals to express as constraints.

Problems with LP

Another problem with LP is its inflexibility. The limits on the secondary goals cannot be violated. Thus, a solution to the BIP problem with $1 million profit and a 9.9 percent share of the market could be considered as infeasible while a solution with $100,000 profit and a 10 percent share of the market could be declared optimal.

Table 9.1 illustrates the major differences between goal programming and linear programming. Goal programming is a technique that offers a different approach to the solution of linear programming types of problems that involve multiple, conflicting goals.

TABLE 9.1
Differences between GP and LP

	Linear programming (LP)	*Goal programming (GP)*
Goals and objectives	One primary—to be maximized or minimized	All objectives are ranked, each with a target
Targets or constraints	Inflexible, no deviations are allowed	Flexible, deviations are acceptable, constraints can be relaxed
Objective function	Maximize (minimize) the value of the primary goal	Minimize the sum of the undesirable deviations (weighted by their relative importance)
Purpose	Optimization	Satisfaction
Theory	Mature	Relatively young, developing
Computer programs	Very efficient, many packages	Inefficient, few computer packages
Applications	Many and varied	Few, but increasing

9.2 THE BASIC IDEA OF GOAL PROGRAMMING

More than an extension

Although GP was developed as an extension of LP, it is much more than a mere extension. It enables the decision maker to analyze multiple goal aspiration levels. It also allows deviations from targets, thus introducing flexibility into the decision-making process. Finally, it incorporates the decision maker's preferences for multiple conflicting goals by allowing changes and trade-offs among the goals.

When a company is faced with multiple conflicting goals, it may not be possible to achieve every goal to the desired extent. For example, the company may not be able to grow at 15 percent a year and make $3 profit per share. The GP model attempts to obtain a satisfactory level of goal attainment that would be the best feasible solution in view of the priorities (relative importance of the goals). Thus, higher-priority goals can be attained at the expense of lower-priority goals.

Goal programming is used to perform three types of analysis:

Three uses

a. Determining the required resources to achieve a set of desired objectives.
b. Determining the degree of attainment of the goals with the available resources.
c. Providing the best satisfying solution under a varying amount of resources and priorities of the goals.

9.3 CONCEPTS FOR GOAL PROGRAMMING

Three important concepts constitute the backbone of GP: *(a)* deviations, *(b)* priorities and weights of the goals, and *(c)* dimensions of the goals.

a. Deviations

Deviations are the amounts by which goals are either overachieved or underachieved. Let us look at three goals:

1. Achieve a profit of at least $300,000 per month.
2. Do not exceed 500 hours of overtime per month.
3. Maintain an inventory level of exactly 20 units.

Overachievement

The **overachievement** deviations measure the extent to which the goals are exceeded; they are labeled by the **deviational variable** d_i^+.

Examples:

If the profit is $320,000, then $d_a^+ = 320{,}000 - 300{,}000 = 20{,}000$
If overtime is 550 hours, then $d_b^+ = 550 - 500 = 50$

The **underachievement** deviations measure the extent by which performance is less than the goal.[1] They are denoted as d_i^-.

Underachievement

Examples:

If profit level is \$290,000, then $d_a^- = 300{,}000 - 290{,}000 = 10{,}000$
If inventory level is 18, then $d_c^- = 20 - 18 = 2$; $d_c^+ = 0$

Note that both d_i^+ and d_i^- must be nonnegative; that is: $d_i^+ \geq 0$ and $d_i^- \geq 0$. As will be seen later, the goal programming model attempts to minimize the weighted sum of the undesirable deviations.

Desirable and undesirable deviations Deviations can be either desirable or undesirable. For example, in the case of profit, d^+ is desirable, while d^- is not. On the other hand, in the case of overtime, d^+ is undesirable, while d^- is desirable. In most cases, we observe the following relationships:

Type of constraint on goal	*Undesirable deviations*
$\geq$	d_i^-
$\leq$	d_i^+
$=$	d_i^+ and d_i^-

According to our definition, *underachievement* is *undesirable* in the case of $\geq$ constraints. Similarly, *overachievement* is *undesirable* in the case of $\leq$ constraints. In the case of equalities, *both* under- and overachievement are undesirable.

b. Prioritizing goals

Goals in GP are prioritized in three different ways: ordinal, cardinal, and a mixture of the two.

1. *Ordinal ranking.* In this method, goals are listed in the order of their importance. P_1 designates the priority level of the most important goal and its undesirable deviation, P_2 designates the second most important goal, and so on.
2. *Cardinal ranking.* In this method, a specific weight is assigned to each of the deviations. These weights show the relative importance of each deviation.
3. *A mix of the two.* This approach will be illustrated later when the objective function's structure is presented.

Priority ranking

[1] In some treatments of goal programming, d_i^- is defined instead as the *undesirable* deviation; for example, underachievement of market share. We follow the more common approach of always defining it as an underachievement, which may or may not be desirable.

The priorities of the goals are expressed in the objective function's coefficients, as will be demonstrated later.

c. Dimensions of the goals

The objective function of the GP attempts to minimize the sum of the undesirable deviations weighted by their importance. Such a summation may make little sense, however, if the dimensions of the deviations are different. For example, d_1 may be profit measured in dollars, while d_2 may be expressed in terms of percent of market share. This problem is most suitable for solution via cardinal ranking. For discussion, see Section 9.4.

9.4 THE STRUCTURE OF GOAL PROGRAMMING

The GP model is composed of four elements:

Four elements

a. Decision variables.
b. System constraints.
c. Goal constraints.
d. Objective function.

a. Decision variables

The decision variables are similar to regular LP decision variables, for example, the number of units to produce each product required, or the amount of each ingredient to blend.

b. System constraints

System constraints are identical to LP constraints. They represent absolute restrictions and do not allow any deviations. For example, the space in the warehouse cannot be increased, it is impossible to work more than 21 shifts (7 × 3) each week, and it is necessary to follow governmental regulations. These constraints are expressed as regular LP constraints. System constraints must be satisfied before *any* of the goal constraints can be considered.

c. Goal constraints

Aspiration levels

Goal constraints represent aspiration levels or target values to be achieved.

Example 1 Achieve a profit of at least $200,000. The decision variables are the products to include in the product mix. Product *A* brings a $5 profit contribution, product *B* nets a $7 profit contribution, and product *C* brings a $3 profit contribution. The total profit is:

$$5A + 7B + 3C$$

In regular LP, we attempt to maximize this function. In GP we write it as:

$$5A + 7B + 3C \geq 200{,}000$$

However, since we allow deviations, the constraint is written instead as:

$$5A + 7B + 3C + d_1^- - d_1^+ = 200{,}000$$

where d_1^- is the underachievement of profit and d_1^+ is overachievement.

Example 2 Each unit of product A (above) requires two hours of labor, each unit of B requires six hours, and each unit of C requires three hours. The labor supply during regular hours is 500 hours. The constraint is:

$$2A + 6B + 3C + d_2^- - d_2^+ = 500$$

Example 3 Overtime, in Example 2, should not exceed 50 hours:

$$2A + 6B + 3C - 500 + d_3^- - d_3^+ = 50$$

Deviation signs

The signs in front of the deviations The reader will notice that a d^+ deviation is always preceded by a minus sign, while a d^- deviation is always preceded by a plus sign. The reason for this is shown in the following example. Assume that we have a profit constraint:

$$5x_1 + 7x_2 \geq 10{,}000$$

In GP terms, we change it to:

$$5x_1 + 7x_2 + d^- - d^+ = 10{,}000$$

Three cases may occur in the solution:

a. The profit $5x_1 + 7x_2$ will be exactly 10,000. In such a case, both d^- and d^+ must equal zero.

b. The profit $5x_1 + 7x_2$ will be less than \$10,000 (underachievement), say, \$9,000. In this case we will get:

$$9{,}000 + d^- - d^+ = 10{,}000$$

that is,

$$d^- - d^+ = 10{,}000 - 9{,}000 = 1{,}000$$

Solving, we get:

$$d^- = 1{,}000, \quad d^+ = 0$$

Note: the deviations cannot be negative. Thus:

$$9{,}000 + (d^- = 1{,}000) + 0 = 10{,}000$$

c. The profit is larger than 10,000; say, 12,000. The equation will then be:

$$12{,}000 + d^- - d^+ = 10{,}000$$

Solving, we get:

$$d^+ = 2{,}000, \quad d^- = 0$$

Again, this is because the deviations cannot be negative.

It is possible to have a GP problem with only one goal. In this case, we use the GP formulation to analyze the deviations from this single goal. Most times, however, GP deals with multiple, conflicting goals.

d. Objective function

The objective function in GP is formulated to minimize the weighted sum of the undesirable deviations. Therefore, the structure of such a function depends on the weighting system. The following variations exist:

1. Single objective problem In such a case, the objective function is:

$$\text{minimize } z = d_1^+ \tag{9.1}$$

where d_1^+ is undesirable or d_1^- if d_1^- is undesirable).

Single and multiple objectives

2. Multiple objectives, ordinal ranking In each case the objective function is written as:

$$\text{minimize } z = P_1 d_1^- + P_2 d_2^+ + P_3 d_3^- + \cdots \tag{9.2}$$

where the P_i indicates the importance of the goal ($i = 1$ is first in importance). For example, $P_1 d_1^-$ means that d_1^- is an undesirable deviation with priority level 1.

There is one variation to this situation: the case when two undesirable deviations exist for one goal. In such a case, we can use *two* approaches.

First, a situation such as $P_1 d_1^- + P_2 d_1^+$ means that the negative deviation is much more important than the positive one. Such a designation is somewhat confusing, since P_2 is generally used to designate another, second, goal. Another way to overcome this problem is discussed later, under item 4.

Preemptive sequence

In solving this type of goals presentation, the computer employs a "preemptive" philosophy. This approach allows pursuing the objectives in an ordinal sequence, but based on their importance. The most important objective (labeled P_1) is pursued first until it is either attained as fully as desired (i.e., its undesirable deviation $= 0$) or found to be unattainable. Then, the deviation of the second most important goal, P_2, is driven to zero (or as close to zero as possible) within the solution space defined by the first priority goal and the system constraints. This process continues until all goals have been considered. This process can be expressed as:

$$P_1 >>> P_2 >>> P_3 >>> P_4 >>> \ldots \tag{9.3}$$

where $P_i >>> P_{i+1}$ means that multiplication of the deviation by any number, however large it may be, cannot make P_{i+1} more important than P_i.

Sooner or later it is usually not possible to fully satisfy all the goals. As a result, there will be undesirable deviations from some of the goal targets. These deviations are analyzed in GP through a sensitivity analysis. Priorities can be changed, for example, and the impact on the solution observed (see Section 9.7).

3. ***Multiple goals, use of a cardinal scale*** In this case, a specific weight is assigned to *each* undesirable deviation. This approach is especially important when the dimensions of the deviations are different. An objective function in such a case may look like this:

$$\text{minimize } z = 16d_1^- + 10d_2^+ + 1d_3^- + 4d_3^+ + 5d_5^-$$

There are two problems with this approach. First, people in general have difficulty assigning specific weights to goals. Second, in this case, the problem is even more difficult, since the weights express both the relative importance of the goals and the dimensional relationship of the deviations.

Cardinal and ordinal scales

4. ***Multiple goals, use of cardinal and ordinal scales*** This is an extension of the ordinal scale for a case where there exist two undesirable deviations for one goal. Let us assume that this happened in the third goal. In such a case, weights are assigned to determine which deviation is more important within the same priority level. The objective function in such a case will look like this:

$$\text{minimize } z = P_1d_1^+ + P_2d_2^+ + 3P_3d_3^- + 2P_3d_3^+ + P_4d_4^+$$

That is, the negative deviation of the third goal is $3/2 = 1.5$ times more important than the positive one.

This situation can be extended to more than two deviations in one goal. As a matter of fact, it pertains to any number of deviations within the same priority level. For example, a function may look like this:

$$\text{minimize } z = P_1d_1^+ + P_2d_2^- + P_3(5d_3^+ + 2d_3^- + 3d_4^- + 1d_4^+ + d_5^-)$$

This means that deviations 3 through 5 are all at the same priority level and **weights** are assigned to the **goals** (as well as to the deviations).

5. ***Multiple goals that are equally important*** If all the goals are equally important, then the objective is simply to minimize the sum of the undesirable deviations. For example, the objective function for the manufacturing example in Section 9.8 will look like this:

$$\text{minimize } z = d_1^- + d_2^+ + d_3^+ + d_4^-$$

subject to the same constraints.

Weight if different units

Note: It should be emphasized that such a formulation makes sense only if the deviations are measured in the same units (e.g., dollars). Otherwise, weights must be used.

9.5 FORMULATION: THE BIRCH PAPER CO.

As the reader may recall, the Birch Paper Company (BIP) is composed of three divisions. Figure 9.1 presents the product relationships among the divisions.

FIGURE 9.1
BIP production flow process

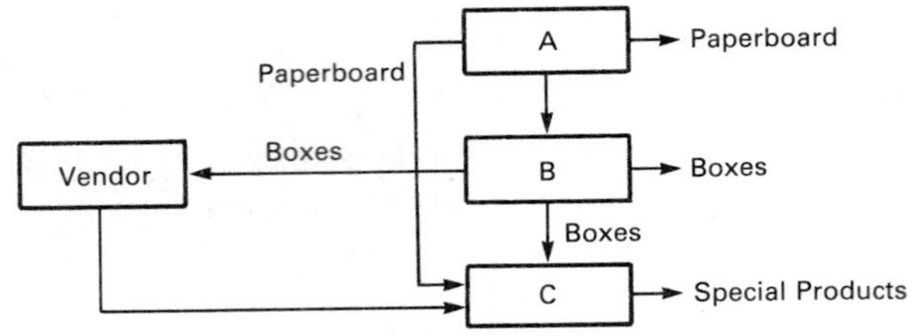

Division C sells up to 150 units a week of two specialty paper products to Sears: x_3 = quantity of product I and x_4 = quantity of product II. The division can acquire the materials necessary for production from two sources: either internally (divisions A and/or B) or from an outside vendor. However, the vendor will provide the materials if and only if division B agrees to provide them with boxes at prices they stipulate. As stated earlier, both A and B can also sell their products on the open market.

The data that are relevant here are shown in Table 9.2.

TABLE 9.2
Data for the BIP Company

Product	*Quantity*	*Selling price per unit*	*Cost per unit*	*Profit margin*
Paperboard	x_1	280	168	112
Boxes	x_2	450	288	162
Special product I	x_3	480	288	192
Special product II	x_4	480	391	89

Find the weekly schedule

The initial problem is to determine the optimal weekly production schedule. That is, find the values of x_1, x_2, x_3, and x_4 that maximize the profit margin. The LP formulation follows.

Objective function:

$$\text{maximize } z = 112x_1 + 162x_2 + 192x_3 + 89x_4$$

subject to the following constraints, which were derived based on certain technological relationships between the divisions and the products:

$$x_1 + x_2 + x_3 + .333x_4 \leq 100 \quad \text{(To be called C5)}$$
$$x_2 + x_3 + .143x_4 \leq 100 \quad \text{(to be called C6)}$$
$$x_3 + x_4 \leq 150 \quad \text{(to be called C7)}$$

The linear programming solution for this problem is:

$$x_1 = 0,\ x_2 = 50,\ x_3 = 0,\ x_4 = 150;\ \text{profit} = \$21{,}450 \text{ per week}$$

This production schedule was utilized before the following new financial requirements were added:

$$\begin{array}{ll}(\text{C1}) & 168x_1 + 288x_2 + 288x_3 + 391x_4 \geq 67{,}000 \text{ (cash on hand)} \\ (\text{C2}) & 150x_1 + \ \ 80x_2 + \ \ 86x_3 + \ \ 70x_4 \geq 16{,}000 \text{ (net working capital)}\end{array}$$

The linear programming solution to this new problem is now:

$$x_1 = 21.44,\ x_2 = 28.55,\ x_3 = 0,\ x_4 = 150$$

for a total profit of $20,948 per week.

When the cash-on-hand requirements were later increased to $72,000, the linear programming computer package signaled a *nonfeasible* solution. Management was unable to use the LP any longer and a negotiated production plan was introduced to meet the financial requirements. However, meeting the requirements resulted in some overtime and reduced profit, a situation that caused the resignation of the former CEO. The new CEO, Ms. Beer, heard about GP and decided to try it.

The GP approach

The system constraints

The capacity constraints of the LP problem are technological in nature and cannot be changed. Therefore, they appear in an identical format as in the original LP problem, namely:

$$\begin{array}{ll} 1x_1 + 1x_2 + 1x_3 + .333x_4 \leq 100 & \text{(constraint C5)} \\ 0x_1 + 1x_2 + 1x_3 + .143x_4 \leq 100 & \text{(constraint C6)} \\ 0x_1 + 0x_2 + 1x_3 + \qquad 1x_4 \leq 150 & \text{(constraint C7)} \end{array}$$

The goal constraints

In addition to the original goal of profit, there are two financial requirements: cash and net working capital. The goals are expressed in GP terms (in descending order of importance) as:

$$\begin{array}{ll}(\text{C1}) & 168x_1 + 288x_2 + 288x_3 + 391x_4 + d_1^- - d_1^+ = 72{,}000 \text{ (cash—most important)} \\ (\text{C2}) & 150x_1 + \ \ 80x_2 + \ \ 86x_3 + \ \ 70x_4 + d_2^- - d_2^+ = 16{,}000 \text{ (working capital)} \\ (\text{C3}) & 112x_1 + 162x_2 + 192x_3 + \ \ 89x_4 + d_3^- - d_3^+ = 23{,}000 \text{ (profit)}\end{array}$$

The profit target of 23,000 is slightly higher than the old plan, but management wanted to see the degree to which this goal can be attained.

Finally, a marketing requirement was added:

$$x_1 = 20$$

which becomes:

$$\text{(C4)} \quad x_1 + d_4^- - d_4^+ = 20$$

The initial GP objective function (including only the undesirable deviations) is:

$$\text{minimize } z = P_1 d_1^- + P_2 d_2^- + P_3 d_3^- + P_4 d_4^- + P_4 d_4^+$$

Since there are two undesirable deviations within the fourth priority level (a result of the fourth constraint being $x_1 = 20$), it is advisable to set weights on the deviations; these were set as 2 on d_4^- and 9 on d_4^+.

That is: minimize $z = P_1 d_1^1 + P_2 d_2^- + P_3 d_3^- + 2P_4 d_4^- + 9P_y d_y^+$

9.6 COMPUTERIZED SOLUTION TO THE BIP CASE

GP problems with two decision variables can be solved graphically (see Section 9.10) but larger problems must be solved by a variant of the simplex method, usually with a computer (for details see Ignizio[2] and Lee[3]).

The solution to BIP's problem is shown in Table 9.3. It was derived by a micro-based program (Lee and Shim[5]).

TABLE 9.3
Solution to BIP problem

a. Analysis of deviations

Constraint	RHS value	d+	d−
C 1	72000.00	0.00	0.00
C 2	16000.00	0.00	875.10
C 3	23000.00	0.00	1985.40
C 4	20.00	0.00	11.13
C 5	100.00	0.00	0.00
C 6	100.00	0.00	37.37
C 7	150.00	0.00	0.00

b. Analysis of decision variables

Variable	Solution value
X 2	41.18
X 1	8.87
X 4	150.00

c. Analysis of the objective function

Priority	Nonachievement
P 1	0.00
P 2	875.10
P 3	1985.40
P 4	22.26

Interpretation of the printout

Part a: Analysis of deviations

Goal constraints (constraints C1–C4 in the printout):

(C1) The most important goal is fully met (cash reserve)
(C2) The working capital was short by $875
(C3) Profit: A deviation of $1,985 exists; that is, the profit is only $21,015
(C4) The solution is $x_1 = 8.87$, that is, there is a negative deviation of 11.13

Interpreting the results

System constraints (C5–C7 in the printout):

(C5) The constraint is fully utilized
(C6) A slack of 37.37 exists
(C7) The constraint is fully satisfied

Notice that in a less-than-or-equal-to type system constraint, a slack is equivalent to a d^-. (A surplus of d^+ will appear in a larger-than-or-equal-to type constraint.)

Part b: Analysis of decision variables

Similar to a regular LP solution, the values of x_1, x_2, and so on are computed.

Part c: Analysis of the objective function

This part lists the *undesirable* deviations multiplied by their importance index. This is labeled as "nonachievement." For example, for priority level 4 we get:

$$11.13 \text{ (the } d^- \text{ of C4) times 2 (the weight for } d_4^-) = 22.26$$

9.7 SENSITIVITY ANALYSIS

Sensitivity analysis techniques for GP are not as well developed as those for LP. Although the questions may be similar, the techniques to find the answer are not as readily available. Most of the analysis is performed by interactively re-solving the problem with new input data. Let us examine some sensitivity analysis possibilities.

Switching priorities

A manager may want to know the effect of changing the order of the priorities. Sometimes such a change will not alter the solution. In other cases, deviations will be switched (or be changed in magnitude).

In the BIP case, we made the following changes:

Priority changes

a. The priorities of the second and fourth goals were reversed. This resulted in no change in the solution.
b. The priorities of the first and third goals were switched. The solution changed as follows:

$$x_2 = 50; \quad x_4 = 150$$

The goals' attainments were:

(1) Cash requirement goal was overachieved (by $1,064.40).
(2) Working capital level was $14,504 or $1,496 short.
(3) Profit increased only slightly, from $21,104 to $21,458.10 (i.e., a deviation of $1,541.90). It seems that profit is very insensitive.

The requirement of making 20 units of product x_1 was completely sacrificed. That is, $d_4^- = 20$; with a weight of 2, this translates to 40 units of nonachievement.

Changing the targets (right-hand side)

If a solution indicates an attainment of the most important goals, one may want to examine the possibility of increasing the targets. Such a change may result in deviations in the most important goals, or in larger deviations in the less important goals.

Cash requirement

In the BIP case, we changed the cash requirement to $75,000. At the same time we reduced its priority to second (working capital was changed to first priority). This resulted in the following solution: $x_1 = 21.37$, $x_2 = 28.68$, and $x_4 = 150$. The cash requirement was not met (70,500 instead of 75,000) and nonachievement was scored in all goals, except the first one.

Changing the weights

Once a solution is observed, it may be desirable to try changing the weights assigned to the goals. Assigning a larger weight to a goal may result in a smaller (or no) deviation.

Relaxing the system constraints

There is a sizable dual in the regular linear programming solution to the BIP problem on one or more of the fully utilized constraints. In such a case, it may be advisable to relax the constraints (e.g., add capacity).

Goal seeking

If a solution to GP includes undesirable deviations in some of the goals, then one may ask, "What would be required in order to eliminate some or all of these deviations?" The answer may be more resources or the increase of deviations in other goals; thus, it is possible to trade off deviations between goals.

Setting up a minimum goal level (or a maximum deviation)

Examining the solution in Table 9.3, management may find the deviation of 11.13 on x_1 to be unacceptable. Adding a system constraint $x_1 \geq 15$, for example, guarantees a solution with at least 15 units of x_1. In such a case, we obtain a solution with $x_2 = 35$ and the profit declines.

Adding a constraint

Other changes

Other changes may include adding or deleting constraints, changing the technology coefficients (left-hand-side of the constraints) and adding or deleting decision variables.

By experimenting with these "what if" scenarios, the analysis may reduce conflict among the managers and help in restoring the corporate image and success.

9.8 EXAMPLES OF APPLICATIONS

a. Advertising (integer GP)

The marketing department of E&D, Inc., uses TV and magazines for advertising. The problem is how to budget advertising if the following goals are to be pursued:

An advertising budget

Goal 1. The funds spent on advertising should not exceed the $200,000 budget. This goal is the most important and is labeled P_1.

Goal 2. The total exposure, measured by the number of people (audience) expected to see the advertising, should be at least 20 million. This is the second highest priority goal, labeled P_2.

Goal 3. The effective exposure, that is, the audience that is assumed to be *influenced* by the advertising, should be at least 5 million, labeled P_3.

Goal 4. There should be at least eight TV inserts, each of which costs $15,000, labeled P_4.

Goal 5. There should be at least five magazine inserts, each of which costs $10,000, labeled P_5.

A TV insert reaches 2 million people, of which 800,000 are influenced. A magazine insert is read by 1 million people, of which 300,000 are influenced.

The problem is to find out how many TV inserts and how many magazine inserts to place in order to attain the above goals.

Formulation

The decision variables

x_1 = The number of TV inserts to be used
x_2 = The number of magazine inserts to be used

The goal constraints

$$
\begin{aligned}
&(1) & 15{,}000x_1 + 10{,}000x_2 + d_1^- - d_1^+ &= 200{,}000 && \text{(budget constraint)}\\
&(2) & 2{,}000{,}000x_1 + 1{,}000{,}000x_2 + d_2^- - d_2^+ &= 20{,}000{,}000 && \text{(exposure constraint)}\\
&(3) & 800{,}000x_1 + 300{,}000x_2 + d_3^- - d_3^+ &= 5{,}000{,}000 && \text{(effectiveness constraint)}\\
&(4) & x_1 + d_4^- - d_4^+ &= 8 && \text{(minimum TV inserts)}\\
&(5) & x_2 + d_5^- - d_5^+ &= 5 && \text{(minimum magazine inserts)}
\end{aligned}
$$

The system constraints

This is an integer programming problem, and therefore the values of x_1 and x_2 are restricted to whole numbers. No other system constraints exist.

The objective function

Considering only the *undesirable deviations* we have:

$$\text{minimize } z = P_1d_1^+ + P_2d_2^- + P_3d_3^- + P_4d_4^- + P_5d_5^-$$

***b.* Manufacturing**

A company is planning the monthly production of three products: A, B, and C. The fabricating department can process 10 units of A in an hour, or 15 of B. Part C is fabricated in five minutes. The department has 250 hours available each month beyond which overtime is required, at a cost of $15 per hour. Painting the products is also required, with times of: 20 minutes per unit of A, 24 minutes per unit of B, and 30 minutes per unit of C. There are three painters in the department, each working 200 hours per month.

Production requirements

The company cannot sell more than 3,000 units of all products, combined, in a month. It is the company's policy to produce at least 200 units of product B each month. The products' contributions to profit are $20, $28, and $40 for A, B, and C, respectively. The company's priorities, in order of importance, are: (1) a desired monthly profit level of $120,000; (2) overtime of $1,000 allowed in the fabricating department; (3) painting hours should not exceed 1,200 each month; and (4) at least 200 units of B should be produced.

Formulation

The decision variables

x_1 = Quantity of product A
x_2 = Quantity of product B
x_3 = Quantity of product C

The system constraints

$$x_1 + x_2 + x_3 \leq 3{,}000$$

The goal constraints

1. Profit: $20x_1 + 28x_2 + 40x_3 + d_1^- - d_1^+ = 120{,}000$.
2. Overtime: The demand on time (in minutes) is: $6x_1 + 4x_2 + 5x_3$. The supply is 250 hours $\times$ 60 minutes = 15,000 minutes. Overtime will be paid after 15,000 minutes, that is: Overtime = $(6x_1 + 4x_2 + 5x_3) - 15{,}000$. The cost of overtime is: \$15 per hour or \$0.25 per minute. The constraint is thus:

   $$0.25\,[(6x_1 + 4x_2 + 5x_3) - 15{,}000] + d_2^- - d_2^+ = 1{,}000$$
   $$\text{or } 1.5x_1 + 1x_2 + 1.25x_3 + d_2^- - d_2^+ = 4{,}750.$$
3. Painting time: $20x_1 + 24x_2 + 30x_3 + d_3^- - d_3^+ = 1{,}200 \times 60 = 72{,}000$ minutes.
4. Production of product B: $x_2 + d_4^- - d_4^+ = 200$.

The objective function

$$\text{minimize } z = P_1d_1^- + P_2d_2^+ + P_3d_3^+ + P_4d_4^-$$

Only undesirable deviations are listed.

c. Recreational Facility Funding (Integer GP)

Community services

A city parks and recreation department has been authorized a special construction budget of \$3 million to expand its public recreation facilities. Four different types of facilities have long been requested by the public: basketball courts, baseball fields, tennis courts, and swimming pools. The demand by various communities within the city has been for 6 basketball courts, 4 baseball fields, 10 tennis courts, and 12 swimming pools. The information about the facilities is summarized in Table 9.4.

TABLE 9.4
Recreational facilities information

Facility	*Cost*	*Required acres per unit*	*Average usage (people per week)*
Basketball courts	\$250,000	3	600
Baseball fields	100,000	10	1,200
Tennis courts	50,000	2	500
Swimming pools	200,000	2	1,000

The park management has located 45 acres of land for construction and, for public image reasons, established the following list of prioritized goals:

P_1: The department would like to spend the total budget.
P_2: The park department desires the additional facilities to be used by 10,000 people or more weekly.
P_3: The department wants to avoid using land other than the 45 acres presently available.
P_4: If the department must secure more land, they desire to limit it to 10 acres.
P_5: The department would like to meet all the demands of the public for the new facilities. However, this priority should be weighted according to the number of people estimated to use each facility.

Finally, the department *must* build at least 14 facilities altogether; this goal cannot be violated.

Formulation

Decision variables

x_1 = Number of basketball courts
x_2 = Number of baseball fields
x_3 = Number of tennis courts
x_4 = Number of swimming pools

System constraints

(1) $x_1 + x_2 + x_3 + x_4 \geq 14$
(2) $250{,}000x_1 + 100{,}000x_2 + 50{,}000x_3 + 200{,}000x_4 \leq 3{,}000{,}000$

Goal constraints

P_1: $250{,}000x_1 + 100{,}000x_2 + 50{,}000x_3 + 200{,}000x_4 + d_1^- - d_1^+ = 3{,}000{,}000$ (Note that d_1^+ must be zero because of system constraint number 2; d_1^- is undesirable.)
P_2: $600x_1 + 1{,}200x_2 + 500x_3 + 1{,}000x_4 + d_2^- - d_2^+ = 10{,}000$
d_2^- is undesirable
P_3: $3x_1 + 10x_2 + 2x_3 + 2x_4 + d_3^- - d_3^+ = 45$
d_3^+ is undesirable
P_4: This priority can be expressed in two ways, either:
$(3x_1 + 10x_2 + 2x_3 + 2x_4) - 45 + d_4^- - d_4^+ = 10$
or: $d_3^+ + d_4^- - d_4^+ = 10$
We will use the second formulation; d_4^+ is undesirable.
P_5: This goal is expressed in term of four goal constraints. The number of users is estimated to be most for baseball fields, second for the swimming pools, and so on.

$x_1 + d_5^- - d_5^+ = 6$ (d_5^- is undesirable)
$x_2 + d_6^- - d_6^+ = 4$ (d_6^- is undesirable)
$x_3 + d_7^- - d_7^+ = 10$ (d_7^- is undesirable)
$x_4 + d_8^- - d_8^+ = 12$ (d_8^- is undesirable)

The objective function

$$\text{minimize } z = P_1d_1^- + P_2d_2^- + P_3d_3^+ + P_4d_4^+ + P_5d_5^- + P_5d_6^- + P_5d_7^- + P_5d_8^-$$

The deviations in goal 5 now receive weights, according to the number of users of each facility (in hundreds):

$$\text{minimize } z = P_1d_1^- + P_2d_2^- + P_3d_3^+ + P_4d_4^+ + 6P_5d_5^- + 12P_5d_6^- + 5P_5d_7^- + 10P_5d_8^-$$

Integer constraints

Finally, x_1, x_2, x_3, and x_4 must be integer numbers.

Notes:

a. The integer requirements make the solution of this problem difficult.
b. For goal 5, we established four sets of deviations and prioritized them.

d. Investment maximization

An investment firm's typical customer earns a salary of $25,000 and has $5,000 of that available to invest. The firm has a variety of opportunities available in which to invest its customers' funds, as shown below:

Decision variable	*Alternative*	*Expected annual return (percent)*
x_1	IRA (retirement)	7.4
x_2	Employer's retirement plan	18.8
x_3	Deferred income (retirement)	24
x_4	RST mutual fund	9
x_5	ABC mutual fund	32
x_6	Money market A	12
x_7	Money market B	13
x_8	Credit union savings account	11
x_9	Bank savings account	8
x_{10}	Investment club	15

The firm's policies, in order of priority, are as follows:

Investment priorities

1. Invest not less than 2 percent but not more than 5 percent of the "typical" individual's annual salary of $25,000 in the employer's retirement plan.
2. Invest at least $150 per year in the investment club.
3. Also fulfill the club's requirement of investing no more than 15 percent of the total amount invested by all club members to date ($5,000).
4. Invest 60 percent of the amount invested in the money market in mutual funds, 20 percent in the savings accounts, and 20 percent in the investment club.
5. Allot no more than 30 percent of the total moneys available for retirement.

6. The total nonretirement moneys invested should be at least 70 percent of the total moneys available.
7. Maximize the return on the sum of all the investments, with a target of 20,000.
8. Invest all the moneys available.

Formulation

The decision variables are the x_i given in the problem.

System constraints

$$x_1 + x_2 + x_3 + x_4 + x_5 + x_6 + x_7 + x_8 + x_9 + x_{10} \leq 5{,}000$$

Goal constraints

$x_2 - d_1^- = 500$ (2 percent of 25,000)
$x_2 + d_2^+ = 1{,}250$ (5 percent of 25,000)
$x_{10} - d_3^- = 150$
$x_{10} + d_4^+ = 750$ (15 percent of 5,000)
$x_4 + x_5 - .6x_6 - .6x_7 - d_5^+ + d_5^- = 0$
$-.2x_6 - .2x_7 + x_8 + x_9 - d_6^+ + d_6^- = 0$
$-.2x_6 - .2x_7 + x_{10} - d_7^+ + d_7^- = 0$
$x_1 + x_2 + x_3 + d_8^+ = 1{,}500$
$x_4 + x_5 + x_6 + x_7 + x_8 + x_9 + x_{10} - d_9^- = 3{,}500$
$.074x_1 + .188x_2 + .24x_3 + .09x_4 + .32x_5 + .12x_6 + .13x_7 + .11x_8 + .08x_9 + .15x_{10} - d_{10}^+ + d_{10}^- = 20{,}000$
$x_1 + x_2 + x_3 + x_4 + x_5 + x_6 + x_7 + x_8 + x_9 + x_{10} + d_{11}^- = 5{,}000$

Objective function

$$\text{minimize } z = P_1d_1^- + P_1d_2^+ + P_2d_3^- + P_3d_4^+ + P_4d_5^- + P_4d_5^+ + P_4d_6^+ + P_4d_6^- + P_4d_7^+ + P_4d_7^- + P_5d_8^+ + P_6d_9^- + P_7d_{10}^- + P_8d_{11}^-$$

9.9 PROBLEMS FOR PART A

1. Products A and B are considered for production. Each unit of A requires two hours of labor, three hours of machine time, and \$20 capital. Each unit of B requires three hours of labor, two hours of machine time, and \$25 in capital. There are available 2,000 hours of labor capacity and 2,200 hours of machine time. The profit on product A is \$110; on product B it is \$120.

Management's objectives, in descending order, are:

P_1: No idle labor.
P_2: Produce at least 400 units of product A.
P_3: Produce at least 400 units of product B.
P_4: Total overtime should not exceed 250 hours.
P_5: Make a profit of at least \$120,000.
P_6: Utilize machine time fully. However, underutilization is one half as desirable as overutilization.

Formulate as a goal programming problem. Solve (use a computer).

2. A production order of 300 units of product A must be executed within a week by AAA Manufacturing Company. Two production lines are available, each for 30 hours during the week.

Production line 1 can produce five units per hour. Using production line 2 it takes 15 minutes to produce each unit. Line 1 costs $9 per hour to operate, and line 2 costs $11 per hour. Overtime is available for line 1 at $15 per hour and for line 2 at $12 per hour.

Management goals, in decreasing order of importance, are:

P_1: Produce 300 units.
P_2: Maximum allowable overtime of four hours for line 1.
P_3: The cost of overtime must not be greater than $800.
P_4: Underutilization of either line during the regular working hours must be avoided. Assign weights to underutilization in direct proportion to their production capability.
P_5: Producing over 300 is twice as undesirable as producing under 300.

Formulate as a goal program in order to find the best production plan.

3. Formulate a goal program to help Atlanta BanCorp invest $5 million. The company is considering investing in stocks, bonds, CDs (certificates of deposit), and gold. The anticipated annual returns are listed below.

Stocks: 5 percent dividends plus 7 percent capital gains.
Bonds: 9 percent interest plus 1 percent capital gains.
CDs: 10 percent interest.
Gold: 13 percent capital gains.

The firm's investment policies, in decreasing order of importance, are:

P_1: The amount to be invested cannot, under any circumstances, exceed $5 million.
P_2: Do not invest more than 10 percent in gold.
P_3: Make at least $500,000 total profit.
P_4: Invest no more than $1 million in stocks.
P_5: Invest at least $200,000 in CDs, for liquidity.
P_6: Derive at least $200,000 from capital gains (tax advantage).

The firm also has the following current investment guidelines:

a. Profit is twice as important as the ceiling limit on investment in stocks.
b. The limitations on stocks and CDs are considered just as important as their proportional contribution to profits.
c. The capital gains target is half as important as the CD restriction.

4. Given a computer printout of GP (* designates a deliberately deleted item of information):

Data Entered

$$\text{minimize } z = P_1d_1^- + P_2d_2^+ + P_3d_3^- + P_4d_4^+ + 7P_5d_5^- + 3P_5d_5^+$$

subject to:

$$\begin{aligned}
(1)\quad & 1x_1 + 1x_2 + d_1^- - d_1^+ = 80\\
(2)\quad & 2x_1 + 3x_2 + d_2^- - d_2^+ = 120\\
(3)\quad & 1x_1 + 0x_2 + d_3^- - d_3^+ = 75\\
(4)\quad & 5x_1 + 2x_2 + d_4^- - d_4^+ = 100\\
(5)\quad & 0x_1 + 1x_2 + d_5^- - d_5^+ = 45\\
(6)\quad & 5x_1 + 2x_2 \le 200
\end{aligned}$$

The solution is:

***** PROGRAM OUTPUT *****

Analysis of decision variables

Variable	Solution value
× 2	66.67
× 1	13.33

Analysis of the objective function

Priority	Nonachievement
P 1	0.00
P 2	*
P 3	61.67
P 4	100.00
P 5	65.00

Analysis of deviations

Constraint	RHS Value	d+	d−
C 1	80.00	0.00	0.00
C 2	120.00	106.67	0.00
C 3	75.00	0.00	*
C 4	*	100.00	0.00
C 5	45.00	*	*
C 6	200.00	0.00	*

Answer the following questions:

a. What are the undesirable deviations on constraints C2 and C3?

b. What are the values of d^+ and d^- on constraint C5?

c. What is the slack (surplus) on constraint C6?

d. What is the total value of the GP objective function?

e. What is the RHS value of C4 in the optimal solution?

5. Consider a case of a single objective function in which the objective is to produce exactly 20 units. Both overachievement and underachievement are undesirable. Write the objective function for such a case.

6. A company produces two products: alpha, which sells for \$30 and costs \$20; and beta, which sells for \$50 and costs \$35. Profit is the most important goal of the company and the target for this year is \$1.0 million.

The second most important goal for the company is the manufacturing budget of \$800,000 a year (maximum).

The products are produced by a machine shop that has a capacity of 40,000 hours a year. Each unit of alpha takes 20 minutes to produce, while beta requires 24 minutes. The machine shop capacity can be expanded. However, the company prefers not to do it. It is a third-priority goal, *not* to expand.

Fourth, for each unit of beta produced, the company would like to produce at least .7 of alpha.

Finally, marketing is an extremely important issue; however, the most the company can sell is 50,000 units of alpha in a year and 60,000 units of beta. These limits *cannot* be exceeded at all.

The company puts the following weights on their objectives: If the least important goal has a weight of 1, then the next one will be twice as important. The next goal in the ladder will then be twice as important as the second from the bottom (or four times more important than the least important), and so on.

a. Formulate as a goal program.

b. Solve, use a computer.

PART B: EXTENSIONS

9.10 GRAPHICAL SOLUTION

Goal programming problems with two decision variables (or two constraints) can be solved graphically. To illustrate the technique, let us examine a simple product-mix problem:

minimize $z = P_1d_1^- + P_2d_2^+ + P_3d_3^+ + P_4d_4^-$
subject to:

(1)	$20x_1 + 30x_2 + d_1^- - d_1^+ = 120$	(profit)
(2)	$10x_1 + 3x_2 + d_2^- - d_2^+ = 30$	(capacity, machine A)
(3)	$7x_1 + 8x_2 + d_3^- - d_3^+ = 56$	(capacity, machine B)
(4)	$1x_1 + 0x_2 + d_4^- - d_4^+ = 5$	(marketing)

The problem is to find the quantities of x_1 and x_2 to be produced.

Solution

To illustrate the process, we will construct the first three constraints, one at a time.

Figure 9.2 shows the profit constraint:

$$20x_1 + 30x_2 + d_1^- - d_1^+ = 120$$

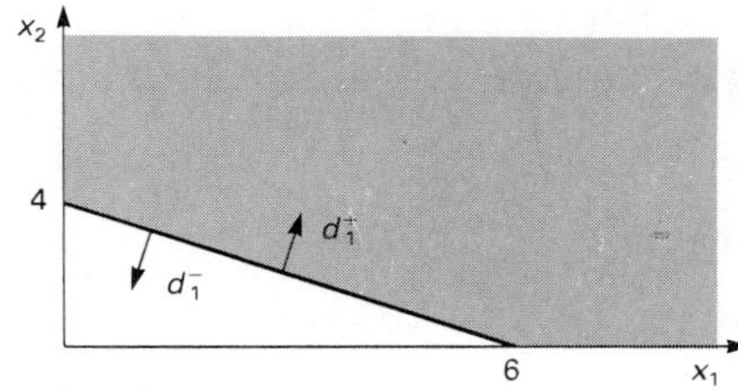

FIGURE 9.2
The profit constraint

Notice that the deviational variables are ignored. Since we are attempting to minimize (or eliminate) d_1^-, it is clear that the feasible area must be on right side of the line, where d_1^+ is.

The second and third priority goals are superimposed on the profit goal, as shown in Figure 9.3.

The shaded area, *ABCD*, designates a feasible solution for the first three constraints. Any point inside this area will fully meet the requirement of no deviations in these three constraints.

No feasible solution space

Now we consider the fourth goal (produce at least five units of product 1). In order to achieve this goal, it is necessary to eliminate the area to the left of the line $x_1 = 5$. However, that cannot be done without violating constraints 2 and 3. That is, in a regular LP situation, a nonfeasible solution would arise. In GP, however, there is a way out! We want, then, to find a solution point that will satisfy the first three goals, yet also come as

FIGURE 9.3
The goal constraints

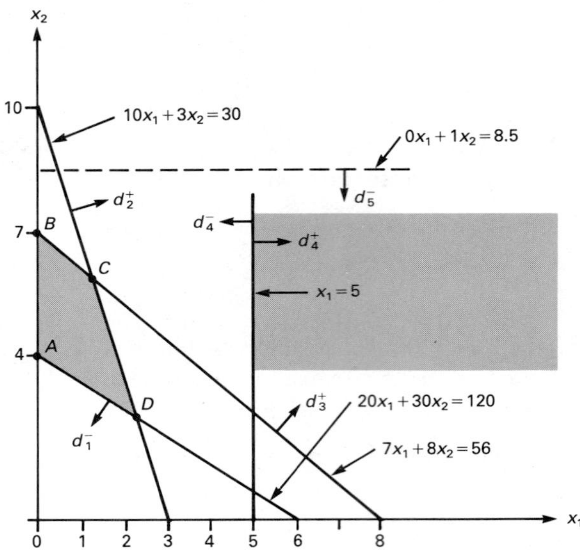

close as possible to achieving the fourth goal. Such a point can be found by observation: point *D*. Its coordinates are:

$$x_1 = 2.25;\ x_2 = 2.5$$

Substituting these values into the goal constraints, we find that the first two goals are fully met (intersection at the solution).

$$\text{Goal 3: } 7(2.25) + 8(2.5) = 35.75$$

That is:

$$d_3^+ = 0;\ d_3^- = 56 - 35.75 = 20.25 \text{ (slack)}$$

This slack is *not* an undesirable deviation.

$$\text{Goal 4: } d_4^+ = 0;\ d_4^- = 5 - 2.25 = 2.75$$

This is the only undesirable deviation.

Another goal

Now let us assume that an additional goal is added:

$$0x_1 + 1x_2 + d_5^- - d_5^+ = 8.5$$

and the undesirable deviation is d_5^-. If we add this goal to Figure 9.3 (broken line), we see that a deviation on goal 5 is imminent. The closest feasible point to the new constraint is *B* and not *D*. However, since d_4^- has higher priority, the optimal solution is to stay at *D*. If, instead, we set weights on the deviations, then we would multiply the distances from a candidate solution point (such as *B*, *C*, or *D*) to the two goals by the weights, total them, and select the solution that minimizes the total deviations. (See problem no. 9.)

The graphical solution to GP has the same drawbacks LP has; namely, it can only handle problems with two variables and not too many constraints. For larger problems, it is necessary to use the modified simplex method. In addition, for a graphical solution, all system and goal constraints must be expressed in terms of x_1 and/or x_2.

9.11 SPECIAL SITUATIONS

Deviational variable goal constraint

Let us assume that we have a machine time constraint:

$$2x_1 + 5x_2 \leq 50$$

where 50 is the amount of machine time available. This can be written in GP terms as:

$$2x_1 + 5x_2 + d_1^- - d_1^+ = 50$$

Now, a new goal is added: that machine overtime can be provided, up to eight hours. This additional goal can be introduced as:

$$(2x_1 + 5x_2) - 50 \leq 8$$

or:

Two methods for a new constraint

$$2x_1 + 5x_2 + d_1^- - d_1^+ = 58$$

Another way to express this new goal is to add a "deviational variable goal constraint":

$$d_1^+ + d_2^- - d_2^+ = 8$$

The new deviation is then considered in the objective function by adding a P_2d_2 term.

9.12 SETTING UP GOALS

The success of a GP approach depends on an appropriate determination of the goals, their priorities, and the targets (the right-hand side (RHS) values of the constraints). In a real-world GP situation, all goals may not be achieved. That is, there will be undesirable deviations in the less important goals. This fact may have a psychological impact on the people responsible for attaining these goals. Specifically, they would not like to be labeled "nonachievers." For this reason, and because of the fact that in many cases there will be rewards attached to achievements, people may attempt to set the goals too low.

Negotiation for goal setting

Goal setting, in many cases, is a negotiated process. Methods such as management by objectives (MBO) extensively utilize negotiated goals. During a negotiation session, the employee responsible for the attainment of the goal (e.g., a department chairperson) may try to set the goal at a low level, while his or her superior may try to increase it. If the goals are set too low, then the GP solution will indicate that all of them can be fully achieved. This can be an easy political escape, but it is usually a poor resource allocation solution.

Recognizing this fact, companies are using a "stretching" strategy. According to this strategy, the initial goals are set through the regular negotiation process. Then, those involved in the GP situation are called into a meeting, where they are briefed about GP and told that the goals are not tight enough. The participants are assured that undesirable deviations are acceptable and rewards will be made based on the GP solution. Then, the stretching process begins, where the goals are tightened as much as possible. Only then should the GP model be initiated.

9.13 CONCLUDING REMARKS

Goal programming can expand the applicability of linear programming into many real-life situations that involve multiple, conflicting goals. For such situations to be treated by GP it is necessary to rank (prioritize) the goals and, preferably, assign weights that indicate their relative importance. In addition to its ability to handle multiple goals, GP permits deviations from the desirable levels of the goals. However, an attempt is made to minimize the sum of the *undesirable* deviations.

The GP approach is currently applied efficiently only to linear situations (linear objective function and constraints). However, the "what if" procedures used during the application of GP make it a very attractive tool for the practicing manager. Furthermore, this can be used to support a group of decision makers with diverse interests.

GP was not a popular tool until rather recently because it required a mainframe computer for its execution. Several micro packages are now available, and others are in a developmental stage.

GP is the newest addition to the family of mathematical programs. Our next chapter deals with much older members of this family—the transportation and assignment models.

9.14 PROBLEMS FOR PART B

7. Given a GP problem:

minimize $z = P_1d_1^- + P_2d_2^- + P_3d_3^+ + P_4d_4^- + P_5d_5^-$

subject to:

$1x_1 + 1x_2 + d_1^- - d_1^+ = 40$ (most important)

$2x_1 + 0x_2 + d_2^- - d_2^+ = 40$

$0.8x_1 + 1x_2 + d_3^- - d_3^+ = 50$

$5x_1 + 4x_2 + d_4^- - d_4^+ = 200$

$0x_1 + 1x_2 + d_5^- - d_5^+ = 32$

a. Solve graphically.

b. Solve by a computer.

8. Given a GP problem:

P_1: $1x_1 + 1x_2 + d_1^- - d_1^+ = 60$ (profit)

P_2: $1x_1 + 1x_2 + d_2^- - d_2^+ = 75$ (capacity)

P_3: $1x_1 + 0x_2 + d_3^- - d_3^+ = 45$ (at least 45 to be produced)

P_4: $0x_1 + 1x_2 + d_4^- - d_4^+ = 50$ (d_4^- is undesirable)

P_5: $1x_1 + 0x_2 + d_5^- - d_5^+ = 10$ (d_5^+ is undesirable)

a. Write the objective function.
b. Identify the conflicting goals.
c. Solve graphically.

9. Refer to Section 9.10. Assume the importance of goals 4 and 5 are given in the objective function as $5d_4^- + 8d_5^-$. Find the optimal solution (point B, C, or D?).

10. Goal Analysis Exercise

a. Identify five *short-term goals* (i.e., to be completed in not more than a year) for the department (unit) for which you work (or in your own career). List these goals. Tell how the information was solicited.

b. For each goal, describe how the goal's attainment can be measured and how the information is to be collected.

Example 1

Provide timely bus service to the City of Hope. Measurement: 95 percent of all buses will leave scheduled departure points no later than five minutes after the scheduled time.
Collect information through self-logging of drivers, sample survey done by supervisor, or install automated vehicle monitoring system.
The goal this year is to improve the service level to 95 percent from 92 percent last year.

Example 2

Provide quality service at the information desk. Measurement: Customers' satisfaction. Ask one question: "Is the service provided to you:"

(5) Excellent; (4) Very good; (3) Good;
(2) Fair; (1) Poor

Survey a sample of 200 customers.
The goal is to improve average satisfaction level from 3.7 to 3.9.

Example 3

Earnings per share: $2.

Example 4

Reject rate: 1 percent.

Example 5

Sales volume: $5 million for next year.

c. Prioritizing the goals.
Use any method you wish (see Chapter 4) to prioritize the goals. Make sure that at least three individuals participate in this part, including your boss and one of your subordinates. Describe the process of *soliciting information* and how different opinions (if they existed) were handled.

d. What have you learned from this exercise? (one-half page)

9.15 CASE

CARTOY INTERNATIONAL

Cartoy International is a large multinational corporation with automobile manufacturing and assembly plants scattered worldwide. The company has recently developed a new model named Zentz. The Zentz will be produced in three forms: sedan, sport, and luxury. The company plans to use excess capacity available in Tokyo (3,000 cars per week), Fremont, California (1,200 cars per week), and Djakarta (2,000 cars per week).

Cartoy is primarily interested in profits, of course; however, the company would also like to minimize idle capacity, because fully utilized facilities increase the employment level in the same areas that the company sells its cars. In addition, high capacity utilization reduces hiring and firing cost, as well as giving a better distribution of fixed costs.

Due to the international nature of the company, it is also necessary to consider distribution constraints. The cars are shipped by boat about once a month. Therefore, it is necessary to store the products in the manufacturing plants. A sedan requires 40 square feet, a sports car 34 square feet, and the luxury model 50 square feet. Storage capacity for one month (four weeks) is available as follows: In Tokyo, 400,000 square feet, in Fremont, 300,000 square feet, and there is no limit on the number of cars that can be stored in Djakarta.

The estimated profit contributions of the cars are: sedan—$680, sport—$1,100, luxury—

$2,200. The anticipated weekly worldwide demand is 4,000 sedans, 1,300 sports cars, and 1,800 luxury.

Top management has announced the following goals and priorities (P_1 is the highest-priority goal):

P_1: To utilize plant capacity in a balanced way. This means that once the new model capacities are assigned, the leftover capacity will be the same, in number of cars, in the three countries. This goal is essential to avoid a feeling of discrimination among the different countries.

P_2: Utilize excess capacity in Djakarta twice as intensively as Tokyo or Fremont (due to the lower labor cost).

P_3: Sell as many luxury cars as possible, due to their larger contribution margin.

P_4: Do not exceed the current storage capacity.

P_5: Produce as many cars of each type as the market can absorb.

P_6: Utilize plant capacity for the new cars in proportion to the available capacity. This goal attempts to balance utilization in terms of percent idle space.

P_7: Maximize profit.

Sen Yokota, the vice president for corporate manufacturing, was displeased with these goals and priorities. Although he was delighted about the decision to produce the Zentz, he had difficulty scheduling its production. So he called the corporate president, Su-nu, and they had the following discussion.

Sen: I do not like these goals. They impose too many restrictions and some of them clearly contradict each other.

Su-nu: Calm down, Sen. You know that we have an international responsibility.

Sen: True, but we have shareholders, too.

Su-nu: We must also consider markets, employees, international distribution, and the like.

Sen: OK, but why is profit the least priority?

Su-nu: I think that we can make a good profit even if it is the last priority. Furthermore, some of the other goals were designed to increase the profit margin.

Sen: But you are not sure how much profit we will make.

Su-nu: No, not until I see the production plan.

Required:

a. Identify the contradictions among the goals.

b. Formulate as a linear program with profit maximization as the only goal. Solve.

c. Formulate as a GP.

9.16 GLOSSARY

Deviational variables The variables that measure the deviations from the goals; d^+ measures the deviation above the goal; d^- the deviation below the goal.

Deviations (from goals) The values by which the goals are either overachieved or underachieved.

Goal constraints These constraints express the desired organizational goals when deviations (d^+ and/or d^-) are tolerable.

Goal programming A mathematical programming extension where several goals can be treated in the model if they are ranked according to their importance. The objective is to minimize the undesirable deviations from the goals.

Multiple goals A situation in which the decision maker must simultaneously consider several, usually competing, objectives.

Overachievement A variable that measures by how much a goal is exceeded.

System constraints Requirements and constraints that must be met in full. No deviations are permitted, usually due to some physical limitation (e.g., space, time). These are identical to LP constraints.

Underachievement A variable that measures the difference between a given target and a performance lower than the standard.

Weighted goals The relative importance of the goals as expressed by explicit weights placed on the deviations.

9.17 REFERENCES AND BIBLIOGRAPHY

1. Charnes, A., and W. W. Cooper. *Management Models and Industrial Applications of Linear Programming*. New York: John Wiley & Sons, 1961.
2. Ignizio, J. P. *Goal Programming and Extensions*. Lexington, Mass.: Lexington Books, 1976.
3. Lee, S. M. *Goal Programming for Decision Analysis*. Philadelphia: Auerbach, 1972.
4. Lee, S. M. *Management by Multiple Objectives*. Princeton, N.J.: Petrocelli Books, 1981.
5. Lee, S. M., and J. P. Shim. *Micro Manager*. Dubuque, Iowa: Wm. C. Brown, 1986. (A software package.)
6. Lev, B., and H. J. Weiss. *Introduction to Mathematical Programming*. New York: Elsevier North-Holland Publishing, 1982.
7. Schniederjans, M. J. *Linear Goal Programming*. New York: Petrocelli Books, 1984.
8. Spronk, J. *Interactive Multiple Goal Programming*. Boston: Martinus Nijhoff, 1981.
9. Zeleny, M. *Multiple Criteria Decision Making*. New York: McGraw-Hill, 1982.

10

PART A: BASICS

10.1 The transportation problem—characteristics and assumptions.
10.2 The transportation method.
10.3 Applications.
10.4 The assignment problem.
10.5 Concluding remarks.
10.6 Problems for Part A.

PART B: EXTENSIONS

10.7 The modified distribution procedure (MODI).
10.8 Degeneracy.
10.9 Use of computers.
10.10 Problems for Part B.
10.11 Case I—Northeastern Blood Bank.
Case II—Greenhill's Federal Grant.
10.12 Glossary.
10.13 References and bibliography.

Distribution problems are a special type of linear programming problem. There are two main types of distribution problems: the transportation problem and the assignment problem.

The transportation problem deals with shipments from a number of sources to a number of destinations. Typically, each source is supply limited, each destination has a known demand, and the shipping costs between sources and destinations are given. The object is to find the cheapest shipping schedule that satisfies demand without violating supply constraints.

The assignment problem deals with finding the best one-to-one match for each of a given number of "candidates" to a number of "positions." Typical situations include assigning workers to machines, teachers to classes, and so on. Different benefits or costs are involved in each match, and the goal is to maximize the total reward or minimize the total expense.

Due to their special structure, these problems can be solved by special computational procedures in an efficient manner.

Distribution models

LEARNING OBJECTIVES

The student should be able to:

a. Identify a transportation problem and state its assumptions.
b. Formulate the problem in a transportation matrix.
c. Write the equivalent LP problem.
d. Generate an initial feasible solution by the Northwest Corner and the least-cost methods.
e. Employ the stepping-stone solution procedure.
f. Identify the assignment problem and state its assumptions.
g. Write the equivalent LP problem.
h. Solve, using the Hungarian method.

Extensions

i. Solve transportation problems using the MODI method.
j. Resolve degeneracy.
k. Solve transportation problems using the computer and interpret the results.

PART A: BASICS

Bill Grout, Tuff's operations manager, knew he would have to face this problem sooner or later, and here it was, finally, on his desk. Tuff Cement Company had opened a new warehouse in New York to serve the fast-growing demand for cement in that region. Management now wondered which plants should supply it and to what extent. As manager of operations, Bill was responsible for making those decisions. Although the problem did not look complicated, he was having trouble matching demand to supply. The situation was as follows.

Tuff Cement Company has two processing plants, one in Allentown, Pennsylvania (A), with a supply capacity of 100 tons per day, and one in Baltimore, Maryland (B), with a supply capacity of 110 tons a day. Tuff now has three warehouses: R in Easton, Pennsylvania, S in Philadelphia, and the newly added T on Long Island in New York. The warehouses need, if possible, 80, 120, and 60 tons of cement each day, respectively, to meet their distribution demands.

The shipping costs from each plant to each warehouse are given below:

From	*To*	*Cost per ton*
A (Allentown)	R (Easton)	1
A (Allentown)	S (Philadelphia)	2
A (Allentown)	T (New York)	3
B (Baltimore)	R (Easton)	4
B (Baltimore)	S (Philadelphia)	1
B (Baltimore)	T (New York)	5

Tuff's distribution scheme is shown in Figure 10.1.

Bill's problem is to plan the shipments at the least possible cost. The managerial tool that will assure him of a least-cost solution is called the *transportation* model.

10.1 THE TRANSPORTATION PROBLEM—CHARACTERISTICS AND ASSUMPTIONS

Tuff's transportation situation is typical of a class of distribution problems that exhibit the following characteristics:

1. *The supply. A limited quantity* of one commodity such as cement, oil, or oranges is available at certain **sources** (or origins) such as factories, refineries, or groves.
2. *The demand.* There is a demand for the commodity at several **destinations** such as warehouses, distribution centers, or stores.
3. *The quantities.* The quantities of *supply* at each source and the demand or *requirements* at each destination are constant.

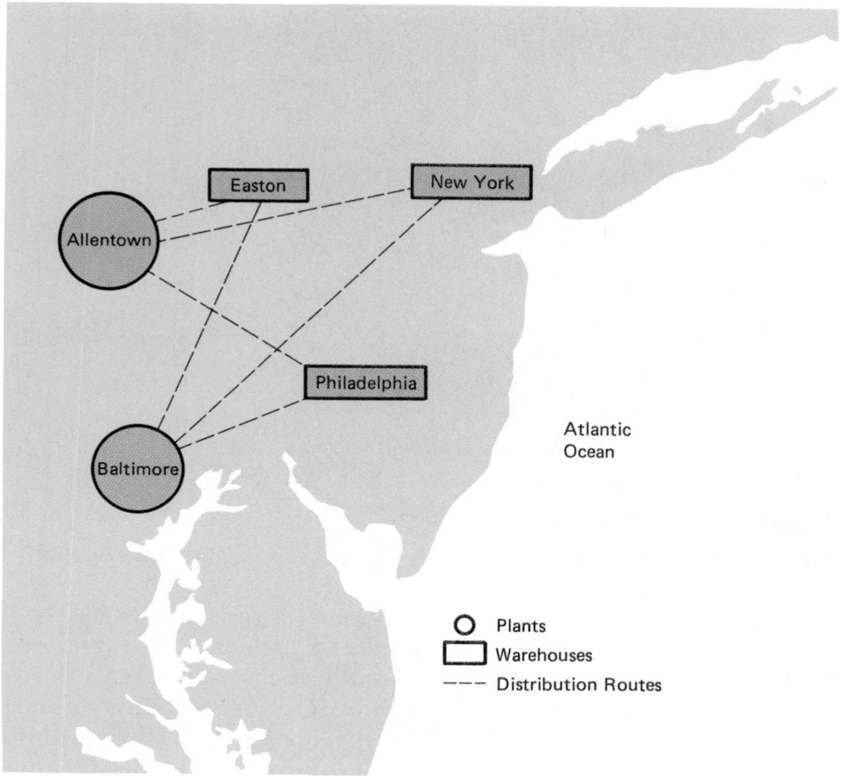

FIGURE 10.1
Tuff's distribution problem

4. *The shipping cost.* The per unit costs of transporting the commodity from each source to each destination are assumed to be constant (e.g., $5 per ton). Usually they are based on the distance between the two points. Moving companies and the post office are examples of users of a similar cost system in their deliveries.

Transportation—a special type of distribution problem

5. *It is assumed* that no shipments are allowed between sources or between destinations. Allowing such transshipments would require special adjustments in the model. (For details, see Wagner [8]).
6. *All supply and demand* quantities are given in whole numbers (integers).
7. *The problem* is to determine how many units should be shipped from each source to each destination (i.e., what routes to use and in what capacity) so that all demands are satisfied (if possible) at the minimum total shipping cost.

Find the best shipment plan

Presentation in a tabular form

Transportation problems are presented in tabular form because it is a convenient form for applying special solution procedures. Table 10.1 shows Tuff's distribution problem.

TABLE 10.1
Tabular presentation of Tuff's problem

From plant \ *To warehouse*	Easton R	Philadelphia S	New York T	*Supply*
Allentown (A)	x_{AR} [1]	x_{AS} [$c_{AS} = 2$]	x_{AT} [3]	$b_A = 100$
Baltimore (B)	x_{BR} [4]	x_{BS} [1]	x_{BT} [5]	$b_B = 110$
Demand	$d_R = 80$	$d_s = 120$	$d_T = 60$	210 ← *Total supply* / 260 ↑ *Total demand*

Using a tabular form

Explanation of the table

Left side. The sources of supply (plants) are listed on the left. Each source is represented by a row.

Top. The destination points (warehouses) are listed at the top. Each destination is represented by a column.

Right side. This column designates the capacity (supply) at the sources.

Bottom. The requirements (demand) of each destination are listed here.

Center. The center of the table is composed of "cells." In this case, there are six. Each is designated by the letter of its row and column; for example, cell AR is in row A and column R. The corresponding shipping costs (per ton) are in the upper right-hand corner of each cell. For example, the shipping cost from plant A to warehouse S is 2. In each cell there is also a decision variable. For example, in cell AR the variable is x_{AR}. This variable designates the quantity to be shipped from plant A to warehouse R.

Presentation as a linear program

Formulation as an LP

Any transportation problem can be presented in the form of a linear programming problem. As such, it includes an objective function and constraints.

The objective function The objective function calls for minimization of the total shipping cost, which is computed by multiplying the quantity shipped from each source i to each destination j (labeled x_{ij}), by its per unit shipping cost, c_{ij}, and totaling the results.

For example, using the data of Table 10.1, the objective function can be written as:

$$\text{minimize } z = 1x_{AR} + 2x_{AS} + 3x_{AT} + 4x_{BR} + 1x_{BS} + 5x_{BT}$$

In general, the objective function can be written as:

$$\text{minimize } z = c_{11}x_{11} + c_{12}x_{12} + \cdots + c_{21}x_{21} + c_{22}x_{22} + \cdots + c_{mn}x_{mn} \quad (10.1)$$

where:

m = Number of sources
n = Number of destinations

The supply and demand constraints We consider three possible problem situations involving the supply and demand constraints: Either the total supply is less than, the same as, or more than the total demand.

a. *Total supply < total demand:* In this case (Table 10.1), all the supply (b_i) will be shipped from all points i, but not all demand (d_j) will be satisfied for all destinations j. Such a situation can be expressed as:

$$x_{i1} + x_{i2} + \cdots + x_{in} = b_i \text{ for each supply point } i \quad (10.2)$$

$$x_{1j} + x_{2j} + \cdots + x_{mj} \le d_j \text{ for each demand point } j \quad (10.3)$$

In our example, this results in:

$$\left.\begin{array}{l} x_{AR} + x_{AS} + x_{AT} = 100 \\ x_{BR} + x_{BS} + x_{BT} = 110 \end{array}\right\} \text{supply constraints}$$

$$\left.\begin{array}{l} x_{AR} + x_{BR} \le 80 \\ x_{AS} + x_{BS} \le 120 \\ x_{AT} + x_{BT} \le 60 \end{array}\right\} \text{demand constraints}$$

b. *Total supply = Total demand:* In this situation, all the constraints are equalities (=).

c. *Total supply > Total demand:* In this case, the demand constraints are equalities and the supply constraints are of the ≤ form (i.e., there will be an excess supply in the optimal solution).

Note: Most transportation problems are really integer problems, but they can be solved by linear programming because the theory guarantees an integer solution when using the simplex algorithm.

Solving the transportation model

Many, many solutions

A transportation problem has a very large, sometimes infinite, number of feasible solutions. For example, consider the simple problem given in Table 10.2. Five feasible solutions are shown in Table 10.3. There are many others.

Some solution approaches

Solution method: Complete enumeration One approach is to generate solutions, as was done in Table 10.3, and then find and compare the total cost of each solution. But even if only nonfractional solutions are considered,

TABLE 10.2
An example problem

Source \ *Destination*	1	2	Supply
A	6	8	60
B	10	7	70
Demand	80	50	130 / 130

TABLE 10.3
Feasible solutions to Table 10.2

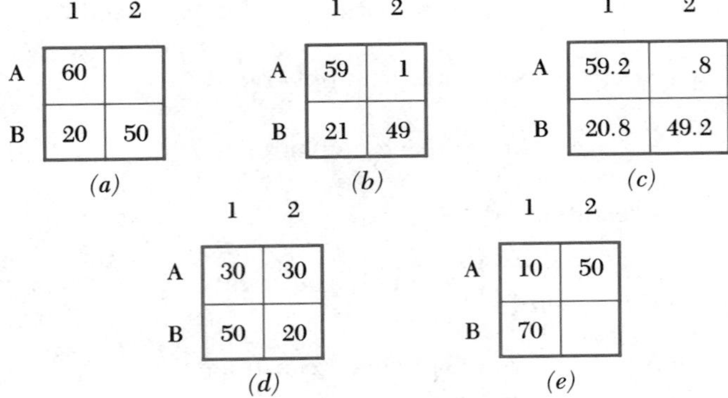

(*a*)

	1	2
A	60	
B	20	50

(*b*)

	1	2
A	59	1
B	21	49

(*c*)

	1	2
A	59.2	.8
B	20.8	49.2

(*d*)

	1	2
A	30	30
B	50	20

(*e*)

	1	2
A	10	50
B	70	

there may still exist a large number of them.[1] Therefore, this could be a cumbersome and time-consuming job.

Solution method: Linear programming Since the transportation problem is indeed a linear programming problem, it can be solved as such. However, presentation of a large transportation problem in a linear programming format results in considerable computational effort, significantly more than the special transportation method. For example, if we have 50 sources and 30 destinations, we will have $50 \times 30 = 1{,}500$ decision variables and $50 + 30 = 80$ constraints.

Solution method: Transportation method The **transportation method** provides a computationally efficient procedure for solving large transportation problems. Section 10.2, which follows, presents the method.

[1] In transportation problems, if the supply and demand are whole (integer) numbers, then the optimal solution *must* also be integer. Therefore, only integer feasible solutions should be considered.

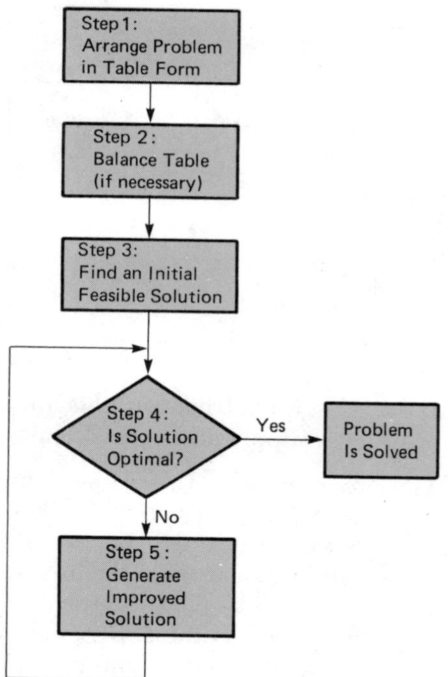

FIGURE 10.2
Steps in solving the transportation problem

10.2 THE TRANSPORTATION METHOD

A five-step procedure

The transportation method is a search and evaluation algorithm, very similar to that of the simplex method in linear programming. The process involves the following five steps, as shown in Figure 10.2.

Step 1. Arrange the data in tabular form

The transportation problem must first be arranged in tabular form. An example of such an arrangement for Tuff's problem was given in Table 10.1 with an explanation.

Step 2. Balance the table

Balance—a must

The use of the transportation solution technique requires that the problem be **balanced**; that is, the *total supply* must equal the *total demand*.[2]

[2] This requirement can be written as:

$$\sum_{i=1}^{m} b_i = \sum_{j=1}^{n} d_j$$

TABLE 10.4
Unbalanced table (excess supply)

Source \ Destination	R	S	T	Supply
A	1	2	3	200
B	4	1	5	100
Demand	80	120	60	260 / 300

If the table is not balanced, this must first be done. Two causes of imbalance are excess supply and excess demand.

1. *Excess supply*. Table 10.4 shows an example of an unbalanced table, where the total supply of 300 exceeds the total demand of 260. In this case, there will be 40 unshipped units. Such a table is balanced by adding an artificial destination column to "absorb" the excess supply (sometimes labeled a "dummy" destination). The amount in this **dummy column** equals the excess supply, as shown in Table 10.5. The cost of "shipments" to the dummy is usually set at zero, since no real shipment implies no real cost. However, in some cases, no shipment may still incur a cost, such as with idled production. In this case, the penalty cost should be entered.

Adding a dummy destination

TABLE 10.5
Balanced table

Source	R	S	T	D (dummy)	Supply
A	1	2	3	0 x_{AD}	200
B	4	1	5	0 x_{BD}	100
Demand	80	120	60	40 (excess supply)	300 / 300

2. *Excess demand*. When the total demand exceeds the total supply, as in Tuff's problem (see Table 10.6), a **dummy** source **row** is added to "meet" the extra demand (50, in this case). Again, the per unit shipping costs for the dummy row are set to zero. The results are shown in Table 10.7. Once the table is balanced, an initial feasible solution is generated.

Adding a dummy source

TABLE 10.6
Unbalanced table (excess demand)

Source \ Destination	R	S	T	Supply
A	1	2	3	100
B	4	1	5	110
Demand	80	120	60	260 \ 210

TABLE 10.7
Balanced table

Source \ Destination	R	S	T	Supply
A	1	2	3	100
B	4	1	5	110
D (dummy)	0	0	0	50 (excess demand)
Demand	80	120	60	260 \ 260

Step 3. The initial feasible solution

An initial feasible solution can be found by any of several available procedures.[3] Two of these are demonstrated next.[4]

Northwest Corner Rule

1. ***Initial assignment by the Northwest Corner Rule***
   a. Starting with the northwest corner (left, uppermost in the table), allocate the *smaller amount* of either the row supply or the column demand.
   b. Subtract from the row supply *and* from the column demand the amount allocated.
   c. If the column demand is now zero, move to the cell next on the right; if the row supply is zero, move down to the cell in the next

[3] An initial feasible solution is any feasible solution used to start the computations.

[4] A third method that gives an efficient initial solution is the Vogel approximation method (VAM). For details, see any text in the references and bibliography section of this chapter.

TABLE 10.8
Initial solution by the Northwest Corner Rule

Source \ Destination	R	S	T	Supply	Remaining supply
A	[1] 80	[2] 20	[3]	100	~~20~~ 0
B	[4]	[1] 100	[5] 10	110	~~10~~ 0
D (dummy)	[0]	[0]	[0] 50	50	0
Demand	80	120	60	260	
Remaining demand	0	~~100~~ 0	~~50~~ 0		

row. If both are zero, move first to the next cell on the right, then down one cell.[5]

d. Once a cell is identified as per step *(c)*, it becomes a northwest cell. Allocate to it an amount as per step *(a)*.

e. Repeat the above steps *(a)*–*(d)* until all the remaining supply and demand is gone.

Purely mechanical

The advantage of this rule is that it is a simple mechanical process. The problem presented in Table 10.1 is balanced in Table 10.8 and serves as an example to illustrate an assignment by the Northwest Corner Rule.

Initially, an amount of 80 tons is allocated to cell AR, out of the 100 available in source A, meeting all the demand of destination R.[6] The remaining supply of 20 tons at source A is then allocated to cell AS. The capacity of row A has now been exhausted, but the demand of S has not yet been fully satisfied. Therefore, 100 tons of the 110-ton supply of source B is allocated to cell BS, in order to meet the entire demand of destination S. Then, moving to the right in row B, the remaining supply of B (10 tons) is allocated to cell BT. This exhausts the supply in row B, but the destination T still needs 50 units. Moving down column T, the remainder (50 tons) is allocated to cell DT. In this fashion, the entire supply has been used and the entire demand has been satisifed. Cells that receive allocations are called *occupied* cells to distinguish them from the remaining empty or unoccupied ones.

The initial solution shown in Table 10.8 calls for shipments of:

---

[5] Case of degeneracy, see discussion in Section 10.8.

[6] If the supply of source A were smaller than the demand of R, then the entire supply of A would have been allocated to cell AR.

Compute total cost

80 tons from A to R at a cost of 80 × 1 =	$ 80
20 tons from A to S at a cost of 20 × 2 =	40
100 tons from B to S at a cost of 100 × 1 =	100
10 tons from B to T at a cost of 10 × 5 =	50
50 tons from D to T at no cost =	0
Total cost	$270

Note that warehouse T supposedly obtains 50 tons from D (dummy); that is, there is a shortage (unsatisfied demand) of 50 tons at warehouse T.

Good initial solutions by least-cost

2. The least-cost (largest profit) method The least-cost method yields not only an initial feasible solution but also one that is close to optimal in small problems. The method is "heuristic" (see Chapter 16) in nature. To illustrate the method, another example, using cost data, is shown in Table 10.9.

Solution The least-cost method prescribes that the first allocation be made to the cell with the lowest cost (the highest profit in a maximization case). In this example, there is an additional consideration, since cells AD and CE both have the lowest cost of $1. Cell AD is selected first because more units can be allocated to it (70) than to cell CE (50). Thus, an allocation of 70 is made to cell AD. As a result, the supply of A is reduced to 30 and the demand at D is completely satisfied. *Note:* If a dummy is added, start with one of the dummy cells with a cost of zero.

Next, an allocation of 50 (maximum possible) is made to cell CE, reducing the supply of C to 70. The process continues in this fashion, seeking the unoccupied cell with the lowest cost. The next search yields BF and CF, which each have a cost of $2. (BE is not considered because E is satisfied already.) Cell CF is filled in first, since a larger quantity (120 − 50 = 70) can be placed there. Then the remaining requirement

TABLE 10.9
Initial solution by the least-cost method

Source \ *Destination*	D	E	F	G	Supply
A	[1] 70	[5]	[3]	[4] 30	100
B	[4]	[2]	[2] 30	[5] 30	60
C	[3]	[1] 50	[2] 70	[4]	120
Demand	70	50	100	60	280 \ 280

of 30 for column F is allocated to cell BF and source B's supply is reduced to 30.

Next, an allocation is made to cells with a cost of \$4, since assignment to the cells with a cost of \$3 is not possible under the supply and demand constraints. The only cell with a cost of \$4 to which an assignment can be made is AG. The maximum possible quantity of 30 is assigned there. Finally, the remaining demand (30 in column G) is assigned to BG to complete the initial solution.

Once an initial solution is achieved (by any method), a test for optimality is conducted.

Step 4. Testing for optimality

The purpose of the optimality test is to see if the proposed solution just generated can be improved or not.

"Basic" variables in the occupied cells

The procedure for testing optimality is analogous to that of the simplex method. A distinction is made between *basic* variables, those associated with the occupied cells, and *nonbasic* variables, those associated with the empty cells. For each empty cell, the effect of changing it to an occupied cell is examined. If any of these changes are favorable, the solution is not optimal and a new solution must be designed.[7]

Two procedures for calculating the effect of such a change are:

1. Stepping-stone (discussed next).
2. Modified distribution (MODI) (discussed in Part B).

Degeneracy

Note: In both cases, the solution to be checked for optimality must be nondegenerate; that is:

the number of occupied cells must be $m + n - 1$

where m = number of sources and n = number of destinations. The reason for this and a method to handle degeneracy are given in Section 10.8.

The stepping-stone procedure

Example (Tuff's problem) Table 10.8 (reproduced in Table 10.10) presents the initial (Northwest Corner) solution to Tuff's problem.

The **stepping-stone procedure** executes the final *two steps* of the transportation method.

Step 4: Testing for optimality. This is done by calculating the **cell evaluators** for all the empty cells.

[7] A favorable change means an increase in the value of the objective function in maximization problems or a decrease in minimization problems.

TABLE 10.10
Table 10.8 reproduced

Source \ Destination	R	S	T	Supply
A	[1] 80	[2] 20	[3]	100
B	[4]	[1] 100	[5] 10	110
D (dummy)	[0]	[0]	[0] 50	50
Demand	80	120	60	260

Step 5: Improving a nonoptimal solution. This is done by:

1. Identifying the incoming cell.
2. Designing an improved solution.

Finding the cell evaluator from a closed loop

Details of Step 4: Start with building a path that forms a closed loop. A cell evaluator for an empty cell is a number designating the cost change that results from occupying that cell (that is, shipping one unit through it) rather than one of the currently occupied cells. In order to occupy an empty cell, a transfer has to be made from a currently occupied cell. Such a transfer, subject to the supply and demand constraints, will affect an even number of four or more cells. The evaluator is calculated by determining the overall effect on the total cost of shifting *one unit* to that empty cell. The signs of the cell evaluators enable us to test for optimality.

TABLE 10.11
Evaluation of cell AT

Source \ *Destination*	R	S	T	Supply
A	[1] 80	(19) [2] 20 −	(1) [3] + ⇒ Start	100
B	[4]	(101) [1] 100 +	(9) [5] 10 −	110
D (dummy)	[0]	[0]	[0] 50	50
Demand	80	120	60	260

Shifting one unit

Gaining and losing cells

In Table 10.11 a demonstration is given of how to calculate the cell evaluator for the empty cell AT using either cell AS or BT. Using AS to demonstrate, one unit is moved from the occupied cell AS to AT (follow the top double arrow). Cell AT is called the *gaining cell* and a "+" sign is placed there; cell AS is labeled the *losing cell* and a "−" sign is placed there. However, since one unit is moved to cell AT, column T will now have 1 + 10 + 50 = 61, which is more than the 60 required. Therefore, in order to maintain the demand requirement, one unit is moved from the occupied cell, BT, to occupied cell BS (follow bottom double arrow). The new number of units in each cell is now circled.

As a result of this transaction, the row supply requirements are maintained:

For row A: 80 + (19) + (1) = 100
For row B: (101) + (9) = 110

and so are the column demands:

For column S: (19) + (101) = 120
For column T: (1) + (9) + 50 = 60

For entire movement process is indicated by a **closed loop** of arrows. Such a closed loop will involved at least four, and sometimes more, cells. *Note:* The direction of all arrows can be reversed by moving the one unit from BT to AT.

Stepping over cells

Rule for drawing each closed loop

When tracing a closed loop, start with the empty cell to be evaluated and, going clockwise, draw an arrow from it to an *occupied cell* in the same row (or column). Next, move vertically or horizontally (but never diagonally) to another *occupied* cell, "stepping over" unoccupied or occupied cells (if necessary) without changing them. Follow the same procedure to other occupied cells until returning to the original empty cell. At each turn of the loop (the loop may cross over itself at times), plus and minus signs are alternately placed in the cells, starting with a + sign in the empty cell. One further important restriction is that there must be exactly one cell with a + sign and exactly one cell with a − sign in any row or column in which the loop turns. This restriction is imposed to ensure that the requirements of supply and demand will not be violated when the units are shifted. Note that an even number of at least four cells must participate in a loop and the occupied cells can be visited once and only once. Also, in a nondegenerate problem, there is only one possible way of drawing the loop for each empty cell. Finally, remember that all cells that receive a + or −, except the first one, must be occupied.

Evaluation of Cell AT. Let us calculate the cost effect of the changes arising from the decision to ship one unit to the empty cell AT. In cells AT and BS, one unit is added, so the additional cost is 3 + 1 = 4. In cells BT and AS, one unit is deleted, and the cost is reduced by 5 + 2 = 7. Thus, by executing this exchange, we simultaneously *increase* the total cost by 4 and *reduce* the total cost by 7; that is, we alter the total cost by 4 − 7 = −3.

This value of −3 is then the *cell evaluator* of cell AT. The minus sign indicates a *possible cost reduction;* that is, the solution tested is improvable and therefore not optimal.

Cell evaluator

How to find the value of a cell evaluator

The value of a cell evaluator is the sum of the per unit shipping costs in the gaining cells less the sum of the per unit shipping costs in the losing cells of the closed loop.

This evaluation process must now be extended to *all* unoccupied cells.

Evaluation of Cell DR (involving six cells). In Table 10.12, the test is applied to cell DR. This time six cells participate in the evaluation.

TABLE 10.12
Evaluation of cell DR

Source \ Destination	R	S	T	Supply
A	[1] ~~80~~ (79) −	[2] ~~20~~ +(21)	[3]	100
B	[4]	[1] (99) − ~~100~~	[5] (11) + ~~10~~	110
D (dummy)	[0] (1) + Start	[0]	[0] ~~50~~ −(49)	50
Demand	80	120	60	260

A move of one unit to DR will result in the addition of one unit to AS and BT and deletion of one unit each from AR, BS, and DT. The total cost impact of this closed loop is:

Gaining (+) cells	Added cost	Losing (−) cells	Saved cost
DR	0	AR	1
AS	2	BS	1
BT	5	DT	0
Total	7	Total	2

Thus, such a move will add to the value of the objective function a cost of 7 (from the gaining cells) and subtract a cost of 2 (from the losing cells). The value of the cell evaluator DR is hence $7 - 2 = +5$. The plus sign indicates that a transfer to this cell increases cost and is *not* favorable since it will *increase* the value of the objective function by 5.

Another way to interpret this situation is: A gaining cell (cell with a + sign) means an *increase* in the value of the objective function and a losing cell (− sign) means a *decrease*. Since the total increase (7) is larger than the total decrease (2), the value of the objective function will *increase* by $7 - 2 = 5$, an undesirable case in *minimization*.

Cost analysis. By drawing these closed loops, *all* the empty cells of Table 10.12 can be evaluated. The results (details not shown) are:

Empty cell	Cell evaluator
AT	−3
BR	+4
DR	+5
DS	+4

Test of optimality. Once the cell evaluators for *all* the empty cells have been computed, their signs are examined.

Test for a minimization (cost) problem:[8]

If one or more of the cell evaluators is negative, the existing solution is not optimal.[9]

A minus evaluator means a possible cost reduction

The logic for this test is that an empty cell (not presently part of the solution) with a negative cell evaluator will reduce the total cost if it becomes occupied. The present solution is thus *improvable* and therefore not optimal.

[8] The test of optimality for a maximization (profit) case is reversed; that is, if any cell evaluator is positive, the solution is not optimal. A positive profit evaluator would mean an empty cell could thus increase the profit.

[9] A cell evaluator of 0 indicates the existence of another solution just as good as the current solution. Thus, in the final solution, if cell evaluators of 0 exist, this indicates the existence of multiple optimal solutions.

In the example just presented, cell AT has a negative evaluator. Thus, the initial solution of Table 10.8 is *not optimal*.

Note: Two options exist for the analysis:

1. Check empty cells until you find an improvable one and improve it. This option is less efficient than the next.
2. Check *all* the empty cells and select for improvement the one with the *largest* improvement potential. This second option is particularly efficient in large problems.

Step 5. Improving a nonoptimal solution

Having discovered that a solution is *not* optimal, the next step in the transportation method is to find a better solution. The operations in this step are:

1. Identify the "incoming" cell (empty cell to be occupied). In a minimization case, the "incoming" cell is located by identifying the *most negative* cell evaluator.[10] In the example, the incoming cell is AT (since only one cell has a negative evaluator).
2. *Design an improved solution*. Once the "incoming" cell has been identified, an improvement is made by shifting *as many units as possible*, along the closed loop, into that empty cell. The quantity limit to this shifting process is reached when one of the "losing" cells becomes empty.[11] In our case, of the two "losing" cells in Table 10.11, AS and BT, cell BT becomes empty first, when 10 units are shifted around the closed loop (10 from BT to BS, 10 from AS to AT).

Shifting units from cell to cell

Rule for shifting units

In general, compare the number of units among all losing cells (−) in the loop of the most improvable empty cell (AT in our case). Select the *smallest* number (10 in this case). Add this number to all cells with a + sign and subtract it from all cells with a − sign. The result here is given in Table 10.13.

Once an improved solution is generated, the optimality test (step 4) is repeated.

Optimality test The evaluators of all the empty cells are again computed for the improved solution of Table 10.13. The results (details not shown) are:

---

[10] If two or more cells have the same value, then either may be selected.

[11] If two or more of the "losing" cells contain the same number of units, both will become empty simultaneously and a "degenerate" solution will result (see discussion in Part B of this chapter).

TABLE 10.13
Improved solution

Source \ Destination	R	S	T	Supply
A	[1] 80	[2] − 20 − 10 = 10	[3] + 0 + 10 = 10	100
B	[4]	[1] + 100 + 10 = 110	[5] − 10 − 10 = 0	110
D (dummy)	[0]	[0]	[0] 50	50
Demand	80	120	60	260

Empty cell	*Cell evaluator*
BR	+4
BT	+3
DR	+2
DS	+1

Since *all* the empty cells have nonnegative cell evaluators, an optimal solution has been obtained. This optimal solution calls for a shipment of:

The total cost

80 units from A to R at a cost of \$1/ton, total	\$ 80
10 units from A to S at a cost of \$2/ton, total	20
10 units from A to T at a cost of \$3/ton, total	30
110 units from B to S at a cost of \$1/ton, total	110
50 units from dummy to T at no cost	0
Total cost	\$240

This, compared with the original solution, represents a reduction in cost of \$30. Notice that the demand requirements of destination T have, in reality, not been completely satisfied, since 50 units are shipped to T out of the dummy source D.

The maximization case If a transportation problem involves maximization, the same method can be used. The only difference is the test of optimality. A *positive* cell evaluator points to an improvement. An optimal solution will show no positive cell evaluators.

MODI for large problems

The stepping-stone method is efficient for small-sized transportation problems. For larger problems, however, the **MODI** method is recommended (see Part B).

Summary of the stepping-stone method

1. Compute the cell evaluators for all empty cells. This is done by subtracting the total cost of the losing cells from that of the gaining cells in the closed loop.
2. If *all* cell evaluators are nonnegative (in a minimization case), then the solution is optimal. Otherwise an improvement (or alternate solution in the case of 0 evaluators) is possible.
3. Generating an improved solution involves identifying the incoming cell (that cell with the largest cost reduction potential for minimization problems) and transferring *as much as possible* to it. Once this has been done, a new solution is generated by adjusting the quantities in all losing and gaining cells along the loop.
4. The improved solution is then tested. If it is not optimal, another improvement is made. Eventually, an optimal solution (if one exists) will be reached.

Some notes on transporation problems

Prohibited or impossible transportation routes There are cases where shipments from a certain source to a certain destination are not possible, due to a physical or legal obstacle. In this case, the appropriate cell may either be completely crossed out or a *very large* per unit transportation cost assigned to it *(M)*. (In maximization problems assign $-M$; see Problem 13 for an example.)

Multiple optimal solutions A solution to a transportation problem can be either *unique* or multiple. An example of a multiple optimal solution (minimization) is given below.

30 (cost 6)	20 (cost 8)	50
(cost 5)	40 (cost 7)	40
30	60	

or:

(cost 6)	50 (cost 8)	50
30 (cost 5)	10 (cost 7)	40
30	60	

These situations are indicated when the value of one of the cell evaluators is zero.

Transshipment In a typical transportation problem, we do not allow shipments between sources, between destinations, or from destinations to sources. If such shipments are permissible, we have a *transshipment* problem.

"Capacited" transportation problems In some cases, there are upper capacity limits on the amounts that can be shipped by a certain route. In other cases, a minimum amount must be shipped from some source to some destination. In these situations, the problem should be transformed into a regular LP problem and the additional requirements added as constraints.

10.3 APPLICATIONS

The commonality of transportation-type problems

Several production planning problems, routing problems, and scheduling problems can be formulated as transportation problems, thus increasing the applicability of the model.

Example 1: Production scheduling Three garment plants are available for monthly production of four styles of men's shirts. The capacities of the three plants are 45,000, 93,000, and 60,000 shirts. The number of shirts required in styles *a* through *d* are 28,000, 65,000, 35,000, and 70,000, respectively. The profits, in dollars per shirt, at each plant for each style are shown in Table 10.14.

TABLE 10.14
The garment plants' profits

Plant \ *Style*	*a*	*b*	*c*	*d*
1	8	12	−2	6
2	13	4	3	10
3	0	7	11	8

Find how many shirts to produce in each plant of each type, so that profit is maximized.

Formulation as a transportation problem. Let the plants be considered as "sources" and the styles as "destinations." The capacities of the plants are the supply, and the required number of shirts of each style are the demand. The transportation table that describes the production scheduling problem is shown in Table 10.15. Note that this is a *maximization* problem.

A maximization problem

Solution. Solving by the stepping-stone method, the results are:

Plant 1	manufactures 45,000 of style *b*
Plant 2	manufactures 28,000 of style *a* and 65,000 of style *d*
Plant 3	manufactures 20,000 of style *b*, 35,000 of style *c* and 5,000 of style *d*
Total profit	$2,119,000

TABLE 10.15

Plant \ *Style*	a	b	c	d	Supply
1	8	12	−2	6	45,000
2	13	4	3	10	93,000
3	0	7	11	8	60,000
Requirements	28,000	65,000	35,000	70,000	198,000

Example 2: International trade Three countries, the United States, the Soviet Union, and the United Kingdom, all both use and grow rice, soybeans, and corn. It is known how much labor is needed to produce one ton of each crop per acre in each country. What is the best domestic planting and import program for each country that makes most efficient use of labor but also satisfies all demand?

The data are given in Table 10.16, where the data in the upper right-hand boxes are the labor costs per ton per acre. Each x_{ij} in the final solution will give the amount of crop i to be raised by country j so as to gain the greatest "comparative advantage" with respect to labor (tariffs and transportation costs are not considered). This is a minimization problem, of course.

Solution. The United States should grow 44 million acres of rice, 16 of soybeans, and 30 of corn. The Soviet Union should grow 12 million acres of soybeans, and the United Kingdom should grow 48 million acres of rice. The total labor cost of all three countries is 1,208 (million).

Example 3: Multiperiod production scheduling The transportation method can be applied to certain multiperiod problems. As an example, consider a production situation where we are dealing with a single plant and a single commodity, but different methods of producing the commodity

TABLE 10.16
International trade

Crop \ *Country*	U.S.	USSR	U.K.	Demand (millions of acres)
Rice	8	13	9	92
Soybeans	7	11	9	28
Corn	6	12	8	30
Acres available (millions)	90	12	48	150

and different periods of demand. The formulation of the transportation matrix is shown in Table 10.17. The objective is to minimize the costs of monthly production plus storage, subject to the constraints of meeting monthly sales demands, capacity limitations, and desired initial and ending inventory levels.

The "sources" are the different production methods in the various periods and can include such methods as regular time production, overtime production, subcontracting, extra shifts, back ordering, and inventory stockpiling between periods. Constraints on productive capacity may also be included but the problem then may require a regular LP formulation (see Problem 18). The "destinations" are the different monthly demands, where September represents the required ending August inventory. A dummy

TABLE 10.17
Multiperiod scheduling

		June	July	August	(September)	Unused	Available
	Beginning Inventory	0	2	4	6	0	200
June	Regular time	50	52	54	56	0	500
	Overtime	60	62	64	66	0	100
	Subcontract	65	67	69	71	0	300
July	Regular time	55	50	52	54	0	500
	Overtime	65	60	62	64	0	100
	Subcontract	70	65	67	69	0	300
August	Regular time*	60	55	50	52	0	250
	Overtime*	70	65	60	62	0	50
	Subcontract	75	70	65	67	0	300
	Demand	1,000	700	500	150	250	2,600

*Two-week vacation in August.

column ("Unused") picks up any slack in the productive abilities of the sources, shown in the far right column as "available."

The cost of using each supply source for each of the month's sales is shown in the appropriate cell. Note that backordering is possible (e.g., July production for June), but at a cost of 5 extra per unit per month. Subcontracting is also possible for future months, but with an inventory carrying charge of 2 per unit per month, as with regular production.

The solution to the example is assigned as a problem in Section 10.6 (Problem 19).

10.4 THE ASSIGNMENT PROBLEM

A second type of distribution problem is the "assignment" problem. Let us illustrate with an example.

Example

The management of a utility company wants to assign three service teams to three geographical zones, one team to each zone. Because of each team's differing familiarity with each zone, there are differences in the efficiency of each team, a fact that is reflected in the different service costs, that are shown in Table 10.18. For example, assigning team S_2 to zone Z_3 will result in a cost of $33,000. The problem is to find that assignment that minimizes the total cost.

Find the least-cost match

TABLE 10.18
Service costs of different team assignments ($ in thousands)

Service team \ *Zone*	Z_1	Z_2	Z_3
S_1	20	15	31
S_2	17	16	33
S_3	18	19	27

Characteristics of the assignment problem

The problem just presented is typical of a class of managerial problems with the following characteristics:

1. The objects under consideration, such as service teams, jobs, employees, or projects, are finite in number.
2. The objects have to be assigned on a *one-to-one* basis to other objects. **One-to-one basis**
3. The result of each assignment can be expressed in terms of payoffs such as costs or profits.

TABLE 10.19
The assignment table

Service team \ *Zone*	Z_1	Z_2	Z_3	Supply
S_1	20	15	31	1
S_2	17	16	33	1
S_3	18	19	27	1
Demand	1	1	1	

4. The aim is to assign all objects (if possible) in such a way that the total cost is minimized (or the total profit is maximized).

Assignment—a common problem

Several practical allocation problems can appear as assignment-type problems. For example, a supervisor assigns subordinates to various jobs every morning, an employment agency matches employees and employers, a real estate agency matches houses to potential buyers, and teachers are assigned to classes.

Presentation of the assignment problem

Assignment problem is a type of transportation problem

1. *Table form.* The assignment problem is usually arranged in a tabular form. For example, Table 10.19 presents the utility company problem of Table 10.18. The assignment table is very similar to the transportation table. Indeed, the assignment problem is considered as a special transportation problem in which the supply at each source and the demand at each destination are always one unit.[12] As in the transportation problem, assignment problems can be balanced or not. In a balanced case, the number of objects to be assigned equals the number of objects to which they are assigned. Unbalanced problems can be balanced by adding a dummy (or dummies) with zero cost coefficients.

2. *Presentation as a linear program.* The assignment problem can also be presented as a linear programming problem with the following formulation.[13]

---

[12] Since the supply and demand are always equal to one unit in each row and column, there is no need to write them in the assignment table.

[13] Let c_{ij} be the *cost* associated with an assignment of i to j. The assignment problem can then be stated as follows:

$$\text{minimize } z = \sum_{i=1}^{m} \sum_{j=1}^{n} c_{ij} x_{ij}$$

subject to the linear constraints (in a balanced case):

The decision variables Let x_{ij} be an assignment of the ith source (i.e., service team) to the jth destination (i.e., zone). Each of these decision variables can take only one of two values: zero or one. We assign the value of $x_{ij} = 1$ if there is a match between i and j. The value $x_{ij} = 0$ means no match. No other value can be assigned.

The objective function The objective function expresses the total cost (or profit) of the assignment.

The constraints There are two types of constraints: supply and demand.

Example The utility company's problem is presented as a linear program.

$$\text{minimize } z = 20x_{11} + 15x_{12} + 31x_{13} + 17x_{21} + 16x_{22} + 33x_{23} + 18x_{31} + 19x_{32} + 27x_{33}$$

subject to:

$$\left.\begin{aligned} x_{11} + x_{12} + x_{13} &= 1 \\ x_{21} + x_{22} + x_{23} &= 1 \\ x_{31} + x_{32} + x_{33} &= 1 \end{aligned}\right\} \quad \text{(supply constraints)}$$

and to:

$$\left.\begin{aligned} x_{11} + x_{21} + x_{31} &= 1 \\ x_{12} + x_{22} + x_{32} &= 1 \\ x_{13} + x_{23} + x_{33} &= 1 \end{aligned}\right\} \quad \text{(demand constraints)}$$

and: x_{ij} either 0 or 1 for all i, j.

Since all x_{ij} can be either 0 or 1, there will be only one assignment in each supply constraint and one assignment in each demand constraint.

Unbalanced problems

Balancing an assignment problem

Notice that the constraints in the linear programming formulation are given as equations. The reason this can be done is that the problem is balanced. In an unbalanced problem, the number of items to be assigned differs from the number of objects to be assigned to and must be balanced before proceeding. The balancing is done by adding dummy supply or demand items. For example, if there are three jobs to be done on five machines, two dummy jobs must be added. A machine matched with a dummy job will, of course, in actuality be matched with nothing. Therefore, the cost (or profit) of such a match is considered to be zero.

$$\sum_{j=1}^{n} x_{ij} = 1 \qquad i = 1,2,\ldots, m$$
$$\sum_{i=1}^{m} x_{ij} = 1 \qquad j = 1,2,\ldots, n \qquad (9.4)$$

and x_{ij} can take either the value of 1 or the value of zero.

TABLE 10.20
Assignment alternative solutions (by enumeration)

Alternative	*Combination*	*Total cost*	
1	S_1Z_1 S_2Z_2 S_3Z_3	20 + 16 + 27 = 63	
2	S_1Z_1 S_3Z_2 S_2Z_3	20 + 19 + 33 = 72	
3	S_2Z_1 S_1Z_2 S_3Z_3	17 + 15 + 27 = 59	← *Minimum*
4	S_2Z_1 S_3Z_2 S_1Z_3	17 + 19 + 31 = 67	
5	S_3Z_1 S_2Z_2 S_1Z_3	18 + 16 + 31 = 65	
6	S_3Z_1 S_1Z_2 S_2Z_3	18 + 15 + 33 = 66	

Balancing of the problem is only required for the **Hungarian method** (to be presented next). If a conversion to linear programming is used, the following rules apply.

If there are more rows (items) to be assigned than columns, then all the supply constraints will be of the ≤ type and all the demand constraints will be of the = type (i.e., not all items will be assigned). If there are more columns, then all the demand constraints will be of the ≤ type and all the supply constraints will be of the = type.

Methods for solving assignment problems

n! solutions

Complete enumeration The assignment problem is usually a balanced problem with n items to be assigned to n objects. As such there are $n!$ (n factorial) different solutions to the problem. One way to find the optimal solution is to list and compare *all* $n!$ solutions. This is called a complete enumeration approach. However, it is often impractical because the number of solutions for even a relatively small problem is unmanageably large.[14] For the problem presented in Table 10.19, there are only 3! or 6 solutions. These are listed in Table 10.20. Comparing all the possibilities indicates that alternative 3, which yields 59 (i.e., $59,000), is the optimal solution.

The simplex method The simplex method can be used, but it is rather inefficient for solving the assignment problem.[15]

The transportation model Any assignment problem can be solved by the transportation method, since the assignment problem is a special case of the transportation problem. However, there are more efficient methods.

"Near-optimal" methods Various computational methods are available for arriving at a near-optimal solution in a rapid way. These are mainly heuristic in nature (see Chapter 16).

Branch and bound In Chapter 8 there is an illustration of how the branch and bound method can be used to solve the assignment problem.

[14] For example, for $n = 10$, $n! = 3{,}628{,}800$. These can be enumerated in seconds by a high-speed computer. However, for a larger n, say 20, even a computer is overwhelmed.

[15] For example, an assignment problem of 10 × 10 will be transformed to a linear program with 100 variables, 20 constraints, and 20 slack (or artificial) variables resulting in a large matrix. The simplex method is much slower than the Hungarian method.

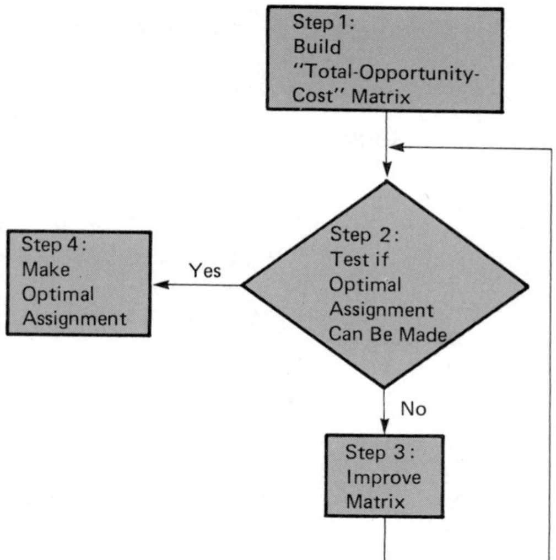

FIGURE 10.3
Solution steps for the assignment problem

The Hungarian method The Hungarian method is the most efficient way of solving large assignment problems.[16]

The Hungarian method

First, balance the matrix

The Hungarian method is a fast, efficient solution procedure for solving large, balanced assignment problems. The procedure is based on the following theorem:

> If one subtracts (or adds) a constant number from all entries in any row or column of the assignment matrix, then the total cost of each of the *n!* possible assignments is reduced (or increased) by the constant number subtracted (or added).

Therefore, one can make these additions or subtractions to rows or columns without changing the ultimate optimal assignment. The total costs are changed, but not the *relative* ones. The Hungarian method is next illustrated for the case of *cost* minimization.

The procedure The solution procedure involves four major steps, as shown in Figure 10.3.

Example The method will be illustrated with the example in Table 10.19.

[16] Named after the Hungarian mathematician Konig, who first proved (1916) a theorem necessary to the development of the method.

A total opportunity cost matrix

Step 1: Build the "total opportunity cost" matrix. This step involves the transformation of the cost matrix to what is termed a *total opportunity cost* matrix. It involves two operations.

First, the element with the lowest value (including zero and negative numbers, where negative numbers represent profit, in a cost table, or cost, in a profit table) in each row is subtracted from all the other elements in that row. All negative numbers *disappear* in this step. For example, in the first row of Table 10.19, the lowest element is 15. The entire operation is shown in Table 10.21.

TABLE 10.21

20 − 15 = 5	15 − 15 = 0	31 − 15 = 16		5	0	16
17 − 16 = 1	16 − 16 = 0	33 − 16 = 17	→	1	0	17
18 − 18 = 0	19 − 18 = 1	27 − 18 = 9		0	1	9

New Matrix

Second, the smallest element (including zero) in each column of the new matrix is subtracted from all the elements of that column. The result is the total-opportunity-cost matrix as shown in Table 10.22.

TABLE 10.22
Total opportunity cost matrix

5 − 0 = 5	0 − 0 = 0	16 − 9 = 7		5	0	7
1 − 0 = 1	0 − 0 = 0	17 − 9 = 8	→	1	0	8
0 − 0 = 0	1 − 0 = 1	9 − 9 = 0		0	1	0

Notice that this matrix now contains *at least* one zero in each row and column

Step 2: The optimality test. Since all entries in the total opportunity cost matrix are nonnegative, the minimum value of the objective function (i.e., total cost) *cannot* be negative, no matter what assignments are made. Hence, the *minimum possible* cost is zero in the relative terms of the new table; the *real* cost with the *real* solution will, of course, be greater. Therefore, *if* a feasible assignment with a total opportunity cost of zero is found, this assignment must have the *lowest possible cost;* that is, it is optimal.

The "lowest possible cost" can be achieved if all the values in the cells where assignments are made are zeros. Thus, in testing for optimality, one needs to know whether there are enough zeros in the table to permit a "zero" assignment for each row and each column.

Rather than using the trial and error approach, we use a simple procedure that tests whether this can be done.

Draw the minimum number of lines

1. Draw the *minimum* necessary number of straight lines, horizontally and vertically, so that all zeros in the matrix are covered. Draw the lines by trial and error but always try to cover two or more zeros with one line.
2. Count the number of these lines. If it equals n (the number of rows or columns), an optimal assignment can be made. If it is smaller than n, an improvement is possible.

Note: In some cases, there are several alternative ways of drawing the minimum number of lines. Any of these may be chosen.

Let us find the minimum number of lines necessary to cover all the zeros in our case. The total opportunity cost matrix of Table 10.22 is reproduced in Table 10.23.

TABLE 10.23
The optimality test

Service team \ *Zone*	Z_1	Z_2	Z_3
S_1	5	0	7
S_2	1	0	8
S_3	0	1	0

Note that the table has four "zero" cells. It is possible to cover all the zeros with two lines (shown as dashed lines in Table 10.23); one through row S_3 and the other through column Z_2. According to the optimality test, since only two lines are needed to cover all the zeros, an optimal assignment cannot be made at this stage and an improved solution is possible.

Step 3: Improve the total opportunity cost matrix. An improved total opportunity cost matrix is derived by the following three operations:

An improved solution

1. Find the *smallest* entry in the *uncovered* cells (cells with no lines through them) and subtract it from *all* entries in the uncovered cells. In our case, the lowest entry is 1 (cell S_2Z_1).
2. Add the same *smallest* entry to those cells in which the lines intersect (cells with two lines through them). In our case, there is only one such cell, S_3Z_2.
3. Cells with one line through them, such as S_1Z_2, are transferred unchanged to the improved table.

The result is the *first improved total opportunity cost matrix*, Table 10.24. The *optimality test* is now applied to this matrix. Using the line-

TABLE 10.24
First operation for the improved matrix

Service team \ Zone	Z_1	Z_2	Z_3
S_1	$5 - 1 = 4$	0	$7 - 1 = 6$
S_2	$1 - 1 = 0$	0	$8 - 1 = 7$
S_3	0	$1 + 1 = 2$	0

TABLE 10.25
First improved total opportunity cost matrix

Team \ Zone	Z_1	Z_2	Z_3
S_1	4	[0]	6
S_2	[0]	0	7
S_3	0	2	[0]

drawing procedure of step 2, a minimum of *three* lines is needed to cover all the zeros in Table 10.25. This means that an optimal assignment can now be made.

In those problems where the first improvement *does not yield* an optimal solution, we *keep on* improving the solution (by repeating step 3) until an optimal solution is achieved.

Step 4: Make an optimal assignment. An optimal assignment should be made to cells with a zero entry, maintaining the one-to-one requirement. If only one solution exists, a fast procedure for finding it is to locate a row or column with only one zero in it and make that assignment. Then drop that row and column from the matrix and repeat the procedure. If the solution is *not* unique, there will be two or more zeros in a column or row to choose from. The choice, then, is arbitrary.

Multiple solution are possible

The optimal assignment for our example is shown in Table 10.25 (squares around the zeros): S_1 to Z_2, S_2 to Z_1, and S_3 to Z_3. The total cost in this case is $15 + 17 + 27 = 59$ (thousand dollars). If more than one optimal solution exists, a trial-and-error approach can be used to find all possible combination assignments in the zero cells.

The maximization case

Convert to minimization

The example just demonstrated was a minimization one. In maximization cases, a convenient solution procedure involves transforming the prob-

TABLE 10.26

	R	S	T
A	8	6	10
B	11	9	6
C	4	7	5

a. Maximize (before transformation)

	R	S	T
A	11 − 8 = 3	11 − 6 = 5	11 − 10 = 1
B	11 − 11 = 0	11 − 9 = 2	11 − 6 = 5
C	11 − 4 = 7	11 − 7 = 4	11 − 5 = 6

b. Minimize (after transformation)

lem into a minimization problem (an opportunity loss table) by the following procedure (see example in Table 10.26).

1. Find the largest profit coefficient in the entire table (11 here).
2. Subtract each entry in the original table from the largest profit coefficient (see Table 10.26b).

Once the transformed table is constructed, the Hungarian method can then be employed to solve the problem. Once a solution is obtained, the total profit can be computed using the original profit coefficients in the original table.

The process of the Hungarian method is summarized in Figure 10.4.

Notes

Impossible assignment If a certain match is not feasible, assign a large cost (M) to this cell. In maximization, a large loss (−M) is assigned.

Multiple solutions These are very common in assignment problems and occur when there are alternative ways to assign the zeros.

Line drawing The following is an alternative procedure that guarantees that the minimum number of lines are drawn and simultaneously identifies unique allocations: Draw lines at right angles to unique zeros, progressively reducing the matrix of uncovered zeros, until no more unique zeros remain, leaving either the unique optimal solution or alternative solutions (pairs).

10.5 CONCLUDING REMARKS

The transportation and assignment models introduced in this chapter are special cases of linear programming. However, formulation and solution of such problems in the format of linear programming is too cumbersome. Due to their special structure, these problems are formulated as special algorithms that are extremely efficient when compared to the linear programming format. The larger the problem, the greater is the advantage of the special algorithms.

In addition to actual transportation problems, there are several production and scheduling problems that can be formulated as transportation-type problems, thus increasing the applicability of the model.

FIGURE 10.4
Flowchart of the Hungarian method

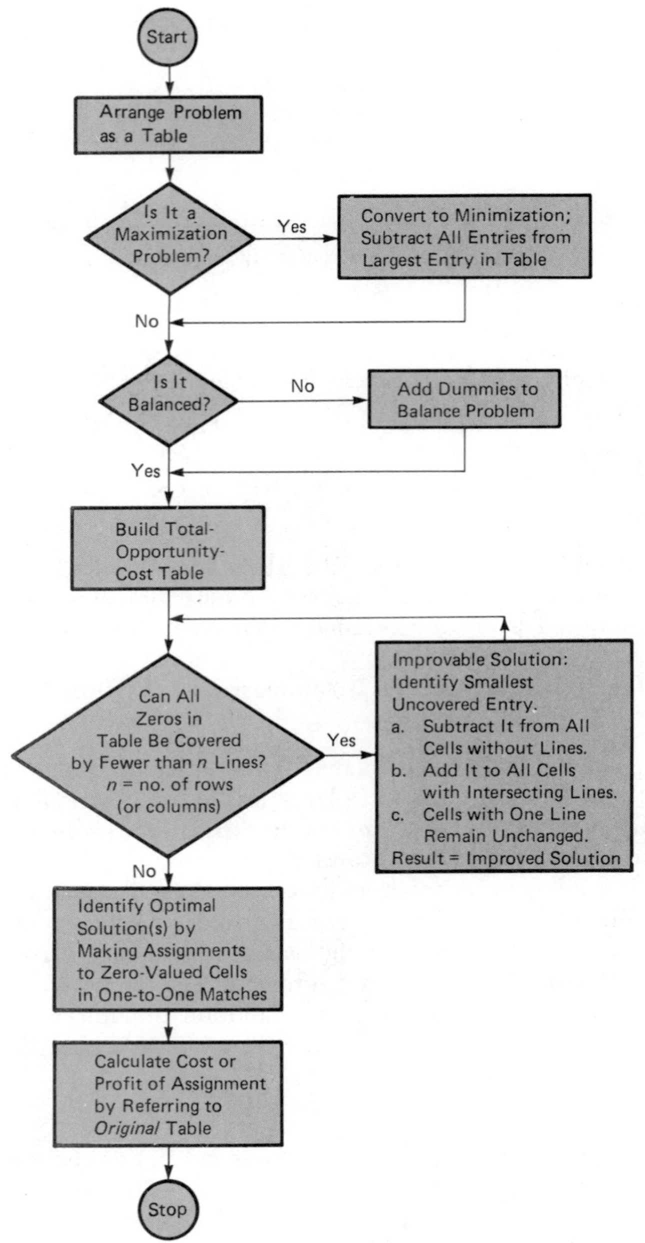

10.6 PROBLEMS FOR PART A

1. Solve the transportation problem (with cost coefficients).

From \ To	1	2	3	Supply
A	67	42	51	250
B	61	24	39	400
C	29	47	60	300
D	43	31	42	200
Demand	400	150	600	1150

   a. Find an initial solution using the least-cost method.
   b. Find the optimal solution (use the stepping-stone method).

2. Given a transportation problem (with cost coefficients):

Sources \ Destinations	1	2	3	4	Supply
A	1	5	3	4	100
B	4	2	2	4	60
C	3	1	2	4	120
Demand	70	50	100	60	280

   a. Find an initial solution by the Northwest Corner Rule.
   b. Find an initial solution by the least-cost method.
   c. Find an optimal solution by the stepping-stone method: Start with the results of part *(a)*.
   d. Are there any other optimal solutions?
   e. Based on findings of part *(d)*, comment on the number of occupied cells in an optimal solution.

3. The Aztec Silver Mine has two operating mines in Chile and three distributing warehouses located in different parts of South America. The company ships the ore by trucks. The capacity of mine 1 is 500 tons a week and that of mine 2 is 1,300 tons per week. The weekly sales potential of the three warehouses is 1,200 tons, 500 tons, and 700 tons. The shipping cost per ton from each mine to each warehouse is given below:

From mine number	*To warehouse number*	*Shipping cost (pesos per ton)*
1	1	8
1	2	13
1	3	9
2	1	11
2	2	14
2	3	5

Find the best shipment schedule if the company's objective is to minimize the transportation cost.

   a. Formulate as a transportation model.
   b. Solve the problem (start with northwest corner).

4. Given below a transportation problem with *profit* coefficients:
   a. Find the best solution (start with the northwest corner).
   b. Present as a linear programming problem (do not solve).

From \ To	1	2	Supply
A	6	4	50
B	3	5	80
C	8	7	60
D	5	9	40
Demand	80	100	

5. Continental Electric Company buys fuel once a month for its five operational zones. Demand (in hundreds of thousands of drums) in each of the zones is given below:

Zone	Demand
A	28
B	60
C	36
D	45
E	16
Total	185

There are three bidders who wish to supply the demand: one in Texas, one in California, and one in Canada. The prices per drum (FOB) and the maximum quantities available (in hundreds of thousands of drums) are given below:

	Price	*Maximum supply*
California	$10.00	80
Texas	11.50	60
Canada	9.50	120

Transportation costs between each bidder and each zone are given below (in $ per drum):

From \ *To zone*	A	B	C	D	E
California	1.8	1.6	1.3	.6	.3
Texas	1.6	1.2	.9	.2	.6
Canada	.8	1.0	1.1	1.2	1.6

Bids can be accepted for the entire quantity or for portions of it. Continental Electric's objective is to supply all demand in all zones at minimal total cost. Find the contract award policy that Continental Electric should follow.

6. The Pollution Control Board of Prado Province has 100 employees: 20 live in city A, 35 in City B, and 45 in city C. The employees have interchangeable skills and are to be assigned to various laboratories. The Water Laboratory requires 40 employees, the Air Lab requires 30 employees, the Solid Waste Lab requires 20 employees, and the Central Lab requires 10 employees. The distance between the cities and the labs is shown on the map below (in miles along the available streets).

   Workers travel by the shortest available route along the streets shown. What worker-to-lab arrangement minimizes the total distances traveled by all the employees?

   a. Formulate as a transportation problem.

   b. Solve.

   c. What assumptions are necessary in this case?

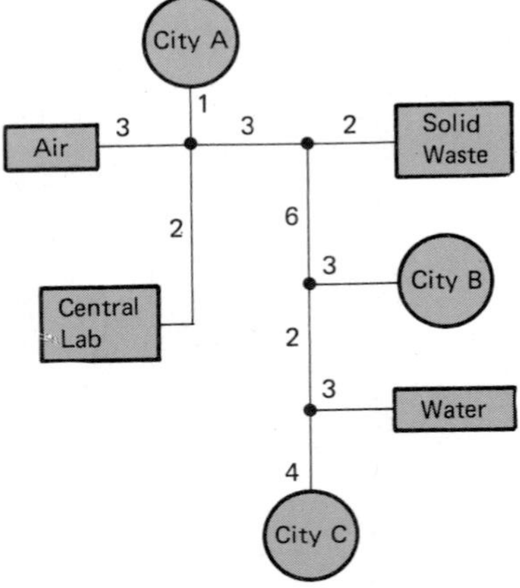

7. A firm owns facilities at five geographically remote locations. It has manufacturing plants at points *A* and *B* with daily production capacities of 60 and 40 units, respectively. At points *C*, *D*, and *E* it has warehouses with daily demands of 20, 30, and 50 units, respectively. Shipping costs between these points are exactly proportional to the distances between them, which are indicated in miles below:

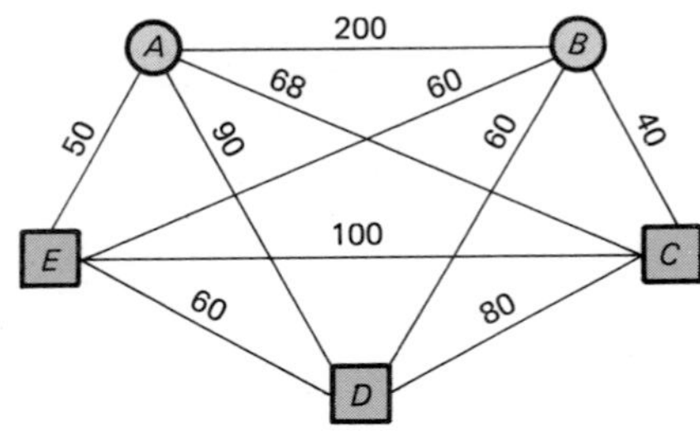

   a. Given that the firm wishes to minimize its total transportation costs, formulate as a transportation problem.

   b. Find the optimal solution; use the least-cost method to generate an initial solution.

   Note: Shipments between plants, and also between warehouses, are prohibited.

8. The energy czar is planning shipments of gasoline from two sources to three destinations. Per ton transportation costs are given in the following table:

From \ To	C	D	E
A	6	7	9
B	9	4	6

There are 1,000 tons available at A and 1,300 available at B. Since the destinations want as much as possible, the czar has decided to ship out *all* available quantities. His object is to minimize total shipment cost.

a. Formulate as a transportation problem.
b. Solve.
c. Formulate in a linear programming format.

9. Taiwan Electronics produces three models of CB radios; A, B, and C. The estimated demand for the three models is 10,000, 12,000, and 7,000 units, respectively. The radios can be produced on one of four available production lines: Q, R, S, and T, whose production capacities are: 6,000, 15,000, 20,000, and 5,000 units, respectively. The manufacturing costs vary among the production lines and are shown in the table below (in $ per unit):

	Production line			
Model	Q	R	S	T
A	60	53	61	50
B	80	75	81	70
C	75	70	75	65

The company's objective is to meet all estimated demand at the lowest possible manufacturing cost. Use the transportation model to find the best production schedule.

10. The cost of assigning jobs A, B, and C on machines M, N, O, and P is shown below:

Job \ Machine	M	N	O	P
A	6	7	5	9
B	8	5	6	7
C	10	8	6	6

a. Use the Hungarian method to find the least-cost assignment.
b. Formulate as a linear program.
c. Formulate as a transportation problem.

11. In a small job shop department there are three tasks to be assigned to three workers. The table below indicates the weekly profit achieved by assigning each worker to each job. (For example, assigning worker B to job III brings $3 profit.) Find the assignment that will maximize profit.

Worker \ Job	I	II	III
A	5	4	7
B	6	7	3
C	8	11	2

a. Solve by complete enumeration.
b. Solve by the Hungarian method.
c. Formulate as a linear program.

12. Fraser City has a group of five social workers. The director of the group wishes to assign each of the workers to a residential area in the "best possible" manner. It was suggested that workers be rotated in the various areas for a few weeks and their efficiency measured by the number of complaints received. The table below gives the number of complaints in each area against each worker in one month of service.

Worker \ Zone	I	II	III	IV	V
A	3	5	4	8	2
B	9	4	3	6	7
C	11	6	8	10	9
D	6	10	4	12	5
E	3	5	6	4	9

a. Suggest the best assignment of workers to zones. Solve by the Hungarian method. (*Hint:* Attempt to minimize the total number of complaints.)

b. Specify the necessary assumptions.

13. Given below is a table that shows the cost of the row personnel doing the column job. The cost figures in the matrix reflect the effectiveness of the person for the particular job weighted by his rate of pay.

Personnel \ Job	Bed making	Patient care	Patient examination
Physicians	—	20	11
Nurses	14	6	30
Nurses aids	5	11	—

Find the optimal assignment of personnel to jobs. Use the Hungarian method.

Note: Some assignments are not feasible (e.g., physicians do not make beds). In such a case, simply ignore the cell.

14. Indian Electronics, Ltd., manufactures computers in two plants. The capacities of the plants are: plant A, 150 units per month; plant B, 120 units a month. The company has three buyers who distribute the product to a chain of stores. Demand is deterministic at the following constant rate:

Buyer I	60 units
Buyer II	120 units
Buyer III	80 units

Transportation costs are given in the table below (in rupees per unit).

From plant	To buyer I	II	III
A	27	40	60
B	35	28	42

Find the quantities to be shipped from A and B to I, II, and III so as to minimize the total transportation costs.

a. Solve by the transportation method.

b. Formulate as a linear program. Solve (use a computer).

15. AMA's maintenance shop has three groups of employees who have varying proficiencies in their skills: Group G-1, three skilled employees; group G-2, four semiskilled; and group G-3, with two specialists. Six jobs to be performed are relatively easy and three are complex (nine jobs total). Assigning one worker per job, find the best assignment schedule if the objective is to minimize total cost.

The table below gives the cost of the repairs:

If done by worker of group	*Easy repair*	*Complex repair*
G-1	10	24
G-2	9	28
G-3	12	20

a. Formulate as a transportation problem.

b. Solve.

c. Formulate (do not solve) as an assignment problem. (*Hint:* Nine variables are required.)

16. The Tilt Lumber Company has four lumberyards, A, B, C, and D, with the following capacities:

A	3,000 tons
B	2,000 tons
C	1,800 tons
D	6,000 tons

The company has received a contract to supply lumber for three construction projects: Project 1, with a maximum demand of 5,200 tons and a selling price of $70 per ton; Project 2, with a maximum demand of 10,000 tons and a selling price of $50 per ton; and Project 3, with a maximum demand of 10,000 tons and a selling price of $45 per ton.

Transportation costs in dollars per ton are given in the table below.

Lumber-yard	*Project 1*	*To project 2*	*Project 3*
A	10	15	30
B	18	12	20
C	25	10	25
D	35	20	12

Find the best schedule for the Tilt Lumber Company. Start with the least-cost method, proceed with the stepping-stone method.

17. A firm that markets one product has four salespersons, A, B, C, and D, and three customers I, II, and III. The firm's profit for selling one unit of its product to customer I is $100, to customer II is $120, and to customer III is $150. Sales of the firm's product to each customer depend on the salesperson-customer rapport. The probability matrix for the sale of a unit of the product to each customer by each salesperson is as follows:

Salesperson \ *Customer*	I	II	III
A	.7	.6	.6
B	.5	.7	.7
C	.4	.8	.5
D	.8	.6	.4

(For example, the probability that salesperson B can sell a unit of product to customer III is 0.7.) If only one salesperson can be assigned to each customer, what is the optimal assignment?

18. Without balancing the profit situation below, formulate as a linear program. Solve as a linear program by computer.

	I	II
A	6	9
B	12	5
C	4	13
D	11	8

19. Solve the problem formulated in Table 10.17 and comment on the result.

PART B: EXTENSIONS

10.7 THE MODIFIED DISTRIBUTION PROCEDURE (MODI)

MODI as the LP dual

An efficient procedure for solving large transportation problems is the **MODI (modified distribution) procedure,** which is based on the *dual* to the transportation problem. The reader will recall that every linear programming problem has a dual. The transportation problem, being a special case of linear programming, has its own dual.

When the dual is solved, its solution yields two types of variables:

Implicit costs

u_i = Implicit cost (or shadow price) of source i, (value of one more unit at source i)

v_j = Implicit cost of destination j, (value of one more unit at j)

The MODI procedure uses the values of u_i and v_j to find the cell evaluators.[17] Let us demonstrate.

The theoretical basis of MODI

In an *optimal solution* for a transportation problem, Equations 10.5 and 10.6 must hold by definition:

$$c_{ij} - u_i - v_j \geq 0 \tag{10.5}$$

where c_{ij} is the per unit shipping cost between i and j, and:

$$x_{ij}(c_{ij} - u_i - v_j) = 0 \tag{10.6}$$

where x_{ij} is the quantity to be shipped between i and j.

Two cases may occur

These two conditions imply that when optimality is reached, one of two things may occur:

Case a If $x_{ij} \neq 0$ (an occupied cell), then $c_{ij} - u_i - v_j = 0$, or $c_{ij} = u_i + v_j$, which means that an allocation i to j will be made if, and only if, the actual cost of transportation c_j is equal to the sum of the implicit cost of source i plus the implicit cost of destination j. In such a case, x_{ij} is called a basic variable;[18] that is, cell ij is occupied.

Case b If $x_{ij} = 0$, then one of two things may happen:

1. $c_{ij} > u_i + v_j$. In this case, an allocation i to j is *not* made, because the actual cost is larger than the sum of the implied costs of the source i and the destination j.

---

[17] u_i and v_j can be found by transforming the problem to a linear program and solving it by the simplex method. However, the MODI procedure *does not require,* as will be shown, the transformation to a linear program in order to find u_i and v_j.

[18] Or a nonbasic variable that has the potential of being in the basis as an alternative optimal solution; that is, when the cell evaluator equals zero.

2. $c_{ij} = u_i + v_j$. In this case, the nonbasic variable has the potential of being in the basis as an alternative optimal solution.

Note: c_{ij} *cannot* be smaller than $u_i + v_j$ without violating Equation 10.5.

The conditions just presented are the foundation for the modified distribution procedure (MODI). The MODI procedure follows the same solution steps as the stepping-stone procedure:

The MODI steps

Step 1. Find an initial feasible solution.
Step 2. Calculate the cell evaluators and test for optimality. If the solution is not optimal, improve it (next step).
Step 3. Identify the "incoming" cell and design an improved solution.
Step 4. Recycle until an optimal solution is obtained.

The major difference between MODI and the stepping-stone procedure is in the optimality test, which involves a different approach for calculating the cell evaluators.

The concept of cell evaluators

Let K_{ij} denote the cell evaluator, defined as:

$$K_{ij} = c_{ij} - (u_i + v_j) = c_{ij} - u_i - v_j \qquad (10.7)$$

The cell evaluator from the implicit costs

The cell evaluator, thus, is the difference between the actual cost of shipping one unit from i to j, c_{ij}, and the sum of the implicit costs of source i and destination j.

Let us investigate the concept of the cell evaluators by examining in Table 10.27 the initial solution of a previous example. In the initial feasible solution there are five occupied cells. It can be shown that the evaluator of each of the *occupied* cells is zero.

TABLE 10.27
Table 10.8 reproduced

Source \ *Destination*	R	S	T	Supply
A	[1] 80	[2] 20	[3]	100
B	[4]	[1] 100	[5] 10	110
D (dummy)	[0]	[0]	[0] 50	50
Demand	80	120	60	260

Now, if one assigns a complete set of row auxiliary numbers, u_i (to be placed at the extreme right-hand side of the table), and a complete set of column auxiliary numbers, v_j (to be placed at the bottom of the table), in such a way that the shipping cost per unit of *each* of the *occupied* cells equals the sum of its *row and column auxiliary numbers*, that is:

$$u_i + v_j = c_{ij} \tag{10.8}$$

then the condition that the cell evaluator of each occupied cell be zero will be satisfied. Further, for the *empty* cells, the sum of the row and column auxiliary numbers will normally be different from the actual cost of the cell, c_{ij}. This difference is the value of the cell evaluator.

Assigning auxiliary row and column numbers

From each *occupied* cell, u_i and v_j are selected so that c_{ij} equals the sum of u_i and v_j. For the occupied cell AR, for example, u_1 and v_1 are chosen so $c_{11} = u_1 + v_1$. Similarly, for the occupied cell AS, u_1 and v_2 are selected so $c_{12} = c_1 + v_2$. This process must be carried out for *all* the occupied cells.

One arbitrary value

To determine all the row and column auxiliary numbers, one *arbitrary*[19] number, serving as either a row or a column number, must first be chosen.[20] Then, the rest will be determined from the occupied cells by using the relationship $c_{ij} = u_i + v_j$. Insofar as *any* arbitrary number can be chosen to represent one of the u_i's or v_j's, we shall follow the practice of *making* u_1 *take the value zero.*[21]

An example of MODI

To illustrate the steps of MODI, the problem presented in Table 10.27 is used.

Step 1: Find an initial solution The initial solution shown in Table 10.27 will be used.

Step 2: Calculate the cell evaluators for all the empty cells and test for optimality Arbitrarily, a value of zero for u_1 is chosen. The next question is: What value must be given to v_1 so that for the first occupied cell AR, $c_{11} = u_1 + v_1$, or $1 = 0 + v_1$? Obviously, v_1 must take a value of 1. Again, what value must be given to v_2 so that $c_{12} = u_1 + v_2$, or $2 = 0 +$

---

[19] The use of an arbitrary number means that the values of u_i and v_j are not the actual shadow prices as could have been generated if the simplex was employed. However, the *relative* relationship between all these shadow prices is being maintained.

[20] This is necessary because there is one less occupied cell $(m + n - 1)$ than the number of auxiliary variables $(m + n)$.

[21] It is even more efficient to let the u_i or v_j of the row or column with the most occupied cells take the value zero.

v_2? The value of v_2 must be 2. We can skip cell AT because it is unoccupied. Now, what value must be given to u_2 so that $c_{22} = u_2 + v_2$, or $1 = u_2 + 2$? Obviously, $u_2 = -1$. In a similar manner, v_3 is found to be 6 and u_3 to be −6.

All the row and column numbers are entered in Table 10.28 in the new row v_j and the new column u_i.

TABLE 10.28
Finding the implicit costs

Destination / *Source*	R	S	T	*Supply*	u_i
A	[1] 80	[2] 20	[3]	100	$u_1 = 0$
B	[4]	[1] 100	[5] 10	110	$u_2 = -1$
D (dummy)	[0]	[0]	[0] 50	50	$u_3 = -6$
Demand	80	120	60	260	
v_j	$v_1 = 1$	$v_2 = 2$	$v_3 = 6$		

Computing the cell evaluators. Let us now calculate the cell evaluator for the empty cell BR. For cell BR, the cell evaluator, according to Equation 10.7, is $K_{21} = c_{21} - u_2 - v_1 = 4 + 1 - 1 = 4$. Similarly, the cell evaluators of the other empty cells are calculated and summarized below:

Empty cell	*Cell evaluator K_{ij}*
BR	$c_{21} - u_2 - v_1 = 4 + 1 - 1 = 4$
AT	$c_{13} - u_1 - v_3 = 3 - 0 - 6 = -3$
DR	$c_{31} - u_3 - v_1 = 0 + 6 - 1 = 5$
DS	$c_{32} - u_3 - v_2 = 0 + 6 - 2 = 4$

Test of optimality. The optimality test is identical to that of the stepping-stone method. Namely, an optimal solution requires that all cell evaluators be nonnegative (in minimization).

Since the cell evaluator of AT is negative, the solution of Table 10.27 is *not optimal.* An improved solution is thus called for.

Shifting units along a closed loop

Step 3: Identify the "incoming" cell and design an improved solution The "incoming" cell for a minimization case is located by identifying, as in the stepping-stone method, the most negative cell evaluator.[22] In this case, the "incoming" cell is AT. The improved solution is obtained

[22] The largest positive evaluator in the case of maximization.

by shifting as many units as possible around a closed path into AT without violating the demand and supply requirements.[23] The improved solution is shown in Table 10.29.

TABLE 10.29
First improved solution

Source \ *Destination*	R	S	T	Supply	u_i
A	[1] 80	[2] 10	[3] 10	100	0
B	[4]	[1] 110	[5]	110	−1
D (dummy)	[0]	[0]	[0] 50	50	−3
Demand	80	120	60	260	
v_j	1	2	3		

Step 4: Recycle (until optimality is achieved) The next step is to test the solution of Table 10.29 for optimality. All cell evaluators for the empty cells are computed by first recalculating the u_i's and v_j's. This is accomplished by again using the equation $c_{ij} = u_i + v_j$ for the *occupied* cells.

The new u_i's and v_j's are entered in Table 10.29. The cell evaluators for the empty cells of Table 10.29 are calculated as:

Empty cell	*Cell evaluator*
BR	+4
BT	+3
DR	+2
DS	+1

Since *all* cell evaluators are positive, the solution in Table 10.29 is optimal.

Economic interpretation of u_i and v_j. The variables u_i and v_j used in the MODI procedure have an interesting economic interpretation. They are, in effect, the dual variables and, as such, represent implict costs associated with the i sources and j destinations:

u_i is the value of one unit of the product at source i. In other words, u_i represents the *implicit cost of source i*.

[23] A loop like the one in the stepping-stone method with pluses and minuses is helpful in this operation.

v_j is the value of one unit of the product delivered at destination j. In other words, v_j is the *implicit cost of the destination j*.

Since, in this procedure, one value of u_i (or v_j) is assigned arbitrarily, the values u_i and v_j are *relative* rather than absolute. Hence, u_i measures the *comparative locational disadvantage* of the various sources. Similarly, v_j measures the comparative disadvantage of the various destination locations.

u_i and v_j are *relative* costs

For example, in the optimal solution:

$$v_1 = 1 \text{ (for warehouse R)}$$
$$v_3 = 3 \text{ (for warehouse T)}$$

This means that if the demand of warehouse T is increased by 1 ton and, at the same time, the requirement of warehouse R is decreased by 1 ton, then the total shipment cost will be *increased* by 2 ($v_3 - v_1 = 3 - 1 = 2$). In other words, warehouse T is less efficient. The policy implication is that if it is impossible to meet all the demand, warehouse T should be supplied only after all the demand at R is met.

Similarly, comparing v_2 and v_3, it can be seen that warehouse S is more efficient than warehouse T. This explains why, in the optimal solution (Table 10.29), the demand for warehouse T is not fully satisfied. It receives only 10 of the required demand of 60 tons.

Summary of MODI

Preparation: MODI requires a balanced transportation table.

Step 1. Derive an initial solution.

Step 2. Use equation $c_{ij} = u_i + v_j$ to compute all implicit costs of the occupied cells. Then compute the cell evaluators of all empty cells using equation $K_{ij} = c_{ij} - u_i - v_j$. Test for optimality as in the stepping-stone method.

Step 3. Identify an incoming cell and design an improved solution in the stepping-stone method.

Step 4. Recycle the process until an optimal solution is found.

10.8 DEGENERACY

A transportation problem has m supply constraints and n demand constraints, or a total of $m + n$ constraints. Since transportation problems are either balanced to begin with or, if not, can be converted to a balanced problem, the total demand is assumed to equal the total supply. As a result of such equality, it is possible to express one of the constraints in terms of the others: thus, one constraint is always redundant. Therefore,

$m+n-1$ occupied cells

there are only $m + n - 1$ active constraints. This suggests that the transportation problem should have $m + n - 1$ active variables (occupied cells) in every *basic feasible solution* as well as in the *optimal solution.* For example, in a 3×3 problem, only five of the nine cells are normally occupied.

Whenever the number of occupied cells is *less than* $(m + n - 1)$ the solution is called *degenerate.* To handle **degeneracy,** the previous solution techniques must be slightly modified.

Two types of degeneracy

Degeneracy can develop in one of two ways. First, it can appear in the initial assignment, if the supply equals demand for any cell in which an assignment is to be made.[24] Table 10.30 presents such a case (see cell AR). Note that the number of occupied cells in Table 10.30 is three instead of four; that is, $m + n - 1 = 2 + 3 - 1 = 4$.

Degeneracy can also develop during the improvement of solutions. If the quantities of two or more "losing" cells of a nondegenerate solution are the same, they will become empty simultaneously when an incoming variable is introduced. The resultant solution will then be degenerate.

TABLE 10.30
Degenerate solution

Source \ *Destination*	R	S	T	Supply
A	100 [1]	[3]	[6]	100
B	[5]	30 [3]	40 [2]	70
Demand	100	30	40	170 / 170

Degeneracy impedes the optimality test

A degenerate solution cannot be tested for optimality by the methods previously outlined. Therefore, a special treatment is called for.

How to resolve degeneracy

***E* is nil**

Case 1: Degeneracy in the very first assignment In this case, an extremely small amount, designated by E, (almost zero) of the commodity to be shipped is allocated to one (or more) of the empty cells of the first solution to bring the number of occupied cells to $m + n - 1$. In a minimization problem, E is allocated to the empty cell with the lowest cost and that still allows the optimality check (in maximization problems, to the

[24] More generally, the remaining supply (after some assignment) equals the remaining demand.

cell with the highest profit coefficient).[25] The problem is then solved as if it were nondegenerate.

Example. Table 10.31a is a minimization example of a transportation problem (with cost data) in which degeneracy will develop when the initial solution is generated by the Northwest Corner Rule (Table 10.31b). The solution of Table 10.31b cannot be checked for optimality since the test requires $m + n - 1$ occupied cells (i.e., $2 + 2 - 1 = 3$). The requirement can be met by adding the quantity E to the low-cost cell AS. It is then possible to test for optimality, whereupon it will be found that the solution is not optimal. One improvement gives the solution shown in Table 10.31c, which is both optimal and nondegenerate.

TABLE 10.31a
A degenerate problem

From \ To	R	S	Supply
A	[3]	[3]	50
B	[4]	[6]	30
Demand	50	30	80

TABLE 10.31b
Initial solution (degenerate)

From \ To	R	S	Supply
A	50 [3]	E [3]	50
B	[4]	30 [6]	30
Demand	50	30	80

TABLE 10.31c
Optimal solution (nondegenerate)

From \ To	R	S	Supply
A	20 [3]	30 [3]	50
B	30 [4]	[6]	30
Demand	50	30	80

[25] The assignment of E should be made so the solution permits a check on optimality. If the configuration of occupied cells is such that after assigning E to the lowest cost cell, and now having $m + n - 1$ occupied cells, a check on optimality is not possible, then E should be assigned to the second lowest cost cell instead, and so on.

Case 2: Degeneracy in intermediate solution stages In this case, E is assigned to one (or more) of the *newly vacated* cells. As mentioned earlier, the assignment must be made so that $m + n - 1$ cells will be "occupied" and an optimality check is possible.

Where to place E

Example. Table 10.32a contains an initial solution for a minimization problem (cost data). It is not optimal, and AT is the incoming cell. Table

TABLE 10.32a
Initial solution

From \ *To*	R	S	T	Supply
A	50 [5]	20 [4]	[2]	70
B	[6]	30 [3]	20 [2]	50
C	[1]	[5]	10 [1]	10
Demand	50	50	30	130

TABLE 10.32b
First improved solution (degenerate)

From \ *To*	R	S	T	Supply
A	50 [5]	[4]	20 [2]	70
B	[6]	50 [3]	E [2]	50
C	[1]	[5]	10 [1]	10
Demand	50	50	30	130

TABLE 10.32c
Second improved and optimal solution (degenerate)

From \ *To*	R	S	T	Supply
A	40 [5]	[4]	30 [2]	70
B	[6]	50 [3]	E [2]	50
C	10 [1]	[5]	[1]	10
Demand	50	50	30	130

10.32b shows the first improved solution. The solution is degenerate. In order to test optimality, E is added to cell BT (the newly vacated cell with the lowest cost coefficient). The solution of Table 10.32b is not optimal; and hence a second improved solution, Table 10.32c is derived. The second improved solution is still degenerate, but on checking, turns out to be optimal. To interpret the final solution, the value E is ignored. The total cost is 420.

10.9 USE OF COMPUTERS

The transportation problem, especially if it is not too large, can easily be solved by the computer.

Example. The Tuff Cement Co. problem, presented in the beginning of this chapter, was solved by computer.[26] The computer inputs and results are given below.

SOLUTION MATRIX
The total cost of this solution is: $240.00

SOURCES	DESTINATIONS R	S	T	SUPPLY
A	80.00	10.00	10.00	100.00
B	0.00	110.00	0.00	110.00
Dummy	0.00	0.00	50.00	50.00
Demand	80.00	120.00	60.00	260.00

Note: In this package it is not necessary to balance the matrix; it is done automatically by the computer.

The results are: 80 from A to R, 10 from A to S, 10 from A to T, and 110 from B to S. The dummy source "ships" 50 to T. The total cost (called the *payoff*) is $240.

Assignment packages

Assignment packages are less common than transportation packages. However, any assignment problem can easily be solved using a transportation package by simply balancing the problem and setting all supply and

[26] Using the MSS package that accompanies this text.

demand constraints to unity (1). A computer printout of the assignment problem, solved in Section 10.4, is given below, solved with the MSS package (where "1.00" means an assignment is made and 0 means no assignment).

SOLUTION
The total cost of this solution is: $59.00

SOURCES	DESTINATIONS a	b	c	SUPPLY
A	0.00	1.00	0.00	1.00
B	1.00	0.00	0.00	1.00
C	0.00	0.00	1.00	1.00
DEMAND	1.00	1.00	1.00	3.00

Note: The MSS package treats the assignment as a transportation problem.

10.10 PROBLEMS FOR PART B

20. Solve Problem 2 by MODI. Start with the Northwest Corner Rule.

21. In the transportation problem below, the data in the cells are profits per unit shipped. The objective of the company is profit maximization. Find the best shipment schedule(s).

Note: Start with the northwest corner solution; use the stepping-stone method. Watch for degeneracy.

From \ *To*	I	II	Capacity
A	6	4	60
B	3	5	100
C	7	2	80
Requirement	60	150	

22. Given the transportation cost table:

Ware-house \ *Store*	A	B	C	D	E	Capacity
1	4	7	3	9	6	200
2	3	2	4	6	5	400
3	5	6	2	5	3	600
4	8	4	5	7	3	700
Requirement	600	400	500	100	300	

a. Find the initial solution by the Northwest Corner Rule.

b. Find the transportation schedule that will minimize total shipping cost. Use MODI.

Hints: Watch for degeneracy and for more than one optimal solution.

23. Swedish Bakeries make three types of bread: small, standard, and large. These are baked in each of their four shops. The daily demand for the three types of bread and the selling prices are given below:

Type	*Daily demand*	*Selling price (krona)*
Small	500	24
Standard	1,200	29
Large	800	37

Each bakery shop is capable of baking up to 1,000 loaves of each type daily. The cost per loaf, including transportation, is given below. The difference in costs is due to baking technology and travel distances.

Shop \ *Bread*	Small	Standard	Large
A	12	15	20
B	13	17	19
C	11	17	22
D	14	16	18

Find how many loaves of each type of bread to bake in each shop to maximize profit.

a. Formulate as a transportation problem.
b. Solve by MODI. Start with the least-cost method.
Note: Watch for degeneracy.

24. Eastern Railroad Company serves five cities, A–E. The distances between the cities are shown below:

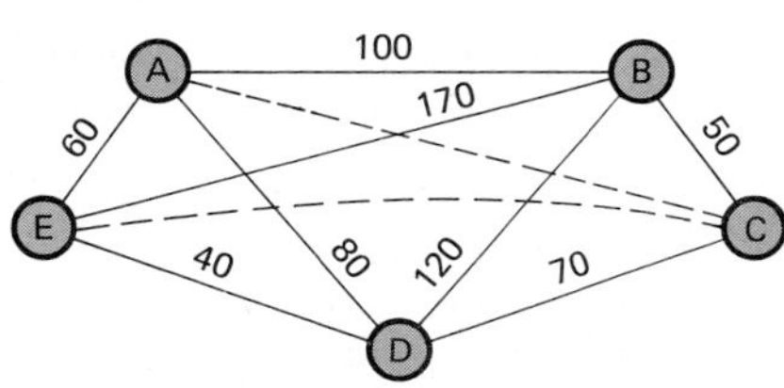

At the present time there is no connection between cities A and C, and E and C, due to maintenance work on the rails.

On Sunday afternoon, the company has 200 identical cars at the following cities: A—40, B—60, C—70, D—30.

By Monday, empty cars are needed in the following cities: B—40, D—50, and E—40.

The company wants to minimize the mileage traveled. All demands of Monday must be met. Find the best routing plan. Use MODI; start with the least-cost method.

25. Westcan Machine Shop produces three products (A, B, and C) using its four automatic machines (1, 2, 3, and 4). Each is capable (unless otherwise specified) of making the product in one operation.

The table below shows the output, in units per hour, of each machine, for each product (*X* implies impossible combinations).

Product \ *Machine*	1	2	3	4
A	16	10	*X*	6
B	8	20	10	9
C	12	*X*	14	1

The monthly demand for the three products is 2,000, 2,500, and 2,200, respectively. The products sell for \$6, \$4, and \$8.20, respectively. The machines are available at a cost of \$24, \$30, \$28, and \$18 per hour. Each machine is capable of making up to 2,500 units per month. Find the optimal monthly production plan.

a. Formulate as a transportation problem.
b. Solve by MODI; start with the least-cost method. *Hint:* Watch for degeneracy.

26. Formulate and solve Problem 10 as a transportation problem.

27. The town of Beersheba must determine how to deploy its four ambulances among its four regions in the most effective manner. The teams differ in their abilities and the special equipment at their disposal. An accurate measure of the health cost in each region would be the average

weekly dollar loss owing to illness and death. Based on historical records and judgment, the table below shows the expected monetary loss that could be prevented if each of the four ambulances were to be assigned to each of the four regions (in 1,000 shekel per week). Determine the optimal assignments.

Ambulance team	*Region* A	B	C	D
1	12	8	10	6
2	6	6	4	8
3	10	10	8	12
4	12	10	12	10

28. The French army is testing four antitank missiles against five targets. At its proving ground in Toulouse, the "effective damage" ratings shown below were ascertained. If each missile is devoted to only one type of target, what would be the best assignments?

Antitank missile	*Target* A	B	C	D	E
Python	26	36	40	30	28
Rattler	18	50	34	40	22
Asp	28	40	30	42	20
Coral	20	30	36	32	18

10.11 CASE I

NORTHEASTERN BLOOD BANK

Northeastern General is the only hospital in a small mountain community in Wales. Dr. Alton, the chief surgeon, just completed the list of patients to be operated on the next morning, specifying the blood that will be required during the operations.

Eight patients are on the list below with their blood type and quantity required.

Patient	*Blood type*	*Quantity (pints)*
Able	AB	3
Brook	B	2
Cock	A	6
Dean	O	3
Elm	B	4
Flint	AB	2
Gloss	A	2
Hope	O	2

The hospital's blood bank currently has the following blood inventory. (Blood comes in 1-pint containers.)

Blood type	*Inventory (pints)*
A	4
B	10
O	11
AB	7

A patient with blood type AB is considered a universal recipient; that is, he or she can receive any type of blood. A blood type O is considered acceptable for transfusion to any type of patient.

Ann White, the director of the hospital's blood bank, has just received the list and computed the demand for blood as:

Type	*Pints in demand*	*versus*	*Pints in stock*
A	8		4
B	6		10
O	5		11
AB	5		7

Ann realizes that she is short by four pints of type A. However, this shortage can be covered by four pints of type O.

As she was ready to deliver the blood, she remembered the meeting she had with the hospital administrator last Friday. The meeting went as follows:

John Par (the administrator): Ann, the doctors are happy with your work. The patients always receive the required amount of the proper type of blood. There is only one problem.

Ann: What do you mean?

John: Well, the cost of acquiring blood is ever increasing, and the expenses of your department are increasing much faster than those of the other departments.

Ann: What can I do about the situation? I can't buy cheaper blood; we belong to a regional blood bank and can't negotiate prices.

John: That's true, but I understand that the cost of the different types of blood isn't the same, especially when the cost of transportation and special orders is added.

Ann: I just completed a study on this. Here are the figures: Type A = \$30/pint; type B = \$36/pint; type O = \$35/pint; and type AB = \$40/pint.

John: This is interesting. It looks as though you might be able to save some money by substituting blood types.

Ann: That's possibly true, but what will the physicians say if we increase the rate of blood substitutions?

John: I don't know. Let's check and find out.

a. Find the *least* total cost blood allocation plan. Use a transportation type model.
b. How much can Ann save by following the optimal solutions, as compared to her present policy of "matching blood to needs as close as possible"?
c. Even though substitutions may be safe from a clinical point of view, the physicians may not be too happy with the optimal solution. Why?

CASE II

GREENHILL'S FEDERAL GRANT

The Greenhill's public hearing meeting turned stormy. Citizens from four suburbs were gathered at city hall to try to get the city's federal funds for their own suburbs.

The government recently awarded \$750,000 to the city for road improvements. The city requested bids and five contractors submitted bids for work in the four suburbs. The bids are listed below (in thousands of dollars):

	Suburb			
Contractor	*1*	*2*	*3*	*4*
A	210	242	202	243
B	222	232	205	250
C	205	225	244	210
D	265	206	200	270
E	215	211	253	212

Since under the terms of the federal grant the work must be completed fairly soon, none of the contractors are large enough to perform more than one job. That is, it will be necessary to use a different contractor for each suburb's job.

From the bids it was clear to Greenhill's city council that the federal funds would not cover road improvements in all four suburbs. As they began to analyze the situation, they realized they needed some hard facts. Therefore, they called the finance director of Greenhills and requested the following information:

a. What is the *minimum* amount of money that the city must add to the government grant such that work may be done in all four suburbs?
b. What is the best contractor-to-suburb match?
c. Which of the contractors should not receive a job contract?
d. If the city cannot come up with any supplementary funds, only three suburbs will be repaired. Based on dollars and cents, which three suburbs should be selected such that the surplus from the government grant is maximized?

The director of finance asked you, a newly appointed assistant, to use some management science tools to answer these questions. What will your answers be?

10.12 GLOSSARY

Balancing Equating total supply to total demand by adding dummy sources of supply or dummy destinations for demand.

Cell evaluator The opportunity cost involved in shipping one unit through a route that is not currently used. This route corresponds to a *cell* in the transportation table, since a cell is at the intersection of the source and destination of that route.

Closed loop A path showing the transfer of units in a revised transportation table.

Degeneracy (degenerate solution) A solution to a transportation problem in which there are fewer than $m + n - 1$ occupied cells in the transportation table.

Destination A place a shipment is directed to.

Dummy row(s), column(s) Row(s) or column(s) that are added to the transportation and assignment tables to equalize total supply and total demand (in the case of transportation) or to equalize the number of rows and columns (in the case of assignment).

Hungarian method An algorithm used to efficiently solve an assignment problem.

MODI (modified distribution procedure) An algorithm used to efficiently solve a transportation problem.

Northwest Corner Rule A procedure used to find an initial feasible solution to a transportation problem.

Source A place a shipment originates from.

Stepping-stone procedure An algorithm used to test a transportation solution for optimality.

Transportation method An algorithm to efficiently solve transportation problems.

10.13 REFERENCES AND BIBLIOGRAPHY

1. Bazaraa, M., and J. J. Jarvis. *Linear programming and Network Flows*. New York: John Wiley & Sons, 1977.
2. Ford, L. R., and D. R. Fulkerson. *Flows in Networks*. Princeton, N.J.: Princeton University Press, 1962.
3. Frazer, J. R. *Applied Linear Programming*. Englewood Cliffs, N.J.: Prentice-Hall, 1968.
4. Gass, S. I. *Linear Programming: Methods and Applications*. New York: McGraw-Hill, 1969.
5. Harvey, C. *Operations Research, An Introduction to Linear Optimization and Decision Analysis*. New York: Elsevier North-Holland Publishing, 1979.
6. Loomba, N. P. *Linear Programming*. 2nd ed. New York: Macmillan, 1976.
7. Taha, H. A. *Operations Research: An Introduction*. New York: Macmillan, 1987.
8. Wagner, H. M. *Principles of Operations Research with Applications to Managerial Decisions*. 2nd ed. Englewood Cliffs, N.J.: Prentice-Hall, 1975.

11

PART A: BASICS

11.1 Introduction to PERT and CPM.
11.2 Formulation: The basic inputs to PERT/CPM.
11.3 Solving PERT and CPM.
11.4 Event analysis.
11.5 Activity analysis.
11.6 Analysis and application.
11.7 Problems for Part A.

PART B: EXTENSIONS

11.8 Estimate of activity time in PERT.
11.9 Finding the probabilities of completion in PERT (risk analysis).
11.10 The critical path method (CPM): Cost-time relationships.
11.11 Other network methods.
11.12 Minimal spanning tree.
11.13 Shortest route.
11.14 Maximum flow.
11.15 Computerization.
11.16 Concluding remarks.
11.17 Problems for Part B.
11.18 Case—The Sharon Construction Corporation.
11.19 Glossary.
11.20 References and bibliography.

Managerial situations involving a complex of interrelated activities can be modeled as "networks." Typical of these are large construction projects (dams, bridges) consisting of a number of subtasks; transportation networks connecting a number of cities; utility and piping systems; computer systems; the organization of a company; and similar cases in which a complex of branches connects, either literally or figuratively, a set of locations. A systematic analysis of these situations enables the manager to plan, monitor, and reorganize resources so that objectives can be attained efficiently and on schedule.

Of special interest among the network models are the Program Evaluation Review Technique (PERT) and the Critical Path Method (CPM). Other networks discussed in this chapter are the minimal spanning tree, the shortest route, and the maximum flow.

Network models

LEARNING OBJECTIVES

The student should be able to:

a. Describe the characteristics of a project and project management.
b. List and discuss the special terms developed for this chapter, namely: activity, event, slack, dummy activity, critical activity, critical path, network, crash time.
c. Describe the purposes and advantages of PERT/CPM.
d. Construct a simple PERT/CPM network.
e. Identify critical events, activities, and paths (using event analysis).
f. List the eight steps in the PERT/CPM procedure.
g. Describe the major inputs and outputs to PERT/CPM analysis.
h. Compute slacks on activities and on events.
i. Perform a PERT/CPM activity analysis.
j. Describe the use of PERT as a control tool.
k. Describe the issue of resource allocation and how it is handled.

Extensions

l. Compute weighted average times, t_e, in PERT.
m. Compute the chance of completing PERT projects at various completion dates.
n. Describe the functions and characteristics of CPM.
o. Construct a CPM network, crash a CPM network, and perform a cost analysis.
p. Define, formulate, and solve a minimal spanning tree problem.
q. Define, formulate, and solve a shortest route problem.
r. Define, formulate, and solve a maximum flow problem.
s. Describe computerized PERT/CPM.

PART A: BASICS

The morning mail held exciting news for Judi Kosen, special projects manager for Restoration, Inc. As she anxiously opened the letter from the Proposal Review Committee, Environmental Projects Branch, Department of the Interior, her eyes spotted the words ". . . most cost-effective bid . . . ," ". . . are pleased to award you. . . ." With a whoop she yelled, "We won! We won!!" Then, to be sure there was no mistake, she reread the good news. After reading the letter four times, Judi settled back in her chair to contemplate the task before her.

Four months ago, Restoration, Inc. submitted a competitive bid to the Department of the Interior to revitalize Moose Lake in the northern part of the state. The company had developed a new technique to combat water pollution by increasing the basic amount of oxygen in a lake, called oxygenation.

Oxygenation of a lake is a very complex project involving several of the company's departments as well as outside suppliers. It requires specialized equipment and supplies and specially trained personnel. The contract was for a period of more than a half a year, a long enough time for significant changes to occur in the economy, in prices, and in the availability of resources. The Department of the Interior wanted the project to be completed on time. Therefore, the contract contained a $2,000 penalty clause for each week beyond the agreed-upon 30-week completion time. Judi realized that there were many factors that could cause a delay in such a complex project. She wondered if it were possible to plan the project so there would be as few delays as possible. Furthermore, she realized the discovery of any delay should be made as soon as possible, before it is too late to catch up or rectify the problem.

As she examined all of the various factors, operations, and activities involved in the project, she felt that planning, monitoring, and controlling this job could be staggering. Just then she remembered a required course in operations management she had taken several years ago. The professor talked about the planning and control of large, complex projects. He explained some special managerial tool that had a long name and had to be abbreviated. It finally came back to her; yes—it was PERT.

11.1 INTRODUCTION TO PERT AND CPM

Characteristics of project management

Project versus production management

The Moose Lake situation is an example of *project management*. Project management is distinguished from production management primarily by the nonrepetitive nature of the work; a **project** is usually a one-time effort. Although similar work may have been done previously, or may be done in the future (Restoration, Inc., may receive a contract for the oxygenation of other lakes), it is not usually repeated in the identical manner of cars or TV sets being manufactured on a production line. The management of projects is more complicated than the management of a production line due to the following characteristics, generally typical of all projects to a greater or lesser degree.

The complexity of projects

1. The duration of a project lasts weeks, months, or even years. During such a long period many changes may occur, most of which are difficult to predict. Such changes may have a significant impact on project costs, technology, and resources. The longer the duration of the project, the more uncertain are the execution times and costs.
2. A project is complex in nature, involving many interrelated activities and participants from both within the organization and outside it (e.g., suppliers, subcontractors). (Our example is highly simplified for the purpose of easier demonstration.)
3. Delays in completion time may be very costly. Penalties for delays may amount to thousands of dollars per day. Completing projects late may result in lost opportunities and ill will as well.
4. Project activities are sequential. Some activities cannot start until others are completed.
5. Projects are typically a unique undertaking, something that has not been encountered previously.

As a consequence of the above, the management of projects is rather complicated. Figure 11.1 summarizes their major characteristics. Until just a few years ago, there were no generally accepted formal techniques to aid in project management. Each manager had his or her own management

FIGURE 11.1
Project management characteristics

Characteristics	*Factors*	*Symptoms*
Uniqueness	Uncertainty	Cost overruns
Extended duration	Uncontrollable	Schedule slippage
Complexity	Need for coordination	Insufficient technical performance
Significant outside participation	Need for priorities	Contract problems
Extensive interactions	Difficult planning	Communication difficulties, finger pointing
Multiple dependencies	High visibility	Uncoordination, foul-ups
High risk	Attention by top management	Big failures, public attention, anxiety
High profit potential	Attention by top management	Competition, external interest

scheme. However, the need for formal tools soon became apparent. Two of the best known tools that fill this need are **PERT (Program Evaluation Review Technique)**[1] and **CPM (Critical Path Method).**[2]

PERT versus CPM

Definitions used in PERT and CPM

In order to explain the purpose, structure, and operation of PERT and CPM, it is helpful to define the following terms:

Activity An effort that requires resources and takes a certain amount of time for completion. Examples of activities are: studying for an examination, designing a part, connecting bridge girders, or training an employee.

Activity: A time-consuming task

Event A specific accomplishment at a recognizable point in time; a milestone, a checkpoint; for example, passing a course at a university, submission of engineering drafts, completion of a span on a bridge, or the arrival of a new machine. Events *do not* have a time duration per se. To reach an event, all the activities that precede it *must* be completed. An event can be viewed as a goal attained, while the activities leading to it can be viewed as the means of achieving it.

Event: A milestone

Project A collection of activities and events with a definable beginning and a definable end (the goal). For example: getting a college degree, patenting an invention, building a bridge, or installing new machinery.

Network A logical and chronological set of activities and events, graphically illustrating relationships among the various activities and events of the project.

Critical activity An activity that, if even slightly delayed, will hold up the scheduled completion date of the entire project.

A path A series of adjacent activities leading from one event to another.

Critical path The sequence of critical activities that forms a continuous path between the start of a project and its completion.

The major differences and similarities between PERT and CPM

PERT and CPM are very similar in their approach; however, two distinctions are usually made. The first relates to the way in which activity durations are estimated. In PERT, three estimates are used to form a weighted average of the expected completion time, based on a probability distribution of completion times. Therefore, PERT is considered a probabilistic tool. In CPM, there is only one estimate of duration; that is, CPM is a deterministic tool. The second difference is that CPM allows an explicit estimate of costs in addition to time. Thus, while PERT is basically a tool for planning and control of time, CPM can be used to control both the time and the cost of the project. Extensions of both PERT and CPM allow the user to manage other resources in addition to time and money,

PERT is probabilistic

CPM includes costs

---

[1] Developed by the U.S. Navy with Booz Allen & Hamilton Inc. and Lockheed Corporation to accelerate development of the Polaris in the late 1950s.

[2] Developed by Du Pont Inc. in the same time period as PERT.

to trade off resources, to analyze different types of schedules, and to balance the use of resources.

The purpose of PERT/CPM

Due to the complex nature of most projects, it is very difficult to completely eliminate the delays and the cost overruns. However, with the appropriate management systems for planning, organizing, and controlling, it is possible to reduce them to a reasonable level. The problem is that the cost of implementing and executing such systems can exceed their benefits because of the large amount of monitoring and reporting that is required.

8,000 activities

For example, overhauling a Boeing 727 airplane may involve 8,000 different activities (work orders). To be completely in control, management must plan, organize, monitor, report, and act on each of these 8,000 work orders, either daily or perhaps even on a shift-by-shift basis. This will require an extreme amount of reporting. However, using the concept of "management by exception," management may elect to exercise tight control over only the most critical activities.[3] The number of critical activities may be only 5 percent of the total activities; less control is then exercised over the remaining activities.

"Management by exception"

The major purpose of PERT and CPM is to objectively identify these critical activities. Further, these techniques can tell us how close the remaining activities are to becoming critical. (This available delay is called *slack* or *float*.)

"Float"

Accordingly, any PERT/CPM program provides management with the following information, as a minimum.

1. Which activities are critical.
2. Which activities are noncritical.
3. The amount of slack on each noncritical activity.

Other valuable information may also be provided by computerized programs, as will be shown later, in Section 11.15.

The advantages of PERT and CPM

Detailed planning The use of PERT and CPM forces management to plan in detail and to define what must be done to accomplish the project's objectives on time.

[3] The same idea is used in inventory control, where a method called the A-B-C classification system is used to identify the most critical items that deserve more control (see Chapter 14 for details).

Commitments and communications Management is forced to plan and make commitments regarding execution times and completion dates. The tools also provide for better communication among the various departments in an organization and between suppliers and the client.

Efficient monitoring and control The number of critical activities in a network (especially in a large one) is only a small portion of the total activities. Identification of the critical activities enables the use of an efficient monitoring system (mainly record-keeping and reports) concentrating only on the critical activities.

Identifying potential problem areas The critical activities are also more likely to become problem areas. Once identified, contingency plans may be devised.

Proper use of resources Employing PERT or CPM enables management to use resources more wisely by examination of the overall plan. Resources can be transferred to bottleneck or trouble areas from other activities.

Rescheduling The tools enable management to follow up and correct deviations from schedule as soon as they are detected, thus minimizing delays.

Government contracts Several government agencies (such as the U.S. Navy) require the submission of a PERT or CPM plan with bids.

Easily understood CPM and PERT can be easily understood because they provide a method for visualizing an entire project. Therefore, management can explain the tools to supervisors and employees in such a way that the chances of implementation are increased.

Adaptable to computers PERT and CPM are easily adaptable to computer use. Large projects can be planned by computers in seconds. The computer is even capable of diagramming the networks (see the end of this chapter).

Tools for decision making PERT and CPM allow management to check the effectiveness and efficiency of alternative ways of executing projects by examining possible trade-offs among resources (usually time and cost).

Assess probability of completion (in PERT only) The probabilities of successfully meeting deadlines, finishing early, or finishing late can be assessed by the use of PERT.

Cost-time trade-offs (in CPM only) CPM enables management to evaluate trade-offs between the cost of executing a job in the normal way or rushing activities (called **crashing**) at a higher cost so as to finish earlier.

The PERT and CPM procedure

Three stages

The application of PERT/CPM may be divided into three phases: formulation (inputs), solution (outputs), and analysis and application. Figure 11.2 illustrates the major steps involved in each phase.

11.2 FORMULATION: THE BASIC INPUTS TO PERT/CPM

In order to illustrate the formulation of a PERT or a CPM network, let us return to the oxygenation problem and follow the general steps outlined in Figure 11.2.

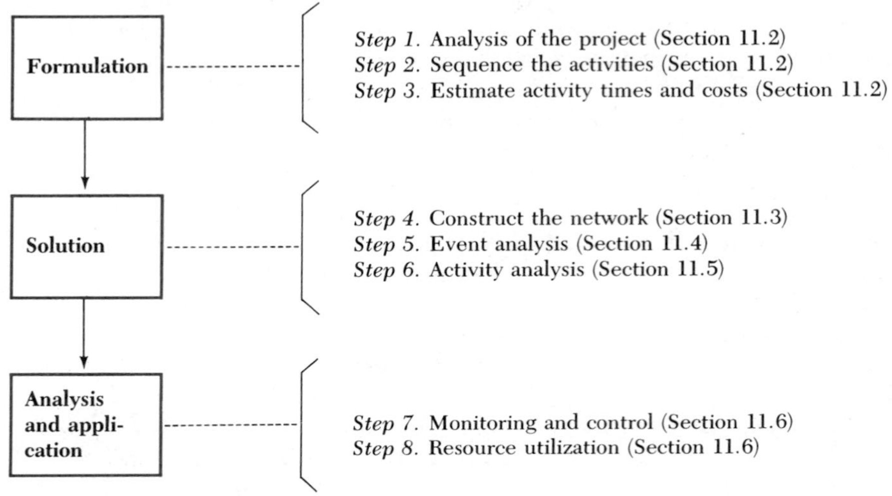

FIGURE 11.2
PERT/CPM procedure

Step 1. Analysis of the project

After consultation with all department heads, a list of activities is agreed upon (see Table 11.1). Each activity is clearly defined and responsibility is assigned to the proper department heads.

TABLE 11.1
Moose Lake project activities

Activity	*Description*	*Duration*	*Required immediately preceding activities*
a	Administrative setup	3	None
b	Hire personnel	4	*a*
c	Obtain materials	4	*a*
d	Transport materials to Moose Lake	2	*c*
e	Gather measuring team	4	*a*
f	Planning	6	*c*
g	Assemble equipment	3	*d, b*
h	Plan evaluation	1	*e*
i	Oxygenation	12	*f, g*
j	Measurement and evaluation	2	*i, h*

Step 2. Sequence the activities

Once the content of each activity is defined, the sequence of execution is determined. For example, personnel cannot be hired before proper authorization is granted (administrative setup) and equipment cannot be assembled before all parts and materials are on site. This information is also shown in Table 11.1 (in the "Required immediately preceding activities" column).

Step 3. Estimate activity times and costs

The next step is to determine the required **duration** (elapsed time) for each activity, designated as t_e, **expected time.** We distinguish two cases: in CPM the activity duration is considered to be deterministic (certain). This assumption occurs when there is a wealth of experience regarding activity times (e.g., in many construction projects). In the case of PERT however, we assume that the duration is unknown, so we use three estimates with an averaging procedure (which is discussed in Part B of this chapter). In both cases we also assume that there are sufficient resources to complete the activities.

Certain or unknown

Note: Other input data In addition to time, we may also enter other information such as cost per activity (labor, parts), trade-offs between time and cost, the availability of resources, and milestone dates. The more information entered, the more information that can be provided to management.

11.3 SOLVING PERT AND CPM

PERT/CPM can be solved manually or by a computer. The manual solution requires the construction of a network. There are two basic network approaches: *event oriented* and *activity oriented.* Both approaches are discussed in this chapter. We will start our presentation by constructing a network and then presenting the two approaches.

Event versus activity

Step 4. Construct the network

The PERT (or CPM) network is a graphical representation of information such as in Table 11.1. It shows the interrelationship among the activities, the events, and the entire project.

To construct a network, start by viewing an activity as an arrow (arc) between two events (circles). For example, the first activity of the Moose Lake Project, the "administrative setup," is shown in Figure 11.3.

An activity as an arrow

The arrow points in the direction of the time flow, but its length is *not* related to the duration of the activity, rather it is arbitrarily set at a suitable length for drawing the diagram. The number circled in front of the arrow, **1,** in Figure 11.3, is the event that *precedes* the activity. The number circled after the arrow, **2,** in Figure 11.3 is the *succeeding* event.

An event as a node

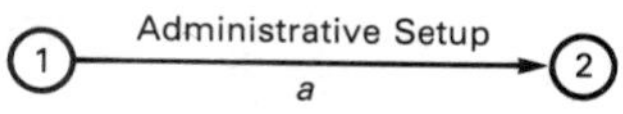

FIGURE 11.3
An activity

FIGURE 11.4
Precedence requirements

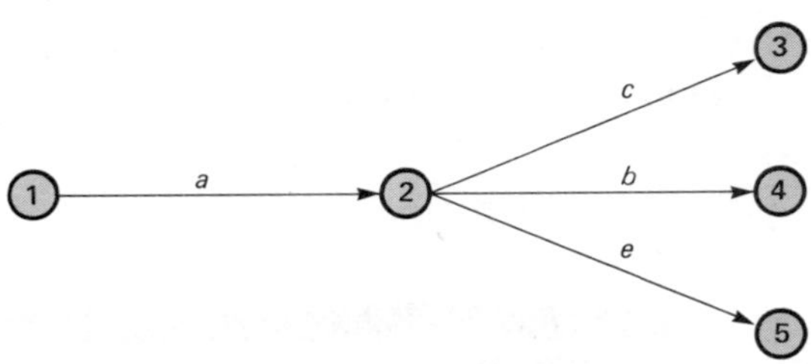

The numbering of the events is somewhat arbitrary—several methods are used in real-life projects. The activity between events **1** and **2** is labeled *a*. It can also be labeled **1–2.**

The construction of the network starts with event **1** (the beginning of the project), which precedes the first activity, *a*. This will always be the activity (or activities) that *does not* require any preceding activity. It is placed at the left side of the diagram (similar to the start of a decision tree); the event before this activity is marked **1,** and the one after it is marked **2.** Next, the data show that activities *b, c,* and *e* must all be preceded by activity *a,* whose conclusion is event **2.** Therefore, all of these activities can start only after **2** has been "declared" (occurs). This is shown in Figure 11.4.

At the end of each activity, a number is assigned to designate the forthcoming event. The assignment of the numbers **3, 4,** and **5** is made as the network progresses, from left to right. The representation in Figure 11.4 shows that activities *b, c,* and *e* can be conducted simultaneously, but none can start until activity *a* has been completed. Note that activity *c* was placed above activity *b* in the diagram; this was done merely as a matter of convenience for drawing the remaining diagram.

Project grows to the right

The construction of the entire network continues in the same manner. Out of event **3**, succeeding activities *d* and *f* are extended (Figure 11.5). Out of event **4** the succeeding activity *g* is drawn, and out of event **5** the succeeding activity *h* is drawn. The diagram grows to the right until all activities and events are depicted.

Dummy activities for proper sequencing

Dummy activities In the construction of a network, care must be taken to assure that the activities and events are in proper sequence. One device that helps proper sequencing is **dummy activities.** Dummy

FIGURE 11.5
PERT network for Moose Lake project

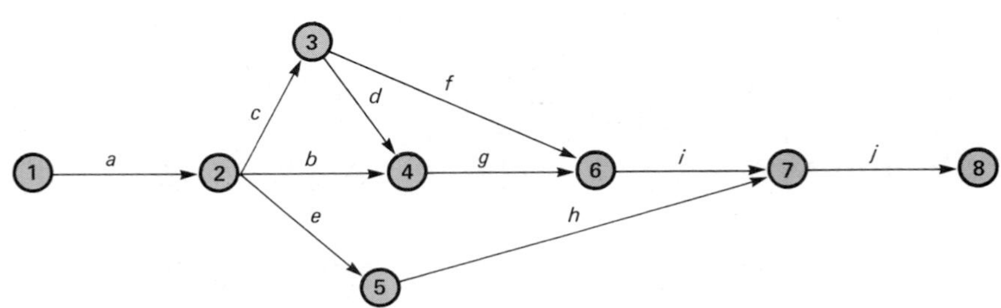

activities are characterized by their use of zero time and zero resources; their function is to designate a precedence relationship. Graphically, such activities are shown as broken lines.

Example. Given the network:

Activity	*Required preceding activities*
a	None
b	None
c	*b*
d	*a, c*
e	*a*
f	*d, e*

To diagram this network it is necessary to use a dummy activity, as shown in Figure 11.6.

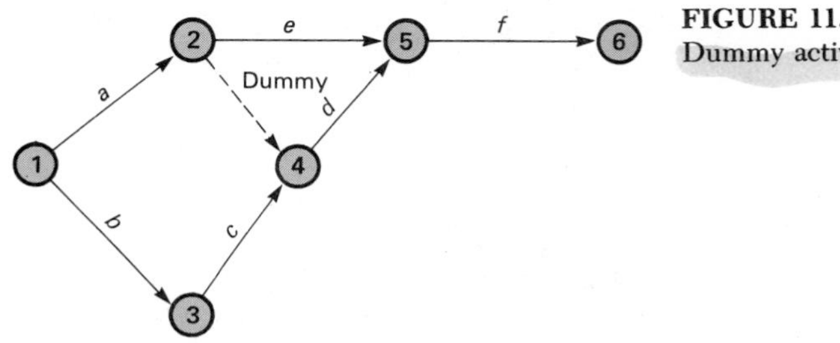

FIGURE 11.6
Dummy activity

Similar complex network relationships are illustrated in Figure 11.7.

Networks without events

It is possible to draw a network composed of activities only. Figure 11.8 shows such a network (a) and its equivalent event-oriented network (b). The activity-oriented network is more cumbersome. It is used mainly in computer analysis where events are not used at all.

Time-scaled networks

A time-scaled network is one in which the activities and events are located by a time scale along the horizontal border. The estimated duration of the activity is shown as a bar whose length is proportional to the duration. Figure 11.9 illustrates a PERT network and its equivalent bar chart. PERT can be viewed as an extension of a simple bar chart. The bar chart in Figure 11.9 shows that all activities in this project can be completed by time 6. Activity **2–4** does not start until activity **1–2** has been completed, and activity **3–4** does not start until **1–3** has been completed. Activities

FIGURE 11.7
Network relationships

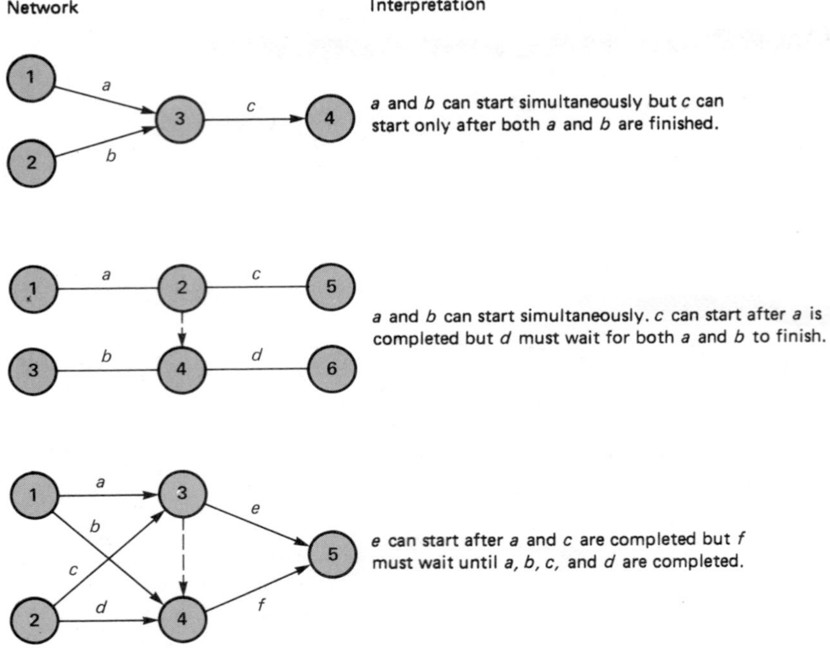

1–2 and **2–4**, however, can take place at the same time that **1–3** and **3–4** are taking place, as long as the precedence relationships are maintained.

Computer programs produce bar charts with dates inserted instead of elapsed time. There are several ways to locate the activities on a chart depending on when the activities are scheduled to "start," if they are not critical.

FIGURE 11.8
Activity- and event-oriented networks

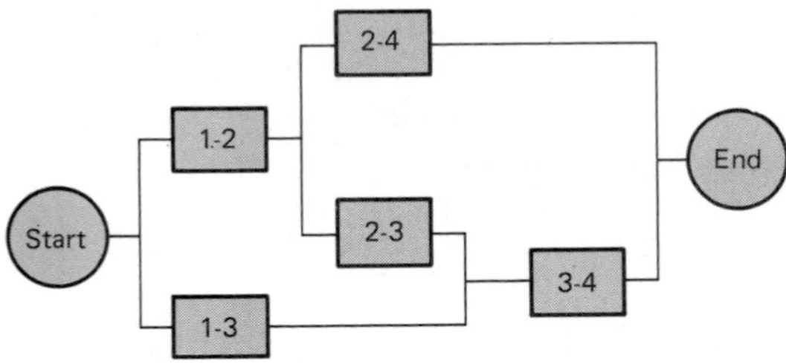

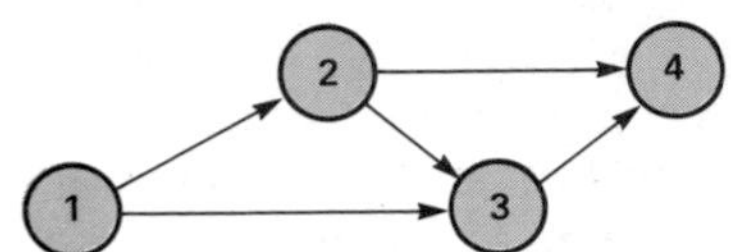

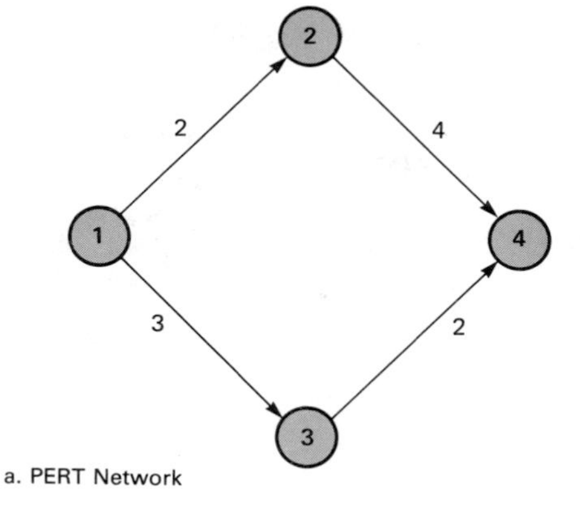

a. PERT Network

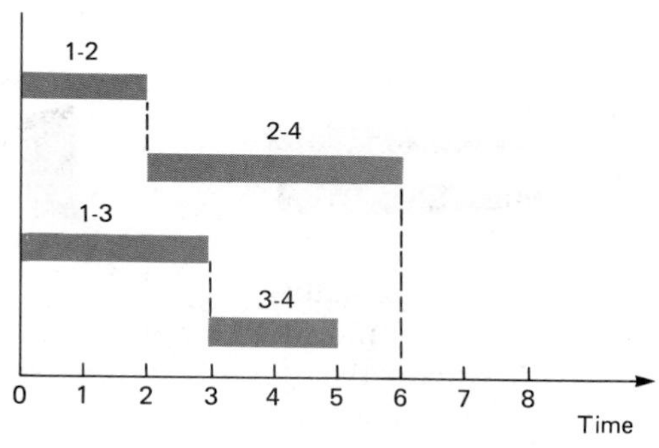

b. Equivalent Bar Chart

FIGURE 11.9
Comparison of PERT and a bar chart

11.4 EVENT ANALYSIS (STEP 5)

Event-oriented analysis is used primarily in PERT since it is especially convenient for risk analysis involving probabilities of completion. Several methods are available for executing event analysis. Two are presented here: first, an analytical method, then complete enumeration. The following procedure is used in event analysis.

a. Enter time estimates on the network.
b. Compute the earliest and latest dates for all events.
c. Find the slack on the events and identify critical events.
d. Find the slack on the activities and identify critical activities.
e. Find the critical path.

The details of this procedure are illustrated below.

a. Enter time estimates on the network

Once the network is completed, the t_e activity durations are entered on the diagram (in parentheses, above the arcs or arrows) as shown in

Figure 11.10. (For a discussion of time estimates in PERT, see Section 11.8.)

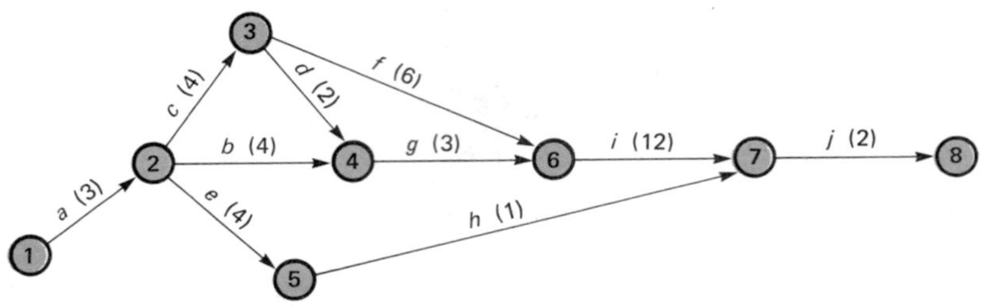

FIGURE 11.10 Time estimates for the project

b. Compute the earliest and latest dates

This approach is based on two important concepts:

- The earliest possible event date—T_E (or ET).
- The latest allowable event date—T_L (or LT).

Earliest date of latest activity

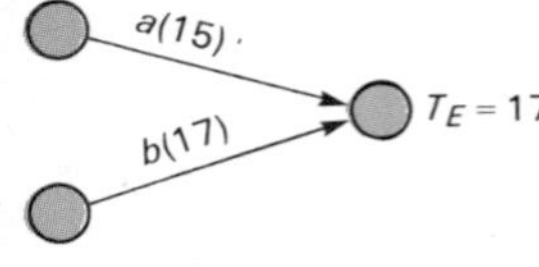

The earliest date: T_E By definition the **earliest date, T_E,** for an event to occur, is immediately after *all* the preceding activities have been completed. For example, if a certain event is preceded by two activities, and the earliest date that activity *a* can be completed is 15 weeks, and the earliest date that activity *b* can be completed is 17 weeks, then the earliest time that the event can occur is at the conclusion of 17 weeks. Since this rule is true for every event including the last one, then *the earliest possible date for completing the entire project is the earliest date of the last event.*

Latest date without delay

The latest allowable date: T_L The **latest allowable date** for each event, T_L, is the latest date that an event can occur *without causing a delay* in the already-determined project's completion date. The completion date for the project can be either the earliest possible completion date, or any other agreed-upon date. Unless otherwise stated, we will use the earliest possible completion date for our calculations. The computation is done as follows.

Forward pass

1. Forward pass: Find T_E for each event. In order to compute T_E for an event, the duration of each path leading to the event is computed. If several paths lead to an event, then the path with the *largest elapsed* time is considered.

Example. We will now find T_E for all events. To begin with, Figure 11.10 is reproduced as Figure 11.11.

Path with the longest time

Event **1:** This is the event at the beginning of the project. The T_E for this event is set to zero. This information is written above the event (Figure 11.11). *For event* **2:** There is only one activity from event **1** to **2;** its duration is three weeks. The T_E for event **2** is thus 3. Similarly, T_E for event **3** is seven weeks and for event **5** is seven weeks.

For event **4:** Note that T_E is to be determined by the longest (timewise)

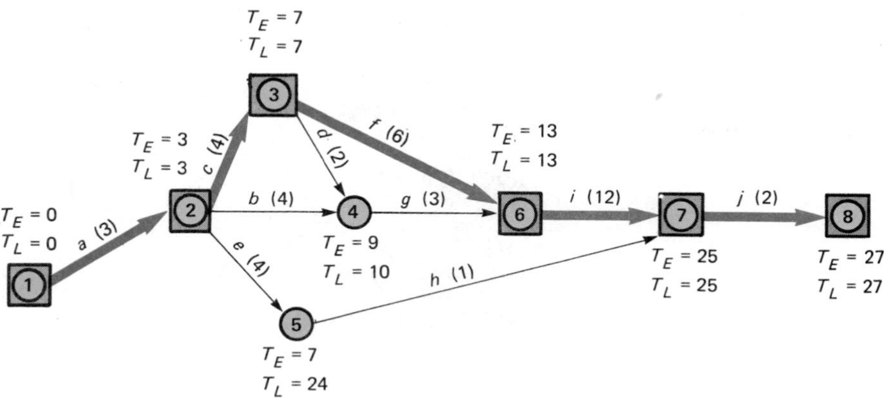

FIGURE 11.11
Computation of T_E and T_L

path leading to an event. However, it is not necessary to return to the beginning of the network to compute all paths leading to an event to figure the longest one; use can be made of existing information, using the following formula:

> Length of a path = Duration of the last activity on the path + T_E of the preceding event

Figure 11.12 shows the portion of the network leading to event **4**. For event **4** to be declared, both activity d and activity b must be completed. Now, the length of the path **1–2–3–4** is determined as:

T_E for event **3** =	7
+ duration of activity d =	2
Total	9

The length of path **1–2–4** is determined as:

Length of a path

T_E for event **2** =	3
+ duration of activity b =	4
Total	7

Now, all paths leading to the event are compared. Since 9 is the larger number, T_E for event **4** will be 9.

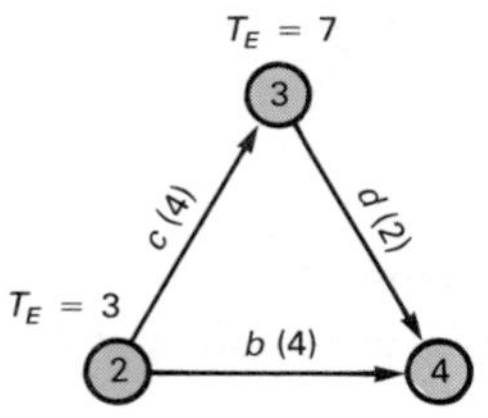

FIGURE 11.12
Event 4

Event **6:** Two paths are considered:

path **1–2–3–6**

whose length is:

$$T_E = 7 \text{ (for event 3)} + 6 = 13$$

and

path **1–2–3–4–6**

(path **2–3–4** is longer than **2–4**) whose length is:

$$9 + 3 = 12$$

Thus, the larger is 13 weeks.

The rest of the earliest start values are obtained in the same manner (shown in Figure 11.11). Event **8** designates the *end* of the project, since no activities emerge from it. Therefore, the earliest date for this event, 27 weeks, is the earliest date that the entire project can be completed. (This is good news for Judi as project director since the agreed-upon completion time was 30 weeks.)

Backward pass

2. *Backward pass: Find T_L for each event.* (Refer to Figure 11.11.) To compute each T_L, start from the last event (**8**) and work backward all the way to event **1**.

For event **8:** T_L for the last event is set equal to the computed earliest completion time of the project (27 weeks).

For event **7:** Since the latest that event **8** can occur is 27 weeks, and since it takes 2 weeks to complete activity *j*, then the latest allowable date that event **7** can occur is $27 - 2 = 25$ weeks.

For event **6:** Since the latest that event **7** can occur is 25 and since activity *i* lasts 12 weeks, then the latest time for event **6** is $25 - 12 = 13$.

Working backward to find T_L

For event **5:** In a similar manner, T_L is found to be 24 (T_L for **7** is 25 minus 1 week for activity $h = 24$).

For event **4:** In a similar manner, T_L is computed as 10.

For event **3:** Here, two activities, *d* and *f*, must be considered. Since activity *d* lasts 2 weeks, and since it must be completed no later than the 10th week (the latest allowable time for event **4**), then activity *d* must start not later than $10 - 2 = 8$. Activity *f* takes 6 weeks; it must be completed, at the latest, by week 13 (which is T_L for event **6**). Therefore, activity *f* must be started *not later* than $13 - 6 = 7$.

Now, to enable both activities to start on time so that there will be no delay in the entire project, event **3** must occur, *at the latest,* by week 7, which is the *smaller* of the two T_L's. Computation is continued in the same manner, event by event, until event **1** is reached. Of special interest is event **2**. Here, three T_L's and activities must be considered. For *c*,

$7 - 4 = 3$; for b, $10 - 4 = 6$; and for e, $24 - 4 = 20$. The *smallest one*, three weeks, is selected as T_L for event **2**. For event **1**, T_L is zero.[4]

Summary

The T_E's are computed starting from the left; this is called a **forward pass.** The T_L's are computed starting from the right side of the network, called a **backward pass.**

c. **Find the slack on the events and identify critical events**

The difference between the T_L and the T_E, for each event, is defined as **slack** (S).

$$S = T_L - T_E \tag{11.1}$$

Two cases are distinguished:

Two cases of slack

1. *When $T_L = T_E$ for the last event (the end of the project).* In this case, slacks in the network can either be zero, whereupon the events are called *critical events,* or larger than zero, whereupon the events are considered to have positive slack.

   In our example (Figure 11.11), we assumed $T_L = T_E$ for the final event and all critical events, which have zero slack. These are shown with a box around them to aid in quick recognition. Note that only events **4** and **5** are not critical here.
2. *When $T_L \neq T_E$ for the last event.* In this case, the *critical* events are defined as those events with the *minimum slack,* which *can* be negative (when $T_L < T_E$).

Critical events

What is the meaning of slack? Since T_E is the earliest that an event can be reached and T_L is the latest that the event can occur without delaying the entire project, then the difference, the slack, tells how long the event can "linger" *without* delaying the entire project. Any delay in a critical event will cause a delay in the entire project.

Slack as allowable delay

Let us examine event **5.** For this event, the slack is: $T_L - T_E = 24 - 7 = 17$ weeks. The meaning of this is that although event **5** can be reached in 7 weeks, management has the flexibility to reach this event at any time during the ensuing 17 weeks (up to the 24th week) without causing a delay in the entire project.

[4] For the first event, T_L must be zero if $T_E = T_L$ for the last event.

d. Find the slack on the activities and identify critical activities

Similar to the slack on an event, there is also slack on activities. This slack tells us how long the activity can linger without delaying the entire project. Equation 11.2 can be used to find the amount of slack:

$$\text{Activity slack} = \underset{\substack{\text{at the end}\\ \text{of the}\\ \text{activity}}}{T_L \text{ for the event}} - \underset{\substack{\text{at the}\\ \text{beginning}\\ \text{of the}\\ \text{activity}}}{T_E \text{ for the event}} - \underset{\substack{\text{duration}\\ \text{of the}\\ \text{activity}}}{t_e} \tag{11.2}$$

Total float and free float

This slack is also called **total float (TF).** It is distinguished from a type of slack called **free float (FF)**, which will be discussed later. In our example, we get the following results:

Activity	T_L minus	T_E minus	t_e =	*Slack (TF)*
a	3 −	0 −	3 =	0
b	10	3	4	3
c	7	3	4	0
d	10	7	2	1
e	24	3	4	17
f	13	7	6	0
g	13	9	3	1
h	25	7	1	17
i	25	13	12	0
j	27	25	2	0

Again, two cases are distinguished:

1. *When $T_L = T_E$ for the last event.* In this case, an activity with zero slack is defined as a *critical activity.*
2. *When $T_L \neq T_E$ for the last event.* In this case, the activities with the *minimum slack* are the critical ones.

e. Find the critical path

The critical activities and events constitute the critical path

The critical path is the path(s) in the network, leading from the beginning of the project to its end, *all* of whose activities and events are critical.

This definition implies that if $T_L = T_E$ for the last event, then there is *zero slack* on the critical path. Otherwise, the critical path is that path with the minimum slack on it.

The critical path has certain additional characteristics:

1. There can be more than one critical path in the network.
2. The critical path is the longest (timewise) path in the network.

In our example, the critical path is:

1–2–3–6–7–8

The importance of identifying the critical path is that it points out those activities and events that are critical and, as such, must be carefully monitored and controlled. Before getting into these topics, however, let us note some additional characteristics of the PERT/CPM network.

Monitoring the critical path

11.5 ACTIVITY ANALYSIS (STEP 6)

The previous method identified the critical events by computing their earliest and latest times. From this information we derived the critical path, critical activities, and the slack. The following method can be used as an alternative for arriving at the same output. Let:

ES = **Earliest start** for an activity. This time is equivalent to the T_E of the event from which the activity starts. We assume that all predecessor activities started at their earliest times and have been completed.

EF = **Earliest finish** time for an activity. Assuming the activity started at its ES and lasted its planned duration t_e, then:

$$EF = ES + t_e \tag{11.3}$$

LF = **Latest finish** time for an activity. This is the latest time by which an activity can be completed without delaying the project. It is equal to the T_L of the event at the end of the activity.

LS = The **latest start** for an activity. This is the latest an activity can start without jeopardizing the project's deadline.

$$LS = LF - t_e \tag{11.4}$$

Graphical presentation

ES, EF, LF, and LS may be presented in different ways. Three common ways are shown in Figure 11.13 on page 454. Also, an event-oriented picture, (d), is included.

Example

Given: the network shown in Figure 11.14 on page 454.

Computing ES and EF (forward pass) The procedure starts from the left and moves to the right. Let the earliest start for the project be zero. (In a real-life situation, an actual date may be used.)

Rule for computing the ES: The earliest time for an activity is equal to the *largest value* of the earliest finish (EF) for all activities ending at the event from which the activity starts.

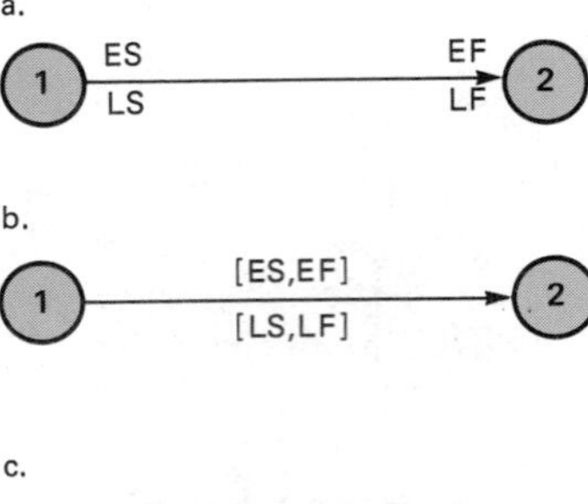

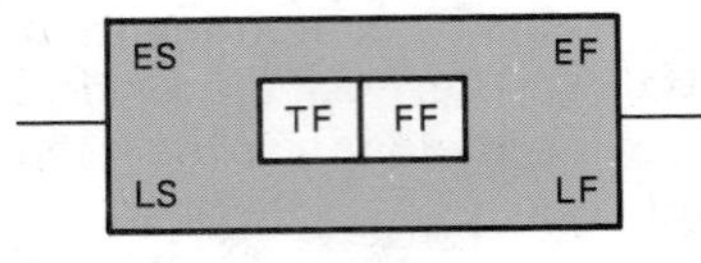

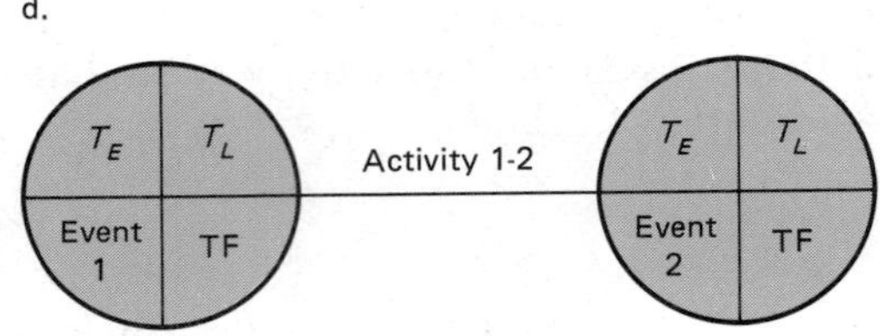

d.

T_E T_L Activity 1-2 T_E T_L

Event 1 TF Event 2 TF

FIGURE 11.13
Alternative ways of presentation

The computations are shown in Table 11.2.

We start with event **1.** The ES for activities **1–2, 1–4,** and **1–3** is zero, since these are the starting activities. Next, we figure EF for these three activities using the formula EF = ES + t_e. Then, we find ES for activities **2–4** and **3–4** using the rule above. Last, we figure EF for these two activities using Equation 11.3.

Computing LF and LS (backward pass) Once all ESs and EFs are computed, we start by setting the LF of all final activities to the *largest* EF (9 in our example). Alternatively, a desired finish date (larger than the largest EF) may be used, as we will discuss later.

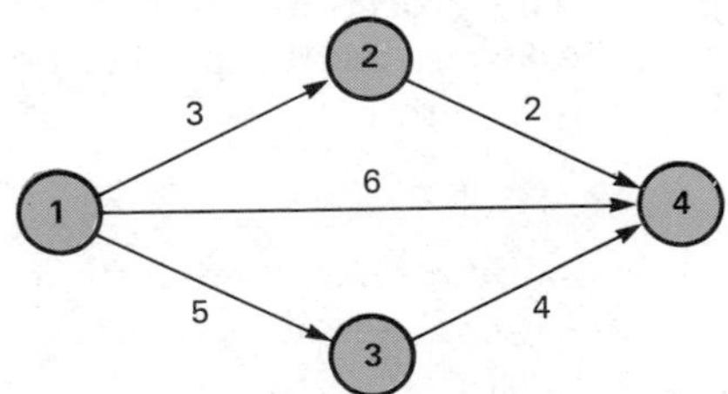

FIGURE 11.14
An example network

TABLE 11.2 Finding the ES and EF values

Activity	*ES*	*EF (Eq. 11.3)*
1–2	0	0 + 3 = (3)
1–4	0	0 + 6 = 6
1–3	0	0 + 5 = (5)
2–4	3	3 + 2 = 5
3–4	5	5 + 4 = 9

Rule for computing the LF: The latest finish time for an activity entering a particular event is equal to the *smallest value* of the LSs for all activities starting from this event.

The computations are shown in Table 11.3, following a backward pass.

TABLE 11.3 Finding the LF and LS values

Activity	*LF*	*LS (Eq. 11.4)*	*ES*	*TF (slack)*
2–4	9	9 − 2 = 7	3	4
1–4	9	9 − 6 = 3	0	3
3–4	9	9 − 4 = 5	5	0
1–2	7	7 − 3 = 4	0	4
1–3	5	5 − 5 = 0	0	0

First, we figure the LSs for activities **2–4, 1–4,** and **3–4** using Equation 11.4 and the designated LFs. Then, we compute LF for the remaining two activities using the rule above. Finally, we compute (with Equation 11.4) the LSs for activities **1–2** and **1–3.**

Computation of the slack The regular slack, also called the total float (TF), is computed as

$$\text{TF} = \text{LS} - \text{ES} \tag{11.5}$$

The computations are shown in Table 11.3.

Some additional characteristics

Regular slack (total float)

Such a case is shown in Figure 11.15. Activity **1–3** has a duration of 6 weeks, while the path **1–2–3** has a duration of 13 weeks. Therefore, activity **1–3** can linger 13 − 6 = 7 weeks; that is, there is a 7-week slack on the activity. Regular slack denotes the *maximum* amount of slack available, some of which may be shared.

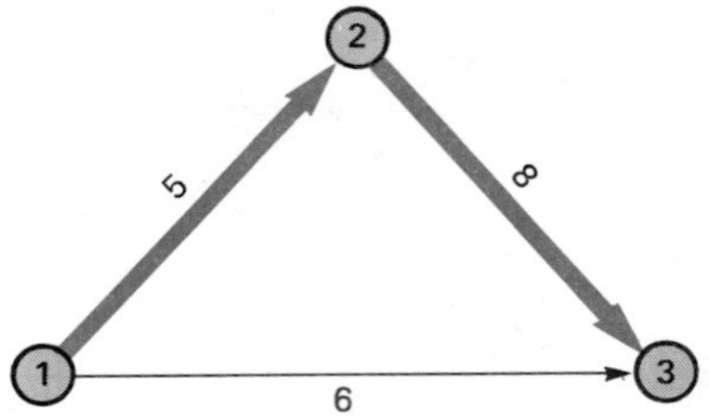

FIGURE 11.15
Regular slack

Shared slack (slack on a noncritical path)

Whenever there are two or more noncritical activities, or noncritical events connected in a series, their slack is called **shared.** An example of shared slack is shown in Figure 11.16, where activities *e* and *h* are connected in series. The critical portion of the path between events **2** and **7** requires 22 weeks.

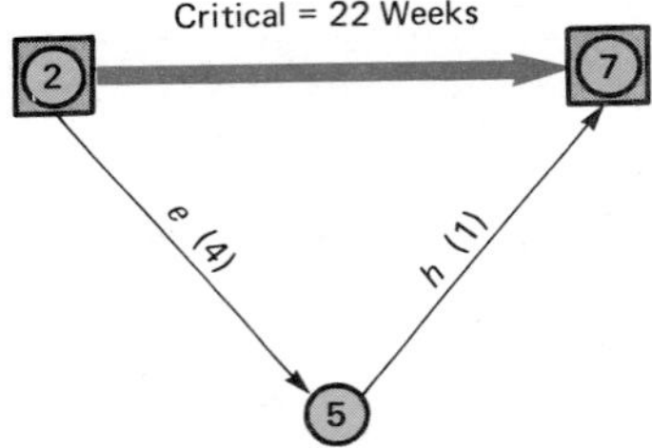

FIGURE 11.16
Shared slack, example 1

Activity *e* requires four weeks and activity *h* requires one week, a total of five weeks. Therefore, there is a slack of 22 − 5 = 17 weeks, which can be distributed between *e* and *h* in any combination. For example, a slack of 17 on *e* and zero on *h*, 16 on *e* and 1 on *h*, and so on.

Another example of shared slack. Figure 11.17 shows a situation with two noncritical events, **2** and **3**, and three noncritical activities *a*, *b*, and *c*. Activities *a*, *b*, and *c* together require 3 + 4 + 5 = 12 weeks. Therefore, there is a regular slack of 30 − 12 = 18 on both events **2** and **3** (e.g., 18 on **2**, zero on **3**; 17 on **2** and 1 on **3**, and so on). That is, there is a shared slack of 18 on events **2** and **3.**

There is also a regular slack of 30 − 12 = 18 on each of *activities a*, *b*, and *c*, which is shared among the three. Again, one may use the 18

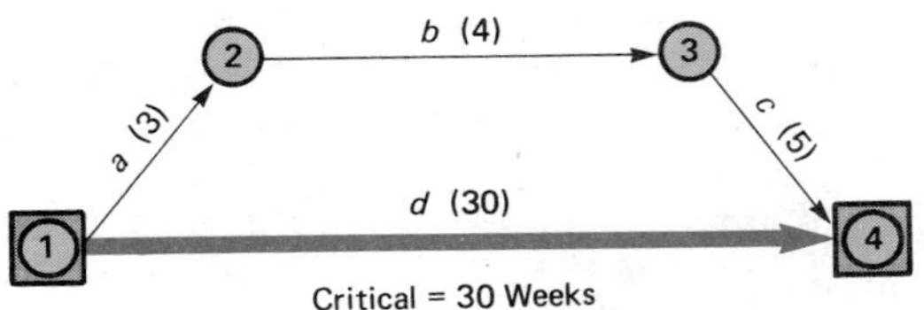

FIGURE 11.17
Shared slack, example 2

on activity *a* alone, or six weeks on each activity, and so on. (There are as many possibilities as there are ways of allocating 18 among three recipients.)

In a situation of shared slack, it can be viewed as being on a path, rather than on an individual activity. For example, in Figure 11.17 there is a slack of 18 on path **1–2–3–4.**

Free float

Free float (FF) is a slack that represents the time any activity can be delayed before it delays the earliest start time of any activity immediately following. For example, in Figure 11.15, the slack of 7 on **1–3** is free, as is the slack of 17 on **5–7** in Figure 11.16. Notice that the free float on activity *e* in Figure 11.16 is zero. In general, if there are several noncritical activities in a series, only the last one will have a free float.

Free float is important in the case of shared slack. It means that if a slack has not been shared, it can all be used in the last sharing activity. Computer printouts typically give both the TF and the FF for each activity, as will be demonstrated later. Basically, the free float on an activity can be calculated as the early start of the successor event, minus the early finish of the activity.

The case when $T_L \neq T_E$ for the project

In the previous computations, we assumed that $T_L = T_E$ for the last event. However, this may not always be the case.

If T_L is larger than T_E for the last event, then the slack for the last event will be positive.

Example. In the Moose Lake project, Judi can consider T_L as 30 (the agreed-upon completion time). Thus, the slack on event 8 will be 30 − 27 = 3, and so will the slacks on all critical events. Further, the slack on all noncritical events will be three weeks larger, too. For example, for event **5** the new $T_L = 27$; since $T_E = 7$ (unchanged), then the slack for event **5** = 27 − 7 = 20 weeks.

If T_L is smaller than T_E for the last event, a *negative slack* will result, indicating that the desired date cannot be achieved and a delay of the magnitude of the negative value is expected. Similar logic can be used for the case of starting LF calculations in an activity-oriented analysis.

Negative slack—a delay

A critical path leading to an event

The critical path procedure outlined previously can also be used to find the critical path leading to any desired event. For example, the critical path to event **4** is: **1–2–3–4.**

Use of complete enumeration

In small problems, like the one in the example, the critical path may be identified by listing all possible paths leading from the beginning

Compare and select the longest path

of the project to its end. The path with the *largest* duration is the critical path (composed of all critical activities and events). The reason for this is that in order to complete the project, all activities *must* be accomplished. Since the longest path is longer than any other, its completion gives enough elapsed time to complete *all other paths*. This guarantees that every single activity in the network will be accomplished. In the Moose Lake example, the following four paths are identified:

		Total duration (weeks)	
Path 1	1–2–3–4–6–7–8	26	
Path 2	1–2–3–6–7–8	27	←*Maximum*
Path 3	1–2–4–6–7–8	24	
Path 4	1–2–5–7–8	10	

When *all* paths are compared (complete enumeration approach), the longest path is found to be Path 2, with a duration of 27 weeks.

In large, complex networks with hundreds of activities, especially when continuous updating is required, the complete enumeration approach may take a long time. In such cases, the analytical approach is used.

Multiple critical paths

In this example, there is a single critical path for the project. However, in other problems, multiple paths may occur. For example, if activity *d* were three weeks, there would have been *two* critical paths. The one already identified:

1–2–3–6–7–8

and another one:

1–2–3–4–6–7–8

Several starting events

The examples given so far exhibit a single starting event. However, this is not necessary and real projects often do have multiple starting events (e.g., see Problem 9).

11.6 ANALYSIS AND APPLICATION

The previous sections showed how to construct a network and find the critical activities, the noncritical activities, and the slack. Based on this information, and using the principle of management by exception, it is possible to construct a management system with tighter control over the critical activities and less control over the noncritical activities. Alternatively, one can use very tight control over critical activities, less control on activities with small slack, and the least control over activities with large slack. PERT/CPM can also be used to generate additional information, as will be discussed in the remainder of this section and again in Part B of this chapter.

Step 7. Monitoring and control

Suppose that the Moose Lake project started on schedule. However, the very first activity, the administrative setup, is delayed. Although the duration of this critical activity had been estimated as three weeks, it is now clear that it will take four weeks to handle all the administrative details. Thus, when the time comes for event **2**, its T_E will be 4, rather than 3. The slack in event **2**, according to Equation 11.1, will be:

$$S = T_L - T_E = 3 - 4 = -1$$

That is, the slack has a negative value and is labeled as *negative slack*. A negative value for a slack means that the project is behind schedule. If T_E's are now computed for all the remaining critical events, including the ending event, there will be a negative slack of 1. This implies that the *entire project* will be delayed by one week. What can management do about this?

Dealing with a delay

Look, for a moment, at event **5**, which is not critical. The previous slack for this event was computed as 24 − 7 = 17; now it will be 24 − 8 = 16, still a positive slack.

Activities *b, d, e,* and *h* likewise possess positive slack. This means that these activities can still be delayed without delaying the entire project. Slowing down noncritical activities may release resources (such as labor, tools, and equipment) that may then be transferred to one (or more) of the critical activities. If such a transfer could reduce the completion time of any critical activity by one week, the delay could be eliminated and the project would still be completed on schedule.

Transferring resources

A similar situation may develop if a noncritical activity such as *g* requires six rather than three weeks for completion. The T_E for event **6** would then be 15 weeks, and a negative slack of 2 would be formed at event **6.** Notice that the critical path will be changed to **1–2–3–4–6–7–8**, and activities *d* and *g* will become critical. In general, any deviation of the actual time from the computed duration should be reported to the project director, who in turn will recompute the critical path. Previously noncritical events and activities may become critical, and vice versa.

In addition to transferring resources to critical activities, management may correct delays by some other actions such as:

- Relaxing (making less strict) the technical specifications or the required quality.
- Changing the scope of the project by reducing the desired goals and consequently the amount of work.

Other ways to correct delays

- Changing the sequencing of activities.
- Pouring additional resources into the project.
- Expediting activities by various incentives.
- Starting activities while preceding ones are still being completed.

Step 8. Resource utilization

The regular PERT/CPM analysis is limited to planning the elapsed time. Since the planning is done prior to actual project execution, it is not always possible to know the precise resource availability, so we assume that there are sufficient resources for executing the activities as planned.

Competing for one resource

Suppose, however, that a project includes two activities that have the same early start date. In addition, they both are noncritical with three days slack and a duration of seven days. Assume that each activity requires a bulldozer throughout the duration, and it is then discovered that only one bulldozer is available. It is therefore apparent that both activities *cannot* proceed simultaneously. Since neither of them is critical, neither has a priority, and since there is not sufficient slack, then either one must be postponed, a second bulldozer obtained, or the network must be rearranged to move one of these activities forward in time. In other words, the way that the company allocates one of its resources may affect the critical path and the completion date.

This example can be extended to cover other resources (e.g., labor, money). In general, whenever several activities need a limited resource, it is necessary to decide on how to allocate this resource. Since the regular PERT/CPM analysis essentially contains only early and late start dates for the activities, the project manager is free to decide on an actual start date between these limits. In contrast, a resource allocation schedule contains a scheduled start date for every activity, taking into consideration the availability of resources.

Example

The following example involves the management of labor. Assume that a project is given as shown in Figure 11.18 (times in weeks). The critical path is shown on the network; the earliest and latest dates for

FIGURE 11.18
Example of a project

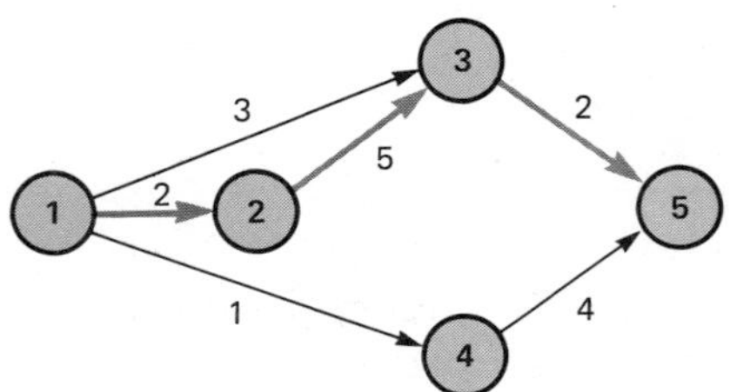

each activity are given in Table 11.4. The last column of the table lists the number of employees required each week to work on each activity. For simplicity, we assume that all the employees possess the same skill.

TABLE 11.4
Earliest and latest dates

Activity	*Earliest start*	*Latest start*	*Slack (TF)*	*Employees*
1–2	0	0	0	2
1–3	0	4	4	2
1–4	0	4	4	3
2–3	2	2	0	2
3–5	7	7	0	1
4–5	1	5	4	2

Solution

The project shown in Figure 11.18 is transferred to a bar chart in Figure 11.19 with each activity at its earliest starting time. In Figure 11.20, the weekly labor requirements identify an *unbalanced demand* for labor, ranging from one to seven employees per week, that may be difficult to arrange. A more leveled schedule can be derived by delaying the noncritical activities **1–3, 1–4,** or **4–5.** Such an arrangement is shown in Figure 11.21. This arrangement reduces the peak manpower requirements to five without affecting the completion date of the project. But if only four employees are available, it would be necessary to delay the completion date of the entire project or use overtime (at an increased cost). A trial-and-error approach is used.

Finding the best schedule—a trial-and-error approach

The reader may note that there are several different five-employee schedules with a duration of nine weeks. Similarly, more than one schedule will give the four-employee duration. Because of this fact, the computer program that performs resource scheduling uses a trial-and-error approach with heuristics, as well as given priority rules to find the *minimum* duration. Existing programs are also able to handle multiple projects with thousands of activities that simultaneously compete for resources and to schedule within specified machine, facility, and manpower limitations.

Trial-and-error approach

Heuristic programs for resource scheduling usually take one of two forms.

1. ***Resource leveling*** An attempt is made to reduce peak resource requirements and to smooth the weekly (daily) requirements within a constraint on project duration.

2. ***Resource allocation*** For a desired resource level (e.g., five employees), find the shortest possible project schedule. Examples can be found in references [9], [10] and [14].

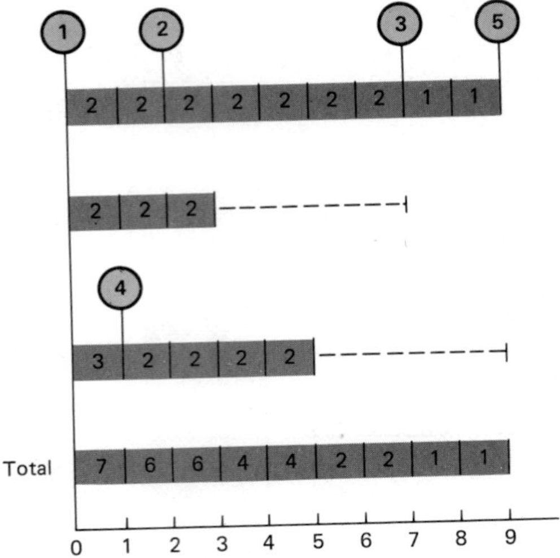

FIGURE 11.19
Earliest start schedule

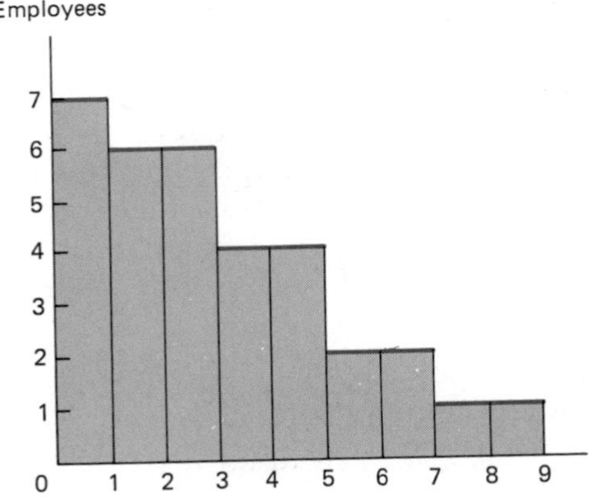

FIGURE 11.20
Manpower requirement

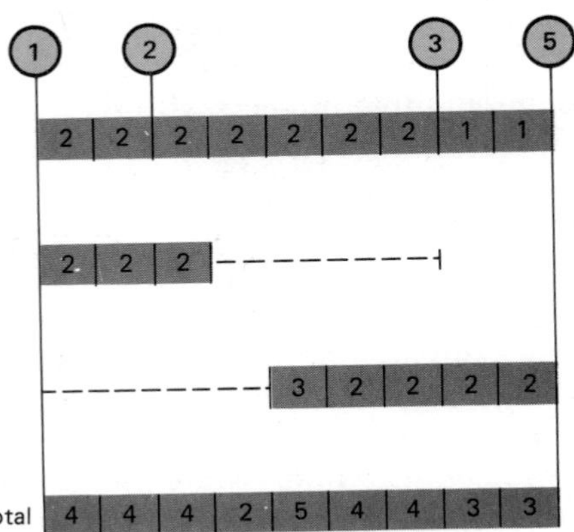

FIGURE 11.21
Leveled schedule of labor demands

Summary

The example in this section dealt with manpower as a resource. Similar analyses can be made with money (cost of activities), multiple skills, or any other resource.

Multiple projects

In this chapter we have presented a case of a company managing a single project. However, companies commonly execute several projects at the same time. For example, an airline may overhaul six airplanes simultaneously and a construction company may build 10 buildings at the same time. If there are dependencies among projects, such as resource constraints, their management becomes very complex. Resources may be shared between projects, and employees may continuously be transferred from lower- to higher-priority activities. Fortunately, several computer programs exist to help manage multiproject activities (e.g., by Unisys, GE, and IBM), as will be discussed in Section 11.15.

Actual dates

Most real-life PERT/CPM programs are executed with actual dates (excluding weekends and holidays, if necessary) rather than elapsed time. Examples will be given in Section 11.15.

11.7 PROBLEMS FOR PART A[5]

1. The events of the project below are designated as 1, 2, and so on.
   a. Draw the network.
   b. Find the critical path by complete enumeration.
   c. Find, for all events, the earliest and latest dates.
   d. Find the slacks on all the events and activities.
   e. Find the critical path using the T_E's and T_L's.

Activity	*Preceding event*	*Succeeding event*	t_e *(weeks)*	*Preceding activities*
a	1	2	3	none
b	1	3	6	none
c	1	4	8	none
d	2	5	7	*a*
e	3	5	5	*b*
f	4	5	10	*c*
g	4	6	4	*c*
h	5	7	5	*d, e, f*
i	6	7	6	*g*

2. Given the following PERT network (times are in weeks):

[5] Unless stated otherwise, slack means total float (TF).

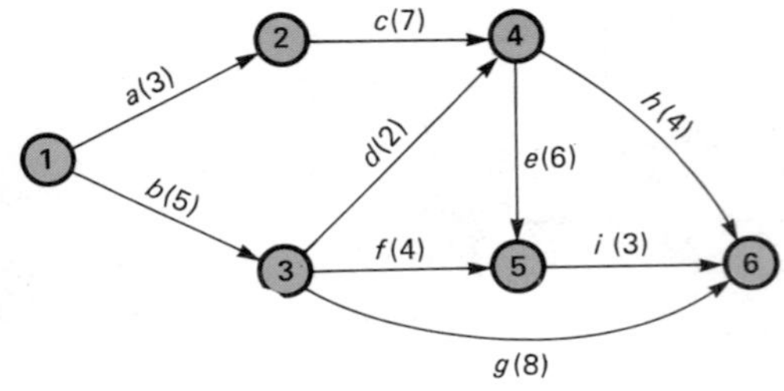

Determine:

a. The T_E and T_L for each event.
b. The slacks on all events and activities.
c. The critical activities and path.
d. The shared slacks.

3. Suppose that management has a contract to finish the project in Problem 2 in 22 weeks.
Determine:

a. The slack on event **3.**
b. The slack on activity *g.*

4. Given the following schedule for a liability work package done as part of an accounting audit in a corporation:

	Activity	Duration (days)	Preceding activities
a.	Obtain schedule of liabilities	3	None
b.	Mail confirmation	15	*a*
c.	Test pension plan	5	*a*
d.	Vouch selected liabilities	60	*a*
e.	Test accruals and amortization	6	*d*
f.	Process confirmations	40	*b*
g.	Reconcile interest expense to debt	10	*c, e*
h.	Verify debt restriction compliance	7	*f*
i.	Investigate debit balances	6	*g*
j.	Review subsequent payments	12	*h, i*

Find:

a. The critical path.
b. The slack time on "process confirmations."
c. The slack time on "test pension plan."
d. The slack time on "verify debt restriction compliance."

5. In the project network shown in the figure below, the number alongside each activity designates the activity duration (t_e) in weeks.

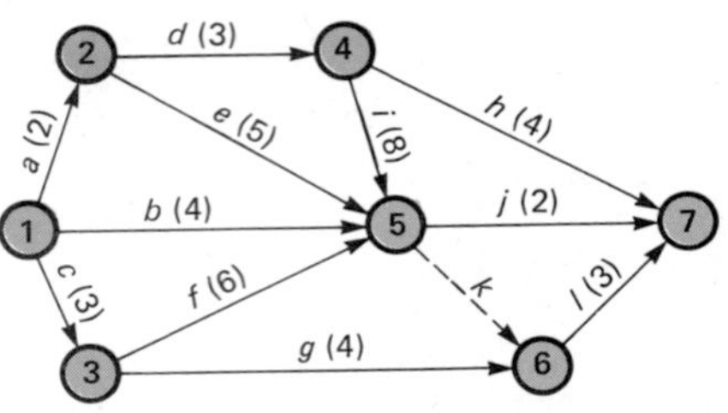

Determine:

a. The T_E and T_L for each event.
b. The earliest time that the project can be completed.
c. The slack on all events and activities.
d. The critical events and activities.
e. The critical path.
f. The shared slacks.

6. Given the following information regarding a project:

Activity	t_e (weeks)	Preceding activities
a	3	none
b	1	none
c	3	*a*
d	4	*a*
e	4	*b*
f	5	*b*
g	2	*c, e*
h	3	*f*

a. Draw the network.
b. What is the critical path?
c. What will the scheduled (earliest completion) time for the entire project be?
d. What is the critical path to event **4** (end of activities *c* and *e*)? What is the earliest time that this event can be reached?
e. What is the effect on the project if activity *e* takes an extra week? Two extra weeks? Three extra weeks?

7. Construct a network for the project below and find its critical path. (Use a complete enumeration approach.)

Activity	t_e *(weeks)*	*Preceding activities*
a	3	None
b	5	*a*
c	3	*a*
d	1	*c*
e	3	*b*
f	4	*b, d*
g	2	*c*
h	3	*g, f*
i	1	*e, h*

8. Construct a network for the project:

Activity	t_e *(weeks)*	*Preceding activities*
a	3	None
b	5	None
c	14	*a*
d	5	*a*
e	4	*b*
f	7	*b*
g	8	*d, e*
h	5	*g, f*

a. Draw the network.
b. Find the critical path by complete enumeration.
c. Assume activity *a* took five weeks. Replan the project.
d. From where would you suggest transferring resources, and to what activities, such that the original target date may be maintained?

9. Given a PERT network:

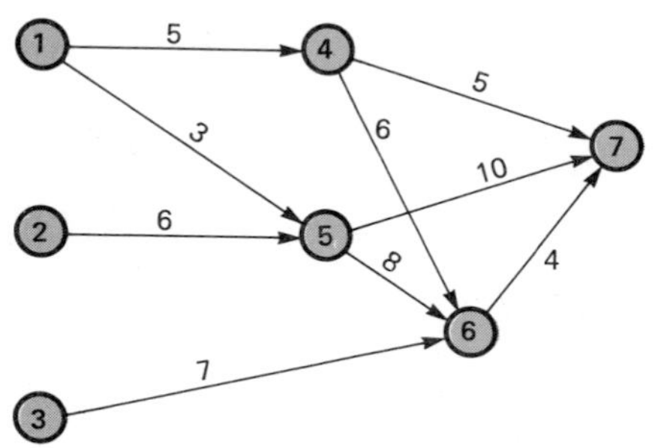

Note that three activities can start immediately. *Find:*

a. The critical path.
b. The earliest time to complete the project.
c. The slack on activities **4–6, 5–6,** and **4–7.**

10. For the project in Problem 2, find:
a. ES, EF, LS, LF for all activities.
b. TF for all activities.
c. The critical path.
d. FF for all activities.

11. For the project in Problem 7, find ES, EF, LS, LF, TF, and FF for all activities.

12. Given the project network below:

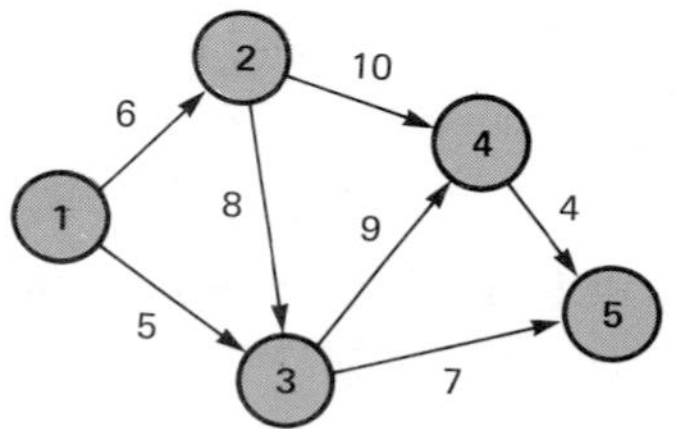

a. Draw an activity-oriented equivalent (without events).
b. Draw a bar chart; start at the *latest* possible time for all activities.

13. Assume that in Problem 2 you need two employees for each of the activities **1–2, 1–3,** and **5–6;** three employees for each of the activities **4–5** and **3–6,** and one employee for each of the remaining activities:
a. Prepare the labor demands if all activities start at their earliest times.
b. Prepare a plan that will level the labor demand over time, as much as possible. Do not "split" jobs. Once started, they must be completed.

14. Solve the maintenance work project network on page 466. (Use a computer.) Find the critical path, ES, LS, EF, LF, and regular slack.

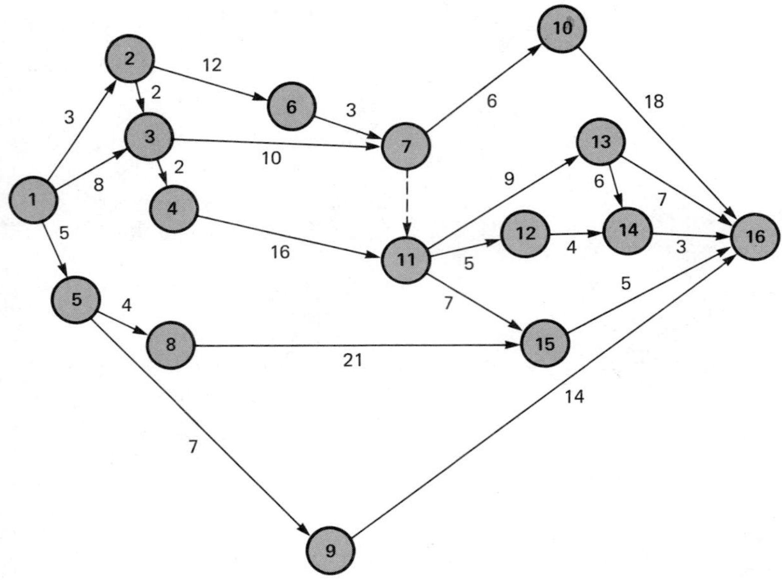

15. Build a PERT network (do *not* use dummy activities) given the following:

Activity	Time	Immediately preceding activity
Drill	2	None
Cut	1	None
Punch	3	Drill
Bend	2	Drill
Inspect	6	Cut, punch
Assemble	3	Cut, punch
Test	1	Assemble
Paint	2	Bend, inspect, test

PART B: EXTENSIONS

11.8 ESTIMATE OF ACTIVITY TIME IN PERT

Since the Moose Lake project was an experimental project, it is suitable for a PERT analysis. Judi asked each department to submit three estimates of duration time for each activity the department was responsible for, using the following guidelines:[6]

Three time estimates

Optimistic estimate (t_o): An estimate of the *shortest possible time* (duration) in which the activity can be accomplished. The probability that the activity will take less than this time is 0.01.

Most likely estimate (t_m): The duration that would occur most often if the activity were repeated under exactly the same conditions many times. Equivalently, it is the time that would be estimated most often by experts.

Pessimistic estimate (t_p): The longest time that the activity could take "when everything goes wrong." The probability that the activity will exceed this duration is 0.01.

All three estimates are entered in Table 11.5. Notice that in some cases $t_o = t_p = t_m$; that is, the exact time duration is known.

Computing the weighted average

Once the three time estimates are obtained, their weighted average is computed. This average, which is called the mean time of an activity,

TABLE 11.5
Moose Lake project activities (weeks)

Activity	*Description*	t_o *(optimistic)*	t_m *(most likely)*	t_p *(pessimistic)*	t_e *(weighted average)*
a	Administrative setup	1	3	5	3
b	Hire personnel	1	3	11	4
c	Obtain materials	3	4	5	4
d	Transport materials to Moose Lake	1	2	3	2
e	Gather measuring team	3	3	9	4
f	Planning	2	5	14	6
g	Assemble equipment	2	3	4	3
h	Plan evaluation	1	1	1	1
i	Oxygenation	12	12	12	12
j	Measurement and evaluation	1	2	3	2

[6] Projects are usually measured with a week as the logical unit of time. However, PERT analyses also use days, shifts, or even hours, especially in short-term projects.

t_e, is a *weighted average* of the three time estimates. It is computed using Equation 11.6:

$$t_e = \frac{t_o + 4t_m + t_p}{6} \tag{11.6}$$

where t_e is the expected duration of the activity.

Note: In CPM, t_e designates the duration time that is considered to be known with certainty.

A weighted average

The formula gives four times more weight to the most likely estimate than to the pessimistic or optimistic estimates. The division by 6 is to obtain a weighted average of 1 + 4+ 1 = 6 weights.[7]

For example, in Table 11.5, for activity *a*, the weighted average is:

$$t_e = \frac{1 + 4\ (3) + 5}{6} = 3 \text{ weeks}$$

and for activity *b* the weighted duration is:

$$t_e = \frac{1 + 4\ (3) + 11}{6} = 4 \text{ weeks}$$

This information is then added to the original data in the t_e column (Table 11.5).

11.9 FINDING THE PROBABILITIES OF COMPLETION IN PERT (RISK ANALYSIS)

The consideration of risk

PERT has more capabilities than just as a planning and control tool. It can also be used to give management an indication of risk in terms of project delay. This is a crucial analysis that considers the chance of completing the project on, before, or after scheduled dates.

The three estimates of activity duration in PERT, t_o, t_m, and t_p, are assumed to follow a probability distribution called the Beta distribution, shown in Figure 11.22 for activity *b* as an example ($t_o = 1$, $t_m = 3$, $t_p = 11$, and their average $t_e = 4$).

Approaching the normal distribution

Only 50 percent chance of completion by earliest chance

Even though estimates of each activity duration follow the Beta distribution, the estimate of the combined duration of several activities (such as those on the critical path) approaches the *normal* distribution. The project estimated completion time, *TS*, is computed as the expected time, T_E, for the last event. (The T_E for the last event is the same as the sum of the t_e's along the critical path if the project starts at time 0. Therefore, there is a 50 percent chance that the *entire* project will be completed by its earliest projected time (27 weeks in our example from Part A). However,

[7] This is based on the assumption that the Beta distribution is the probability distribution of duration times. Other weights are used in real-life problems based on experience.

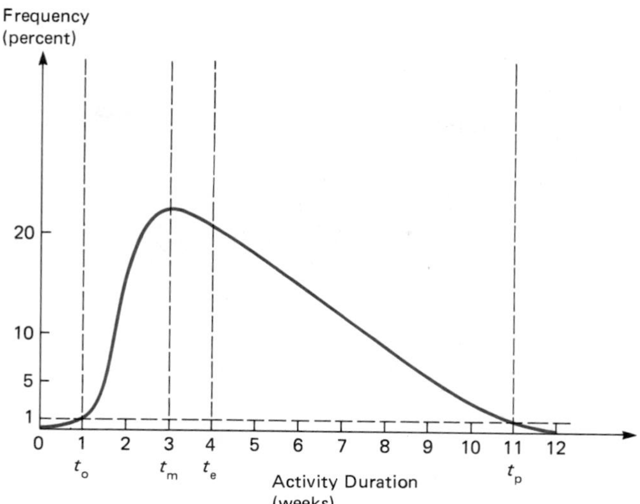

FIGURE 11.22
Activity time distribution for activity *b*

a "50 percent chance" is usually too low a confidence level for managerial planning. Management may want to know the chances of completing the project in a given amount of time, say 25 or 30 weeks. To answer such questions, an analysis involving the probability associated with the duration times is conducted.

Since each activity's duration involves three estimates, it is possible to calculate a *standard deviation* for the activity. The standard deviation of the Beta distribution of activity durations is given by Equation 11.7.

$$\text{Standard deviation of an activity} = \sigma = \frac{t_p - t_o}{6} \tag{11.7}$$

The variance of the activity's distribution is given by Equation 11.8.

$$\text{Variance of activity} = \sigma^2 = \left(\frac{t_p - t_o}{6}\right)^2 \tag{11.8}$$

For example, for activity b, the standard deviation is:

$$\sigma_b = \frac{11 - 1}{6} = 1.67 \text{ weeks}$$

and the variance is:

$$\sigma_b^2 = 1.67^2 = 2.79 \text{ weeks}$$

For activities h and i, the variance is zero, since $t_p = t_o$ for these activities. This means that no uncertainty is involved in their estimates. The larger the variance, the greater the degree of uncertainty involved in estimating the duration of the activity.

Assuming that the durations of the activities are independent of each other, the variance of a *group* of activities (designated by V) can be computed by adding the variances of the activities in that group. The value of V is then expressed by Equation 11.9.

$$V = \sigma_1^2 + \sigma_2^2 + \cdots \sigma_n^2 \tag{11.9}$$

where n is the number of activities in the group.

The variance along the critical path

Of special interest are the activities that comprise the *critical path*. For example, in the Moose Lake project, the variance for the critical path is given as:[8]

$$\begin{aligned} V &= \sigma_a^2 + \sigma_c^2 + \sigma_f^2 + \sigma_i^2 + \sigma_j^2 \\ &= .44 + .11 + 4.00 + 0 + .11 = 4.66 \end{aligned}$$

A critical path to each event

The value of V can be computed, in a similar manner, for *any event* in the network by considering the group of activities along the critical path leading to that event.

Note: The method described here is valid only if the following three assumptions hold: (1) there is a large number of activities (at least 25) on the critical path; (2) the activities' completion times are independent of each other; and (3) the noncritical paths are not relevant (i.e., we are not checking the degree of risk there). If the above assumptions are not valid, simulation must be used for the risk analysis.

Managerial applications

The managerial questions raised at the beginning of this section—the chance of completing the project in a certain desired time and the duration necessary for obtaining any desired probability of completion—can now be answered. Let:

TS = Earliest project completion time. It is the earliest time (T_E) computed for the last event, 27 weeks in the example.

D = The desired completion time, 30 weeks in the example.

Z = The number of standard deviations of a normal distribution (see Appendix C, Table C1) corresponding to the probability of completing the project by the desired completion time.

$$Z = \frac{X - \mu}{\sigma} = \frac{D - TS}{\sqrt{V}} \tag{11.10}$$

[8] If more than one critical path exists, then V should be computed for *all* such paths. Use the path with the largest V to compute probabilities of completion for dates *after* the expected completion time; use the smallest V for probabilities of completion for dates *before* the expected completion time.

Note: The justification for the use of the normal distribution is based on the *central limit theorem:* the sum of *n* independent variables tends to be normally distributed as *n* approaches infinity.

"What if . . ."

Example 1: Finding the probability of completion within a desired time, D Management wishes to know the probability of completing the Moose Lake project, *on or before* the 30th week, as specified in the contract.

Thus: $D = 30$, $TS = 27$ (as computed), $V = 4.66$ (as computed). Therefore:

$$Z = \frac{30 - 27}{\sqrt{4.66}} = \frac{3}{2.16} = 1.39$$

Using the normal distribution

The probability equivalent to $Z = 1.39$ can be found in Table C1 in Appendix C as .9177: Therefore, there is a 91.77 percent chance of completing the Moose Lake project within 30 weeks. (Remember that there is a 50 percent chance of completing the project by 27 weeks.) Figure 11.23 depicts the situation.

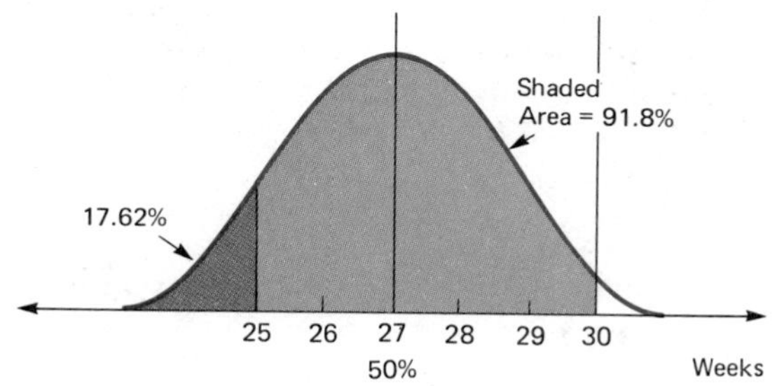

FIGURE 11.23
Chance of completing the project in 25, 27, and 30 weeks

In a similar manner, the Z for completing the project within 25 weeks is:

$$Z = \frac{25 - 27}{2.16} = -.93$$

If the normal distribution tables included negative numbers, the probability could be read directly from them. Since this is usually not the case, the probability for $Z = +.93$ is read first (which is .8238). This value is then subtracted from 1.0 (the total area under the curve); that is, $1 - .8238 = .1762$. Thus, there is only a 17.62 percent chance of completing the project in 25 weeks (see Figure 11.23).

Note: If Z is negative, the corresponding probability is always less than 50 percent. If Z is positive, the corresponding probability is always more than 50 percent; and if Z is 0, the corresponding probability is exactly 50 percent.

Goal-seeking analysis

Example 2: Finding the duration associated with a desired probability In the previous example, a chance of 91.77 percent of completing the project in 30 weeks was computed. Suppose that management would like to know for what duration they can be 80 percent sure of completion.

To do so, Table C1 in Appendix C is consulted. The value of Z associated with 80 percent is searched for. The answer is Z = .845. Using Equation 11.10, with D as the unknown, we obtain Equation 11.11:

$$D = Z\sigma + TS \tag{11.11}$$

$$D = .845 \times 2.16 + 27 = 28.83 \text{ weeks}$$

That is, there is an 80 percent chance of completing the project within 28.83 weeks. The computation of D enables management to make delivery commitments knowing the degree of risk assumed.

The variance of a noncritical path

The danger of noncritical paths

The probability of completing a project was found to be related to the variance of the critical path (Equation 11.10). Suppose, however, that there is a noncritical path whose variance V is *larger* than, or even similar in magnitude to, the variance of the critical path. What might its effect be on the probability of completion? If Equation 11.10 is used for the new path, then the probability of completion by the desired time might very well be *lower* than that computed using the critical path. Therefore, in PERT analysis, it is wise to also consider noncritical paths with large variances.

11.10 THE CRITICAL PATH METHOD (CPM): COST-TIME RELATIONSHIPS

Expediting projects

CPM analysis is used to evaluate various alternatives of executing projects in those cases where it is possible to *expedite* the execution of some or all of the project's activities. Expediting activities requires additional resources, which means increasing the cost of the project. However, considerable savings may be realized in projects finished ahead of schedule. An example of such a case was observed in Palm Beach, Florida, where two builders constructed two large condominium projects. With the economic slump of 1975, the demand for condominiums dropped considerably. One of the builders decided to expedite construction, at a considerable cost, in order to finish first. He sold 240 units in a short time, exhausting the demand. When the second builder completed his project, he could not sell the units and was forced to file for bankruptcy.

Thus, the decision of how much to expedite may be of great importance to management. The tool that enables such an analysis is CPM.

The basic idea

Normal or crash?

Figure 11.24 presents the relationship in CPM between cost and time. An activity can be performed in a *normal manner* (normal point in

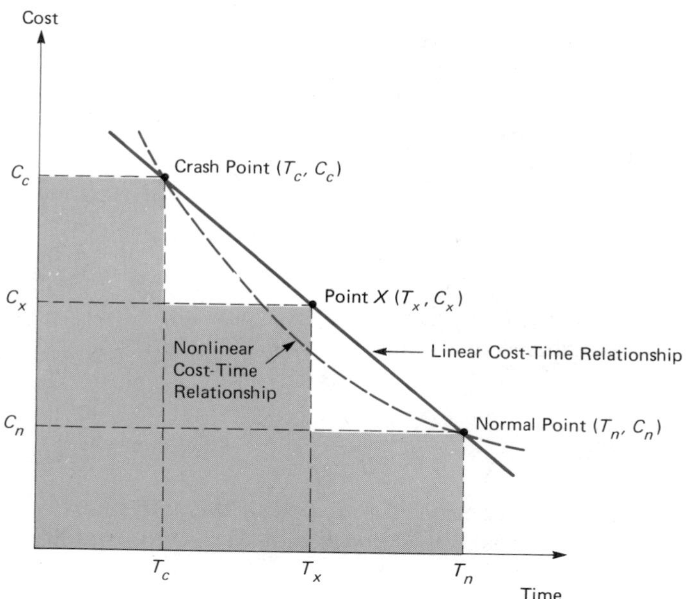

FIGURE 11.24
CPM cost-time trade-offs for an activity

Figure 11.24) requiring T_n units of time and C_n units of money (where n designates *normal*). In an extreme case, the activity can be performed on a *crash* basis (e.g., using overtime, special services, extra tools) at a time T_c and a cost C_c (where c designates *crash*). No activity can be executed in less time than T_c or more than T_n, but can take any value between.

The crash point and the normal point can be connected by a *straight line*. Any intermediate point X on the straight line will involve T_x time and C_x cost. The relationship between time and cost is given by the slope of the straight line (Equation 11.12).

$$\text{Slope} = \frac{C_c - C_n}{T_n - T_c} \qquad (11.12)$$

The slope as a trade-off

The slope gives us the *cost increase* associated with a reduction of one unit of the activity duration.[9] The assumption of a linear relationship between cost and time is not valid in all cases. In some cases, the relationships are described by a nonlinear function (the broken curve in Figure 11.24) and the solid line only approximates the broken line. In other cases a stepwise curve is applicable. It is customary to write the normal and crash data for each activity directly on the diagram as shown in Figure 11.25

[9] The true slope will actually be a negative number since the direction of the line is from northwest to southeast; however, Equation 11.12 yields a *positive* number that we use as a cost *increase*.

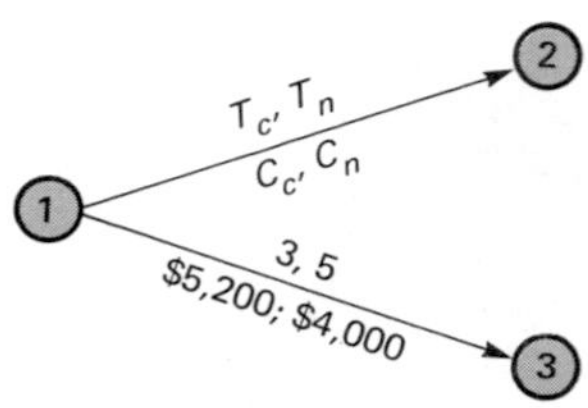

FIGURE 11.25
CPM labeling

(time above the line, cost underneath). For example, for activity **1–3,** the normal time is five weeks at a cost of \$4,000; the crash time is three weeks at a cost of \$5,200.

The slope of activity **1–3** is:

$$\frac{\$5,200 - \$4,000}{5 - 3} = \$600 \text{ per week}$$

This is the cost required to expedite the activity by one week. The linear relationship means that it will cost \$1,200 to expedite the activity by two weeks, to the crash point.

The CPM analysis

The CPM analysis examines the total cost involved in executing the project at various scheduled times, starting with either the lowest cost–longest duration alternative or with the higher cost–shortest duration alternative. The additional cost of expediting the project can then be compared with the possible savings from the expedited completion (e.g., a client may pay a bonus for completion ahead of schedule).

Solve the problem twice

The CPM analysis starts by solving the problem twice. First, attention is paid only to **normal times.** Using the procedure outlined in Part A of this chapter and assuming that the normal times are the t_es, a solution is derived, and its cost is also computed. Second, by considering only the crash times as t_es, another solution is derived, and its cost is also computed.

Once the two solutions are computed, the cost-time trade-offs are used to find the least-cost plan for any number of weeks (days) between the *all crash* and *all normal* plans. This cost can then be compared with the anticipated benefits.

Example A network of activities[10] for a maintenance project is shown in Figure 11.26. The problem is to find the least-cost plan for various project durations.

The normal time (in days) and cost as well as the crash time and cost are shown in Table 11.6. The column "Cost slope" indicates the incre-

[10] The broken line from event **3** to event **4** designates a requirement that event **4** cannot occur before event **3.** The activity *H* is a dummy activity. Note that activities can also be designated by the number of the preceding and succeeding events.

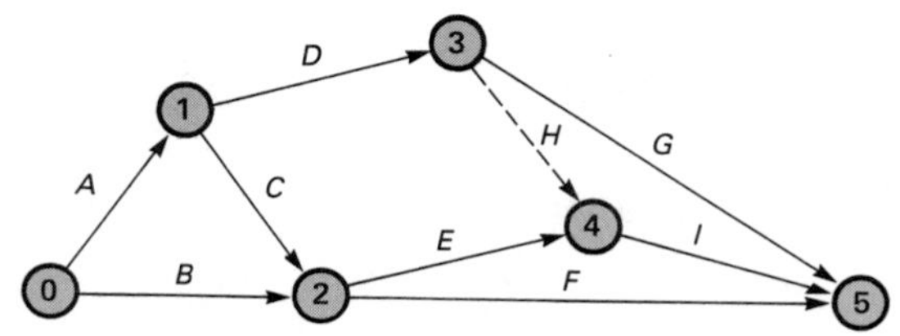

FIGURE 11.26
A maintenance project

mental *increase* in cost when the duration of the project is decreased by one day, computed from Equation 11.12. For example, for activity *D:*

$$\text{Slope} = \frac{340 - 280}{9 - 7} = \frac{60}{2} = \$30 \text{ per day}$$

TABLE 11.6
Time and cost information

	Normal		Crash		
Activity	*Time*	*Cost*	*Time*	*Cost*	*Cost slope*
A	5	$ 100	4	$ 140	40
B	9	200	7	300	50
C	7	250	4	340	30
D	9	280	7	340	30
E	5	250	2	460	70
F	11	400	7	720	80
G	6	300	4	420	60
I	8	80	6	140	30
Total		$1,860		$2,860	

Solution The first observation that can be made from Table 11.6 is that if all activities are performed in the normal duration, the total cost will be $1,860. Second, if all activities are performed on a crash basis, the total cost will be $2,860. The *times* required to complete the project on an *all-normal* basis and on an *all-crash* basis should be determined next.

All normal—least cost—longest time

All-normal basis Considering first *all-normal* times (disregard the normal costs, the crash time, and the crash cost) the critical path can be computed using the procedure shown in Part A of this chapter. The results are shown in Figure 11.27. The critical path is **0–1–2–4–5** for a duration of 25 days and a cost of $1,860.

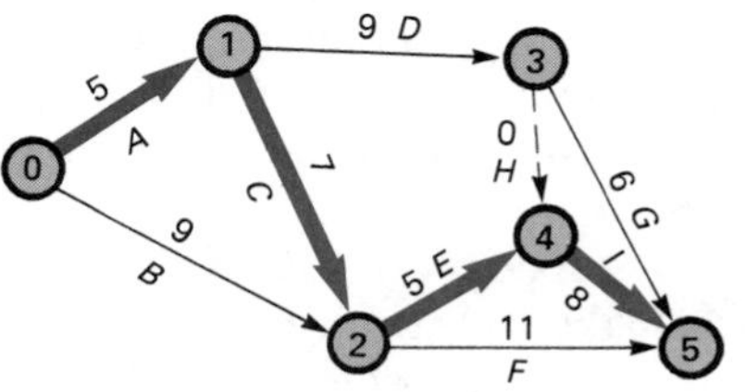

FIGURE 11.27
All-normal solution, 25 days

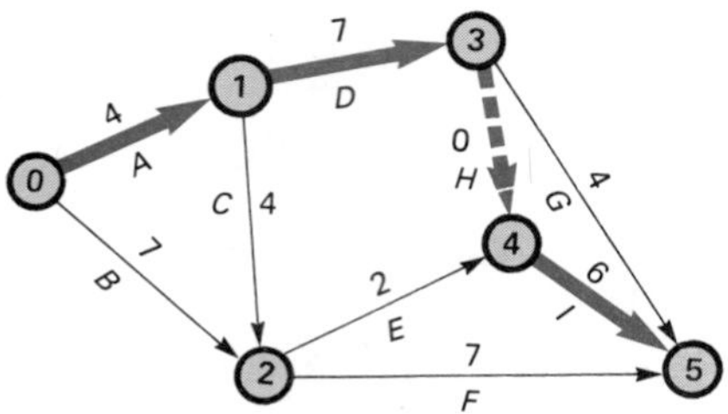

FIGURE 11.28
All-crash solution, 17 days

All crash—most expensive—shortest time

All-crash solution In a similar manner, the critical path of *all-crash* duration is computed (Figure 11.28).

The critical path is **0–1–3–4–5** for a duration of 17 days and a cost of $2,860.

At this stage, the following analysis is performed:

a. Determine the *minimum* cost for the crash time of 17 days.
b. Determine the least-cost plan for any desired number of days, between all-normal to all-crash.

Find the minimum cost for the crash time

So far it was found that it is possible to perform the project in 17 days at a cost of $2,860. The question is whether it is possible to perform the project in 17 days but at a lower cost.

To achieve a cost reduction, the noncritical activities could be performed at a slower pace. (This is called *expanding* the activities.) There is a simple procedure for this.

Step 1: All *noncritical* activities found in Figure 11.28 are listed with their appropriate cost slopes:

Noncritical activities	*Cost slope*
B: **0–2**	50
C: **1–2**	30
E: **2–4**	70
G: **3–5**	60
F: **2–5**	80

Step 2: The activity with the *largest* slope is selected (activity *F*) first. The largest savings can be made if this activity is expanded first. It would be desirable to expand it *as much as possible* to achieve as large a cost reduction as possible. Since activity *F* is on two noncritical paths **0–1–2–5** and **0–2–5,** it can be expanded until one of these becomes critical.

Since path **0–2–5** now takes 14 days, it can be expanded by 3 days to make it critical, up to 17 days. However, path **0–1–2–5** now takes 15 days and therefore only 2 days can be added to it to make it critical.

Therefore, the maximum number of days that can be added to activity F is two (the smaller of the two).

There is another point that should be checked in expanding an activity. The crash time of activity F is seven days. The normal time is given as 11 days. Therefore, expansion by two days is feasible. In other cases it *may not be feasible* to expand up to the maximum length allowed by the length of the noncritical path because of the normal time limitations that are imposed on an individual activity. (In other words, it is assumed that the normal time is the *slowest* execution time of an activity.)

Check for feasibility

The expansion of activity F now yields an additional critical path **0–1–2–5** that will take 17 days at a cost reduction of $160.

Step 3: Activity E, which has the *second largest* cost reduction potential, is expanded next. Here, an expansion of only one day is possible at a $70 saving. In a similar manner, the expansion of activity G by two days will yield an additional $120, and finally activity B can be expanded by one day, resulting in a $50 saving. Notice that since activity F has been expanded to nine days, the maximum that activity B can be expanded is to eight days ($17 - 9 = 8$). It is impossible to expand activity C, since it became *critical* as a result of the expansion of activity F.

The total cost savings are: $160 + 70 + 120 + 50 = 400$. Thus, the revised plan calls for a 17-day project, at a total cost of $2,860 − $400 = $2,460.

This new schedule is shown in Figure 11.29. Notice that all activities are now *critical;* that is, no further expansion is possible.

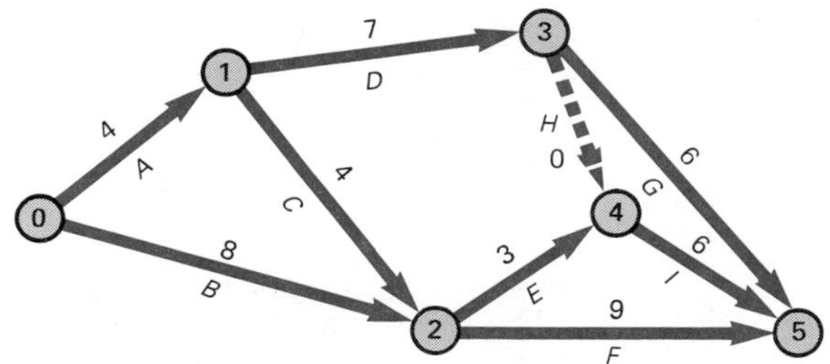

FIGURE 11.29
Least-cost, crash schedule of 17 days ($2,460)

The information is then entered into a cost-time diagram (Figure 11.30) as point A.

Determine the least-cost plan for any desired number of days

The normal schedule is the *longest* (slowest) schedule for carrying out the project, and costs the *least*. On the other hand, the all-crash schedule is the *fastest* but is also the most expensive. In certain cases, management needs to know the cost of carrying out the project at some point between the fastest and the slowest. Such a situation may develop, for example, when a customer offers to pay a certain amount as a bonus for finishing ahead of schedule.

Example: Least-cost plan for 22 days. Let us assume that manage-

FIGURE 11.30
Cost-time trade-offs

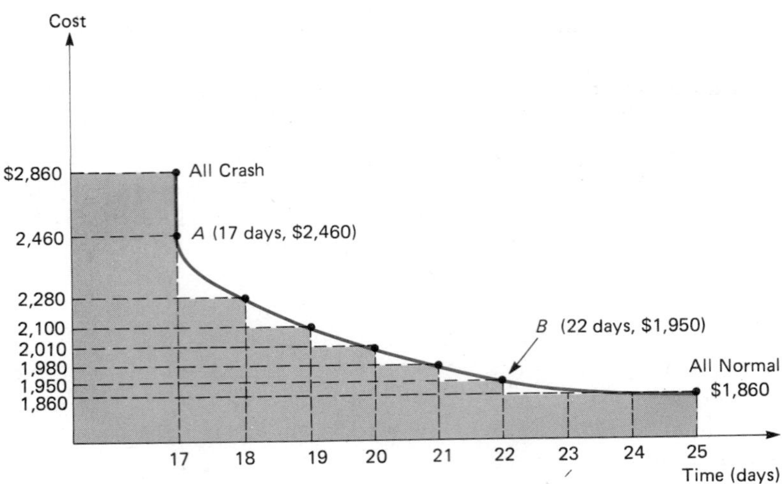

ment would like to find the least-cost plan for 22 days. Two approaches are available: either *compressing* the project from 25 days (all normal) to 22 days, or *expanding* the project from 17 days (all crash) up to 22. The former approach will be illustrated here.

Compress or expand?

The first step is to list all *critical activities* of the all-normal schedule (Figure 11.27). The list of these activities and their slopes follows:

Critical activity	*Slope*
A: **0–1**	40
C: **1–2**	30
E: **2–4**	70
I: **4–5**	30

The activity with the *least* slope will be compressed first, since decreasing the project time by one day will result in the smallest increase in cost. In the example, either activity *C* or activity *I* can be selected, since both have the smallest slope (lowest cost). Arbitrarily, activity *C* is selected.

Multiple critical paths

How much can activity *C* be compressed? The most an activity can be compressed is up to its *crash time* (four days here). However, such a reduction may create one (or more) additional critical paths. The minute an additional critical path is created, the compression should be stopped and a cost reevaluation made. In the example, two additional critical paths are formed after activity *C* is reduced from seven to four days. Thus, the maximum project compression is to 22 days (see Figure 11.31) at a cost of $1,860 + 90 = $1,950 (point *B* in Figure 11.30).

Notice that the compression to 22 days also tells us that the best plan for achieving 24 days is to cut one day from activity *C* and the best plan for 23 days is cutting two days from activity *C*.

Compression to 20 days. In a similar manner, the best plan for 21 days can be found. Starting with 22 days, the *critical* activity *I* (Figure 11.31) is expedited, since its cost increase is now the smallest. Compressing by one day yields a 21-day schedule with a cost of $1,980. This activity could be compressed by two days to its crash time of six days. After compressing it by two days, we get a 20-day schedule at a cost of $2,010 (see Figure 11.32). This information is now entered in Figure 11.30. Note that the entire network is now critical.

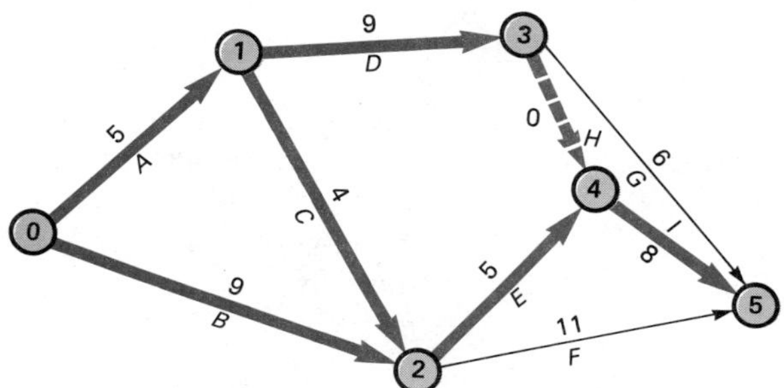

FIGURE 11.31
A 22-day, least-cost schedule

Additional compression. At this stage, a single activity can no longer be considered by itself, since there are several critical paths involved. For example, if activity *D* is reduced by one day, the critical path **0–1–3–5** will be reduced to 19 days, but other critical paths will also have to be reduced by one day. In this case, activities *E* and *F* have to be compressed by one day each and the cost effect will be felt in two places. Therefore, it is necessary to check all combinations of possible reductions to make sure that the smallest total cost is added. This is done by taking the smallest slope on a path (rather than an activity) first and adding the resultant cost impact to the other paths.

Check all possibilities

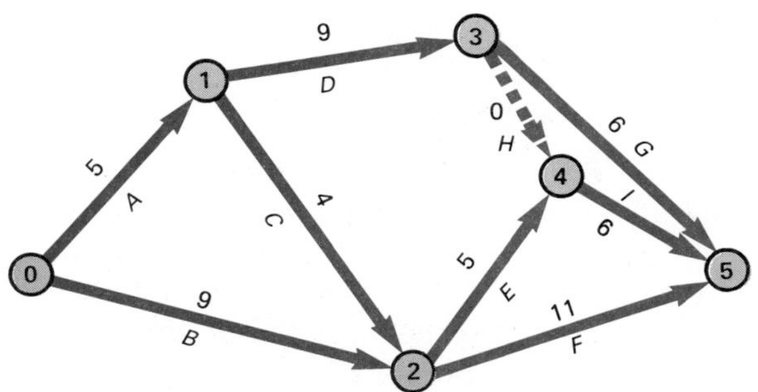

FIGURE 11.32
A 20-day, least-cost schedule

Then a computation is made for the least slope on the next path, taking into consideration the impact on the resultant cost, and so on. Finally, all alternatives are compared and the one with the least-cost increase is selected. In the example, a compression of activities *A* and *B* by one day results in a 19-day schedule at a cost of $2,010 + 40 + 50 = $2,100 (see Figure 11.33).

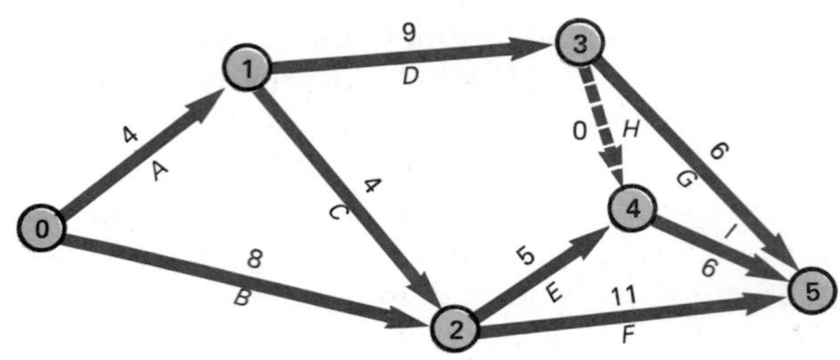

FIGURE 11.33
A 19-day, least-cost schedule

Further compression is done in the same manner. An 18-day schedule can be obtained with a cost of $2,280, and a 17-day schedule has a cost of $2,460.

All these results are entered in Figure 11.30 for the purpose of evaluation of the anticipated benefits.

Project crashing with linear programming

Linear programming can be used to find the best crashing schedule. The total cost of a project is minimized subject to the precedence relationship in the network. This formulation will not be discussed here due to lack of space. See Whitehouse [15] for further details.

11.11 OTHER NETWORK METHODS

Nonproject networks, too

Over the years, several other network techniques have been developed. Some of these are modifications and extensions of PERT and CPM. Various techniques can be classified as either project or nonproject oriented.

Project-oriented techniques

PERT/Cost The PERT technique is a time-oriented method that helps plan and control a project's direction. **PERT/Cost** is an extension that permits the planning and control of both time and cost. The basic concept of PERT/Cost is that costs are to be measured and controlled primarily on a project basis rather than, say, on a departmental basis. Thus, individual activities (or groups of activities) form cost centers for both accounting purposes and managerial control. This is in contrast to conventional cost methods, where organizational units such as departments are the cost centers. There are several variations of PERT/Cost. For further details see Wiest and Levy [14].

Other techniques Several other planning techniques such as PERT II, PERT III, PERT IV, LESS, TOPS, COMET, PROPT, and the like (all extensions or modifications of PERT or CPM) are available (see [4]).

Graphical evaluation and review technique (GERT) The application of PERT assumes that all activities must be completed before an event can be realized, that events cannot be repeated, that all activities in the network must be completed, that estimates follow the Beta distribution, and that the critical path is the one with the longest elapsed time (sum of mean activity times), even though variances from those mean times exist. GERT is an extension of PERT, where all of the above assumptions are relaxed; that is, they are not imposed any longer. (For details, see [1] and [15]).

Nonproject-oriented network techniques

The next three sections concern three special nonproject-oriented network models, all of which are recognized for their simplicity and solution efficiency. A *network* is a collection of nodes connected by arcs. Figure 11.34 depicts a general network. Another example is a decision tree (Chapter 4) or a PERT (event-oriented) diagram.

Many managerial problems can be represented by networks even though they may not physically appear to be networks. Examples include inventory decisions and scheduling problems.

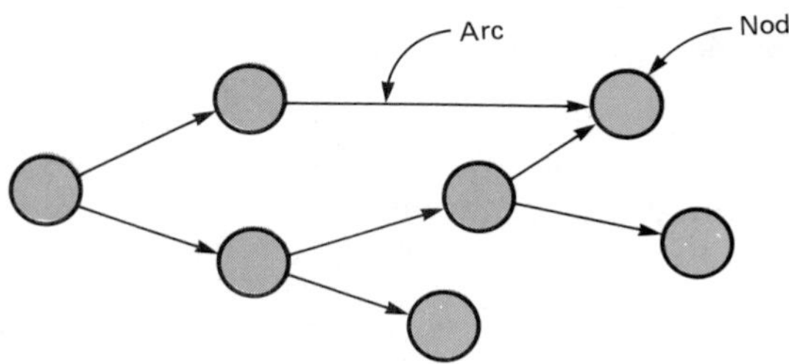

FIGURE 11.34
A general network

11.12 MINIMAL SPANNING TREE

We will illustrate this topic through an example.

Example

The Northwood Telephone Company is planning a network of telephones for a small, high-class shopping center. Figure 11.35 shows the desired location of the phones (circled and lettered). The lines to every telephone must be buried to maintain the posh image of the center. The telephone company wishes, of course, to minimize the necessary digging, but due to existing electrical and utility lines, it is not possible to dig just anywhere. Figure 11.35 also shows the feasible underground lines with the distances (in feet). The problem is to determine which of these lines to dig such that the total distance is minimized, yet every phone is connected to the network.

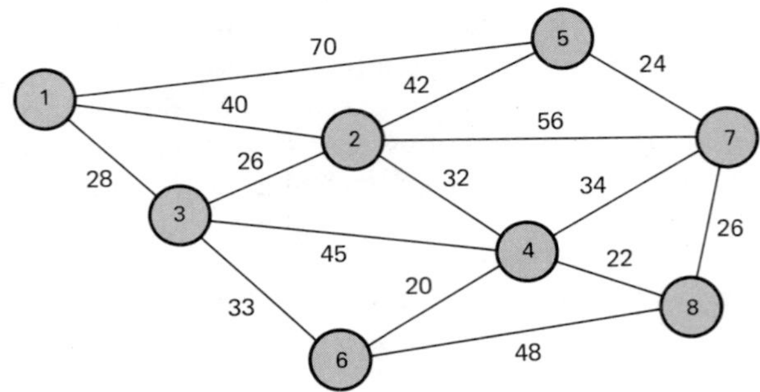

FIGURE 11.35 The telephone problem

The example just presented is typical of many network problems that will be illustrated in the forthcoming sections. In this case, the objective is to select a set of arcs in a network, from a feasible larger set of arcs, that will span (connect) *all* the nodes of the network, yet minimize the sum of the arc lengths (which equate to cost). This problem is called the **spanning tree** problem. In solving this problem, we are searching for the *minimal* spanning tree.

Solution using the greedy algorithm

The best solution method is usually referred to as the **greedy algorithm,** since simply joining to the closest node at each iteration of the solution turns out to be the optimal procedure.

First, arbitrarily select any node and connect it to the nearest node. We will start with **1** and connect it to **3,** the closest node. From the connected nodes **1** and **3** (both must be considered), we search for the shortest distance to any unconnected node, **3** to **2** in our example, and connect the two. We repeat this process, always considering *all* connected nodes when searching for a new node to connect, until all nodes are connected. In our example:

From **2** to **4.**
From **4** to **6.**
From **4** to **8.**
From **8** to **7.**
From **7** to **5.**

The optimal solution is shown in Figure 11.36 with a total distance of 178.

Notes:

1. There may be more than one optimal solution.
2. The total number of connecting segments is always $n - 1$, where n is the number of nodes.

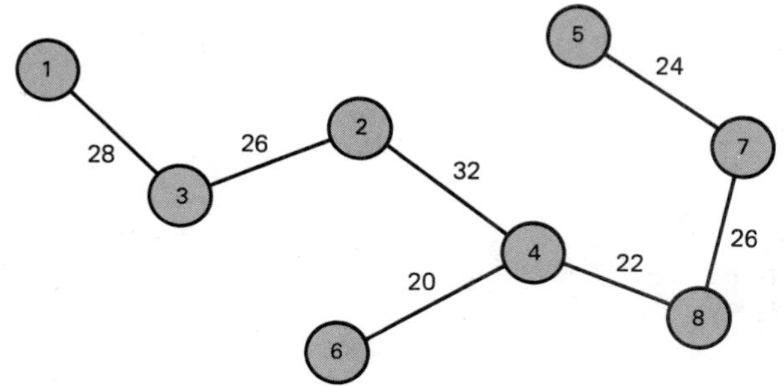

FIGURE 11.36
The optimal solution

3. A more complicated problem is one in which there are *limits* on the capacities that can be transmitted along the arcs (a *capacitated* spanning tree).

11.13 SHORTEST ROUTE

The **shortest route** problem can be stated as follows: Find the shortest route (in terms of distance, time, or money) from a given node in a network to any (or all) of the nodes in the network.

Example

A bank has six branches and a headquarters in the greater Los Angeles metropolitan area (see map, Figure 11.37). The distances along the streets are shown on the map. Some routes, such as from **1** directly to **6**, are not possible because of an intervening airport, railroad, or park. Note that the arcs are *not* directed; that is, they permit travel in either direction. Bank employees frequently travel from headquarters **1** to the branches. The problem is to find the shortest distance from headquarters to each branch.

Solution

The algorithm used is iterative in nature. In each iteration, the shortest distance to one node is determined. Therefore, the optimal solution will be reached in $n - 1$ iterations, where $n =$ the number of nodes.

Step 1: Determine the distance from headquarters **1** to every node that can be reached directly. Label each such destination node according to the following code:

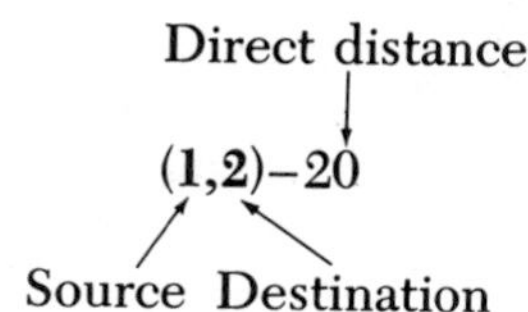

FIGURE 11.37
The bank route problem

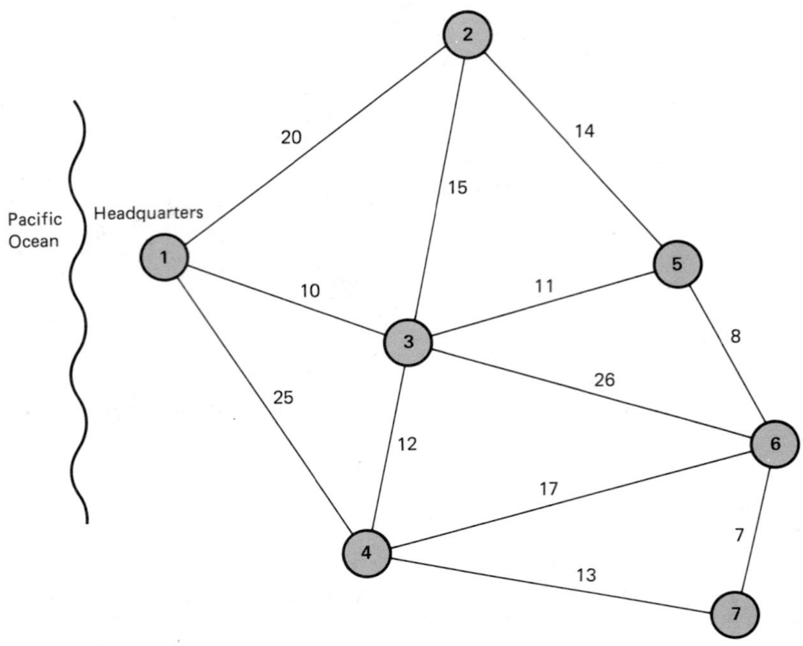

Step 2: Box the initial node, then box the closest node to the initial node (**3** in our case). The results are shown in Figure 11.38.

Step 3: We now have three types of nodes:

a. Those that are boxed (**1** and **3**).
b. Those that are labeled (**2** and **4**).
c. Those that are not labeled (**5, 6,** and **7**).

Start from the latest boxed node **3** and check the distance to all unlabeled direct nodes. Since **5** and **6** are unlabeled, label them, using the distance from the initial node **1** *through* node **3.**

For **5:** the label is (**3, 5**)–21

For **6:** The label is (**3, 6**)–36

Step 4: Check the labeled nodes, **2** and **4,** for possible improvement.

For node **2:** Two alternatives exist: **1–2** for a distance of 20, or **1–3–2** for a distance of 25. Since no improvement can be achieved by going through **3,** we conclude that **1–2** is the shortest way. Therefore, **2** is boxed.

For node **4:** The previous label indicated a distance of 25. However, following route **1–3–4** results in a shorter path of 10 + 12 = 22. Therefore, the node is relabeled (**1, 3**)–22. (Refer to Figure 11.39.)

Step 5: Step 4 is repeated for node **2.** At this iteration, the label of **5** is checked and stays unchanged. Node **4** is boxed, since no improvement is possible.

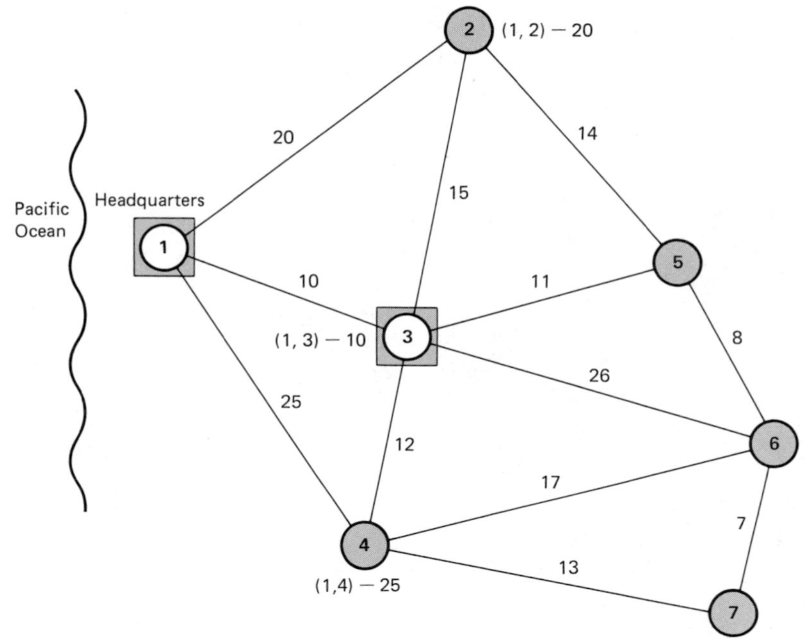

FIGURE 11.38

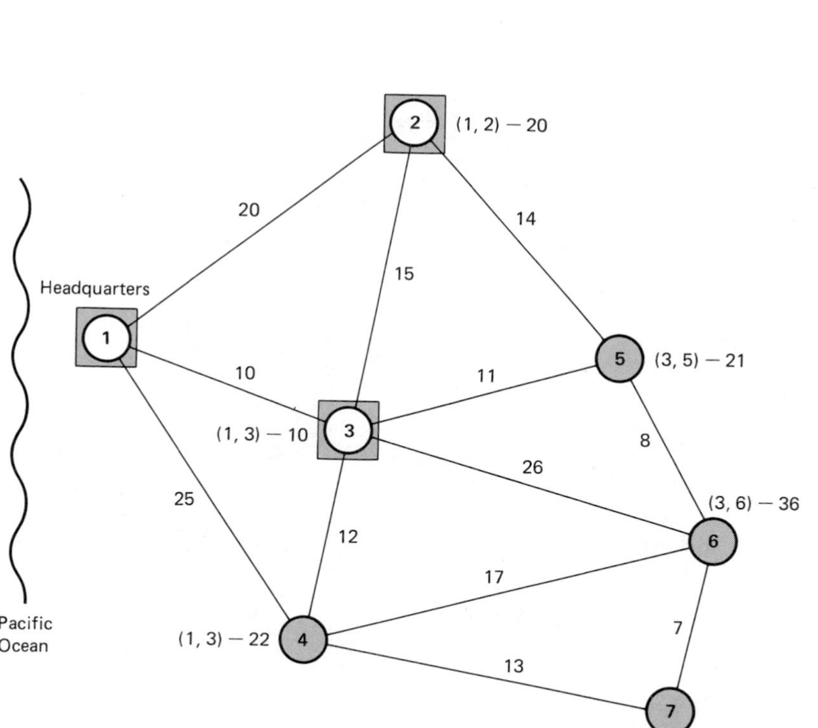

FIGURE 11.39

FIGURE 11.40

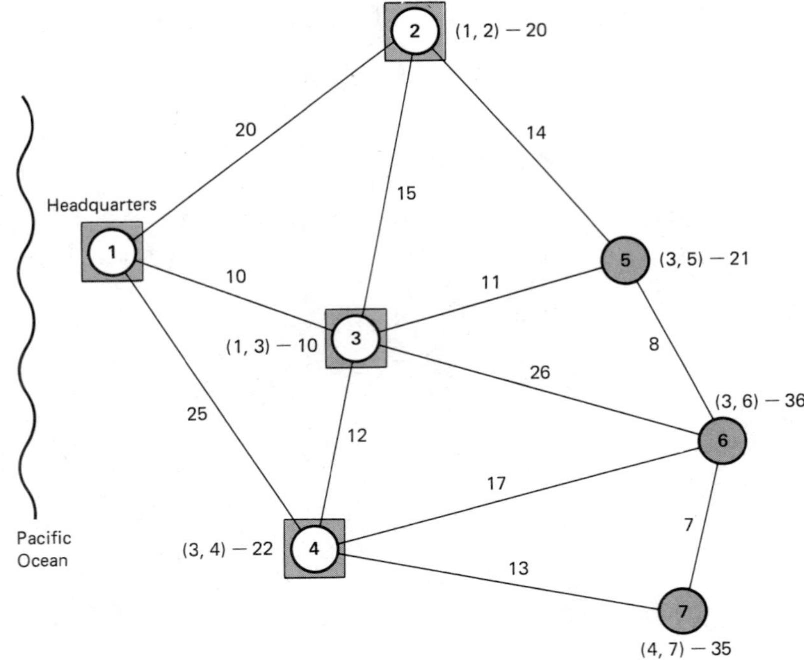

FIGURE 11.41

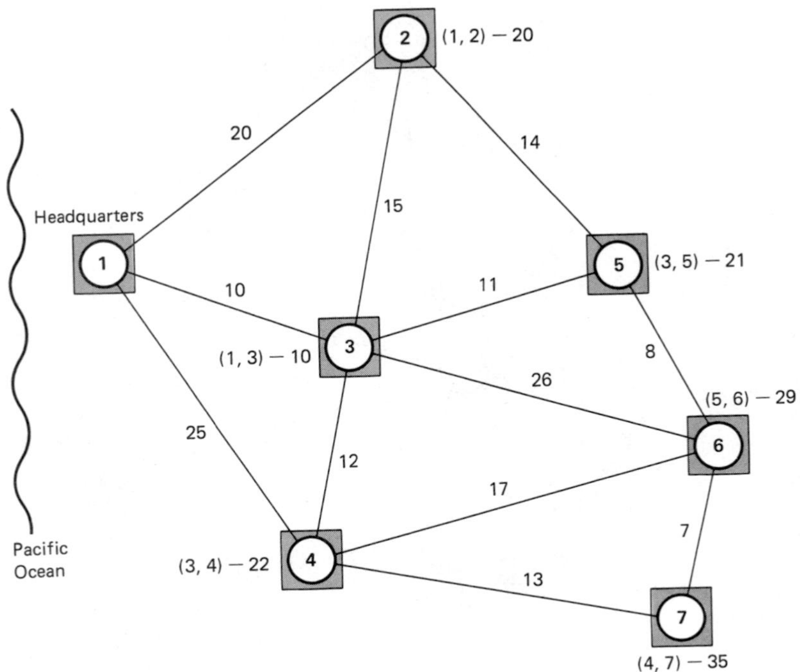

Step 6: Step 4 is repeated for node **4.** The results are shown in Figure 11.40.

Step 7: Step 4 is repeated for node **5.** No improvement is possible, so the node is boxed.

Step 8: Step 4 is repeated for node **6.** Improvement is possible: (**5, 6**)—29 so it is boxed. Finally, we check node **7.** No improvement is possible, so we box it too. (See Figure 11.41.)

The optimal solution is then read from the labels. From **1,** the shortest paths are:

To	*Path*	*Distance*
2	1-2	20
3	1-3	10
4	1-3-4	22
5	1-3-5	21
6	1-3-5-6	29
7	1-3-4-7	35

11.14 MAXIMUM FLOW

The objective in this problem is to find the **maximum** amount of **flow** of fluid, traffic, information, and so on, that can be transported through a capacitated (capacity limited) network. Such a network is composed of a **source** and a **sink** and connecting arcs and nodes. Flow in each individual arc (e.g., a water pipe) is measured by the amount that can be transported during a unit of time (e.g., six gallons per minute). Flow can be one-way only, as shown by the arrows in Figure 11.42. It is also possible to have two direct arcs between nodes; for example, points **2** and **3** in Figure 11.42.

Solution procedure

Step 1: Trace a continuous path from the source to the sink; for example, **1–2–3–4.** (Do not consider any path where there is one or more arcs with a *zero*-flow capacity.)

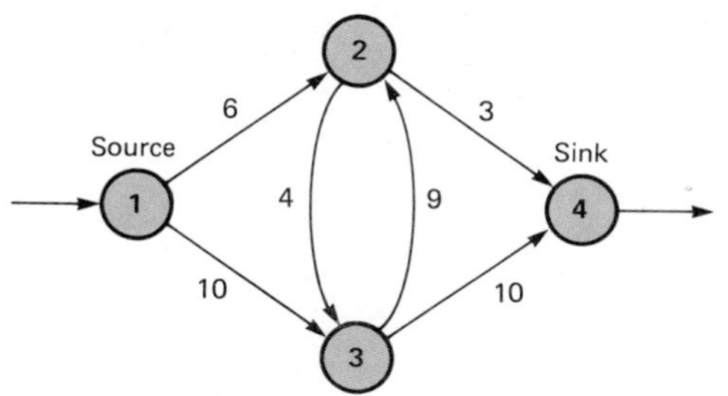

FIGURE 11.42
A capacitated network

Step 2: In this continuous path, determine the arc with the *minimum* flow capacity. In our example it is arc **2–3** with a flow of 4. The most we can transport through path **1–2–3–4** is 4.

Step 3: Reduce all the quantities along this path by 4 (the maximum amount transported). The result is shown in Figure 11.43.

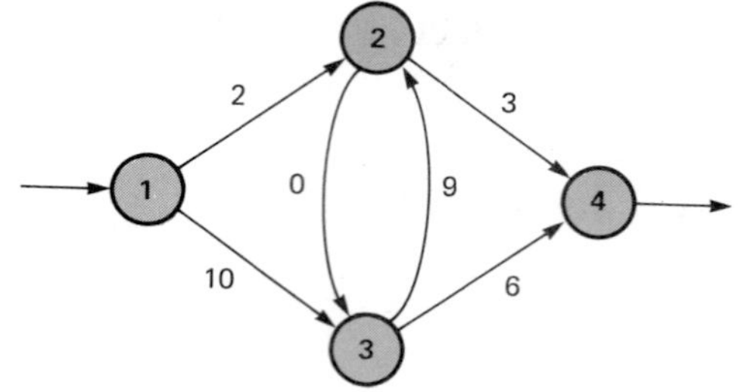

FIGURE 11.43
Network after iteration 1

Iteration 2. Repeat steps 1 through 3. This time, the path **1–3–4** is considered. (Note that the *order* in which paths are considered does not matter.) The minimum quantity is 6. The result is shown in Figure 11.44.

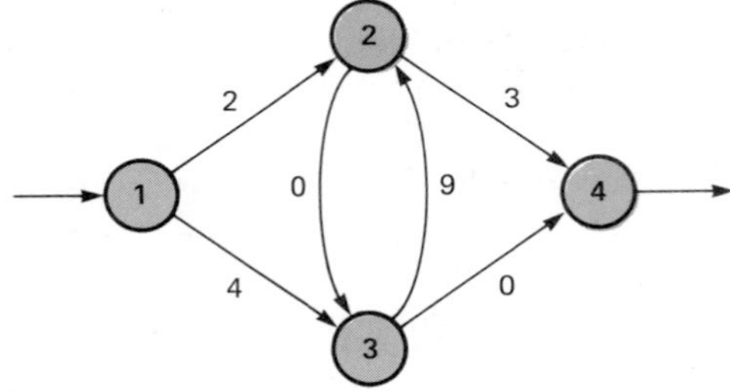

FIGURE 11.44
Network after iteration 2

Iteration 3. Repeat steps 1 through 3. This time, path **1–3–2–4** is considered. The minimum flow is 3. The result is shown in Figure 11.45.

Step 4: Since all the paths have at least one arc with a zero capacity, we stop. The maximum flow is 4 + 6 + 3 = 13.

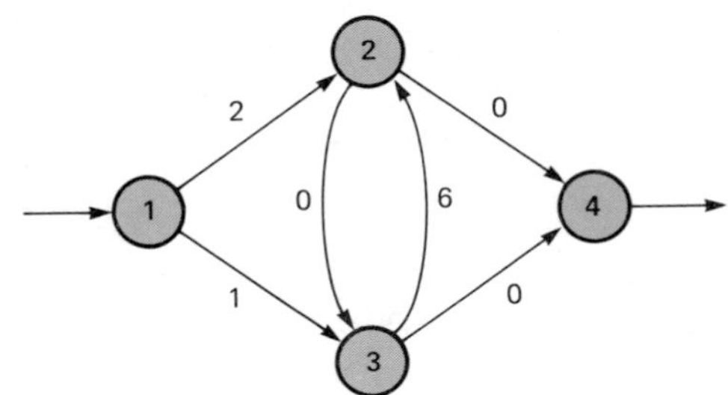

FIGURE 11.45
Network after iteration 3

11.15 COMPUTERIZATION

PERT/CPM networks are usually very large and require frequent replanning or updating for changes. Therefore, many computer programs have been developed to perform partial or complete network analyses. A typical computer program will have the input-output structure shown in Figure 11.46. An example data printout of the Moose Lake project presented in Part A is shown in Figure 11.47.

FIGURE 11.46
Computerized network models

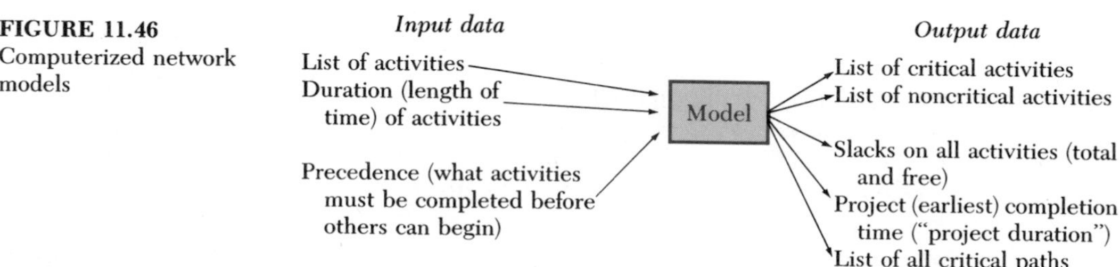

This example also includes the risk analysis for the project. The input-output information for a typical risk analysis is shown in Figure 11.48. The printout for the Moose Lake project is shown in Figure 11.49. Note

FIGURE 11.47
Moose Lake data printout

Project Name: PEL
Completion Time: 27
Max. Path Variance: 4.666667

Problem Type: PERT-Stochastic
No. of Critical Paths: 1
Min. Path Variance: 4.666667

Name	DESCRIPT	ES	EF	LS	LF	SLACK	Te	STD. DEV	CRITICAL
A		0.00	3.00	0.00	3.00	0.00	3.00	0.67	YES
B		3.00	7.00	6.00	10.00	3.00	4.00	1.67	NO
C		3.00	7.00	3.00	7.00	0.00	4.00	0.33	YES
D		7.00	9.00	8.00	10.00	1.00	2.00	0.33	NO
E		3.00	7.00	20.00	24.00	17.00	4.00	1.00	NO
F		7.00	13.00	7.00	13.00	0.00	6.00	2.00	YES
G		9.00	12.00	10.00	13.00	1.00	3.00	0.33	NO
H		7.00	8.00	24.00	25.00	17.00	1.00	0.00	NO
I		13.00	25.00	13.00	25.00	0.00	12.00	0.00	YES
J		25.00	27.00	25.00	27.00	0.00	2.00	0.33	YES

CRITICAL PATHS

NO.	PATH ACTIVITY NAMES	VARIANCE
1	A→C→F→I→J	4.666667

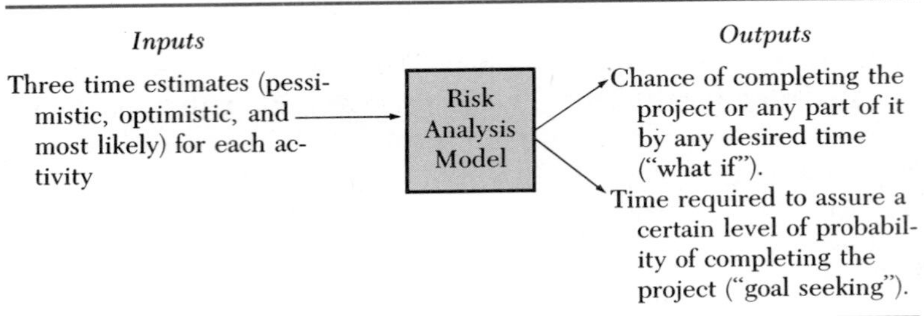

FIGURE 11.48
Risk analysis model

that the MSS program monitors all critical paths and considers the one with the largest variance (in our example there is only one such path).

Also note that the program is capable of conducting an interactive "what if" analysis. The user enters the desired completion times (we entered four values: 30, 26, 31, and 32) and the program computes the probability of completion for each of them, as shown in Figure 11.49.

FIGURE 11.49
Moose Lake risk analysis

Project completion time: 27		No. of critical paths: 1	
Maximum path variance: 4.667		Minimum path variance: 4.667	
		Time	*Probability*
Probability of completion by what time?		30	.917
		26	.322
		31	.968
		32	.990

Critical path method

The MSS package also includes a routine for CPM. For example, entering the input data from Table 11.6 results in the output shown in Figure 11.50. The program also allows for a least-cost "what if" analysis similar to what is shown in the text. The least-cost crash solution is found in four iterations:

Expanding activity:	F by 2:	2,700
	E by 1:	2,630
	G by 2:	2,510
	B by 1:	2,460

Least-cost crash: 17 and 2,460

FIGURE 11.50
CPM results of Table 11.6

Normal Project		All Crash Project	
Duration	25	Duration	17
Cost	1860	Cost	2460

More sophisticated computer programs

Project management software for mainframes and minis is available for all types of hardware. Typical packages are PAC II™ and PAC III™ (from AGS Management Systems), Quicknet™ (Project Software and Development Inc.), and Artemis™ (Metier Management Systems).

Micro-based projects range in price from $50 to over $5,000. They range in their capabilities from entry level to professional applications. A representative list is provided in Table 11.7.

TABLE 11.7 Representative PC-based project management software

Product	*Vendor*
Advanced Project 6™	Softcorp. Inc, Clearwater, Fla.
Harvard Project Manager™	Software Publishing Co., Mountain View, Calif.
MacProject™	Apple Computer, Inc., Cupertino, Calif.
Microsoft Project™	Microsoft Corp., Northup Way, Bellvue, Wash.
Milestone™	Digital Marketing Corp., Walnut Creek, Calif.
Planning Pro™	Kepner-Tregoe Inc., Princeton, N.J.
Project Scheduler Network™	Scitor Corp., Foster City, Calif.
PC MIS™	Davis and Associates, Atlanta, Ga.
Project Manager IBM™	Institute of Industrial Engineering, Norcross, Ga.
Project Workbench™	Applied Business Technology Corp.
Scheduling and Control™	Softext Publishing Co.; New York, N.Y.
Superproject Plus™	Computer Associates International, San Jose, Calif.
The Project Manager™	Wiley Professional Software, New York, N.Y.
VisiSchedule™	Paladin Software Corp., Santa Clara, Calif.

Capabilities of the packages Listed below are some of the capabilities of these computer software packages.

- Drawing network and/or Gantt charts.
- Controlling several resources: time, labor, money, and so on.
- Resource leveling.
- Conducting risk analyses.
- Providing an on-line tutorial.
- Mainframe/micro interfacing.
- Windowing.
- Providing detailed cost analyses.
- Conducting "what if" analyses.
- Calculating job requirements, salaries, skill levels.
- Report writing.

FIGURE 11.51
Cost and labor control

Job $4, Develop Work Manual

Duration = 14 days
Work completed = 0 days
On critical path = No
Slack time = 25 days
Prerequisites = none
Manpower skills = Skill #1, Personnel (U.S.), 4.0 @ 150$ per man-day
Skill #2, Management (U.S.), 1.0 @ 250$ per man-day
Skill #3, Spanish liaison, 2.0 @ 200$ per man-day
Total effort = 98.0 man-days
Manpower cost = $17500.0
Direct cost = $5000

Earliest start = 1/2/88
Earliest finish = 1/20/88
Latest start = 2/6/88
Latest finish = 2/27/88

- Displaying leveled manpower requirements.
- Calculating labor, cost, time, and other trade-offs.

Examples Figure 11.51 presents the printout of a more sophisticated program. The analysis involves both cost and labor control. Powerful graphical capabilities are available in most new packages. For example, the MSS program generated the bar chart shown in Figure 11.52. An example of a computer-drawn network is shown in Figure 11.53.

FIGURE 11.52
Bar charting graphical capabilities

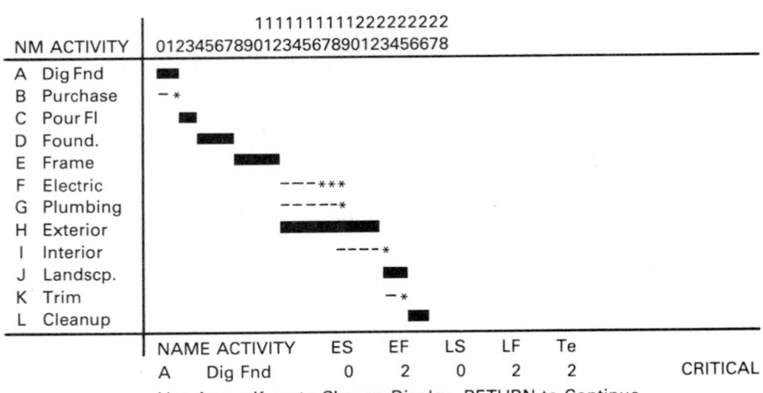

Notes: solid bar ■ designates a critical activity
dashed line --- runs from early start to early finish for non critical activities
asterisks ****** represent slack time

FIGURE 11.53
A computer drawn network

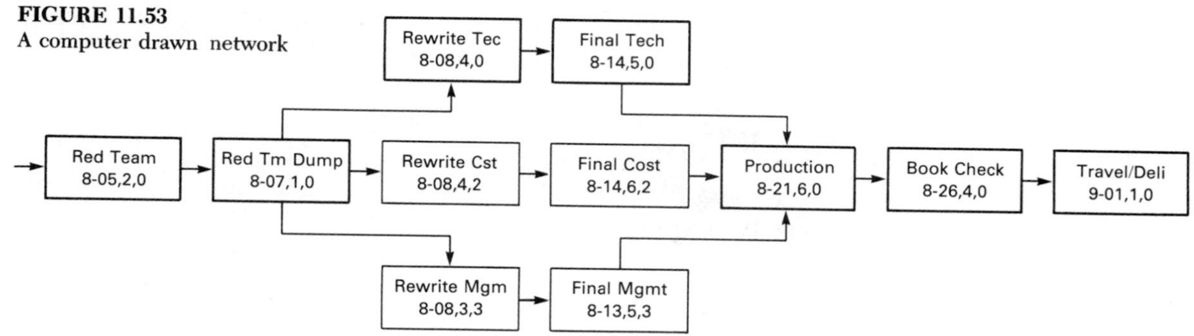

Nonproject network programs

Computer programs are also available for nonproject-oriented networks such as minimal spanning tree, shortest route, and maximum flow. Figures 11.54, 11.55, and 11.56 illustrate the computer solutions to the corresponding manually solved examples in Section 11.12, 11.13, and 11.14.

FIGURE 11.54
Minimal spanning tree solution

ARC	STARTING NODE	ENDING NODE	COST	ARC	STARTING NODE	ENDING NODE	COST
1	1	2	40	2	1	3	28
3	1	5	70	4	2	3	26
5	2	4	32	6	2	5	42
7	2	7	56	8	3	4	45
9	3	6	33	10	4	6	20
11	4	7	34	12	4	8	22
13	5	7	24	14	6	8	48
15	7	8	26				

SOLUTION: MINIMAL SPANNING TREE

Problem Name: ms1

STEP	CONNECT NODE	TO	NODE	DISTANCE	STEP	CONNECT NODE	TO	NODE	DISTANCE
1	1		3	28	2	3		2	26
3	2		4	32	4	4		6	20
5	4		8	22	6	8		7	26
7	7		5	24					

TOTAL DISTANCE: 178

Note that the program can allow for travel in both directions (called *symmetric*) or in only one direction (called *asymmetric*).

11.16 CONCLUDING REMARKS

PERT and CPM are tools for planning, monitoring, and controlling large, complex projects.

FIGURE 11.55
Shortest route solution

SHORTEST ROUTE

Problem Name: sr1 Type: Symmetric

ARC	STARTING NODE	ENDING NODE	COST	ARC	STARTING NODE	ENDING NODE	COST
1	1	2	20	2	1	3	10
3	1	4	25	4	2	3	15
5	2	5	14	6	3	4	12
7	3	5	11	8	3	6	26
9	4	6	17	10	4	7	13
11	5	6	8	12	6	7	7

SHORTEST ROUTE SOLUTION SUMMARY

Problem Name: sr1
Type: Symmetric
Solution Steps Required: 6

NODE	DISTANCE	SHORTEST ROUTE
2	20	2 ← 1
3	10	3 ← 1
4	22	4 ← 3 ← 1
5	21	5 ← 3 ← 1
6	29	6 ← 5 ← 3 ← 1
7	35	7 ← 4 ← 3 ← 1

FIGURE 11.56
Maximum flow solution

MAXIMUM FLOW

Problem Name: NONE

ARC	STARTING NODE	ENDING NODE	CAPACITY S → E	CAPACITY S ← E	ARC	STARTING NODE	ENDING NODE	CAPACITY S → E	CAPACITY S ← E
1	1	2	2	0	2	1	3	10	0
3	2	3	0	9	4	2	4	3	0
5	3	4	6	0					

SOLUTION

Problem Name: mf1

STEP	MAX FLOW	PATH SELECTED
1	2	1 → 2 → 4
2	1	1 → 3 → 2 → 4
3	6	1 → 3 → 4

MAXIMUM TOTAL FLOW: 9

MAXIMUM FLOW SOLUTION
Problem Name: MF2

STEP	MAX FLOW	PATH SELECTED
1	3	1 → 2 → 4
2	10	1 → 3 → 4

MAXIMUM TOTAL FLOW: 13

Formulation

The project under consideration can be presented graphically as a network. Such a presentation is based on the following assumptions:

The assumptions

1. The project can be subdivided into a set of predictable, independent activities, each of which has a clear beginning and end.
2. Each activity can be sequenced as to its predecessors or successors. An activity cannot start until all its predecessors are completed.
3. The network is not cyclical; that is, each activity is executed once and only once during the life of the project. Any repeating activity is considered a different activity.
4. Activity times may be estimated, either as a single-point estimate (CPM) or as a three-point estimate (PERT).
5. The durations of the activities are independent of each other.

In addition, special assumptions are made with respect to:

PERT

a. Activity duration is assumed to follow the Beta distribution.
b. The variance of the length of the project is assumed to be equal to the sum of the variances of the activities on the critical path.

CPM

a. Duration of an activity has a negative linear relation to its execution cost.
b. The normal time for an activity is the slowest. Executing an activity in a normal time costs the least.

As with any other models, here, too, not all the assumptions hold in all cases. However, most of these assumptions hold, at least for the short run, for many complex projects. (For further discussion, see Wiest and Levy [14].) The relaxation of some of these assumptions leads to more complicated network models such as GERT. (See [1] and [15].)

Methodology and solution approaches

The major objective of PERT and CPM analyses is to identify the *critical activities* of a project. The search for these activities can be done through a comparison of all paths in the network (complete enumeration), looking for the longest path (which is labeled the critical path), or through a special algorithm that computes the slack times in the network. In the algorithm case, all events with no slack are situated on the critical path. PERT and CPM can also be presented as linear programming models (a presentation that makes the computations rather cumbersome). The interested reader is referred to Wiest and Levy [14].

It is also possible to use simulation to enlarge the scope of PERT/

CPM analyses. For example, using simulation, it is possible to find the probabilities of any noncritical path being delayed or becoming critical for any desired discrete or continuous distribution of the activity times.

PERT versus CPM

The distinction between PERT and CPM centers around two areas. In PERT, a three-point estimate of time is used, which introduces a probabilistic element into the results. In CPM, a cost-time relationship is exhibited and the cost of shortening the project's completion time is evaluated.

Application

PERT and CPM are powerful and flexible tools for decision making. Specifically, they can be used in planning, monitoring, and controlling large projects. Due to their graphical presentation and simple conceptual basis, they are relatively easy to explain and therefore easy to implement. Further assistance in implementation is achieved through adaptability to computers. A wide range of preprogrammed computer routines is available from many computer manufacturers.

Identification of critical events and activities enables management to exercise better control of the project, using a management-by-exception philosophy. In addition, control becomes even more effective since the corrective actions and replanning can take effect as soon as deviations in critical activities are reported.

In summary, PERT and CPM can be most effective amplifiers of managers' skills.

11.17 PROBLEMS FOR PART B[11]

16. Given a project with the following information:

Activity	*Standard deviation*	*Critical?*	*Duration*
a	2	yes	2
b	1		3
c	0	yes	4
d	3		2
e	1	yes	1
f	2		6
g	2	yes	4
h	0	yes	2

Find:

a. The probability of completing this project in 12 weeks (or less).

b. The probability of completing this project in 16 weeks (or less).

c. The probability of completing this project in 13 weeks (or less).

d. The number of weeks required to assure a 92.5 percent chance of completion.

17. Given the following project:

a. Find all "earliest dates," including project completion (T_E's for all events).

b. Find all "latest dates" (T_L's for all events).

c. Determine the critical path and the event slack values.

d. What is the critical path leading to event **5?**

[11] Slack here refers to "total slack/float."

e. What will happen if activity **4–5**'s actual time slips to 9?

f. What will be the slack on activity **3–5** if activity **4–5** slips to 9 weeks and activity **5–7** takes 6 weeks?

	Times (weeks)		
Activity	*Optimistic*	*Most likely*	*Pessimistic*
1–2	5	11	11
1–3	10	10	10
1–4	2	5	8
2–6	1	7	13
3–6	4	4	10
3–7	4	7	10
3–5	2	2	2
4–5	0	6	6
5–7	2	8	14
6–7	1	4	7

18. *a.* Find the probability of finishing the project in Problem 17 in 19 weeks. In 17 weeks. In 24 weeks.

b. What is the probability of completing event 5 in Problem 17 by 9 weeks?

c. If management wants to be 80 percent sure that the project will be completed by a "guaranteed" date, what date should be quoted?

19. The following event completion times have been estimated by a contracting firm:

	Times		
Activity	*Optimistic*	*Most likely*	*Pessimistic*
1–2	3	6	9
1–3	1	4	7
3–2	0	3	6
3–4	3	3	3
3–5	2	2	8
2–4	0	0	6
2–5	2	5	8
4–6	4	4	10
4–5	1	1	1
5–6	1	4	7

If the firm can complete the project within 14 days, it will be given a $20,000 bonus. If not, it must pay a penalty of $3,500. Should the firm accept the contract? What other factors are probably relevant? Are there any noncritical paths whose variance might become important?

20. Given a PERT network:

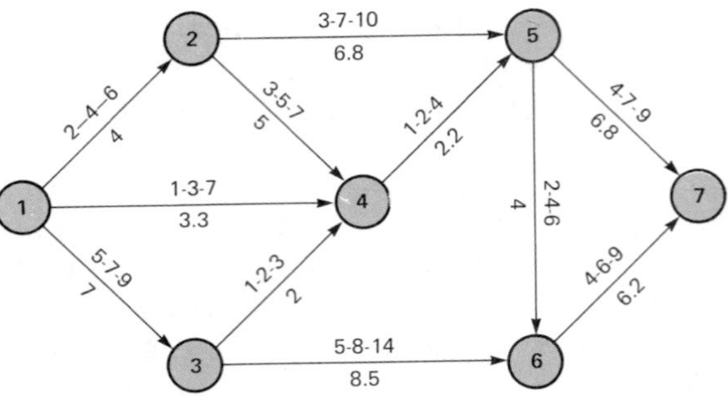

Find:

a. The estimated project completion time.

b. The critical path.

c. The slack on events **2** and **3**.

d. The slack on activities **1–4**, **2–5.**

e. The probability the project will be completed in 20 weeks or less.

f. The probability the project will be completed in 30 weeks or less.

g. The number of weeks required to complete the project with 95 percent certainty.

21. The following data were obtained from a study of the times required to overhaul a chemical plant:

	Crash schedule		Normal schedule	
Activity	*Time*	*Cost*	*Time*	*Cost*
1–2	3	6	5	4
1–3	1	5	5	3
2–4	5	7	10	4
3–4	2	6	7	4
2–6	2	5	6	3
4–6	5	9	11	6
4–5	4	6	6	3
6–7	1	4	5	2
5–7	1	5	4	2

Note: Costs are given in thousands of dollars; time in weeks.

a. Find the all-normal schedule and cost.

b. Find the all-crash schedule and cost.

c. Find the total cost required to expedite all activities from all-normal (case *a*) to all-crash (case *b*).

d. Find the *least-cost* plan for the all-crash time schedule. Start from the all-crash problem (*b*).

e. Find the least cost for an intermediate time schedule of 17 weeks.

22. Reconsider Problem 1 under the constraint that the project *must* be completed in 16 weeks. This time, however, activities *c*, *f*, *h*, and *i* may be crashed as follows:

Activity	*Crash time (weeks)*	*Additional cost per week*
c	7	40
f	6	20
h	2	10
i	3	30

Find the best schedule and its cost.

23. The CPM network below has a normal time and a fixed cost of $90 per day.

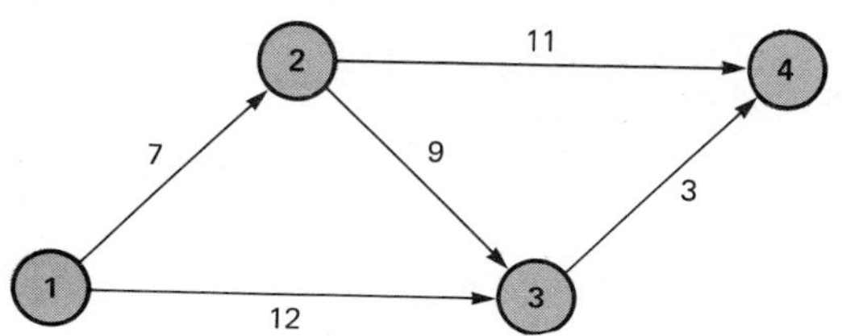

The various activities can be reduced up to their crash time with the additional costs shown:

Activity	*Crash time*	*Cost increase, per day reduction*
1–2	4	30 first day, 50 second, 70 third
2–3	6	40 first day, 45 second, 65 third
1–3	10	60 each
2–4	9	35 first, 60 second
3–4	3	—

Find the least-cost schedule.

Hint: Start with the normal time of 19 days (**1–2–3–4**). The total cost there is 19 × 90 = $1,710. Then start cutting to 18. You save $90 fixed cost but have a cost increase of $30 when you cut activity **1–2** by 1 day. Continue until no further reductions are possible or the cost climbs.

24. Given a network with normal times and crash time (in parentheses), find the optimal time-cost plan. Assume indirect costs are $100 per day. The data are:

Activity	*Time reduction direct cost per day*
1–2	$30 first, $50 second
2–3	$80 each
3–4	$25 first, $60 second
2–4	$30 first, $70 second, $90 third

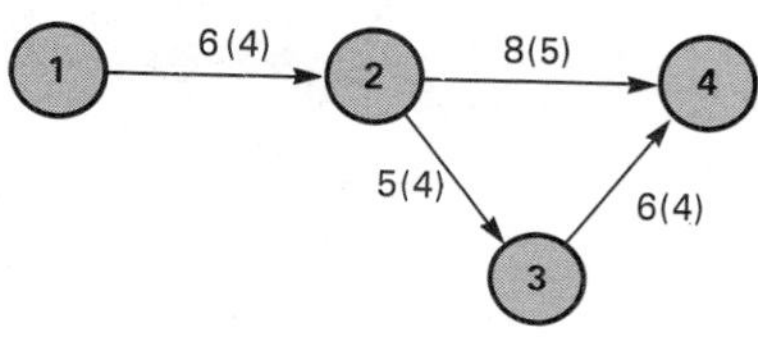

25. Given a proposed water system with the feasible distances shown below, find the optimal layout of pipes such that water will reach all points from the pump to F.

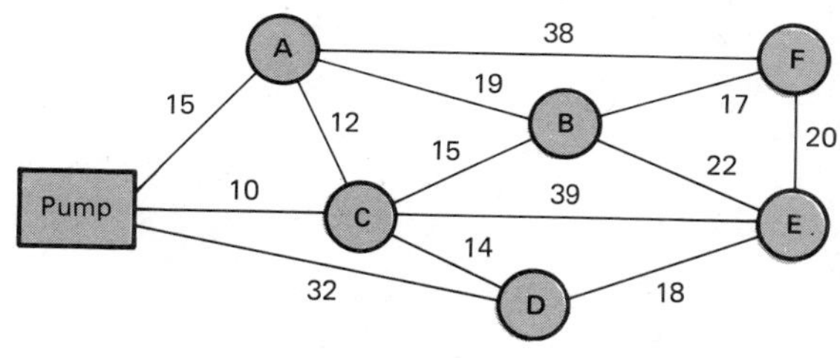

26. Your company plans to install a telecomputing system composed of a mainframe computer and seven terminals. The computer may be connected directly to a terminal or a terminal may be connected to another terminal that is connected to the computer. The matrix of distances is given below (an *X* means no direct connection is possible), as well as the map of terminal and computer locations. Find the optimal installation plan.

	Computer	*Terminal Number*						
		T1	*T2*	*T3*	*T4*	*T5*	*T6*	*T7*
Computer	—	20	48	25	61	21	37	60
T1	20	—	30	32	60	50	65	85
T2	48	30	—	22	33	40	x	73
T3	25	32	22	—	36	18	x	x
T4	61	60	33	36	—	67	52	40
T5	21	50	40	18	67	—	x	x
T6	37	65	x	x	52	x	—	x
T7	60	85	73	x	40	x	x	—

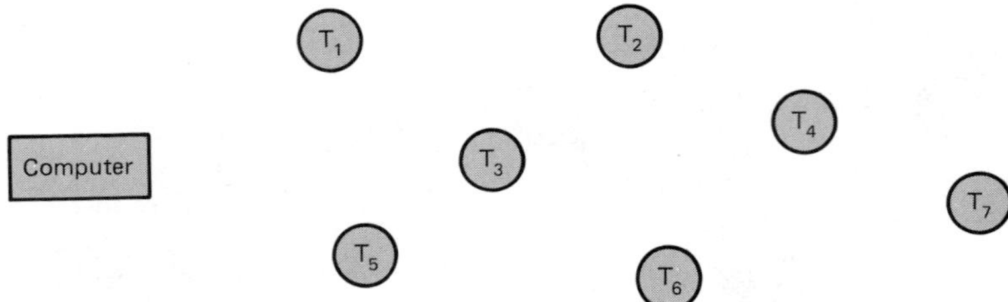

27. Find the maximum flow in the following networks.

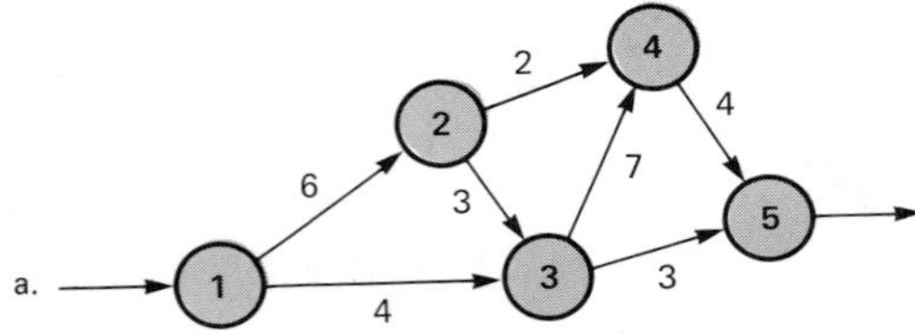

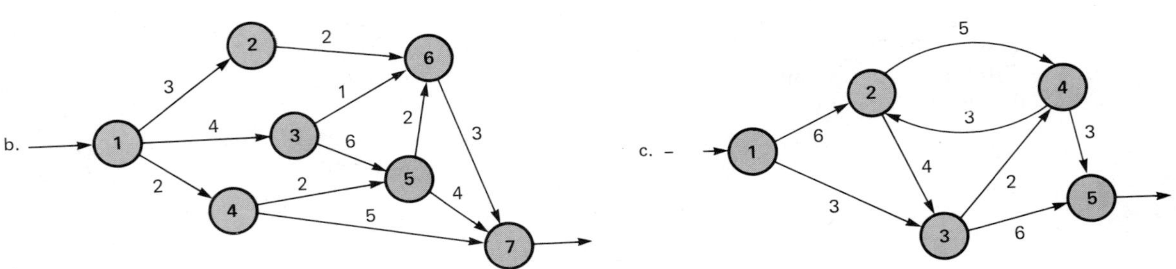

28. Find the shortest route from 1 to all the nodes.

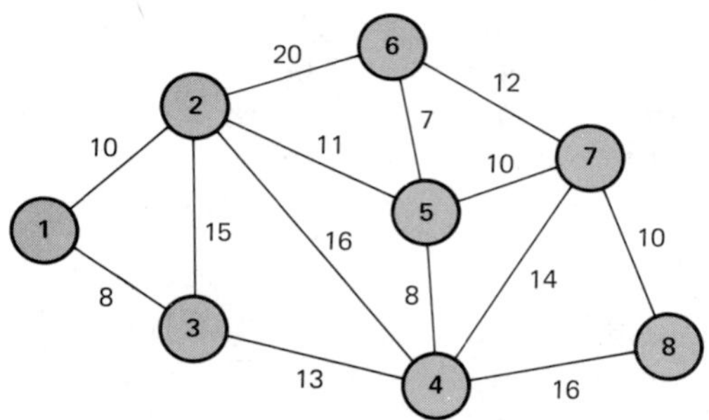

29. Find the minimum spanning tree for the previous problem.

11.18 CASE

THE SHARON CONSTRUCTION CORPORATION

The Sharon Construction Corporation has been awarded a contract for the construction of a 20,000-seat stadium. The construction must start by February 15 and be completed within one year. A penalty clause of $15,000 per week of delay beyond February 15 of next year is written into the contract.

Jim Brown, the president of the company, called for a planning meeting. In the meeting he expressed great satisfaction at obtaining the contract, revealing that the company could net as much as $300,000 on the project. He was confident that the project could be completed on time, with an allowance made for the usual delays anticipated in such a large project.

Bonnie Green, the director of personnel, agreed that in a normal year only slight delays might develop due to a shortage of labor. However, she reminded the president that for such a large project, the company would have to use unionized employees and that the construction industry labor agreements were due to expire on November 30. Past experience indicated a 50–50 chance for a strike.

Jim Brown agreed that a strike might cause a problem. Unfortunately, there was no way to change the contract. He inquired about the prospective length of a strike. Bonnie figured that such a strike would last at least 8 weeks (70 percent chance) and possibly 12 weeks (30 percent chance).

Jim was not too pleased with these prospects. However, before he had a chance to discuss contingency plans, he was interrupted by Jack White, the vice president for engineering. Jack commented that an extremely cold December had been predicted. This factor had not been taken into consideration during earlier estimates, since previous forecasts called for milder weather. Concrete pouring in a cold December would require, in one out of every three cases (depending on the temperature), special heating that costs $500 per week.

This additional information did not please Jim at all. The chances for delay were mounting. And an overhead expense of $500 per week would be incurred in case of any delay.

The technical details of the project are given in the appendix to this case.

The management team was asked to consider alternatives for coping with the situation. At the end of the week, five proposals were submitted.

1. Expedite the pouring of seat gallery supports. This would cost $20,000 and cut the duration of the activity to six weeks.
2. The same as proposal 1, but in addition, put a double shift on the filling of the field. A cost of $10,000 would result in a five-week time reduction.
3. The roof is very important, since it precedes several activities. The use of three shifts and some overtime could cut six weeks off the roofing, at an additional cost of only $9,000.
4. Take no special action until December 1. Then, if December is indeed cold, defer the pouring until the cold wave breaks, schedule permitting, and heat whenever necessary. If a strike occurs, wait until it is over (no other choice) and then expedite *all* remaining activities. In that case, the duration of any activity could be cut to no more than one third of its normal duration. The additional cost per activity for any week that is cut would be $3,000.
5. Do not take any special action at all; that is, hope and pray that no strike and no cold December occur (no cost).

Analyze the five proposals and make recommendations.

Appendix: Technical details of the stadium

The stadium is an indoor structure with a seating capacity of 20,000. The project begins with clearing the site, an activity that lasts eight weeks. Once the site is clear, the work can start simultaneously on the structure itself and on the field.

The work in the field involves subsurface drainage that lasts eight weeks, followed by filling for the playing field and track. Only with the completion of the filling (14 weeks) can the installation of the artificial playing turf take place, an activity that consumes 12 weeks.

The work on the structure itself starts with excavation, followed by the pouring of concrete footings. Each of these activities takes four weeks. Next comes the pouring of supports for seat galleries (12 weeks), followed by erecting precast galleries (13 weeks). The seats can then be poured (four weeks), and are ready for painting. However, the painting (three weeks) cannot begin until the dressing rooms are completed (four weeks). The dressing rooms can be completed only after the roof is erected (eight weeks). The roof must be erected on a steel structure that takes four weeks to install. This activity can start only after the concrete footings are poured.

Once the roof is erected, work can start simultaneously on the lights (five weeks) and on the scoreboard and other facilities (four weeks). Assume that there are 28 days in February and that February 15 falls on a Monday.

11.19 GLOSSARY

Activity A specific job or task that is part of a project and requires time and resources for completion.

Backward pass Solving a network problem by starting at the end first.

CPM (critical path method) A tool that plans and monitors both time and cost where expediting of activities (crashing) is possible.

Crashing Expediting an activity so that it will be completed in less than its normal time up to the minimum possible duration.

Critical activity Any activity on the critical path. All of these activities have either zero slack or the same amount of minimum slack in the network.

Critical path The longest path(s) in the network. This path has the least slack in the network. It is wholly composed of critical activities and critical events.

Dummy activity A fictitious activity that requires no time for completion. Its main purpose is to establish the precedence relationship in a network.

Duration Time required to complete an activity.

Earliest date (T_E) The earliest time (counted from the beginning of the project) at which an event, or activity, may be finished.

Earliest finish (EF) The earliest time an activity can be completed, provided it started at its ES.

Earliest start (ES) The earliest calendar time that an activity can start.

Event A specific accomplishment at a recognizable point in time; a milestone, a checkpoint. An event occurs when *all* preceding activities have been completed. Events use neither time nor resources.

Expected time (t_e) Average duration time for an activity.

Forward pass Solving a network problem by starting at the beginning and proceeding forward.

Free float (FF) A slack that represents the time that an activity can be delayed without delaying the early start time of an immediately following activity.

Graphical evaluation and review technique (GERT) An extension of PERT that relaxes several of PERT's assumptions, making it more realistic (and more complex).

Greedy algorithm A solution method that incrementally solves a problem by selecting the next best element in the set.

Latest allowable date (T_L) The latest date (counted from the beginning of the project) at which an event can occur without holding up the project's earliest completion date.

Latest finish (LF) The latest an activity can be finished without delaying the project.

Latest start (LS) The latest an activity can start without delaying the project.

Maximal flow Finding the distribution of flows through a network that permits the greatest amount to flow from the source to the sink.

Most likely time estimate (t_m) An estimate of an activity duration time that is considered to be the most likely (modal value).

Network A graphical presentation of a project showing the sequential relationship of activities. It consists of nodes representing events, and arcs representing activities.

Normal time The lowest cost activity times in a CPM network.

Optimistic time estimate (t_o) An estimate of an activity's duration under ideal conditions; the shortest possible time to complete the activity. Such conditions occur only 1 out of 100 times.

Path (in the network) A sequence of activities (described by arcs) leading from the beginning of the project to its end.

PERT (program evaluation review technique) A planning and monitoring technique for projects based on three time estimates for each activity's duration.

PERT/Cost An extension of PERT that allows the planning and control of both time and cost in a project.

Pessimistic time estimate (t_p) An estimate of the activity's duration under the worst possible conditions that may occur in only 1 out of 100 cases.

Project A collection of activities with a definable beginning and a definable end (the goal).

Shared slack Slack shared by two or more noncritical activities.

Shortest route Finding the shortest path from one point to another in a network.

Sink A destination where all flows end.

Slack The extra time that an activity (or an event) can be held up without delaying the project's completion.

Source The point where all flows begin.

Spanning tree A network where every node may be reached from every other node through one or more arcs.

Total float (TF) The extra time an activity or event can delay without delaying the project completion, assuming that the slack is not used by another activity already.

11.20 REFERENCES AND BIBLIOGRAPHY

1. Clayton, E. R., and L. J. Moore, "PERT vs. GERT." *Journal of Systems Management* 23 (1972), pp. 11–19.
2. Cleland, D. I., and W. R. King. Eds. *Project Management Handbook*. New York: Van Nostrand Reinhold, 1983.
3. Davis, E. W. *Project Management: Techniques, Applications, and Managerial Issues,* 3rd ed. Norcross, Ga.: American Institute of Industrial Engineers, 1983.
4. Elmaghraby, S. B. *Activity Networks: Project Planning and Control by Network Models*. New York: John Wiley & Sons, 1977.
5. Ford, L. R., and D. R. Fulkerson. *Flows in Networks*. Princeton, N.J.: Princeton University Press, 1962.
6. Gray, F. C. *Essentials of Project Management*. New York: Van Nostrand Reinhold, 1981.
7. Harrison, F. L. *Advanced Project Management*. Hants, England: Gower Pub., 1981.
8. Kerzner, H. *Project Management for Executives*. New York: Van Nostrand Reinhold, 1981.
9. Meredith, J. R., and S. J. Mantel, Jr. *Project Management: A Managerial Approach*. New York: John Wiley & Sons, 1985.
10. Moder, J. J.; C. R. Phillips, and E. W. Davis. *Project Management with CPM, PERT, and Precedence Diagramming,* 3rd ed. New York: Van Nostrand Reinhold, 1983.
11. Rosenaw, M. D. *Successful Project Management*. Belmont, Calif.: Wadsworth Publishing, 1981.
12. Spinner, H. *Elements of Project Management,* Englewood Cliffs, N.J.: Prentice-Hall, 1981.
13. Stuckenbruck, L. C. Ed. *The Implementation of Project Management: The Professional's Handbook*. Reading, Mass.: Addison-Wesley Publishing, 1981.
14. Wiest, J., and F. Levy. *Management Guide to PERT-CPM*. 2nd ed. Englewood Cliffs, N.J.: Prentice-Hall, 1977.
15. Whitehouse, G. E. *Systems Analysis and Design Using Network Techniques*. Englewood Cliffs, N.J.: Prentice-Hall, 1973.

12

Dynamic programming

PART A: BASICS

12.1 The nature of dynamic programming.
12.2 The stagecoach problem.
12.3 Terminology and structure.
12.4 Allocation processes.
12.5 Concluding remarks.
12.6 Problems for Part A.

PART B: EXTENSIONS

12.7 Probabilistic problems.
12.8 Mathematical presentation and optimization techniques.
12.9 The knapsack problem.
12.10 Computerization.
12.11 Problems for Part B.
12.12 Case—The personnel director.
12.13 Glossary.
12.14 References and bibliography.

The managerial problems presented in the previous chapters dealt with situations involving a single decision. Management, however, must frequently consider a *sequence* of decisions where each decision affects future decisions. The tool used for solving certain types of such sequential decision problems is called dynamic programming.

No single model for solving dynamic programming problems exists. Therefore, these problems are classified into groups, each with its own formulation and method of solution. However, the basic approach and logic for solving all dynamic programming problems is the same. In Part A of the chapter, the basic structure and terminology of dynamic programming are discussed. Some examples are also given to illustrate the prototype problems and their solution approaches.

In Part B of the chapter, the mathematics of the dynamic programming method are formulated and additional examples are given.

LEARNING OBJECTIVES

The student should be able to:

a. Describe the philosophy of DP.
b. Define the terms *states, stages, rewards, rollback analysis,* and *prototype problems.*
c. Solve simple DP problems of the allocation and stagecoach types.
d. Define the principle of optimality.
e. Describe the relationship between states, stages, and rewards.

Extensions

f. Solve simple probabilistic problems.
g. Describe the recursive relationship and general formulas of DP.
h. Solve knapsack-type problems.

PART A: BASICS

Jeff knew that he was in trouble. It had been only three days since he received the job he had waited so long for, a dinner cook at the prestigious Queen's Hotel. The recipe for dinner that evening called for 7 ounces of wine; but Jeff, new on the job, could only find a 5-ounce cup and an 8-ounce cup. The problem was that dinner time was quickly approaching, and no time remained to search for other measuring cups or to buy or borrow one.[1] Jeff was tempted to use the 8-ounce cup, filling it not quite to capacity; but as a good cook he knew that accuracy in the use of wine was very important.

Jeff did some quick thinking. Clearly, if 7 ounces of wine were to be contained in one of the cups, it must be the 8-ounce cup. The problem then became one of getting 7 ounces into the 8-ounce cup. Proceeding in the same manner, he realized that if 2 ounces of wine were already in the 8-ounce cup, his problem would have been solved. He could then use a full 5-ounce cup of wine to add to the 2 ounces. How then could he pour 2 ounces of wine into the 8-ounce cup? Presumably by filling one of the cups and then pouring some out. Using the 8-ounce cup meant filling it up and pouring out 6 ounces. Using the 5-ounce cup, it would be necessary to pour out 3 ounces. In either case, he needed a 6-ounce or a 3-ounce cup, but he had neither. Which alternative should he explore further? Jeff felt that he was getting nowhere, and dinner time was almost at hand. The problem, however, intrigued him, and he considered it a bit longer.

After a moment of reflection he was sure that his problem could be solved. If 5 ounces of wine were in the 8-ounce cup (which could be accomplished by filling the 5-ounce cup and pouring it into the 8-ounce cup) and he then refilled the 5-ounce cup and poured it into the 8-ounce cup until the latter was full, then there would be *exactly 2 ounces* left in the 5-ounce cup! All that was left to do then was to empty the 8-ounce cup, pour the 2 ounces from the 5- to the 8-ounce cup, refill the 5-ounce cup and add it to the 2 ounces in the 8-ounce cup to get exactly the required 7 ounces.

"Eureka!" cried Jeff. Only a minute or so was required to pour *exactly* 7 ounces of wine over the dinner beef. Jeff did not realize that his thinking followed the general thought process of perhaps the most fascinating tool of management science—*dynamic programming* (DP).

[1] This problem is adapted from a similar one given in Nemhauser [11].

12.1 THE NATURE OF DYNAMIC PROGRAMMING

Jeff's approach to the solution of his problem is typical of dynamic programming (developed by Bellman [2]), which has the following characteristics:

Segmentation

Jeff approached the problem as follows: Since he could not solve the problem in one shot, he asked himself if there was any intermediate position which, if achieved, could take him to his target of 7 ounces. He soon realized that if 2 ounces were already in the 8-ounce cup, then he could solve his original problem. At this point, two things actually happened:

1. Jeff *created* and *solved* a second problem; namely, if there were 2 ounces of wine in the 8-ounce cup, then, in order to get 7 ounces, all that remained to do was to add 5 ounces from the second cup to the 2 ounces.
2. Jeff *created* a third problem; namely, how to place 2 ounces of wine in the 8-ounce cup.

Two problems from one

Overall, the original problem was **segmented** into two smaller ones. Once the two smaller problems were solved, the solution to the original problem was achieved.

Each problem a stage

The segmentation of the complex problem into smaller problems resulted in a *sequence of decisions.* Jeff actually made two decisions. Each of the smaller problems created is labeled a **stage.**

In a multistage decision problem, a sequence of interrelated decisions either exists already or must be constructed. For example, the decision about how much preventive maintenance to give to an automobile this year is interrelated with the maintenance (or replacement) decision to be made next year. If the intent is to sell or replace the car next year, less maintenance will probably be prescribed this year. However, if the intent is to keep the car for several years, more extensive maintenance may be recommended.

Rollback approach

Start from the end first

Jeff started the analysis by first solving the last of the newly created problems. Namely, how to achieve the goal of 7 ounces, once 2 ounces were in the cup. Only then did he proceed to solve the next to last problem; namely, how to get 2 ounces in the cup. Such an approach is called the **rollback** or backward approach, since the problem closest to the target is solved first. Most dynamic programming (DP) problems are solved in this manner. There are, however, certain DP problems that are solved "forward"; that is, starting with the problem farthest from the goal first. The approach to be selected depends on the convenience and speed of computation.

Problems solved by dynamic programming

DP for segmented problems

Dynamic programming can solve problems that can either be segmented into a sequence of decisions (such as Jeff's problem) *or* are composed of a series of small problems to begin with.

Before considering the general structure and terminology of dynamic programming, the **sequential decision-making** process is illustrated in more detail with another example.

12.2 THE STAGECOACH PROBLEM

In the good old days, stagecoaches were the only means of public transportation. A traveling salesman, living in San Francisco, decided to cross the country to New York. Figure 12.1 depicts the available stagecoach routes. Each circle on the map represents an exchange point. At an exchange point, the traveler moved to another stagecoach, since the horses needed to rest. The exchange points are numbered from **1** to **11** as a matter of convenience. The distance in "travel days" is marked above the routes. The problem is to find the route from San Francisco to New York that requires the fewest days of travel.

Solution by complete enumeration

There are only eight possible routes as shown in Table 12.1. Thus, by complete enumeration, route **1 → 2 → 5 → 8 → 11** (doubled in Figure 12.1 by a broken line) is found to be the fastest, requiring only 15 days.

FIGURE 12.1
The stagecoach problem

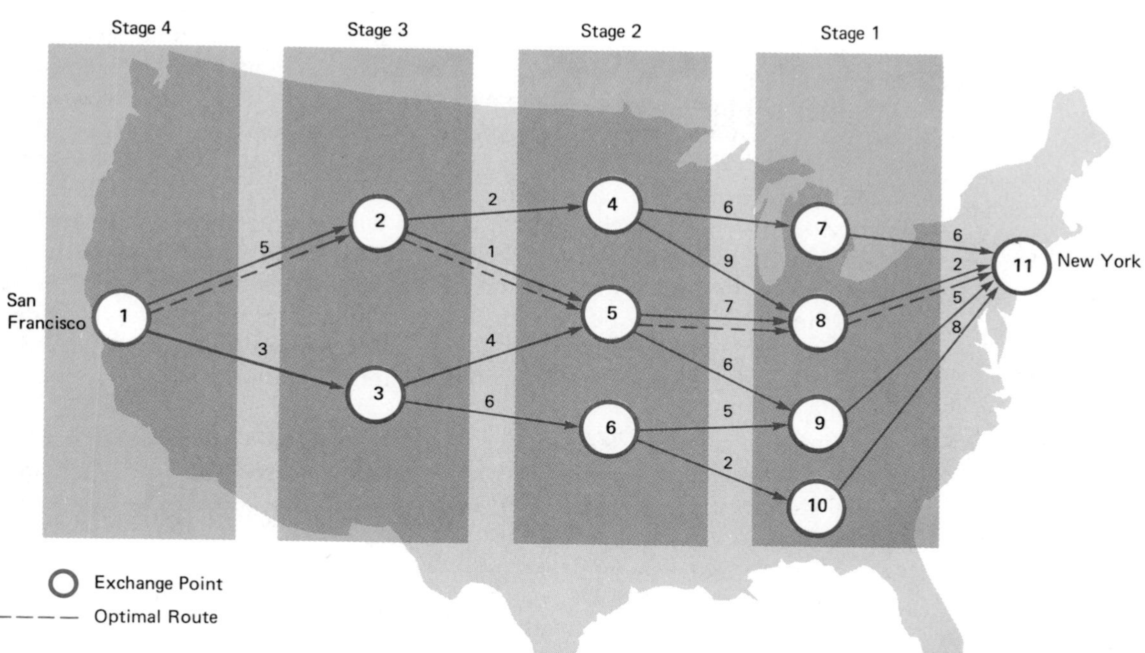

TABLE 12.1
Possible routes and days of travel—complete enumeration

Route	Days of travel	
(1) → (2) → (4) → (7) → (11)	19	
(1) → (2) → (4) → (8) → (11)	18	
(1) → (2) → (5) → (8) → (11)	15	←*Minimum*
(1) → (2) → (5) → (9) → (11)	17	
(1) → (3) → (5) → (8) → (11)	16	
(1) → (3) → (5) → (9) → (11)	18	
(1) → (3) → (6) → (9) → (11)	19	
(1) → (3) → (6) → (10) → (11)	19	

The problem with enumeration

In large travel networks, a complete listing and computation of all possible routes may be cumbersome, especially when constraints on travel (e.g., fares and probability of delays) are taken into consideration. Also, the problem may be more complicated when additional objectives (such as safety and fun) are taken into consideration. For those cases, dynamic programming is prescribed.

Solution by dynamic programming (DP)

The first step of dynamic programming is the segmentation of the given problem into smaller problems or *stages*. A stage, in this example, is a decision point where the traveler must decide which stagecoach to take next. This segmentation is done as follows: In San Francisco, the traveler must decide on going to either **2** or to **3**. Once the traveler gets to either **2** or **3**, he must make another decision that will get him to either **4**, **5**, or **6**. A decision at **4**, **5**, or **6** will take him to **7**, **8**, **9**, or **10**, from which he may then travel directly to New York, **11**. Thus, no matter which route the traveler selects, he will travel in *four stagecoaches*. Therefore, the problem can be broken into four smaller problems, each made at a zone (stage) regarding what stagecoach to take next. The stages are marked backward, from 4 to 1, for convenience in employing the rollback concept.

Four stagecoaches, 11 states

In each stage the decision maker can be at one and only one exchange point. The exchange points in these examples correspond to what are called **states** in DP. A state is the condition that a system, or the problem, can occupy in a particular stage.

DP eliminates some routes

The use of dynamic programming eliminates the need to investigate *all* possible routes, as is done in complete enumeration. In this example, the computational work involved in DP is larger than that involved in complete enumeration. However, for large DP problems, the savings over complete enumeration can be substantial.

Details of the solution

Starting from the end

The solution procedure uses a rollback analysis; that is, the end of the problem is analyzed first. The salesman thus first assumes that he is in New York. The salesman then considers the question of how to proceed from any given exchange point (state) to New York so as to minimize the travel time. This computation begins with the *last* stage, which is labeled 1. Once this decision is made, the traveller considers another question; namely, how to get, in the best manner, to each of the possible exchange points of stage 1. The process then is repeated until San Francisco is reached.

Stage 1 Once the traveler is in New York, he has reached his goal. Immediately before that, he must be in one of the exchange points **7, 8, 9,** or **10.** These points are the states of stage 1. Note that there is *only one* possible way of getting from each of these points to New York. That is, if the traveler is, for example, in exchange point **7,** then the *best* and only choice for him is to travel by route **7 → 11** in order to reach New York. In other words, it does not matter how the traveler reached exchange point **7;** once he is there, he should travel by route **7 → 11** to New York. A similar analysis is made for all other exchange points at stage 1. The results are shown in Table 12.2, and should be treated on an "if-then" basis (e.g., *if* the traveler is at exchange point **7,** *then* the best way to continue traveling is **7 → 11,** for six days of travel).

TABLE 12.2
The first stage

State	*Alternative route*	*Days of travel to New York*	*Best route (days)*
7	(7)→(11)	6	6
8	(8)→(11)	2	2
9	(9)→(11)	5	5
10	(10)→(11)	8	8

The computation of this stage can be summarized in the following manner:

The evaluation of the effectiveness in this case is based on "days of travel." The smaller the number of days, the better. The number of days of travel is the payoff or the **reward.**

The reward

Stage 2 In order to reach any of the stage 1 exchange points—**7, 8, 9,** or **10**—the traveler must be in one of the stagecoaches that started at exchange points **4, 5,** or **6.** Hence, these exchange points are the states of *stage 2.*

TABLE 12.3
The second stage

State	*Alternative route*	*Distance to stage 1*	*Best distance from stage 1 to New York (from Table 12.2)*	*Total distance*	*Best route*
4	(4)→(7)	6	6	12	
	(4)→(8)	9	2	11	←
5	(5)→(8)	7	2	9	←
	(5)→(9)	6	5	11	
6	(6)→(9)	5	5	10	←
	(6)→(10)	2	8	10	←

From each of these states, the best possibility of getting to New York is examined. However, instead of enumerating all routes to New York, only the routes to the states of stage 1 are examined. This is done because it is *already known* how to get from each state in stage 1 to New York in the best way.

Considering state **4** first, there are two alternative ways of reaching stage 1: **4** → **7** or **4** → **8.** The former requires 6 days plus the optimal time to New York, computed in stage 1 as 6, for a total of 12. The latter requires 9 days + 2 days = 11 days. Of the two, the better is **4** → **8** with 11 days. Similar computations are executed for states **5** and **6.** The results are shown in Table 12.3. Notice that the best solution is computed for each state independently.

Stage 3 In order to get to either exchange point **4, 5,** or **6,** in the previous stage, it is necessary to exchange stagecoaches at points **2** or **3.** These points are the states of stage 3.

Table 12.4 summarizes the computations for the third stage. Note

TABLE 12.4
The third stage

State	*Alternative route*	*Distance to stage 2*	*Best distance from stage 2 to New York (from Table 12.3)*	*Total distance*	*Best route*
2	(2)→(4)	2	11	13	
	(2)→(5)	1	9	10	←
3	(3)→(5)	4	9	13	←
	(3)→(6)	6	10	16	

that the best results found in stage 2 above are used as an input for computing stage 3.

Stage 4 Finally, the traveler is at the initial point. There are two alternatives here: either go to exchange point **2** or to exchange point **3.** There is only one state to be examined, state **1.** The computations are shown in Table 12.5.

TABLE 12.5
The fourth stage

State	*Alternative route*	*Distance to stage 3 (immediate reward)*	*Best distance from stage 3 to New York (from Table 12.4)*	*Total distance (reward)*	*Best route*
1	①→②	5	10	15	←
	①→③	3	13	16	

Now it is possible to reconstruct the optimal solution for the entire problem, this time going forward. In stage 4, the solution is route **1** → **2.** In stage 3, we know that *if* one is at state **2,** it is best to go to state **5** (Table 12.4). In stage 2, we know that if one is at state **5,** it is best to go to state **8** (Table 12.3). Finally, Table 12.2 tells us that from state **8** the best way to get to New York is **8** → **11.** The optimal travel route is:

1 → **2** → **5** → **8** → **11**

for a total of 15 travel days (Table 12.5 gives this total).

Note that in each of the stages and for each state the following computations were executed (see Table 12.5):

a. Total distance (reward) = Distance to previous stage (immediate reward) + Best distance from previous stage to New York (optimal reward in previous stage).
b. Best route (optimal reward) = Smallest total distance (reward).

These two computational procedures are the backbone of dynamic programming.

12.3 TERMINOLOGY AND STRUCTURE

The stagecoach example will be used to help define the major terms and concepts of dynamic programming.

Stages The stagecoach problem was solved by breaking it into four subproblems, each of which is considered a *stage.* Thus, the first step in any dynamic programming solution is to divide the problem into stages, if it is not originally so divided.

A stage as a decision point

> *Definition:* A stage refers to a particular decision point on the solution route. For example, each time a decision about the next stagecoach has to be made, a stage is encountered.

A state as an exchange point

States At each stage, the traveling salesperson could have been in one (and only one) of several possible exchange points, each of which is considered a *state*. As the salesperson traveled along the route, he moved from state to state.

The decision process A DP solution is viewed as a process of moving from stage to stage, making a decision at each. The direction of the move can be either forward (sometimes called a *forward pass*), from the *initial* to the *final* stage, or backwards, which is termed *rollback* (or *backward pass*), from the *final* to the *initial* stage. At each stage, a decision about what state to move to is made. However, in some DP problems, the system may not change its state even though it goes through several stages. For example, a machine may remain in good condition for several weeks in the case where each stage is considered to be one week, and the possible conditions of the machine are the states.

Three types of rewards

Reward The dependent variable in the stagecoach example was the "days of travel." In dynamic programming the dependent variable is called the *reward.* Three types of rewards are distinguished:

1. *Immediate reward.* This is the reward associated with a move between two adjacent stages. For example, in Table 12.5, the column "Distance to stage 3" designates the reward. This reward is an **immediate reward** for each alternative route (state to state) between two adjacent states.

2. *The total reward.* An examination of Tables 12.3, 12.4, and 12.5 indicates that at each stage, and *for each state in that stage,* the total reward (i.e., the total distance from each state to New York) was derived as the sum of the *immediate reward* (distance to previous stage), plus the *optimal reward* obtained in the previous stage.

3. *Optimal total reward.* In each stage, and for each state, there are usually several alternatives to reach the next stage and eventually the goal. For each alternative, the total reward is computed (according to 2). The best of all total rewards in each state, for each given stage, is the *optimal total reward.*

In terms of the stagecoach example, the optimal total reward for each exchange point (state) is the shortest route from that exchange point to New York.

Notice that the optimal total reward from the final decision state (San Francisco) gives the optimal solution for the original unsegmented problem.

The recursive relation

The recursive relation The function that ties together the immediate reward, the total reward, and the optimal total reward is called the **recursive**

relation. This function will be discussed in more detail in Part B. This relationship is derived from the **principle of optimality.**

Policy A **policy** in DP refers to a complete, predetermined plan for selecting a course of action under every possible circumstance. In addition to solving the original problem, DP solves several subproblems. The solution to these is in the form of a policy. For example, in the stagecoach problem, the solution in Table 12.4 says: *if* you are at state **2,** it is best to go to **5;** *if* you are at state **3,** go also to **5.** Overall, dynamic programming dictates an *optimal policy* to follow, which is the *best* of all possible policies for the entire problem, derived from the collection of policies for the subproblems.

A policy as a contingency plan

The basic idea—the principle of optimality In dynamic programming, the analysis is based on Bellman's *principle of optimality* [2], which states:

> An optimal policy has the property that whatever the initial state and initial decision are, the remaining decisions must constitute an optimal policy with regard to the state resulting from the decision.

In the stagecoach example, this principle implies that:

> If an exchange point is on the optimal route, then the shortest path from that exchange point to New York is also on the optimal route.

The implication of the principle of optimality is that, starting at a current stage, the optimal policy (decision) for the remaining stages depends only on the state at the current stage and not on the means that the system used in arriving at that state. (That is, the optimal policy is independent of the policies [decisions] adopted at prior stages.)

The basic principle of DP

The structure of dynamic programming

To illustrate the general structure of a DP problem, let us visualize what happened in an *intermediate stage* (3) of the stagecoach problem (Table 12.4) by viewing it as an input-output system.

Assume that we arrived at any point (state) in stage 3 somehow; then, a question may be asked: What is the best route to go from *each* of these points to stage 2? (Remember, this is exactly how Jeff approached his problem: "Assume that 2 ounces are in the large cup, what is the best way to get 7 ounces in that cup?")

The answer to such a question depends on what state we are in at stage 3. If we are in state **2,** then route **2** → **5** will be selected. If we are in state **3,** then route **3** → **5** will be selected.

The actual location (state **2** or state **3**) can be determined only after stage 4 is analyzed (see Table 12.5). Therefore, the ultimate *input* to stage 3 is the *output* of stage 4. In a similar manner, the *output* of stage 3 is the *input* to stage 2. In graphical terms, this is shown as follows:

Input-decision-reward-output

Let:

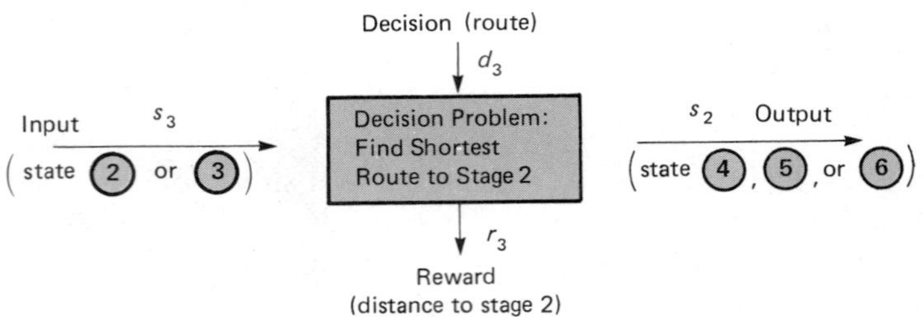

FIGURE 12.2
Stage 3 input and output

s_3 = Input into stage 3 (state **2** or **3**)
d_3 = Decision at stage 3
r_3 = Reward at stage 3
s_2 = Output to stage 2 (state **4, 5,** or **6**)

Then, the input-output relationship can be viewed as a diagram, as shown in Figure 12.2.

Diagrams like that of Figure 12.2 can be drawn for every stage in the problem. Since the stages are connected, the entire DP process can be shown as a chain of input-output relationships. The stagecoach problem is displayed in this manner in Figure 12.3.

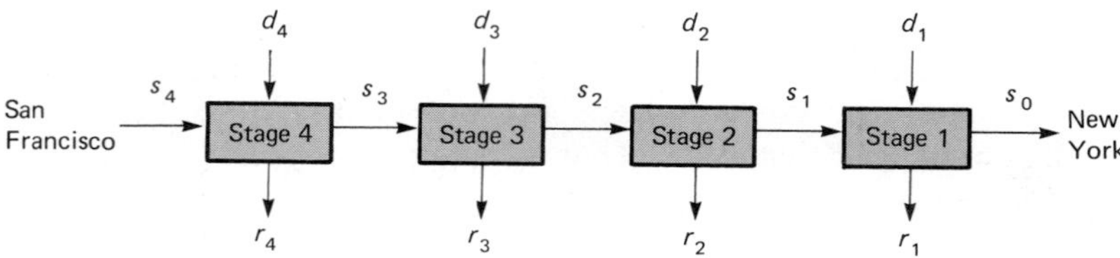

FIGURE 12.3
The stagecoach problem

Diagramming the DP problem in this manner helps its formulation in mathematical terms, as will be shown in Part B.

Prototype dynamic programming problems

Families of DP problems

Unlike most other mathematical models, no *standard* recursive relation exists for DP. Therefore, it is impossible to use a general computational tool (such as the simplex method in linear programming). However, it is possible to classify DP problems into "families" (or prototypes) and build a special computational procedure for each. While these prototypes differ in their structures and computational procedures, they share the general approach of DP. These prototypes are:

1. *Allocation processes.* These processes (to be discussed in the next section) are segmented into smaller allocation problems.
2. *Multiperiod processes.* These processes are originally segmented, having two or more time periods. These are also known as smoothing or scheduling processes.

3. *Network processes.* PERT and other networks can often be viewed as DP problems and solved as such. The stagecoach problem is one example of a network process.
4. *Multistage production processes.* These problems arise in industrial production situations.
5. *Feedback control processes.* Feedback problems occur in electronics, aerospace, and automated production.
6. *Markov decision processes.* Markovian situations are discussed in Chapter 13.

The remainder of this chapter is primarily devoted to illustrating some of these prototype problems; other examples can be found in Bellman and Dreyfus [3].

12.4 ALLOCATION PROCESSES

The allocation of resources among potential recipients is a major problem of organizations. In cases with a linear objective function and constraints, the problem may be presented as a linear programming problem. However, in many cases, the mathematical programming formulation leads to integer or nonlinear models that require difficult or costly solution procedures. Dynamic programming offers a better way to handle some of these complicated cases.

An investment example

The management of the Southern Corporation is considering the allocation of $4 million among its three plants. It has already been decided that the allocation per plant is to be either $0, $1, $2, $3, or $4 million. (An investment is made in whole units of $1 million.)

DP for investment decisions

Each plant has submitted its forecast of yearly returns corresponding to different levels of money invested. The forecast returns are given in Table 12.6. For example, an initial investment of $2 million in plant A will yield an annual return of $.5 million. The problem is to determine the optimal allocation of money to each plant in order to maximize the overall expected annual return. This problem cannot be solved as a linear

TABLE 12.6
Southern Corporation investment alternatives

Amount allocated (in million $)	*Annual return (reward) ($ million) to:*		
	Plant A	*Plant B*	*Plant C*
0	0	0	0
1	.2	.3	.4
2	.5	.6	.9
3	1.5	1.2	1.1
4	1.4	1.5	1.6

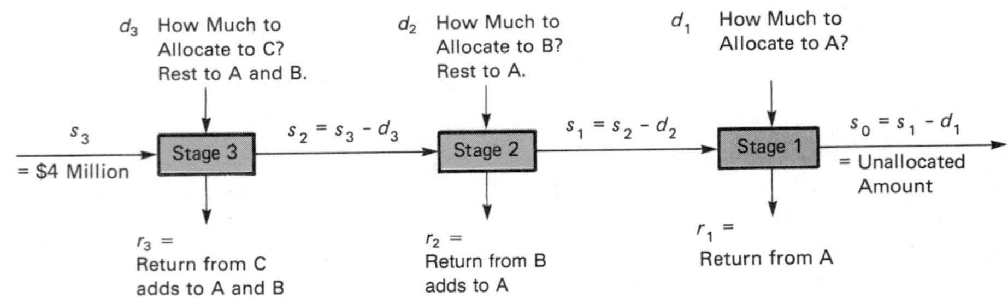

FIGURE 12.4
An allocation problem

program, first, because it is an integer programming problem and, moreover, because the returns are nonlinear.

Formulation In order to solve this problem, it will be segmented into three stages; each stage represents an allocation to one plant. That is, the process will be viewed as a sequence of decision-making subproblems. The relationship between the stages is shown in Figure 12.4. Again, a rollback approach will be followed. First, an allocation will be made to plant A (arbitrarily considered the "last" plant), then to B, and then to C.

States In each stage there are five possible states; allocate either 0, 1, 2, 3, or 4.

Solution

Stage 1 In this stage, either $0, $1, $2, $3, or $4 million will be available for allocation to plant A. The computed returns from the investment in plant A are given in Table 12.7. The amount available (0, 1, 2, 3, or 4) is designated s_1. The optimal policy is: If 0, 1, 2, or 3 are available, the best solution is to allocate all the money. But if $4 million are available, then it is best to allocate only $3 million, since the optimal return from $3 million is larger than the return from $4 million (a situation that is unusual but possible). This information is shown in Table 12.7; the last column is composed of the highest reward (optimal) in each row. The numbers that are shaded are the highest, and they point to the optimal policy (decision).

Stage 2 At this stage, it is necessary to determine how to split the available dollars between A and B. Let us designate the amount available for allocation to both A and B as s_2.

Thus, of the allocated amount s_2, plant B gets d_2, while the remaining $s_2 - d_2 = s_1$ is made available for allocation to plant A in the best possible way, as already computed in stage 1.

For each value of s_2 (0, 1, 2, 3, or 4), there are several alternatives for allocation; they must all be considered. This is done by examining all five possible states.

For state $s_2 = 0$. No allocation, no return.

TABLE 12.7
Stage 1: Allocation to plant A

Amount s_1, available for plant A	*Decision d_1: How much to give to plant A, by state*					Optimal reward
	0	*1*	*2*	*3*	*4*	
0	0					0
1	0	.2				.2
2	0	.2	.5			.5
3	0	.2	.5	1.5		1.5
4	0	.2	.5	1.5	1.4	1.5

For state $s_2 = 1$. Either 1 to B and 0 to A (total return of .3 + 0 = .3) or 0 to B and 1 to A (total return of 0 + .2 = .2). It is clear that 1 to B is a better allocation. That is, *if* \$1 million is ever left to be allocated between A and B, B should get it. This information is then entered in Table 12.8. Table 12.8 includes the computations for all the remaining states. In each state, the optimal total reward is computed.

Amount s_2, available for plants A and B	*Decision d_2: How much to allocate to B; the remainder goes to A in an optimal matter*					*Optimal reward*
	0	*1*	*2*	*3*	*4*	
0	0					0
1	0 + .2 = .2	.3 + 0 = .3				.3
2	0 + .5 = .5	.3 + .2 = .5	.6 + 0 = .6			.6
3	0 + 1.5 = 1.5	.3 + .5 = .8	.6 + .2 = .8	1.2 + 0 = 1.2		1.5
4	0 + 1.5 = 1.5	.3 + 1.5 = 1.8	.6 + .5 = 1.1	1.2 + .2 = 1.4	1.5 + 0 = 1.5	1.8

In general, the computations in the body of the table are those of the *total reward,* which is the sum of the immediate reward plus the optimal reward from stage 1.

Example for state $s_2 = 3$. Row 3 in Table 12.8 was computed as shown in Table 12.9. Once all total rewards are computed for each row, then the *highest* one is selected and designated as the "optimal total reward."

TABLE 12.9
Detailed computation of $s_2 = 3$

d_2 Allocation to B	*Remainder to allocate to A*	*Immediate reward*	*Optimal from stage 1*	*Total reward*	*Optimal total reward*
0	3	0	1.5	1.5	←
1	2	.3	.5	.8	
2	1	.6	.2	.8	
3	0	1.2	0	1.2	

TABLE 12.10
Stage 3: Allocation to plant C, state $s_3 = 4$

s_3, *amount available for plants A, B, and C*	*Amount allocated to C, d_3*					*Optimal total reward*
	0	*1*	*2*	*3*	*4*	
4	0 + 1.8 = 1.8	.4 + 1.5 = 1.9	.9 + .6 = 1.5	1.1 + .3 = 1.4	1.6 + 0 = 1.6	1.9

Stage 3 In this stage, an allocation decision is made to C, and the remaining amount is then *best allocated* between A and B, according to the policy described in stage 2. At this final stage, only one state will be shown: $s_3 = 4$.[2] The computations are shown in Table 12.10 in the standard manner used before, and in a somewhat more detailed manner in Table 12.11. Thus, the best allocation is: $d_3 = 1$, $d_2 = 0$, $d_1 = 3$; that is, 1 to C and 3 to A, with a return of $1.9 million.

TABLE 12.11
Stage 3, state $s_3 = 4$

Alternatives	*Reward to C*	*Reward from best allocation among A and B (as computed in stage 2)*	*Optimal total reward*	
d_3 = 4 to C, 0 to A & B	1.6	0	1.6	
d_3 = 3 to C, 1 to A & B*	1.1	.3 (1 to B)	1.4	
d_3 = 2 to C, 2 to A & B	.9	.6 (2 to B)	1.5	
d_3 = 1 to C, 3 to A & B	.4	1.5 (3 to A)	1.9	←*Maximum (best)*
d_3 = 0 to C, 4 to A & B	0	1.8 (1 to B, 3 to A)	1.8	

* Allocated between A and B in an optimal manner, as computed in stage 2.

Some observations

Several valuable observations can be made from the example shown here.

1. For every value of *s*, at every stage, the optimal return is computed in the analysis.
2. The marginal return for a given allocation policy, as *s* is increased (decreased) in units of $1 million, can easily be observed from previously computed tables.
3. A sensitivity analysis can easily be performed. For example, if management decides to consider only two plants, then the optimal solution can be found in the intermediate computations. (For example, if only

[2] The other states are inferior and therefore are omitted.

A and B are considered, the best solution is read from Table 12.8 as: $d_2 = 1$ and $d_1 = 3$, for a total return of $1.8 million.)

4. The dynamic programming procedure also identifies the *second* best alternative. In this case, it is (Table 12.10): $d_3 = 0$; that is, allocate nothing to C, 1 to B, and 3 to A, with an expected profit of $1.8 million. Similarly, the third best solution, and so on, can be found. These solutions are frequently important when qualitative factors have to be considered.

DP advantages and characteristics

5. Adding a new plant to the problem merely adds an additional stage to the computations.
6. Adding more money to be allocated merely adds more states to the computations.
7. The dynamic programming process required 18 calculations for this problem. A solution by complete enumeration would have required only 15 calculations. Again, there is no saving of computational effort in such small problems. However, the savings would have been large had the problem been larger.

12.5 CONCLUDING REMARKS

Dynamic programming is an approach for finding an optimal solution to a problem by breaking it into smaller subproblems, each labeled a *stage*. In each stage, that is, for each subproblem, there exist several *states*, or positions, that the system under study can occupy.

The dynamic programming procedure considers one subproblem (stage) at a time, usually beginning from the *ending* stage. For each stage, a set of optimal solutions is derived for each state in that stage, with the aid of complete enumeration, or using an algorithm such as linear programming. This set is then used for the stage next in line. The process continues until all the subproblems are solved. The solution to the subproblems then leads to an optimal solution for the original problem.

Some limitations of DP

The curse of dimensionality

The application of dynamic programming is limited by two factors. First, the approach has to be tailored for each different type of problem. Every time a problem differs slightly, then a new formulation must be designed. Second, while DP can be used to solve complex problems where other tools fail, it suffers from the "curse of dimensionality." The primary effect of this "curse" is an exponential growth in the amount of computation with problem size; that is, if the problem doubles in size, the amount of computation quadruples. Despite the meager number of applications of DP, it has tremendous potential due to its ability to attack difficult problems that other optimization tools fail to solve.

12.6 PROBLEMS FOR PART A

1. Given the following network:

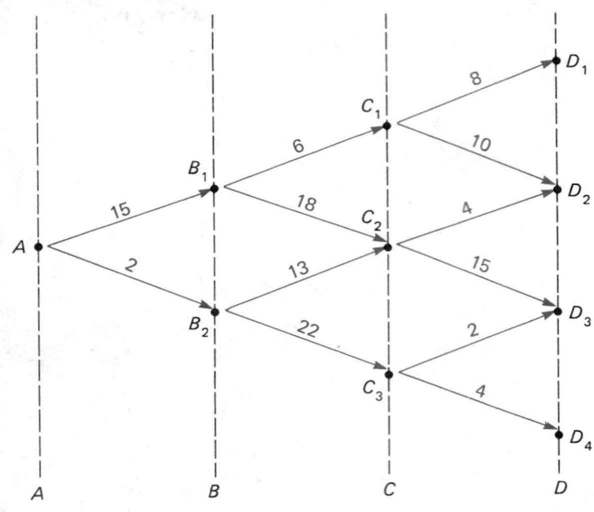

Determine the shortest path in the network going from point *A* to *any* point on the line *D*. Use dynamic programming.

2. XYZ Publishing Company divides the country into two zones: eastern, with headquarters in Philadelphia; and western, with headquarters in Los Angeles. Regional sales centers in the eastern zone are in Atlanta, Boston, and Chicago. Regional sales centers in the western zone are in Seattle, Denver, Houston, and Reno.

The president wants to fly from Philadelphia to Los Angeles and stop in one eastern and one western sales center. The estimated travel expenses from Philadelphia to the eastern centers (assuming that the eastern center is visited first), are: Boston, \$100; Atlanta, \$130; Chicago, \$110. The estimated travel expenses between the eastern centers and the western centers are:

	Denver	*Reno*	*Houston*	*Seattle*
Boston	160	150	180	180
Atlanta	80	130	110	200
Chicago	130	100	140	150

The travel expenses from each of the western centers to Los Angeles are: Seattle, \$230; Denver, \$190; Houston, \$140; Reno, \$180.

Find which cities the president should visit in order to minimize travel expenses (use dynamic programming).

3. Tijuana Auto Repair Shop, Inc., has three departments: metal, painting, and testing. Cars are repaired through all three departments. The metal department has three parallel workstations: M, N, and O. The painting department has two parallel workstations: P and Q. And the testing department has three parallel workstations: T, U, and V.

Whenever a car is towed in, its repair costs are estimated. This morning a car was brought in, and management would like to know through which stations the car should be processed to minimize the cost.

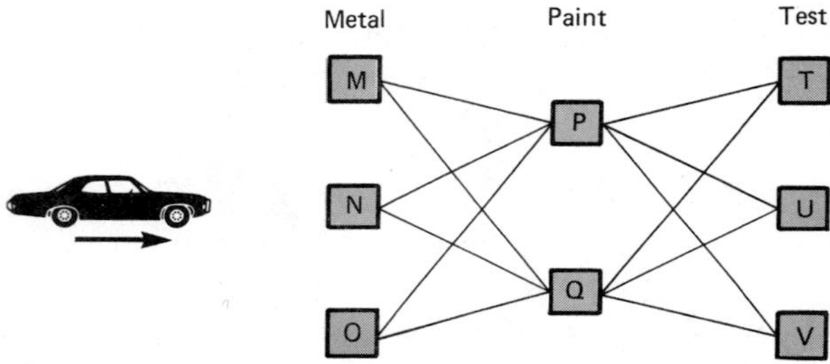

The costs at stations M, N, and O are 200, 220, and 230 million pesos, respectively. The cost at painting and testing depends on what happened in the previous stations. For example, if the metal work is not perfect, as is frequently the case in station M, the painting cost is slightly higher. The conditional cost relationships are:

Cost in the painting department (million pesos)

If car moved from	to	P	Q
	M	95	92
	N	80	85
	O	85	88

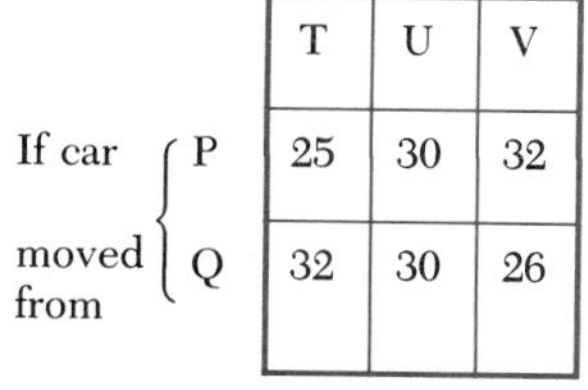

		T	U	V
If car moved from	P	25	30	32
	Q	32	30	26

Find the sequence of stations that will minimize the repair cost (use dynamic programming).

4. Phillipine Electric Corporation produces and sells CB radios. A new model has just been developed with an estimated life of four years. The company must decide on an initial price that, in order to be competitive, must be either 90, 100, or 110 thousand pesos. The company's policy is to change prices, if necessary, only once a year. When a change is made (up *or* down), it is a 10 peso change.

   The anticipated yearly profit from making and selling the CB radios, for each price/year combination, is given in the following table (in millions of pesos):

Price \ *Year*	*1*	*2*	*3*	*4*
90	20	18	30	24
100	24	18	35	28
110	25	15	32	31

   For example, if the price in the third year is 90 pesos, then the company will make 30 million pesos.

   Find the optimal prices the company should set each year. Use dynamic programming. *Hint:* Stages are years; states are price levels. Assume the price levels are either 90, 100, or 110 pesos all the time.

5. ABC Development Corporation plans to use one or more of three subcontractors to build six cooling units. The corporation would like to determine the best allocation of cooling units to subcontractors.

   The table below shows the bids submitted by each subcontractor. The data are in thousands of dollars.

Units (number)	*Subcontractor A*	*Subcontractor B*	*Subcontractor C*
1	5	4	5
2	10	8	9
3	14	11	12
4	17	18	18
5	20	25	24
6	27	30	30

   For example, subcontractor A would build two units for $10,000 and three units for $14,000. Differences in the bids result from locational considerations and other such variations.

   Use dynamic programming to determine the best allocation of six cooling units among the subcontractors.

6. A sales manager must decide how to allocate her four available salespersons among three districts in her territory. The sales results (in thousands of dollars per month) are shown below as a function of the number of salespeople assigned to a district.

   a. Use dynamic programming to find that assignment of salespersons to districts that will maximize sales.

District \ *Salespeople assigned*	*0*	*1*	*2*	*3*	*4*
A	5	10	13	15	17
B	6	10	14	17	15
C	4	9	11	15	18

   b. Without resolving the problem, find the second best assignment.

   c. Without resolving the problem, find the best solution if only three salespeople are available.

7. A fancy Jamaican restaurant operates a fleet of vans for deliveries. A new van costs $10,000. It is estimated that in the future the vans will

continue to cost $10,000. The operating cost and the resale value as related to the age of the van are given below:

Age of van	*Operating cost ($)*	*Resale value ($)*
1	2,000	7,000
2	2,500	5,000
3	3,000	3,500
4	3,700	2,200
5	4,500	1,000
6	5,500	600

All the data, including the cost of new vans, are given in present values and are assumed to remain constant in the future.

Replacement decisions are made once a year. The restaurant buys only new vans. Find the replacement policy (i.e., at what age a van should be replaced) that minimizes the total cost.

PART B: EXTENSIONS

12.7 PROBABILISTIC PROBLEMS

The previous two examples of DP dealt with deterministic situations. DP, however, can deal effectively with probabilistic problems as well.

DP can deal with risk

Example: The purchasing agent's problem

A purchasing agent must buy, for her company, a special beryllium alloy in a market that trades only once a week, and the weekly prices are independent. Each week there is a 20 percent chance that the alloy will cost \$10,000; 50 percent that it will cost \$11,000; and 30 percent that it will cost \$12,000. At the present time, the agent knows that in order to meet the company's production schedule, the alloy must be bought within the next month (four trading weeks). The agent worries that if she waits too long, price rises may force her to buy the alloy at a premium. On the other hand, if she buys early, future prices may be lower and she may miss an opportunity to economize. Thus, the timing of the purchase poses a delicate managerial problem.

Formulation The agent's decision of "when to buy" can be viewed as a sequence of decisions. In each of the four trading weeks, a decision must be made between two alternatives: either to buy or to wait. The analysis starts from the final week and proceeds *backwards* in time.

Stages. Each week is considered a stage; therefore, there will be four stages.

States. There are two states in each week, to buy or to wait.

Reward. The expected (average) price is used as the criterion. It is labeled r_i, where i designates the stage.

Solution

Stage 1. Rolling back, the first stage occurs at week 4. At that time, there is no choice; if the alloy has not already been bought, it *must* be bought then. The expected price of the alloy is computed as the expected value, designated by $E(r_1)$.

$$E(r_1) = .2 \times \$10,000 + .5 \times \$11,000 + .3 \times \$12,000 = \$11,100$$

This situation is shown in a decision tree presentation in Figure 12.5.

Stage 2 (third week). The agent can either *buy* at the price prevailing that week (either \$10,000, \$11,000, or \$12,000) or she can *wait* until the fourth week. The decision is based on the following criterion:

If the prevailing price at the third week is *more* than the expected price in the last week (already calculated as \$11,100), the agent should *wait* until the final week. If the prevailing price is *less* than the expected price in the final week, the agent should buy. If the prices are the same,

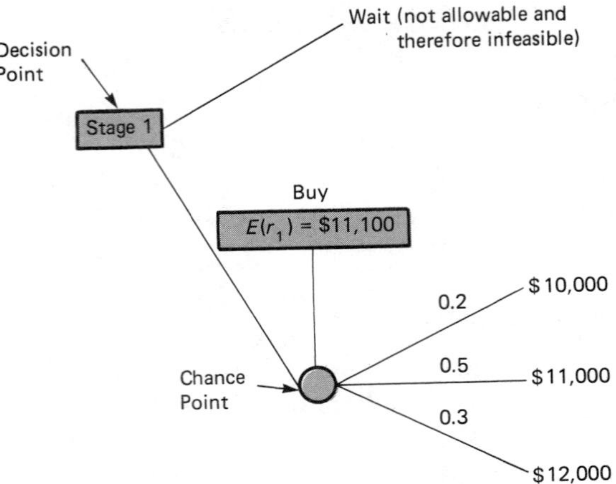
Wait (not allowable and
therefore infeasible)
Decision
Point
Stage 1
Buy
$E(r_1)$ = $11,100
0.2
$10,000
0.5
$11,000
0.3
$12,000
Chance
Point

FIGURE 12.5
Decision at stage 1

the agent is indifferent between the two alternatives. The agent may now extend the decision tree (Figure 12.6) for the analysis.

Since the price at any week can take only three possible values, it is possible to compute the expected reward in much the same way as was done for stage 1:

- There is a 30 percent chance of waiting, in which case the reward will be $11,100, realized in week 4.
- There is a 20 percent chance of buying at $10,000.
- There is a 50 percent chance of buying at $11,000.

The expected reward at stage 2 is therefore:

	Immediate reward	Best reward from previous stage

$$E(r_2) = .2(\$10{,}000) + .5(\$11{,}000) + .3(\$11{,}100) = \$10{,}830$$

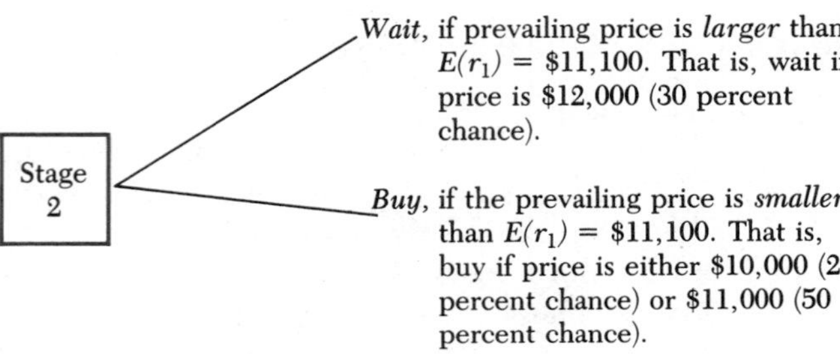
Stage
2
Wait, if prevailing price is *larger* than $E(r_1)$ = $11,100. That is, wait if price is $12,000 (30 percent chance).
Buy, if the prevailing price is *smaller* than $E(r_1)$ = $11,100. That is, buy if price is either $10,000 (20 percent chance) or $11,000 (50 percent chance).

FIGURE 12.6
Decision at stage 2

Stage 3 (second week). The agent will buy if the price is less than $E(r_2)$ and wait if it is more. The situation is shown in Figure 12.7. The expected reward is:

If *wait* (80 percent): the expected price will be \$10,830.
If *buy* (20 percent): the price will be \$10,000.

$$E(r_3) = .2(\$10{,}000) + .8(\$10{,}830) = \$10{,}664$$

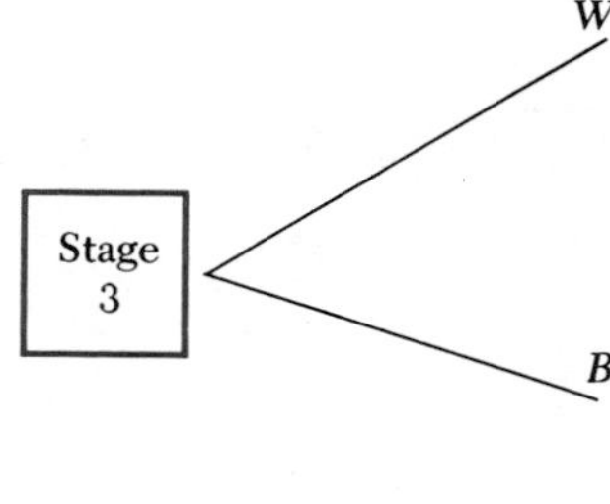

Wait, if the prevailing price is *more* than $E(r_1)$ = \$10,830. That is, wait if the price is \$11,000 (50 percent chance) or \$12,000 (30 percent chance). Total 80 percent chance of waiting.

Buy, if the prevailing price is *less* than $E(r_2)$ = \$10,830. That is, buy if the price is \$10,000 (20 percent chance).

FIGURE 12.7
Decision at stage 3

Stage 4 (initial week). The agent will buy if the price at the first week is smaller than $E(r_3)$, otherwise she will wait. Figure 12.8 shows this situation.
The expected reward is:

$$E(r_4) = .2(\$10{,}000) + (.5 + .3)(\$10{,}664) = \$10{,}531$$

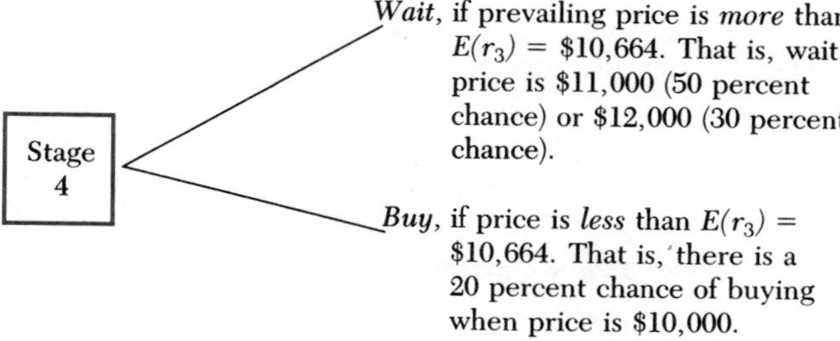
Stage 4
Wait, if prevailing price is more than E(r3) = $10,664. That is, wait if price is $11,000 (50 percent chance) or $12,000 (30 percent chance).
Buy, if price is less than E(r3) = $10,664. That is, there is a 20 percent chance of buying when price is $10,000.

FIGURE 12.8
Decision at stage 4

Summary

If the purchasing agent pursues the *optimal policy,* then the expected price she will pay is \$10,531. The decision rules for each week are summarized in Figure 12.9.

FIGURE 12.9
Decision rules for the purchasing agent

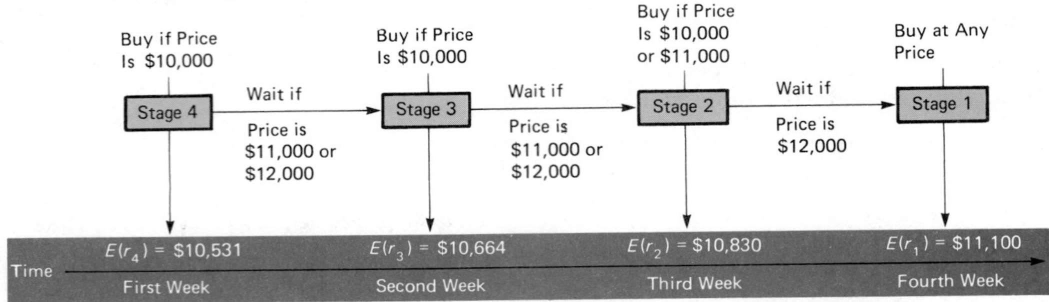

12.8 MATHEMATICAL PRESENTATION AND OPTIMIZATION TECHNIQUES

The recursive relation

In all previous examples, we avoided mathematical symbols whenever possible. However, we stated over and over again that the relationship between the reward at each stage and the optimal reward is the key to the DP process. This reward relationship is called the *recursive relation.* In dynamic programming it is necessary to write a recursive relation for each problem. Once such an equation has been written, it is much easier to execute the DP computations. The recursive relation expresses the notion that an optimal reward, at any given stage, for any given state, is given as the value of the best alternative, when each alternative includes the total of the immediate reward and the optimal reward computed in the previous stage.

General formulation

Let:

n = Index for current stage. This index tells how many stages exist from the current stage to the end of the process (problem)

$n-1$ = Previous stage

s_n = State of the system in the current stage for which the recursive relations hold

s_{n-1} = State in the previous stage

$f_n(s_n)$ = Total reward realized for each alternative, starting from state s_n in stage n to the end of the process

$f^*_n(s_n)$ = Optimal total reward; that is, the best $f_n(s_n)$ from state s_n in stage n

$f^*_{n-1}(s_{n-1})$ = Optimal total reward obtained in the previous stage

$r_n(s_n, d_n)$ = Immediate reward realized in stage n, when decision d_n is made for a specific value s_n of the state variable

d_n = Decision among alternatives made at stage n in the state under consideration

The recursive relation (minimization) for state s, at stage n, is then:

$$f_n^*(s_n) = \min_{d_n} [r_n(s_n, d_n) + f_{n-1}^*(s_{n-1})] \tag{12.1}$$

We will fit this formulation to a DP problem in Section 12.9.

Optimization techniques

The basic approach of dynamic programming is to reduce a complex problem into a series of simpler subproblems. However, once such a reduction has been performed, it is still necessary to solve the subproblems. The following methods can be used in solving these subproblems:

Enumeration In many cases, complete enumeration is very efficient, since the number of possible solutions in the subproblems is usually finite and small. In some cases, it is possible to approximate an infinite number of possible solutions by using a finite number (e.g., replace a continuous function by a discrete one) and then employ enumeration.

Classical calculus The classical calculus methods can be used for certain nonconstrained optimization problems, as well as for simple cases of constrained optimization.

Lagrange multipliers and the Kuhn-Tucker conditions Equality constraints can be handled with the aid of the Lagrangian function. Inequality constraints are treated with the help of the Kuhn-Tucker conditions. (Refer to [9] or [12].)

Mathematical programming In certain cases, the subproblems are actually linear, integer, or nonlinear programming problems, and can be solved as such.

Sequential search In some cases, iterative procedures may be used where the solution is improved step by step (e.g., see Nemhauser [11]).

Other techniques Several other **optimization techniques** can be used. See Nemhauser [11] and Gluss [8] for details.

12.9 THE KNAPSACK PROBLEM

What should go in the knapsack?

Consider the following problem. A knapsack or a container has a limited weight and/or volume capacity. It is to be loaded with different items, each with a given weight (or volume). Each item has a certain value. The problem is to find what items to include in the knapsack to maximize the total value.

An example of a **knapsack problem** is a spaceship where weight is limited. The problem is: What instruments to include so that the scientific utility of the mission is maximized.

Another example involves production scheduling. Suppose that it is necessary to determine how many units to produce, among several possible products, on one machine. The value of the products is known, and so is their use of machine time, which is limited. The problem is: What products to produce and in what quantities (integer) so that the value is maximized. The knapsack problem appears in various forms and can often be formulated as an integer programming problem. Integer programming problems are, however, often difficult to solve, especially if they are nonlinear. Therefore, dynamic programming is used.

Example

Four types of items are considered for loading on an airplane with an unlimited supply of each type. The weights and values of the types of items are given in Table 12.12. Find which items should be loaded on the plane, and in what quantities, if the maximum capacity of the plane is 11 tons and the objective is to maximize the value of the shipment.

TABLE 12.12
Knapsack items

Item	*Weight (tons)*	*Value*
A	2	18
B	4	25
C	5	30
D	3	20

Mathematical presentation

Let

n = The stage (item) under consideration
x_n = Number of items of type n to load
v_n = Value of one type n item
w_n = Weight of one type n item
K = Maximum available capacity
s_n = State (remaining weight available) at stage n

Integer programming formulation The problem can be presented as:

$$\text{maximize } z = \sum_{n=1}^{4} v_n x_n$$

subject to: (12.2)

$$\sum_{n=1}^{4} w_n x_n \leq K$$

and x_n is a nonnegative integer.

For our example:

$$\text{maximize } z = 18x_1 + 25x_2 + 30x_3 + 20x_4$$
subject to:
$$2x_1 + 4x_2 + 5x_3 + 3x_4 \leq 11$$

and x_1, x_2, x_3, x_4 are nonnegative integers.

Dynamic programming formulation This problem is an extension of the allocation problem discussed in Section 12.4.

Stages. Each type of item is considered a stage.

States. The remaining capacity (in integer tons) available for allocation; that is, the states are 0, 1, 2, . . . , 11.

The decision at each stage. How many units of each item to include in the optimal mix.

The recursive relation. The recursive relation for this problem is:

$$f^*_n(s_n) = \max_{x_n} [v_n x_n + f^*_{n-1}(s_n - w_n x_n)] \tag{12.3}$$

where:

s_n = The amount of the remaining weight available for allocation.

$v_n x_n$ = Immediate reward

$f^*_n(s_n)$ = Optimal total reward starting at stage n, for state s_n

$f^*_{n-1}(s_n - w_n x_n)$ = Optimal reward at the previous stage

Solution Since there are four items, there will be four stages.

Stage 1 (item D). Table 12.13 shows the states on the left side. On the top, the possible number of units of D that can be loaded are

TABLE 12.13
Stage 1: Item D

State s_1 (tons available for allocation to item D)	$f_1(s_1) = v_1x_1 = 20x_1$ (number of D units to load at 3 tons each)				
	$x_1 = 0$	$x_1 = 1$	$x_1 = 2$	$x_1 = 3$	$f^*_i(s_1)$
0	0				0
1	0				0
2	0				0
3	0	20			20
4	0	20			20
5	0	20			20
6	0	20	40		40
7	0	20	40		40
8	0	20	40		40
9	0	20	40	60	60
10	0	20	40	60	60
11	0	20	40	60	60

shown. Since the weight of D is 3 tons, then either 0, 1, 2, or 3 units can be loaded. The body of the table gives the reward computed by the formula given at the top of the table.

Mathematical statement of stage 1 The reward function is given by $v_1 x_1 = 20x_1$, where x_1 designates the number of units of D.

The optimal solution column is designated by $f_1^*(s_1)$ = maximum $[v_1 x_1]$, where $f_1^*(s_1)$ is the optimal reward starting from state s_1 and using an optimal policy from stage 1 to the end.

Stage 2 (item C). At this stage, an allocation is made to item C, with the remaining weight utilized according to the best policy recommended in stage 1. Table 12.14 shows the rewards for the various states. The total rewards are $f_2(s_1) = 30x_2 + f_1^*(s_2 - 5x_2)$; and the optimal reward is the maximum of $f_1(s_2)$. For example, in state 10, if 10 tons are available, then the following three alternatives are available:

a. Zero to C, then 10 goes to D. From Table 12.13 we know that the optimal allocation of 10 to D yields 60.

b. One to C, then there are 5 tons remaining. The best allocation of 5 (from stage 1) yields 20 plus the 30 achieved from the allocation of one to C, for a total yield of 50.

c. Two to C, this takes 10 tons; that is, nothing remains. Therefore, the reward is $2 \times 30 = 60$.

The computations are similar to the allocation problem of Section 12.4.

TABLE 12.14
Stage 2: Item C

State s_2 (tons available for C and D)	$f_2(s_2) = 30x_2 + f_1^*(s_2 - 5x_2)$ (number of C units at 5 tons each)			$f_2^*(s_2)$
	$x_2 = 0$	$x_2 = 1$	$x_2 = 2$	
0	0			0
1	0			0
2	0			0
3	20			20
4	20			20
5	20	30		30
6	40	30		40
7	40	30		40
8	40	50		50
9	60	50		60
10	60	50	60	60
11	60	70	60	70

Stage 3 (item B). The results are shown in Table 12.15. The total reward function is:

$$f_3(s_3) = 25x_3 + f_2^*(s_3 - 4x_3) \text{ and } f_3^*(s_3) = \max f_3(s_3)$$

Optimal Solution The starting state is $s_4 = 11$, and its solution is the solution to the entire problem. The optimal solution is read as: $x_4 =$

TABLE 12.15
Stage 3: Item B

State s_3 (tons available for B, C, and D)	$f_3(s_3) = 25x_3 + f^*_2 s_3 - 4x_3)$ (number of B units at 4 tons each)			$f^*_3(s_3)$
	$x_3 = 0$	$x_3 = 1$	$x_3 = 2$	
0	0			0
1	0			0
2	0			0
3	20			20
4	20	25		25
5	30	25		30
6	40	25		40
7	40	45		45
8	50	45	50	50
9	60	55	50	60
10	60	65	50	65
11	70	65	70	70

4; that is, four units of A (weighing 8 tons). The remaining 11 − 8 = 3 tons are allocated in the optimal manner according to stage 3 (Table 12.15). Thus, $x_3 = 0$, and no units of B are included. The check then continues to stage 2 (Table 12.14). According to this table, $x_2 = 0$. Moving finally to stage 1 (Table 12.13), the optimal solution for 3 tons is $x_4 = 1$.

Therefore, the best solution is:

$$x_4 = 4 \text{ units of A}$$
$$x_1 = 1 \text{ unit of D}$$

The total reward is:

$$18 \times 4 + 20 \times 1 = 92$$

The knapsack problem has several variations. For example, it may be required that at least one unit of each item be included. Another variation is that no more than one unit of each item is to be included. Cost minimization can be the objective. Additional constraints may also be added, such as volume limits. Some of these variations are given in the problem section.

Stage 4 (item A). The results for stage 4 are shown in Table 12.16. The optimal policy is given by $f^*_4(s_4) = \max\,[18x_4 + f^*_3(s_4 - 2x_4)]$.

TABLE 12.16
Stage 4: Item A

State s_4 (tons available for A, B, C, and D)	$f_4(s_4) = 18x_4 + f^*_3(s_4 - 2x_4)$, (number of A units at 2 tons each)						$f^*_4(s_4)$
	$x_4 = 0$	$x_4 = 1$	$x_4 = 2$	$x_4 = 3$	$x_4 = 4$	$x_4 = 5$	
11	70	78	81	84	92	90	92

12.10 COMPUTERIZATION

Due to the special structure of dynamic programming, it is difficult to design a standard dynamic program for computers. Either a special program must be built for each problem, or else a special option selected from an extremely large variety of options of some standardized structure.

12.11 PROBLEMS FOR PART B

8. You own 1,000 shares of a certain company that you *must* sell, for tax reasons, on or before the end of the fifth forthcoming trading day. The price of a share fluctuates between $20 and $22. At any given day, there is a chance of 25 percent of selling the shares at $20, 45 percent of selling them at $21, and 30 percent of selling them at $22.
   a. Suggest an optimal policy. Assume that all shares are sold in one trade (use dynamic programming).
   b. How much money will you receive for your shares if the commission is 25 cents per share?
9. Reconsider Problem 1. Suppose that the result of the choice made at each node is probabilistic. Namely, when one selects a route, there is only a 60 percent chance of pursuing that route. For example, if a decision made at node A was to go to B_1, the actual result would be 60 percent at B_1 and 40 percent at B_2. Use DP to find the path with the lowest expected value of the sum of the numbers along the arcs.
10. Suppose you own an option to buy 100 shares of the ABC Corporation at a certain price. Such options are traded on Mondays through Fridays on the American and Chicago exchanges. Today is Monday, and your option will expire on Friday; at that time, you will be able to sell it for $175. From your experience, you know that the price movement of this type of option during the last week of expiration will behave in the following manner:

Monday:	60 percent chance for $300, 40 percent chance for $200.
Tuesday:	40 percent chance for $350, 40 percent chance for $250, 20 percent chance for $150.
Wednesday:	20 percent chance for $400, 60 percent chance for $200, 20 percent chance for $150.
Thursday:	50 percent chance for $300, 50 percent chance for $200.
Friday:	100 percent chance for $175.

The reason for such sharp movements is that in the last days before the expiration date, some traders who sold the option short must buy it back. Also, the stock itself moves up and down quickly.

The commission for selling an option is $25, regardless of its price. Use dynamic programming to find the best trading policy for options of this type.

11. A truck can carry a total of 10 tons. Three types of boxes are available for shipment. The boxes weigh 2, 1, and 3 tons, respectively, and their value is $50, $30, and $70, respectively. The truck delivers 10 times a day. It is required that at least one unit of each type of box be delivered in each shipment.
    a. Use dynamic programming to determine the loading policy that will maximize the value of the shipments.
    b. Find the daily dollar value of the shipment.
    c. Formulate as an integer programming problem.
12. Peru Trucking Company delivers four types of containers between two cities. The company wants to load *at least* 14 tons on each truck. The weight and the handling cost that is paid to porters for each type of container is given as:

Container	Weight (tons)	Handling cost (sols)
A	4	20
B	2	15
C	5	23
D	3	18

Find how many containers of each type should be loaded on each truck in order to minimize the total handling cost.

a. Formulate as an integer program.
b. Formulate and solve by dynamic programming.

13. Formulate the recursive relations for *(a)* the allocation example of Section 12.4, *(b)* the stagecoach problem of Section 12.2, and *(c)* the purchasing agent problem of Section 12.7.

12.12 CASE

THE PERSONNEL DIRECTOR

Bud Friendly, personnel director for Glades Corporation, was on the phone explaining his problem to the manager of marketing research:

"Mrs. Rich, with only three days to hire that customer rep, we won't be able to interview many applicants. It takes a full day to screen each one, including interviews, reference checks, and appraisals, so the most we can consider is three applicants. Obviously, if the first or second candidate is excellent, we will hire that candidate, but what if they're not?"

"Look, Bud. In the past we have found that of every 10 candidates you screen, 3 are 'excellent', 5 are 'good', and 2 are 'poor'. Surely in three days you can come up with a superior candidate."

"But Mrs. Rich, if I delay an early decision on a 'good' candidate, hoping to find an 'excellent' one, he or she might take another job instead and then we might have to settle on a 'poor' candidate on the last day."

"Well, I don't know what to advise you. I can say this though. A 'good' candidate is worth twice as much as a 'poor' one and an 'excellent' candidate is worth twice that again. Good luck, Bud."

Questions for discussion:

1. Use dynamic programming to advise Bud on a hiring policy.
2. What will be the candidate's expected worth if an optimal policy is followed?

12.13 GLOSSARY

Immediate reward The reward resulting from a move between two adjacent stages. It is the value added to the objective function when moving from stage to stage.

Knapsack problem A classical allocation problem that determines the optimal mix of items to be put in a limited space (knapsack, bag, container) such that the total value of the items is maximized.

Optimization techniques Mathematical techniques that can be used to optimally solve subproblems.

Policy A complete, predetermined choice plan under every possible circumstance.

Principle of optimality Bellman's principle, which is the basis for solving dynamic programming problems.

Recursive relation The function used in dynamic programming to compute the value of the objective function.

Reward The payoff or the value of the objective function.

Rollback ·A solution approach in which the subproblems that are closest to the end point are solved first.

Segmentation Breaking up a complex problem into a sequence of smaller subproblems.

Sequential decision making A decision-making process involving two or more interrelated decisions that are made one after the other.

Stage A decision point in a sequence of decisions. A subproblem.

State A condition or a possible alternative for each subdecision or stage. The possible condition for the system (or process) at each stage.

12.14 REFERENCES AND BIBLIOGRAPHY

1. Beckmann, Martin, J. *Dynamic Programming of Economic Decisions*. New York: Springer-Verlag, 1968.
2. Bellman, R. *Dynamic Programming*. Princeton, N.J.: Princeton University Press, 1957.
3. Bellman, R., and S. E. Dreyfus. *Applied Dynamic Programming*. Princeton, N.J.: Princeton University Press, 1962.
4. Bertsekas, D. P. *Dynamic Programming and Stochastic Control*. New York: Academic Press, 1976.
5. Cooper, L. *Introduction to Dynamic Programming*. Elmsford, N.Y.: Pergamon Press, 1981.
6. Denardo, E. V. *Dynamic Programming Models and Applications*. Englewood Cliffs, N.J.: Prentice-Hall, 1982.
7. Dreyfus, S., and A. M. Law. *The Art and Theory of Dynamic Programming*. New York: Academic Press, 1977.
8. Gluss, Brian. *An Elementary Introduction to Dynamic Programming: A State Equation Approach*. Boston: Allyn & Bacon, 1972.
9. Hastings, N. A. J. *Dynamic Programming with Managerial Applications*. New York: Crane, Russak & Co., 1973.
10. Jensen, P. *Microsolve—Operations Research*. San Francisco: Holden-Day, 1983.
11. Nemhauser, G. L. *Introduction to Dynamic Programming*. New York: John Wiley & Sons, 1966.
12. Norman, J. M. *Elementary Dynamic Programming*. New York: Crane, Russak & Co., 1975.
13. Ross, S. *Introduction to Stochastic Dynamic Programming*. New York: Academic Press, 1983.
14. White, D. J. *Dynamic Programming*. San Francisco: Holden-Day, 1969.

13

Markov analysis

PART A: BASICS

13.1 Markov systems.
13.2 Input data: Transition probabilities and initial conditions.
13.3 State probabilities.
13.4 Steady state (equilibrium).
13.5 Managerial applications.
13.6 Concluding remarks.
13.7 Problems for Part A.

PART B: EXTENSIONS

13.8 Absorbing states.
13.9 Managerial application.
13.10 Use of computers.
13.11 Problems for Part B.
13.12 Case—Springfield General Hospital.
13.13 Glossary.
13.14 References and bibliography.

A Markov analysis is a procedure that can be used to describe the behavior of a system in a dynamic situation. Specifically, it describes and predicts the movement of a system, among different system states, as time passes. This movement is done in a probabilistic (stochastic) environment.

Movements of people, inventories, monetary accounts, and even taxicabs are a few examples of situations that can be described by Markov processes. To be able to predict the future movements and condition of such a system would clearly be of value to management. This is basically the goal of a Markov analysis.

Markov analysis makes predictions such as:

1. The probability of finding a system in any particular state at any given time.
2. The long-run probabilities of being in each state.

The use of such predictions as a basis for managerial decision making is illustrated throughout the chapter.

LEARNING OBJECTIVES

The student should be able to:

a. Describe the Markov process and its assumptions.
b. Discuss the transition movements and transition probabilities.
c. Discuss the characteristics predicted by the Markov chains.
d. Compute state probabilities.
e. Compute steady state probabilities.
f. Recognize managerial applications in marketing, finance, and production.

Extensions

g. Formulate problems involving absorbing states.
h. Solve problems involving absorbing states.
i. Use a canned software program.

PART A: BASICS

John Byer, director of product planning for P&C Chemical Corporation, felt somewhat satisfied as he scanned the latest marketing research results of last year's big gamble. The argument, as he recalled the meeting of the executive committee, centered around the question of competing with one's own product. P&C's original entry, known inside the company by the code Brand A in the already well-established household detergents market, had been well accepted by the market until two years ago, when a competitor moved in with a flashy promotional campaign and began luring P&C's customers away. John's suggestion to the executive committee was to bring out an improved detergent (Brand B) with a countering advertising campaign stressing the quality of the new brand based on P&C's experience in the area with the successful Brand A.

But the executive vice president, Bill Harmon, was deeply worried that Brand B might compete more with P&C's own Brand A than with the competitor's brand. Other members of the committee pointed out that these buyers would probably be customers P&C would have lost to the competition anyway, but this did not seem to appease Bill. Finally, John pointed out how common it was in the detergent market for companies to offer multiple brands, in stark contrast to their chemicals market. He argued that detergents, being in the consumer market, were totally unlike industrial chemicals.

The executive committee finally decided to go along with John's idea, but they were not completely convinced. Thus, the first year's report took on special importance for John. At the time of the introduction of Brand B a year ago, P&C held 40 percent of the market and the competitor had 60 percent. The 12-month report summary now indicated that Brand A's share had dropped to 27.5 percent, but that the competitor's share had almost been halved, now standing at 35 percent, the losses in each case going to the new Brand B, currently holding 37.5 percent of the market.

The detailed report showed month-to-month "brand loyalty" (brand switching) figures from the date of introduction of Brand B until this last month. Initially, the rate of shifting between brands changed every month, but it has now settled down to the general situation illustrated in Figure 13.1. Customers were still being drawn from Brand A to the competitor (Brand C) to the extent of 60 percent of them each month (the remainder divided evenly at 20 percent each between switching to B and staying with A). However, half of the competitor's market (Brand C) would return to A in any particular month, with another 20 percent switching from C to B, resulting in the competition maintaining only 30 percent of its customers. Of particular interest was the response to Brand B, with half of B's purchasers remaining loyal to B and only 40 percent switching to C.

John felt that these figures substantiated his words from a year earlier

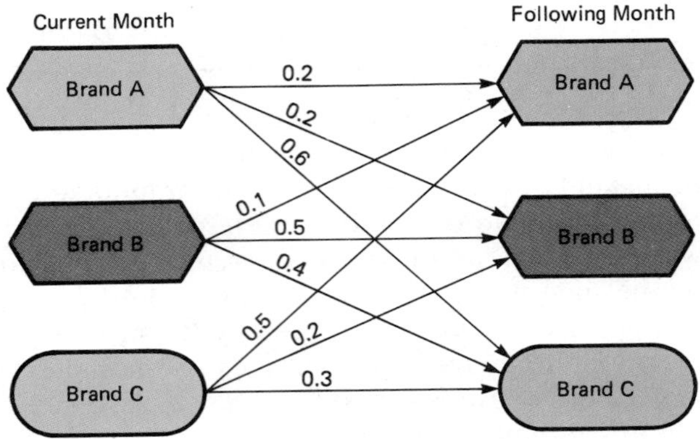

FIGURE 13.1 Month-to-month switching

and saved P&C from failing in this new market venture. Although John realized that the competition might upset this delicate balance at any moment with a new product introduction or a new marketing campaign, he wondered how the market shares would shift in the coming months, given the brand switching results above. In particular, he wondered what the ultimate market shares would be if conditions ever settled down.

13.1 MARKOV SYSTEMS

The situation presented in the preceding incident is concerned with the prediction of market shares in a dynamic market. Such predictions are based on what is termed a *Markov analysis* and can be used as a basis for determining market strategies and product planning.[1] Notice that John Byer is not asking about how to determine the *best* marketing strategy, but rather he wishes to determine or predict the *behavior* of the "system" (the household detergent purchasers in this case). Thus, for the first time in this book, we deal with a **descriptive** rather than with a **normative** analysis. Other features of the incident are:

Markov analysis is descriptive—not normative

1. The situation occurs in a chance environment consisting of two or more possible outcomes (three here) that occur at the end of a well-defined, usually fixed period. Such a process is referred to as a **stochastic** (or probabilistic) process. Thus, we are now dealing with analysis and prediction under risk.
2. The situation involves a multiperiod (monthly here) case. The customer's brand-switching propensities are followed for many months. The

[1] In honor of the Russian mathematician A. Markov, who developed the technique in 1907.

probabilities of switching (shown in Figure 13.1) are termed the **transition probabilities** of the stochastic process.

3. The situation is dynamic in nature since the customers make a sequence of decisions.[2]
4. The process is observed after each transition and is governed by a matrix of transition probabilities.

Transition probabilities

Markov processes

As stated before, the customer's brand switching is a *stochastic process.* If a customer's brand choice in any given month depends *only* on his or her choice the month before (i.e., not on the choice two, three, or more months previously), the stochastic process is called a **Markov process.** In addition, if the transition probabilities of a customer's switching from one brand *(state)* to another remain constant over time, then the Markov process is called a homogeneous **Markov chain.**[3]

Stochastic process, Markov process, Markov chain

The characteristics of a Markov analysis

A Markov analysis is conducted on a system that can usually be interpreted in two different ways: either as *the fraction of a group* (e.g., percentage of Brand A sold) or *the probability of an individual* (e.g., the chance of a customer purchasing Brand A). To familiarize the reader with both of these (equivalent) interpretations, we will use both quite frequently in this chapter.

Two interpretations

As a *descriptive tool,* the major objective of Markov chain analysis is the prediction of the future behavior of managerial systems.[4] A prediction can be achieved, in some cases, by other tools such as decision trees (coupled with complete enumeration) or simulation. The advantage of Markov chain analysis is that the computational work is relatively uncomplicated and can be carried out very rapidly. Small problems can be solved manually; for larger problems, a standard computer package can be used (see Section 13.10).

Advantage of simple manipulations

Necessary assumptions

In the Markov chains discussed in Part A of this chapter, the following assumptions are made:

1. The system has a finite number of discrete states, none of which is "absorbing" (a state that, once entered, cannot be left).

---

[2] Markov analysis is related to dynamic programming. Markov analysis can also be used to solve certain types of dynamic programming problems (e.g., see Howard [5]).

[3] This chapter deals only with homogeneous Markov chains.

[4] A "system" in this chapter can be a person, an organization, the demand for a product, a machine, or other such entity.

2. The system's condition (state) in any given period depends only on its condition in the preceding period and on the transition probabilities.
3. The transition probabilities are constant over time.
4. Changes in the system may occur once and only once each period (once a month in the example).
5. The transition periods occur with regularity.

The assumptions as reflected in the detergent incident

Finite number of states, none of which is absorbing In this example, the *condition* of the system was limited to three **states** (brands). If there was a brand from which a customer *never* switched, then this would be termed an **absorbing state.** It is assumed here that none of the states is absorbing.

Present brand choice is dependent on the previous month's choice It was assumed that the brand choice in any given month was influenced *only* by the choice in the previous month. This may or may not be a realistic assumption, depending on the circumstances.

Constant transition probabilities It may well be that the transition probabilities will change over time. If so, a more complicated analysis is required (consult reference [6]).

One change (transition) per period This requirement is usually satisfied by choosing a natural time period for the system. For example, consumers commonly shop once a month for detergent.

Regular transition periods This assumption is satisfied since the brand purchases are monitored on a monthly basis. If purchases change faster, the time period can be shortened (e.g., a week rather than a month). Note that the periods need not be of the same time lengths; for example, classes are frequently offered on a Tuesday–Thursday basis with a cycle of one day off and then four days off.

Information flow in the Markov analysis

The Markov model is based on two sets of input data (both discussed in Section 13.2), the transition matrix and the existing (initial) conditions, as shown in Figure 13.2. From these inputs, the model makes two predictions, usually expressed as vectors:

FIGURE 13.2
Information flow

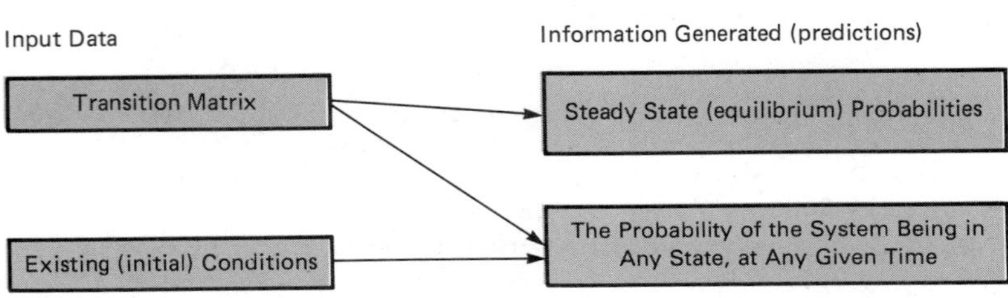

a. The probabilities of the system being in any state, at any given future time (Section 13.3).

b. The long-run (steady state) probabilities (Section 13.4). Note that the transition matrix is necessary for *both* predictions but the initial conditions are only needed for the former.

13.2 INPUT DATA: TRANSITION PROBABILITIES AND INITIAL CONDITIONS

The transition probabilities

The Markov process describes the movement of a system from a certain condition (or state) in the current stage (time period) to one of n possible states in the next stage.[5] The system moves in an uncertain environment. All that is known is the probability associated with any possible move (transition). This probability, termed the *transition probability*, p_{ij}, is the likelihood that the system, currently in state i, will move to state j in the next period. The transition probability concept is the key to Markov analysis.

Transition probabilities—the key

Transition diagram

Let us return to the detergent example. Figure 13.3 illustrates the three possible brand choices of the customers. The arrows show the probabil-

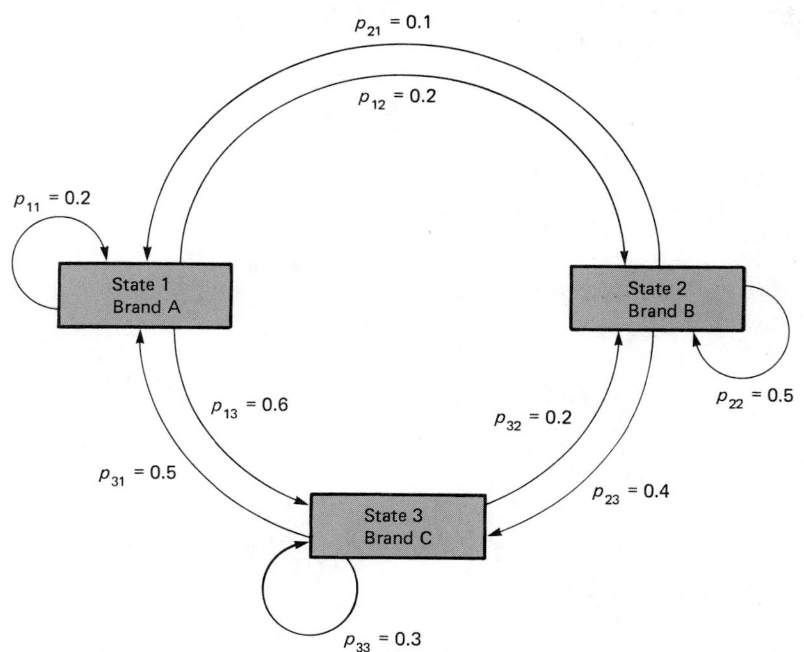

FIGURE 13.3
Transition diagram of the Markov process

[5] As in dynamic programming, here too, stages do not have to be time periods, though they usually are.

TABLE 13.1
The transition matrix P

Current month's brand choice \ Next month's brand choice	P&C's brand A	P&C's brand B	Competitor's brand C
P&C's brand A	.2	.2	.6
P&C's brand B	.1	.5	.4
Competitor's brand C	.5	.2	.3

ities of a customer (or the fraction of detergent purchasers) moving from state to state (brand to brand), as computed by the available historical data.

The transition matrix

Another way of expressing the system's movement is in tabular or matrix form, as shown in Table 13.1. Such a table is called a *transition matrix* (denoted by P).[6]
Note that the sum of the probabilities in every row is 1.0. That is, the customers must choose one of the three brands the next month, since these are the only brands available. (That is, there are a finite number of states.) Formally, for any row *i:*

$$p_{i1} + p_{i2} + \cdots + p_{in} = 1 \qquad (13.1)^7$$

[6] The general structure of a transition matrix is:

$$\begin{array}{ll} & \text{To} \\ & \text{State at the next period} \\ \text{From} & \\ \downarrow & \end{array}$$

$$\text{State in the current period} \quad \begin{array}{c} \\ s_1 \\ \cdot \\ \cdot \\ \cdot \\ s_i \\ \cdot \\ \cdot \\ \cdot \\ s_n \end{array} \begin{array}{c} \begin{array}{ccccccc} s_1 & s_2 & \cdots & s_j & \cdots & s_n \end{array} \\ \begin{bmatrix} p_{11} & p_{12} & \cdots & p_{1j} & \cdots & p_{1n} \\ \cdot & \cdot & & \cdot & & \cdot \\ \cdot & \cdot & & \cdot & & \cdot \\ \cdot & \cdot & & \cdot & & \cdot \\ p_{i1} & p_{i2} & \cdots & p_{ij} & \cdots & p_{in} \\ \cdot & \cdot & & \cdot & & \cdot \\ \cdot & \cdot & & \cdot & & \cdot \\ \cdot & \cdot & & \cdot & & \cdot \\ p_{n1} & p_{n2} & \cdots & p_{nj} & \cdots & p_{nn} \end{bmatrix} \end{array} = P$$

[7] In abbreviated form:

$$\sum_{j=1}^{n} p_{ij} = 1$$

where p_{ij} is the probability of being in state j in the next period, given it is now in state i (i.e., the *conditional* probability).

The set of transition probabilities across any row (current state) is called a *probability vector* and represents all possibilities of moving from one state in the current period to one of the n states in the next period. For example, the vector [.2 .2 .6] means that there is a chance of .2 of moving *from* A *to* A, .2 from A to B, and .6 from A to C.

The transition matrix as a set of probability vectors

The transition probabilities can be obtained in a number of ways. One is through market research—asking people about their preferences and seeing how they change over time. Another is to simply monitor their actions over time. Alternatively, the flow of products can be monitored directly.

The initial conditions

The initial conditions describe the situation the system is currently in. For example, the market share is divided 27.5 percent to A, 37.5 percent to B, and 35 percent to C. These conditions are usually described by a row vector: [.275 .375 .350]. Initial conditions such as [0 1 0] mean that the market is totally held by brand B; or, a *given* customer has currently purchased brand B.

13.3 STATE PROBABILITIES

A Markov analysis can make several predictions (see [4]). Two are discussed here: The probability q of the system being in state i in period k, called the *state probability;* and the long run (steady state) probability of finding the system in a particular state i. The state probability is denoted as $q_i(k)$ where k denotes the period; $k = 0$ is *now* and i, the index, specifies the particular state.

State probability

Since the system must occupy one and only one of the possible states at any given period, including period 0, then the sum of all q_i values must equal 1. Formally:

$$q_1(k) + q_2(k) + \cdots + q_n(k) = 1 \qquad \text{for every } k \qquad (13.2)$$ [8]

where:

n = Number of states
k = Number of transitions (periods ahead) = 0, 1, 2, . . .

[8] Equation 13.2 can be expressed as:

$$\sum_{i=1}^{n} q_i(k) = 1$$

Example Let us consider the detergent example to illustrate the determination of these $q_i(k)$ probabilities. The states of the system—Brands A, B, and C—are designated as 1, 2, and 3, respectively. The probability $q_1(0)$ represents the probability of a customer choosing Brand A this month (time zero); $q_1(1)$ represents the probability of choosing Brand A after "one transition"; that is, after one month, and so on.

State probabilities. The probability distribution of the customer choosing any given brand (1, 2, 3) in any given month (k), can be written as a row vector:[9]

$$Q(k) = [q_1(k), q_2(k), q_3(k)] \tag{13.3}$$

In general, for n states we can write:

$$Q(k) = [q_1(k), q_2(k), \ldots, q_n(k)] \tag{13.4}$$

Initial conditions are expressed as $Q(0)$.

Initial state probabilities in the detergent example. Let us denote the month in the example as the initial state, labeled $k = 0$. The initial state probabilities were given in the case as:

$q_1(0) = .275$ current share of the market for Brand A
$q_2(0) = .375$ current share of the market for Brand B
$q_3(0) = .350$ current share of the market for Brand C

These values can be summarized as:

$$Q(0) = [q_1(0), q_2(0), q_3(0)] = [.275, .375, .350]$$

The transition matrix. To compute the state probabilities we will use the transition matrix P of Table 13.1 (reproduced as Table 13.2). The states are labeled Brand A = 1, B = 2, and C = 3.

TABLE 13.2
Transition matrix for the detergent example (Table 13.1 reproduced)

From \ To	1	2	3
1	.2	.2	.6
2	.1	.5	.4
3	.5	.2	.3

$= P$

Three ways to choose Brand A

Computing the state probabilities the next month (k = 1). The value of $q_1(1)$ is first computed. This is the probability that the customer will choose Brand 1 (A) after one month. There are three ways for this to occur:

[9] For a review of matrix algebra, see Appendix A.

1. A customer who last purchased Brand A could continue to purchase Brand A (probability of .2).
2. A customer could switch to Brand A from Brand B (probability of .1).
3. A customer could switch to Brand A from Brand C (chance of .5).

Conditional probabilities

Note: all the above probabilities are *conditional* probabilities. That is, each depends on the customer's last purchase. Therefore, the chance of choosing Brand A in the next month, $q_1(1)$, is the sum of the following probabilities:

1. The probability of continuing to choose Brand A *given that* the customer last purchased Brand A. This probability is computed as $q_1(0)p_{11} = .275\ (.2)$.
2. The probability of choosing Brand A given that the customer last purchased Brand B. It is computed as: $q_2(0)p_{21} = .375\ (.1)$.
3. The probability of choosing A given that the customer last purchased C. It is given by $q_3(0)p_{31} = .350\ (.5)$.

Formally:

$$q_1(1) = .275(.2) + .375(.1) + .350(.5) = .2675$$

This is the sum of the chance of being in each state times the chance of switching from there to Brand A. In vector notation this can be written as:

$$q_1(1) = [Q(0)] \begin{bmatrix} .2 \\ .1 \\ .5 \end{bmatrix} = [.275\ .375\ .350] \begin{bmatrix} .2 \\ .1 \\ .5 \end{bmatrix} = .2675$$

That is: Multiply the $Q(0)$ row vector times the first column vector (Brand A) in the transition matrix P.

Similarly, the values of $q_2(1)$ and $q_3(1)$ are:

$$q_2(1) = [Q(0)] \begin{bmatrix} .2 \\ .5 \\ .2 \end{bmatrix} = .275(.2) + .375(.5) + .350(.2) = .3125$$

$$q_3(1) = [Q(0)] \begin{bmatrix} .6 \\ .4 \\ .3 \end{bmatrix} = .4200$$

Generalization. It is the probability $q_1(1)$ together with $q_2(1)$ and $q_3(1)$ that are the components of $Q(1)$. In matrix notation, $Q(1)$ is computed as the product of $Q(0)$ and P:

$$Q(1) = [q_1(1)\ q_2(1)\ q_3(1)] = Q(0)P \tag{13.5}$$

or:

$$[q_1(1) \quad q_2(1) \quad q_3(1)] = [q_1(0) \quad q_2(0) \quad q_3(0)] \times P$$

where P is the transition probability matrix of the system. Thus:

$$Q(1) = Q(0)P \tag{13.6}$$

and by similar reasoning it can be shown that:

$$Q(2) = Q(1)P \tag{13.7}$$

Introducing the value of $Q(1)$ from Equation 13.6 into Equation 13.7 results in:

$$Q(2) = Q(1)P = Q(0)PP = Q(0)P^2 \tag{13.8}$$

Similar computations can be performed for $Q(3)$, $Q(4)$, . . . In general:

$$Q(k) = Q(k-1)P = Q(k-2)P^2 = \cdots = Q(k-k)P^k = Q(0)P^k \tag{13.9}$$

John Byer's first question

Using Equation 13.9, John Byer could address his first question; namely, what the market shares will be the first, second, and third month from now, and so on. For example, for the first two months:

$q_3(1)$ = The probability of choosing Brand C (state 3) one month from now. This was already computed as .42 (or 42 percent).
$q_3(2)$ = The probability of choosing Brand C two months from now.

In order to find $q_3(2)$, Equation 13.9 is used with $k = 2$: $Q(2) = Q(0)P^2$. Thus, P^2 must first be calculated:

$$P^2 = P \times P = \begin{bmatrix} .2 & .2 & .6 \\ .1 & .5 & .4 \\ .5 & .2 & .3 \end{bmatrix}^2 = \begin{bmatrix} .2 & .2 & .6 \\ .1 & .5 & .4 \\ .5 & .2 & .3 \end{bmatrix} \times \begin{bmatrix} .2 & .2 & .6 \\ .1 & .5 & .4 \\ .5 & .2 & .3 \end{bmatrix}$$

$$= \begin{bmatrix} .36 & .26 & .38 \\ .27 & .35 & .38 \\ .27 & .26 & .47 \end{bmatrix}$$

Since $q_3(2)$ is the third entry in the row vector $Q(2) = [q_1(2), q_2(2), q_3(2)]$, it can be found by multiplying the third column of P^2 by $Q(0)$; that is:

$$q_3(2) = Q(0) \times [\text{the Brand C (third) column vector of } P^2]$$

$$= [.275 \quad .375 \quad .350] \begin{bmatrix} .38 \\ .38 \\ .47 \end{bmatrix}$$

$$= .275(.38) + .375(.38) + .35(.47) = .4115 \quad \text{or 41.15 percent.}$$

In a similar manner, it is possible to find $q_1(k)$, $q_2(k)$, and $q_3(k)$ for any desired k.

Tree presentation The relationship between the transition and state probabilities can be seen in a probability tree presentation (Figure 13.4). The tree presentation may be clearer for small problems, but its computations become very tedious for large problems.

FIGURE 13.4
Tree presentation of transition and state probabilities

Initial Month (k = 0)
State Probabilities
Brand Choice
Transition Probabilities
Next Month (k = 1)
Brand Choice
State Probabilities
Customers
q_1 (0) = .275
q_2 (0) = .375
q_3 (0) = .350
A
B
C
p_{11} = 0.2
p_{12} = 0.2
p_{13} = 0.6
p_{21} = 0.1
p_{22} = 0.5
p_{23} = 0.4
p_{31} = 0.5
p_{32} = 0.2
p_{33} = 0.3
(1) .0550 .0375 .1750 A
(2) .0550 .1875 .0700 B
(3) .165 .150 .105 C
q_1 (1) = 0.550 + 0.375 + .1750 = .2675
q_2 (1) = .0550 + .1875 + .0700 = .3125
q_3 (1) = .165 + .150 + .105 = .4200
q_1 (1) + q_2 (1) + q_3 (1) = 1

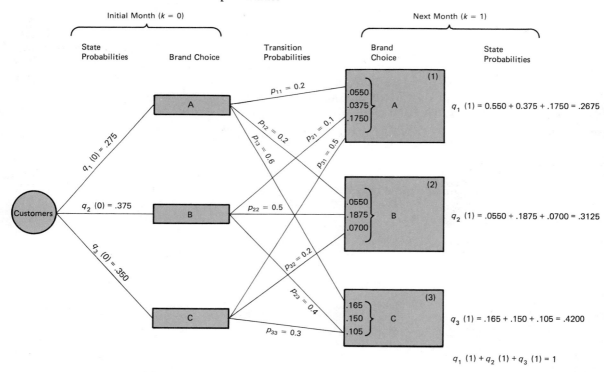

Computation without matrix algebra From k = 1, we can move in a similar fashion to the month after next, k = 2, as shown in Figure 13.5.

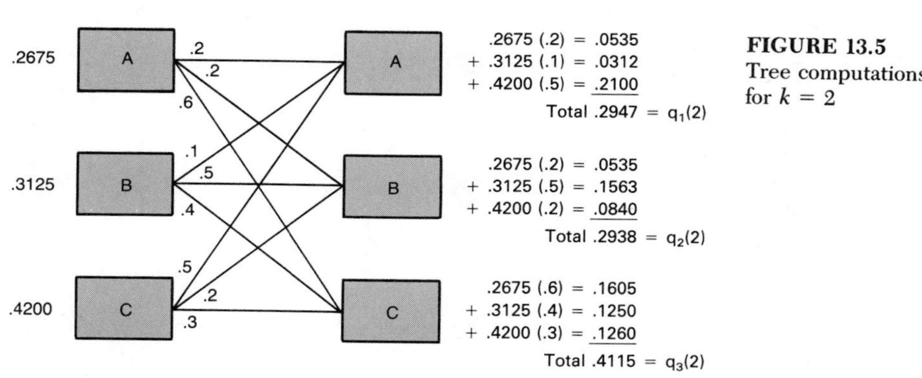

FIGURE 13.5
Tree computations for k = 2

That is, the market share distribution is predicted to be:

A: 29.47 percent
B: 29.38 percent
C: 41.15 percent

State probabilities given the system is in a specific state

In the previous discussion, the state probabilities (i.e., market shares) were interpreted in terms of the fraction of the group of detergent purchasers. However, in some instances, management may be interested in finding out the state probabilities in terms of the chances of a particular purchaser buying a particular brand, *given* that he or she previously purchased Brand X. These are called *conditional state probabilities*.

Conditional state probabilities

Example A customer last purchased Brand B (state 2). Find the probability that she will purchase Brand C (state 3) in two months ($k = 2$).

Solution Let us use a tree diagram (Figure 13.6) to follow the customer's possible purchases. The tree first shows the chances of switching from

FIGURE 13.6
Tree diagram for brand B purchaser

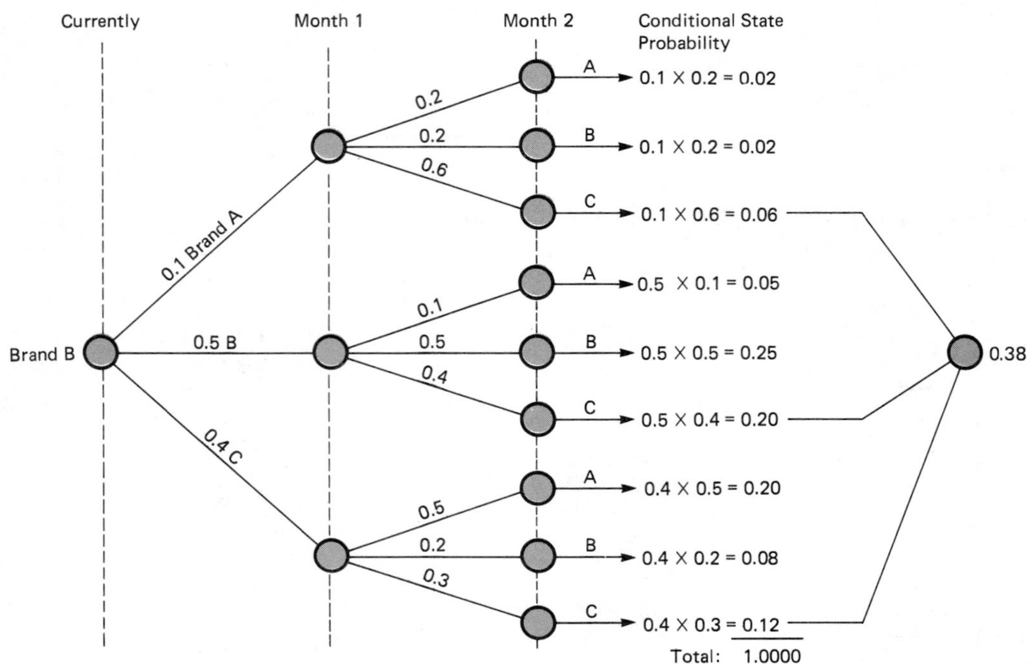

Brand B to either A, B, or C after one month. Then it shows the probabilities of switching among these brands in month 2. For example, the probability that the customer will purchase Brand C in month 2 is the sum of the following three probabilities:

	.06	(switch from A to C at month 2)
	.20	(switch from B to C at month 2)
	+ .12	(stay with C at month 2)
Total	.38	

Similarly, the chance for the Brand B customer to purchase Brand A after two months is:

$$.02 + .05 + .20 = .27$$

and the chance of purchasing Brand B again is:

$$.02 + .25 + .08 = .35$$

Note also that the total probabilities of the purchases sum to 1.0 (.38 + .27 + .35 = 1).

Conditional state probabilities

Generalization *Conditional state probabilities* can be expressed as $q_{ij}(k)$;[10] that is, the probability of being in state i, *given* initial condition j, after k transitions. Thus, $q_{32}(2)$ means: the probability of buying Brand C given that Brand B was initially purchased, after two transitions.

Mathematical presentation. The computation of the decision tree can be done with matrix algebra as follows:

1. Multiply the transition matrix by itself k times. For example, in the detergent case, for $k = 2$:

$$P^2 = \begin{bmatrix} .2 & .2 & .6 \\ .1 & .5 & .4 \\ .5 & .3 & .3 \end{bmatrix}^2 = \begin{bmatrix} .36 & .26 & .38 \\ .27 & .35 & .38 \\ .27 & .26 & .47 \end{bmatrix}$$

2. Each initial condition (j) is equivalent to a row, each final state (i) to a column. Note that this is the *reverse* of the usual interpretation of i and j. For example:

$$q_{32}(2) = .38$$
$$q_{13}(2) = .27$$

The computation of the state probabilities provides management with valuable descriptive information about the system's behavior. Additional valuable information is provided by analyzing the system in a "stabilized" (steady state) condition, which is discussed next.

---

[10] Note that:

$$\sum_i q_{ij}(k) = 1, \quad \text{for } j = 1,2, \ldots$$

13.4 STEADY STATE (EQUILIBRIUM)

Steady state—long-run stability

One of the major properties of Markov chains is that, in the long run, the process usually stabilizes. A stabilized system is said to approach **steady state** or **equilibrium** when the system's state probabilities have become independent of time.

The phenomenon of equilibrium probabilities is expressed as:

$$Q(k) = Q(k-1) \tag{13.10}$$

That is, the state probabilities in period k are identical to those in the previous period. Introducing expression 13.10 into Equation 13.9, the following formulation for the steady state is obtained:

$$Q(k) = Q(k)P \qquad \text{or} \qquad Q = QP \tag{13.11}$$

Equilibrium probability

where the deletion of the index k denotes *equilibrium* probabilities. Equation 13.11 can also be presented as:

$$Q = [q_1, q_2, \ldots, q_n]\begin{bmatrix} p_{11} & p_{12} & \cdots & p_{1n} \\ p_{21} & p_{22} & \cdots & p_{2n} \\ \vdots & \vdots & & \vdots \\ p_{n1} & p_{n2} & \cdots & p_{nn} \end{bmatrix} \tag{13.12}$$

The matrix multiplication shown in Equation 13.12 results in a system of n simultaneous linear equations, as per Equation 13.13.[11]

$$\begin{aligned} q_1 &= p_{11}q_1 + p_{21}q_2 + \cdots + p_{n1}q_n \\ q_2 &= p_{12}q_1 + p_{22}q_2 + \cdots + p_{n2}q_n \\ &\vdots \\ q_n &= p_{1n}q_1 + p_{2n}q_2 + \cdots + p_{nn}q_n \end{aligned} \tag{13.13}$$

Replacing a redundant equation

In Equation 13.13, it so happens that one equation is redundant and hence the system of equations cannot be solved for a unique solution;[12] therefore a replacement equation must be added. Using Equation 13.2

[11] Equation 13.13 can also be expressed as:

$$q_j = \sum_{i=1}^{n} p_{ij}q_i, \quad \text{for } j = 1, 2, \ldots, n$$

[12] A redundant equation presents the same information as that given by another equation in a different form. For example: $x_1 + 2x_2 = 50$ and $2x_1 + 4x_2 = 100$ are redundant.

$$\sum_{i=1}^{n} q_i = 1$$

as a replacement, it is possible to derive a solution for the steady state vector Q.

Before returning to the problem of finding Q in the detergent example, let us consider some additional examples:

The case of two states

The simplest case is that of a 2×2 transition matrix. In this case, Equation 13.12 is expressed as:

$$\begin{bmatrix} q_1 \, q_2 \end{bmatrix} = \begin{bmatrix} q_1 \, q_2 \end{bmatrix} \begin{bmatrix} p_{11} & p_{12} \\ p_{21} & p_{22} \end{bmatrix} = \begin{bmatrix} q_1p_{11} + q_2p_{21}; \; q_1p_{12} + q_2p_{22} \end{bmatrix} \quad (13.14)$$

Solving this equation and the equation $q_1 + q_2 = 1$ we obtain:

$$q_1 = \frac{p_{21}}{1 - p_{11} + p_{21}}$$

Example 1 Given a transition matrix:

$$\begin{array}{c} \\ A \\ B \end{array} \begin{array}{c} \begin{array}{cc} A & B \end{array} \\ \begin{bmatrix} .2 & .8 \\ .3 & .7 \end{bmatrix} \end{array}$$

Find the steady state probabilities utilizing Equation 13.14:

1. $q_1 = p_{11}q_1 + p_{21}q_2 = .2q_1 + .3q_2$
2. $q_2 = p_{12}q_1 + p_{22}q_2 = .8q_1 + .7q_2$
3. Also, it is known that $q_1 + q_2 = 1$

This system can be solved by considering either Equations 1 and 3, or Equations 2 and 3 (since one of the first two equations is redundant and can be dropped).

Solution, using Equations 1 and 3.[13] Equation 3 can be rewritten as $q_1 = 1 - q_2$. Introducing this value into Equation 1: $1 - q_2 = .2(1 - q_2) + .3\,q_2$. Solving for q_2, the solution $q_2 = 8/11$ is obtained. Introducing this value into Equation 3 yields the solution for q_1; $q_1 = 3/11$. Thus, *in equilibrium* there is a chance of 3/11 that the system will be in state A, and a chance of 8/11 that it will be in state B.

Example 2 Given a transition matrix:

$$\begin{bmatrix} .3 & 0 & .7 \\ 0 & .2 & .8 \\ .5 & .4 & .1 \end{bmatrix}$$

[13] For methods of solving simultaneous linear equations, see Appendix A.

Find the steady state probabilities.

Equation 13.12 is utilized to find the steady state vector:

$$Q = [q_1 \quad q_2 \quad q_3] = [q_1 \quad q_2 \quad q_3] \times \begin{bmatrix} .3 & 0 & .7 \\ 0 & .2 & .8 \\ .5 & .4 & .1 \end{bmatrix}$$

Executing the multiplication, a system of three simultaneous linear equations is obtained:

$$\begin{aligned} &(1) \quad q_1 = .3q_1 + 0q_2 + .5q_3 \\ &(2) \quad q_2 = 0q_1 + .2q_2 + .4q_3 \\ &(3) \quad q_3 = .7q_1 + .8q_2 + .1q_3 \end{aligned}$$

In addition, Equation 13.2 for three states contributes:

$$(4) \quad q_1 + q_2 + q_3 = 1$$

To solve this system, any two of the first three equations, plus the fourth one, may be considered. The following solution then is obtained:

$$q_1 = \frac{10}{31}, \quad q_2 = \frac{7}{31}, \quad q_3 = \frac{14}{31}$$

A simple test can be employed to assure that an equilibrium solution has been obtained. Check if Equation 13.11 holds; that is, if $Q = QP$. In the above example:

$$\underset{Q}{\begin{bmatrix} \frac{10}{31} & \frac{7}{31} & \frac{14}{31} \end{bmatrix}} \times \underset{P}{\begin{bmatrix} .3 & 0 & .7 \\ 0 & .2 & .8 \\ .5 & .4 & .1 \end{bmatrix}} = \underset{Q}{\begin{bmatrix} \frac{10}{31} & \frac{7}{31} & \frac{14}{31} \end{bmatrix}}$$

Thus, it does check.

The following example will help clarify the process through which steady state is achieved.

Example 3 One half of Glade County's population lives in the city and one half in the suburbs. The initial condition of this system can therefore be described as:

$$Q(0) = [.5 \quad .5]$$

Exodus to the suburbs

There is an 80 percent chance that a suburban resident will remain in the suburbs and a 20 percent chance that he or she will move to the city within the next year. A city dweller has a 50–50 chance of staying in the city or moving to the suburbs. The transition matrix describing this process is:

$$\text{Today:} \begin{array}{l} \textit{Suburb} \\ \textit{City} \end{array} \overset{\begin{array}{c}\text{Next Year:} \\ \textit{Suburb} \;\; \textit{City}\end{array}}{\begin{bmatrix} .8 & .2 \\ .5 & .5 \end{bmatrix}} = P$$

Using Equation 13.9, the population distribution after any desired number of years can be found. Results are shown in Table 13.3.[14]

TABLE 13.3
The approach to steady state

(k) Year	$q_1(k)$* Percentage in suburbs	$q_2(k)$ Percentage in city	Formula used
0	50	50	$Q(0)$ Given
1	65	35	$Q(1) = Q(0)P$
2	69.5	30.5	$Q(2) = Q(1)P$
3	70.85	29.15	$Q(3) = Q(2)P$
4	71.255	28.745	.
.	.	.	.
.	.	.	.
.	.	.	.
n (large)	71.4286	28.5714	$Q = QP$

* q_1 and q_2, the probabilities of an individual being in the suburbs or in the city, respectively, also correspond to the percentage of the population in the suburbs and in the city. For example, after one year, 35 percent of the total population will be in the city.

The probability distributions $q_1(k)$ and $q_2(k)$ of Table 13.3 show that as equilibrium is approached, the changes in the probability distribution become smaller. In the long run, about 71.43 percent of the population will reside in the suburbs and 28.57 percent in the city. Note that the same results are achieved regardless of the initial conditions. The reader is encouraged to test this statement with the extreme initial conditions $q_1(0) = 1$, $q_2(0) = 0$.

Market shares in equilibrium

Let us return now to the detergent example. With the equilibrium Equation 13.11, John Byer's second question concerning the ultimate market shares can be addressed. The equilibrium probabilities are computed (to three decimal-place accuracy) as:[15]

$$Q = [.297 \quad .286 \quad .417]$$

This means that once steady state has been achieved, the market shares of A, B, and C in any given month are 29.7 percent, 28.6 percent, and 41.7 percent, respectively.

Summary: How a steady state situation is recognized

As seen earlier, the state probabilities changed over time. In the detergent example we found that:

[14] The reader is encouraged to derive this table for him- or herself. Note in this example that we are using the Markov interpretation of the "fraction of a group," rather than the "probability of an individual."

[15] The reader is encouraged to derive these probabilities for him- or herself, using Table 13.1 and Equation 13.12.

Initially $Q(0) = [.2750 \quad .3750 \quad .3500]$
After a month $Q(1) = [.2675 \quad .3125 \quad .4200]$

That is, $Q(0) \neq Q(1)$.

A steady state condition is recognized when the state probabilities remain *unchanged* from period to period.

Formally, such a condition is expressed by Equation 13.10, namely: $Q(k) = Q(k - 1)$.

Characteristics of the steady state situation

From Equation 13.11 it can be seen that the steady state conditions can be expressed by a set of probabilities, Q, that are called the steady state (or equilibrium) probabilities. These probabilities are constant state probabilities, and they depend only on the transition matrix. In contrast, state probabilities that are *not* in (or close to) equilibrium *do* depend on the initial conditions. In a nonabsorbing situation, steady state is approached in a finite number of transitions.

13.5 MANAGERIAL APPLICATIONS

Markov analysis to test "what if" questions

Markov analysis is used to predict a system's behavior. Therefore, it is considered a descriptive tool that provides information that can be used as a basis for making decisions by either complete enumeration of all alternatives *or* through additional optimization models. The relationship between the Markov analysis and the managerial analysis is shown in Figure 13.7.

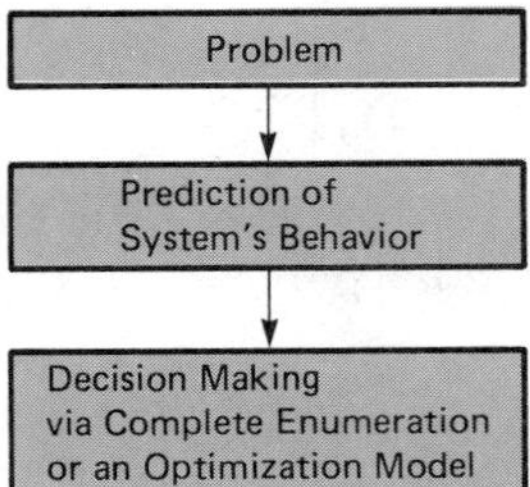

FIGURE 13.7
Managerial analysis using Markov chains

In this section, an extension of the detergent example is given. Other examples are given in the problem sections of 13.7 and 13.11.

Promotional policy planning

P&C is considering two alternative policies for promoting its products.

1. Promote brand A only. This will cost \$150,000 invested in a lump sum and is expected to change the transition matrix to:

From \ To	A	B	C
A	.6	.2.	.2
B	.4	.4	.2
C	.6	.1	.3

2. Promote brand B only. This will cost $280,000 (lump sum, one shot) and is expected to change the transition matrix to:

From \ To	A	B	C
A	.1	.5	.4
B	.2	.8	.0
C	.3	.5	.2

Find:

1. Which policy will bring larger increases in P&C's total share of the market in the long run?
2. Which policy will be more efficient (gain per dollar invested) in the long run?
3. Assume that each percentage of increased share in the total market is worth $10,000 to P&C; which policy (if any) should P&C take?
4. What is the break-even point for each of the two possible policies? That is, at what dollar value of worth, for each percentage gain, will the policies start to be profitable, disregarding interest rates?

Solution:

1. If only brand A is promoted, the following market equilibrium (using the new transition matrix) is obtained:

   A = .555, B = .223, D = .223 (rounded)

   The total of brands A + B increases from .297 + .286 = .583 to .778 (or 77.8 percent of the market). If only brand B is promoted, the equilibrium (using the third transition matrix) is: A = .190, B = .715, C = .095, for a total of .905 to A + B. Thus, promoting B only is preferable, since it will result in a larger share of the market.

2. Promoting A only is more efficient since promoting A yields a 19.5 percent increase for a $150,000 investment = .13 percent per $1,000 investment;[16] promoting B yields a 32.2 percent increase for a $280,000 investment = .115 percent per $1,000 investment.
3. For promoting A: $10,000 × 19.5 = $195,000; less $150,000 (cost) = $45,000. For promoting B: $10,000 × 32.2 = $322,000, less $280,000 (cost) = $42,000. Thus, promoting A is better. This solution was expected since the same answer was obtained earlier in part 2, but here it is in absolute terms.
4. In promoting A only, let x be dollars per 1 percent gain. To break even, the total gain must equal the expenses; that is, $19.5(x) = \$150{,}000$. Solving:

   $$x = \$7{,}678, \text{ for each 1 percent gain}$$

   If only B is promoted, $32.2\ (x) = \$280{,}000$. Solving:

   $$x = \$8{,}685 \text{ for each 1 percent gain.}$$

   Thus, promoting A is better, since its break-even point is lower.

Other predictions

Markov chain analysis can also give other information of managerial interest. (See [4] for the formulas.)

Mean first passage times The average number of periods that will elapse before a customer of one brand first switches to another *specified* brand.

Equilibrium first passage times The average number of periods that will elapse before a customer of one brand first switches to *any* of the other brands.

Expected recurrence times The average number of periods that will elapse before a customer of one brand again purchases that *same* brand.

In these definitions, *brand* refers to *state* in general. The computer printout in Section 13.10 provides the values of these predictions for our P&C brand-switching example.

13.6 CONCLUDING REMARKS

Markov analysis is a descriptive tool designed to predict the behavior of a system over time. The analysis applies in a dynamic, probabilistic environment where most other management science tools are inadequate.

What information is provided?

The analysis can provide information about the chances of a system occupying any state at any future time. Such information can be used by

[16] .778 − .297 − .286 = .195.

management to determine the *effectiveness* of a system under various operating conditions. This enables management to compare various policies and projects by considering each relevant transition matrix.

Determining system effectiveness

Difficulties in application

A key difficulty in the application of Markov chain analysis is that of obtaining the transition matrix. Historical data can serve this purpose in some cases. In other cases, the subjective beliefs of management may be used.

Using historical or subjective data

Markov chain analysis can be applied as an auxiliary tool to a host of managerial problems that are dynamic in nature, such as replacement, maintenance, brand loyalty, investment evaluation, and management of ecology. In addition, it is used in dynamic programming [5]. Ultimately, the extent of the applications of Markov chains will depend on the ability to relax the restrictive assumptions and to solve the modified models efficiently.

13.7 PROBLEMS FOR PART A

1. A survey of textile machines in the ABC Corporation indicated the following condition of the machines:
   January 1: Two hundred in excellent condition, 80 in good condition, 20 in fair condition.
   February 1: Of those found in excellent condition on January 1, 180 are still in excellent condition, 20 in good. Of those found in good condition in January, 60 are still in good condition, 16 are in excellent condition (maintenance is given routinely), and 4 are in fair condition. Of those found in fair shape in January, 2 are in good condition and 18 are in fair condition.
   Construct the transition matrix.
2. Given the following transition matrix:

$$P = \begin{array}{c} \\ s_1 \\ s_2 \end{array} \begin{array}{c} \begin{matrix} s_1 & s_2 \end{matrix} \\ \begin{bmatrix} .2 & .8 \\ .6 & .4 \end{bmatrix} \end{array}$$

   The system is now in state s_2 (i.e., $q_2(0) = 1$). Find the probability vector $Q(3)$ after three periods.
3. A survey of a two-brand market indicates that 80 percent of brand A's customers remain loyal to their brand (state 1) and 20 percent switch to brand B (state 2) each period (say, a week). It is also known that 40 percent of B's customers are loyal and that 60 percent switch to A. This information is presented as a *brand-switching* (transition) matrix:

$$\begin{array}{c} \\ \text{This A} \\ \text{week B} \end{array} \begin{array}{c} \text{Next week} \\ \begin{matrix} A & B \end{matrix} \\ \begin{bmatrix} .8 & .2 \\ .6 & .4 \end{bmatrix} \end{array} = P$$

   Assume that a consumer is currently buying product B. Find:
   a. The probabilities that the consumer will buy products A and B after one week.
   b. The probabilities that the consumer will buy products A and B after two weeks.
   c. The equilibrium (steady state) probabilities.
4. Continental Corporation operates a large fleet of cars for which an extensive preventive maintenance program is utilized. The cars can be classified in one of three states: good (G), fair (F), and poor (P). The transition matrix of these cars is given below:

$$\begin{array}{c} \\ \text{G} \\ \text{From F} \\ \text{P} \end{array} \begin{array}{c} \text{To} \\ \begin{matrix} G & F & P \end{matrix} \\ \begin{bmatrix} .6 & .3 & .1 \\ .2 & .6 & .2 \\ .1 & .4 & .5 \end{bmatrix} \end{array}$$

a. Assume that currently there are 100 cars in good shape, 60 in fair shape, and 20 in poor shape. How many cars will be found in each condition next week?

b. How many cars will be found in each condition once the process stabilizes (steady state)?

5. Buckaday Rent-A-Car has a fleet of 1,000 cars. The company has three rental offices, A, B, and C. Cars can be picked up at and returned to any office. Customers return cars to each of the offices according to the following probabilities:

Picked up at \ Returned to	A	B	C
A	.7	.1	.2
B	.3	.5	.2
C	0	.2	.8

a. How many cars should the company keep in each office and why? What special assumption must be made in order to answer this question?

b. Near which office should the maintenance facilities be located and why?

6. A university's service department is considering leasing one of two possible computers. A computer can be found in operating condition O or nonoperating condition NO. The daily transition matrix of the two computers under identical maintenance is given below:

Computer A

	O	NO
O	.95	.05
NO	.90	.10

Computer B

	O	NO
O	.98	.02
NO	.85	.15

a. Which computer should the university lease if the leasing charges are the same?

b. If charges are not the same, what additional information is necessary to determine which computer to lease? Under what conditions should the university lease computer A and under what conditions computer B?

7. Given below are two transition matrices.

Matrix 1

	A	*B*	*C*
A	.8	.1	.1
B	0	.4	.6
C	0	.6	.4

Matrix 2

	A	*B*	*C*
A	.2	.1	.7
B	0	1.0	0
C	0	.6	.4

a. Analyze these matrices and explain their uniqueness.

b. Predict the steady state probabilities. *Do not* set up any equations; use logic!

8. A company's job rotation program shows the following rotations among its employees between March and April 1988.

Dept.	*March*	*Gains* From checking	From loans	From savings	*April*
Checking	18	0	3	2	20
Loans	12	2	0	1	10
Savings	10	1	2	0	10

a. What would you expect the June results to be?

b. What assumptions were necessary in (a) above?

9. A yearly follow-up of a certain metropolitan area residents' mobility showed that 6 percent of the residents in the city move to the suburbs. At the same time, 3 percent of the suburbs' residents move to the city. Assume that the moving percentages remain unchanged and the total number of people in the combined area remains constant (500,000). The average yearly taxes paid by a city dweller is $100 per capita, and by a suburb dweller $200 per capita.

a. How much tax will the metro government collect (assume 100 percent collection) two years from now if 40 percent of the population currently live in the suburbs.

b. The metro government proposed to induce people to stay in the city by reducing yearly taxes for city dwellers (only) to $50 per capita. As a *result* of this change, population movement from the city to the suburbs will be reduced from 6 percent to 5 percent, while population movement from the suburbs to the city will be changed from 3 percent to 5 percent. How much tax would be collected each year in the long run (steady state) if the proposal is rejected; that is, if the existing tax structure remains unchanged?

c. How much tax will the metro government lose each year, in the long run, if the proposal is accepted?

d. If the total number of people in the metropolitan area is changing due to additions from other metropolitan areas, what pattern of change should be assumed in order to employ the Markov chain approach?

10. Three major oil companies compete in a certain marketing zone. Company A runs a promotion campaign 50 percent of the time, and Company B runs one 30 percent of the time. Company C does no advertising. All campaigns are run on a weekly basis. The average buyer shows the following purchasing habit:

a. If only one company advertises, a buyer will buy from that company.

b. If no one advertises, a buyer will buy from C.

c. If *both* A and B advertise, the buyer will review the previous week's decision. If in the previous week the buyer bought from A, he or she will do so again. If in the previous week the buyer bought from B, he or she will buy from B again. However, if in the previous week the buyer bought from C, the product will be selected at random from either A, B, or C (each with a one-third chance of being selected).

Find the long-run market distribution among the three oil companies.

11. Carefully read the following statement:

Why Worry?
There are only two things to worry about—either you are well or you are sick. If you are well, then there is nothing to worry about. But if you are sick, there are two things to worry about. Either you will get well or you will die. If you get well, there is nothing to worry about. If you die, there are only two things to worry about—either you will go to Heaven or to Hell. If you go to Heaven, there is nothing to worry about. But if you go to Hell, you'll be so damn busy shaking hands with friends, you won't have time to worry!

a. Assume that the chances of moving among the events described are known and constant. Would it be possible to describe this process as a Markov process? Why or why not?

b. If the answer to part *(a)* is no, would it be possible to make certain assumptions that will turn the answer to *(a)* into yes? Name these assumptions.

c. Is it possible to describe the process as a decision tree (assuming that the probabilities of the events are known)? If the answer is no, explain why. If the answer is yes, draw the decision tree and comment on the relationship between Markov chains and decision trees.

12. The Chamber of Commerce of the city of MidAmerica conducted a study on the size of new, high technology businesses. Companies were classified as small (S), medium (M), or large (L). One survey was taken on January 1, 1988. It showed 400 companies, of which 200 were small, 150 were medium, and 50 were large. At the end of the year another survey of the 400 companies was taken. This time there were 160 small, 180 medium and 60 large corporations. The gains and losses in terms of number of companies between the two surveys are given below:

	Gains from			*Loss to*		
Size	*S*	*M*	*L*	*S*	*M*	*L*
S	0	5	2	0	42	5
M	42	0	1	5	0	8
L	5	8	0	2	1	0

a. Construct the transition matrix.

b. State all the assumptions necessary to answer the following questions if a Markov chain is to be used.

c. Predict how many small, medium, and large companies will exist on January 1, 1990.

d. Predict the number of companies in each category in the long run.

13. A production line has 0.4 probability of failure during any one day. Seventy percent of the time the failure can be fixed in exactly one day; otherwise it requires two days. Assume that failures occur at the end of a day and that downtime costs $450 per day.

a. Formulate this situation as a Markov chain, describe the states and assumptions, and develop the transition matrix for the situation.

b. For $200 per day, extra tooling can be rented so that a failure is always repaired in one day. Should this be done?

14. The air in Mexico City is classified as being in one of nine levels of pollution. Observations show that the following transition probability matrix exists. (Consider one day as a period.)

From \ To	1	2	3	4	5	6	7	8	9
1	.22	.28	.20	.15	.10	.05	0	0	0
2	.10	.20	.30	.20	.10	.10	0	0	0
3	.10	.10	.20	.40	.10	.05	.05	0	0
4	.05	.10	.10	.20	.40	.10	.05	0	0
5	0	0	.10	.10	.20	.30	.20	.10	0
6	0	0	0	.07	.08	.15	.40	.20	.10
7	0	0	0	.05	.10	.15	.36	.20	.14
8	0	0	.05	.07	.08	.10	.15	.30	.25
9	0	0	.06	.06	.08	.10	.15	.25	.30

For how many days during the year (365 days) is the air polluted at each level? (Use of a computer is recommended.)

15. Hopeful Hospital is using volunteer help in three departments. On May 1, there were 20 volunteers in departments A, 16 in B, and 14 in C. Volunteers are free to move between departments once a month.

The table below shows the *gains* in volunteers, in each department, on June 1.

Department	*Gains* From A	From B	From C	*Volunteers on June 1*
A	16	0	1	17
B	3	12	1	16
C	1	4	12	17

a. Write the formulas that will show the long-run probability distribution of volunteers among the three departments.

b. Solve the equations to find the probabilities.

16. Taxi-cab of Miami has 100 cabs; currently, 70 are located at the airport and 30 are at the beach. The probability that a car located at the beach will be called for a trip to the airport is 80 percent. The net profit of such a trip is $5. Otherwise, the cab will be called for a local trip where a profit of $2 is realized.

The probability that a cab located at the airport will be called to the beach is 90 percent. The net profit is $5 for such a trip. There is a 10 percent chance that the cab will be called for a trip to the airport. In this case, the cab will return to the airport parking, netting $3.

Note: Once a trip is completed, the cabs return to the port nearest to their unloading point.

Find:

a. What assumption should be made so that a Markov chain approach can be used for this problem.

b. How many cabs will be at each location after three periods.

c. The per period profit for the company in a steady state situation.

d. Cab 135 (nicknamed Fair Lady) is currently parked at the airport. What is the chance of this cab being located at the beach after two trips?

PART B: EXTENSIONS

13.8 ABSORBING STATES

A system is said to be in an absorbing state if, once there, it cannot exit to some other state. There are numerous practical examples of absorbing states. A bankrupt business, a river or lake irreversibly destroyed by pollution and sediment, and a building destroyed by fire are examples of absorbing state situations.

Examples of absorbing states

Analysis of absorbing Markov chains can provide management with answers to at least four important questions:

1. What is the average number of periods that the system will be in *each* nonabsorbing state before it is absorbed?
2. How long is the system expected to stay in nonabsorbing states before it is absorbed?
3. What is the probability of moving into each absorbing state starting from each nonabsorbing state?
4. What proportion will be absorbed in each absorbing state?

Answers to four questions

Such information has an important practical value for managerial decisions in areas such as replacement of equipment, marketing, and maintenance, as will be demonstrated in the following personnel management example.

A labor training program

Participants in a certain labor training program can be found in one of four given states: s_1, no service (not in the training program); s_2, discharged; s_3, in training; and s_4, employed. Table 13.4 shows the proportion

TABLE 13.4
A training problem

	Status on February 1, 1988									
	s_1 *No service*		s_2 *Discharged*		s_3 *In training*		s_4 *Employed*		*Total*	
Status on January 1, 1988	*No.*	*Percent*	*No.*	*Percent*	*No.*	*Percent*	*No.*	*Percent*	*No.*	*Percent*
s_1 No service	10	10.0	60	60.0	30	30.0	0	.0	100	100.0
s_2 Discharged	0	.0	100	100.0	0	.0	0	.0	100	100.0
s_3 In training	60	20.0	60	20.0	150	50.0	30	10.0	300	100.0
s_4 Employed	0	.0	0	.0	0	.0	500	100.0	500	100.0

of the program population that has changed categories (states) in the most recent month.

The first step is to construct the *transition matrix* (assuming that the transition probabilities are constant over time). The numbers in the matrix below (derived from Table 13.4) represent the fraction of people who have transferred from one category to another during the month. States s_2 and s_4 are defined as *absorbing states* since all the entries in rows s_2 and s_4 are zero except the one corresponding to the *same* state, which has the value of one. *If a system is in an absorbing state, there is a zero probability of moving from that state to any other state.* For example, once employed or discharged, movement to another state is not possible.

From \ *To*	s_1	s_2	s_3	s_4
s_1	.1	.6	.3	0
s_2	0	1.0	0	0
s_3	.2	.2	.5	.1
s_4	0	0	0	1.0

The fundamental matrix

After the transition matrix is constructed, it is *rearranged* by placing the absorbing states first. This enables us to partition the matrix and identify four submatrices **I, O, A,** and **N,** as shown in Figure 13.8.

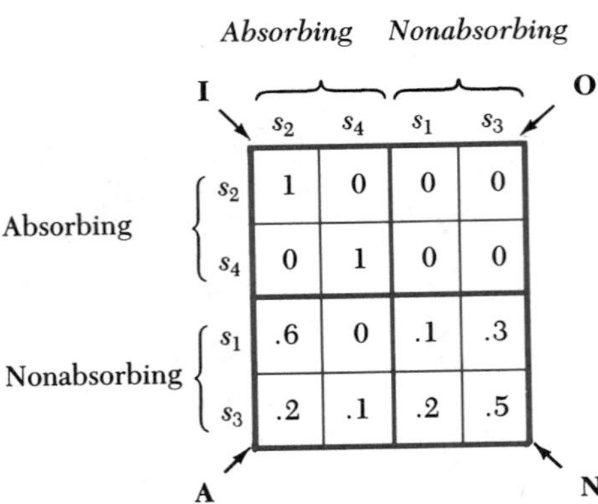

FIGURE 13.8
A partition of the transition matrix

These four matrices are:

I = Unit (identity) matrix[17]
0 = All zero (null) matrix
A = Absorbing matrix
N = Nonabsorbing matrix

Fundamental matrix

Next, we define a new matrix, termed the *fundamental matrix (F)*, according to Equation 13.15:

$$F = (I - N)^{-1} \qquad (13.15)$$

where the −1 exponent stands for the *inverse* of the matrix (see Appendix A). In our case:

$$F = \left(\begin{bmatrix} 1 & 0 \\ 0 & 1 \end{bmatrix} - \begin{bmatrix} .1 & .3 \\ .2 & .5 \end{bmatrix}\right)^{-1} = \begin{bmatrix} .9 & -.3 \\ -.2 & .5 \end{bmatrix}^{-1} = \begin{matrix} \\ s_1 \\ s_3 \end{matrix} \begin{matrix} s_1 & s_3 \\ \left[\begin{matrix} \frac{50}{39} \\ \frac{20}{39} \end{matrix}\right. & \left.\begin{matrix} \frac{30}{39} \\ \frac{90}{39} \end{matrix}\right] \end{matrix}$$

The meaning of the entries in the fundamental matrix

The entries in the fundamental matrix give the *average number of periods* (months in our case) *the system will be in each nonabsorbing state until it gets absorbed.* If an employee started in state s_1, then he or she will spend $50/39 = 1.28$ months (on the average) in state s_1 *and* $30/39 = .77$ months in state s_3 before being absorbed; that is, either employed (state s_4) or discharged (state s_2). If the employee was in s_3, then he or she will spend $20/39 = .51$ months in state s_1 *and* $90/39 = 2.31$ months in state s_3 before being absorbed into either s_4 or s_2.

Time to absorption To find the average number of periods to absorption, add the entries in the rows of matrix F:
If an employee starts in state s_1, it will take, on the average:

$$\frac{50}{39} + \frac{30}{39} = \frac{80}{39} = 2.05$$

months until he or she is absorbed into either s_2 or s_4. If the employee starts in state s_3, it will take $110/39$ or 2.82 months until he or she is absorbed, on the average.

Conditional probabilities It is of interest to find the probabilities of moving from any nonabsorbing state to each absorbing state. These probabilities are given by a matrix B whose formula is:

$$B = FA \qquad (13.16)$$

[17] A unit or identity matrix contains zeros in all elements except the diagonal from upper left to lower right, which is filled in with ones (see Appendix A).

In our case:

$$B = \begin{bmatrix} \frac{50}{39} & \frac{30}{39} \\ \frac{20}{39} & \frac{90}{39} \end{bmatrix} \begin{bmatrix} .6 & 0 \\ .2 & .1 \end{bmatrix} = \begin{matrix} \\ s_1 \\ s_3 \end{matrix} \begin{matrix} s_2 & s_4 \\ \left[\begin{matrix} \frac{36}{39} & \frac{3}{39} \\ \frac{30}{39} & \frac{9}{39} \end{matrix}\right] \end{matrix}$$

Interpreting the results

These results may be interpreted as follows: If an employee is in state s_1, there is a probability of $36/39$ or .92 that he or she will be absorbed by state s_2 (i.e., discharged) and $3/39$ or .08 by state s_4 (i.e., employed). Similarly, if an employee starts from s_3, there is a $30/39 = .77$ chance that he or she will be absorbed by state s_2, and $9/39 = .23$ chance of being absorbed by state s_4. Note again that the sum of the probabilities in each row is 1.

The final proportion in each of the absorbing states can now be found. As the reader may recall, the initial conditions were $s_1 = 100$; $s_3 = 300$ (numbers in each nonabsorbing state). If we multiply these numbers by matrix B, we can find the total number of employees (again, the alternate Markov interpretation) in each absorbing state; namely:

$$B = \begin{matrix} \\ s_1 \\ s_3 \end{matrix} \begin{matrix} s_2 & s_4 \\ \left[\begin{matrix} .92 & .08 \\ .77 & .23 \end{matrix}\right] \end{matrix}$$

Total in s_2: $100(.92) + 300(.77) + 100 = 423$ discharged
Total in s_4: $100(.08) + 300(.23) + 500 = \underline{577}$ employed
Grand total 1000

The proportion in s_2 is thus 42.3 percent and in s_4 is 57.7 percent. That is, in the long run, 42.3 percent will be discharged and 57.7 percent employed.

The results obtained in the above analysis can be compared to desired standards, or to results obtained from alternative training programs. Different programs will result in different movements of employees from category to category. In other words, each program will result in a different transition matrix. Given the monthly costs of each program, the administration can determine the cost-benefit relationship of different labor training programs.

13.9 MANAGERIAL APPLICATION

Accounts receivable analysis

Markov chains with absorbing states have been applied to business situations dealing with accounts receivable analysis. Many businesses extend credit to customers. Some of the customers pay late, others do not pay at all (a situation called a *bad debt*). The typical business will classify such accounts according to their age; once an account reaches a certain age, it will often be transferred to a collection agency (which takes a certain percentage of the successful collections) or perhaps simply written off as a bad debt.

Consider a department store that classifies its accounts as:

S_1 = 0–30-day age
S_2 = 31–90-day age
S_3 = In collection agency
S_4 = Bad debt
S_5 = Paid

Past experience indicates the following one-month transition matrix is appropriate (in terms of dollars):

	S_1	S_2	S_3	S_4	S_5
S_1	0	.8	0	0	.2
S_2	0	.7	2	0	.1
S_3	0	0	.4	.2	.4
S_4	0	0	0	1	0
S_5	0	0	0	0	1

The current situation in the department store is as follows:

$$S_1 = \$100{,}000;\ S_2 = \$150{,}000;\ S_3 = \$50{,}000$$

It would be of interest to management to know the following:

1. The long-run "fate" of a dollar currently in S_1, S_2, and S_3.
2. The average number of months it will take an account now in the hands of the collection agency to be either paid or closed.
3. The probability that an account now in category S_2 will be paid.

The solution to this problem, by computer, is given in the next section.

13.10 USE OF COMPUTERS

Markov chain problems can be easily programmed for computers. Several statistical packages include Markov chain computations such as multiplication of a matrix by a vector, or multiplication of a matrix by itself n times (raising it to the nth power). The input to the computer includes the transition matrix, the initial conditions (if applicable), and the number of regular and absorbing states.

Two examples of computer printouts are given below. The first one is the solution to the earlier P&C brand-switching example in Section 13.3. Note that the solution includes:

a. The steady state (equilibrium) probabilities.
b. Equilibrium first passage times.
c. Expected recurrence times.
d. Mean first passage times.
e. The transition matrix after n transitions (three in our case).
f. The state probabilities after n (3 here) periods (labeled *market share*).

a. STEADY STATE PROBABILITIES

STATE	MARKET SHARE
Br. A	0.29670
Br. B	0.28571
Br. C	0.41758

b. EQUILIBRIUM 1ST PASSAGE TIMES

STATE	TIME
Br. A	2.247
Br. B	3.571
Br. C	1.223

c. EXPECTED RECURRENCE TIMES

STATE	TIME
Br. A	3.370
Br. B	3.500
Br. C	2.395

d. MEAN 1ST PASSAGE TIMES

	TO		
FROM	Br. A	Br. B	Br. C
Br. A	0.00000	5.00000	1.84211
Br. B	4.07407	0.00000	2.36842
Br. C	2.59259	5.00000	0.00000
MKT.SHR.	0.29408	0.28813	0.41780

e. TRANSITION MATRIX AFTER 3 TRANSITIONS

FROM	TO Br. A	Br. B	Br. C	ROW TOT
Br. A	0.28800	0.27800	0.43400	1.00000
Br. B	0.27900	0.30500	0.41600	1.00000
Br. C	0.31500	0.27800	0.40700	1.00000
f. MKT.SHR.	0.29408	0.28800	0.41780	

The second example is the solution to the accounts receivable problem, including absorbing states. The absorbing states ("paid" and "bad debt") are arranged first (states 1 and 2) while the nonabsorbing states are arranged last (states 3, 4, and 5). The solution includes:

a. The fundamental matrix *F*.
b. The time to absorption.
c. The conditional probabilities.

** *INFORMATION ENTERED* **

NUMBER OF STATES :5
NUMBER OF ABSORPTIVE STATES:2

TRANSITION MATRIX

STATES					
PAID	1	0	0	0	0
BAD DEBT	0	1	0	0	0
D 0–30	.2	0	0	.8	0
D 31–90	.1	0	0	.7	.2
COLLECTION	.4	.2	0	0	.4

** *RESULTS* **

a. *FUNDAMENTAL MATRIX*

STATES

FROM	D 0–30	TO D 31–90	Coll.
D 0–30	1.00000	2.66667	0.88889
D 31–90	0.00000	3.33333	1.11111
Coll.	0.00000	0.00000	1.66667

b. ABSOR.TM 4.55556 4.44444 1.66667

c. *CONDITIONAL PROBABILITIES*

FROM	TO Paid	Bad db.	ROW TOT
D 0–30	0.82222	0.17778	1.00000
D 31–90	0.77778	0.22222	1.00000
Coll.	0.66667	0.33333	1.00000

Interpretation

Notice that the transition matrix had to be rearranged with the absorbing states first. Also, we named the states.

The *fundamental matrix* is given first. The cells of this matrix indicate the average time that an account will be in any nonabsorbing state, given that the account is in a nonabsorbing state. For example, an account now in state 0–30 days will be 2.666 months in the state 31–90 days.

Absorption time This is the average time (number of periods) that it will take for an entry to be absorbed by either one of the absorbing states. For example, for a 0 to 30-day account, it will take 4.555 months, on the average, to either be paid or closed (bad debt).

Conditional probabilities This is the probability that each account in a nonabsorbing state will be absorbed in a particular absorbing state. For example, the collection agency collects .66667 (66.667 percent) of all accounts submitted to it.

With this information, one can answer the three questions posed by management.

Question 1

a. Of the $100,000 in 0–30 days, $82,222 will be paid, $17,778 will become bad debt.

b. Of the $150,000 in the 31 to 90-day category, 77.778 percent (or $116,667) will be paid, while 22.22 percent ($33,333) will become bad debt.

c. Of the $50,000 currently in the collection agency, 66.67 percent (or $33,334) will be paid, while $16,667 will become bad debt.

Thus, of the $300,000: $82,222 + $116,667 + $33,334 = $232,223 will be paid.

Question 2 On the average, it will take the collection agency 1.66667 months to collect an account, or to close it.

Question 3 The probability that an account, now in the 31 to 90-day category, will be paid is 77.778 percent.

13.11 PROBLEMS FOR PART B

17. Given the transition matrix below, find the appropriate *fundamental* matrix.

$$\begin{bmatrix} 1.0 & 0 & 0 & 0 \\ .3 & .2 & .5 & 0 \\ .1 & .6 & .1 & .2 \\ 0 & 0 & 0 & 1.0 \end{bmatrix}$$

18. Assume that a machine is currently maintained in either good (G), fair (F), or poor (P) condition. Suppose that management decides to stop all preventive maintenance and let the machine fail. If preventive maintenance stops, the machine will have a new state, complete failure (D). The transition matrix under these conditions is given below:

From \ To	G	F	P	D
G	.4	.3	.2	.1
F	0	.5	.3	.2
P	0	0	.1	.9
D	0	0	0	1

Assuming the machine is presently in good condition, management wants to know:

a. How many weeks the machine is expected to go before it fails.

b. How many weeks (on the average) it will operate in good, fair, and poor condition before it fails.

c. What its probability of failing is. What would this probability be, given that the machine was in fair condition to start? In poor condition?

19. Suppose a new labor training program became available. What information would you need to determine if it were better or worse than the program described in Section 13.8? If you wished to determine the cost-benefit of both programs, what information would you need and how would you conduct the analysis?

20. A department store classifies its accounts as: S_1 = Paid in full, S_2 = Current, S_3 = Delinquent, S_4 = Bad debt. The following information is given regarding the accounts:

Transactions during October

Category	S_1	S_2	S_3	S_4
S_1	500,000	0	0	0
S_2	400,000	500,000	100,000	0
S_3	50,000	0	100,000	50,000
S_4	0	0	0	100,000

The amounts on October 1 were: \$500,000 in S_1; \$1,000,000 in S_2; \$200,000 in S_3, and \$100,000 in S_4.

Find:

a. How much money will be in each category on November 1 and on December 1.

b. In the long run, how much money will be classified as paid.

c. What allowance should be prepared for the possible bad debt.

d. What is the average number of months that it will take a current account to be closed.

21. A computer printout of a Markov chain is shown below. Cells marked with * were deliberately deleted. Answer the following questions:

a. For a person now in state 4:
   (1) How long will it take to be absorbed (on the average)?
   (2) How long will he or she stay in that state (on the average)?

b. Of the 10,000 people currently in state 4, how many will be absorbed by state 1?

c. Of the 20,000 people in state 5, how many will be absorbed by state 1? By state 2?

d. There are 15,000 in state 3, 50,000 in state 1, and 100,000 in state 2. How many will be in each of the five states at the end?

FUNDAMENTAL MATRIX

FROM	TO 3	4	5
3	3.67347	0.20408	0.81633
4	1.42857	2.85714	1.42857
5	1.02041	0.61224	*
ABSOR.TM	4.69388	*	4.08163

CONDITITIONAL PROBABILITIES

FROM	TO ABSORB 1	ABSORB 2	ROW TOT
3	0.44898	0.55102	1.00000
4	*	0.71429	1.00000
5	0.34694	*	1.00000

13.12 CASE

SPRINGFIELD GENERAL HOSPITAL

Dr. Bill Parker, medical director of Springfield General Hospital, has just been informed that an ambulance is rushing in an accident victim who may require surgery using the heart-lung machine. This hospital has only one such expensive machine, which is not in use now but is heavily scheduled for surgeries in the next few days. Dr. Parker has called the management science unit to provide him with estimates of the following:

a. The likelihood that the victim will require service on the heart-lung machine during each of the next few days.
b. The prognosis for such cases.

After quickly reviewing their records, the management science analysts compiled the following information:

1. In the past, 112 such victims entered the hospital. At admittance, 72 were found to be in satisfactory condition, 24 were diagnosed as fair, and 16 were considered to be in critical condition, requiring the heart-lung machine.
2. Of the 72 in satisfactory condition, 63 (87.5 percent) were still in satisfactory condition the following day, while the condition of 9 (12.5 percent) had deteriorated due to complications and these persons were considered to be in fair condition. None had deteriorated to the point of being in critical condition.
3. Of the 24 in fair condition, 12 (50 percent) were still in the same condition the following day, while 8 (33.3 percent) had improved to satisfactory condition; but 4 (16.7 percent) had deteriorated so much they were classified as critical.
4. Of the 16 in critical condition, 10 (62.5 percent) had improved to fair by the following day, 4 (25 percent) were still in critical condition, and 2 (12.5 percent) had improved significantly to the level of satisfactory.

With this information on hand, the management analysts can answer Dr. Parker's questions.

Questions for discussion

1. What is the likelihood of the patient requiring the heart-lung machine today or in the next two days?
2. What are the steady state transition probabilities?
3. Assume now that in addition to the 112 victims listed in the records, there were another 8 found who were discharged. Six of these were discharged alive from "satisfactory" sta-

tus and two had expired from "critical" status.

4. Starting from each nonabsorbing state, what is the average number of days in each state and to "discharged"?
5. From each nonabsorbing state, what is the probability of expiring, as opposed to being discharged alive?

13.13 GLOSSARY

Absorbing state A state that, once entered, cannot be left.

Descriptive Illustrating a system and how it reacts.

Equilibrium (see Steady state).

Markov chain A Markov process with constant transition probabilities.

Markov process A stochastic process whose probability of being in any state depends only on its previous state and the transition matrix.

Normative Prescriptive; that is, what *should* be done.

State A condition that a system may be in.

Steady state A point where the chances of finding a system in any particular condition are unchanged from period to period.

Stochastic Probabilistic; that is, with an exhaustive set of probabilities or chances of outcomes.

Transition probability The chance of a system moving from one state to another.

13.14 REFERENCES AND BIBLIOGRAPHY

1. Derman, C. *Finite State Markov Decision Processes*. New York: Academic Press, 1970.
2. Ethier, S. N. *Markov Processes*. New York: John Wiley & Sons. 1986.
3. Freedman, D. *Markov Chains*. San Francisco: Holden-Day, 1971.
4. Hillier, F. S., and G. J. Lieberman. *Introduction to Operations Research*. 3rd ed. San Francisco: Holden-Day, 1980.
5. Howard, R. A. *Dynamic Probabilistic Systems*. Vols. 1 and 2. New York: John Wiley & Sons, 1971.
6. Kemeny, J. G., and J. L. Snell. *Finite Markov Chains*. Englewood Cliffs, N.J.: Prentice-Hall, 1960.
7. Kemeny, J. G., A. Schleffer, Jr., J. L. Snell, and G. L. Thompson. *Finite Mathematics with Business Applications*. 2nd ed. Englewood Cliffs, N.J.: Prentice-Hall, 1972.
8. Martin, J. J. *Baysian Decision Problems and Markov Chains*. New York: John Wiley & Sons, 1967.
9. Mine, H., and S. Osaki. *Markovian Decision Processes*. New York: Elsevier North-Holland Publishing, 1970.

14

Inventory models

PART A: BASICS

14.1 Production/inventory systems.
14.2 The structure of the inventory system.
14.3 Inventory costs.
14.4 The economic order quantity model.
14.5 Application of the EOQ model.
14.6 Discussion of the EOQ assumptions.
14.7 Inventory systems.
14.8 Concluding remarks.
14.9 Problems for Part A.

PART B: EXTENSIONS

14.10 Quantity discounts.
14.11 Production runs: Economic lot size (ELS).
14.12 Single-period inventories.
14.13 Material requirements planning (MRP).
14.14 Planned shortages.
14.15 Safety stocks and service levels.
14.16 Use of computers.
14.17 Concluding remarks.
14.18 Problems for Part B.
14.19 Case I—Visutech.
Case II—Emco Corporation.
14.20 Glossary.
14.21 References and bibliography.

The use of mathematical models to determine the best inventory level to maintain and the best time to reorder merchandise is one of the oldest techniques of management science.

Part A of this chapter is directed toward determining a proper balance between the cost of holding an inventory and the cost of placing an order. The result is the classical "economic order quantity" (EOQ) model. Part A also covers the applicability and limitations of this model and closes with a discussion of some practical inventory systems.

The most common extension of the EOQ model is the "economic lot size" (ELS) production model, presented in Part B. Also presented there are the quantity discount model, the establishment of safety stock, MRP, single period inventories, computerization, and the treatment of shortages.

LEARNING OBJECTIVES

The student should be able to:

a. List the characteristics of the inventory problem.
b. Distinguish various types of inventories and their purposes.
c. Describe the various components of an inventory system (inventory level, reordering, depletion, lead time, shortage, safety stock).
d. Analyze the relevant costs.
e. Develop the EOQ formula.
f. Solve problems using the EOQ formula.
g. Solve problems using extensions to the EOQ model.
h. Evaluate the sensitivity of the model.
i. Distinguish several practical inventory systems and their characteristics.
j. Describe the A-B-C classification system and its importance.

Extensions

k. Solve problems using the economic lot size formula.
l. Discuss the concept of quantity discounts and solve problems with EOQ and discounts.
m. Discuss the concepts of safety stocks and service levels and solve appropriate problems.
n. Solve problems with planned shortages.
o. Describe the nature of single period inventory problems and solve them by marginal analysis.
p. Describe the workings of MRP systems and solve MRP problems.

PART A: BASICS

As Jed Stowe, the director of materials, walked out of the vice president's office, it was clear that Jed felt frustrated. Just last month, Jed recalled, the vice president had complained about the secretaries "wasting time filling out requisition (order) forms for materials." Almost in the same breath, he mentioned the possibility of an inventory shortage due to an impending strike against their major supplier. In the face of those comments, Jed thought that a simple solution for both of the vice president's concerns was to order materials in larger amounts, but less frequently. Thus, the number of orders would be reduced (less work for the secretaries) and protection would exist in the event of a strike against the supplier. This strategy carried the additional advantage of allowing the company to obtain discounts given by the supplier on large orders.

Yesterday, however, the previous month's operating cost report came out and the cost of keeping the inventory had jumped to a record high. Jed was summoned to the vice president's office, where he learned that the additional inventory cost due to his larger orders caused a cash flow problem to the company. Jed concluded that there was simply no way to win.

14.1 PRODUCTION/INVENTORY SYSTEMS

Characteristics of the situation

Two conflicting costs

Jed Stowe's plight illustrates a typical inventory dilemma. An inventory is any stock of economic resources that is stored for future use. Jed's case called attention to the following dilemma: If a commodity is ordered frequently, then the costs of ordering (paperwork, secretarial time) are high. On the other hand, ordering more units less frequently saves on ordering costs but increases the expense of keeping a larger inventory. Thus, the proper ordering policy is a dilemma. The management problem in this case is: *How frequently should materials be ordered?*

How frequently to order supplies?

This is a problem for management because the dilemma exists for many of the items in stock, sometimes tens of thousands of items. Further, due to continuous changes in prices, the solution should be updated periodically. What makes the situation even more complicated is that there are many (theoretically infinite) possible solutions to the problem. An item may be ordered on a daily basis, or once every 10 years or so.

For all these reasons, a trial-and-error solution is not practical. Management science provides models that execute the search for an *optimal* solution rather quickly.

Inventories in the production system

Several types of inventories are maintained by organizations. Some of the major inventories are:

1. Raw materials.
2. Finished goods.
3. Semifinished products.
4. Spare parts and supplies.

Some specific examples of inventories are:

- Items on the shelves of department and food stores.
- Unused telephone numbers the phone company is holding.
- Cash on hand at the bank (reserves).
- Blood in blood banks.
- Standby pilots and stewardesses employed by airlines.
- Empty space in a warehouse for incoming shipments.

Blood, cash, spaces

The general production process is illustrated in Figure 14.1. As shown, vendors supply raw materials, supplies, spares, and even semifinished parts to the firm. These inventories then enter the production process where parts are fabricated, some of which temporarily reenter the storeroom as semifinished parts, and then are sent on to assembly where finished goods are produced for sale. The finished goods may be temporarily stocked in the storeroom or a warehouse, or go directly to a customer. The former

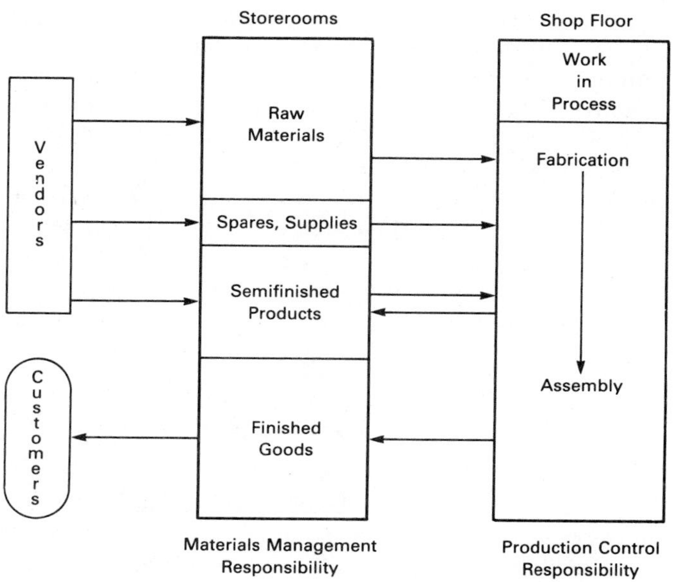

FIGURE 14.1 The production/inventory process

are called "made-to-stock" goods and the latter are called "made-to-order" goods. In some cases, products are fabricated "to stock" and then, as customer orders come in, assembled "to order," thereby cutting down on the lead time to customers.

The purpose of inventory

Many reasons for inventory

The following is a list of the major reasons for maintaining an inventory:

Protection against fluctuating demand Inventories are kept to meet peak demand. For example, blood is stored in hospitals in quantities sufficient to meet the needs of a major accident.

Protection against delayed supply A strike by the supplier's employees is one reason why deliveries may not arrive on time. Lack of material at the supplier level, strikes in the transportation network, or a snowstorm are other possible causes for shortages. Inventories are kept as a buffer that can be used until late deliveries arrive.

Protection against inflation Inventories are often kept as a hedge against inflation. In this case, inventories are built up in anticipation of a price increase. This speculative practice is especially common in the commodity markets (such as wheat or gold).

Benefits of large quantities Purchasing large quantities of an item often entitles the buyer to a price *discount* (lower per unit price). Similarly, in the case of manufacturing of large production lots, the utilization of more efficient automated equipment can be justified by the reduction in the per unit manufacturing cost.

Primary basis for business Retail operations involving customer perusal and selection require fully stocked shelves and complete inventories.

Savings on ordering cost Ordering in large quantities reduces the number of times that an order must be placed and processed. Since a fixed cost is associated with placing each order, the fewer times one places an order, the lower the total cost of ordering will be.

Other reasons Inventories are kept for several other reasons: An inventory may improve the bargaining power of a firm with a supplier (or with its own employees) by making the company less vulnerable to delays or stoppages. Inventories also are kept so that machines can be shut down for overhauls. An inventory of labor is maintained to meet fluctuating production demands in order to reduce hiring, firing, and training costs.

The importance of inventory management

Proper inventory management may be one of the most important functions of management. Tracing several bankruptcies of construction firms and agricultural machinery manufacturers has shown that overstocking was the major contributor to failure. As another example, grocery stores have a profit margin of only about 1 percent of sales; thus, saving $20,000 in inventory costs is equivalent to a sales increase of $2 million. High technology companies must often write off expensively produced inventories because of technological obsolescence.

Excess inventories are costly to store, but insufficient inventories may result in loss of market share or idle employees. The task of inventory control is a part of a management function named *materials management,* which is concerned with acquisition, distribution, storage, and disposal of materials and parts in organizations. In this text we will only address the topic of inventory management.

Materials management

14.2 THE STRUCTURE OF THE INVENTORY SYSTEM

The inventory models described in the remainder of this chapter pertain only to an *individual* item in stock. This means, for example, that with an inventory system for three different items, the model must be employed three times.

An inventory system involves *a cyclical process,* which is assumed to run over several periods, whose major characteristics are described next.

Inventory ordering—a cyclical process

Inventory level

An item is stocked in a warehouse, store, or any other storage area. This stock constitutes an *inventory.* The size of the inventory is called the *inventory level* (or the inventory *on hand*).

Demand and depletion

The inventory is *depleted* as *demand* occurs. Assume that one starts with an inventory of 100 units, as shown in Figure 14.2. As time passes, the inventory level declines due to the demand for the item in stock.

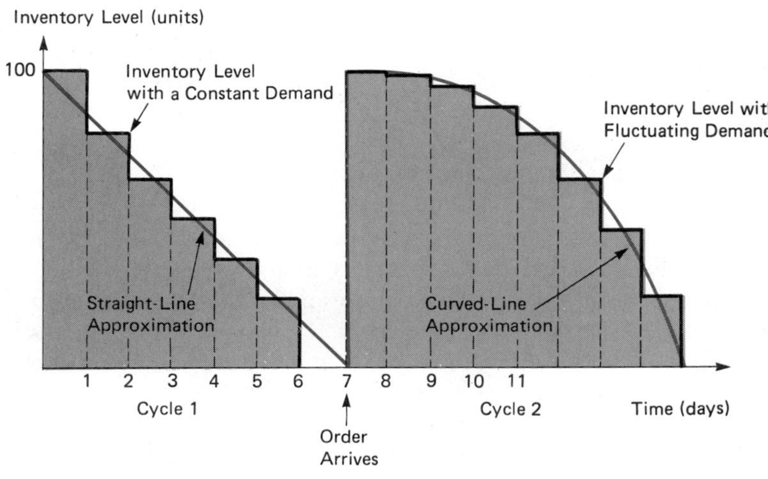

FIGURE 14.2
An inventory system

Constant or fluctuating demand

The *rate of demand* determines the **depletion** rate and the inventory level. The higher the rate of demand, the quicker the inventory is reduced. The rate of demand can be constant (e.g., five units per day), or may fluctuate (e.g., three units on the first day and seven on the second). A *constant demand* reduces the inventory level in equal steps. Graphically, it is shown as a stairway (see cycle 1 in Figure 14.2). The steps of the constant demand can be approximated by a straight line. A *fluctuating* (variable) *demand* is shown by unequal steps, as in cycle 2 of Figure 14.2, and can be approximated by a curve.

Reordering

Reorder points and lead times

To rebuild an inventory, the item is replenished periodically. When the inventory level is reduced to a certain level called the **reorder point,** a **replenishment** order is placed (see Figure 14.3). The time between reordering and receiving the shipment is called the **lead time.**

FIGURE 14.3
Reordering, replenishment, and a shortage

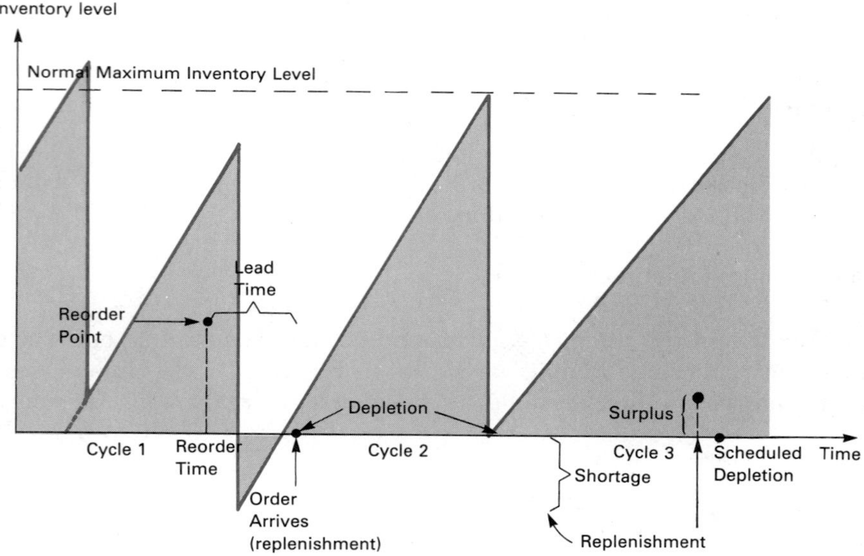

Replenishment, shortages, and surpluses

In some basic inventory models, it is assumed that the reordering is scheduled so that the replenishment will arrive exactly when the inventory level reaches zero. Such an assumption holds if the demand is constant (as shown in cycle 1 of Figure 14.3). However, if the demand fluctuates and/or the lead time varies, the shipment may arrive either before or after the stock is completely depleted; that is, the depletion and replenishment do not coincide. In such a case, a surplus or a shortage will occur. If the shipment arrives *after* depletion, then the demand cannot be met

Shortages result from demand fluctuation or lead time variation and a **shortage** (or **stockout**) will occur. This is shown by the second cycle of Figure 14.3. When the shipment arrives *prior* to depletion, an inventory level larger than zero, or a *surplus*, exists, as demonstrated by the third cycle of Figure 14.3.

Safety stock

Shortages can be eliminated or reduced by establishing a *buffer* or **safety stock.** This topic is discussed in detail in Section 14.15.

The average inventory

For purposes of inventory decision making, as well as for other managerial uses such as insurance and taxation, the concept of an **average inventory** is used. To illustrate, let us assume that during a five-day period the inventory levels are as follows:

Monday	*Tuesday*	*Wednesday*	*Thursday*	*Friday*
16	12	8	4	0

The average inventory is then:

$$\frac{16 + 12 + 8 + 4 + 0}{5} = 8 \text{ units}$$

This is shown in Figure 14.4.

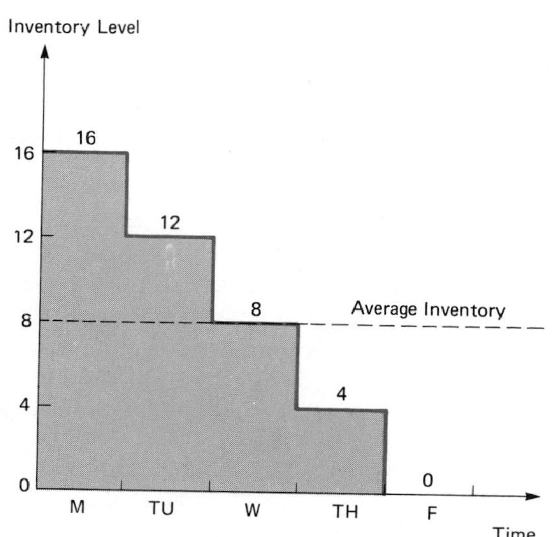

FIGURE 14.4
Average inventory

Average inventory as one half the maximum

If the demand is *constant,* the average inventory can be computed by adding the inventory at the beginning of a cycle (16 in this example) to the inventory at the end of the cycle (0 in this case) and dividing it by 2. If the inventory at the end of the cycle is 0 (as in this example), the *average inventory equals exactly one half of the initial* (or *maximum*) *inventory.* If the demand is not constant, a more complicated formulation is required.

Inventory problems and decisions

The major problem of inventory management is determining the *appropriate inventory level.* This problem is related to the problem of "how much" to order, since the amount ordered determines, in part, the inventory level. Also related is the problem of "when" to order. These three issues appear together in most models. A fourth issue that will affect the inventory level concerns the creation of a safety stock.

Other inventory decisions

Other inventory decisions are often made by management, but they will not be discussed in this text.[1] Some of these decisions are:

- Where to stock.
- How the inventory system should be staffed.
- Whether the inventory system should be computerized.

The most common criteria considered in inventory analysis are inventory-related costs. Inventory models compute these costs, total them, and then search for a policy or an alternative solution that *minimizes* the total cost. Before presenting the models, it is necessary, therefore, to discuss these costs.

14.3 INVENTORY COSTS

Inventory problems are usually examined from a cost rather than from a profit standpoint. The major types of inventory costs are:

Ordering cost

Ordering cost includes all the necessary expenses of placing orders. It is assumed to be a fixed cost per order; that is, each time an order is placed, the same expenses occur regardless of how many units are ordered. Included in the ordering cost are the clerical and paperwork expenses of purchasing, inspection, receiving, bookkeeping, and data processing that

[1] Such decisions are discussed in texts specializing in inventory management. See Green [5], Lewis [10], Silver [16], and Tersine [18].

are directly related to ordering, as well as the expenses of delivery, postage, and the related overhead (such as direct telephone charges). The cost of ordering can be computed by dividing the total annual cost related to ordering by the number of orders processed that year.

Example A typical ordering cost calculation is:

Expense category	*Annual expense for 2,000 orders*	*Annual expense for 5,000 orders*
Department head	$ 25,000	$ 25,000
Clerks (at $13,000 each)	26,000	39,000
Buyers (at $18,000 each)	18,000	36,000
Secretary	12,000	12,000
Receiving clerks (at $14,000)	14,000	28,000
Bookkeeping (accountant)	15,000	20,000
Supplies	1,200	2,000
Phone, postage, miscellaneous	800	1,000
Overhead	20,000	25,000
Total	$132,000	$188,000

If the company processes 2,000 orders, then the average cost per order is 132,000/2,000 = $66. At a volume of 5,000 orders, the cost is 188,000/5,000 = $37.60. The *incremental cost,* however, is:

$$(188{,}000 - 132{,}000)/(5{,}000 - 2{,}000) = \$18.67$$

If our system is at 2,000 orders, and we change to 5,000 orders, then the incremental cost is only $18.67 per order, and this cost must be considered in the analysis. Note that some of the ordering costs are fixed or semifixed, while others are variable.

Holding (carrying) cost

The expenses of holding or carrying the inventory include such components as:

- *Cost of capital:* The interest paid on the capital invested in inventories or the opportunity cost of doing something else with the money.
- *Storage:* Cost of maintaining the storage space. This includes rental fees, lights, heat, security, and janitorial services.
- *Storekeeping operations:* Expenses such as record-keeping and taking of physical inventory.
- *Insurance and taxes.*
- *Obsolescence and deterioration* of the items stored.

Two holding cost expressions

All **holding (carrying) costs** are totaled and expressed either in terms of *dollars per item per year,* or in *percentage of the value of the inventory.*

Example A chair costs $40. To keep the chair in inventory for one year will cost H = $10. Alternatively, we can say that the holding cost is 25 percent of the value of the item (25 percent of $40 is $10).

Shortage (or stockout) cost

Shortage costs occur when an item is out of stock and demand is unsatisfied. Depending on the item under consideration, shortage costs may include the following:

In the case of raw materials: costs of idled production, spoilage of products or materials, and the cost of placing and fulfilling special expediting orders.
In the case of finished goods: cost of "ill will" to the seller (the loss of customers) due to inability to deliver or due to late deliveries.[2]
In the case of replacement parts: costs of idle machines, idle labor, spoilage of materials, and delays in shipment.
In other cases: the shortage of blood or ambulances may cost a life; and a shortage of fire engines may result in excessive damage caused by a fire.

Back orders versus lost sales

Shortages may be temporary (**back orders**), in which case they are eliminated when the supply arrives; or permanent, in the sense that sales are lost.

Item cost

Quantity discounts

Item (or unit) cost is the price paid for one unit of the commodity under consideration. It is not a direct inventory cost, as the items must eventually be procured anyway, but it may be influenced by inventory decisions. For example, ordering large quantities may result in a lower per unit price due to **quantity discounts.**

14.4 THE ECONOMIC ORDER QUANTITY MODEL

How much to order

The **economic order quantity (EOQ)** model, which was developed prior to World War I, is the most elementary of all inventory models. Its objective is to determine the *optimal quantity to order*. It answers the following questions:

1. How much should be ordered each time?
2. When should it be ordered?
3. What will the total cost be?

[2] The cost of ill will or the loss of goodwill reflects the anticipated loss of future profits due to customers' dissatisfaction.

4. What will the average inventory level be?
5. What will the maximum inventory level be?

Assumptions

The EOQ model assumes the following:

- The demand for the item is constant over time (e.g., two units per day).
- Within the range of quantities to be ordered, the per unit holding cost and ordering cost are independent of the quantity ordered.
- The replenishment is scheduled in such a way that shipments arrive exactly when the inventory level reaches zero. Therefore, there will never be a shortage or a surplus.
- Since only one item is being considered, orders for different items are independent of each other.

The behavior of the inventory level under the above assumptions is shown in Figure 14.5. An examination of the figure indicates that all cycles are equal, that orders arrive exactly when the inventory level reaches zero, that the order quantity Q is equal in all cycles, and that the maximum inventory level is also Q.

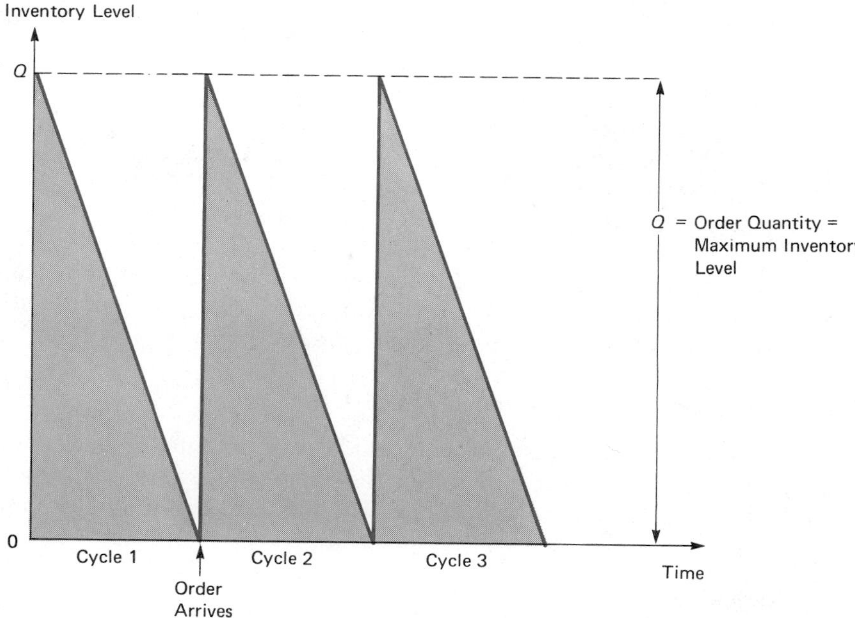

FIGURE 14.5
The inventory process

Example

Everglades University uses 1,200 boxes of typing paper each year. The university is trying to determine how many boxes to order at one time. The information it considers is:

$$\text{Annual demand, } D = 1{,}200 \text{ boxes}$$
$$\text{Ordering cost, } K = \$5 \text{ per order}$$
$$\text{Holding cost, } H = \$1.20 \text{ per box, per year}$$

The problem is to find the quantity to be ordered, Q. (As we shall see, finding this quantity will also tell us how often to order.)

Figure 14.6 demonstrates three possible ordering policies: annually, quarterly, and monthly. Let us examine these:

1. Annual policy: Order once a year, therefore, $Q = 1{,}200$ boxes.
2. Quarterly: Order once a quarter, four times a year. $Q = 1{,}200/4 = 300$ boxes at a time.
3. Monthly: Order once a month, 12 times a year. $Q = 1{,}200/12 = 100$ boxes at a time.

FIGURE 14.6
Inventory level under three different ordering policies

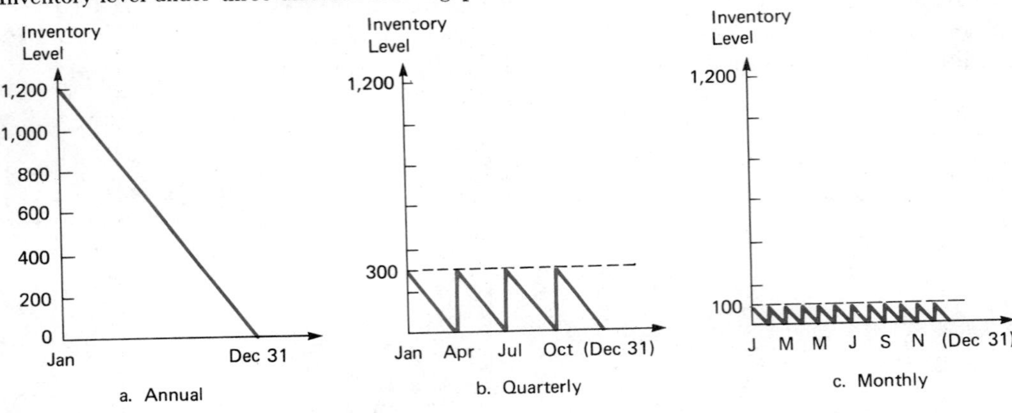

Other ordering policies could also be considered; for example, once a week, semiannually, or once every two years. The problem faced by management is: *Which ordering policy is the best?*

Which policy costs less?

Solution using a trial-and-error approach

One way of solving this problem would be to compute the incremental total annual inventory cost for each of the suggested policies. The policy with the lowest total cost is the best one. The total cost is given by Equation 14.1.[3]

[3] The total annual inventory cost includes only the relevant (incremental) costs. Therefore, such factors as the cost of the units and the cost of the analysis (which can be considered equal for all alternative policies) are not included in the model.

$$TC = T_O + T_H$$

$$\begin{Bmatrix}\text{Total annual}\\ \text{inventory cost}\end{Bmatrix} = \begin{Bmatrix}\text{Total annual}\\ \text{ordering cost}\end{Bmatrix} + \begin{Bmatrix}\text{Total annual}\\ \text{holding cost}\end{Bmatrix} \quad (14.1)$$

Let us execute the calculation step by step:

Step 1. Find total annual ordering cost, T_O The total annual ordering cost is given as the number of times an order is placed, N, multipled by the ordering cost, K. This is expressed in Equation 14.2.

$$T_O = NK \quad (14.2)$$

But, the number of times an order is placed during a year is given by the total yearly demand, D, divided by the order quantity, Q:

$$N = \frac{D}{Q} \quad (14.3)$$

Thus, the equation for T_O is:

$$T_O = NK = \frac{D}{Q}K \quad (14.4)$$

T_O in the three proposed policies is:

Annual:	$N = 1,$	$K = 5,$	$T_O = 1(5) = \$\ 5$
Quarterly:	$N = 4,$	$K = 5,$	$T_O = 4(5) = \$20$
Monthly:	$N = 12,$	$K = 5,$	$T_O = 12(5) = \$60$

The above values are entered in Figure 14.7, as points a (for the annual policy), b (for quarterly), and c (for monthly). Points a, b, and c are then connected, resulting in a *total annual ordering cost* curve. The curve indicates that as the order quantity, Q, increases, the total annual cost of ordering decreases. The reason for this is that the larger the order size, the fewer the number of orders placed per year.

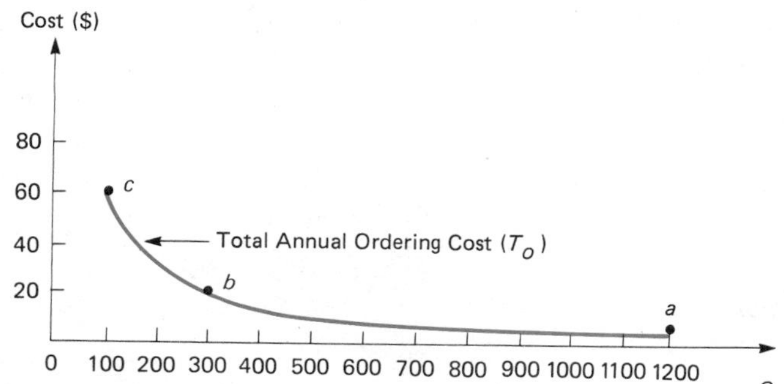

FIGURE 14.7
The total annual ordering cost curve

Step 2. Find total annual holding cost, T_H The total annual holding cost can be computed by multiplying the holding cost (measured in dollars per item per day), H, by the *number of units in inventory* each day of the year, and summing. However, since the inventory level is changing from day to day, the number of units in inventory fluctuates over time. Thus, it is easier to solve this problem by using the **average inventory** on hand. When the demand is constant, the average inventory is the midway point between the highest and the lowest inventory level. Since one of the EOQ assumptions requires that the lowest inventory level be zero, the average inventory equals exactly one half of the maximum inventory. However, in the EOQ model, the maximum inventory equals the order quantity, Q. Consequently, the average inventory equals one half of Q:

$$\text{Average inventory} = \frac{Q}{2} \tag{14.5}$$

Therefore, the total annual inventory holding cost, T_H, will be:

$$T_H = H\frac{Q}{2} \tag{14.6}$$

The total annual inventory holding cost for the three proposed ordering policies is:

$$\text{Annual:} \quad Q = 1{,}200, \quad T_H = 1.20\left(\frac{1{,}200}{2}\right) = \$720$$

$$\text{Quarterly:} \quad Q = 300, \quad T_H = 1.20\left(\frac{300}{2}\right) = \$180$$

$$\text{Monthly:} \quad Q = 100, \quad T_H = 1.20\left(\frac{100}{2}\right) = \$\ 60$$

It is evident that the value of Q will be in direct proportion to the value of T_H. This information is shown graphically in Figure 14.8.

Step 3. Compute total annual inventory cost, TC Using Equation 14.1 the total annual cost (designated TC, or sometimes TC[Q]) for the proposed policies is:

Policy	$T_O + T_H = TC$	
Annual	5 + 720 = 725	
Quarterly	20 + 180 = 200	
Monthly	60 + 60 = 120	←*Minimum*

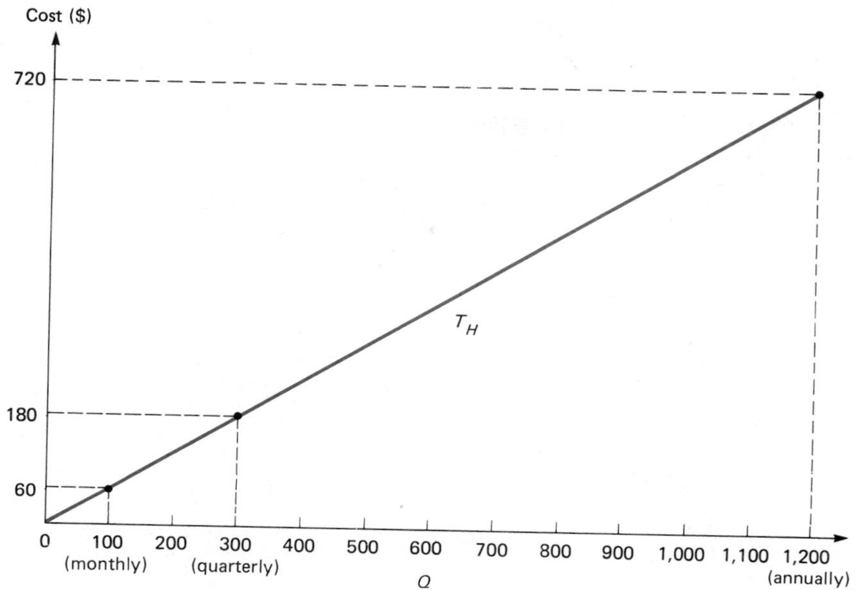

FIGURE 14.8
Total annual holding cost (T_H)

Comparing the three alternatives, the best ordering policy is "Monthly," since it has the lowest total cost of \$120. However, since other possible ordering policies (e.g., semiannually, weekly) were not checked, no assurance exists that monthly ordering is indeed the *optimal* policy. To check *all* possible policies may involve much computational work, especially since these calculations must be made and continuously updated for every item in the stock. Therefore, a more efficient method is provided through the economic order quantity (EOQ) formula.

Checking other possible policies, too

The EOQ Formula

It was shown previously that the total cost, TC, can be expressed as:

$$TC = T_O + T_H = \frac{DK}{Q} + \frac{HQ}{2} \tag{14.7}$$

where D is the annual demand, K is the ordering cost, H is the holding cost, and Q is the quantity to be ordered. The problem is to find that Q for which TC is the minimum.

Graphical solution One way to find TC is to combine T_O and T_H graphically and then to find a minimum point on the combined curve.

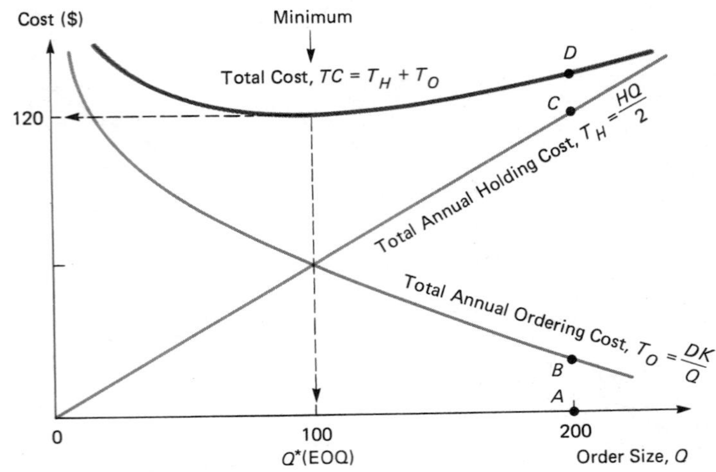

FIGURE 14.9 Ordering, holding, and total cost variation with order size

Figure 14.9 shows TC as the summation of T_O and T_H.[4] The minimum value of TC occurs at the intersection of T_H and T_O,[5] that is, where T_H equals T_O. This approach is very cumbersome.

Analytical solution Through calculus, the optimal value of Q (designated Q^*) can be found analytically.[6] It occurs where the total annual holding cost equals the total annual ordering cost:

$$\frac{HQ^*}{2} = \frac{KD}{Q^*} \tag{14.8}$$

EOQ: The *optimal*

By manipulation of Equation 14.8 it is possible to compute the *optimal* value of Q;[7] that is, the EOQ.

---

[4] Summation of two curves is done as shown in Figure 14.9 for $Q = 200$ (point A). Take the distance A to B and add it to the distance A to C. The result is the distance A to D.

[5] With other forms of cost curves, the minimum point on the total cost curve may occur at a point other than the intersection.

[6] The EOQ can also be obtained through calculus: $TC = HQ/2 + KD/Q$. Setting the first derivative to 0:

$$\frac{dTC}{dQ} = \frac{H}{2} - \frac{KD}{Q^2} = 0 \quad \text{or} \quad Q^* = \sqrt{\frac{2KD}{H}}$$

To verify that this is a minimum point, we check for a positive second derivative:

$$\frac{d^2TC}{dQ^2} = \frac{2KD}{Q^3} > 0$$

Since the second derivative is positive (K, D, and Q can take only positive values), the point is a minimum point indeed.

[7] Multiply each side by Q; then divide each side by $H/2$.

$$(Q^*)^2 = \frac{2KD}{H} \quad \text{or} \quad Q^* = \sqrt{\frac{2KD}{H}} \qquad (14.9)$$

where K is the ordering cost (in dollars), D is the annual demand (in units), and H is the holding cost (in dollars per unit per year).

Solution to the example

$$Q^* = \sqrt{\frac{2(5)(1{,}200)}{1.20}} = 100 \text{ boxes}$$

The optimal solution calls for an order size of 100 boxes at a time. For a yearly demand of 1,200, this means 12 orders per year, or once a month. Thus, the monthly order policy is indeed optimal.

Additional information provided by EOQ

In addition to the size of the order to be placed, the EOQ can be used to provide the following information:

a. *The best number of orders* to be placed in a year. Using Equation 14.3 we find:

$$N = \frac{D}{Q^*} = \frac{1{,}200}{100} = 12 \text{ times}$$

b. *The maximum inventory on hand, and the average inventory level.* The maximum inventory is equal to Q^* or 100 in the example. The average inventory is one half of Q^*, which is 50 in the example.

c. *The number of days' supply.* The computation of the EOQ also helps provide the number of **days' supply,** d. This information tells management the length of each inventory cycle. This is given in Equation 14.10.

Other information from the EOQ

$$d = \frac{365}{N} \qquad (14.10)$$

In the example:

$$d = \frac{365}{N} = \frac{365}{12} = 30.4 \text{ days}$$

Note: If the company works less than 365 days a year, use the actual number of days worked.

d. *The dollar value of an optimal order and of the average inventory.*[8] Sometimes it is useful to know the dollar value of the EOQ; this is

[8] This information is important since the dollar value of the average inventory is useful for such purposes as cash flow determination, tax assessment, and calculation of depreciation.

obtained by multiplying Q^* by the unit cost. Assume in the example that the cost of one box of paper is \$10. Thus, Q in dollars is 100(10) or \$1,000. That is, the university orders \$1,000 worth of supplies at a time. Similarly, the dollar value of the average inventory is:

$$\frac{100}{2}(10) = \$500$$

e. *The total annual cost.* Using Equation 14.7, the total annual cost (excluding the cost of the goods themselves) can now be computed.

$$TC = \frac{DK}{Q^*} + \frac{HQ^*}{2} = \frac{(1{,}200)5}{100} + \frac{1.2(100)}{2} = 60 + 60 = \$120$$

$T_H = T_O$ in the optimal solution

Notice that the two components of the total cost, the ordering cost and the holding cost, *must equal* each other whenever the optimal Q is used (\$60 each in the example.)[9]

14.5 APPLICATION OF THE EOQ MODEL

In applying the EOQ formula the following points may be helpful:

Holding cost given as a percentage of value

It is sometimes common to express the holding cost as a percentage of the value in inventory. For example, it may be stated that the inventory holding costs are 30 percent per year. This means that if the item is worth \$20, then $H = .3 \times \$20 = \$6$ per item, per year. In general, $H = IC$ where I = Annual percentage and C = Per item cost.

With a 10–15 percent cost of capital (interest per year) it is not unusual to find that the cost of holding inventory is 30 percent or even higher.

When the demand is given in dollars

Demand in dollars

In some cases, the demand for an item is given in terms of dollars rather than in units. Two cases are then distinguished:

[9] If for some reason Q^* is known, *the input variables* can be found as:

The ordering cost: $$K = \frac{Q^{*2}H}{2D} \quad (14.11)$$

The annual demand: $$D = \frac{Q^{*2}H}{2K} \quad (14.12)$$

The holding cost, per unit per year: $$H = \frac{2KD}{Q^{*2}} \quad (14.13)$$

1. *The unit cost is given.* In this case, simply convert the demand to units by dividing the annual dollar amount by the unit cost.
2. *The unit cost is not given.* In such a case, the holding cost *must* be expressed as a percentage.

Example A recreation department's annual budget for supplies is \$200,000. The ordering cost is \$50, and the holding cost is 20 percent of the value of the item. Find the EOQ, the optimal number of orders, and the total inventory costs.

Given:

D: Annual *dollar value* of demand = \$200,000
K: Ordering cost, in dollars = \$50
H: Holding cost = .2 (i.e., 20 percent)

Solution:

Using the EOQ formula (Equation 14.9):

$$Q^* = \sqrt{\frac{2KD}{H}} = \sqrt{\frac{2(50)(200{,}000)}{0.2}} = \$10{,}000$$

Thus, the optimal policy is to order \$10,000 worth of supplies at a time. Because the yearly demand is \$200,000, there will be N = 20 orders per year (Equation 14.3).

The total annual inventory costs are:

$$TC = \frac{KD}{Q^*} + \frac{Q^*H}{2} = \frac{50(200{,}000)}{10{,}000} + \frac{10{,}000(.2)}{2} = \$2{,}000$$

Sensitivity Analysis: The cost impact of deviations from the EOQ

Sensitivity analysis

In some situations, it is not convenient to actually order the EOQ. For example, the standard package size may differ from the EOQ, or there may be insufficient funds to purchase the EOQ amount. Using the university's supply situation in Section 14.4 as an example, the EOQ calls for 100 boxes, but suppose that they are packed 40 to a case. In such an event, it is possible to buy either 80 or 120 boxes, but not 100. Let us examine the effect of overordering (120), versus underordering (80).

For 80 boxes The total annual cost for an order of 80 will be (use Equation 14.7 with Q = 80):

$$TC = \frac{DK}{Q} + \frac{HQ}{2} = \frac{(1{,}200)5}{80} + \frac{(1.2)80}{2} = \$123$$

Compared with the cost of \$120 for the EOQ of 100 (as previously computed), there is an increase of only \$3, which is about 2.5 percent, even though the order quantity was decreased by 20 percent.

For 120 boxes:

$$TC = \frac{5(1{,}200)}{120} + \frac{120(1.2)}{2} = \$122$$

Thus, overordering by 20 percent caused the total annual inventory cost to rise by less than 2 percent.

Cost insensitive to order quantity

In a similar manner, it can be shown that a change of 10 percent in the order quantity increases the total inventory cost by only about 0.5 percent. In other words, TC in the EOQ formula is *relatively insensitive to changes in the order quantity.* This property gives management greater flexibility in implementing the EOQ since the theoretical order quantity can be changed by as much as 20 percent with only a slight impact on the total inventory cost.

Note that the sensitivity for decreasing the EOQ is *larger* than the sensitivity for increasing it (cost increase of $3 on the downside versus cost increase of $2 on the upside for a change of 20 units from EOQ). Another example is that changing the EOQ from 100 to 50 (deviation of 50), will increase the total cost from $120 to $150 (an increase of 25 percent). A look at Figure 14.9 shows us why this is so. The curve of total cost increases faster when Q decreases, especially when Q is very small.

The sensitivity of the EOQ to changes in input data

Let us examine the EOQ formula:

$$Q^* = \sqrt{\frac{2KD}{H}}$$

One can see that the quantity Q^* is proportional to the square root of the input data (K, D, and H). This means that if K or D quadruples, for example, then Q^* will be doubled, and if H quadruples, then Q^* will be halved. Table 14.1 compares the original university purchasing problem with three changes: change 1, quadruple D; change 2, quadruple K; change 3, quadruple H. In all three cases, the total cost doubled.

TABLE 14.1
Cost effect of data changes

	Original problem	*Change* ①	Change ②	Change ③
Given	$D = 1{,}200$ $K = 5$ $H = 1.20$	$D = 4{,}800$ $K = 5$ $H = 1.20$	$D = 1{,}200$ $K = 20$ $H = 1.20$	$D = 1{,}200$ $K = 5$ $H = 4.80$
Computed	$Q^* = 100$	$Q^* = 200$	$Q^* = 200$	$Q^* = 50$
Total cost	$TC = \$120$	$TC = \$240$	$TC = \$240$	$TC = \$240$

The managerial implication of the sensitivity of the EOQ is that the order quantity should *not* be increased or decreased in direct proportion to the changes in the input data. Some managers make the mistake of doubling their EOQ when the demand doubles. Instead, they should increase it only by $\sqrt{2} = 1.41$, since the EOQ is directly proportional to the *square root* of the demand.

Nonproportional changes

When to order (the reorder point)

The decision *when* to order does not depend on the optimal value of Q. Rather, it is a function of the demand and the lead time to resupply. For example, if the demand is 50 per week and the lead time is two weeks, then the order should be placed when the inventory level is 100 units (two weeks' supply). The reorder point (designated ROP) is a practical concept used in many inventory systems.

Rounding the result

The computed EOQ may be noninteger; for example, 6.3 units. In such a situation, the result may be rounded to 6 or 7. The total cost for 6 should be calculated and compared to that for 7 to decide whether to round down or up. Rounding is often done to comply with required bulk quantities, such as six cartons per case.

14.6 DISCUSSION OF THE EOQ ASSUMPTIONS

In order to derive the EOQ, a list of assumptions was outlined in Section 14.4. These assumptions enabled us to develop a rather simple inventory formula. These assumptions were:

Constant demand In the EOQ model, a constant demand was assumed (e.g., five units per day). In reality, demand may fluctuate. In such a case, it is necessary to modify the EOQ formulation (e.g., by using safety stock as shown in Section 14.15 or by using special stochastic models (see Lewis [10]).

Constant unit price The EOQ analysis that assumes constant unit price can be extended to include variable prices due to discounts as larger quantities are ordered. This procedure is discussed in Section 14.12.

The EOQ assumptions

Constant holding cost It is assumed that the holding cost is constant. However, as the level of inventory increases, the holding cost may decrease (e.g., due to storage efficiency) or increase (e.g., due to higher capital costs). Such a situation can be handled by a procedure similar to the one used for quantity discounts.

Constant ordering cost This assumption is usually valid for limited ranges of order quantities. For exceptional cases, the EOQ model can be modified by computing different values for different ordering costs. Again, this situation resembles the quantity discount case discussed in Part B of this chapter.

No shortages The assumption is made that all demand is immediately supplied and therefore there will never be a shortage. As long as the demand is constant and delivery time is either constant or zero, the assumption will hold. Otherwise, a safety stock should be added or a modified model with a shortage (Section 14.14) can be used.

Instantaneous (or fixed) delivery time It is assumed that deliveries are received on a desired date. This can be assured by instantaneous delivery; for example, if the supplier happens to be in the same area and can deliver quickly on short notice. Alternatively, if the lead time and the demand are both constant, an order can be placed so that the delivery will arrive exactly on a desired date. But in the case of variations in the lead time or the demand, the EOQ must be modified as shown in Part B.

Joint ordering

Independent orders Quite often, several items are purchased from the same supplier, and the ordering cost can be reduced by ordering several items in one order. This saves paperwork, transportation costs, and may also result in discounts. Special models have been developed to deal with situations where several items are ordered together, a practice known as **joint ordering.** (See Tersine [18].)

Single goal of cost minimization This assumption is not always true. Sometimes, for example, the service level is more important (e.g., in blood inventory).

Summary

The EOQ model is summarized in Figure 14.10.

FIGURE 14.10
Summary of the EOQ model

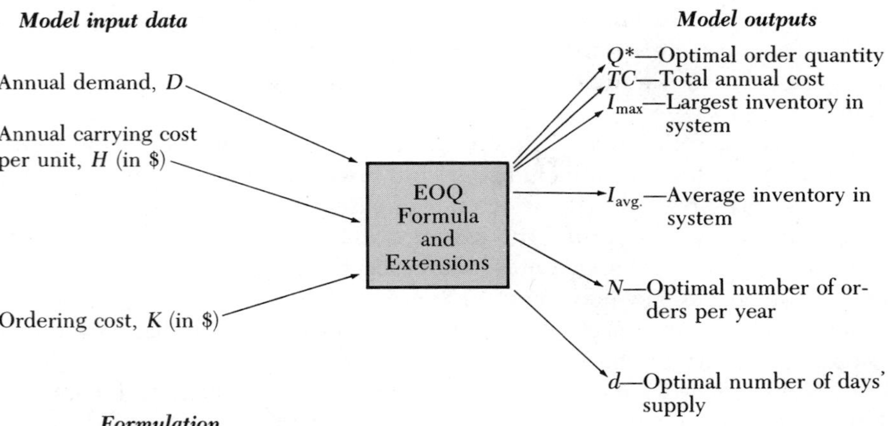

14.7 INVENTORY SYSTEMS

The A-B-C classification system

Some organizations carry such a large number (thousands) of items in inventory that it would be impractical to try to exercise control over every single item, using the EOQ analysis. Remember that each time any input (such as demand or ordering cost) is changed, the EOQ has to be recomputed.

One method frequently used to identify the items that deserve tight control is called the **A-B-C classification system** or the *value-volume analysis.*[10]

A-B-C, value-volume, 80–20

The A-B-C classification system segregates all items in stock into three groups, A, B, and C, based on the annual dollar inventory value of the items.[11]

The A group Group A usually includes a small (e.g., 10) percent of the items that account for a large (e.g., 70) percent of the total annual inventory cost for the company (see Figure 14.11).[12] Special attention should be paid to every item in this group, and application of the EOQ formula is recommended for every one of the items.

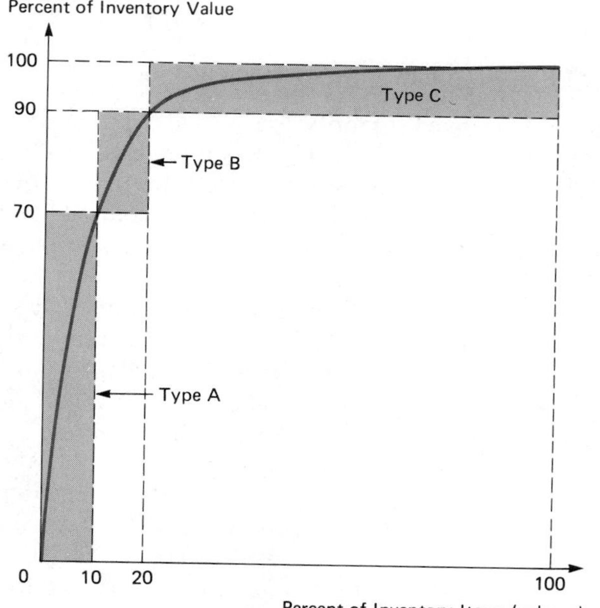

FIGURE 14.11
A-B-C inventory categories

[10] Other names are the *Pareto* analysis and the "80–20" method. The idea is based on the economic phenomenon observed by Pareto, an Italian economist (1848–1923), that a few items usually account for the majority of the value.

[11] Other possible criteria for classifying items are the cost, amount of use, or importance of the items.

[12] The percentages of the A, B, and C categories and their inventory value may vary according to the situation.

The B group Items in this group constitute another small (e.g., 10) percent in inventory volume, but are worth only 20 percent or so of the total value. Accordingly, items in this group merit somewhat less control than those in group A. For example, an EOQ may still be used, but updating due to changes in input data may be done only once a year.

Adding the groups A and B together shows that perhaps 20 percent of the items account for possibly 90 percent of the dollar value of the inventory.

The C group The remaining 80 percent or so of the items account for perhaps only 10 percent of the inventory dollar value. These are small usage items such as nuts, bolts, and nails. Control over such items should be minimal since the potential saving rarely justifies the expense of the control exercised.

Different amounts of control

Classification into three categories is traditional but not mandatory. Classification into two, four, or even more categories can be found in some companies. What is important to remember is that some items in inventory deserve detailed and continuous planning and control, whereas others do not merit such consideration. Thus, different classes of items should be subjected to different inventory systems, as discussed next.

The fixed-quantity (perpetual) system

Safety stock

The **fixed-quantity (perpetual) system** dictates that a fixed-quantity order be placed each time the inventory level reaches the reorder point. The fixed quantity could be determined by the EOQ formula. A safety stock is usually added (at a level determined by experience or by computation, as shown in Section 14.15). This system is used mainly for type A items.

The two-bin system

A special, less expensive to administer version of the fixed-quantity system, called the **two-bin system,** is frequently used for type B and C items. The inventory is stored in a large bin, with the exception of a safety stock kept in a smaller bin. Demand depletion of the large bin acts as a signal to reorder. While awaiting replenishment of the large bin, demand is supplied from the small bin. When the shipment arrives, the smaller bin is refilled first and the remainder then goes into the larger bin. The amount to be ordered can be based on the EOQ, but is usually based on experience. This system is practical if the stock can be conveniently separated into two bins; if not, a perpetual auditing (counting) of the amount on hand (balance) is required, increasing the cost substantially.

The fixed-time (periodic or s,S) system

s,S system

The **fixed-time (periodic or s,S) system** involves a periodic auditing (e.g., once a month) of the inventory. If at that time the stock of an item is below the predesignated level, s, an order is placed to return the inventory level to another predetermined, maximum level S.[13] Although amounts ordered each cycle will vary, as shown in Figure 14.12, this system allows *joint reordering* of items in the same period at a substantial savings. The major disadvantages of the s,S system are:

Joint reordering possible

1. A large safety stock may be needed to reduce the possibility of shortages.
2. The nonuniform order sizes may be inconvenient to fill. The method is used mainly for group A items and sometimes for group B items.

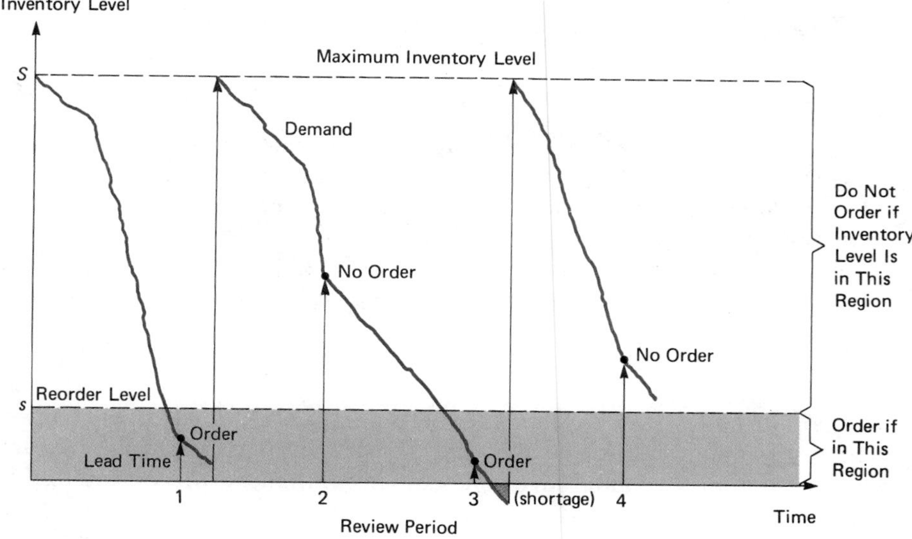

FIGURE 14.12
Periodic (s, S) inventory system

A version of this method is the so-called **base-stock system,** in which orders are placed as soon as demand occurs, *regardless of the inventory level,* to bring the inventory back to its maximum level, S. This method is especially useful where the number of units in inventory is very small (e.g., 1–5), the units are expensive, and the ordering cost is negligible.

The base-stock system

Rule of thumb systems

Type C items are typically of such low value that the effort required either to determine the EOQ or audit frequently cannot be economically justified. Thus, these items are typically ordered on the basis of experience or when stock is depleted. The control imposed on such items is minimal.

Computerized systems

Inventory systems in medium- and large-sized organizations are usually computerized. The computer system follows the inventory level in a

Computer use is common

[13] The levels of s and S can be determined by a mathematical model or by experience.

manner similar to that of a computerized banking system following a cash balance. All transactions are recorded, and the balance is computed immediately. Whenever the inventory level is at or below the reorder point, the computer signals to place a new order. The same computer may issue and print the purchasing orders. The reorder point and the order quantity can be computed with the aid of one of the models presented in this chapter, by the aid of more complicated models such as MRP (see Part B), with the use of simulation (see example in Chapter 16), or by using a trial-and-error approach. In addition, computers (Section 14.16) are used to prepare management reports concerning the overall inventory system.

"Zero-inventory" systems and the Japanese approach

Zero inventory

With the high cost of capital (interest rates near 20 percent) in 1981, inventory holding costs became so high that some companies decided to adopt a "no-inventory" policy. The concept behind this system is called *total life cycle* (from acquisition to disposition), and an attempt is made to minimize or even eliminate inventories. In addition to saving holding costs, there is a savings in internal material handling as well. For example, several hospitals are using this system by having daily deliveries from large suppliers located in the same city. (For the story, see reference [15]).

Just-in-time

While no-inventory systems are becoming more common in the United States, their equivalent, "just-in-time" or JIT, is very popular in Japan, the classic example being Toyota's "Kanban" system [6]. According to this approach, only the necessary products are made, at the necessary time, in the necessary quantities. Thus, stock on hand is held down to a minimum.

The impetus behind JIT in Japan is different than in the United States, however: it is to eliminate waste, particularly in facility space, which is scarce in Japan. Stores of unused materials are perceived as using up precious space. The goal, then, is to turn every production system into a continuously flowing system of materials, where items pass through the system one by one and are never in storage.

But the JIT system has produced many unexpected side benefits for the Japanese as well. With no stores of material sitting idle, there is little inventory cost, of course. And with each worker passing his or her completed item to the next worker, defects are caught immediately and the reason corrected. Scrap also becomes immediately apparent and, thus, efforts are made to eliminate it. And without bins of material to store, locate, and move, the scheduling and management process is much simpler. For further details see Huang [7], Schonberger [12,13], or Walleigh [19].

14.8 CONCLUDING REMARKS

The models presented in this chapter deal with the simplest inventory situations. Yet they are widely applied in inventory control systems and give satisfactory results even in places where real-life conditions do not conform exactly to the models' formats and the underlying assumptions. The insensitivity of the models provides management with more flexibility, enabling deviation from optimal solutions at a small cost.

Inventory models are one of the most common applications of management science. This is partly due to their insensitivity, but mainly attributable to the possibility of realizing quick and significant savings. Further, since the application of such models only affects people minimally, human resistance to implementation is not much of a problem.

The models are basically cost models attempting to minimize the total inventory expense. This inventory expense may be extremely high in some instances and thus, so are the potential savings.

14.9 PROBLEMS FOR PART A

1. The Elco Company needs 10,000 lamps annually. It costs $45 to place one order and 10 cents to store each lamp for a year.
   Find:
   a. The economic order quantity.
   b. The total inventory cost per year.
   c. How many orders will be placed each year.
2. Sunshine Corporation uses 840,000 bags of fertilizer each year for its orange groves. It costs the company $100 to place an order and 50 cents to store a bag for a year. How many month's supply should the company purchase at one time using the economic order quantity formula?
3. Columbia City buys office supplies for $500,000 each year. It costs $80 to place one order. Annual per item holding costs are 20 percent.
   a. What is the dollar value of the EOQ?
   b. How many times should orders be placed each year?
   c. What is the total annual ordering cost?
   d. What is the total annual carrying cost?
4. Eastwood State Park uses 1,000 bags of food each month. It costs $30 to place a purchase order, and the carrying cost is $1.125 per bag per year.
   a. Find the economic order quantity.
   b. How many months' supply of food are contained in one order?
5. Assume an inventory system where a demand of 2,500 units per year must be supplied and where orders are shipped immediately.
   a. Find how often orders should be placed (how many times a year) if the ordering cost is $40 per order, and the cost of the product is $1 per unit. The annual per unit carrying cost is 20 percent of the value of the product.
   b. Find the total carrying and ordering cost.
   c. What will happen to the EOQ if demand increases to 10,000 units? What will happen to the total inventory cost?
6. American Department Store sells 4,050 vacuum cleaners a year. One cleaner occupies 6 square feet of storage space. Each cleaner costs $50, and the annual per unit holding cost is 16 percent of each cleaner. Placing an order costs $32. There is presently an area of 900 square feet for storage. Using the EOQ, would it be profitable for the store to increase the storage area if it costs 50 cents a square foot per year?
7. The Costly Company buys its raw materials 10 times a year, 100 units each time. It is known that this purchasing policy is an optimal one (most economic). The company pays $50 per unit. Annual carrying cost is 20 percent of the value stored.
   Find:
   a. The cost of placing one order (ordering cost).
   b. The total cost (ordering, carrying, and parts) for one year.
   c. Assume that the yearly demand has increased from X to $4X$, all other conditions

remain the same; what will the new economic lot size be? What general conclusions may you arrive at?

8. Producers Company is using $200,000 of a certain material per year. The inventory holding cost is 20 percent. The cost of placing an order is $50.
   a. How often should an order for the material be placed?
   b. What is the total inventory cost involved?
   c. The company wants to place four orders a year; how much more than the optimal solution found in parts *(a)* and *(b)* will it cost the company?
   d. After establishing the optimal policy, it was found that there is a price increase of 10 percent in the material. What ordering policy would you suggest now?
   e. What will the effect on the total inventory cost be if the company orders once a month? (Compare to part *(b)* of this problem.)

9. Find the reorder point (number of units still remaining in stock) for the following three situations:

	Annual demand	*Lead time*
Case A	5,200	2 weeks
Case B	60	1 month
Case C	600	17 days

Assume 50 working weeks and 300 working days per year.

10. The following data give expenditures for carrying light bulbs in a department store.

Annual sales (units)	10,000
Annual cost of capital	$1,200.00
Insurance (per unit)	.05
Taxes and licenses (per unit)	.03
Rent, maintenance (per unit)	.12
Annual paperwork	800.00

Find H, the annual carrying cost per unit.

11. Northwest Hospital currently buys surgical gloves in lots of 1,200 boxes once every four months. The carrying cost per box is $12.50 per unit per year, and the ordering cost is $100 per order.
   Find:
   a. The economic order quantity.
   b. The annual inventory cost. Compare it to the annual cost under the existing purchasing policy.
   c. Suppose that it is possible to buy only in lots of 100 boxes. How many boxes should the hospital buy?

12. CORDON Industries produces 7,200 energy conserving devices each year. The company sells these units at $10 apiece. CORDON's objective is to produce these units at the least possible cost. One option is to produce all the units once a year. Alternatively, the company may produce several times during the year. Each such production period is called a "run" and these runs are equal in size. Assume that the start-up cost for each product run is $300 and the holding cost is computed at 30 percent.
   Find:
   a. The annual cost of one run per year.
   b. The optimal size and cost of the production run.
   c. The optimal number of production runs per year.

13. For what household items do you use: *(a)* a perpetual, *(b)* a periodic, or *(c)* a rule of thumb inventory system?

14. Which items in a typical household would be classified as type A items? Which as type C items (in an A-B-C classification system)?

15. What would the modification be to the EOQ formula if the carrying charge is a function of the *maximum* inventory level rather than the average?

16. Compare the concept of the A-B-C classification system with the concept of the critical path in PERT/CPM.

17. A company has sales offices in Miami, Tampa, and Jacksonville. The annual unit sales in these cities are 40,000, 8,000, and 16,000, respectively. The company is considering opening a central inventory warehouse instead of the three existing regional warehouses.

    Inventory holding costs, which are $10 per unit per year, are estimated to be 20 percent lower in the central location. Ordering cost, $30 per order, is expected to stay the same. It is further expected that there will be an additional transportation cost of 10 cents per unit under the proposed centralization. Should the company use a centralized warehouse? What assumption *must* be made in order to answer this question?

PART B: EXTENSIONS

14.10 QUANTITY DISCOUNTS

Sellers frequently offer buyers a price discount for purchasing large quantities ("cheaper by the dozen"). There may be several price intervals (or price breaks) such as \$10 each unit for quantities up to 99, \$9 each unit for 100 to 499, \$8 each unit for 500 up to 999, and \$7 each unit for 1,000 and over.

"Cheaper by the dozen"

The practice of quantity discounts is widely spread since it offers advantages to both buyer and seller. These are listed, together with some possible disadvantages, in Table 14.2.

TABLE 14.2 Quantity buying considerations

	Advantages	*Disadvantages*
Buyer	Lower unit price Less paperwork Cheaper transportation Fewer stockouts Uniform goods (coming from same shipment) Security (against such factors as strikes, price increases)	Larger inventories Higher holding cost Risk of deterioration and obsolescence Older stock on hand
Seller	Cheaper transportation Less paperwork Larger production runs (thus, lower production costs per unit)	Lower unit prices Less bargaining power with buyers

We distinguish two cases of discounting:

Two types of discounts

a. A discount is offered at one price level.
b. A discount is offered at several levels (price breaks).

Example 1—Discount offered at one level

A conditional discount

The city of Northstar uses 100 replacement lamps a month for its streetlights. Each lamp costs the city \$8. Ordering costs are estimated at \$27 per order and the holding costs (primarily the cost of capital) are 25 percent. The city currently orders according to the EOQ. The supplier has now offered the city a 2 percent discount *if* the city will buy 600 lamps at a time. Should the city accept the offer?

Solution

Given:

$D = 100$ units per month $\times$ 12 months $= 1{,}200$ units per year
$H = .25 \times 8.00 = \$2.00$ per lamp per year
$K = \$27$ per order

$$EOQ = \sqrt{\frac{2 \times 27 \times 1{,}200}{2}} = 180 \text{ lamps}$$

The current total annual inventory cost is:

$$TC = \frac{27 \times 1{,}200}{180} + \frac{180 \times 2}{2} = \$360 \text{ per year}$$

To this cost should be added the item cost, which is relevant when discounts on the item cost are considered. If we let P_i be the item cost at the ith price break, then,

$$\text{Annual cost of items} = P_iD = \$8 \times 1{,}200 \text{ lamps} = \$9{,}600 \quad (14.14)$$

Thus, the total *system* cost is $360 + $9,600 = $9,960.

Review of the discount offer. The analysis is conducted on an annual basis. The offer to buy 600 units at a 2 percent discount will reduce the item cost, the holding cost will be higher since the city will buy 600 units instead of 180, and the ordering cost will decrease with fewer orders. The analysis is shown in Table 14.3 and illustrated in Figure 14.13.

Conclusion. The discount offer should be rejected. The city will be at a disadvantage to accept it. A higher discount rate should be negotiated instead (e.g., a 5 percent discount is favorable).

TABLE 14.3
Cost comparision on an annual basis

No discount		*Discount*	
$Q^* = 180$ $K = 27$ $D = 1{,}200$ $H = 2.00$		$Q = 600$ (given) $K = 27$ $D = 1{,}200$ $H_d = 1.96$, (2 percent less than previous H)	
Total annual ordering cost = $	180	$\frac{KD}{Q} = \frac{27 \times 1{,}200}{600} =$	$54
Total annual holding cost =	180	$\frac{QH}{2} = \frac{600 \times 1.96}{2} =$	588
Total annual unit cost =	9,600	2 percent off	9,408
Total cost	9,960		10,050

Note: H has been changed in the proportion of the discount. The reason for this is that the major portion of H is the cost of capital. Since the unit cost decreases, the cost of capital will decrease also. The new H is subscripted with d = discount, i.e., H_d.

Example 2—Discounts at several price breaks

General Hospital buys a certain antibiotic from a large supplier. The drug can be bought at the following prices:

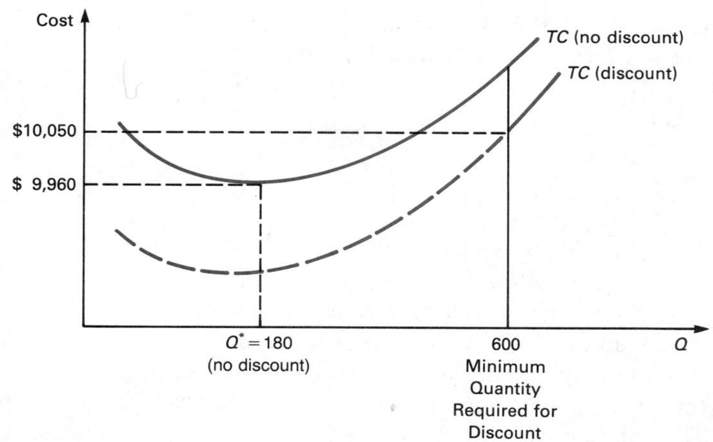

FIGURE 14.13
Northstar quantity discounts situation

For quantities of 1 up to 4,999—$2.75 a unit.
For quantities from 5,000 to 9,999—$2.60 a unit.
For quantities over 10,000 units—$2.50 a unit.

The demand (D) for the drug in the hospital is 50,000 units a year. There is an ordering cost (K) of $50 per order and a holding cost (H) of 20 percent of the cost of the item, per unit, per year. The problem is to find the optimal purchasing policy for the hospital.

Solution

Step 1 Find the EOQ (labeled Q_1^*) for the *lowest price level* ($2.50 in our case). Using the EOQ formula we get:

$$Q_1^* = \sqrt{\frac{2KD}{H}} = \sqrt{\frac{2 \times 50 \times 50{,}000}{.5}} = \sqrt{10{,}000{,}000} = 3{,}163 \text{ units}$$

[Note that H = 20 percent of 2.50 = .2(2.5) = $0.5]

Step 2 Compare Q_1^* to the quantity required for the price break (10,000 in our case). If Q_1^* is *larger* than this quantity, the problem is solved. If it is *smaller*, the solution is *not feasible* and the search for the lowest cost ordering quantity continues (in this example 3,163 is smaller than 10,000).

Step 3 Select the next higher item cost ($2.60 in this example) and calculate Q_2^*, using the EOQ formula:

$$Q_2^* = \sqrt{\frac{2 \times 50 \times 50{,}000}{.52}} = \sqrt{9{,}615{,}385} = 3{,}101 \text{ units}$$

[Notice that H has been changed to .2(2.60) = $0.52.]

Step 4 Repeat step 2. Compare Q_2^* to the range that is required for the equivalent price. In this example, the price of $2.60 is for the range of 5,000–9,999. Since Q_2^* is not within this range, the solution is *not feasible* and the search continues.

Step 5 Compute the EOQ for the next higher price ($2.75 in the example):

$$Q_3^* = \sqrt{\frac{2 \times 50 \times 50{,}000}{.2 \times 2.75}} = \sqrt{9{,}090{,}910} = 3{,}015$$

Step 6 Repeat step 2. This time Q_3^* is within the appropriate range for the price of $2.75. Therefore, it is a *feasible* solution.

Step 7: Cost comparison (on an annual basis) Now a cost comparison is executed. The total annual cost is computed for the feasible EOQ. Then it is compared with the total annual cost of each of the minimum quantities required for each price break. (These are 10,000 units and 5,000 units.) The total annual cost is computed according to Equation 14.15:

$$TC = \text{Ordering cost} + \text{Holding cost} + \text{Units cost}$$

$$TC = \frac{DK}{Q} + \frac{HQ}{2} + P_iD \tag{14.15}$$

Computing the total cost, TC, we get

$$TC_1(\text{for } 10{,}000) = \underbrace{\frac{50{,}000}{10{,}000}(50)}_{\text{Ordering cost}} + \underbrace{\frac{.2(2.5)10{,}000}{2}}_{\text{Holding cost}} + \underbrace{50{,}000(2.5)}_{\text{Units cost}}$$

$$= \$127{,}750 \text{ (minimum)}$$

$$TC_2(\text{for } 5{,}000) = \frac{50{,}000}{5{,}000}(50) + \frac{.2(2.6)5{,}000}{2} + 50{,}000(2.6)$$

$$= \$131{,}800$$

$$TC_3(\text{for } 3{,}015) = \frac{50{,}000}{3{,}015}(50) + \frac{.2(2.75)3{,}015}{2} + 50{,}000(2.75) = \$139{,}158$$

Therefore, an order for 10,000 units at a time should be placed since it exhibits the lowest total cost of $127,750 per year.

The process of solving for the EOQ with quantity discounts is shown in Figure 14.14.

Note: Quantity discounts may not apply in all cultures. *Time* magazine (October 25, 1982, p. 80) reports that a western trader wanted to make a deal with an Eskimo, offering to buy several identical wooden figures for a discount. The Eskimo replied: "It is not working this way; you will have to pay *more* per piece and not less, since the job is more boring."

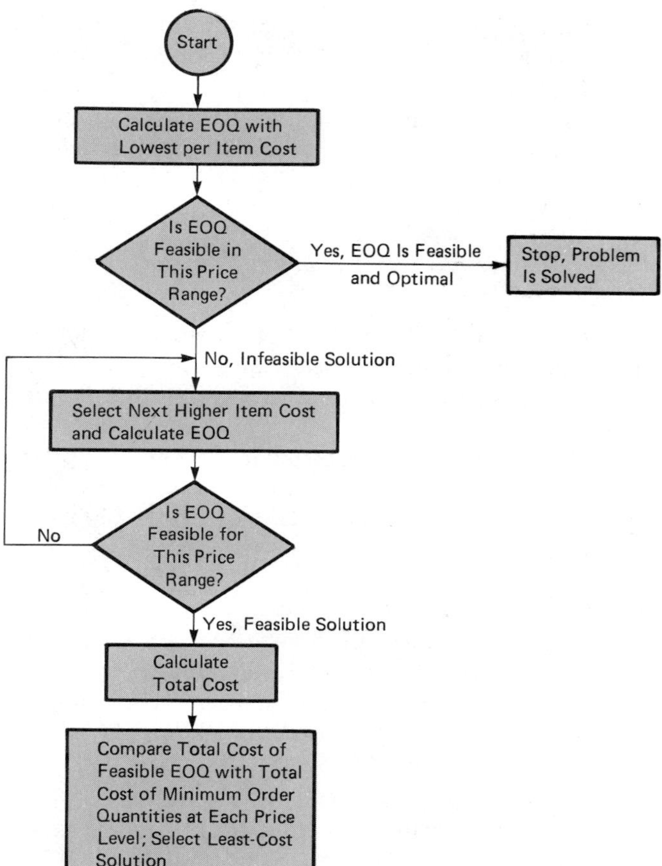

FIGURE 14.14
Flow diagram for quantity discounts of EOQ

14.11 PRODUCTION RUNS: ECONOMIC LOT SIZE (ELS)

ELS a modification of EOQ

The EOQ model has an interesting extension in the production area, where items are often produced in large lots rather than in small lots that exactly meet demand. When more is produced than demanded, an inventory is accumulated. When the accumulated inventory is large enough, a period of no production occurs. The demand then is met from stocks as long as they last. When these are depleted, another large lot is produced and so on. The EOQ assumptions hold for this model as well.

Advantages

The major advantage of producing large lots ("batches") is that savings of the **setup cost** can be realized. Setup cost includes the expense required to "tear down" the machines from a previous production run, as well as that of preparing the machines for the upcoming run. It also includes the cost of processing the necessary paperwork. The larger the production run, the fewer times it will be repeated each year, and therefore fewer setups will be required. Another advantage is the reduction in the *unit production cost* due to the possibility of buying expensive but efficient tools and machines for producing large quantities.[14] Also, better control over quality may be expected.

Disadvantages

The major disadvantage of producing large lots is that the accumulated inventory has a holding cost. Thus, the production of lots that are too large may result in additional inventory costs larger than the setup costs saved.

Management is interested in finding the production quantity for a lot that minimizes the sum of the holding inventory and setup costs. Such a problem is called the **economic lot size (ELS)** problem.

Example

Energy Sol Corp. produces a certain energy-saving device. The demand for the device, D, is 1,800 units per year (or 6 units each day, assuming 300 working days in a year). The company can produce at an annual rate, P, of 7,200 units (or 24 per day). (P is the *maximum* rate when the line is running, *not* an average daily rate.) Setup cost, S, is \$300. (Setup cost is the cost of preparing for a production run and is similar to the ordering cost K in the EOQ.) There is an inventory holding cost, H, of \$36 per unit, per year. The problem is to find the economic lot size, which is designated by L.

Schematic illustration The process is shown in Figure 14.15. As in the regular EOQ illustration, the time axis is divided into cycles, each with the following elements:

The production period T_1. Let us assume that Energy Sol Corp. produces in economic lots of 72; that is, $L = 72$. Since the production rate is 24 per day, it will take 72/24 = 3 days to produce one lot. This period is called T_1. In general, the length of the production period is given by Equation 14.16:

$$T_1 = \frac{L}{P} \tag{14.16}$$

Note: If P is expressed in years, T_1 will be also. If P is in days, so will be T_1. And so on.

---

[14] A reduction in unit production cost is equivalent to a *quantity discount* and can be treated as such (see Section 14.10).

FIGURE 14.15
Inventory level for ELS model

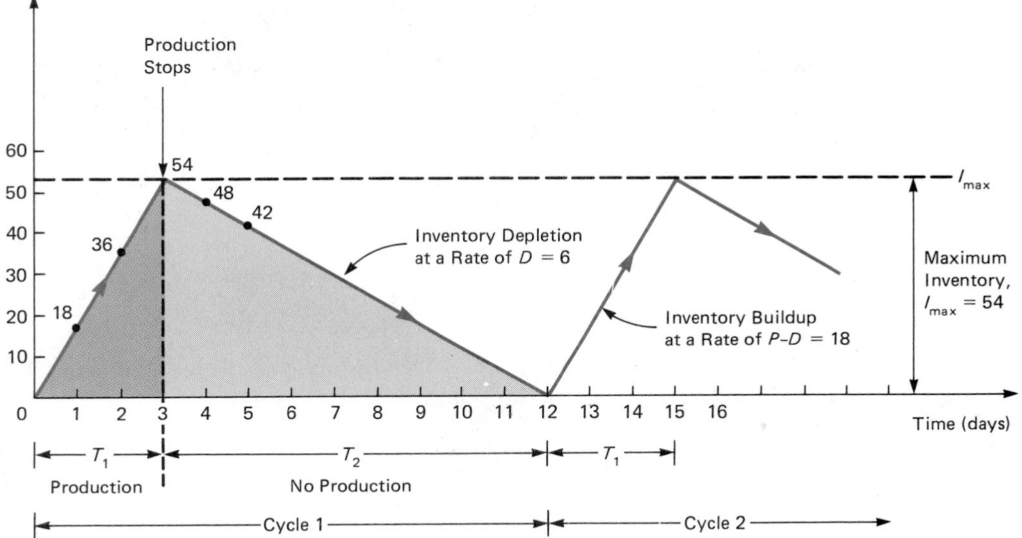

Inventory buildup. During the first day within period T_1, Energy Sol will produce 24 units, but will also *use* 6. Thus, the inventory level at the end of the day will be (daily P) – (daily D) = 24 – 6 = 18. At the end of the second day there will be 36 units in inventory and at the end of the third day, 54. (See Figure 14.15.) At that time, production will stop.

The maximum inventory. The maximum inventory will be reached when the production stops, at the end of the third day (end of T_1). Equation 14.17 can be used to compute this level.

$$I_{max} = (P - D)T_1 = (P - D)\frac{L}{P} \qquad (14.17)$$

$$= (24 - 6)3 = 54$$

The depletion period (T_2). Once production stops, demand is provided from the inventory during the "depletion" period, T_2. With an initial 54 units of inventory at the end of T_1, there is enough to supply 54/6 = 9 days (days 4–12 in Figure 14.15) of demand. In general, T_2 is given by Equation 14.18.

$$T_2 = \frac{I_{max}}{D} = \frac{(P - D)L}{PD} \qquad (14.18)$$

A cycle

A cycle. The time between two consecutive production runs in called a **cycle,** and is composed of:

$$\text{Cycle} = T_1 + T_2 \tag{14.19}$$

Other performance variables

Using the information given we can find some additional performance variables as well.

The average inventory (I_{avg}). As in the EOQ case, the average inventory here also equals half the maximum inventory:

$$I_{avg} = (1/2)I_{max} = \frac{(P - D)L}{2P} \tag{14.20}$$

Number of cycles per year. The number of cycles per year, N, is determined from the annual demand D and the lot size L.

$$N = \frac{D}{L} \tag{14.21}$$

Cost analysis

The annual holding cost. The annual holding cost is given, as in the regular EOQ, by the product of the average inventory and the annual holding cost per unit *(H)*:

$$\text{Annual holding cost} = \frac{H(P - D)L}{2P} \tag{14.22}$$

The annual setup cost. The setup cost per cycle is given as S. Therefore, the total annual setup cost is the product of S times the number of cycles. That is:

$$\text{Annual setup cost} = \frac{SD}{L} \tag{14.23}$$

The total annual cost. The total annual cost is again equal to the sum of the total holding cost and the total setup cost:

$$TC = \frac{H(P - D)L}{2P} + \frac{\text{SD}}{\text{L}} \tag{14.24}$$

Finding the ELS The optimal lot size, L^*, is found by taking the first derivative of Equation 14.24 and setting it to zero, with the result:

$$L^* = \sqrt{\frac{2PSD}{H(P - D)}} \qquad (14.25)$$

Solution to Energy Sol's problem

Given:

Annual demand, $D = 1{,}800$
Annual production capability, $P = 7{,}200$
Setup cost, $S = \$300$
Holding cost per unit per year, $H = \$36$

Inserting the data given into Equation 14.25:

$$L^* = \sqrt{\frac{2PSD}{H(P - D)}} = \sqrt{\frac{2(7{,}200)(300)(1{,}800)}{36(7{,}200 - 1{,}800)}}$$

$$= 200 \text{ units per production run}$$

Using Equations 14.16 through 14.23:

$$T_1 = \frac{L^*}{P} = \frac{200}{7{,}200} = .0278 \text{ years;}$$

assuming 300 working days, this will be 8⅓ days.

$$I_{max} = (P - D)T_1 = 5{,}400 \times .0278 = 150 \text{ units}$$

$$I_{avg} = \frac{I_{max}}{2} = 75 \text{ units}$$

$$T_2 = \frac{I_{max}}{D} = \frac{150}{1{,}800} = .0833 \text{ years, or 25 working days}$$

A cycle $= T_1 + T_2 = .0278 + .0833 = .111$ years, or 33⅓ working days

The above information is entered on Figure 14.16. Additional information

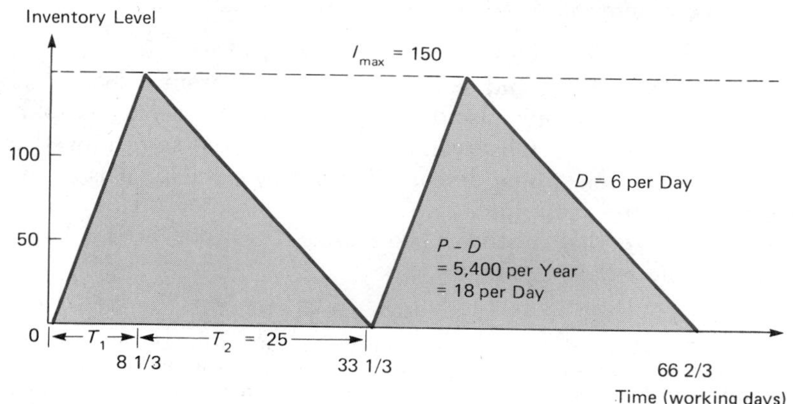

FIGURE 14.16
The Energy Sol production process

that can be derived is:

$$N = \frac{D}{L^*} = \frac{1,800}{200} = 9 \text{ cycles per year}$$

$$\text{Annual holding cost} = \frac{36 \times (7,200 - 1,800)200}{2 \times 7,200} = \$2,700$$

$$\text{Annual setup cost} = \frac{300(1,800)}{200} = \$2,700$$

Note: These two costs *must* be equal in an optimal solution.

Total annual cost = Annual setup + Annual holding cost = $5,400

14.12 SINGLE-PERIOD INVENTORIES

The "Newsboy" problem

There exist some situations where the inventory question is a one-period problem due to the product's high degree of perishability or obsolescence. This problem is classically known as *the Newsboy problem,* since day-old newspapers are considered worthless. Similar one-period situations are: church bake sales, Christmas tree sales, and Easter bunnies at the pet store. Seasonal products such as holiday greeting cards, spring dresses, and certain holiday foods and flowers are other examples of the one-period problem.[15]

Underorder or overorder?

The common element in all these situations is that the product is only ordered once, and there is a penalty associated with underordering as well as a penalty associated with overordering. The underordering penalty is the loss of potential profit (opportunity cost) plus a possible loss of customer goodwill. The overordering penalty is primarily the cost of the leftover product. There may additionally be disposal costs that add to the penalty or a salvage value that decreases the penalty.

A discrete demand distribution example

Calexico Produce buys tomatoes from Mexico once a week. A crate of tomatoes costs $6 and sells for $11 (i.e., a profit of $5 per crate sold). Any crates remaining unsold at the end of the week are sold as animal food for $2 a crate. Observations show that past sales ranged from 16 to 20 crates a week. Since demand is relatively stable, it is assumed it will continue at the same rate.

Suppose that a study, taken over the sales of the last 50 weeks, showed the following results:

[15] The same problem with a modified structure is the situation of those firms and people who must accept reservations or appointments for their services. This category consists of such services as motels and hotels, restaurants, airlines, doctors, and hairdressers.

Number of crates demanded	*Number of weeks*
16	4
17	10
18	12
19	15
20	9
Total	50

The problem is to find how many crates Calexico Produce should order each week so that the profit will be maximized.

Solution using a decision table Since demand ranges between 16 and 20, there is no sense in ordering less than 16, nor more than 20. Therefore, there are only five alternatives of ordering: 16, 17, 18, 19, and 20 crates. There are five possible states of nature (demand); they are given with their respective probabilities below.

Five alternatives

16 crates with a chance of 4 out of 50 = 8 percent = .08
17 crates with a chance of 10/50 = .20
18 crates with a chance of 12/50 = .24
19 crates with a chance of 15/50 = .30
20 crates with a chance of 9/50 = .18

The information can be arranged in a decision table form (Table 14.4). To demonstrate the calculation of the numbers in the table, if 16 crates are ordered and the demand is 16 or more, a profit of \$5 × 16 = \$80 will be realized. It is assumed here that there is no cost for unsatisfied customers (cost of "ill will"). If 17 crates are ordered and there is only a demand for 16, 16 crates will be sold for \$80 profit, and the 17th crate

TABLE 14.4
Calexico Produce decision table

	Demand					
Probabilities →	.08	.20	.24	.30	.18	
Alternatives	16	17	18	19	20	*Expected value of profit (\$)*
16	80	80	80	80	80	80.00
17	76	85	85	85	85	84.28
18	72	81	90	90	90	86.76
19	68	77	86	95	95	87.08 ←*Maximum*
20	64	73	82	91	100	84.70

will be sold at a $6 - 2 = \$4$ loss; that is, the total profit is $80 - 4 = \$76$. For every crate overordered, a loss of $4 is recorded. Thus, if 20 crates are ordered and the demand is 16, the profit will be $64: $80 - (4 \times 4) = \$64$.

Solution Using expected value as a criterion, the best strategy is: order 19 crates each week at an expected profit of:

$$.08(\$68) + .20(\$77) + .24(\$86) + .30(\$95) + .18(\$95) = \$87.08$$

Note that, as with the EOQ, the solution is not highly cost sensitive.

Solution by marginal analysis

Excessive number of alternatives

Small inventory problems can be solved using the decision table approach rather quickly. However, the solution of problems with dozens or hundreds of possible alternatives requires excessive computations. To overcome this difficulty, marginal analysis can be used. Marginal analysis can also be used for the solution of more complicated problems involving continuous demand distributions and costs due to ill will.

The basic idea of marginal analysis is to compare two opposing costs, the cost of overordering (including holding and spoilage) and the cost of underordering (primarily shortage cost), on an "additional-unit" basis. Let us demonstrate. Let:

p = Probability of selling *at least* one more (the *marginal*) unit
This is the *cumulative* probability of demand exceeding the current level
$1 - p$ = Probability of *not* selling one more unit
MP = Profit realized from selling that additional unit (marginal profit)
ML = Loss realized if the additional unit is not sold (marginal loss)

General formulation

The expected profit is equal to the probability of selling the unit times its marginal profit:

$$\text{Expected profit} = p\,(\text{MP})$$

Similarly, the expected loss is given as:

$$\text{Expected loss} = (1 - p)\,\text{ML}$$

Keep ordering more until . . .

To find out whether or not an additional unit should be ordered (at a given level of ordering), it is necessary to compare the expected profit versus the expected loss of the next unit. As long as the expected profit is *larger* than the expected loss, a unit should be added. Units will be added, one at a time, until the point where the *expected profit* equals the *expected loss*. (Ordering more than this will produce a loss.) This condition is expressed mathematically as:

$$p\,(\text{MP}) = (1 - p)\,\text{ML}$$

Solving for p, the critical fraction:

$$p = \frac{\text{ML}}{\text{ML} + \text{MP}} \tag{14.26}$$

In other words, in order to justify ordering (or stocking) a unit, the probability of selling that unit must be *at least* equal to p. The problem now is how to find that last (optimal) unit.

Application to the discrete probability example:

$$\text{MP} = 11 - 6 = \$5$$
$$\text{ML} = 6 - 2 = \$4, \text{ therefore: } p = \frac{4}{4+5} = .444$$

Cumulative probability

It is necessary now to relate p to the *cumulative probability of demand;* that is, the probability that one *or more* crates will be sold. For example, the probability of selling 19 or more crates (that is, 19 or 20) is .18 + .30 = .48 (see Table 14.5).

TABLE 14.5
Cumulative probability of demand

Number of crates, N	*Probability of demand*	*Cumulative probability (of selling N or more)*
16	.08	1.00
17	.20	.92
18	.24	.72
19	.30	.48
20	.18	.18

Note that the cumulative probability for 19 crates is .48, more than p = .444, and, hence, 19 should be stocked; but at 20 crates .18 is less than .444 and, hence, 20 cannot be justified. Therefore, the optimal order policy is 19 crates.

Application to continuous probability situations

The same approach can be applied to situations involving continuous probability distributions such as normal, triangular, or uniform demand distributions. In these cases, 1.0 − cumulative probability distribution function is set equal to the critical fraction, p, to find the optimal ordering level. For example, in the last situation with Calexico Produce, if the demand was uniformly distributed over 16–20 crates (i.e., each had a .20 probability), the optimal number of crates to order would be found as follows:

$$1.0 - .2(x - 16) = .444$$
$$x = 18.78 \text{ crates}$$

14.13 MATERIAL REQUIREMENTS PLANNING (MRP)

Independent versus dependent demand

Lumpy dependent demand

The EOQ inventory control system assumes that demand is essentially constant. This is often the case for items that are *independently* demanded, such as finished goods, supplies, and spare parts. However, many inventoried items consist of subassemblies whose **demand,** being **dependent** on the demand for finished goods, is **lumpy** rather than constant. For example, in producing a batch of tables, the demand for table legs occurs at a high rate for a very short time—immediately prior to assembling the top and apron to the legs. To constantly hold all these legs in inventory to meet a peak demand that rarely occurs would cost a lot of money. Therefore, the EOQ is not useful in this case. It would be much better to have the legs arrive in inventory *just prior* to the time when they are needed. This is the major purpose of **materials requirements planning (MRP),** a computer-based production planning and inventory control system. Table 14.6 compares the characteristics of MRP with EOQ systems.

TABLE 14.6
MRP versus EOQ system characteristics

Characteristic	*MRP systems*	*EOQ systems*
Demand	Dependent	Independent
Item flow	Lumpy, discontinuous	Continuous
Lead time basis	Time point	Reorder point (in units)
Reorder basis	Future demand	Historical demand
Safety stock	Finished goods only, not components	All items
Item focus	Finished goods	All parts

MRP requires computer power

MRP as one part of MRP II

Each product typically consists of several subcomponents—for a company with many products, the number of subcomponents and parts may reach tens of thousands. To keep track of all these parts on a *finished product* basis clearly requires a computer. Therefore, until the advent of economical computer power in the 1960s, MRP was not feasible for many situations. In actuality, MRP is only one component in a production planning and control system known as manufacturing resource planning (MRP II) that includes other computer components to schedule production jobs, purchase materials, check capacity requirements, forecast product demands, and so on.

MRP—basic overview

Let us assume that a company produces a walnut table in three sizes: large, medium, and small. Also, the company produces other tables (e.g., oak, teak) as well as a variety of wooden chairs. Each of the finished products includes a *bill of materials* (Figure 14.17) that details what it takes to make the product, and can be represented by a *product tree* (Figure 14.18) that shows how the materials go together to make the product.

It frequently happens that some of the materials in the products are common to a number of tables, for example, screws and anchors. The

Top		(one)	manufactured
Walnut veneer	15 ft^2	(one)	purchased
Particle board	½″ × 15 feet	(one)	manufactured
Veneer strip	½″ × 17 feet	(one)	purchased
Apron		(one)	manufactured
Veneer strip	3″ × 15 feet	(one)	purchased
Particle board	3″ × 5½ feet	(two)	manufactured
Particle board	3″ × 2 feet	(two)	manufactured
Wood screws	1½″ flathead	(eight)	purchased
Legs		(four)	manufactured
Walnut	1½″ × 1½″ × 2′	(one)	manufactured
Anchors		(one)	manufactured
1/16″ steel ribbon		(one)	purchased
6–32 screws		(two)	purchased
6–32 nuts		(two)	purchased

FIGURE 14.17
Bill of materials for walnut table

MRP system is then executed for each product and aggregates common parts and subassemblies from the several sources according to their unique, time-phased requirements for purchase and manufacture.

The elements of MRP

Three sets of data requirements

The MRP system is composed of four data elements (Figure 14.19):

1. A master production schedule.
2. A bill of materials file.
3. An inventory master file.
4. Lead times.

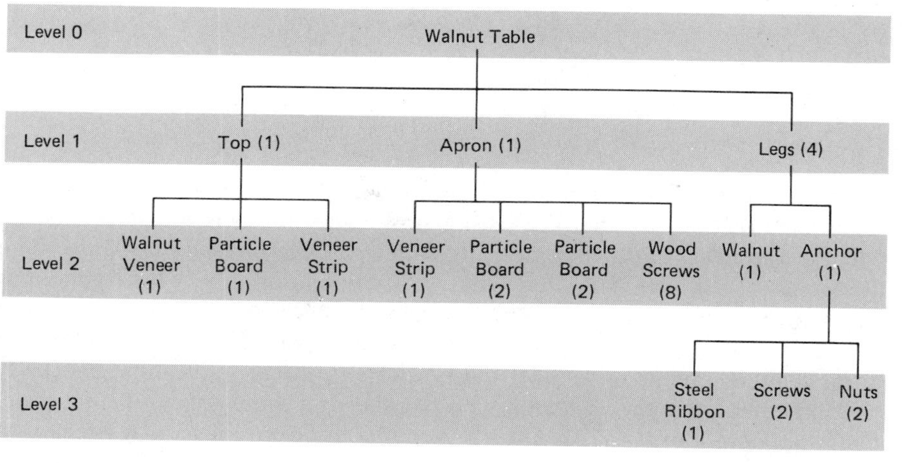

FIGURE 14.18
Walnut table product tree

FIGURE 14.19
The MRP data elements

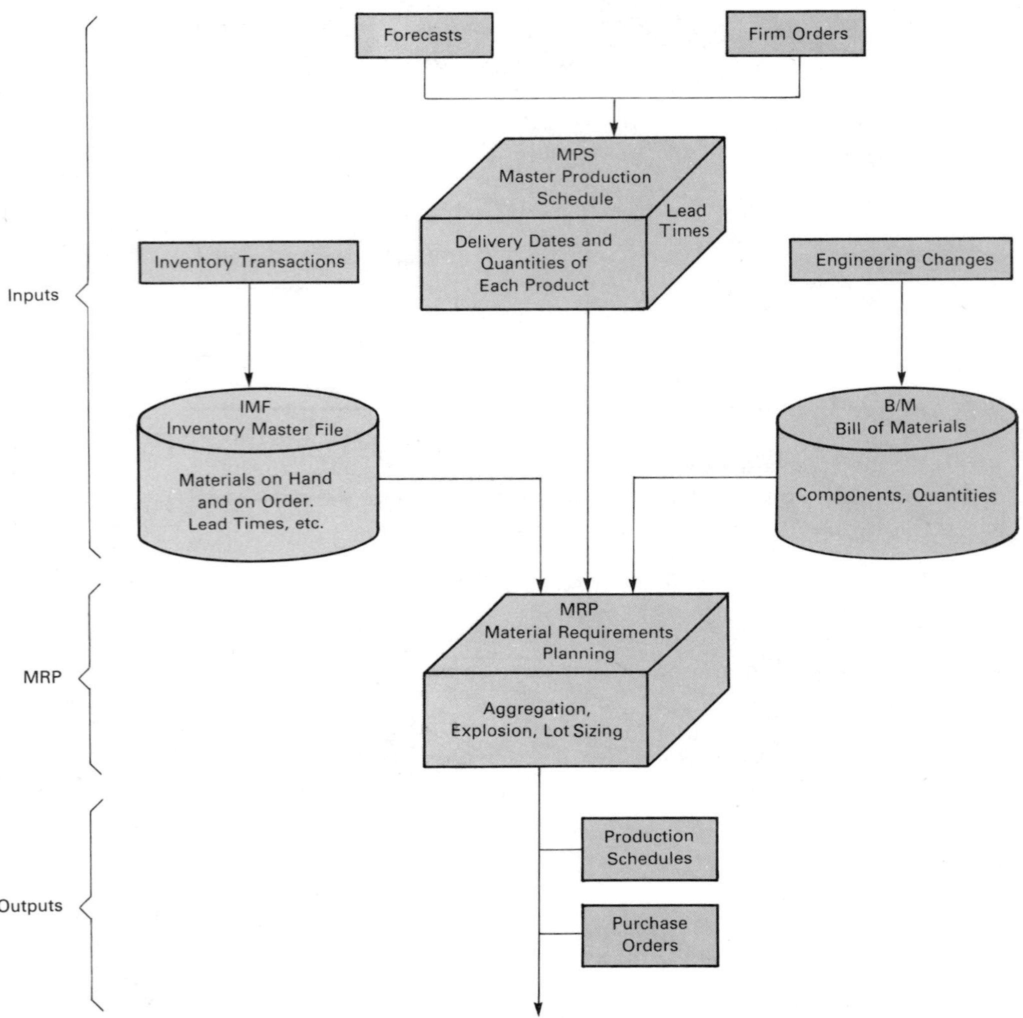

The master production schedule (MPS) The **master production schedule (MPS)** is a schedule listing how many of each finished product will be required and when; this is called a *time-phased* schedule. The items may be finished goods, parts, or subcomponents. The demand is based on both forecasts and actual customer orders to date.

"Parent" or "Level 0" items in the MPS

It is the MPS that drives the MRP system. To assemble the end items (called **parent** or **level 0 items**) the subcomponents must be ready on time. To have the subcomponents ready for final assembly on time, *their* subcomponents (parts) must be produced, or purchased, by the necessary date. And so on. The time it takes to get these subcomponents is called their *lead time*. The MRP system takes these lead and assembly times into account in determining when to release work orders and purchase requisitions. An example of an MPS will be given soon.

The bill of materials (B/M) The MRP system knows what items constitute each end product and each subassembly from the **bill of materials (B/M).** The B/M includes all of the raw materials, components, and subassemblies, (and their quantities) required to produce the item.

The inventory master file (IMF) The **inventory master file (IMF)** contains detailed information on the lead times to make, assemble, or purchase each item and the number of items on hand in inventory, on order with suppliers, and previously committed to production items. If sufficient items are available, the system commits them to use; if not, purchase or work orders are scheduled for release at the proper time so that items will be available when needed with the least possible inventory.

Inspecting the IMF for material availability

The MRP computation process

As an order is entered into the MPS, the MRP system **explodes** the B/M to determine what subcomponents will be required in what quantities in what time periods. The "explosion" simply consists of stepping down through the B/M levels and determining the quantity and lead times of subcomponents to support the purchase, manufacture, or assembly at each level. The result is a time-phased set of production requirements to support the parent order.

Exploding the B/M to determine time-phased material requirements

An example is given in Table 14.7 for a delivery schedule of 100 tables in week 15 and 70 tables in week 18. Note that because of an on-hand inventory of 90 tables and planned receipts of 30, only (100 + 70) − 90 − 30 = 50 are exploded through the B/M.

TABLE 14.7
Level 0 MPS for walnut table (two-week lead time)

	Week							
	12	*13*	*14*	*15*	*16*	*17*	*18*	*19*
Gross requirements				100			70	
On hand	90	90	120	120	20	20	20	0
Net requirements							50	
Planned receipts		30						
Planned releases					50 ← 2-week lead time			

The levels 1, 2, and 3 exploded schedules for a portion of the B/M are shown in Table 14.8. The gross requirements at any level are based on the planned releases at the previous level. Notice, however, that gross requirements can be accumulated for several products; for example, the anchors and screws have externally generated demands on them as well. (They are also used in oak tables whose schedule is not illustrated here.)

Externally generated demands also

TABLE 14.8
B/M explosion for subcomponent requirements

a. Level 1: Legs (one-week lead time)

	Week							
	11	*12*	*13*	*14*	*15*	*16*	*17*	*18*
Gross requirements						200		
On hand	130	130	130	130	130	130	0	0
Net requirements						70		
Planned receipts								
Planned releases					70			

× 1 =

b. Level 2: Anchors (one-week lead time)

	Week							
	11	*12*	*13*	*14*	*15*	*16*	*17*	*18*
Gross requirements			10		70		40	
On hand	35	35	60	50	50	0	0	0
Net requirements					20		40	
Planned receipts		25						
Planned releases				20		40		

× 2 =   × 2 =

c. Level 3: Screws (three-week lead time)

	Week							
	11	*12*	*13*	*14*	*15*	*16*	*17*	*18*
Gross requirements		50		40		80		40
On hand	80	80	30	30	0	0	0	0
Net requirements				10		80		40
Planned receipts								
Planned releases	10		80		40			

Work and purchase order releases

The planned release of work orders for 50 tables in week 16 (Table 14.7) generates a gross requirement of 4 × 50 = 200 legs in week 16. Since 130 are already in stock (Table 14.8a), only 70 need be released in week 15. This generates a gross requirement for 70 anchors in week 15 (Table 14.8b). Considering other external requirements for anchors (e.g., 10 in week 13), inventory on hand, and planned receipts, two work orders are released in weeks 14 and 16 for more anchors. These work orders generate, in turn, requirements for twice as many screws, since there are two screws in an anchor, and purchase orders are thus placed for screws in weeks 11, 13, and 15 (Table 14.8c).

The lot-sizing problem

Note in Table 14.8b that work orders were released for anchors in weeks 14 and 16 (and purchase orders for screws in weeks 11, 13, and 15). Clearly, it may well be worthwhile to consider combining these orders and avoiding an extra setup or ordering charge. But, how many orders ahead should be included? This is known as the **lot-sizing problem.**

Lot sizing

The best approach to the lot-sizing problem is still an unresolved question in the research literature. An acceptable trial-and-error approach is shown next.

Produce to demand In this straightforward approach, the firm simply produces or purchases to meet demand and keeps no inventories. Holding costs are thus minimized, but the production fluctuations and possible capacity problems are a severe disadvantage. If the cost of ordering screws in Table 14.8c is \$5 each time, and the holding cost is \$0.01 each per week, the total cost of this policy would be \$15 from ordering three times.

Produce for the entire time horizon In this approach, all the parts known to be needed over the horizon of demand are produced or ordered at the same time. Thus, in Table 14.8c, the firm would order 10 + 80 + 40 = 130 screws. The resulting inventory cost would be:

Carry 80 units for two weeks: $.01 \times 80 \times 2 = \$1.60$
Carry 40 units for four weeks: $.01 \times 40 \times 4 = \$1.60$

for a total of \$3.20, added to the one-time ordering cost of \$5.00, results in a total cost for the horizon of \$8.20.

Trial-and-error approach

Produce in intermediate lots In this situation, different lot sizes, corresponding to different horizons, can be tried to determine the most cost-effective approach. For example, the firm can order 90 in week 11 and then 40 in week 15, or 10 in week 11 and 120 in week 13, and so on.

Summary

MRP has emerged as the best inventory control sytem for job lot production with a dependent demand. It allows a *near zero* inventory level since the inventory is closely coordinated with the production schedule. In contrast to the EOQ that controls one item at a time, MRP can control several products simultaneously when they share common components or parts. Therefore, most MRP systems are large in size and require a computer for processing. A number of software firms offer industrial MRP packages, for example, IBM, Arista, Burroughs, and Cincom, typically as one module in their complete MRP II system for planning and controlling production.

14.14 PLANNED SHORTAGES

As discussed earlier, safety stock is used as a protection against shortages. However, safety stock increases the inventory level and may result in excessive holding cost. Therefore, it may be better to allow shortages

Allowing shortages

to occur (**planned shortages**) rather than to build up a safety stock. The penalty may be a continuing temporary (backlogged) charge or a permanent one-time (lost sales) charge. In either case, there is a penalty. If the cost continues for the duration of the shortage, such as would be incurred with expediting, for example, then this is akin to an inventory holding charge. This is the assumption we will make in this section.

The problem to be addressed now is to find the economic order quantity in a case in which a shortage is allowed and safety stock is not considered. A situation of this type is shown in Figure 14.20.

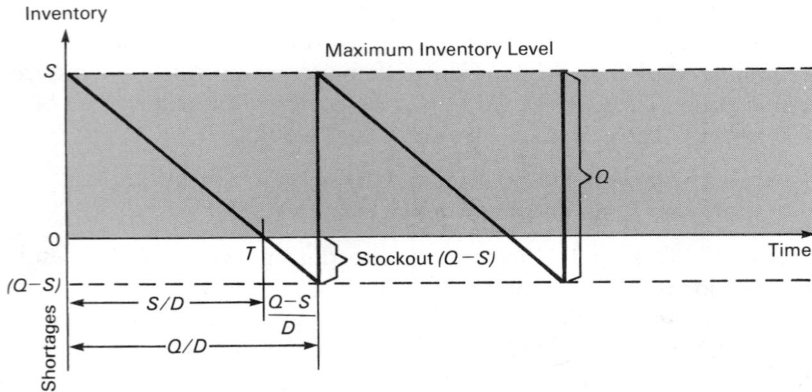

FIGURE 14.20
An inventory situation with planned shortages

The symbols to be used in this section, some of which are shown in the figure, are:

Q = Order quantity
D = Annual demand
K = Order cost
S = Maximum inventory level
H = Holding cost (per unit per year)
S/D = Time during which inventory is positive (no stockout)
Q/D = Time of one cycle
G = Shortage cost (per unit per year) that continues for the duration of the stockout

Computation of costs

In this situation, there are three relevant costs: an *ordering cost,* a *holding cost,* and a *shortage cost.*

Total annual ordering cost As in the regular EOQ: KD/Q.

Total annual holding cost The annual holding cost, however, is not $HQ/2$ or even $HS/2$, corresponding to the regular EOQ, since during the time duration of the shortage period there is *no inventory at all.* The average inventory level is calculated from the total "unit years" of inventory in a cycle, divided by the total length of a cycle *(Q/D)*. The number of unit years is given by Equation 14.27:[16]

$$\text{Unit years of inventory (per cycle)} = \frac{1}{2}\left(\frac{S}{D}\right) S = \frac{S^2}{2D} \qquad (14.27)$$

Thus, the average inventory is:

$$\text{Average inventory} = \frac{S^2/2D}{Q/D} = \frac{S^2}{2Q} \qquad (14.28)$$

and the holding cost is:

$$\text{Annual holding cost} = \frac{HS^2}{2Q} \qquad (14.29)$$

The shortage cost Applying the same type of analysis for the calculation of the annual shortage cost, where G is the annual cost per unit of being out of stock, the total shortage cost is expressed by Equation 14.30:

$$\text{Annual shortage cost} = \frac{G(Q-S)^2}{2Q} \qquad (14.30)$$

The total relevant cost, TC The total cost is the sum of all three costs:

$$TC = \frac{KD}{Q} + \frac{HS^2}{2Q} + \frac{G(Q-S)^2}{2Q} \qquad (14.31)$$

The optimal ordering quantity is:[17]

$$Q^* = \sqrt{\frac{2KD}{H}\left(\frac{G+H}{G}\right)} \qquad (14.32)$$

[16] Equation 14.27 is derived from the area of the triangle *OST* (Figure 14.20).

[17] In order to find the minimum *TC*, partial derivatives with respect to both Q and S are taken and are set to 0:

$$\frac{\partial TC}{\partial Q} = -\frac{KD}{Q^2} - \frac{HS^2}{2Q^2} + \frac{G(Q-S)}{Q} - \frac{G(Q-S)^2}{2Q^2} = 0$$

$$\frac{\partial TC}{\partial S} = \frac{HS}{Q} - \frac{G(Q-S)}{Q} = 0$$

When these are solved simultaneously, Equations 14.32 and 14.33 result.

with a maximum inventory level:

$$S = \sqrt{\frac{2KD}{H}\left(\frac{G}{G+H}\right)} \tag{14.33}$$

Example Using the data of the problem from Section 14.4:

$K = \$5$
$H = \$1.20$ per unit per year
$D = 1{,}200$ units

Also given:

$G = \$2.40$ per unit per year

Solution According to Equations 14.32 and 14.33:

$$Q^* = \sqrt{\frac{2(5)1{,}200}{1.20} \times \left(\frac{2.4 + 1.2}{2.4}\right)} = 122 \text{ units}$$

$$S = \sqrt{\frac{2(5)1{,}200}{1.20} \times \left(\frac{2.4}{2.4 + 1.2}\right)} = 81.5 \text{ units}$$

The previous no-shortage solution was $Q^* = 100$, and the maximum inventory was the same, namely, 100. Now the quantity ordered has increased by about one fifth, but the maximum inventory level is only about four fifths the previous level.

In conducting this type of analysis, it is important to compute the total cost after Q^* is established and compare it to the cost of using safety stock instead.

Planned shortages and ELS

Planned shortages can be applied to the ELS situation as well. We will not derive the formulas for this case. However, in Section 14.16 is an example of a computer printout in which a shortage cost is added to the ELS example of Section 14.11.

14.15 SAFETY STOCKS AND SERVICE LEVELS

Stockout

So far, it has been assumed that the demand and the lead time are constant. As a result, it was possible to adopt an inventory policy whereby an item would *never be out of stock*. Running out of stock (a *stockout* or a *shortage*) implies that demand cannot be filled on time. Stockouts result from either delays in deliveries and/or from unexpected rises in demand during the lead time. These situations are depicted in Figure 14.21. Though models exist for each of these situations, the model below is applicable to both, either individually or combined.

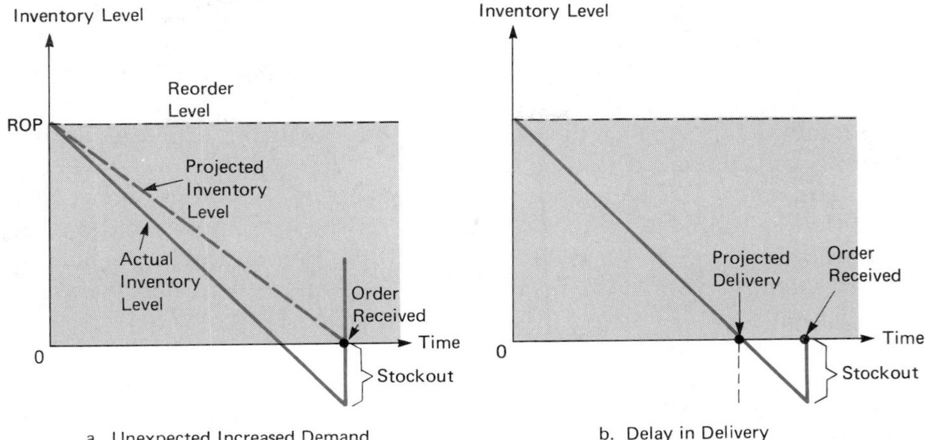

FIGURE 14.21
Factors contributing to an inventory stockout

What level of safety stock?

For protection against a stockout, an order can be computed and placed so that the delivery will arrive when a certain level of inventory is still remaining, rather than at the scheduled depletion of the stock. The managerial problem is *determining the proper level* of this safety stock (SS).

Example

Assume an average demand of 10 units per day and a lead time of six days. In such a case, there is an average demand during the lead time (DDLT) of 10(6) = 60 units. Now assume that protection against a stockout (safety stock) of up to SS = 50 units is desired. The reorder point will be: ROP = 60 + 50 = 110 units. In general, the following relationship exists between the reorder point and the safety stock:

$$\text{ROP} = \text{DDLT} + \text{SS} \qquad (14.34)$$

The concept of service level

To build up a safety stock that would prevent shortages in *all* cases could be very expensive. The cost of incurring a once-a-year shortage may be much smaller than the cost of maintaining the safety stock. Therefore, management may wish to maintain a safety stock that will protect against a shortage not in all cases but, say, 80 percent of the time. The percentage of time that all demand is met (in this example, the 80 percent) is called the **service level.** The service level is defined as the probability of *not* running out of stock, that is:

The service level

$$\text{Service level} = 1 - \text{Probability of running out of stock} \qquad (14.35)$$

The higher the service level, the higher the required safety stock with its associated inventory cost, and the lower the chance of a shortage and its consequences. Service levels are usually determined by management policies but may also be determined mathematically in such a way that the total cost of keeping the safety stock and incurring expenses during shortages is minimized. Let us show how.

The normal distribution

Example The average demand for product G is 10 units a day. The lead time is known to be six days. Therefore, the *average* demand during the lead time is 6 × 10, or 60. The lead time demand follows a *normal distribution* (see Appendix B, Section B3) with a *standard deviation*, σ_d, of 8.59 units.

With a normal distribution there is exactly a 50 percent chance that the demand during the lead time will be more than the average of 60 units. Using the tables for the area under the normal curve (see Table C1 in Appendix C), the relationship between a desired service level (which is equivalent to the area under the normal curve) and the safety factor (number of standard deviations), Z, can be found. For example, for a 50 percent (.50) service level, Z = 0; for a 67 percent (.67) service level, Z = .44; for a 90 percent service level, Z = 1.28.

Suppose that management is interested in providing a 90 percent service level. To find the safety stock required for such a level we invoke the definition of Z (see Appendix B, Section B3):

$$Z = \frac{X - \mu}{\sigma}$$

In our case:

$$Z = \frac{\text{ROP} - \text{DDLT}}{\sigma_d} = \frac{\text{SS}}{\sigma_d}$$

or:

$$\text{Safety stock} = Z \times \sigma_d \qquad (14.36)$$

where Z is the number of standard deviations equivalent to the desired service level and σ_d is the standard deviation of the demand during the reorder period (8.59 in this case). For this example:

$$\text{Safety stock} = 1.28 \times 8.59 = 11 \text{ units}$$

This information is shown in Figure 14.22.

Note that in addition to the average demand for 60 units needed during the lead time, there is a need for a safety stock of 11 to ensure a service level of 90 percent; that is, 71 total units is the reorder point. In a similar manner it can be found that in order to ensure a 95 percent service level, a safety stock of 14 units is required; and to ensure a 99.9 percent service level, 26.5 units of safety stock are needed.

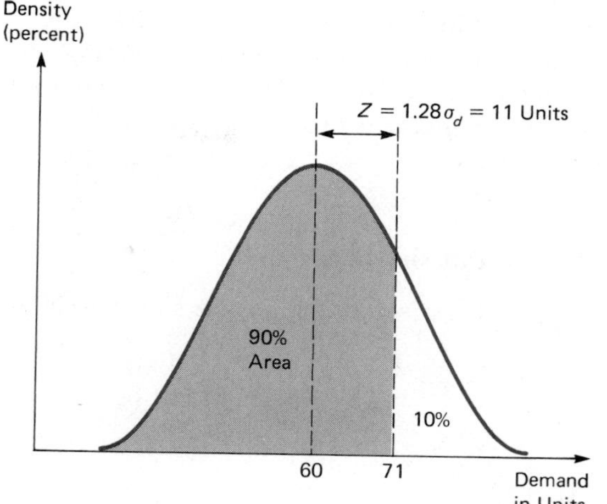

FIGURE 14.22
Service level of 90 percent

Finding the best level of safety stock

Equation 14.36 tells management what amount of safety stock is required in order to maintain a desired service level. However, management may also be interested in knowing the cost of maintaining a desired service level. The establishment of a safety stock involves two costs:

1. The expected cost of a shortage, which declines as the safety stock increases.
2. The expected cost of keeping the safety stock, which increases as the safety stock increases.

The total cost that management is interested in is the sum of the two (see Figure 14.23). Management may be interested in finding the

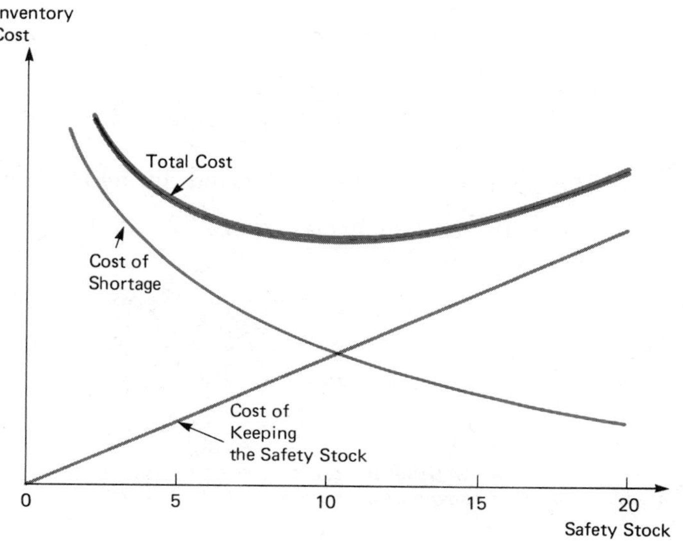

FIGURE 14.23
Safety stock costs

relationship between this total cost and the service level. Management may also be interested in determining the service level for which the total cost is the lowest. The following computations illustrate such an analysis, assuming that orders are spread out enough that only one order may be outstanding at any given point in time.

The cost of shortage

The expected cost of the shortage is given by Equation 14.37:

$$\text{Annual cost of shortage} = \frac{\pi BD}{Q} \tag{14.37}$$

where:

π = The probability of shortage (which equals 1 minus the service level)
B = Average cost of one shortage[18]
D = Annual demand
Q = Order quantity
$\frac{D}{Q}$ = The number of cycles per year

The cost of holding safety stock

The expected cost of holding safety stock is given by Equation 14.38:

$$\text{Annual holding cost} = H \times (\text{safety stock}) = HZ\sigma_d \tag{14.38}$$

where:

H = Holding cost, per unit per year
Z = Number of standard deviations required to maintain a desired service level
σ_d = The standard deviation of demand during the lead time

The sum of the cost in Equations 14.37 and 14.38 is the total relevant cost for each service level:

$$TC = \frac{\pi BD}{Q} + \text{HZ}\sigma_d \tag{14.39}$$

[18] We have used the *average* cost per shortage here for the sake of simplicity. In Problem 14.26 we show a case with a cost per unit short.

To find the best level of safety stock, the total relevant cost, TC, is computed for several desired service levels (e.g., 80 percent, 90 percent, 95 percent, 99 percent) and the lowest one is chosen.

Example In the example of product G, the following data are given:

Lead time = 6 days
Demand = 10 units per day or 2,500 per year (with 250 working days)
Standard deviation = 8.59 units during the lead time
K = Order cost = \$160 per order
H = Holding cost = \$20 per unit per year
B = Shortage cost = \$100 per shortage

Management insists that a service level of at least 90 percent be maintained.

The problem is to find the cost of maintaining this 90 percent service level and whether there is one above it that would cost less.

Solution First, the EOQ is computed disregarding shortages and safety stock.

$$\text{EOQ} = \sqrt{\frac{2KD}{H}} = \sqrt{\frac{2(160)2{,}500}{20}} = 200 \text{ units per order}$$

Computation for 90 percent service level. It was shown earlier that a safety stock of 11 units will guarantee a 90 percent service level. The total annual holding cost of a safety stock of 11 units is:

$$H \times (\text{safety stock}) = 20(11) = \$220$$

The total annual shortage cost (according to Equation 14.36) is:

$$\text{Shortage cost} = \frac{\pi BD}{Q^*} = \frac{.1(100)(2{,}500)}{200} = \$125$$

Therefore, the *total relevant costs* are 220 + 125 = \$345. Using a trial-and-error approach, the analyst now searches for a possible lower cost service level above 90 percent.

Try a service level of 95 percent. It was mentioned earlier that the necessary safety stock for a 95 percent service level is 14. Thus, the total annual holding cost of safety stock is (14)(20) or \$280, and the total annual shortage cost = .05 × 100 × 2,500/200 = \$62.50. Therefore, the *total relevant costs* are 280 + 62.50 = \$342.50.

Try a service level of 99.9 percent. The necessary safety stock for 99.9 percent was stated to be 26.5. Rounding to 27 units, the total annual holding cost of safety stock is 27(20) or \$540 and the total annual shortage cost is:

$$.001 \times 100 \times \frac{2{,}500}{200} = \$1.25$$

The *total relevant costs* are:

$$540 + 1.25 = \$541.25$$

Comparing the three service levels, 95 percent is the best. However, this process could have been continued in the same manner for any other desired service level (e.g., 91 percent) until an even lower total cost level might have been found.

Notes:

1. If the demand during the lead time follows a distribution other than the normal (e.g., Poisson, negative exponential), the appropriate statistical methodology for the standard deviation and safety factor calculations must be followed.
2. If both the demand and the lead time are stochastic (variable) a Monte Carlo simulation may be used to determine the best safety stock (see Chapter 16).

Shortage cost on a per unit basis

To conduct a cost analysis with per unit shortage costs, it is necessary to determine the average number of units short. Table 14.9, developed by Brown [1], relates the average number of units short $E(K)$ to the service level. To find $E(K)$ the second column must be multiplied by σ_d. For our earlier example, $E(K)$ for a 90 percent service level = 0.0473 × 8.59 = 0.406 units. In general, the annual shortage cost will be:

$$\text{Shortage cost} = (D/Q^*)(G)E(K)\sigma_d \qquad (14.40)$$

where G is the cost per unit short.

Example If G = \$10, then:

$$\text{Annual cost of shortage} = (2{,}500/200)(10)(.406) = \$50.75$$

TABLE 14.9
Unit shortage as a function of service level

Service level	$E(K)/\sigma_d$
99	0.00441
95	0.02089
90	0.04730
85	0.07776
80	0.11156

Source: R. G. Brown, *Decision Rules for Inventory Management* (New York: Holt, Rinehart & Winston, 1967).

14.16 USE OF COMPUTERS

There probably exist more computerized programs for inventory management than for any other management science model. Several computer printout examples are included in this section. The first is a regular EOQ applied to the problem presented in Section 14.4. Notice that the program computes the reorder level when the lead time is input.

```
  ** INFORMATION ENTERED **

DEMAND                  : 1200
ORDERING COSTS          : 5
HOLDING COSTS           : 1.2
LEAD TIME (DAYS)        : 10
WORKING DAYS            : 300

OPTIMAL ECONOMIC ORDER QUANTITY (EOQ): 100 UNITS
AVERAGE INVENTORY LEVEL: 50

TOTAL ANNUAL INVENTORY COSTS
                        HOLDING COST:          $60.00
                        ORDERING COSTS:        $60.000
                                 TOTAL:        $120.00

OPTIMAL REORDER POINT: 40 UNITS
OPTIMAL NUMBER OF ORDERS PER YEAR: 12 TIMES
OPTIMAL INVENTORY CYCLE TIME: 25 days
```

The second example involves the ELS problem of Section 14.11.

```
  ** INFORMATION ENTERED **

DEMAND                     : 1800
ORDERING COSTS             : 300
HOLDING COSTS              : 36
LEAD TIME                  : 0
WORKING DAYS               : 300
PRODUCTION RATE            : 7200
```

```
OPTIMAL ECONOMIC LOT SIZE: 200 UNITS

ANNUAL INVENTORY COSTS
                    HOLDING COSTS:        $2,700.00
                    SETUP COSTS:          $2,700.00
                              TOTAL:      $5,400.00

MAXIMUM INVENTORY: 150

OPTIMAL NUMBER OF PRODUCTION RUNS PER YEAR: 9

TOTAL INVENTORY CYCLE TIME
                    PRODUCTION:           8.333334 DAYS
                    NO PRODUCTION         25 DAYS
                              TOTAL       33.33333 DAYS
```

The next example is a modification of the example given in Section 14.15. The input data include a lead time of 6 days with an average demand of 60 during this time and a standard deviation of 8.59. The penalty cost is $20 per unit per year. The results are:

```
   ** INFORMATION ENTERED **

DEMAND              : 2500
ORDERING COSTS      : 160
HOLDING COSTS       : 20
LEAD TIME           : 6
WORKING DAYS        : 250
SERVICE LEVEL       : 95%
MEAN DEMAND         : 60
STANDARD DEV        : 8.59
PENALTY COST        : 20

** RESULTS **


ECONOMIC ORDER QUANTITY (EOQ) =                 200
SAFETY STOCK LEVEL  =                           14.1735 UNITS

EXPECTED NUMBER OF UNITS SHORT =                .1783714
REORDER POINT (ROP) =                           74.17 UNITS
ANNUAL HOLDING COSTS FOR SAFETY STOCK =         283.47
```

```
ANNUAL SHORTAGE COSTS FOR SAFETY STOCK = 44.59285
TOTAL ANNUAL SAFETY STOCK COSTS =        328.0628
ANNUAL ORDERING COST                     2000.00
ANNUAL HOLDING COST                      2000.00

** END OF ANALYSIS **
```

Notice that the reorder level is not just usage times lead time, but also includes safety stock (of 14).

The last example is that of marginal analysis (the one solved manually earlier).

```
                MARGINAL ANALYSIS (NEWSBOY)
 PROBLEM NAME:
 NO. OF DEMAND LEVELS          5

DEMAND LEVEL               PROBABILITY

     16                        .08
     17                        .2
     18                        .24
     19                        .3
     20                        .18

 MARGINAL PROFIT               5
 MARGINAL LOSS                 4
                MARGINAL ANALYSIS (NEWSBOY)

 PROBABILITY OF SELLING THE MARGINAL UNIT: .4444444

                CUMULATIVE PROBABILITY TABLE
```

DEMAND	PROBABILITY OF DEMAND	CUMULATIVE PROBABILITY (OF SELLING N OR MORE)	EXPECTED PROFIT
16	0.080	1.000	80
17	0.200	0.920	84.28
18	0.240	0.720	86.76
19	0.300	0.480	87.08 <---BEST
20	0.180	0.180	84.7

OPTIMAL INVENTORY LEVEL: 19 UNITS

The MSS package includes several other inventory models.

Computerized MRP It is estimated that more than 1,000 U.S. companies use computerized MRP packages. In the last few years, a large number of these packages were micro-based. This development makes the use of MRP economically feasible for almost any size of company. Such systems can immediately reflect the effects of changes, delays, or cancellations on production schedules. It is a virtual necessity to use a computer for MRP calculations. IBM, Xerox, Markem Corp., and several others have developed MRP programs. For a discussion, see reference [3].

14.17 CONCLUDING REMARKS

This chapter has presented a variety of basic inventory models, each of which is appropriate for a different set of circumstances. There exist many more inventory models based on other characteristics of demand, supply, and the costs involved. There are even dozens of variations of the basic models presented here. With the increased complexity of many of the advanced models, it is necessary to use a computer to apply them.

14.18 PROBLEMS FOR PART B

18. Canographic Corporation produces computer plotters for the West Coast. The monthly demand for the plotters is 20 units. The company has a production capacity of 80 units per month. There is a setup cost of \$750 per production run. Each plotter kept in stock for one month costs \$25 in holding cost. Management's policy is to supply *all* demand; thus, no shortage is allowed.

a. Show the inventory cycle graphically (without any data).

b. Find the best production plan (i.e., how many units to produce each production run). A whole number of units must be produced in each run. A production run may involve a fraction of a day.

c. How many days of production will there be in each cycle (assume 20 manufacturing and demand days per month)?

d. In part *(a)*, find the length of the total cycle and the maximum inventory level.

e. Assuming that the company produces 60 units in each production run, what will the effect on the total monthly cost be? (Compare to the minimum cost.)

19. Union Machine Corporation operates a punch press that produces 20 units of product M each hour. The press is in operation five hours a day. In order to set up the press for product M, it is necessary to shut down for two hours. Setup time costs the company \$15 per hour.

The demand for product M is 40 units a day, during 250 operating days in a year. The inventory carrying cost, for each unit of product M, is \$1 per year.

Determine:

a. The optimal production lot.

b. The production and no-production periods.

c. The total annual inventory cost.

20. Amerland Corporation produces industrial air cleaners in the *most economical way,* in lot sizes of 600 units. Each unit costs \$300. The company operates 360 days a year and is capable of producing 30 units daily. The demand rate is 300 units per month. Inventory carrying cost is 25 percent of the value stored.

Find:

a. The length of a production run.

b. The maximum inventory, in units.

c. The length of the "no-production" periods.

d. The total yearly inventory cost.

21. Central Airlines buys special valves at \$10 apiece. The company uses 24,500 valves each year. It costs \$20 to place an order, and the unit carrying cost per year is considered to be 20 percent of the value stored.

a. Find how many valves should be purchased at a time (using EOQ).

b. Should the company accept an offer of a 2 percent discount on the valves if they are purchased quarterly?

22. Given an inventory system with the following data:

Yearly demand = 120 units
Ordering cost = \$45
Price of unit = \$200
Annual carrying cost = 24 percent of value stored

Determine:

a. The economic order quantity.
b. The supplier offered a 1 percent discount on the unit price if the items are purchased in lots of 100 at a time. Should management accept the offer?
c. The minimum percentage discount that will make the offer attractive.

23. Dee's Department Store sells 25,000 type A shirts a year. The supplier offers a generous quantity discount. His price list is given below:

Quantity	*Price per shirt for entire quantity*
0–999	\$2.50
1,000–1,749	2.00
1,750–2,499	1.50
2,500 and over	1.00

Given: Order cost, \$20. Inventory carrying cost, 20 percent of the value of the item.

Find the EOQ for each price level and check its feasibility. In the infeasible cases, compute cost data for the closest possible limit. Compare total cost at all quantity levels and suggest the best inventory policy for Dee's.

24. Formulate an algorithm (set of decision rules) to solve the quantity discount problem when only one price break exists.

25. A company uses a certain product that is demanded at an average rate of 10 units a working day. The company operates on a five-day-a-week schedule.

Replenishment occurs once every six weeks. Storage cost per unit is \$6 (paid only if the unit is stored for the entire six-week period). Shortage cost is \$30 per unit per week. The table below gives the probability of demand during the six weeks.

Quantity demanded	*Probability*
60	.05
150	.10
240	.15
300	.40
360	.15
450	.10
540	.05

Find the best safety level. Use the trial-and-error approach to check safety levels of 0, 60, 150, and 240.

26. Westcan Electric Corporation distributes large industrial transformers in the West Coast. Demand is known to be 60 units per month. The company can order transformers any time and delivery from the plant is instantaneous. There is a fixed cost of \$800 associated with each order. The company can store the product in its warehouse in an attempt to reduce the fixed cost per order by increasing the order size; however, this creates a holding cost per unit of \$150 per month. If demand is not satisfied, the company loses \$250 (loss of goodwill) per unit demanded each month (assume 30 days per month).

a. Find the quantity the company should order each time in order to minimize its total relevant inventory cost.
b. Find the minimum cost per cycle if the optimal ordering policy is used.
c. How many units of demand will be supplied late each period?
d. How often should an order be placed?
e. What are the possible consequences of this policy in the long run?

27. The lead time for a product is 10 days. The demand for the product is 20 units per day. It is known that the standard deviation of the demand during the lead time is 15 units. Assume a normal distribution for the demand.

Management would like to provide a service level of 85 percent or 90 percent, whichever is less expensive.

The company orders 10 times a year, and the holding and shortage costs are:

H = \$20 per unit per year
G = \$80 per unit short per year

Should the company use the 85 percent or the 90 percent service level?

28. Tampa Electric Corp. wishes to determine the number of special batteries it should maintain. Each time the company runs out of batteries it costs the company $700. The holding cost of a battery is $80 per year. The company now orders four times a year. The following historical data on inventory levels and stockouts is available.

Inventory level	*Probability of stockout*
20	.60
30	.30
40	.20
50	.10

Find:

a. The total annual inventory and stockout cost for an inventory level of 20 batteries.

b. Which of the given inventory levels will be the most desirable?

29. A company can produce 10 units of product M per day, during 250 working days per year. The cost of producing one unit is $10. The cost of setting up one production run amounts to $100. The inventory carrying cost, per year, is 30 percent of the value stored. The company sells 1,500 units of product M each year. The company's objective is profit maximization.

Find:

a. The economic lot size.

b. The annual number of production runs.

c. The total annual cost of carrying inventory.

d. The production time (T_1).

e. The maximum inventory level.

f. The depletion period (T_2).

g. The company is considering producing a two-year supply in one production run. If they do so they will be able to cut production cost by 10 percent. Show whether such an alternative will be profitable.

30. I produce parts for $5 each. If I run out of spares I must make a special run and they will cost $15 each. If my probability of demand for spares is constant (discrete) between 1 and 10, how many spares should I produce?

31. Ambulances cost $50,000 each. Goodwill loss due to a death is X. The chance of needing two ambulances is 1 in a 100 and three is 1 in a 1,000. If the hospital buys three ambulances, what is the minimum value of X?

32. You run a restaurant with room for 100 tables that are available on a reservations-only basis. If you accept N reservations you will actually get N-19, N-18, . . . N customers with a probability of .05 each. For each unavailable table you lose a profit of $9. Rent, and so on, is $10 per table. Each customer who must be turned away because of overreserving costs you $6 in damages and $5 in bad publicity. If you accept 100 reservations, how many tables should you rent? If you *buy* 100 tables, how many reservations should you accept? (*Hint:* $Q^* = 100$).

33. Given the following MPS, IMF, and product tree, determine the planned releases for item 1342.

Item	*Lead time*	*On hand*	*Demand in week (number)* 11	12	13	14	15
19	1 week	100	100	0	100	200	0
1342	2 weeks	200	0	500	0	0	0
102	1 week	0	50	0	0	0	0
312	2 weeks	0	5	0	0	10	0

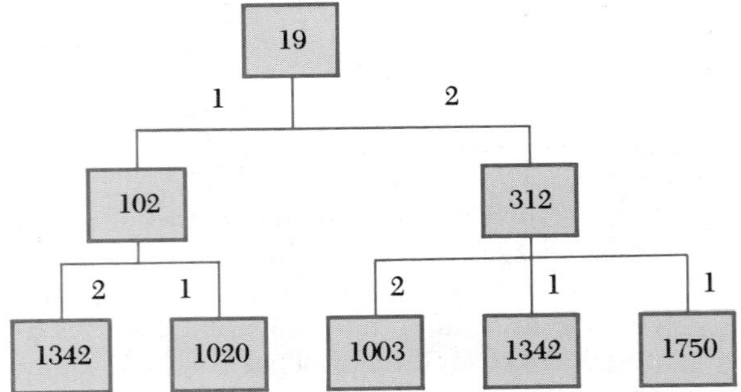

34. In part-period lot sizing, a lot size is selected that comes closest to equating the holding cost to the ordering cost. Conduct a part-period lot sizing for table legs given the following demand schedule. Holding a leg in inventory costs $1 per week. Ordering/shipping costs $100 for any size order. Lead time is virtually instantaneous.

Week	*Demand for table legs*
10	85
11	40
12	25
13	40

Week	Demand for table legs
14	105
15	75
16	80

35. Resolve the example following Equation 14.38 if the shortage cost is given as $10 *per unit* short. Consider service levels of 90, 95, and 99 percent.

36. Several airlines offer their passengers a selective food menu (e.g., fish, beef, chicken). The flight attendents admit that sometimes some passengers do not get the meal of their choice, but the vast majority of passengers do get what they ask for. Relate this situation to the concept of "service level."

37. The lead time to make a special gear is four weeks. There are currently four gears available and two due to be finished in two weeks. The gross requirements for the gear over the next eight weeks are as follows:

Week	1	2	3	4	5	6	7	8
No. of units	3	1	2	0	1	3	2	1

If the ELS is 2 units, when should orders be released for the year?

38. Given a schedule for planned releases as derived by MRP for a plant that works on a 50-week production schedule:

Date	January 3	January 10	January 17	January 24	January 31	February 7
Quantity	50	—	120	80	40	140

The ordering cost is $100.
The item cost is $500.
The holding costs are 20 percent per unit per year.
Find the optimal lot size (ordering policy).

39. Given an MRP system with the following information:

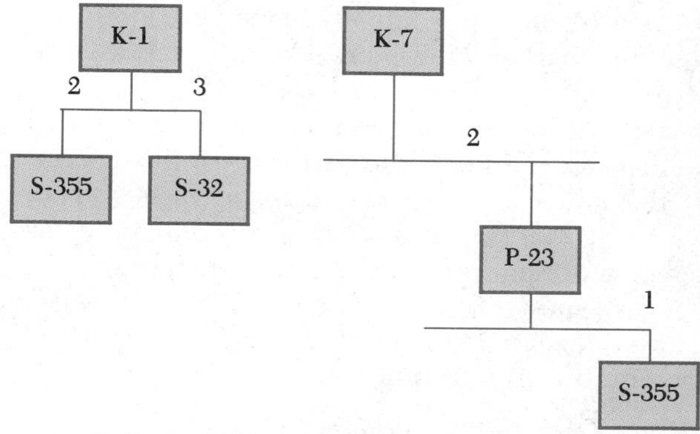

Delivery Schedule:

Item	*Lead time*	*On hand*	*November 5*	*November 12*	*November 19*	*November 26*	*December 3*
K-1	2 weeks	0		20	—	50	—
K-7	1 week	20	10	—	30	40	—
P-23	1 week	0	—	—	—	—	—
S-32	2 weeks	30	—	—	—	—	—
S-355	2 weeks	100	—	—	—	—	—

Existing Orders:

K-7 (complete): 10 units to arrive on November 12

Find the planned releases for part S-355.

14.19 CASE I

VISUTECH

Visutech is a manufacturer of industrial cameras that are currently selling for $4,200 a unit. The demand for the product is stable in the quantity of 6,000 units per year.

The company had little competition up to last year. At that time, two Japanese companies entered the market. Visutech sales started to drop. In order to boost sales, the company decided not to increase prices even though inflation pushed up the production cost by 11 percent. As a result, the company gained back its share of the market. However, earnings decreased significantly.

At present, the company produces at a rate that exactly meets the demand. In this manner, the unit cost is estimated to be $4,000. There is a $6,000 setup cost for each production startup and monthly production is 500 units per lot.

The company's cost containment committee met last Monday. Two proposals were submitted to the committee:

a. Change the frequency of production to produce the most economic lot sizes. The company's production capacity is estimated at 2,000 units per month.

b. Buy subassemblies in Korea and assemble them at the plant. The Koreans can ship the parts in lots of 1,000 once every two months. The cost of each subassembled unit is $3,000. The assembly work requires no setup cost; it is done continuously at a cost of $1,010 per unit. The Korean supplier will offer a 3 percent discount if Visutech is willing to receive shipments twice a year.

Being a management scientist working for the cost containment committee, what would you advise them to do? (*Hint:* Consider the alternative of no change.)

General information

The company computes its inventory carrying cost at an annual rate of 25 percent. Ordering cost for vendor's work is considered to be $60 per order. An order must be prepared for every shipment.

CASE II

EMCO CORPORATION[19]

The Emco Corporation, a midwestern manufacturer of desk calculators, has the public image of a well-managed corporation in a growth industry. If the company is able to maintain its present rate of growth, it will be number one in its field within a few years. Emco has sales offices in approximately 100 cities in the United States. Emco calculators are sold or rented to both large and small customers in a number of different industries. Exhibit 1 shows the firm's income statement for the past five years.

The company has always followed a policy of giving liberal trade-ins on Emco and non-Emco equipment to increase sales in this competitive industry. About 10 years ago, Mr. E. Miller, a former salesman, showed management that there was a market for these trade-ins. He was then put in charge of the used equipment department. His job was to maintain an orderly market in used equipment—maintaining high prices on the used units sold so as not to cut into the sales of new calculators. The department staff, which was composed mostly of former salesmen, grew from 10 to 45 over a 10-year period. It was discovered that there was a market for machines that had been used as floor demonstrators in the sales offices. Thus, today, the two major sources of used equipment are trade-ins and former demonstrators.

Some of the machines are sold, while others

[19] This case was prepared by Dean Harold Lazarus, School of Business Administration, Hofstra University, and John D. McGarr of the Graduate School of Business Administration of New York University, for class discussion.

EXHIBIT 1

EMCO CORPORATION
Income Statement
For the Past Five Years
($ in thousands)

	1987	*1986*	*1985*	*1984*	*1983*
Gross income	$599,000	$450,000	$330,000	$315,000	$290,000
Cost of goods sold	200,000	150,000	120,000	115,000	140,000
Gross profit	339,000	300,000	210,000	200,000	150,000
Net income	55,000	45,000	33,000	27,000	15,000

are directed into a used rental program. Those sold to wholesalers or dealers are in either an as-is or reconditioned state. The as-is units are sold from any 1 of 10 regional headquarters when a large quantity is accumulated. All non-Emco trade-ins are sold as-is. The reconditioned units are sold from the factory, where they have been collected by company vans from the sales offices on a quarterly basis.

The machines in the used rental program have all been reconditioned. Once they have been reconditioned, they are shipped to regional headquarters to await renting for periods ranging from two weeks to one year.

All Emco products have a seven-digit serial number which is used for inventory classification purposes. The inventory of used equipment is broken down into Emco trade-ins, non-Emco trade-ins, former demonstrators, and reconditioned calculators in the used rental program. Machines are classified as Emco trade-ins and non-Emco trade-ins at the time when a customer receives his new Emco unit. When the sales offices receive new calculators for demonstration purposes, the old demonstrators are then considered former demonstrators. The demonstrators are replaced on a yearly cycle. Machines are transferred to the used rental program at the discretion of the used equipment department.

Mr. S. Carlson, the controller of Emco, recently set up a profit analysis area within the finance department. The objective of this new area is to evaluate the profitability of the firm's various operations.

The profit analysis area was called upon by the controller to make an analysis of a proposal put forth by Mr. Miller. He proposed that the firm put new machines into the high profit used rental program for six months and then sell them in the used market. Mr. Miller reasoned that the demand for machines in the used market was greater than the present inventory or the forecasted additions to inventory, for the remainder of the year.

Mr. A. Ernst, a financial analyst, received this proposal. In order to get some background, Mr. Ernst first computed income statements for the past five years. Exhibit 2 shows these statements, while Exhibit 3 gives a breakdown of Exhibit 2 into the sales and rental programs of used equipment.

The statements puzzled Mr. Ernst since

EXHIBIT 2

Income Statements
Used Equipment
(in thousands)

	1987	*1986*	*1985*	*1984*	*1983*
Gross income	$25,600	$19,020	$14,150	$9,100	$5,000
Net earnings before taxes	(2,504)	500	(1,700)	(1,800)	(1,000)

EXHIBIT 3

Income Statements
Used Equipment by Source
(in thousands)

	1987	*1986*	*1985*	*1984*	*1983*
Sales					
Gross income	$19,000	$14,000	$11,100	$7,000	n.a.
Net earnings before taxes	(4,514)	(1,630)	(2,900)	(2,900)	n.a.
Rental					
Gross income	6,600	5,020	3,050	2,100	n.a.
Net earnings before taxes	2,010	2,130	1,200	1,100	n.a.

everyone was under the impression that the used equipment department was a profitable operation.

The factory inventory classification report for June 1988 is shown in Exhibit 4.

The used equipment department had made a forecast of trade-ins and former demonstrators which they expected to be added to the inventory for the rest of the year. They also forecasted their sales for the remainder of the year. This data is shown in Exhibit 5.

At first Mr. Ernst thought it obvious that there were enough machines in inventory and incoming flows to cover the forecasted demand. Mr. Ernst then checked the factory on the physical inventory. He called the factory and, after speaking with several managers in the inventory area who didn't know where this information was or even if the factory had it, he finally received the June 1988 report on physical inventory. The report is shown in Exhibit 6.

When Mr. Ernst called Mr. Miller to ask about the discrepancies in the inventory figures, he found that Mr. Miller was on a trip to Los Angeles. Mr. Ernst spoke, instead, to a former salesman who had recently joined the used equipment department. The former salesman,

EXHIBIT 4
Inventory classification report—June 1988

	Units
Emco trade-ins	17,586
Non-Emco trade-ins	9,987
Former demonstrators	29,543
Total	57,116
Used rental program	20,437*

* 4,543 machines in district office warehouses awaiting rental.

EXHIBIT 5
Used equipment department forecast—June 1988

	Units
July–December 1988 additions to inventory	
Emco trade-ins	19,642
Non-Emco trade-ins	7,679
Former demonstrators	23,113
Total	50,434
Sales forecast	70,445
Forecast addition to used rental program	2,000

EXHIBIT 6
Used equipment physical inventory report—June 1988

	Units		
	At sales office	*At plant*	*Total*
Emco trade-ins	5,843	2,894	8,737
Non-Emco trade-ins	3,435	1,015	4,450
Former demonstrators	7,364	6,775	14,139
Total			27,326

when asked about the inventory figures, told Mr. Ernst, in a laughing manner, that some salesmen would "misplace" demonstrators and others would forget that customers had machines to trade in when the new calculators were installed. The former salesman related that he had just received a letter from the New York sales office manager asking what he should do about 150 demonstrators, still in factory packaging, that had been accumulating in the office warehouse. The average age of these demonstrators was three years.

After this conversation, Mr. Ernst collected his figures (Exhibits 2–6), went to the used equipment department to pick up a copy of the letter from the manager of the New York sales office, and went to Mr. Carlson's office. After hearing Mr. Ernst's presentation, Mr. Carlson agreed to permit Mr. Ernst to make a full study of this department. The two men then began to formulate a strategy for the investigation of this operation.

Analyze this case and ascertain the nature of Emco's problem. Where are the missing calculators?

14.20 GLOSSARY

The A-B-C classification system Inventory items are classified into three groups: A (high value, small quantity), B (medium value, larger quantity), C (small value, many items—the nuts and bolts). Classification is made for control purposes.

Average inventory The average amount of inventory, usually on a one-year period. It is equal to one half of the maximum inventory of the EOQ model.

Back order A temporary shortage. Items that will be delivered (or produced) later.

The base-stock system An inventory system in which an order is placed as soon as a unit is taken from stock.

Bill of materials (B/M) The list of raw materials, components, and subassemblies (and their quantities) needed to produce an item.

Carrying cost Same as holding cost.

Cycle time The length of time between placing (or receiving) two consecutive orders.

Days' supply The length of time (days) that an inventory will last without renewal (replenishment or stockout).

Dependent demand Demand for items that are parts of items whose production is already planned.

Depletion Reduction of the inventory to a zero point of no inventory.

Economic lot size (ELS) A manufacturing lot or batch size that will minimize the total annual costs of setup and holding inventory.

Economic order quantity (EOQ) A quantity of an item that, if purchased at one time, will minimize the total annual inventory ordering and holding costs.

Explode Stepping down through the bill of materials levels to determine what parts will be required, in what quantities, and when.

The fixed quantity (perpetual) system An inventory system where orders for fixed amounts are placed whenever an agreed-upon reorder point is reached (i.e., order whenever stock is down to 10 units).

The fixed time (periodic or *s,S*) system An inventory system where varying-sized orders are placed periodically (e.g., once a month).

Holding cost Costs associated with storing inventory, such as cost of capital, insurance, renting storage space, and taxes.

Inventory master file (IMF) The computer file that contains a listing of on-hand, on-order, and committed inventory.

Joint ordering Placing orders for different items (usually with one supplier) as one combined order.

Lead time The time between placing an order and its delivery.

Level The stage of subcomponent assemblies in the bill of materials, the finished product being designated as level 0.

Lot sizing Determining the best amount of items to produce or purchase at a given time.

Lumpy demand Demand that comes in groups, with little or no demand occurring between the groups.

Master production schedule (MPS) The time-phased list of products (and their quantities) that are to be produced.

Material requirements planning (MRP) An inventory control system for dependent demand items.

Ordering cost The costs of placing one order for an item, including paperwork, inspection of the incoming order, and telephone calls.

Parent item The finished product (level 0).

Planned shortage Allowing shortages to occur from time to time rather than keeping a large inventory.

Quantity discount A discount on the unit cost offered by the supplier to a buyer willing to buy in large lots.

Reorder point The inventory level at which an order for an item is placed.

Replenishment Describes the arrival of a shipment or renewal of the inventory.

Safety stock Inventory maintained specifically to reduce shortages when demand is high or when the lead time is too long.

Service level The percent of time that all demand is met on request. The probability of *not* running out of stock.

Setup costs Expenses incurred to start up a production run (paperwork, tool preparation, and clean up).

Shortage Inability to provide the item from stock. Available inventory is insufficient to meet demand.

Stockout Same as shortage.

The two-bin system An inventory system where items are stored in two bins: large and small. Demand is satisfied from the large bin first. Depletion of the large bin signifies the need to reorder.

14.21 REFERENCES AND BIBLIOGRAPHY

1. Brown, R. G. *Decision Rules for Inventory Management.* New York: Holt, Rinehart & Winston, 1967.
2. Buffa, E. S., and J. G. Miller. *Production Inventory Systems: Planning and Control.* 3rd ed. Homewood, Ill.: Richard D. Irwin, 1979.
3. Davis, E. W. *Case Studies in MRP.* Washington, D.C.: American Production and Inventory Control Society, 1978.
4. Fuchs, Jerome H. *Computerized Inventory Control Systems.* Englewood Cliffs, N.J.: Prentice-Hall, 1978.
5. Green, J. H. *Production and Inventory Control Handbook.* New York: McGraw-Hill, 1970.
6. Hall, R. W. *Zero Inventories.* Homewood, Ill.: Dow Jones-Irwin, 1983.
7. Huang, P. Y., L. P. Rees, B. W. Taylor, III. "A Simulation Analysis of the Japanese JIT Technique." *Decision Sciences* 14, (July 1983), 326–44.
8. Johnson, L. A., and D. C. Montgomery. *Operations Research in Production Planning, Scheduling and Inventory Control.* New York: John Wiley & Sons, 1974.
9. Larson, S. *Inventory Systems and Controls Handbook.* Englewood Cliffs, N.J.: Prentice-Hall, 1976.
10. Lewis, C. D. *Demand Analysis and Inventory Control.* Lexington, Mass.: Lexington Books, 1975.
11. Orlicky, J. *Material Requirements Planning.* New York: McGraw-Hill, 1975.
12. Schonberger, R. J. *Japanese Manufacturing Techniques: Nine Hidden Lessons in Simplicity.* New York: Free Press, 1982.
13. Schonberger, R. J. "Some Observations on the Advantages and Implementation Issues of JIT Production Systems." *Journal of Operations Management* (November 1982), pp. 1–12.
14. Schroeder, R. G., et al. "A Study of MRP Benefits and Costs." *Journal of Operations Management* 2 (October 1981), pp. 1–10.

15. Shanoff, C. S. "*No Inventory Systems.*" *Purchasing Administration,* August 1978.

16. Silver, E. A., and R. Peterson *Decision Systems for Inventory Management and Production Planning.* 2nd ed. New York: John Wiley & Sons, 1985.

17. Smolik, D. P. *Material Requirements of Manufacturing.* New York: Van Nostrand Reinhold, 1983.

18. Tersine, J. R. *Principles of Inventory and Materials Management.* 2nd ed. New York: Elsevier North-Holland, 1982.

19. Walleigh, R. C. "Getting Things Done: What's Your Excuse for Not Using JIT." *Harvard Business Review,* March–April 1986.

15

Waiting lines

PART A: BASICS

15.1 The queuing situation.
15.2 The managerial problem.
15.3 The methodology of queuing analysis.
15.4 The arrival process.
15.5 The service process.
15.6 The waiting line.
15.7 Queuing models and solution approaches.
15.8 The basic Poisson-exponential model.
15.9 Cost analysis of queuing systems.
15.10 Managerial applications of Poisson-exponential queuing systems.
15.11 Concluding remarks.
15.12 Problems for Part A.

PART B: EXTENSIONS

15.13 Multifacility queuing systems.
15.14 Other queuing situations.
15.15 Serial queues.
15.16 Use of computers.
15.17 Problems for Part B.
15.18 Case I—Newtown Maintenance Division.
Case II—A queuing case study of drive-in banking.
15.19 Glossary.
15.20 References and bibliography.

The more society becomes interdependent psychologically, economically, and technically, the more individuals encounter waiting lines, or queues, in their daily lives. People queue at doctors' offices, supermarkets, gasoline stations, and tollbooths. Waiting lines may also involve nonhumans as customers: airplanes circling airports and machines waiting for repairs. The problem of managing waiting lines is complex, since the cost of providing services of all kinds is rapidly increasing.

The objective is to determine the appropriate level of service. The method of analyzing waiting line problems illustrated in this chapter is called queuing theory.

In Part A of this chapter the queuing problem is formulated and a solution using equations for simple problems is derived. In Part B, more complex queuing systems are addressed, and tables substituting for formulas are presented to facilitate the analysis of these systems. For even more complex queuing systems, the technique of simulation, presented in Chapter 16, is necessary.

LEARNING OBJECTIVES

The student should be able to:

a. Define a service–waiting line system and identify its major components.
b. Describe the managerial problems involved in such a system.
c. List the *costs* that are involved in such a system.
d. List the major measures of performance of a service system.
e. Describe the arrival process and its measurement.
f. Describe the service process and its measurement.
g. Discuss the formation of waiting lines, the queue discipline, and the customer's behavior in the queue.
h. Formulate and solve deterministic situations.
i. Formulate and solve simple problems of the Poisson-exponential single facility system, using formulas.

Extensions

j. Solve multichannel problems using a table.
k. Solve finite source queuing problems using a computer.
l. Solve queuing systems with a maximum queue length, using a computer.
m. Solve queuing systems with a constant service time and Poisson arrivals, using a computer.
n. Solve Poisson-exponential serial queues.

PART A: BASICS

All American Aviation Company has a specialized machine shop that serves the airlines in Plain City. At the present time the shop employs about 400 mechanics. Willie Davis, the materials manager, just returned, troubled, from the regular Monday executive committee meeting. It was only a week ago that he placed his best employee, John, in the "toolroom," the machine shop's center for distributing specialized tools. He took this action after continuous complaints from the production manager about long waiting lines there. It appeared to Willie that the toolroom was the scapegoat for everything that went wrong with production.

This week Willie was sure that the problem of the waiting lines had been solved, because John seemed to be handling the situation well. However, in the morning's meeting, Willie was again under the gun. He therefore started wondering if it might be necessary to add a second clerk. He reasoned that with two clerks, the waiting time at the toolroom would be reduced by one half. However, he was not sure that such a reduction would justify the additional cost.

Willie's reasoning that doubling the capacity of the toolroom would decrease the waiting time by one half seemed so logical and obvious that it didn't occur to him that it might be incorrect. His error will be analyzed later in this chapter.

15.1 THE QUEUING SITUATION

Characteristics of waiting line situations

Fluctuating demand

The incident at the All American Aviation Company is typical of a situation that arises in the delivery of services. On the one hand, the demand for services is unstable; there are some foreseeable fluctuations during certain time periods (e.g., rush hours at the beginning and the end of shifts at the toolroom). In addition, there are unforeseeable changes in the pattern of demand. On the other hand, the length of service may vary, due to particular requirements of those requesting the service. The result is difficulty in meeting demand immediately on request, especially during rush hours.

Expensive to meet peak demand

The only way that demand can be immediately supplied, all the time, is to build a high service capacity that can always meet peak demand. Such a situation can be observed in an electric utility company. However, the balancing of demand and supply at an electric company is relatively easy, since capacity can be added or deleted as needed, at relatively low cost once the generators have been constructed. In other areas, it is *very expensive* to build, operate, and maintain a service facility so that all demands will be met, all the time, on request. It may also be expensive to constantly change the capacity in an existing service facility to fit the demand, especially when people provide the service. Instead, service facilities are usually designed so that their capacity is less than the maximum demand. As a result, whenever demand exceeds capacity, a *waiting line*, or a **queue**, is formed; that is, the customers do not get service immediately on request, but must wait. On other occasions, the service facility will be idle. Thus, at a high level of service capacity, the people served will have only a limited wait, but the service facility will frequently be idle (at considerable expense). At a lower, less expensive level of service capacity, there will be less idle time but people will have to wait longer.

Formation of a queue

The management of services is indeed complicated. While management would like to satisfy the customer ("the customer is always right"), it is very expensive, sometimes even impossible, to satisfy everyone immediately, all the time. Therefore, management is interested in finding the *appropriate level of service*. The theory applied to this problem is called *queuing* or *waiting line* theory.

Pioneered by A. K. Erlang, a Danish engineer in the telephone industry in the early 1920s, queuing theory was extended in application, especially after World War II, to a large number of situations; for example:

Erlang pioneers queuing theory

- Determining access to telecommunications networks.
- Determining the capacity of an emergency room in a hospital.
- Determining the number of runways at an airport.
- Determining the number of elevators in a building.
- Determining the number of traffic lights and their frequency of operation.
- Determining the number of flights between two cities.
- Determining the number of first-class seats in an airplane.
- Determining the size of a restaurant.
- Determining the number of employees in a storeroom, in a typing pool, or in a nursing team.
- Scheduling work in large computer systems.

The structure of a queuing system

A queuing system (Figure 15.1) is composed of the following parts:

The customers and their source (Section 15.4) Customers are defined as those in need of service. Customers can be people, airplanes, machines, or raw materials. The customers are generated from a *population* or a **source.** For example, a hospital's "population" would be the residents in the surrounding community and the "customers" would be those sick people in the population requiring hospitalization.

The source

The arrival process (Section 15.4) The manner in which customers show up at the service facility is called the arrival process.

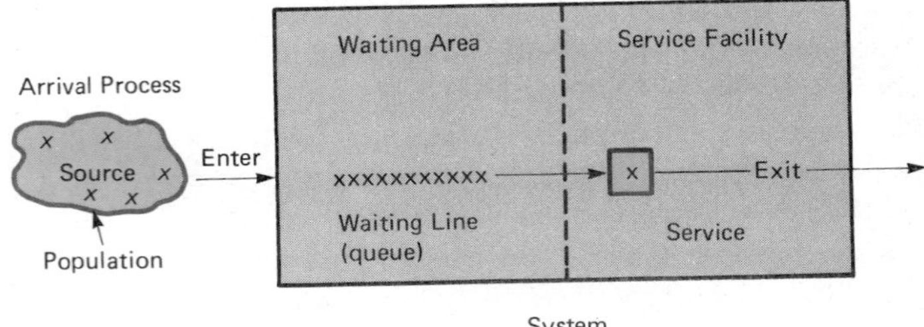

FIGURE 15.1
The major components of a queuing system

The service facility

The service facility and the service process (Section 15.5) The service is provided by a **service facility** (or facilities). This may be a person (a bank teller, a barber), a machine (elevator, gasoline pump), or a space (airport runway, parking lot, hospital bed), to mention just a few. A service facility may include one person or several people operating as a team.

The queue (Section 15.6) Whenever an arriving customer finds that the service facility is busy, a *queue*, or waiting line, is formed.

Examples of queuing systems

The following table lists some examples of queuing systems:

System	*Queue*	*Service*
Computer	Jobs	Process facilities
Bank	People	Tellers
Telephone	Callers	Switchboards
Library	Books to be shelved	Librarian's assistants
Freeway	Automobiles	Tollbooths
Airplane	People	Seats, flights
Airport	Circling planes	Runways

15.2 THE MANAGERIAL PROBLEM

The basic queuing problem: What level of service?

Looking at Willie Davis's situation, it is now possible to understand the managerial problem of waiting lines. As a responsible manager, Willie realizes that he must satisfy his customers. On the other hand, there is a cost attached to the provision of this service. In general, the basic problem of the management of waiting lines is: What is an "appropriate" level of service?[1]

[1] In addition to this basic decision, management will have to make several related decisions regarding such factors as the priorities of service and the operating hours. These decisions will not be discussed in this text. The interested reader is referred to texts on queuing theory such as Cooper [3], Newell [9], and White [13].

Decisions about an appropriate level of service are:

a. If only one service station exists, then the decision involves the *speed* of service, which can be increased by adding more personnel and/or equipment, or using *faster* personnel or equipment.

b. If additional service stations can be added, then the decision is: How many more is best?

Decision variables

Cost considerations

In making such decisions, the objective would be to minimize total cost. Management must consider both the cost of providing the service and the cost of customers' waiting (lost time, loss of goodwill, lost sales, and so on). Unfortunately, these costs are in direct opposition to each other, as shown in Figure 15.2[2] That is, the cost of providing the service increases with the service level, while the waiting time (and its cost) declines with the service level.[3] Unfortunately, the cost of waiting, in many cases, cannot be expressed in terms of dollars. This issue is discussed later.

Opposing costs

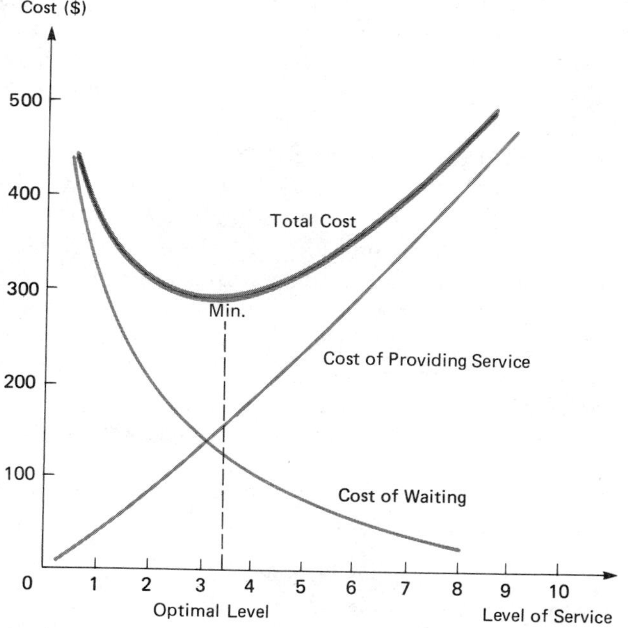

FIGURE 15.2
The queuing system

[2] Observe the resemblance of Figure 15.2 to the one associated with the EOQ model (Figure 14.9, Chapter 14).

[3] The service level may be measured by the capacity (number of facilities or speed) of the service.

The costs involved in a queuing situation

The facility cost The cost of providing a service includes:

1. Cost of construction (capital investment) as expressed by interest and amortization.
2. Cost of operation: labor, energy, and materials required for operations.
3. Cost of maintenance and repair.
4. Other costs: insurance, taxes, rental of space, and other fixed costs.

The cost of waiting customers In some cases, it is easy to assess the waiting cost. For example, when employees are waiting in line to use a copying machine or get tools, the cost is their wasted wages. This is the typical cost when the customers belong to the same organization as the one providing the service.

In other situations, such as retail sales, external customer ill will may be involved. Then the cost of waiting time is more difficult to assess and involves several components. For example, a waiting customer may get impatient and leave, thus resulting in a loss of revenue and possible loss of repeat business due to his or her dissatisfaction. There may also be an ill-will cost incurred; that is, when talk is spread about the poor service given at a facility, other customers may not come. A more extreme situation would be that of a patient waiting for surgery. If the patient waits too long, he or she may die. In addition to the loss of revenue to the hospital and the cost of ill will, there is an additional cost to the customer; in this case, the loss of his or her life.

Ill-will costs

Internal versus external customers

The difficulties in expressing the cost of waiting are especially severe in cases where the customers are *external* to the organization providing the service and the provider of the service is a nonprofit organization. In such a case, one may raise such questions as: "Cost to whom (e.g., to the patient, to the doctor, or to society)?" Or, "Is the cost directly proportional to the waiting time?" The answer to such questions is not simple, since it involves personal values, social priorities, and other qualitative factors. For this reason, decisions concerning queuing systems are often made from one of the two perspectives described below.

Management objectives

Management may hold either or both of the following objectives when making decisions about an appropriate service level.

Cost minimization In cases where it is possible to ascribe a cost to the waiting time (usually when a company is serving its own employees or equipment), management will provide a service level such that the total cost of waiting *and* service is minimized. This approach is demonstrated in Section 15.9.

Achieving a specified performance level (service goal) Instead of (sometimes in addition to) minimizing costs, management will strive to achieve a certain level of service. For example:

- Telephone companies want to repair 99 percent of all inoperative telephones within 24 hours.
- Fast-food restaurants advertise that you will not have to wait more than three minutes for breakfast.
- Banks try to avoid having more than six cars in any lane of their drive-in windows at a time.
- Service facilities should be in use at least 60 percent of the time.

Service policies

Determining the "best" level of service is a matter of organizational policy and is influenced by external factors such as competition and consumer pressures.

15.3 THE METHODOLOGY OF QUEUING ANALYSIS

Queuing is a descriptive tool

Predicting operating characteristics

The queuing methodology is basically a *descriptive* tool of analysis. As such, it is similar to a Markov analysis. As the reader may recall, the major objective of the Markov analysis was *prediction* of a system's behavior. Here, too, the major objective of waiting line theory is *prediction* of the behavior of a system as reflected in its *operating characteristics* or *measures of performance*. This information is needed by management to determine the most appropriate service level of the system. Although queuing theory is basically descriptive, it can also be used at times to determine the optimal number of service facilities or the optimal speed of a facility. Such normative applications are, however, limited.

The managerial application of waiting line theory involves the use of computed measures of performance for selecting an alternative solution to a queuing problem, usually among small numbers of alternatives. The entire process involves three steps:

a. Establish the measures of performance (or the operating characteristics) of the queuing system.
b. Compute the measures of performance (result variables).
c. Conduct an analysis.

a. Establish the measures of performance of the system

Measures of performance

In this step, a model of the problem is constructed and the *measures of performance* are decided on. Examples of such measures are:

- The average waiting time per customer.
- The average number of customers in the waiting line.
- The utilization of the service facility, or else its idle time.

b. Compute the measures of performance

Once the problem has been formulated, one of two solution methods is employed to find the measures of performance:

1. For problems in which certain theoretical statistical distributions can describe the actual data, formulas (Section 15.8) or equivalent tables (Section 15.13) can be used.
2. For other problems, simulation (see Chapter 16) is used.

The measures of performance are then computed for every course of action under consideration.

c. The analysis

In queuing analysis, there are usually only a small number of alternatives to be evaluated. For example, in a decision about the number of elevators to be constructed in a new building, 10 possibilities would be a realistic consideration, but not 5,000. The number of feasible alternatives in a service system is usually small because of human, technical, financial, and legal constraints. Alternatives may differ in the size of the facility, the number of servers, the speed of service, the priorities given to customers, or in the operating procedures. For each alternative, the measures of effectiveness must be computed.

Limited alternatives

Comparing the alternatives

The alternative solutions are then compared on the basis of their overall effectiveness. One approach is the use of a total cost curve, as shown in Figure 15.2. The major problem in this step may be the cost assessment. A queuing system usually involves several measures of performance, and it is necessary to establish a common denominator (such as total cost or total utility) to quantitatively compare the alternatives.[4] In some cases, a qualitative comparison of the alternatives is performed and no attempt is made to perform a cost analysis.

In a limited number of cases, the comparative analysis leads to an optimal solution—for example, a decision regarding the choice of the proper number of identical service facilities (see Example 2 in Section 15.13). In such cases, an explicit dollar value for the cost of waiting must be specified.

But most frequently the analysis involves the assessment of performance levels under different system configurations. For example, if waiting time per customer is important, it is useful to know, for each alternative configuration, how long customers must wait.

But before conducting such an analysis, let us examine the structure of a service system. As the reader may recall, a service system is composed of arrivals (Section 15.4), a service facility (Section 15.5), and a waiting line (Section 15.6).

15.4 THE ARRIVAL PROCESS

Description of arrivals

Arriving customers are classified according to the following:

Finite or infinite?

Source: Finite versus infinite Two cases are of primary interest: when the source (population) is basically *infinite* (or unlimited), such as the number

[4] Methods discussed in Chapter 4 can be utilized here.

of people visiting Niagara Falls, or when it is *finite*, as when a repair crew in a factory is responsible for maintaining a dozen machines.[5] Unless otherwise specified, *queuing theory assumes an infinite population.*

Batch versus individual arrivals Customers may arrive in *batches* (such as the arrival of a family to a restaurant) or *individually* (such as the arrival of an airplane at an airport). In this text, *individual arrivals are assumed* in all cases.

Scheduled versus nonscheduled arrivals Customers arrive at a service facility either on a scheduled basis (by appointment) or without prior notification. If they come without prior notification, their arrival time is not exactly known, but historical data enables us to describe arrivals by some *frequency distribution* (see Appendix B).

Quantitative measures of arrivals

Scheduled or unexpected arrivals?

Arrival rate and interarrival time

As indicated earlier, arrivals may be either scheduled or unexpected. In both cases, the arrival process can be described by either the average **arrival rate** (the average number of arrivals per unit of time) or by the average **interarrival time** (the reciprocal of the average arrival rate). The difference is that in scheduled arrivals, the arrival rate is relatively predetermined, while in unscheduled arrivals, the times are **random variables** and we must therefore talk about **averages** and **frequency distributions** of the times.

The arrival rate and the interarrival times (unscheduled arrivals)

The arrival process can be described by either the *mean arrival rate* or by the *mean interarrival time*. As an example, consider the situation at a toolroom (an area for storage and dispersal of tools) between 7 and 8 A.M. Figure 15.3 shows that seven employees arrived during the hour. Therefore, the *arrival rate* is seven per hour. The times between two consecutive arrivals vary. For example, there are eight minutes between the first arrival and the second, while there are two minutes between the second and third arrivals. These times between arrivals are called the *interarrival times*. The *average* (or *mean*) interarrival time during the first hour is $60/7$ = 8.6 minutes = $1/7$ of an hour. Let us examine these times through examples.

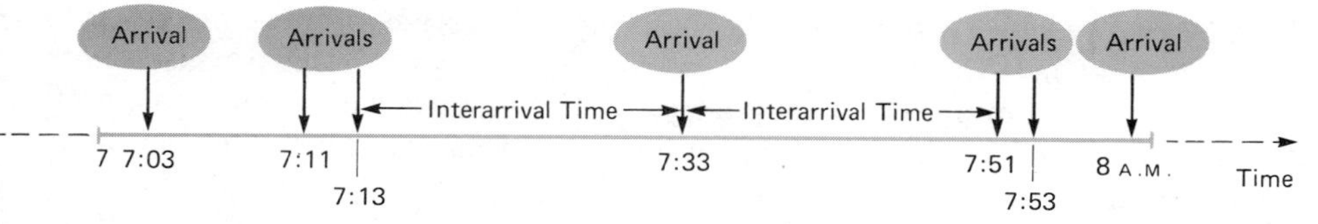

FIGURE 15.3
Arrivals at the toolroom

[5] No population is really infinite. What is meant is that the population is large enough that the probability of a second arrival is not significantly changed by the first arrival.

The average arrival rate (unscheduled arrivals), λ

Assume that the arrival times of employees to the toolroom were recorded over a period of 100 hours. Of these 100 hours, there were 5 hours within which there were 0 arrivals (5 percent of all cases), 6 hours where there was only 1 arrival, and so on. Such results can be described in the form of a frequency distribution or *histogram*, as shown in Figure 15.4. The shape of Figure 15.4 is very similar to the theoretical **Poisson** distribution (see Appendix B). Such a distribution is very common in queuing systems.

Poisson arrivals

FIGURE 15.4
The frequency distribution of arrivals

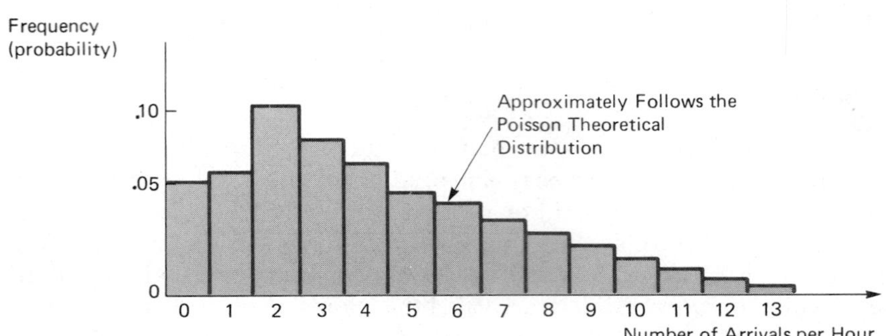

When customers, in a given period of time, arrive *at random*, the distribution of arrivals has been shown to follow the *Poisson* distribution. Random arrival means that even if the mean number of arrivals in a time period is known, the exact moment of arrival cannot be predicted. Thus, each moment in the time span has the same chance of having an arrival. Such behavior is observed when arrivals are independent of each other; namely, when the arrival time is unaffected by preceding or future arrivals. Examples of such arrivals are customers to gasoline stations and failures of machines. The *average* arrival rate is usually designated by the Greek letter "lambda," λ.

The average interarrival time (unscheduled arrivals), $1/\lambda$

As an alternative to the arrival rate, the interarrival time can also be used. In Figure 15.5, an interarrival frequency distribution is shown. After many observations of a certain service system, it may be possible to say that in 15 percent of the cases the time between two consecutive arrivals was 5 minutes, in 12 percent of the cases it was 7 minutes, in 10 percent of the cases it was 17 minutes, and so on. This information is recorded by the dots in Figure 15.5.

If the arrival rate of Figure 15.4 follows the Poisson distribution, then the interarrival times of Figure 15.5 are distributed according to

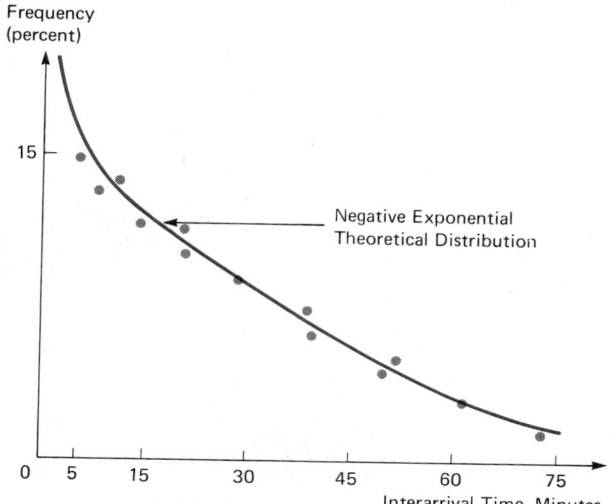

FIGURE 15.5
The interarrival times

Exponential interarrival times

the **negative exponential** distribution (see Appendix B).[6] The average interarrival time is designated by $1/\lambda$; for example, if $\lambda = 5$ per hour, then the average interarrival time will be $1/5$ of an hour or 12 minutes.

15.5 THE SERVICE PROCESS

Several basic arrangements of service facilities exist:

1. Single facility (such as a dentist's chair).
2. Multiple, **parallel,** *identical* facilities (**multifacility**), either with a single queue (as in the post office) or with multiple queues (as in a gasoline station).
3. Multiple, parallel, but *not identical* facilities (such as express and regular checkout counters in a supermarket).
4. Service facilities that are arranged in a series (**serial** arrangement). The customer enters the first facility and gets a portion of the service, then moves on to the second facility, and so on, as though he or she is on an assembly line. An example of such an arrangement is the registration process at a university, or a restaurant where you may wait first for a table, then for the food, and finally at the cashier.
5. Combinations of the above.

Figure 15.6 illustrates some of these possible service arrangements. The arrows into the boxes represent arriving and waiting customers, the boxes

[6] Notice that in Figure 15.5, the distribution is described by a curve "connecting" the points. Such a distribution is a continuous distribution. The distribution of Figure 15.4, on the other hand, is composed of intervals and is called a discrete distribution.

FIGURE 15.6
Different arrangements of service facilities

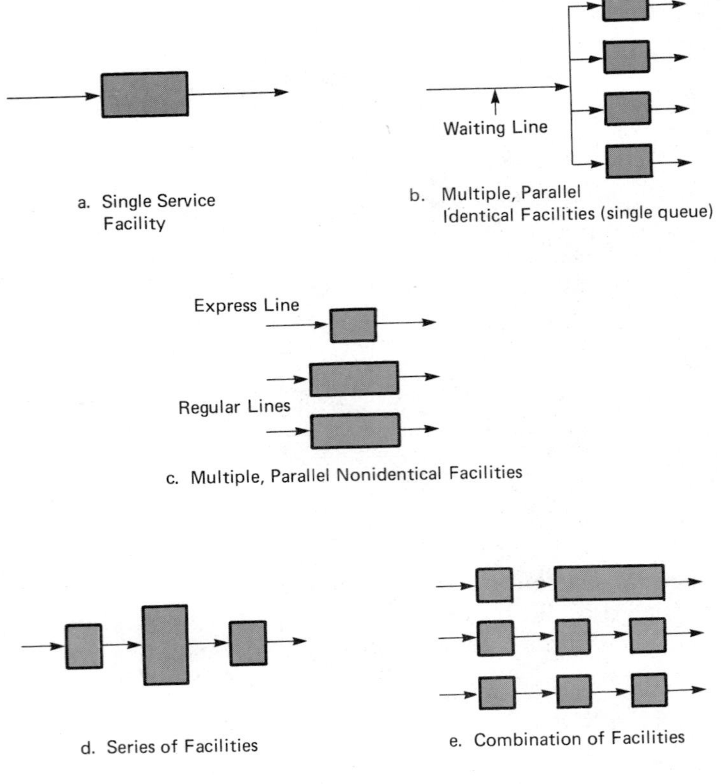

represent the service facilities, and the arrows out represent served customers.

Description of the service time

Constant versus fluctuating service

The service given in a facility consumes time. The length of time of the service may be *constant* (e.g., exactly 10 minutes for each service), or it may *fluctuate*.[7] A fluctuating service time may be described by a frequency distribution.

There are two ways of describing fluctuating service times. One is to describe the *average length of the service* (e.g., 15 minutes, on the average); the other is the average **service rate** or how many customers can be served, on the average, each hour (e.g., four per hour).

[7] Service times may, in actuality, be affected by the length of the waiting line. If the line is long, the servers may work faster because of psychological and social pressures. In this text, the length of the line is assumed *not* to affect the service rate.

The average length of service (service time), $1/\mu$

A fluctuating service time may follow one of several statistical distributions. Most common is the *negative exponential* (as in Figure 15.5). For example, the length of telephone calls is distributed in this fashion. A less common distribution is the *normal distribution* (Appendix B), such as might be used in describing the time required for repairing a car. The average service time is usually designated by $1/\mu$, where the Greek letter "mu," μ, designates the average service rate.

Exponential service time

The average service rate, μ

The service rate measures the service capacity of the facility in terms of customers per unit of time. The mean service rate, μ, is the *inverse* of the mean service time. For example, if the average service time is one half of an hour, then the mean service rate is $1 \div \frac{1}{2} = 2$ customers per hour. If the service time is exponentially distributed, then the service rate can be shown to be Poisson distributed. Other service time distributions also exist, such as constant, Erlang, or "arbitrary" (which means that the mean service time and its standard deviation are known). For further discussion, see Cooper [3].

Inverse relationship

15.6 THE WAITING LINE

A queue is formed whenever customers arrive and the facility is busy. The characteristics of the queue depend on rules and regulations that are termed the **queue discipline.**

The queue discipline

Queue discipline

The queue discipline describes the policies that determine the manner in which customers are selected for service. Examples of some common disciplines are:

A priority system Priority is given to selected customers. For example, those with ten items or less in a supermarket can go to the express lane. The handicapped and passengers with small children board airplanes first.

Some priority systems

Emergency (preemptive priority) systems An emergency (**preemptive priority**) system is one in which an important customer not only has priority in entrance, but can even interrupt a less important customer in the middle of his or her service. For example, in an emergency case in a hospital, the doctor may leave the regular patient in the middle of the treatment. That is, the regular patient is *preempted* by the emergency one.

Last-come, first-served (LCFS) Last arrivals are served first. This system is commonly used with parts and materials in a warehouse, since it reduces handling and transportation.

First-come, first-served (FCFS) Customers that arrive first are served first.

In this text, the FCFS queue discipline is assumed.

The organization of the queue

Queues may be organized in various ways. For example, customers may be screened at a main gate and then referred to one of several lines (such as in some theaters or banks), depending on the service and the queue discipline. In some cases, there is one line for several parallel service facilities. This is the organization generally assumed here. Arrangements may also depend on the physical area available for the queue.

The behavior in a queue

Some interesting observations of human behavior in queues are:

Human behavior

1. **Balking**—Customers refusing to join the queue, usually because of its length.
2. **Reneging**—Customers tiring and leaving the queue before they are served.
3. **Jockeying**—Customers switching between waiting lines (a common scene in a supermarket).
4. **Combining or dividing**—Combining or dividing queues at certain queue lengths (e.g., in a supermarket when a counter is closed or opened).
5. **Cycling**—Returning to the queue immediately after obtaining service. (Children taking turns at a playground or ore cars cycling at a mine.)

In this text, we assume that a customer enters the system, stays in the line (if necessary), receives the service, and leaves. If a customer behaves otherwise (according to any of the above observations), the queuing system becomes very complex, requiring simulation for its analysis.

15.7 QUEUING MODELS AND SOLUTION APPROACHES

Queuing models

Due to the large number of possible queuing systems, a notation set was developed by D. G. Kendall in 1953. This notation system is commonly used today to label queuing models. Six items of information are necessary to completely define a queuing system. The arrival process, service process, and number of servers in the system are first defined. The way in which arriving units are accepted for service (the queue discipline), the maximum size permitted for the queue, and the number of people (or units) in the population served by the queuing system are then specified. The symbols are shown below. These are also used in the MSS package.

Item	*Value*	*Notation Used*
Arrival process	Poisson	*M*
	Erlang, shape parameter-*k*	*Ek*
	Constant	*D*
	Normal	*N*
	Uniform	*U*
	Only mean and variance known	*G*
Service process	Exponential	*M*
	Erlang, shape parameter-*k*	*Ek*
	Constant	*D*
	Normal	*N*
	Uniform	*U*
	Only mean and variance known	*G*
Number of servers	1 or more	*K* (actual number)
Queue discipline	First-come first-served	*FCFS*
	Nonpreemptive priority	*PRI.*
Maximum queue length	No limit	∞
	Finite limit	*n* (actual number)
Calling population size	Infinite	∞
	Finite	*n* (actual size)

When a system is described, its symbols are summarized using a simple two-part system based on Kendall's notation. The items are shown in two sets of three items, separated by slashes. For example, a system with a Poisson arrival process, exponential service time distribution, two servers, first-come, first-served discipline, no queue size limit, and serving a large (presumed infinite) population would be labeled *M/M/*2 *FCFS/∞/∞*. The most common queuing systems are listed below.

Descriptive label		*Comments*
*M/M/*1	*FCFS/∞/∞*	Standard single server model
M/M/K	*FCFS/∞/∞*	Standard multiserver model
*M/Ek/*1	*FCFS/∞/∞*	Single Erlang service model
*M/G/*1	*FCFS/∞/∞*	Service time distribution unknown
*M/M/*1	*PRI./∞/∞*	Priority service
M/M/K	*PRI./∞/∞*	Multiserver priority service
*M/M/*1	*FCFS/n/∞*	Finite queue, single server
M/M/K	*FCFS/n/∞*	Finite queue, multiserver
*M/M/*1	*FCFS/∞/n*	Limited source, single server
M/M/K	*FCFS/∞/n*	Limited source, multiserver

There are many variations of queuing situations, for example, truncated queues, queues with priorities, cyclic queues, and others that will not be treated here. See Cooper [3] for more discussion.

Solution approaches

There are two basic approaches to the solution of queuing problems: analytical and simulation.

Simulation versus analytical approach

The analytic approach The measures of performance are determined through the use of formulas. Unfortunately, many queuing situations are so complex that the analytic approach is completely impractical or even impossible.

Simulation For those situations in which the analytic approach is unsuitable, the procedure of simulation can be used. The process of solving queues by simulation will be deferred to Chapter 16 where the necessary theory is presented first.

In either of the above cases, computers are now the most practical approach to solving complex queuing problems. This will be discussed further in Section 15.16.

Information flow in waiting line models

As discussed earlier, it is helpful to use some measures of performance when evaluating service alternatives, particularly when a cost approach (Section 15.9) is planned. Therefore, a *solution* to a queuing problem means computing certain measures of performance. These measures are computed from three input variables:

λ, the mean arrival rate
μ, the mean service rate
K, the number of servers

Figure 15.7 summarizes the relationship between the input variables and the major measures of performance for most queuing models. For other models there may be additional input and/or output variables. Detailed explanations of these measures of performance will be given in the next section.

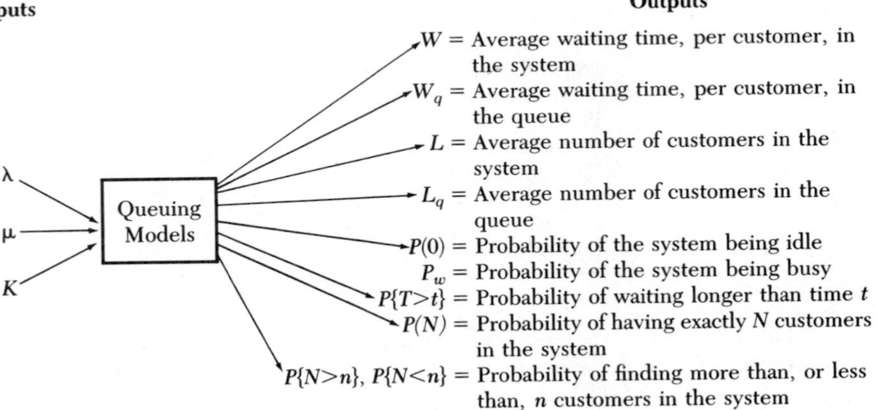

FIGURE 15.7
Information flows

Deterministic queuing systems

The simplest and the rarest of all waiting line situations involves constant arrival rates at predetermined times and constant service times. Three cases can be distinguished:

Three situations

1. *Arrival rate equals service rate.* Assume that people arrive every 10 minutes, to a single server, where the service takes exactly 10 minutes. Then the server will be utilized continuously (100 percent utilization), and there will be no waiting line.
2. *Arrival rate larger than service rate.* Assume that there are six arrivals per hour (one every 10 minutes) and the service rate is only five per hour (12 minutes each). Therefore, one arrival cannot be served each hour, and a waiting line will build up (at a rate of one per hour). Such a waiting line will grow and grow as time passes and is termed an **explosive queue.**
3. *Arrival rate smaller than service rate.* Assume that there are again six arrivals per hour but the service capacity is eight per hour. In this case, the facility will be utilized only $6/8$ = 75 percent of the time. There will never be a waiting line (if the arrivals come at equally scheduled intervals).

Note that in case 1, there is no waiting line and no idle facility. In the second case, the facility is fully utilized but a waiting line is formed. In the third case, there is no waiting line but the facility is not fully utilized. *In all these cases, there cannot be a waiting line and underutilization in the same situation.* However, when nonscheduled arrivals are involved, it is common to have *both* idle facilities at times and waiting lines at other times in the same service system, as will be shown later.

15.8 THE BASIC POISSON-EXPONENTIAL MODEL (*M*/*M*/1 *FCFS*/∞/∞)

The classical and probably best known of all waiting line models is the **Poisson-exponential single-server system.** It exhibits the following characteristics:

Arrival rate The arrival rate is assumed to be random and is thus described by the *Poisson* distribution. The *average* arrival rate is designated by the Greek letter "lambda," λ.

Service time The service time is assumed to follow the *negative exponential distribution.* The *average* service rate is designated by the Greek letter "mu," μ, and the *average* service time by $1/\mu$.

The *major assumptions* for the operation of such a single server system are:

Some assumptions

1. Infinite source of population.
2. First-come, first-served treatment.
3. The ratio λ/μ is smaller than 1. This ratio is designated by the Greek letter "rho," ρ. The **ratio** is a measure of the **utilization** of the system.

If the utilization factor is equal to or larger than 1, the waiting line will increase without bound (will be *explosive*), a situation which is unacceptable to management.

4. Steady state (equilibrium) exists.[8] A system is in a "transient state" when its measures of performance are still dependent on the initial conditions, otherwise it is in a standby state. Our interest is in the "long-run" behavior of the system, commonly known as *steady state*. A steady state condition occurs when the system measures become *independent of time*.
5. Unlimited space for the waiting line exists.

Measurements of performance (operating characteristics)

A queuing system is usually evaluated by one or more of the following measures of performance (given with their respective formulas). These measures depend on only two given variables, λ and μ, which must be stated in the same time dimensions.

The average waiting time, W The average time a customer spends in the system—waiting for the service *and* being served.

$$W = \frac{1}{\mu - \lambda} = \frac{1}{\mu(1 - \rho)} \tag{15.1}$$

The average waiting time in the queue, W_q This is the average time a customer will wait, in the queue, before the service starts

$$W_q = \frac{\lambda}{\mu(\mu - \lambda)} = \frac{\rho}{\mu(1 - \rho)} \tag{15.2}$$

The average number of customers in the system, L The average number of customers in the system, that is, counting those in the queue and those being served, is:

$$L = \frac{\lambda}{\mu - \lambda} = \frac{\rho}{1 - \rho} \tag{15.3}$$

The average number of customers in the queue, L_q The average number of customers in the queue measures the average length of the waiting line.

$$L_q = \frac{\lambda^2}{\mu(\mu - \lambda)} = \frac{\rho^2}{1 - \rho} \tag{15.4}$$

[8] For a discussion, refer to the chapter on Markov chains (Chapter 13). Notice the resemblance between the two techniques.

The probability of an empty facility, P(0) The probability that there are no customers in the system (that the facility is idle) is:

$$P(0) = 1 - \frac{\lambda}{\mu} = 1 - \rho \tag{15.5}$$

The probability of the system being busy, P_w The probability of the system being busy, P_w is the same as the probability of *not* finding an empty system, that is:

$$P_w = 1 - P(0) = \frac{\lambda}{\mu} = \rho \tag{15.6}$$

The probability of being in the system (waiting and being served) longer than time t The probability is:

$$P\{T > t\} = e^{(\lambda - \mu)t} \tag{15.7}$$

where:

e = 2.718 (the base of the natural logarithms)
t = Specified time
T = Time in the system

The probability of waiting (before service starts) a period of time T', which is *larger* than a designated time t', is:

$$P(T' > t') = \rho\, e^{-(\mu - \lambda)t'} \tag{15.8}$$

The probability of finding exactly N customers in the system, P(N)

$$P(N) = \rho^N(1 - \rho) \tag{15.9}$$

The probability that the number of customers in the system, N, will be larger than a specified number of customers, n.

$$P\{N > n\} = \rho^{n+1} \tag{15.10}$$

Note that:

$$P\{N < n\} = 1 - P\{N > (n - 1)\} \tag{15.11}$$

For example:

$P\{N < 3\}$ means $N = 0$, 1, or 2 and $P\{N > 2\}$ means $n = 3, 4, \ldots$

Thus:

$$P\{N < 3\} = 1 - P\{N > 2\}$$

The following relationships, developed by J. D. C. Little, are extremely important because they hold for *any* queuing system and enable us to find, L, L_q, W, and W_q as soon as one of these is computed.

$$L = \lambda W$$
$$L_q = \lambda W_q \qquad (15.12)$$
$$W = W_q + \frac{1}{\mu}$$

Managerial use of the measures of performance

Some of these measures can be used in a cost analysis, as is shown in the next section. Others are used to aid in determining service level policies. For example:

Example service policies

a. A fast-food restaurant wants to design its service facility such that a customer will not wait, on the average, more than two minutes (i.e., $W_q \leq 2$ minutes) before being served.
b. A telephone company desires that the probability of any customer being without telephone service more than two days be 3 percent (i.e., $P\{T > 2 \text{ days}\} = .03$).
c. A bank's policy is that the number of customers at its drive-in facility will exceed 10 only 5 percent of the time (i.e., $P\{N > 10\} = .05$).
d. A city information service should be busy at least 60 percent of the day (i.e., $P_w \geqslant .6$).

The use of the various measures of performance is further demonstrated in the examples throughout this chapter, in the problems at the end of the chapter, and in Section 15.10.

15.9 COST ANALYSIS OF QUEUING SYSTEMS

In certain situations, it is possible to express the waiting costs in terms of dollars and cents. Queuing systems can then be compared on the basis of their total cost *(TC)*, which is composed of two components: the facility cost (C_F) and the total cost of waiting customers (C_W).

$$TC = C_F + C_W \qquad (15.13)$$

Costs are computed on one of two bases: either as "cost per unit of time (hourly, daily)," or as "cost per customer served." In this text, the cost-per-unit-of-time basis is used.

Computing the cost of waiting

Two different cost structures can be distinguished, as noted earlier. First, the total wait *(W)*, including the time during service, may be of relevance, for example, in industrial settings where employees are being paid for the total time they are away from their work. In the second case, typical of retail situations, only the time while waiting in the queue (W_q) is relevant, since consumers harbor virtually no ill will while being served in a normal fashion. Here we will assume that the waiting cost (regardless if it is linked to W or W_q) is *proportional* to the waiting time; that is, if the cost of waiting for an hour is $12, then the cost of waiting two hours is 2 × 12 = $24.

Cost is proportional to time

Let C be the cost of one customer waiting one unit of time. Then the *waiting cost* per unit time for the queuing system as a whole is given by:

$$C_W = W\lambda C = LC \tag{15.14}$$

where W is the average time in the system *per customer* (use W_q if the cost is directly proportional to the time in the queue) and λ is the average arrival rate per unit of time under consideration.

The cost of service

The cost incurred by providing the service, C_F, is typically composed of both fixed and variable costs. The annual fixed cost (amortization, insurance, taxes) and the variable (hourly) cost must both be converted into the same time units as used in Equation 15.14 so that the cost components can be added together.

The cost of service can be given in the following ways:

a. Per hour (or other time unit) of service (e.g., $20 per hour).

b. Per customer served (e,g., $5 per customer). If four customers are typically served during the hour, then the hourly cost is 4 × $5 = $20.

The costs of service

c. Per unit capacity of service. For example, $2 for each customer that can be served. If the facility is capable of serving 10 customers per hour, then the hourly cost will be $2 × 10 = $20.

15.10 MANAGERIAL APPLICATIONS OF POISSON-EXPONENTIAL QUEUING SYSTEMS

Example 1. The toolroom problem

The All American Aviation Company toolroom is staffed by one clerk who can serve 12 production employees, on the average, each hour.[9] The

[9] A toolroom is a storeroom where large and special tools (sometimes also parts and materials) are stored. The tools are borrowed by employees who need them. We assume here that the population of 400 production employees is so great that the arrival process is essentially Poisson-distributed.

production employees arrive at the toolroom every six minutes, on the average. Find the measures of performance expressed in Equations 15.1–15.12.

Solution

It is necessary first to change the time dimensions of λ and μ to a common denominator; λ is now given in minutes, μ in hours. We will use hours as the common denominator.

The problem states that $\mu = 12$ per hour. For λ, the arrival of one customer every six minutes means one customer every 1/10 of an hour. Therefore, the arrival rate, λ, is 10 customers per hour.

Thus, in all the following formulas we shall use: $\lambda = 10$, $\mu = 12$.

1. Toolroom utilization:

$$\rho = \lambda/\mu = 10/12 = .833$$

2. Average waiting time in the system (toolroom):

$$W = \frac{1}{\mu - \lambda} = \frac{1}{12 - 10} = .5 \text{ hours, per employee}$$

3. The average waiting time in the line:

$$W_q = \frac{\lambda}{\mu(\mu - \lambda)} = \frac{10}{12(12 - 10)} = .417 \text{ hours, per employee}$$

4. The average number of employees in the toolroom area:

$$L = \frac{\rho}{1 - \rho} = \frac{.833}{.167} = 5 \text{ employees}$$

5. The average number of employees in the line:

$$L_q = \frac{\rho^2}{1 - \rho} = \frac{(.833)^2}{.167} = 4.17 \text{ employees}$$

6. The probability that the toolroom clerk will be idle:

$$P(0) = 1 - \rho = 1 - .833 = .167$$

7. The probability of finding the system busy:

$$P_w = \rho = .833$$

8. The chance of waiting longer than 30 minutes in the system. That is, $t = 1/2$:

$$P\{T > t\} = e^{(10-12)1/2} = \frac{1}{e} = .368$$

9. The probability of finding four employees in the system, $N = 4$:

$$P(4) = \rho^N(1 - \rho) = (.833)^4(1 - .833) = .0814$$

10. The probability of finding more than three employees in the system:

$$P\{N > 3\} = \rho^{n+1} = (.833)^4 = .488$$

In the following example, it will be shown how to use such measures of performance in a comparative analysis.

Example 2. The duplicating machine

The Comtec Corporation is considering leasing one of two possible self-service duplicating machines. The Mark I is capable of duplicating, on the average, 20 jobs each hour, at a cost of \$50 per day. Alternatively, the Mark II can duplicate, on the average, 24 jobs per hour, at a cost of \$80 per day. The duplicating center is open 10 hours a day with an average arrival of 18 jobs per hour. The duplication is performed by employees arriving from various departments, whose average hourly wage is \$5. Should the company lease Mark I or Mark II?

Solution

To assess the alternatives, it is necessary to compute the same measures of performance in both systems;[10] we will compute the measures shown in Table 15.1.

TABLE 15.1 Comparing measures of performance

	Mark I	*Mark II*
λ, given per hour	18	18
μ, given per hour	20	24
ρ, utilization $= \frac{\lambda}{\mu}$	$\frac{18}{20} = .9$	$\frac{18}{24} = .75$
W(Equation 15.1) hours per customer	$\frac{1}{20-18} = \frac{1}{2}$	$\frac{1}{24-18} = \frac{1}{6}$
L(Equation 15.3) customers	$\frac{18}{20-18} = 9$	$\frac{18}{24-18} = 3$
$P(0)$(Equation 15.5)	$1 - .9 = .1$	$1 - .75 = .25$

Cost comparison on a daily basis

Mark I Since each employee will spend $W = ½$ hour in the duplicating center, and since 180 persons arrive at the center each day (18 per hour times 10 hours), there will be a total waiting time of ½(180) = 90

[10] We will assume that the service rate for the duplicating jobs is random. In essence this implies that the number of copies is random. However, if exactly one (or n) copies were needed per job, then the service time would be constant, a case discussed in Part B of this chapter.

employee-hours, each day. At \$5 an hour, this waiting time will cost the company 5(90) = \$450 a day. The total cost is thus \$450 + \$50 daily machine cost = \$500 per day (see Table 15.2).

TABLE 15.2
Cost comparison for the duplicating machine

System	Facility cost, C_F	Cost of waiting				TC (\$ per hour)	TC (\$ per day)
		λ	W	C	$C_W = \lambda WC$		
Mark I	\$50 per day = \$5 per hour	18	½	5	½ × 18 × 5 = 45	5 + 45 = 50	500
Mark II	\$80 per day = \$8 per hour	18	⅙	5	⅙ × 18 × 5 = 15	8 + 15 = 23	230

Mark II With W = ⅙ hour per employee, there will be a total wait of ⅙(180) = 30 employee-hours each day. The cost is now only 5(30) = \$150. Add to this the \$80 cost of renting Mark II for a total cost of \$150 + \$80 = \$230, or \$270 per day lower than the Mark I.

Note that even though Mark II is only utilized 75 percent of the time, it is still the "better" machine to lease (considering costs only).

Note: In comparing Mark I and Mark II, notice that Mark II is only 20 percent faster (i.e., its service capacity is 1.2 times that of Mark I). Yet the waiting time was cut down by almost 67 percent (from one half to one sixth of an hour). This is one indication that a "commonsense" approach (such as, double the service rate so the waiting time will be cut in half) is incorrect in queuing situations, which exhibit *nonlinear* characteristics.

Example 3. Truck loading

A plant distributes its products by trucks. The average loading time is 20 minutes per truck. Trucks arrive at an average rate of two each hour. Management feels that the existing loading facility is more than adequate. However, the drivers complain that they have to wait "more than half the time." Analyze the situation and find how much money the company can save by speeding up loading if the waiting time of a truck is figured at \$10 per hour and the plant is in operation eight hours each day.

Solution

Given $\lambda = 2$ and $\mu = 3$ (20 minutes service means 3 per hour). Using Equation 15.6, the chance of having to wait in line is equal to ⅔ or 66.7 percent, so the drivers' complaints are legitimate. Using Equation 15.2, the average waiting time for a driver in the line is:[11]

$$W_q = \frac{2}{3(3-2)} = \frac{2}{3} \text{ hours} = 40 \text{ minutes}$$

Since there are 2 × 8 = 16 loads a day, there is a waiting time of 2(16)/3 = 10⅔ hours, each day, which costs the company, at $10 an hour, a total of $106.67. Therefore, the company should consider alternatives that could reduce this cost.

Automatic device The reader is encouraged to examine the following situation: An automatic device that can load 10 trucks an hour is available at a cost of $90 per day over the cost of the existing facility. Should management replace the existing facility? [Solution: Yes, W_q is reduced to .025 hours and the daily cost of waiting to $4. Total daily savings $106.67 − (90 + 4) = $12.67.]

The results are summarized in Table 15.3.

TABLE 15.3
Cost comparison for the truck loading problem

System	*Facility cost,* C_F	*Cost of waiting*				*TC* *($ per hour)*	*TC* *($ per day)*
		λ	W	C	C_W		
Existing system	Irrelevant	2	⅔	$10	13.33	$13.33	106.67
Proposed (automatic)	$90 per day = $11.25 per hour	2	.025	$10	0.50	11.25 + .50 = $11.75	94.00

15.11 CONCLUDING REMARKS

Waiting line (queuing) theory is a tool used mainly for computing measures of performance of systems providing services. This information is used by management to design service systems and to improve their operations.

How waiting lines are formed

The main reason a queue forms when the average service rate is *faster* than the average arrival rate is that both are fluctuating in an unpre-

[11] The problem can also be solved using W rather than W_q yielding the same conclusion. The reason for using W_q is that this is basically a wasted time to the truck drivers and the source of their complaints.

dictable manner. As a result, there are short-term variations in both the arrival and service rates. This leads to idle capacity at some points in time (which is usually lost since it cannot be accumulated) and to periods of waiting at other times. This sporadic variation in arrival and service rates results, for example, in a bank teller being idle for a while and then swamped with customers a little later.

Loss of capacity

Recognition of the distributions

The models discussed so far, as well as some of those to be discussed in the extensions of this chapter, assume Poisson arrival rates and exponential service times. The question now is how to find out if a certain arrival rate or a certain service time indeed follows these distributions.

Data are required

Stable conditions

To begin with, one must collect data. This can be done through continuous observation, through a sample observation, or through an analysis of historical (logged) data (e.g., arrival times to emergency rooms are usually recorded). The first step is to determine how much data to collect. This question can be answered with the aid of statistical theory. Next, one should check if λ and μ remained unchanged throughout the period of data collection (again, statistical methods are available). It is necessary that these measures be stable, otherwise the formulas cannot be applied.

Once λ and μ are found to be stable, frequency distributions (Appendix B) can be constructed. The general shape and the amount of spread around the mean of the distributions should suggest certain standard probability distributions.

Check mean and standard deviation

A quick way to check a distribution is to compute its mean and standard deviation. In the exponential distribution, the mean and the standard deviation must be equal, and in the Poisson the mean must equal the variance. Such a test can rule out distributions that are not Poisson or exponential. However, in order to be sure, the chi-square goodness of fit (Kolmogorov-Smirnov) test should be applied. This is another measure of the goodness-of-fit of a theoretical frequency distribution to an actual distribution. It is a simple, yet powerful, nonparametric test particularly useful for judging how close the observed frequency distribution is to the expected frequency distribution. (For the application of such a test, see the texts listed in Appendix B.) Graphical examination of the histograms and comparison with probabilities in statistical tables can be used an an approximation.

Solution approaches

"Commonsense" solutions are least desirable in waiting line situations. For example, most managers are likely to assume that to obtain the most efficient operations, they must make the average service rate approximate the average arrival rate, that is, have a utilization close to 1.0. Such a design will ordinarily be far from efficient when arrivals and service times are subject to chance variations. "Doubling the speed will cut waiting time in half" is another commonsense fallacy. Therefore, the use of models for queuing situations is very important.

In the event that the arrival rate and the service time follow certain theoretical distributions, formulas and/or charts can be used to compute the operating characteristics of queuing systems. However, if the theoretical distributions are not close to reality, or if the system is complex, then the technique of simulation must be used.

15.12 PROBLEMS FOR PART A[12]

1. The number of customers arriving at the loan department of the Swiss National Bank was logged over a period of 100 hours. The following table indicates the number of customers that arrived each hour:

Customers per hour	*Number of times observed*
0	10
1	20
2	30
3	15
4	15
5	10
Total	100

Compute:

a. The average arrival rate per hour.

b. The average interarrival time in minutes.

Graph the distribution of arrivals.

2. Given below is the distribution of repair times, as recorded for 550 repairs:

Hours per repair	*Number of times recorded*
1	110
2	165
3	165
4	85
5	25
Total	550

Determine:

a. The average repair time in hours.

b. The average number of repairs per day (24 hours).

Graph the distribution of service times.

3. A physician schedules checkup patients at the rate of one every 15 minutes. Assume that the patients arrive exactly on schedule. Assume a constant checkup rate of four patients per hour.

a. Calculate the waiting line that is likely to be generated after four hours.

b. Assume that the physician can see five patients in an hour. What will be the waiting time after four hours, and what will be the physician's rate of utilization?

c. What will happen if the physician can see only three patients an hour. How long will the line be after four hours?

4. Identify the customers and the servers in the following systems:

a. Telephone booth.
b. Airport runways.
c. Parking lot.
d. Secretarial pool.
e. Maintenance center.
f. Hospital.
g. Automobile assembly line.
h. Elevators in a building.
i. Traffic lights.

5. Vic's Vending Corporation operates vending machines in one town. The machines break down at an average rate of two per hour. An hour of downtime of a machine is considered as a loss of \$13. Currently, the machines are serviced by the company maintenance crew, which is capable of repairing each machine in 24 minutes. The hourly cost of the maintenance team is \$20. A maintenance contractor offered to take over the maintenance work. The contractor can repair three machines each hour, with an hourly charge of \$40. Should management accept the contractor's offer?

6. A service system has an average interarrival time

[12] For the problems in this section, unless otherwise stated, assume random arrivals (Poisson) and a negative exponential service time.

of two minutes and an average service rate of 60 per hour.

Find:

a. The probability that a customer will have to wait.

b. The probability that four persons are in the system.

c. The probability of finding more than three in the system.

d. The probability of waiting more than three minutes for service.

e. The probability that fewer than four are in the system.

f. The probability of being through the system within 10 minutes.

7. A toolroom clerk at British Light Industries, Ltd. is serving a maintenance department with a large number of employees who earn £8 per hour. The clerk earns £5 per hour. The workers arrive at the toolroom at an average rate of 6.2 per hour. The average service time is eight minutes.

a. What is the probability of finding no workers at the toolroom (either waiting or being served)?

b. What is the average waiting time (before being served) per worker?

c. What is the average number of workers waiting in line (excluding the one being served)?

d. Would you recommend installing an incentive plan that will reduce the average service time to 6.4 minutes and will cost the company £2 per hour?

e. Another clerk can be hired at £5 per hour. The two clerks will operate as a single team serving one line with an average service time of four minutes. Would you recommend hiring the additional clerk? (Assume no incentives.)

f. If you had the alternative of installing the incentive plan with the existing system or hiring a second clerk, which one would you recommend?

g. Two more clerks can be hired (at £5 each per hour) to help the single clerk, reducing the average service time to two minutes. Would you recommend this over hiring one more clerk? Why (or why not)?

8. Given an arrival rate $\lambda = 3$, find values of L_q and W_q for the following values of μ: 3.1, 3.5, 4, and 6. When does serving efficiency become important?

9. Given a waiting line system with:

1. Average interarrival times of six minutes.
2. Space necessary for accommodating a waiting customer = 5 square feet.
3. Cost per hour of waiting time per customer = \$2.
4. It was also observed that the facility is idle 20 percent of the time.

Find:

a. The area necessary to accommodate the average waiting line.

b. Is it profitable to invest \$5 an hour in the facility if the service rate can be doubled (twice as fast)?

10. Sunny Engineering Corporation is designing a special machine for processing chickens. The chickens arrive from the farms on trucks, in cages, at a rate of 10 trucks per hour. If the chickens are kept in the cage in the waiting area more than three hours, they will start to dehydrate, lowering their quality and causing damage to the processor. Determine the minimum average processing rate (in truckloads per hour) that must be designed for the machine, in order to ensure that the cages will be processed on the average, in three hours or less. That is, waiting and processing time is three hours or less.

11. Lima Airport currently operates with one runway for landings. The average landing time is three minutes. Airplanes arrive at the airport at the rate of 17 per hour. The estimated average fuel consumption for an airplane waiting for a landing is 10 liters per minute. A liter of fuel costs 2 thousand Peruvian sol.

Find:

a. The average number of airplanes circling the airport in a "holding pattern," that is, waiting for permission to land. Do not include the landing plane.

b. The average cost of fuel "burned" by an airplane waiting to land.

c. The chance of finding less than three airplanes in the airport vicinity (in the waiting line and landing).

d. The utilization of the runway.

12. Five cars arrive at an emissions testing station each hour. The average service time is six minutes. The station can accommodate only three cars (waiting and being served). Any car that cannot be accommodated in the station is parked in a No-Parking area on the street, where there is a 40 percent chance of being fined $10. The owner of the station pays the fines. The station is in operation 48 hours per week. Cars completed are picked up immediately by the customers.

    Find the weekly fines collected (in $).

13. The Jamaican Pelican is a one-man yogurt shop where people arrive at the average rate of 20 per hour. Big Joe, the proprietor, serves a customer, on the average, in two minutes. During the noontime rush, the arrival rate increases to one arriving customer every two minutes. *Find:*
    a. How fast must Big Joe work to ensure that a noontime customer will not wait for service, on the average, more than 10 minutes?
    b. What is the probability that six or more people are in the shop during the nonrush period?
    c. What is the average waiting time during the regular hours?

14. Customers arrive at a service facility every 12 minutes, on the average. The average service time is 10 minutes. The operation of the existing system costs $5 an hour. The facility is in operation eight hours a day.
    Find:
    a. If the waiting (prior to service) area, that can accommodate three customers, is sufficient 70 percent of the time.
    b. It is proposed to speed up the service so 10 customers can be served in an hour. The additional cost of this higher speed is $24 per day. If an hour waiting time (prior to service), per customer, is worth $1, is the investment justified?

15. Customers arrive at a one-person barbershop with an average interarrival time of 20 minutes. The average time for a haircut is 12 minutes.
    a. The owner wishes to have enough seats in the waiting area so that no more than 5 percent of the arriving customers will have to stand. How many seats should be provided?
    b. Suppose there is only sufficient space in the waiting area for five seats. What is the probability that an arriving customer will not find a seat?

16. The industrial engineering department of First National Bank conducted a study to determine the effectiveness of its two drive-in stations. These stations operate independently of each other and each has its own waiting line. The study involved random observations of the number of cars in a line (including the one being served). The results of the first day of study are given below:

Time	*Cars in station 1*	*Cars in station 2*
9:12	3	2
9:37	5	3
10:04	2	2
11:30	0	4
11:58	4	2
12:20	3	3
12:39	2	2
1:23	5	1
1:37	4	5
2:06	2	3
2:19	1	0
2:46	3	4

In addition, it was noted that line 1 served 84 customers and was open six hours, while line 2 served 79 customers and was open six hours and 15 minutes. Find the utilization of each line and which is better utilized.

17. The following are observations taken at South London Bank Drive-in regarding the number of cars in the waiting line (prior to service):

Time	*Cars in line*
10:30	6
10:37	7
10:53	2
11:06 (0 in service)	0
12:12	1
12:44	4
1:20	3
1:40	6
1:50 (1 car in service)	0
2:06	5
2:50	2
3:00	8

The Drive-in opened at 10:30 and at 3:00 no more cars are allowed to join the line. The last car left at 3:20

Find:

a. The average number of cars in the system.

b. The average number of cars in the waiting line.

18. Refer back to Problem 14. An alternative solution suggests three parallel, identical facilities serving one line. Each facility is capable of serving three customers per hour at a cost of $2 per hour per facility. Analyze this alternative. Would you recommend it?

PART B: EXTENSIONS

15.13 MULTIFACILITY QUEUING SYSTEMS *(M/M/K FCFS/∞/∞)*

The multifacility (multiserver, multichannel) queuing systems considered here are composed of several identical and parallel service facilities. Such a situation is depicted in Figure 15.8. Note that only one waiting line exists that feeds the mutliple service facilities. Whenever a server is free, the first customer in the queue goes to that service facility. An example of such a situation is an IRS (Internal Revenue Service) office, where arrivals get a number as they arrive and then the numbers are called sequentially as the examiners become free. Another example is airplanes circling a large airport with two runways; whenever a runway becomes free, an airplane is directed to that runway.

"Take a number please"

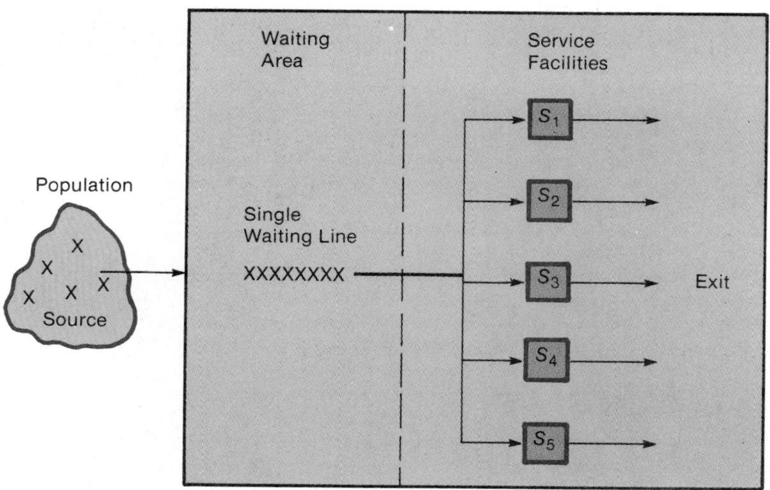

FIGURE 15.8
The multifacility waiting line system

There are several managerial problems in a multifacility system. For example, management is concerned with determining the proper number of servers, whether to use identical or nonidentical servers (e.g., whether or not to open an express lane in the supermarket), and the organization of the waiting line (one line for all servers, one line per server). Such decisions are based on the computation of the *measures of performance.*

An express lane?

In this section, the simplest multiserver system is analyzed. In such a system, the following assumptions are made:

1. Poisson-exponential systems, as described in Part A of this chapter.
2. Identical service facilities.
3. One waiting line exists.
4. The arrival rate λ is smaller than the combined service rate $(K\mu)$ of all K service facilities.

Formulas for computing the measures of performance

Let:

λ = Mean arrival rate
μ = Mean service rate of *each* facility
K = Number of servers (service facilities)
ρ = Utilization factor $\frac{\lambda}{\mu}$ as in the single facility system
$\bar{\rho}$ = Utilization factor of the entire system:

$$\bar{\rho} = \frac{\rho}{K} = \frac{\lambda}{K\mu} \tag{15.15}$$

Assuming that $\lambda < K\mu$ (a necessary condition to avoid an explosive queue), then some of the most common measures of performance are:

1. The probability of finding no customers in the system (an "idle" system):

$$P(0) = \frac{1}{\frac{\rho^K}{K!(1-\bar{\rho})} + \sum_{i=0}^{K-1} \frac{\rho^i}{i!}} \tag{15.16}$$

where i = Index of summation.

2. The probability of finding exactly N customers in the system:

$$P(N) = \begin{cases} P(0)\frac{\rho^N}{N!} & \text{when } N \leq K \\ \frac{P(0)\bar{\rho}^N K^K}{K!} & \text{when } N > K \end{cases} \tag{15.17}$$

3. The average number of customers in the waiting line:

$$L_q = \frac{P(0)\rho^K\bar{\rho}}{K!(1-\bar{\rho})^2} \tag{15.18}$$[13]

4. The average number of customers in the system:

$$L = L_q + \rho \tag{15.19}$$

---

[13] Given L_q, this equation yields the following for $P(0)$:

$$P(0) = \frac{L_q K!(1-\bar{\rho})^2}{\rho^K \bar{\rho}}$$

5. The average waiting time per customer, before service:

$$W_q = \frac{L_q}{\lambda} \tag{15.20}$$

6. The average time a customer spends in the system (waiting and service):

$$W = \frac{L}{\lambda} = W_q + \frac{1}{\mu} \tag{15.21}$$

Use of a table to solve multifacility problems

In order to save computational time, a table of $P(0)$, Table 15.4, can be used. The process, illustrated in Figure 15.9, is simple: $P(0)$ is read from the table for various values of λ, μ, and K. Then L, L_q, W, or W_q can be computed.

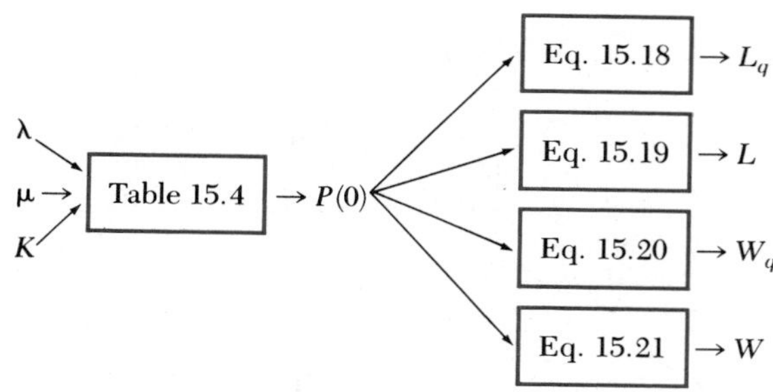

FIGURE 15.9
The multifacility solution process

Table 15.4
P(0) for the multichannel queue

$\frac{\lambda}{K\mu}$	*Number of channels, K*								
	2	*3*	*4*	*5*	*6*	*7*	*8*	*10*	*15*
.02	.9608	.9418	.9231	.9048	.8869	.8694	.85214	.81873	.74082
.04	.9231	.8869	.8521	.8187	.7866	.7558	.72615	.67032	.54881
.06	.8868	.8353	.7866	.7408	.6977	.6570	.61878	.54881	.40657
.08	.8519	.7866	.7261	.6703	.6188	.5712	.52729	.44933	.30119
.10	.8182	.7407	.6703	.6065	.5488	.4966	.44933	.36788	.22313
.12	.7857	.6975	.6188	.5488	.4868	.4317	.38289	.30119	.16530
.14	.7544	.6568	.5712	.4966	.4317	.3753	.32628	.24660	.12246
.16	.7241	.6184	.5272	.4493	.3829	.3263	.27804	.20190	.09072
.18	.6949	.5821	.4866	.4065	.3396	.2837	.23693	.16530	.06721
.20	.6667	.5479	.4491	.3678	.3012	.2466	.20189	.13534	.04979

Table 15.4 *(concluded)*

$\frac{\lambda}{K\mu}$	*Number of channels, K*								
	2	*3*	*4*	*5*	*6*	*7*	*8*	*10*	*15*
.22	.6393	.5157	.4145	.3328	.2671	.2144	.17204	.11080	.03688
.24	.6129	.4852	.3824	.3011	.2369	.1864	.14660	.09072	.02732
.26	.5873	.4564	.3528	.2723	.2101	.1620	.12492	.07247	.02024
.28	.5625	.4292	.3255	.2463	.1863	.1408	.10645	.06081	.01500
.30	.5385	.4035	.3002	.2228	.1652	.1224	.09070	.04978	.01111
.32	.5152	.3791	.2768	.2014	.1464	.1064	.07728	.04076	.00823
.34	.4925	.3561	.2551	.1812	.1298	.0925	.06584	.03337	.00610
.36	.4706	.3343	.2351	.1646	.1151	.0804	.05609	.02732	.00452
.38	.4493	.3137	.2165	.1487	.1020	.0698	.04778	.02236	.00335
.40	.4286	.2941	.1993	.1343	.0903	.0606	.04069	.01830	.00248
.42	.4085	.2756	.1834	.1213	.0800	.0527	.03465	.01498	.00184
.44	.3889	.2580	.1686	.1094	.0708	.0457	.02950	.01226	.00136
.46	.3699	.2414	.1549	.0987	.0626	.0397	.02511	.01003	.00101
.48	.3514	.2255	.1422	.0889	.0554	.0344	.02136	.00820	.00075
.50	.3333	.2105	.1304	.0801	.049	.0298	.01816	.00671	.00055
.52	.3158	.1963	.1195	.0721	.0432	.0259	.01544	.00548	.00041
.54	.2987	.1827	.1094	.0648	.0831	.0224	.01311	.00448	.00030
.56	.2821	.1699	.0999	.0581	.0336	.0194	.01113	.00366	.00022
.58	.2658	.1576	.0912	.0521	.0296	.0167	.00943	.00298	.00017
.60	.2500	.1460	.0831	.0466	.0260	.0144	.00799	.00243	.00012
.62	.2346	.1349	.0755	.0417	.0228	.0124	.00675	.00198	.00009
.64	.2195	.1244	.0685	.0372	.0200	.0107	.00570	.00161	.00007
.66	.2048	.1143	.0619	.0330	.0175	.0092	.00480	.00131	.00005
.68	.1905	.1048	.0559	.0293	.0152	.0079	.00404	.00106	.00004
.70	.1765	.0957	.0502	.0259	.0132	.0067	.00338	.00085	.00003
.72	.1628	.0870	.0450	.0228	.0114	.0057	.00283	.00069	.00002
.74	.1494	.0788	.0401	.0200	.0099	.0048	.00235	.00055	.00001
.76	.1364	.0709	.0355	.0174	.0085	.0041	.00195	.00044	
.78	.1236	.0634	.0313	.0151	.0072	.0034	.00160	.00035	
.80	.1111	.0562	.0273	.013	.0061	.0028	.00131	.00028	
.82	.0989	.0493	.0236	.0111	.0051	.0023	.00106	.00022	
.84	.0870	.0428	.0202	.0093	.0042	.0019	.00085	.00017	
.86	.0753	.0366	.0170	.0077	.0035	.0015	.00067	.00013	
.88	.0638	.0306	.0140	.0063	.0028	.0012	.00052	.00010	
.90	.0526	.0249	.0113	.0050	.0021	.0009	.00039	.00007	
.92	.0417	.0195	.0087	.0038	.0016	.0007	.00028	.00005	
.94	.0309	.0143	.0063	.0027	.0011	.0005	.00019	.00003	
.96	.0204	.0093	.0040	.0017	.0007	.0003	.00012	.00002	
.98	.0101	.0045	.0019	.0008	.0003	.0001	.00005	.00001	

Example

Given $\lambda = 36$ per hour, $\mu = 10$ per hour, and $K = 5$. Find $P(0)$, L, L_q, W, and W_q.

Solution

Step 1. Find $\bar{\rho} = \lambda/K\mu = 36/50 = 0.72$

Step 2. From the table, the value of $P(0)$ that corresponds to $K = 5$ is $P(0) = 0.0228$.

Step 3. From $P(0)$ compute the other variables, using Equations 15.18–15.21. For our example:

$$\rho = 36/10 = 3.6$$

$$L_q = \frac{P(0)\rho^K\bar{\rho}}{K!(1-\bar{\rho})^2} = \frac{0.0228(3.6)^5.72}{5!(1-.72)^2} = 1.055$$

$$L = 1.055 + 3.6 = 4.655$$

$$W_q = 1.055/36 = 0.029$$

$$W = 4.655/36 = 0.129$$

Example 1 Parishioners arrive randomly to church for confession, at an average rate of 5.8 per hour. Father Bailey estimates that an average confession lasts 10 minutes. However, he is worried about the possibility of a long queue and wonders if he should ask more priests to hear confessions.

Solution In this problem, it is given that:

$$\lambda = 5.8 \text{ per hour}$$

$$\frac{1}{\mu} = 10 \text{ minutes} = \frac{1}{6} \text{ hour}$$

$$\mu = 6 \text{ per hour}$$

If only one priest hears confession, then it is a system with a single server and, therefore, the equations in Section 15.8 can be used to generate the following information:

$$L = \frac{\lambda}{\mu - \lambda} = \frac{5.8}{.2} = 29 \text{ parishioners in the church}$$

$$L_q = \frac{\lambda^2}{\mu(\mu - \lambda)} = \frac{5.8(5.8)}{6(.2)} = 28.03 \text{ parishioners in the waiting line}$$

$$W = \frac{1}{\mu - \lambda} = \frac{1}{.2} = 5 \text{ hours average time in the church (waiting and service) per parishioner}$$

$$W_q = \frac{\lambda}{\mu(\mu - \lambda)} = \frac{5.8}{6(.2)} = 4.83 \text{ hours average wait in the queue, per parishioner}$$

The results above certainly corroborate Father Bailey's anxieties: an expected line length of 28 parishioners and a total time of five hours before they may leave for home. Let us now examine the result of having a second priest to hear confessions.

Solution with two priests For this situation, Table 15.4 will be used. Using the values $\rho = .967$ and $\bar{\rho} = .484$ with $K = 2$ in Table 15.4 (round $\bar{\rho}$ to .48), we find $P(0) = .3514$:

$$L_q = \frac{.3514(.967)^2.484}{2!(.516)^2} = .216$$

$$L = .216 + .967 = 1.183$$

$$W_q = .216/6 = .036 \text{ hours (or 2.16 minutes)}$$

$$W = 1.183/6 = .197 \text{ hours (or 11.82 minutes)}$$

Not a commonsense result at all

Notice that adding just one more priest to hear confessions did not cut the queue length and waiting time just in half (that would have resulted in a line of 14 parishioners and a total time of 2.5 hours); instead, the results indicate an average waiting line of only .2 persons and an average waiting time prior to the confession of only 2.16 minutes. This amazing result is due to the *randomness* of the arrivals, and that fact that idle service time between arrivals cannot be stored, resulting in an excessive queue in the case of one priest.

Example 2 Star Oil service station is considering how many of its eight identical gasoline pumps to staff during the night. Past experience indicates that there are an average of 16 random arrivals per hour during the 9 P.M.–7 A.M. period. Each customer brings the station a revenue of \$1.50. The service time takes three minutes on the average, and follows a negative exponential distribution.

Long waiting lines create ill will. In addition, customers may not enter the station if they see long lines. Therefore, the management of Star Oil estimates that each total customer-hour of waiting time in the service station effectively costs \$3. The operating cost of manning each pump is \$5 per hour. Find how many pumps should be manned so that the total profit is maximized.

Solution In this system, $\lambda = 16$, $\mu = 60/3 = 20$. The waiting time of interest is W_q, since this is a retail situation.

How many pumps are best?

For one pump:

$$W_q = \frac{\lambda}{\mu(\mu - \lambda)} = \frac{16}{20(20 - 16)} = \frac{16}{20(4)} = \frac{16}{80} = .2 \text{ hours per customer}$$

Since there are 16 customers each, the cost of ill will is 16(.2)(\$3) = \$9.60 per hour.

The total profit per hour is:

Gross income: 16 customers × 1.5 = \$24
Less operating expenses = \$5
Less ill-will expense = \$9.60
Profit = 24 − (5 + 9.6) = \$9.40 per hour

Two pumps

To compute W_q for two pumps, Table 15.4 is used, with $\rho = 0.8$, $K = 2$, and $\bar{\rho} = 0.4$. The result is $P(0) = 0.4286$. Thus:

$$L_q = \frac{0.4286(0.8)^2 0.4}{2(0.6)^2} = 0.152$$

and the cost of ill will is:

$$(W_q\lambda)\text{ Cost} = L_q(\text{Cost}) = 0.152(3) = \$0.46$$

The profit is 24 − 5(2) − 0.46 = \$13.54, which is considerably better than the case of one pump.

Three pumps

From Table 15.4 $P(0) = 0.2941$:

$$L_q = \frac{0.2941(0.8)^3 0.4}{3!(0.6)^2} = 0.028$$

and the cost of ill will is 0.028(3) = \$0.084, the profit is thus 24 − 5(3) − 0.084 = \$8.92, which is less than either one or two pumps.

Four pumps or more

There is no need to check; since the cost of ill will is minimal, then adding more pumps (attendants) will increase total costs.

Comparison These computations are summarized in Table 15.5. The best number of pumps is two, with an hourly net profit of \$13.54.

TABLE 15.5
Optimal number of service facilities

Number of pumps	*Facility cost*	L_q	*Cost of waiting* ($L_q \times \$3$)	*Total cost*	*Net profit = \$24 − total cost*	
1	5	3.2	\$9.60	\$14.60	\$ 9.40	
2	10	0.152	.46	10.46	13.54	←*Maximum*
3	15	0.028	.084	15.08	8.92	
4	20	negligible	negligible	20.00	4.00	

15.14 OTHER QUEUING SITUATIONS

Finite source queuing systems (*M/M/*1 *FCFS/*∞*/n*)

If the number of customers is limited

All waiting line situations discussed thus far assumed an infinite population source. However, in some real-life situations, the number of customers is small and cannot be considered infinite. For example, there may be only 9 production employees coming to the toolroom, or the number of airplanes arriving at a small airport each day may be limited to 12. Another very common situation is the so-called machine repair problem:

Companies often have maintenance teams whose primary function is to repair certain machines used for production when they break down. For instance, there may be one service person and five bottling machines. Another example is a production employee who supervises 15 textile machines. In such cases, the machines are viewed as the "customers" that require service.

Let M denote the finite number of customers in the source and λ denote each (identical) customer's individual average arrival rate (*not* the group of all M customers). The basic formulas, assuming a Poisson-exponential system and a *single* server, are:

$$P(0) = 1/\sum_{i=0}^{M}\left[\frac{M!}{(M-i)!}(\rho)^i\right] \qquad (15.22)$$

where i = Summation index

$$P_N = P(0)\,\rho^N \frac{M!}{(M-N)!} \qquad (15.23)$$

$$L_q = M - \frac{\lambda+\mu}{\lambda}(1 - P(0)) \qquad (15.24)$$

$$L = L_q + (1 - P(0)) \qquad (15.25)$$

$$W_q = \frac{L_q}{\mu(1 - P(0))} \qquad (15.26)$$

$$W = W_q + \frac{1}{\mu} \qquad (15.27)$$

These equations could be applied to a situation such as the following.

Example The ABC Bottling Corporation has five machines. Each breaks down once every 2½ weeks, on the average. Thus, λ = 1/2.5 =

.4 per week. The repair capacity is one machine per week: $\mu = 1$. Find the operating characteristics of the system.

Rather than manually solving the equations, employing a computer program that already has been programmed with the above equations is faster and less susceptible to error. Equations for the multiple server case, which are even more complex, can be included as well. This will be demonstrated in Section 15.16, "Use of Computers."

Queuing systems with a maximum queue length (*M/M/*1 *FCFS/n/*∞)

In all the previous situations, no limits were set on the size of the waiting line. In the real world, however, there are many situations where the storage capacity of the waiting line or entire system is limited. For example, at some gas stations, there is only so much room for cars to wait. Another example is a parking lot. Any customers that arrive while the waiting area is full will leave the system permanently without being served (called the *balking rate*).

Limited queue

The maximum capacity of the system (including both the waiting line and the customers that are being served) is designated by n. Again, a Poisson-exponential system is assumed. The equations will not be presented here (see Hillier and Yu [7]). Instead, we will rely on the computer approach in Section 15.16.

Queuing systems with a constant service time and Poisson arrivals (*M/D/*1 *FCFS/*∞/∞)

In some situations, the service time can be considered as constant. For example, automated servers such as vending machines perform service at essentially a constant rate. Also, humans servicing nonhuman customers (an "oil change" on a car) frequently perform at an approximately constant rate.

Human-machine systems

The equations for this case are also complex and we will rely again on the computer approach of Section 15.16.

15.15 SERIAL QUEUES

In certain service situations, a customer or a product receives service at a number of stations. The customer (product) moves from station to station and possibly from queue to queue. This is known as a *serial* or *multiphase* queue. Under certain assumptions, such a process may be analyzed rather easily. Multiple servers may even be included in the process.

Service in stages

The first two necessary assumptions are that the source is infinite and the queues in each station are not limited in length. Second, in the case of multiple servers, within each station, all servers must have the

Poisson in . . . Poisson out

same exponential service time distribution. Third, the customers at the first station arrive randomly (Poisson). Finally, $\lambda < K\mu$ at every station, where K = Number of servers, so that an explosive queue is not formed somewhere in the system. Under the above assumptions, the output from each station will also be Poisson, with the average rate λ. Since each station has Poisson arrivals, it may be treated independently of the others, and Table 15.4 can be used for computing the measures of performance throughout the entire process.

Example

Consider a three-station process, where the arrival rate $\lambda = 5$ per hour. The number of servers are:

$$K_1 = 1 \text{ (for station 1)}$$
$$K_2 = 3 \text{ (for station 2)}$$
$$K_3 = 2 \text{ (for station 3)}$$

The service rates per hour per server are:

$$\mu_1 = 6 \text{ (for station 1)}$$
$$\mu_2 = 2 \text{ (for station 2)}$$
$$\mu_3 = 4 \text{ (for station 3)}$$

The problem is shown schematically in Figure 15.10. Find the waiting times within the process.

FIGURE 15.10
A serial queue situation (combined with parallel servers)

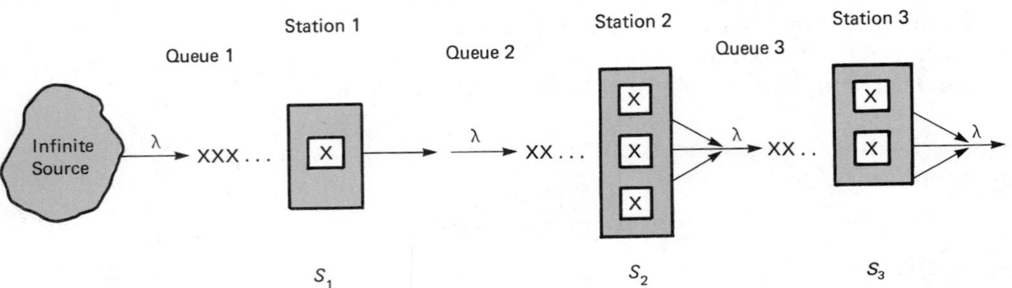

Solution (all times are given in hours)

Station 1 (Single server, use formulas of Section 15.7)

$$\frac{\lambda}{\mu_1} = .833, \quad L_{q_1} = 4.5; \quad W_{q_1} = \frac{4.5}{5} = .90$$

Station 2 (Multiple servers, use Table 15.4)

Given:

$$\lambda = 5,\ \mu_2 = 2,\ K_2 = 3$$

$$\rho_2 = \lambda/\mu_2 = 5/2 = 2.5$$

Compute: $\bar{\rho}_2 = 5/(3 \times 2) = 0.833$ (round to 0.84)

From Table 15.4: $P(0) = 0.428$:

$$L_{q_2} = \frac{0.0428(2.5)^3 0.833}{(3 \times 2)(1 - 0.833)^2} = 3.33$$

$$W_{q_2} = L_{q_2}/\lambda = 3.33/5 = 0.66$$

Station 3 (Multiple servers, use Table 15.4):

$$\rho_3 = 1.25$$

$$\bar{\rho}_3 = 5/8 = 0.625 \text{ (round to 0.62)}$$

From Table 15.4: $P(0) = 0.2346$:

$$L_{q_3} = \frac{0.2346(1.25)^2 0.625}{2(0.375)^2} = 0.815$$

$$W_{q_3} = 0.815/5 = 0.16$$

The total waiting time for service is:

$$W_q \text{ (system)} = 0.90 + 0.66 + 0.16 = 1.72 \text{ hours}$$

15.16 USE OF COMPUTERS

As mentioned earlier, computers are ideal for queuing computations. Below are examples of computer printouts, using the MSS program, for several models; some include a cost analysis. In all the computer analyses, the waiting cost is based on W, not W_q and all data are on a per-hour basis.

Example 1 Single server ($M/M/1$).

Average Time Between Arrivals: .05 Average Arrival Rate: $\lambda = 20.0$
EXPONENTIAL Distribution
Average Time for Service: .04 Average Service Rate: $\mu = 25.0$
EXPONENTIAL Distribution

Number of Servers: 1
Queue Discipline: First Come, First Served
Maximum Queue Length: ∞
Source (Population) Size: ∞
Service Cost: 18
Waiting Cost: 5

QUEUING MODEL RESULTS

PROBLEM NAME: q1 SOLUTION METHOD: ANALYZE MODEL

ITEM	SYMBOL	ANALYSIS
Average Waiting Time in the System	W	0.200
Average Waiting Time in the Queue	Wq	0.160
Average No. of Units in the System	L	4.000
Average No. of Units in the Queue	Lq	3.200
Utilization Rate	P	0.800
Probability the System is Idle	P(0)	0.200
Total System Cost	TC	38.00

The probability of finding exactly 3 units in the system:

P(3) = 0.102400

The probability that more than 3 units are in the system:

P(n > 3) = 0.409600

The probability of being in the system longer than .2:

P(W > .2) = 0.367879

The probability of waiting for service longer than .15:

P(Wq > .15) = 0.377893

Example 2 Single server (*M*/*M*/1) with queue limitation of six in the system (see Section 15.14). (*Note:* the balking rate refers to the percentage of customers that do *not* join the queue). The remaining input data are the same as for Example 1.

ITEM	SYMBOL	ANALYSIS
Average Waiting Time in the System	W	0.115
Average Waiting Time in the Queue	Wq	0.075
Average No. of Units in the System	L	2.140

Average No. of Units in the Queue	Lq	1.400
Utilization Rate	P	0.746927
Probability the System is Idle	P(0)	0.253073
Total System Cost*	TC	28.70
Balking Rate Percentage	P(n > M)	6.634

* This figure does not include the cost of balking if relevant. For an example where it is included, see Problem 32.

Example 3 Multiple server *(M/M/K)*.

Average Time Between Arrivals: .1 — Average Arrival Rate: 10.0
EXPONENTIAL Distribution
Average Time for Service: .25 — Average Service Rate: 4.0
EXPONENTIAL Distribution

Number of Servers: 3
Queue Discipline: First Come, First Served
Maximum Queue Length: ∞
Source (Population) Size: ∞
Service Cost: 8
Waiting Cost: 12

QUEUING MODEL RESULTS

PROBLEM NAME: q3 — SOLUTION METHOD: ANALYZE MODEL

ITEM	SYMBOL	ANALYSIS
Average Waiting Time in the System	W	0.601
Average Waiting Time in the Queue	Wq	0.351
Average No. of Units in the System	L	6.010
Average No. of Units in the Queue	Lq	3.510
Utilization Rate	P	0.955056
Probability the System is Idle	P(0)	0.044944
Total System Cost	TC	96.12

15.17 PROBLEMS FOR PART B

Note: Assume a Poisson-exponential system unless otherwise specified.

19. One branch of the post office in Calcutta would like to know how many windows to staff so the average number of customers waiting for service does not exceed eight. The average service time is three minutes and the post office uses a single queue system, as illustrated below. How many windows should the post office staff on Monday mornings when the average arrival rate is 60 customers per hour?

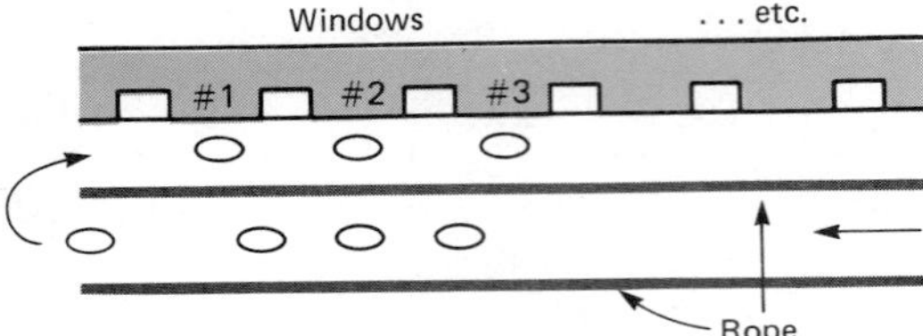

20. Mrs. Grouch and Mr. Mean each have a private secretary who can type letters at the average rate of four per hour. The letters are generated by each manager at the average rate of three per hour. The managers have been wondering if they would benefit by pooling the two secretaries. What would you suggest? (Show calculations.)

21. The supervisor of the maintenance department of Everglade City is faced with a decision regarding maintenance of the city's heavy equipment. He is considering three alternatives:

a. Hire a first-class mechanic, which will cost the city $14.20 per hour (including fringe benefits). Such a mechanic can repair five units per eight-hour day.

b. Hire two second-class mechanics, each of whom will cost the city $11.50 per hour and would work separately. If the two serve one waiting line, they can each fix four units a day.

c. Subcontract the maintenance to ABC Engineering at a cost of $50 per unit repaired. The average repair time is one hour.

The quality of repairs in all three alternatives is considered the same. Currently, there is an average of four units of heavy equipment requiring daily repair (assume random arrivals). A unit of heavy equipment not in operation costs the city $25 per hour, since the city must lease alternative equipment. Find the total daily cost of the three alternatives.

22. Trucks are loaded by forklifts at a rate of four per hour. An hour of forklift operation costs $10. The trucks arrive at an average rate of one every 20 minutes. An idle hour (waiting for loading) for a truck is estimated to cost $16. Find how many forklifts should be used. Assumption: Only one forklift can be used per truck.

23. The keen competition in the successful fast-food industry has forced the management of Burger Corporation to study the operation of their various restaurants. At their Northwestern restaurant, where they receive the most complaints, an analysis revealed the following:

During rush hours, customers arrive at an average rate of one every minute. The attendants can serve, on the average, 66 customers per hour. Burger's president cannot understand why there are so many complaints about the Northwestern restaurant. As the president states: "Why do they complain? We can serve even 10 percent more without any problems."

a. Explain to the president why you think there are so many complaints.

b. What will happen if the average number of customers grows by 10 percent?

c. It was proposed that two teams, each with an hourly serving capacity of 33 customers, replace the existing team, which can serve 66 customers per hour. If there is no additional cost involved in such a change, would you recommend it? Show why or why not. (Assume that the two teams serve a single waiting line.)

Hint: Assume that the number of complaints is a function of waiting time per customer.

24. Hong Kong Machine Company has a toolroom with two clerks. Both clerks issue spare parts and tools to maintenance workers. Maintenance workers arrive at the rate of 20 per hour, each wanting either a part (40 percent) or a tool (60 percent), but not both. The average issuing time is five minutes per order (service by one clerk).

Each clerk currently issues both parts and tools. A maintenance worker not at his or her bench costs the company $5 per hour. It was proposed that the two clerks be specialized, namely: One will issue spare parts only, and the other will issue tools only.

a. Would you advise specialization of the clerks if the service time does not change?

b. Would you advise specialization if the service time is reduced to four minutes per order?

Hint: Treat the current situation as a multiple station system with two servers. Treat the specialization as two single stations.

25. Toulouse Bakeries serves 480 customers during eight hours of operation. The average service time per customer is four minutes. Currently there are five servers at the bakery serving one line.

Find:

a. The utilization of the bakery.

b. The average number of customers at the bakery.

c. The average waiting time (prior to service) in the bakery (per customer), in minutes.

d. The average number of customers being served.

e. The probability of finding no customers in the bakery.

f. The probability of finding exactly three customers in the bakery.

26. A mechanic-operator services five machines. When a machine needs an adjustment, it is shut down. An adjustment takes 15 minutes, on average. Each machine needs an adjustment, on the average, once every two hours. Use a computer.

Compute:

a. The average number of operating machines.

b. The average number of inoperative machines.

c. The utilization rate of the machines.

d. The probability that all five machines are working.

e. The weekly cost of inoperative machines if one hour of downtime costs $10 and the machines are in operation eight hours each day five days a week.

27. Five factory servicepersons maintain 20 old machines that break down at an average rate of 15 per week. If the machines are repaired, one by each serviceperson, at an average rate of two per week, what is the expected line length of inoperative machines? Use a computer.

28. A gasoline station is served by one employee, who is capable of serving 30 customers per hour. There is a maximum space for five cars in the station (served and in line). Cars arrive at the station at an average rate of one every three minutes. Cars that do not have parking space leave and do not return. Use a computer.

Find:

a. The average number of cars *waiting* for service.

b. The average waiting time in line per car.

c. The probability of finding the station without any cars.

d. The probability of finding three cars in the station.

e. It was proposed to increase the space so that 10 cars could be accommodated. The investment in such a case is $0.50 per car space per hour. A car that leaves the station means a loss of $1 profit. Should the space be enlarged or not?

29. A restaurant with an 85-seat capacity has a bar that can accommodate 15 additional waiting customers. Customers who cannot be seated in the bar leave the restaurant. There are 10 waitresses at the restaurant, each capable of serving three customers per hour. Customers arrive at the restaurant at a rate of 29 per hour.

Find the average number of customers waiting for service in the restaurant and bar. Assume that all customers go into the restaurant on arrival if room is available. Use a computer.

30. A five-stage manufacturing process receives raw materials (in units) randomly and must process an average of 12 units each day (eight hours). The data of the system are as follows:

Stage	*No. of parallel servers in stage (K)*	*Service capabilities (per eight-hour day, per server)*
1	2	7
2	1	15
3	5	3
4	3	4.5
5	1	30

a. Find the *expected time* that a unit will spend in the entire processing system (from arrival until finished in stage 5).

b. Find the average waiting time prior to entering the processing system.

c. The cost of a server in the system is $6 per hour. Unit waiting time costs $1 per hour. Would it be profitable to add more servers to the system? If yes, in what stage(s) should they be placed?

d. As an alternative to adding more servers, would a transfer of servers among stages be profitable?

Assume:

(1) The arrival rate cannot be changed.

(2) Servers are paid on an hourly basis, and if they work a portion of an hour they are paid proportionally.

31. Team Oil is a gas station with four pumps selling unleaded gasoline. The arrival rate during rush hours is 60 per hour. The service time is three minutes. What is the chance that an arriving customer will find no cars in the station? (Assume one waiting line.)

32. Refer to computer examples 1 and 2 in Section 15.16.

a. Assume the system is in operation 300 days a year, 10 hours a day. Find the difference in the annual cost and comment on it.

b. Use a computer to find out the cost impact of increasing the waiting space from six to seven units (on an annual basis).

33. Access to the freeway system in Los Angeles is controlled by a signaling system. The system permits one car to enter the freeway every few seconds. The time is constant (e.g., three seconds). However, it is changed during rush hours to a larger value.

a. Explain in queuing terminology the reason for such an arrangement.

b. Devise a freeway system with three lanes and use your own numbers to prove your point.

34. A system has the following input data: $\lambda = 10$, $\mu = 12$, service costs $150 per hour, and waiting costs $35 per hour.

a. Find the total cost if the maximum number of customers in the system is four. Find the cost for five. For six. If the cost of balking is $10 per person who balks, which alternative is the least expensive?

b. Which alternative is the least expensive if the cost of balking is $1 per customer?

Note: In both cases, ignore any additional cost associated with adding more waiting space.

35. Given the computer printout of two service systems, A and B, below; data are for one hour of operation. The company operates 2 shifts, 5 days a week, 50 weeks per year, 8 hours per shift. The company operates now with system A. It is estimated that each customer that leaves the line (balks) costs the company $1.50. System B is a proposed system that is faster. Replacing the system requires $1 million. The company uses a two-year payback as a criterion for determining the acceptability of capital budgeting (investment) projects. Namely, the savings should return the investment in two years or less. Based on the computer printouts, show the calculations and the recommended action. Note: $\lambda = 35$; $\mu = 50$ for A, 60 for B. Max. No. in system = 5.

System A

```
BALKING RATE (PERCENT) 5.7
EXPECTED NUMBER IN SYSTEM 1.53
EXPECTED NUMBER IN QUEUE .87
EXPECTED TIME IN SYSTEM .046
EXPECTED TIME IN QUEUE .026

ECONOMIC ANALYSIS RESULTS (PER HOUR)
COST OF SERVICE  : 48
COST OF WAITING  : 244.8
      TOTAL COST : 292.8
```

System B

```
BALKING RATE (PERCENT) 2.9
EXPECTED NUMBER IN SYSTEM 1.15
EXPECTED NUMBER IN QUEUE .59
EXPECTED TIME IN SYSTEM .034
EXPECTED TIME IN QUEUE .017

ECONOMIC ANALYSIS RESULTS (PER HOUR)
COST OF SERVICE  : 48
COST OF WAITING  : 184
      TOTAL COST : 232
```

15.18 CASE I

NEWTOWN MAINTENANCE DIVISION

The city of Newtown, like many other cities today, is caught in a severe financial squeeze. Up to now, previous city managers have taken a short-term approach to Newtown's maintenance and repair services in the expectation that future tax receipts would improve. However, Newtown's voters have just rejected the fourth proposed tax increase on the ballot for city services in as many years, and the expected relief of future tax revenues now looks hopeless.

The new city manager has decided that a long-term policy must finally be established that recognizes the reality of continued low funding for city services. One portion of this problem is the manner of making daily repairs to the city's streets. Calls for repairs arrive randomly at the average rate of two per day. It is the mayor's declared policy that the city will respond to all calls for street repairs within one week (five eight-hour working days) of the call.

The city manager has two alternatives for servicing street repairs:

1. He can use any number of standard city crews which cost $79 per hour and can each repair a street, on the average, in 10 hours.
2. He can lease special heavy-duty street repairing equipment and use smaller crews, resulting in an hourly cost of $90 per crew. These special crews can repair the average street in only seven hours.

Make a recommendation to the city manager concerning these two alternatives. How soon can the city respond to calls under the cheapest of the above two policies? What would happen if the mayor insisted that the response time be reduced to *two* working days?

CASE II

A QUEUING CASE STUDY OF DRIVE-IN BANKING[14]

This case is a summary of the efforts of two students in the Applied Operations Research course taught in the University of Oklahoma School of Industrial Engineering in the fall of 1972. The case involved the effort of a local bank to expand their drive-in facilities. Two options were basically available: a "robo-window" system and a traditional expansion of the current system which involved teller stations approximately 8 feet by 8 feet stationed on a traffic lane. The robo system involved a small cube approximately 3 feet in each dimension which had a speaker system and a pneumatic tube to deliver cartridges back to a central location. Space was at a premium and expansion of the present system was limited to five teller stations (they now have three), whereas up to seven stations were available if the robo system was used. The robo station was, of course, much cheaper (by about one half) than an 8 foot by 8 foot room for a teller.

The bank was less concerned about the costs than the quality of customer service. Our team was called in to assess the two systems.

The first concern was finding a measure of performance. Interviews with bank officials rapidly dismissed total costs as a consideration. The prime consideration was lost customers due to poor service. Bank officials then defined poor service as causing a customer to wait longer than five minutes. This choice was not as arbitrary

[14] B. L. Foote, *Interfaces* 6, no. 4 (August 1976), pp. 31–36, copyright 1976, The Institute of Management Sciences.

as it sounds, as further questions showed that customers base their impatience on the movement of the minute hand between two marks, which on most watches represents five minutes. Bank officials then set four minutes as the maximum waiting time. The team then suggested a risk level of approximately .05 and this was agreed to.

The team also suggested that the cost criterion should be evaluated as a backup piece of information, and suggested that for any design the imputed cost of waiting should be determined and submitted to bank officials for their judgment. This was agreed to. The team cheerfully set to work with a set of formulas.[15] Time studies were immediately taken, using two observers to facilitate data collection. (Initial tests disclosed that observing the cars, operating the watch, and reordering were too much for one student to do without substantial error.) Table 1 and similar tables were computed for various days and time intervals.

TABLE 1
Friday 2:15–6:30

Interval (seconds)	*Observed frequency*	*Expected frequency*	*Chi Square ($\lambda = .03$ arrivals per second)*
0–19	208	206	.019
20–39	109	113	.142
40–59	64	62	.016
60–79	33	34	.029
80–99	19	19	0
100–119	13	10	.9
120+	10	12	.333
	456	456	1.439

The expected frequency computations assumed that interarrival times were distributed exponentially. Since $\chi^2_{.01}$ with five degrees of freedom is 15.086, this looked like a good fit.

Other tables had similar results. A plot of the arrival rates in Exhibit 1 gave rise to some second thoughts. The queue was obviously always in a state of flux and the theory of the transient behavior of queues was probably needed. A look at some basic references was discouraging. The formulas were so complex that elaborate programming or simulation seemed to be called for in order to compute the probability of waiting in the system longer than four minutes. Further, the team could find no solid information on how long the "transient" state of a queue lasted. Someone remembered reading something about four hours. References were examined with no solid information found.

The bank operated by adding tellers as the waiting line grew. When about four were waiting, another window opened up. This rule of thumb would be used in the new system, so the team thought perhaps that this might "smooth out" the transient behavior and perhaps some simple formulas could still be used.

The team next studied the service time. Since waiting times can be lessened either by adding servers or decreasing service times, the layout of the workstation was studied and service times during busy periods were taken. No improvements in layout or work methods could be seen. Further, service times also were textbook fits of the χ^2 distribution. However, a fortunate observation was made. The service time of the system and the service time of the teller were two different times. The service time of the system consisted of the following events: realizing the car in front had moved, move to the teller window, give the teller instructions or requests plus material items, teller actions, move out. On three of these actions the teller was forcibly idle. The total of the five actions the team called block time. The block time was 72 seconds and service time was 48 seconds. These were average figures, of course. A little machine interference speculation was conducted. Perhaps two tellers could serve three lanes. Two tellers could sit in a teller station and serve the station lane and two robo lanes.

Exhibit 2 shows a sample of the machine

[15] H. A. Taha, *Operations Research* (New York: Macmillan, 1971).

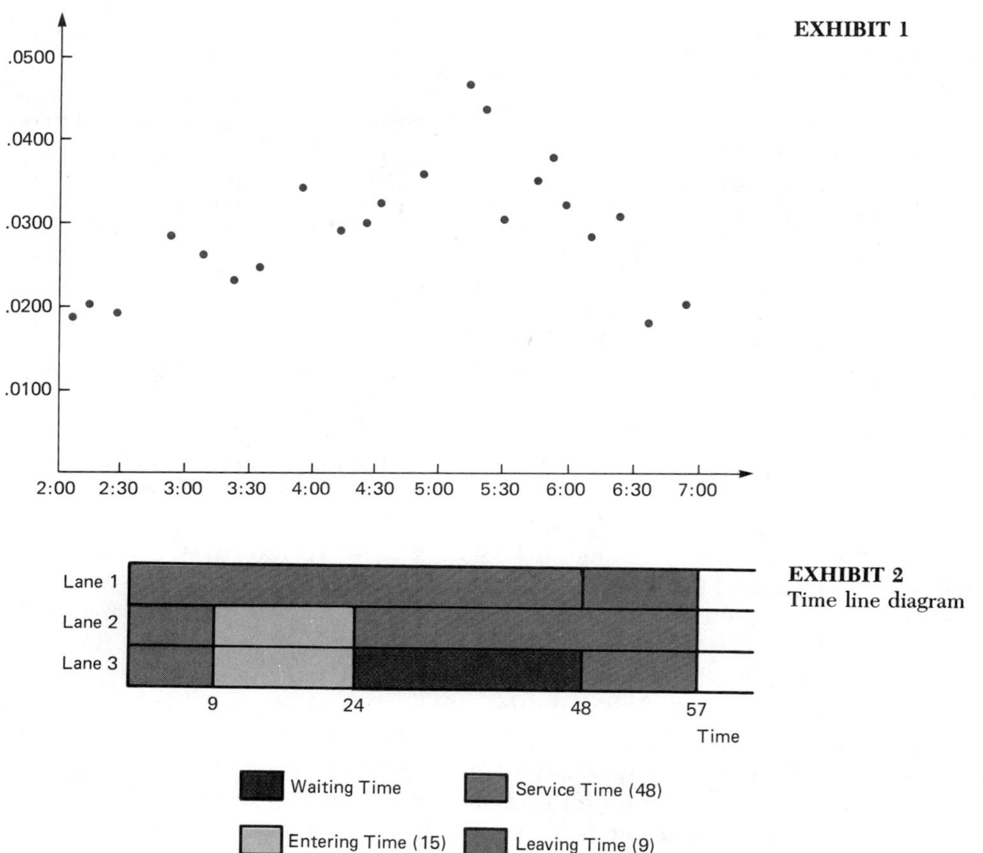

EXHIBIT 1

EXHIBIT 2
Time line diagram

interference diagramming done. The conclusion was that this assignment was a possibility. Of course, the diagram was idealized based on averages, but it was felt that short service times would balance out in this case. When the time line was extended the waiting times vanished. The time of vanishing of waiting time (115 seconds) was used as an estimate of transient state time. The relationship between 72 and 48 was too good to be true, but rechecks verified the figures.

The team then began calculations to see if the formulas[16] could predict average waiting times. About two minutes after a window opened, observations were taken. One, two, and three server cases were observed. Table 2 gives the results.

Table 2 and tables like it were intriguing. The predictions seemed good except for one "outlier." Further, the last calculation was *very* interesting. It seemed a variable teller window number policy could be approximated by formulas based on the maximum number of windows open at all times. Upon reflection, this seemed very reasonable.

If we assume the cost of a server[17] is constant (probably not true), Taha gives an inequality that can be used to estimate imputed cost of waiting per hour.

[16] Ibid.

[17] Ibid.

TABLE 2
Predicted versus observed system average waiting times

Ws (*seconds*) *observed*	*Ws* (*seconds*) *predicted*	
89	85	(1 Teller, $\lambda = .0214$, $\mu = .0138$)
106	86	(3 Tellers, $\lambda = .0216$, $\mu = .0138$)
100	174	(2 Tellers, $\lambda = .0211$, $\mu = .0138$)
90	94	(3 Tellers, $\lambda = .025$, $\mu = .0138$)
208	202	(3 Tellers, $\lambda = .0356$, $\mu = .0138$)
125*	124*	(3 Tellers, $\lambda = .0305$, $\mu = .0138$)

λ = Arrival rate per second.
μ = Service rate per second.
Ws = Average waiting time in system.
* Observed and expected values for *Ws* for the entire period, assuming three open windows at *all* times.

TABLE 4
$\alpha = 2$

Interval	*Observed frequency*	*Expected frequency*	χ^2
I	56	67	1.81
II	112	88	6.55
III	56	66	1.52
IV	24	30	1.20
V	13	13	0
VI	7	8	.13
VII	8	4	4.00
Totals	276	276	15.21

These calculations showed the bank's current policy-imputed customer waiting time at somewhere between $3 and $24 per hour. These figures seemed acceptable to bank officials. The important calculation was still to come.

The formulas were good for expected times, but what about the waiting time distribution? For the transient case the waiting time distribution is not known explicitly. For the steady state case, the distribution has the form of a gamma distribution. It was hoped that using steady state as an approximation would work here also. Using Table 3, some empirical tests were made.

The gamma distribution depends on two parameters α, β where $\alpha\beta$ = mean value. For convenience, α was chosen as 1, 2, 3, . . . since, if α is noninteger, we no longer have $(\alpha - 1)!$ in the function definition, but a very complicated evaluation. β was determined by $\alpha\beta = W_s$; $\alpha = 2$ and $\alpha = 3$ are tested in Tables 4 and 5. $\chi^2_{.005} = 16.750$. $\alpha = 2$ was chosen, of course.

The team then set to work. They calculated W_s for various combinations of c; $1 \le c \le 7$. Using $\alpha\beta = W_s$, $\alpha = 2$, they computed $P(W_s \le 4)$ by integration.

These evaluations "showed" the new system could handle the projected arrival rates in the future with some room to spare. An expansion to five lanes with two robos added to the current three lanes was recommended, with an assurance that adding a teller when the waiting line exceeded three or four would handle the projected volume and a customer would run less than a 5 percent chance of waiting more than four minutes.

TABLE 3
Observed system waiting times

Interval	*Seconds*	*Observed frequency*
I	0–50	56
II	51–100	112
III	101–150	56
IV	151–200	24
V	201–250	13
VI	251–300	7
VII	300+	8

TABLE 5
$\alpha = 3$

Interval	*Observed frequency*	*Expected frequency*	χ^2
I	56	48	1.33
II	112	105	.47
III	56	69	2.45
IV	24	37	4.57
V	13	9	1.78
VI	7	6	.17
VII	8	2	18.00
Totals	276	276	28.77

The students happily handed in their report knowing they would be gone before the robo lanes would be built, and the instructor waited for the results of the bank decision.

Epilogue

The robo lanes were built and worked as predicted. There was an exception. The phenomenon of jockeying is well known in queuing systems. Here we had a single lane that emptied into one or two car queues in front of each of the tellers. This was a departure from the basic single queue multichannel service system which was used to model the system. The system worked fine as long as customers in the single queue drove to the empty lane. But, on occasion, customers would go into a nonempty queue in front of a teller station rather than a shorter queue on a robo lane (see Exhibit 3). Waiting times, of course, expanded. Now, as the system continues to be used, the robo lanes have become more popular as the customers have become used to them, and the system is functioning normally.

EXHIBIT 3
Layout of final system

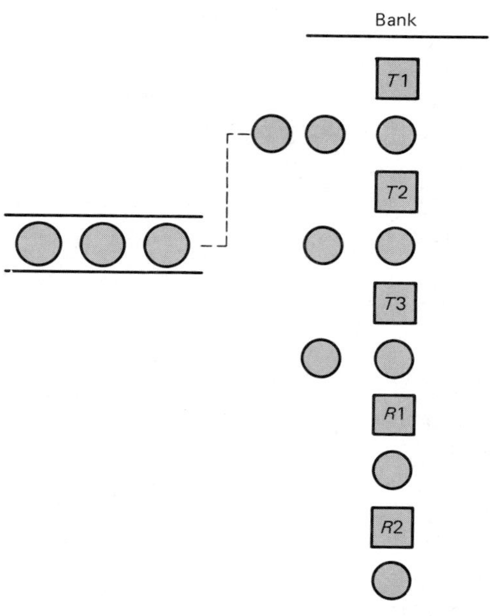

Questions for discussion

1. What measure of performance was used in the queuing model in this situation? Can you suggest additional measures of performance that would be appropriate in this case?
2. What is the purpose of applying the chi-square test to the distribution of interarrival times?
3. Discuss the concept of *imputed cost*. Is it possible to calculate the imputed cost of waiting in a queue?
4. In the context of queuing models, what is meant by the *transient case* and by the *steady state case*?
5. Can you think of, or glean from the literature, situations where the application of standard queuing theory would be extremely limited?

15.19 GLOSSARY

Arrival rate The number of units arriving at the service facility for service.

Balking Refusing to join a waiting line.

Calling population See Source.

Cycling Returning to the queue following service.

Explosive queue A situation where the customers arrive faster than the service and the queue builds up without a decrease.

FCFS The first-come, first-served service discipline.

Interarrival time The time between customer arrivals at the service facility.

Jockeying Shifting back and forth between queues.

LCFS Last-come, first-served; a priority system used in warehouses and stores.

Multifacility A service facility with multiple service stations in parallel, each providing the same service.

Negative exponential A type of continuous statistical distribution.

Parallel Providing service at the same time; simultaneous.

Poisson A type of discrete statistical distribution.

Poisson-exponential system The elementary queue with random arrivals and services.

Preemptive priority When one can interrupt an ongoing service.

Queue A waiting line.

Queue discipline The policy of selecting customers for service.

Random Based completely on chance; not deterministic.

Reneging Leaving the system before service; backing out.

Serial One following the other.

Service rate The number of units that can be served in a unit of time.

Service facility The station where recipients are served.

Source The population of customers for a queue.

Utilization ratio The fraction of time the server is busy.

15.20 REFERENCES AND BIBLIOGRAPHY

1. Bhat, U. N. "Sixty Years of Queuing Theory." *Management Science* 15 (1969), p. B–280.
2. Cohen, J. W. *The Single-Server Queue. New York: Elsevier North-Holland Publishing, 1969.*
3. Cooper, R. B. *Introduction to Queueing Theory.* 2nd ed. New York: Elsevier North-Holland Publishing, 1981.
4. Erikson, W. J., and O. P. Hall, Jr. *Computer Models for Management Science.* Reading, Mass.: Addison-Wesley Publishing, 1983.
5. Gross, D., and C. N. Harris. *Fundamentals of Queuing Theory.* New York: John Wiley & Sons, 1974.
6. Hillier, F. S., and G. J. Lieberman. *Introduction to Operations Research.* 3rd ed. San Francisco: Holden-Day, 1979.
7. Hillier, F. S., and O. S. Yu. *Queuing Tables and Graphs.* New York: Elsevier North-Holland Publishing, 1981.
8. Jaiswal, N. K. *Priority Queues.* New York: Academic Press, 1968.
9. Newell, G. F. *Application of Queueing Theory.* London: Chapman and Hall, 1971.
10. Panico, J. A. *Queuing Theory.* Englewood Cliffs, N.J.: Prentice-Hall, 1969.
11. Peck, L. G., and R. N. Hazelwood. *Finite Queuing Tables.* New York: John Wiley & Sons, 1958.
12. Solomon, S. L. *Simulation of Waiting Line Systems.* Englewood Cliffs, N.J.: Prentice-Hall, 1983.
13. White, J. A., and J. W. Schmidt. *Analysis of Queuing Systems.* New York: Academic Press, 1975.

16

Simulation

PART A: BASICS

16.1 The general nature of simulation.
16.2 The methodology of simulation.
16.3 Types of simulation.
16.4 The Monte Carlo methodology.
16.5 Time independent, discrete simulation.
16.6 Time dependent, discrete simulation.
16.7 Risk analysis.
16.8 The role of computers in simulation.
16.9 Issues in simulation.
16.10 Problems for Part A.

PART B: EXTENSIONS

16.11 Complex queuing situations.
16.12 Simulation with continuous probability distributions.
16.13 Visual interactive simulation.
16.14 Heuristic programming.
16.15 Business games.
16.16 Corporate and financial planning models.
16.17 System dynamics.
16.18 Other simulation models.
16.19 Concluding remarks.
16.20 Problems for Part B.
16.21 Case—Express A.G.
16.22 Glossary.
16.23 References and bibliography.

The application of the management science tools described in the earlier chapters is frequently limited to relatively simple managerial problems. When managerial problems become complex, they often no longer fit the standard problem classifications that are solved by the standard tools. Development of special optimization models to handle such problems may be too costly in terms of dollars and time or the task may even be impossible. For such cases, simulation models are useful. A simulation model involves trial-and-error experimentation with a mathematical model in order to describe and evaluate the system's behavior. Six types of simulation models will be discussed in this chapter: Monte Carlo, visual simulation, heuristic programming, business games, corporate planning, and system dynamics.

LEARNING OBJECTIVES

The student should be able to:

a. Define simulation and understand its role in management science.
b. Describe the major characteristics of simulation.
c. Distinguish between time-dependent and time-independent simulation.
d. Distinguish between continuous and discrete simulation.
e. Use simulation in risk analysis.
f. Define Monte Carlo.
g. Describe the role of random numbers in simulation.
h. List the various methods of generating random numbers.
i. Formulate simple problems to be simulated by Monte Carlo, write flowcharts, and solve the problems.
j. Describe the concept of stability and the determination of sample size.

Extensions

k. Solve problems involving normal and Poisson probability distributions.
l. Describe how simulation is used in corporate planning.
m. Solve problems using heuristic programming.
n. Describe the process of playing management games.
o. Simulate waiting line situations, using Monte Carlo.
p. Simulate events with a normal distribution.
q. List the major advantages and disadvantages of simulation.
r. Define visual simulation and its role in management.
s. Define heuristic programming and its role in management.
t. Define operational gaming and its role in management.
u. Define system dynamics.

PART A: BASICS

Sunny Goldman was delighted with her new job as director, Tourist Information Center, for the city of Miami Beach. She had completed her graduate work in the Hotel and Entertainment Services program of a highly rated college in New York and accepted the offer for the new position from her former internship employer, the city of Miami Beach.

The city manager, Cy Bushnell, had been impressed with Sunny's analytical skills during her summers as an intern working at the Senior Citizens Center. There she had been instrumental in instituting programs that raised the quality of the center's services while simultaneously cutting their costs. Cy had been straightforward in his expectations when offering Sunny the permanent position of director for this new center: the budget was severely underfunded, yet the city council had high expectations for the center. If the first year was successful, the center would be much better funded the second year. If not, the city council might well cancel the entire concept.

Sunny saw her first task as determining the needs for service at the center. This required statistics concerning the tourists' arrival rates, their waiting times, and the service times they required to meet their needs. Following this, Sunny would look into more detail concerning the variety of services the tourists required. Special brochures and posters might handle a significant portion of their information requirements, for example. Or perhaps some form of "express line" for commonly asked questions or senior citizens was desirable.

We will return to Sunny's situation and describe some tools that Sunny might find helpful a bit later in the chapter.

16.1 THE GENERAL NATURE OF SIMULATION

The example just presented is a simple case of one server (possibly more) in a waiting line situation. Unfortunately, as we will show, the case cannot be solved by the formulas in Chapter 15 because the arrival rate does not follow the Poisson distribution, nor is the service time exponential.

Sunny's first approach to the data collection problem was to log tourist arrivals and services in the facility. Her results for the first 10 tourists are shown in Table 16.1.

Based on this quick preliminary sample, Sunny concluded that the average tourist waited 7/10 of a minute and the employee was busy during 41/50 minutes or 82 percent of the time. Several questions came to Sunny's mind:

How long should she clock the operation of the information clerk?
How do the employees feel about being clocked?

TABLE 16.1
Tourist Information Center data

Tourist number	*Arrival time*	*Start of service*	*End of service*	*Tourist waiting from–to*	*Employee idle from–to*
1	9:02	9:02	9:08	—	9:08–9:10
2	9:10	9:10	9:14	—	—
3	9:12	9:14	9:17	9:12–9:14	—
4	9:13	9:17	9:20	9:13–9:17	—
5	9:20	9:20	9:23	—	—
6	9:22	9:23	9:28	9:22–9:23	9:28–9:31
7	9:31	9:31	9:34	—	9:34–9:35
8	9:35	9:35	9:40	—	—
9	9:40	9:40	9:45	—	9:45–9:48
10	9:48	9:48	9:50	—	—
Total				7 minutes	9 minutes

How do the tourists feel about being clocked?
What other kinds of measurements should she take?

What Sunny did not know then was that she can conduct all her experiments on a model of the Tourist Agency, and that she can get answers to all her questions by using the technique of simulation. (The solution to Sunny's problem is given in Section 16.6.)

War games and Monopoly

Simulation is not limited to waiting line problems. Other familiar simulations are the mock war games that national armies regularly schedule, primarily for their reservists, and Monopoly, the real estate game. Other, not so familiar, simulations are:

- Simulation models of urban systems.
- Corporate organizational (policy) models.
- Business games used for training.
- Flights to the planets and the moon.
- Plant and warehouse location models.
- Determination of the proper size of repair crews.
- Econometric models of national economies.
- Network models of traffic intersections to determine the best sequencing of traffic lights.
- Queuing models of airport runway takeoffs and landings.
- Air basin models to determine pollution sources, concentrations, and dynamics.
- Dam and river basin models to determine the effect of weather and operating policies on the hydroelectric output and water supply.
- Financial models (short and long run).

A flexible tool

From the above list, it can be seen that simulation is one of the most flexible techniques in the tool kit of management scientists. It can be applied to many different types of problems and yields a great deal of information concerning the effectiveness of different operating policies under various conditions and assumptions.

What is simulation?

Simulation has many meanings, depending on the area where it is being used. To *simulate,* according to the dictionary, means to assume the appearance or characteristics of reality. In management science, it generally refers to *a technique for conducting experiments with a digital computer on a model of a management system over an extended period of time.*[1]

Major characteristics

Imitation—not just representation

To begin, simulation is not strictly a type of model; models in general *represent* reality, while simulation *imitates* it. In practical terms, this means that there are fewer simplifications of reality in simulation models than in other models.

Conducting experiments

Second, simulation is a technique for *conducting experiments.* Therefore, simulation involves the testing of specific values of the decision variables in the model and observing the impact on the output variables.

Simulation is a *descriptive* rather than a normative tool; that is, there is no automatic search for an optimal solution. Instead, a simulation describes and/or predicts the characteristics of a given system under different circumstances. Once these characteristics are known, the best among several policies can be selected, though an optimum, as analytic models yield, may be considerably better, but was not selected for testing. The simulation process often consists of the repetition of an experiment many, many times to obtain an estimate of the overall effect of certain actions. It can be executed manually in some cases, but a computer is usually needed.

Finally, simulation is usually called for only when the problem under investigation is too complex to be treated by analytical models (such as EOQ) or by numerical optimization techniques (such as linear programming). Complexity here means that the problem either cannot be formulated mathematically (e.g., because the assumptions do not hold, as in Sunny's case) or the formulation is too involved for a practical or economic solution.

Advantages and disadvantages of simulation

The increased acceptance of simulation at the higher managerial levels is probably due to a number of factors:

[1] In rare cases, it is possible to conduct optimization in simulation.

1. Simulation theory is relatively straightforward.
2. The simulation model is simply the aggregate of many elementary relationships and interdependencies, much of which is introduced slowly by request of the manager and in a patchwork manner.
3. Simulation is descriptive rather than normative. This allows the manager to ask "what if" type questions (especially when used with an on-line computer). Thus, managers who employ a trial-and-error approach to problem solving can do it faster and cheaper with less risk, using the aid of simulation and computers.

"What if" questions

4. An accurate simulation model requires an *intimate* knowledge of the problem, thus forcing the management scientist to constantly interface with the manager.
5. The model is built from the manager's perspective and in his or her decision structure rather than the management scientist's.
6. The simulation model is built for one particular problem and, typically, will not solve any other problem. Thus, no generalized understanding is required of the manager; every component in the model corresponds one to one with a part of the real-life model.
7. Simulation can handle an extremely wide variation in problem types such as inventory and staffing, as well as higher managerial level functions like long-range planning. Thus, it is "always there" when the manager needs it.

Always there

8. The manager can experiment with different variables to determine which are important, and with different policies and alternatives to determine which are the best. The experimentation is done with a model rather than by interfering with the system.
9. Simulation, in general, allows for inclusion of the real-life complexities of problems; simplifications are not necessary. For example: simulation utilizes the real-life probability distributions rather than approximate theoretical distributions.
10. Due to the nature of simulation, a great amount of **time compression** can be attained, giving the manager some feel as to the long-term (1 to 10 years) effects of various policies, in a matter of minutes.

Time compression

11. The great amount of time compression enables experimentation with a very large sample (especially when computers are used). Therefore, as much accuracy can be achieved as desired at a relatively low cost.

The primary disadvantages of simulation are:

No guarantee of optimality

1. An optimal solution cannot be guaranteed.
2. Constructing a simulation model is frequently a slow and costly process.
3. Solutions and inferences from a simulation study are usually not transferable to other problems. This is due to the incorporation in the model of the unique factors of the problem.
4. Simulation is sometimes so easy to apply that analytical solutions that can yield optimal results are often overlooked.

16.2 THE METHODOLOGY OF SIMULATION

Simulation involves setting up a model of a real system and conducting repetitive experiments on it. The methodology consists of a number of steps (Figure 16.1). The following is a brief discussion of the process.

Problem definition The real-world problem is examined and classified. Here we should specify why simulation is necessary. The system's boundaries and other such aspects of problem clarification (see Chapter 2) are attended to here.

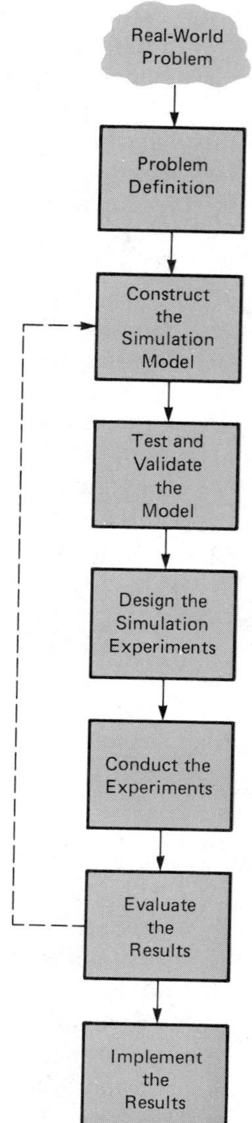

FIGURE 16.1
The process of simulation

Construction of the simulation model This step involves gathering the necessary data. For example, in Sunny's case, information is needed about arrivals, the Center's policies, and the nature of the service process. In many cases, a flowchart (to be discussed in Section 16.8) is used to describe the process. Then, if the simulation is to be conducted by a computer, a program is written, often in a special computer language. A manual simulation may be conducted instead and involves the creation of a summary table and a description of the appropriate functional relationships.

Testing and validating the model The simulation model must properly imitate the system under study. This involves the process of validation, discussed in Section 16.9.

Design of the experiment Once the model has been proved valid, the experiment is then designed. Included in this step is determining how long to run the simulation (when to stop the experiment) and whether to consider all the data or to ignore the transient start-up data. This step thus deals with two important and contradictory objectives: *accuracy* and *cost*. These, as well as other issues of design, are discussed in Section 16.9.

Conducting the experiments There are several types of simulation (see Section 16.3). Conducting the experiment may involve issues such as random number generation, stopping rules, and derivation of the results. These issues are also discussed in Section 16.9.

Evaluating the results The final step, prior to implementation, is the evaluation of the results. Here, we deal with issues such as: "What constitutes a significant difference?" "What do the results mean?" In addition to statistical tools, we may also use a sensitivity analysis (in the form of "what if" questions). At this stage, we may even change the model and repeat the experiment.

Implementation The implementation of simulation results involves the same issues as any other implementation. However, the chances of implementation are better since the manager is usually more involved in the simulation process than with analytical models.

16.3 TYPES OF SIMULATION

There are several types of simulation. The major ones described in this book are:

Probabilistic simulation In this type of simulation one or more of the independent variables (e.g., the arrival rate in a waiting line problem, or the demand in an inventory problem) is probabilistic. That is, it follows a certain probability distribution. Two subcategories are recognized: *discrete distributions* and *continuous distributions.*

Discrete or continuous?

1. *Discrete distributions* involve a situation with a limited number of events (or variables that can only take on a finite number of values. See Appendix B).

2. *Continuous distributions* refer to a situation with an unlimited number of possible events that follow density functions such as the normal distribution (see Appendix B).

The two types of distributions are shown in Table 16.2.

TABLE 16.2
Discrete and continuous distributions

Discrete		*Continuous*
Daily demand	*Probability*	
5	.10	Daily demand is normally distributed with a mean of 7 and a standard deviation of 1.2
6	.15	
7	.30	
8	.25	
9	.20	

Probabilistic simulation is conducted with the aid of a technique called Monte Carlo (Sections 16.4–16.7, 16.11, 16.12, and 16.16). Deterministic simulation is discussed in Section 16.18.

Time dependent and time independent simulation **Time independent** refers to a situation where it is not important to know exactly when the event occurred. For example, we may know that the demand is three units per day, but we do not care *when* during the day the item was demanded. Or in some situations, such as financial or organizational simulation, time may not be a factor in the simulation (see Sections 16.7, 16.15, and 16.18). On the other hand, in waiting line problems, it is important to know the precise time of arrival (to know if the customer will have to wait or not). In this case, we are dealing with a **time dependent** situation. Time dependent simulation is presented in Sections 16.6 and 16.11, while time independent is demonstrated in Sections 16.5 and 16.7.

Visual simulation This graphic display of computerized results is one of the more successful new developments in computer-human problem solving. It is described in Section 16.13.

Heuristic programming Presented in Section 16.14, this type of simulation is used for more complex managerial problems and situations.

Business games The simulation of competitive decision making, which may also involve probabilistic simulation, is presented in Section 16.15.

Large system simulation Complex simulations of corporations or even national economies are possible. These methods are presented in Sections 16.16–16.18.

16.4 THE MONTE CARLO METHODOLOGY

Sampling from the probability distributions

Managerial systems of decisions under risk exhibit chance elements in their behavior. As such, they can be simulated with the aid of a technique called **Monte Carlo** (named after the famous gambling kingdom). The technique involves random *sampling* from the probability distributions that represent the real-life processes.

Recall that in the Tourist Information Center case, we timed the arrivals and lengths of service. These two variables are usually probabilistic (the service time may sometimes be constant, as we have seen in Chapter 15). What the Monte Carlo method does is to generate *simulated* arrival times and service times from a given distribution by use of *random sampling*.

Thus, the Monte Carlo mechanism is not a simulation model per se, although it has become almost synonymous with probabilistic simulation. It is a mechanism used in the process of probabilistic simulation. Before we show how this is done, let us define some basic terms.

Uniform distribution A uniform distribution is one where each value of the variable has exactly the same chance of occurring (see Table 16.3). This distribution is shown graphically in Figure 16.2.

TABLE 16.3
An example of the uniform distribution

Demand	*Probability*
5	.25
6	.25
7	.25
8	.25

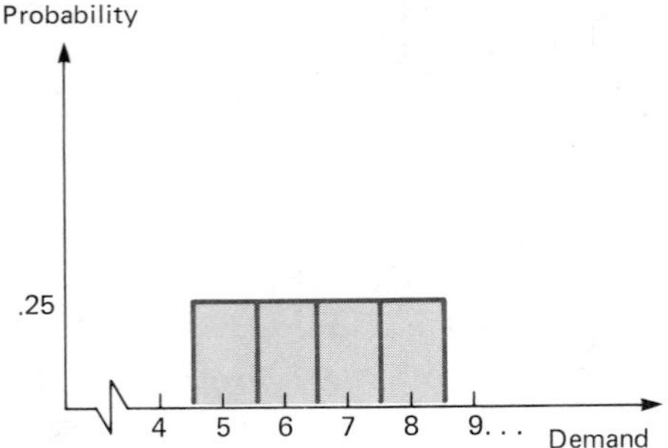

FIGURE 16.2
A uniform distribution shown graphically

Selecting an RN

Random number A **random number** (RN) is a number picked, at random, from a population of uniformly distributed numbers. That is, each number in the population has an equal probability of being selected. Random numbers can be arranged in various ways, depending on the population:

Population	*RN*
0 to 1	Decimal—.62 or .87
0 to 9	Single digit—6, 8, 0, 3
00 to 99	Two digits—16, 83, 42
000 to 999	Three digits—123, 306, 027, 815

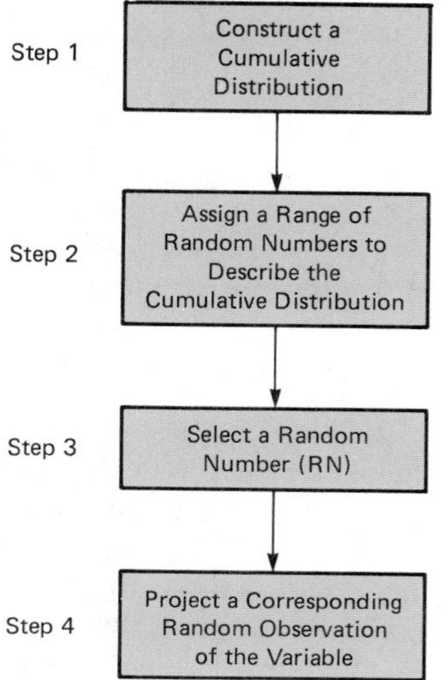

FIGURE 16.3
The Monte Carlo process

The process

The Monte Carlo process involves the four steps shown in Figure 16.3.

Example

Let us return to Sunny's problem. Assume that through more historical data, a time study, or estimation it is possible to express the service time in the Tourist Information Center by the probability distribution shown in Table 16.4.

TABLE 16.4
Probability distribution of service time

Length of service (minutes)	*Probability*
3	.156
4	.287
5	.362
6	.195

Step 1. Construct the cumulative probability distribution This is done in Table 16.5.

The cumulative distribution is obtained by adding the probabilities in Table 16.4 to the previous cumulative probabilities in Table 16.5. This is shown in Figure 16.4.

At this point, the process can continue either graphically (steps 3 and 4; step 2 has been eliminated here since the graph provides the RN range assignments), or using a tabular approach (steps 2, 3, and 4).

Graphical or tabular approach?

TABLE 16.5
Cumulative probability distribution of service time

Length of service	*Cumulative probability distribution*
3	.156
4	(.156 + .287=) .443
5	.805
6	1.000

The graphical approach

Step 3. Generate a random number A random number may be selected in several ways (see Section 16.9). A convenient way is to use a table of random numbers, such as Table C2 in Appendix C. The first number is 7823. Since we are working with three-decimal accuracy we need only a three-digit RN (782), and since we are in the 0 to 1 population we will label it 0.782.

Step 4. Project a service time This is done with the aid of the cumulative distribution, Figure 16.4.

a. Locate the RN = .782 on the cumulative probability axis.
b. Go horizontally to the cumulative probability, point *K*.

FIGURE 16.4
Cumulative probability distribution shown graphically

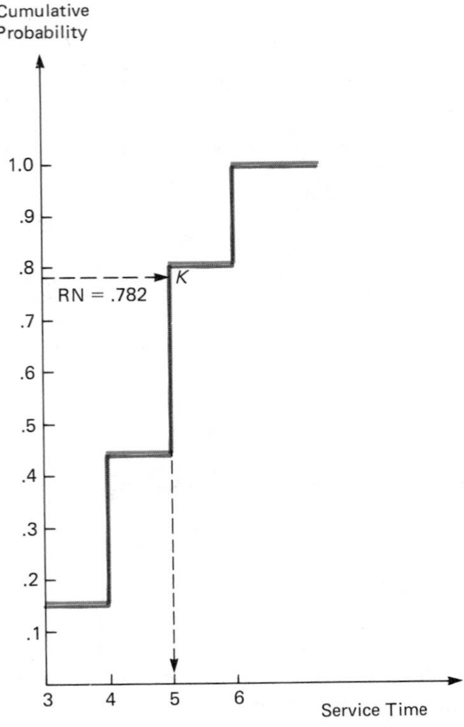

c. Turn downward, go vertically until the "Service Time" axis is reached.
d. Read the value of service time: 5 in our case.

The tabular approach

This approach starts with step 2.

Step 2. Assign a range of RNs Using the cumulative probability (Table 16.5) as a guide, a representative range (or interval) is assigned to every value of the "service time" variable. This is done as follows (refer to Table 16.6). Since this case involves three-digit data, the numbers 000 to 999 shall be used.

TABLE 16.6
Assigning a range of RNs

Service time	*Probability*	*Cumulative probability*	*Range of RNs*
3	.156	.156	000–155
4	.287	.443	156–442
5	.362	.805	443–804
6	.195	1.000	805–999

Maintain proportionality

The assignment of representative numbers must be such that the *proportion* of the various states of nature (the number of minutes of service in this case) be maintained. For example, the assignment for three minutes service time requires 156 three-digit numbers. This is because the proportion of three minutes is .156 and out of *all* existing three-digit numbers (1,000), .156 translates into 156 (i.e., 1,000 × .156). The numbers to be used in each category are somewhat arbitrary. *Any* 156 three-digit numbers can be used. For the sake of uniformity one can start with 000. Starting with 000 and counting 156 numbers, one will end with the number 155. However, since it does not make any difference which numbers are used, one can also use the numbers 001 to 156.

In assigning the representative numbers, it is common to use, as an auxiliary instrument, the *cumulative* probability distribution. Notice, then, that the *lower limit* of the representative numbers (say 156, in the case of four minutes) corresponds to the cumulative probability of three minutes (observe the arrows in Table 16.6).

Step 3. Generate a RN This is done in exactly the same manner as in the graphical method.

Step 4. Predict a specific value of the variable of interest (make a random observation) Take the generated RN (782 in our case, dropping the unneeded digit 3) and find the range in which this number falls. In Table 16.6, the range is 443–804. Therefore, the RN 782 is said to correspond to five minutes service time. In a similar fashion, the Monte Carlo method will generate a sequence of random service times from a corresponding sequence of RNs (see Table 16.7). These values are then used in the simulation process.

TABLE 16.7
Generating random service times

RN (from Table C2):	782	430	922	871	477
Service time:	5	4	6	6	5

Simulation experimentation: A preview

Eight steps in simulation

The simulation experimentation in this book involves cases of risk and, therefore, the Monte Carlo mechanism is used constantly. However, in deterministic simulation, the Monte Carlo method is omitted. The following is a list of the eight steps involved in the simulation experimentation (including Monte Carlo):

1. Describe the system and obtain the probability distributions of the relevant probabilistic elements of the system. This is a crucial step requiring intimate familiarity with the system. Frequently incorrect assumptions are made at this point that invalidate the rest of the simulation.
2. Define the appropriate measure(s) of system performance. If necessary, write it in the form of an equation(s).
3. Construct cumulative probability distributions for each of the stochastic elements.
4. Assign representative numbers in correspondence with the cumulative probability distributions.
5. For each probabilistic element, take a random sample (generate a number at random or pick one from a table of random numbers).
6. Derive the measures of performance and their variances.
7. If steady-state results are desired, repeat steps 5 and 6 until the measures of system performance "stabilize" (discussed in step 7 of Section 16.5).
8. Repeat steps 5–7 for various managerial policies. Given the values of the performance measures and their confidence intervals, decide on the appropriate managerial policy.

The above procedure will next be demonstrated with an inventory control example.

16.5 TIME INDEPENDENT, DISCRETE SIMULATION

Note: Some of the material presented in this section and the next, as well as the corresponding homework problems, are simple enough to be handled by analytical models. More complex examples would unnecessarily complicate and extend the presentation. In addition, we sometimes use simulation because it is faster and easier than deriving analytical solutions.

Marin's Service Station sells gasoline to boat owners. The demand for gasoline depends on weather conditions and fluctuates according to the following distribution.

Weekly demand (gallons)	*Probability*
2,000	.12
3,000	.23
4,000	.48
5,000	.17

Shipments arrive once a week. Since Marin's Service Station is located in a remote place, it must order and accept a fixed quantity of gasoline every week. Joe, the owner, faces the following problem: If he orders too small a quantity, he will lose, in terms of lost business and goodwill, 12 cents per gallon demanded and not provided. If he orders too large a quantity, he will have to pay 5 cents per gallon shipped back due to lack of storage. For each gallon sold he makes 10 cents profit. At the present time, Joe receives 3,500 gallons at the beginning of each week before he opens for business. He feels that he should receive more, maybe 4,000 or even 4,500 gallons. The tank's capacity is 5,500 gallons. The problem is to find the best order quantity.

This problem can be solved by trial and error. That is, the service station can actually order each quantity for, say, 10 weeks, then compare the results. However, simulation can give an answer in a few minutes and a simulated loss is only a loss on paper.

Solution by simulation To find the best ordering quantity, it is necessary to compute the profit (loss) for the existing order quantity (3,500 gallons) and for other possible order quantities. For example, 4,000 and 4,500 (as suggested by Joe) or any other desired figure (e.g., 3,600, 3,750, 3,800, and so on) may be tried. Each quantity is a proposed solution, and the first seven out of eight steps must be executed for each; the eighth step then concludes the analysis. Assume that today is the first day of the week, a shipment has just arrived, and there is now an inventory of 3,800 gallons.

Using a flowchart

Before constructing a simulation, particularly if computerized, it is wise to construct a **flowchart** or flow diagram of the tasks. A flowchart is a schematic presentation of all computational activities used in the simulation. Its major objective is to help the computer programmer in writing the computer program. Figure 16.5 shows a flowchart for the inventory problem. We will discuss the equations a bit later, but the logic flow for the simulation process is clear. Therefore, let us begin the eight steps for the simulation and then follow the steps in the flowchart.

Step 1: Describe the system and determine the probability distributions. There is only one probability distribution in this case. It describes

FIGURE 16.5
Flow diagram for the inventory example

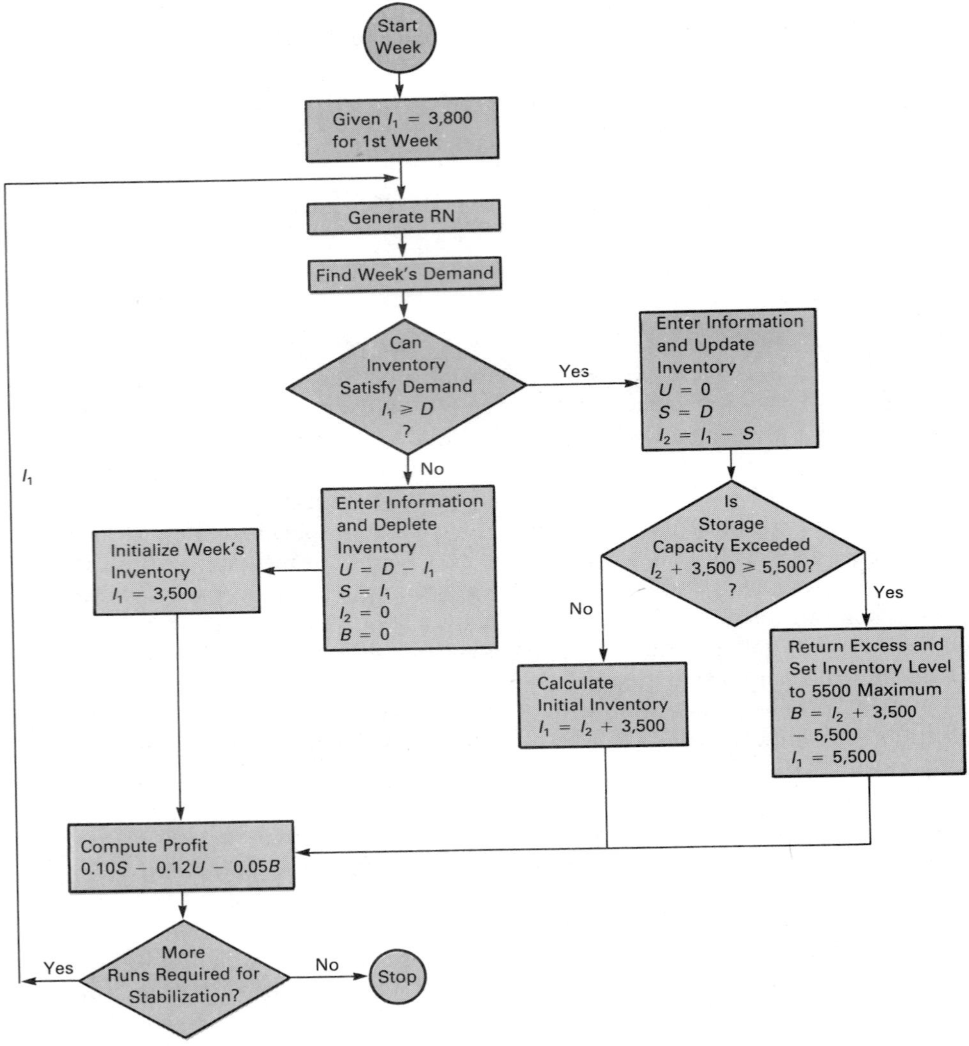

the demand. In more complicated Monte Carlo simulations there are several distributions involved.

Step 2: Decide on the measures of performance. The primary measure of performance is the *average daily profit,* which is computed as (all quantities are in gallons):

$$\text{Average daily profit} = 10¢ \times (\text{Sales}) - 12¢ \times (\text{Unsatisfied demand}) - 5¢ \times (\text{Quantity shipped back}) \quad (16.1)$$

Several less important measures such as the average shortage are discussed at the end of this example.

TABLE 16.8
Assignment of representative numbers

(A) Weekly demand	(B) Probability	(C) Cumulative probability	(D) Representative numbers (range)
2,000	.12	.12	01–12
3,000	.23	.35	13–35
4,000	.48	.83	36–83
5,000	.17	1.00	84–00

Step 3: Compute cumulative probabilities. The cumulative probabilities are computed in Table 16.8.[2]

The cumulative probability column indicates the chance for a certain demand or less to occur. For example, there is a .35 chance for a demand of 3,000 or less.

Representative ranges

Step 4: Assign **representative ranges of numbers.** For each possible demand, a range of representative numbers is assigned in proportion to the probability distribution. For example, there is a chance of .12 for a demand of 2,000 to occur. Therefore, out of 100 numbers (all two-digit numbers), 12 will be assigned to represent a demand of 2,000.[3] An easy way of doing this is to assign the numbers 01, 02, 03, . . . , 12. (This information is entered in Table 16.8.) Next, the demand of 3,000 is represented by 23 numbers, since it has a .23 chance of occurring. Since the numbers 01–12 have already been used, it is logical to use the next 23 two-digit numbers, 13–35.

Step 5: Generate random numbers and compute the system's performance. The first inventory system that will be considered is the current order policy of 3,500 gallons per week. For purposes of demonstration, step 5 is repeated here only 10 times to simulate 10 weeks. In reality, it should continue until the measure of performance (average weekly profit) achieves *stability,* as will be explained later in step 7. The detailed computations are shown in Table 16.9 and are executed as follows:

Column 1 designates the simulated week. In this example, only 10 weeks are simulated.

Column 2 is a list of random numbers (RNs), taken from the righthand side of Table C2 in Appendix C.[4] Here, we are interested in two-digit

---

[2] Columns *(A)* and *(B)* are given; column *(C)* is computed from column *(B)*, and column *(D)* is assigned according to column *(C)*.

[3] In this case, a two-digit random number is used. If the probability of demand were given by three-digit figures, for example, .115, then three-digit random numbers would have to be used.

[4] The table of RNs is entered at some random location, not necessarily the top-left corner, and the digits read in *any* direction: horizontally, downwards, diagonally, and so on. This procedure results in a set of random numbers because the table is generated in such a manner that every numeric location has the same chance (10 percent) of being occupied by a zero, or a one, up to a nine. That is, no digit has a preferred chance of being included in the table *or* of occupying any particular location. The table, thus, represents a *uniform distribution* of the digits 0 through 9.

TABLE 16.9
The simulation for 10 weeks

(1) Week number	(2) RN	(3) Inventory at beginning of week $I_b = I_e + 3{,}500$	(4) Simulated demand D	(5) Sold S	(6) Inventory at end of week $I_e = I_b - S$	(7) Unsatisfied demand $U = D - I_b$	(8) Shipped back B	(9) Weekly profit	(10) Average weekly profit
1	32	3,800	3,000	3,000	800			300.00	300.00
2	08	4,300	2,000	2,000	2,300			200.00	250.00
3	46	5,500	4,000	4,000	1,500		300	385.00	295.00
4	92	5,000	5,000	5,000	0			500.00	346.25
5	69	3,500	4,000	3,500	0	500		290.00	335.00
6	71	3,500	4,000	3,500	0	500		290.00	327.50
7	29	3,500	3,000	3,000	500			300.00	323.57
8	46	4,000	4,000	4,000	0			400.00	333.12
9	80	3,500	4,000	3,500	0	500		290.00	328.33
10	14	3,500	3,000	3,000	500			300.00	325.50
Total	—	40,100	36,000	34,500	5,600	1,500	300	3,255.00	—
Average per week	—	4,010	3,600	3,450	560	150	30	325.50	325.50

numbers, so the first and second of the four-digit numbers are used, starting with 32, then the next two, 08, and so on.

Column 3 represents the inventory at the beginning of each week (I_b). The column is computed by adding the 3,500-gallon shipment to the inventory at the end of the previous week (I_e). The *maximum inventory* is 5,500 gallons, due to limited storage capacity. Thus, $I_b = I_e + 3{,}500$ (up to 5,500 as an upper limit).

Column 4 represents the forecasted demand, D, based on the RN in column 2 and the range of RNs in Table 16.8. For example, the first RN, 32, falls in the representative range of 13–35, which is equivalent to a weekly demand of 3,000. Once the second column (RN) is generated, the entire fourth column can be computed quickly.

Two sales possibilities

Column 5 represents the amount sold. Two cases may occur.

1. The demand, D, is equal to or smaller than the inventory on hand, I_b. In this case, sales equal demand (i.e., $S = D$ as in weeks 1, 2, 3, and 4).
2. Demand is *larger* than the inventory on hand. In this case, sales are limited to the inventory on hand, I_b (i.e., $S = I_b$). The difference between the demand and the inventory on hand, $D - I_b$, is thus the unsatisfied demand, U (column 7). For example, in week 5 there is a demand of 4,000, but an inventory of 3,500. Therefore, the sales are 3,500 and there is an unsatisfied demand of 500.

In Column 6 the inventory at the end of each week, I_e, is listed. It is computed by subtracting the amount sold (column 5) from the beginning inventory (column 3), $I_e = I_b - S$.

Column 7 designates the unsatisfied demand, U. This column shows the difference between the demand and the beginning inventory whenever demand is larger (e.g., in week 5). Thus, $U = D - I_b$.

Column 8 designates the amount shipped back, B. Such a situation occurs when the "end-of-the-week inventory" plus the shipment (3,500 gallons in the system under study) exceed the 5,500-gallon tank capacity. In this case, the excess supply is shipped back and the beginning inventory is 5,500. For example, in week 3, the shipment of 3,500, added to the weekend inventory of week 2 of 2,300, gives a total of 5,800 gallons. Therefore, 5,800 − 5,500 = 300 gallons are shipped back.

Column 9: The measure of performance in this problem is profit. The profit is calculated, every week, according to the formula:

$$\$ \text{ profit} = .10S - .12U - .05B$$

For example:

In week 1: $S = 3{,}000$, $U = 0$, $B = 0$. Profit $= .1(3{,}000) = \$300$
In week 3: $S = 4{,}000$, $U = 0$, $B = 300$. Profit $= .1(4{,}000) - .05(300) = \$385$

The resulting values are plotted in Figure 16.6a and compared to a "theoretical" continuous distribution that may, in reality, be the underlying distribution of weekly profit.

Column 10: The *average* weekly profit at any week is computed by totaling the weekly profits up to that week (cumulative profit) and dividing it by the number of weeks. The results are shown in Figure 16.6b. For example:

In week 3: Cumulative profit = \$300 + \$200 + \$385 = \$885
Weekly average: \$885/3 = \$295

Step 6: Computing the measures of performance. Each simulation run is composed of multiple **trials.** The question of how many trials to have in one run (or finding the *length* of the run) involves statistical analysis. The longer the run, the more accurate are the results, but the higher the cost. This issue concerns what are labeled *stopping rules*. The stopping rules are usually built into the simulation program. For example, the run could be terminated when a desired standard error in the measures of performance is attained. These measures are computed continuously during the simulation, since they determine stability and the stopping time.

The simulation performed thus far indicated an average weekly profit of \$325.50. In addition to total profit, some other measures of performance can be computed.[5]

[5] The number of simulation trials that was close to sufficient for the average profit is still too small for the other measures of performance.

FIGURE 16.6
Profit results

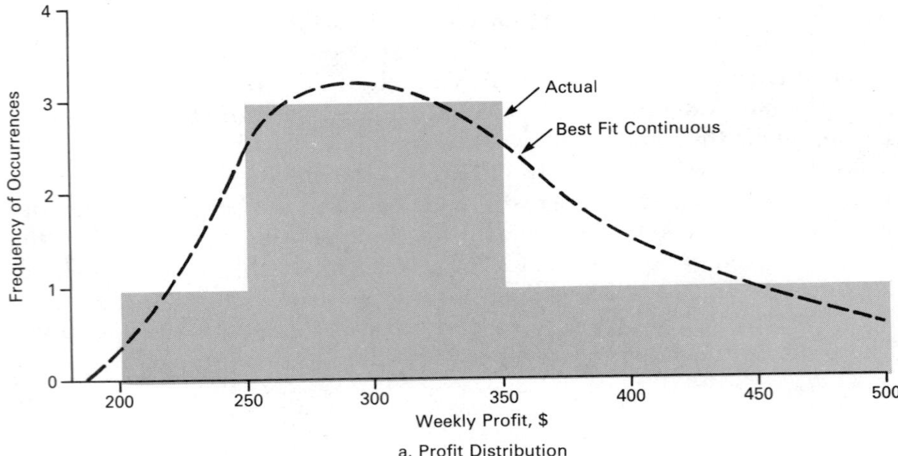

a. Profit Distribution

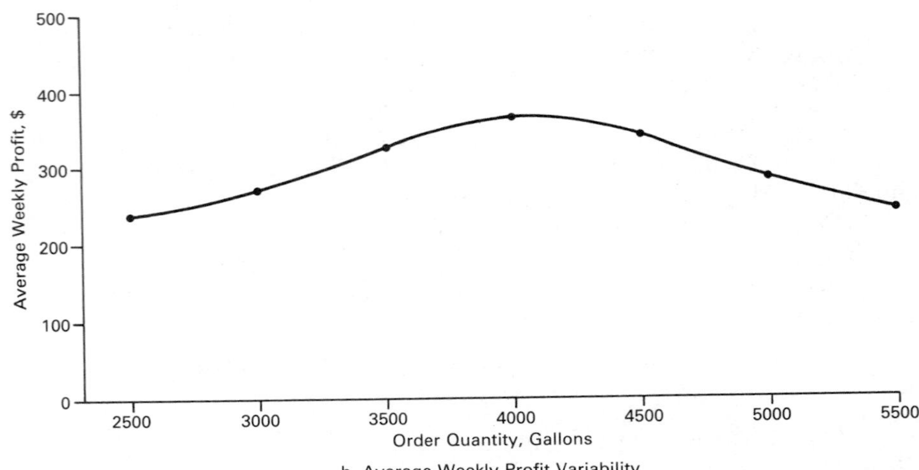

b. Average Weekly Profit Variability

a. *The probability of running short and the average shortage.* In 3 out of the 10 weeks there was an unsatisfied demand. Therefore, there is a 3/10 = 30 percent chance of running out of stock. The average shortage, per week, is 1,500/10 = 150 gallons.

b. *The probability of shipping back and the average quantity shipped back.* In 1 out of the 10 weeks some gasoline was shipped back. On the average there is a 1/10 = 10 percent chance of shipping back; the average amount is 300/10 = 30 gallons per week.

Multiple measures of performance

c. *The average demand.* The average weekly demand is computed as 3,600, which is close to the expected value of the demand (from Table 16.8) of 3,700. (In a stabilized process, these two numbers will be very close.)

d. *The average beginning inventory* is computed as 4,010 gallons.
e. *The average weekly sales* are computed as 3,450 gallons.
f. *The average ending inventory* is computed as 560 gallons.

Step 7: Stabilization of the simulation process. In all the examples in this text and the homework problems, we use *all* the data generated by the simulation to achieve brevity in presentation, even if the measures of performance have not stabilized. In reality, however, we recognize that the simulation begins to represent reality only after stabilization has been achieved. Stabilization is equivalent to what we called *steady state* in Markov analysis. Therefore, we distinguish a *start-up transient* period during which the data results are not yet valid. Usually, though not always, the decision maker is interested in finding the long-run, steady-state average values of the performance measures, rather than the short-run, transient values.

Examination of column 10 in Table 16.9 indicates that the process, although close to stabilizing, has not yet stabilized (see Figure 16.7). That is, the *average* weekly profit is still fluctuating. Notice, however, that after seven weeks, the differences are becoming very small. The end of this transient, start-up period is determined from estimates of "serial correlation" in the measure of performance. Once this period is determined, *then* simulation runs are made to extend past this point into the stabilization period, and the measures of performance and their variances are recorded to determine their average value, and confidence intervals.

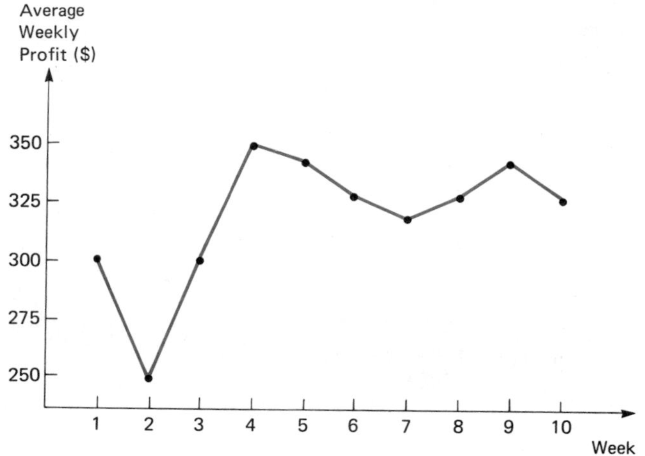

FIGURE 16.7 Stabilization of the simulation process

If there exist several measures of performance, then the stabilization analysis must be performed for *each* measure. Only after stabilization is achieved in *all* measures of performance (or at least in *all important* measures) should the simulation be stopped.

Step 8: Find the best ordering policy. Steps 5, 6, and 7 are now repeated for other ordering policies in order to find the best. In the example just presented, the ordered quantity Q was 3,500; other values of Q (e.g., 3,300, 3,700, 4,000) should next be considered. Each Q constitutes an independent system for which the various measures of effectiveness such as average profit, average sales, and unsatisfied demand are computed. Each such experiment is called a **simulation run.** The results for average weekly profit are shown in Figure 16.6b; the best results seem to occur at about 4,100 gallons.

In this case, the most important measure of performance has been assumed to be the average profit, and therefore the policy with the highest average profit will be selected (lack of space prevents us from showing the computations or calculating a 99 percent confidence interval). In other systems, two or more measures of performance may have to be compared using a multiple objective method such as presented in Chapter 4.

16.6 TIME DEPENDENT, DISCRETE SIMULATION

A waiting line example

Sunny has now collected the following information: The Tourist Information Center is manned by one employee and is open from 9 A.M. to 5 P.M. The length of service required by tourists varies according to the following probability distribution:

Length of service (minutes)	*Probability (percent)*
3	15.6
4	28.7
5	36.2
6	19.5

Tourists arrive at the center according to the following probability distribution:

Time between two consecutive arrivals (interarrival time, minutes)	*Probability (percent)*
3	20.2
4	23.6
5	31.2
6	18.4
7	6.6

Sunny now wishes to find:

a. The average waiting time per tourist, in minutes.
b. The percentage of time that the employee is busy (the utilization).

c. The aveage number of tourists in the center.
d. The probability of finding two tourists in the center.

Analysis

This is a waiting line problem, but it cannot be solved by the models of Chapter 15 because the assumptions of Poisson arrivals and exponential service times do not hold.

For illustrative purposes, we will simulate 10 arriving tourists (including the first arrival, we assume, at 9 A.M.) using the following random numbers for arrivals: 826, 058, 489, 643, 781, 321, 590, 187, 962; and the following random numbers for service: 242, 318, 876, 408, 630, 027, 716, 203, 130, 297.[6]

The simulation

Step 1. Assign representative numbers for the two distributions (cumulative probabilities omitted):

For arrivals:

Interarrival time	*Probability*	*Representative numbers*
3	20.2	000–201
4	23.6	202–437
5	31.2	438–749
6	18.4	750–933
7	6.6	934–999

For service:

Time in minutes	*Probability*	*Representative numbers*
3	15.6	000–155
4	28.7	156–442
5	36.2	443–804
6	19.5	805–999

Step 2. Generate arrival and service times (in minutes). This is done in Table 16.10.

Explanation

Table 16.10 is divided into 11 columns: The first four deal with arrivals, the next four with service, and the last three with measures of performance. The time of the first arrival is given as 9:00. Next, a random number is

[6] The simulation *should,* of course, only use the stabilized measures of performance.

TABLE 16.10
Simulation of tourist information center

	Arrivals			*Service*				*Measures of performance*		
Tourist number	*RN (1)*	*Interarrival time (2)*	*Time arriving (3)*	*RN (4)*	*Length (minutes) (5)*	*Start (6)*	*End (7)*	*Wait (min.) (8)*	*Idle (min.) (9)*	*No. in center (10)*
1	—	—	9:00	242	4	9:00	9:04	—	—	1
2	826	6	9:06	318	4	9:06	9:10	—	2	1
3	058	3	9:09	876	6	9:10	9:16	1	—	2
4	489	5	9:14	408	4	9:16	9:20	2	—	2
5	643	5	9:19	630	5	9:20	9:25	1	—	2
6	781	6	9:25	027	3	9:25	9:28	—	—	1
7	321	4	9:29	716	5	9:29	9:34	—	1	1
8	590	5	9:34	203	4	9:34	9:38	—	—	1
9	187	3	9:37	130	3	9:38	9:41	1	—	2
10	962	7	9:44	297	4	9:44	9:48	—	3	1
							Total (performance):	5	6	
							Average per tourist:	5/10		

selected to predict the length of service (242 is in the 156–422 range, meaning four minutes of service). The second tourist is predicted to arrive six minutes after the first one, since the first RN of 826 is in the range of 750 to 933, which corresponds to six minutes interarrival time.

In a similar manner, we compute all arrival and service times. Next, we compute the starting time for service (column 6). If the employee is busy with the previous customer, the tourist will have to wait, as happened to tourist 3 who waited from 9:09 until 9:10. If no one is in the center, the employee is idle, as is the situation between 9:04 and 9:06.

Analysis of the measures of performance

The average waiting time. For the 10 arriving tourists, only five minutes of waiting were recorded. Thus, the average waiting time per tourist was 5/10 = 0.5 minutes.

The utilization of the service facility. The center was simulated during 48 minutes (from 9:00 to 9:48). During this period, there were six minutes of idle time; thus, 48 − 6 = 42 minutes of utilization or 42/48 = 87.5 percent utilization.

The average number of tourists in the center. During six minutes there were no tourists in the center, while during five minutes there were two (during times of waiting). During the remaining 37 minutes (48 − 6 − 5 = 37) there was one tourist.

On the average, there were:

$$\frac{0(6) + 1(37) + 2(5)}{48} = .98 \text{ tourists}$$

This is a weighted average that corresponds to L in Chapter 15.

The probability of finding two tourists in the center. This situation happened in 5 out of the 48 minutes, or 10.4 percent. In a similar manner, it is possible to find other measures of performance for this service system.

Time-dependent, continuous distributions

Continuous distributions

In the case above, both the interarrival times and the service times followed discrete distributions. If one or both of these follow a continuous distribution, we must use the procedure outlined in Section 16.12 to generate the times of arrival and the lengths of service. Other than that, the procedure is identical (see Problem 33).

16.7 RISK ANALYSIS

In Chapters 3 and 4, we presented simple examples of risk analysis in the form of a decision tree or a decision table. Simulation can deal with much more complicated risk analysis problems. The example we use here is fairly simple, but it will illustrate the application of simulation in risk analysis.

Simulation for risk analysis

Let us assume that we want to predict the profit from product M-6. The profit is given by the following formula:

$$\text{Profit} = (\text{Unit price} - \text{Unit cost}) \times \text{Volume sold} - \text{Advertising cost}$$

Now, let us assume that the unit selling price can assume three levels: either \$5, \$5.50, or \$6, depending on market conditions. We also assume that the probabilities of these market conditions are known. Similarly, the unit cost may assume several levels (depending on the commodity markets). The volume is a function of the economic conditions, and the advertising cost depends on competitors' actions. All this information is summarized in Table 16.11.

TABLE 16.11
Data for simulation risk analysis, product M-6

Selling price	*Probability*	*Unit cost*	*Probability*	*Volume*	*Probability*	*Advertising cost*	*Probability*
\$5.00	.20	\$2.50	.35	15,000	.30	\$20,000	.50
5.50	.50	3.00	.50	18,000	.45	25,000	.30
6.00	.30	3.50	.15	20,000	.25	30,000	.20

Using RNs, we can simulate the four random variables and compute the profit, or any other measure of performance. First, a RN range is assigned (Table 16.12).

TABLE 16.12 Assigning ranges

Selling price	*RN range*	*Unit cost*	*RN range*	*Volume*	*RN range*	*Advertising cost*	*RN range*
5.00	00–19	2.50	00–34	15,000	00–29	20,000	00–49
5.50	20–69	3.00	35–84	18,000	30–74	25,000	50–79
6.00	70–99	3.50	86–00	20,000	75–00	30,000	80–99

The simulation is conducted with RNs taken from Table C2 in Appendix C. The first 10 trials are shown in Table 16.13.

TABLE 16.13 First 10 trials

	Price		*Cost*		*Volume*		*Advertising*		
Trial	*RN*	*Prediction*	*RN*	*Prediction*	*RN*	*Prediction*	*RN*	*Prediction*	*Profit*
1	17	5.00	91	3.50	42	18,000	82	30,000	−3000
2	05	5.00	89	3.50	31	18,000	17	20,000	7000
3	21	5.50	17	2.50	60	18,000	51	25,000	29,000
4	66	5.50	94	3.50	71	18,000	44	20,000	16,000
5	43	5.50	85	3.50	76	20,000	75	25,000	15,000
6	54	5.50	44	3.00	55	18,000	58	25,000	20,000
7	11	5.00	62	3.00	52	18,000	41	20,000	16,000
8	61	5.50	09	2.50	38	18,000	38	20,000	34,000
9	35	5.50	66	3.00	59	18,000	29	20,000	25,000
10	39	5.50	37	3.00	97	20,000	61	25,000	25,000

Based on the simulation we can find:

a. The average profit.
b. The probability of having a loss.
c. The probability of having a profit.
d. The probability of making $10,000 or more.
e. The probability of losing $20,000 or more.

A risk profile

This information is then summarized in a *risk profile* probability distribution function and a cumulative probability distribution, such as in Figure 16.8. Such functions are extremely important in risk analysis. What these figures show is that the range of profit varies between a *loss* (actually −$3,000) and $50,000 profit. The mean is $18,820 and the standard deviation is $9,706, rather large. If we compute the *most likely profit* (based on the most likely values of the variables) we would get:

$$(5.50 - 3.00)18{,}000 - 20{,}000 = \$25{,}000$$

a $6,180 difference compared to the long-run mean. The cumulative probability curve also shows us that there is a 2 percent chance of *losing* money on this product and a 14 percent chance of making less than $10,000. On the other hand, there is a 15 percent chance of making over $30,000 and a 5 percent chance of making more than $40,000. For further discussion, see Hertz [19].

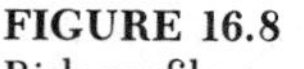

FIGURE 16.8
Risk profile

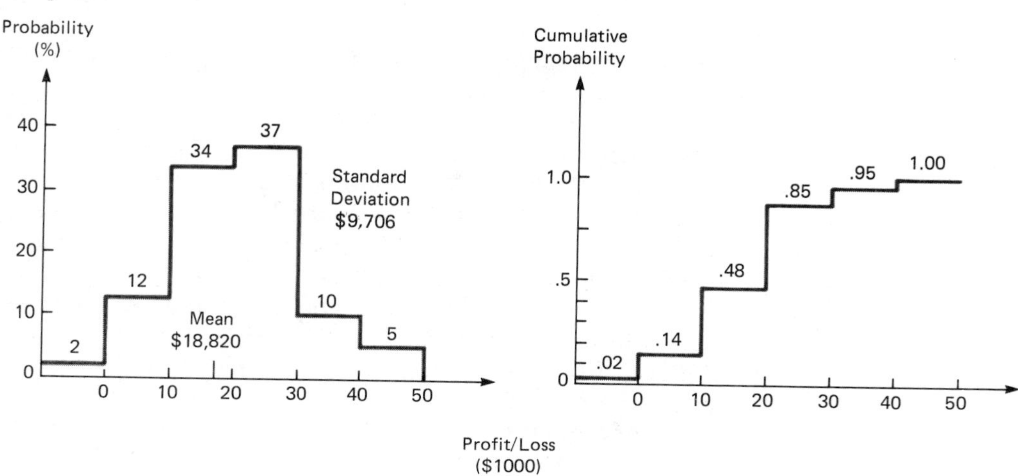

16.8 THE ROLE OF COMPUTERS IN SIMULATION

Since simulation models involve as few simplifications of the real system as possible, then the function expressing the internal relationships is frequently quite complex. In addition, each simulation run involves a large number of trials, as required for stabilization. On top of that, the entire simulation must be repeated each time a change is made in some of the input data. It is necessary to frequently check dozens of different system configurations. The end result of all the above is the necessity of a huge computational effort. Therefore, computers are desired and frequently necessary for conducting simulation studies. Simulation problems can be programmed for computers with relative ease, since there is no need to develop algorithms or optimize functions. Also, special simulation languages can speed up the construction.

The need for a computer

Simulation languages

Once a simulation problem is formulated, it is usually followed by a flowchart as a basis for computer programming. As with other models, the program may be written in a general-purpose language such as BASIC or Pascal, but this process can be very lengthy and expensive for large simulation problems. For this reason, there are several *special-purpose* simulation languages.

The best known commercially available languages are **DYNAMO, SLAM II, EZQ, GASP, GPSS, SIMSCRIPT II.5** and **SIMULA.** The highlights of these languages are:

DYNAMO™. Developed at MIT, it is especially suited to large-scale system dynamics models for entire corporations, national economies, and so on. A microcomputer version is also available.

EZQ™. Developed by Acme Software Arts, this package is available only for the Apple II series computers.

Special languages

GASP™. Developed at U.S. Steel, this is a set of computer subroutines written in FORTRAN. Several versions are available. Its major advantage is the flexibility resulting from its subroutine structure.

GPSS™. Developed by IBM, it is mainly a flowchart-oriented simulation technique. It is simple to use since it does not require a knowledge of computer programming.

SIMSCRIPT™. A generalized simulation and programming language, SIMSCRIPT was developed by RAND Corp. It exists in several versions (e.g., SIMSCRIPT II.5, a micro-based version from CACI, Inc.) and is one of the more powerful, efficient, and flexible languages. It also assists the user in the conceptualization and design of the simulation model.

SIMULA™. Developed in Norway as a generalized simulation language, it is similar to the early version of SIMSCRIPT.

SLAM II™. Developed by Pritsker and Associates, this is a micro-based version of the powerful mainframe SLAM package.

16.9 ISSUES IN SIMULATION

To fully understand simulation, it is helpful to elaborate some of the major issues involved.

Model validation The **validation** of simulation models involves practical as well as theoretical questions concerning the use of simulation techniques. How do we know that a model represents the process under study? How are we to understand what is going on in a model of a complex system? How do we use the results to yield predictions that are empirically accurate?

Validation concerns

Analogies between wind tunnel models and simulation models are frequently drawn, but these analogies break down when one considers the complex underlying structure. The same fundamental laws of nature govern the behavior of an airplane model in a wind tunnel as govern the full-scale airplane. But a simulation model is usually a numerical representation of a system and is not governed by any physical laws that make it behave similar to the system that is being modeled.

A valid simulation model should behave similar to the underlying phenomena. This is a necessary validation condition, but by itself may not be sufficient to allow us to rely on its predictive abilities. Theoretical insights into the underlying phenomena that govern the behavior of the business, economic, and social system that is being simulated are critical to the construction of a valid model. There is, however, little consensus on the proper method to validate a simulation model.

Once a model is constructed, validating it may be viewed as a two-step process. The first step is to determine whether the model is internally correct in a logical and programming sense. The second is to determine whether it represents the phenomena it is supposed to represent.

Interval versus external validity

When a model is intended to simulate a new or proposed system for which no actual data are available, there is no good way to verify that the model, in fact, represents the system. Under these circumstances, there is little choice but to test the model thoroughly for logical or programming errors (especially at extreme values of the data) and to be alert for any discrepancies or unusual characteristics in the results obtained from the model.

Experimental designs Some simulation models are very complex to design because the number of runs that are required to test all the feasible alternatives is very large.

For example, consider investment problems (like our risk analysis example), with 10 possible investment alternatives (e.g., stocks, bonds), each of which may assume only five values. All together there are 5^{10} different possibilities (close to 10 million). To simulate 10 million runs is very time-consuming and costly. The design of simulation experiments is similar to the usual design of experiments. Issues such as the *structure, sample size, cost, quality,* and the use of *statistical tools* to analyze the results are some of the issues involved. Other issues are: What constitutes a *significant difference* between alternatives? What is the *relative importance* of the different independent variables? For further discussions, refer to Naylor [24] or Hicks [20].

Design issues

Length of the run The longer the run, the more accurate the results, but the costlier the experiment. "Stopping rules" have been developed (using statistical theory) to determine the most appropriate run size. (See references [22] or [24]). With the minimal cost of computer time, it is worthwhile to make longer runs.

Variance reduction In order to save time, it is possible to design the simulation so that the greatest precision is achieved for a given sample size, or equivalently, the sample size needed to achieve a desired level of accuracy is reduced to the minimum. Several techniques are available for decreasing the variance of the distribution of the measures of performance. An example is *stratified sampling,* where the data are divided into portions (called *strata*) and each stratum is individually sampled. Again, see references [22] or [24].

Stratified sampling

Generating random numbers For teaching purposes, we use random number tables to conduct the simulation. These tables were originally generated by a physical device (such as a spinning disk or an electronic randomizer). In real-life simulation, instead of feeding a table of random numbers into the computer, the computer itself generates the random numbers. There are many methods for doing this. The numbers generated by a computer are not called random numbers (strictly speaking) since they are *predictable* and *reproducible*. Rather, they are called **pseudorandom numbers,** but for our simulation purpose, they are as good as the usual random numbers.

Start-up conditions It is usually necessary to wait until the model stabilizes before conducting the simulation, whereupon the start-up data is discarded. If the start-up period is short and the simulation run is long, the impact of the start-up will be minimal.

16.10 PROBLEMS FOR PART A

1. Given a distribution of daily demand:

Daily demand	*Probability*
6	.15
7	.25
8	.38
9	.22

a. Construct a cumulative probability distribution.
b. Show the cumulative probability graphically.
c. Graphically predict the demand for the following RNs: 91, 06, 85, 57, 31, 72.

2. Assign ranges of RNs to the daily demand in Problem 1 (start with 00). Predict the demand that corresponds to the following RNs: 43, 90, 12, 36, 51.

3. A community in South Florida is composed of 15 percent blacks, 40 percent Cubans, and 45 percent "others." Use random numbers to indicate the races of the first 10 people from the community to enter a room. Use the following RNs: 23, 74, 50, 96, 82, 79, 40, 06, 67, 31.

4. There is a 30 percent chance that a company will sell 100 units, 50 percent that they will sell 110 units, and 20 percent chance they will sell 120 units. The profit per unit is $14.
a. Use simulation to find the average profit. (Use 15 trials: random numbers are: 4, 7, 3, 6, 0, 9, 8, 2, 1, 1, 8, 6, 5, 7, 3, 0, 9, 4, 6, 8. Start the representative numbers from 1.)
b. Compare it to the results of the expected value.

5. The U.S. Department of Agriculture estimates that the yearly yield of limes per acre is distributed as follows:

Yield in bushels per acre	*Probability*
350	.10
400	.18
450	.50
500	.22

The estimated average price per bushel is $7.20.
a. Find the expected annual per acre lime crop yield generated over the next 10 years. (Use simulation; compare to the theoretical expected value results. Use RNs: 37, 23, 92, 01, 69, 50, 72, 12, 46, 81, 31, 89. Start the representative numbers from 00.)
b. Find the average yearly revenue.

6. The following information is known to you:
A rainy day in Paris has a 40 percent chance of being followed by a rainy day. A nonrainy day has an 80 percent chance of being followed by a nonrainy day.
a. Use simulation to predict what the weather is going to be over the next 20 days. (Today is a nonrainy day.) Use two-digit RNs from Table C2 in Appendix C. Start at the top left and go down the columns. Start the representative numbers from 01.
b. Based on the information collected in part *(a)*, estimate the number of rainy days in Paris in one year (365 days).

7. A company has two cars. Car 1 is in use 40 percent of the time, and car 2, 30 percent of the time. The president wishes to go somewhere; what is the chance that there will be a car available?
a. Draw a simulation flowchart.
b. Manually simulate for 20 periods. (Use the following RNs: 7, 4, 9, 8, 4, 8, 8, 2, 0, 1, 5, 5, 0, 1, 4, 7, 0, 3, 2, 2, 7, 1, 0, 9, 8, 1, 4, 5, 4, 8, 6, 1, 2. Start the representative numbers from 0.)

c. Find the theoretical answer (use conditional probabilities) and compare with the simulation results.

d. Show graphically the stabilization process for 20 runs. What are your conclusions?

e. If a company car is unavailable, a cab is used, with an average cost of $15 per ride. Find the annual cost if the president makes 100 trips per year.

8. The B & T car dealership has a salesperson that sells 13 cars, on the average, each week. The sales statistics show that of all cars sold, 20 percent are small, 45 percent are of medium size, and the remainder are large. The profit from the sale of the cars and the commission paid are shown in the following table:

Type of car	*Price per car*	*Per car profit to dealership*	*Per car commission paid to salesperson*
Small	$5,200	$310	$62
Intermediate	6,050	425	70
Large	7,800	500	80

Find, with the aid of simulation (simulate for one week):

a. The size of the last car sold during the week.

b. The commission the salesperson will make in an average week.

c. The total dollar sales volume generated in one month (four weeks).

d. The chance of selling two large cars in a row.

e. The weekly profit to the car dealership.

Use the following RNs: 08, 48, 16, 78, 37, 91, 82, 31, 54, 25, 69, 94, 41. Start the representative numbers from 00.

9. A newscarrier sells newspapers and tries to maximize profit. The exact number of papers purchased daily by customers can't be predicted. An elaborate time study was performed on the demand each day, and the following table was developed (for 125 days):

Demand per day	*Number of times*
15	10
16	20
17	42
18	31
19	12
20	10
Total	125

The following ordering policy was used by the newscarrier: The amount ordered each day is equal to the quantity demanded the preceding day. Assume that demand the previous day was 18.

A paper costs the carrier 15 cents; the carrier sells it for 30 cents. Unsold papers are returned, and the carrier is credited 8 cents per paper out of the 15 cents paid. An unsatisfied customer is estimated to cost 7 cents in goodwill.

Determine the average daily profit if the newscarrier follows the ordering policy. Also determine the average loss of goodwill. Simulate for 15 days; use three-digit RNs: 782, 430, 922, 871, 477, 838, 872, 276, 198, 520, 076, 452, 702, 042, 297. Start the representative numbers from 00.

10. Kojo Corporation stocks small motors for their textile machines. The weekly demand for the motors follows the distribution below:

Demand	5	6	7	8
Probability	.2	.3	.4	.1

Motors arrive at the end of each week (after the plant is closed for the weekend) either 6 in a package (60 percent chance) or 10 in a package (40 percent chance).

Simulate 15 weeks of operation to find:

a. The average inventory on hand (at the beginning of the week).

b. The probability of stockout (in terms of number of times).

c. The inventory at the end of 15 weeks (before the last shipment arrives).

d. If the process has stabilized (check for the inventory level situation).

e. Comment on the existing inventory policy.

Assume:

(1) The current inventory, at the beginning of week 1, is 5.

(2) Unsatisfied demand is provided from stock whenever a supply arrives.

(3) RNs for demand: 7, 8, 1, 6, 9, 0, 5, 9, 3, 2, 5, 4, 0, 4, 1, 7, 9, 3, 8, 2.
RNs for arrivals: 3, 1, 8, 0, 6, 7, 2, 4, 9, 0, 2, 8, 3, 5, 1, 9, 5, 7, 0, 4.
Start the representative numbers from 1.

11. Customers arrive at a service facility according to the following distribution:

Number of arrivals per hour	*Probability*
4	.22
5	.68
6	.10

The service time is always exactly 11 minutes. The facility opens for service at 8 A.M. At the opening time, the first customer is there waiting.

Simulate for 15 customers. Start the representative numbers with 00. RNs: 73, 06, 62, 45, 93, 15, 69, 54, 37, 81, 26, 18, 81, 96, 31. *Find:*

a. Average waiting time, W_q.
b. Average time in the system, W.
c. Average number of customers in the system.
d. The utilization ratio.

12. Icon Airline has 15 daily flights from Miami to New York. The average profit per flight is $6,000. Each flight requires one pilot. Flights that do not have a pilot are canceled (passengers are transferred to other airlines). Since pilots get sick from time to time, the airline has a policy of keeping three reserve pilots on standby to replace sick pilots. The probability distribution of sick pilots on any given day is given as:

Number sick in one day	*Probability*
0	.20
1	.25
2	.20
3	.15
4	.10
5	.10

Use Monte Carlo simulation to simulate 10 days. Use the following random numbers: 24, 57, 77, 68, 64, 88, 98, 50, 91, 55. Start assigning representative numbers from 01.

Note: The answers to the questions must be derived by *simulation* and not by statistics. The reserve pilots are drawn from a pool (so they cannot be considered to be sick).
Find:

a. The average daily utilization of the reserve pilots (in percent).
b. The average daily lost revenue due to canceled flights caused by lack of pilots (in dollars).
c. The chance that one or more flights will be canceled in a day.
d. The utilization of the aircraft (in percent).

13. A special medical diagnosis and treatment machine contains three identical radiation devices, which cost $2,000 each. If any of the devices fail, the machine is shut down for one hour and the failed device is replaced. Management considers each hour of downtime as having an opportunity loss of $1,000. The life expectancy of the radiation devices, in hours of operation, is listed below.

Life expectancy (hours)	*Probability*
500	.05
550	.08
600	.12
650	.15
700	.21
750	.14
800	.10
850	.07
900	.05
950	.03

Management is considering three replacement policies:

a. Replace each device when it fails.
b. Replace *all* the devices whenever *one* fails.
c. Replace a failed device and at that time check the life of the other two. If a device has been in use 850 hours or more, replace it, too.

The replacement costs are:

Replacing one device: $30 labor and 1 hour downtime.

Replacing two devices at a time: $40 labor, 1 hour and 20 minutes downtime.

Replacing all three devices at one time: $45 labor, and 1 hour and 30 minutes downtime.

Replaced devices with some remaining life are sold to a South American hospital for $15 each, regardless of age.

a. Write a flow chart for this problem.
b. Write a computer program.
c. Run each policy for approximately 10,000 hours of operation.
d. What are the results?

14. Conduct a risk analysis for Fiji Corporation's new portable computer. The price can be set at either $300 or $400; it is believed that the lower price will increase sales by 30 percent. The fixed cost is $1 million and the variable costs are a function of the number of shifts used. If one shift is used, the variable cost is expected to be either $200 or $250 with a 50 percent chance of each. With two shifts the variable cost will be either $250 or $270, again with a 50 percent chance of each. With one shift the maximum volume is 40,000 units; with two shifts the maximum volume is 60,000 units. Assuming a $400 price, there is an equal chance of achieving either 20,000, 30,000, or 40,000 units of sales. What should Fiji's decision be concerning price and shifts?

PART B: EXTENSIONS

16.11 COMPLEX QUEUING SITUATIONS

Simulation for waiting lines

One of the most useful roles of Monte Carlo simulation is for solving waiting line problems. Analytical solutions, such as demonstrated in Chapter 15, become extremely difficult, or even impossible, when the waiting line system increases slightly in complexity; for example, when the arrival or the service rate does not follow a standard distribution (such as the Poisson), or when priorities are considered. In Part A of this chapter we gave one example. The following example is more complicated. (Again, we skip the calculation of the confidence intervals for brevity.)

The toolroom problem

Manufacturing firms use a central toolroom to lend out tools to employees. Consider a typical situation with one clerk in the toolroom. Two different types of employees are served by it: production employees and maintenance employees. Each has a different rate of arrival, as shown in Table 16.14. Note that the arrival rates do not follow standard distributions. The table also shows the assigned numbers that are required for the simulation. The number of employees in both groups is large enough so that the source may be assumed infinite.

TABLE 16.14
The arrival rates

Production employees			*Maintenance employees*		
Time between arrivals (hours)	*Probability*	*Assigned numbers*	*Time between arrivals (hours)*	*Probability*	*Assigned numbers*
.2	.1	0	.4	.25	01–25
.3	.1	1	.6	.60	26–85
.5	.4	2–5	1.0	.15	86–00
.8	.3	6–8			
1.0	.1	9			

Currently, the production employees have priority over the maintenance employees; that is, a production employee will always be placed at the head of the waiting line. However, if a maintenance employee is being served, the service will continue uninterrupted (i.e., the production employee has a regular priority and not a "preemptive" priority over the maintenance employee).

Table 16.15 gives the distribution of service times, assuming that service can take only three time values: .1, .2, and .3 hours. The table also includes the assigned numbers required for the simulation.

TABLE 16.15
Service times

Length of service time (hours)	*Probability*	*Assigned numbers*
.1	⅓	001–333
.2	⅓	334–666
.3	⅓	667–999

Skip some numbers

Note that an *exact* duplication of the ⅓ to ⅓ to ⅓ ratio is achieved by assigning only 999 out of all 1,000 three-digit numbers.[7] The assignment of three digits was arbitrary in this case (one digit is actually sufficient).

The toolroom clerk earns $4 per hour. A production employee earns $5 per hour, and a maintenance employee earns $6 per hour. The problem is to find the optimal number of clerks in the toolroom. Management also wishes to know if the existing priority system should be maintained.

Solution

Simulating the arrivals. For the purpose of presentation, the time between arrivals of 15 employees of each type is simulated, using random numbers from Table C2 in Appendix C. The results are shown in Table 16.16. The table also indicates the clock time of arrivals.

For example, assume that employee 1 arrived at opening time, 7 A.M. Then, for arrival 2, the one-digit RN 5 is selected as the first RN

TABLE 16.16
Generating arrivals (number 1 arrives at time zero)

	Production employees			*Maintenance employees*		
Arrival number	*Random number*	*Time between arrivals (hours)*	*Clock time*	*Random number*	*Time between arrivals (hours)*	*Clock time*
2	5	.5	7:30	52	.6	7:36
3	2	.5	8:00	02	.4	8:00
4	0	.2	8:12	73	.6	8:36
5	2	.5	8:42	48	.6	9:12
6	7	.8	9:30	06	.4	9:36
7	3	.5	10:00	15	.4	10:00
8	4	.5	10:30	94	1.0	11:00
9	8	.8	11:18	12	.4	11:24
10	0	.2	11:30	95	1.0	12:24
11	6	.8	12:18	87	1.0	1:24
12	1	.3	12:36	04	.4	1:48
13	5	.5	1:06	99	1.0	2:48
14	9	1.0	2:06	40	.6	3:24
15	4	.5	2:36	98	1.0	4:24

[7] If we do not assign some numbers (such as 000 in this case), then when such numbers appear as RNs, they are skipped over.

from Table C2. According to Table 16.14 for production employees, an RN of 5 is in the assigned numbers 2–5, which corresponds to .5 hours between arrivals. Since the process starts at 7:00, then the clock time is 7:30. The generation of arrivals then continues. For the third production employee, an RN of 2 is selected. The equivalent time between arrivals is again .5 hours, and the clock time is therefore 7:30 + 30 minutes = 8:00. The process continues for as many arrivals as desired (15 in the example) or for a specific period of time. Once the generation of the production employees is completed, the generation of the maintenance employee arrivals is conducted. The only difference in the process is the use of two-digit RNs instead of one-digit RNs.

Simulating the length of service. The lengths of service are generated using three-digit RNs and Table 16.15. The process is similar to the generation of arrivals. The results are shown in Table 16.17, where 30 services are generated. A different set of random numbers is used this time.

Simulating the process. Figure 16.9 presents what happened during the first six hours of operation. Assume that at 7 A.M. a production employee

TABLE 16.17
Generating 30 services

Service number	*RN*	*Length of service (hours)*
1	782	.3
2	309	.1
3	194	.1
4	308	.1
5	421	.2
6	392	.2
7	283	.1
8	682	.3
9	871	.3
10	744	.3
11	244	.1
12	773	.3
13	264	.1
14	283	.1
15	879	.3
16	978	.3
17	477	.2
18	752	.3
19	016	.1
20	579	.2
21	260	.1
22	241	.1
23	643	.2
24	056	.1
25	861	.3
26	565	.2
27	029	.1
28	970	.3
29	958	.3
30	713	.3

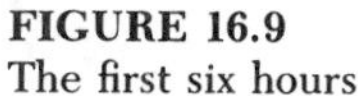

FIGURE 16.9
The first six hours

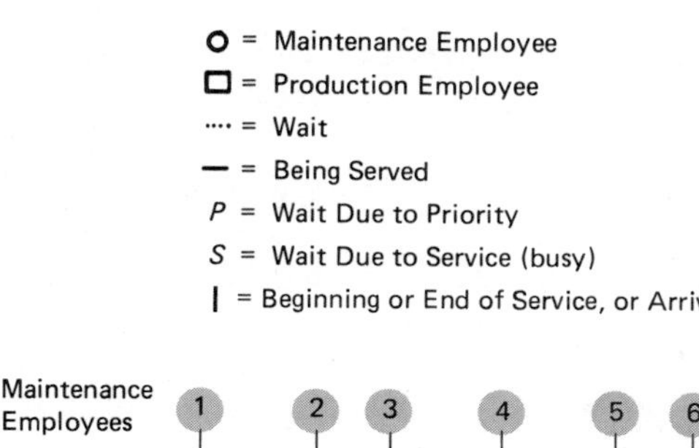

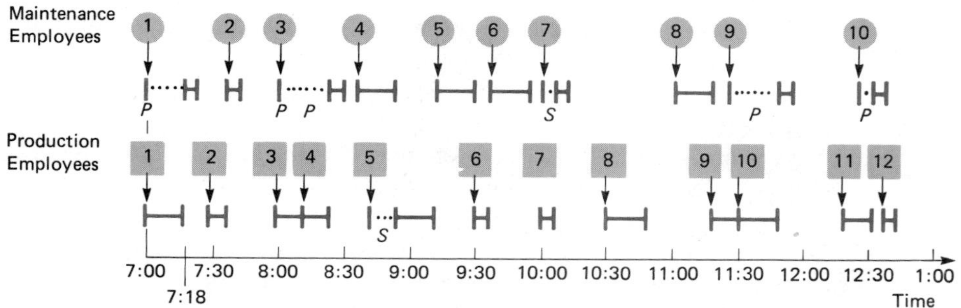

and a maintenance employee are waiting at the toolroom. The production employee is served first (has priority). Table 16.17 indicates (based on the first random number of 782) a service of .3 hours (18 minutes) from 7:00 to 7:18. During this time, the maintenance employee waits. The second production employee arrives after .5 hours at 7:30 (according to Table 16.16).

The first maintenance employee will start receiving service at 7:18. This service will be completed at 7:24 (random number of 309 for a service time of .1 hours = 6 minutes, in Table 16.17). The second production employee arrives at 7:30 and is served from 7:30 to 7:36. The second maintenance employee arrives at 7:36 (random number 52 indicates that the second maintenance employee arrives .6 hours after the first one, Table 16.16). Since the toolroom is free, this employee is served immediately (length of service is .1 hours as per Table 16.17). The third production employee and the third maintenance employee arrive at 8 A.M. (check Table 16.16 for computed time of arrival). Due to priority, the production employee is served first. Production employee 3 is served for .2 hours, 8:00 to 8:12 (according to Table 16.17). Then production employee 4 arrives (check Table 16.16) and due to priority, is served before maintenance employee 3. Figure 16.9 shows the process for the first six hours. (This process could also be shown in an equivalent tabular form.)

Computing the characteristics and measures of system effectiveness

The process that was simulated for six hours should be continued until stabilization is achieved. However, for the purpose of demonstration, let us examine the results of the six hours of simulation.

Arrivals Ten maintenance employees arrived, or 10/6 = 1.67 each hour, on the average. Twelve production employees arrived, or 12/6 = 2 per hour.

Service All 22 arrivals were served. The total service time was 4.2 hours. This means that the toolroom clerk was busy 4.2/6 = 70 percent of the time. The average service time was 4.2/22 = .19 hours.

Policy measures

Probability of waiting Of the 10 maintenance workers 5 had to wait for service. Thus, the probability of a maintenance worker having to wait is 5/10 = 50 percent. There was only one production employee out of 12 (8.34 percent probability) who had to wait.

Length of wait Total waiting time was 1.5 hours. Thus, on the average, an employee waited 1.5/22 = .07 hours (about four minutes). However, the average waiting time for a maintenance employee was 1.3/10 = .13 hours, versus .2/12 = .02 hours for a production employee.

The total cost of waiting

For production employees	= .2 hours × $5	= $1.0,	for the 6-hour period
For maintenance employees	= 1.3 × $6	= $7.8	
Total		$8.8	

$$\text{Waiting cost per hour} = \frac{8.8}{6} = \$1.47$$

Priorities In four cases (40 percent of all maintenance employees), priorities were utilized by the production employees.

Conclusion In this case, the system seems to be efficient. The cost of waiting is only $1.47 per hour. There is no sense in adding a second clerk to the toolroom at a cost of $4 an hour, since the maximum possible saving is only $1.47. The priority for the production employees is questionable. A second simulation run on a first-come, first-served basis should be taken to compare the results. Also, a third simulation, giving priority to maintenance employees could be run. (They earn more!) Results should then be compared.

Under a different system, it could have been possible for the waiting line to be longer, and the cost of waiting very high. In such a system, a simulation run should be conducted to check if two or even three clerks were justified. Also, if one or more clerks are added, they could operate in various configurations. For example, each clerk could serve one group only, or both could serve one customer at one time (one doing the paperwork, one doing the material handling), and so on. Simulation can handle all such cases readily.

16.12 SIMULATION WITH CONTINUOUS PROBABILITY DISTRIBUTIONS

The simulation procedure described so far involved random variables with discrete distributions. However, real-life situations may involve random variables whose probability density functions are continuous. The problem, then, is how to generate random values (demand, sales, and so on) from the continuous distributions. Two approaches exist.

a. The graphical method

The graphical method involves plotting the *cumulative probability* function. This method can be used for any distribution, *including a discrete distribution,* as long as we can plot the cumulative distribution. Once the distribution is plotted (see Figure 16.10 for an example) we use the following procedure:

Graphical or formula approach

A random number between 0 and 1.0 is first obtained from a uniform distribution such as the table of random numbers (C2), putting a decimal point in front of the number. For example, if the RN is 8, then we use .8. Next, we go to the cumulative probability axis (Figure 16.10) and find the value 0.8. Next, we draw a *horizontal* line over to the cumulative function until the line hits the curve (point *K*), make a 90° turn, and go straight down to the random observation axis and read off the desired value. In our case, point *L* reads approximately 58.

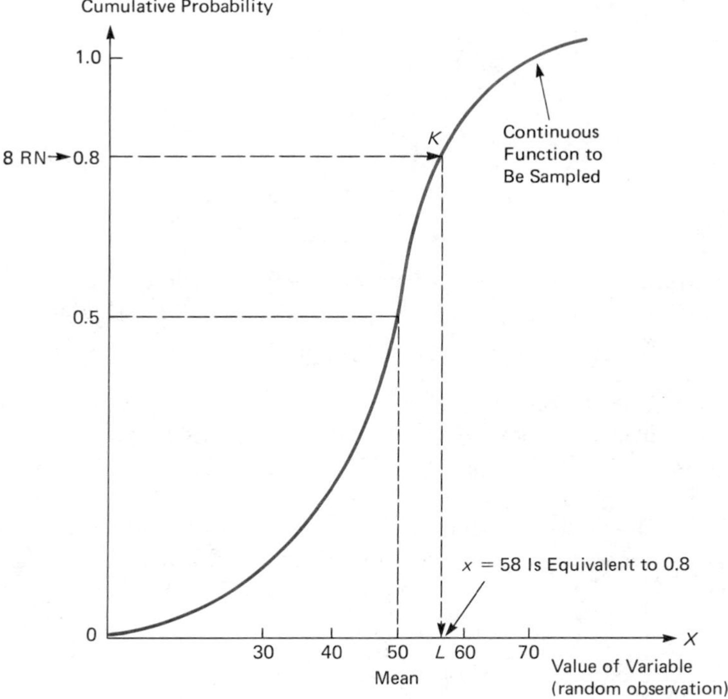

FIGURE 16.10
A cumulative distribution

b. The use of a formula

If it is possible to write the equation of the cumulative distribution function (or to use a table or chart) that describes it, then the following process can be followed. Construct a cumulative distribution function:

$$F(x) = P(X \leq x) \tag{16.2}$$

where x is the random variable of interest. Next, generate a random number (RN) between 0 and 1. Finally, set $P(X \leq x) =$ RN and solve for x.

The following examples will illustrate both approaches: Tables will be used for the normal distribution and a formula for the exponential distribution. For further discussion, see Meier et al. [23].

Use of tables: Normal distribution

To illustrate, consider a variable that is normally distributed with mean $\mu = 100$ and standard deviation $\sigma = 10$.

Step 1 Generate an RN. Let us assume that the three-digit random number 695 is selected from a table.

Step 2 Put the decimal point in front of the RN, that is, the 695 is changed to .695.

Using tables

Step 3 Use Table C1 in Appendix C, the "area under the normal curve." Since it is known that:

$$Z = \frac{X - \mu}{\sigma} \tag{16.3}$$

then:

$$X = \mu + Z\sigma \tag{16.4}$$

The number .695, when spotted in the middle of Table C1, is equivalent to Z = .51. Using Equation 16.4 with $\mu = 100$ and $\sigma = 10$:

$$X = \mu + Z\sigma = 100 + .51 \times 10 = 105.1$$

Since Table C1 includes only numbers larger than .5, it is necessary to subtract any RN that is less than .5 (after the decimal point is added) from 1.0. For example, the RN of 273 is changed to .273 and then 1.0 − .273 results in .727.

The corresponding value of Z is then found in Table C1 (Z = .605 is equivalent to .727), and then Equation 16.5 is used to find X,

$$X = \mu - Z\sigma \tag{16.5}$$

That is, $X = 100 - .605 \times 10 = 93.95$.

Use of a formula

Exponential formula

The exponential distribution is extensively used in waiting line problems (both for the interarrival times and the service rate). The distribution is described in Appendix B. Its density function is:

$$f(t) = \lambda e^{-\lambda t} \qquad 0 \leq t \leq \infty \tag{16.6}$$

where t is the time, and λ is the mean arrival rate. The mean of this distribution is $1/\lambda$. Also, remember that the exponential distribution for arrival time describes the same thing as the Poisson distribution for arrivals per unit of time.

To generate random interarrival times, we can use Equation 16.7:

$$t = (-1/\lambda)\log_e(\text{RD}) \tag{16.7}$$

where RD = Random decimal (between 0 and 1) generated from a uniform distribution, and $\log_e$ = Natural logarithm.

Example Generate arrival times for a waiting line system if $\lambda = 6$ per hour. Use the RNs 828, 135, 619, 430, and 015.

Solution

Since $\lambda = 6$ per hour, then $1/\lambda = 1/6$ of an hour, or 10 minutes. This type of simulation is done in minutes (round results to the nearest minute). Thus $t = -10 \log_e \text{RD}$. Table 16.18 presents the results.

TABLE 16.18
Random arrival times

RD	*$\log_e$ (RD)*	*Interarrival time, t*	*Time of arrival*
.828	− .1887	1.88 ≃ 2	2
.135	− 2.000	20	22
.619	− .4790	4.78 ≃ 5	27
.430	− .8440	8.44 ≃ 8	35
.015	−4.2000	42	77

16.13 VISUAL INTERACTIVE SIMULATION

VIS with computers

One of the most interesting developments in computer graphics is visual interactive simulation (VIS). The technique, also known as visual interactive modeling, or visual interactive problem solving, has been used in the area of management science with unusual success.

VIS uses computer graphic displays to present the impact of various managerial decisions, thereby differing from regular computer graphics that use the screen simply as a communication device for presenting numeric data. Also, VIS can represent either a static or dynamic system. Static models display a visual image of the result of one decision alternative at a time. (With computer windows, several results can be compared on one screen.) Dynamic models display systems that *evolve* over time, the evolution being represented by animation.

Decision simulation

VIS is a decision simulation using visual interactive modeling. The end user watches the progress of the simulation in an animated form on a graphics terminal and interacts with and alters the simulation through various decision strategies.

Benefits

Conventional simulation does not usually allow a decision maker to *see* how a solution to a complex problem is developing through time, nor does it give him or her the ability to interact with it. The simulation only gives statistical answers at the end of a set of particular experiments. As a result, the decision maker is not an integral part of the simulation, and his or her experience and judgment cannot be used to directly assist in the analysis. Thus, any conclusions obtained by the model must be taken on faith. If the conclusions do not agree with the intuition or practical judgment of the decision maker, a confidence gap will exist about the model. The very nature of simulation studies means that a significant part of the analysis must appear to the manager as a "black box." For this reason, a solution derived by simulation may not be implemented.

A black box

The basic philosophy of VIS is that, since decision makers can watch the simulation of problem situations develop through time, they can also contribute to the validation of the model. Decision makers will have more confidence in its use because of their own participation. They are also in a position to be able to use their knowledge and experience to interact with the model in order to explore alternative strategies.

Testing the model

Simulation can be interactive at the design stage, the execution stage, or both. In order to gain insight into how systems operate under different conditions, it is important to be able to interact with the model while it is running so that alternative suggestions or directives can be tested. VIS has also been used in conjunction with artificial intelligence. The integration of the two techniques adds several capabilities that range from the ability of graphically building systems to learning about the dynamics of the systems.

A simple example of VIS is its application in the area of waiting lines (queuing). Complex waiting line problems typically require simulation, and the VIS can display the size of the waiting line or the value of the waiting time as it changes during the simulation runs. The VIS can also graphically present the answers to "what if" questions regarding changes in the input variables.

Commercial software

General-purpose, dynamic VIS software is commercially available for both mainframe and microcomputers (e.g., see Bell et al. [11]). Examples are SEE WHY™ (from BLSL, Inc.), SIMAN™ (from System Modeling Corporation), 1 DDS™ (from Pritsker and Associates, Inc.), PC Model™

(from Simulation Software Systems, Inc.), SIMFACTORY™ (from CACI), and SIMKIT™ (from Intellicorp).

How VIS helps a manager[8]

The first exposure to VIS sets the manager on unfamiliar ground. A large color screen lights up with a graphic display that may include moving icons and blinking colors. The first response is usually a comparison to a videogame and, indeed, the program creating the display has much in common with game software. The comparison is, however, short-lived. The power of the technique emerges in stages.

Stage 1 The manager recognizes the screen display as a graphic representation of a familiar process or situation.

Stage 2 The manager observes the screen carefully, perhaps also several other screen displays, and accepts the picture(s) as a sufficiently detailed image of the real process, with any motion showing realistic process evolution.

Stages of acceptance

Stage 3 The manager interacts with the model and observes that the screen image responds in accordance with his or her understanding of the real system.

Stage 4 Through experimentation and observation, the manager gains confidence in the visual model and becomes convinced that the model producing the displays is a valid representation of the real system.

Stage 5 Once convinced of the validity of the visual model, the manager can begin to ask "what if" questions and the visual model becomes a powerful decision-making aid.

The power of VIS as a decision-making tool comes from the confidence in the model that grows as the manager sees the model confirm his or her understanding of the real system. Managerial validation of the model occurs because:

- A picture is recognizable as a model of the real world more readily than a table or set of numbers—a street map of a city is easier to recognize as a city than a list of the coordinates of street intersections.
- A visual model is not a "black box." The interior workings of the model are in full view and nothing has to be taken on trust.
- Dynamic visual models show the same transient behavior of the process that the manager sees every day, rather than average behavior over a long period of time.
- VIS enables the manager to interact directly with the model rather than working with a mathematical model through an analyst.

Validation

Once confidence in the visual model is achieved, VIS provides the manager with a decision-making environment very much like that of a

[8] This subsection is adapted from Bell [11].

scientist working in a laboratory. The manager chooses experiments to be conducted and evaluates them using results provided by the model. Explicit measures of the quality of alternative solutions can be incorporated into the model. For example, in a bus-routing problem, it may be desirable to keep the routes as short as possible and so, after changing stops around, the total length of the routes can be computed and displayed. Optimizing procedures can also be built into the model. When a stop is moved from one route to another, the routes can be redrawn so that the distance traveled is a minimum.

Flexibility of VIS

VIS is particularly powerful when the decision maker has multiple decision criteria, or where decision criteria are implicit or difficult to formalize. VIS allows the decision maker to choose a best solution, using whatever criteria are deemed appropriate. VIS is also a powerful training device, allowing the exposure to operations that appear to be very real—a flight simulator, for example, is an advanced form of VIS application.

Log-cutting decisions at Weyerhaeuser Company

Weyerhaeuser Company (of Tacoma, Washington) is a large timber processor. The company developed several applications of visual interactive simulation (VIS) that have contributed approximately $7 million per year to the firm's profits. One of these involves the log-cutting decision.

Timber processing involves harvesting trees, which are then delimbed and topped. The resulting "stems" are crosscut into logs of various lengths. These logs are allocated among different mills, each of which makes a different end product such as plywood, lumber, or paper. For each tree there may be hundreds of reasonable cutting and allocating combinations. The cutting and allocation decisions are the major determinant of revenues of the company and its profitability. The decisions are made on a stem-

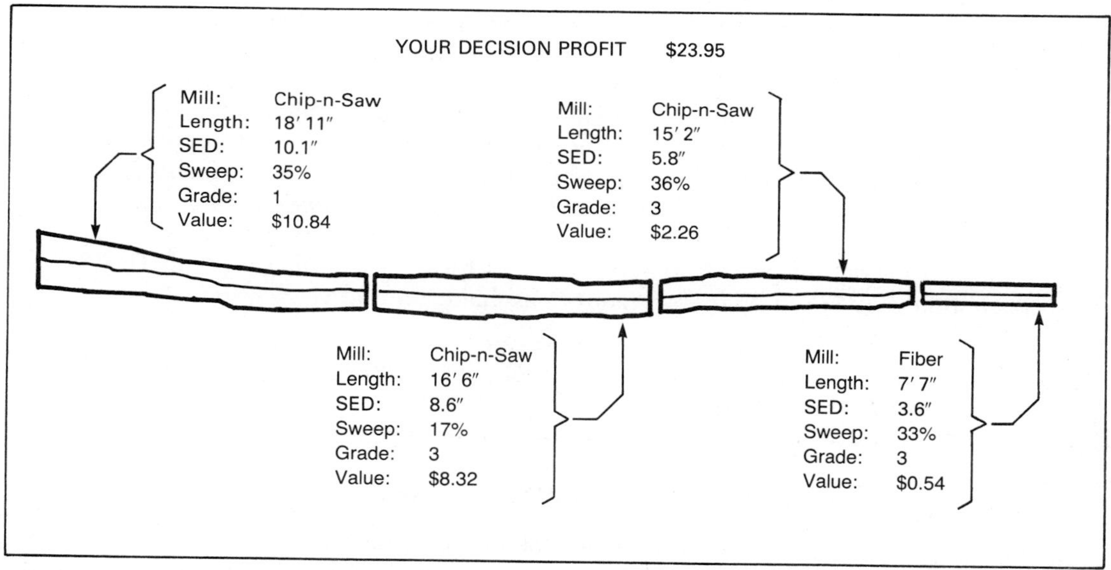

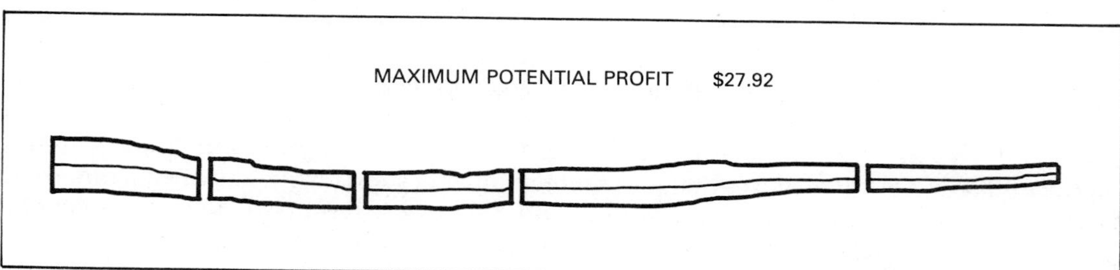

Graphic Display of User's Profit vs. Model's Profit

by-stem basis since each tree is physically different from every other tree. Many variables determine the manner in which a stem is to be cut, but these decisions usually do not affect cost significantly; thus, the larger the revenue generated, the larger the profit.

Management scientists developed a theoretical optimization model for the cutting and allocating decisions, using the technique of dynamic programming. However, the employees in the field were reluctant to use solutions that resulted from an unfamiliar, somewhat intimidating "black box" algorithm. Furthermore, like any other mathematical model, this one too is based on several assumptions that do not always fit reality. Therefore, the recommended solutions proved to be, on occasion, inferior to the solutions suggested by the operators. Thus, the operators had a legitimate reason for not following the computer's recommendations.

The VIS now allows the operators to deal with the proposed solutions on their own terms. This is done by letting them simulate on a video display a realistic representation of each stem (see exhibit). The simulator allows the operator to roll, rotate, cut, and allocate each stem the way he wants, on the computer screen, of course. He can *see* the end product and the resultant profit contribution of his suggested solution. He then can compare it with the profit resulting from the recommendation of the dynamic programming model. If not satisfied, the operator can recut the same stem repeatedly (on the screen) to explore alternate decisions. The final decision, how to cut, is always made by the operator; therefore, the system is nonthreatening. Furthermore, the repeated cutting experimentation on the screen improves the operator's decision-making skill. The system is also used by management to evaluate alternative stem-processing strategies.

Source: M. R. Lembersky and U. H. Chi, "Decision Simulators Speed Implementation and Improve Operations," *Interfaces*, July–August 1984, pp. 1–15.

16.14 HEURISTIC PROGRAMMING

The determination of optimal solutions to some complex decision problems could involve a prohibitive amount of time and cost, or it may even be an impossible task. In such situations, it is sometimes possible to arrive at *satisfactory* solutions more quickly and less expensively by using *heuristics*, frequently within a simulation routine. Though not a form of simulation itself, this technique is so common we include a discussion of the approach in this chapter on simulation.

Good rather than optimal

Heuristics (from the Greek word for "discovery") are step-by-step procedures that, in a finite number of steps, arrive at a *satisfactory* solution. (Note that an algorithm also progresses step-by-steptoward a solution, but an *optimal* one). It is important to note the difference between heuristics and **rules of thumb.** A rule of thumb is usually developed as a result of a trial-and-error experience. It does not possess any analytical foundation.

Rules of thumb

Heuristics, on the other hand, are rules that are developed on the basis of a solid and rigorous analysis of the problem, possibly with designed experimentation.

While heuristics are used primarily for solving ill-structured problems, they can also be used to provide satisfactory solutions to certain complex, well-structured problems much more quickly and cheaply than algorithms. The main difficulty in using heuristics is that they are not as general as algorithms. Therefore, they can normally be used only for the specific situation for which they were intended.

Heuristic programming is the approach of employing heuristics to arrive at feasible and "good enough" solutions to such complex problems, similar to the use of heuristic rules in expert systems (Chapter 18). "Good enough" is usually in the range of 90–99.9 percent of the true optimal solution (depending on the problem and the proposed heuristic). Heuristic programs are usually executed by a computer, although a manual execution is possible in simple cases.

Heuristic programming

For example, in evaluating investments in the stock market, the investor may have rules such as this: "Only companies whose assets are at least three times larger than their liabilities should be considered." The employment of several similar rules may reduce the number of feasible investment alternatives from thousands to a dozen.

In studying examples of applied heuristic programming, one can observe that the computer attempts to reduce the amount of search for a satisfactory solution. In such a search, the computer is "taught" how to explore only relatively fertile paths and ignore relatively sterile ones. The computer choices are made by using heuristics that can be improved in the course of the search (through learning, as with expert systems).

Heuristic programming has been used for helping solve problems such as:

Problems addressed with heuristics

- Sales forecasting.
- Investment decisions (portfolios of stock).
- Facilities location.
- Job shop scheduling.
- Work force and production level determination.
- Plant layout.
- Large project scheduling.
- Inventory control.
- Balancing assembly lines.

With the reduction in cost of using computers, there is an increased tendency to use heuristics as an alternative to optimization methods (e.g., see Zanakis and Evans [4]). Heuristics can be fun to develop and use. What is required is an understanding of the nature of the problem and some ingenuity, as illustrated in the next example.

Example: Heuristic sequencing of jobs through a machine

The cost of setups

An interesting sequencing problem occurs when several different jobs must be processed through a single production facility such as a printing press, boring mill, or a computer. The facility must be shut down after finishing each job in order to prepare it for the next job. The time periods that the facility is shut down are frequently referred to as *setup* or *changeover* times. While the processing time of the jobs is usually independent of the sequence used, the setup times may depend on both the job being removed and the job being introduced. The setup times depend on the physical similarities between the jobs; similar jobs require less changeover time. Management desires to sequence the jobs that are required to be processed in such a way that the total setup time will be minimized.

The difficulty in solving such a problem is that the sequencing can be done in many different ways; to be exact, n different jobs can be sequenced in $n!$ different ways.[9] For example, if there are only 10 jobs, there will be $10! = 3,628,800$ different sequencing alternatives.

Unfortunately, there is no simple analytical model that can tell us which sequence is the best. One way to find the best sequence is to compare all alternatives (complete enumeration). The complete enumeration of as few as 20 jobs may take a long time, even with the aid of computers. Heuristic rules, although they do not guarantee an optimal solution, can usually identify a satisfactory solution very quickly.

Assume the following situation.[10] A manager has three jobs assigned to a printing press in a certain day. The press is currently empty. The setup times for the jobs are indicated in Table 16.19. In this simplified case there are only six possible alternatives; therefore, it is possible to enumerate all of them rather easily. The results are given in Table 16.20.

TABLE 16.19
Setup times in minutes

From job \ *To job*	*1*	2	3
Empty	25	20	30
1	0	35	20
2	50	0	45
3	45	10	0

[9] $n!$ (called n factorial) means $1 \times 2 \times 3 \times \ldots = n$. For example, $4! = 1 \times 2 \times 3 \times 4 = 24$.

[10] The example is based on Gavett [3].

TABLE 16.20
Enumeration results

Sequence job number	*Setup times*	*Total (minutes)*	
1–2–3	25 + 35 + 45	105	
1–3–2	25 + 20 + 10	55	← *Minimum*
2–3–1	20 + 45 + 45	110	
2–1–3	20 + 50 + 20	90	
3–1–2	30 + 45 + 35	110	
3–2–1	30 + 10 + 50	90	

By complete enumeration it is shown that the sequence 1–3–2 is the best, with a minimum total setup time of 55 minutes.

The next best rule

In many practical cases, workers do not enumerate the alternatives, even when only a small number of jobs is involved. Instead, they use an interesting rule of thumb, called the *next best rule*. According to this rule, the worker sorts all jobs and selects, as the first job to be processed, the job that requires the least setup time from the "empty" condition (job 2 in the example, with only 20 minutes setup time). Then, the employee searches for that job that will require the *least* setup time from job 2 (job 3 in this case) and so on, until all jobs are sequenced.

Next job with least time

In this case the selected sequence 2–3–1 will result in 110 minutes of setup time, a solution that is far from the best. On the average, however, as studies by Gavett [3] show, a savings of 8 percent to 76 percent over a random selection can be realized. Much *better results* were achieved by using another rule: the next best rule with adjustments.

The next best with adjustments

According to this rule, the original setup time matrix is modified as follows: The minimum time in each column is subtracted from all other times in that column. (Ignore the zero values.) This calculation is shown in Figure 16.11.

FIGURE 16.11
Decision matrix using "next best with adjustments" rule
(Minimum column values circled.)

Original matrix (*To*):

From	1	2	3
Empty	(25)	20	30
Job 1	0	35	(20)
Job 2	50	0	45
Job 3	45	(10)	0

→ Reduction process (*To*):

From	1	2	3
Empty	25 − 25 = 0	20 − 10 = 10	30 − 20 = 10
Job 1	X	35 − 10 = 25	20 − 20 = 0
Job 2	50 − 25 = 25	X	45 − 20 = 25
Job 3	45 − 25 = 20	10 − 10 = 0	X

→ Resultant (reduced) matrix (*To*):

From	1	2	3
Empty	0	10	10
Job 1	X	25	0
Job 2	25	X	25
Job 3	20	0	X

Develop a new matrix

Once the reduced matrix is constructed, the regular next best rule is employed on it. Thus, from "empty," the least setup time is for job 1 with a value of 0. From 1, the least setup time is to number 3, from 3 one goes to 2. The solution is sequence 1–3–2 with 55 minutes of setup time (the optimal solution).

Both rules are relatively simple and can be used manually by the employees themselves.

16.15 BUSINESS GAMES

An oligopoly

Business games are simulation models involving several participants who are engaged in playing a game that simulates a realistic competitive situation. Typically, a number of teams are organized as an **oligopoly,** each team trying to maximize its own profit by making periodic decisions in areas such as production, inventory, marketing, investment, maintenance, research, and financing.[11] Similar games exist for the services and nonprofit sectors. For example, hospital games [9] allow the examination of decisions concerning staffing, room rates, expansion, and fund drives.

The two primary purposes of games are for *training* and *research.*

Training

Operational games

Operational gaming, or more generally, **management games,** have been very popular for training—both in industry and in the academic setting. The advantages claimed are: (1) that learning is much faster and more permanent when the participant is active in the training process than when he or she is passive, and (2) the game introduces interfunctional dependencies (such as the relationship between production and marketing) in the organization, in a congenial manner.

A great advantage of games, as in any other simulation, is the time compression factor—many years of operating experience can be obtained over the duration of a short period. This gives the participants an opportunity to test unusual tactics that they would not be able to try in real organizations.

Research

Games are used for research purposes to provide insight into the behavior of organizations, the decision-making process, and the interactions within a team. When used to study managerial decision making, the manager's rate of learning as he or she continues to play the game is also analyzed.

[11] An oligopoly is a market where only a small number of sellers operate.

Observing the dynamics of team decision making sheds light on important research areas such as the roles assumed by individuals, the effect of personality types and managerial styles, the emergence of "politics," and team conflict and cooperation.

Politics and conflict

Example: A business game

A business game typically uses a computer to simulate an industry in which there are a few companies (oligopoly) manufacturing and selling one product. Participants are organized into teams that manage their hypothetical companies in competition with each other. Decisions are made at regular intervals (e.g., "quarterly" decisions that may require 45 minutes in the game), and the outcome is determined by the interactions between the teams and the framework of the economic structure programmed into the computer. The models are basically deterministic, but the results may also be affected by probabilistic elements, since chance events and luck are also sometimes programmed into the process.

Teams usually make decisions concerning the following:

Decisions, decisions

- Price of product.
- Marketing budget.
- Research and development budget.
- Maintenance budget.
- Production volume scheduled.
- Investment in plant and equipment.
- Purchase of materials.
- Dividends declared.
- Financing.

A typical decision sheet, filled out by each of the firms each decision period (usually simulating a quarter of a year), is shown in Figure 16.12. When decisions have been made, they are entered into the computer system. The computer, having been programmed to simulate the industry's operations, computes the financial and operational results and prints this information, as well as other useful reports, for each firm, each quarter,

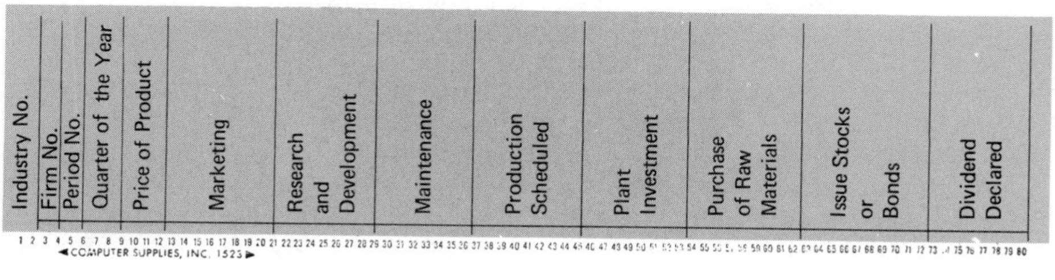

Industry No.	Firm No.	Period No.	Quarter of the Year	Price of Product	Marketing	Research and Development	Maintenance	Production Scheduled	Plant Investment	Purchase of Raw Materials	Issue Stocks or Bonds	Dividend Declared

◄COMPUTER SUPPLIES, INC. 1523►

FIGURE 16.12
Decision sheet (80-column punch card)

FIGURE 16.13
Typical game printout

```
                          EXECUTIVE GAME
MODEL 2 PERIOD  3 JFM PRICE INDEX 101.2 FORECAST,ANNUAL CHANGE  5.5 0/0
SEAS.INDEX   90 NEXT QTR.  100  ECON.INDEX  110 FORECAST,NEXT QTR.  113

              INFORMATION             ON              COMPETITORS
           PRICE            DIVIDEND      SALES VOLUME          NET PROFIT
  FIRM 1   $  6.19      $    100000          794363        $      150120
  FIRM 2   $  6.30      $    200000          950000        $      335424
  FIRM 3   $  6.20      $         0          350091        $      -53503
  FIRM 4   $  6.15      $    200000         1314660        $      275325
  FIRM 5   $  6.10      $    100000          741021        $       39519
  FIRM 6   $  6.15      $    100000          462704        $       53713
  FIRM 7   $  6.15      $    150000          522485        $      -34884
  FIRM 8   $  6.10      $     30000          519784        $       22190
  FIRM 9   $  6.15      $    100000          830413        $      179052

                            FIRM 7 5
                      OPERATING STATEMENTS
   MARKET POTENTIAL                                741021
   SALES VOLUME                                    741021
   PERCENT SHARE OF INDUSTRY SALES                     11
   PRODUCTION,THIS QUARTER                         820000
   INVENTORY,FINISHED GOODS                        147336
   PLANT CAPACITY,NEXT QUARTER                     431593
                        INCOME STATEMENT
   RECEIPTS,SALES REVENUE                                         $  4520230
   EXPENSES,MARKETING                          $   900000
     RESEARCH AND DEVELOPMENT                      200000
     ADMINISTRATION                                419762
     MAINTENANCE                                   120000
     LABOR(COST/UNIT EX.OVERTIME $ 1.43)          1176310
     MATERIALS CONSUMED(COST/UNIT  1.55)          1269597
     REDUCTION,FINISHED GOODS INV.                -239218
     DEPRECIATION(2.500 0/0)                       221630
     FINISHED GOODS CARRYING COSTS                  74218
     RAW MATERIALS CARRYING COSTS                   63590
     ORDERING COSTS                                 50373
     SHIFTS CHANGE COSTS                           100747
     PLANT INVESTMENT EXPENSES                          0
     FINANCING CHARGES AND PENALTIES                    0
     SUNDRIES                                       90348            4447357
   PROFIT BEFORE INCOME TAX                                            72873
   INCOME TAX(IN.TX.CR.   7 0/0,SURTAX   0 0/0)                        33354
   NET PROFIT AFTER INCOME TAX                                         39519
   DIVIDENDS PAID                                                     100000
   ADDITION TO OWNERS EQUITY                                          -60481
                           CASH FLOW
   RECEIPTS,SALES REVENUE                                         $  4520230
   DISBURSEMENTS,CASH EXPENSE                  $  3195348
     INCOME TAX                                     33354
     DIVIDENDS PAID                                100000
     PLANT INVESTMENT                                   0
     MATERIALS PURCHASED                          1350000            4678702
   ADDITION TO CASH ASSETS                                           -158472
                       FINANCIAL STATEMENT
   NET ASSETS,CASH                                                $   204863
     INV. VALUE,FINISHED GOODS                                        445307
     INVENTORY VALUE,MATERIALS                                       1352205
     PLANT BOOK VALUE(REPLACE.VAL.$   8912324)                       8643557
   OWNERS EQUITY(ECONOMIC EQUITY)    10914699)                      10645932
```

Source: Reprinted from R. C. Henshaw and J. R. Jackson, *The Executive Game*, 3d ed. (Homewood, Ill.: Richard D. Irwin, 1978). © 1978 by Richard D. Irwin, Inc.

as in Figure 16.13. In addition, there is an "annual report" after every four quarters.

After a certain number of periods have been simulated, the game is stopped and the instructor discusses the policies used by the firms, their results, the techniques of analysis employed or employable, and so on. A number of specialized games exist for financial management, banking, marketing management, production management, and maintenance, to name just a few.

Specialized games

16.16 CORPORATE AND FINANCIAL PLANNING MODELS

One of the most important applications of simulation is in corporate planning, especially the financial aspects. Corporate planning involves both long- and short-range plans. These simulation models can be considered to be the first generation of early decision support systems (see Chapter 17). The development of corporate models differs from corporation to corporation. Some of them are *deterministic* (see Section 16.18) in nature, while others allow for risk analysis. Over the past few years, many large corporations (e.g., Sears, GM, J.C. Penney, New York Times, Eli Lilly, Monsanto, AVCO, United Airlines, and Kraft) have developed corporate simulation models. These models integrate production, finance, and marketing modules into one model (see Figure 16.14).

Long-range planning

FIGURE 16.14
An integrated corporate planning model

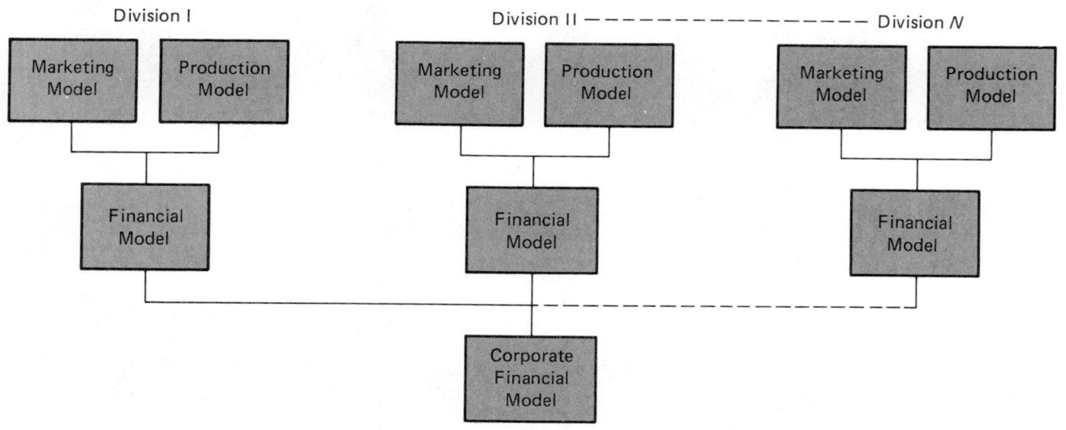

The development of a corporate model usually starts with determining the appropriate planning horizon (e.g., five years), then goals and objectives are determined, and only then is simulation used to project activities (such as sales, production levels, or cash flow). Once the long-range plan is completed, the short-run (one year) plan can be generated. (Such a process is demonstrated in the cases of Chapter 17.) The model enables management to examine the impact of various policies, to conduct a sensitivity ("what if") analysis, and to perform a risk analysis.

Short-run plans

The financial planning submodel is usually the center of the corporate planning model. An example of such a model is given in Section 16.18. The example there shows the possibility of combining optimization with simulation, which is where simulation interfaces with decision support

Financial hub

FIGURE 16.15
A corporate planning model (from [18]).

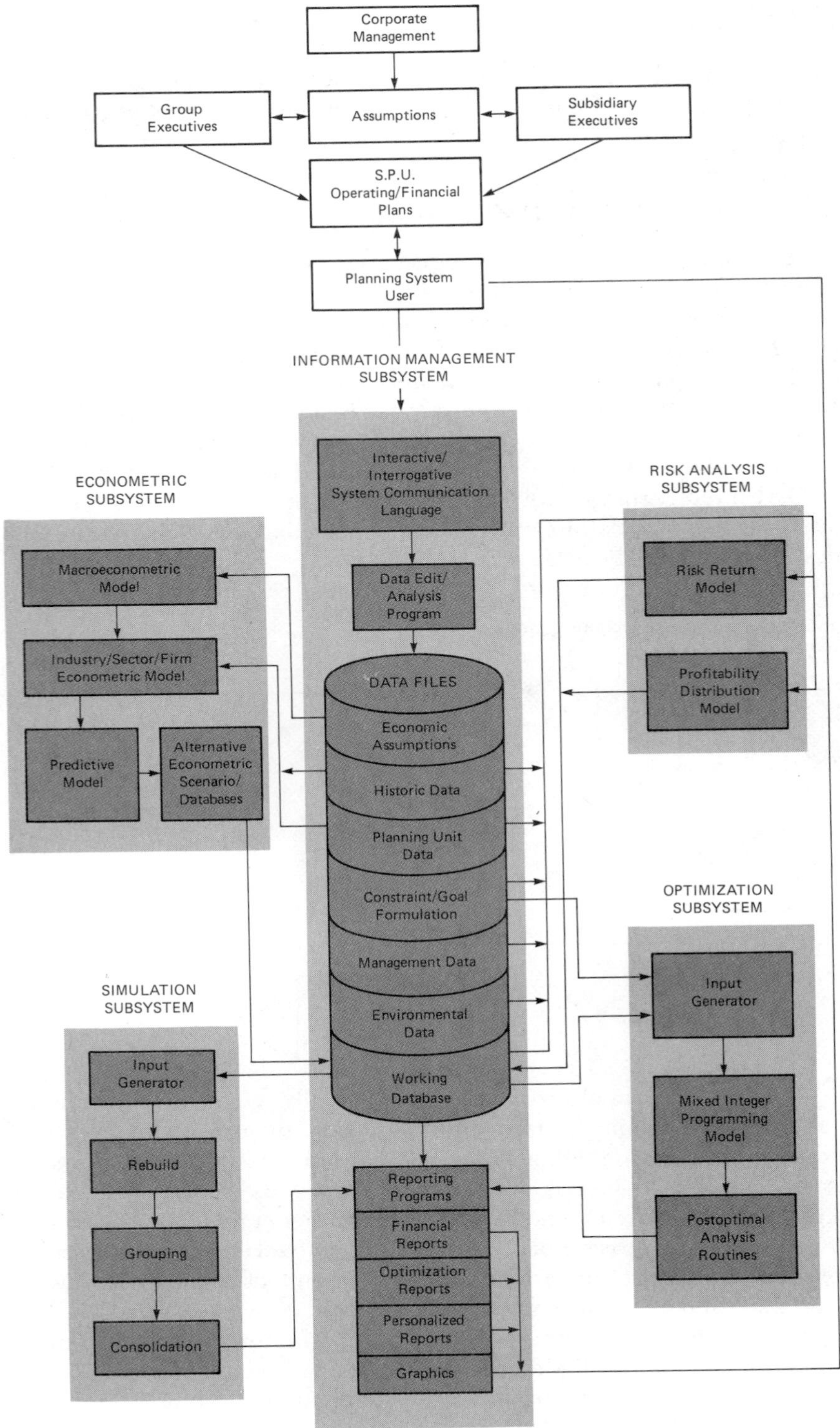

systems. A comprehensive conceptual corporate planning model was developed by Hamilton and Moses [18]. The schematic presentation of this model is shown in Figure 16.15. This classical model is considered to be an early decision support system.

A simple example of a corporate operational planning model is given next.

Simulation of a paper manufacturer

The simulation starts with the raw materials: the existing forest timber and used paper available for recycling (see Figure 16.16). A set of equations effectively "translates" the timber into available pulp. Another set of equations does the same thing for the used paper. The plant itself is then simulated by equations that "translate" the conversion of pulp into paper and waste. Lag times between pulp input and paper output are included, as well as the lag time for shipping to distributors and wholesalers, from there to customers, and from customers to waste or back into the plant as used paper.

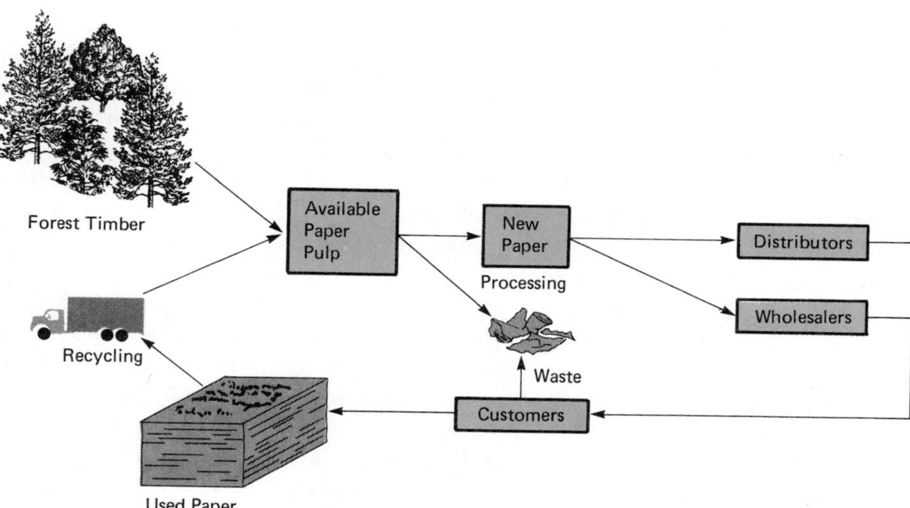

FIGURE 16.16 Paper manufacturer system dynamics

Under this system simulation, management can test the effect of varying environmental conditions such as:

Test various conditions

- Fire destruction of timberland,
- Decreased customer demand,
- Increased land values, and
- Transportation strikes.

on such dependent variables as annual costs, profits, revenues, reserve timberland, and total assets. In addition, the impact of various managerial (controllable) policies on the dependent variables can be tested. These include:

Test various policies

- Alternative uses of the timberland,
- Increased prices,
- Decreased production,
- Faster transportation,
- Earlier knowledge of customer demand.

The result is a significantly improved basis for managerial decision making. Risk can be evaluated against potential profits. Frequently, the system simulation also gives the manager greater insight into the dynamic workings of the system itself, thus further improving his or her managerial decision-making ability. A detailed discussion of the dynamic aspects is presented in the next section.

16.17 SYSTEM DYNAMICS

Non-equilibrium models

One of the most interesting types of simulation is **system dynamics.** Regular simulation models, as we have seen, are most commonly meant to be evaluated in steady state (equilibrium) conditions. The same applies to Markov chains, queuing models, inventory, and almost all other management science models. But the real world is not static, it continuously changes; therefore, a model is needed that will allow for dynamic behavior.

Industrial dynamics

Initiated in the 1960s by J. W. Forrester [13] under the name **industrial dynamics,** this engineering-oriented method is based on the concept that complex systems are usually composed of chains of causes and effects known as *feedback loops.* A decision or policy in one area (the cause) produces a result (effect) in another area, which in turn produces the need for another decision or creates another result. Two types of loops are considered: *positive,* where an increase in the cause results in an *increase* in the effect; and negative, where an *increase-decrease* relationship is observed (see Figure 16.17).

Positive versus negative loops

Disaster!

Forrester used the system dynamics model to study the effects of population growth on the use of natural resources. The results of his model indicated a potential disaster for the human species. Population was predicted to reach a peak in the year 2020 and then decline rapidly. Additional computer runs were made involving other assumptions, such as doubling the estimate of natural resource reserves; unlimited resources; population controls; pollution controls and increased agricultural productivity; and perfect birth control. Although the timing varies, all runs eventually ended with disaster.

System dynamics has been used to encompass social, political, corporate, governmental, and even world systems. As with any other simulation, the method permits experimentation with a model of the system under study. However, in contrast to the other simulation models, which are

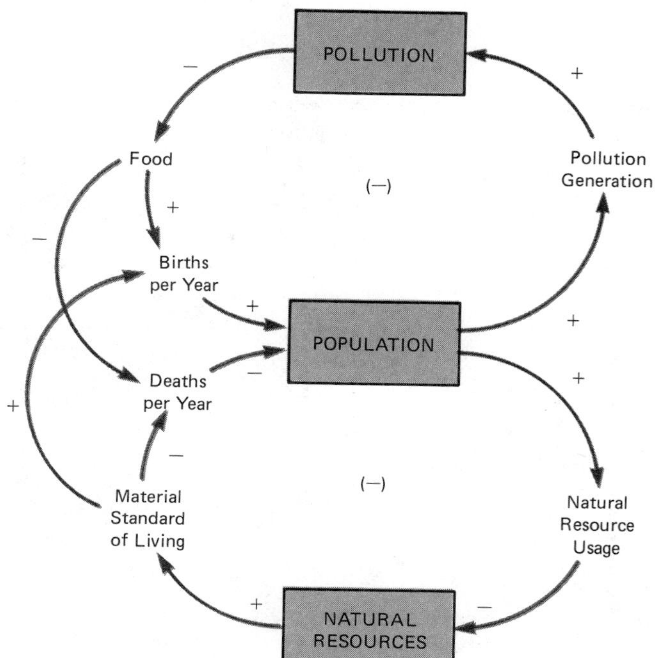

FIGURE 16.17
System dynamics feedback loops (adapted from Forrester [13])

more precise and deal with decision-making situations, system dynamics deals with policies. For example, a policy might state that our company will reduce the price whenever our major competitor reduces price. A *decision* would be the *specific amount* of price reduction (e.g., 5 percent). Thus, the focus here is on policymaking rather than decision making. System dynamics models allow the manager to formulate several different policies and observe their effect through the feedback loops. However, a precise impact is not given, only the *general* directions (e.g., if price is increased, the sales volume will decline). The model, therefore, provides the manager with new insight about the system and its relationship with the environment.

Policymaking

System dynamics is composed of flowcharts coupled with equations that describe how the various elements of the system interact. An example of an industrial firm is shown in Figure 16.18. Note, that in addition to the feedback loops (shown as information flows — — →), other flows are also shown. Note that inventory, inventory reorders, backlog, and manufacturing form a closed loop. The policy that we might test is whether to manufacture or to supply a backlog from existing inventory. Questions such as how to stabilize the employment level can also be analyzed through this diagram.

System dynamics models are generally associated with large computer simulations (via the special language DYNAMO). However, the method does not necessarily require a computer to develop insight into problems. For further discussion, see Roberts [30].

FIGURE 16.18
System dynamics flowchart

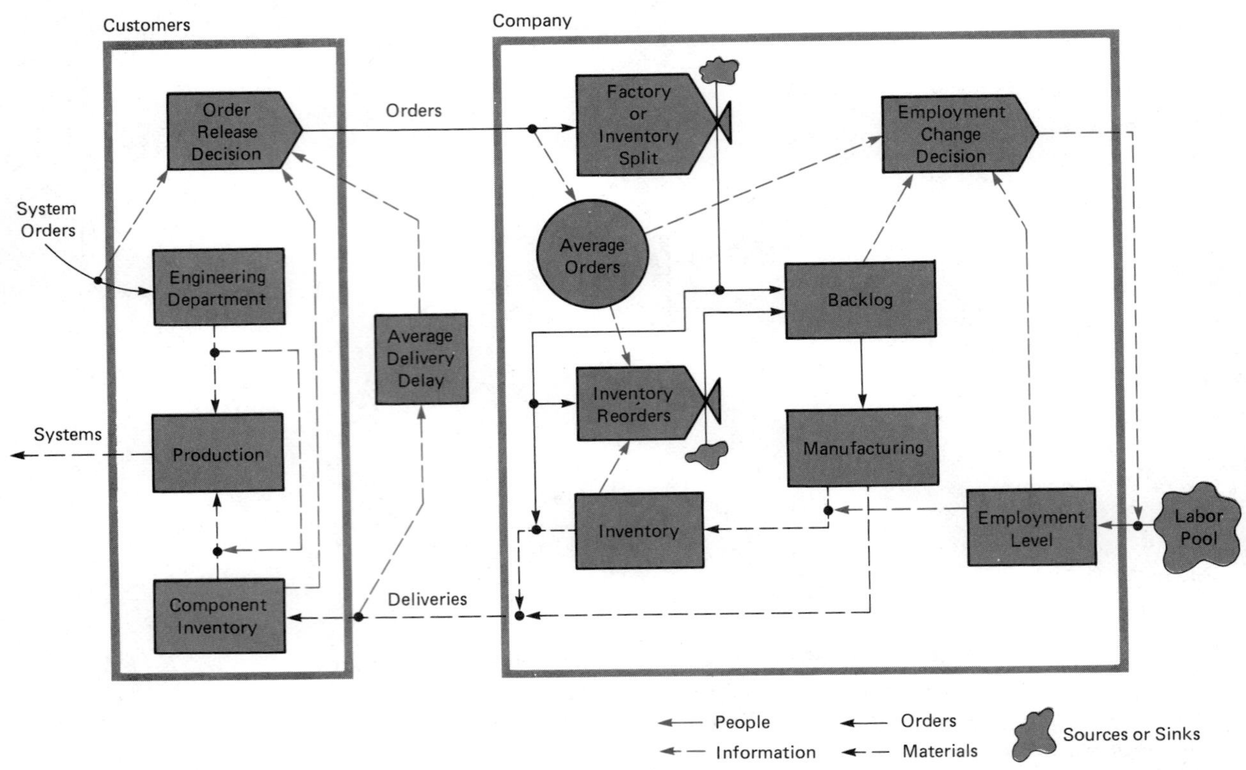

Source: Reproduced from Decision Sciences, vol. 8 (1977), with permission.

16.18 OTHER SIMULATION MODELS

There are many other simulation models in use. In this section we will present two *deterministic* models.

Deterministic models

Most of the examples presented in this chapter were of a probabilistic nature. In some cases, however, simulation is strictly deterministic, where all the variables are assumed to be certain. Several of the corporate planning models, especially financial models, are deterministic. In contrast to Monte Carlo simulation, the operating characteristics and relationships of the situation under study are *explicitly specified* rather than being random. Deterministic simulation models are normally less accurate than analytic representations of a system, but the additional simplification of ignoring the random elements is frequently justified and thereby results in a less complex, faster solution. These models are used to predict the impact of changes or to compare alternative courses of action or policy. Most of the more advanced models involve the "what if" capability and provide the foundation for some of the decision support system models described in Chapter 17.

TABLE 16.21
An inventory simulation

	January	*February*	*March*	*April*	*May*	*June*
Projected demand	310	250	110	420	450	150
Starting inventory	500	190	500	390	500	450
Ending inventory	190	0	390	0	50	300
Shortage	0	60	0	30	0	0
Regular orders	0	500	0	500	450	0
Emergency orders	0	60	0	30	0	0
Cost						
Ordering		200		200	200	
Shortage		1,200		600		
Holding	1,900	0	3,900	0	500	3,000
Total	1,900	1,400	3,900	800	700	3,000

Example A An example of a deterministic inventory model is given in Table 16.21.

The current inventory policy is to replenish the stock whenever the month-end inventory drops below 100 units. In that case, the order size is the difference between the existing level and 500 units. The lead time is one month. The ordering cost is $200 and carrying cost is figured at $10 per unit per month charged on the end-of-month inventory. Stockouts are figured at $20 per unit (emergency purchasing).

The simulation starts by projecting demand ahead for several months. We assume that the starting inventory is 500. The simulation is similar to Monte Carlo, the only difference being that the demand is given as certain. The average cost per month can then be computed ($1,783 per month). Then, a second run is made for a different ordering rule, the total cost is recomputed, and so on until the best policy is identified.

Example B A large, fast-food corporation is interested in examining various capital-spending policies. More specifically, the company can:

a. Own and operate a store.
b. Own the store but lease it.
c. Form a joint venture.
d. Use a complete franchised arrangement.

The problem is to determine the percentage of the 200 new stores planned for next year in each category.

The simulation will involve two stages. First, a financial projection is made for each type of ownership (per store). An example of a five-year projection for company-owned stores is shown in Table 16.22. (The same procedure is repeated for the other three alternatives.)

In stage two, different combinations can be tested (e.g., 50 company-owned, 50 leased, 50 joint venture, and 50 franchised). Total costs and other measures of performance can then be compared. In this case, the second stage may involve an analytical model such as integer or goal programming to optimize the mix.

TABLE 16.22
Simulation of the financial impact of a company-owned store

		YEAR 1	YEAR 2	YEAR 3	YEAR 4	YEAR 5
SALES		865.7	943.6	1028.5	1121.1	1222.0
COST OF SALES (37%)		320.3	349.1	380.6	414.8	452.1
GROSS PROFIT (63%)		545.4	594.5	648.0	706.3	769.9
COST OF LABOR (27.4%)		237.2	258.5	281.8	307.2	334.8
MAINTENANCE (1.9%)		16.4	17.9	19.5	21.3	23.2
UTILITIES (4%)		34.6	37.7	41.1	44.8	48.9
ADVERTISING (6%)		51.9	56.6	61.7	67.3	73.3
OTHER (3.9%)		33.8	36.8	40.1	43.7	47.7
SG&A (3%)		26.0	28.3	30.9	33.6	36.7
SOP (16.8%)		145.4	158.5	172.8	188.3	205.3
START-UP		20.0				
SOP BEFORE DEPREC		125.4				
LESS: DEPRECIATION						
BUILDING		17.5	17.5	17.5	17.5	17.5
EQUIPMENT		32.2	32.2	32.2	32.2	32.2
REPL EQUIP			3.6	7.5	11.6	16.0
REMODEL						
TOTAL DEPRECIATION		49.7	53.3	57.2	61.3	65.7
PBIT		75.7	105.2	115.6	127.0	139.6
LESS: INTEREST		91.6	88.6	85.3	81.8	84.7
PBT		−15.9	16.6	30.3	45.2	54.9
PAT		−7.9	8.3	15.2	22.6	27.4
ADD: DEPRECIATION		49.7	53.3	57.2	61.3	65.7
CASH FLOW		41.8	61.6	72.4	83.9	93.1
NPV		955.5				
INVESTMENT						
LAND	196.8					
BLDG	350.3					
EQUIP	225.5	25.2	27.0	28.9	30.9	33.0
W.C.	3.0					
TOTAL	775.6					
AVG INV CAP		763.4	738.0	710.7	681.3	705.9
ROIC		9.9%	14.3%	16.3%	18.6%	19.8%
IRR		18.1				

16.19 CONCLUDING REMARKS

The advances in computer technology, combined with their reduced cost, makes simulation one of the most popular techniques of management science, especially for top management. The more complex the problems and the more departments involved, the more likely is the use of simulation. Further, simulation is one of the foundations for decision support systems (Chapter 17). Complex organizational problems are often composed of many interacting variables, with the possibility of several uncontrollable chance variables also affecting the situation. Therefore, optimization models are usually not very helpful. Simulation thus allows management science to widen its scope and tackle problems in corporations, government organizations, and social agencies.

Simulation is a much more complicated task than using an analytical model such as EOQ or linear programming. The formulation is very complex and lengthy, and the programming may take weeks or even months to complete. Yet it is one of the most flexible management science tools.

16.20 PROBLEMS FOR PART B

15. Identify which types of simulation can be used in each of the following tasks:

a. Writing poetry.
b. Analyzing biblical passages to determine the author.
c. Determining the effect of monetary policy on a national economy.
d. Locating the most profitable sites for a chain of restaurants.
e. Learning how to run a blast furnace.
f. Imitating a controller's bond purchasing decision.

16. Describe visual interactive decision making and explain its contribution to improved problem solving.

17. Give some examples of heuristics.

18. How can a "hospital game" make a nurse aware of interdependencies in her hospital that she never knew existed?

19. You are looking for syrup in a new grocery store. What heuristics do you employ?

20. You have the following weekend jobs facing you:

Hanging a picture
Mowing a lawn.
Walking a dog.
Tuning up the car.
Cleaning out the garage.

In what order would you choose to do these? What heuristic decision rules did you employ to choose this order?

21. Heuristic problem: Little Billie is famous as the best junior burgler in Beverly Hills. He only robs from the "filthy" rich and is very selective in what he is willing to "lift" (because his "goodies sack" will only hold 27 cubic feet). Also, being small, he can only carry up to 92 pounds in his pack. On this particular night, he has the following items from which to choose.

Item	*Value ($)*	*Volume ($ft.^3$)*	*Weight (lb.)*
A	300	2	25
B	100	1	10
C	500	3	20
D	900	5	30
E	600	5	15
F	400	1	35
G	200	2	10
H	300	3	15
I	500	4	15
J	700	8	10
K	200	4	20
L	800	7	20

Clearly, he wishes to maximize his "haul," but isn't sure which items to choose first. Test each of the following heuristic rules and advise Little Billie on their soundness:

a. If smaller items are chosen first, after they are gone, there might not be enough room for the bigger, more valuable items, and the sack may have to be left partly empty. Therefore, since value is somewhat proportional to volume, fill the sack with the largest items first, tucking in the smaller items as space allows.
b. By the same reasoning, perhaps the heaviest items should be chosen first.
c. Choose the items in order of their value.
d. Choose the items in order of their value per unit volume.
e. Choose the items in order of their value per unit weight.
f. Choose the items in order of their value per unit volume per unit weight.

22. Find the best sequence by using "next best" and "next best with adjustments" rules. The times are setup times.

From \ To	1	2	3	4	5	6	7	8
Initial condition	9	29	9	14	29	34	18	16
1	0	23	30	15	18	17	11	24
2	24	0	22	8	22	10	24	16
3	7	7	0	8	33	26	20	25
4	7	18	11	0	27	18	6	34
5	4	15	22	10	0	22	30	35
6	26	33	26	9	22	0	35	15
7	23	19	29	33	7	24	0	30
8	31	24	19	28	10	21	19	0

23. A doctor has the following patients waiting to see him with the corresponding projected treatment times. The doctor wishes to schedule them to minimize average waiting time. Formulate two heuristic rules and compare them with taking the patients in the order given.

Patient	*Treatment time (hours)*
A	1.0
B	.2
C	2.0
D	1.5
E	.1
F	.7

24.[12] People arrive at an elevator in groups once every three minutes (there is a pedestrian crossway in front of the building with a traffic light that switches every three minutes), with the following frequencies:

Number of people in group	*Probability P(x)*
3	.10
4	.15
5	.35
6	.25
7	.15

The elevator can accommodate at most five persons. It takes the elevator an average of two minutes to go and return to the ground floor if it doesn't go beyond the eighth floor. If it goes beyond the eighth floor, it takes an average of four minutes to return. In 75 percent of the trips, the elevator does not go beyond the eighth floor.

If a person waits for an elevator and the elevator returns, that person takes it *without* waiting for the next group to arrive.

Simulate for 10 arriving groups until all people are accommodated. The elevator is at the ground floor at the beginning of the simulation and should return to the ground floor at the end of the simulation.

Find (by simulation):

a. The average number of people arriving each time.
b. The average number in an elevator ride.
c. The average time a person has to wait for the elevator.

[12] Developed by Professor Dieter Klein, Worchester Polytechnic University, in 1974.

d. The probability that a person will have to wait for the elevator.
e. The utilization of the elevator.
f. How many trips the elevator will make in *one hour*.

Use the following RNs:

I. For arrivals: 15, 81, 22, 55, 91, 48, 06, 58, 37, 74, 26, 87.
II. For the elevator: 09, 28, 93, 65, 31, 71, 42, 18, 68, 80, 52, 22, 60, 03.

Assign representative numbers from 01.

25. Of all the customers entering Swiss National Bank, 20 percent go to the receptionist, 15 percent to the loan department, 55 percent to the cashier windows, and 10 percent to the credit card department.

Of all who see the receptionist, one half then go to the loan department, one fourth go to the credit card department, and one fourth leave the bank.

Of all those who go to the cashier windows, 80 percent leave the bank and 20 percent go to the loan department.

Of all those who go to the credit card department, 50 percent will leave the bank and 50 percent will go to the cashier windows.

Of all those who go to the loan department, 50 percent will go to the cashier windows, 15 percent will go to the credit department, and 35 percent will leave the bank.

Simulate the paths of five customers going through the bank. Assume that a customer may return to a service area more than once. Use the following random numbers: 78, 54, 16, 24, 58, 03, 90, 88, 48, 42, 59, 94, 80, 86, 14, 29, 36, 63, 12, 37, 89, 41. (Start the first customer with the first random number, the second customer with the second random number, and so on.)

Find:

a. In how many service areas each of the customers will stop.
b. How many times the first customer will show up at the cashier windows.
c. The average time at the receptionist's desk is 2 minutes, at the cashier windows it is 3 minutes, and at the loan and credit card departments it is 10 minutes. Estimate how the *workload*, in terms of minutes of service, is divided among the four service areas.
d. How many visits were paid, in total, to the cashier windows.
e. The floor area of the bank is 5,000 square feet. How would you allocate this area to the various service areas if the area needed is considered proportional to the number of visits?

26. Pump-It-Yourself, Inc., is an independently owned and operated service station. As such, it does not receive regular deliveries from the local wholesale gasoline distributorship, which is controlled by a major oil company. Instead, the station has the opportunity of purchasing any or all of the excess gasoline remaining on the distributor's truck after all regular deliveries have been made each day. The delivery truck stops each day *after* the station has closed for business. The amount of gasoline remaining on the truck is a random variable with the following distribution:

Gallons remaining	*Probability*
0	.20
500	.25
1,500	.30
2,500	.15
3,500	.10

The station has a 3,000-gallon storage capacity, and the demand for gasoline varies according to the following distribution:

Gallons demanded	*Probability*
660	.10
1,200	.20
1,800	.30
2,400	.25
3,000	.15

Assume that unsatisfied demand is lost (customer goes to a competitor). Simulate the activities involving the supply and demand of gasoline for 12 days. Start with an inventory on hand of 2,100 gallons. Use the following random numbers:

RNs for demand: 79, 25, 03, 19, 28, 91, 58, 52, 68, 13, 46, 67.
RNs for supply: 69, 07, 95, 41, 49, 76, 08, 37, 83, 57, 12, 29.

Given:

Profit from a gallon sold = 20 cents
Cost of ill will = 5 cents per gallon
Cost of shipping back = 2 cents per gallon

Determine:

a. The average daily demand for gasoline (compare to the "expected value").
b. The percentage of time that storage capacity will not be sufficient for taking all gasoline from the truck.
c. The percentage of time that demand can not be met.
d. The average daily beginning inventory.
e. The average daily ending inventory.
f. The average daily loss of unmet demand.
g. The percentage of times that sales equaled demand.
h. The daily net profit.

27. Given an inventory system with the following information:

- Replenishment arrives at the beginning of the week (Monday).
- Demand occurs during the week.
- Inventory is taken at the end of the week (Friday) and orders are placed at that time.
- Lead time: Orders are placed at the *end* of a week and are delivered at the beginning of the week after next (nine days lead time).

Ordering policy:
If inventory on hand at the end of a week is I (can be negative for shortage) and replenishment due in the beginning of the following week is R, then: If $I + R \leq 5$, order so that $I + R + Q = 10$, where Q is the size of the order. If $I + R \leq 5$, do not order.

The probability of demand in each given week is shown below:

Number of units	*Probability*
3	.05
4	.20
5	.35
6	.25
7	.15

Start with an inventory of six at the beginning of the first week (after replenishment arrived). Then:

1. Write a simulation flowchart.
2. Manually simulate for 20 weeks (use RNs from Problem 26).

Find:

a. The percent of times the system will be in a stockout.
b. The average number of units stocked out per week.
c. The percent of times the system will have a zero inventory at the end of the week.
d. The frequency of placing replenishment orders.
e. The average inventory on hand.

28. Assume that in Problem 27 the cost of a stockout is $50 per unit per occurrence, and the storage (holding) cost is $5 per unit per week. Explain how you would simulate to find if a different inventory policy is more profitable.

29. Dr. X has an appointment schedule where patients are scheduled to come every 20 minutes. The office is open from 9 A.M. to noon, four days a week. The last patient is scheduled at 11:40 A.M. each day. Assume that patients arrive exactly on time. The time required for treatment or examination is distributed as follows:

Minutes	*Percent*
10	14
15	25
20	41
25	20

The doctor will see all patients that are scheduled. Simulate for *two days* to find:

a. The average waiting time (prior to treatment) per patient (in minutes).
b. The average utilization of the physician (the percentage that working time is of the total time in her office). *Note:* If the physician completes her examinations before noon, she will stay in the office until noon.
c. The average overtime *(in hours)* worked by the physician each week. Overtime is considered any time beyond noon.

d. The length of the last treatment on the second day (in minutes).

e. The average number of breaks the physician will have in a day, between seeing patients.

f. The exact time the doctor will finish the treatment of the last patient on the second day.

RNs for the simulation: 52, 02, 73, 48, 06, 15, 94, 12, 95, 87, 04, 99, 40, 98, 58, 68, 08, 81. Start assigning RN with 00.

30. Mexivalve, Inc., produces valves on a weekly schedule. Shipments are made to two customers, A and B. The customers enter orders by phone every Friday, after their weekly maintenance inspection is completed, and they want immediate delivery. Past experience indicated the following demand pattern: customer A orders either 15 valves (35 percent of the time) or 20 valves (65 percent of the time). Customer B orders 25 valves in 20 percent of the cases, 30 valves in 40 percent of the cases, and 35 valves in the remaining cases.

The company would like to be able to meet all demand at least 95 percent of the time. The production manager thinks that he can do it with a weekly production schedule of 48 valves. Valves not demanded on Friday are used as safety stock, which currently stands at five units. Demand that cannot be met from production is met from the safety stock. Demand that cannot be met at all is considered a lost opportunity.

Simulate for 12 weeks.

RNs for customer A: 63, 87, 06, 51, 33, 93, 15, 75, 26, 68, 41, 58.
RNs for customer B: 34, 66, 12, 87, 43, 04, 53, 92, 27, 72, 49, 81.

Start assigning RNs from 00.

Find:

a. Is the production level of 48 sufficient to meet the company's service policy? Why?

b. What is the average weekly profit if one valve brings 27.50 pesos?

c. What will be the safety stock at the end of the 12th week?

d. The average weekly number of valves demanded that are considered as a lost opportunity.

31. A certain service time is normally distributed, averaging 15 minutes with a standard deviation of 2. Three RNs were generated: 386, 628, 953. Find the length of service time of the first three services.

32. Demand for a perishable liquid product is known to be normally distributed, with an average daily demand of 23 gallons and a standard deviation of 4 gallons.

a. Generate demand for 10 days. Use RNs: 783, 430, 922, 871, 477, 838, 872, 276, 198, 520

b. Round the average daily demand found in part *(a)* to one decimal point (e.g., 25.2). Assume that an inventory of 23.6 gallons is being kept daily. If demand in a given day is more than the inventory on hand, the company incurs a loss of $100 for each gallon short (proportion of $100 for fraction of a gallon). If there is some left over, the company's demurrage is $120 per gallon (proportion for a fraction). Find the average daily profit (loss) if each gallon sold contributes $50 to profit.

c. Based on the result of part *(b)*, estimate the chance of not meeting the demand on any specific day.

33. Solve the waiting line problem of Section 16.6, using the following data:

a. The interarrival time is five minutes, on the average, with a standard deviation of 1.0 minutes (normally distributed).

b. The service time is constant, five minutes. Use the same RNs as in the example.

34. *Given:*

1. A waiting line situation with Poisson arrivals of $\lambda = 10$ per hour.
2. The service time is four minutes (exponentially distributed).

Simulate for 12 arrivals to find:

a. The average waiting time.

b. The utilization of the system (round to the nearest whole minute).

Use RNs from Table C2; column 1 for arrivals, column 2 for service. Use three-digit RNs.

35. A survey of 100 arriving customers at a drive-in window of North Eastern Bank resulted in the following information:

Time between arrivals (minutes)	*Frequency*
.5	6
1.0	10
1.5	15
2.0	18
2.5	20
3.0	15
3.5	12
4.0	4
	100

The service time (from the time the car enters the service position until the car leaves) was distributed as follows:

Service time (minutes)	*Frequency*
1.0	12
1.5	18
2.0	30
2.5	25
3.0	15

a. Convert the distributions to cumulative probability distributions.

b. Use the graphical approach to generate 12 arrivals:

RNs for arrivals: 81, 13, 66, 58, 43, 76, 06, 33, 96, 50, 88, 39

RNs for service: 26, 48, 04, 62, 98, 17, 51, 58, 73, 86, 21, 35.

c. Find the average waiting time, per customer.

d. Find the utilization (in percent) of the drive-in window.

36. Moscow University has an information center staffed by one employee. Historical data indicate that people arrive at the center according to the following distribution:

Interarrival time (minutes)	*Frequency*
4	.223
5	.481
6	.275
7	.021

The time of service is normally distributed with an average of five minutes and a standard deviation of one minute. The center opens at 8:30 and the first person arrives at 8:30 sharp. Simulate for 12 customers (including the first one). Use the following RNs:

For arrivals: .621, .326, .907, .698, .018, .434, .715, .246, .168, .540, .992.

For service: .319, .625, .428, .912, .037, .446, .721, .173, .268, .819, .396, .527.

Note:

1. Round the minutes to the nearest whole minute.
2. Round all other numbers to the nearest possible figure.
3. End the simulation after the last customer is served.

Find:

a. The utilization of the center.

b. The average number of customers in the center (waiting and/or being served).

c. The probability that a customer will have to wait.

d. The probability that a customer will be in the center more than five minutes in total.

e. The average waiting time, W_q, in the queue.

37. The demand for Orange Microcomputer II for the next 10 weeks is known (from existing orders) as: 520, 314, 618, 240, 590, 806, 430, 180, 300, 250. It takes two weeks to receive micros from the factory. The current inventory on hand is 600; an additional 400 will arrive next week. The costs are:

Ordering costs are \$300 plus \$5 per unit.
Carrying cost is \$10 per unit per week.
Shortage cost is \$30 per unit short (special rush shipment).

The existing ordering policy is to order 500 units whenever the inventory is 100 units or less.

a. Simulate for the period of 10 weeks.

b. Calculate the average inventory and shortage cost per week.

c. Design a better ordering rule and find how much money you can save.

16.21 CASE

EXPRESS A.G.[13]

In early October, Mr. Hans Huber, operations manager of Express A.G., received a request from Mr. Max Retter, the traffic manager at Stuttgart, for an increase in the number of dispatchers assigned to the Stuttgart operation from two (the present number) to four. Mr. Retter claimed that with only two dispatchers the delivery van drivers were spending too much idle time waiting to report in and to receive new instructions. When Mr. Huber asked Retter how he had arrived at "four dispatchers" as the appropriate number, Retter replied, "Based on my observations, four dispatchers should clear up most of the waiting time." Mr. Huber then promised to look into the matter and to advise Retter of his decision.

The delivery van operations of Express A. G.

Express A. G. was an integrated transportation company operating throughout western Germany. Its headquarters were at Frankfurt, and other major operations centers were at München, Stuttgart, Hamburg, Bremen, and Aachen. An important segment of Express's business was the delivery van operation. In each major center, Express operated a fleet of delivery vans that served the metropolitan area around the center. The delivery vans made home deliveries for many of the large department stores. In addition, the vans delivered goods locally that were brought into the metropolitan area warehouses by the large transcontinental trucking firms.

For each trip, the driver of the delivery van received instructions from the dispatcher as to the particular requirements of the assignment. Upon return to the motor pool, the driver reported to the dispatcher either the successful completion of his assignment or any difficulties that he may have encountered. At the completion of the "trip report," the dispatcher would assign the driver to a new job.

The operation at Stuttgart

Following the receipt of Mr. Retter's request, Mr. Huber became quite concerned. He felt that Retter's request should not be looked upon in isolation—if, as Retter claimed, the number of dispatchers at Stuttgart was inadequate, then it was probable that most of the other delivery van centers were also understaffed. Therefore, he decided to send Felix Stamm, a staff operations analyst, to Stuttgart to investigate the problem.

EXHIBIT 1
Information about delivery van operation at Stuttgart

Number of dispatchers	2
Number of delivery vans	30
Average length of trip	2 hours
Arrival rate per hour at dispatcher's office	Random, approximately normally distributed, with mean = 15 and standard deviation = 4.*
Time with dispatcher	Random, approximately normally distributed, with mean = 8 minutes and standard deviation = 3 minutes. Minimum service time = 1 minute.
Wage rate per hour—dispatchers	12 DM†
Wage rate per hour—drivers	10 DM
Billing rate (revenue) per hour for van with driver	30 DM

* Within the hour, the arrivals appear to follow a completely random pattern.

† DM stands for the German currency deutsche mark.

[13] This case was prepared by Professor A. A. Robichek, Stanford University, Graduate School of Business.

Mr. Stamm spent several days at Stuttgart and then returned to Frankfurt. He showed Mr. Huber the data he had gathered about the Stuttgart operation (see Exhibit 1) and promised to prepare a report within the next few days.

Questions for discussion

1. What is the optimal number of dispatchers for Stuttgart under each of the following assumptions:
   a. While the driver is waiting to see a dispatcher, the van is being serviced by the service department.
   b. The van and the driver are both idle during the waiting period.

   (In resolving this problem, make any additional assumptions you consider necessary.)
2. What additional information would have been of assistance in resolving this problem?

   Notes:
   a. Simulate for two hours. Use the waiting times for the second hour to arrive at a decision (waiting time for the first hour is too far from a stabilized condition).
   b. Round the time to whole minutes.
   c. Simulate the exact minute of arrival by using the formula: random number × (60/100). After computing the average number of arrivals within an hour, arrange by the "order of arrivals."
   d. Use Table C2 for estimated service time and arrival rate values.

16.22 GLOSSARY

Business games Operational games that deal with decision making at the top of a business corporation.

DYNAMO A special-purpose simulation language for system dynamics.

Flowchart (or diagram) A schematic presentation of all computational activities used in the simulation written in a symbolic language.

GASP A simulation language written in FORTRAN.

GPSS A flowchart-oriented simulation language.

Heuristic programming A step-by-step procedure using heuristics that, in a finite number of steps, arrives at a satisfactory solution.

Heuristics Decision rules that are developed on the basis of logical problem analysis and, possibly, designed experimentation.

Industrial dynamics A computerized system simulation of a whole company or industry.

Monte Carlo simulation Simulation that uses a random number mechanism to describe the behavior of systems with probabilistic elements.

Oligopoly A market where only a small number of sellers operate.

Operational (management) games Simulation of a competitive situation arranged in the form of a game. Participants make periodic decisions and the results are then analyzed. Such games are used mainly for training purposes.

Pseudorandom number A random number generated by a mathematical process.

Random number Numbers sampled from a uniform distribution. Each number has the same chance of being drawn.

Random number generation A process of generating random numbers, usually by a computer. Can be done manually by drawing pieces of papers with numbers from a hat or from a specially constructed table (Table C2 in Appendix C in this text).

Representative range of numbers A range of numbers with the same number of digits (e.g., 00–19) that corresponds to the frequency distribution of the factor under consideration.

Rules of thumb Rules of decision making that are based on trial and error and that yield acceptable solutions for managerial problems.

SIMSCRIPT A special computer programming language.

SIMULA A generalized simulation language.

Simulation A procedure that involves the use of a mathematical model that imitates reality for the purpose of conducting experiments on the model. These trial-and-error-type experiments intend to *predict* the behavior of the system under different situations.

Simulation runs A simulation run is one simulation experiment with one set of input data.

System dynamics Simulation of large systems that allow for dynamic behavior. Used mainly for policy analysis.

Time compression The ability to simulate years of operations in seconds or minutes of computer time.

Time dependent Simulation where the exact time of each event is required and tracked.

Time independent Simulation where the exact time of each event is *not* needed.

Trial One period in a simulation run. A run is composed of many trials.

Validation Determining how closely the model predicts the behavior of the system.

Variance reduction A technique for increasing the precision for a fixed sample size (or decreasing the sample size required to obtain a desired level of precision).

Visual simulation Visual interactive decision making in real time using simulaiton and computer graphics.

16.23 REFERENCES AND BIBLIOGRAPHY

Heuristic programming

1. Findler, N., and B. Meltzer. *Artificial Intelligence and Heuristic Programming*. New York: Elsevier North-Holland Publishing, 1971.
2. Foulds, L. R. "The Heuristic Problem-Solving Approach." *Journal of the Operational Research Society*," October 1983.
3. Gavett, J. W. "Three Heuristic Rules for Sequencing Jobs to a Single Production Facility." *Management Science* 11 (1965), pp. B166–76.
4. Zanakis, S. H., and J. R. Evans. "Heuristic Optimization: Why, When and How to Use It." *Interfaces*, October 1981, pp. 84–91.

Gaming

5. Bartion, R. F. *The Imaginit Game: A Creative Business Decision Simulation*. Lubbock, Tex.: Active Learning Pub., 1978.
6. Bartion, R. F. *Primer on Simulation and Gaming*. Englewood Cliffs, N.J.: Prentice-Hall, 1972.
7. Horn, R. E., and A. Clearas. *The Guide to Simulation and Games*. 4th ed. Beverly Hills, Calif.: Sage Publications, 1980.
8. Graham, R. G., and C. F. Gray. *Business Games Handbook*. New York: American Management Associations, 1969.
9. Meredith, J. *The Hospital Game*. Cincinnati, Ohio: Shasta Publications, 1978.

Simulation

10. Banks, J., and J. S. Carson. *Discrete Event System Simulation*. Englewood Cliffs, N.J.: Prentice-Hall, 1984.
11. Bell, P. C., et al. "Visual Interactive Problem Solving—A New Look at Management Problems." *Business Quarterly*, Spring 1984.
12. Bulgren, W. *Discrete System Simulation*. Englewood Cliffs, N.J.: Prentice-Hall, 1982.
13. Forrester, J. W. *Industrial Dynamics*. Cambridge, Mass.: MIT Press, 1961.
14. Forrester, J. W. *World Dynamics*. Cambridge, Mass.: Write-Allen Press, 1971.
15. Frazer, J. *Introduction to Business Simulation*. Englewood Cliffs, N.J.: Prentice-Hall, 1978.
16. Graybeal, W., and U. W. Pooch. *Simulation: Principles and Methods*. Cambridge, Mass.: Winthrop Publishers, 1980.

17. Guetzkow, H., et al. *Simulation in Social and Administrative Science*. Englewood Cliffs, N.J.: Prentice-Hall, 1972.

18. Hamilton, W. F., and M. A. Moses. "A Computer-Based Corporate Planning System." *Management Science,* October 1974, pp. 148–59.

19. Hertz, D. G. "Risk Analysis in Capital Investment." *Harvard Business Review,* January–February 1964, pp. 95–106.

20. Hicks, C. R. *Fundamental Concepts in the Design of Experiments*. New York: Holt, Rinehart & Winston, 1973.

21. Jacoby, S. L. S., and J. S. Kowalik. *Mathematical Models with Computers*. New York: Prentice-Hall, 1980.

22. Law, A. M., and W. D. Kelton. *Simulation Modeling and Analysis*. New York: McGraw-Hill, 1982.

23. Meier, R. C.; W. T. Newell; and H. L. Pazer. *Simulation in Business and Economics*. Englewood Cliffs, N.J.: Prentice-Hall, 1969.

24. Naylor, T. H. *Computer Simulation Experiments and Models of Economic Systems*. New York: John Wiley & Sons, 1971.

25. Naylor, T. H. *Simulation Models in Corporate Planning*. New York: Praeger Publishers, 1979.

26. Payne, J. A. *An Introduction to Simulation*. New York: McGraw-Hill, 1982.

27. Pidd, M. *Computer Simulation in Management Science*. New York: John Wiley & Sons, 1984.

28. Pritsker, A. B., and D. Pegden. *Introduction to Simulation and SLAM*. West Lafayette, Ind.: Systems Publishing Corp., 1979.

29. Richardson, G. P., and A. L. Pugh. *Introduction to System Dynamics Modeling with Dynamo*. Cambridge Mass.: MIT Press, 1981.

30. Roberts, E. D., ed. *Managerial Applications of System Dynamics*. Cambridge, Mass.: MIT Press, 1978.

31. Watson, H. J. *Computer Simulation in Business*. New York: John Wiley & Sons, 1981.

PART III

Up to this point, the foundations and tools of management science have been presented. In this third part of the text, attention is directed to applying the results of the analysis. This aspect of management science is probably the most difficult in practice.

The first two chapters in this part explore the new technologies of decision support systems (DSS, Chapter 17) and expert systems (ES, Chapter 18) and their effect on management. Chapter 19 then deals with implementation of the MS recommendations as related to both the specific project itself and to the factors that are independent of any individual project.

To give the reader an opportunity to grapple with real-world issues, nebulous goals, and data problems, a case analysis, solved by three different MS models, is included in Chapter 20. The text then ends with a discussion of the outlook for applications of management science in the future and in the general direction of development and growth of the field.

APPLICATIONS

A preview to chapters 17 and 18

The management science techniques presented so far (with the exception of simulation) are designed to deal with relatively structured situations. Assumptions such as constant demand, linear objective functions, and the presence of certain probability distributions made it possible to employ a variety of models and derive, in many cases, optimal solutions. For more complex situations, the approach of simulation was suggested.

However, even the simulation approach may not work in all cases. The execution of simulation is fairly complex. Writing computer programs for simulations, validating them, and debugging them can be a lengthy process. Furthermore, making changes in a simulation may take a long time when executed by the traditional approach. Finally, all our previous models involved numerical analysis and were not efficient or even feasible in situations involving symbolic manipulation. The introduction of symbols to replace or supplement numbers can significantly increase the range of problems that can be solved by management science.

Decision support systems (DSS) and expert systems (ES) are approaches designed to rectify the deficiencies mentioned above. Both methods are gaining recognition in the management science community. They clearly extend the boundaries of management science by allowing many complex problems to be scientifically analyzed.

Chapter 17 is devoted to DSS. A decision support system is a computerized system designed to deal with managerial problems that are not structured. It is an end user–oriented approach that incorporates various management science and other quantitative models (e.g., statistical, financial) in combination with a computer database, in an attempt to create an extremely flexible and adaptable management support system.

Expert systems (ES), presented in Chapter 18, are applied Artificial Intelligence (AI) techniques designed to capture human expertise and store it in the computer. This knowledge can be used by nonexperts to solve problems that are so complex that they require considerable expertise. Furthermore, ES are also used as training devices and productivity improvement tools. Finally, ES can even deal with symbolic representation and incomplete information.

17

Decision support systems

17.1 Introduction and definitions.
17.2 A framework for decision support.
17.3 DSS characteristics and benefits.
17.4 The evolution of decision support systems.
17.5 The structure of decision support systems.
17.6 The capabilities of DSS.
17.7 Construction considerations.
17.8 A group decision support system (GDSS).
17.9 Examples of applications.
17.10 Example of a DSS generator: IFPS.
17.11 Concluding remarks.
17.12 Review questions.
17.13 Glossary.
17.14 References and bibliography.

Prior to the development of this DSS it seemed to take months to get the needed reports. Today I can just sit and generate them myself in minutes.

An anonymous DSS user, 1980

The mystique surrounding computers and quantitative models has resulted in a significant *gap* between existing technology and its use by the practicing manager. A decision support system (DSS) is a flexible, easy-to-use, interactive, computerized system that may significantly reduce this gap. This chapter presents the characteristics, structure, and capabilities of DSS as well as several case studies of actual applications.

LEARNING OBJECTIVES

The student should be able to:

a. Define DSS and describe its major characteristics.
b. Describe the evolution of DSS and its relation to MIS.
c. List the major components of DSS and describe their content and interaction.
d. Describe the capabilities of DSS.
e. Define "what if" analysis and discuss its importance.
f. Define goal-seeking analysis.
g. Discuss the major factors affecting DSS construction.
h. Describe the major characteristics of IFPS.
i. Describe a group DSS.

Houston Minerals Corporation was interested in a proposed joint venture with a local petrochemicals company to develop a chemical plant. Houston's executive vice president responsible for the decision wanted an analysis of the risks involved in the areas of supplies, demands, and price. Bob Sampson, manager of planning and administration, and his staff built a DSS model in a few days by means of a specialized planning language. The results strongly suggested the project should be accepted.

Then came the real test. Although the executive vice president accepted the validity and value of the results, he was worried about the potential downside risk of the project—the chance of a catastrophic outcome. As Sampson tells it, his words were something like this:

"I realize the amount of work you have already done, and I am 99 percent confident with it. I would like to see this in a different light. I know we are short on time and we have to get back to our partners with our yes or no decision." Sampson replied that the executive could have the risk analysis he needed in less than an hour's time. Sampson concluded, "Within 20 minutes, there in the executive boardroom, we were reviewing the results of his 'what if?' questions. Those results led to the eventual dismissal of the project, which we otherwise would probably have accepted."

DSS to apply management science

The Houston Minerals Corporation case just presented demonstrates some of the major features of **decision support systems (DSS)**, an emerging concept in the application of management science/quantitative analysis. The case demonstrates that the analysis started with the application of simulation modeling, which was the first cut, based on the decision maker's initial definition of what was needed. Then, the executive vice president, using his experience, judgment, and intuition, felt that the model should be modified. The initial model, although mathematically correct, was incomplete. With regular modeling, a modification would have taken a long time, but the DSS provided a *very quick* analysis. Furthermore, the DSS was flexible and responsive enough to allow managerial intuition and judgment to be followed in the end.

How can a thorough risk analysis be performed so quickly for a proposed major plant? How can the judgment factors be elicited, quantified, and worked into a model? How can the results be presented meaningfully and convincingly to the manager? For the answers to these and some other questions of this nature, the reader is invited to explore one of the most important recent approaches in managerial decision making—*decision support systems*.

17.1 INTRODUCTION AND DEFINITIONS

Management decision systems

The concepts involved in DSS were first articulated in the early 1970s by Scott-Morton (see [4]) under the term *management decision systems*. He defined such systems as "interactive computer-based systems, which help decision makers utilize *data* and *models* to solve unstructured problems." Another classical definition of DSS, provided by Keen and Scott-Morton [5], follows:

> Decision support systems couple the intellectual resources of individuals with the capabilities of the computer to improve the quality of decisions. It is a computer-based support system for management decision makers who deal with semistructured problems.

The foregoing definitions indicate the four major characteristics of DSS:

Four characteristics

- DSS incorporate both data and models.
- They are designed to *assist* managers in their decision processes in *semistructured* or *unstructured* tasks.
- They *support*, rather than *replace*, managerial judgment.
- The objective of DSS is to improve the *effectiveness* of the decisions, not the *efficiency* with which decisions are made.

It should be noted that DSS is a "content free" expression; that is, it means different things to different people. There is no universally accepted definition of DSS. In many cases, DSS are described through their characteristics and benefits (see Section 17.3).

17.2 A FRAMEWORK FOR DECISION SUPPORT

Before describing DSS, it will be useful to present a classical framework for decision support. This framework will provide us with several major concepts that will be used in the definitions of DSS and ES. It will also help us in discussing several additional issues, such as the relationship between management science, expert systems (ES), and DSS. This framework was proposed by Gorry and Scott-Morton [4], who combined and integrated the work of Simon [10] and Anthony [2]. The details of this framework are as follows.

According to Simon, decision-making processes fall along a continuum that ranges from highly structured (sometimes referred to as *programmed*) to highly unstructured *(nonprogrammed)*. *Structured* processes are used for routine and repetitive problems for which standard solutions exist. *Unstructured* processes are for "fuzzy," complex problems for which there are no standard solution methods.

Fuzzy problems

The focus on decision making also requires an understanding of the *human* decision-making process. This process is divided by Simon into three phases:

1. *Intelligence*—searching for conditions that call for decisions.
2. *Design*—inventing, developing, and analyzing possible courses of action.
3. *Choice*—selecting a course of action from those available.

A *fully structured* problem is one in which *all* these phases are structured. A structured phase is a phase whose procedures are standardized, whose objectives are clear, and whose input and output are clearly specified.

An *unstructured* problem is one in which none of the three phases is structured. Decisions where some, but not all, of the phases are structured, are referred to as *semistructured* by Gorry and Scott-Morton [4].

In a structured problem, the procedures for obtaining the best (or at least a good enough) solution are known, as shown by the various models described in Part II of this book. Whether the problem involves finding an appropriate inventory level or deciding on an optimal investment strategy, the objectives are clearly defined. The manager can thus use the support of management science people.

Using intuition

In an unstructured problem, human intuition is still the basis for decision making. Typical unstructured problems include planning of new services to be offered or hiring an executive. The semistructured problems fall between the structured and the nonstructured, involving a combination of both standard solution procedures and individuals' judgment. Keen and Scott-Morton [5] give the following examples for semistructured problems: trading bonds, setting marketing budgets for consumer products, and performing capital acquisition analyses. Here, a decision support system can improve the quality of the information on which the decision is based (and, consequently, the quality of the decision) by providing not only a solution but a range of alternate solutions.

The second half of this framework is based on Anthony's taxonomy [2], which defines three broad categories that encompass all managerial activities:

1. *Strategic planning*—the long-range goals and policies for resource allocation.
2. *Management control*—the acquisition and efficient utilization of resources in the accomplishment of the organizational goals.
3. *Operational control*—the efficient and effective execution of specific tasks.

Nine cell framework

Anthony's and Simon's taxonomies are then combined in a nine-cell table (see Figure 17.1) to create a decision-support framework. The right-hand column indicates the tools needed to support the various decisions. Gorry and Scott-Morton suggested that, for the semistructured and unstructured decisions, conventional management science models were insufficient. They proposed the use of a "supportive" information system, which they called a "decision support system." Expert systems (Chapter 18), introduced several years later, are most suitable for supporting tasks requiring human expertise. Such problems can be semistructured or unstructured, but usually fall in a very narrow problem area.

FIGURE 17.1
Decision support framework

Type of Decision / Type of Control	Operational Control	Managerial Control	Strategic Planning	Support Needed
Structured	1 Accounts Receivable, Order Entry	2 Budget Analysis, Short-Term Forecasting, Personnel Reports, Make or Buy Analysis	3 Financial Management (investment), Warehouse Location, Distribution Systems	Management Science and Other Quantitative Models
Semistructured	4 Production Scheduling, Inventory Control, Production Scheduling	5 Credit Evaluation, Budget Preparation, Plant Layout, Project Scheduling, Reward Systems Design	6 Build New Plant, Mergers, Acquisitions, New Product Planning, Compensation Planning, Quality Assurance Plans	DSS ES
Unstructured	7 Selecting a Cover for a Magazine, Buying Software, Approving Loans	8 Negotiation, Recruiting an Executive, Buying Hardware, Lobbying	9 R & D Planning, New Technology Development, Social and Responsibility Planning	DSS ES

17.3 DSS CHARACTERISTICS AND BENEFITS

Ability to support the solution of complex problems A DSS enables the solution of complex problems that ordinarily cannot be solved by other computerized approaches (or can be solved, but at a much slower pace).

Fast response to unexpected situations that result in changed inputs A DSS enables a thorough, quantitative analysis in a very short time. Even major changes in a scenario can be evaluated objectively in a timely manner.

Ability to quickly and objectively try several different strategies under different configurations As demonstrated in the preceding case, a complete "what if" analysis was carried out to examine the downside risk of the Houston Minerals Corporation project. This analysis, which took 20 minutes, would have taken days or weeks with other computerized systems.

What if . . .

New insights and learning The user can be exposed to new insights through the composition of the model and an extensive sensitivity/"what if" analysis. The new insights can help in training inexperienced managers and other employees as well.

Facilitates communication Data collection and model construction/experimentation are executed with active users' participation, thus greatly facilitating communication among managers. The objectivity and logic of the decision process can also make employees more supportive of organizational decisions. The "what if" analysis can be used to satisfy skeptics and, in turn, improve teamwork.

Improved management control and performance Decision support systems can increase management control over expenditures and improve the performance of the organization.

Cost savings Routine applications of DSS may result in considerable cost reduction or in reducing (eliminating) the cost of wrong decisions.

Objective decisions The decisions derived from DSS are more consistent and objective than complex decisions that are made intuitively. Also, they are based on a thorough analysis and executed with greater participation of the individuals who are affected by the decisions. Therefore, the decisions are of better quality and have a greater chance of success.

Consistent objective

Improving managerial effectiveness All of the above capabilities can improve managerial effectiveness (and personal efficiency) by allowing managers to perform a task in a way that uses less time and effort. DSS provide managers with more "quality time" for analysis, planning, and implementation by reducing the need for number crunching.

Support to individuals and/or groups Decision support systems can be used to support either individual managers and/or groups of managers.

Graphical display Decision support systems provide a graphical display of the information needed by managers. Computer graphics enable a user to view the data in several forms such as bar graphs, scatter diagrams, or pie charts. Such a presentation helps managers to view, analyze, and understand large amounts of data.

Extensive range of support Decision support systems can support managers in all steps of decision making. Conventional management science models are limited to only one or two steps in the process. For a discussion of how DSS interface with the decision-making steps, see Sprague [11] and Turban [14].

FIGURE 17.2
Attributes of information system performance according to performance level

	Levels			
	Lower			*Higher*
Attributes	*Basic data processing systems*	*Integrated data processing systems*	*Management information systems*	*Decision support systems*
Applications	Payroll, inventory and personnel record-keeping	Production scheduling, sales analysis	Production control, sales forecasting, some long-range strategic planning	Long-range strategic planning and ad hoc analysis with "what if" capabilities
Database	Unique to each application, batch update	Common to tasks within a system, batch update	Interactive access by programmers	Database management systems, interactive access by managers, and extensive use of shared information
Decision capabilities	No decision models	Simple decision models	Management science models	Integrated management science and operations research models
Types of information	Summary reports	Summary reports, operational information	Scheduled and demand reports, management-oriented information, structured information flows	Information to support specific decision-making responsibilities
Highest organizational level served	Submanagerial levels, lower management	Lower management	Middle management	Top management

Note: Only the most sophisticated attributes of each level are listed. Many lesser attributes of lower levels are also found on higher levels. In fact, overlapping attributes exist in most cases.

Source: Adapted from H. J. Watson, R. H. Sprague, Jr., and D. W. Kroeber, "Computer technology and information system performance," *MSU Business Topics*, Summer 1977.

17.4 THE EVOLUTION OF DECISION SUPPORT SYSTEMS

Changing the decision process

The past 25 years have witnessed the rapid growth of management and information sciences. This development is beginning to have a significant effect on the ways in which managers make and implement their decisions. Specifically, managers are beginning to incorporate these tools, using the computer-information system to assist them in making decisions. (For example, see Rockart and Treacy [9].) As shown in Figure 17.2, the synthesis of these two sciences is one of the major characteristics of DSS.

Four stages of development

Figure 17.2 also shows the development of information systems in four levels, starting with data processing systems and ending with DSS. Five attributes are correlated with the four levels. Attributes on higher levels (such as DSS or MIS) may include attributes of the lower levels. For example, DSS are not limited to top management nor do they exclude the management science models and production control applications listed under MIS. However, attributes of a higher level are particular only to that level.

Watson et al. [15] view DSS as a natural development of computer-information system technology. In addition, while information systems stress structured information flows, the focus of DSS is on the use of decision models to support decision making. The major differences between the traditional management science techniques and DSS are summarized in Table 17.1.

TABLE 17.1
Comparing management science and decision support systems

Operations Research/Management Science

The impact has mostly been on structured problems (rather than tasks), where the objective, data, and constraints can be prespecified.

The payoff has been in generating better solutions for given types of problems.

The relevance for managers has been the provision of detailed recommendations and new methodologies for handling complex problems.

Decision Support Systems

The impact is on decisions in which there is sufficient structure for computer and analytic aids to be of value, but where managers' judgment is essential.

The payoff is in extending the range and capability of managers' decision processes to help them improve their effectiveness.

The relevance for managers is the creation of a supportive tool, under their own control, that does not attempt to automate the decision process, predefine objectives, or impose solutions.

Source: P. G. W. Keen and M. S. Scott-Morton, *Decision Support Systems, An Organizational Perspective* (Reading, Mass.: Addison-Wesley Publishing, 1978.)

17.5 THE STRUCTURE OF DECISION SUPPORT SYSTEMS

A decision support system is composed of the following major components (see Figure 17.3):

a. The database and its management.
b. The model base and its management.
c. The hardware.
d. The user-system interface.

FIGURE 17.3
A conceptual model of DSS

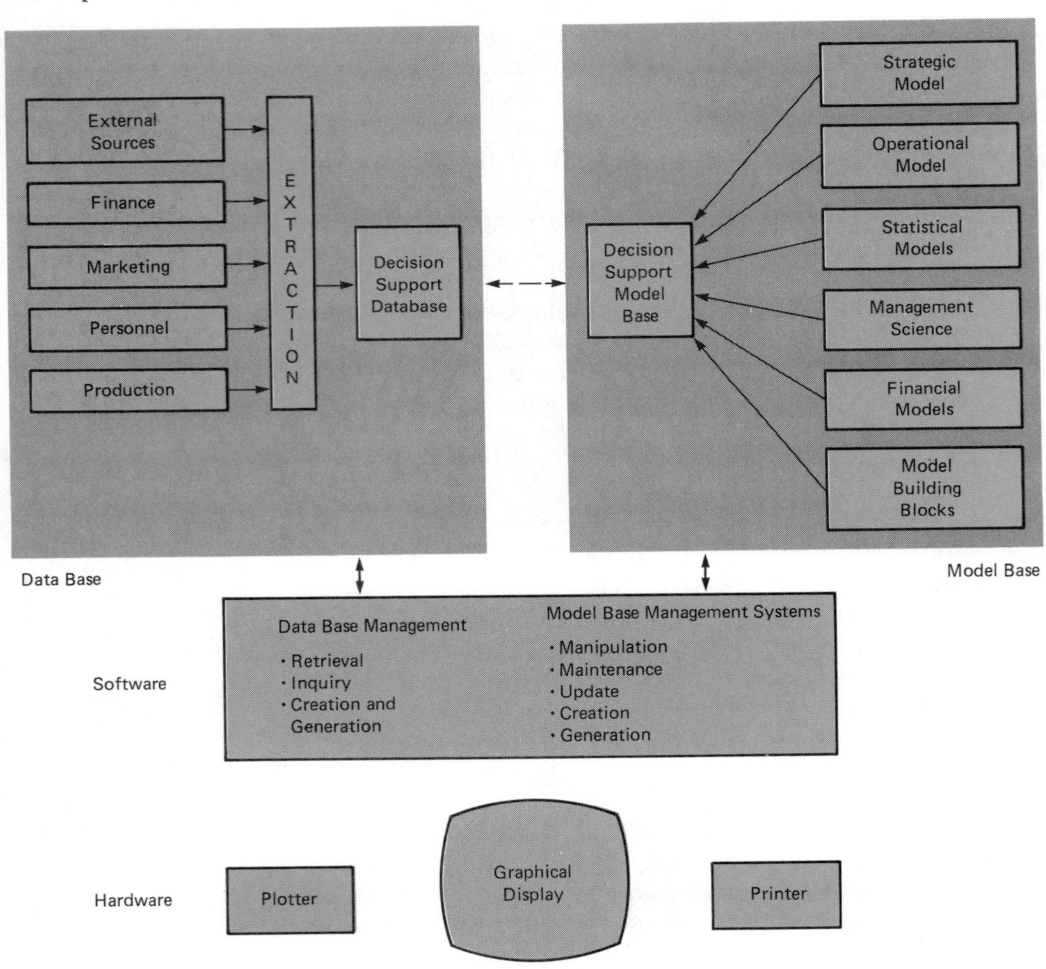

a. The database and its management

A **database** is a collection of data that is organized in such a way that it corresponds to the needs and structure of a company and can be used for more than one application. In order to understand what a database is, we should first talk about information that is kept in files. A file contains information regarding one application. For example, a company may have a personnel file, listing all employees; a customer file, listing all customers; and so on. Each such file may contain extensive information such as addresses, telephone numbers, and volume of purchases for each customer. In a computerized system, a file can be on an auxiliary storage device such as a tape or disk. Companies indeed store thousands of files in the form of libraries. Each file is usually used for a different purpose; however, the data within each file may be *interrelated.*

Interrelated files

Example Let us assume that a company has four files: a parts inventory file, a product file, a parts usage file, and a customer file. Although each file is used for a different purpose, the data within the files are interrelated. For example, the parts usage file (quantity used) is required in the monthly inventory report (to compute the quantity on hand). The purchase of products recorded in the customer files relates to the product monthly demand.

In addition, management may require special reports from time to time (called **ad hoc reports**) that will be based on information available in two or more files. In some companies, as much as 80 percent of all reporting is nonroutine; that is, for ad hoc reports and special analyses. In the past, programmers and system analysts had to sort files, create new programs, and manipulate data to meet management's needs, at tremendous cost and time. The solution to this problem is the concept of a general database.

Ad hoc reports

A database is a collection of interrelated data stored together with a minimum of redundancy to serve multiple applications, with the data stored so that it is *independent* of the computer program that uses it and the type of hardware on which it is stored. The database is organized in a special manner that enables retrieval of the data on request. For example, instead of the four separate files described earlier, there will be one database. In the file structure, item data is listed only once. This, of course, is very important when information is updated, in addition to the saving of storage space and the time of retrieving information.

Database management system (DBMS)

The database is created, accessed, and updated by a **database management system (DBMS)**. The DBMS is a series of *software programs.* DBMS provides six major features:

1. Capability of obtaining answers to queries.
2. Establishing data relationships.
3. Achieving data independence.

Six DBMS features

Six DBMS features

4. Quick retrieval (recovery) of data.
5. Quick updating of data.
6. Comprehensive data security.

The development and control of a database is a difficult and complex task. The DBMS software consolidates and standardizes large and complex files through an activity called **extraction.** DSS may include several databases, some of which are external to the company. In addition to internal and external files that are included in the database, it is possible to add managers' own files.

b. The model base and its management

The **model base** is divided into two major parts:

Two parts to model base

1. Prewritten computer programs (or packages). These may include standard mathematical and statistical models such as linear programming or regression analysis, as well as special programs developed for an individual manager, an organization, or an industry. Notable are strategic, long-range planning models, financial planning models, and tactical and operational models. In addition, the model base includes simulation programs and sensitivity analysis routines.
2. Model building block. Some of the prewritten programs and subroutines can be used to *construct* additional ad hoc routines.

The model base management system (MBMS)

The model base management system (MBMS) is a software system whose functions are model creation using subroutines and other building blocks to generate new routines and reports, model update and change, and data manipulation. The MBMS is capable of interrelating models with the appropriate linkages through the database.

c. The hardware

Large DSS are typically run on mainframe computers. Many user-constructed DSS, however, are installed on microcomputers. The system's **hardware** typically includes a CRT screen for graphic display and printer and/or plotter. For managerial use, the graphic display is of tremendous value. Charts, graphs, diagrams, and even three-dimensional pictures can be produced in color.

d. The user-system interface

This component includes the computer languages and the means by which information is entered into the computer and displayed. The following parts are included.

1. Query languages A key factor in the development of a DSS is the ease of communication between the manager and the computer. Since most managers are uncomfortable in procedural languages such as BASIC or COBOL, communication should be in an English-like language. Today there are several software packages that allow direct communication in a natural language (English, Spanish, and so on). Such languages have been developed mainly for the financial modeling and planning areas. Examples are: Interactive Financial Planning System™ (IFPS), developed by EXECUCOM (see Section 17.10); NOMAD 2,™ developed by National CSS; and EXPRESS,™ developed by Tymshare, Inc.

English-like communication

Special-purpose languages have also been developed for specific industries such as university administration (a language called EFPM), airlines, and hospitals. These **query languages** are also nonprocedural, which means that statements in the model may be entered in any order, while the system itself determines the proper sequence of the solution. The problem with these languages is that currently they are less efficient in execution than the procedural languages. However, DSS are not intended to have high efficiency, but rather to provide a convenient and effective tool for managers to support decisions.

2. Entry and display DSS are constructed **on-line** with the computer. This arrangement allows:

(a) Immediate response to questions (**interactive** communication) and the timely preparation of analysis and reports, even during a management meeting. Results can be displayed on a large CRT in a company's decision room.

(b) Quick policy experimentation and sensitivity analysis.

(c) Monitoring and controlling production processes in real time (important in production and quality control decisions). Entry and display capabilities depend on the availability of supporting graphical display processor subsystems and the appropriate software.

On-line benefits

A key idea in DSS is that the user can play an active role in the development and implementation of the analysis. Emphasis is placed on ease of use, flexibility, and quick response—all of which are necessary in practical decision-making situations.

The manager (user) communicates with the computer via the terminal. Ideally, he or she turns on the terminal in the office and, in an English-like language, commands the computer to execute some tasks. The computer accesses the database and uses the model base as instructed. The results are then displayed.

17.6 THE CAPABILITIES OF DSS

The characteristics of DSS outlined earlier helped in defining what DSS are. However, they do not describe the specific tasks and functions that a DSS can perform for the manager. The latter are:

1. Update or manipulate the database, the model base, the report format, and so on. Also, select data from the database.

2. Create special (ad hoc) reports in a desired format. These reports, once constructed, may be stored in the model base for future use.
3. Perform standard mathematical calculations and execute the aggregation of data.
4. Produce reports, memos, letters, and resumés from information available in the database.

Task and functions of a DSS

5. Signal exceptions (e.g., job execution times that exceed 5 percent of the standard) and analyze any data that warrant further investigation.
6. Construct simple mathematical models that describe a problem or situation as visualized by the user.
7. Perform financial analyses (e.g., consolidate financial statements) in spreadsheet form, if desired.
8. Perform analyses either with standard mathematical models (e.g., regression analysis, time-series analysis) or with specially created models.
9. Conduct optimization. DSS may use analytical methods that can be embedded in a command that makes sense to the manager. DSS may include optimization models such as linear programming. Experience indicates that nonanalytical users of DSS have no difficulty in accepting a highly complex analytical methodology when it is embedded in a DSS that is under the manager's control.[1] Thus, DSS are able to translate complex models into usable techniques for decision making. Further, if the user disagrees with the model, he or she can change it.
10. Perform simulation. One of the major advantages of DSS is the ease with which simulation can be performed. Several DSS include a prewritten routine to conduct a Monte Carlo risk analysis or a corporate planning analysis (see Chapter 16). Special simulation planning languages such as SIMPLAN™ can be incorporated into DSS.

Several other activities can be performed at the wish of the manager: special ratio analyses, comparative analyses, or the consolidation, equilization, separation, or summarization of information. All are intended to support the manager in making his or her decisions. But the greatest advantage of a DSS is the ease with which it performs a "what if" analysis.

"What if" analysis

One of the major arguments against the use of quantitative analysis in management is that the models are "unrealistic." A model is a simplification of reality. The model builder makes predictions and assumptions regard-

---

[1] For example, a DSS for setting school attendance boundaries includes a complex multiobjective linear programming optimization model. The users of the model (parents, school officials) had no difficulty in accepting the highly analytical methodology, whether or not they understood what was occurring within the DSS. (P. G. W. Keen, "Decision Support Systems: Translating Analytic Techniques into Useful Tools," *Sloan Management Review*, Spring 1980.)

ing the input data, many of which deal with the assessment of uncertain futures. When the model is solved, the results depend, of course, on these data. Sensitivity analysis attempts to check the impact of changes in the input variables on the proposed solution (the dependent variable). This type of sensitivity analysis is called **"what if"** analysis, since it is structured as: "*What* will happen to the solution *if* an input variable, an assumption, or a parameter value, is changed?"

Sensitivity analysis

Sensitivity analysis is very important since it can be used to improve confidence in the model and thus increase the rate of application and implementation of quantitative analysis. In a regular, computer-based decision system it is difficult to conduct such an analysis because the prewritten routines usually present only a limited opportunity for "what if" questions.

Sensitivity analyses may appear in several ways. For example:

- "What is the impact on the total inventory cost if there is a 10 percent change in carrying cost?"
- "What is the impact on the economic order quantity if there is a 5 percent change in ordering cost?"

The manager can ask these types of questions in English. Furthermore, he or she can change the percentage or any other data in the question as desired.

Goal seeking

Goal seeking is a property that is similar to the "what if" analysis. It has the capability of a "backward" solution of a model; that is, the manager is able to set a goal such as profit, and adjust another variable such as sales. For example, let us say that our initial analysis yielded a profit of $2 million. Management would then like to know what sales volume is necessary to generate a profit of $2.5 million, or what market share is required to achieve a 15 percent growth rate by 1990.

Backward solutions

17.7 CONSTRUCTION CONSIDERATIONS

Over the last few years, we have witnessed a slow initial implementation of DSS. In the mid 1970s, DSS were mainly used in the academic world, in industrial R&D, and in some large corporations. In the early 1980s, DSS were also found in some medium-sized organizations. Today, thanks to the microcomputer revolution, there are thousands of DSS in almost every type of organization (see Turban [14]).

Installing a large DSS requires the support of top management. In some cases, a DSS is a companywide project, not limited to one functional area such as finance. As a matter of fact, DSS are comprehensive with regard to the types of decisions supported and may be simultaneously useful for operations, finance, marketing, and other functional areas.

Two ways to construct a DSS

There are two basic approaches to the construction of a DSS. One is to do it from scratch, and the other is to construct the specific DSS from an existing DSS generator. The former approach is extremely expensive and may take a long time, while the latter is limited to existing DSS generators. The major advantage of using an existing generator is the tremendous saving in time (it may take only a few weeks) and the low cost. The cost depends on the extent of the modifications and the cost of the existing DSS generator. DSS installed on microcomputers are usually constructed with DSS generators and other such tools.

Constructing DSS from a DSS generator

Specific DSS can be constructed from a *DSS generator* supported by special *DSS tools* (see Figure 17.4).[2]

FIGURE 17.4
Constructing a DSS

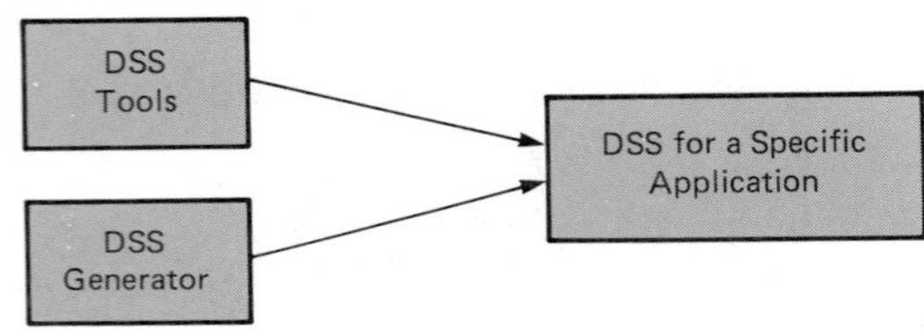

Police patrol redesign

As an example, let us look at an application of a DSS for a police patrol redesign. This system, which was implemented in San Jose, California, allows a police officer to display a map outline and call up data by geographical zone, showing police calls for service, response times, and activity levels. The officer can manipulate the map, zones, and data, and experiment with a variety of police patrol alternatives. This application, which yielded superior results (in terms of acceptance by the users and fitness to reality) over a standard linear programming model, was built from a DSS generator called geodata analysis and display system (GADS) (for details see [1] and [5]).

DSS generators

A DSS generator is a package of related hardware and software used to build a specific DSS application. For example, IBM's GADS displays a map showing the location of equipment, machines, inventories, and materials. It also shows workload by territory. In addition to the police patrol redesign application, it has been used for setting school attendance boundaries, establishing sales territories, planning equipment for fire stations, and routing copier repairmen. All the specific applications are special cases of the type of geographical resource allocation problems for which GADS was constructed.[3]

---

[2] For a complete discussion, see Turban [14], and Sprague and Carlson [12].

[3] This powerful system is still experimental and not commercially available at this time.

DSS tools

The construction of a DSS application and/or the creation of a DSS generator is facilitated by special hardware and software elements called DSS tools. These tools include special-purpose languages (such as IFPS™ and EXPRESS™), color graphics hardware, and supporting software. For example, GADS was written in FORTRAN using an experimental graphics subroutine, a laboratory enhanced color monitor, and a powerful interactive data extraction DBMS.

Special-purpose languages

Some of the DSS tools are so sophisticated that they approach an ideal DSS generator. For example, planning languages, which used to be basically modeling tools, now have strong database management capabilities. Products such as 1–2–3® from Lotus®, Symphony® from Lotus®, Framework®, and PC Express™ run on microcomputers with capabilities and features similar to (or even exceeding) those of the mainframe generators of the 1970s such as GADS. For further information, see Turban [14] and McLeod [7].

DSS software

DSS **software** is developing in several directions. One is industry oriented; for example, for hospitals (reimbursement and financial planning), banks (portfolio management), and airlines (planning and control). The other direction is functional; for example, finance, marketing, and operations management. The first category is more limited and more difficult to modify and adapt for specific use. The second category is more general. The most advertised software in this class is Interactive Financial Planning System, **IFPS**™ (see [8]).

Cost-benefit analysis

Decision support systems, as with any other new management tools, have many intangible benefits that are difficult to measure. Even tangible benefits from DSS are still difficult to assess. Therefore, a cost-benefit approach to a decision regarding the use of DSS will be almost impossible. The costs-benefits of DSS generators will probably be systemized in the near future. In other cases, the analysis must be qualitative in nature. Therefore, it is necessary to acquire top-management support for the use of DSS.

Despite the apparent success of DSS, there are reports of difficulties because of people's desire to do things as they were done in the past. Some managers would rather do things by hand; they seem afraid of using the computer directly. Therefore, implementation must be done very carefully. For a lengthy discussion on the introduction of DSS and tips for implementation, see Alter [1], especially Chapters 5–7. Supplementary discussion is given by Keen and Scott-Morton [5]. Some of these aspects are discussed in Chapter 19 of this book.

Computer fear

17.8 A GROUP DECISION SUPPORT SYSTEM (GDSS)[4]

A **group decision support system (GDSS)** is an interactive, computer-based system that facilitates solution of unstructured problems by a set of decision makers working together as a group. Components of a GDSS include hardware, software, people and procedures. These components are arranged to support a group of people, usually in the context of a decision-related meeting. Important characteristics of a GDSS can be summarized as follows:

GDSS characteristics

1. The GDSS is a specially designed system, not merely a configuration of already existing system components.
2. A GDSS is designed with the goal of supporting groups of decision makers in their work. As such, the GDSS should improve the decision-making process and/or decision outcomes of groups over that which would occur if the GDSS were not present.
3. A GDSS is easy to learn and easy to use. It accommodates users with varying levels of knowledge regarding computing and decision support.
4. The GDSS may be specific (designed for one type of problem) or general (designed for a variety of group-level organizational decisions).
5. The GDSS contains built-in mechanisms that discourage development of negative group behaviors such as destructive conflict, miscommunication, or "group think."

The definition of GDSS is quite broad and, therefore, can apply to a variety of group decision situations, including committees, review panels, task forces, executive board meetings, remote workers, and so forth. Appropriate settings for a GDSS range from an executive group meeting that occurs in a single location for the purpose of considering a specific problem (such as a merger/acquisition decision), to a sales managers' meeting held via telecommunications channels for the purpose of considering a variety of problems (such as hiring of sales representatives, product offerings, and sales call schedules).

Group information needs

Because the contexts of group decision making vary so greatly, it is useful to think of a GDSS in terms of the common group activities that, therefore, are in need of computer-based support. These are: *information retrieval,* which includes selection of data values from an existing database, as well as simple retrieval of information (including attitudes, opinions, and informal observations) from other group members; *information sharing,* which refers to the display of data to the total group on a viewing screen, or sending of data to selected group members' terminal sites for viewing; and *information use,* which involves the application of software technology (such as modeling packages or specific application programs), procedures, and group problem-solving techniques for the purpose of reaching a group decision.

---

[4] Condensed from DeSanctis and Gallupe [3].

17.9 EXAMPLES OF APPLICATIONS

AAIMS (an analytic information management system)

A classical DSS that was developed in the early 1970s is AAIMS™. It is used by several airlines for a cross section of operations, planning, marketing, and financial airline problems. For example, AAIMS has proven to be an invaluable management tool in areas such as productivity measurement, seating configuration, aircraft utilization, and load factor and operating statistics.[5] It is basically a data retrieval and forecasting system designed initially to reduce clerical work.

The *database* (Figure 17.5) includes collections of data on virtually all U.S. scheduled airlines and on over 300 major airports in the world. Data on traffic, fuel consumption, maintenance schedules, flight time, and operating expenses, for example, are available for all major types of aircraft.

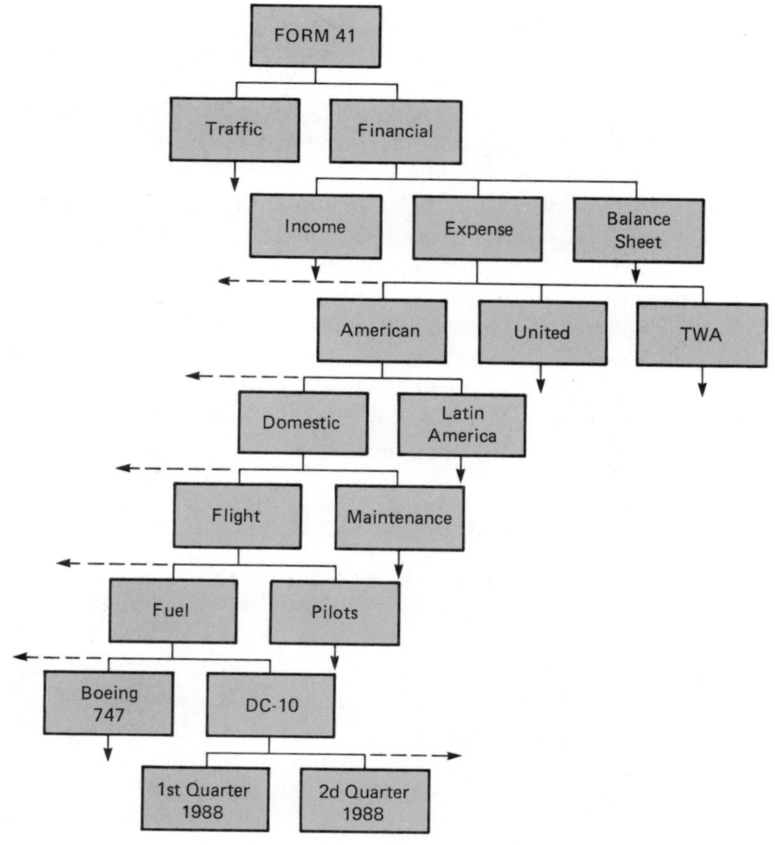

FIGURE 17.5
The data base for AAIMS

[5] For a detailed description, see Klass [6] or Alter [1]. AAIMS was developed by American Airlines and is being marketed through APL Services, Inc. (a time-sharing vendor).

In addition, the database includes financial data for the participating airlines. The primary sources for the data are the reports submitted periodically to the Civil Aeronautics Board (called Form 41).

In addition, the database includes individual users' private files. Thus, users may enter their own data, perform manipulations on it independent of, or in conjunction with, the industry files. The 1977 database contained more than 150,000 items; the database is updated monthly.

A DSS for airlines

The *model base* includes several forecasting models (such as regular and multiple regression, econometric models, moving averages, time series, trend analysis, and period over period ratios).

The AAIMS is written in APL, a flexible language that allows easy additions to the DSS software. Further, APL allows the formation of higher level languages or special-purpose "dialects" that are used to write new DSS or expand existing ones. As with most other DSS, a graphic display is an integral part of the system.

In addition to standard reports and graphs (such as "operating expenses as a percent of revenue"), it is possible to construct ad hoc reports and to get an answer to questions. For example, "What is American Airlines' domestic yield, as defined by passenger revenue divided by revenue passenger-miles, from January 1975 to date?" An interesting application of AAIMS is the collection of corporate performance and productivity indicators that include over 100 graphs, tables, ratios, and trends. In addition, a special analysis was performed in 1976–1977 in anticipation of airline deregulation. Another special analysis was the evaluation of a proposed merger. The system also monitors fuel usage; for example, trends in fuel use characteristics are compared. This DSS is also used to monitor total factor productivity. The productivity model includes inputs such as labor, maintenance, interest, and purchased goods and services, and enables management to evaluate proposals for productivity improvement as well as proposals for price and schedule changes. Data limitations thus far prevent completion of the proper mix of inputs that would maximize return on investment.

Gotaas-Larsen Shipping Corp. (GLSC)[6]

One of the most promising uses of DSS is in the area of corporate planning and control, especially in strategic (long-range) planning.

Strategic planning

Strategic planning is one of the most difficult tasks of modern management. It involves all the functional areas in the organization and several outside factors, a fact which complicates the analysis, especially when one deals with the uncertainties of the long run. With the advances in computer technology and simulation, it is possible to find more and more corporations that use some kind of quantitative analysis in their strategic management process. However, regular MIS-type systems are less effective than DSS, since they lack the "what if," on-line capabilities of DSS.

[6] Condensed from Alter [1], p. 47.

GLSC, a subsidiary of International Utilities that operates cargo ships all over the world, developed a comprehensive decision support system for executing both short- and long-term planning.

The *database* includes both external data (such as port or canal characteristics, competition, and prices) and internal data (such as existing plans, availability of resources, and individual ships' characteristics).

A DSS for shipping

The *model base* includes standard accounting financial analysis models (such as cash flow computations, pro forma income and expenses) organized on a per ship, voyage, division, and entire company basis. These models enable elaborate financial analyses. A simulation model is used to analyse alternative short- and long-term plans and projects. In addition, the system interfaces with commercially available time-sharing programs for analyzing individual voyages (time-charter analysis).

A highly decentralized, 15-month operational planning and control document is prepared within the framework of the long-term, strategic plan. This 15-month document is used as a basis for detailed goal formation for the various ships and the individual voyages. A detailed monitoring and control mechanism is also provided, including a regular variance report and diagnosis analysis. In addition, a detailed performance tracking report is executed (by voyage, ship, division, and for the entire corporation).

Charter analyses

Threat assessment

Once the assessment of the opportunity of individual projects (such as buying a ship or contracting a voyage) is examined by a charter analysis, an aggregation is performed. The objective is to determine whether a series of individually profitable projects add up to a feasible and desirable long-range plan. The DSS utilizes a simulation model that examines various configurations of projects in an attempt to conduct a "fine-tuning" of the aggregate plan. Specifically, when several projects are executed, the resources (such as financial arrangements) might be insufficient. Therefore, modifications in scheduling and financial arrangements, for example, might be necessary. This fine-tuning provides a trial-and-error approach to feasibility testing and sensitivity analysis. The "what if" capabilities of the DSS are especially important in this case. The strategic plan of GLSC is very detailed and accurate because of the contractual nature of both the sales and some of the expenses. The model is geared to a traditional business policy structure that helps in assessing the threats and risks in the general operating environment and enables an examination of the impact of new opportunities on existing plans.

Pfizer Pharmaceutical, Inc.[7]

Ten years ago, Rachelle Laboratories, Inc., Long Beach, California, a competitor of Pfizer, began selling an antibiotic called Doxychel, which appeared to be the same drug as Pfizer's Vibramycin. Pfizer contended that its patent had been violated.

[7] Condensed from M. Lasden, *Computer Decisions,* November 1983.

The disagreement came to a head in the winter of 1983 in a district court in Honolulu. Throughout the six-week trial, however, Pfizer had an edge over Rachelle. Pfizer had a DSS. Jeffrey Landau, manager of DSS at Pfizer, recalls: "We put together a team of lawyers, system-staff professionals, and others, and built a model." The model, he says, looked at one key: "what if." If Rachelle hadn't started selling Doxychel, how much more money would Pfizer have made? The answer, of course, depended on two assumptions. One was that all Rachelle's sales were at Pfizer's expense. The other was that, without Rachelle as a competitor, Pfizer could have sold its antibiotic at a higher price.

A DSS war room

Armed with these assumptions, the Pfizer team set up, three blocks from the courthouse, a DSS war room, complete with terminals, printers, plotters, and high-speed communication to a DEC System-10 mainframe in Connecticut. With the system in place, the opposition could not stall for time by requesting additional information. Pfizer's system accessed the requested information instantly.

When the trial got under way, however, Pfizer's decision support system was really put to the test. "We could measure the impact of claims witnesses made about the market. Using the information provided, the lawyers would yield on points that were determined to be insignificant. If the other side made a claim that had big monetary implications, our lawyers would fight it." In effect, the Pfizer team used the model to plan its legal tactics.

$55.8 million

The result: On June 30, 1983, Judge Martin Pence, who frequently alluded to Pfizer's model, awarded Pfizer $55.8 million. It was the largest judgment on a patent-infringement suit in U.S. history.

17.10 EXAMPLE OF A DSS GENERATOR: IFPS

The Interactive Financial Planning System (IFPS)™ is a comprehensive general DSS generator that enables planning as an extension of normal management thought processes.[8] The system was initially developed for financial and Monte Carlo simulation modeling. In practice, however, its applicability has become more general than that.

The structure of IFPS

IFPS consists of five subsystems: the executive subsystem, the modeling language subsystem, the report generator subsystem, the data file subsystem, and the command file subsystem.

The *executive subsystem* is the highest level of IFPS operation. It is used to accomplish the following activities:

---

[8] Developed by EXECUCOM System Corp. (Austin, Texas).

- Specify permanent files.
- List models and reports.
- Delete models and reports.
- Combine models.
- Consolidate models and data files.
- Copy models and reports.
- Call other subsystems.

Executive subsystem

The *modeling language subsystem* is called by issuing a MODEL command. The modeling language subsystem is the primary vehicle for analyzing the situation of interest to the IFPS user. The following activities are performed in the modeling language subsystem.

- Create new models.
- Edit models.
- Produce solutions to the model.
- Plot model results.
- Print complete reports.
- Ask "What if" questions.
- Perform goal seeking.
- Perform risk analysis.

Modeling subsystem

The *report generator subsystem* is called by issuing a REPORT command. This subsystem is used for the following purposes:

- Creation of special report definitions.
- Editing of special report definitions.

Report subsystem

The *data file subsystem* is entered by using a DATAFILE command. The data file subsystem is used for:

- Creation of IFPS data files.
- Editing and maintenance of IFPS data files.

Data subsystem

Command subsystem

The *command file subsystem* is entered by issuing a CMDFILE command. This subsystem allows the user to create stacks of commands that may be called with a single command.

Figure 17.6 gives a schematic of IFPS flow and a partial list of commands. Some typical IFPS applications are:

IFPS applications

Balance sheets	Project investment analysis
Income statements	Plant expansion
Cash budgets (cash flow projections)	Real estate evaluation
Operating budgets	Bidding analysis
Current or pro forma financial reports	Risk analysis
Spread sheet information	Discounted cash flow analysis

Forecasting
Lease versus purchase
Strategic planning
Merger and acquisition analysis
Profit planning
Budget planning
Planning market strategies
R&D project selection
Engineering cost estimation
Make or buy decisions
Cash flow projections
Capital budgeting

FIGURE 17.6
IFPS system structure and commands

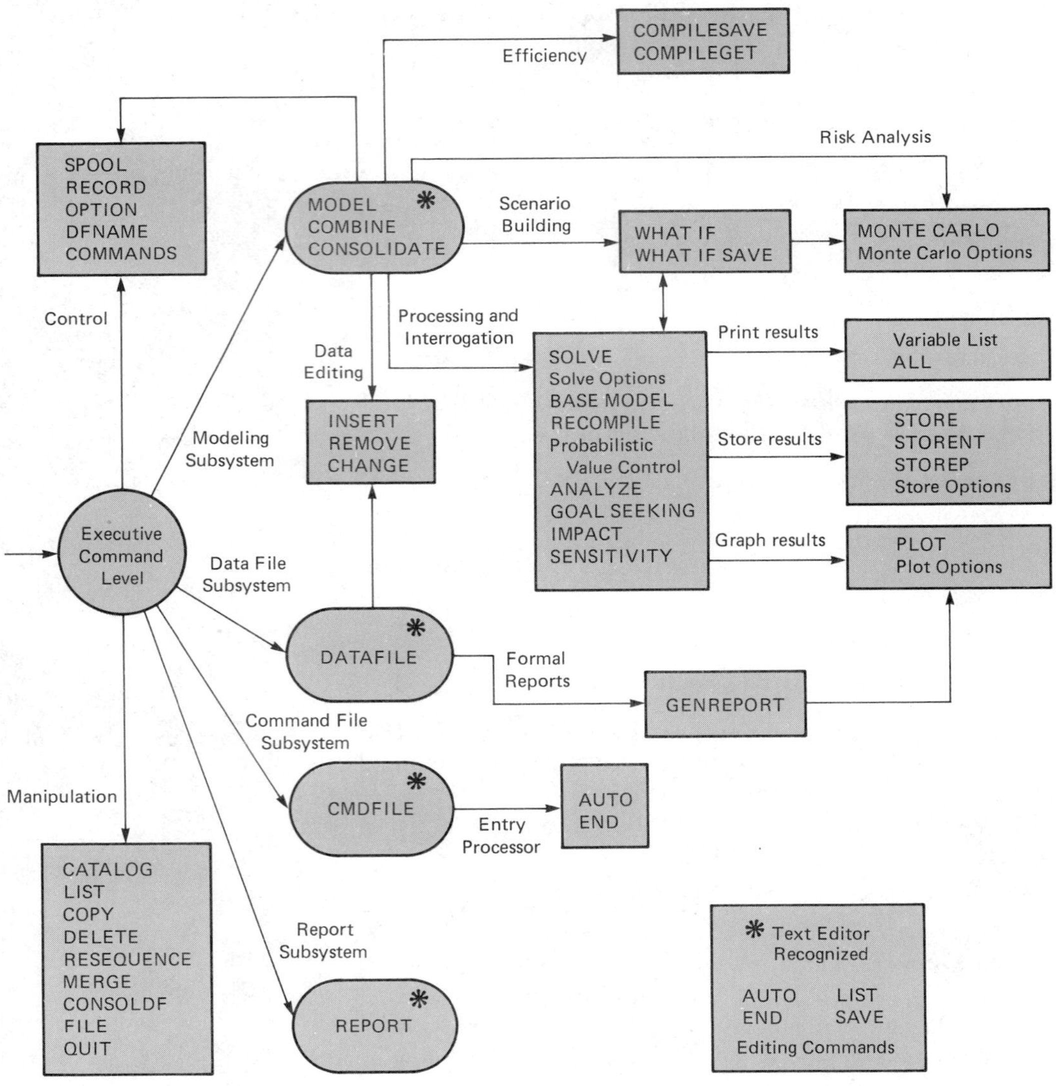

17.11 CONCLUDING REMARKS

Decision support systems can be viewed as a philosophy and a new approach to information systems design and applications. It is not at the present time a well-defined methodology with specific features and techniques. DSS can be viewed as a conceptual breakthrough because they integrate and incorporate the disciplines of MIS, management science, and management theories. As such, they should be embedded in the guidelines and policies of both information system design/evolution and mathematical model building. It is not surprising, therefore, to find a chapter on DSS both in new texts in management science and in texts on information systems and system design. The present and future capabilities of DSS will help in implementing more and more computer systems to support managerial decision making, especially at the higher levels.

DSS use management science analytical models, other quantitative models, and possibly simulation in conducting an analysis. Traditional management science and other quantitative techniques operate quite well outside DSS in many organizations. However, DSS can greatly increase the extent of applications of these techniques.

This chapter provided some guidelines as to what DSS are and their potential for management. DSS could lead eventually to the extensive use of computerized quantitative analysis in management and to the realization of John Dearden's prediction of a paperless office where the manager uses a personal computer to support his or her decisions.

17.12 REVIEW QUESTIONS

1. Define DSS.
2. List the major characteristics of DSS.
3. Trace the evolution of DSS and comment on its relation to MIS.
4. What are the major components of DSS?
5. What is a database?
6. Compare a file organization to a database.
7. Define database management system (DBMS).
8. Discuss the major capabilities of DSS.
9. What are the two options of building a DSS?
10. List the three phases of the decision-making process (according to H. A. Simon [10]).
11. List five major benefits of DSS.
12. Define structured, semistructured, and unstructured decisions.
13. Categorize managerial activities (according to Anthony [2]).
14. Discuss the major differences between DSS and MS/OR.
15. Give additional examples for each of the cells in the DSS framework.
16. Survey the literature of the last three months. Find one application each of DSS and Management Science. Summarize each application on one page, then compare the two applications.
17. Observe an organization with which you are familiar. List five decisions it makes in each of the following categories: *strategic planning; management control* (and tactical planning); and *operation planning and control.*

17.13 GLOSSARY

Ad hoc reports Reports for special purposes, nonroutine.

Database A collection of interrelated data stored together with minimum redundancy to serve multiple applications.

Database management system (DBMS) The software to establish, update, or query a database.

Decision support systems (DSS) An advanced, interactive computer system that is easy to use and quick to respond.

Extraction Organizing data from files into a database.

Goal seeking The capability of asking the computer what values certain variables must have in order to attain desired goals.

Group DSS (GDSS) A situation where a group makes decisions using a DSS.

Hardware The electrical, electronic, transistor, mechanical, and other parts of the computer and peripheral equipment.

IFPS Interactive financial planning system.

Interactive The capability of both the user and computer to ask questions and to reply to questions while the user is on-line.

Model base A collection of computer programs of various mathematical models.

On-line Connected directly to the computer.

Query language A language provided as part of a DBMS for easy access to data in the database.

Software Programs written for a computer system.

"What if" The capability of "asking" the computer what the effect will be of changing some of the input data.

17.14 REFERENCES AND BIBLIOGRAPHY

1. Alter, S. L. *Decision Support System, Current Practice and Continuing Challenges.* Reading, Mass.: Addison-Wesley Publishing, 1980.
2. Anthony, R. N. *Planning and Control Systems: A Framework for Analysis.* Boston: Harvard Business School, 1965.
3. DeSanctis, G., and B. Gallupe. "Group Decision Support Systems: A New Frontier." *Data Base,* Winter 1985.
4. Gorry, G. M., and M. S. Scott-Morton. "A Framework for Management Information Systems." Sloan Management Review, Fall 1971.
5. Keen, P. G. W., and M. S. Scott-Morton. *Decision Support Systems, An Organizational Perspective.* Reading, Mass.: Addison-Wesley Publishing, 1978.
6. Klass, R. L. "A DSS for Airline Management." *Data Base,* Winter 1977.
7. McLeod, R. Jr. *Decision Support Software for IBM Personal Computers.* Chicago: SRA, 1985.
8. Plane, D. R. *Quantitative Tools for Decision Support Using IFPS.* Reading, Mass.: Addison-Wesley Publishing, 1986.
9. Rockart, J. F., and M. E. Treacy. "The CEO Goes On-Line." *Harvard Business Review.* January–February 1982.
10. Simon, H. A. *The New Science of Management Decision.* New York: Harper & Row, 1960.
11. Sprague, R. H., Jr. "A Framework for the Development of Decision Support Systems." *M.I.S. Quarterly,* December 1980.
12. Sprague, R. H., Jr., and E. D. Carlson. *Building Effective Decision Support Systems.* Englewood Cliffs, N.J.: Prentice-Hall, 1982.
13. Sprague, R. H., Jr., and H. J. Watson, eds. *Decision Support Systems: Putting Theory into Practice.* Englewood Cliffs, N.J.: Prentice-Hall, 1986.
14. Turban, E. *Decision Support Systems and Expert Systems.* New York: Macmillan, 1988.
15. Watson, H. J.; R. H. Sprague, Jr.; and D. W. Kroeber. "Computer Technology and Information System Performance." *MSU Business Topics,* Summer 1977.

18

18.1 Introduction and basic concepts.
18.2 The structure of expert systems.
18.3 How an expert system works.
18.4 The benefits of expert systems.
18.5 The limitations of expert systems.
18.6 Expert systems and management science.
18.7 Expert systems applications.
18.8 Concluding remarks.
18.9 Review questions.
18.10 Glossary.
18.11 References and bibliography.

Decision support systems increase the boundaries of management science by permitting the analysis of unstructured complex problems. Expert systems (ES), the newest tool in the management scientist's arsenal, allow the treatment of complex problems that require human expertise for their solution. Furthermore, expert systems add a new dimension to management science by introducing symbolic processing as a substitute for, and/or complement to, numerical analysis.

Expert systems

LEARNING OBJECTIVES

The student should be able to:

a. Comprehend the basic structure of expert systems.
b. Understand and describe how expert systems work.
c. Describe the benefits and limitations of these systems.
d. Explain how management science relates to and is being aided in its implementation by ES.
e. Discuss a number of applications of ES and the benefits they have brought.
f. Sketch the general distribution of expertise in the population.
g. List the names of a variety of ES and their uses.
h. Identify the many capabilities of expert systems.

The problem

GE's top locomotive field service engineer, David I. Smith, had been with the company for more than 40 years. He was the top expert in troubleshooting diesel-electric locomotive engines. Approaching retirement, Mr. Smith was very busy traveling throughout the country to places where locomotives were in need of repair, to determine what was wrong and to advise young engineers about what to do. Being very busy, he had little time to train a successor. Should Smith retire, GE would have to rely on a younger, less trained generation of engineers, some of whom, being less loyal to the company, could move to another employer as soon as they were trained.

The traditional solution

GE's traditional approach to such a situation was to create teams that paired senior and junior engineers. The pairs worked together for several months or years, and by the time the older engineers finally did retire, the young engineers had absorbed enough of their senior's expertise to carry on troubleshooting or other tasks. This practice proved to be a good short-term solution, but GE still wanted a more effective and dependable way of disseminating expertise among its engineers and preventing valuable knowledge from retiring with the worker. Furthermore, having railroad service shops throughout the country required extensive travel, or moving the locomotives to an expert, since it was not economically feasible to have an expert in each shop.

The expert system

In 1980, GE decided to build an expert system to model the way a human troubleshooter would work. The system builders spent several months interviewing Mr. Smith and transferring his knowledge to a computer. The computer programming was developed over a three-year period, slowly increasing the information and the number of decision rules stored in the computer. Finally, the system was able to "reason" much the way an experienced locomotive engineer reasons.

The new diagnostic technology enables a novice engineer or a technician to uncover a fault by spending only a few minutes at the computer terminal. The system can also *explain* to the user the logic of its advice, thus serving as a teacher as well. Furthermore, the system can lead its users through the required repair procedures, presenting a detailed computer-aided drawing of parts and subsystems, and providing specific "how to" instructions.

The system is based on a flexible, human-like thought process rather than rigid procedures expressed in flowcharts or decision trees. The system, which was developed on a PDP 11/23 but operates on a microcomputer, is currently installed at every railroad repair shop served by GE, thus eliminating delays and boosting maintenance productivity.

Source: Condensed from P. P. Bonissone and H. E. Johnson, Jr., "Expert System for Diesel Electric Locomotive Repair." *Human Systems Management* 4 (1985).

18.1 INTRODUCTION AND BASIC CONCEPTS[1]

An **expert system (ES)** employs human knowledge captured in a computer to solve problems that ordinarily require human expertise. Well-designed systems imitate the reasoning processes of experts in solving specific problems. They can be used by nonexperts to improve their problem-solving abilities. They can also be used by experts as knowledgeable assistants. Expert systems (ES) are used to propagate scarce knowledge resources for improved, consistent results. Ultimately, such systems could function better than any single expert in making judgments in a specific, usually narrow, area of expertise (referred to as the *domain*). This possibility may have a significant impact both on advisory professionals (financial analysts, lawyers, tax advisers, and so on) and on organizations and management.

ES impact on management

The GE case introduced six basic concepts of expert systems: *expertise, experts, transferring expertise, reasoning, rules,* and *explanation capability.* These concepts will be defined in this section, with the remainder of the chapter devoted to a more detailed description and discussion of these concepts and their integration into an expert system.

Expertise

Expertise is the extensive, task-specific knowledge acquired from training, reading, and experience. The following types of knowledge are examples of what is included in expertise:

[1] Most of the material in this chapter was adapted from Turban [18] with permission.

Examples of expertise

- Facts about the problem area
- Theories about the problem area
- Hard-and-fast rules and procedures regarding the general problem area
- Rules (heuristics) of what to do in a given problem situation (i.e., rules regarding problem solving)
- Global strategies for solving these types of problems
- Metaknowledge (knowledge about knowledge)

These types of knowledge enable experts to make better and faster decisions than nonexperts in solving complex problems. It takes a long time to become expert and novices do it only incrementally.

Experts

Expert knowledge

It is difficult to define what an expert is since we usually talk about a *degree* (or a level) of expertise. Nevertheless, it has been said that the nonexperts outnumber experts in any field by a ratio of 100 to 1. Also, the distribution of expertise appears to be of the same shape regardless of the type of knowledge being evaluated. Figure 18.1 represents a typical distribution of expertise. The top 10th performs three times better than the average, and 30 times better than the lower 10th. This distribution suggests that the overall effectiveness of human expertise can be significantly increased if we can somehow make top-level expertise available to other decision makers.

The characteristics of a human expert Typically, human expertise includes a constellation of behavior that involves the following activities:

FIGURE 18.1
Distribution of expertise, percent successes achieved per decile

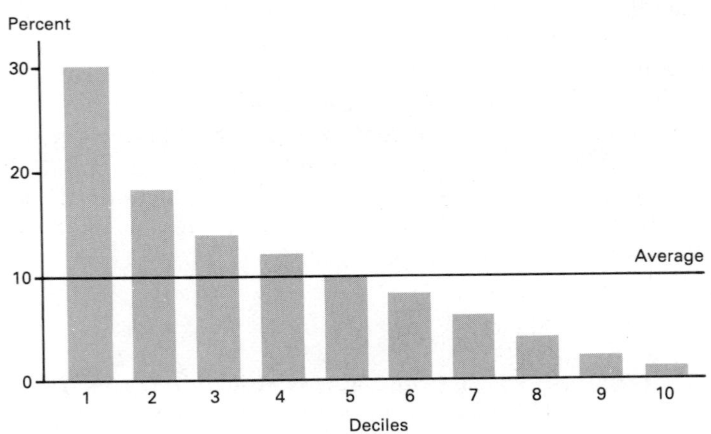

Source: Adapted from N. R. Augustine, "Distribution of Expertise," *Defense System Management*, Spring 1979.

- Recognize and formulate the problem
- Solve the problem fairly quickly
- Explain the solution
- Learn from experience
- Restructure knowledge
- Break rules
- Determine relevance
- Degrade gracefully

Expert's behavior

Experts can take a problem stated in some arbitrary manner and convert it to a form that lends itself to a fast or effective solution. Problem-*solving* ability is necessary, but not sufficient by itself. An expert should be able to *explain* the results, to *learn* new things about the domain, to *restructure knowledge* whenever needed, to *break rules* whenever necessary (i.e., know the exceptions to the rules), and to determine whether his or her expertise is *relevant*. Finally, experts *"degrade gracefully,"* meaning that as they get close to the boundaries of their knowledge, they gradually become less proficient at solving problems. All these activities must be done efficiently (fast and at a low cost) and effectively (with high-quality results).

Graceful degradation

To mimic the human expert it is necessary to build a computer that will be able to exhibit all these characteristics. To date, work in ES has primarily explored the second, third, and fourth of these activities.

Transferring expertise

The objective of expert systems is to transfer expertise from the expert to the computer, and then transfer the knowledge and advice from the machine to other humans. This process involves two activities: *knowledge acquisition* (from the experts) and *knowledge representation* (in the computer). The knowledge is stored in the computer in a component called a *knowledge base*. Two types of knowledge are distinguished: *facts* and *procedures* (usually rules) regarding the problem domain.

Reasoning

A unique feature of an expert system is its ability to reason. Given that all the expertise is stored in the knowledge base, the computer is programmed so that it can make inferences from that knowledge. The reasoning is performed in a component called the *inference engine*, which includes procedures regarding problem solving, by an approach called **symbolic reasoning.**

The inference engine

Symbolic reasoning[2] When human experts solve problems, particularly the type we consider appropriate for expert systems, they don't do it by solving sets of equations or performing other laborious mathematical computations. Instead, they choose symbols to represent the problem concepts and apply various strategies and rules to manipulate these symbols. An expert system also represents knowledge symbolically, as sets of symbols that stand for problem concepts. In **artificial intelligence (AI)** jargon, a *symbol* is a string of characters that stands for some real-world concept. Examples of symbols are:

Artificial intelligence

Product
Defendant
0.8

These symbols can be combined to express relationships between them. When these relationships are represented in an AI program, they are called *symbol structures*. The following are examples of symbol structures:

(DEFECTIVE product)
(LEASED-BY product defendant)
(EQUAL (LIABILITY defendant) 0.8)

These structures can be interpreted to mean "the product is defective," "the product is leased by the defendant," and "the liability of the defendant is 0.8."

Symbol manipulation

To solve a problem, an expert system manipulates these symbols. This is not to say that expert systems don't do math; rather the emphasis is on manipulating symbols.

Rules

Most commercial ES are rule-based; that is, the knowledge is stored mainly in the form of rules, as are the problem-solving procedures. A simple rule is structured in an if-then format. A rule in the GE case may look like this: "*IF*, the engine is idle, and the fuel pressure is less than 38 psi, and the gauge is accurate, *THEN*, there is a fuel system fault." There are about 600 such rules in the GE system.

If-then

Explanation capability

Another unique capability of an ES is its ability to explain its advice or recommendations and even to justify why a certain action was not recom-

[2] Condensed from Waterman [19].

mended. The explanation and justification is done in a subsystem called the *justifier* or the explanation subsystem. It enables the system to examine its own reasoning and to explain its operation.

Justifier

18.2 THE STRUCTURE OF EXPERT SYSTEMS

Expert systems can be viewed as composed of two major parts: the **development environment** and the **consultation environment** (see Figure 18.2). The expert system development environment is used by the ES builder to *introduce* expert knowledge into the ES knowledge base. The consultation environment is used by a nonexpert to *obtain* the expert knowledge and advice.

The following components exist in a sophisticated expert system:

ES components

- Knowledge acquisition (expert and knowledge engineering).
- Knowledge base.
- Inference engine.
- Blackboard (workplace).
- User interface.
- Explanation (justifier).
- Reasoning capability improvement (knowledge refinement).

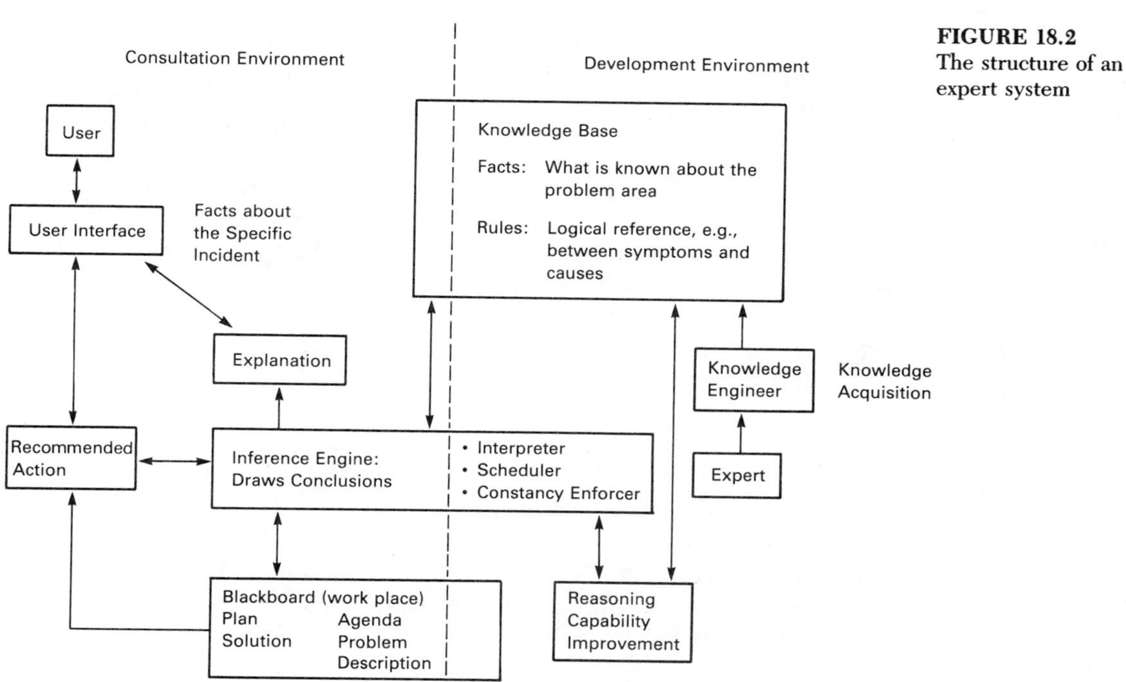

FIGURE 18.2
The structure of an expert system

Most existing expert systems do not contain the knowledge refinement component. Also, there are very large variations in the *content* and *capabilities* of each component.

A brief description of these components follows.

Knowledge acquisition subsystem

Knowledge acquisition is the accumulation, transfer, and transformation of problem-solving expertise from some knowledge source to a computer program for constructing or expanding the knowledge base. Potential sources of knowledge include human experts, textbooks, databases, special research reports, and the user's own experience.

The knowledge engineer

Acquiring the knowledge from experts is a complex task that often is a bottleneck in ES construction. The state of the art today requires a **knowledge engineer** to interact with one or more human experts in building the knowledge base. Typically, the knowledge engineer helps the expert structure the problem area by interpreting and integrating human answers to questions, by drawing analogies, posing counterexamples, and bringing to light conceptual difficulties (see Hart [6]).

The knowledge base

Heuristics

The information in the knowledge base is everything that is necessary for understanding and formulating the problem and then solving it. The knowledge base includes two basic elements: (1) *facts* (the database), for example, the problem situation and theory of the problem area; and (2) **heuristics** or rules that control the use of knowledge to solve problems in a particular domain. The heuristics express the informal judgmental knowledge of an application area. Global strategies, which can be both heuristics and a part of the theory of the problem area, are usually included in the knowledge base. Knowledge, not mere facts, is the primary material of expert systems. In addition, the knowledge base may include standard problem-solving and decision-making models. The information in the knowledge base is incorporated into a computer program by a process called **knowledge representation.**

The inference engine

The brain

The "brain" of the ES is the **inference engine,** also known as the *control structure* or the *rule interpreter* (in rule-based ES). This component is essentially a computer program that provides a methodology for reasoning about information in the knowledge base and in the blackboard, and for formulating conclusions. This component makes decisions about how to use the system's knowledge by developing the *agenda* that organizes and controls the steps taken to solve current problems.

The workplace (blackboard)

The **workplace** is an area of working *memory* set aside for description of a current problem, as specified by the input data. It is also used for recording intermediate results. Referred to as a **blackboard,** the workplace records intermediate hypotheses and decisions.

The blackboard

User interface

Expert systems contain a language processor for friendly, problem-oriented communications between the manager-user and the computer. This communication is best carried out in a *natural language,* and in some cases it is supplemented by graphics.

Explanation subsystem (justifier)

The ability to trace responsibility for conclusions to their sources is crucial both in the transfer of expertise and in problem solving. The **explanation subsystem (justifier)** can trace such responsibility and explain the ES behavior by interactively answering questions such as:

- *How* was a certain conclusion reached?
- *Why* was a certain alternative rejected?
- *What* is the plan to reach the solution? For example, what remains to be established before a final diagnosis can be determined?

Knowledge refinement

A human expert can analyze his or her own performance, learn, and improve it for future use. Similarly, such evaluation is necessary in computerized learning so that the program will be able to analyze the reasons for its success or failure. This could lead to improvements resulting in a better knowledge base and more effective reasoning. This component, **knowledge refining,** is not available in commercial expert systems at the moment. However, it is being researched as a component in experimental ES at several universities.

Self-improvement

18.3 HOW AN EXPERT SYSTEM WORKS

Three major activities take part in ES development and use: development, consultation, and improvement.

Development

The development of an expert system involves the construction of a *knowledge base* by acquiring knowledge from experts and/or from docu-

Declarative versus factual knowledge

mented sources. As stated earlier, the knowledge is both *declarative* (factual) and *procedural*. In contrast, non-AI computer-based systems include only declarative knowledge. The development activity includes the construction (or acquisition) of an inference engine, a blackboard, and an explanation facility.

The major participants in this phase are the domain expert, the knowledge engineer, and possibly information system programmers (especially if there is a need to program from scratch). The knowledge is represented in the knowledge base such that the system can draw conclusions by emulating the reasoning process of human experts.

Consultation

Bidirectional conversation

Once the system is developed, it is transferred to the users. When the user wants advice,, he or she comes to the ES, which conducts a bidirectional conversation with the user. The system asks the user to provide *facts* about the specific incident. Based on the user's answers, the ES attempts to reach a conclusion. This effort is done by the inference engine, which "decides" which heuristic search techniques should be used to determine how the rules in the knowledge base are to be applied to the problem. The user can ask for explanations (e.g., why a certain question was asked by the computer, and how certain conclusions were derived). The quality of inference capability is determined by the knowledge representation method used and by the power of the inference engine.

Improvement

The improvements include the addition of new rules (to deal with unique cases), modification of rules (to deal with changing conditions or to correct rules), and deletion of rules that are no longer relevant. The improvement task is similar to the initial development task. However, this time, the user participates in the process.

18.4 THE BENEFITS OF EXPERT SYSTEMS

Expert systems can provide major benefits to users. Potential benefits are:

Cost reduction Human expertise is very expensive when compared to a frequently used expert system.

Increased output ES can work faster than humans. For example, XCON™ (see Section 18.7) has enabled Digital Equipment Corporation (DEC) to increase fourfold the throughput of VAX computer orders. Increased output means fewer people and reduced costs.

94 percent error reduction

Improved quality ES can improve quality by providing consistent advice and reducing the error rate. For example, XCON reduced the error rate of configuring computer orders from 35 to 2 percent.

Reduced downtime Many operational ES are being used for diagnosing malfunctions and prescribing repairs. By using ES, it is possible to significantly reduce the downtime. For example, one day of lost time on an oil rig can cost as much as $250,000. (A system called "Drilling Advisor" was developed to find troubles in oil rigs.)

Capturing scarce expertise Scarce expertise is evident where there are not enough experts, the expert is about to retire or leave, or expertise is required in widespread geographical locations.

Flexibility The availability of ES could provide flexibility in providing services and making products. For example, DEC tries to make each VAX order fit the customer's needs as closely as possible.

Equipment operation ES make complex equipment easier to work with. For example, STEAMER™ is an ES intended to train inexperienced people to operate complex ships' engines.

Use of less expensive equipment There are many cases where a human must rely on expensive instruments for monitoring and control. ES can perform the same tasks with instruments of lower cost.

Operation in hazardous environments There are many tasks that require humans to operate in a hazardous environment. ES can enable the human to stay outside of the hazardous environment.

Reliability ES are reliable, they do not become tired or bored, call in sick, go on strike, or talk back. Also, ES will consistently pay attention to all details and not overlook relevant information and potential solutions.

Never tired, bored, or sick

Response time ES will respond, in some cases, much faster than a human would, especially when it is necessary to go over a large volume of data.

Working with incomplete and uncertain information In contrast to conventional computer systems, ES can, like human experts, work with incomplete information. The user can usually give a "don't know" or "not sure" answer to one of the system's questions during a consultation and the expert system will still be able to produce an answer, although it may not be a certain one.

Educational benefits ES can provide training. Novices who work with ES become more and more experienced. The explanation facility can also be used as a teaching device.

Enhancing problem solving ES enhance problem solving by allowing the integration of top experts' judgment into the analysis. ES also increase users' understanding through explanation. The systems are compatible with many managers' decision styles because of their use of judgment and symbolic, rather than numeric, information processing.

Solving complex problems in a narrow domain Expert systems can be used to solve problems whose complexity exceeds human ability. Also, some ES have been able to solve problems where the required scope of knowledge exceeds any one individual's breadth of knowledge.

The list of potential benefits is rather impressive. However there exist several limitations to the wide use of ES.

18.5 LIMITATIONS OF EXPERT SYSTEMS

Available ES methodologies seem to be straightforward and effective only for relatively simple applications in about a dozen generic categories (see Table 18.1). For applications of even modest complexity, most expert systems code is generally hard to understand, debug, extend, and maintain. Other factors and problems that slow down the commercial spread of ES are:

ES problems

- Knowledge is not always readily available.
- Expertise is hard to extract from humans.
- The approach of each expert to situation assessment may be different, yet correct.
- It is hard, even for a highly skilled expert, to abstract good situational assessments when he or she is under time pressure.
- ES work well only in a narrow domain, in some cases very narrow.
- Most experts have no independent means of checking whether their conclusions are reasonable.
- The vocabulary that experts use for expressing facts and relations is frequently limited.
- Help is frequently required from knowledge engineers who are rare and expensive, a fact that makes ES construction costly.
- The cost and/or the time of development may be a prohibitive factor.

There is currently extensive research under way to overcome the above limitations.

TABLE 18.1
Generic categories of expert systems

Category	*Problem addressed*
Interpretation	Inferring situation descriptions from sensor data
Prediction	Inferring likely consequences of given situations
Diagnosis	Inferring system malfunctions from observations
Design	Configuring objects under constraints
Planning	Developing plans to achieve goal(s)
Monitoring	Comparing observations to plan vulnerabilities, flagging exceptions
Debugging	Prescribing remedies for malfunctions
Repair	Executing a plan to administer a prescribed remedy
Instruction	Diagnosing and correcting student performance
Control	Interpreting, predicting, repairing, and monitoring system behavior

Source: F. Hayes-Roth, D. A. Waterman, and D. B. Lenat, *Building Expert Systems* (Reading, Mass.: Addison-Wesley Publishing, 1983).

18.6 EXPERT SYSTEMS AND MANAGEMENT SCIENCE

One of the most challenging sessions at the May 1984 national meeting of The Institute of Management Sciences in San Francisco was titled: "Will

Artificial Intelligence (AI) Provide the Rebirth of Management Science (MS)?" The session was chaired by Karl M. Wiig, who presented the following beliefs:

MS rebirth

- MS needs to be reborn.
- Expert Systems and natural language processors are the major branches of AI technology that will affect managerial decision making.
- MS needs ES and AI to automate decision support systems.
- MS will be combined with ES, mainly in such complex decision areas as long-range planning, socioeconomic models, and complex operational support (e.g., job shop scheduling).

In summary, Wiig concluded that ES (and other AI technologies) can and will provide the rebirth of MS.

The following issues will be discussed here:

- Expert systems as a consultant and assistant to the management scientist.
- Expert systems as a modeling tool and intelligent DSS.
- ES as a management science consultant to the manager.
- ES as a tutor.

ES as a consultant and assistant to the management scientist

Expert systems can serve the MS consultant in several ways. First, the consultant can use the computer as a source of information. Second, he or she can use the ES as a tutor, to learn the expertise of top specialists in MS or in related fields whenever a certain unique expertise is needed by the researcher. That is, in addition to (or instead of) referring to a book or an expert, the MS person will be able to consult the machine. Finally, the ES can be used as a personal assistant to execute routine activities (e.g., provide answers to routine questions and/or conduct standard training).

The consultant's consultant

Expert systems as a modeling tool and intelligent DSS

Expert systems can be used as a tool to help the researcher in modeling; for example, in constructing simulation models (see Schell [13]), in conducting a complex PERT analysis by providing estimates (see Marcus [9], or by conducting a statistical analysis (see Hand [5]).

Expert systems can be used to model situations involving symbolic processing as well as analysis. The latest support is called an "intelligent DSS" or DSS-ES.

A DSS-ES

There are many ways that an expert system can be integrated with management science models and/or a DSS. For an overview, see Turban and Watkins [17]. Some examples of such integration are described below.

Logistics Management System (LMS) Sullivan and Fordyce [16] report that IBM has constructed several integrated systems. One such system is called the *Logistics Management System* (LMS). LMS combines ES, simulation, traditional DSS, and computer-based information systems. In addition, the system includes computer-aided manufacturing and distributed data processing. The system provides IBM Burlington's manufacturing management a tool to assist in resolving a "crisis" (e.g., down machines) and in planning.

DSS/Decision Simulation (DSIM) DSIM is the outcome of combining traditional DSS, management science, statistics, database management, query capabilities, and AI. AI, especially the natural language interfaces and expert systems, provides three capabilities to DSIM:

DSIM capabilities

a. Easing the communication of pertinent information to the computational algorithm or display unit.
b. Assisting in finding the appropriate model, computational algorithm, or data set.
c. Finding a solution to a problem where the computational algorithm(s) alone is not sufficient, appropriate, or applicable.

The PAD system An ES called PAD (Procurement Assembly and Distribution), developed at the Intelligent Computers Systems Research Institute (University of Miami, Miami, Florida), integrates management science models (especially dynamic programming) into an expert system. The system provides analysis and advice for the procurement of parts for the production of PCs, assignment of plants for PCs, and assembly and allocation of finished products to worldwide distribution centers for a five-year planning horizon.

Expert systems as an MS consultant to the manager

Interesting work is being done at Oregon State University, where Goul et al. [4] have developed a DSS-ES system that replicates a manager-consultant-machine team that operates as follows: The computer attempts to diagnose the manager's problem by determining the general nature of the problem (e.g., allocation, inventory, investment—Step 1 in Figure 18.3). Once the general nature of the problem has been determined, the characteristics of the situation are analyzed and a model is jointly constructed (Step 2). For example, if Step 1 diagnosed an allocation problem, Step 2 will attempt to construct the objective function and the constraints.

The third step is the suggestion of the specific MS tool (e.g., linear programming or dynamic programming).

In Step 4, the computer uses the tool to solve the problem. Finally, a "what if" analysis can be conducted (Step 5).

A tutor

It is assumed that the decision maker is not an MS expert; therefore, the ES acts also as a nonhuman tutor with the ability to explain terminology, concepts, and computational procedures. Further, the computer can pro-

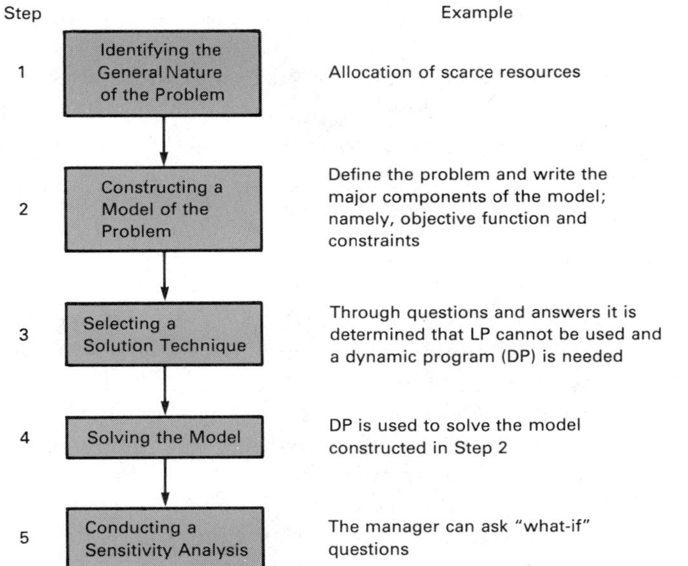

Step
Example
1
Identifying the General Nature of the Problem
Allocation of scarce resources
2
Constructing a Model of the Problem
Define the problem and write the major components of the model; namely, objective function and constraints
3
Selecting a Solution Technique
Through questions and answers it is determined that LP cannot be used and a dynamic program (DP) is needed
4
Solving the Model
DP is used to solve the model constructed in Step 2
5
Conducting a Sensitivity Analysis
The manager can ask "what-if" questions

FIGURE 18.3 Expert system as a consultant

vide a supportive bibliography, examples of typical applications, and other information as requested by the manager. In addition, the system can explain why a certain model was used and discuss the underlying assumptions.

During the man-machine interaction, the user may disagree with the logic of "why a certain action was undertaken." In such a case, the user can change the decision rules that generated the specific action.

The type of consultation given by the computer in these situations will probably be limited to fairly structured problems. For more complex problems, a combination of a manager, a human expert, and a computer will be needed, using a DSS approach.

Expert systems as a tutor

Computer aided instruction

Expert systems are intended to transfer the expert's knowledge to the computer and then to the nonexpert. It makes sense that an instructor can be viewed as an expert, while the students are not. This idea is being implemented in the area of Intelligent Computer Aided Instruction (ICAI), which is based on AI. In the past 20 years, there has been considerable progress in the area of CAI (e.g., see Kearsley et al. [8]). Lately, we have seen some evidence (e.g., [10] and [11]) of tutoring MS via expert systems.

In addition to classroom teaching, ES can be used as an on-site tutor; for example, the experience of GE's locomotive-fault ES indicated that the less experienced engineers use it as a tutor during actual field consultation.

The major advantage of an expert system as a tutor is that it can make learning an active, as opposed to a passive, process. It also can be designed to adapt to the requirements of the individual learner (e.g., speed of learning, terminology used).

18.7 EXPERT SYSTEMS APPLICATIONS

XCON (expert VAX system configuration)

Digital Equipment Corporation (DEC) has always offered its customers a very wide range of minicomputer system configurations. It is not uncommon to have thousands of customer orders on hand, each one involving different needs. This wide range of combinations creates a very complex business environment involving many interdependent decisions and tasks for processing the orders, scheduling the necessary manufacturing and other operations, and distributing computer systems to the customers in a timely manner.

Until XCON became available, the computer system configuration task was accomplished manually. Technical editors in manufacturing reviewed all customer orders for technical correctness and order completeness. This was an extremely difficult task, requiring many knowledgeable people. A dramatic increase in productivity of the technical editors has occurred due to the implementation of XCON. By 1985, all VAX family system orders in U.S. and European plant operations were configured by XCON.

Traditionally trained manufacturing technical editors required 20–30 minutes to configure each system order. In contrast, XCON can configure extremely complex systems in less than a minute. XCON also provides additional functions and capabilities not formerly performed by the traditional technical editors, such as defining the exact cable length for all cables required between each system component.

In the past, a large portion of the system orders being scheduled for the factory floor had numerous configuration errors and lacked completeness; with the use of XCON, orders have accurate configurations 98 percent of the time. Manufacturing operation benefits from accurate system configurations include an increased throughput order rate, fewer shipments delayed due to system configuration errors, and better use of materials on hand.

$15 million annual savings

DEC's system of highly skilled senior technicians has been redeployed, allowing them to address more technically difficult tasks. Cost savings to DEC are estimated at about $15 million each year. Plant management is extremely satisfied with the emerging Artificial Intelligence methodologies, and they are participating in this pioneering effort with great enthusiasm.

The company is now developing related expert systems (as shown in Figure 18.4). These systems are:

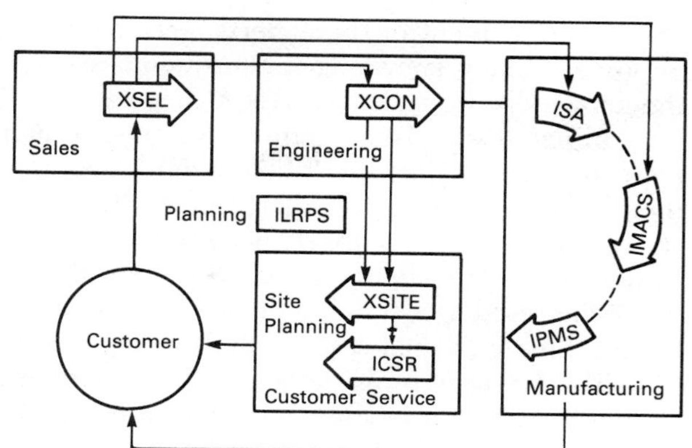

FIGURE 18.4
Expert systems network

XSEL—This system checks orders for consistency, such as making sure that the power supplies match the equipment being shipped.
XSITE—This system provides a site plan for a customer's machine room and lists the equipment needed.

Other systems are:

ISA—to aid scheduling.
IMACS—to aid manufacturing.
ILRPS—to aid long-range planning.
IPMS—to aid in project management.
ICSR—to aid in customer service.

For more information, see O'Connor [12].

A multinational insurance underwriting system

American International Group, Inc. (AIG) (New York, New York) is the nation's seventh largest insurance company (more than $11 billion in assets). The company operates in 130 countries, primarily writing tailor-made policies for major corporations. Many clients (such as aerospace companies) encounter unusual risk problems. Therefore, underwriting the policies requires experienced individuals with flexible thinking capabilities.

Development of the system The ES was developed by Syntelligence, Inc. (an AI vendor in Sunnyvale, California) for the American Home Inland Marine division. The division operates 14 offices worldwide and insures literally "anything that moves," from telecommunications signals to registered mail. When the system is fully implemented, it will be equivalent to having another top underwriter in each of the 14 offices.

Insuring anything that moves

The prototype was initially done on one product which deals with an insurance policy that covers all types of perils, including earthquakes and floods. The development took about a year, with numerous iterations, each of which improved the system's performance. By late 1985, the system covered 95 percent of the experts' knowledge and it is continually being improved. Many knowledge acquisition sessions were required to extract the knowledge from the top risk managers.

Capabilities The system is designed to help the company's staff explore how a risk manager should think about insurance risks and *price* them—which is basically what underwriters do. The AIG ES can think as top experts at AIG think. The system advises, for example, whether or not to accept a client and what the premium should be. The system is also being used as a training device for new underwriters, who work with the machine on actual cases under the supervision of a top expert.

The ES uses probabilities in its recommendations. In addition, the system takes into account geographical differences. It knows, for example, how AIG experts think about earthquake chances in Los Angeles as compared with San Francisco.

More than 100 AIG people with PCs will be able to tap into the company's mainframe and use the ES once it is completed.

Facts, issues, and lessons This is what has been learned:

- The system cost about $2 million, with a 2½-year payback period (salary savings of 14 senior risk managers at $60,000 a person).

Increase capacity instead of laying off

- Risk managers will not be fired; rather, the computer enables AIG to handle a substantially increased volume of business with existing personnel.
- Senior managers who were skeptical at the beginning now think the system is great and has much potential.
- Eight special-area experts were interviewed to ensure that expertise in diversified topics is covered.
- Once this application is operational, the company will produce prototype product lines.
- Some employees fear that ES will replace the need for human experts. Management is dealing both with the apparent fear and the possible reassignment of employees.
- Expert systems speed up corporate decision making and make it more consistent.

For further information, see Shamoon [14].

How expert systems can perform useful tasks

Suppose you manage an engineering firm that bids on many projects. Each project is, in a sense, unique. You can calculate your expected cost, but that's not sufficient to set up your bid. You have background information on your likely competitors and their bidding strategies. Something is known about the risks—possible technical problems, political delays, material shortages, or other sources of trouble. An experienced proposal manager can put all this together and, generally, arrive at a sound judgment concerning terms and bidding price. However, you do not have that many proposal managers who have the time to concentrate on preparing and negotiating major proposals.

This is where expert systems become useful. A knowledge-based bid support system can capture the lines of thinking the experienced proposal managers follow. It can also catalog information gained on competitors, local risks, and so on, and incorporate your policies and strategies concerning risk, pricing, and terms. It can even help your younger managers work through to an informed bid consistent with your policy.

Suppose you are a life insurance agent and a very good one; however, your market has changed. You are no longer competing only with other insurance agents. You also are competing with banks, brokers, money market fund managers, and the like. Your company is now pushing a whole array of products, from universal life insurance to venture capital funds. Your clients have the same problems as ever, but they are more inquisitive, more sophisticated, and more conscious of tax avoidance and similar considerations. How can you give them advice and put together a sensible package for them when you are more confused than they are?

Financial planning systems and estate planning guides have been part of the insurance industry's marketing kit for a long time. However, sensible financial planning takes more skill than the average insurance agent has or can afford to acquire. This is one reason why the fees of professional planners are as high as they are. A number of insurance companies are currently investing heavily in artificial intelligence techniques in the hope that these techniques can be used to build sophisticated, competitive, knowledge-based financial planning support systems to assist their agents in helping their clients.

Source: Publicly disclosed project description of Arthur D. Little, Inc.

18.8 CONCLUDING REMARKS

Expert systems can be viewed as a powerful tool in the arsenal of the management scientist. But they are much more than that. The integration of an intelligent component into MS could provide the catalyst to revitalize the MS field, which will emerge as an even more prominent and rewarding discipline with many benefits to organizations. It seems that there is an evolution of management science toward DSS and continuing toward expert systems. This evolution, which is discussed by Wynne [20], could greatly expand the scope of MS operations. Using ES, the MS field could deal with complex problems of strategy that are of great interest to top executives. Further, as Wynne concluded, we should view the MS-DSS-ES relationship as sequential steps along the same path, with each step dominating some parts of the previous one. For example, DSS dominate MS by moving less structured situations from the MS world into the framework of DSS. Similarly, expert systems will dominate DSS in applications where human judgment needs to be extended rather than merely regularized.

Since the aims of MS and ES are similar (supporting decision making), there is a potential for cooperation and cross fertilization. Indeed, there exist several research topics that are of mutual interest to both MS and ES; for example, multicriteria objectives, combining probabilistic information, rule-based situation/action, and real-time systems operations. Thus, joint research should be developed between management scientists and ES specialists.

18.9 REVIEW QUESTIONS

1. Explain how ES can distribute (or redistribute) the available knowledge in an organization.
2. Based on Figure 18.1, estimate the percentage of knowledge that is possessed by the top 30 percent of experts.
3. List the types of knowledge that are included in "expertise."
4. List and describe the eight activities that human experts perform. Which activities are performed well by current expert systems?
5. Which component of the ES is primarily responsible for reasoning capability?
6. List and define the major components of an ES.
7. List and discuss three characteristics of expert systems.
8. List and discuss three benefits of expert systems.
9. What is the function of the justifier?
10. List the four types of potential users of an ES.
11. Define the ES development environment and contrast it with the consultation environment.
12. Explain why it is said that ES make mistakes; what kind of mistakes do they make and why?
13. Define symbolic reasoning and contrast it with nonsymbolic reasoning.
14. Describe the manner in which ES can assist the management scientist.
15. Describe the manner in which ES can be used as a modeling tool.
16. "Expert systems, being a consultant to the manager, may replace the management scientist." Speculate on such a possibility.
17. Explain how ES is used for training.

18.10 GLOSSARY

Artificial intelligence The behavior of a computer programmed to react to situations in much the same manner as a human being would.

Blackboard A globally accessible database used in expert systems for recording intermediate, partial results of problem solving.

Consultation environment The part of the expert system that is used by the nonexpert to obtain expert knowledge and advice. It includes the workplace, inference engine, explanation facility, recommended action, and user interface.

Development environment The part of the expert system that is used by the builder. It includes the knowledge base, the inference engine, and improving reasoning capability. The knowledge engineer and expert are considered a part of this environment.

Expert systems (ES) Computer systems that achieve high levels of performance in task areas that, for human beings, require years of special education and training.

Expertise The set of capabilities that underlies the high performance of human experts, including extensive domain knowledge and heuristic rules that simplify and improve approaches to problem solving.

Explanation subsystem (justifier) The component of an expert system that can explain the system's reasoning and justify its conclusions.

Heuristics The informal, judgmental knowledge of an application area that constitutes the "rules of good judgment" in the field. Heuristics also encompass the knowledge of how to solve problems efficiently and effectively, how to plan steps in solving a complex problem, how to improve performance, and so forth.

Inference engine The component of an expert system that controls its operation by selecting (in a rule-based system) the rules to use, accessing and executing those rules, and determining when an acceptable solution has been found. This component sometimes is called the "control structure" or the "rule interpreter."

Knowledge acquisition The extraction and formulation of knowledge derived from experts and documented sources.

Knowledge engineer An AI specialist responsible for the technical side of developing an expert system. The knowledge engineer works closely with the domain expert to capture the expert's knowledge in a knowledge base.

Knowledge refining The ability of the program to analyze its own performance, learn, and improve it for future consultations.

Knowledge representation A formalism for representing, in the computer, facts and rules about a subject or specialty.

Symbolic reasoning Use of symbols rather than numbers combined with rules of thumb (or heuristics), in order to process information and solve problems.

Workplace See Blackboard.

18.11 REFERENCES AND BIBLIOGRAPHY

1. Augustine, N. R. "Distribution of Expertise." *Defense System Management,* Spring 1979.
2. Bonissone, P. P., and H. E. Johnson, Jr. "Expert System for Diesel Electric Locomotive Repair." *Human Systems Management* 4 (1985).
3. Feigenbaum, E., and P. McCorduck. *The Fifth Generation*. Reading, Mass.: Addison-Wesley Publishing, 1983.
4. Goul, M., et al. "Designing the Expert Component of a Decision Support System." Paper presented at the ORSA/TIMS meeting, San Francisco, May 1984.
5. Hand, D. J. "Statistical Expert Systems: Design." *Statistician,* December 1984.
6. Hart, A. *Knowledge Acquisition for Expert Systems*. New York: McGraw-Hill, 1986.
7. Hayes-Roth, F., D. A. Waterman, and D. B. Lenat. *Building Expert Systems*. Reading, Mass.: Addison-Wesley Publishing, 1983.
8. Kearsley, G., et al. "Two Decades of Computer-Based Instruction Projects: What Have We Learned?" *T.H.E. Journal,* January 1983.
9. Marcus, R. "An Application of Artificial Intelligence to Operations Research." *Communications of the ACM,* October 1984.
10. Miller, M. "Learning-Oriented Expert Systems." Paper presented at the ORSA/TIMS meeting, Dallas, November 1984.
11. Movassaghi, K., and C. Vinyangkoon. "Computer-Aided Instruction in Linear Programming: CALIP." Paper presented at the ORSA/TIMS meeting, Dallas, November 1984.
12. O'Connor D. E. "Using Expert Systems to Manage Change and Complexity in Manufacturing." in *Artificial Intelligence Application for Business,* ed. Reitman W.N.J.: ABLEX Publishing, 1984.
13. Schell, G. P. "Developing Expert Systems for Simulation." Paper presented at the ORSA/TIMS meeting, Dallas, November 1984.
14. Shamoon, S. "The 'Expert' that Thinks Like an Underwriter." *Management Technology,* February 1985.
15. Simon, H. A. *The Sciences of the Artificial*. Cambridge, Mass.: MIT Press, 1981.

16. Sullivan, G., and K. Fordyce "The Role of Artificial Intelligence in Decision Support Systems." Paper presented at the International Meeting of TIMS, Copenhagen, Denmark, June 1984.

17. Turban, E., and P. Watkins. "Integrating Expert Systems and Decision Support Systems." *MIS Quarterly,* June 1986.

18. Turban, E. *Decision Support and Expert Systems.* New York: Macmillan, 1988.

19. Waterman, D. A. *A Guide to Expert Systems.* Reading, Mass.: Addison-Wesley Publishing, 1985.

20. Wynne, B. "A Domination Sequence—MS/OR; DSS; and the Fifth Generation." *Interfaces,* May–June 1984.

19

Implementation

19.1 What is implementation?
19.2 Project viability.
19.3 Other project particulars.
19.4 Organizational factors.
19.5 Operational factors.
19.6 Behavioral factors.
19.7 Implementation failure: A case study.
19.8 Concluding remarks.
19.9 Review questions.
19.10 Case—Sunrise Electronics.
19.11 Glossary.
19.12 References and bibliography.

The success of implementation depends first of all on the value of the project itself. The following factors, or particulars, that determine the value of the project are discussed in the first half of this chapter.

1. The economic viability of the project.
2. Its priorities and timing.
3. The availability of financing (cash flow).
4. The organization of the project and the operations involved.

The second half of the chapter discusses those organizational factors relating to implementation that are independent of the particular project at hand. The organizational aspects are divided into three parts: those relating solely to the organization, those relating to operations, and behavioral factors. Together, these constitute what is called the implementation climate. The chapter ends with a brief case illustrating some of the real-life difficulties in implementation.

LEARNING OBJECTIVES

The student should be able to:

a. Define the term *implementation.*
b. List and discuss the roots of the implementation problem.
c. Define the terms *project particulars* and *implementation climate.*
d. Describe the concept of project viability.
e. Describe the operational aspects of implementation.
f. Realize the importance of top-management support.
g. Recognize the mode and structure of MS units in organizations.
h. Describe the supportive role of computers.
i. Define the concept of life cycle in implementation.
j. Define the concept of organizational validity.
k. Recognize the role of politics and ethics in implementation.
l. Describe the relationship between the management scientist and the manager.
m. Define the term *cognitive style.*
n. Recognize the behavioral factors that have an impact on implementation.
o. Define the term *innovation boundary* and its relationship to implementation.

19.1 WHAT IS IMPLEMENTATION?

Machiavelli astutely noted over 400 years ago that there was "nothing more difficult to carry out, nor more doubtful of success, nor more dangerous to handle, than to initiate a new order of things." The implementation of a proposed MS solution is, in effect, the initiation of a new order of things, or in modern language—*the introduction of a change.* The difficulties pointed out by Machiavelli are the major concern of this chapter.

The introduction of change

The definition of implementation is somewhat complicated, since implementation is a long and involved process whose boundaries are vague. In a simplistic manner, *implementation* can be defined as putting a recommended solution to work. Implementation can also be defined as "the manner in which the results of scientific effort may come to be used by the manager."

There is a distinction between two classes of implementation. First, there are the routine, programmed problems for which prototype models exist. These include, for example, certain allocation problems that are solvable with the aid of linear programming. For such problems, implementation means a commitment to routine and frequent use of the model, or **institutionalization.**

Institutionalization

Second, for ill-structured, one-shot–type decisions, implementation means simply the one-time use of the recommended solution.

One way to treat implementation is to view it not as an independent topic but as a *continuing step* in the MS approach to decision making and problem solving; that is, the activities performed from the time a study is begun by the management scientist to the time the recommendation is executed.

Is implementation a problem?

Several researchers (e.g, Huysmans [16]) believe that managers often receive little or no benefit from management science. One reason is that there exists a significant gap between MS recommendations and their actual execution.

No benefit?

Not all analysts share this view. Some believe that there is no real problem. Wagner, for example, believes that implementation is much easier than it was in 1960 ([36]), and that the only factor really needed for successful MS applications is the joint exercise of good judgment by both executives and analysts.

There is very little evidence to substantiate the real extent and magnitude of the implementation problem. Actual information on the subject is a closely held secret in organizations, expecially when thousands of dollars have been spent on unimplemented projects.

Of the available evidence, the results published by Turban [35], in his study of corporate headquarters, indicated that 35.4 percent of all projects were completely implemented, 21.4 percent were mostly implemented, 20.4 percent had some parts implemented, 4.4 percent had very few implemented parts, 11.4 percent were not implemented, and 7 percent were not yet clear. These findings show that one should talk in terms of *degree* of implementation rather than complete success or failure.

The degree of implementation

Whose problem is implementation?

Is implementation a problem of the management scientist or the manager? Implementation may not appear to be of direct concern to the scientist, but it should be. As Churchman et al. point out [6], adjustments, frequently essential for implementation of MS solutions, should not be entrusted to those who do not have a thorough understanding of the problem and its mode of solution!

Implementation should be important to scientists for another reason. The lower the rate of successful implementation, the smaller the chances are for the scientist to develop or even to survive. For this reason, implementation is an integral part of many MS projects, even in the initial stages.

Approaches to the study of implementation

The major difficulty of studying implementation is its dependence on a multiplicity of interrelated factors. A survey by Watson and Marett [37] identified 10 categories of such factors (see Table 19.1). The majority of the studies of implementation deal with only one or, at most, a few of these factors, which can be classified into two primary groups:

TABLE 19.1
Categories of implementation problems

	Problems in implementing management science	*Percentage of respondents*
1.	Selling MS methods to management.	35
2.	Lack of adequate educational background by top and middle management to appreciate MS methods.	34
3.	Lack of good clean data.	32
4.	Insufficient time to analyze a real problem with sophisticated methods.	23
5.	Lack of understanding by users.	22
6.	Difficulty in defining problems for applications.	19
7.	Sufficient existing payoff for unsophisticated methods.	16
8.	Shortage of personnel.	12
9.	Poor reputation of management scientists as problem solvers.	11
10.	Individuals feeling threatened by MS.	10

Source: H. J. Watson and P. G. Marett, "A Survey of Management Science Implementation Problems," *Interfaces,* August 1979, p. 125.

Two groups of factors

1. Those aspects directly related to an individual project or problem (labeled *project particulars*).
2. The general conditions surrounding implementation in an organization. These conditions are termed the *implementation climate.*

In general, the degree and/or probability of implementation is a function of both. The major elements of each of these two perspectives are shown in Figure 19.1.

Project particulars

Of the various project particulars that are discussed in this chapter, the project viability (Section 19.2) is probably the most important. Other factors, discussed in Section 19.3, are timing and priority, availability of financing, and operations.

The implementation climate

Climate is project independent

Implementation climate, as viewed in this text, includes all those factors that determine the success of implementation but are not related to a *particular* project. These factors are divided into three classes:

Organizational factors (Section 19.4)

1. The support of top management.
2. The place of MS in the organizational structure.
3. The size of the MS unit.
4. The internal structure of the unit.
5. The information system and the availability of computers.

FIGURE 19.1
The implementation process

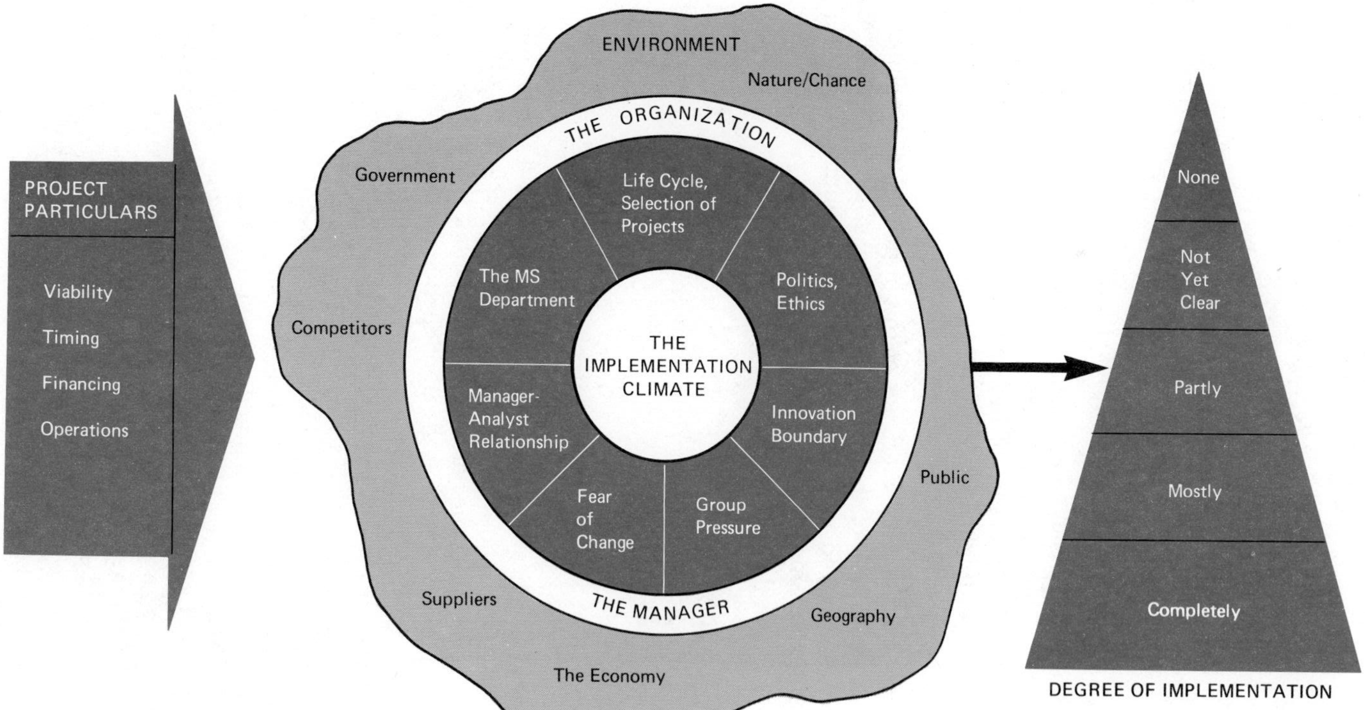

Operational factors (Section 19.5)

1. The selection of projects—life cycle.
2. The selection of projects—organizational validity.
3. Organizational politics.
4. Values and ethics.

Behavioral factors (Section 19.6)

1. The analyst-manager relationship.
2. The fear of change.
3. The pressure of the work group.
4. Individual innovation.
5. The role of computerized management information systems.

The characteristics of the implementation climate are much broader than those of the usual *organizational climate*. Organizational climate can be viewed as a *part* of the implementation climate; it is basically the expression of behavioral factors and can be defined as:

> A set of properties of the work environment perceived directly[1] or indirectly[2] by the employees therein. Climate appears to be an influential force.

19.2 PROJECT VIABILITY

An MS proposal can be viewed as a course of action recommended by the analyst for implementation. As such, it should show a clear advantage over any other alternative, including that of "doing nothing." Therefore, implementation is greatly dependent on the ability to show such advantage.

Each alternative requires an investment of resources (including money) which can be viewed as the costs in the system, in exchange for some expected benefit(s) yielded.

Cost-benefit analysis

The **project viability** is determined by comparing the costs with the anticipated outputs. This comparison is termed a **cost-benefit** (or *effectiveness*) **analysis.** In practice, such an analysis may become rather complicated. One or more of the following reasons may account for this.

1. Cost valuation The cost of a project seems, at least at first sight, easy to identify and quantify. In practice, it is often difficult to relate costs to projects in an exact way. Allocation of overhead cost is an example. Should it be allocated by volume, activity level, or value? What about future costs? A well-known "game" is to show the advantages of a certain

---

[1] This can be measured through attitudes; for example, by questionnaires (see Litwin and Stringer [21]).

[2] Examples of indirect measures of climate are turnover rate, absenteeism rate, and number of complaints.

alternative "neglecting" future costs. There are additional accounting complications such as the impact of taxation and the selection of a proper interest rate for present value analyses.

Neglecting future costs

2. ***Benefit valuation*** The assessment of costs is not easy, but the assessment of benefits is even more difficult. First, some benefits are intangible. Second, one frequently cannot precisely relate a benefit to a single cause. Third, results of a certain action may be felt over a long period, showing up in different times and quantities. Fourth, a valuation of benefits includes the assessment of both quantity and quality. The latter is difficult to measure, especially when services are involved. Fifth, the multiplicity of consequences can pose a major problem for quantification. Also, some consequences, such as goodwill, inconvenience, waiting time, and pain are extremely difficult to valuate. (What is the cost of a trouble that "ages you by a year" overnight?).

3. ***Partial implementation*** Also, decisions are frequently made on the basis of the return shown if *total* implementation is achieved rather than the more likely 90, or even 70, percent effective implementation. Clearly this will be misleading to management. The general reason for less than 100 percent implementation is that a change introduced at one point in a system usually precipitates a compensatory change (or changes) elsewhere. This may thus force management to drop some parts of the proposal.

70 percent effective

4. ***Payback period*** Management often will insist on a very short payback period (e.g., two years), which only considers the tangible benefits. Ignoring longer term intangible benefits, such as competitive advantage, can do permanent harm to a firm.

19.3 OTHER PROJECT PARTICULARS

Timing and priorities

Two important factors in implementation are the timing and the priority of the project. For example, the analyst may find that an issue of prime importance at the time the study was undertaken is not as important at implementation time for several reasons. First, changes in the surrounding environment may have an impact on the importance of the problem, the costs, or the benefits involved. Second, errors could have been made in an initial assessment. Finally, other studies may indicate that more urgent or more profitable projects should be considered first.

Timing and priority are almost uncontrollable factors as far as the analyst is concerned. For example, energy-saving projects developed in 1981 were canceled in 1983 due to the oil glut. However, the analyst may be able to predict some of the problems and defer or adjust the implementation of the project. On the other hand, timing may help implementation. For example, a project to increase the capacity of a refinery

Oil shortage, oil glut

that was rejected in 1973 was implemented in 1974 due to the energy crisis.

Availability of financing

All required financing, cash flows, identification of sources, and assurances of funds should be planned in advance. Commitments should be secured so that money will be available when needed. Lack of appropriate financing is cited by many analysts as a major obstacle to implementation.

Operations and resources

Several practical questions should be answered regarding the project prior to its implementation. For example:

Some questions

- Who will be responsible for executing each portion of the project?
- When must each part be completed?
- What resources (in addition to money) will be required?
- What information is needed?

In brief, a complete planning document for implementation should be prepared. Based on the answers to these questions, operating procedures can be designed and any necessary training and transitions can be planned beforehand so that they do not become problems to implementation later.

19.4 ORGANIZATIONAL FACTORS

The aware organization may well ask "What's the best way of organizing our MS department to aid in achieving successful implementation?" Certain areas, described next, can be identified that will help provide an answer.

The support of top management

Top support crucial

Top-management support is demonstrated by the status and backing given by the president and senior officers to the MS unit, their willingness to wait for results, and by the resources allocated to the MS operation. Without sufficient support, the cooperation of the affected operating managers is difficult to obtain and the fate of MS is questionable.

The place of MS is the organizational structure

The management science unit is usually a staff unit. The higher the status accorded it, the better the chances for successful implementation. One possibility is to organize MS with information systems as a systems department that reports to a senior vice president or to the president.[3] It could also be included in the research and development department, in the industrial engineering department, or in the finance and control department.

The size of the department

A safe rule for the size of the department is "a few at first." Too large a group appears a luxury to budget-minded managers. Growth should come with success, but before either occurs, a natural flow of communication and a proper allocation of work should be decided within the group. **A few at first**

For many companies starting an MS unit, an experienced employee supervising one or perhaps two other employees would constitute an effective group. A one-person MS group is probably too small for effective action, since only one person usually lacks the interdisciplinary expertise required.

The internal structure of the MS unit and its mode of operation

The leader of the MS unit and the way the unit is organized and operates are of utmost importance. In a study conducted in large U.S. corporations [35], it was found that about one third of all the directors of MS units hold a doctorate degree. Competency and high educational level are necessary not only for the directorship; management science should be viewed as a unit of experts. Internally, the unit should be flexible, with an organized communication system and a clear delegation of authority and responsibility. The mode of operations should be efficient, planning and control procedures should be clear, and customers should receive first-class treatment. **PhD director**

The relationship to the information system and computers

The MS unit should be integrated into the organization's *information system.* The information system must be capable of providing current as well as historical data to the analyst. By continuously monitoring the information flow to detect changes in basic model assumptions, managerial priorities, environmental constraints, and other pertinent information, the analyst can increase the likelihood of implementation significantly.

The nature of the information system is also important to implementation; typically, an accounting information system does not provide sufficient data for MS purposes. Of more use are *decision support systems* (DSS,

[3] A study [35] of MS units in the headquarters of large corporations showed that 10 percent of the MS directors report directly to the president and 75 percent to vice presidents. The study also indicated that 23.4 percent of all MS departments in large U.S. corporations are part of the information systems division.

Tied in to the MIS

discussed in Chapter 17), *expert systems* (ES, Chapter 18), and *management information systems* (MIS) whose purpose is to generate, collect, store, process, retrieve, and report data as required by management.

One of the most important properties of DSS is their ability to translate complex analytical models into usable techniques for the decision maker. This is done through:

a. The interactive structure of DSS, which allows the manager to ask questions.
b. The ability to graphically display results and conduct a sensitivity analysis on the screen.
c. The *participation* of the manager in the decision process through dialogue between the user and the system.

An important part of DSS and MIS, especially to the MS analyst, is the computer. The computer allows the analyst to quickly solve very large problems that were previously impossible (or impractical) to solve by hand. In addition, many general computer packages are available either from the manufacturer or through SHARE for such models as linear programming, inventory control, and PERT.[4] Also, hundreds of micro-computer programs are now available off-the-shelf at reasonable cost. To facilitate model building, some specialized codes are also available. The best known of these are the simulation languages: GPSS,™ SIMSCRIPT,™ and DYNAMO™ (micro versions are also available).

GIGO

For all the advantages of computers, there are shortcomings. If the input data is inaccurate, the output data will also be—a phenomenon responsible for the acronym GIGO (garbage-in, garbage-out). This becomes particularly important in view of the human tendency to believe anything on a computer printout. Furthermore, the superior capabilities of the computer do sometimes result in correspondingly super mistakes. Thus, the large likelihood of a person making a small error has been replaced with the smaller likelihood of a computer making a gigantic one (as evidenced by the occasional clerk whose weekly payroll check suddenly jumps to $175,000).[5]

19.5 OPERATIONAL FACTORS

The selection of projects—life cycle

Proper *project selection* can be an important determinant of the success of implementation. In many cases, MS units have a certain degree of freedom in selecting and/or soliciting problems for study. Researchers at Northwestern University (see Radnor et al. [29]) have described the relation-

[4] SHARE is a national library of computer programs.

[5] Computers actually do not make mistakes. The mistakes are made by the programmers or the operators.

ship between the selection of projects and the integration of an MS unit into the organization in terms of the three phases of a "life cycle," as explained below.

Life cycle

Introductory phase In this phase, the MS unit is accepted by management only on a trial basis. It is apparent that success is a "must" in this critical phase if the unit is to survive. As a result, only projects with a high probability of success should be selected. That is, projects that take a relatively short time to complete, are technologically simple, and demonstrate high potential cost savings. The primary objective is to impress both top management (the sponsors) and line management (the users) with results that are immediate and highly visible. Another motivation for selecting relatively small problems is that these usually require a smaller task force and fewer demands on management, thus facilitating the establishment of initial communications.

Transitional phase Based on initial success, the MS unit can continue on a full-scale basis. No formal commitments have been made yet, although the attitude toward it is somewhat less skeptical than in the previous phase. This time, however, the expectations are higher and small results will not be sufficient to provide the necessary "push" toward the third phase of the life cycle. Since somewhat larger and possibly less visible projects are involved, the group must educate both users and sponsors in what to expect. By working together with the MS unit, line and top managers learn about different ways of thinking about problems and may begin to appreciate some of the MS concepts being used. In turn, the joint work benefits the analysts in assessing management's needs. If significant results are obtained, and functional channels of communications have been established, a further gain in status results.

Permanent phase At the successful completion of the transitional phase, the MS group is now established as a formal, permanent part of the organization. The immediate pressure to perform is off, and more difficult projects may be attempted. However, it is advisable to maintain a "portfolio concept"; that is, have a balance of projects that require various amounts of time and resources and are visible and difficult to different degrees. Only then will the group always have a "recent success" on hand to help justify longer term projects.

Portfolio concept

The selection of projects—organizational validity

The concept of **organizational validity** developed by Schultz and Slevin [32] implies that for an MS project to be implemented, it must be compatible with, or "fit," that organization. This fit *must* occur at three levels: individual, small group, and organizational. If an MS project requires an extraordinary amount of change in individual attitudes, small group dynamics, or organizational structure (i.e., there is no fit), then the probability of successful implementation will be reduced. Of the three, individual attitudes are

Organizational fit

the most difficult to measure, but this can be done, in part, with the aid of a special questionnaire that Schultz and Slevin developed.

Organizational politics

Of all the factors that determine implementation, the most interesting and, in many cases, the most important one, is organizational politics—present in any organization. This is often underestimated or ignored. The Research Institute of America [30] reports that office politics is on the increase, at a tremendous cost to the individual as well as the organization. Chew [5] notes that "surveys show that organizational politics are becoming more and more ruthless—and back stabbing is an accepted hazard of an executive's life."

Back stabbing

Organizational growth usually results in an initial allocation of power, influence, and authority, followed by a temporary stability (similar to "detente"). The implementation of an MS project often threatens this equilibrium by giving some individual(s) and/or group(s) greater power or status. Therefore, those who think that the balance of power will be changed to their disfavor will oppose the project.

This is where "politics" frequently enters the picture. The most insidious and detrimental, but best camouflaged politics are typically played at the upper levels of management. The reasons are usually to maintain divisions of power, or cover the fact that the executive has become incompetent in a position where the job has outgrown him or her. Politics are also employed at lower levels of the organization, of course. Here, however, the younger employees are typically involved for reasons of self-interest such as money, prestige, or job security.

To some extent, it thus appears that the analyst may be well advised to become involved, learn the rules, and find where the power centers and cliques are in order to gain support. An important question the analyst may eventually have to face is whether or not he or she can even remain neutral.

Is neutrality possible?

In summary, politics, due to established managers' natural resistance to change, may be the greatest force opposing the implementation of any MS project. However, such politics appear to be minimal in hard-driving, low-overhead companies, since less time is available and power positions are less solidified. There is also the possibility that some managers will play politics to *help* implement a project because they see it as an opportunity to fulfill their own interests. Playing politics is always a dangerous tactic, however.

Values and ethics

The researcher, as a human being, should consider the ethics and values that are involved in implementing an MS project. The following points are of importance:

*1. **Goals of the MS project*** Since the process of implementation is an attempt to attain certain goals, the analyst should decide in his or her own mind whether the ultimate goals desired are ethical. For example, Japan's attempt to acquire IBM's secrets was prosecuted as a criminal case and Toshiba's recent sale of highly advanced, restricted computerware to the Soviets required a public apology to the American people. The analyst should also check if the goals are ethical to those people crucial to the implementation process.

Secrets and apologies

*2. **Implementation process*** Another question the analyst should address is whether he or she considers it ethical to effect the implementation. That is, the goals may be ethical, while the implementation process itself is not. Examples are attempting to attain a sales goal via violation of government antitrust law; dumping toxic materials; bribes; and so on.

Bribes

*3. **Possible impact on the system and on other systems*** The probable impacts on other systems should also be considered. That is, the goals and process may both be ethical, but the probable outcome of the implemented project on the system of interest, or on another system, may not be. For example, a public transit system may drive a railroad company out of business.

Before undertaking a project, the analyst should be certain he or she understands what the manager's goal *really* is and whether the project involved will actually fulfill it. For example, if the proposed project is a new rapid transit system for a city, is the mayor motivated by a desire to improve the traffic flow in the city or is the mayor really interested in bringing a "progressive" image to the administration? Assuming the former is indeed the case, could the traffic flow be improved by merely rerouting certain streets or is the proposed project in order?

19.6 BEHAVIORAL FACTORS

This is an extensive field in its own right and we will only touch upon some of the high points. For further information consult the bibliography [3, 7, 8, 9, 16, 20, 33, 34].

Analyst-manager relationships

Churchman and Schainblatt [8] have laid out a matrix that helps to explain the type of relationship that may exist between the analyst and the manager. Four possibilities, represented by the four cells of the matrix in Table 19.2, may be considered.

Position $A'B'$ is called the *separate function position*. This position represents the approach that it is up to the analyst to present a project (or a change) with detailed instructions on how to implement it. The manager then takes the analyst's plan and should be able to apply it if the instructions given are adequate. The functions of the parties are entirely separate; the job of one begins where that of the other ends.

Separate function

TABLE 19.2
Relationship types

Manager is— \ Analyst is—	*Responsible* *B*	*Not responsible* *B′*
Responsible *A*	Mutual understanding	Communication
Not responsible *A′*	Persuasion	Separate function

Persuasion position

Position A′*B* is called the *persuasion position.* It holds that implementation rests to a great extent on the skill of the analyst in understanding the problems of the manager. That is, the obligation is on the analyst, who must understand the essence of the manager's personality and overcome *resistance* using basically a persuasion approach. This position stresses the psychological and social factors of implementation.

Communication position

Cell *AB′* is called the *communication position.* This position holds that the solutions suggested by the analyst are not accepted because the manager does not "understand" them.

Mutual understanding

The fourth position, *AB*, is called the *mutual understanding position.* Here, implementation is considered to be a function of the type of relationship that exists between two responsible parties, and this position represents the *most desirable* kind of relationship. The ingredients of the relationship have been summarized in the concept of "trust" discussed by Churchman and Schainblatt [8]:

"Trust"

- The two parties have faith in each other's recommendations.
- Each party is sensitive to the motivation, aspirations, and values of the other.
- Each party understands his or her own decision-making process, as well as that of the other.
- The party responsible for implementation is also involved in the formulation of goals in order that his or her recommendations bear a relationship to the needs of the recipients. For continuity, the same party is involved in formulation and implementation.
- The recipients are involved in the preparation of plans and programs so that they bear a relation to their own needs and values. This ensures input of the recipients' values and needs.

The implementation matrix has been profitable in focusing attention on particular aspects of the relationship between the manager and the analyst. Some of these aspects are outlined below.

Communication One frequently hears people say that "if only management scientists could learn to talk in a language that managers could understand, their recommendations would be accepted more readily." This relates to the fact that the quantitative nature of management science does not appear to be understood by most managers who, therefore, have to accept such recommendations as an act of faith.

However, experimentation conducted by Churchman and Schainblatt [8]) indicates that lack of communication per se *does not* appear to be a major barrier to implementation. They found that no matter how the necessary information was communicated to the manager, there was no evidence that the *mode of communication* made any significant difference. Of couse, poor communication did not help implementation; but even when the project recommendations were made in terms that the manager could apparently understand, the project was still frequently not implemented. It seems, therefore, that lack of communication is used as an excuse, in most cases, and the real reasons for resistance are different.

Mode of communication irrelevant

Differences in cognitive styles Frequently, the so-called communication barrier is symptomatic of a more basic reason for nonimplementation: a difference in *cognitive styles* between the manager and the analyst. **Cognitive style** refers to the fact that people differ in the approach they take in solving problems. The differences in style may reflect underlying differences in personality, education, culture, or combinations of such traits. Two basic styles are distinguished: some people are *analytically oriented* and tend to solve problems by seeking out cause-effect relationships in a step-by-step manner. Others are *intuitively oriented* and tend to utilize common sense and subconscious feelings in arriving at solutions.

Analytical versus intuitive styles

While it is difficult to generalize, it is probably true that, on the whole, MS analysts tend to be analytically oriented, while managers incline toward the intuitive end of the scale. This being the case, one would imagine that the manager and the analyst would have a great deal of difficulty working together, not because of a difficulty in understanding each other's language, but because the way in which they analyze and solve problems is different.

Huysmans [16] has carried out a series of experiments designed to test the impact of cognitive style differences on proposal implementation. He labeled the two classes of cognitive styles as *analytical* and *heuristic*. Analytical reasoning is defined as being directed toward detecting underlying causal relationships and manipulating quantifiable variables so that some "optimal" solution is reached with respect to the objectives. On the other hand, heuristic reasoning is based on common sense and intuition.

The results of Huysmans' experiments strongly suggest that cognitive style may operate as an important constraint on implementation. In particular, he found that heuristic subjects, with few exceptions, rejected—completely or in part—the MS recommendations when they were supported by an analysis of the technical problems, even though the recommendations were supported by persuasive arguments as well.

The analytical subjects, on the other hand, responded much more favorably to the MS proposals if the more technical approach was used. Furthermore, when the heuristic subjects received their recommendations from the analyst utilizing the more intuitive approach, they generally reached a level of implementation just as high as analytical subjects who received their recommendations via the technical approach.

Thus, to foster implementation, proposals should be couched in the manager's style.

Participation One of the best ways to encourage implementation is via participation of the people involved. The importance of participation has been demonstrated by the classic Coch and French experiment [9]. These researchers worked with four comparable groups of clothing factory operators. Each was exposed to a change in work procedures. The groups differed mainly in the *method* by which they were exposed to this change.

No participation

Group 1. The change was introduced by a "no participation" method. The operators *were notified* about the nature of the change, as well as the reasons for the change.

Group 2. This group was introduced to the work change by a "participation through representation" method. In this variation, the operators elected representatives who were allowed to participate with the scientists in determining the nature of the change.

Total participation

Groups 3 and 4. The third and fourth groups were introduced to the work change through a "total participation" procedure. All the members of these groups met with the scientists, who in turn demonstrated the need for cost reduction. The operators were then given an opportunity to influence the formulation of new work methods. Groups 3 and 4 were identical in nature.[6]

Coch and French reported a marked difference between the results achieved by the methods of introducing the change. The most striking difference was between group 1 (the "no participation" group) and groups 3 and 4 (the "total participation" groups). Immediately after the change was implemented, the output of group 1 dropped to about two thirds of its previous level and resistance developed. Marked expressions of aggression against management occurred, such as conflict with the methods engineer, hostility toward the supervisor, deliberate restriction of production, and lack of cooperation with the supervisor. Seventeen percent of the group quit in the first 40 days.

17% quit

In contrast, the output in groups 3 and 4 showed a smaller initial drop, followed by a very rapid recovery to a level which exceeded that prior to the change. The researchers found no sign of hostility toward the staff or toward the supervisors in these groups, and no one quit during the experimental period.[7]

---

[6] The reason for having two identical groups was to increase the reliability of the results by showing that the results for the two groups were the same.

[7] The results for group 2 were between group 1 and groups 3 and 4.

Findings such as these suggest that participation is helpful for overcoming resistance to at least certain types of change.

The fear of change

The implementation of an MS project can be viewed as an introduction of change into an organization. The change can be social, technical, psychological, or structural (or a combination).

When the manager (or employee) resists the logical arguments presented in defense of an MS proposal, he or she may not be resisting the technical aspects of the proposed change as much as the perceived social ramifications. Managers often feel threatened by modern techniques of analysis and sense that a proposed project, with the help of high-speed computers, may take over or jeopardize their job. This fear of change may originate from various sources: that the job will be eliminated, that previous performance will be proven inefficient relative to the new technique, or that the new technique will result in a downgrading in the status or intrinsic satisfaction of the job.

Of course, the analyst may think that such beliefs are absurd. The important point, however, is that what governs the manager's behavior is not so much the real threat as the *perceived* threat.

Perceived threat

The best way for the analyst to cope with the fear of change is to eliminate the perceived threat. The problem is that some of the perceived threat is probably real (e.g., workers may be laid off and the importance of certain managers may be reduced). Furthermore, some of the consequences of the change are uncertain.

Managers sometimes are not afraid of the organizational and social ramifications as much as the changes in the actual job responsibilities. If the job's content and meaning are changed, managers may not be too sure of how they will perform. They may foresee more responsibility (which many like to avoid), more control, and more accountability than they are used to. While managers may not like their job more challenging, they may not like it more routinized than what they were used to, either.

Retraining

The apparent solution here is retraining. However, this may not be an easy task. For example, some managers think of themselves as complete failures in mathematics, just because they had problems with it 30 years ago in school.

Overcoming resistance to change Many theories of overcoming resistance to change have been developed by behavioral scientists. For example, one of the best known theories regarding organizational change comes from Lewin [20] who identifies the various organizational forces resisting change. In order to overcome this resistance and ensure long-term effectiveness, the implementation process must be considered as a three-step procedure consisting of unfreezing, changing, and refreezing. "Unfreezing" refers to overcoming resistance to change by introducing disequilibrium into the present stable equilibrium. "Changing" refers to the exposure and

Unfreezing

Changing

acceptance of new information, attitudes, and theories in order to achieve new perceptions and learn new behavioral patterns. "Refreezing" refers to the reinforcement, confirmation, and support of new behavior based on the implementation. The Lewin theory stresses the sequential nature of these activities.

Refreezing

Sorensen and Zand [34] conducted an empirical investigation in which the Lewin theory was used to explain the variability in the success of 280 MS projects. Their major hypothesis (which was supported by the experiment) was that, in general, high levels of unfreezing, changing, and refreezing caused high implementation success and low levels were less successful.

The pressure of the work group

Few factors have a more pronounced influence on an employee's behavior than the pressures of formal and informal work groups. This is as true at the managerial level, where these groups tend to take on the characteristics of political coalitions, as it is in the lower echelons of the organization.

Work groups can influence employee behavior in a variety of ways. Asch [3] has found, for example, that groups can influence the perception of their members. In one of his experiments, five out of six group members were told to insist that two lines drawn on a blackboard were of *unequal* size, when in fact they were not. In more than half of the cases, the sixth member, when asked to compare the length of the lines, although at first insisting for several minutes that the lines were of *equal* size, gradually conformed to the group consensus, even though it was obviously incorrect.

Peer pressure

Furthermore, group pressure is an important determinant of its members' output.[8] In particular, group pressure generally results in the reduction in variation in members' output; that is, there is a significant amount of pressure for conformity.

Individual innovation

For several decades, scientists from psychology, economics, marketing, and organization theory have studied the conditions under which an individual chooses to try something new. One result is Slevin's theory of the **innovation boundary** [33], which suggests that two zones of innovation exist. In one zone, individuals will choose to innovate or try new things, while in the other, they will not. Between the two zones lies the innovation boundary.

Innovation boundary

Slevin developed a mathematical model that describes the formation of the boundary as a function of four variables: current success level (S),

[8] An important aspect here is the role of unions, which frequently determine the methods, quality, and speed of work.

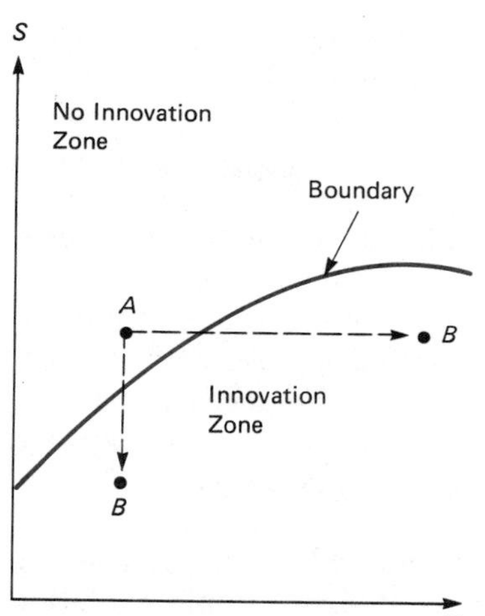

a. Change in an *individual's* position due to an increase in aspiration level (*T*), or a decrease in current success level (*S*)

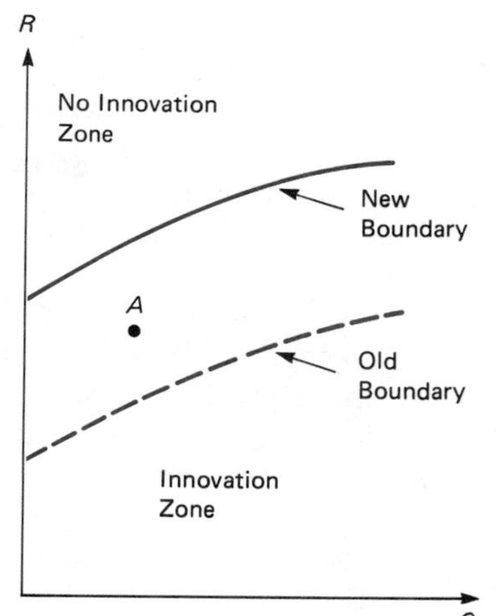

b. Change in the *boundary* due to a decreased cost (*C*), or an increased reward (*R*)

FIGURE 19.2
The innovation boundary

target aspiration level (T), the cost of innovation (C), and the reward for successful performance (R).

Through experimentation and questionnaires it is possible to predict the location of individuals in the zones; it is also possible to analyze means of transforming an individual from the "no innovation" zone to the "innovation" zone. Figure 19.2 shows such situations with: (1) a potential move from point *A* (no innovation) to point *B* (innovation), and (2) a potential move of the innovation boundary in such a way that location *A*, which was previously in the no innovation zone, is now in the innovation zone.

The role of computerized management support systems

Both DSS and ES are likely to increase the chance of successful implementation for the following reasons:

a. DSS provide an extremely easy way to conduct "what if" and other types of sensitivity analyses. This feature can greatly increase the confidence of the user in the models.

b. MS generates, in many cases, recommendations that are independent of the perceptions and activities of the users. Further, MS largely ignores the decision process and the individual characteristics of the decision maker. In contrast, expert systems draw conclusions principally through a logical or plausible inference, as managers commonly do. Since many practicing managers can be classified as having a heuristic cognitive style, it is only natural to assume that they will be more receptive to recommendations of an ES (or a DSS with an expert system component) than to the recommendations of the management science analytical approach.

Decision makers use a wide variety of decision-making processes, since they differ in styles, skills, and knowledge. A computerized system is more likely to be used if it supports multiple decision-making processes and if there is a fit between the user and the system.

As pointed out by Wiig [38], MS models, with the exception of simulation, are used very little by managers for a variety of reasons, ranging from "the models are not understood by the decision makers" to "the models have too many unrealistic assumptions." ES can improve the implementation success rate since they eliminate several of these causes.

Finally, the explanation capability of ES, which enables asking questions such as why, how, and why not, could make implementation much easier.

c. A recent survey (Mittman & Moore [26]) indicated that senior executives use computers in support of decision *implementation* activities *significantly more often* than in decision making. Implementation activities involve explanation, justification, and communication, all of which are provided by ES to a much larger extent than by any other computerized tool. Thus, the chance of implementing recommended solutions can be much higher if expert systems are used.

d. Several recent studies indicate that the graphical capabilities of DSS, especially when used in conjunction with visual simulation, can ease the implementation problem. The Weyerhaeuser Co., for example, reported an increased use of dynamic programming models when the users were permitted to simulate the solution suggested by the dynamic programming model and compare it to their intuitive beliefs (see Lembersky & Chi [18]).

19.7 IMPLEMENTATION FAILURE: A CASE STUDY

In 1974, a community hospital was approached with a proposed MS project that could have reduced the hospital's operating cost by about $4 per patient-day (about $365,000 a year). The administrator of the hospital was very candid in explaining his objections to the project, which were:

1. The hospital would gain nothing from the saving; the operating budget of the hospital would simply be reduced (this was a public hospital).
2. Showing lower cost than other community hospitals might be interpreted as either low health care quality rendered in the hospital or an inability of the administrator to use the budget effectively.
3. If the hospital could operate on a reduced budget, then the administrator might be viewed as incompetent, since the previous situation was allowed to last for four years.

4. The administrator had no faith in the model since the analyst was unable to show the administrator a similar situation (in a hospital in a similar condition) that was successful.
5. The proposed project required the use of a computer, which the hospital did not have. Under no circumstances would the administrator bring the "monster" in. The use of an outside computer was out of the question. How could the administrator trust an outsider when many insiders could not be trusted?

This case illustrates some of the implementation aspects discussed in this chapter. The problem for management scientists is to consider all the implementation aspects together to improve the chances of success.

19.8 CONCLUDING REMARKS

Implementation is the process of translating the models' results into operating instructions and carrying them out. Many management analysts see this as the major part of their task; it certainly is one of the most difficult aspects of the profession.

The tendency of some researchers to leave the "dirty" work of implementation to the manager, as well as the tendency of some managers to try to keep the management analyst out of the field during this final phase, may lead to the failure of implementation. Churchman, Ackoff, and Arnoff ([6], p. 616) conclude that it is *necessary* that the researcher be actively involved throughout.

This chapter has identified several aspects of projects that may pose a problem for implementation: the participants involved, the cost involved, the benefits accruing and their utility to management, the timing and priority of the project, the financing of the project, and operational difficulties that may develop as the project unfolds.

A positive climate is essential to the success of implementation. While the project particulars can be viewed as "seeds," the implementation climate can be viewed as the "weather." The better the seeds and the weather, the better is the chance for success.

However, good seeds and weather, although necessary, are not the only criteria. The management analyst and the methods of "cultivation" used also will affect implementation.

19.9 REVIEW QUESTIONS

1. In what way can implementation be viewed as "institutionalization"?
2. Propose some measures of cost and benefit for:
   a. Automating a production line.
   b. Introducing a labor-saving machine in a hospital.
   c. Scheduling visits of welfare agency employees.
3. How might the analyst attempt to circumvent timing and priority difficulties?
4. Explain the concept of "degree of implementa-

tion" through an example and differentiate it from "probability of implementation."

5. What are the major reasons given for analysts *not* participating in implementation? Why is it important for them to participate?
6. How would one assess the benefits of installing a computerized inventory system?
7. Why is the availability of financing considered by some as the *most important* condition for implementation?
8. What implementation difficulties may be encountered if a complete operational plan of implementation is not prepared beforehand?
9. What is the danger of an MS group reporting to a line manager? Are there any advantages?
10. This chapter concerned the implementation climate of the entire organization. What points would be relevant concerning the internal organizational climate of the MS group itself?
11. What other parts of the "information flow" should the MS group be integrated into besides the management information system (MIS)? How important are they?
12. Give an example of an MS project that is incompatible with an organization.
13. Describe your own cognitive style; what type of reasoning is most persuasive to you?
14. Participation is considered to be one of the strongest factors to aid in implementation. Explain why this might be so.
15. Describe a project where the following would not be ethical to you:
    a. The goal.
    b. The implementation.
    c. The results.
16. Are group pressures stronger at lower levels of an organization or at higher levels? Why?
17. Give some examples of how to move a manager into the innovation zone by changing:
    a. S.
    b. *T.*
    c. *C.*
    d. *R.*
18. How would you argue with the hospital administrator's reasons for not implementing the project (Section 19.7)?

19.10 CASE

SUNRISE ELECTRONICS

Sunrise Electronics manufactures cordless telephones (CTs), which are sold both through the company's retail outlets and in department stores. The company's policy for the past several years has been to emphasize sales and advertising with one goal in mind: increasing their share of the expanding market. During 1987 and 1988, the company's earnings were soaring. However, in the last quarter of 1988 the company incurred a loss; its first in the last eight years. Although the change in profitability was attributed in part to increased competition, the company also realized that quality control and cost control had become extremely important. In addition, large inventories and high interest rates contributed to increased expenses.

The president of the company had been considering the idea of initiating a management science (MS) department because he had heard favorable reports on cost reductions achieved with the aid of management science techniques. In the weekly meeting of the executive committee he suggested starting an MS department on an experimental basis. Most of the vice presidents, especially the old timers, rejected the idea, claiming that such an experiment was not justified at this time.

After long deliberation, the president decided to form an MS group within the existing industrial engineering department. Thus far, this department had been primarily engaged in methods improvements, work studies, and incentive schemes. John Green, the director of the department, had been pushing for years to get additional personnel to expand activities into management science.

The first step in the organization of the MS group was the recruitment of Bill Swan. Bill had a Master of Science degree in Management Science from a leading university and work experience of three years in an established MS department with a large oil company.

The first project that John and Bill conceived was in the materials management area. They felt that the company's mode of operations was heavily dependent on proper inventories of raw materials, semifinished components, and finished goods. The materials management department was headed by Dave Wilkes, who had been running the department for more than 15 years and had been with the company for 22 years, since its inception. Dave was considered a competent, hard-working department head. Although he had only a high school education, he had taken some management development courses and had considerable experience.

The latest changes in the company's CT models caused tremendous inventory problems and Dave had been working 12 hours a day or more to straighten things out. Dave did not like the idea of the MS group "poking into" *his* department and suggested they start in "any other place." He believed Bill to be a "good, sincere man" but that he did not understand the realities. Furthermore, Bill had never dealt with materials management of CTs. "Inventories of oil differ from inventories in electronics; there is too much complexity in our inventories for mathematical models."

It was obvious that without top management's support, the project would not move. Finally, John and Bill talked with the president, who then called Dave and requested that he cooperate.

In the initial stages of the study, Bill found that Dave ran the department in a very autocratic manner. Most decisions regarding purchasing, inventory levels, storage, and usage were made by Dave, usually on the spot.

The only documentation that Bill found was in the finance and the accounting departments for billing and tax purposes. This document was not suitable for the data needs of an inventory model. When Dave was approached for the necessary information, he seemed to have trouble remembering. The more Bill attempted to extract the information, the more defensive Dave became.

After spending three months on the project, Bill suggested scrapping it and moving on to another department. "I am sure that some of the more up-to-date managers will be only too glad to participate."

Questions for discussion

1. What were the major factors that determined the failure of the MS project?
2. What steps could have been taken in the early stages that might have improved the chances of success for the project?
3. What alternatives are open to John now? Analyze all of them and recommend one.

19.11 GLOSSARY

Cognitive style The manner in which people solve problems. Can be either *analytical* or *intuitive*.

Cost-benefit analysis A comparison of the costs and benefits of each project or alternative, often expressed as a ratio.

Implementation Putting a recommended solution into effect. The manner in which the results of scientific effort may come to be used by the manager.

Implementation climate The environmental factors that have an impact on the chance of implementing an MS project. This is in contrast to the specific factors ("project particulars") that impact specific projects.

Innovation boundary A line or a graph that divides those who are willing to try a change from those who resist it.

Institutionalization A permanent change. Routine and frequent use of the change.

Organizational validity The fitness between a project and an organization and its people.

Project viability Projects whose benefits are larger than their cost and that have a clear advantage over other alternatives.

19.12 REFERENCES AND BIBLIOGRAPHY

1. Ackoff, R. L. "The Art and Science of Mess Management." *Interfaces,* February 1981, pp. 20–26.
2. Anderson, J. C., and T. R. Hoffmann. "A Perspective on the Implementation of Management Science." *Academy of Management Review,* July 1978.
3. Asch, E. "Effects of Group Pressure on the Modification and Distortion of Judgment." In *Readings in Social Psychology,* ed. E. E. Maccoby, T. M. Newcomb, and E. L. Hartley. New York: Holt, Rinehart & Winston, 1958.
4. Berman, P. "The Study of Macro- and Micro-Implementation." *Public Policy,* Spring 1978.
5. Chew, P. T. "New Rules for Office Politics." *The Miami Herald,* February 24, 1974.
6. Churchman, C. W.; R. L. Ackoff; and E. L. Arnoff. *Introduction to Operations Research.* New York: John Wiley & Sons, 1957.
7. Churchman, C. W., and A. H. Schainblatt. "Commentary on 'The Researcher and the Manager: A Dialectic of Implementation.'" *Management Science* 12 (1965), pp. B2–B39.
8. Churchman, C. W., and A. H. Schainblatt. "The Researcher and the Manager: A Dialectic of Implementation." *Management Science* 11 (1965), pp. B-69–B-87.
9. Coch, L., and J. R. P. French, Jr. "Overcoming Resistance to Change." *Human Relations* 1 (1948), pp. 512–32.
10. Davis, M. W., and P. E. Robinson. "The Pits of OR/MS and Gamesmanship to Skirt the Rim." *Interfaces,* April 1981, pp. 53–61.
11. Doktor, R., et al., eds. *The Implementation of Management Science.* New York: Elsevier North-Holland Publishing, 1981.
12. Ginzberg, M. J. "Steps toward More Effective Implementation of MS and MIS." *Interfaces,* May 1978, pp. 57–63.
13. Graham, R. J. "The First Step to Successful Implementation of Management Science." *Columbia Journal of World Business,* Fall 1977.
14. Henderson, J. L., et al. "The Implementation of OR/MS Techniques." *IEEE Transactions on Engineering Management,* February 1980.
15. Hesse, R. "Management Science or Management/Science?" *Interfaces,* February 1980, pp. 104–109.
16. Huysmans, J. H. B. M. *The Implementation of Operations Research: An Approach to the Joint Consideration of Social and Technological Aspects.* New York: John Wiley & Sons, 1970.
17. Konczal, E. D. "New Demands for Managing Management Science." *Journal of Systems Management,* November 1979.
18. Lembersky, M. R., and U. H. Chi. "Decision Simulator Speeds Implementation and Improves Operations." *Interfaces,* July–August 1984, pp. 1–15.
19. Levitt, T. "A Heretical View of Management Science." *Fortune,* December 18, 1978.
20. Lewin, K. "Group Decision and Social Change." In *Readings in Social Psychology,* ed. E. E. Maccoby et al. New York: Holt, Rinehart & Winston, 1958.
21. Litwin, G. H., and R. A. Stringer, Jr. *Motivation and Organizational Climate.* Boston: Harvard Business School, 1968.
22. Lucas, H. C., Jr. "Unsuccessful Implementation: The Case of a Computer-Based Order Entry System." *Decision Sciences,* October 1978.
23. Meredith, J. R. "The Importance of Impediments to Implementation." *Interfaces,* August 1981, pp. 71–74.

24. Meredith, J. R. "The Implementation of Computer-Based Systems." *Journal of Operations Management* 1 (October 1981), pp. 11–21.

25. Mintzberg, H. "Beyond Implementation: An Analysis of the Resistance to Policy Analysis." *INFOR,* May 1980.

26. Mittman, B. S., and J. H. Moore. "Senior Management Computer Use." *Proceedings DSS84,* Dallas, April 1984.

27. Morris, W. T. *Implementation Strategies for Industrial Engineers.* Columbus, Ohio: Grid, 1979.

28. Pidd, M., and R. N. Woolley. "Four views on Problem Structuring." *Interfaces,* February 1980, pp. 51–54.

29. Radnor, M.; A. H. Rubenstein; and D. A. Tansik. "Implementation in Operations Research and R&D in Government and Business Organizations." *Operations Research* 18 (1970), pp. 967–97.

30. Research Institute of America. *Coping with Office Politics.* New York: Selectron Report, 1971.

31. Schultz, R. L., and M. J. Ginsberg, eds. *Management Science Implementation.* Greenwich, Conn.: JAI Press, 1985.

32. Schultz, R. L., and D. P. Slevin, eds. *Implementing Operations Research/Management Science.* New York: Elsevier North-Holland Publishing, 1975.

33. Slevin, D. P. "The Innovative Boundary" (two articles). *Administrative Science Quarterly* 16 (1971), pp. 515–31, and 18 (1973), pp. 71–75.

34. Sorensen, R. E., and D. E. Zand. *Improving Implementation of OR/MS Models by Applying the Lewin-Schein Theory of Change.* Paper presented at the National Research Conference on Implementation, Pittsburgh: University of Pittsburgh, November 15–17, 1973.

35. Turban, E. "A Survey Sample of Operations Research Activities at the Corporate Level." *Operations Research,* May–June 1972, pp. 708–21.

36. Wagner, H. M. *Principles of Operations Research,* 2nd ed. Englewood cliffs, N.J.: Prentice-Hall, 1975.

37. Watson, H. J., and P. G. Marett. "A Survey of Management Science Implementation Problems." *Interfaces,* August 1979, pp. 124–28.

38. Wiig, K. "Will Artificial Intelligence Provide the Rebirth of Operations Research?" Paper presented at ORSA/TIMS National Meeting, San Francisco, May 1984.

39. Zanakis, S. H., L. M. Austin, D. C. Nowading, and E. A. Silver. "From Teaching to Implementing Inventory Management: Problems of Translation." *Interfaces,* December 1980.

40. Zmud, R. W., and J. F. Cox. "The Implementation Process: A Change Process," *MIS Quarterly,* June 1979.

20

20.1 Brunswick Corporation.
20.2 Analysis.
20.3 Solution by incremental analysis.
20.4 Solution by decision tree.
20.5 Solution by simulation.
20.6 Review questions.
20.7 References and bibliography.

In learning management science, it is necessary to spend the great majority of time studying the techniques. Of equal, and perhaps even greater, importance is obtaining experience in applying these techniques to real-world problems, which are usually more complex than the examples given in the textbook. Unfortunately, the techniques must come before the applications and most curricula simply cannot devote that much time to the latter.

The case in this chapter is included specifically to help alleviate this problem and fill the gap between theory and reality. It communicates a sense of reality for practicing MS applications. Moreover, it illustrates the fact that there are typically several ways to solve the same problem, though some are easier than others. The case also points up the importance of having the appropriate data and how often data is incomplete, or even contradictory.

A case application

LEARNING OBJECTIVES

The student should be able to:

a. Better understand the application of MS models to real-world situations.
b. Realize that there is more than one way to attack a problem.
c. Understand that different ways of approaching a problem will entail different amounts of both conceptual and computational difficulty.
d. Appreciate the importance of qualitative factors in decision making.
e. Realize that decision problems involve complex, and sometimes even contradictory, inputs.

20.1 BRUNSWICK CORPORATION[1]

Part (A)

In mid-April 1967, Gerry O'Keefe, vice president for marketing of Brunswick Products, was trying to decide how many Snurfers he should request the manufacturing plant to produce for the 1967–68 winter season.

The Snurfer was a new item, first introduced to the consumer market by Brunswick during July and August 1966; but because of the difficulty of predicting the actual sales requirements, the factory had produced more Snurfers than were eventually sold. Mr. O'Keefe was anxious to avoid the same situation occurring in the 1967–68 selling season.

The Snurfer The Snurfer was a surfboard-like device designed for use on snow. It consisted of a molded wooden plank 48 inches long by 7 inches wide upon which the rider stood and skied/surfed down snow-covered slopes. The company in its specification brochure described the Snurfer:

> Snurfing is the all-new and exciting winter fun sport. Children, teens, and young adults can now combine the many thrills and skills of surfing and skiing on the new Brunswick Snurfer. It's really maneuverable, fun-filled, and easy to learn. Goes on a minimum of snow—where saucers and sleds won't go. The Snurfer is just the thing for action-packed snow outings! Also fun for sand surfing.[2]

The Snurfer was produced in two types, the regular and the super. Exhibit 1 shows the regular model. The regular model consisted of a molded laminated wood shell, painted yellow with black stripes, which used metal staples as foot grips. The Super Snurfer was the same basic shape as the regular but incorporated a metal keel for greater maneuverability. In place of the painted finish the super had a genuine natural wood surface, included

---

[1] This case was made possible by the cooperation of the Brunswick Corporation. It was prepared by Richard G. C. Hanna, research assistant, under the supervision of Associate Professor Paul A. Vatter.

[2] 1967 sales brochure.

EXHIBIT 1
Standard Snurfer

Source: Company sales brochure.

deluxe metal traction button-type Snurf treads (foot grips), was decorated with an official red racing stripe and was sold complete with Snurf-Wax. The wax allowed the bottom surface to be polished for even greater speeds.

The development of the Snurfer, January 1966–March 1967 The idea for the Snurfer had originated in Muskegon, Michigan, in early 1966. A plumbing supply salesman had converted a water ski for his children to use in the snow. The idea interested him, and he experimented with different sizes and shapes and coined the name Snurfer.

During February, the product came to the notice of a Brunswick employee who felt that the item might be of interest to the corporation. On April 1, 1966, after some negotiation, Brunswick bought both the rights to the design and the registered name from the Muskegon salesman. The contract involved a lump-sum payment and a royalty that was based on Brunswick's gross sales of the product. The royalty was not to become effective, however, until a set number of Snurfers had been sold.

Following the signing of the contract, the Brunswick engineers commenced a careful study aimed at optimizing the shape of the Snurfer. Many samples were made, and field tests were conducted on the rapidly disappearing snow fields. By the end of April, the design had been finalized and the engineers were ready to turn the project over to the production personnel.

While the engineers had been working on the design, Noel Biery, a product manager, and Mr. O'Keefe, the marketing vice president, had been attempting to determine the size of the potential market and to settle upon channels of distribution. Because the product had been proved to be more readily usable by children than adults, Brunswick had decided to distribute the product through toy channels. After making rather slow progress with the local toy stores and jobbers, the decision was made to show the Snurfer at the New York Toy Show in late March. Only one prototype Snurfer was available at that time, yet the response at the show was encouraging. During the show, manufacturers' representatives covering 38 states were appointed. The product at this time, which consisted of only a single model (which later became the regular), was sold at a factory price of $3.60 with a suggested retail price of $5.95. During the second week in April, engineering prototypes together with specification sheets were sent to all representatives and Brunswick asked them to sound out the market and push for orders during the remainder of April.

By the end of April, Mr. O'Keefe had to make the decision whether or not to continue with the Snurfer and, if so, to decide how many units he would order from the factory. The Brunswick production people were insistent that if the units were to be produced in time for the winter selling season, they must have the firm annual production requirements for the Snurfer by the end of April. With only one firm order for 3,000 units, Mr. O'Keefe decided to go ahead with the project and ordered 60,000 units from the factory for delivery during the 1966–67 winter season. Fifty thousand units were to be the regular Snurfer and 10,000 units the super.

The tooling, capable of producing up to 150,000 units, was ordered at a cost of $50,000, and production scheduled to commence in early September.

By June, no further orders of note had been received and both Mr. Biery and Mr. O'Keefe became concerned as to what action should be taken. Brunswick's own full-time representative in New York was asked to investigate the reasons why the Snurfer was not being sold. With this assignment, and a Snurfer in hand, he visited several sporting good stores, as distinct from toy shops, and found the reaction to be very good. By July, Mr. Biery realized that the original decision to sell through toy jobbers and manufacturers' representatives had probably been a mistake; consequently the original distribution channels were closed down and Brunswick made an all-out effort to generate interest through their own dealer salespersons. However, by this time most sporting good stores had completed their winter buying; and although a good reaction was forthcoming, many stores were unwilling to order in quantity for the current season because of the late date. During August the decision was made to retrench, and the factory managed to cut back production from 60,000 to just over 50,000 units. In addition they agreed to change the product mix between regulars and supers.

The total number of Snurfers sold during the 1966–67 season only reached 35,000 units, with the ratio between supers and regulars being approximately 40:60. By mid-March 1967 there were nearly 17,000 Snurfers in inventory, consisting of 12,000 regulars and 5,000 supers.

The production decision—April 1967 Because of the difficulties and setbacks that they had experienced during 1966, Mr. O'Keefe and Mr. Biery were anxious to ensure that the plans for 1967 were firmly based on what they had already learned.

In reviewing the situation, they had reason to believe that most of the early problems had arisen from their decision to class the Snurfer as a toy. Experience had shown that a considerable degree of skill could be developed by Snurfer enthusiasts and that speeds in excess of 30 miles per hour were attainable. This fact coupled with the good, although somewhat late, response received from the sporting goods shops suggested that by careful distribution and promotion, 1967 sales were potentially well in excess of the 1966 predictions. Although both Mr. Biery and Mr. O'Keefe were convinced that the immediate prospects for the Snurfer were excellent, they were uncertain as to the actual market demand for the coming year and as to the share of this market that would be taken by the Super Snurfer. They were certain, however, that in order to maximize the overall profitability of the product they would have to estimate the size of the production order in a careful and systematic manner. The factory order for the 1967–68 production run had to be in the hands of the production people by the end of April.

As a first step in determining this quantity Mr. Biery decided to review the new cost estimates for the two Snurfer models. The production department advised him that the existing tooling, which had been purchased at a cost of $50,000, was in good shape and would be capable of producing a total of 150,000 units per year in any mix of models. To produce anywhere between 150,000 and 200,000 units would require an additional $15,000 of tooling. To increase the production above 200,000 units per year would require yet another $55,000 in addition to the extra $15,000 already mentioned. This latter step-up in tooling would allow the factory to produce up to 500,000 Snurfers a year. In calculating costs, Mr. Biery planned to amortize tooling completely during the year in which it was ordered.

After consultation with the salespersons, it had been decided to sell the Snurfers in 1967 at an average price from the factory (quantity discounts were involved) of $4.30 for the standard and $5.50 for the super. Brunswick's direct costs for these items were $2.50 and $3.20, respectively. In addition to direct costs, Mr. Biery estimated that 9 percent of the gross margin for both models would be required for selling expenses, royalties, and discounts, while a further 3 percent would be allocated to advertising and promotion. Also, there would be a penalty for overproduction in the form of an inventory-carrying cost that was charged at the rate of 2 percent per month based on Brunswick's direct costs. Mr. Biery estimated that any excess inventory could be considered as being carried for an average of six months.

Having outlined the costs involved, Mr. Biery turned his attention to the question of demand. Although he was uncertain as to what figure he should choose, he believed that it was unlikely that there would be any major intrusion into the 1967 market from competitive manufacturers. In addition, he realized that the Snurfer was something of a novelty item, and as such, might follow the trend of the skate board or Hula-Hoop™ with sales rising extremely rapidly for one or two years and then tailing off just as quickly. Because of the extreme uncertainty arising from these factors, he determined to concentrate solely on the demand for the 1967–68 season.

To help in ascertaining the demand he called on Mr. O'Keefe, and together they considered the possible sales figures for Brunswick's Snurfers. They finally decided that the median demand was 150,000 units. They were certain that the demand would not be below 50,000 or above 300,000 units, and they believed that there was one chance in four that demand would be at least 190,000 units, and three chances in four that the demand would be at least 125,000 units.

In order to decide on what quantity of units to order from the factory, Mr. O'Keefe felt that they should estimate how this demand would be broken down between the super and standard model Snurfers. This was necessary because the factory had to order raw materials well in advance, and Mr. O'Keefe didn't want to be left carrying standard Snurfers in inventory while the market was demanding supers, or vice versa. Both Mr. Biery and Mr. O'Keefe believed that this breakdown of demand between models was independent of the overall level of demand. They reasoned that the consumer would purchase either the standard or the super entirely on each one's distinctive selling features, and this decision as to which to purchase would in no way be influenced by the total number of Snurfers being sold.

Mr. Biery and Mr. O'Keefe felt that the Super Snurfer would most likely account for 40 percent of the total Brunswick demand, although it might rise to as high as 60 percent of the demand. In no circumstances, they believed, would it fall below 30 percent. In addition they considered there was a 75 percent chance that the share would be 45 percent of demand and a 25 percent chance that the supers would account for 36 percent of the total demand for Snurfers.

Possible production quantities Mr. Biery now felt that he had all the information necessary to decide how many standard and super Snurfers he should order.

Part (B)

To help in determining what production quantities he should consider, Mr. Biery decided to look at the suggestions he had received from the various people associated with the project. He prepared the following summary of recommendations from letters and memos that he had in his files:

> Field sales personnel argued that the gross margins on both standard and super Snurfers far outweighed the storage costs if some were left unsold. They requested that a total quantity of 225,000 be ordered. This was to be made up of 130,000 regulars and 95,000 supers.
>
> On the other hand, the production manager advised total production of 150,000 units split 70,000 super and 80,000 regulars. He argued that until the Snurfer caught on, there was no point in incurring an additional investment cost. Realizing the Super sales contributed a higher gross margin, he had suggested raising the proportion of supers to around 47 percent rather than at the level of 40 percent which was more in line with previous selling experience.

Mr. Biery himself felt that each of these arguments had its merits but suspected that a production quantity of 200,000 units, split 85,000 supers and 115,000 regulars, might decrease the cost of lost sales without incurring too high an investment cost in tooling. To ensure that he made the correct decision, however, he decided that he would analyze all three alternatives in order to determine which suggestion formed the best course of action.

20.2 ANALYSIS

Review of the case

The vice president of marketing and the product manager of a new product must decide on the production levels for two versions of a new product. Sales of the new product in the previous year were less than anticipated but finally encouraging, given a new distribution network. The vice president had overproduced in the previous year and did not want to repeat that mistake. However, the product was of a type similar to Hula-Hoops™—in that it might suddenly "catch on," then boom for two seasons or so, and die. In those circumstances, the company certainly did not want to be caught short on inventory of finished product in the midst of a boom they had created themselves.

The estimate of the proportion mix between the two versions was in considerable error the previous year, and also had to be reconsidered. Profit margins on each version were known, but depended on production levels. (Of course, production levels depended on profit margins as well.) Assuming the product was not of the boom-bust type, some feel for the distribution of demand for each version was available.

Overview points of note

1. Mr. O'Keefe desired to avoid overproducing as he had done in 1966–67; such a situation would have cast him in a bad light.

2. Factory price increased between 1966–67 and 1967–68 from \$3.60 to \$4.30, or about 20 percent.
3. We do not find out what the New York representative learned about toy store sales. Since response at the toy show was good, it seems there may exist an unexploited opportunity here.
4. Distribution through sporting goods stores allowed the firm to use their own full-time representatives instead of outsiders.
5. Based on (4) above, Biery and O'Keefe estimated that 1967–68 sales could be "well in excess of the 1966 predictions." Normally, this phrase would probably be interpreted to mean "anywhere between 20 to 100 percent over the 60,000 value," or therefore 72,000–120,000 units.
6. Even if the equipment is amortized in the year it is ordered, it would still be useful in following years, or at least have a significant salvage value.
7. If inventory is carried an average of six months, then the assumption is that it *will* be sold in the next snow season.
8. The "no competition" assumption appears reasonable.
9. The boom-bust possibility is a serious assumption. If this is indeed that type of product, all demand projections could be extremely low for 1967–68. Following any final conclusion, this possibility should be checked.
10. The demand distribution given is not symmetric and hence not normal. Based on the figures given and the interpretation of the case (boom-bust possibility), a Beta distribution appears more reasonable.
11. The same comments as in (10) hold for the proportion of supers. Here, however, we have a definite market result to go by (40 percent).

Cost data

	Regular	*Super*
Inventory cost:		
.02 × 6 × DC		
(if overproduced)	\$ .300	\$ .384
Factory price	4.300	5.500
Direct cost (DC)	2.500	3.200
Gross margin	1.800	2.300
Selling expenditures		
royalty, discount (9%)	.162	.207
Promotion, ads (3%)	.054	.069
Net margin*	\$1.584	\$2.024

* Net margin is used throughout this case rather than the more common "profit." The difference is that the net margin can be applied toward fixed costs and is a more meaningful term to managers than profit where some unknown allocation has already been made for fixed costs.

Probability distributions

Regardless of what method is selected to analyze this case, the probability distributions of demand and fraction of supers (or regulars) must be determined. The data in the case are as follows:

Demand, D:

Median: 150,000
Lower limit: 50,000
Upper limit: 300,000
$P(D \geq 190{,}000) = .25$
$P(D \geq 125{,}000) = .75$
1967 sales: 14,000 supers; 21,000 regulars
Inventory: 5,000 supers; 12,000 regulars

Fraction supers, F (independent of demand):

Mode (most likely):* 40 percent
Upper limit: 60 percent
Lower limit: 30 percent
$P(F \leq .45)^* = .75$
$P(F \leq .36)^* = .25$

Beta, Gamma, or lognormal distribution?

From the above data the demand and fraction distributions can now be approximated. Because of the given form of the data (upper and lower limits) and the fact that the distributions are nonsymmetrical, a Beta distribution (see Chapter 11) appears to be a reasonable form to try. Other possibilities are a Gamma or a lognormal distribution. Each of these could be checked with a statistical goodness-of-fit test to see how close it matched the given data at the upper and lower quartile points and, if acceptable, the best fit taken.

Invoking a piecewise linear approximation

Such a procedure is beyond the scope of this textbook, however, and a simpler approximation will be used here instead. Exhibits 2 and 3 display the cumulative probability functions for the demand and fraction, with the given data marked by the dots. (The mode is used here as an estimate of the median for the fraction distribution.) The approximation will be to simply join the dots with a straight line of the form $P = a + bR$, where R is either demand, D, or fraction, F, depending on which distribution is being approximated.[3]

For a straight line, the values of a and b are given by:

$$b = \frac{P_1 - P_2}{R_1 - R_2}; \qquad a = P_1 - bR_1$$

* Notice Mr. Biery's poor phrasing of these probabilities in the case. Literally the case states that the *point* probabilities $P(F = .45) = .75$ and $P(F = .36) = .25$. If true, these would be the *only* values that F could attain and the "most likely" value of .40 could never occur.

[3] A piecewise quadratic approximation would allow a smoother curve, especially at the tails, but this is also beyond the scope of this text.

EXHIBIT 2
Demand

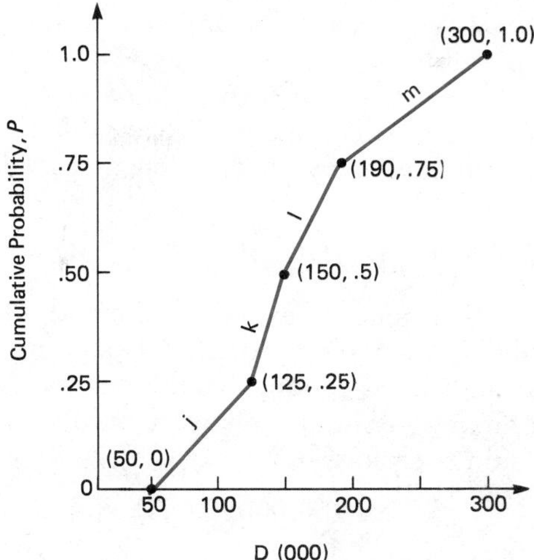

EXHIBIT 3
Fraction of supers

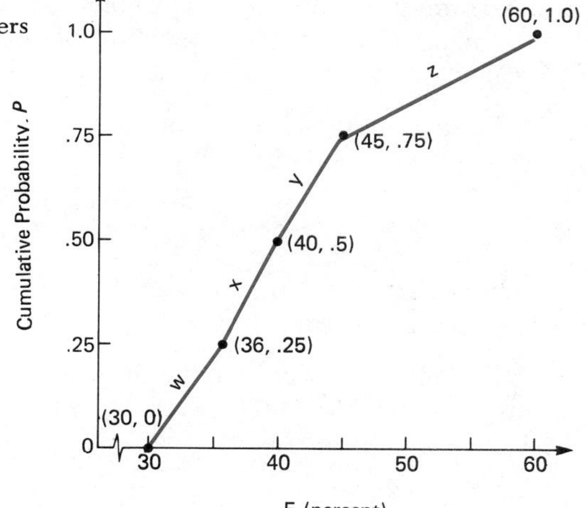

EXHIBIT 4
Line segment coefficients

Segment	$b = \dfrac{P_1 - P_2}{R_1 - R_2}$	$a = P_1 - bR_1$
j	.25/75 = .00333 per 1,000	.25 − .00333 (125) = −.16625
k	.25/25 = .010 per 1,000	.50 − .010 (150) = −1.0
l	.25/40 = .00625 per 1,000	.75 − .00625 (190) = −.4375
m	.25/110 = .00227 per 1,000	1.0 − .00227 (300) = .319
w	.25/6 = .04167 per 1%	.25−4.167 (.36) = − 1.25
x	.25/4 = .06250 per 1%	.50 − 6.25 (.40) = − 2.0
y	.25/5 = .0500 per 1%	.75 − 5.0 (.45) = − 1.5
z	.25/15 = .01667 per 1%	1.0 − 1.667 (.60) = 0

Let us now calculate each of the line segments j, k, l, m, w, x, y, z in Exhibit 4.

Now that the distributions have been approximated, analyses of the case may be conducted. Three different approaches are illustrated here: incremental analysis, decision tree analysis, and simulation.

20.3 SOLUTION BY INCREMENTAL ANALYSIS (see Chapter 14)

The net margin at median demand

The median expected demand was 150,000 units, with a most likely split of 40 percent supers/60 percent regulars. At this production level, no additional tooling would be necessary. The total net margin to the company (assuming all were sold and the 17,000 inventory maintained) would therefore be:

$$.4(150{,}000)(2.024) + .6(150{,}000)(1.584) = \$264{,}000$$

Sensitivity analysis

Before proceeding to the optimal production level analysis, we might look at the sensitivity of the margin to product-mix demand.

a. Assuming the products will *not* substitute for each other, a 1 percent demand *decrease* in proportion of supers *reduces* the year's margin calculated above by:

$$\binom{\text{Reduction in super net margin}}{(.01)(150{,}000)(2.024)} + \binom{\text{Overproduction inventory cost}}{(.01)(150{,}000)(.384)} = \$3{,}612$$

and a 1 percent *increase* in supers (or reduction in regulars) would reduce the margin by:

$$\binom{\text{Reduction in regular net margin}}{(.01)(150{,}000)(1.584)} + \binom{\text{Overproduction inventory cost}}{(.01)(150{,}000)(.300)} = \$2{,}826$$

b. If the products *will* substitute for each other, the corresponding reductions are:

$$(.01)(150{,}000)(2.024) - (.01)(150{,}000)(1.584) = 3{,}036 - 2{,}376 = \$660$$

and, by symmetry, $-\$660$

respectively. This latter figure of $-\$660$ means that if customers buy supers when regulars are out of stock, our "reduction" is really an *increase* in net margin (per 1 percent change in product mix).

The anticipated impact of producing one more unit

Incremental analysis is also known by many other names, such as *critical fractile*, *newsboy problem*, and *marginal analysis*. The idea is to see if increasing the production by *one unit* will improve or hurt the present situation. At the median demand:

$$\text{Expected increase in margin} = (\text{Probability of sale, } 1 - P)(\text{Average net margin}) - P(\text{Average "loss" from carrying inventory})$$
$$= (.5)[.4(2.024) + .6(1.584)] - .5[.4(.384) + .6(.300)]$$
$$= .5(1.76) - .5(.333)$$
$$= .88 - .167$$
$$= .713$$

where P is the cumulative probability in Exhibit 2 of demand *not* reaching the level D; that is, not selling one more unit and then having to carry it in inventory until the following season.

Thus, the expected rewards of having one more Snurfer available for sale are considerably greater than the expected losses, when we are starting at the median demand figures. Note that the calculations assumed a hypothetical Snurfer that exhibited the margin and inventory cost characteristics of the super and regular models in the 40/60 proportion expected. Also note that the loss figures assumed no substitutability between the two models, and thus the loss was in holding the Snurfer in inventory for the next season (when it would be sold).

The critical probability

Clearly, at some point in the demand distribution, the probability of not selling the next unit is so large that the expected return (M) doesn't compensate for the probable loss (L). Calling this critical probability P^*:

$$(1 - P^*)M = P^*L$$

or:

$$P^* = \frac{M}{M + L}$$

$$= \frac{1.76}{1.76 + .333} = .84$$

Using the line segment m in Exhibit 2, with P given and solving for D, results in:

$$.84 = .319 + .00227D$$

or:

$$D = 229 \text{ (thousand units)}$$

Justifying the extra tooling

Since there are 17,000 units in inventory already, this then implies a *production* level of 229 − 17, or 212 (thousand units). But will the anticipated increase in returns at this production level justify the cost of the additional tooling? To reach 200,000 production units from 150,000 requires $15,000 in extra tooling. To go beyond 200,000 units requires another $55,000. It certainly seems doubtful that it would be worth the extra $55,000 to produce 12,000 more units, since the net margin is only about $2, but the $15,000 investment might be worthwhile.

This can be checked by calculating how much extra return the \$15,000 tooling can generate. *Without* the tooling, demand (sales) up to 150,000 + 17,000 = 167,000 units could be satisfied. *With* the tooling, an extra 50,000 units could be produced, or a maximum of 217,000 *sold*. Both line segments *l* and *m* in Exhibit 2 will have to be used to calculate the expected increase in net margin. This would be the probability of a sale $(1 - P_D)$ times the margin (M_D) less the probability of not making the sale (P_D) times the loss (L_D) for every thousand units (D) from 167 to 217. Average margins and losses based on the 40/60 product mix are again assumed.

Expected increase in margin:

$$= \sum_{D=167}^{190} [(1 - P_D)M_D - P_D L_D] \qquad \text{(segment } l\text{)}$$

$$+ \sum_{D=191}^{217} [(1 - P_D)M_D - P_D L_D] \qquad \text{(segment } m\text{)}$$

$$= \sum_{167}^{190} [(1 + .4375 - .00625\,D)1.76 - (-.4375 + .00625\,D).333]$$

$$+ \sum_{191}^{217} [(1 - .319 - .00227\,D)1.76 - (.319 + .00227\,D).333]$$

$$= \sum_{167}^{190} (2.6757 - .01308\,D) + \sum_{191}^{217} (1.0923 - .00475\,D)$$

$$= (2.6757)24 - .01308 \sum_{167}^{190} D + (1.0923)(27) - .00475 \sum_{191}^{217} D$$

$$= 64.217 - .01308\left(\frac{167 + 190}{2}\right)24 + 29.492 - .00475\left(\frac{191 + 217}{2}\right)27$$

$$= 11.51 \text{ thousand dollars}$$

Qualitative considerations and risk

It is, therefore, concluded that the extra tooling is *not* worth the cost. However, it is *almost* worth the cost and faith in the probability distribution of demand is not strong, particularly if the Snurfer becomes a fad item. Thus, for another \$3,500, Brunswick can obtain "insurance," so to speak, so that they aren't left out in the cold if the Snurfer "catches on."

The optimal product mix

Still to resolve is the question of the best production mix, because it is clear that the demand will not be *exactly* 40 percent–60 percent. Since each product results in different net margins, an *optimal* mix between the two models will give the highest expected yield. Again, marginal analysis can be used to find this mix. Since Brunswick expects to lose more, at the median mix, by a 1 percent decrease in proportion of supers available for customers (\$3,612 versus \$2,826 for regulars), the proportion of supers should be *increased* until the expected loss from each model is the same:

$$(1 - P^*)3{,}612 = (P^*)2{,}826$$

Solving:

$$P^* = \frac{3{,}612}{3{,}612 + 2{,}826} = .56$$

where P^* is the probability of not selling at least one more super model. Using line segment y from Exhibit 3 results in the optimal product mix:

$$.56 = -1.5 + .05F$$

or:

$$F = 41.2 \text{ percent supers}$$

Therefore, Brunswick should have available for sale:

$$.412(167{,}000) = 68{,}804 \text{ supers}$$
$$.588(167{,}000) = 98{,}196 \text{ regulars}$$

Since Brunswick already has 5,000 supers and 12,000 regulars in stock, they should *produce:*

63,804	supers
86,196	regulars
150,000	total

Note: previous calculations based on the median 40/60 mix should now be "corrected"; but since the correction is small (.2 percent for the margin), it is treated as not significant here.

20.4 SOLUTION BY DECISION TREE (see Chapter 3)

Here the approach is to handle the variability of demand by "discretizing" it into branches of a decision tree. If the number of branches is sufficiently large, the discrete approximation will be accurate enough for practical purposes. The method is illustrated with only a few branches.

A bivariate distribution

The joint probabilities of the bivariate level/mix distribution are formed from the marginal probabilities. We work with only four branches, each with a probability of (.5)(.5) = .25:

1. Demand of 125,000; fraction of supers of .36.
2. Demand of 125,000; fraction of supers of .45.
3. Demand of 190,000; fraction of supers of .36.
4. Demand of 190,000; fraction of supers of .45.

Four or 16 branches?

This simplification assumes that the given values properly represent the range of values they replace, akin to an "expected value." For example, 190,000 units with a probability of .5 represents from 150,000 to 300,000. A better approximation would have been to use all four segments of Exhibit 2 with each of the four segments of Exhibit 3, resulting in 16 branches.

Three policies to consider

The number of alternatives to consider are very large: a production level anywhere between 0 and 500,000, and a mix from 0 percent supers to 100 percent. Let us consider the three alternatives of Part (B) since they generally fall at natural break points in demand. Then the decision

EXHIBIT 5
Decision tree

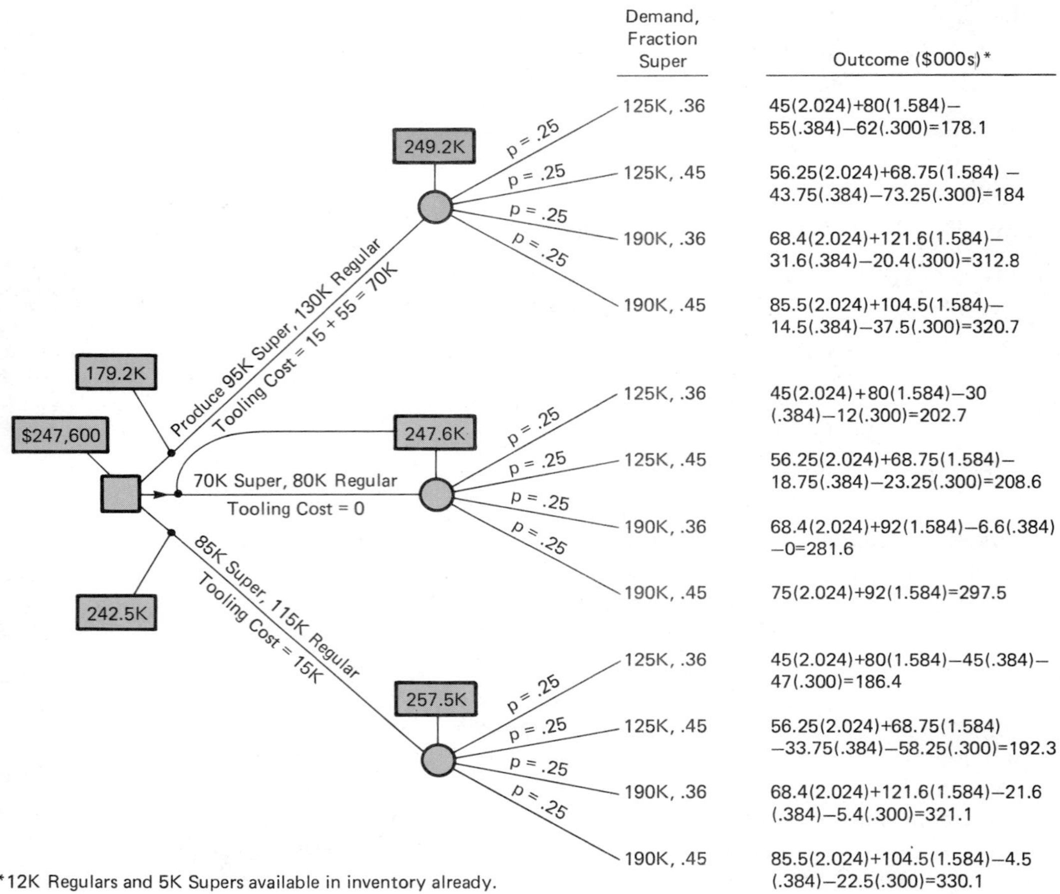

*12K Regulars and 5K Supers available in inventory already.

tree appears as shown in Exhibit 5, assuming no costs for shortage (such as ill will). The tree assumes the use of the available existing inventory.

Calculating the first outcome

The outcomes listed in the far-right column of Exhibit 5 are calculated in the following manner. Consider the first outcome, where 95,000 supers and 130,000 regulars are produced; 100,000 supers and 142,000 regulars are available for sale; and (125,000) .36 = 45,000 supers and 80,000 regulars are demanded and, since they are available, are sold (in some cases the number demanded are not available, so sales are limited). On each super, the margin is $2.024, and on each regular $1.584. There remains unsold 100,000 − 45,000 = 55,000 supers and, similarly, 62,000 regulars, each at a storage cost of $.384 and $.300, respectively. The outcome is $178,100.

Same answer as before

The result of the decision tree is the same as that by incremental analysis—by keeping the current tooling and only producing 150,000 units, the expected outcome is $5,100 better than spending the $15,000 and producing 200,000 units. The incremental analysis showed $3,500 better; but the product mix was quite different also: 41 percent supers instead of the 46.6 percent here (70,000/150,000 = .466).

The pros and cons of the three proposals

The pros and cons of the three proposals are as follows. The extra tooling cost for the 225,000-unit proposal simply cannot be justified on the basis of the 25,000 extra units produced. On the other hand, if this is a hula-hoop–type product, then O'Keefe would certainly be glad they had the extra capacity. The advantage of the 150,000-unit proposal is the lack of a necessity to put more money into tooling without something definite to show for it. Up to now, they have only sold 35,000 units. In addition, O'Keefe didn't wish to repeat his previous overproduction mistake. However, with the high profit potential of the units and low costs of storage of any overproduction, it would appear a greater mistake on O'Keefe's part to underorder. In that case, he would look even more foolish than just being an optimist—he would have overordered when the demand *wasn't* there, and then underordered when the demand *was* there. The last proposal may be the best compromise. It requires a small additional investment but generates a sufficient amount of extra capacity to minimize risk if high demand should occur.

20.5 SOLUTION BY SIMULATION (see Chapter 16)

Determining the actual distribution of net margin, stockouts, and so on

The procedure here would be to try several different policies (such as the three alternatives Mr. Biery is considering) with a computerized simulation. Each trial would constitute one possible reaction of the market. Repeating the process many many times would then give distributions for the variables of interest: net margin, shortages, sales mix, remaining inventory to carry over, and the like.

A PL/1 simulation

Such a simulation was programmed in PL/1 for an IBM 370 computer and run for 500 trials. The three proposals described in Part (B) of the case were then tested (where K is 000's):

Alternative	*Production strategy*
I	70K super, 80K regular, no extra tooling
II	85K super, 115K regular, $15K tooling
III	95K super, 130K regular, $70K tooling

It was also assumed that there was no substitution by customers of regulars for supers and vice versa. This assumption is relaxed later.

Stabilization of the measures

The stabilization history of three measures of performance are illustrated in Exhibit 6. In the lower section of the figure, the average net margins of the three alternatives jump around quite a bit for the first 40

EXHIBIT 6
Stabilization of the simulation

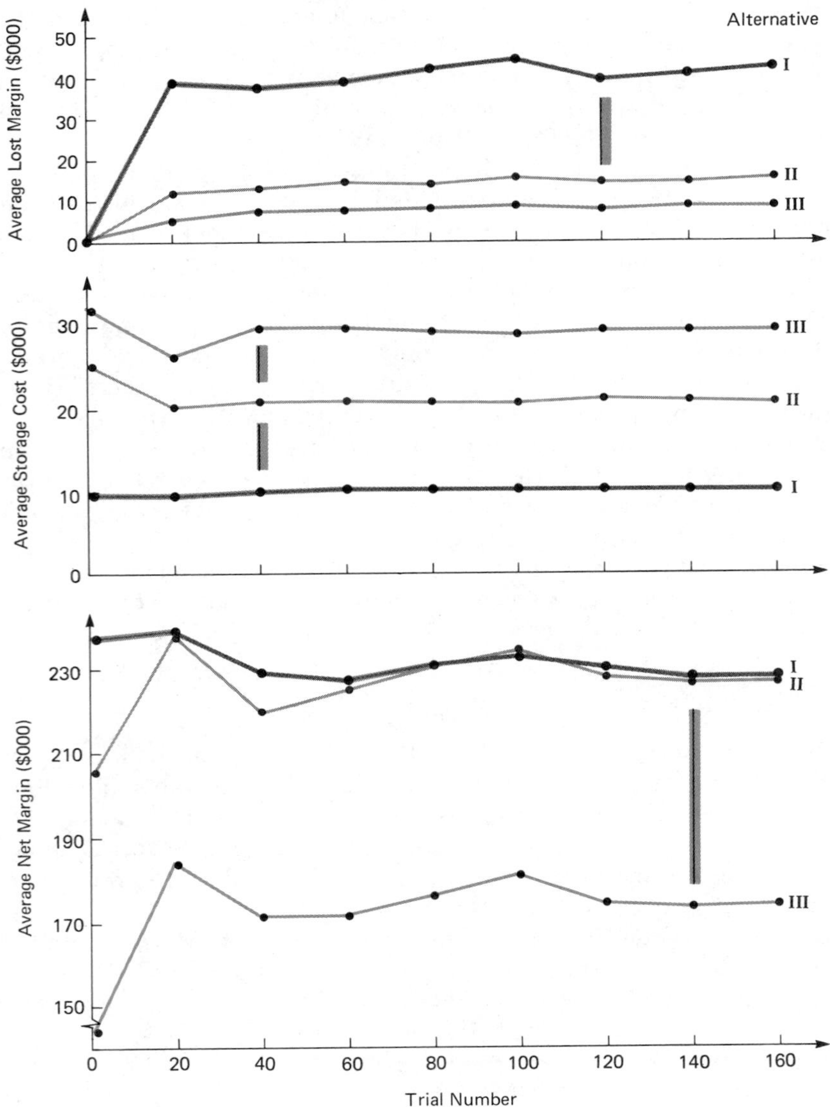

Stable by trial #140

trials. The graphs only show every 20th trial, so the true variation can't be seen; but the average net margin for Alternative III goes from \$144,000 in trial 1 (as shown) to \$133,000, to \$208,000, to \$228,000 in trial 4. Thus, between trials 2 and 4 the average ranged through \$95,000 (that is, 228,000 − 133,000). Note in the figure that between trials 100 and 120 the difference shown is only \$7,000. By trial 140 the variations are almost completely damped out for all three alternatives (as indicated by the vertical line at trial 140).

Average storage cost has much less variation and is essentially stable for all three alternatives in Exhibit 6 by trial 40. At the top of the exhibit, the average lost margin (by not having specific Snurfer models available when demanded) stabilizes for Alternatives II and III by trial 40, but Alternative I doesn't stabilize until about trial 120.

Considering all three measures of performance, the number of trials needed was probably only 140 or so. Using 500 trials, however, allowed plotting more accurate frequency distributions of the three measures of performance for each of the alternatives, as shown in Exhibits 7, 8, and 9.

Plotting the distributions

The most important measure, net margin, is graphed first. On a trial-by-trial basis, 64 percent of the time Alternative I had the highest net margin, and 36 percent of the time II was best. Alternative III was never best—the $70,000 tooling investment for Alternative III was always a heavy penalty at the demand levels that were observed.

Net margin: I is best, III is never best

As can be seen in Exhibit 7, Alternative I has a distribution whose mode is at a significantly higher net margin than II, which is itself higher than III. Furthermore, fully 30 percent of I's margins are at this mode ($280,000–$320,000), whereas only 20 percent of II's and III's margins are at their modes. The result is that the mean and median margins are highest for I, then II, and lastly III.

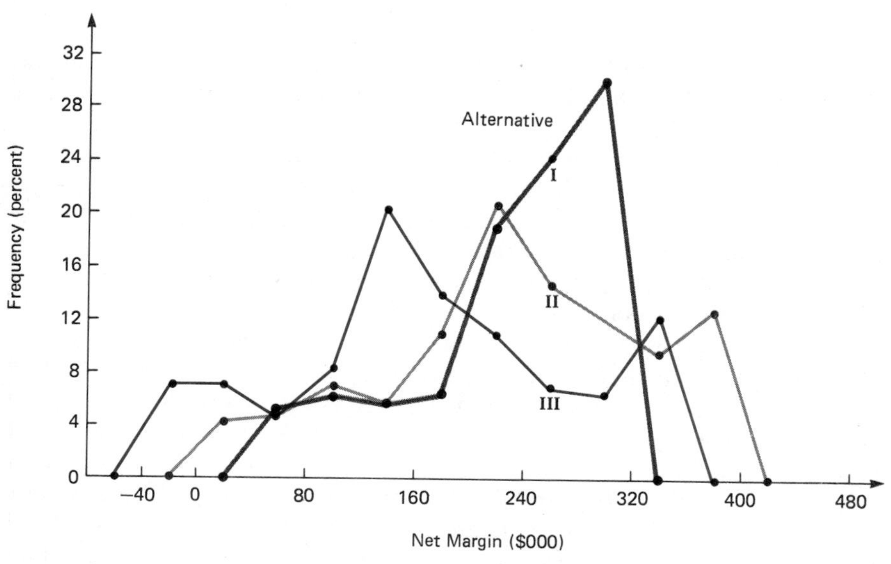

EXHIBIT 7
Distribution of net margins

The assumption of no substitution between Snurfer models was also relaxed. When this was done, Alternative I was even more superior, being favored in 71 percent, rather than 64 percent, of the trials. Again, Alternative III was never best.

Exhibit 8 illustrates the storage cost distributions of the three alternatives. As shown in the exhibit, Alternative I's highest frequency is near zero storage cost. Alternative II is the "more even" of the three distributions,

Storage cost: I is best again

EXHIBIT 8
Storage cost distributions

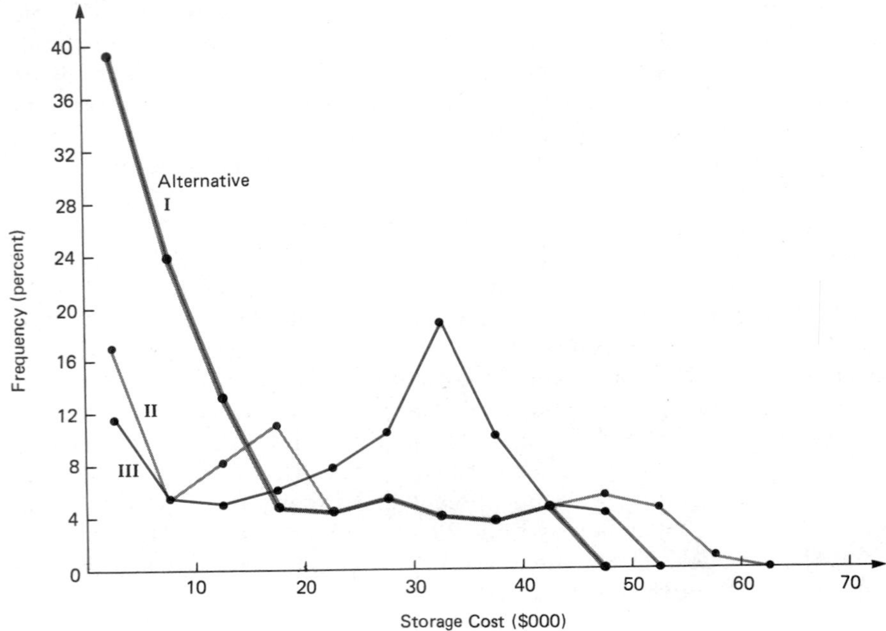

with a lesser downward trend than I. And III's highest frequency is beyond the $30,000 cost. In terms of storage cost, the preferred order of alternatives is, again, I, II, and III.

Lost Margin: III is best

Exhibit 9 illustrates the distributions of margins lost due to insufficient production. The majority of the time very little is ever lost, and all three alternatives look much the same up to about $35,000. Beyond this, Alternative I, which produces only 150,000 Snurfers, has a fairly constant (3 percent) distribution of loss up to $220,000. Alternative II drops off quickly, with no loss beyond $130,000, and III drops off even faster.

Use II for "insurance"

In summary, the simulation verifies the conclusion reached by the other two procedures: that Alternative I is the best of the three. The incremental analysis indicates Brunswick could increase their expected margin somewhat by reducing the number of supers in Alternative I from 70,000 to 64,000 and substituting the difference with regulars. It is seen from the net margin distributions in Exhibit 7 that Alternative I is superior for the majority of possible outcomes of demand, except for very high demands. At 175,000 total demand, Alternative II is about equivalent to Alternative I and, at 300,000 demand, II is $70,000 better than I. There is about a 37 percent chance of demand exceeding 175,000 (see Exhibit 2). The question then becomes: Is it worthwhile to spend $15,000 to try to gain this amount (computed earlier as an expected value of $11,510)? The answer: No, unless the money is important for some other reason (such as not looking like a fool again), or unless there is a good chance of this becoming a boom product. Then the $15,000 tooling is "insurance."

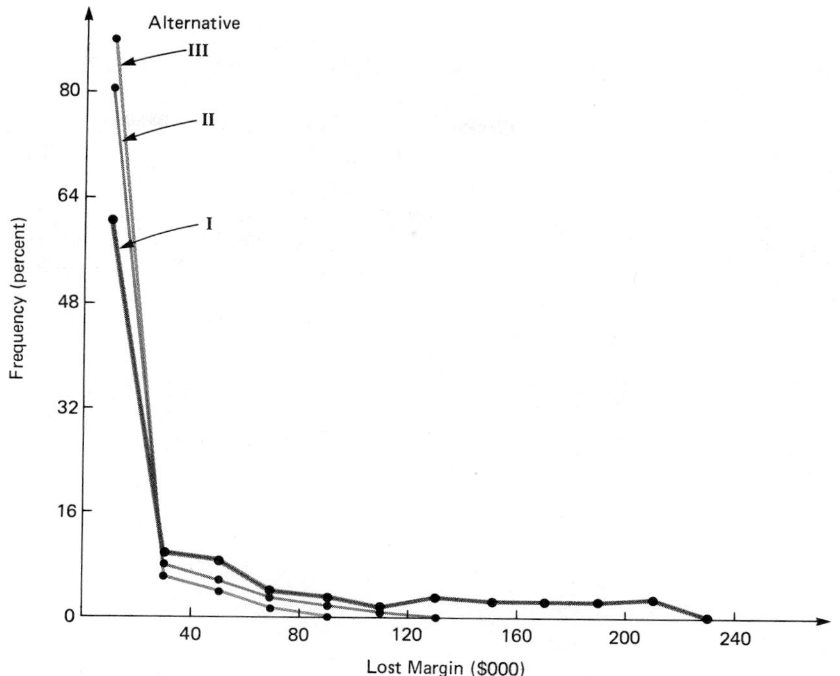

EXHIBIT 9
Distributions of lost margins

To conclude, all three analyses gave essentially the same answers. Some of the analyses were more direct, some required more approximations, and some took more effort. Yet, the model results in all cases could not be applied unthinkingly or uncritically. Other factors played important roles as well, such as regret, behavioral considerations, resource constraints, risk propensities, and the like. Probably the most important contribution of the model in a case such as this is to identify the poor alternatives and quantify the trade-offs among the better alternatives so management can make a choice based on other relevant criteria.

20.6 REVIEW QUESTIONS

1. How would you respond to the arguments of field sales and the production manager in Part (B) of the case, given the quantitative analyses just presented?
2. Given the price of the Snurfer, how substitutable do you feel the two models are for each other?
3. What are the important nonquantitative factors in this case?
4. Which quantitative approach is most conceptually straightforward? Which is simplest? Which is the most difficult? Which is the most accurate? Which do *you* prefer?
5. What are the key elements in this case that make the decision abnormally difficult?
6. How does the "boom or bust" aspect of the product complicate Mr. Biery's decision?
7. What decision is best for Brunswick? For Mr. O'Keefe? What would you decide in this situation?

20.7 REFERENCES AND BIBLIOGRAPHY

1. Aggarwal, R., and I. Khera. *Management Science, Cases and Applications*. San Francisco: Holden-Day, 1979.
2. Berry, W. L., et al. *Management Decision Sciences: Cases and Readings*. Homewood, Ill.: Richard D. Irwin, 1980.
3. Dyer, J. S., and R. D. Shapiro. *Management Science/Operations Research: Cases and Readings*. New York: John Wiley & Sons, 1982.
4. Newson, P. *Management Science and the Manager: A Casebook*. Englewood Cliffs, N.J.: Prentice-Hall, 1980.
5. Render, B., and R. M. Stair, Jr. *Cases and Readings in Quantitative Analysis for Management*. Boston: Allyn & Bacon, 1982.
6. Turban, E. and P. Loomba. *Cases and Readings in Management Science*. Plano, TX: BPI, 1982.
7. von Lanzenauer, C. H. *Cases in Operations Research*. San Francisco: Holden-Day, 1975.

21

21.1 The past: Requirements for growth.
21.2 The present: Extensions of MS.
21.3 The future: Effectiveness and computerized management support systems.
21.4 Research opportunities.
21.5 Concluding remarks.
21.6 References and bibliography.

This chapter assesses the growth and trends in the field of management science. The stages in the field's development are discussed, and it is concluded that the field is currently in a "maturing" stage—solidifying its areas of usefulness and moving into the realm of delivering human services where problems are more nebulous and ill-structured.

It appears that linear programming is still the most useful normative technique, but computerized decision, expert, and management support systems, many of which include normative techniques, are becoming the most popular tools with managers. This is because they better aid the manager in dealing with ill-defined, unstructured problems, and thus improve the manager's effectiveness in dealing with problems and making decisions. With the advent of such computerized systems, the future of management science looks extremely exciting.

The future of management science

LEARNING OBJECTIVES

The student should be able to:

a. Describe the history of management science.
b. Understand the requirements for growth of the field.
c. Be aware of the current extensions of the field into all types of public and private organizations.
d. Comprehend the future role for the field, the forces behind its development, and the importance of computerized support systems in the future of management science.

MS—a newcomer

Management science, as a field, is about 40 years old, a relative newcomer. The early years of development have witnessed significant growth and changes in the field. Magee [10] identifies three separate stages of this development.

The *Primitive* stage (1950s)

Small problems—outside experts

The earliest stage of management science was characterized by a focus on small, well-defined "tactical" problems that could be "optimally" solved by consideration of only quantitative aspects. Typical model examples were economic order quantity inventory models and linear programming. The experts in the field were often from other disciplines such as economics and mathematics; academic programs in management science and operations research were very limited.

The *Academic* stage (1960s)

Growth of theory and techniques

The emphasis in this intermediate stage was on the "technical," rather than any managerial, aspects of problems. Thus, the theory behind the models blossomed. Solid progress in techniques of analysis was being made as a foundation for further growth. An appreciation was being gained for the proper role of management science and its strengths and weaknesses. As a result, the number of formal academic programs at major universities increased, and trained management scientists as well as students exposed to the techniques were entering the business world and making firms aware of the emergence of a new discipline.

The *Maturing* stage (the 1970s and 1980s)

This stage witnessed the expansion of some trends of the 60s, such as:

1. An interest in the nature of real-life managerial problems and their environments.
2. A more realistic appreciation of the strengths and limitations of management science.

3. More emphasis on the nonquantitative aspects: behavioral, functional, interrelationships, assumptions.
4. More of a "systems" orientation with integration of the quantitative and qualitative problem aspects through computerized managerial support systems.

More problem orientation

Additionally, more emphasis has been placed on the problem rather than on the theory. This more realistic perspective, in turn, has led analysts to think in terms of dynamic, continually evolving solutions to ongoing problems.

Fuzzy problems

There has also been a trend toward analyzing more ill-structured ("fuzzy") problems [13] such as exist in the public service area (urban development, transportation, health, education) as well as at top corporate levels. Such problems involve nonquantitative elements and thus indicate a possible expansion of management science toward other disciplines such as psychology and anthropology.

21.1 THE PAST: REQUIREMENTS FOR GROWTH

In 1961, Magee and Ernst [11] set out some general requirements for the growth of management science:

Requirements for growth

1. A need for it must exist.
2. Management must perceive its problems as potentially amenable to management science techniques.
3. Management science must prove itself in the eyes of the manager.

The assumption inherent in the requirements above was that, to survive as a discipline, management science must have a sponsor in the "real world." Magee and Ernst warned that the field must not turn inwards, continually finding better and better answers to a set of ever narrowing problems, or else it will stop growing and occupy only a niche in the manager's sphere of acquaintance, as did "time and motion study" in previous eras.

A field of esoterics?

Their advice was of extreme importance, because it is only too obvious from a cursory examination of the journals in management science that entire tomes could be written on such topics as: "A Hundred Different Types of EOQ Models" or "The Thousand Variations of the Queuing Problem." This would clearly have been a continuation of the "academic stage" described earlier. However, if management science had completely adopted this orientation, it would have become a field of esoterics talking to themselves. Fortunately, this did not occur.

It should be mentioned that the first two requirements of Magee and Ernst appear currently to be fulfilled; progress on the third item is slow. After an initial "oversell" to management, with the naturally resulting failures and disappointments, both sides are taking a more realistic view of the potential (and limitations) of management science. Thus, a foundation for further growth appears to be forming.

21.2 THE PRESENT: EXTENSIONS OF MS

Radnor and Neal [14] have closely studied the use of management science in business firms and have come to the following conclusions:

MS is spreading

1. Management science capabilities are diffusing throughout firms.
2. At the same time, a "core" MS group is establishing itself within firms as a separate entity.
3. MS is spreading into smaller organizations as well.
4. MS is still in a transitional state.

Outside of the industrial firm, it appears that MS is spreading into several other disciplines as well: economics, public affairs, sociology, engineering, and all areas of business [8]. This expanded base of operations appears to confirm Magee's contention that management science is currently in a "maturing stage." Zahedi [19] corroborates this view in his report on the extensive development of the field. He summarizes the considerable literature on theory versus application, education in the MS field, career paths in the field, research, research topics, application guidelines, and teamwork. Clearly, MS has achieved a state of acceptance as a field of its own.

Thus, it appears that management science is finally being accorded some recognition by management, but probably not to the extent envisioned by scientists. Dearden and Lastanica [3] summarize studies that show that linear programming is still, in general, the most common normative technique for solving problems with a large number of variables. Such techniques as game theory and dynamic programming, about 30 years old, have had virtually no evidence of significant practical application. Management apparently views such techniques as useful *aids* to decision making but not of overwhelming importance. This may not hold for some other techniques however (such as interactive modeling and simulation), as discussed below.

21.3 THE FUTURE: EFFECTIVENESS AND COMPUTERIZED MANAGEMENT SUPPORT SYSTEMS

And what of the future? It seems clear that the "maturing" stage will continue for some time. As younger managers, whose education has included management science techniques, take over higher positions, and as computers become more powerful and less expensive, management science seems sure to play an even larger role in private and public firms.

A larger role for MS?

Operational problems

Clearly, management science will play a substantial role in the various functional business areas (such as production, marketing, accounting and finance) where routine planning, organizing, directing, and controlling are performed. This would amount to an expansion of MS on an already existing base. And given the pace of world competition today, it is clear that MS will be increasingly used in the international realm for such decisions as factory locations, allocation of goods, and so on. As Dearden and Lastanica [3] point out, most of the techniques are primarily useful for operational problems in business. Thus, one may expect to see increasing analysis of policies in areas such as inventories, staffing, scheduling, and allocation.

An accelerating factor in broadening the management science base may possibly be an enlarging role for interactive modeling on the computer terminal to help solve complicated sequencing and scheduling problems of lower and middle management:

> Most of the really important problems are complex and messy and thus their systematic treatment requires substantial subjective inputs: value judgments, opinions, personal goals and feelings. The decision maker's mind becomes an integral part of an analytical algorithm, its main interactive subroutine. This symbiotic, intricate, and elegant cooperation of manager and management scientist leads to a stagewise, adaptive procedure where mutual learning helps to understand what the solutions should be and why. Men and machines cooperate rather than compete [20].

Symbiotic cooperation

Ill-structured problems

Just as important is the trend in management science toward the tackling of ill-structured problems. Zeleny [20] points out the task:

> As managerial concerns advance from simple, well-structured, static and deterministic problems toward more complex, fuzzy, dynamic and stochastic problems, the optimal working framework of the human mind changes from logical, rational, sequential, and quantitative, to perceptive, intuitive, simultaneous and qualitative. . . .
>
> The development of new tools, aimed at the enhancement of *intuitive* powers of managers, is the main task for management science today.

A *new* task for MS

This trend is an outgrowth of the increasing problem orientation, rather than technique orientation, among management scientists. And this has been fostered, in large part, by the development of simulation and computerized management support systems.

Simulation

The importance of simulation

Simulation, which goes hand in hand with advances in computer capabilities (at lower cost), has been a primary management science development with great potential beyond the operational level of business firms. The acceptance of simulation at the higher managerial levels is probably due primarily to the four following factors:

- Simulation, being descriptive, requires the manager to interact with the model by asking "what if" questions and then directing modifications in the model.

- To build the model accurately, the management scientist must constantly communicate with the manager.
- The model is built from the manager's perspective, rather than from the management scientist's.
- Simulation is an integral part of many decision support systems.

Thus, as a model, simulation *requires* that the analyst act in a manner as if he or she were trying to guarantee implementation of the results: *involve those responsible and work with them on the problem.*

Computerized management support systems

MS integration with ES and DSS

Perhaps the most significant change in the MS field in the future will be its integration with decision support systems (DSS) and expert systems (ES). This integration could result in a much broader base for support of managerial decisions ranging from structured to completely unstructured decisions. As will be discussed in Section 21.4, the research opportunities involving the use of DSS and ES in the MS field will be considerably enhanced.

The computerized management support systems of the future will include:

Future capabilities

a. Integration of MS models into complex decision situations.
b. The use of expert systems as a tutorial for MS.
c. The use of expert systems as a front-end to model bases for the purpose of selecting appropriate models.
d. The use of expert systems to help in problem diagnosis.
e. The use of expert systems to enhance the use of both simulation and analytical techniques.
f. Increasing utilization of MS models in DSS.
g. The integration of MS models, DSS, ES, and other artificial intelligence technologies.

With the increased capabilities and decreased cost of computer hardware and software, it is only natural to assume that managers will use more and more computerized support systems, especially those that are user friendly. And the introduction of intelligence into the decision support system will increase the boundaries of the problem areas addressed by both management and management scientists. Clearly, the economic capabilities of computers will continue to increase, further opening up the scope and research opportunities of managerial problems.

The Firestone Tire & Rubber Co.

Firestone explained its reasons for implementing a decision support system to the press:

- An unstable economy.
- Increasing foreign and domestic competition.
- Increasing difficulty tracking their numerous business operations.
- Inadequate support of the firm's business objectives.

Firestone explained that the company's existing computer systems would not support their objectives of increased efficiency, higher profitability, and successful entry into new markets. "The Data Processing Department could not begin to address the diversity of the company's needs or management's ad hoc inquiries, and business analysis functions were not inherent within the existing systems."

Source: *Computerworld,* September 27, 1983.

Other sectors

MS outside the firm

The expansion of management science outside the industrial firm will continue to occur. To some extent, multiple-firm projects are appearing, such as cooperation between producers, wholesalers, and retailers, and information sharing, as now exists among the airlines.

The service and public sectors

The movement into the services and the public sectors will significantly increase. Problem areas such as pollution, transportation, health, social services, fire/police/rescue services, insurance, education, and labor relations are typically ill-structured; but the solution of problems in these areas can also be much more rewarding. Again, simulation, DSS, and ES appear to be making the most headway on these types of problems. Government agencies are also utilizing management science techniques throughout their areas of responsibility. In these areas, it is imperative that the management scientist maintain a problem orientation, since much of what must be dealt with cannot be addressed from a technique perspective.

21.4 RESEARCH OPPORTUNITIES

Little [9] reports on the research opportunities provided by the initiation of the Decision and Management Science Program in the National Science Foundation. He classifies the opportunities into four major categories: operational processes, choice theory, decision support and expert systems, and complexity.

Operational processes research is subdivided into two areas: phenomenological processes and organization and managerial processes. The former includes processes such as technology transfer, spread of epidemics, growth of networks and systems, production flows, information flows, and urban emergency service systems. The research goal in this area is to develop classes of models that capture the functioning of these processes.

In the second area, organization and managerial processes, major research opportunities exist in organizational design for decision making, organizational support systems, and strategic management. Research is needed here to relate decision outcomes to organizational forms and outcomes and performance to decisions, plans, and actions.

Choice theory includes individual choice, values, judgments, and risk behavior, as well as group choice and decision making. Included here is research investigating normative behavior theory compared to actual behavior, bias in decision and risk, crisis decision making, and customer behavior, including the relations between preferences, intentions, and choice. In the group area, research opportunities lie with modeling the generation of alternatives, the structuring of values, information generation and representation, the resolution of conflict, preference and judgment, organizational implementation, and feedback and time effects.

Decision support and expert systems have been discussed at length previously (Chapters 17 and 18), but the research opportunities here are seen to lie in three areas: (1) the interplay between expert systems, decision analysis, models, and humans; (2) the dynamics of the person/machine interactions and the resulting performance; and (3) the impact on the organizational and decision-making structure of the firm.

Last, complexity offers three separate sets of research opportunities. The first is in prescriptive complexity—the determination of optimal behavior in complex and noisy settings. The second is in descriptive complexity—modeling the individual and group decision-making processes in realistic settings. The third is communicative complexity—conducting research across interdisciplinary lines and fields.

21.5 CONCLUDING REMARKS

It appears that the broad industrial sponsorship of management science in the operational areas will continue to grow from an already well-established base. Additionally, interactive modeling through computerized management support systems may begin to play a much more important role in that growth.

Continuing a trend from the 1970s, management science will make further inroads in the services and public areas as public agencies and governmental units adopt MS techniques. These applications, as well as further developments in theory, will be increasingly reported in the growing range of journals devoted to this field such as *Operations Research, Management Science, Interfaces, Omega, Computers and Operations Research, Decision Sciences, IIE Transactions*, and many others.

There is currently strong pressure within the field itself to emphasize applications and implementation instead of development of new and extended models. The use of decision support and expert systems further supports this trend. This thrust is a healthy sign; it indicates that the field will continue growing and not become an esoteric endeavor. Those following the "applications" orientation will have to "get their hands dirty" trying to solve social issues, juggle political constraints, and deal with other such nonmathematical details. Those with a theoretical bent will also continue to advance that side, considering "fuzzy" managerial problems and qualitative and intuitive aspects of issues. Indeed, each faction may well be very interested in the other, and there will undoubtedly be some few individuals who can embrace both camps.

Computerized management support systems will continue growing rapidly in the late 1980s and will be used to address both standard and unstructured problems. It has been estimated that by 1990, about 40 percent of all computer applications will be in the area of supporting managerial decision making.

Finally, the rate of expansion of management science will depend on successful implementation. This text is intended to help in closing the gap between the sponsor-managers and the management scientists, in order to increase the successful implementation of MS projects, thus advancing management science as a discipline.

21.6 REFERENCES AND BIBLIOGRAPHY

1. Ackoff, R. L. "The Future of Operational Research Is Past." *Journal of the Operational Research Society* 30, no. 2 (1979).
2. Ackoff, R. L. "Resurrecting the Future of Operational Research." *Journal of the Operational Research Society* 30, no. 3 (1979).
3. Dearden, J., and J. Lastanica. "New Directions in Operations Research." *Financial Executive* 38 (1970), pp. 24–33.
4. Fiksel, J. "Winning Is Not Everything: The Midlife Crisis of Operations Research." *Interfaces,* April 1980, pp. 106–7.
5. Gray, P. "Is OR/MS Everywhere?" *Interfaces* 9 (November 1979), pp. 129–34.
6. Hall, J. R., Jr., and S. W. Hess. "OR/MS Dead or Dying? RX for Survival." *Interfaces* 8 (May 1978), pp. 42–44.
7. Halsey, J. J. "Management Science: A Complement of Information Services." *Interfaces,* June 1981, pp. 12–15.
8. Larson, R. C., and A. R. Odoni. *Urban Operations Research*. Englewood Cliffs, N.J.: Prentice-Hall, 1981.
9. Little, J. D. L. "Research Opportunities in the Decision and Management Sciences." *Management Science* 32 (1986), pp. 1–13.
10. Magee, J. F. "Progress in the Management Sciences." *Interfaces* 3 (February 1973), pp. 35–41.
11. Magee, J. F., and M. L. Ernst. "The Challenge of the Future." In *Progress in Operations Research,* ed. R. L. Ackoff. New York: John Wiley & Sons. 1961.
12. McClure, R. H. "Educating the Future Users of O.R." *Interfaces,* October 1981, pp. 108–12.
13. Negeita, C. V. *Fuzzy Systems*. Philadelphia, Penn.: Heyden & Sons, 1981.
14. Radnor, M., and R. D. Neal. "The Progress of Management Science Activities in Large U.S. Industrial Corporations." *Operations Research* 21 (1973), pp. 427–50.
15. Rowse, J. "A Midlife Crisis for Operations Research? New Fundamental Challenges for the Profession? Another View." *Interfaces,* February 1981, pp. 27–30.
16. Simon, H. A. *The New Science of Management Decisions*. 3rd ed. Englewood Cliffs, N.J.: Prentice-Hall, 1977.
17. Turban, E. *Decision Support Systems and Expert Systems*. New York: Macmillan, 1988.
18. Walker, W. E. "Models in the Policy Process: Past, Present, and Future." *Interfaces,* October 1982, pp. 91–100.
19. Zahedi, F. "A Survey of Issues in the MS/OR Field." *Interfaces,* March–April 1984, pp. 57–74.
20. Zeleny, M. "Notes, Ideas, and Techniques: New Vistas of Management Science." *Computers and Operations Research* 2 (1975), pp. 121–25.
21. Zeleny, M. "The Last Mohicans of OR: Or, It Might Be in the Genes." *Interfaces* 9 (November 1979), pp. 135–41.

Appendixes

A—MATHEMATICS

The purpose of this appendix is to review the mathematical concepts that are used in this text.

A1 DEFINITIONS

Some notation is used throughout the text, independent of subject, and the student should be intimately familiar with these symbols:

! "Factorial": $n! = n(n-1)(n-2) \ldots (1)$

Example: $5! = 5 \cdot 4 \cdot 3 \cdot 2 \cdot 1 = 120$

$\sum$ Summation

$\sum_i$ Sum over all values of the index i:

$$\sum_i x_i = x_1 + x_2 + \cdots + x_n, \quad \text{where} \quad i = 1,2, \ldots, n.$$

Alternatively, the symbol $\sum_{i=1}^{n} x_i$ can be used.

$\sum\sum$ Double summation

Example:

$$\sum_{i=1}^{3} \sum_{j=1}^{2} x_{ij} = x_{11} + x_{12} + x_{21} + x_{22} + x_{31} + x_{32}$$

Constant: A constant is a quantity that always maintains a fixed value.

Parameter: A parameter is usually constant throughout a problem but may change from problem to problem.

Variable: A variable is a quantity whose value may change throughout a problem.

Continuous variable: The variable may assume *any* value (e.g., 14.7638 . . .) within its acceptable range.

Discrete variable: The variable may only take on certain (countable) values (e.g., 1/7, 2/7, 3/7, and so on), but usually the integers (1, 2, 3, . . .).

Independent variable: In an equation, this variable is known. It is usually shown on the X-axis of graphs.

Dependent variable: In an equation, this variable, whose value is desired, is unknown. It is usually shown on the Y-axis of graphs.

Example:

In the equation for a circle's circumference, $C = \pi D$:

C = A continuous dependent variable
π = A constant (3.14159)
D = A continuous independent variable (the diameter)

A2 CONCEPTS

Functions

A function is a mathematical expression that states a relationship between at least two variables. The expression $y = f(x)$ is read as follows: y is a function of x. This means that given a value for x, then y can be determined, although $y = f(x)$ does not tell us how. It states that some relationship exists. This relationship may take the form of a table or an equation. For example, $C = \pi D$ means that C is a function of D. That is: given D, it is possible to determine C. This example demonstrates a *single-valued* function, because for each value of D there exists only one value of C. Similarly, the equation $y = 4 + x^2$ is a single-valued function. However, the equation $y^2 = 4 + x$ is an example of a *multiple-valued* function because y, *the dependent variable,* may take on more than one value for each value of the *independent variable* x (if $x = 0$, then $y = 2$ or -2).

In the above examples, y was a function of the single variable x. However,
in expressions like $y = f(x, z) = x^2 + 3z$, y is a function of *several variables.* Again, x and z would be the independent variables and y the dependent variable.

The *slope* of a function measures how much the dependent variable changes for a small amount of increase in each of the independent variables. If the function is a straight line, then the slope of the function is the same everywhere. However, for functions that are not straight lines, it is necessary to specify *where* the slope is to be measured and in what direction, because it may be different at different values of the independent variables. If the dependent variable *increases (decreases)* with small increases in the independent variables, then we say that the function is *positively (negatively) sloped.*

Continuous and discrete functions

In a manner similar to continuous and discrete variables, there exist continuous and discrete functions also. Examples of continuous functions are:

$$y = x^2 + 2x$$
$$y = 5$$

Some examples of discrete functions are:

$$y = 5x \qquad \textit{where } x = 0,1,2, \ldots$$

$$y = \begin{cases} 10 + 3x & \text{for} \quad 0 \le x \le 2 \\ 14 + x & \phantom{\text{for}} \quad x \ge 2 \end{cases} \quad \text{and } x \text{ integer.}$$

Equalities

Functional relationships where the value of the dependent variable *equals* certain values of the independent variable are termed *equations*. For example, $y = 4x$.

Inequalities

If functional relationships cannot be written as equations but it is known that one exceeds the other, then they must be unequal and can be expressed as inequalities.

Such relationships can be designated by the symbols $\neq$. For example $y \neq 5x$ means that y is *not* equal to $5x$.

When relationships are not equal they can take *one* of four possible forms:

Form	*Symbol*	*Example*
Smaller than	$<$	$y < 6x + 2$
Smaller than or equal to	$\leq$	$y \leq 4x - 1$
Larger than	$>$	$y > 2x + 9$
Larger than or equal to	$\geq$	$y \geq 5x$

A3 LINEAR EQUATIONS

One of the most important functional relationships is the *linear equation*, due to its simplicity and wide range of applicability. A linear equation of two variables (one dependent, one independent) is a straight line. A linear equation of three variables is a plane, in three dimensions. The general form of a linear equation is:

$$y = a_1x_1 + a_2x_2 + \cdots + a_nx_n + b = \sum_i a_ix_i + b \tag{A1}$$

where the a_i and b are constants and the x_i are different variables. A linear equation always satisfies the following rule:

> If kV_i is substituted for each variable V_i in the original equation,[1] $y = f(V_i)$, where k is a constant, then the result will be ky.

Mathematically:

$$\text{If } y = f(V_i) \text{ is linear, then } f(kV_i) = ky \tag{A2}$$

Example Is the function $y = 5x + 3(w - 4z)$ linear?
Solution Substitute k times each variable in the equation and find:

[1] V_i designates each variable; that is, $x_1, x_2, \ldots, x_n$.

$$5(kx) + 3[kw - 4(kz)] = 5kx + 3k(w - 4z) = ky$$

Thus, the equation is linear.

The slope of a linear equation

The slope of a linear equation is constant at all points of the function. In general, the equation of a straight line is given as:

$$y = ax + b \tag{A3}$$

where a and b are constants. The slope of such a line is always a. The constant b also has a special name: the *intercept*. This is because when x is set to 0 (which is where the line "intercepts" the y-axis), the value of y equals b. The slope and intercept for the equation $y = 2x + 2$ are shown in Figure A1. Also shown in the figure are parts of the linear functions $y = 2$ and $y = 2x$, both of which differ from $y = 2x + 2$. The slope of $y = 2$ is 0, and its intercept is 2. The slope of $y = 2x$ is 2 and its intercept is 0.

FIGURE A1
Slope of linear functions

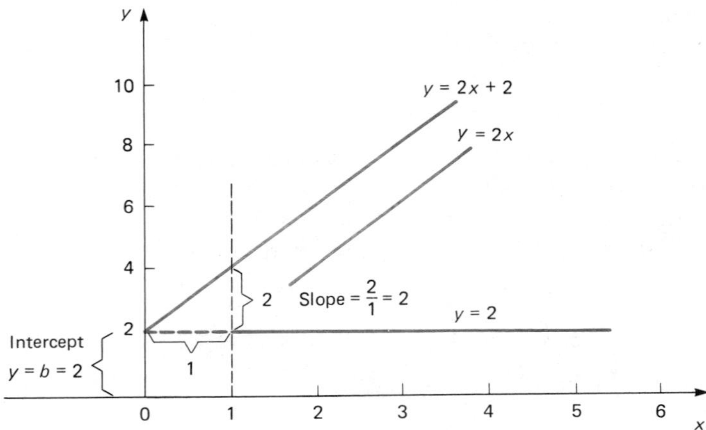

Nonlinear functions

Any function that does not meet the linearity requirement is considered *nonlinear*.

A4 RULES OF MANIPULATION

Inequalities

The rules of manipulation of inequalities are the same as for equations with one exception: when multiplying or dividing the inequality by a negative number, the inequality sign is reversed.

For example, given:

$$3 \geq -5$$

Multiplying by -1:

$$-3 \leq 5$$

As another example:

$$-4y + 10x \geq 2x - 8$$

Dividing by -2:

$$2y - 5x \leq -x + 4$$

Exponents

The definition of x^n (called x to the nth power) is x multiplied together n times, where n is called the *exponent*. The rules for manipulating exponents are:

1. ***Rule of multiplication:***

$$x^a \bullet x^b = x^{a+b} \tag{A4}$$

For example, $x^2 \bullet x^3 = x^5$.

2. ***Rule of division:***

$$x^a/x^b = x^{a-b} \tag{A5}$$

The second rule holds for cases where $b > a$ as well. This states, for example, that $x^3/x^4 = x^{3-4} = x^{-1}$. Invoking rule 1, it is possible to work backwards through cross-multiplication to obtain:

$$x^4 \bullet x^{-1} = x^{4-1} = x^3$$

3. ***Implications:***

a.

$$x^n/x^n = x^o = 1 \tag{A6}$$

for any nonzero value of x.

b. It can be seen that $1/x^2 = x^0/x^2 = x^{0-2} = x^{-2}$; that is, in general:

$$x^{-a} = 1/x^a \tag{A7}$$

c.

$$(x^a)^b = x^{a \cdot b} \tag{A8}$$

Example: $(x^2)^3 = (x \cdot x)(x \cdot x)(x \cdot x) = x^{2 \cdot 3} = x^6$.

d.

$$\sqrt[b]{x^a} = x^{a/b} \tag{A9}$$

Example: $\sqrt[3]{x^6} = x^{6/3} = x^2$

A5 SIMULTANEOUS EQUATIONS

Frequently, in management science, sets of simultaneous equations are encountered that must be solved in order to determine the optimal answer to a problem. Sets of *linear* equations are particularly frequent, as in linear programming. A general set of *simultaneous linear equations* is indicated below, where there are m equations and n unknown variables x_i.

$$\begin{array}{l} a_{11}x_1 + \ldots + a_{1n}x_n = b_1 \\ \cdot \qquad\qquad\qquad\qquad \cdot \\ \cdot \qquad\qquad\qquad\qquad \cdot \\ \ldots + a_{ij}x_j + \ldots = b_i \\ \cdot \qquad\qquad\qquad\qquad \cdot \\ \cdot \qquad\qquad\qquad\qquad \cdot \\ \cdot \qquad\qquad\qquad\qquad \cdot \\ a_{m1}x_1 + \ldots + a_{mn}x_n = b_m \end{array} \tag{A10}$$

This system can be written as:

$$\sum_{j=1}^{n} a_{ij}x_j = b_i \qquad \text{for } i = 1, \ldots, m$$

The a_{ij} terms are the *coefficients* (constants) of the x variable in the ith row and jth column, x_j. Note that there are only n unknown x variables, one for each of j columns. There are also m right-hand constants, b_i. If all the b_i are zero, the linear system is called *homogeneous.*

There are a number of techniques for solving a system of linear equations if, indeed, a solution exists. On the other hand, sometimes more than one solution exists.

Solution methods

A common method is the *Gauss-Jordan* technique. Consider the following set of linear equations:

1. $3x_1 + x_2 = 6$
2. $x_1 - 2x_2 = -1$

The Gauss-Jordan solution procedure aims to eliminate x_j from all equations except the jth equation and to give x_j a coefficient of unity in that equation. Starting with x_1, Equation 1 is divided by 3:

1′. $$x_1 + \frac{1}{3}x_2 = 2$$

Next, the new Equation 1′ is subtracted from Equation 2 (a rule of algebra states that a multiple of one equation can be added to, or subtracted from, another equation without affecting the functional relationship):

2. $$x_1 - 2x_2 = -1$$

1′. $$-\left(x_1 + \frac{1}{3}x_2 = 2\right)$$

The result is that x_1 has been eliminated:

2′. $$0 - 2\frac{1}{3}x_2 = -3$$

The new set of equations is thus:

1′. $$x_1 + \frac{1}{3}x_2 = 2$$

2′. $$-2\frac{1}{3}x_2 = -3$$

Now consider the variable x_2. In order to have a coefficient of 1 for x_2, Equation 2′ is divided by $-2\frac{1}{3}$. The result is Equation 2″:

2″. $$x_2 = \frac{9}{7}$$

Next, one third of Equation 2″ is subtracted from 1′ to eliminate x_2 in Equation 1′:

1′. $$x_1 + \frac{1}{3}x_2 = 2$$

$$-\left(\frac{1}{3}x_2 = \frac{3}{7}\right)$$

The result is:

1″ $$x_1 \qquad = \frac{11}{7}$$

Thus, the answer is:

$$x_1 = \frac{11}{7} \quad \text{and} \quad x_2 = \frac{9}{7}$$

Note: These solutions can be derived faster but our aim was a step-by-step explanation.

Other solution methods involve the use of matrices or determinants. For discussion, see any text in the bibliography for this appendix.

A6 MATRIX ALGEBRA

Matrices

A *matrix* is a rectangular (or square) array of numbers in m rows and n columns. Matrices are typically designated by capital letters. Alternately, small bracketed letters with two subscripts (the first refers to the row and the second to the column) to indicate elements of the matrix can be used. The general format of a matrix is:

$$A = [a_{ij}] = \begin{bmatrix} a_{11} & a_{12} & \cdots & a_{1n} \\ a_{21} & a_{22} & \cdots & a_{2n} \\ \cdot & \cdot & & \cdot \\ \cdot & \cdot & & \cdot \\ \cdot & \cdot & & \cdot \\ a_{m1} & \cdots & \cdots & a_{mn} \end{bmatrix} \tag{A11}$$

A is a matrix with m rows and n columns, or a matrix of $m \times n$ *dimension*. If $m = n$, the matrix is said to be a *square* matrix of *order n*. Each element in the matrix has an address designated by its row and its column. For example, a_{36} means a number in the third row and the sixth column. (For more than nine rows or columns, separate the subscript with a comma.)

Row and column vectors

If a matrix has only one row and two or more, say n, columns, it is called an n-dimensional *row vector;* if there is one column and two or more rows, it is called a *column vector*. Vector's elements are also designated by brackets [ ].

Examples:

Three-dimensional row vector:

$$S = [a_1 \quad a_2 \quad a_3] = [3 \quad 1 \quad -2]$$

Three-dimensional column vector:

$$T = \begin{bmatrix} a_1 \\ a_2 \\ a_3 \end{bmatrix} = \begin{bmatrix} 5 \\ 2 \\ 6 \end{bmatrix}$$

A matrix can be represented as a set of row or column vectors.

Example:

Given:

$$V = \begin{bmatrix} a_{11} \\ a_{21} \\ a_{31} \end{bmatrix} \quad W = \begin{bmatrix} a_{12} \\ a_{22} \\ a_{32} \end{bmatrix}$$

and:

$$X = [a_{11} \quad a_{12}] \qquad Y = [a_{21} \quad a_{22}] \qquad Z = [a_{31} \quad a_{32}]$$

then:

$$A = [VW] = \begin{bmatrix} X \\ Y \\ Z \end{bmatrix} = \begin{bmatrix} a_{11} & a_{12} \\ a_{21} & a_{22} \\ a_{31} & a_{32} \end{bmatrix}$$

The null (zero) vector and unit vector

Two special vectors of importance are the *null vector*, with all elements zero; that is, [0 0 0 0], and the *unit vector*, with all elements zero except one element, whose value is unity (1); that is, [0 0 1 0].

The null matrix and unit matrix

Similar to the null vector and unit vector there also exist the *null matrix*, with all elements zero, and the *unit (or identity) matrix*, denoted by I, with all elements zero except for ones along the main (top-left to bottom-right) diagonal:

$$I = \begin{bmatrix} 1 & 0 & 0 \\ 0 & 1 & 0 \\ 0 & 0 & 1 \end{bmatrix} \tag{A12}$$

The transpose of a matrix

The *transpose* of a matrix, A^T, is the matrix obtained by interchanging the rows and columns of the original matrix, A.

$$\text{If:} \quad A = \begin{bmatrix} a_{11} & a_{12} & a_{13} \\ a_{21} & a_{22} & a_{23} \\ a_{31} & a_{32} & a_{33} \end{bmatrix} \qquad \text{Then:} \quad A^T = \begin{bmatrix} a_{11} & a_{21} & a_{31} \\ a_{12} & a_{22} & a_{32} \\ a_{13} & a_{23} & a_{33} \end{bmatrix} \tag{A13}$$

Matrix manipulations

Addition and subtraction In order to add or subtract matrices, they must be exactly of the same size. Then the corresponding elements in each matrix are added or subtracted. For example in a 2 × 2 matrix:

$$\begin{bmatrix} a_{11} & a_{12} \\ a_{21} & a_{22} \end{bmatrix} + \begin{bmatrix} b_{11} & b_{12} \\ b_{21} & b_{22} \end{bmatrix} = \begin{bmatrix} a_{11} + b_{11}, & a_{12} + b_{12} \\ a_{21} + b_{21}, & a_{22} + b_{22} \end{bmatrix} \qquad \text{(A14)}$$

Example:

$$\begin{bmatrix} 4 & 2 \\ 3 & 1 \end{bmatrix} + \begin{bmatrix} 5 & 3 \\ 0 & 4 \end{bmatrix} = \begin{bmatrix} 9 & 5 \\ 3 & 5 \end{bmatrix}$$

Multiplication To multiply a matrix by a constant (called a *scalar*) it is necessary to multiply every element of the matrix by the constant. For example:

Given:

$$A = \begin{bmatrix} a_{11} & a_{12} \\ a_{21} & a_{22} \end{bmatrix}$$

then:

$$kA = \begin{bmatrix} ka_{11} & ka_{12} \\ ka_{21} & ka_{22} \end{bmatrix} \qquad \text{(A15)}$$

Multiplying a matrix by a matrix is somewhat more complex. Let us use an example to demonstrate. Suppose that it is desired to multiply matrix A by matrix B where:

$$A = \begin{bmatrix} a_{11} & a_{12} \\ a_{21} & a_{22} \\ a_{31} & a_{32} \end{bmatrix} \qquad B = \begin{bmatrix} b_{11} & b_{12} \\ b_{21} & b_{22} \end{bmatrix}$$

Note that the number of columns of matrix A must equal the number of rows of matrix B. Otherwise they are not "comformable" for multiplication.

The product of $A \times B$ is:

$$C = \begin{bmatrix} a_{11} & a_{12} \\ a_{21} & a_{22} \\ a_{31} & a_{32} \end{bmatrix} \times \begin{bmatrix} b_{11} & b_{12} \\ b_{21} & b_{22} \end{bmatrix} = \begin{bmatrix} a_{11}b_{11} + a_{12}b_{21} & a_{11}b_{12} + a_{12}b_{22} \\ a_{21}b_{11} + a_{22}b_{21} & a_{21}b_{12} + a_{22}b_{22} \\ a_{31}b_{11} + a_{32}b_{21} & a_{31}b_{12} + a_{32}b_{22} \end{bmatrix} \qquad \text{(A16)}$$

$$= \begin{bmatrix} c_{11} & c_{12} \\ c_{21} & c_{22} \\ c_{31} & c_{32} \end{bmatrix}$$

In general:

An element in the resultant matrix C is the sum of the products of the elements of the ith row of A and the jth column of B. A simple way to derive the solution of a matrix multiplication is as follows. First, represent the left matrix (A) by *row* vectors:

$$A = \begin{bmatrix} A_1 \\ A_2 \\ A_3 \end{bmatrix}$$

where A_1, A_2, and so on, are each a row vector: ($A_1 = [a_{11}\ a_{12}\ a_{13} \ldots]$). Then, represent the right matrix (B) by column vectors:

$$B = [B_1 \quad B_2]$$

where B_1, B_2, and so on, are each column vectors:

$$B_1 = \begin{bmatrix} b_{11} \\ b_{21} \\ \cdot \\ \cdot \\ \cdot \end{bmatrix}$$

Then combine the matrices by forming the appropriate products:

$$A \times B = \begin{bmatrix} A_1 \times B_1 & A_1 \times B_2 \\ A_2 \times B_1 & A_2 \times B_2 \\ A_3 \times B_1 & A_3 \times B_2 \end{bmatrix} \qquad \text{(A17)}$$

Note that this final matrix has as many rows as matrix A and as many columns as matrix B. The remaining step is to multiply each of the A_iB_j vectors together, element by element, and sum.

Examples:

a. $$\begin{bmatrix} 2 & 3 \\ 4 & 1 \\ 1 & 5 \end{bmatrix} \times \begin{bmatrix} 6 & 7 \\ 8 & 0 \end{bmatrix} = \begin{bmatrix} 2 \times 6 + 3 \times 8 = 36 & 2 \times 7 + 3 \times 0 = 14 \\ 4 \times 6 + 1 \times 8 = 32 & 4 \times 7 + 1 \times 0 = 28 \\ 1 \times 6 + 5 \times 8 = 46 & 1 \times 7 + 5 \times 0 = 7 \end{bmatrix} = \begin{bmatrix} 36 & 14 \\ 32 & 28 \\ 46 & 7 \end{bmatrix}$$

b. $$\begin{bmatrix} 2 \\ 4 \end{bmatrix} \times [6 \quad 7] = \begin{bmatrix} 2 \times 6 = 12 & 2 \times 7 = 14 \\ 4 \times 6 = 24 & 4 \times 7 = 28 \end{bmatrix} = \begin{bmatrix} 12 & 14 \\ 24 & 28 \end{bmatrix}$$

c. $$[2 \quad 3] \times \begin{bmatrix} 6 \\ 8 \end{bmatrix} = [2 \times 6 + 3 \times 8 = 36] = 36$$

d. $$\begin{bmatrix} 2 \\ 4 \end{bmatrix} \times \begin{bmatrix} 6 \\ 8 \end{bmatrix} = \text{not conformable for multiplication}$$

In general, $A \times B$ does not give the same result as $B \times A$. That is, the cumulative law of algebra *does not* hold with matrices. However, the *associative law* holds; that is:

$$(A \times B) \times C = A \times (B \times C) \qquad \text{(A18)}$$

Also, the *distributive law* holds:

$$A \times (B + C) = A \times B + A \times C \qquad \text{(A19)}$$

The inverse of a matrix

If square matrices A and D exist such that $AD = DA = I$ (the identity matrix), then D is said to be the inverse of A.[2]

$$D = A^{-1} \tag{A20}$$

Inverse matrices are important in solving systems of simultaneous linear equations. A simultaneous linear equation set, such as that of Equation A10, may be expressed in matrix form as follows:

1. All the coefficients a_{ij} are described in a matrix A:

$$A = \begin{bmatrix} a_{11} \cdots a_{1n} \\ \cdot \quad \cdot \\ \cdot \quad \cdot \\ \cdot \quad \cdot \\ a_{m1} \cdots a_{mn} \end{bmatrix}$$

2. All the unknown variables x_j are expressed as a column vector X:

$$X = \begin{bmatrix} x_1 \\ \cdot \\ \cdot \\ \cdot \\ x_n \end{bmatrix}$$

3. The right-hand-side constants, b_i, are expressed as a column vector B:

$$B = \begin{bmatrix} b_1 \\ \cdot \\ \cdot \\ \cdot \\ b_n \end{bmatrix}$$

4. The entire system is expressed as:

$$AX = B \tag{A21}$$

With matrix algebra, it is possible to solve for the vector X by multiplying the inverse of the vector A times B:

$$X = A^{-1}B$$

[2] A matrix whose determinant (to be presented soon) equals zero is called a *singular* matrix and it does not have an inverse.

Finding the inverse

Several methods are available for finding the inverse of a matrix, but one that works for *any* sized matrix utilizes the Gauss-Jordan system:

Example:

Given a matrix:

$$A = \begin{bmatrix} a_{11} & a_{12} \\ a_{21} & a_{22} \end{bmatrix}$$

find the inverse.

Step 1. Append an identity matrix to the right side of the original matrix, A.

$$\begin{bmatrix} a_{11} & a_{12} & 1 & 0 \\ a_{21} & a_{22} & 0 & 1 \end{bmatrix}$$

Step 2 Manipulate the rows via the Gauss-Jordan method such that the identity matrix appears on the left side:

$$\begin{bmatrix} 1 & 0 & d_{11} & d_{12} \\ 0 & 1 & d_{21} & d_{22} \end{bmatrix}$$

The resulting right-hand matrix:

$$D = \begin{bmatrix} d_{11} & d_{12} \\ d_{21} & d_{22} \end{bmatrix}$$

will then be the inverse of A:

$$D = A^{-1}$$

As an example, let us use the Gauss-Jordan coefficients of Section A5:

$$A = \begin{bmatrix} 3 & 1 \\ 1 & -2 \end{bmatrix}$$

Step 1.

$$\begin{bmatrix} 3 & 1 & 1 & 0 \\ 1 & -2 & 0 & 1 \end{bmatrix}$$

Step 2. Divide the first row by 3:

$$\begin{bmatrix} 1 & 1/3 & 1/3 & 0 \\ 1 & -2 & 0 & 1 \end{bmatrix}$$

Subtract row 1 from row 2:

$$\begin{bmatrix} 1 & 1/3 & 1/3 & 0 \\ (1 - 1 = 0) & (-2 - 1/3 = -2\tfrac{1}{3}) & (0 - 1/3 = -1/3) & (1 - 0 = 1) \end{bmatrix}$$

Divide row 2 by $-2\frac{1}{3}$:

$$\begin{bmatrix} 1 & \frac{1}{3} & \frac{1}{3} & 0 \\ 0 & 1 & \frac{1}{7} & -\frac{3}{7} \end{bmatrix}$$

Subtract one third of row 2 from row 1:

$$\begin{bmatrix} (1-0=1) & (\frac{1}{3}-\frac{1}{3}=0) & (\frac{1}{3}-\frac{1}{21}=\frac{2}{7}) & (0+\frac{1}{7}=\frac{1}{7}) \\ 0 & 1 & \frac{1}{7} & -\frac{3}{7} \end{bmatrix}$$

The inverse is thus:

$$\begin{bmatrix} \frac{2}{7} & \frac{1}{7} \\ \frac{1}{7} & -\frac{3}{7} \end{bmatrix}$$

Check:

$$\begin{bmatrix} 3 & 1 \\ 1 & -2 \end{bmatrix} \begin{bmatrix} \frac{2}{7} & \frac{1}{7} \\ \frac{1}{7} & -\frac{3}{7} \end{bmatrix} = \begin{bmatrix} 1 & 0 \\ 0 & 1 \end{bmatrix}$$

A7 PRESENT VALUE

Many managerial decisions must reflect the value of time: "time is money." Thus, a dollar today is worth more than a dollar in the future (especially with inflation). This time value is accounted for by an interest rate (or, equivalently, a discount factor). The following formulas present the basic mathematical notions of annuities, compound interest, and present value.

Formulas for value and compound interest factors

Let:

A = Future worth
P = Present value
A = Annuity, equal payments, of \$A each payment
n = Number of years
i = Interest rate

1. *To find P, given F, single payment.* The present worth of a single sum F, payable n years from now:

$$P = \frac{F}{(1+i)^n} \qquad \text{(A22)}$$

2. *To find P, given A:*

$$P = A\left[\frac{(1+i)^n - 1}{i(1+i)^n}\right] \qquad \text{(A23)}$$

This is the present value of a series of uniform end-of-year payments, each of value A, for n years.

This information is usually given in the form of tables in many finance, economics, and accounting texts.

A8 BIBLIOGRAPHY

1. Adams, B. *Fundamentals of Mathematics for Business, Social, and Life Sciences.* Englewood Cliffs, N.J.: Prentice-Hall, 1979.
2. Churchman, C. W.; L. Auerbach; and S. Sadan. *Thinking for Decisions: Deductive Quantitative Methods.* Chicago: Science Research Associates, 1975.
3. Draper, J., and J. S. Klingman. *Mathematical Analysis.* New York: Harper & Row, 1967.
4. Hohn, F. E. *Elementary Matrix Algebra.* 2nd ed. New York: Macmillan, 1964.
5. Kemeny, J. G., A. Schleffer, Jr., J. L. Snell, G. L. Thompson. *Finite Mathematics with Business Applications.* 2nd ed. Englewood Cliffs, N.J.: Prentice-Hall, 1972.
6. Mason, R. D. *Programmed Learning Aid for College Mathematics.* Homewood, Ill.: Learning Systems, 1971.
7. Owen, G. *Finite Mathematics.* Philadelphia: W. B. Saunders, 1970.
8. Peck, L. C. *Basic Mathematics for Management and Economics.* Glenview, Ill.: Scott, Foresman, 1970.
9. Theodore, C. A. *Applied Mathematics: An Introduction.* 3rd ed. Homewood, Ill.: Richard D. Irwin, 1975.
10. Vazsonyi, A. *Finite Mathematics, Quantitative Analysis for Business.* New York: John Wiley & Sons, 1977.

B—STATISTICS

This appendix includes a condensed presentation of the basic concepts of statistics and probability theory as related to this text. For more detailed explanations, the reader is referred to the bibliography for this appendix. Material here is divided into three main categories: probability, statistics, and distributions.

B1 PROBABILITY

The essence of probability is estimating the "odds," "risks," or "the long-run chances" of certain events occurring. An *event* is an *uncertain outcome*. The probability of a given event occurring is designated on a scale of 0 to 1. If the event *cannot* occur, then its probability is zero. If, on the other hand, the event is certain to occur, then its probability is one. Probability values other than 0 to 1 (expressed as a decimal fraction) represent an estimate of the random effect of chance. They measure the degree of belief that an event will occur. For example, a probability of .4 of showers today means that there is a .4 chance (or 40 percent chance) of rain.

Whenever probabilities are stated, a time frame must be specified. There is a certain chance for showers *today*, which may differ from the chances tomorrow, or over a week's duration. The classical definition of probability is given below.

The probability of an occurrence is the relative frequency of an event when a situation is repeated many times under identical circumstances.

Formally, it is expressed as:

$$P(\text{event } A) = \frac{\text{Number of occurrence of the event } A}{\text{Total number of occurrences}} \tag{B1}$$

Basic concepts

Range Probabilities range between 0 and 1 and can never assume a negative value. Formally: $0 \le P(A) \le 1$, where $P(A)$ is the probability of event A.

Frequency and probability The terms *frequency* and *probability* express the same idea in slightly different ways. For example, it can be said that the frequency of a "head" in a coin toss is one out of two. The same information is given by saying that the *probability* of a "head" in a coin toss is .5, or 50 percent. The two terms are used interchangeably.

Example. Suppose that you are in a hurry driving on a crowded street. You have driven down this street 80 times before. Out of these 80 times, you estimate, as best as you can, the relative frequency of occurrence of different speeds of traffic (events) on this street, as shown in Table B1.

Table B1 shows the frequency of the seven events. The table also shows the cumulative probability.

TABLE B1
Probability distribution of traffic speeds

Speed MPH (event)	*Number of times observed*	*Relative frequency (percent)*	*Cumulative probability (percent)*
20	6	6/80 = 7.5	0 + 7.5 = 7.5
25	14	14/80 = 17.5	7.5 + 17.5 = 25.0
30	25	25/80 = 31.3	25 + 31.3 = 56.3
35	18	18/80 = 22.5	56.3 + 22.5 = 78.8
40	11	11/80 = 13.7	78.8 + 13.7 = 92.5
45	5	5/80 = 6.3	92.5 + 6.3 = 98.8
50	1	1/80 = 1.2	99.8 + 1.2 = 100.0
Total	80	80/80 = 100.0	100.0

Cumulative probability The last column of Table B1 shows the probability of two or more events occurring on a cumulative basis. For example, the probability of traveling at 25 miles per hour or less is: 7.5 percent + 17.5 percent = 25.0. The *cumulative probability for all the events* is 100 percent, by definition. This property helps us to compute cumulative probabilities. For example, let us compute the cumulative probability of traveling faster than 40 MPH. Since the cumulative probability of traveling 40 MPH or less is 92.5 percent, then the probability of going faster than 40 MPH is 100 percent − 92.5 percent = 7.5 percent. The same result is achieved if the probability of 45 MPH is added to that of 50 MPH: 6.3 percent + 1.2 percent = 7.5 percent.

Assessment of probabilities Probabilities may be assessed in two ways: subjectively and objectively.

1. Subjective probability. If the chances of an event occurring are estimated by an individual, based on his or her beliefs and experience, but without hard data to back this belief, then the probability is termed *subjective*.

2. Objective probability. If the probability is based on hard facts, then it is termed *objective*. Three cases are distinguished:

a. Probability that is *based on logic*. For example, the probability of a "head" in a coin toss is reasoned to be 50 percent.

b. Probability that is *based on historical data*. For example, if 17 of the last 100 years had more than 3 inches of rain in April, then the probability of having more than 3 inches of rain in April is assessed as 17/100 = 17 percent.

c. Probability that is *based on experimentation*. For example, in order to find out the reliability of a new product, one may test 100 units of the new product to find out how many of these will work.

Random variable A variable whose value is determined by chance is referred to as a random variable. For example, the traffic speed in Table B1 is a random variable.

Event relationships

Independent and dependent events Events are classifed as *independent* if the occurrence of one has no effect on the probability of others, and vice versa. Events are considered *dependent* if the occurrence of one of them *does* affect the probability of the others.

Mutually exclusive events If the occurrence of an event *precludes* the occurrence of another event (that is, the two *cannot* occur together) then the events are said to be mutually exclusive.

Collectively exhaustive events A set (collection) of events is called *collectively exhaustive* if one of them *must* occur.

Union of events An outcome that occurs whenever *any* event in a set of events happens is called the *union* of those events. It is expressed, for the case of two events, as:

$$(A \text{ or } B)$$

Such a situation occurs when the occurrence of either A, or B, or both together result in the same outcome (e.g., a successful product).

Joint (intersection of) events An outcome that occurs only whenever *all* events occur (together) is called the *intersection* of events. These are referred to as *joint* events. For the case of two events this situation is written as:

$$(A \text{ and } B)$$

Probability relationships

Designations Let:

$$P(A) = \text{Probability of } A \text{ occurring}$$
$$P(B) = \text{Probability of } B \text{ occurring}$$

And so on.

Conditional probabilities The probability of two mutually exclusive events A and B occurring at the same time is zero, by definition. However, if A and B are *not mutually exclusive,* then it is possible to talk about the probability of A occurring *given* that B *has occurred* and vice versa. That is, if B happens first, what is the chance of A happening? The probability of A occurring, given that B has occurred, is called the *conditional* probability of A, given B, and is denoted $P(A|B)$. Similarly, $P(B|A)$, denotes the conditional probability of B, given that A has occurred.

Joint probabilities The probability of two or more events occurring jointly is labeled the *joint probability* of the events and is designated as $P(A \text{ and } B)$ for the case of two events.[1]

Laws of probability[2]

Multiplication The multiplication rule is used to find the probability of the *joint occurrence* of two or more events. Two cases are distinguished:

1. Dependent events. For the case of two events:

$$P(A \text{ and } B) = P(A) \times P(B|A) = P(B) \times P(A|B) \tag{B2}$$

The relationship between conditional and joint probabilities:

It is possible to compute the conditional probability of two events if the probability of each event and their joint probability are given.

$$P(A|B) = \frac{P(A \text{ and } B)}{P(B)} \tag{B3}$$

2. *Independent events.* If the events are independent, then the outcome of one has no effect on the outcome of the other, and therefore the conditional probabilities are identical. For two events, this can be expressed as:

$$P(A|B) = P(A) \quad \text{and} \quad P(B|A) = P(B) \tag{B4}$$

Inserting these values in Equation B2, we get a simplified multiplication law for independent events:

$$P(A \text{ and } B) = P(A) \times P(B) \tag{B5}$$

This law can be extended to any number of independent events; that is:

$$P(A \text{ and } B \text{ and } C \text{ and } \ldots) = P(A) \times P(B) \times P(C) \times \ldots \tag{B6}$$

Addition This law predicts the chances of a *union* of events occurring. Three cases are distinguished:

1. Nonexclusive joint events. In such a case, the formula is (for two events):

$$P(A \text{ or } B) = P(A) + P(B) - P(A \text{ and } B) \tag{B7}$$

---

[1] Also written as $P(A,B)$.

[2] These laws are given here for two events. They can be extended, as shown in some cases, to any number of events.

2. *Mutually exclusive events.* The joint occurrence of mutually exclusive events is impossible (by definition). Thus, $P(A \text{ and } B) = 0$.

Therefore, Equation B7 becomes:

$$P(A \text{ or } B) = P(A) + P(B) \tag{B8}$$

3. *Mutually exclusive and collectively exhaustive events.* If a set of events is both mutually exclusive and collectively exhaustive, then the *union* of these events *must occur* (by definition); that is, the probability of (A or B or . . .) is certain (equal to one). This property can be expressed as:

$$P(A \text{ or } B \text{ or } \ldots) = P(A) + P(B) + \ldots = 1 \qquad \text{(B9)}[3]$$

B2 STATISTICS

Definitions

Statistics The word *statistic* generally is taken to mean an estimate of a population characteristic or a summarized presentation of a mass of data. There are two subtopics of statistics: *descriptive* and *inferential.*

Descriptive statistics is the methodology that reduces a large mass of data into a few summary statistics. The most common are: the *central tendency,* the *dispersion,* and the *frequency distribution.*

Inferential statistics is the methodology for inferring the characteristics of a large mass of data based on the examination of a sample.

Population and samples The description of data depends on what type of measurement is used. In general, two approaches exist: (1) measuring the entire population and (2) measuring a sample.

Population A population is a complete set of individuals, objects, or measurements, having some common observable characteristics. The observation of the entire population is normally more expensive and takes more time than the observation of a sample. On the other hand, observing the population generally yields more accurate results.

Samples. A sample is a small portion of data drawn from a larger group (the population). If properly drawn, it is possible to make reasonably accurate conclusions about the entire population from the study of the sample. This ability provides a powerful device for getting the information required for decision making cheaply and quickly.

Frequency distribution A frequency distribution is a function telling how many times each of a set of random events, x_i, occurred. In other

[3] Probabilities of events can be designated as p_i = Probability of event i. Then Equation B9 is written as:

$$\sum_{1}^{n} p_i = 1$$

words, given a set of mutually exclusive and collectively exhaustive events (such as shown in Table B1), then the set of relative frequencies of all events is called the *frequency distribution function*. Frequency distribution functions can be shown graphically as histograms (such as Figure B1) or curves (Figure B2). These figures and a detailed discussion of the most common frequency distribution functions used in this text are given in Section B3 of this appendix.

Measures of central tendency

The most common statistic is the central tendency, or the average. The purpose of the average is to represent a group of individual values in a concise manner. The most common measures of central tendency are: the *mean*, the *median*, and the *mode*.

The population mean The population mean is given as:

$$\mu = \sum_i x_i P(x_i) \qquad \text{(B10)}$$

where:

x_i = The value of the variable
$P(x_i)$ = The probability of obtaining the value x_i (or the relative frequency of x_i) in the population[4]
μ = A Greek letter (pronounced mu) that designates the mean

The expected value The mean and expected value of a random variable are conceptually and numerically the same. The two are completely interchangeable. An expected value is designated by $E(x)$ (read as: the expected value of x).

The median The *median* is the middle value of the distribution. That is, if the number of observations is odd, then 50 percent of the observed data is smaller than the median and 50 percent is larger than the median. If the number of observations is even, then we average the middle two. For example, in Table B1, both the 40th and the 41st observations (which are 50 percent of the total of 80 observations) are 30 MPH. Thus, 30 MPH is the median speed.

The mode The *mode* is that data value with the highest frequency (there may be more than one). In Table B1, it is 30 MPH (25 observations). In this distribution, the median and mode fell in the same speed value, but that need not necessarily be true in other cases. Also, although the mode is always physically a realizable integer data point, the mean and

[4] If the frequency of all values is the same, the formula is:

$$\mu = \frac{\Sigma x_i}{n} \qquad \text{(B11)}$$

the median may *not* be. For example, the mean family size in the United States is about 4.3 people. The mean, median, and mode apply both to the populations and to samples.

Measures of dispersion

Measures of dispersion are measures of scatter around an average, or how data are scattered around the mean. The most important measure of dispersion in the context of this book is the standard deviation.

Standard deviation and variance of the population The standard deviation is designated by the Greek letter sigma (σ).

The formula for populations involving frequency distributions is:[5]

$$\sigma = \sqrt{\sum_i (x_i - \mu)^2 P(x_i)} \tag{B12}$$

The value σ^2 is known as the population *variance*.

Sample distributions

The mean Data such as those presented in Table B1 (a sample of 80 observations) can be described by a sample mean (denoted by $\bar{x}$) according to the following formula:

$$\bar{x} = \sum_i x_i \frac{f_i}{n} \tag{B14}$$

The meaning of this notation can be explained by using the data of Table B1: x_i is the ith speed, f_i is the number of occurrences of that speed, and n is the sample size (80 in this case). The term f_i/n is the frequency of speed i.

The standard deviation and variance The sample standard deviation s, is calculated from Equation B15.

$$s = \sqrt{\sum_i (x_i - \bar{x})^2 \frac{f_i}{n-1}} \tag{B15}$$

The value s^2 is known as the sample *variance*.

---

[5] If the frequency of all values is the same, the formula simplifies to:

$$\sigma = \sqrt{\frac{\Sigma(x_i - \mu)^2}{n}} \tag{B13}$$

where n is the population size.

Sample error Once $\bar{x}$ has been determined, it is possible to estimate the population mean. The difference between μ and $\bar{x}$ is termed the *sampling error.*

The law of large numbers Sampling is governed by the following law:

> *As the size of a sample increases toward infinity, the difference between the true population mean and the sample mean tends toward zero.*

Thus, it may be assumed that the sample mean is a good estimate of the population mean if the sample is "large enough" (30 is often considered the dividing point between a "small" and a "large" sample).

The central limit theorem It is possible to assess the *error* in estimating the population mean, indirectly, with the aid of the *central limit theorem.* The *central limit theorem* tells us that if one continues to take random samples of size n, from *any population distribution* with a standard deviation of σ, then the distribution of the *means of the samples* will tend to be normally distributed (the normal distribution is discussed in the next part of this appendix), with mean μ and standard deviation $\sigma/\sqrt{n}$, as n approaches infinity. Again, for practical purposes, if $n \geq 30$ ("large enough"), then a normal distribution of the samples' means can be assumed.

B3 PROBABILITY DISTRIBUTIONS

Discrete and continuous probability distributions

If a random variable may take only certain specific numerical values, such as integer numbers, then the probability distribution that characterizes the process which generated that random variable is called a *discrete distribution.* However, if the random variable may take *any* value (within a specified interval), then the probability distribution is labeled *continuous.* In this appendix, the following distributions will be discussed: the Poisson (a discrete distribution) and the normal and exponential (continuous distributions).

The Poisson distribution

The Poisson distribution describes situations where the number of occurrences per unit of time is constant; however, the timing of occurrence is random. In other words, occurrences have an equal chance of happening during any moment in the time interval under study. The distribution is shown in Figure B1.

The formula for the Poisson distribution is:

$$P(x) = \frac{\lambda^x e^{-\lambda}}{x!} \qquad \text{(B16)}$$

FIGURE B1
The Poisson probability distribution

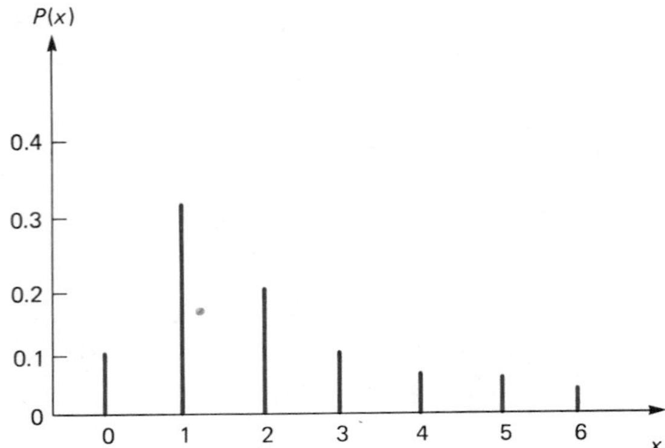

where:

λ = The average number of occurrences per unit of time
e = 2.718 (the base of the natural logarithms), approximately
x = A variable that assumes integer values (such as $x = 0, 1, 2, \ldots$)
$P(x)$ = Relative frequency of each value of x

The mean and standard deviation of this distribution are:

$$\text{Mean} = \lambda \tag{B17}$$

$$\text{Standard deviation} = \sqrt{\lambda} \tag{B18}$$

Values of $e^{-\lambda}$ are tabulated in Table C3 of Appendix C.

The normal distribution

The normal distribution is a continuous distribution discovered over 200 years ago. It was then considered to be the law governing distributions of natural phenomena. This belief has been modified as other distributions were discovered; however, the distribution is still the most common in statistics.

The normal distribution is shown in Figure B2 and its formula is:

$$f(x) = \frac{1}{\sigma\sqrt{2\pi}}\left[e^{-\frac{1}{2}\left(\frac{x-\mu}{\sigma}\right)^2}\right] \tag{B19}$$

where:

$f(x)$ = The relative frequency of variable x
μ = The mean of the distribution
σ = The standard deviation of the distribution
π = 3.14 (approximately)

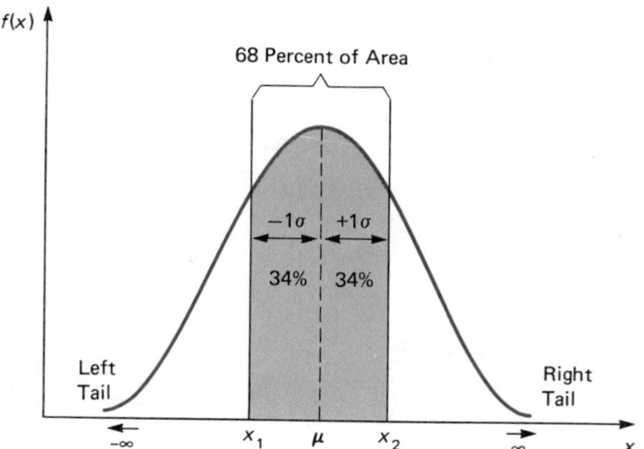

FIGURE B2
The normal distribution

Note that in contrast to the Poisson distribution, we talk here about $f(x)$ being the relative frequency of point x, in the range of $-\infty$ to ∞. (In contrast, the $P(x)$ in the Poisson was the *probability* of x having a *particular value*.)

Note also that the values of μ and σ are necessary and sufficient to describe the normal curve.

The area under the normal curve. Since the normal distribution is symmetrical, its midpoint is the mean. All x values (on the x-axis) are measured as deviations from the mean in standard deviation units.

The area under the normal curve describes the proportion of the total distribution between two points on the x-axis. For example, in Figure B2, the shaded area between point x_1 (which is one standard deviation to the left of the mean) and point x_2 (which is one standard deviation to the right of the mean) is 68 percent of the total area. The area from point $-\infty$ (left side) to point x_2 is 84 percent (34 percent plus the mean, which is exactly at 50 percent). It is known that 95.4 percent of the curve lies between $\pm 2\sigma$ around the mean and 99.7 percent lies between $\pm 3\sigma$.

The standard normal distribution A normal distribution whose mean is zero and whose standard deviation is one is called a *standard* normal distribution. Such a distribution was used for the construction of Table C1, in Appendix C, which lists the area under the curve as a function of the number of standard deviations, Z. This table is extremely useful since it enables one to find the probabilities for *any* given normal distribution, using the relationship:

$$Z = \frac{x - \mu}{\sigma} \qquad \text{(B20)}$$

where x is the value of the measured variable. Note that *if* in Equation B20, $\mu = 0$ and $\sigma = 1$, then $z = x$.

The use of the table of the area under the normal curve (Table C1) Tables that give the area under the normal curve appear in two alternative forms (Figure B3).

FIGURE B3
Alternative presentation of the area under the normal curve

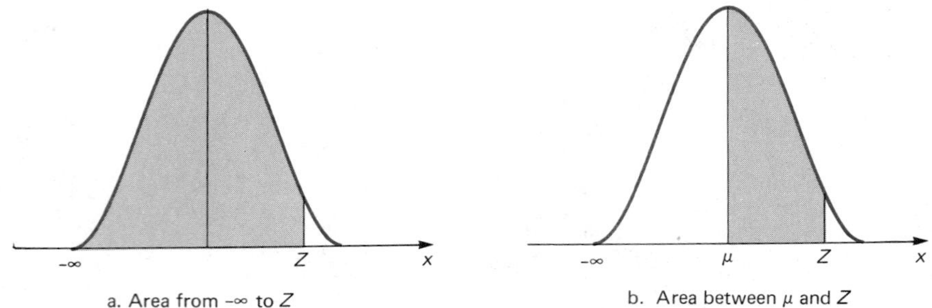

Alternative a. The entries in a table of this type represent the proportion of the total area under the normal curve (shaded) that falls between $-\infty$ and Z standard deviations to the right of the mean.

Alternative b. The entries in a table of this type represent the proportion of the total area under the normal curve (shaded) that falls between the mean and Z standard deviations to the right of the mean.

The difference between the same entry in the two tables is .5; that is, each entry in table type *a* is exactly .5 larger than that of type *b*. In this text, Table C1 is a type *a* table.

Using Table C1

Example 1. Find the area between $-\infty$ and $Z = 1.43$ standard deviations to the right of the mean. First, find the entry in row $Z = 1.4$ that intersects with column .03; the reading is .9236 (that is, 92.36 percent of the area is covered).

Example 2. Find the area between the mean and .45 standard deviations to the *left of the mean.*

Solution. Find the entry equivalent to $Z = .45$ (row $Z = .4$, column .05), which is .6736. Then subtract .5 from this value. The result $.6736 - .5 = .1736$ means that the solution is 17.36 percent of the area.

See Figure B4 for a graphical presentation of these two examples.

FIGURE B4
Graphical presentation of the two examples

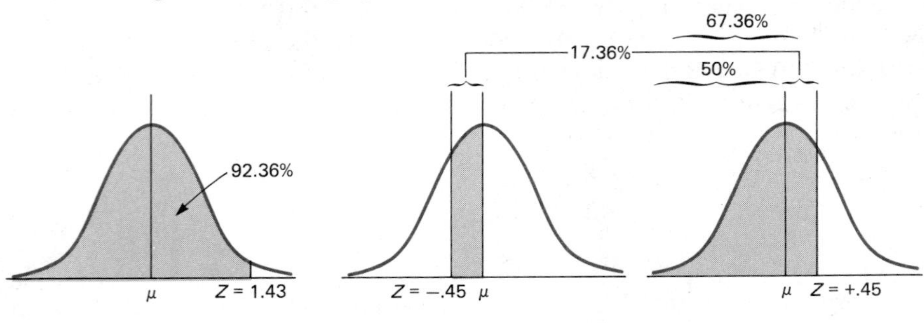

The negative exponential distribution

The negative exponential distribution describes the probability "that it will take x time before the first occurrence of an outcome."

The formula for the distribution is:

$$f(x) = \lambda e^{-\lambda x} \quad \text{for } \lambda \geq 0 \tag{B21}$$

where λ = The average number of occurrences per unit of time (e.g., service rate).

The statistics of this distribution are:

$$\text{Mean} = \frac{1}{\lambda} \tag{B22}$$

$$\text{Standard Deviation} = \frac{1}{\lambda} \tag{B23}$$

The distribution is shown in Figure B5 and $e^{-\lambda}$ is tabulated in Table C3.

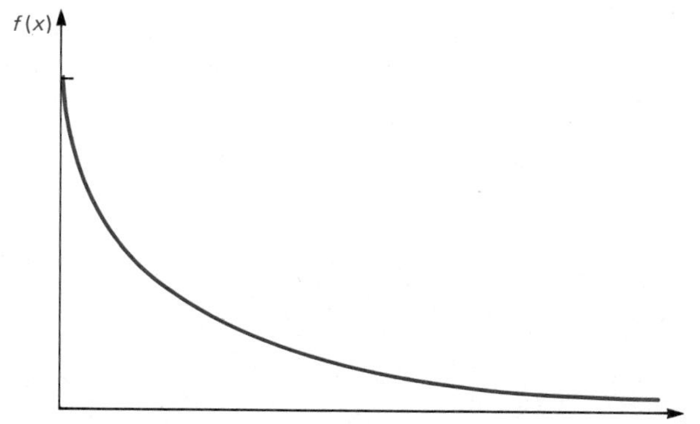

FIGURE B5
The negative exponential distribution

B4 BIBLIOGRAPHY

1. Celland, R. C.; J. S. deCani; and F. F. Brown. *Basic Statistics with Business Applications.* 2nd ed. New York: John Wiley & Sons, 1973.
2. Daniel W. W., and J. D. Terrell. *Basic Statistics.* Boston: Houghton Mifflin, 1975.
3. Gulezion, R. C. *Elements of Business Statistics.* Philadelphia: W. B. Saunders, 1979.
4. Madsen, R. W., and M. L. Mueschberger. *Statistical Methods for Business and Economics.* Englewood Cliffs, N.J.: Prentice-Hall, 1980.

5. Mason, R. D. *Programmed Learning Aid for Business and Economic Statistics*. Homewood, Ill.: Learning Systems, 1974.
6. Mullen, K., and H. J. Malik. *Applied Statistics for Business and Economics*. Reading, Mass.: Addison-Wesley Publishing, 1975.
7. Sanders, D. H., A. F. Murph, R. J. Eng. *Statistics—A Fresh Approach*. 2nd ed. New York: McGraw-Hill, 1980.
8. Spirer, H. F. *Business Statistics*. Homewood, Ill.: Richard D. Irwin, 1975.
9. Spurr, W. A., and C. P. Bonini. *Statistical Analysis for Business Decision*. Homewood, Ill.: Richard D. Irwin, 1973.
10. Stockton, J. R., and C. T. Clark. *Introduction to Business and Economic Statistics*. 5th ed. Cincinnati: South-Western Publishing, 1975.
11. Wonnacott, T. H., and R. J. Wonnacott. *Introductory Statistics for Business and Economics*. New York: John Wiley & Sons, 1972.

C—TABLES

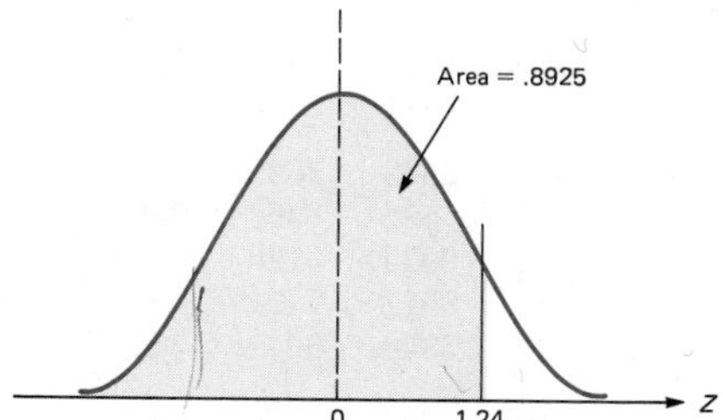

TABLE C1
Cumulative probabilities of the normal probability distribution (areas under the normal curve from $-\infty$ to Z)

Z	.00	.01	.02	.03	.04	.05	.06	.07	.08	.09
.0	.5000	.5040	.5080	.5120	.5160	.5199	.5239	.5279	.5319	.5359
.1	.5398	.5438	.5478	.5517	.5557	.5596	.5636	.5675	.5714	.5753
.2	.5793	.5832	.5871	.5910	.5948	.5987	.6026	.6064	.6103	.6141
.3	.6179	.6217	.6255	.6293	.6331	.6368	.6406	.6443	.6480	.6517
.4	.6554	.6591	.6628	.6664	.6700	.6736	.6772	.6808	.6844	.6879
.5	.6915	.6950	.6985	.7019	.7054	.7088	.7123	.7157	.7190	.7224
.6	.7257	.7291	.7324	.7357	.7389	.7422	.7454	.7486	.7517	.7549
.7	.7580	.7611	.7642	.7673	.7704	.7734	.7764	.7794	.7823	.7852
.8	.7881	.7910	.7939	.7967	.7995	.8023	.8051	.8078	.8106	.8133
.9	.8159	.8186	.8212	.8238	.8264	.8289	.8315	.8340	.8365	.8389
1.0	.8413	.8438	.8461	.8485	.8508	.8531	.8554	.8577	.8599	.8621
1.1	.8643	.8665	.8686	.8708	.8729	.8749	.8770	.8790	.8810	.8830
1.2	.8849	.8869	.8888	.8907	.8925	.8944	.8962	.8980	.8997	.9015
1.3	.9032	.9049	.9066	.9082	.9099	.9115	.9131	.9147	.9162	.9177
1.4	.9192	.9207	.9222	.9236	.9251	.9265	.9279	.9292	.9306	.9319
1.5	.9332	.9345	.9357	.9370	.9382	.9394	.9406	.9418	.9429	.9441
1.6	.9452	.9463	.9474	.9484	.9495	.9505	.9515	.9525	.9535	.9545
1.7	.9554	.9564	.9573	.9582	.9591	.9599	.9608	.9616	.9625	.9633
1.8	.9641	.9649	.9656	.9664	.9671	.9678	.9686	.9693	.9699	.9706
1.9	.9713	.9719	.9726	.9732	.9738	.9744	.9750	.9756	.9761	.9767
2.0	.9772	.9778	.9783	.9788	.9793	.9798	.9803	.9808	.9812	.9817
2.1	.9821	.9826	.9830	.9834	.9838	.9842	.9846	.9850	.9854	.9857
2.2	.9861	.9864	.9868	.9871	.9875	.9878	.9881	.9884	.9887	.9890
2.3	.9893	.9896	.9898	.9901	.9904	.9906	.9909	.9911	.9913	.9916
2.4	.9918	.9920	.9922	.9925	.9927	.9929	.9931	.9932	.9934	.9936
2.5	.9938	.9940	.9941	.9943	.9945	.9946	.9948	.9949	.9951	.9952
2.6	.9953	.9955	.9956	.9957	.9959	.9960	.9961	.9962	.9963	.9964
2.7	.9965	.9966	.9967	.9968	.9969	.9970	.9971	.9972	.9973	.9974
2.8	.9974	.9975	.9976	.9977	.9977	.9978	.9979	.9979	.9980	.9981
2.9	.9981	.9982	.9982	.9983	.9984	.9984	.9985	.9985	.9986	.9986
3.0	.9987	.9987	.9987	.9988	.9988	.9989	.9989	.9989	.9990	.9990
3.1	.9990	.9991	.9991	.9991	.9992	.9992	.9992	.9992	.9993	.9993
3.2	.9993	.9993	.9994	.9994	.9994	.9994	.9994	.9995	.9995	.9995
3.3	.9995	.9995	.9995	.9996	.9996	.9996	.9996	.9996	.9996	.9997
3.4	.9997	.9997	.9997	.9997	.9997	.9997	.9997	.9997	.9997	.9998

TABLE C2
Random numbers

7823	9505	7863	2976	4536	0062	2757	3281
4308	3826	1329	8318	5829	0986	2765	0874
9228	9903	9793	6938	9344	2120	1306	4629
8717	5407	0187	3141	7651	9415	2893	9213
4773	8866	4966	3964	8718	9311	5954	6955
8387	4641	6280	4467	4578	2349	7635	7109
8728	4950	9218	2101	8320	1526	8462	2968
2768	3615	2529	2812	3783	0934	3126	4600
1988	5102	1837	3864	1161	8517	7101	8024
5202	0158	0715	9539	4229	3874	6042	1437
9763	5760	9080	5720	1216	7843	5890	2789
7025	2332	6238	8043	1373	5162	6336	7402
6020	5070	7485	5620	3081	4854	8759	8005
0526	8974	8545	8541	6886	5014	2012	1843
5078	8581	1215	2189	8128	9536	5357	5700
5801	3622	6441	5059	8871	3844	7643	8809
8691	0747	7648	9165	7648	5068	5216	9526
6272	9181	7511	3217	8037	9114	8365	3502
9208	4589	5428	8676	3424	2980	7001	0478
0693	0665	0855	7396	5297	4919	1061	3722
0363	1856	9196	6949	6230	9456	9558	5963
5238	3367	2373	5890	6273	4141	4451	6709
1907	6029	5227	6050	2698	8500	1478	5049
3057	3784	1807	2634	8159	3015	9813	0030
2926	0519	2181	5244	1046	5367	5901	7474
0456	0663	0756	4094	4418	7953	4044	7590
4124	4389	1198	5571	6119	6540	7273	2009
9376	3496	0902	9923	2789	4477	6797	1870
1543	7954	9548	1232	4219	0236	6777	0342
2739	5811	1642	5979	2059	8088	3391	3480
0682	0604	2051	1375	8191	2566	3162	2572
0535	0605	6357	8278	3078	6929	5224	9124
7782	3184	4504	5879	3238	4159	5676	0418
0805	5265	6536	6506	9487	6087	9420	9063
6262	7289	3310	8731	3921	2095	5837	4218
8508	3313	2976	5658	3616	3361	9396	5188
6248	3796	5543	2582	2832	1983	4747	9837
5220	0327	3268	4413	3040	6358	8106	0776
5193	3007	3666	8084	1389	5026	2680	1549
2652	1375	4799	8832	3241	0752	5649	3029

TABLE C3
Poisson values of $e^{-\lambda}$

λ	$e^{-\lambda}$	λ	$e^{-\lambda}$	λ	$e^{-\lambda}$	λ	$e^{-\lambda}$
0.1	0.90484	2.6	0.07427	5.1	0.00610	7.6	0.00050
0.2	0.81873	2.7	0.06721	5.2	0.00552	7.7	0.00045
0.3	0.74082	2.8	0.06081	5.3	0.00499	7.8	0.00041
0.4	0.67032	2.9	0.05502	5.4	0.00452	7.9	0.00037
0.5	0.60653	3.0	0.04979	5.5	0.00409	8.0	0.00034
0.6	0.54881	3.1	0.04505	5.6	0.00370	8.1	0.00030
0.7	0.49659	3.2	0.04076	5.7	0.00335	8.2	0.00027
0.8	0.44933	3.3	0.03688	5.8	0.00303	8.3	0.00025
0.9	0.40657	3.4	0.03337	5.9	0.00274	8.4	0.00022
1.0	0.36788	3.5	0.03020	6.0	0.00248	8.5	0.00020
1.1	0.33287	3.6	0.02732	6.1	0.00224	8.6	0.00018
1.2	0.30119	3.7	0.02472	6.2	0.00203	8.7	0.00017
1.3	0.27253	3.8	0.00237	6.3	0.00184	8.8	0.00015
1.4	0.24660	3.9	0.02024	6.4	0.00166	8.9	0.00014
1.5	0.22313	4.0	0.01832	6.5	0.00150	9.0	0.00012
1.6	0.20190	4.1	0.01657	6.6	0.00136	9.1	0.00011
1.7	0.18268	4.2	0.01500	6.7	0.00123	9.2	0.00010
1.8	0.16530	4.3	0.01357	6.8	0.00111	9.3	0.00009
1.9	0.14957	4.4	0.01228	6.9	0.00101	9.4	0.00008
2.0	0.13534	4.5	0.01111	7.0	0.00091	9.5	0.00007
2.1	0.12246	4.6	0.01005	7.1	0.00083	9.6	0.00007
2.2	0.11080	4.7	0.00910	7.2	0.00075	9.7	0.00006
2.3	0.10026	4.8	0.00823	7.3	0.00068	9.8	0.00006
2.4	0.09072	4.9	0.00745	7.4	0.00061	9.9	0.00005
2.5	0.08208	5.0	0.00674	7.5	0.00055	10.0	0.00005

D-ANSWERS TO EVEN-NUMBERED PROBLEMS

CHAPTER 2

2. *a.* $A \leq 400$
b. $A + B \geq 540$
c. $A + B \leq 720$
d. $800A + 1{,}150B \leq 50{,}000$

CHAPTER 3

2. Insure, 50,000 deductible: Expected cost = $825
4. *b.* 2.45 cars per day
c. $174,195
6. Do not play; expected loss of playing is $0.167 per play
8. *a.* Select a_1: Expected profit 6.1, EOL = 1.1
b. Select a_1: Expected profit 4.5, EOL = 1.6
c. Select a_1: Expected profit 2.0, EOL = .3
10. Choose alternative *c* for a cost of $7,300
12. *a.* Order 11 crates
b. Average daily profit $15.60
14. Convert now; expected cost 2,500 pesos
16. *a.* a_2
b. $0.272 \leq s_1 \leq 0.615$
18. Do not insure: expected cost = $80
20. Do not repair: expected cost = $1,370
22. Attend at random: expected value is 1.74
24. Expand: expected present value = $695,000
26. Use no preparation: expected cost = $130.20
28. $.825 per day
30. Table 1:
a. a_1
b. a_3
c. a_1
d. a_3
e. a_3
Table 2:
a. a_2 or a_3
b. a_2
c. a_3
d. a_2
e. a_2
32. *a.* a_2
b. a_2
c. a_3
d. a_2
e. a_2
34. 77.6 percent chance of purchase by the government
38. *c.* 0.62
d. No, value is only 2,083
40. *a.* EVPI = 7; purchase
b. No, value of 2,850
42. *a.* 3.50
b. Vendor A (2.07 net profit vs. 1.94 for B)
c. .09
d. .32
f. .17, .58, 0, .25, 0

CHAPTER 4

2. U(1000) = 25; $1400
4. Since U($3000) is about .75 and the expected utility of the investment is only .662, she should *not* invest
6. *a.* A = 20 percent, B = 20 percent, C = 33 percent, D = 27 percent
b. A = 15 percent, B = 20 percent, C = 39 percent, D = 26 percent
8. The best year was 1978 with the highest index of 250
10. Spain
14. *b.* A should advertise; B should cut prices; game value = −1
16. *a.* A use a_1 one sixth of the time, a_2 five sixths of the time
B use b_1 one half of the time, b_2 one half of the time
b. 0.5 percent increase to A at B's expense
c. Yes

18.

	b_1	b_2	b_3
a_1	−3	4	3
a_2	2	1	4
a_4	1	6	−4

20. *a.* A: Advertise in evening
B: Advertise once in the evening and once in the afternoon, or else twice in the evening
b. 25 percent to A; 75 percent to B

22. 2. Farmer should plant on a large scale to guarantee at least $2,500
3. Everyone plant on a small scale and each make $10,000

24. 1.

	E	N	W
E	180	220	220
N	220	180	282.5
W	220	157.5	180

2. Both companies play 50 percent E and 50 percent N

3.

	E	N
E	18,000	22,000
N	22,000	18,000

CHAPTER 5

2. Final moving averages:

Order, n	*Value*
3	3.3
4	3.0
5	3.0

4. Alpha of 0.05: 30.5
Alpha of 0.60: 19.2

6.

Alpha	*MAD*	*BIAS*
.05	16.5	9.9
.60	20.3	7.3

8. Overall MAD averages 2.85
10. MAD = .532
Bias = 0
Mean % deviation = 0
Mean absolute % deviation = 18.07
Mean square deviation = .3585
Standard error of intercept = .166
Standard error of slope = .048
12. $T = 4 + 0.167X$
$S_1 = 1.22$
$S_2 = 0.96$
$S_3 = 0.72$
$S_4 = 1.10$
14. 5.44
MAD = 0.165
Bias = −0.0125
16. *a.* D = 3,361.3 − 56.33S
2122 tires
MAD = 1743
Bias = 0
b. D = − 810.1 + 112.6S
1960 tires
MAD = 445
Bias = 0
18. Winter: 58,800
Spring: 87,120
Summer: 97,100
Fall: 121,680
20. Forecast (period 45) = 551.19
Regression equation: $T_e = 484.79 + 1.67x$
Seasonal indexes: 96.27, 109.91, 96.78, 97.04

CHAPTER 6

2. Two optimal solutions give $z = 95$; $x_1 = 12.6$, $x_2 = 6.4$; $x_1 = 8$, $x_2 = 11$
4. *c.* $x_1 = 9$, $x_2 = 7.5$
d. 117
e.

Constraint	*Slack*	*Surplus*
1	0	0
2	0	0
3	0	12
4	25	0

f. $x_1 = 10.67$, $x_2 = 3.33$, $z = 105.34$
6. *a.* 600 pants, 1,200 shirts, z = $4,200 per day
b. The price of shirts must exceed $6 per unit
8. 37.5 hours (150 units) on line 1
170 hours (850 units) on line 2
Total cost = 1,150,000 won
10.

	Case a	*Case* b
a.	#1	#6
b.	#4, #1	#4, #5
c.	None	#1

12. *b.* 5 (the number of constraints)
c. If degenerate
d. Bread 750.9 grams; carrots 135.8 g.; halibut 111.6 g.; eggs 325.4 g. Cost: .92 pesos per day
e. 56.36 grams of protein
f. Beef 169.6 grams; butter 62.8 g.; bread 500 g.; carrots 130.4 g.; halibut 70.1 g.; eggs 200 g. Cost: 1.085 pesos, 52.5 grams of protein
14. *a.* $x_1 = 10$, $x_2 = 8$, $z = 82$
b. Solution is degenerate
e. Additional solution: $x_1 = 11.45$, $x_2 = 6.18$, $z = 82$
16. $x_1 = 1$, $x_2 = 3$, $z = 14$
18. $x_1 = 1$, $x_2 = 3$, $z = 14$
20. Unbounded solution in x_2

CHAPTER 7

2. $x_1 = 6\frac{2}{3}$
$x_2 = 1\frac{2}{3}$
$x_3 = 1\frac{2}{3}$
$z = 103\frac{2}{3}$

4. $x_1 = 1{,}000$
$x_2 = 1{,}235.3$
$x_3 = 352.9$
$z = \$4{,}588.20$

8. *a.* Maximize $z = .25x_a + .32x_b + 15x_c + .28x_d$
subject to:
$$\begin{aligned} x_a + x_b + x_c + x_d &\le 500 \\ x_a &\le 250 \\ x_b &\le 250 \\ x_c &\le 250 \\ x_d &\le 250 \\ x_b &\ge 50 \\ x_a - 2x_c &\le 0 \end{aligned}$$

10. $x_1 = \$3{,}400$
$x_2 = 9{,}350$
$x_3 = 4{,}250$
$z = 223{,}550$ customers

12. Maximize $z = .4x_1 + .23x_2 + .48x_3 + .31x_4$
subject to:
$$\begin{aligned} x_1 + x_3 &\le 4{,}200{,}000 \\ x_2 + x_4 &\le 504{,}000 \\ x_1 + x_3 &\ge 1{,}000{,}000 \\ x_2 + x_4 &\ge 600{,}000 \\ x_1 + x_2 &\ge 2(x_3 + x_4) \\ .1x_1 &= .9x_2 \\ .13x_3 &= .87x_4 \end{aligned}$$

a. 4,200,000 and 504,000
b. 3,584,000 and 1,120,000
c. \$4,564,000
d. \$1,879,808

16. For (a): minimize $x_1 + x_2$
subject to $7x_1 + x_2 \ge 1$
$8x_2 \ge 1$

Solution: $x_1 = \frac{1}{8}$
$x_2 = \frac{1}{8}$
Play b_1 ½ and b_2 ½
Play a_1 $\frac{4}{7}$ and a_2 $\frac{3}{7}$
Value of the game = 1

CHAPTER 8

2. $u_1 = 1\frac{2}{3},\ u_2 = \frac{1}{3},\ u_3 = u_4 = 0,\ w = 132$

4. *a.* Minimize $50u_1 - 20u_2 + 26u_3 - 26u_4$
subject to:
$$\begin{aligned} 5u_1 \qquad\quad + 2u_3 - 2u_4 &\ge 5 \\ 3u_1 - 2u_2 + 3u_3 - 3u_4 &\ge 3 \\ -\ 1u_2 - 1u_3 + 1u_4 &\ge 1 \end{aligned}$$

b. Minimize $-50u_1 + 20u_2 - 20u_3 + 45u_4$
subject to:
$$\begin{aligned} -3u_1 + 1u_2 - 1u_3 + 2u_4 &\ge -6 \\ -4u_1 + 2u_2 - 2u_3 + 3u_4 &\ge 2 \end{aligned}$$

6. *a.* $x_1 = .4,\ x_2 = .1,\ z = 200$
b. The first, third, and fourth
c. 1. None
2. None
3. None
4. None
5. Reduce cost by 50(.5) = \$25
6. Infeasible

8. *a.* $2{,}666.67 \le x_1 \le 8{,}000$
$2{,}500 \le x_2 \le 7{,}500$
b. No nonbasic variables
c. $-\infty \le b_1 \le 11.50$
$-16.50 \le b_2 \le \infty$
$102.86 \le b_3 \le 240$
$120 \le b_4 \le 233.33$
$60 \le b_5 \le \infty$

10. *a.* $x_1 = 0.5,\ x_2 = 0,\ z = 350$
b. Coefficient of x_2 must exceed 35
c. Can decrease by 3.5
d. Coefficient can increase up to $2\frac{1}{3}$
e. Infeasible solution

12. *a.* Yes, \$916 > \$120 cost
b. 16.10
c. 66.3 percent
d. 1, 3, and 4
e. No, violates constraint 5
f. No, violates constraint 4
g. 36,956.3
h. Decreasing the RHS will not help

14. *a.* 335.23
b. 0
c. x_1
d. 45.703
e. 234
f. 0
g. 4.297
h. Slack exists
i. Constraints not fully utilized
j. #4 not fully utilized; #5 is
k. 15.65
l. 10% = nothing; 20% = no more x_4

16. *a.* Either $x_1 = 1,\ x_2 = 2$ *or* $x_1 = 2,\ x_2 = 1$; $z = 3$
b. LP solution $x_1 = \frac{5}{3},\ x_2 = \frac{5}{3},\ z = \frac{10}{3}$

c. Rounding gives the two solutions in *(a)*
d. ⅓

18. Minimize $600x_1$ (M-1 flights) $+ 8{,}000x_2 + 10{,}000x_3$
Subject to
$100x_1 + 180x_2 + 270x_3 \geq 3{,}200$
$4x_1 + 12x_2 + 17x_3 \leq 140$
$x_1 \leq 15$
$x_2 \leq 12$
$x_3 \leq 6$
x_i integer

20. *a.* $x_1 = 13⅓$, $x_2 = 23⅓$, $z = \$9{,}250$
b. $x_1 = 13$, $x_2 = 23$, $z = \$9{,}075$

22. See Problem 16 solution

28. *a.* $x_1 + x_2 + x_3 + x_4 = 2$
b. $x_1 - x_3 = 0$
c. $x_1 - x_3 \leq 0$ where $x_i = 0$ or 1

CHAPTER 9

2. x_1 = hours on line 1
x_2 = hours on line 2
1) $5x_1 + 4x_2 + d_1^- - d_1^+ = 300$ (produce 300 units)
2) $x_1 - 30 + d_2^- - d_2^+ = 4$ (overtime)
3) $15(x_1 - 30) + 12(x_2 - 30) + d_3^- - d_3^+ = 800$ (overtime cost)
4) $(30 - x_1) + (30 - x_2) + d_4^- - d_4^+ = 0$
5) $5x_1 + 4x_2 + d_5^- + d_5^+ = 0$
Minimize $z = P_1d_1^- + P_2d_2^+ + P_3d_3^+ + 5P_4d_4^- + P_5d_5^-$

4. *a.* 106.67 and 61.67
b. 21.67
c. 40
d. 333.44
e. 100

6. 50,000 units of alpha, 42,857 units of beta

8. $x_1 = 45$, $x_2 = 30$, profit = 75

CHAPTER 10

2. *a.* Cost = \$700
b. Cost = \$560
c. Optimal solution cost = \$560
d. Yes, many

4. *a.* Optimal profit = \$1,260
b. Maximize $6x_{11} + 4x_{12} + 3x_{21} + 5x_{22} + 8x_{31} + 7x_{32} + 5x_{41} + 9x_{42}$
subject to:
$x_{11} + x_{12} \leq 50$
$x_{21} + x_{22} \leq 80$
$x_{31} + x_{32} \leq 60$
$x_{41} + x_{42} \leq 40$
$x_{11} + x_{21} + x_{31} + x_{41} = 80$
$x_{12} + x_{22} + x_{32} + x_{42} = 100$

6. *b.* Several optimal solutions with a distance of 885 miles

8. *b.* Optimal minimum cost = \$11,200; $x_{AC} = 1{,}000$; $x_{BD} = 1300$
c. Minimize $6x_{AC} + 7x_{AD} + 9x_{AE} + 9x_{BC} + 4x_{BD} + 6x_{BE}$
subject to $x_{AC} + x_{AD} + x_{AE} = 1{,}000$
$x_{BC} + x_{BD} + x_{BE} = 1{,}300$

10. *a.* A–O, B–N, C–P, Minimum cost = \$16

12. *a.* Several optimal solutions with minimum complaints of 21

14. *a.* $x_{AI} = 60$, $x_{AII} = 80$, $x_{BII} = 40$, $x_{BIII} = 80$, Cost = 8,500 rupees

16. $x_{A1} = 3{,}000$, $x_{B1} = 2{,}000$, $x_{C1} = 200$, $x_{C2} = 1{,}600$, $x_{D3} = 6{,}000$, Profit = \$555,000

18. $x_1 = 0$, $x_2 = 1$, $x_3 = 1$, $x_4 = x_5 = 0$, $x_6 = x_7 = 1$, $x_8 = 0$; $z = 45$

20. See answer to Problem 2

22. *a.* Degenerate, cost = 6,400
b. $x_{1A} = 200$, $x_{2A} = 400$, $x_{3C} = 500$, $x_{3D} = 100$, $x_{4B} = 400$, $x_{4E} = 300$, Cost = 6,000

24. $x_{AE} = 40$, $x_{CD} = 20$, minimum mileage = 3,800

26. See Problem 10

28. P to *E*, R to *B*, A to *D*, C to *C*, *A* uncovered
Maximum damage = 156

CHAPTER 11

2. *a.*

Event	T_E	T_L	*Slack*
1	0	0	0
2	3	3	0
3	5	8	3
4	10	10	0
5	16	16	0
6	19	19	0

b. (See *(a)* also).

Activity	*Slack*
a	0
b	3
c	0
d	3
e	0
f	7
g	6
h	5

c. Critical path: *a–c–e–i*
d. 3 on *b–d*
7 on *b–f*
6 on *b–g*

4. *a.* *a–d–e–g–i–j*
b. 20 days
c. 61 days
d. 20 days

6. *b.* *b–f–h*
c. 9 weeks
d. *a–c;* 6 weeks
e. 1 extra week: No effect
2 extra weeks: Second critical path *b–e–g*
3 extra weeks: One week delay and new critical path *b–e–g*

8. *b.* *b–e–g–h*
c. new critical path *a–d–g–h*
d. From *c* and *f* to *d,* then to *g,* lastly to *h*

10.

	ES	*EF*	*LS*	*LF*	*TF*	*FF*
a	0	3	0	3	0	0
b	0	5	3	8	3	0
c	3	10	3	7	0	0
d	5	7	8	10	3	3
e	10	16	10	16	0	0
f	5	9	12	16	7	7
g	5	13	11	19	6	6
h	10	14	15	19	5	5
i	16	19	16	19	0	0

Critical path is *a–c–e–i.*

14. Critical path is **1–3–4–11–13–14–16.**

16. *a.* 36.9 percent
b. 84.1 percent
c. 50 percent
d. 17.32

18. *a.* 20.8 percent, 5.2 percent, 89 percent
b. 0
c. 23.057 weeks

20. *a.* 21.7 weeks
b. **1–3–6–7**
c. .3, 0
d. 6, 0.7
e. 17.88 percent
f. 100 percent
g. 24.728 weeks

22. Cost 130

24.

Date	*Cost*
17	0
16	25
15	55
14	105
13	165
12	245

26. Total distance = 271

28. Total distance = 156

CHAPTER 12

2. P→A→H→LA, cost = \$380

4.

Year	*Price (thousands pesos)*
1	110
2	100
3	100
4	110

6. *a.* 1 to *A,* 2 to *B,* 1 to *C;* \$33,000 per month
b. 2 to *A,* 1 to *B,* 1 to *C;* \$32,000 per month
c. 1 to each; \$29,000 per month

8. *a.* Sell on any day (exept the fifth) if the price is ≥ 22; otherwise, wait. On the fifth day, sell at any price
b. Net return = \$21,526

10. Mon: Wait
Tues: Sell if 350, otherwise wait
Wed.: Sell if 400, otherwise wait
Thurs: Sell

12. *a.* Minimize $z = 20A + 15B + 23C + 18D$
Subject to:
$4A + 2B + 5C + 3D \geq 14$
$A, B, C, D \geq 0$ and integer
b. 1*A* and 2*C;* Cost = \$66

CHAPTER 13

2. $Q(3) = [.456 \quad .544]$

4. *a.* 74 good; 74 fair; 32 poor
b. 52.68 good; 83.42 fair; 43.90 poor

6. *a.* *P*(A operates) = .948; *P*(B operates) = .977; lease B
b. If the lease for A is less than (.948 ÷ .977) × lease for B, then A should be leased; otherwise, lease B

8. *a.* 21.74 in checking; 8.53 in loans, 9.72 in savings

10. 42.3 percent to A; 19.8 percent to B; 36.9 percent to C

12. *a.* $\begin{bmatrix} .765 & .210 & .025 \\ .033 & .913 & .053 \\ .040 & .020 & .940 \end{bmatrix}$

c. 131, 199, 70

d. 54, 170, 176

14.

Level	*Days*
1	7.01
2	10.50
3	24.05
4	40.15
5	50.50
6	51.47
7	77.35
8	59.80
9	44.17
Total	365.00

16. *b.* 39 at airport, 61 at beach

c. $458.80

d. 27 percent

18. *a.* 3.37 weeks

b. 5/3 weeks in good condition; 1 week in fair condition; 19/27 weeks in poor condition.

c. In the long run, 100 percent. Within a week, 10 percent if in good condition, 20 percent if fair, and 90 percent if poor

20. *a.*

		Paid	*Bad*	*Current*	*Delinq.*
		(in thousands)			
a.	Nov. 1	950	150	500	200
	Dec. 1	1,200	200	250	150

b. 1.5 million

c. 300,000

d. 2 months in current + .4 months in delinq. = 2.4

CHAPTER 14

2. 18,330 bags, .262 month's worth

4. *a.* 800 bags

b. 0.8 month's worth

6. No, the cost would be $1,530, compared to $1,464 by ordering only 150 units (for which space is available

8. *a.* Order $10,000 worth 20 times per year

b. $2,000

c. $3,200 more per year

d. Order $10,488 worth

e. $266.67 more per year

10. $.32 per unit per year

12. *a.* $11,100

b. 1,200 units; $3,600

c. 6

18. *b.* 40

c. 10 days

d. 40 days
30 units maximum inventory

e. Increases the cost from $750 to $812.50

20. *a.* 20 days

b. 400

c. 40 days

d. $30,000 per year

22. *a.* 15

b. No, total cost is $1,470 higher

c. 7 percent

26. *a.* 32

b. $1,600 per cycle

c. 12

d. Every 16 days (.533 months)

28. *a.* $3,280

b. 30

30. 7

32. 106 if rent; 109 if buy

34. Order 150 in week 10, 145 in week 13, and 155 in week 15

38. Order 50 for Jan. 3, 120 for Jan. 17, 120 for Jan. 24, 140 for Feb. 7; TC = $480.

CHAPTER 15

2. *a.* 2.545 hours

b. 9.44 repairs

6. *a.* 50 percent

b. 3.12 percent

c. 6.25 percent

d. 22.3 percent

e. 93.75 percent

f. 99.32 percent

8.

μ	L_q	W_q
3.1	29.04	9.68
3.5	5.13	1.71
4	2.25	.75
6	0.5	.167

10. 10.33 truckloads per hour

12. $60

14. *a.* No, only 60 percent of the time

b. Yes, since the investment will reduce the total hourly cost of the system from $9.17 to $8.50

16. Line 1 utilization is best: 73.9 percent
18. Using the table, $L_q = .375$, $TC = \$8.04$
20. Unpooled $W = 1$ hour; pooled $W = 35$ minutes
22. Use 2 forklifts: Total cost = $21.92 per hour
24. *a.* No, an explosive queue forms for tools
    b. Yes, a savings of $2.62 per hour
26. *b.* 3.68
    b. 1.32
    c. 73.6 percent
    d. 48 percent
    e. $127
28. *a.* 0.8
    b. 2.5 minutes
    c. 36.5 percent
    d. 11 percent
    e. No, the savings is only 0.6¢
30. *a.* 2.235 days
    b. 0.383 days
    c. No, since the savings of $45.89 per day doesn't justify the daily cost of $48
    d. Not in this case
32. System #1 (without limitation) costs $27,900 more; but there is no balking. System #2 has 6.6% balking.
34. *a.* 4 spaces is the cheapest; TC = $241.78/hr.
    b. 4 spaces is the cheapest; TC = $239.27/hr.

CHAPTER 16

2. 8, 9, 6, 7, 8
4. *a.* 108 units for $1,512 average profit
   b. 109 units
6. *b.* 109.5 days
8. *a.* Intermediate
   b. $944
   c. $342,800
   d. 15.4 percent
   e. $5,670
10. *a.* 13.27 units
    b. 20 percent
    c. 17 units
    d. No, inventory is increasing
12. *a.* 80 percent
    b. $3,000
    c. 30 percent
    d. 96.6 percent
14. One shift is better for either price; the $400 price is *much* more profitable
22. *NB* rule: 3–2–4–7–5–1–6–8 for total of 73
    NBWA rule: Same as above.
24. *a.* 5 people
    b. 3.846 people
    c. 0.94 minutes
    d. 54 percent
    e. 97 percent
    f. 25.2 trips
26. *a.* 1,755 compared to $E(V) = 1{,}890$
    b. 8.33 percent
    c. 41.67 percent
    d. 1,816.67 gallons
    e. 441.67 gallons
    f. $22.75 due to ill will; $91.00 due to opportunity loss of 20¢ gallon
    g. 66.6 percent
    h. $260.00 − 0.83 (shipped back) = $259.13. Opportunity loss of $22.75 might also be deducted
30. *a.* Unit demand was met (97.6%) but weekly demand was not (66.7%)
    b. 1,331.45 pesos
    c. Zero
    d. 1.16 valves per week
32. *b.* $830.50 profit per day
    c. 50 percent
34. *a.* 1.33 minutes per customer (prior to service)
    b. .762
36. *a.* .967
    b. 1.02
    c. 9.272
    d. .545
    e. .272

Index

A

A-B-C classification system, 597, 641
Absorbing states, 563, 573
Algorithm, 40, 50, 242
Allocation problems, 44, 209, 269
Analog model, 27, 50
Artificial intelligence, 800, 814
Artificial variables, 245, 269
Assignment models, 405
  balancing, 407
  characteristics, 405
  complete enumeration, 408
  formulation, 406
  optimality test, 410
  presentation as a linear program, 406
  solution methods, 408
  total-opportunity-cost matrix, 410
Assignment problem, 63, 339–41, 405

B

Basic feasible solution, 249
Bayes' theorem, 96, 121
Bias, 177, 207
Blending problems, 214, 217, 218, 234, 247, 270
Branch and bound, 335, 338, 350
Business (operational) games, 705, 745–49

C

Cognitive style, 831
Complete enumeration, 64, 334, 350, 408, 529
Computers, use, 16
  in management science, 866–88
Constant service time, 683
Controllable (decision) variables, 32–33, 218, 220
Corporate planning models, 749
CPM (Critical Path Method), 472–80, 437–63, 497, 502
  advantages, 440
  construction, 441–43
  crashing time analysis, 473–80
  definition, 440
  identifying critical path, 452
  objectives, 440
  slacks, 455–57
  use as control tool, 459
Crash time, 473, 502
Cycle, 187

D

Decision making, 21–22, 58–59
Decision support systems (DSS), 770–94
  capabilities, 781
  cases, 787
  characteristics, 774–75

Decision support systems (DSS)—*Cont.*
construction, 783–85
data base, 779, 787
definition, 772
evolution, 777
generator, 784
group, 786
model base, 780
structure, 777–79
Decision tables, 58–60
Decision theory, 58, 125
Decision trees, 8, 72–82, 100, 121, 544–49, 855
Decision variables; *see* Controllable (decision) variables
Decisions under
certainty, 61, 64, 121
conflict, 142, 157
risk, 62, 65, 122
uncertainty, 62, 102, 122
Degeneracy, 261, 270, 425, 434
Delphi, 172, 207
Dependent variables, 32, 50, 214
Descriptive models, 50
Deterministic models, 61, 121, 754
Deviational variables, 356, 380
Dominance, 121, 149, 163
Duality, 301
Dummy, in transportation and assignment, 390, 434
Dummy activity in PERT/CPM, 444, 502
Dynamic programming, 505
allocation, 517
general formulation, 528
nature of, 507
optimization techniques, 529
probabilistic problems, 525
reward, 514
rollback approach, 508
sensitivity analysis, 520
stagecoach problem, 509
stages, 508, 513, 536
states, 514, 536
structure, 515
DYNAMO, 723–24

E

Economic lot size (ELS), 607, 624, 641
Economic order quantity (EOQ), 641
assumptions, 585
model, 584
Expected monetary value (EMV), 69, 121
Expected utility (EU), 163
Expected value, 67, 121
Expert systems, 795–816
and management science, 806
applications, 810
basic concepts, 797
benefits, 804
development, 803
limitation, 806
structure, 801–03
Exponential distribution (negative), 655
Exponential smoothing, 173, 176, 207

F

Feasible area of solutions, 223, 229, 270
Financial planning models, 749
Forecasting, 167
causal, 170, 182
counting methods, 169, 173
decomposition, 186
errors, 177
factors, 170
judgment methods, 168, 172
methods, 168
seasonal, 188
time series, 169, 181
Fundamental matrix, 564

G

Game theory, 142–57
dominance, 149, 163
format, assumptions, 144
graphical solution, 155
mixed strategy, 150, 163
normal form, 144
presentation as a linear program, 156, 287
pure strategy, 146, 163
General Purpose System Simulator (GPSS), 724
Goal programming, 138, 352, 380
concepts, 356
deviations, 356, 380
examples, 367
graphical, 375
structure, 358
Goal seeking, 783
GPSS; *see* General Purpose System Simulator
Graphical Evaluation and Review Technique (GERT), 481, 503
Greedy algorithm, 482, 503
Group DSS, 786

H

Heuristic programming, 742–45, 765
Heuristics, 40, 50
Hungarian method, 409, 434
Hurwicz criterion, 106

I

Iconic model, 27, 50
IFPS, 790
Ill-structured problems, 31
Implementation, 44, 817–41
  behavioral factors, 829
  climate, 820
  definition, 818
  operational factors, 826
  organizational factors, 824
  politics, 828
  project particulars, 820
  resistance to change, 833
  support of top management, 824
  values and ethics, 828
  viability, 822
Independent variables, 33
Industrial dynamics; *see* Systems dynamics
Integer programming, 331
  definition, 270, 333
  methods of solution, 334
Interdisciplinary approach, 26
Inventory costs, 582
Inventory models, 574
  average, 580
  characteristics, 576
  computers, 631
  decisions, 581
  functions, 578
  replenishment, 580
  safety stock, 580, 624
  sensitivity analysis, 593
  shortage, 580, 621, 628, 642
  simulation of, 710–18
  stockout, 642
  structure, 579
Isocost lines (equations), 235, 270
Isoprofit lines (equations), 231, 270
Iteration, 270

K–L

Knapsack problem, 336, 529, 535
Laplace's criterion, 103
Life cycle, 186, 207
Linear programming, 213
  advantages, 222
  applications, 273–87
  assumptions, 222
  basis, basic solutions, 247
  constraints, 220, 225
  feasible area of solutions, 223, 229, 270
  formulation, 214, 220
  graphical method, 224, 242
  incremental analysis, 852
  limitations, 222
  multiple solutions, 264
  nature of, 213
  objective function, 220
  sensitivity analysis, 311
  simplex method, 242
  unbounded solutions, 262

M

MAD (Mean Absolute Deviation), 177, 207
Management science
  characteristics, 6, 20
  definition, 6
  extent of use, 10
  future of, 864–71
  historical development, 9
  limitations, 10
  process, 21
  research, 869
  tools, 7, 21, 46
Managerial problems (prototype), 44
Markov analysis, 537
  absorbing states, 541, 563
  assumptions, 542
  characteristics, 541
  definition, 541, 573
  equilibrium, 552, 573
  steady state, 552, 573
  transition matrix, 543, 546
Material requirements planning, 616, 642
Mathematical models, 27, 32–34, 50
Mathematical programming, 301
Maximal flow, 487, 503
Maximax, 105
Maximin, 104
Minimax, 104, 147, 163
Minimal spanning tree, 481
Minimax regret, 106, 121
Minimin, 105
Modified distribution method (MODI), 420, 434
Monte Carlo simulation, 705–10
Moving average, 173, 207
Multiple goals, 134, 163, 380

N

Network models, 435, 503
  activity, 438, 502
  critical activity, 439, 502
  critical path, 439, 502
  events, 438, 503
  projects, 439, 503
Nonlinear programming, 344
Nonnegativity constraints, 220, 270
Nonzero-sum games, 146, 163

Normative models, 36, 50, 573
Northwest corner rule, 391, 434

O

Objective probability, 121
Operational gaming; *see* Business games
Opportunity loss (regret), 67, 69, 121
Optimization, 36, 50, 535

P

Payoffs, 60, 121, 144
Perfect information, value of, 93, 121
Planned shortages inventory model, 621, 642
Poisson distribution, 654
Principle of optimality, 535
Probabilistic models; *see* Stochastic models
Product-mix problem, 213, 215, 270
Production scheduling, 263, 403
Program Evaluation and Review Technique (PERT), 437, 503
  advantages, 440
  construction, 441
  definition, 439
  identifying critical path, 452, 458
  objectives, 439
  PERT/cost, 480, 503
  probabilities of completion, 468
  slacks, 451, 455, 503
  time estimates, 443, 467
  use as control tool, 459
Programmed decisions, 6, 15, 31

Q

Quadratic programming, 345
Quantity discount inventory models, 603, 642
Queue behavior, 657
Queue discipline, 657–58
Queueing; *see* Waiting lines

R

Random numbers (RN) generation, 706, 708, 725, 735–36
Recursive relations, 536
Regret; *see* Opportunity loss
Revised probabilities, 122
Risk, 62, 122
Risk analysis, 202, 721–23

S

Safety stock inventory analysis, 624, 642
Satisficing, 37, 51
Savage's criterion; *see* Minimax regret
Scientific approach, 22
Seasonal variation, 187, 197, 207
Sensitivity analysis, 311, 351
  concept of, 43, 51
  for goal programming, 365
  for linear programming, 311
Sequential decisions, 536
Serial queue, 683–85
Service level, 642
Shadow prices, 307
Shortage (stockout), 580, 621, 628
Shortest route, 483, 503
Simplex method, 242
SIMSCRIPT, 723, 724
Simulation, 698–766
  advantages and disadvantages, 701, 702
  of continuous distributions, 734–37
  definition, characteristics, 699–704
  flow chart, 712
  measures of performance, 715–16
  methodology, 703–04, 724–26
  of inventory, 710–18
  of waiting lines, 718–23, 730–34
  risk analysis, 721–23
  stabilization, 636
  types of, 613
  use of computers, 633
  validation, 724–25
Slack in PERT/CPM, 451, 503
Slack variable, in linear programming, 236, 270, 309
Stage, definition, 508, 536
States of nature, 122
Stepping-stone method, 394, 434
Stochastic models, 122, 573
Subjective probability, 122
Suboptimization, 36, 51
Surplus variables, 236, 237, 270, 309
Symbolic reasoning, 800
System simulation, 749–52
Systems, 22, 51
Systems dynamics, 752–54

T

Time series analysis, 169, 181, 207
Transition probabilities, 543, 545
Transportation models, 384
  assumptions, 384
  balancing, 389, 434
  cell evaluators, 397, 421, 434
  characteristics, 384
  degeneracy, 425, 434
  least cost method, 393
  presentation as a linear program, 386
  transportation-type problems, 402
Trend, 186, 207
Two-person zero-sum games, 146

U–V

Utility, 71, 125, 137, 163
Utility curves, 129
Visual simulation, 737–42, 705

W–Z

Waiting lines, 646–696
  applications, 665–69, 677–81
  arrival process, 652, 654
  characteristics, 647
  computers, 685–87
  costs, 649–50, 664–65
  interarrival time, 654
  measures of performance, 662–64
  methodology, 651–52, 669–77
  models, 658–60, 682–85
  multiple (multichannel) facility, 675–85
  Poisson-exponential system, 661–74
  service process, 655
"What-if" analysis, 782
Zero-one model, 335
Zero-sum games, 145, 146, 163